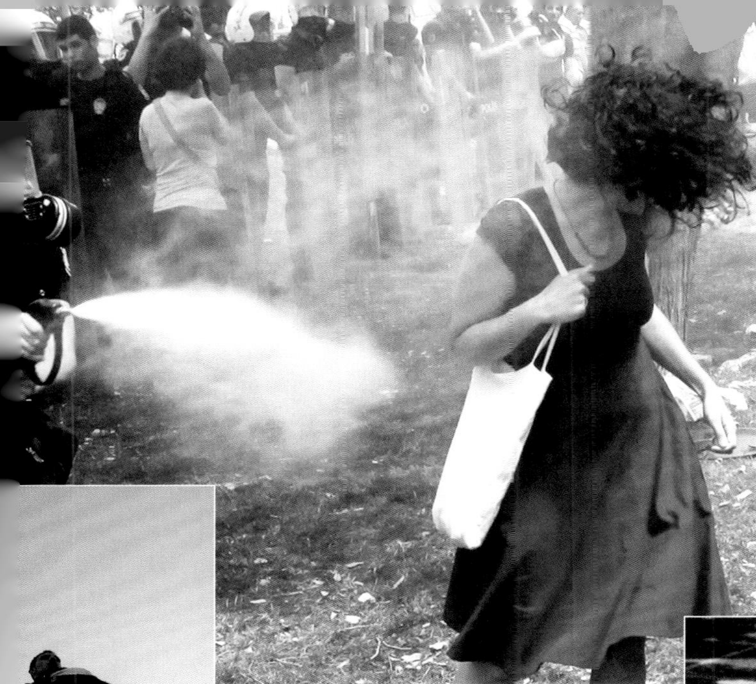

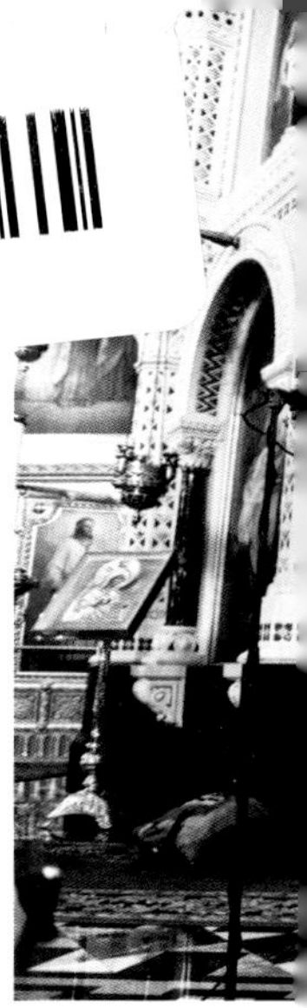

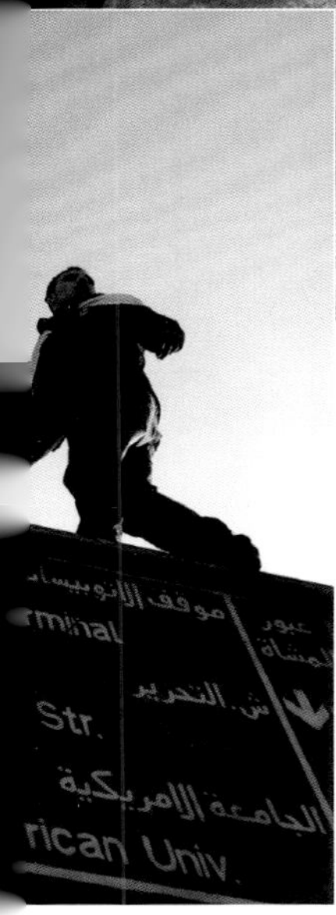
ش. التحرير
Str.
الجامعة الامريكية
rican Univ.

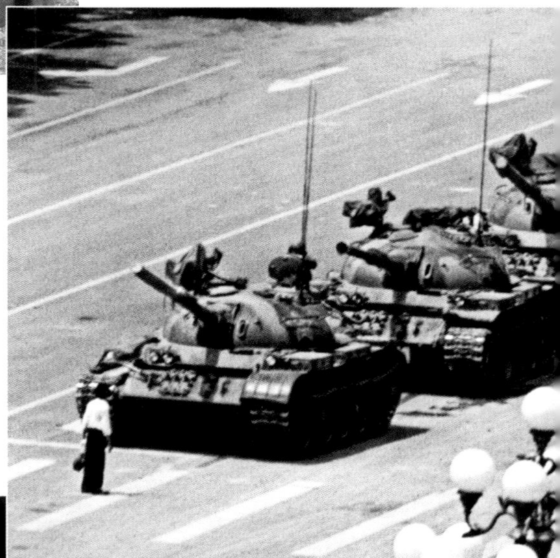

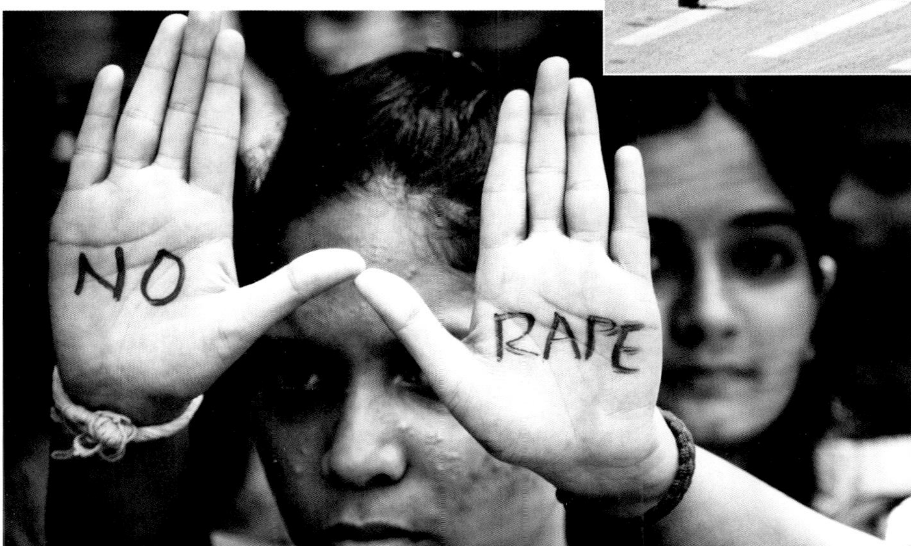
NO
RAPE

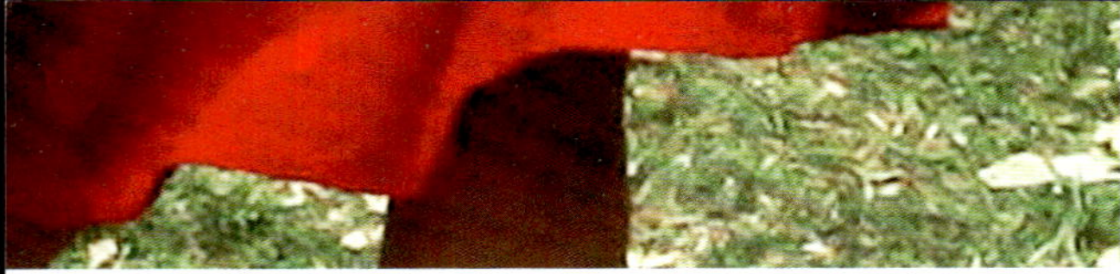

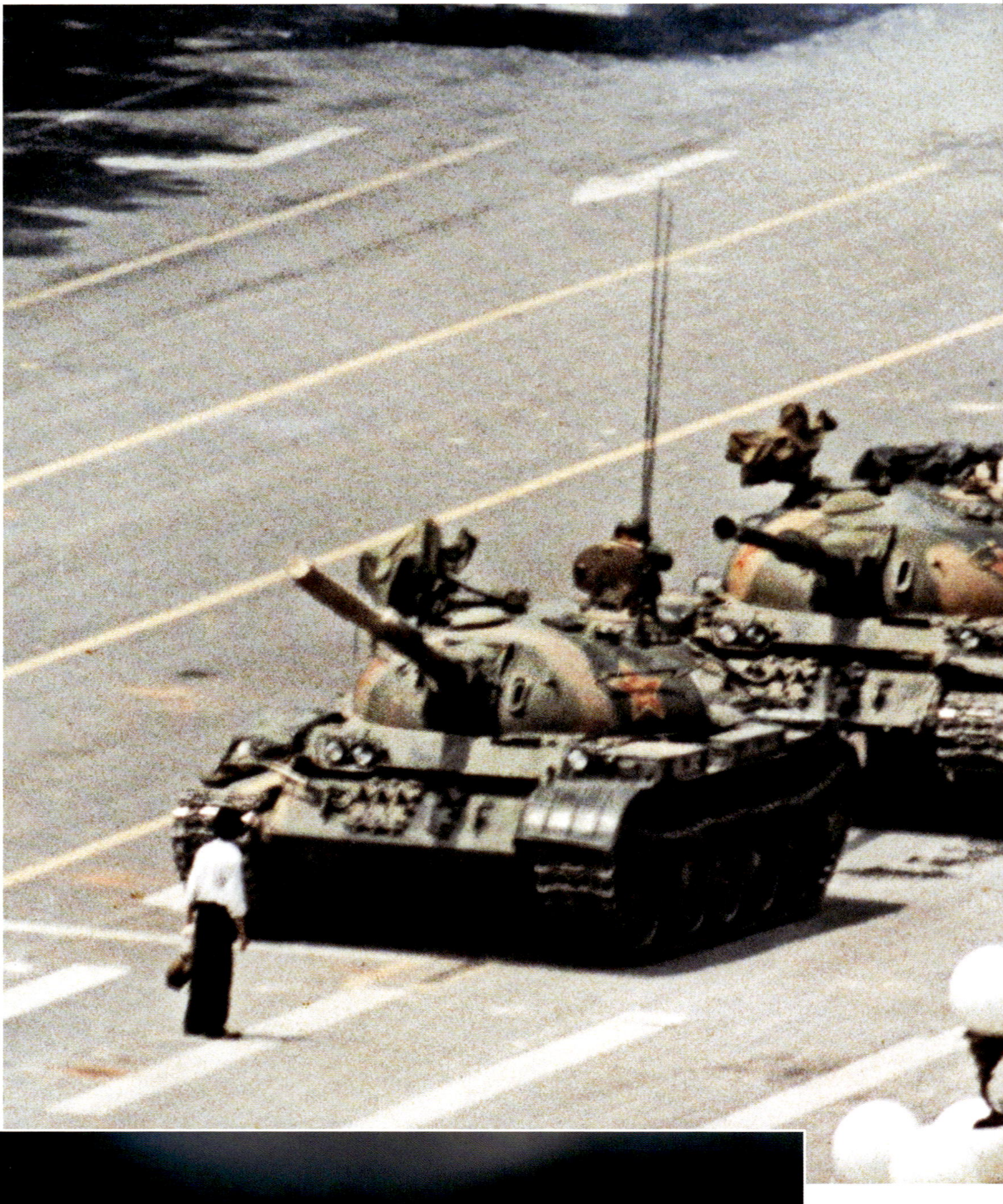

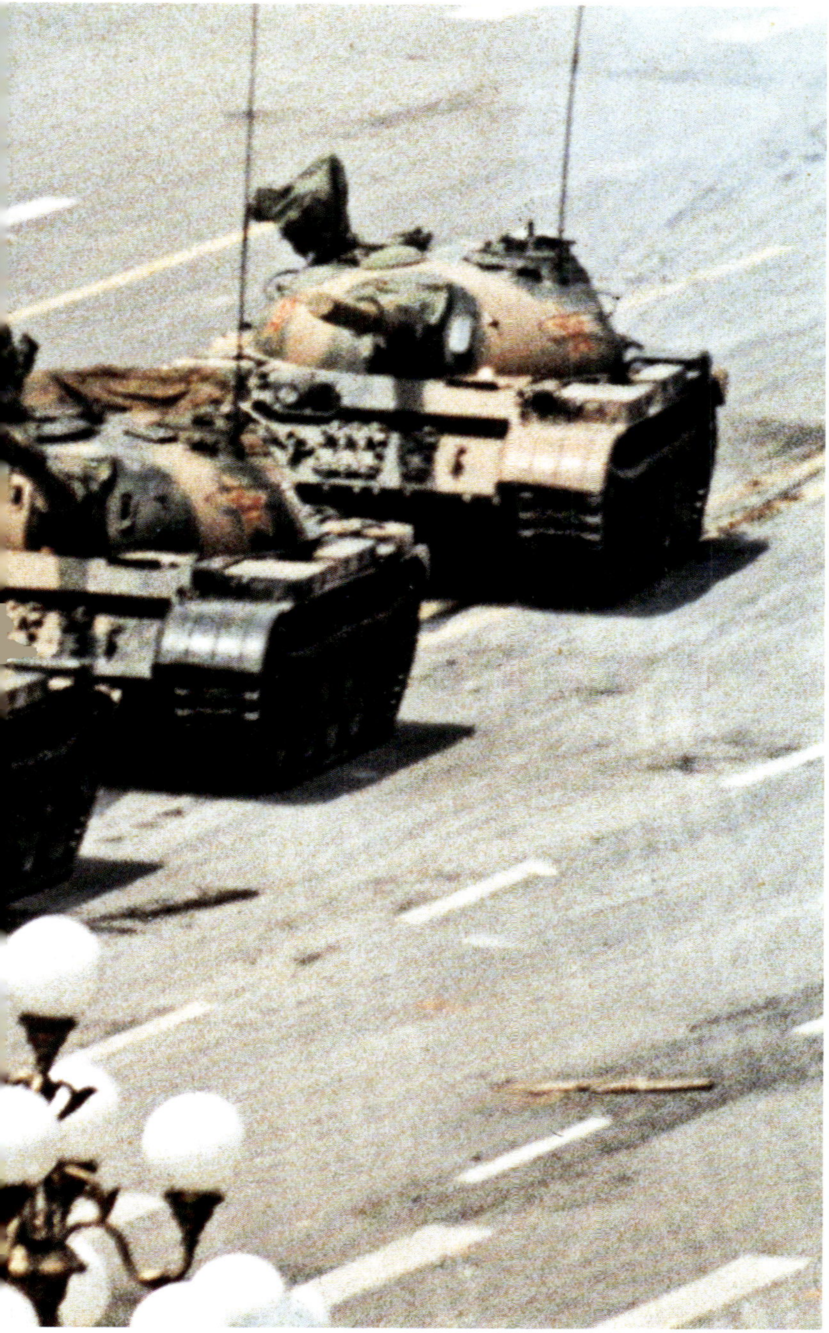

China

Jeff Widener's photo of the man standing in front of a tank ("Tank Man") has become a symbol of the popular uprising in Beijing and the violent suppression of the Chinese democracy movement in 1989.

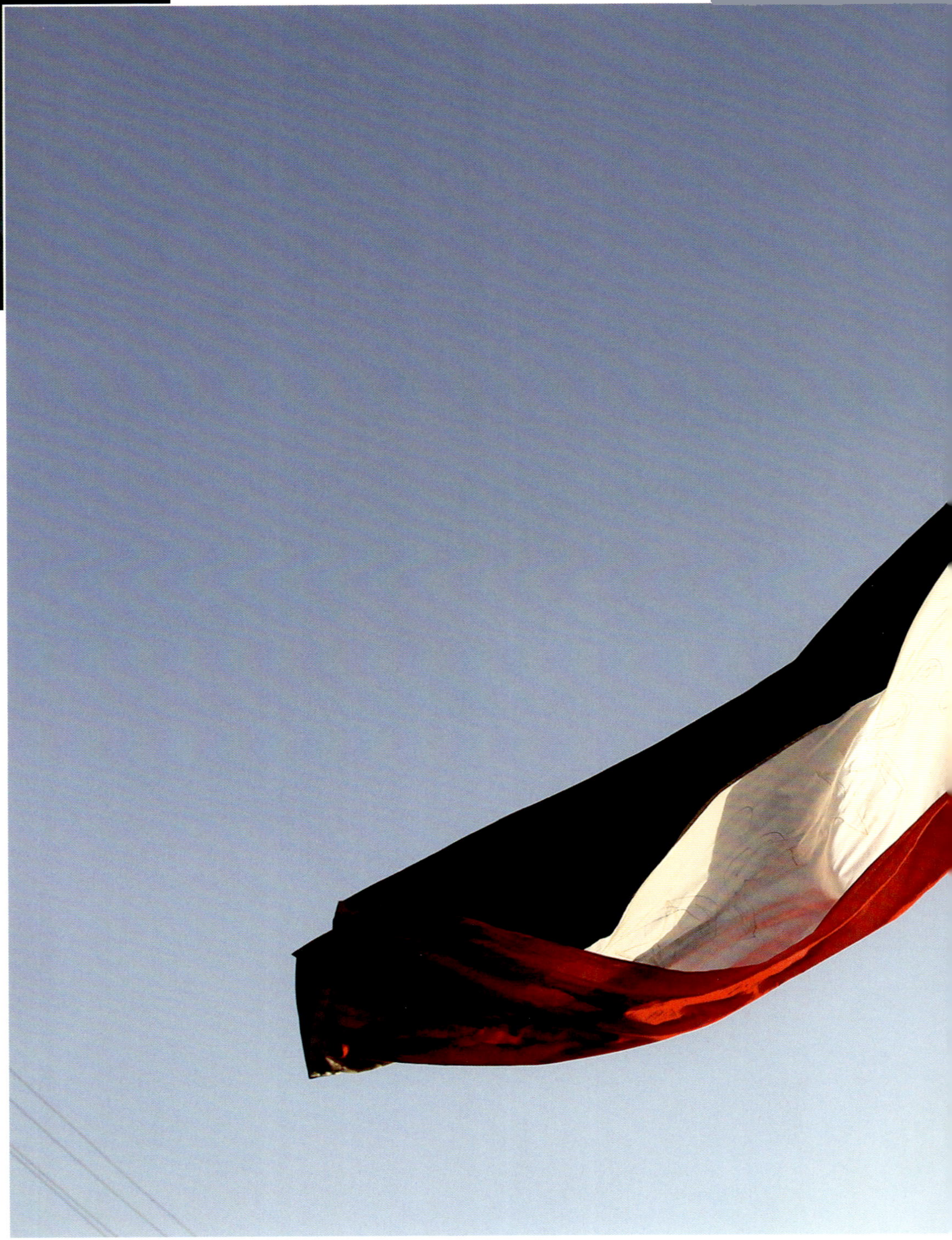

Egypt

Protesters wave an Egyptian flag atop a street sign at Tahrir Square in Cairo on January 29, 2011. Egypt's former president Hosni Mubarak gave the first indication that he was preparing an eventual handover of power by naming a vice president for the first time in thirty years after protests that had rocked the foundations of the state.

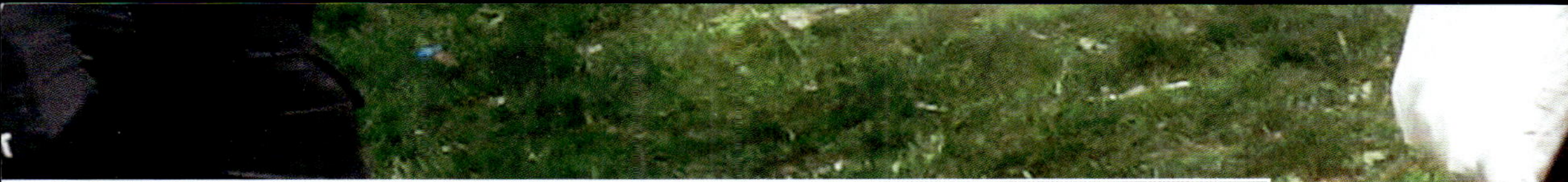

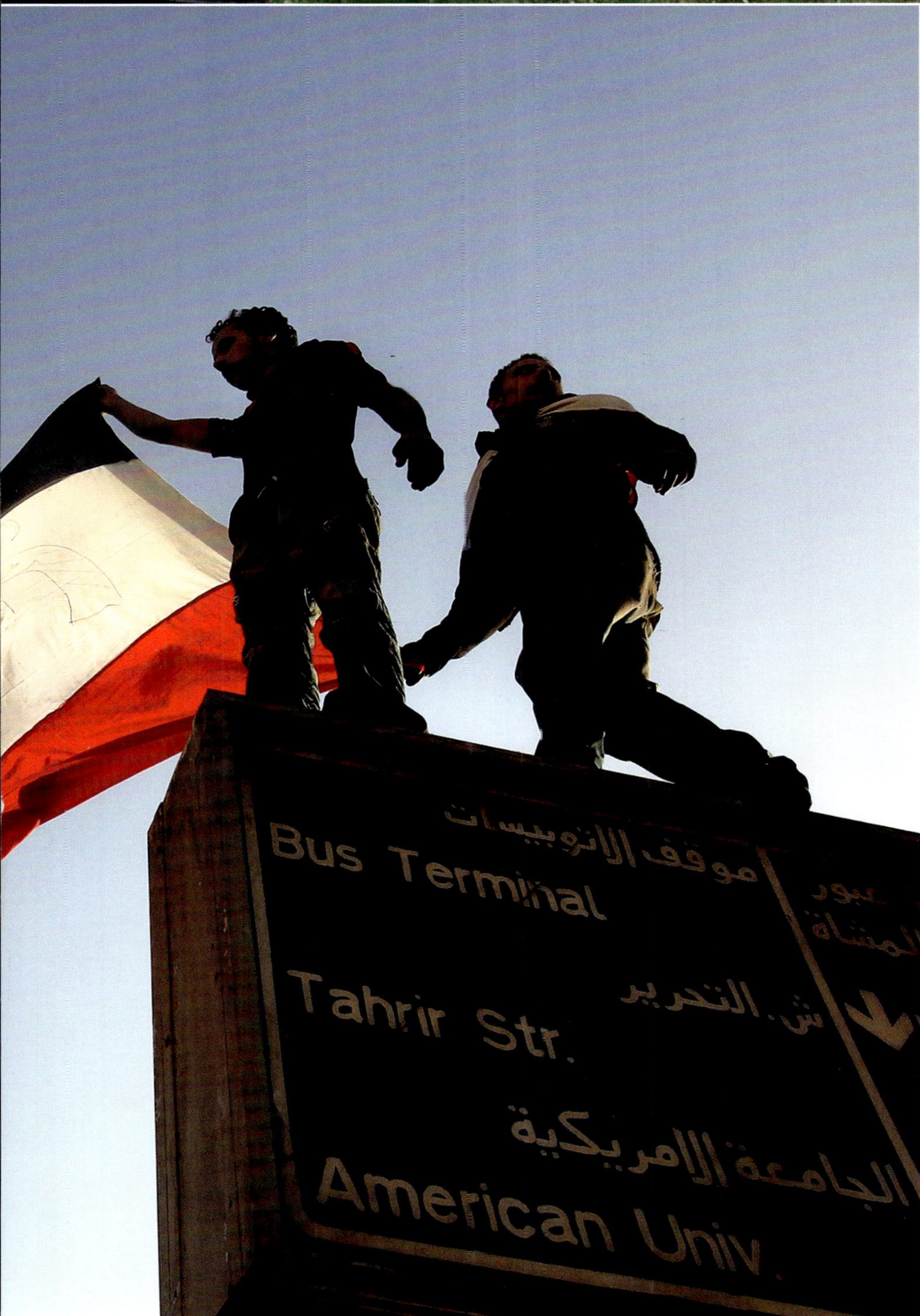
موقف الاتوبيسات
Bus Terminal
ش. التحرير
Tahrir Str.
الجامعة الامريكية
American Univ.

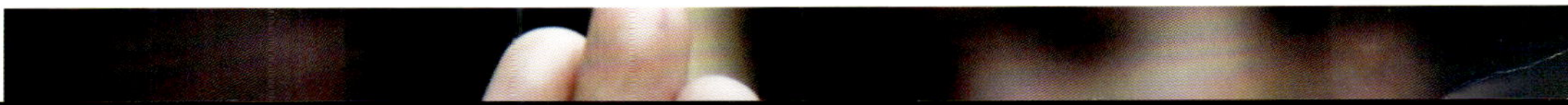

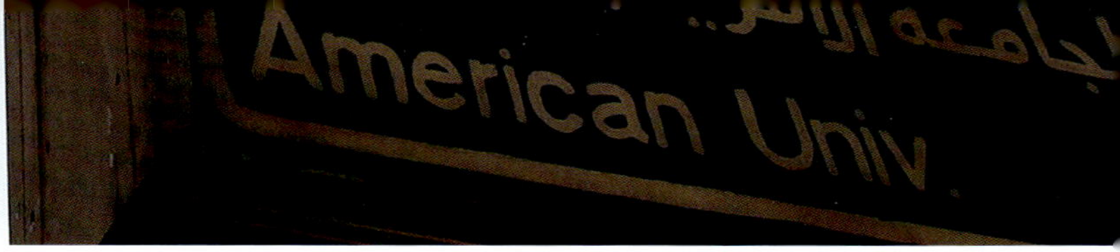
American Univ

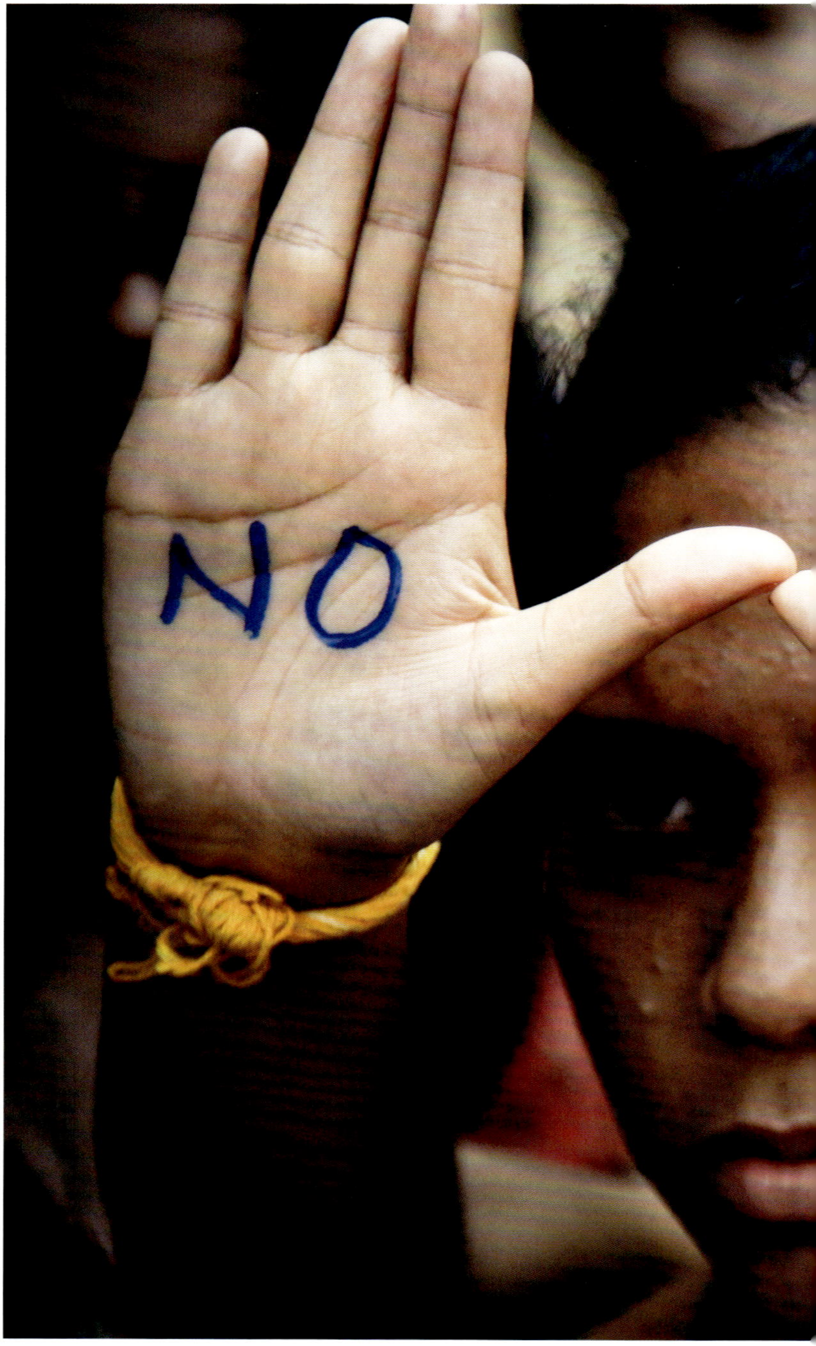
NO

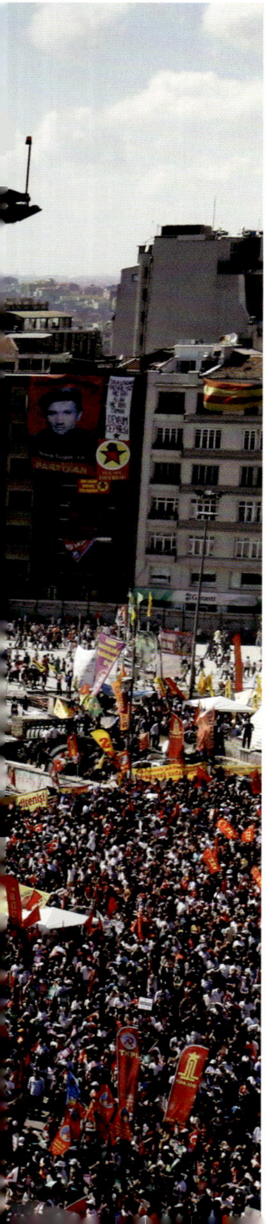

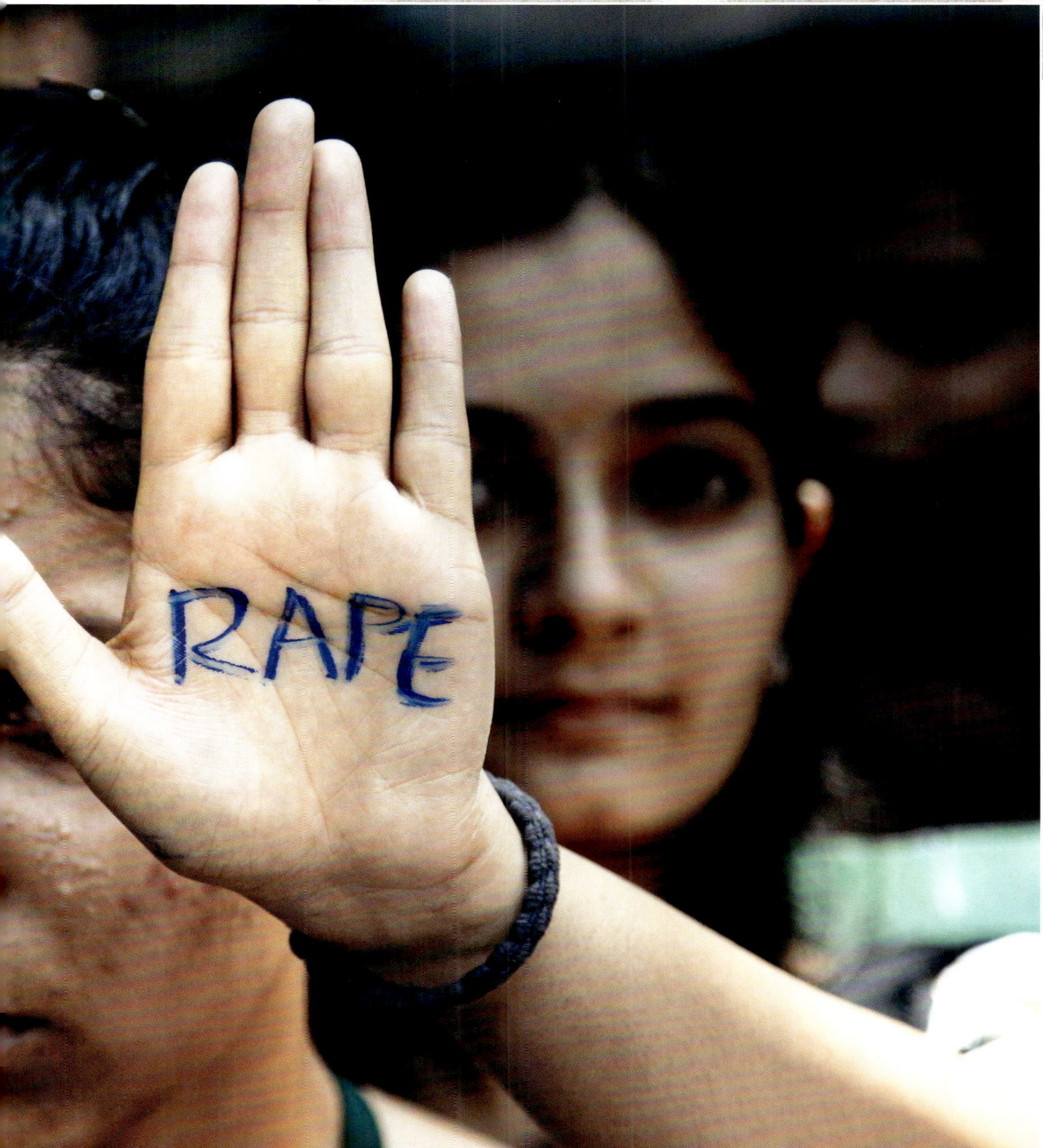

India

An Indian student displays the message "NO RAPE" painted on her hands during a demonstration in Hyderabad, India, on September 13, 2013 to demand the death sentence for four men convicted of the rape and murder of a student on a moving bus in New Delhi in 2012. A judge sentenced all four to the gallows for the brutal attack that left the young woman with such severe internal injuries that she died two weeks later.

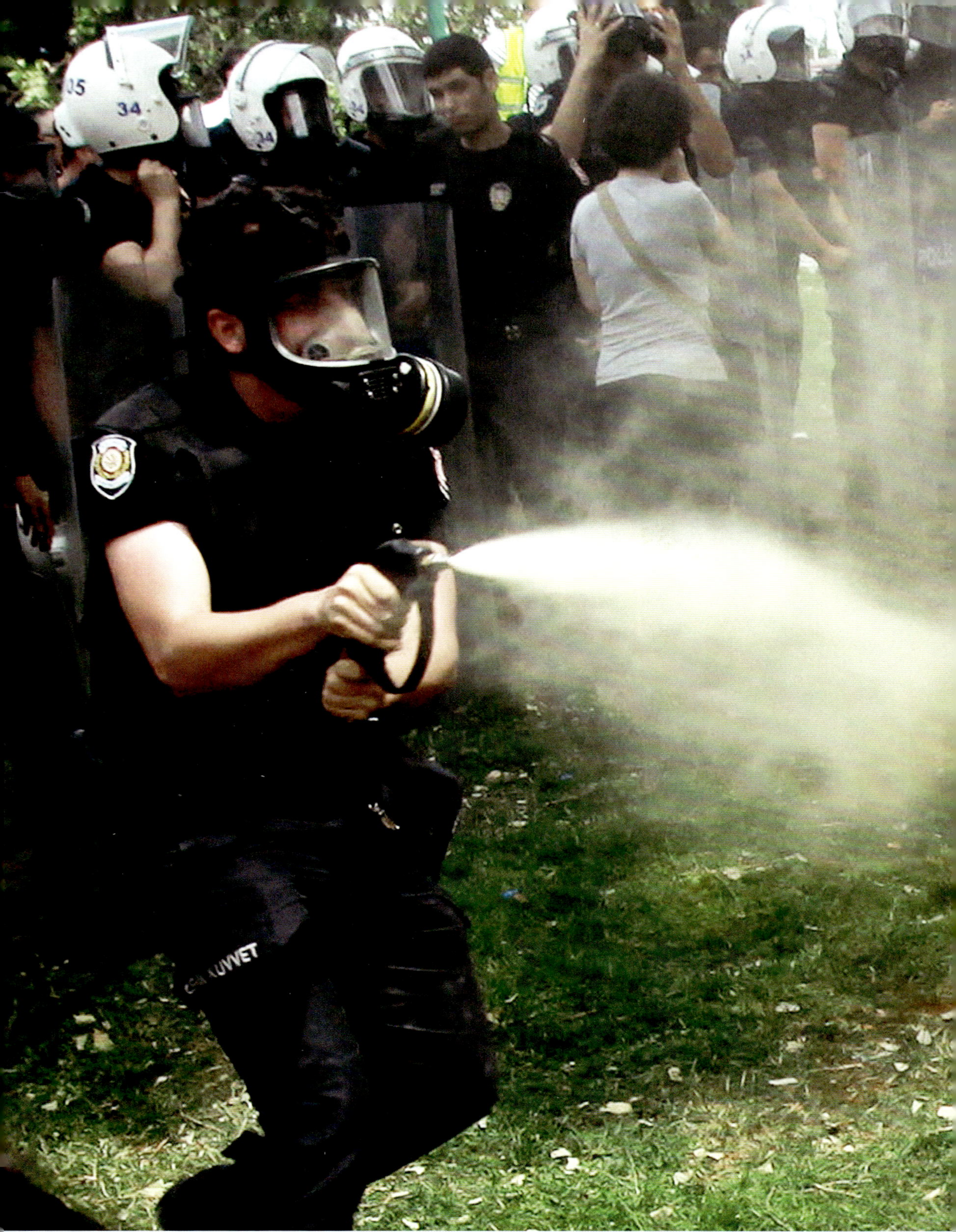

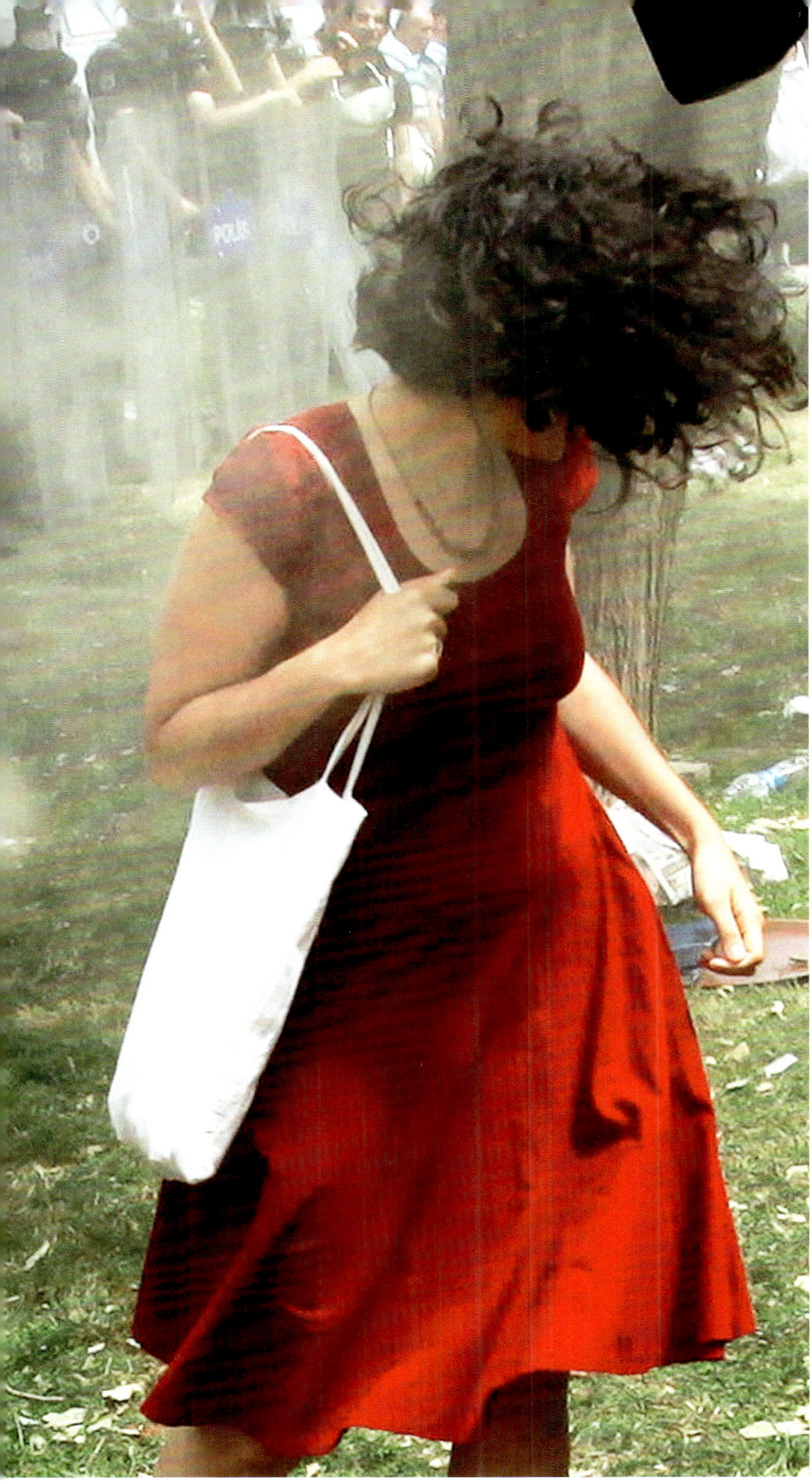

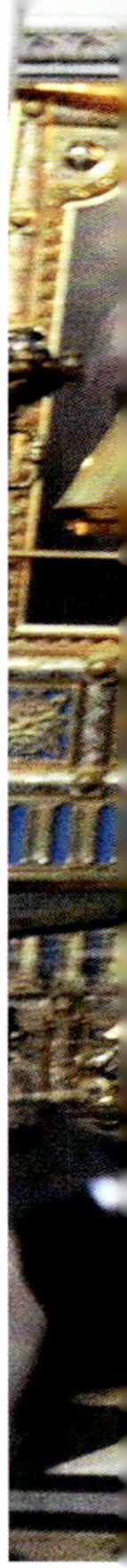

Turkey

A Turkish riot policeman uses tear gas against a woman as people protest against the destruction of trees in Gezi Park for a pedestrian development project in Taksim Square in central Istanbul on May 28, 2013. Endlessly shared on social media and replicated as a cartoon on posters and stickers, the image of the woman in red became the leitmotif for female protesters during the days of violent antigovernment demonstrations in Istanbul.

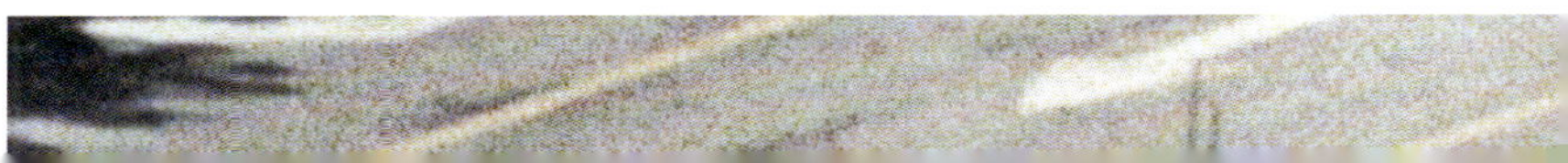

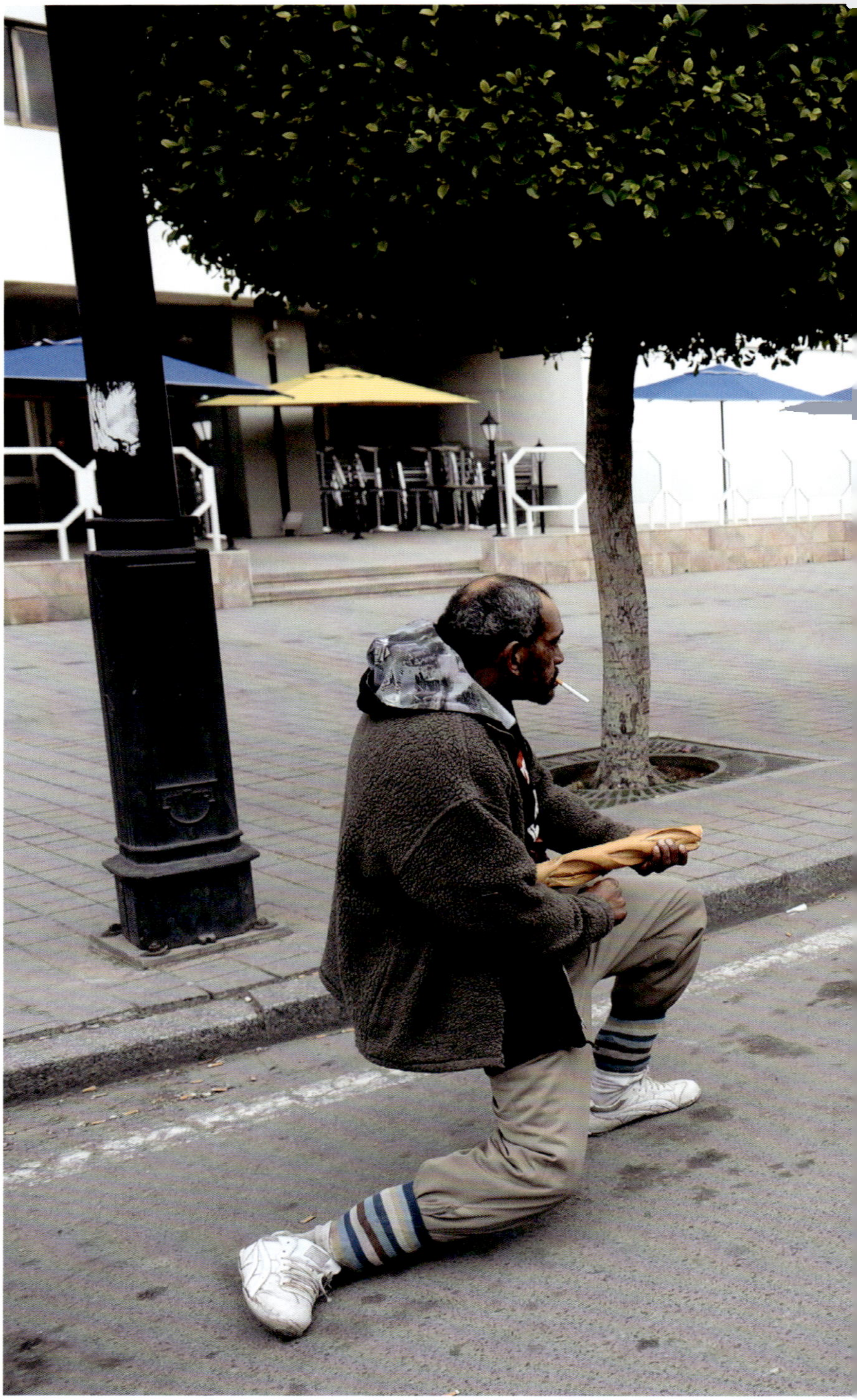

Tunisia

A Tunisian demonstrator holds his bread stick like a weapon in front of riot policemen during a protest against the country's new government in Tunis on January 18, 2011. About 180,000 Tunisians followed on social networks the adventures of a character called Captain Khobza [Captain Bread], inspired by this picture.

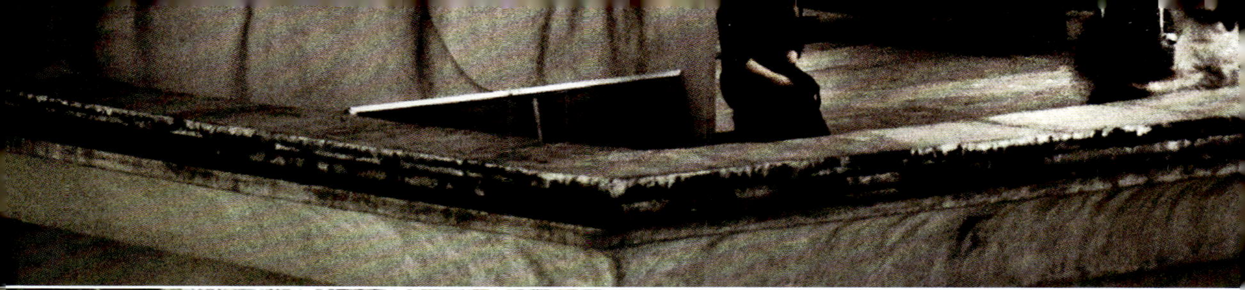

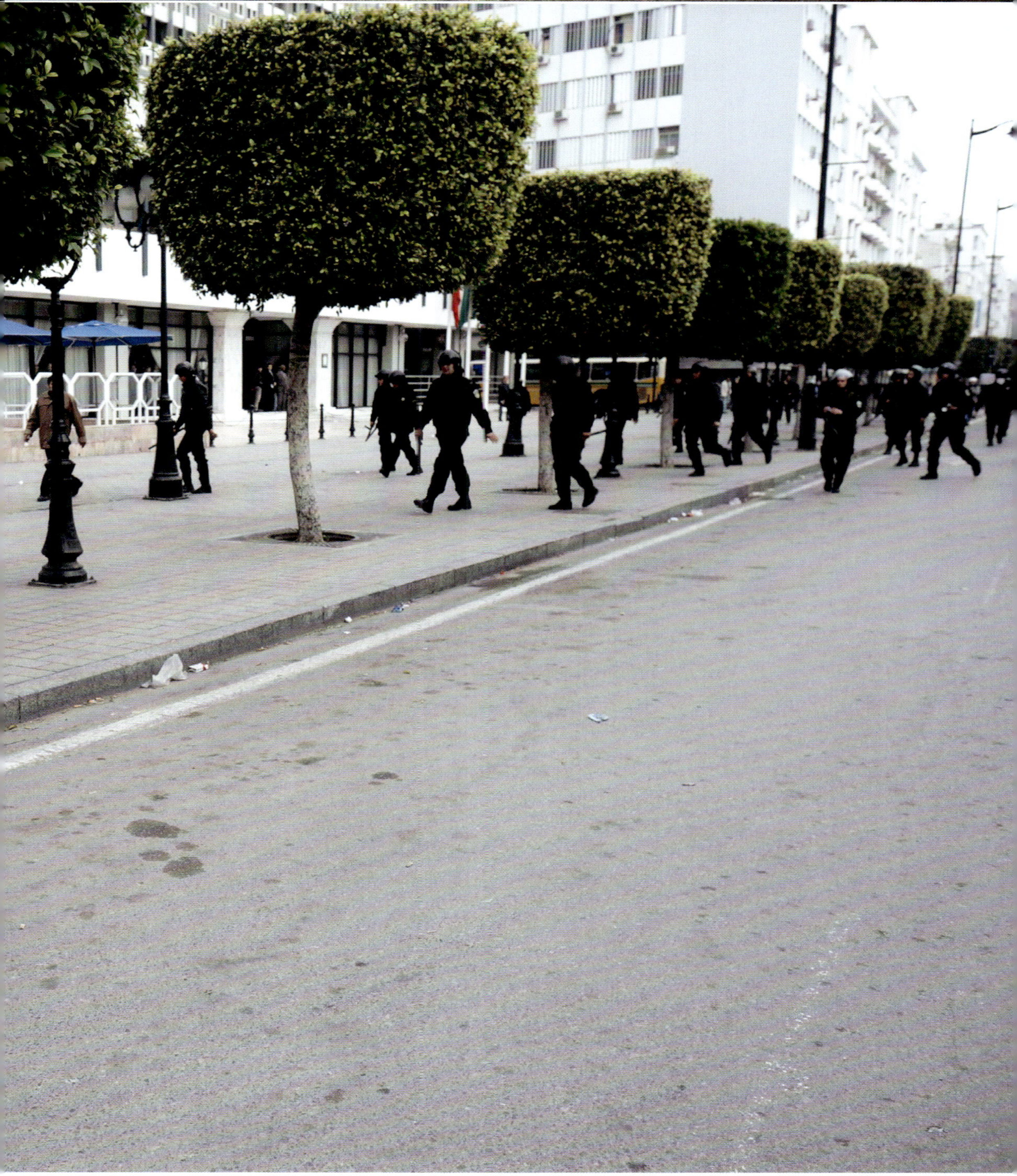

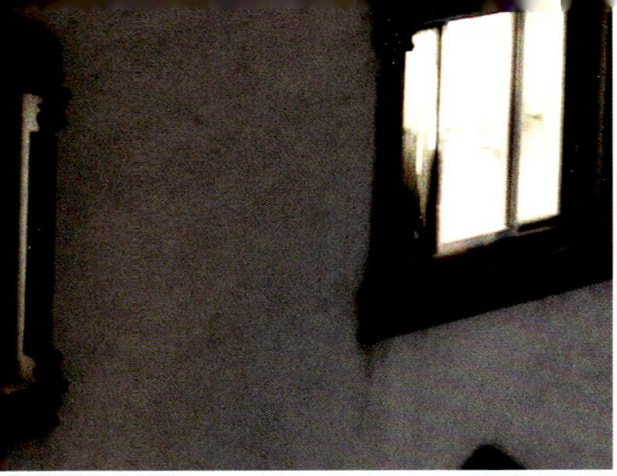

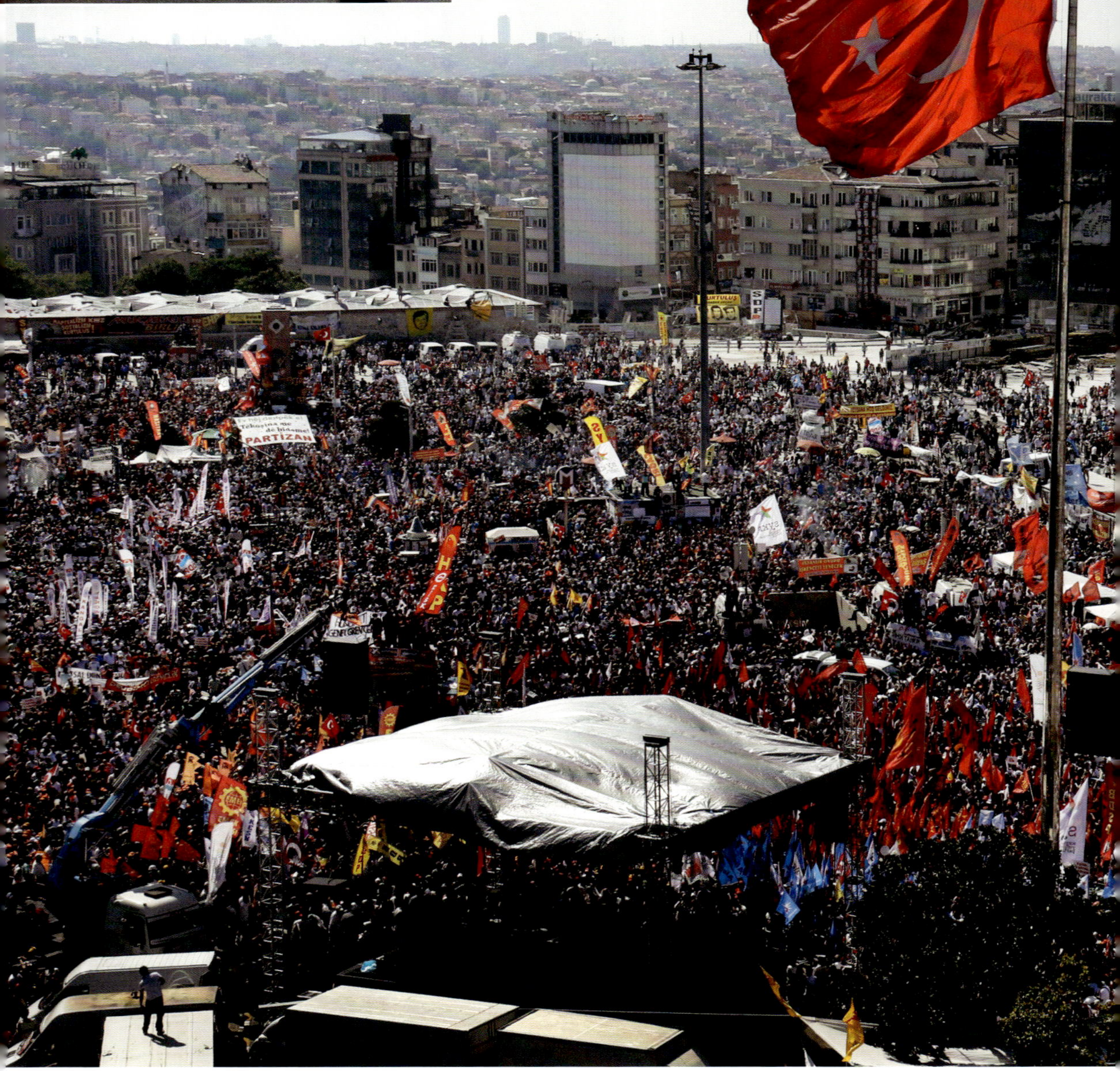
PARTIZAN

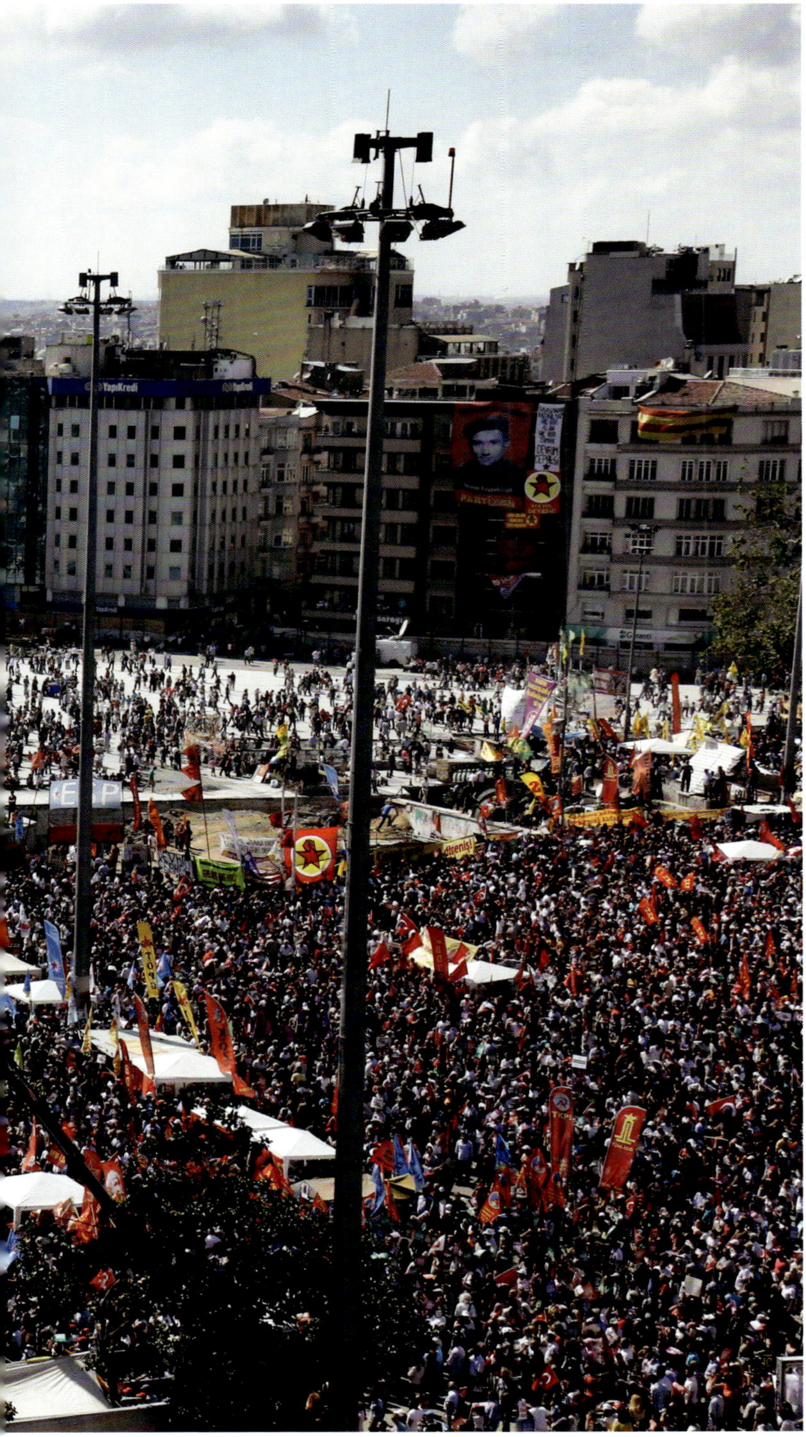

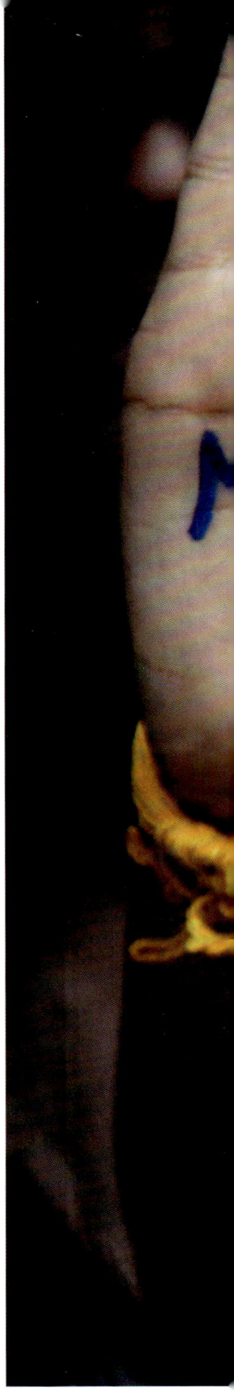

Turkey

Antigovernment protesters gather during a rally in Istanbul's Taksim Square on June 9, 2013. Turkish protest organizers called for a demonstration to keep up pressure on the government to sack those responsible for a violent police crackdown and to abandon plans to redevelop the central Istanbul square.

Iran

Iranian women hold up a picture and banners for the Iranian protester named Neda, killed during a protest against the Iranian elections, outside the Federal Building in Los Angeles on June 22, 2009. A video of blood-drenched Neda, purportedly killed in the Tehran protests, has become an Internet symbol of the demonstrations and it increased pressure on Iran in its battle with foreign media. The video, showing blood pouring from the nose and mouth of the young woman, was posted online and has since been viewed hundreds of thousands of times around the world.

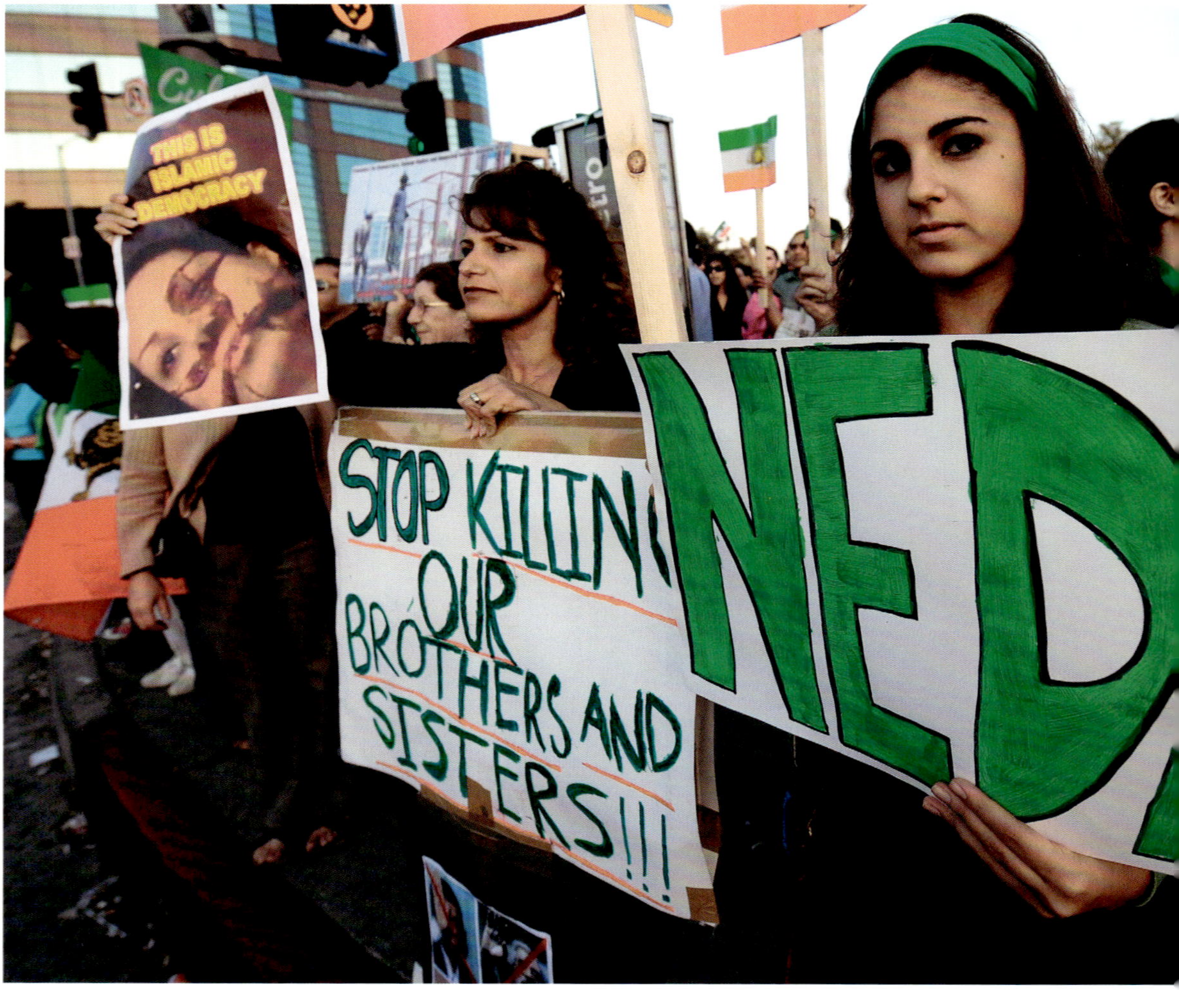

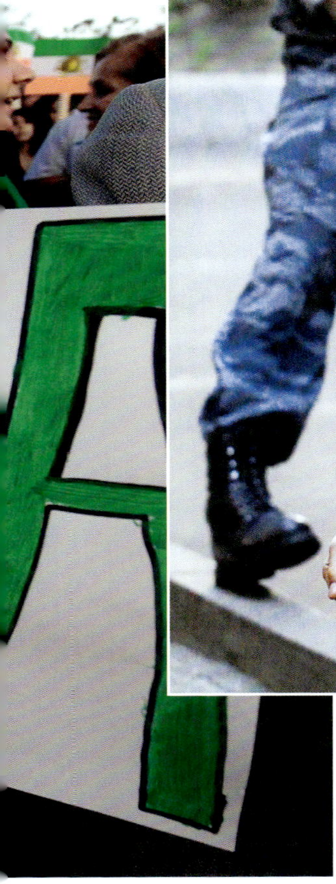

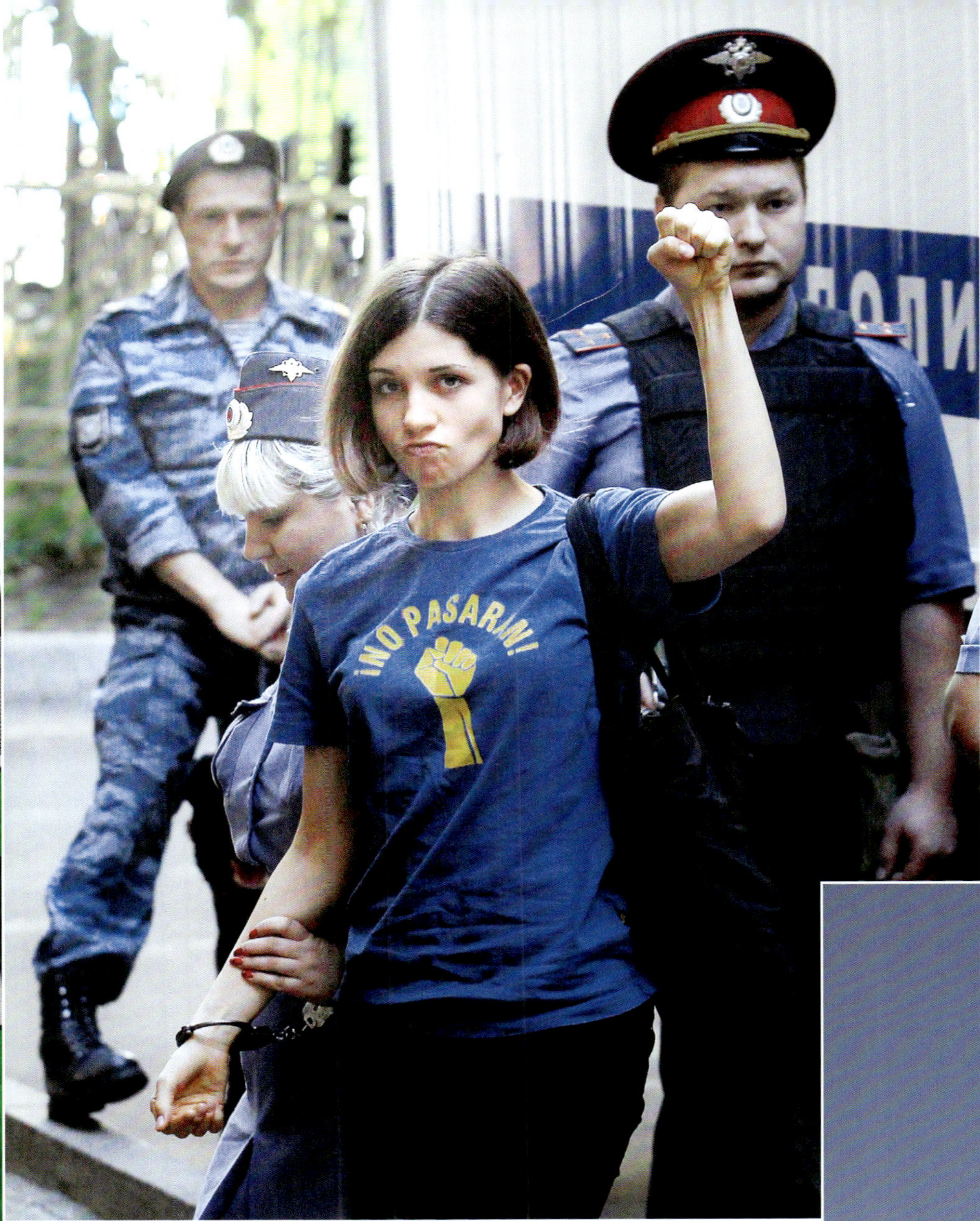

Russia

Pussy Riot punk group member Nadezhda Tolokonnikova gives a clenched fist salute to supporters as she is taken to Khamovnichesky district court in Moscow, Russia, on August 8, 2012. Three Pussy Riot members were accused of hooliganism in the Cathedral of Christ the Savior, where the group had played a protest song against the participation of Vladimir Putin in the presidential elections.

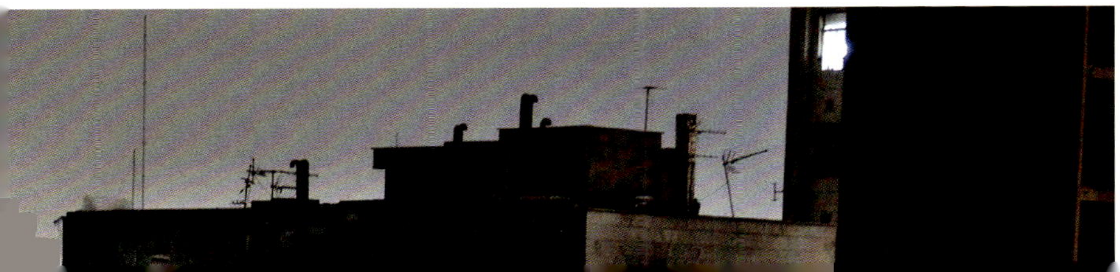

global activism

Art and Conflict in the 21st Century

edited by Peter Weibel

published by
ZKM | Center for Art and Media Karlsruhe, Germany
The MIT Press, Cambridge, MA / London, England

This book was published on the occasion of the exhibition
global aCtIVISm at the ZKM | Center for Art and Media Karlsruhe
December 14, 2013–March 30, 2014

2 Icons of Revolution
23 Peter Weibel, *Preface*
29 Peter Weibel, *People, Politics, and Power*

Chapter I
Activism and the Citizen

65 Robin Celikates, *Learning from the Streets: Civil Disobedience in Theory and Practice*
73 Bruno Latour, *War and Peace in an Age of Ecological Conflicts*
85 Ugo Mattei, *Institutionalizing the Commons: An Italian Primer*
100 Antonio Negri, *Living in a Time of Crisis*
111 Peter Sloterdijk, *Last Exit Indignation: On Neutralizing Civilians in Democracies*
119 Karl-Peter Sommermann, *The Right of Resistance: Approaches in Legal Philosophy*
129 Slavoj Žižek, *Don't Fall in Love with Yourselves*

Adbusters 132 — Amnesty International 134 — Anonymous 136 — Attac 137 — Olaf Bertram-Nothnagel, *lowercase d: Getting There* 138 — Nadir Bouhmouch 140 — Noam Chomsky 142 — Hassan Darsi 144 — Muath Freij 146 — Sacha Goldman 148 — Régis Debray, *Lead to Believe* 148 — Greenpeace 150 — Stéphane M. Grueso 152 — Stéphane Hessel, *The Hope of Continuity* 154 — Jim Hubbard 156 — Human Rights Watch 158 — Kein Mensch ist illegal 160 — Jan Jaap Kuiper and Katja Sokolova 162 — Lynn Lauterbach 164 — Let's Do It! World 166 — Museum of the Revolution 168 — No TAV 170 — Protests against Stuttgart 21 172 — rabble 174 — Resist 176 — Mykola Ridnyi 178 — Robin Wood 180 — Faten Rouissi 182 — Stop the Traffik 184 — Tanya Sushenkova 186 — Terre des Hommes 188 — The Yes Men 190 — Transparency International 192 — Malala Yousafzai 194 — Wango 196 — The Damascus Bureau 197 — Yezzi 197

Chapter II
Public and Private Sphere

201 Can Altay, *A Public Presence versus Greed, Brutality, and Control: Gezi Park*
207 Korhan Gümüş, *Liberating Public Spaces: Where to Start?*
211 Walter D. Mignolo, *Re:emerging, Decentring, and Delinking: Shifting the Geographies of Sensing, Believing, and Knowing*
225 Dimitris Papadopoulos, Vassilis Tsianos, and Margarita Tsomou, *Athens: Metropolitan Blockade – Real Democracy*
233 Slavoj Žižek, *Freedom in the Clouds*

!Mediengruppe Bitnik 242 — #StopWatchingUs 246 — Paolo Cirio 248 — Creative Commons 252 — Hedonist International 253 — Julia "Butterfly" Hill 254 — Mikaela 256 — Surveillance Camera Players 258 — Thomson & Craighead 260 — Troika 264 — Cyber Guerilla 266 — We Are the 99 Percent 267

Chapter III

How to Do Activism

271 Youness Belghazi and Hadeer Elmahdawy, *"Arab Spring Is Not Over, but Continues in a Different Way."*
279 Sarah Maske, *Activist Women's Rights Groups: Demands and Methods*
289 Rita Raley, *The Ordinary Arts of Political Activism*
298 Martha Rosler, *The Artistic Mode of Revolution: From Gentrification to Occupation*
315 Guido Strack, *Whistle-blowing as a Global Protest Movement and Its Relationship with the Law*
325 Bo Zheng, *Nearby Facts to Trouble the Emperor: A Note from China*

Zanny Begg 332 — John Beieler 334 — Campact 336 — Canvas 338 — Ralf Christensen 340 — Isabelle Fremeaux and John Jordan 342 — Sasha Kurmaz 344 — Julia Leser and Clarissa Seidel 346 — Partizaning 348 — Oliver Ressler 352 — The Riahi Brothers, *Everyday Rebellion: A Cinema Documentary, a Web Platform, and a Smartphone Application* 360 — Sandra Schäfer 366 — Kreativer Straßenprotest 368 — Politics Outdoors 368 — Take the Square 369

Chapter IV

Tactical, Social, and Global Media

373 Graham Meikle, *Distributed Citizenship and Social Media*
384 Marcus Michaelsen, *Beyond the "Twitter Revolution": Digital Media and Political Change in Iran*
396 Zixue Tai, *Finger Power and Smart Mob Politics: Social Activism and Mass Dissent in China in the Networked Era*

Johanna Domke and Marouan Omara 408 — Electronic Disturbance Theater 410 — Sharon Hayes 412 — kanalB 414 — MootiroMaps 416 — Taryn Simon and Aaron Swartz 418 — Tweets from Tahrir 420 — UK Uncut 424 — Christoph Wachter and Mathias Jud, *Crossing the Bosphorus with Tin Cans: How Global Networking Compels Self-Criticism* 426 — "We are all Majid" 436 — #occupygezi 438 — 0. 438 — Actipedia 439 — Anonymous News Germany 439 — Martin Balluch 440 — Facebook 440 — Freedom of the Press Foundation 441 — Independent Media Center (Indymedia) 441 — International Encyclopedia of Revolution and Protest 442 — Iranian Riots 442 — Meetup 443 — Meta-Activism 443 — Solitary Watch 444 — Twitter 444 — WikiLeaks 445 — YouTube 445

Chapter V
"Artivism" – Art and Activism

449 Sruti Bala and Veronika Zangl, *Humor's Opponents: Artistic Activism and the Ludic Aesthetic*
455 Tatiana Bazzichelli, *Networked Disruption: Connecting Art, Hacktivism, and Business in Political Struggles*
462 Dietrich Heissenbüttel, *Protest Everywhere?*
483 Sarah Lewison and Dan S. Wang, *In the Back of the Beyond: "What Time Is It on the Clock of the World?"*
493 André Mesquita, *Noises in the Concrete: Artistic Activism in São Paulo*
511 Joulia Strauss, *Demonstrations Are Performances*
515 Tatiana Volkova, *The Chronicles of Russian Activist Art*
531 Ahmad Zatari, *How the Jordanian Music Scene Missed the Arab Spring*
535 M. Ragıp Zık, *Raising Resistance: Reinterpreting Art within the Gezi Movement*

Ammar Abo Bakr and Ganzeer, *Street Art War in Egypt: An Interview* 544 — G.M.B. Akash 552 — ArtLeaks 554 — Bombily 556 — Ángela Bonadies and Juan José Olavarría, *La Torre de David* 558 — Osman Bozkurt 564 — Chim↑Pom 566 — Chto Delat? 568 — Colectivo Etcétera 570 — Enmedio 572 — Ramy Essam 574 — Noah Fischer 576 — Floating Lab Collective 578 — Jakob Gautel and Jason Karaïndros 582 — Erdem Gündüz, *The Meaning of Freedom–Excerpts from an Interview with the Turkish Artist Erdem Gündüz* 584 — Ed Hall 590 — Brian Haw and Mark Wallinger 592 — Idis Hartmann and Peter Weibel, *State Britain: Activist Art vs. Artistic Activism* 592 — Niklas Hoffmann and Rebecca Meining 598 — Alexey Iorsh 600 — Just Do It. 602 — Amadou Kane Sy 604 — Thomas Kilpper 606 — Kiss my Ba 610 — Mischa Kuball 612 — Christopher LaMarca 614 — Mohammed Laouli 616 — Viktoria Lomasko 618 — Renzo Martens 620 — Masasit Mati 622 — MediaImpact 624 — MindBomb 626 — Carlos Motta 628 — MTL 630 — Nitasha Dhillon, Amin Husain, and Yates McKee, *#Occupy Wallst: A Possible Story* 631 — Neozoon 640 — Christof Nüssli and Christoph Oeschger 642 — Jean-Gabriel Périot 644 — Platform 646 — Pussy Riot 648 — R.E.P. 650 — Itamar Rose and Yossi Atia 652 — Bahia Shehab 654 — SOSka group 656 — Joulia Strauss with Moritz Mattern 658 — Jackie Sumell, *The Best Activism Is Always Equal Parts Love and Equal Parts Anger* 660 — Teatro Valle Occupato 666 — Ugo Mattei, *The Valle Theater Commons Foundation: How to Deploy the Law in Current and Future Struggles* 667 — Patricia K. Triki and Christine Bruckbauer 682 — Voina 684 — Alexander Volodarsky 686 — Aalam Wassef 688 — Peter Weibel 690 — Yomango 692

694 Appendix
720 Icons of Revolution

Peter Weibel

Preface

For some years now, we have been seeing the rise of a new activism among critical citizens[1] all over the world, which was the focus of the *global aCtIVISm* exhibition that ran from December 14, 2013 to March 30, 2014 at the Museum of Contemporary Art at ZKM | Karlsruhe. The exhibition documented the approaches, tactics, strategies, and methods used in this "performative democracy," and by means of photos, films, videos, blogs, social media, and other documents disseminated through the mass media charted a first map of this global activism. The "artivism" that arises from the combination of activism and art is perhaps the twenty-first century's first new art form.

With *global aCtIVISm* ZKM continued its series of exhibitions which addresses the political and social changes brought about by new media that began with *[CTRL SPACE]. Rhetorics of Surveillance. From Bentham to Big Brother* (2001/2002), *Iconoclash. Beyond the Image Wars in Science, Religion and Art* (2002) through to *Making Things Public. Atmospheres of Democracy* (2005). The exhibition *Cross-border. Contemporary Female Artists from the Arabian Mediterranean Region* (2013), which documented the heroic struggle of female artists in this region, was what then prompted us to devise *global aCtIVISm*.

Global activism is a consequence of both globalization and technological advances. Globalization occurred in two phases: first, in the industrial, machine-driven revolution from 1800, and second, in the data-based information revolution since 1900. Digitization, the transition from an alphabetic to a numeric code, laid the technical foundations for the personalization of the media and the global networking of individuals. In the age of the monopolistic mass media (a product of the industrial revolution) each person became a recipient and only later, in the age of social media (a product of the information revolution), a broadcaster or sender. The Internet gave rise to new horizontal and transversal social structures.

We no longer live in a small-data environment, in which interaction between people and their surroundings is limited to a few data items, but in a big-data environment in which such interaction takes place more or less by the second. In the stimulus–response behavior between humans and environment not only has the volume of data increased immensely, but so has the frequency. Each person has to

1 See: Pippa Norris (ed.), *Critical Citizens. Global Support for Democratic Government*, Oxford University Press, Oxford, New York (NY), 1999.

process an ever greater volume of data in an ever shorter period of time. All the recipients respond almost simultaneously to every stimulus sent, generating greater communication and performance, and in terms of the "performative turn"[2] we construe this as increasingly changing the world of things by the transmission of signals and the response to them. As a result, we now talk of the Internet of Things.

In sharp contrast to this daily experience of the reciprocal influence of humans and environment via the new media, citizens in most representative democracies only have an opportunity to influence the major political decisions by voting every few years. In the highly technological lifeworld of the twenty-first century, such fundamental changes in both social relationships and in the relationships between humans and their environment are occurring that society seems to be overextended. The only term it knows to describe these changes is the concept of crisis; from climate crisis to financial crisis to the crisis of democracy (Peter Sloterdijk calls this a statist "neutralization of civilians"[3]). Today's protest groups, for example, the *indignados* or the Occupy movement, constitute new "cultures of repair" as it were, which search for ways out of these crises and the partial inability of politics to act.

The new types of spontaneous mass protests by individuals recently showed during the Arab Spring how established power systems can be upended, at least for a brief moment in time. Problems of democracy and the economy, above all corruption, are just as much the target of global activist protests as is the call for human rights to be observed, for peaceful solutions to global conflicts, for immigration policies that emphasize human dignity, for health care, for the protection of animal rights and the environment.

In the Anthropocene epoch we see conflicts between friends and enemies of the globe. For this reason, new tribunals and new contracts are aspired to between humans and nature (for example, in terms of sustainability), between generations and nations, between citizens and the state, and such agreements seem possible especially in a digital society. The first products of this extension of the legal sphere were the NGOs (nongovernmental organizations), which in recent decades have played an immensely important and preparatory role for global activism. One only needs to think of the high-profile campaigns captured in the global media and organized by Greenpeace, Amnesty International, and Transparency International, amongst others. Evidently, large parts of society think that not only does the state not protect civil rights, on the contrary, it actually violates them. For this reason, citizens have created new forms of organization to perform this task themselves. In the wake of the global city[4] and global governance[5] we are now witnessing a new form of social action centered around "global citizens." They represent the survival interests of all humanity and of the Earth itself which are disregarded by individual states. Global activism thus arises on the bedrock of "global citizenship."

Performance-based interventions by artist collectives and individuals combined with distribution through the mass media have shown how activists can make a real contribution to overcoming crisis situations by being unequivocal about problematic conditions, often using artistic means to do so. The practices of artistic performances and the participation of the audience, which have existed in art since the 1960s, are now making inroads into the sphere of politics. The expansion of the arts associated with the "exit from the image"[6] has spelled its entry into politics. The participation of the audience in art has morphed into the participation of the citizens in the sphere of politics. Global activism not only relies on "classical" basic rights, such as freedom of assembly, or the instruments of direct democracy, such as citizens' initiatives, but also on artistic, performative practices. A new form of public art is emerging, namely public politics. We are witnessing the evolution of a "performative democracy," a social model that was already anticipated in the performative and interactive (media) arts. The *global aCtIVISm* exhibition and, moreover, the present publication, highlight the parallels between performative, interactive, and participative art forms and global activism.

The present publication is divided into five main themes, each of which is addressed in extensive essays and numerous positions adopted by artists and activists.

Chapter I, "Activism and the Citizen," provides the theoretical foundation. The authors discuss the state of the modern *res publica* as well as the very different varieties of participative democracy, ranging from civic participation to participation in political opinion formation and decision-making, and to resistance and civil disobedience. The focus is on elaborating the right to resistance in terms of the philosophy of law, as well as social perspectives, such as the idea of the commons.

Chapter II, "Public and Private Sphere," outlines how activism asserts and establishes a new form of public sphere by inverting traditional relationships. Increasingly we are seeing the occupation of public spaces by private persons, as well as the publication of

2 See: John Langshaw Austin, *How to Do Things With Words*, The Clarendon Press, Oxford, 1962.

3 Peter Sloterdijk, "Last Exit Indignation: On Neutralizing Civilians in Democracies," this volume, pp. 111–118; originally published in German: "Der verletzte Stolz," in: *Der Spiegel*, November 8 2010, available online at: www.spiegel.de/spiegel/print/d-74948265.html, accessed 02/09/2015.

4 See: Saskia Sassen, *The Global City. New York, London, Tokyo*, Princeton University Press, Princeton (NJ), 1991.

5 See: The World Commission on Environment and Development, *Our Common Future* (Brundtland Report), Oxford University Press, Oxford, New York (NY), 1987.

6 See: Laszlo Glozer, *Westkunst. Zeitgenössische Kunst seit 1939*, DuMont, Cologne, 1981.

nonpublic information by private persons. The lines dividing the private from the public sphere are blurring. The political debate is shifting away from collectively managed and hierarchically structured institutions, away from parliaments to the press, to the individuals, who either on their own or in large groups seek a public presence, be it in local urban spaces or through the global mass media, in order to articulate global interests and concerns.

Chapter III, "How to Do Activism," offers an idea of how activism is constituted in both specific contexts and specific countries. The authors take a stance, for example, on the Arab Spring, on whistle-blowing, and on women's rights movements, and discuss different sides to activists' practice and the significance of symbolic languages and images. As regards the potential for nonviolent resistance, the immense reach of creative forms of protest and artistic interventions is explored.

Chapter IV, "Tactical, Social, and Global Media," focuses on the role modern communications technologies and social networks can play in the emergence and the actual course of protests, for example, in terms of processes of mobilization, information, and expressing solidarity. Further, selected examples demonstrate how relevant online real-time reporting is, which in many countries, such as Iran, Turkey, and China, has frequently triggered mechanisms such as obstruction or censorship, or led to existing repressive mechanisms being intensified. Innovative, technological, and artistic examples show how simple means can be used to circumvent controls and censorship.

Chapter V addresses the phenomenon of so-called "artivism" – the wide variety of ways of utilizing artistic means to intervene in socially relevant processes. Artivism refers to the interface of art and activism in the sense of a turning away from *l'art pour l'art*, art for art's sake, and also a turning away from twentieth-century art. This had turned its back on reproducing reality in images, that is, representing the world of objects, as early as 1900. Means of representation such as dots, lines, surfaces, and color no longer served to represent the world, but represented themselves. This spawned abstract art. With the banishing of the representation of objects, real objects forced their way into the art system. The result was the self-representation of objects, object art. In the course of the twentieth century everything that was representation was replaced by reality. And now, together with the new media, art for humans' sake is evolving. This art replaces the expansion of the concept of art with an expansion of the concept of the artist. Scientists as well as ordinary citizens can become artists, just as citizens and artists can participate in scientific projects, and artists and scientists can participate as citizens in politics. This is why we speak of "citizen artists" and "citizen scientists."

The exhibition and this book were only made possible by the enthusiasm and passion of the curatorial and organizational team. I would therefore like to thank most cordially the curatorial team of Andreas Beitin, Andrea Buddensieg, Elisabeth Klotz, Joulia Strauss, Tatiana Volkova, Philipp Ziegler, and our committed project manager Sarah Maske, who was ably supported by Sabiha Keyif, Linnea Semmerling, Annika Etter, and Elisa Kaiser. Moreover, I am deeply grateful to the entire team of the ZKM | Karlsruhe that contributed to the development of the exhibition. Our thanks go to Freddy Paul Grunert for pointing us in the direction of and getting us in contact with Teatro Valle Occupato and Ugo Mattei. Parallel to the show in the museum there was also an online exhibition – and here our thanks go first and foremost to Dietrich Heissenbüttel for managing the blog.

I would like to thank the ZKM Publications Department for the editorial work and copyediting of the volume, specifically Martina Hofmann, Katharina Holas, Caroline Jansky, and Eva-Maria Höllerer, headed by Jens Lutz. My special thanks go to the authors of the texts on the artists and activists: Martina Hofmann and Katharina Holas. I am grateful to Idis Hartmann and Anett Holzheid for the invaluable scholarly support provided for my own essay. I would also like to thank The MIT Press, in particular Roger Conover, for choosing to include the present volume in their marvelous publications list. Jan Kiesswetter and Niko Sinnger have created a wonderful innovative graphic design for the exhibition and catalog that most successfully does justice to the themes of both.

We are most grateful to the German Federal Foreign Office, the Goethe-Instituts in Egypt and Tunisia, and the German-Egyptian and the German-Tunisian Transformation Partnership for their financial support and idealism.

And above all I would like to thank the artists, the activists, those who loaned us works, the authors, and the speakers at the accompanying symposium for their marvelous contributions to the exhibition and to the present publication. Without their courage and unwavering sense of purpose, their expertise and intelligence, their humanity and their sense of justice, their commitment and their empathy, the world would look different.

Translated from the German by
Jeremy Gaines.

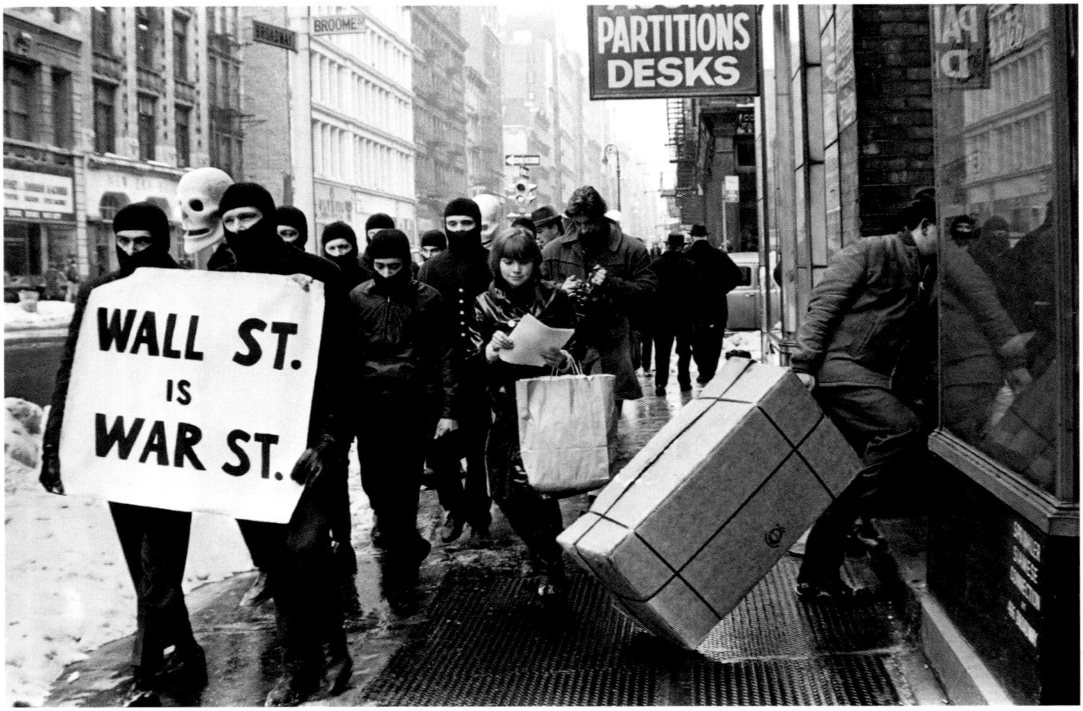

Black Mask, performance on Wall Street, New York, February 10, 1967

Black Mask was an artists' collective, founded by Ben Morea and Ron Hahne (later temporarily joined by Dan Georgakas, Allan Hoffman, Tony Verlaan, Everett Shapiro, etc.), which emerged from Group Center (Aldo and Elsa Tambellini, Don Snyder, Ron Hahne, Ben Morea, Jackie Cassen, Peter Martinez, etc.), a political artistic group, which had organized many subversive actions in New York in the early 1960s. Group Center had also realized various multimedia events like, for instance, *Black Zero* (November 1965).

Black Mask existed from 1966 to 1967, and then became the group Up Against the Wall Motherfucker, whose activities ended in 1969. Black Mask organized a happening-demonstration against the Museum of Modern Art in New York in 1966. In December 1966 they published the magazine *Black Mask*, no. 2 on *The Total Revolution*.

In the January 1967 issue of their leaflet the group stated: "We are creative men – revolutionaries. As creative men we are dedicated to building a new society [...]."* Then, on February 10, 1967, twenty-five masked men marched on Wall Street with the poster "WALL ST. IS WAR ST." This performance of Black Mask anticipated the Occupy Wall Street protests in September 2011. It is an example of how avant-garde artists moved their activities from the galleries into the streets and started social revolutionary movements. The Black Mask demonstration was maybe the model for all the future demonstrations of people in black wearing masks. It also shows the visual influence of art movements on social movements and foreshadows the future confluence of artists and activists.

* "Art and Revolution," in: *Black Mask*, vol. 3, January 1967, p. 3, as quoted in: Gavin Grindon, "Poetry Written in Gasoline: Black Mask and Up Against the Wall Motherfucker," in: *Art History*, vol. 38, no. 3, February 2015, pp. 170–209, here p. 183.

I. The Invention of the Government

Peter Weibel

People, Politics, and Power

"Who governs?" has for millennia been a key issue for all communities. One answer is: "The government." The logical sequence of questions that then follow is: "What kind of government?" and "Who forms the government?" There are many answers to these: the monarch, the dictator, the Pope, the oligarch, the parliament, and – the people. In other words, it is not governance itself that is questioned, but the form it should take. But the very question "Who governs?" needs to be interrogated. We should ask: "So who's asking the question" and "What purpose is behind the question?" Why are there even reasons to ask about this? The question is itself a trap. For the logical answer to the question "Who governs?" can only be: the government. The question predetermines the answer. The answer is part of the question. Question and answer are a tautology. The questions should at least be: "What does *government* mean? Do we need a government? How do we want to be governed?[1] Only anarchists ask whether any form of rule is needed and suggest it is not. Advocates of all other currents in political philosophy only ask what the best form of governance is. Governance itself is therefore not a controversial notion for most of them. Democracy, by contrast, is a form of government that is the object of much controversy.

Today, at a time when democracy is seemingly in crisis, it is all the more urgent that we find an answer to the question "Who governs?" which Robert A. Dahl posed in book form as long ago as 1961.[2] There is much talk of "facade democracy,"[3] simulative democracy,[4] defective democracy,[5] unpolitical democracy,[6] and postdemocracy.[7] The specter of the end and the collapse of democratic systems is thus doing the rounds.[8] This discourse on the crisis in democracy not only stems from a critique of capitalism, neoliberalism, and their structural difficulties and problems of legitimation,[9] but above all from growing ennui with politics, dwindling trust in democratic institutions and parties, and a desire for more participation, that is, for direct, presentistic rather than representative democracy.

On a closer examination of which form of government is criticized most, it emerges that the representative democracy such as exists in the West is the main butt of critique, meaning what is

1

How Do We Want to Be Governed? was the title of an exhibition project in 2004 curated by Roger Buergel in Barcelona on behalf of the Barcelona Museum of Contemporary Art (MACBA), preceded by a series of workshops entitled *Of Direct Action Considered as One of the Fine Arts* in 2002, also organized by MACBA.

2

Robert A. Dahl, *Who Governs? Democracy and Power in an American City*, Yale University Press, New Haven (CT), 1961.

from the Western perspective the most progressive and libertarian form of government. Surprisingly, the semi-democracies and dictatorships of South America, Asia, the Middle East, and Africa are less the subject of critical debate. On the one hand, this observation accords with the nature of the beast. The critical discussion of democracy speaks in favor of that form of governance and the freedom of opinion it provides, and it is clear that in dictatorships and semi-democracies in which there is very little freedom of speech, or indeed where it is dangerous to express an opinion, there is less discussion of the government. On the other, there are different notions of democracy, some more radical, others more moderate, driving the debate on democracy from within. It is thus part and parcel of democracy that it criticizes itself most of all, as the issues are: "What is democracy?" and "What is an ideal democracy or the ideal democracy model?"

We can distinguish between three fundamental models of representative democracies: In the first, the electoral or rather minimalist model, democracy signifies holding free, equal, and secret ballots, which, or so Joseph A. Schumpeter suggested, function like the market, like the interplay of supply and demand.[10] The parties offer their programs like products and the buyers (the citizens) can choose freely between them and after a few years have the opportunity to reassess the products, meaning vote a party back into office or vote it out.

The second, proceduralist democracy model calls not only for free elections, but also guaranteed human, basic, and civil rights.[11] The constitutional state, with its division of executive, legislative, and judiciary, has (since Montesquieu's day) been a core element of democracy. Citizens' political participation here is not meant to be limited merely to casting a vote, with opportunities for participation in the form of referendums, direct grassroots polls, public activities, and debates destined to ensure representation of the various interests in society is not simply left to the political parties.[12]

The third, maximalist democracy model is social democracy, the welfare state, which guarantees social security and justice. As early as 1950 in his essay "Citizenship and Social Class"[13] Thomas Humphrey Marshall highlighted the problematic relationship between the capitalist economy (inequality) and political democracy (equality). In the current debate on civil society and civil rights, people are once again drawing on Marshall's ideas. As part of global protest movements, we are seeing a veritable renaissance of his concept of *social citizenship*, which confers equal civil, political, and social rights on all citizens.

There is no doubt that citizens are expressing their growing discontent with representative, liberal, pluralist democracy – and above all with the totalitarian regimes – and calling for political rights of participation that go far beyond the rights that democratic institutions currently offer them. For this reason they are increasingly joining forces to form social protest movements, NGOs, and interest groups, seeking direct forms of democratic participation and referendums, and calling for the clear participation in political processes, for example, a right to be consulted when it

3 Peter Bofinger, Jürgen Habermas, and Julian Nida-Rümelin, "Einspruch gegen die Fassadendemokratie," in: *Frankfurter Allgemeine Zeitung*, August 3, 2012, no. 180, p. 33, available online at: http://www.faz.net/aktuell/feuilleton/debatten/europas-zukunft/kurswechsel-fuer-europa-einspruch-gegen-die-fassadendemokratie-11842820.html, accessed 04/01/2015; here quoted from: Wolfgang Streeck, *Gekaufte Zeit. Die vertagte Krise des demokratischen Kapitalismus*, Suhrkamp, Berlin, 2013, p. 241.

4 See: Ingolfur Blühdorn, *Simulative Demokratie. Neue Politik nach der postdemokratischen Wende*, Suhrkamp, Berlin, 2013.

5 See: Wolfgang Merkel et al., *Defekte Demokratien*, vol. 1: *Theorien*, Leske + Budrich, Opladen, 2003; vol. 2: *Regionalanalysen*, VS Verlag für Sozialwissenschaften, Wiesbaden, 2006.

6 See: Danny Michelsen and Franz Walter, *Unpolitische Demokratie. Zur Krise der Repräsentation*, Suhrkamp, Berlin, 2013.

7 See: Colin Crouch, *Post-Democracy*, Polity Press, Cambridge, 2004; Jacques Rancière, *Hatred of Democracy*, Verso, London, 2006; Sheldon S. Wolin, *Democracy Incoporated. Managed Democracy and the Specter of Inverted Totalitarianism*, Princeton University Press, Princeton (NJ), 2008.

8 See: Juan J. Linz, *The Breakdown of Democratic Regimes. Crisis, Breakdown, and Reequilibration*, edited by Juan J. Linz and Alfred Stepan, The Johns Hopkins University Press, Baltimore (MD), 1978; John Keane, *The Life and Death of Democracy*, Simon & Schuster, London, 2009.

9 See: Claus Offe, *Strukturprobleme des kapitalistischen Staates. Aufsätze zur Politischen Soziologie*, Suhrkamp, Frankfurt am Main, 1972; James O'Connor, *The Fiscal Crisis of the State*, St. Martin's Press, New York (NY), 1973; Jürgen Habermas, *Legitimation Crisis*, Polity Press, Cambridge, 1988.

10 See: Joseph Alois Schumpeter, *Capitalism, Socialism, and Democracy*, Harper & Brothers, New York (NY), 1942.

comes to planning infrastructure projects. Citizens want not only to vote, but to play a part in governing. The current answer to the question of "Who governs?" is thus: The citizens, too!

The mutual antagonism of capitalism and democracy, and since World War II it has been somewhat pacified by a kind of credit-driven arranged marriage, was subjected at the beginning of the twenty-first century to a renewed dose of conflict by the global financial crisis. There are too many treatises on the financial crisis to quote them all. But most of the authors share the opinion that the trenches between capitalism and democracy are becoming ever deeper and unbridgeable. During the crisis, it was theorists and writers who recited Adam Smith's creed of the invisible hand (i.e., the market's ability to regulate itself) as if it were a mantra, and demonized the state as an enemy of the market, of all people who were to be heard calling for the state to save the banks. The state became the banks' booty by first shouldering their obligations or, with the help of central banks, flooding the markets with money to buttress banks' liquidity.[14]

The hegemonic political-economic system has, and this is particularly true of southern Europe, evidently not found an adequate response to the crisis of capital. Not only the financial elites, the banks, and the hedge funds failed during the 2008 financial crisis and in the Euro crisis that followed, but so did the governments. In addition to the fundamental structural and systemic problems, creditism, corruption, clientele politics, the wastage of public money, and an unjust fiscal system accelerated this failure by the state and the subsequent austerity policies that the rich governments in the north imposed on the poor nations in the south intensified the crisis still further.

The decision-making powers of parties, parliaments, and governmental institutions in the nationstates are currently being eroded in supranational political and financial contexts, from the EU to the World Bank. Central democratic institutions are thus seeing their significance dwindle and the traditional patterns of legitimation, such as general elections, are becoming less important. Citizens' groups enter these gaps in the depoliticized, damaged democracies. Citizens, therefore, set about taking into their own hands the requisite reforms that do not happen because low-income strata are excluded from participation and the high-income strata (at most 1 percent of the population) exert maximal political influence while avoiding social and political responsibility at all costs. Globally active corporations and oligarchs have created parallel worlds through tax havens and financial linkages where they duck almost all political, legal, or economic legitimation and yet possess all the greater influence over governments and the market. The inane way politicians resort to citing the "markets" when justifying their actions points to precisely this state of affairs; namely, that the 1 percent who are the world population's superrich are active beyond the pale of the sphere of politics and the state, and worse still, the politicians do not prevent this happening.

Given the real dwindling political options in a globalized economy and a neoliberal economy, something that considerably reduces the differences between the party programs and in which

11 See: Guillermo O'Donnell, "Horizontal Accountability in New Democracies," in: *Journal of Democracy*, vol. 9, no. 3, July 1998, pp. 112–126; Wolfgang Merkel, "Die Herausforderung der Demokratie," in: Wolfgang Merkel (ed.), *Demokratie und Krise. Zum schwerwiegenden Verhältnis von Theorie und Empirie*, Springer, Wiesbaden, 2015, pp. 7–42, here pp. 7–14.

12 See: Carole Pateman, *Participation and Democratic Theory*, Cambridge University Press, Cambridge (MA), 1970; Benjamin Barber, *Strong Democracy. Participatory Politics for a New Age*, University of California Press, Berkeley (CA), 1984; James S. Fishkin, *Democracy and Deliberation. New Directions for Democratic Reform*, Yale University Press, New Haven (CT), 1991; John S. Dryzek, *Deliberative Democracy and Beyond. Liberals, Critics, Contestations*, Oxford University Press, Oxford, 2000; Mark E. Warren, *Democracy and Association*, Princeton University Press, Princeton (NJ), 2001.

13 See: Thomas Humphrey Marshall, "Citizenship and Social Class," in: Thomas Humphrey Marshall, *Citizenship and Social Class. And other Essays*, Cambridge University Press, Cambridge (MA), 1950.

14 See: Amartya Sen, *Development as Freedom*, Alfred A. Knopf, New York (NY), 1999; Loretta Napoleoni, *Rogue Economics*, Seven Stories Press, New York (NY), 2008; Ulrich Schäfer, *Der Crash des Kapitalismus. Warum die entfesselte Marktwirtschaft scheiterte und was jetzt zu tun ist*, Campus, Frankfurt am Main, New York (NY), 2009; Dani Rodrik, *The Globalization Paradox. Democracy and the Future of the World Economy*, W.W. Norton, New York (NY), 2011; Immanuel Wallerstein, Randall Collins, Michael Mann, et al., *Does Capitalism Have a Future?*, Oxford University Press, New York (NY), 2013.

citizens can therefore no longer distinguish or choose between different alternatives for economic and social policy, the result is factually elections without choice. The real lack of choice is underscored by the fact that those in power, from Margaret Thatcher through Gerhard Schröder to Angela Merkel, constantly claim that "There Is No Alternative," or the TINA principle that Thatcher invented. It becomes the sole justification for their actions and for this reason citizens' thirst for nonelectoral forms of participation, for overcoming a merely electoral, minimalist democracy model intensifies.

Neoliberalism, deregulation, and globalized capitalism have supported the hegemony of antistate economic interests to the detriment of nationstate democracies. This is why many citizens, especially those in marginalized strata, are again asking themselves the question: "Who governs?" Central banks, supranational regimes like the EU, corporations that are global players, lobbies, the international financial markets, the World Bank, the International Monetary Fund, or democratically legitimated institutions? Economists and political scientists, such as Joseph E. Stiglitz, Paul Robin Krugman, Thomas Piketty, Jacob Stewart Hacker, and Paul Pierson, have given disquieting answers.[15] Key areas of financial, trade, and employment policy are assigned to private actors, global companies, and deregulated markets. The deregulation efforts in the USA and Europe in the 1980s and 1990s have squeezed democracies. Since economic parameters are now being set by banks, pension funds, hedge funds, major investors, and supranational financial institutions and not by national governments, economic inequality is on the up, and this threatens to turn into growing political inequality. Will we in future live in democracies in which a minority of the population politically marginalizes the majority of the low-income populace?

Conservative theorists also discern that there is a crisis in democracy, although they attribute the excess strain on democratic states not primarily to the economy, but to democratic mechanisms themselves, and as a result increasingly question whether democracy is the best form of government. Does the excessive strain on the state lead to democratic systems being ungovernable? The conservative question as regards the economic crisis therefore reads: "Is political democracy, as it exists today, a viable form of government […]?"[16] For the first time, the formula of democracy + capitalism = welfare state is being questioned, and some publicly suggest that possibly dictatorships and capitalism are more compatible, as for example in China. Everywhere you look there are signs that capital prefers a dictatorship and leaves democracy in the lurch when it comes to profits. The civil movements attack this, driven by the old chestnut: "Who governs and what is the best form of government?" Global activism has a new supranational answer to this.

Activists' deep dissatisfaction with existing democracies, above all with representative democracy, relate to the fact that they are not able to participate in the political process, or as a slogan by protest marchers would have it: "We have a vote, but we do not have a voice." With their protests they do not aspire to question or reject democracy, but on the contrary to highlight shortfalls in democracy and call for a radicalization of democratic institutions.

15
See: Jacob S. Hacker and Paul Pierson, *Winner-Take-All Politics. How Washington Made the Rich Richer – And Turned Its Back on the Middle Class*, Simon & Schuster, New York (NY), 2011; Paul Krugman, *End This Depression Now!*, W.W. Norton, New York (NY), London, 2012; Joseph E. Stiglitz, *The Price of Inequality. How Today's Divided Society Endangers Our Future*, W.W. Norton, New York (NY), 2012; Thomas Piketty, *Capital in the Twenty-First Century*, The Belknap Press of Harvard University Press, Cambridge (MA), 2014.

16
Michel Crozier, Samuel P. Huntington, and Joji Watanuki, *The Crisis of Democracy. Report on the Governability of Democracies to the Trilateral Commission*, New York University Press, New York (NY), 1975, p. 2.

Chantal Mouffe argues that Western democracies are based on two traditions: Liberalism, with its emphasis on liberty and pluralism, and democracy with its emphasis on equality and the people's sovereignty. Both concepts are essentially incompatible, she argues,[17] and therefore advocates the model of an "agonistic democracy."[18] A liberal, democratic society must offer alternatives and the various actors must be able to debate these. Conflicts should not be eliminated and an opponent must be able to accept defeat in the democratic process. For this reason, on the one hand Mouffe welcomes the civic movements' critique of the neoliberal hegemony that has hollowed out our democratic values, but does not believe that setting up "nonrepresentative" democracies are a solution to the democratic crisis.

It is precisely discontent with representative democracy that the civic movements articulate. Since the institutions of representative democracy have not found any effective measures with which to counter the growing inequality and to curb the influence of banks and investors on government and parliament, democracy has evidently lost position in key areas of its constitutional core.[19] Citizens do not despair as regards democracy, they doubt the ability of the institutions and parties in representative democracy to realize democracy. For this reason, new social movements that are not political parties or trade unions arise. A lack of trust has led to dwindling active support for representative democracy, and increasingly the social middle classes are giving birth to *critical citizens*,[20] who articulate ecological, cultural, and infrastructural interests, not to mention a focus on the politics of democracy. Even if it seemingly is only protest against railway stations, new rail tracks, streets or power lines, nuclear power, and tax increases, in reality these are all symbols of overall social responsibility. They are signals for responsive and responsible behavior. Given the shortcomings in real existing democracies, the protest movements around the world, ranging from the *indignados* in Spain to the Occupy movement in New York, seek to democratize democracy.

The answer to the question whether democracy is in crisis depends on what model of democracy we take as a yardstick. In most cases, critics demand the maximalist model of democracy, a socially just democracy. Since in recent decades social inequality has increased in the extreme, or so the report by British NGO Oxfam in January 2014 has found, according to which 1 percent of the global population has accumulated more wealth than the remaining 99 percent, and central principles of democracy have been damaged. According to Oxfam, the 85 richest people on Earth together own more than the poorer half of the world's population (3.5 billion people).[21]

This destabilization of democracy is also borne out by the philosophers of right. As a result thinkers such as John Rawls (*A Theory of Justice*, 1971), Michael J. Sandel (*Liberalism and the Limits of Justice*, 1982), and Amartya Sen (*The Idea of Justice*, 2009) have each tried to devise a theory of justice steeped in the philosophy of right that can function as the foundations for a politics of justice. In this context, formal studies on the inner consistency of democracies also play an important role. In his book *Numbers Rule*[22] George G. Szpiro

17 See: Chantal Mouffe, *The Democratic Paradox*, Verso, London, New York (NY), 2000.

18 See: Chantal Mouffe, *Agonistics. Thinking the World Politically*, Verso, London, New York (NY), 2013.

19 See the KOF Index of Globalization of the ETH Zurich, the Democracy Barometer – a project of the National Center of Competence in Research (NCCR) "Challenges to Democracy in the 21st Century," funded by the Swiss National Science Foundation – (democracybarometer.org), and Axel Dreher, "Does Globalization Affect Growth? Evidence from a New Index of Globalization," in: *Applied Economics*, vol. 38, no. 10, 2006, pp. 1091–1110.

20 Pippa Norris, *Critical Citizens. Global Support for Democratic Governance*, Oxford University Press, Oxford, New York, 1999.

21 See: Oxfam International, *Working for the few. Political capture and economic inequality*, Oxfam Briefing Paper, no. 178, January 20, 2014, available online at: https://www.oxfam.org/sites/www.oxfam.org/files/file_attachments/bp-working-for-few-political-capture-economic-inequality-200114-en_3.pdf, accessed 05/18/2015.

22 George G. Szpiro, *Numbers Rule. The Vexing Mathematics of Democracy, from Plato to the Present*, Princeton University Press, Princeton (NJ), 2010.

outlines the paradoxes and antinomies of representative democracy, from Condorcet's paradox[23] to the arrow theorem.[24] Majority votes and the allocation of seats in a parliament involve mathematical questions that can be described by simple arithmetic but which are surprisingly difficult, if not impossible to solve.

23 See: Jean-Antoine-Nicolas de Caritat Marquis de Condorcet, *Essai sur l'application de l'analyse à la probabilité des décisions rendues à la pluralité des voix*, Imprimerie Royale, Paris, 1785.

24 See: Kenneth J. Arrow, *Social Choice and Individual Values*, Wiley, New York (NY), 1951.

Democracy and the constitutional state are evidently moving ever further apart, and the discontent with democracy in its existing form is likewise growing. However, we repeatedly witness brief moments when citizens awake, from the above-mentioned idea of *social citizenship* (Thomas Humphrey Marshall, 1949) through to today's *citizen science*, a rekindling of notions from the eighteenth century. The crisis of democracy is essentially a crisis of representative democracy, because its institutions either exceed their constitutional rights or do not discharge their duties. The more dissatisfied citizens are with their governments, the more strongly they gain the impression that their governments are failing, the greater they consider the potential of those NGOs to be which concern themselves with fundamental democratic civil rights and defend these.

Without doubt: We are witnessing disenchantment with democracy. As long as the welfare state is able to deliver on minimum wages and social services by constantly raising tax revenues, peace prevails. For this reason, most political measures restrict themselves to trying to repair the deficiencies in representative democracies. But no party dares change the system of representative democracy, not least because the parties profit from the system and/or only exist on the basis of and within that system. Studies prove, however, that transferring decision-making processes to society strengthen the idea of democracy. It is not prolonging and strengthening the existing formal institutions of democracy that secures democracy's future, but changing them. Only participative innovations by critical citizens, who are often defamed by the press, by the agents of "manufacturing of consent,"[25] secure the future of democracy. Democratic experimentalism in the form of political participation over and above elections and outside of parliaments is the precondition for democracy to grow.

25 See: Edward S. Herman and Noam Chomsky, *Manufacturing Consent. The Political Economy of the Mass Media*, Pantheon Books, New York (NY), 1988.

The next wave of democratization will therefore be a trend towards developing a "performative democracy."[26] Global activism calls for the expansion of political sovereignty to include the citizen. Citizens want to participate in the political arena not just through elections but also by actions, for example, by determining budgets at the communal and national levels. To date, budget decisions have been taken by the local council or the parliament, depending on party majorities. Through party majorities parties control democratic processes. Now citizens no longer want just to be represented and vote, but to participate and to have a say in individual decisions. The civil rights movements and civil activism therefore ask the question "Who governs?" in a new way. They search for new forms of government, and above all prefer those forms that promise to deliver a high degree of participation. Participative democracy in which the citizens are involved in decision-making and are active is thus the new answer to the old question of "Who governs?"

26 See: Peter Weibel, "Von der repräsentativen zur performativen Demokratie. Zum Verhältnis von Kunst und Demokratie," in: *ARCH+*, vol. 204, October 22, 2011, pp. 126–129.

In 1962, linguist John Langshaw Austin defined linguistic utterances in his *How to Do Things with Words* as speech acts that not only describe the world, but also change it and create a new state of affairs. The efficacy of verbal acts is tied here to certain conditions, for example, the institutional context. It is from this that the performative draws its authority. "How to do things with words" was up to now the domain of the professional politician. Through activism, the individual appropriates the authority of the performative without this being coupled to an institution and in doing so acts like an artist. Citizens also want to have the *pouvoir* to do things with words. They want their speech acts to directly influence decisions and actions. Whoever has the power to do things with words rules (through decrees, declarations, laws). In this regard, citizens want to become sovereigns. In the twenty-first century, the performative turn in the humanities has reached the sphere of politics. Politics is likewise undergoing a performative turn, which is why civic activism is the beginning of a performative democracy.

II. The Invention of the People

The dynamics of modern democracy started with the invention of the people. The sweet smell of democracy comes from Greece; the Greek words *dēmos* (the people of a nation) and *kratía* (rulership) describe the government of the people. Yet although the idea and concept originated in Greece, democracy as a form of governance was rejected by Greek philosophers such as Plato or Aristotle. In his renowned book *The Open Society and Its Enemies* (1945) Karl Popper defined Greece as a slave society. In the year 307 BCE, Athens was home to some 21,000 free citizens as opposed to about 400,000 slaves.

Solon, politician and reformer of the Attic polis, divided the inhabitants of Athenian democracy into four classes, of which only three were allowed to participate in government, in the polis in Athens. Citizens in the lowest order, the *thetes*, were permitted to sit in the *ekklesia* (assembly), but not to take part in resolutions.[27] In the fourth and fifth centuries BCE, women, foreigners, and slaves were not considered citizens and were therefore not permitted to participate in government. The Greek form of a polity thus excluded a large part of the population from taking part in it, which does not accord with our notion of democracy today. However, the ruling Greek nobles did not feel any commitment to the ideal of all members of society being equals. And Greek citizenry started to rebel against them as a result.[28] The Greek citizens laid claim to representing the entire polity, and in the process invented the idea of equality as then free citizens were able to rule over the polity and replace the aristocracy at the helm. This championing of the equality of all citizens can be considered the "invention of the people" and served the rise of the bourgeoisie who sought to justify their own political emergence by advocating the equality of all citizens. The representation of citizens in a social ideal of equality ignored the fact that the citizens formed a minority of the inhabitants of a city, excluding the noncitizens (women,

27

See: Roger Osborne, *Of the People, By the People. A New History of Democracy*, Bodley Head, London, 2011, p. 13.

28

See: Christian Meier, *Res publica amissa. Eine Studie zu Verfassung und Geschichte der späten römischen Republik*, Steiner, Wiesbaden, 1966; *Die Entstehung des Begriffs „Demokratie". Vier Prolegomena zu einer historischen Theorie*, Suhrkamp, Frankfurt am Main, 1970; *Die Entstehung des Politischen bei den Griechen*, Suhrkamp, Frankfurt am Main, 1980; *Athen. Ein Neubeginn der Weltgeschichte*, Siedler, Berlin, 1993.

foreigners, and slaves) and thus the majority of the polity. There could be no talk of all members of society being equals.

Greek philosophers Aristotle and Plato were themselves not democrats. Only Democritus, the founder of atomism and empiricism, was a convinced democrat. He was a materialist, a freethinker, and a utilitarian who aligned his general philosophy to the idea of democracy. Plato championed an oligarchy and, according to Diogenes Laertius, was of the opinion that all Democritus' writings should be burned.[29] For Aristotle, the state was a "community of freemen,"[30] but he understood "freemen" only to include free citizens.[31] He defined those forms of government as the true ones, "[...] in which the one [the monarch], or the few [the aristocracy], or the many [the polity], govern with a view on the common interest [...]."[32] With regard to legitimate rule by the majority, Aristotle explicitly commented: "But when the citizens at large administer the state for the common interest, the government is called by the generic name – a constitution."[33] As illegitimate perversions of such forms of state, bad organizations in the service of private interest, he identifies tyranny, oligarchy, and democracy.[34] "For tyranny is a kind of monarchy which has in view the interest of the monarch only; oligarchy has in view the interest of the wealthy; democracy, of the needy: none of them the common good of all."[35] So we see that Aristotle did not have the best opinion of democracy. Rather, he aspired to a mixture of polity and aristocracy in order to neutralize the inconstant rule by the many, which he felt to be prone to manipulation, and the dangers of both extremes (democracy and oligarchy).

29 See: Diogenes Laertius, *Leben und Meinungen berühmter Philosophen*, vol. 2: books VII–X, translated by Otto Apelt, new edition with an introduction and notes by Klaus Reich and Hans Günter Zekl, Meiner, Hamburg, 2008, p. 168.

30 Aristotle, *Politics*, translated by Benjamin Jowett, Indo-European Publishing, Los Angeles (CA), 2009, p. 55 (Book Three, Part VI).

31 See: ibid., pp. 47–48 (Book Three, Part I) and pp. 49–50 (Book Three, Part III).

32 Ibid., p. 56 (Book Three, Part VI).

33 Ibid.

34 See: ibid.

35 Ibid.

Who rules?	**How is rule conducted?**	
	Lawful constitution (in the common good)	Lawless constitution (in the private interest)
One ruler	**Monarchy**	**Tyranny**
A few rulers	**Aristocracy**	**Oligarchy**
Many rulers	**Polity**	**Democracy**

Aristotle's Typology of Government

Aristotle then transposes this political class hierarchy onto the field of knowledge, too, and advocates that a class-structured hierarchy of knowledge be introduced there as well. In his *Nicomachean Ethics* he differentiates between *technê* (craft, art, a knowledge in things) and *epistêmê* (knowledge, scientific knowledge).[36] As regards knowledge, he then distinguishes between various different types, for example, the expert knowledge of the unfree person, wage laborers, and craftsmen (*technites* or *banausos*). The latter, as is clearly stated in his *Politics* come very low in his estimation. The position of the craftsman corresponds to that of limited slavery, which is why craftsmen are not citizens, he opines. In Aristotle's view, the sons of "freemen" should not be too strongly involved in useful activities that could push them down the ladder to the status of *banausos*, as the souls and mindset of craftsmen would obstruct free men in exercising and applying virtue. The handcrafts of arts hurt the body and rob the mind of the leisure required to think. Useful things should therefore only be taught to the extent that they form the basis for something higher. Music, for example, is something an adult free man should only listen to for enjoyment's sake, but should not perform himself, as performances would be something craftsman-like *(banauson)* and thus undignified for a free man. So there is a need for people who as wage laborers or slaves master a craft *(technê)*, but only in the service of others in order to nurture the latters' enjoyment or enable them to engage in a higher activity.[37]

In a very sophisticated study of Athenian democracy, *Democracy and Knowledge,* Josiah Ober declares that the Greek polis had a direct democratic government and attributes its success to democratic knowledge management. His proposition is that:

> "Democratic Athens was able to take advantage of its size and resources, and therefore competed successfully over time against hierarchical rivals, because the costs of participatory political practices were overbalanced by superior returns to social cooperation resulting from useful knowledge as it was organized and deployed in the simultaneously innovation-promoting and learning-based context of democratic institutions and culture."[38]

Moreover, he praises the multistate Greek world and its open-access economy: "there is no authoritative central world government."[39]

As the examples from Ancient Greece show, underlying the principle of the equality of members of a polity is the question: Who is a member of the polity in the first place? For the Greeks, democracy was a polity of selected members. This problem continues to apply today, as it is still not clearly defined who are members of the polity (inclusion) and who are not (exclusion). The Mexican immigrants in the USA and refugees from Africa and the Middle East who have fled to Europe, live in America or Europe but they are not recognized as members of the polity. They have no "membership cards," such as passports, and therefore count as *sans-papier*. Some "civil rights" therefore still only apply to selected members of a society. A distinction is made between

36 See: Aristotle, *Nicomachean Ethics*, translated with an interpretive essay, notes, and glossary by Robert C. Bartlett and Susan D. Collins, The University of Chicago Press, Chicago (IL), London, 2011, pp. 118–122 (Book 6, Chapters 3–6).

37 See: Aristotle 2009, pp. 177–179 (Book Eight).

38 Josiah Ober, *Democracy and Knowledge. Innovation and Learning in Classical Athens*, Princeton University Press, Princeton (NJ), Oxford, 2008, p. 268.

39 Ibid., p. 278.

the new-arrival inhabitants of a country, the natives of the country, the people, citizens, and electorate and stateless people who are members nowhere.

An attempt was made to solve the problem of selective membership by aspiring to universal membership: citizens of the Earth or cosmopolitans rather than citizens of states. But unfortunately even a cosmopolitan can only claim in ideal terms that his/her polis is the cosmos and he/she therefore a universal member, a member of all polities. For no one can be a member of all polities. Being a citizen of the cosmos is of course a contradiction in terms, as the cosmos consists of a whole host of communities. No one can, for example, be a member of different religious communities (e.g., a Protestant, Catholic, and Muslim), as reality teaches us. The world consists of mutually exclusive memberships. Chantal Mouffe rightly explains in *Agonistics* (2013) that cosmopolitans lack the political in its antagonistic dimension. For this reason, cosmopolitanism as a theory of state is only an idealist utopia,[40] and doomed to fail in reality. Possible responses to these antinomian memberships are firstly, *global governance*, which promises the real equality of all the world's inhabitants, and that includes all the animal and plants, or, secondly, at least plurality and multitude,[41] as the world is not a universe but a pluriverse.[42]

After the fall of Athens, in Scandinavia elements of democracy emerged; namely, the formal assemblies that were called a *ding*, *ting*, or *thing*. The best-known among them was the *althing* in Iceland, which was founded in 930 and where the Gothars, the representatives of the various communities, met each year, elected a spokesman and a judge, and decided on laws. In 1130, a first-past-the-post system of voting was introduced in Iceland.[43]

In England, between the fifteenth and seventeenth centuries, nascent forms of democracy evolved, for example, parliamentary organizations and secret ballots for the election of mayors. In the early seventeenth century, the relationship between the English parliament and the monarch was exceedingly complex, particularly as central elements of the modern state, the army and the tax authorities, were not subject to the sovereign's control. Indeed, there were actual battles between the king's troops and parliament's troops. Parliament was able to prevent tax increases and as a result the king had to accord parliament privileges in exchange for its financial and military support. When parliament did not cede to his wishes, the king simply dissolved it. In 1640, the English parliament therefore resolved that only parliament itself could dissolve itself. In fact, 1647 marked another important moment in the history of democracy: *The Putney Debates* on "An Agreement of the People." Essentially, the focus was on a more just distribution of parliamentary seats in terms of inhabitants per county and to distinguish between citizens and inhabitants as well as the issue of enfranchisement.

> "That the people of England, being at this day very unequally distributed by counties, cities and boroughs for the election of their deputies in parliament, ought to be more indifferently

40 See: Isabelle Stengers, *Cosmopolitiques*, 7 vols., La Découverte, Paris, 2003.

41 See: Antonio Negri and Michael Hardt, *Empire*, Harvard University Press, Cambridge (MA), 2001; Antonio Negri and Michael Hardt, *Multitude. War and Democracy in the Age of Empire*, Penguin Books, London, 2004. The authors cite the term "multitude" as used by Spinoza.

42 See the video work *Gesänge des Pluriversums* by Peter Weibel (1986–1988).

43 See: Bruno Latour, "From Realpolitik to Dingpolitik or How to Make Things Public," in: Bruno Latour and Peter Weibel (eds.), *Making Things Public. Atmospheres of Democracy*, ZKM | Zentrum für Kunst und Medientechnologie Karlsruhe, The MIT Press, Cambridge (MA), London, 2005, p. 14–41.

proportioned, according to the number of inhabitants: the circumstances whereof, for number, place, and manner, are to be set down before the end of this present parliament."[44]

44 First proposal of *An Agreement of the People* (1647), as quoted from: Osborne 2011, p. 88.

That champion of civil rights Maximilian Petty was of the opinion that "we judge that all inhabitants who have not lost their birthright should have an equal voice in elections."[45] Others felt that only the propertied should be enfranchised. This stemmed from the fear that those who owned no property could gain more influence through elections and contest the rights the rich had to property. In the battle against the monarchy, judicial proceedings ensued in which Charles I argued in 1649 that there could be no higher authority than that of the king, and therefore the High Court of Justice had not the right to open litigation against him. The decisive contribution as regards establishing democratic principles was made by Chief Judge John Bradshaw, who responded: "Sir, as the law is your superior, so truly sir, there is something that is superior to the law and that is indeed the parent or author of the law – and that is the people of England."[46] Suddenly, the people became the superior class, the legislative, the law itself. This is the moment when the notion of the people is invented. This statement clearly shows what the purpose was behind inventing the people or rather the sovereign people. Greek citizens first invented the people, *demos*, in order to emancipate themselves from the aristocracy and justify their rights. But they were the people, not the women and not the slaves. In England, the invention of the people served to justify the rule of parliament, meaning the rule of the propertied class. The bourgeoisie invented the people in order to abolish and overcome the monarchy. In Ancient Greece, as in seventeenth-century England, the invention of the people served the social ascent of the class advocating it, and thus to secure its rule. With the legitimation in the name of the people, even the king could be dismissed, stripped of his powers, and beheaded. A court citing the authority of the people of England had King Charles I publicly executed on January 30, 1649, paving the way for the French Revolution.

45 Ibid.

46 Ibid., p. 93.

As became clear, the invention of the people was needed to justify one's own actions, to overthrow the powers-that-were, and to buttress one's own new power. This question of legitimacy also gave rise to fundamental treatises on modern political philosophy, on the modern state by Thomas Hobbes (*Leviathan or the Matter, Forme and Power of a Commonwealth Ecclesiastical and Civil,* 1651), John Locke (*Two Treatises of Government*, 1689), Jean-Jacques Rousseau (*The Social Contract*, 1762), and John Stuart Mill (*Considerations on Representative Government*, 1861).

In England, the *Bill of Rights* of 1689 formed the starting point for a series of laws that led to the foundation of a constitutional monarchy, but actually served to keep out the idea of democracy. The monarch retained limited powers in parliament and the latter continued to rule over the country. The old powers shared power. Parliament and not the people was henceforth the sovereign. Europe learned from the English example that parliament could be a major instrument of governance. And we can discern through to the middle of the twentieth century how British politics was shaped by a small elite whose members were often as not related to one another.[47] As in Athens, England was far from being a true democracy. Around 1800, in England there were only 350,000 voters from a total population of some 10 million.

Not until the end of the nineteenth century did the word democracy crop up again in public debates, when in 1890 the manuscripts of the *Putney Debates* were rediscovered in the archive of Worcester College library in Oxford. Not until the labor movement of the late nineteenth century did other parts of the British populace gain access to parliament, that is, to power. Only then was a start made on expanding the privileged and selective power club to include new members.

47 See: Lewis Namier, *Crossroads of Power. Essays on Eighteenth Century England* (The Collected Essays of Sir Lewis Namier, vol. 2), Hamish Hamilton, London, 1962.

The United States, as former British and French colonies, took over the small torch of democracy from them and took it to a new level. Around 1840 every white, male adult was given the vote, but women and blacks remained disenfranchised. Important public offices were made a matter of election, and the express goal was to protect citizens from anyone trying to exert power over them, even if it was the state.

Before this could happen a whole series of trailblazing decisions and developments first had to take place which in the final instance led to the United States population's sociopolitical emancipation from its European roots. A large number of new nonconformist religious communities settled in the first colonies. These communities fled the Old World to escape authoritarian governments. The North American population rocketed in the course of the eighteenth century, from 50,000 around 1650 to 5.3 million around 1800. The annihilation of the Native American population and the forced resettlement of millions of African slaves attest to extreme brutality that was irreconcilable with religious morality and democratic intentions. The war between France and England on American soil changed the political landscape. As in seventeenth-century England, taxation also played a major role here. The British government might have won the war against France, but it had accumulated massive debts in the process and wished to shift repayment of the debts onto the shoulders of its thirteen American colonies by raising taxes. The Sugar Act (1764), the Stamp Act (1765), and the Townshend Acts (from 1767 onwards) imposed taxes on tea, paper, lead, and glass. The American colonies started to rebel against this and 1773 saw the famous Boston Tea Party, when a group of militant Boston citizens dumped a shipment of tea belonging to the East India Trading Company into the sea. Their slogan was "No taxation without representation" – meaning no taxes would be paid without Bostonians being represented in parliament. Less than two years later the War of Independence had already begun. Thomas Paine's pamphlet on *Common Sense* (1776), which claimed for the colonies the right to self-government, was printed in an edition of 500,000 copies. On July 4, 1776 Congress adopted the famous *Declaration of Independence*, mainly penned by Thomas Jefferson.

> "We hold these truths to be self-evident, that all men are created equal, that they are endowed by their Creator with certain unalienable Rights, that among these are Life, Liberty and the pursuit of Happiness. – That to secure these rights, Governments are instituted among Men, deriving their just powers from the consent of the governed, – That whenever any Form of Government becomes destructive of these ends, it is the Right of the People to alter or to abolish it, and to institute new Government, laying its foundation on such principles and organizing its powers in such form, as to them shall seem most likely to effect their Safety and Happiness."[48]

48 Available online at: www.archives.gov/exhibits/charters/declaration_transcript.html, accessed 04/01/2015.

Here, again, we see the efficacy of the idea of inventing a people. The declaration's weakness became clear in practice in particular in the Southern states, which refused to make slaves and women equal with "men" and grant them human rights. For this reason, in 1789 the *Bill of Rights* was approved in the USA, ten Amendments to the constitution, which for the first time guaranteed civil rights. In this way, the citizen was invented basically owing to justificatory legal compulsions. Benjamin Franklin stated in this context: "Our constitution is in actual operation and everything appears to promise that it will last. But in this world, nothing can be certain but death and taxes."[49]

49 As quoted from: Osborne 2011, p. 106.

The USA introduced the division of legislative, executive, and judiciary powers, voting regulations for Congress and for the Presidency, and a Supreme Court to watch over the constitution. The British three-party constitution (Crown, House of Lords, House of Commons) is nevertheless reflected in the U.S. Constitution with the President, Senate, and House of Representatives. Soon, US democrats realized that the key issue of democracy was: "In whose interest do the citizens vote?" In their own interest, in that of the common good, or of the state, and who then puts these interests into practice in a representative democracy? The party system was created in order to turn the utopian dream innate in the *Declaration of Independence* into an operable political system. The father of the *Declaration of Independence*, Thomas Jefferson, did, however, have the following to say about his experience with representative party democracy: "If I could not go to heaven but with a [political] party, I would not go at all."[50]

50 Ibid., p. 112. The structure of political parties also meant so-called common people could take a seat in government. The profession of the politician thus arose (see: Max Weber, *Politik als Beruf* (Geistige Arbeit als Beruf. Vier Vorträge vor dem Freistudentischen Bund, Zweiter Vortrag), Duncker & Humblot, Munich, Leipzig, 1919.

In 1854 Abraham Lincoln and the Republican Party, newly founded by Alvan E. Bovay, had to fight to resolve the issue of slavery at the national level. The Civil War began and in his famous *Gettysburg Address* of November 19, 1863, a speech of only three minutes in honor of those who had fallen at Gettysburg, Abraham Lincoln once again invoked the *Declaration of Independence* and once and for all sealed the invention of the people as an instrument of government.

> "Four score years and seven ago our fathers brought forth on this continent a new nation, conceived in liberty and dedicated to the proposition that all men are created equal. [W]e here highly resolve that these dead shall not have died in vain, that this nation under God shall have a new birth of freedom, and that government of the people, by the people, for the people shall not perish from the Earth."[51]

51 As quoted from: Osborne 2011, pp. 116–117.

The concept of democracy stands and falls with what Edmund S. Morgan has called the "invention of the people."[52] In the U.S. *Declaration of Independence* people are guaranteed inviolable rights and above all that the governments destined to secure these rights shall only possess and retain power with the approval of the people governed. In other words, a democracy thrives on this dynamism between the government and the governed, between the politicians and the people.

52 See: Edmund S. Morgan, *Inventing the People. The Rise of Popular Sovereignty in England and America*, W.W. Norton, New York (NY), 1988.

However, this system of government did not evolve in terms of free people, but the free citizens in the propertied class. The Greek slave society repeated itself in America, and the rights of the U.S. Constitution were only valid for white, male, free citizens. Women and slaves were excluded from the rights of the *Declaration of Independence*. Not until around 1900 did all free whites get the vote in the USA (including women), and not until the second half of the twentieth century were they joined by black citizens.

The French Revolution came about precisely because of all these shortcomings in the early democratic constitutions and their inherent oppression of large parts of the population. In France, as in England and the USA, a three-class regime prevailed. The *Ancien Régime* in eighteenth-century France was an autocratic regime that ruled over a country of 28 million people and divided society into the three so-called Estates-General. The third estate was made up of commoners – craftsmen, farmers, wage-laborers, and bourgeoisie and together they accounted for 98 percent of the population. The second estate consisted of the aristocracy, some 400,000 people, or 1.5 percent of the population, whose primary income derived from landed property. The first estate with about 130,000 members, or 0.5 percent of the population, was the clergy, which likewise owned immense landed property. As long as France gathered enough tax revenue, its agricultural output sufficed to feed the people, and it had sufficient soldiers to defend itself, French kings were more or less able to govern from Versailles. By means of moderate land reforms, progressive taxation, pension schemes, the battle against starvation, state schools, and an acceptable judiciary France survived well on the Continent. However, the spread of printed matter and a culture of reading in clubs and salons gave rise to a new type of citizen: lawyers, merchants, doctors, literary scholars, journalists, all of whom laid claim to political rights. Out of the people the bourgeois emerged and started to participate in the power hitherto reserved for the aristocracy.[53]

53 See: Franco Moretti, *Der Bourgeois. Eine Schlüsselfigur der Moderne*, Suhrkamp, Berlin, 2014.

When taxation no longer sufficed to pay the ruling classes' debts, and agriculture did not produce enough food to feed the population, in 1789 the era of the *Ancien Régime* started to collapse with the Storming of the Bastille. In March 1789 Louis XVI called upon the representatives of the three Estates-General to vote. At the assembly, about 300 representatives each of the clergy and the aristocracy represented 2 percent of the population, with 600 representatives of the third estate representing the remaining 98 percent, the actual body of the people. On June 17, 1789 this third estate proclaimed the National Assembly of France, which Louis XVI refused to recognize. As in England, a war ensued between the royal house and parliament. The deputies in the assembly justified their powers by deriving it from the people who had voted for them. This power, they said, was higher than the authority of either the king or the nobles. As in England, the king could therefore be beheaded in the name of the people. On July 14, 1789 some 8,000 people stormed the Bastille and the French Revolution commenced, seeking to establish a democratic society in keeping with the principles of "Liberté, Égalité, Fraternité" – and thus including all members of society as citizens.

III. The Invention of the State

The idea of justice is an invention, so unreal that from the outset it was not possible to anchor it in earthly matters, but in otherworldliness, at the end of days, the Last Judgment. Originally, the idea of justice in the Old Testament was therefore construed as divine justice. It was evidently inconceivable that people could themselves create justice. For that reason, down through the centuries in the Christian West the idea of justice between people, and later that of state justice, was closely bound up with a belief in divine justice. A just state in which people themselves ensured justice between and with one another, is actually proclaimed in the Bible: "Blessed are those who hunger and thirst for justice" (Matthew 5:6). At the same time, the idea of justice realized by a secular state was rejected as utopian, given experiences with people, and a just divine state considered the ultima ratio. Not in a secular state, but only in one subject to divine rule could justice prevail. So runs the sad conclusion of people about people.

The universal idea of justice and law proved unfulfillable and therefore disintegrated into subsystems, into the individual or special disciplines of law and justice. The result was a pluralism of legal orders (church law, natural law, civil law, public law, penal law, constitutional law, common law). Because, in spite of all its prophets, the just divine state did not materialize, competing types of law evolved and the place of an omniscient god was taken by a more or less omnipresent and omnipotent state. After centuries of religious and political oppression it is finally time to think of a state constitution that focuses on justice in the comprehensive sense. The emergence of the modern state with its division of powers is likewise to be attributed to the secularization of governance. The roots of the Western legal tradition go back, after all, to the struggle between imperial and papist powers. Harold J. Berman terms this the eleventh-century Gregorian Revolution. The division in validity claims between the secular and religious powers is, so he suggests, the most decisive revolution in European history, and he therefore asserts that the modern Western state arose from that Gregorian Revolution.[54] Before Gregory VII ascended the papal throne, the Church had not known terms such as sovereignty and independent law-making that are central to the modern constitutional state. After Gregory VII the Church itself assumed and preempted characteristics of the modern state. It saw itself as a hierarchical, public power that asserted its laws by means of an administrative hierarchy.

54 See: Harold J. Berman, *Law and Revolution. The Formation of the Western Legal Tradition*, Harvard University Press, Cambridge (MA), London, 1983.

The Pope had the right to make laws, but also the executive and juridical powers, which means the distinction between legislative, executive, and judiciary was already acknowledged. Yet the Church was not a modern state, as the main feature of the modern state is its secular character and the division of powers is only its second most important feature.

The modern philosophy of state is indebted, however, less to law and the idea of justice than to fear. Not democracy, but phobocracy, not law and freedom, but punishment and control are the goals of the majority of states today. This can be discerned most clearly in Thomas Hobbes' famous treatise *Leviathan* (1651), one of the founders of the modern philosophy of state. The book's frontispiece visualizes the idea of phobocracy in a composite image from the Arcimboldo school that is attributed to Wenceslaus Hollar and Abraham Bosse. Many faces combine to form the monster of a crowned giant in whose hand lie the bishop's crook and the sword, the symbols of church and state power.[55] Thomas Hobbes assumes that people require a life regulated by the rule of bourgeois laws, a *civitas*, a civil society, a "*common wealth* or state." Just how much Hobbes' philosophy of state rested on fear can be seen from the very title *Leviathan*, the name of the sea monster that God makes appear to doubting Job in an awful storm to reveal God's powers: "Upon earth there is not his like, who is made without fear. He beholdeth all high things: he is a king over all the children of pride." (Job 40:33–34) The frontispiece visualizes this alliance of fear and power, the dominion of power as a response to human fear. In a natural state what rules is "continuall feare, and danger of violent death; And the life of man, solitary, poore, nasty, brutish, and short."[56]

In his *Die Provinz des Menschen* (1973) [*The Human Province*, trans. 1978] Elias Canetti clearly and critically adumbrated the basic principle of fear in Hobbes' justification of state power. Fear is the origin of the modern state. As the philosopher of the sovereign state, Hobbes acutely highlights the linkage of violence, punishment, and fear:

> "Ignorance of the Penalty, where the Law is declared, Excuseth no man: For in breaking the Law, which without a fear of penalty to follow were not a Law, but vain words, he undergoeth the penalty, though he know not what it is; because, whosoever voluntarily doth any action, accepteth all the known consequences of it; but Punishment is a known consequence of the violation of the Lawes, in every Common-wealth; which punishment, if it be determined already by the Law, he is subject to that; if not, then is he subject to Arbitrary punishment."[57]

This nurturing of fear on behalf of the powers of state is familiar in the twentieth century and not just from totalitarian but also from democratic systems.[58] The culture of fear is an indicator of the forward march of authoritarian structures and ideologies in democracies and all other social institutions.

55
See: Herfried Münkler, *Thomas Hobbes*, Campus, Frankfurt am Main, 1993; Herfried Münkler, *Politische Bilder, Politik der Metaphern*, Fischer Taschenbuch, Frankfurt am Main, 1994; Horst Bredekamp, *Thomas Hobbes. Der Leviathan. Das Urbild des modernen Staates und seine Gegenbilder. 1651–2001*, Akademie Verlag, Berlin, 2003.

56
Thomas Hobbes, *Leviathan*, edited with an introduction by C.B. Macpherson, Penguin, Harmondsworth, 1968, p. 186.

57
Ibid., pp. 338–339.

58
See: Barry Glassner, *The Culture of Fear. Why Americans Are Afraid of the Wrong Things: Crime, Drugs, Minorities, Teen Moms, Killer Kids, Mutant Microbes, Plane Crashes, Road Rage, and So Much More*, Basic Books, New York (NY), 1999; Nancy Lusignan Schultz (ed.), *Fear Itself. Enemies Real and Imagined in American Culture*, Purdue University Press, West Lafayette (IN), 1999; Paul Newman, *A History of Terror. Fear and Dread Through the Ages*, Sutton, Stroud, 2000; Robert Alan Goldberg, *Enemies Within. The Culture of Conspiracy in Modern America*, Yale University Press, New Haven (CT), 2001.

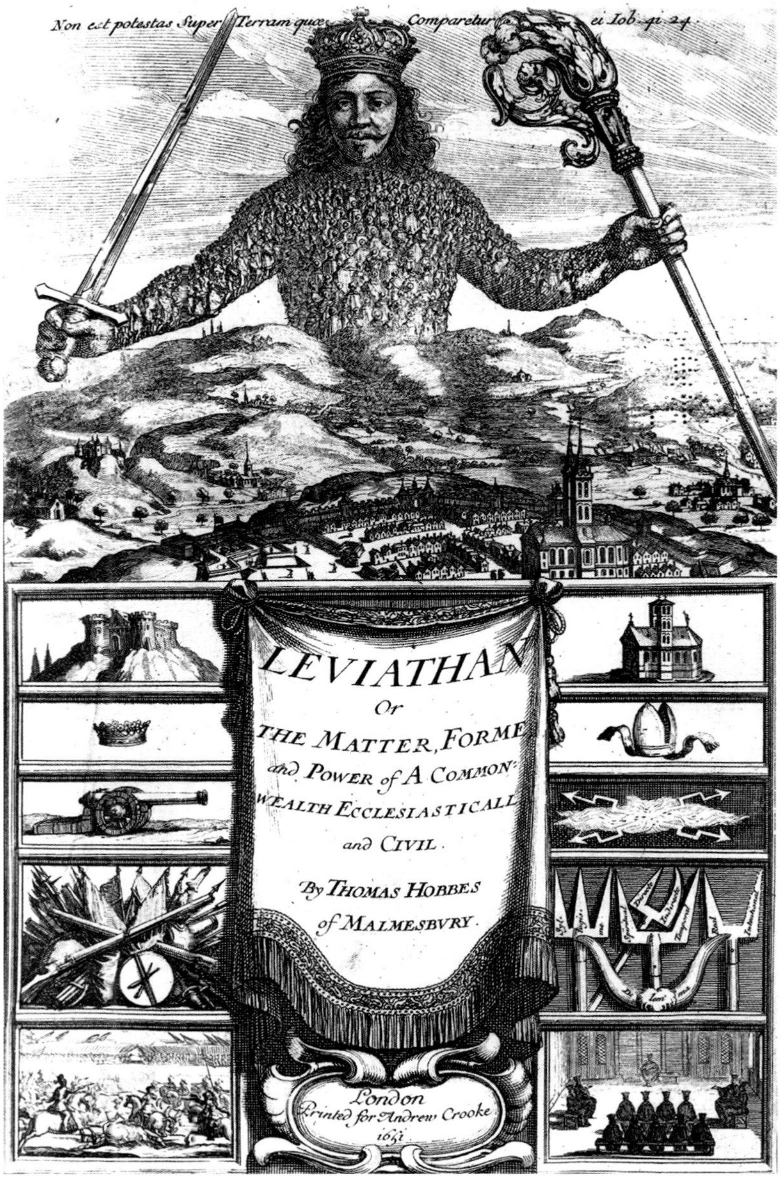

Thomas Hobbes, *Leviathan*, Andrew Crooke, London, 1651, Holmes Collection, U.S. Library of Congress, frontispiece

On the frontispiece of *Leviathan* we saw the awful image of the sovereign state, born from horror and exuding horror. The monster of the state as a giant does not curb violence, it simply monopolizes it. By virtue of the mass subjecting itself to the sovereign, the mass becomes a "person" who has to be represented by a sovereign. The body of the people thus becomes the monarch and not the people are sovereign, but the monarch. The state is the sovereign that represents the people, and thus the people does not rule, but the representatives of the state. The invention of the state substitutes for and liquidates the invention of the people. Aristotle's theorem that "[t]he end of democracy is freedom […]"[59] disappears into the distance.

59
Aristotle, *Rhetoric*, translated by W. Rhys Roberts, unabridged republication of *Rhetoric* from volume nine of *The Works of Aristotle*, originally published by Oxford University Press, London, in 1924, Dover Publications, Mineola (NY), 2004, p. 30 (Book I, Chapter 8).

IV. The Invention of the Public

The concept of the republic stems of course from that of the *res publica*, public things. This shows that the public is a key category of democracy. So we can ask: "Is governing a public matter?", "Is there a functionally viable public?", "Does the public rule?", "Who is the public?"

By creating a public sphere the mass media took on a special task; namely, to manufacture and secure democracy. In the 200 years they have now existed, the newspapers, and later media such as TV and the Internet, have served the construction of the public sphere and thus democracy. The evolution of the press cannot be separated from the emergence of bourgeois society, and democracy for the press was the instrument of power with which the bourgeois class forced through its participation in matters of state and in the powers of state in the early nineteenth century. Just as Greek citizens created the ideals of equality in order to participate in power, the nineteenth-century bourgeoisie created the press and the public sphere to gain access to political power. Without the public media, the bourgeois class would not have been able to participate in political life. Given that around 1900 parliaments were still dominated by members of the aristocracy, rich members of the middle class used publications in the print media to influence decisions in parliament and thus gain access to the decision-making bodies.

This modus operandi still remains in place, as today people still try to influence the powers of state by using public opinion, that is, the press. Parliamentarization that does not take place in parliament is the real essence of public media. Publicist power has established itself alongside the public force of state institutions, such as the legislative, executive, and judiciary, and to this extent people also speak of the fourth power. But who controls this fourth power? In an authoritarian society, the state; in a democratic society, the interests of the ruling class, but in no case is it the people. There is no proletarian public sphere.[60]

60 See: Alexander Kluge and Oskar Negt, *Public Sphere and Experience. Toward an Analysis of the Bourgeois and Proletarian Public Sphere*, University of Minnesota Press, Minneapolis (MN), 1993.

At a very early date, in his *Kritik der öffentlichen Meinung* (1922) sociologist Ferdinand Tönnies (who was sacked from his position in the civil service by the Nazi regime in 1933) criticized the power of public opinion for being a kind of substitute religion. Viewer ratings – and to this day the mass media still genuflect to them – is exactly such an expression of an uncritical, as it were religious veneration of public opinion. In 1922 US publicist Walter Lippmann, who cofounded the magazine *The New Republic* (the new *res publica*) in 1914, summarized his experiences in his famous book *Public Opinion*, where he proposed that the press involves the "manufacture of consent." Information, he suggested, is so filtered by certain rules and agencies that all journalists deliver corresponding reports; in other words, the public assumes that since everyone says it is the case, it must be the case. In his next book *The Phantom Public* (1925) he championed the idea that the public sphere is just a phantom anyway. He accused the democracy theorists of having simply transposed omniscience, omnipotence, and the sovereignty of the state onto the citizen. He criticized that they presume the existence of sovereign and omnicompetent citizens who would be able to create a democracy: "The public is a mere phantom embedded in a mystical notion of society." Lippmann argues that if there is no such thing as the omnicompetent citizen, who forms the basis of any democracy, then there can be no democracy either. He does, however, feel that the general public is empowered to intervene in crisis situations and correct the abuse of political power by bringing the power of public opinion to bear. His model for democracy relies on individuals who are directly involved. However, we know today that it is not the minority of omnicompetent citizens who endanger democracy, but the majority of semi-competent politicians. Philosopher John Dewey responded to Lippman by writing *The Public and Its Problems* (1927) where he points out that democracy can function despite the problem of the public.

The gap between the standards expected of the competent citizen and the range of political institutions in representative democracy is becoming ever wider. As a result, citizens' criticism increases, new forms of protest arise, and participation in the public sphere of the street spreads, because citizens' interests are no longer being represented in parliament or by the government. To this extent, global activism not only spells a critique of defective democracy, but is also a herald of future participative reforms and transformations of democracy.

The political revolution consists not only in introducing government by the people, the invention of the people, but also the invention of the citizen, the definition of the citizen, and this can only read: All individuals are citizens. As we have seen, from ancient Athens to the *Declaration of Independence* not all people were citizens, and women and slaves were excluded from enfranchisement until about 1900. And as also became clear, to this day several mechanisms of exclusion persist, for example regarding refugees' rights. Whenever a human being comes up against a national border, be it Germany or the USA, they have few rights when they are not a citizen of that country, as the fate of immigrants on Lampedusa shows. This is why we need a form of civil activism that fights for the civil rights of all people.

V. The Invention of the Citizen

The *citoyen* (derived from *cité* as in "city," Latin *civitas*, "civic society," "state") designates the citizen or civic member of a nation who takes an active and responsible part in the polity in the tradition and spirit of the Enlightenment, and helps shape it. Jean-Jacques Rousseau highlights a key distinction for the definition of citizens in *The Social Contract* (1762):

> "Each of us puts his person and all his power in common under the supreme direction of the general will, and, in our corporate capacity, we receive each member as an indivisible part of the whole. […] The real meaning of this word [i.e., *polis*, the public person, so formed by the union of all other persons,

formerly took the name of city,] has been almost wholly lost in modern time; most people mistake a town *[ville]* for a city *[cité]*, and a townsman *[bourgeois]* for a citizen *[citoyen]*."[61]

61 Jean-Jacques Rousseau, *On the Social Contract*, translated by G. D. H. Cole, Dover Publications, Mineola (NY), 2003, p. 9 (Book I, Chapter VI).

In his writings, Immanuel Kant likewise makes this important distinction. What is new about political practice today is that the citizen's free will, in the sense of Georg Wilhelm Friedrich Hegel's philosophy of right, must not be reduced to the free choice between several options predefined by politics, but rather consists of proposing to politics what the options for action are. A new language and rhetoric of politics is being developed that is engendered by historical and by new, technologically driven elements. Simply defining this new language as protest is to miss the actual innovation involved for what we are seeing in reality is the "invention of the citizen."

Just as the invention of the people was necessary in order to constitute representative democracy, today the invention of the citizen by the citizen is needed to advance democracy, which is otherwise under threat. The movements emerging globally are therefore not protest movements, but anticipatory movements for democracy. This hinges on the practical and performative advance of the distinction between *citoyen* and *bourgeois*. The politicians in modern democracies tend to confuse the two. But in truth to remain viable, democracy requires the *citoyen*. This is why the American founders of democratic theory, from Walter Lippmann to John Dewey, always emphasized the central function of the *citizen*. The demand of these active *citizens* of today is thus "No Taxation Without Participation," in the wake of the Boston Tea Party slogan of "No Taxation Without Representation" (1773). The new citizen insists on participation not representation, and free will in a participatory or performative democracy then means not only free elections, but free actions, a part in shaping political actions.

The emergence of the idea of the *citoyen* is inseparably bound up with the evolution of the idea of the individual. The individual person who determines his or her own life is only possible as a free and equal member of the civic world of the "polis," democracy. As only the democratic separation of the powers of the legislative, executive, and judiciary guarantees the freedom of the individual, meaning the individual needs a civil constitution in order to be able to express him/herself. Individual and democracy are mutually conditioning. To defend the individual is therefore to defend democracy and citizenship. To defend democracy means to defend the individual, as only a civic republic protects the individual, whereas for a totalitarian regime the individual does not exist and can therefore be destroyed at will. The twentieth century was the century of the absolute loss of inhibition, articulated most clearly in the total devaluation of individual life. The political mass murders from Armenia to China, from Germany to Russia, were only possible because the respective system of governance negated the idea of the individual and the citizen. The more the powers are separated, the more freedom there is, the more individuals: *sola divisione individuum*.[62]

62 See: Odo Marquard, *Individuum und Gewaltenteilung. Philosophische Studien*, Reclam, Stuttgart, 2004.

VI. The Invention of the Individual

Self-experience, self-determination, and self-expression are among the parameters of modern societies and democracy's axiomatic promises. However, these terms assume the existence of a self that was first asserted incisively by René Descartes in the seventeenth century with his *cogito ergo sum*. Between the Renaissance and the Enlightenment, that is, between 1500 and 1800, the human being was discovered as an individual, and paradoxically individualization, subjectivization, and personalization culminated during Enlightenment's opposite pole, Romanticism.

The literary rise of autobiography from the late sixteenth century, reaching perfection in the eighteenth century, confirms the growing importance of the ego and its sensations and perceptions. From the late sixteenth century countless testimonies to explicit self-observation that placed the individual center stage were published. From Gerolamo Cardano (1501–1576) to Michel de Montaigne (1533–1592) numerous such self-descriptions appeared in which the respective authors state that their own biography forms the sole content of the book. Instead of a reference to the world the sole reference is the self, and the biography shows how the author analyzes and constructs his or her self. In Jean-Jacques Rousseau's *Confessions* (1782 and 1789) subjectivism is taken to the point of self-immersion: "I desire to set before my fellows the likeness of a man in all the truth of nature, and that man myself. *Myself alone!*"[63] The uniqueness of the individual, this radical subjectivism that underscores the uniqueness of one's own sensibilities, is the mirror held up to the experience of the world.

63 Jean-Jacques Rousseau, *Confessions*, unabridged republication of a standard edition, Dover Publications, Mineola (NY), 2014, p. 3 (Book I).

In the eighteenth century, the sum total of these autobiographies provided the basis for future sciences such as psychology, physiognomy, anthropology, and ethnology. On the back of self-knowledge as self-description, in diary and in epistolary form, what arises is an account of the human soul. The sixteenth century's discovery of the self is followed by the scientific discovery of the psyche. The exploration of the individual's sensibilities becomes a research topic for experimental psychology in the nineteenth century. In 1863 physicist Hermann von Helmholtz published his *On the Sensations of Tone as a Physiological Basis for the Theory of Music* and in 1886 Ernst Mach *The Analysis of Sensations*. Mach's drawing of self-perception, produced in 1871, is legendary.

It bears noting here that individuality, a consciousness of one's own person, is not given by nature but is the product of social education. The individual arises in the context of social systems and is the result of disciplining by social institutions. For this reason, Friedrich Kittler, drawing on the work of Michel Foucault, spoke of the subject as civil servant.[64] Hard on the heels of the definition of the human as an individual follows the insight that the ego is embedded in social developments and political constellations, and that humans as individuals are defined by society. Then the dialectical struggle ensues between individual and institution, subject and system, with all the consequences, from the challenge to the state to the art myth of the outsider.

64 See: Friedrich Kittler, "Das Subjekt als Beamter," in: Manfred Frank, Gérard Raulet, and Willem van Reijen (eds.), *Die Frage nach dem Subjekt*, Suhrkamp, Frankfurt am Main, 1988, pp. 401–420; Michel Foucault, *Discipline and Punish. The Birth of the Prison*, Pantheon Books, New York (NY), 1977.

On the threshold to the nineteenth century, the emphasis turned to the individual's creative genius and the bourgeois ideal of the autonomous individual emerged, someone whom one must grant individual options for action. In 1794/1795 Johann Gottlieb Fichte began his *Foundations of the Science of Knowledge* with a definition of the ego: "The self [...] is at once the agent and the product of action; the active, and what the activity brings about; action and deed are one and the same, and hence the 'I am' expresses an Act [...]."[65] The sources of current civic activism are to be found in German Idealist philosophy, which defines the self as a form of action. For as an individual the citizen wants to be empowered to act and therefore to be a political activist, and not simply someone who is politically represented.

65
Johann Gottlieb Fichte, *The Science of Knowledge*, edited and translated by Peter Heath and John Lachs, Cambridge University Press, Cambridge, New York (NY), 1982, p. 97.

The invention of the individual is the actual political detonation, the explosive arming modern democracy. With the discovery of the individual as citizen, human and civil rights were discovered as well. The autonomy of the individual as was already alluded to in the literary genre of autobiography is now linked to the concrete demand not only for individual, but also for social freedom of action. This struggle for the individual's scope in society gained momentum in the nineteenth century: the individual, born as a civil servant, wants the power of the sovereign.

In the extreme individualism of Max Stirner and his book *The Ego and Its Own* (1844) we hear not only a radicalized echo of Fichte, but also an absolutization of the ego that Karl Marx criticized sharply in *Sankt Max*. Stirner already uses the term "indignation" albeit in the sense of "to rise up," as liberation from "the afterworld." Following Marx, Hans G. Helms, writer, composer, and thinker stated in his *Die Ideologie der anonymen Gesellschaft* (1966) that the uniqueness of the ego that Stirner proclaims is actually the extreme opportunism of the petit bourgeois and the struggle for supremacy within the middle class. The *société anonyme* is a form of limited liability company because the names of the members of the stock corporation remain anonymous and they are therefore protected in the event of bankruptcy. In this sense, this legal entity protected those responsible from the consequences of their actions, in other words it exonerated them from responsibility. Helms therefore chose the notion of anonymity to describe society under a capitalist state.

In the final instance, the discovery of the individual means nothing more than the paradox process of individualization of social life. As a result, individuality became the central topic of modernity and artistic freedom the mirror of individual freedom. The artist embodies the absolute sovereign. In other words, democracy should also be considered the attempt to institutionalize the individual shaping of biographies and individual development. The modern individual expects social systems to offer living conditions that not only enable her/his individuality, subjectivity, and uniqueness, but enhance it. The subject (from the Latin: *subiectus*, to subject oneself) wishes to no longer be subjugated, but to rise from servant to master. In his *Phenomenology of Mind* (1807), Hegel describes in Chapter 4 on the "Independence and Dependence of Self-Consciousness: Lordship and Bondage" revolutionary consciousness as the consciousness of the subjugated: "The truth of the independent consciousness is accordingly the consciousness of the bondsman."[66]

While the concept of the *people* was a battlecry for upward social mobility, the terms individual and subject subsequently emerged as the battlecry for liberation from rule. Citizens revolted as humans and masters against the aristocracy, from the Greek polis to the nineteenth century. In the twentieth century, the slave, the servant, and the worker revolted against the aristocracy and the bourgeoisie. The state, in particular the welfare state, was supposed to guarantee the individual's claim to realizing its ideas. And democracy for a long time appeared to be the constitution of a state that was best and most able to protect the individual's right to self-realization.[67]

From *Das Ende des Individuums* (Michael Landmann, 1971) to the *Death of the Author* (Roland Barthes, 1967) through to the *Death of Man* (Michel Foucault, 1966)[68] for philosophy it seemed evident that the subject has ended. However, as stated, democracy can only be realized by the individual and, conversely, individuality can only be realized by democracy. The subject is the wrong target to attack. The criticism and concern should be leveled at the end of democracy. A decisive date for the end of a social, just society was the invention of the GmbH, the limited liability company in Germany, in 1892, the country's most successful export commodity, originally meant as a way of limiting a company's legal responsibility for its actions. Today, the GmbH is the model for all of society, and is basically a model for unlimited irresponsibility as poignantly shown by the 2008 bank crisis.

The welfare state was the reconciliation between capital and democracy, bitterly fought for, because as long as there is "prosperity for all,"[69] people chose democracy for justice, equality, and popular sovereignty. At present, however, the rule of capital and economic market mechanisms are undermining these promises of democracy. The twentieth century's hopes that capitalism and democracy would be mutually beneficial appear to be being dashed by the twenty-first century.

VII. The Invention of the User

The crisis of representation in politics runs parallel to the same crisis in art. The crisis of representation in art started in that historic moment when, under pressure from true-to-life images in photography, painting lost interest in representing visible reality. At the beginning of the twentieth century, under the paradigm of photography modernist art redefined the representation of reality or even substituted reality for representation. Painting severed the bond to the reality of the world of objects: With the pure self-representation of the dot, line, plane, and colors (the means of representation hitherto used to represent the world), around 1913 painting became nonfigurative, abstract (Kazimir Malevich).[70] Wassily Kandinsky emphasized the autonomy of painting's individual elements as the trajectory of abstract painting in his treatise on *Point and Line to Plane. Contribution to the Analysis of the Pictorial Elements* (1926).

66 Georg Wilhelm Friedrich Hegel, *Phenomenology of Mind* (1807), translated, with an introduction and notes, by J. B. Baillie (1910), Dover Publications, Mineola (NY), 2012, p. 110.

67 See: Odo Marquard, "Sola divisione individuum. Betrachtungen über Individuum und Gewaltenteilung," in: Marquard 2004, pp. 68–90.

68 Michel Foucault: "[M]an would be erased, like a face drawn in sand at the edge of the sea," in: Michel Foucault, *The Order of Things*, Vintage Books, New York (NY), 1973, p. 387.

69 Ludwig Erhard, 1957; see: Ludwig Erhard, *Prosperity through Competition*, Frederick A. Praeger, New York (NY), 1958.

70 See: Peter Weibel, "Die Geburt der Moderne aus dem Ikonoklasmus: Von der Repräsentation zur Realität – Selbstmord bzw. Selbstauflösung der Kunst?," in: Peter Weibel, Christa Steinle, and Gudrun Danzer, *Modern: Selbstmord der Kunst? Im Spiegel der Sammlung der Neuen Galerie Graz*, exhib. cat., Neue Galerie Graz, Hatje Cantz, Ostfildern, 2011), pp. 56–91, here p. 64.

On the other hand, likewise around 1913, the object as banished from the image was reintroduced into art as a real object (Marcel Duchamp). In the self-representation of objects, the real object morphs into a sculpture. Through the readymade, the real object as artwork, a series of substitutions were set in motion in the course of which in the twentieth century everything that had been representation was replaced by reality: Landscape painting gave way to Land art, painted motion to real movements (kinetics), painted sunlight to real artificial light, and finally the real audience to the audience as part of the piece of art.

As long as the object was only depicted, there was no question about its utility. With the use of real everyday objects in art the question of use moved more to center stage. With his industrial readymades, Duchamp also negated the objects' use. For example, there was no using the urinal on its back (*Fountain*, 1917). Duchamp presented it as an aesthetic object, not as an object for use. Conversely, he provocatively suggested using an artwork, namely, a painting by Rembrandt, as an iron.[71] The Surrealists also rejected utility for their aesthetic objects in order to highlight the purely symbolic function involved. Useful objects, such as Man Ray's *Cadeau* (1921) or Meret Oppenheim's *Fur Cup* (1936), became *objets à fonctionnement symbolique*.

By contrast, Constantin Brâncuşi felt his handmade sculptures had three use functions. A sculpture could serve as the plinth for another sculpture, but also be a stool for sitting on. And a stool could in turn be a plinth for a sculpture or itself be a sculpture or useful object. Around 1920, the Productivists led by Alexander Rodchenko expanded the notion of sculpture to include a use function and produced good chairs for working men's clubs.

Along with objects of use, thereafter instructions of use also entered art. Because most objects cannot be used without them. The instructions for use became instructions for viewers on how to act, turning them into actors. Marcel Duchamp provided exact instructions on how an image should be viewed, and called one of his pieces *A regarder d'un œil, de près, pendant presque une heure* (1918).

In the late 1950s, Yoko Ono started replacing the use of objects with instructions for use. She proposed actions, provided instructions for the reader, viewer, or user.

Franz Erhard Walther fulfilled the call for explicit instructions for use in 1968 with his book *OBJEKTE, benutzen*, in which he showed how his objects, made specially for actions by the viewer, were to be used.[72] At the latest from this point onwards, the user assumed a central role in art. It is the user who perfects the artwork, as it were. For only by using the objects does the artwork come into being and unfold. Fichte's idea that "the self is *solely* active,"[73] is reflected in the mutation of all art forms into forms of action, in the transformation of the passive subject into an active individual, the viewer into a user.

The acceptance of the viewers as actors rested on their having been raised to the status of a reflective and creative subject: "All in all," Duchamp wrote in 1957, "the creative act is not performed by the artist alone; the spectator brings the work in contact with the external world by deciphering and interpreting its inner qualification

71 Marcel Duchamp, *La Mariée mise à nu par ses célibataires, même* (1934), as quoted from: Marcel Duchamp, *Duchamp du signe suivi de Notes*, revised and corrected edition, Michel Sanouillet and Paul Matisse (eds.), Flammarion, Paris, 2008, pp. 62–107, here p. 68 ("READYMADE RÉCIPROQUE / Se servir d'un Rembrandt comme planche à repasser").

72 See: Franz Erhard Walther, *OBJEKTE, benutzen* (1968), 2nd updated and expanded edition, edited by Peter Weibel, Verlag der Buchhandlung Walther König, Cologne, 2014.

73 Fichte 1982, p. 133.

and thus adds his contribution to the creative act."[74] By this definition, the recipient is thus an integral part of the creative act. The viewer morphs into an artist, the consumer into a producer, the viewer into a user who participates directly in the production of art. Art becomes a participatory process, and the participation finally becomes part of the artwork itself. In this way, the model is set for politics. If art, hitherto solely the field of the artist's sovereign actions, becomes a participatory process that includes the viewer, then this should also count for other social processes.

After 1945, in the visual arts and in New Music audience participation emerged as part of the artwork. In "action painting," for example, the panel painting, as the name suggests, served as the arena of the action, and physical actions on a horizontal canvas created painting. These physical actions on the canvas led to painting before the canvas, to show painting in front of an audience (Georges Mathieu) and actions with the body on canvas (Yves Klein), and finally actions completely without a canvas and only with the body, as Action art.

Analogous to the participatory trends in 1950s art (Kinetic art and Op art), New Music of the late 1950s (Earle Brown, John Cage, etc.), who concerned themselves closely with the issue of scores and granted the performer great freedom, was a key root of the stronger emergence of participation and the evolution of instruction art. "In 1957 New Music was the Center of all Arts Movements and Germany was the Center of the New Music," Nam June Paik recollected in 1999. In 1960, composer La Monte Young wrote *Compositions 1960*, which included real non-musical instructions, too. *Composition 1960 #10*, for example, called on the listener to "Draw a straight line and follow it." In 1962 Nam June Paik wrote in his instructions *Read Music – Do It Yourself – Answers to La Monte Young*: "See your right eye with your left eye."

From Cage onwards, the performer's freedom within the instructions for the score was a key theme in New Music. Paik transferred these compositional techniques from the world of tones into the world of images. Through this transfer, the musician was replaced by the audience itself as the performer or participant: "As the next step toward more indeterminacy, I wanted to let the audience (or congregation, in this case) act and play itself," he wrote.[75] His video sculpture *Participation TV* (1963/1966) enabled the audience to change the images on a black-and-white TV using a microphone and signal amplifier – a key piece for the following decades of interactive media art. His piece *Random Access* in the exhibition *Exposition of Music – Electronic Television* (1963) consisted of tapes attached to the wall. The viewer or user was able to pull a mobile audio head across them and create music him/herself, becoming a pianist as it were who navigated along the audio track composing in the process. The birth of media art and its participatory trends was born of the spirit of music around 1960. Action art (happenings, Fluxus, performance) was thus influenced not just by painterly and literary sources, but also by musical considerations.

The trend in the visual arts to transpose participatory principles from acoustic art to the visual arts and thus place the audience on center stage as the artwork's actor sparked the "performative

74 Marcel Duchamp, *The Creative Act*, short lecture in the course of: *Session on the Creative Act, Convention of the American Federation of Arts*, Houston, Texas, April 1957, available online, for example, at: http://danm.ucsc.edu/~dustin/library/Duchamp-the_creative_act.pdf, accessed 05/28/2015; here quoted from: Michel Sanouillet and Elmer Peterson (eds.), *Salt Seller. The Writings of Marcel Duchamp*, Oxford University Press, Oxford, New York (NY), 1973, p. 140.

75 Nam June Paik, "About the Exposition of Music," in: Wolf Vostell (ed.), *Décollage. Bulletin aktueller Ideen*, no. 3, December 1962, n. p.

turn," at a time when John L. Austin and his book *How to Do Things with Words* (1962) and his theory of speech acts likewise initiated a performative turn in philosophy.

As early as 1959 Fluxus artist George Brecht, a student of John Cage, held a solo show called *Toward Events* in New York's Reuben Gallery and coined the term "events": it consisted mainly of binary instructions, so-called event scores. Allan Kaprow's famous concept forming happening *18 Happenings in 6 Parts* (1959) entailed "instructions" for "a cast of participants." In *Cut Piece* (1964) Yoko Ono called on the audience to step up onto the stage and cut the clothes off her body. She transformed the art of instructions for using objects into the art of instructions for people.[76] Another example of the art object being replaced by actions and instructions for them was Wolf Vostell's Action art happening *YOU* (1964) in Long Island, New York. "Basic idea: confront those involved, the audience with a satire of what life puts upon us in the form of a test run for chaos [...] / what I think is not important – but what the audience culls for itself from the processes and my image."[77]

76 See: Jon Hendricks (ed.), *Instructions for paintings by Yoko Ono*, May 24, 1962, Galeria 56, Budapest, 1993.

77 Wolf Vostell, *Happening & Leben*, Luchterhand, Neuwied, Berlin, 1970, p. 263.

In *Nouveau Réalisme* a major role is likewise accorded to calling on the audience to participate in creating the artwork. In the form of *Métamatics*, Jean Tinguely's drawing machines, as of the mid-1950s the audience was able to make drawings itself. With her exhibition *Feu à volonté* (1961) Niki de Saint Phalle invited the audience to take a gun in their hands and shoot her assemblages.

It was not only New Music, Fluxus, happenings, performance, and *Nouveau Réalisme* that discovered the participating viewer, co-creator, and player in the 1960s, for in the 1950s Kinetic and Op art had inserted audience participation into the construction of artworks. In the course of the 3rd Paris Biennale in 1963, the artist collective GRAV (Groupe de Recherche d'Art Visuel) proclaimed in their manifesto:

> "[...] We want to interest the viewer,
> to reduce his inhibitions, to relax him.
> We want to make him participate.
> We want to place him in a situation that
> he triggers and transforms.
> We want him to be conscious of
> his participation.
> We want him to aim towards an interaction
> with other viewers.
> We want to develop in the viewer a strength
> of perception and action.
> A viewer conscious of his power of action,
> and tired of so many abuses and
> mystifications, will be able to make his
> own 'revolution in art.'"[78]

78 As quoted from: Claire Bishop, *Artificial Hells. Participatory Art and the Politics of Spectatorship*, Verso, London, Brooklyn (NY), 2012, p. 89.

The viewer had to move to perceive the optical illusions and phenomena of Op art. She/He was able to set the kinetic image objects and sculptures in motion and change them, thus becoming a user. The works enabled early forms of interactivity.

This turn to the recipient has been radicalized by the technological means of recording: photography, TV, video, computers, and the Internet. The audience participates not only in the production of the artwork, but has itself been declared an artwork. It became content, as in Peter Weibel's video work *Das Publikum als Exponat* (1969), where in a closed-circuit installation real viewers for the first time encountered themselves on "TV" (actually on video) both in real time and with a time lag. Video, computer, and network technology augmented the participatory options in the 1980s and 1990s to the point of interactivity. Media art established the viewer's participation in the creation of the artwork as interactivity between viewer and artwork in terms of mutual physical influence. In the Action and media art of the second half of the twentieth century, the audience practiced intensified participation. Art became a field of action[79] and the viewer the activist or actor. This experience in the field of art had to spill over into the social domain at some point.

79 See: Peter Weibel, *Offene Handlungsfelder. Open Practices*, exhib. cat., Austrian Pavilion at the 48th Venice Biennale 1999, DuMont, Cologne, 1999.

VIII. The Invention of the Net Activist

The most unambiguous form of Action art was 1990s Internet art. It explicitly saw itself as a type of social action and applied its attention to those forces structuring society. Its goal was to shed light on the ways realities are constructed online or to create new types of public life and reality. The artists involved react to the fundamental effects of information technology, which themselves cannot be separated from the global economy. The rise of neoliberalism is based among other things on the global expansion of information technology. In their actions, the artists and Internet culture activists saw the historic opportunity to ensure information and communication technology served emancipated citizens, individuals reendowed with rights – freeing them from the dictates of capital, commerce, and the military.

Net-based art sets out to contribute to the recivilization of global media technology by criticizing the Internet's economic, social, and technological conditions and constraints, by altering software, and by attacking the standardized intermeshing of global computer culture and corporate monopolization of new technologies. These attacks focus on the norms of the new technologies as well as on the companies establishing these norms.

A new generation of artists operates in the networked computer data world, providing crucial insights into the consequences of the processing taking place across the world, on which our society relies. Global information space becomes the new frame of reference, the new arena of action, superseding the frame of the panel painting. New communities are forged through global information technology that are to a certain degree structured homogeneously in social terms but no longer tied to specific localities. Art, having extended its field of action from the image into real space in the mid-twentieth century, now also uses virtual data space. Net-based activism operates at the level of the technical *dispositif* itself, that is, on the Web, for example, by distributing net-based documents or by operating to counteract that backdrop by attacking hardware and software.

So-called whistle-blowers like Edward Snowden now form the vanguard of Net activism. They demonstrate just what kind of power a single individual can have who does not want to bow to a system that violates basic democratic rights. This is why the system is so afraid of code breakers and hackers: the insider knowledge the whistle-blowers expose and share via online media channels provides an enormously important basis for the citizens' movements.

This creates a new equation between press, public, and power. Net activists' early warnings concerning the IT-related military complex that superseded the traditional industrial military complex and which U.S. President Dwight D. Eisenhower had warned about in his valedictory address on January 17, 1961, were initially rejected or marginalized by press and politics and, of course, by the art system. That said, the people, individuals, have begun to use the Web and mobile media for their purposes. The technical opportunities afforded by multimedia that were used and explored by artists as part of their investigations into participation and performance are now being employed by other citizens. What were once purely "visual media" have metamorphosed in the process into the now famous "mobile media." The media that previously merely represented the world in images or text have turned into "social media." Art's individual Net activism has now become a social activity, thereby turning into one of the crucial preconditions of Net-assisted civil activism. The progressive personalization and mobilization of the new media, from PC to smartphone, has also contributed to the advancing individualization of politics, to the increased power held by individuals in social life. Without the online social networks, gatherings by thousands of individuals in public spaces would not have happened on the scale witnessed nor would they have had such a political impact.

Net activists use action in the digital arena to organize real space in a new way and render it dynamic. The Internet is used as a weapon of enlightenment and information against the established power nexus. Artistic projects based on Net activism highlight the technological preconditions of computer-based communication, along with its power structures and its indissoluble interconnect with technology. Here, Philippe Quéau's insights apply. Quéau insists that because all these technologies have a great impact on our lives (comparable to the impact of legislation), we should first test them and then create tools for educating people about their impact.[80]

The global mass circulation of videos online, and this applies to those with both political and artistic content, and the panoptical constitution of our society, in which all data on a "person of interest" can be gathered at any time, have all fundamentally changed the world. They put values such as freedom, equality, the public sphere, privacy, property, in short, our basic values, to the test. Many states and "embedded journalism" now seem to give security priority over freedom, favoring a limited liberalism over democracy. In view of the revelations made by Edward Snowden and the other whistle-blowers it seems as though a new safety Securitate is busy ramping up to dominate the world. And so far, it is only the Net activists who are putting up resistance to this development.

80
See: Philippe Quéau, "Das globale Gemeinwohl. Politische Entscheidungsfindung und Cyberspace," in: Florian Rötzer (ed.), *Megamaschine Wissen. Vision: Überleben im Netz*, Campus, Frankfurt am Main, New York (NY), 1999, pp. 203–222, here pp. 218–219; Philippe Quéau, "Global Governance and Knowledge Societies," in: *Development*, vol. 45, no. 4, 2002, pp. 10–16.

IX. The Invention of the "Artivist"

As the previous sections have shown, the art world has brought about a behavioral change in how artworks are received and has systematically put this change to the test since the 1950s. Creativity has shifted from artist to viewer, with the artist transferring the role of actor to the recipient. Interactive artworks no longer exist autonomously. They only really come into existence by virtue of being used by the recipient. In my view, exiting the image and entering physical action has not only spawned audience participation (as the participation is fostered in particular by interactive media artworks), but has also anticipated corresponding developments in society as a whole. It has, moreover, laid the ground for a stronger participation in the political sphere, precisely in the shape of the global activism we are seeing today.

As a result, even social action, such as interventions carried out in the public sphere, can gain art status. As Joseph Beuys said as early as 1970: "Every human being is an artist." Social media is now also turning all humans into transmitters rather than mere receivers. The art of the twentieth century has made the boundaries between the various actors (architects, designers, artists, scientists, politicians, citizens) and between aesthetic and nonaesthetic objects and events both permeable and invisible. The long-standing distinction between the sphere of highbrow art and lowbrow "everyday" culture, between artist and consumer, between aesthetic communication and social action has become fluid and vague. The field of action replaces the object. This field of action consists of verbal instructions or performative actions, the actors are people and things. The artwork-as-object has been superseded by open-ended events, installations, actions, processes, games, instructions for action, concepts, and environments. The passive viewer has been replaced by the participant, the cocreator, the fellow player.[81]

Millions of people are now using the Internet to exchange photos, texts, videos, and music every day. In this way, all individuals can become transmitters. A newly structured space for the creative expression of millions of people is evolving. Millions of people are finding a platform for communication, creativity, and art online, independently of authorities such as publishing houses, museums, galleries, magazines, radio, TV, and the Hollywood film industry, who traditionally decided on the production and distribution of cultural works. Online, everyone is an author and a publisher, and in the final instance likewise a voter and a politician, because digitally distributed communication can change the state of the social world. This is why the "artivist" is the new type of artist of the twenty-first century. The now ubiquitous term was coined by Italian media researcher Tatiana Bazzichelli, who declared the Internet an artwork in her initiative "AHA:Activism–Hacking–Artivism" in 2001, and who has also contributed a text to this publication.[82]

The field of actors has broadened: with the "artivist," creativity and innovation are democratized. "User innovation" and "user-generated content" no longer influence only the world of mass media, but also the art world. The "creative industries" of the future will be the emancipated users. And art itself will become a "democratized user-centered innovation system."[83] Information and communication

81 See: Peter Weibel and Holger Jost (eds.), *Claus Bremer: mitspiel. Die Aktivierung des Publikums: Vom dynamischen Theater zur Theaterstadt. Dramaturgische Texte 1948–1971*, Alexander Verlag, Berlin, 2014.

82 See: Tatiana Bazzichelli, *Networking. The Net as Artwork*, Digital Aesthetics Research Centre (DARC), Aarhus University, Aarhus, 2008.

83 See: Eric von Hippel, *Democratizing Innovation*, The MIT Press, Cambridge (MA), 2005.

technologies open the gates to a century of the emancipated user who wants to be duly recognized in the worlds of art and politics. Will the individual as historical subject be the deciding factor for the development of civilization and culture in the twenty-first century?

The dream of a direct democracy or a soviet republic as a response to the crisis of the parliamentary democracy arose as early as the 1960s. What we are seeing today is a new type of extra-parliamentary opposition, made up not of a student elite, but of a mass of anonymous individuals. We are experiencing the transition from a parliamentary to a performative democracy. Citizens now want to break the monopoly of a party-political caste and participate in political power. They want to assert their ability to act performatively and make decisions, which means turning rhetoric or votes into action. What is genuinely new about this is the demand for performativity. Performative interventions by artivists coupled with mass media online distribution have shown how citizens can – and want to – play a tangible part in overcoming crisis situations: practices of artistic performance and those of audience participation, which have existed in art since the 1960s, are now descending into the world of politics, as it were. Audience participation in art as a consequence of the performative turn has created the historical preconditions for the new civic involvement in democracy. Interactive media art has anticipated social models.

It is one of the characteristics of today's global society that the state is no longer some artificial entity invented to protect the natural human being as Hobbes wrote. Instead, the modern state has actually become humankind's enemy.[84] The totalitarian systems of the early twentieth century and their wars have prompted people to see the state not as a defender but as a destroyer of man. In the past twenty years, we have seen an increasing accumulation of power and an interweaving of politics, the economy, IT, science, and finally culture, too. It is a combination which threatens the very functioning of political and civic institutions to the same extent as it threatens individual rights.

84
See: Franz L. Neumann, *Behemoth. The Structure and Practice of National Socialism*, Oxford University Press, Oxford, New York (NY), 1942.

Large swathes of society are evidently under the impression that the state does not sufficiently protect citizens', environmental, and animal rights, and on the contrary actually impinges on these rights. This is why they have found new forms of organization, namely NGOs, that are financed by individuals and which shoulder tasks that were originally a government responsibility, such as protecting the environment, safeguarding human rights, or providing humanitarian aid. The actions by Greenpeace, Amnesty International, Doctors Without Borders, and so on come to mind, which has caused a stir worldwide. Protests against nuclear weapons or against the pollution of the Earth's atmosphere first originated in civic movements rather than state organizations, have achieved a degree of success, and in some cases have even led to new political parties being formed. NGOs have played a game-changing role in the rise of global activism.

After the *global city* (Saskia Sassen, *The Global City: New York, London, Tokyo*, 1991) and *global governance* (Brundtland Report, *Our Common Future*, 1987) we are now seeing a new kind of social action emerging, a "performative democracy" centered around the *global citizen*. This *global citizen* recognizes the existential threats to, and interests of, all of humanity that are not contained by national borders. This new type of citizen addresses both local problems (such as unneeded train stations being built) as well as global ones (such as climate protection). Global activism is then constituted on the basis of a "global citizenship."

A new kind of protest, an uprising of the indignant,[85] is currently establishing itself, fed by the powerlessness people are experiencing. This new type of spontaneous, noninstitutional mass protest by individuals is an immense global phenomenon revealing the extent to which people desire social change.

85 See: Stéphane Hessel, *Time for Outrage!*, with a foreword by Charles Glass, Quartet Books, London, 2011.

The new kinds of spontaneous mass protests by individuals take the shape of actions, demonstrations, and operations carried out in the public sphere and have shown, in particular in the context of the Arab Spring, how established power systems can be opposed and disabled, at least for a short moment in history. Deficiencies in democracy and the economy, most notably corruption, are the subject of worldwide activist protests as is the demand for the upholding of human rights and the right to free speech, for peaceful solutions to global conflicts, for stable immigration policies, preventative health care, or animal and environmental protection. In the Anthropocene era we are seeing new conflicts between friends and enemies of the Earth. New pacts, new *contrats socials*, are therefore being sought: between humans and nature (for example, as regards sustainability), between generations, between nations, between citizens and state. These seem more possible than ever before in the digital society.

A new space for negotiation is beginning to open up in the digital age, a space beyond the control-based authority of the state and beyond the authority of state institutions. After the Papal power of God's representatives, after the imperial authority of succession by lineage, and the political authority of representation we are now seeing an individual authority emerge that is founded in performativity and participation. Despite there being talk of a crisis of democracy and even of a postdemocracy, a variety of movements based on civic involvement are multiplying across the world. After the waves of democratization in the twentieth century, a "democratic experimentalism" made up of a conflation of participation, representation, and deliberation has spread, in particular in the new democracies of Latin America. The establishment of local and national councils, participatory town planning, and participatory budgeting has meant first and foremost that we are now seeing not just the middle but also the lower classes involved in political decision-making. Issues relating to pensions, health, telecommunication, and water and electricity supply are now decided by plebiscite procedures. These participatory reforms strengthen the maximalist democracy model. And it is not in the established democracies of the West, let alone those in Eastern Europe, that the most egalitarian types of participatory democracy are being put to the test, but in South America of all places – after the countries there have finally freed themselves from the yoke of years of dictatorship. "There are simply no analogies on a similar scale and depth in North America, Europe, Asia or Africa."[86]

86 Archon Fung, "Reinventing Democracy in Latin America," in: *Perspectives on Politics*, vol. 9, no. 4, December 2011, pp. 857–871, here p. 868.

It is time, then, to test how compatible participatory reforms are with the institutions of representative democracy; this can definitely lead not only to a transformation of the types of political parties we are seeing, but also to a transformation of representational party democracy itself. Political parties and their representatives are mainly known for trying to circumvent control. This is in fact why citizens' movements are protecting democracy from self-destructive forces.

The exhibition *global aCtIVISm* at ZKM | Center for Art and Media Karlsruhe asked how artist-citizens, artivists, express their concern at the current states of affairs in the world. They evidently draw on aspects of the action and performance art of the twentieth century. But in many cases performance art was solely concerned with the cultivation of the self of the artist. It took place, for the main part, in "White Cube" museum spaces, at the behest of the institution. It is only performances in the public sphere of the street, anonymously and without institutional invitation, that are cultivated in activism: with the objective of solving social rather than artistic problems. Activism is the art form of the protest movement. It takes place outside of institutions and has a socially motivated, emancipatory basis. Art has a new agency (Alfred Gell, *Art and Agency. An Anthropological Theory*, 1998) which results in a new kind of activism: artivism.

The artist-citizen then embodies two dreams: the citizen models his political freedom after the artist's freedom. Artistic freedom as a product of civil revolution vouches for the model of political freedom. This is why we are seeing citizens' movements in the twenty-first century whose ephemeral character unsettles traditional political parties and sociologists precisely because what is involved are the mass movements of individuals instead of classes.

The new activism is a war between individual and institution, subject and system. Public mass manifestations, from the Puerta del Sol in Madrid, the Tahrir Square in Cairo, the Tiananmen Square in Beijing to Taksim Square in Istanbul all offer examples not only of the power of the masses, but of the power of otherwise powerless individuals. Historically, mass marches were organized and initiated "from above," with the exception of revolutionary situations. Mass civil protest today is organized and initiated bottom-up. Global activism as a twenty-first century movement is providing the first examples of how mass culture can become critical instead of affirming mass consumerism like pop culture.

The invention of the people created the "bass line"; that is, the outline of democracy. The invention of the citizen gave us representative democracy. But the real challenge and motor of democracy is the invention of the individual. The personalized or individualized version of democracy, which is imposed on society by the ubiquitous personalized technology (from personal computers to personal medical health gadgets), will bring us a performative democracy. The promised freedom of the individual in an open society and the traditional claims of power by the state will clash constantly in the future. This is what global activism is about. The questions "Who governs?" and "Who decides what is real and what is truth?"

will become more and more a battlefield between the state power and the individual subject, who will no longer willingly succumb and be subjugated to the monopoly of the state. This book is a humble monument to the global movements of critical citizens.

The exhibition *global aCtIVISm* was thus predestined to illuminate a new social, political, and artistic phenomenon. It showed global activism to be the first new art form of the twenty-first century: it is an art form founded on the tactical and strategic use of media technologies in the age of the Internet. The exhibition was supplemented by a virtual presentation online. This included a database on art and activism stretching back to include the 1970s, as well as a blog with background information on the participating artists and activists. Exhibition, database, website, blog, and catalog aim to do their part in making the utopia of democracy a reality, which is owed to the dynamics of a democratic citizenry, as can already be seen in the word *CIVIS* (Lat. citizen) in the term *aCtIVISm*.

Translated from the German by Jeremy Gaines.

Further References

Mark Achbar (ed.), *Manufacturing Consent. Noam Chomsky and the Media. The Companion Book to the Award-Winning Film by Peter Wintonick and Mark Achbar*, Black Rose Books, Montreal, New York, 1994.

John S. Ahlquist and Margaret Levi (eds.), *In the Interest of Others. Organizations and Social Activism*, Princeton University Press, Princeton (NJ), Oxford, 2013.

Alain Badiou, *The Rebirth of History. Times of Riots and Uprisings*, translated from the French by Gregory Elliott, Verso, London, Brooklyn (NY), 2012.

Ulrich Beck, *What Is Globalization?*, translated from the German by Patrick Camiller, Polity Press, Cambridge, 2000.

Erica Chenoweth and Maria J. Stephan, *Why Civil Resistance Works. The Strategic Logic of Nonviolent Conflict*, Columbia University Press, New York (NY), 2013.

Noam Chomsky, *Profit Over People. Neoliberalism and the Global Order*, Seven Stories Press, New York (NY), 1999.

Richard van Dülmen, *Die Entdeckung des Individuums. 1500–1800*, Fischer, Frankfurt am Main, 1997.

David Graeber, *The Democracy Project. A History, a Crisis, a Movement*, Penguin Books, London, 2014.

Michael Hardt and Antonio Negri, *Commonwealth*, Harvard University Press, Cambridge (MA), 2009.

Michael Hardt and Antonio Negri, *Declaration*, Argo Navis Author Services, 2012.

David Held, *Global Covenant. The Social Democratic Alternative to the Washington Consensus*, Polity Press, Cambridge, Malden (MA), 2004.

Lutz Hieber and Stephan Moebius (eds.), *Avantgarden und Politik. Künstlerischer Aktivismus von Dada bis zur Postmoderne*, Transcript, Bielefeld, 2009.

Brian Homes, *Unleashing the Collective Phantoms. Essays in Reverse Imagineering*, Autonomedia, Brooklyn (NY), 2008.

Nadia Idle and Alex Nunns (eds.), *Tweets from Tahrir. Egypt's revolution as it unfolded, in the words of the people who made it*, OR Books, New York (NY), 2011.

Henry Jenkins and David Thorburn (eds.), *Democracy and New Media*, The MIT Press, Cambridge (MA), 2003.

Jens Kastner, *Transnationale Guerilla. Aktivismus, Kunst und die kommende Gemeinschaft*, Unrast, Münster, 2007.

Joshua Kurlantzick, *Democracy in Retreat. The Revolt of the Middle Class and the Worldwide Decline of Representative Government*, Yale University Press, New Haven (CT), London, 2013.

Marc James Léger, *Brave New Avant Garde. Essays on Contemporary Art and Politics*, Zero Books, Winchester, Washington (DC), 2012.

Chase Madar, *The Passion of Bradley Manning. The Story Behind the Wikileaks Whistleblower*, Verso, London, Brooklyn (NY), 2013.

Solange Mercier-Josa, *La lutte pour la reconnaissance et la notion de Peuple dans la Première Philosophie de l'Esprit de Hegel*, Inclinaison, Montargis, 2003.

W.J.T. Mitchell, Bernard E. Harcourt, and Michael Taussig, *Occupy. Three Inquiries in Disobedience*, University of Chicago Press, Chicago (IL), London, 2013.

Mahdi Darius Nazemroaya, *The Globalization of Nato*, Clarity Press, Atlanta (GA), 2012.

Lin Noueihed and Alex Warren, *The Battle for the Arab Spring. Revolution, Counter-Revolution and the Making of a New Era*, Yale University Press, New Haven (CT), London, 2012.

Gerald Raunig, *Art* and *Revolution. Transversal Activism in the Long Twentieth Century*, Semiotext(e), Los Angeles (CA), 2007.

Tomáš Sedláček and David Graeber, *Revolution oder Evolution. Das Ende des Kapitalismus?*, Hanser, Munich, 2015.

Richard Sennett, *The Culture of the New Capitalism*, Yale University Press, New Haven (CT), 2007.

Theda Skocpol, *Diminished Democracy. From Membership to Management in American Civic Life*, University of Oklahoma Press, Norman (OK), 2003.

Paolo Virno, *Multitude. Between Innovation and Negation*, Semiotext(e), Los Angeles (CA), 2008.

Loïc Wacquant, *Punishing the Poor. The Neoliberal Government of Social Insecurity*, Duke University Press, Durham (NC), London, 2009.

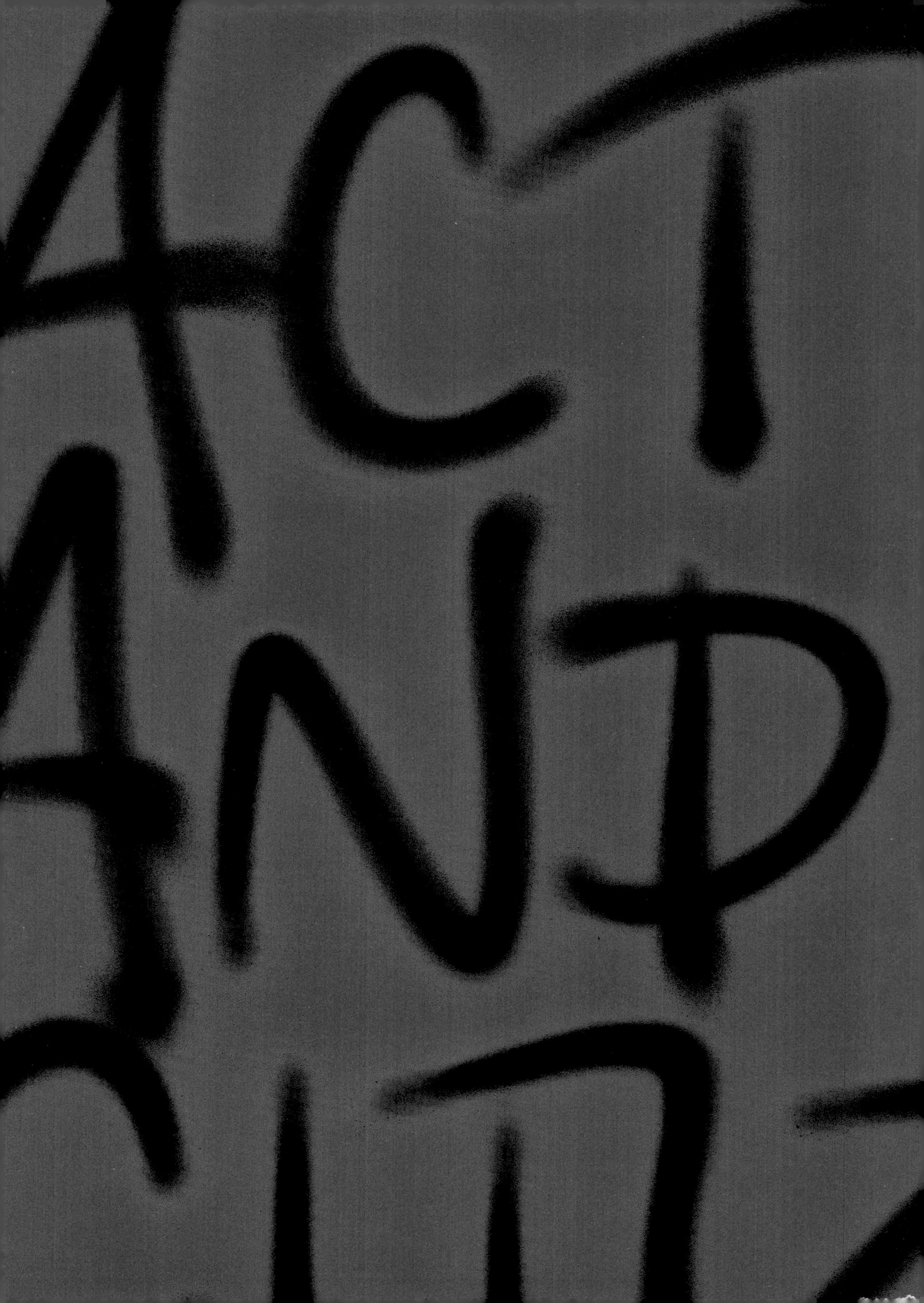

Activism and the Citizen

Chapter I

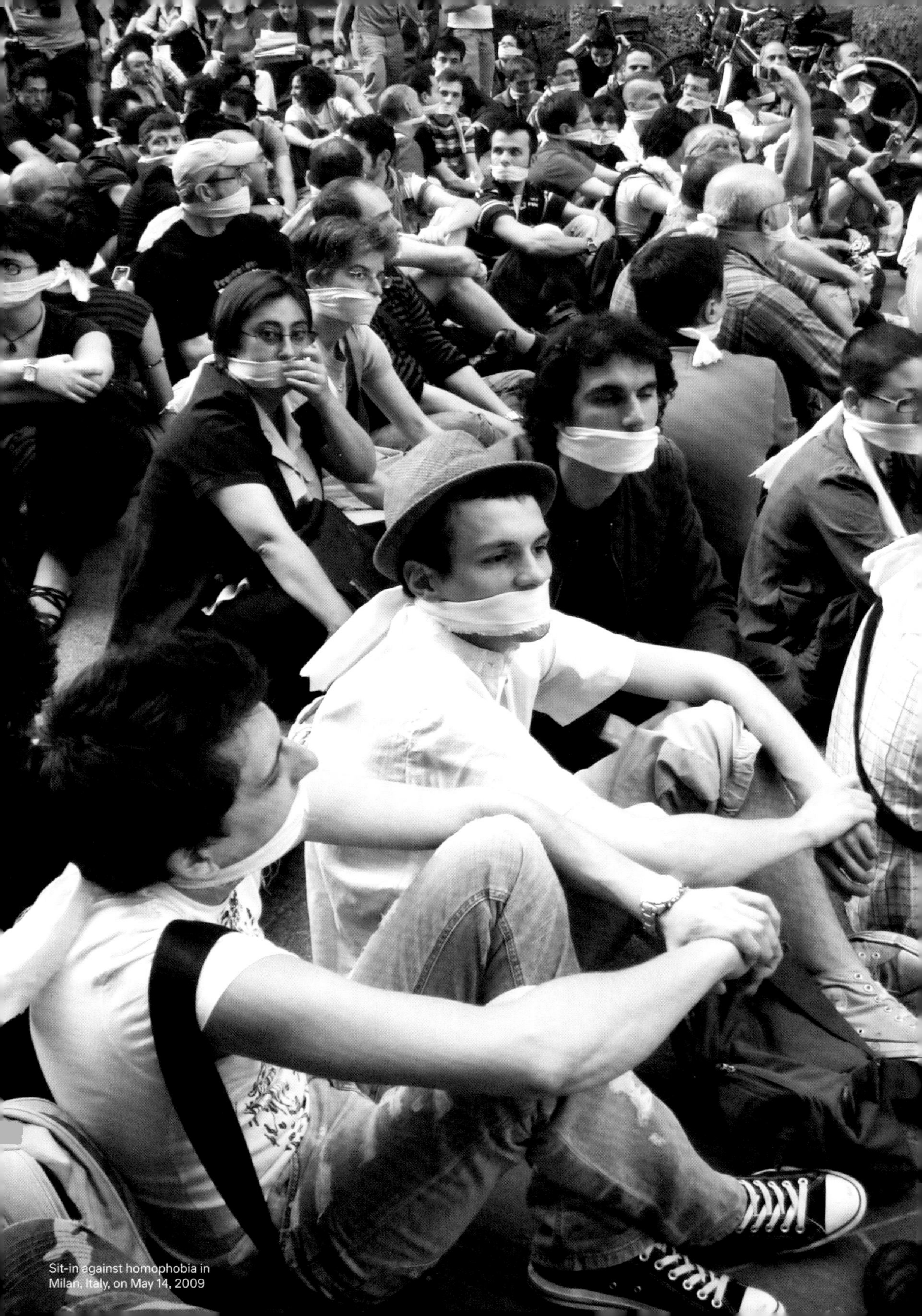

Sit-in against homophobia in
Milan, Italy, on May 14, 2009

Robin Celikates

Learning from the Streets: Civil Disobedience in Theory and Practice

Civil disobedience can be understood as a civic practice of contestation – a noninstitutionalized practice with which citizens (in the broad sense, not necessarily those recognized as such by the state) challenge established and institutionalized forms of vertical authority. What can we learn about this practice from how it is exercised in the real world? How can the activist practice of confronting "low-intensity representative democratic institutions" with "participatory or high-intensity democratic forms of democracy and self-determination"[1] inform the attempt to theorize disobedience? Asking these questions, that is, starting from the practice of dissent "on the streets," is especially relevant in the case of civil disobedience, since the discussion about this political practice – a practice with a rich and contested history that stretches from Henry David Thoreau via Mahatma Gandhi and Martin Luther King, Jr. to Occupy – has been marked by a number of systematic shortcomings. These shortcomings can be seen as stemming from theorists' systematic ignorance of the complex reality of disobedience, leading them to a simplified and depoliticized understanding of this practice.[2] In order to counter this tendency, in what follows I will sketch some theoretical lessons that can be drawn from "the streets," and in particular from the recent uprising in Turkey that started on May 28, 2013, and that has become a prominent episode in the cycle of global protest that started with the so-called Arab Spring. After the protests in Istanbul had first focused on the neoliberal transformation of urban space and its disastrous ecological and social consequences, they spread out socially (in terms of participants), geographically (in terms of cities involved), and politically (in terms of both the substance of the demands that were formulated and the way in which they were formulated) – their political and theoretical significance, however, is even further reaching.[3]

Highlighting some central aspects of these protests will serve to indicate three ways in which the practice of civil disobedience is more complex and also more political than it is suggested by the mainstream understanding of it as a primarily or exclusively symbolic and nonviolent act of protest that involves breaking particular laws without challenging the legitimacy of the existing order. The three aspects I will focus on are: first, the meaning of "civil" in civil disobedience; second, the political mobilization and the essentially collective character of civil disobedience; and third,

1 James Tully, *Public Philosophy in a New Key*, vol. II: *Imperialism and Civic Freedom*, Cambridge University Press, Cambridge (MA), 2009, p. 158, p. 206.

2 This is especially true of the discussion in political philosophy that has been shaped by the writings of John Rawls and, to a lesser extent, Jürgen Habermas. For a more detailed discussion see Robin Celikates, "Civil Disobedience as a Practice of Civic Freedom," in: *On Global Citizenship. James Tully in Dialogue*, Bloomsbury, London, 2014, pp. 207–228.

3 See the symposium Reflections on the Gezi Uprising, available online at: roarmag.org/2014/01/beyond-gezi-future-movement/, accessed 05/15/2014, and, for some documentation, "@showdiscontent. A record of Taksim Gezi Park protest meetings," available online at: showdiscontent.com/archive/gezi-parki/, accessed 05/15/2014.

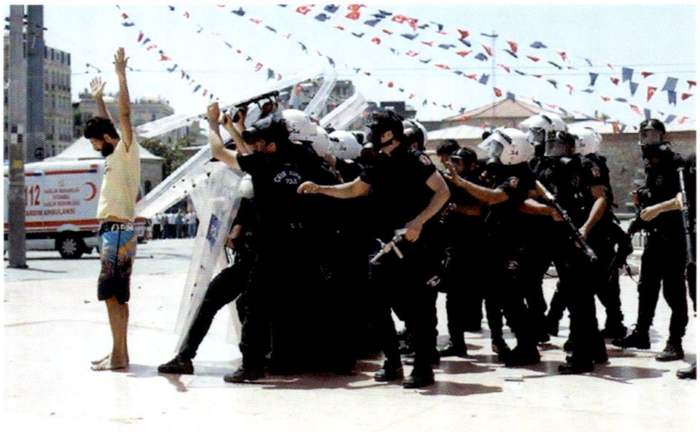

A lone protester faces the police at Taksim Square, Istanbul, 2013.

the inventiveness of the practice of civil disobedience in terms of the repertoire of political action that goes beyond the simple dichotomy of a merely symbolic appeal on the one hand and violent militancy on the other.

So to start with the first point: What is civil about civil disobedience? It is well worth emphasizing the civil and civic character of the protests in Turkey which is all the more remarkable since it is the outcome of massive self-restraint in the face of the enormous aggression and repression exercised by the government and its security forces and the evident power asymmetry they imposed on the movement from the very beginning. Against this background, the civility of the movement should be understood as an expression of political commitment rather than of loyalty to the state or the existing order; in addition, as Gandhi and King already knew, civility in this sense is a significant political achievement and the always precarious outcome of an individual and collective work on the self.[4]

In mainstream discourse, the "civil" in "civil disobedience" is often taken to mean that protesters do not engage in confrontational, aggressive, or violent behavior, that is, it is often identified with (romanticized and one-sided interpretations of) the idea of nonviolence and peacefulness. Whether that is convincing, however, of course depends on how precisely violence is understood, and the problem here is that it is an extremely contested and politicized notion.[5] My point here is not that we should develop a better theoretical definition of violence that can then be applied to practice, but rather that without problematizing how both violence and nonviolence are understood in both theory and practice and without

4

See: *The Moral and Political Writings of Mahatma Gandhi*, vol. 3: *Non-violent Resistance and Social Transformation*, Clarendon Press, Oxford, 1987, pp. 18ff., pp. 88ff.; and King's famous "Letter From Birmingham Jail," April 16, 1963, available online at: www.stanford.edu/group/King/frequentdocs/birmingham.pdf, accessed 05/15/2014.

5

A related problem is that this identification is often based on an extremely one-sided understanding of the activism of King and the broader context of the American Civil Rights Movement, and more recently also of Nelson Mandela and the ANC, that in some cases amounts to historical whitewashing.

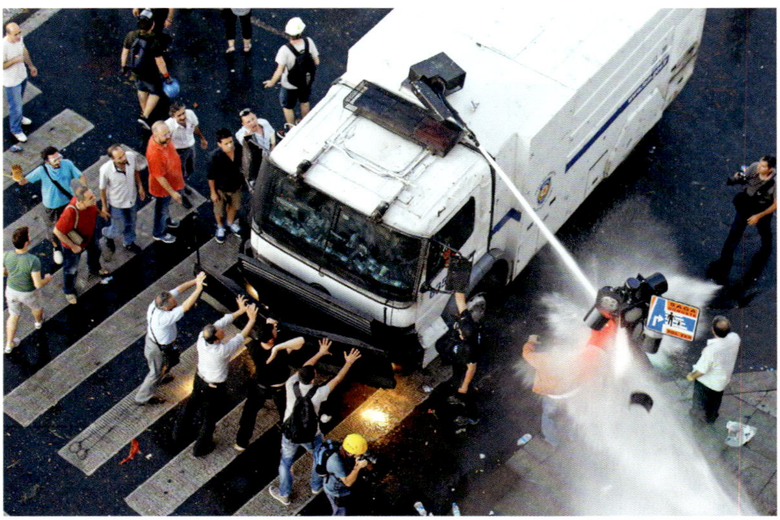

Protesters try to stop an armored crowd control truck from which the riot police fire a water cannon at Taksim Square, Istanbul, June 22, 2013.

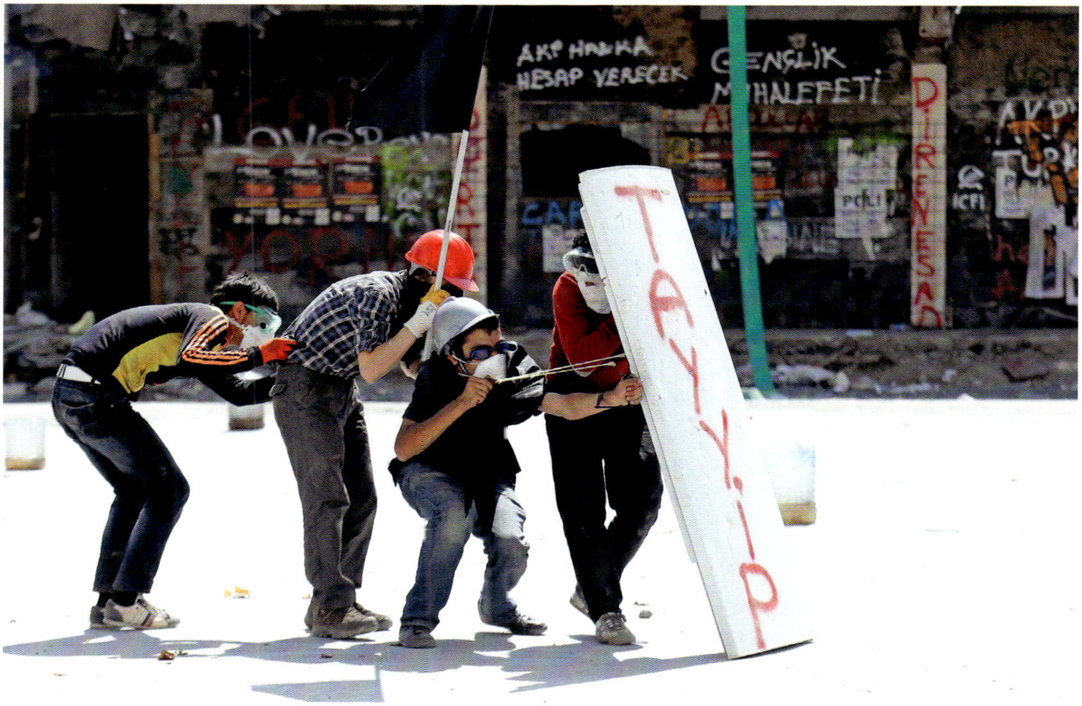

Protesters take cover behind a shield during a protest at Taksim Square, Istanbul, June 11, 2013.

paying more attention to how this distinction is politically instrumentalized, insisting on the necessarily nonviolent character of civil and civic forms of contestation is both politically and theoretically problematic. In this light we have to remind ourselves that in many countries, including Germany and Turkey, it can nowadays count (in public opinion but also in a court of law) as an act of violent coercion to collectively stand in one place, to sit down on the street, or to make fun of the ruling authorities; that often trespassing or damaging private property are subsumed under the notion of violence thus assimilating them to serious violations of the bodily integrity of real persons; and that it is a feature of repressive tolerance, in Herbert Marcuse's sense, that governments pursue a tactic of divide and conquer with regard to protest, portraying and celebrating certain forms of protest as good (good in terms of who protests how and with what aim) and labeling and repressing other forms of protest – often those of marginalized groups – as violent, uncivil, and criminal.[6]

Instead of simply identifying the civil and civic character of collective action with "nonviolence" we should therefore insist that civility is quite compatible with a variety of actions often classified as violent by the media and the state, most prominently violence against oneself (which plays a crucial role in the repertoire of action of protest movements, think of the self-immolation of Mohamed Bouazizi which was a catalyst for the mobilization of the people in Tunisia in December 2010[7]), violence in self-defense (think of relatively minor forms of violence in defense against police aggression), or, maybe even more obviously, the destruction of private or public property which is also often considered as violent.

6

See: Herbert Marcuse, "Repressive Tolerance," in: Robert Paul Wolff, Barrington Moore, Jr., and Herbert Marcuse, *A Critique of Pure Tolerance*, Beacon Press, Boston, 1969, pp. 95–137. A recent illustration of this tendency is the public reaction to the riots in the French banlieues and in London – that even riots that are framed as "issueless" or driven by "consumerist desires" can be seen as a reaction to the violation of civic claims is a point made by Ferdinand Sutterlüty, "The Hidden Morale of the 2005 French and 2011 English Riots," in: *Thesis Eleven*, vol. 121, no. 1, April 2014, pp. 38–56.

7

See: Banu Bargu, "Why Did Bouazizi Burn Himself? Fatal Political Action as Embodied Critique," unpublished lecture, Goethe University Frankfurt am Main, December 2013.

What is decisive for the civility of protest is not that it is nonviolent in a sense that would exclude these forms of action or that it is purely symbolic and remains "peaceful" and "civilized," but rather that it does not follow a military logic and replace civil and civic resistance with armed force aimed at the physical destruction of an (imagined) enemy. Hence, in the case of the Gezi uprising, the civil character of the movement – despite its engagement in sometimes confrontational and even violent forms of action – prominently expresses itself in the radical refusal of seeing the other side as the "enemy" and of playing the established political game of polarization and defamation.[8] As in so many other recent protest movements such as Occupy, in the Turkish uprising civility has therefore also been connected to what is often called prefiguration. Prefigurative politics experimentally anticipates the transformation it seeks to initiate in the way the struggle is organized here and now: in a horizontal, participatory, inclusive, and civil way, thus breaking not only with the authoritarian state and the politics of the right but also with the vanguardist tradition of the left.[9]

The first lesson to be learned is thus that civil and civic forms of resistance are not reducible to purely symbolic means of protest – even occupying a square or an intersection is obviously more than symbolic. In order to retain their effectiveness, civic forms of protest in general and civil disobedience in particular will, in many circumstances, have to be careful not to be reduced to their symbolic dimension, they have to keep a confrontational character as well – not least in order to defend their civil character. Civil disobedience can only function as symbolic protest – as dramatization in Martin Luther King, Jr.'s sense[10] – if it involves moments of real confrontation, such as practices of blockade and occupation but also digital forms of activism such as hacking, and at the same time it can only function as real confrontation if its participants are aware of its irreducible symbolic dimension – the fact that it is always also a performance in need of (and in search of) a stage and an audience.

8 See: Serhat Karakayalı and Özge Yaka, "The Spirit of Gezi: The Recomposition of Political Subjectivities in Turkey," in: *New Formation*, vol. 83, 2014, pp. 117–138.

9 See: Mathijs van de Sande, "The Prefigurative Politics of Tahrir Square – An Alternative Perspective on the 2011 Revolutions," in: *Res Publica*, vol. 19, no. 3, 2013, pp. 223–239.

10 See: King 1963: "Nonviolent direct action seeks to create such a crisis and foster such a tension that a community which has constantly refused to negotiate is forced to confront the issue. It seeks so to dramatize the issue that it can no longer be ignored."

The second lesson theory can learn from practice concerns the question of political mobilization. I do not mean this in the sense of looking for a single set of "objective" causes that can explain why people start to rise up. After the event, social scientists are quick to point to shifting patterns of social mobility, urban transformation, and clashing political cultures as the causes of what happened, but as with the so-called Arab Spring these are largely ex-post rationalizations, since no one was able to predict these events. Importantly, this includes the activists themselves who have been equally surprised by the dynamics of the chain of events they have set in motion. This sense of surprise has to be preserved against the urge to explain and to fit what happened into all-too-familiar historical patterns and narratives. Of course, people have myriads of reasons to protest, but for such politically and socially heterogeneous groups to come together and to be so resilient in the face of repression and criminalization something else has to happen. What is this something else, this unexplainable and unpredictable remainder that seems to drive collective action?

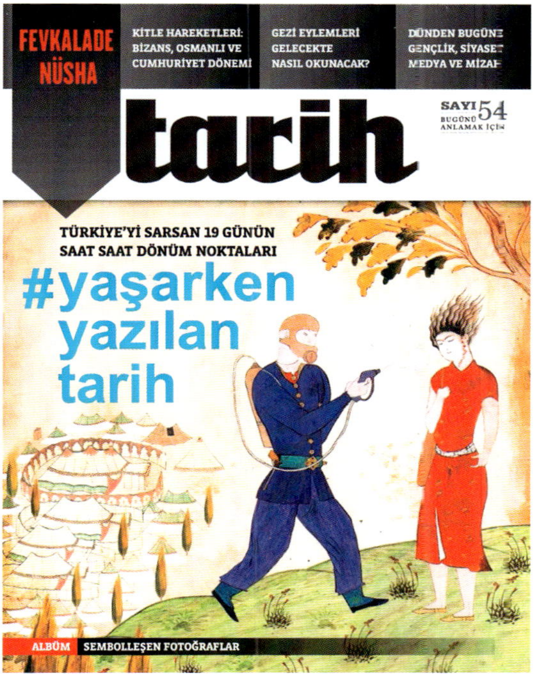

The magazine was closed down by its owners, because a special issue about the Gezi protests was in preparation. Doğuş Holding, owner of the magazine has close ties with the AKP government. The Gezi issue is available online at: www.yasarkenyazilantarih.com, accessed 07/17/2014.

In order to grasp this dimension of the practice of disobedience one has to move beyond the individualist focus of liberal theory and the spotlight the media puts on individual heroes of the rebellion, such as, in the case of Turkey, the famous "woman in red" or "Talcidman" – as important as their role might have been as metaphorical figures that became representatives of the uprising. Instead, we have to take the essentially collective character of civil disobedience into account. The dynamics of collective action is, of course, difficult to theorize but it is an essential aspect of most first-hand accounts and shapes the experience of protesters. When theorists try to capture this dynamic (rather than explain it away or ignore it), they often resort to relatively metaphorical language. Think of the empowering collective experience of overcoming fear and what Hannah Arendt called the joy of acting together and of beginning something new;[11] of Jean-Paul Sartre's marvelous analysis of the storming of the Bastille at what would later become the beginning of the French Revolution in terms of the "groupe en fusion"[12]; or of Michael Hardt and Antonio Negri's multitude in which plurality and creativity come together in the emergence of new political subjectivities – and what is it that these movements exemplify if not the ability of the multitude, usually denied by the state and its representatives, to organize and govern itself?[13]

Without taking this first-person perspective, this phenomenology of protest into account, we – or future social scientists – will never be able to understand why and how people do what they do in an uprising. In contrast to what the liberal mainstream suggests, this is rarely a matter of isolated individuals standing up for their rights or their conscience against the state or the majority: more often, and paradigmatically, civil disobedience is the collective assertion of political agency, which confronts the vertical form of state authority and its institutional realizations with the horizontal and informal power of the association of citizens or the governed, thus creating new political subjectivities both at the individual and collective level that might well turn out to be the most transformative effect of such an uprising.[14]

The third aspect of disobedience about which theory can learn from practice concerns the repertoire of political action. Tahrir, Zuccotti, Syntagma, Taksim ...: Obviously these are very different contexts, in which very different aims, agents, and strategies are involved, but as many commentators have pointed out there still seems to be something like a shared emerging political form: All these protests have prominently involved occupations of public space, that is, democratic acts of reclaiming and reappropriating this space – on a

11
See: Hannah Arendt, "Civil Disobedience," in: *Crises of the Republic*, Harcourt Brace & Company, New York, 1972, pp. 49–102, and Oliver Marchart, *Neu beginnen. Hannah Arendt, die Revolution und die Globalisierung*, Turia & Kant, Vienna, 2005.

12
Jean-Paul Sartre, *Critique de la raison dialectique, Tome I*, Gallimard, Paris, 1960, pp. 391ff.

13
See: Michael Hardt and Antonio Negri, "The Fight for 'Real Democracy' at the Heart of Occupy Wall Street," available online at: www.foreignaffairs.com/articles/136399/michael-hardt-and-antonio-negri/the-fight-for-real-democracy-at-the-heart-of-occupy-wall-street, accessed 05/15/2014.

14
See: Étienne Balibar, "Sur la désobéissance civique," in: *Droit de cité*, PUF, Paris, 2002, pp. 17–22.

more than purely symbolic or metaphorical level – as something that already belongs to the people who use it on an everyday basis but that is threatened by both privatization and state control.[15] Again, these occupations are prefigurative in that protesters organize these spaces by way of political and social relations that the protest is supposed to defend and aim at the same time.

On a general level, there seem to be at least three shared characteristics of how these movements occupy these spaces and of the prefigurative practices realized within them: First, these movements are all committed to plurality in terms of ideological commitments, identities, aims, strategies, and forms of organization and collectivity – in the case of Turkey this is again especially noteworthy against the background of a decidedly antipluralist political culture characterized by widespread patriarchal, nationalist, and paranoid tendencies. Second, its prefigurative politics emphasizes the autonomy of the movement and the way in which it creates its own spaces, independently from the state and the private sector, effectively ignoring their existence (this is the "exodus" component of this form of protest), organizing and protecting in their own way the plurality of bodies that make up the protest movement.[16] This can take a variety of forms that exemplify what it could mean to understand democracy not merely as a set of formal institutions and procedures, but as a form of life, from using the Internet – especially social networks sites such as Twitter and Facebook – to create one's own alternative public sphere[17] via establishing networks of care and support (e.g., in terms of medical assistance and food supply) to building barricades to defend the occupied space against the police. In this respect it is crucial that the prefigurative character mandates a self-reflexive and

15
See: Nilüfer Göle, "Public Space Democracy," available online at: www.eurozine.com/articles/2013-07-29-gole-en.html, accessed 05/15/2014.

16
See: Judith Butler, "Bodies in Alliance and the Politics of the Street," available online at: http://eipcp.net/transversal/1011/butler/en, accessed 05/15/2014; Daniël de Zeeuw, "Engaged Withdrawal: Occupying Politics Beyond Politics," in: *Krisis*, no.1, 2014, available online at: www.krisis.eu, accessed 05/15/2014.

17
On the ambivalence of Internet-enabled activism between empowerment and the state's capacity to control and suppress see: Zeynep Tufekci, "Is the Internet good or bad? Yes. It's time to rethink our nightmares about surveillance," available online at: https://medium.com/matter/76d9913c6011, accessed 05/15/2014.

Below: Antigovernment protesters stand on a barricade during an antigovernment protest in Istanbul, June 3, 2013. Facing page: Emrah Cengiz, *The 10 Days of the Resistance*, infographic, excerpt, 2013

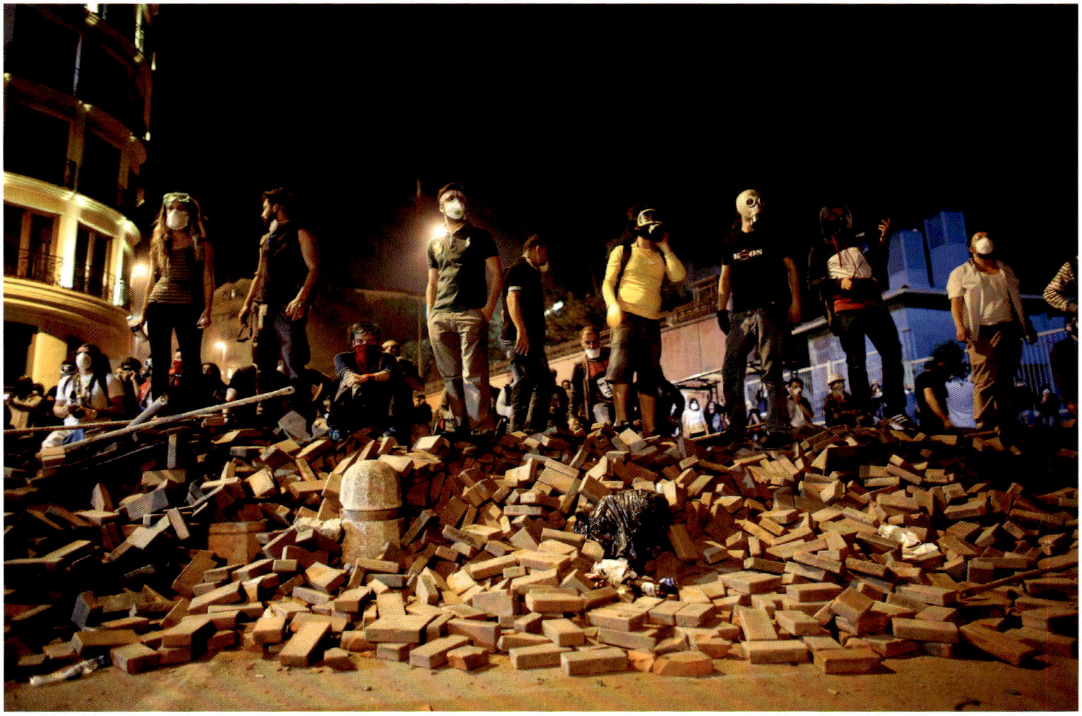

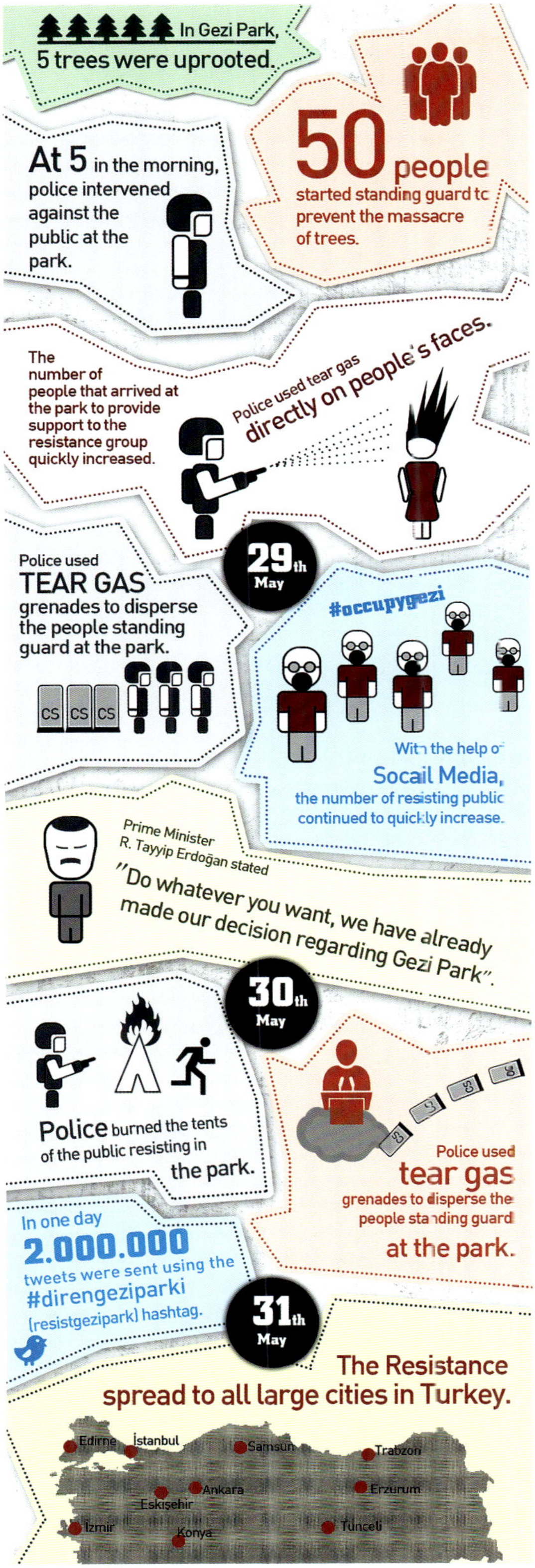

self-critical form of political practice that continually interrogates its own presuppositions, structures, and implications – and this is indeed what, despite all obstacles and challenges in terms of organization, the forum- and assembly-centered non-hierarchical politics of these movements has aimed at approximating.

The third aspect – the creativity of the uprising – has been prominent in media coverage but often represented in a one-sided and trivializing way by isolating specific instances of humorous intervention from the broader context of the movement and its more confrontational tactics. In that context creativity is a form of constantly expanding the repertoire of contestatory collective action.

In the case of Turkey endless examples illustrate that this has happened with an astonishing frequency, from the initial occupation via the barricades and the humor expressed in posters and street graffiti to the "Standing Man" and the proliferation of public park forums. This creativity is important for addressing a variety of problems protest movements are facing, from responding to, and evading, state practices of control and criminalization, via the problem of cooptation and integration into the realm of normalized culture (a.k.a. the commodification of protest – indeed, it did not take long until the first Occupy Gezi T-shirts and coffee mugs were sold on the Web), to the problem of what in social movement studies is called the exhaustion of the repertoire of collective action: the fact that when confronted with protest, people tend to react by saying that they have seen it all before. It is in this political context – and not in collections of funny banners and graffiti in exhibitions or catalogs – that the creativity of global activism has its place.

The lessons one can learn from paying attention to "the streets" are thus manifold. Their general teaching is that in order to generate contestatory power, political movements in general and practices of civil disobedience in particular have to combine new forms of civility that will challenge established assumptions about civil and civic norms, the symbolic and the confrontational, alternative forms of collectivity, and a prefigurative transformation of public space in ways that trigger the dynamics of collective action. Civil disobedience thus emerges as an essentially collective and political practice of contestation, in which structural deficits of the existing system are addressed in ways that go beyond the very limited and often dysfunctional channels of existing institutions. Activist forms of political protest, such as practices of disobedience, should therefore be seen as an essential part of the history and the present of democracy understood in a broader and more radical sense – a democracy-in-the-making and "from below" that is not reducible to its always deficient institutional realization in the state but crucially relies on extra-institutional practices of contestation of which civil disobedience is a prominent example.[18] In this respect, what has been said in response to the question whether the French Revolution of 1789 should be seen as a success might well be true of the most recent cycle of global protest: it is too early to tell…

18
Albert Ogien and Sandra Laugier, *Le principe démocratie. Enquête sur le nouvelles formes du politique*, La Découverte, Paris, 2014.

Bruno Latour

War and Peace in an Age of Ecological Conflicts

Introduction: While politics has always been linked to geography, the Earth itself has largely been seen as playing a backstage role, the mere window dressing for human intention and interest. With the advent of the epoch known as the "Anthropocene," the Earth is no longer in the background, but very much in the foreground, in constant rivalry with human intentionality. In the meantime, human action has taken on a dimension that matches that of nature itself, and consequently the definition of geopolitics has been transformed. Appeals to nature, therefore, do not seem to have the same pacifying and unifying effect that they did in earlier ecological movements. By drawing on anthropological and philosophical literature, this lecture[1] will discuss this new geopolitical framework and show how the extension of politics into nature must modify our views on war and peace in the future.

Let me start with the notion of "conflicts." I think it is fair to say that on all the questions I will deal with tonight, we are divided. Not only are we divided among different parties, different factions, religions, ideologies; but also, and maybe more deeply, each of us is divided inside ourselves. I certainly feel such division. Indeed, it is to this place of internal conflict that I look for the courage to address you tonight.

What I am going to do is attempt to trace with you some of the many lines of dissent that today constitute the warring parties whose disputes require new forms of political attitudes. Or rather new forms of *geopolitical* attitudes, provided you take the prefix "geo" by its etymological meaning of "Earth." As we will see, geopolitics is not about human politics overlaid on the Earth's static frame, but politics concerning contradictory portions, visions, aspects of the Earth and its contending humans. Such is the novel situation for which we don't seem to be intellectually equipped.

Let me start by drawing the first front line. Consider the key issue: that of the facts about the anthropic – that is the human – origin of the quickened pace of global climate variations. Such a fact is not a divisive topic among climate scientists. That is, among those who really work to assemble data on the matter – since, as you know, there is not much remaining controversy on the general picture (and the soon to be released Fifth Assessment Report (AR5) of

1 This text is a transcript of a lecture, held in Vancouver in September 2013.

the United Nations Intergovernmental Panel on Climate Change (IPCC) will confirm the existence of this consensus among experts). Yet there exist two immensely troubling dividing lines that have recently come to define the entire worldview of many people, and not only in the developed world.

In spite of the consensus of the IPCC experts, some scientists (I have to tread carefully here: some scientists say "many scientists"...), most often not themselves specialists in the fields (that is, not publishing in the same journals as those summarized in the IPCC report), wage against their colleagues a vigorous (some say a vicious) attack in the name of Science – capital S – and Reason – capital R. They argue that this consensus is a sham that shows only the opinion (not the facts) of a powerful politico-scientific "lobby" (this is their word) addicted, at least this is the main claim, to computer modeling that has only an uncertain relation to empirical facts. And those dissenting voices argue that to take action based upon such a premature opinion would be an irrational *decision*. (Mark the word "decision," the meaning of which will play a big role in this lecture.)

Now this in itself is not new. Scientific controversies – and controversies about ecology and technology – are as old as science and industry. What is new is the extent and intensity of the dispute where a segment of the "scientific community" (two words to bracket), acting in the name of "skepticism" (itself one of the two highest virtues of science) debunks what other colleagues call "objective certainty" (the second highest virtue of science). While, in return, those colleagues accuse that such a form of skepticism is nothing more than a veil under which "pseudoscientists," in order to protect industrial interests, hide the "denial" – or worse, the "negation" – of what is probably the best-established fact in the whole of natural history. (Since Vancouver is the site of the remarkable DeSmogBlog.com, I don't need to belabor the issue.)

Where this controversy matters is that, whatever the verdict, there is one thing that I, as a citizen, and probably most of you here tonight, cannot take for granted anymore: we cannot hide behind the verdict of the "scientific community" taken as a whole. The novelty is that we have to choose, *inside* the disciplines, *among* the specialties, which segment of the population we will trust more than the other and behind whom we will thrust our weight in the future. This means that we have to get used to a strange type of geopolitics – that is, the geopolitics of science in action – by learning to navigate the various maps of conflicting disciplines, paradigms, instruments, theories, and reports. (In effect, if you look at the maps visualizing the IPCC expert network you see something like a small "parliament" of climate experts, with about 4,000 representatives and a core group of 300 influential people – not a lobby but indeed a parliament.)

The important point here is to realize that the decision about the facts of the matter cannot be delegated to a higher unified authority that would have chosen *in our stead*. Controversies – no matter how spurious they might be – are no excuse to delay the *decision* about which side represents our world *better*. In effect, we have to deal with those conflicts, *horresco referens*, much like we used to in the past with "political" parties. We don't believe nor trust them, but, as the American writer, reporter, and political commentator Walter Lippmann said, we align ourselves behind those who appear less partisan than the others.

This is where I draw the first dividing line: one side of me sees this destruction of the authority of a final verdict upon the laws of nature as a catastrophe (who will, from now on, be the arbiter of our conflicts?). Another side of me, however, considers this situation as a great advance: we cannot any longer hide behind anyone else's decision. We have finally grown up, as far as taking our destiny in our own hands is concerned. On one side of the border, it is the end of the rationalist dream, on the other it is an extension of the great quest for a more rational – or at least a more reasonable – kind of politics: decision about the world in which we live cannot be outsourced.

But then there is a second reason why we are so deeply divided on the question of the anthropic origin of "climate change" (a polemical expression introduced, as you might know, by the infamous Mr. Frank Luntz to replace "global warming" in Republican Party talking points). The reason is that, even once we have thrown our trust behind the IPCC's last report, we still *don't do much* about it; or, if we do something, we remain fully aware that our endeavors are not at the relevant scale or at the relevant level for effective action. In that sense, even if most of you follow the report (I assume that this is the case in the "Green City" of Vancouver and with what is probably a largely "liberal" audience), you are nonetheless all climatosceptics since this knowledge, even if widely shared, does not trigger as much action as is necessary. As the Chinese proverb says: "To know and not to act, is not to know." What does a reader of a review article on the link between smoking and lung cancer really *know* about this fact if he is reading it while smoking a cigar? Is it not fair to say that he knows this connection only vaguely? In a similar way, there is a form of *practical* climatoscepticism very different from the cognitive one.

Even though I decided to align myself behind the IPCC report (not the same thing as "believing" in it), I feel very much that I am a skeptic since I don't know what to do about it, apart from a few pathetic gestures like sorting my rubbish and limiting my carbon footprint (and feeling guilty about it). I *act* as a climatosceptic, or rather, because of this state of relative indecision, I share with those people an attitude that represents most of the developed world right now (including Canada, to the great disappointment of Europeans...), and one that could be called climato-*quietism* (quietism in theology being a laid-back attitude that somehow, without doing anything much, God will take care of our salvation).

This first dividing line on the anthropic origin of climate change (a division exploited with great skill by all sorts of pretty disreputable lobbies) could have been easier to stitch back together but for another source of dispute, this time even more troubling, about what we may expect from science and from its complex institutional machinery of fact-making. This is a tricky point that, in my experience, always triggers fierce passions.

The usual solution when a group of people encounters a new and dangerous issue – an epidemic, a pollution, a depression, a startling piece of news such as, for instance, a dictator who attacks his population with poison gas – is to try to get the facts right *first* and only *then* to formulate a policy about it. If the facts of the matter cannot be readily checked, some research programs have to be launched, and the group mobilized by the issue must wait for the results; if there is a controversy about the data, then they wait for closure of the dispute.

This is sheer common sense: first, an *agreement* about the facts which *by nature*, if they are objective, are one (this is why facts compel all reasonable, unbiased minds to agree); second, many *disagreements* about policies since those are, also *by nature*, based on multiple and irreconcilable values. In such a common sense view, facts divide only the experts and only for the time it takes to complete the research. So what is expected is unity and final closure about facts, followed by discord and then attempts at closure about policy (either by consensus, compromise, or vote). Facts do not divide, except provisionally; policies and values always do, but only for a time, provided an institution has taken charge of the closure. The first closure is objective and final; the second is somewhat makeshift. More importantly, the first closure is based on the nature of things themselves; only the second may rightly be called a "decision." If the word "decision" is applied to the first closure, that of facts, then it is considered illegitimate and arbitrary; that is, as an intrusion of politics into Science.

I have tried to summarize as clearly as I can the rationalist ideal of a division of labor between science and politics. But the fascinating paradox is that if such a view of rationalism had been applied to our topic, then *there should be no climate controversy*. Since, in our case, the consensus of the "scientific community" would indeed have been reached long ago, and we should by now have entered a normal discord about policies. Today, the emphasis should entirely be on reaching some compromise about how to deal with the issue, among dissenting parties having legitimate dissenting interests. We would have progressed as quickly as possible from step one – fact closure – toward step two – policy closure.

Yet we have witnessed exactly the opposite move; that is, a constant *regression* from the urge to quick action to inaction, from urgency to delay, from climate certainty to climate-quietism, from declaration of a state of emergency to a call for appeasement. Every year, while the facts have accumulated at an ever-expanding speed, the general doubt about the urgency and nature of acting on the basis of them has constantly *decreased*. The unanimity that seemed possible at the time of Reagan, Bush I., or Clinton seems impossible at the time of Copenhagen 2009 or, probably, Paris 2015.

What has happened? Many things for sure, but one conceptual one concerns us here tonight: the rationalist theory of action. It becomes a fantasy when applied to a *live connection* between your own action and what you are talking about or trying to know. Let me show you how we may handle this difficult point.

There is a traditional division in philosophy between statements about "natural" phenomena – it makes no difference to them that you know them or not – and "social" phenomena – to know them is to modify them (I put "natural" and "social" in scare quotes for a reason that will be clear in a minute). John Searle has written a whole book about this division: a statement about the boiling point of water has no influence on water, while a statement by the right banking authority about the value of a dollar bill does define how much it is worth. One is called a "constative" statement, the other a "performative" one.

This is why for any action that concerns us in daily occurrences we never – I insist we never – follow the rationalist theory of action. Who, I am asking you, who among you possessed all the facts of the matter *before* deciding to marry, to have children, to invest, to move to Vancouver, to plant a garden, to vote for a party, etc.? We are all aware that acting means taking risks and making bets. This does not mean that all those decisions were arbitrary since you acted on feelings, on many subtle cues, pointers, tastes, and warnings that depended on your having rendered yourselves sensitive to a multitude of unconnected events and tiny perceptions. And this does not mean that you took your decisions *without* any knowledge either. Rather, it means that they had not been made *after* full knowledge had been obtained and consensus reached. But it is fair to say that, once a decision took effect, a lot of *new knowledge* was obtained and many rectifying steps were then taken along the way. The only point I wish to make is that, far from following the pattern: "knowledge and closure first, action second, policy closure third," all our decisions are made without waiting for complete closure – the only closure, as Jean-Paul Sartre could have said, is when clods of earth are thrown by our friends on our coffin!

So, for all the daily decisions we take, we should say that they neither follow undisputable facts (actually, in that case no real "decision" would have to be made since action would just have been *deduced* straight out from the fact) nor are they whimsical arbitrary choices as if we had been throwing dice to decide whom we should marry or what investment to make. Those statements are entering a zone that is based on what I am tempted to call "objective, choice-triggering facts." There exist undisputable statements that, as the name indicates, close any dispute. Period. They are called apodictic. And then there are facts that, even though they are objective, do not close all discussions, but have to be *relayed* by many disputed choices, some of them triggering more accurate and objective data. Those are not followed by a period, but, so to speak, by a colon: discussion begins.

To see how this somewhat innocuous distinction may throw some light on our question, we may think of an event that occupies an intermediary position between daily decisions and huge geopolitical tragedies. Take for instance the Cold War nuclear buildup. Lobbies today fiercely combat climate science because it is still too incomplete and inaccurate to take action. But few would have complained in the 1950s about the lack of quality intelligence the government had about the Soviet threat. A very limited knowledge was enough to trigger momentous choices on how to counteract the threat. This is a perfect case where action and knowledge proceeded in parallel – and reached baroque proportions until the threat all but disappeared.

Now, project the pattern of the present climate controversy over the Cold War nuclear buildup and try to see what the rationalist theory of action would have done to handle this past situation. Imagine that think tanks of various persuasions would have asked the CIA first to provide "undisputed proof" that the Soviets were to attack; then, and only then, proportionate answers could be devised. And, of course, as long as the proof was uncertain, action would have been delayed. This is the great virtue of the rationalist view: if action begins only *after* full knowledge has been acquired, then any doubt, any skepticism is enough to block policy and to delay action! That is exactly why Mr. Luntz (certainly a great rationalist!), introduced into the Republican talking points the necessity of doubting climate data when he wrote:

> "Should the public come to believe that the scientific issues are settled, their views about global warming will change accordingly. Therefore, you need to continue to make the *lack of scientific certainty* a primary issue […]."[2]

2 The Luntz Research Companies, "The Environment: A cleaner, safer, healthier America," in: Frank Luntz, *Memorandum to Bush White House*, 2002, pp. 131–146, here p. 137.

Another Mr. Luntz in the 1950s would have put quite a spoke in the wheel of the great chariot of war: "the lack of scientific certainty about the Soviet threat" would have paralyzed action. Imagine: No nuclear buildup! No threat of annihilation! We would have saved billions of dollars or – this is another plausible outcome – because the USA would have been paralyzed by inaction, we would all be ruled, yes, even here in Vancouver, from Mr. Putin's office under the Red Star flag in the Kremlin…

Of course, we could say that in the case of the Cold War, the rationalist scheme is clearly inapplicable because, first, we deal here with Americans and Russians and not with facts of nature (we are thus dealing with "performative" and not "constative" statements); second, because in the case of the Soviets we were *at war* with them. And as we all know: "The first casualty of war is truth." Well, this is precisely why I choose this example. First, it could well happen that the real nature of ecological conflicts implies performative statements; and, second, we might very well be in a situation of war.

This is the really tricky part of my lecture: it happens that what is in dispute – the "anthropic origin of the quicker pace of global climate variation" – sits exactly *between* the two types of statements that I mentioned earlier. It is a constative statement of fact about sets of action for which those who speak are also the main agents not to say the culprits. This is the heart of the dispute and why the issue is so divisive. If we were talking about a fact of the matter in the traditional sense, that is, bearing on agents that are *indifferent* to our knowledge and action about them, then the rationalist theory of action could say: "Let us wait for closure and *then* we will define policies at our leisure." But if we are dealing with a fact that is more like the Cold War nuclear buildup, that is, about agents that are *far from indifferent* to our action and that react quickly to what we do, what we have done, what we will do, then to apply the rationalist scheme to such a situation is just as silly, not to say criminal, as to wait for the Soviets to have crossed the Bering Strait before taking action.

To make myself completely clear, let me take one of those trivial examples beloved by analytic philosophy: you are on a bus and you see that a rather corpulent, distracted man is going to choose a seat where a little cat in a pink basket is going to be squeezed flat if the man carries out his action. It would be ludicrous to wait for the meowing little kitty before telling the man. However, if you state: "There is a cat in a basket on the seat," *is it a constative or a performative statement*? (Note that the argument does not depend on the tone in which you utter such a statement, whether you scream or articulate it matter-of-factly.) The answer is not that easy.

On the one hand, such a statement is certainly as accurate and objective as one wishes it to be: it describes a state of affairs: "the cat is on the seat." But it is just as clearly a warning directed at shifting a course of action. Thus it happily mixes objective accuracy and an urgent call (in addition it carries a value preference: grown-ups should not be in the habit of squashing little cats with their rear ends). But, more interestingly, it will also be heard by the man in the same mixed register, being understood at once as a call for attention, for information, and for remedial action. Even if you had stated in the utmost matter-of-fact tone, it will be taken by him as a pointer directing attention toward a whole set of successive actions. Here we are clearly dealing with a case of "choice-triggering facts" crossing the fact–value distinction, that is, with what I have called elsewhere "matters of concern" to render more vivid the contrast with "matters of fact."

The point here is that the classical distinction between facts and values is overlaid upon a distinction between "natural" entities (those about which we may speak from afar and in a dispassionate tone) and "social" situations (those inside which we are thoroughly embedded because we are part of the feedback mechanism we attempt to describe while acting upon it at the same time). As you know this division itself is what was supposed to distinguish "natural sciences" from "social" ones – the latter without real objectivity because of the involvement of scientists in their subject matter. Now, here is the new conundrum: you may speak in a disengaged and dispassionate way of the boiling point of water, but can you speak in a disengaged and dispassionate way of the objective measurement that industrial civilization passed 400 ppm of CO_2 in the atmosphere in the Spring of 2013? Is this statement more like "water boils at 100 °C" or like "there is a cat on the seat" or like "the Reds are threatening us with nuclear holocaust"?

This is where the whole distinction between fact and value is falling apart and this is also why those who are most worried and passionate about the objective facts of climate change are precisely those very scientists who are supposed to talk dispassionately about them! It seems that they behave vis-à-vis those facts just as the bus passenger in my trivial example of the man and the cat. It is not the tone that counts, it is the shift in the very character of the statement: not one uttered by an indifferent and disinterested voice speaking about something distant and indifferent, but it is the voice of someone fully engaged in a feedback loop with other agencies which themselves show a distinct "sensitivity" about what we do to them. It is not that those climatologists are not objective (even though this is just what the other party accuses them of being since they are too passionate and too interested!), it is that they are talking about events of which they (and all of you) are parts and parcels, just as was the case for so-called "social" situations in the recent past.

Such is the completely unexpected situation that has been captured in the beautifully disputed term of "Anthropocene," a new label that designates the confusion of geology and human action. For any course of action it has become highly uncertain whether we are considering a human or a non-human agency at work. It is just as impossible to decide on which side you are as when you follow the path of a Mobius strip with your finger. Which means that, on Earth at least, the old distinction (well not so old in the end) between "natural" and "social" factors has become moot.

But of course this is just the point where lies the most intense dispute and what characterizes, for every one of us, the defining moment: Are we or are we not living in the Anthropocene? *Hic est Rhodus, hic est saltus*. There is no way to decide this question on "objective grounds" since it is precisely the very nature of what "objective ground" is that has to be decided. I insist: "objective" and "ground" are at stake here. The fight is a radical one pitting two sides against one another. On the one hand there are those who say: "Of course not, we should behave like normal humans inside a natural frame that might react a bit more surprisingly than expected, but to which the normal rationalist theory of action fully applies: the agents with which we are dealing are so distant and unconcerned by our actions that we should first get the facts of the matter as dispassionately as we can and then it will be time to argue about policy." On the other hand are those who say: "Too late, we are talking objectively and *thus* passionately about matters which are so little distant from us, and so little indifferent to what we do that we are engaged in a frightening and somewhat frenetic feedback loop while remaining in deep ignorance about the exact mechanisms of their reactions as well about policies." To sum up: business as usual on one side, total subversion on the other. Or, as I have sketched the scene elsewhere: on one side "Humans" and on the other "Earthbound." Don't rush to take your side. There is more to come.

The reason to delay your choice of camp is that we have to understand what is implied by the very notion of "decision" that I have used a lot so far. This will lead us to the third and final dividing line I have chosen to draw tonight, the one that is the most damning of all since it literally means war or peace.

It is traditional in political philosophy to contrast *war* with what could be called *policing* or peace-making *operations*. If a burglar is breaking into your neighbor's house, there is no controversy over values and procedures. You call the police. It might be difficult to get the culprit but nobody discusses the legitimate grounds of the police to act. The overall situation has been settled by a referee, an arbiter, in this case the State. Things are entirely different in the case of war – for instance, civil war. Then the decision on *who* is the legitimate authority is precisely what is to be tried out through some decisive encounter. In this case, there is no arbiter, no referee, nor preliminary verdict. This argument should not be misunderstood as a gory version of history: war does not mean necessarily blood and weapons, but it does mean the absence of a referee to settle the matter. Conversely, as Carl Schmitt has shown, police interventions, even peace operations, may lead to extermination since an irrational moron (*inimicus* to use his language) never triggers the same respect as a real enemy *(hostis)*.

The point I want to introduce here is that when people turn to nature or speak about nature or invoke natural laws, they are never really "at war" with anybody – whatever crimes they may commit. Of course they meet people who disagree, but those are not technically – legally – their *enemies*, they are simply more or less irrational people, more or less enlightened persons, more or less educated parties, more or less archaic or backward members of exotic cultures. And this "peaceful" attitude is as common to those who say: "Of course we are living in the epoch of the Anthropocene, it is proven, only reactionary nitwits may still doubt it" as those who say: "Of course the Anthropocene is a fantasy pushed by misguided fanatics, Cassandra scientists, and apocalyptic sects." In both cases they might be able to fight fiercely but still they are not *at war* since the overall question has been *decided elsewhere*, above the parties, by Science, by Reason, by God, by Providence, by the Tribunal of History, by the movement of modernity, it does not matter which. If you believe this, then, at heart, no matter how combative you feel, you are a peacemaker engaged in the task of merely disciplining the remaining morons.

Do you feel the difference? When you engage in a police operation, you act in the name of a higher authority that has *already* settled the conflict and you merely play the role of an instrument of punishment. But when you are at war, it is only through the throes of the encounters that the authority you have or don't have will be decided *depending whether you win or lose.*

Now, I am going to ask you the toughest question of all, the really divisive one: Do you consider that those who are on the opposite sides of the ecological issues in which you are engaged directly or indirectly are irrational beings that should be resisted, disciplined, maybe punished, or at least enlightened and reeducated? That is, do you believe that your commitment is to carry out a police or a peace-making operation of some sort in the name of a higher authority? Or do you consider that *they are your enemies* that have to be won over through a trial the outcome of which is unknown *as long as you have not succeeded*? That is, that neither you nor them can *delegate* to some superior and prior instance the task of refereeing the dispute?

Many of you might not see this as a divisive question, but maybe for the wrong reason! You might have been blinded to it by the habit of believing, when dealing with issues involving nature (especially nature known through science), that whenever you invoke it and its laws, agreement will necessarily ensue. To the point that they are not seen as conflicts since every side considers that once nature has spoken the case has been closed. It is just a question of policing the remaining dissenters. There is a sort of jus-naturalism that is implicit in all sides of ecological disputes. The same people who would deride the papacy for invoking "natural law" to give its decrees a solid foundation will not hesitate a minute to use "what science tells us" to decide anything, from the "absurdity" of a cap and trade bill to the "urgent necessity" of decarbonizing industry, from "saving the biodiversity of the planet" to defunding the instruments that monitor sea level. The problem with such a belief is that it means that there are no politics involved in ecological conflicts, only policing. Everything unfolds as if there existed somewhere *some instance with the capacity and authority of a quasi State* – what could be called a State of Nature! – to settle the disputes. Strangely enough, as I have shown in *Politics of Nature: How to Bring the Science into Democracy* (2004, French original 1999) ecology has always suffered from a lack and not from an excess of politicization. Only those who have enemies do politics. Only those who are not treating their adversaries as irrational or mad or archaic may begin to equip themselves to win in a battle.

"Why insist so much on declaring a state of war, as if we did not have enough sources of conflict?" you might object. "What is to be gained in losing the great arbiter of the laws of nature (of natural law), this final referee who has protected us against the vagaries of politics and internal strifes? Has not the appeal to nature known by science been the only protection against generalized conflicts? We might disagree on anything but at least the boiling point of water is not in dispute. Period." Yes, I know and I am myself divided on this question, but it is exactly this common-sense solution that seems to have run out of steam when dealing with climate issues. The objective statement "industrial civilization passed the 400 ppm of CO_2 threshold in spring 2013" directs toward either action or inaction which is fully *political* not only in the sense of being practical or of mobilizing heads of state, but in that this action or inaction amounts to a kind of – there is no other word for it – *civil war.* Sides have to be taken. Decisions have to be made. Police or politics, you have to choose.

The reason why it is so important to answer my question – "do you fight against enemies or simply against irrational people?" – is that the capacity of natural laws to unify is entirely gone. You might still invoke Science, capital S, as "one and indivisible," but the sad truth is that they are multiple and, it seems, indefinitely divisible. Nature used to be one when we were dealing with a highly simplified version of its components – Galilean objects, not Darwinian organisms. Today any look at the multiplicity of agencies mobilized in any scientific paper will show that the unity of science has always been wishful thinking. The sheer difficulty of modeling the Earth's climate on a computer will show that the *objectivity* of science cannot be confused with the *unity* of its decrees. The former domain of "nature" is neither harmonious nor unified. Nor is it "outside." And the situation is even worse on the side of the formal "social domain." There is no unity to be expected in invoking the "human race." The sheer diversity of interests and situations, the vertiginous differences in wealth and power, the multiplicity of cultures and ways of relating to the soil, all forbid that any appeal to a "universal human interest" will trigger any assent.

Contrary to a superficial reading, the term Anthropocene does not mean the great superior fusion of unified "nature" and unified "human" (as if the two could somehow live harmoniously with one another), but the mind-boggling shattering and dissemination of its components. What used to be "human" and what used to be "natural" are so mixed up that to get back a sense of order one has to do politics all over again – politics understood, that is, as the progressive composition of a common world. And if the world is not common yet, it has to be composed bit by bit, issue by issue, and for that there is no overall master plan – because there is no master. This is why geopolitics take on another dimension altogether; it is not politics inside a stable frame that could be appealed to and relied upon in case of emergency, but it is, so to speak, politics all the way down, including the very components of what the old "Gè" or "Gaia" are made of.

Let me conclude. I have attempted to trace in front of you (or maybe to draw inside yourself!) three lines of dissent that, in my view, make up an important part of political ecology but are not often underlined enough, so strong is the idea – the nostalgia rather – that when nature enters the scene a whole set of global, unified, totalizing, even spherical images immediately come to mind. To counteract this attitude, I have asked you to see both sides of the three following geopolitical struggles:

First:

When dealing with climate controversies do you expect the "scientific community" to come to a final agreement, or have you taken upon yourself to decide which kinds of disciplines and which scientists you have to align behind? Or to put it in other words: are you for Science, capital S, or for scientists and their fact-making institution? This is a dividing line.

Second:

Are the statements about ecological conflicts more like "the boiling point of water" or more like "the Cold War threat"? In other words, are we dealing with a world made of distant matters of fact or a world composed of highly reactive matters of concern? This, too, divides sharply since those on both sides of the border, literally, do not inhabit the same world. To put it too starkly: some are readying themselves to live as Earthbound in the Anthropocene; others have decided to remain as Humans in the Holocene.

Third:

Do you act as the legitimate instrument of a higher authority that has already settled the issue, or do you have enemies who could win if you fail to fight them during an encounter for which there is no higher arbiter? Is there some Tribunal of History to decide the issue or not? In other words: Are we at war with one another, or just in the usual normal disagreement that can be settled by appealing to some sort of Universal State?

I wish I was wrong in drawing these lines, in insisting on division and war. Can you imagine how marvelous life would be if we were to learn from the IPCC report that they had been mistaken all along and that the temperature would not increase as much as they had expected; how relaxing it would be to learn that geo-engineering will take care of the remaining problems and engulf the planet in a safer state of control; how delightful it would be to believe in the progress of Science and Reason, in the prolongation of the frontier spirit, all the way to the fully modernized Earth and beyond to the Moon and to Mars, maybe further to the stars; how charming it would be to believe again in the endless progress of modernization and terraforming; in the globe of Reason encircling the blue planet. I could retire happily nursing the same dreams we shared when I was a little kid, eyes upward trying to detect the blinking sign of Sputnik!

Modern again; human again; eyes wide shut, far away from planet Earth, in the hypnotic utopia of the past. Then we would not have to worry about the angel of geostory: [video clip: *The Angel of Geostory*, Stefany Ganachaud, 2013].

Transcript of a lecture, prepared for the Peter Wall Institute, Vancouver, September 23, 2013

PART I: Political Background. *Indignados* Italian Style

Ugo Mattei

Institutionalizing the Commons: An Italian Primer

This chapter is devoted to what I believe is a rather interesting and unique experiment in transforming indignation into new institutions of the commons. Perhaps this praxis "Italian style" could become an example for a global strategy.[1]

1. A22

The complex and fascinating phenomenon of the political emergence of the commons movement in Italy is something akin to the more noted Spanish *indignados*, known to the rest of the world as 15M (May 15, 2011), the date of the beginning of a long-term protest camp at Madrid's Puerta del Sol.

In Italy, the symbolic date that evokes the three key moments in the recent history of the commons movement is April 22. For three times, by chance, something of crucial importance happened on that date. On April 22, 2008, the Rodotà Commission handed over an Enabling Law Bill[2] to the Minister of Justice at a conference held at the Accademia Nazionale dei Lincei in Rome which contained the first legal definitions of the commons to appear in an official document. Again on April 22, in 2010, the committee for the referendum on "water as a common" collected the first signatures on the forms containing the question drafted by jurists of the aforementioned Rodotà Commission. Thirdly, on April 22 in 2013, the transformation of ARIN[3] S.p.A.[4] into ABC[5] Napoli as a special public "commons" company was finally registered with the Naples' Chamber of Commerce, ending a long political and legal struggle. Thus, the name for Italy's commons movement should be A22!

2. The Rodotà Commission

The triggering of indignation that gave a political soul to the discourse on the commons, until that moment relegated to the margins of political and juridical reflection, arrived on November 19, 2009. With a vote of confidence, the House of Representatives approved the DL 135/2009, popularly known as the Ronchi-Fitto decree from the names of the ministers of Berlusconi's government who proposed it.[6]

1 For an attempt to collect international energies for such a struggle, see: David Bollier and Silke Helfrich (eds.), *The Wealth of the Commons. A World Beyond Market and State*, Levellers Press, Amherst (MA), 2012.

2 An English version of the Rodotà Commission Bill is available online at: http://iuccommonsproject.wikispaces.com/file/view/Rodota+Commission+Bill_+EN.pdf, accessed 08/13/2014.

3 ARIN stands for Azienda Risorse Idriche di Napoli [Water Resources Company of Naples].

4 The S.p.A (società per azioni) is the Italian equivalent of the public limited stock company. On this subject see, for example: Salvatore Settis, *Italia S.p.A.: L'assalto al patrimonio culturale* [Italy S.p.A.: The Assault on the Cultural Heritage], Einaudi, Turin, 2007.

This measure, based on a presumed "European obligation," determined that by the end of December 2011 all local public services and utilities of economic relevance (including the integrated water system) would be auctioned off on the market where private corporations could bid to manage them. This brutal attempt to perpetrate the most radical round of privatizations in Italian history, right at the beginning of the dramatic economic crisis (certainly not produced by the public sector!), generated political resistance far beyond the expectations of its promoters. It was not difficult to foresee that putting an enormous number of public services, mainly natural monopolies, on the market at the same time would cause a sharp drop in their purchase price. These assets, still mostly managed in Italy by companies owned one hundred percent by the public sector, according to the so-called "in-house" model would be transferred at ridiculously low prices to privately owned corporations. The Italians could not and did swallow this new plunder of public resources (worth more than five hundred billion euros according to estimates from the International Monetary Fund).

By chance, on that very same November day of 2009 when in the Chamber of Deputies the vote in favor of the Ronchi-Fitto decree was taking place, in a room at the nearby Senate a ceremony was in progress. Numerous senators from both the government and the opposition parties were in attendance as well as the President of the Academia Nazionale dei Lincei, the Vice President of the Piedmont region, and many members of the Rodotà Commission, including its President. The Piedmont region was introducing a new bill, which reproduced the text of the Rodotà Commission verbatim. According to the Italian constitution, regions have the power to initiate legislation and Piedmont was exercising this power. The first legislative definition of the commons was officially beginning its protracted parliamentary itinerary to become a law of the State.

The Rodotà Commission directly descended from a 2005 scholarly project at the Academia Nazionale dei Lincei. At that prestigious venue, scholars began to rethink the politics of wildcat privatization carried on since the 1990s in Italy. Technical governments dismissed assets worth about 140 billion euros in a very short period of time, making Italy a more intense privatizer than Magaret Thatcher's Britain.[7] These privatizations have been denounced in vain even by the Corte dei Conti, the Italian Court of Auditors, the institution whose task is to safeguard public finances and guarantee that public patrimony is respected.[8] In fact, Italian center-right and center-left governments had taken it upon themselves to liquidate public holdings and place the ensuing capital in the hands of the usual "private" groups. They transferred from the public to the private goods and services worth billions without making any formal declaration of the public utility of these measures, using sub-primary sources of law such as ministerial decisions (no involvement of Parliament), and with no compensation whatsoever. Italian governments have de facto expropriated public and communal assets from the people (who owned them) without respecting any of the basic guarantees that would be due to a private owner in a case of expropriation.[9]

5 ABC stands for Acqua Bene Comune [Water as a Common Good].

6 The decree is available online in Italian at: www.parlamento.it/parlam/leggi/decreti/09135d.htm, accessed 08/13/2014.

7 See: Ugo Mattei, *Contro riforme* [Counterreforms], Einaudi, Turin, 2013

8 See: www.corteconti.it/export/sites/portalecdc/_documenti/controllo/sez_centrale_controllo_amm_stato/2010/delibera_3_2010_g_relazione.pdf, accessed 09/11/2014.

9 See: Ugo Mattei, "Proprietà (nuove forme di)," in: *Enciclopedia del diritto*, vol. 5, Giuffrè, Milan, 2012, pp. 1125–1131, here p. 1127 (note 54 refers to: Ugo Mattei, *Beni comuni. Un Manifesto*).

The very old legal framework (contained in Article II of Book III of the Civil Code) that remains essentially unchanged since the Napoleonic Code (1804), is too outdated to exert any effective legal control over the government. This legal situation explains the continuous dramatic mismanagement of public property carried on by Italian governments, captured by private interests. It explains also the impudent arrogance deployed by the current administration in plundering public assets, as well as the bipartisan refusal even to discuss the proposed legal remedies to this catastrophe.[10]

In an attempt to stop this plunder, which is documented in detail by studies undertaken at the Accademia dei Lincei,[11] Stefano Rodotà, Edoardo Reviglio, and this author were finally received by the Minister of Justice of Romano Prodi's government, Clemente Mastella.

It was June 14, 2007, the birthdate of the commission for reforming Article II of Book III of the Civil Code[12] which was set up by the Prodi government and known as the Rodotà Commission after its president, the eminent legal scholar and well-known politician Stefano Rodotà.[13] (June 14 is another lucky date for the commons movement. Exactly four years later the occupation of the Valle Theater in Rome was initiated.)

The Commission completed its work in February 2008. It produced an Enabling Law Bill to reform the Civil Code in matters of public property. On April 22, at the Accademia dei Lincei, it delivered its work to the new Minister of Justice Luigi Scotti, who succeeded Mastella just prior to the fall of the Prodi government.[14] In the bill of the Rodotà Commission the commons (in Italian *beni comuni*) received the first technical-legislative definition in the following terms:

> "[…]
> (b) Classification of assets into three categories: commons, public properties, private properties.
> (c) Definition of the commons as such goods whose utility is functional to the pursuit of fundamental rights and free development of the person. Commons must be upheld and safeguarded by law also for the benefit of future generations. The legal title to the commons can be held by private individuals, legal persons or by public entities. No matter their title, their collective fruition must be safeguarded, within the limits of and according to the process of law. When the holders are public juridical persons the common properties are managed by public entities and are considered out of commerce; their concession to privates is admitted only in cases allowed by law and for a limited time, without the possibility of extension. Commons are: rivers, torrents and their springs; lakes and other waterways; the air; parks defined as such by law, forests and woodlands; high altitude mountain ranges, glaciers and snowlines; beaches and stretches of coastline declared natural reserves; the protected flora and fauna; protected archaeological, cultural, and environmental properties, and other protected landscapes. The commons legal regime must be coordinated with that of civic uses. Anyone may have

10 See: Ugo Mattei, *Beni comuni. Un manifesto* [Commons. A Manifesto], Laterza, Rome, 2011.

11 See: Ugo Mattei, Edoardo Reviglio, and Stefano Rodotà, *Invertire la rotta. Idee per una riforma della proprietà pubblica* [Change Direction. Ideas for a Reform of Public Property], Il Mulino, Bologna, 2007.

12 See: www.giustizia.it/giustizia/it/mg_2_7_6_1.wp?previsiousPage=mg_7_7, accessed 09/11/2014.

13 See: Stefano Rodotà, *Il terribile diritto. Studi sulla proprietà privata e i beni comuni* [The Terrible Right. Studies on Private Property and the Commons], 3rd ed., Il Mulino, Bologna, 2013.

14 See: Ugo Mattei, Edoardo Reviglio, and Stefano Rodotà (eds.), *I beni pubblici. Dal governo democratico dell'economia alla riforma del Codice Civile* [Public Goods. From the Democratic Government of Economy to the Reform of the Civil Code], Accademia Nazionale dei Lincei, Scienze e Lettere, Editore Commerciale, Rome, 2010.

access to the jurisdictional protection of the rights connected to the safeguard and use of commons. Except for cases prescribed by law for the protection of other rights and interests, only the State may take legal action for damages done to public properties. The State is also entitled to the reversion of profits. The requirements and modalities for legal action mentioned above will be defined by the delegated decree. [...]"[15]

It is enough to read the definition above to verify that water holds the top spot in the hit parade of the commons. Thanks to the contribution of Commissioner Alberto Lucarelli,[16] a legal scholar from the University of Naples, the Commission adopted an approach coherent with that of a bill of a popular initiative, backed by more than 400,000 signatures, on which the Italian water movement was working at the time.[17] This early definition of the commons by the Rodotà Commission became an exceptionally important legal concept in Italy that obtained the highest judicial recognition,[18] as well as at the local normative level, such as local charters of a variety of municipalities (including the city of Naples). Nevertheless, and this is yet another piece of evidence of the terminally ill state of Italian representative democracy, to date the bill of the Rodotà Commission has never been discussed in Parliament.

3. The Genesis of the Water Referendum

It is not difficult to imagine the satisfaction of the more motivated of the ex-commissioners when they were informed that the Piedmont region had adopted the Rodotà Enabling Law Bill as its own proposal to the Senate.[19] It is also easy to understand our outrage when, returning from Rome after the magnificent ceremony in the Senate's Nasiryah Room, we were informed of the passage of the Ronchi-Fitto Decree that prescribed the sale of public properties of unprecedented importance including the entire Italian water management system.

In just a matter of hours, after a few outraged phone calls within a small group of former commissioners, a first draft of the referendum proposal dealing with these points was ready. In only ten days, ex-commissioners Alberto Lucarelli, Ugo Mattei, Stefano Rodotà, and Luca Nivarra with the help of constitutionalists Gianni Ferrara and Gaetano Azzariti finalized the text for being published online.[20] The referendum adventure had begun. The first signatures on the three questions regarding water as a common (fully shared and endorsed by the Italian Forum of Water Movements) began to be collected in notarized form within a remarkable mobilization campaign.

The incredible number of signatures collected (over 1.5 million in three months from April 22, 2010 to July 13 the same year) on a very limited budget and with no help from the media remains legendary.[21] According to Italian law, once the signatures have been collected, the Constitutional Court rules on the admissibility of each single question of the referendum. Two of the three proposals passed, while the Constitutional Court disallowed the third

15 See: www.giustizia.it/giustizia/it/mg_2_7_6_1.wp?previsiousPage=mg_7_7, accessed 09/11/2014; translated from the Italian by Robert Booth.

16 See: Alberto Lucarelli, *La democrazia dei beni comuni* [The Democracy of Commons], Laterza, Rome, 2013.

17 See: www.acquabenecomune.org/raccoltafirme/index.php?option=com_content&view=article&id=1060&Itemid=122, accessed 09/02/2014.

18 See: Supreme Court of Cassation S.U. 02/14/2011, no. 3665, available online at: www.ricercagiuridica.com/sentenze/sentenza.php?num=3471, accessed 09/11/2014.

19 Art. 121 of the Italian Constitution gives regions the power of legislative initiatives at the national parliament.

20 See: www.acquabenecomune.org/spip.php?article7196, accessed 09/02/2014.

21 For a very recent detailed discussion of the legal issues involved in the referendum see: Ugo Mattei and Alessandra Quarta, *L'acqua e il suo diritto*, Ediesse, Rome, 2014.

(decisions 23, 24, 25 2011). The contested issue of admissibility (especially of referendum number 1, the most important one) was the claim by the government attorneys that the Ronchi-Fitto Decree prescribing the auctioning off of public services was itself based on a prescription of European law to member states. Because laws that carry out international obligations cannot be the object of a referendum according to Article 75 of the Italian Constitution, the government argued that the referendum could not be held. The Court, however, completely accepted our argument, which this author personally articulated in front of it (already articulated during the campaign of signature collection), that such an obligation did not exist under European law. The fact that a statute (such as the Ronchi-Fitto one) declares itself to be the execution of an obligation of European law is irrelevant if such an obligation does not actually exist in European law itself. A member state cannot make up its own obligation. The Court held that European law does not mandate member states to privatize or auction off local public services provided "in-house"; it is actually indifferent to the form and the proprietary choices that the member states wish to pursue.

However, the Court rejected the third question (ban on the use of the stock corporation form in the managing of commons), mainly because of a "suicide question" put forward somewhat senselessly by the Italia dei Valori [Italy of Values party]. This party, in retaliation for having been rejected (as all political parties) by the organizing committee of the referendum, presented its own referendum on water by means of a question whose admission could not be granted because of its inherent contradiction with our third question. The Court seized the opportunity to reject both questions to avoid the risk of contradictory results. However, this unfortunate political accident greatly distorted the original design of the entire package. Our idea was to ban the stock corporation (S.p.A. in Italian law) from the management of the commons, especially water. In fact, short-term profit is in the DNA of the stock corporation, an objective that is strongly at odds with the philosophy of commons management. As we shall see, the fact that the Court did not admit the third referendum has determined the current situation, with the city of Naples remaining unique in Italy in attempting genuine institutional experimentation for participatory public management of the commons.

4. The Outcome of the Referendum and the Political Strengths of the Commons

Equally unique in Italian history was the result of the referendum (almost 27 million voted YES to the abolition of the challenged laws) that was proclaimed on June 14, 2011. Despite the government's strategy to postpone the referendum to when schools are closed, right after an administrative vote that had already brought Italians to the polls twice in the previous weeks, the referendum easily exceeded the turnout quorum of 50% of the electorate, a hurdle that is usually sufficient to defeat most referendums in

Italy.[22] Perhaps even more interesting on the political and cultural levels is that the notion of "commons" *(beni comuni)* and the movement surrounding it (sometimes known as *"benicomunismo"* that roughly translates as "commonism") grabbed its place in the sun within the Italian political debate during the referendum's preparation period to become a keyword of Italian politics.[23]

In early 2011 one of the most important trade unions, FIOM (Federazione Impiegati Operai Metalurgici – union of Blue- and White-Collar Metalworkers) organized a major demonstration under the slogan "Labor is a common." The No TAV[24] movement, whose twenty-year struggle against the 56-kilometer tunnel perforating the Alps to Lyon is legendary, also organized its first major demonstration in Turin (attended by 25,000 people) under the slogan "No TAV is a common." Moreover, mass student protests were claiming the "university as a common." Finally, on June 14, 2011, the Teatro Valle (a particularly generative[25] experience discussed in this volume on pp. 666–681 as well) was occupied in Rome and declared a common which spawned a huge occupy movement labeled "Culture is a common." All of these examples and other less well-known episodes have added to the awareness in Italy of the many ways in which the current phase of capitalist exploitation massively affects the commons and has produced a degree of social indignation that, despite its importance, is not enough by itself.

Many Italians have interpreted the notion of commons not only in theory. What emerged in 2010 and 2011 was a unifying political grammar for different actions opposed to different specific neoliberal views.[26] The commons movement in Italy rejects the neoliberal vision of the water service (for profit); of work (as brute exploitation); of the university (as a place of corporate subculture); of rail transport (as a place of plunder founded on the logic of large public works); of the city (as a privatized place); of culture (as show business). After my small book *Beni comuni. Un Manifesto* [Commons. A Manifesto] was published at the right moment, reaching eight editions in a matter of a few months, I had the good fortune to experience firsthand this very real "commonist" insurgence when I was invited all over the country. I witnessed the incredible number of ongoing struggles in Italy against plunder, exclusion, and concentration of power generated by the unholy alliance between the public and the private sector against the commons that characterizes the current European scenario. Thousands of committees all over the country have discovered that their single-issue struggles, having lasted perhaps for years (like, for example, No TAV), are not isolated but connected to numerous others; different in appearance, yes, but in reality sharing objectives, enemies, and goals over long periods in their quest for a better world. Through the theory and praxis of the commons, single-issue indignation can finally see light at the end of the tunnel, something far greater to fight for.

Obviously, the totally unexpected "unofficial" political and cultural success of the theoretical grammar that originated with the Rodotà Commission was amplified by the worsening of the global economic crisis. The same economic issues behind the Spanish 15M and the American occupy movement or perhaps the Arab

22 For more details on the context see: Ugo Mattei, "Protecting the Commons: Water, Culture and Nature. The Commons Movement in the Italian Struggle against Neoliberal Governance," in: *South Atlantic Quarterly*, vol. 112, no. 2, Spring 2013, pp. 366–376; Saki Bailey and Ugo Mattei, "Social Movements as Constituent Power. The Italian Struggle for the Commons," in: *Indiana Journal of Global Legal Studies*, vol. 20, no. 2, Summer 2013, pp. 965–1013.

23 For a variety of experiences see: Paolo Cacciari, Nadia Carestiato, and Daniela Passeri, *Viaggio nell' Italia dei Beni Comuni* [A Journey trough the Italy of Commons], Marotta & Cafiero, Naples, 2012; Gregorio Arena and Christian Iaione (eds.), *L'Italia dei beni comuni* [The Italy of Commons], Carocci, Rome, 2012.

24 TAV stands for Treno Alta Velocità [High-Speed Train].

25 With regard to the use and explanation of the term "generative" in this context see: Marjorie Kelly, *Owning Our Future. The Emerging Ownership Revolution. Journeys to a Generative Economy*, Berrett-Koehler, San Francisco (CA), 2012.

26 See: Giovanna Ricoveri, *Beni comuni vs merci* [Commons vs. Goods], Jaca Book, Milan, 2010.

Spring were also behind the Italian experience. However, the struggles in other Western countries proved on balance far more ephemeral than the Italian one, which was well entrenched in a solid relationship between theoretical-juridical elaboration and the praxis of movements.

5. The Suspension of the Constitutional System after the Referendum

Despite these clear signals of the resistance of a majority of the Italian people to the dominant neoliberal rhetoric, various governments from 2011 onward – in cahoots with the President of the Republic – just responded by intensifying repression, and with pseudo-reformist rhetoric and authoritarian politics. Their implementation of aggressive neoliberal policies and total indifference to the wishes of the people increased to the point of putting the constitutional legitimacy of the current Italian system of power very much in doubt. Attempts by Silvio Berlusconi and Mario Monti, twice halted by the Constitutional Court, to defy the result of the referendum just a few weeks after its outcome was published by passing decrees which reproduced all the statutes that had just been abolished prove this point.

This first attack on the referendum's outcome, the result of a joint letter sent to Berlusconi by the outgoing and the new President of the European Central Bank (Jean-Claude Trichet and Mario Draghi) happened a few days after the August break. It soon became clear that President Napolitano, who should be the Constitution's supreme guarantor, would do nothing to block the Berlusconi decree (subsequently there was an even worse one by Monti), despite an appeal from some of the jurists, who had drafted the said referendum, and a petition with 10,000 signatures that the author collected personally in just a few days via a website.

Eventually the Constitutional Court did justice to the commons movement, and declared both the Berlusconi and the Monti decrees as unconstitutional (decision 199/2012). However, this only happened a year later. The unconstitutional offensive against the commons thus continued for a year after the referendum with very little opposition.[27] The fall of the Berlusconi government in November 2011 did not help the commons movement; in fact, it created a certain vacillation amongst some of the jurists who to that point had sustained the commons. Some of them were so happy about the fall of Berlusconi they needed some time before realizing that, with the Monti administration and the incredible constitutional excess of Giorgio Napolitano's power, Italy had jumped from the frying pan into the fire. Similarly, the commons movement was not helped by an unrealistic attempt to participate in political elections in April 2013 with a list containing some of its leaders (none of them were elected). Nor did the equally reckless use of the slogan "Italy as a common" to name a coalition help, also defeated, in which the lion's share of the candidates belonged to the Partito Democratico (the Democratic Party), whose leadership has been traditionally cosy with the lobby of privatizers at both local

27 Carried on with the "spending review," itself declared unconstitutional in the section opposed to the referendum in the very recent 229/2013 decision.

and national levels. In reality, the party that captured much of the impetus emerging from the commons movement at the 2013 political elections was the Movimento 5 Stelle (M5S, Five Star Movement). This party, founded by a former comedian, had participated widely in many of the grassroots battles of 2010 and 2011. It does not identify itself with either the right or the left, but expresses, at times with quite reactionary arguments, at times with remarkably advanced ecological and economic visions, a sense of indignation about the predatory nature of neoliberal capitalism, of the European Union institutions, and of the Italian political elite. At the April 2013 general election the M5S became the first political party to get more than 24% of the vote, but because of the electoral law and the whim of the Italian President, Mr. Enrico Letta became the new prime minister, a favorite of Napolitano and of the European elite.

Since then, in spite of the Constitutional Court declaring the electoral law unconstitutional, a large coalition that nobody in Italy elected continues to govern the country in full continuity with the dominant European neoliberal vision. Today, the leader of such a coalition is Matteo Renzi, a former mayor of Florence and a favorite of the section of the media industry that is an adversary of Berlusconi.

Meanwhile the de facto transformation of Italy into a semi-presidential constitutional order has been completed with the unprecedented reelection of Mr. Napolitano as president over the M5S candidate Stefano Rodotà (former President of the Commission), who was certainly supported by a very large proportion of the commons movement.

The context outlined above provides an idea of the current suffering of democracy in a country that, after the European Elections of May 2014, plunged into a state of denial regarding the gravity of its current democracy sufferance with the privatization frenzy again high on the agenda of the Renzi government. Aggressive constitutional reforms are attempted by a government that was never elected and by a parliament that the Constitutional Court declared elected with an unconstitutional law.

Shocked by 27 million votes expressed against the will of all the political parties sitting in Parliament, the Italian power elite, under constant pressure from European technocracy, has launched a *constituent phase*, clearly beyond any constitutional legality, as a reaction to the commons referendum. What has been staged is a de facto attempt to constitutionalize an authoritarian transformation of our system, well evidenced by the flamboyant rhetoric of the current Prime Minister.

6. The Repression Directed against the Commons Movement

This is not the place to expose the long list of “legal illegalities”[28] used unscrupulously in our country as a result of the collusion between an arrogant private sphere and a corrupt public one to discourage civic engagement. Suffice to consider the many instances of civil, administrative, and criminal violations perpetrated

28 See: Ugo Mattei and Laura Nader, *Plunder. When the Rule of Law is Illegal*, Blackwell Publishing, Malden (MA), 2008.

against the people by police, prosecutors, and authorities in the Susa Valley in order to defeat twenty years of struggle against a high-speed train (TAV). Or the affair of the Torre Galfa in Milan, a long abandoned and unfinished skyscraper, the property of absentee and criminally indicted tycoon Salvatore Ligresti, which is located near the Central Station. This tower block was occupied by the Macao collective as part of the insurgence for culture as a common with a view to opening it up for an experience of urban commoning which would have included a refuge for homeless people. The occupation, involving hundreds of active citizens and artists, was cleared by police in just a few hours, all under the watchful eye of leftist-leaning "friendly" Mayor Giuliano Pisapia. It soon became known that the son of Interior Minister Annamaria Cancellieri was an executive of the Ligresti group, which explains the hasty intervention of the police with the full political backing of the mayor. Now, more than two years later, Ligresti is in jail, but thanks to the shortsightedness of the political leaders, the tower is still empty and hundreds of Syrian refugees, including women and children, sleep rough in Milan Central Station. Other Italian examples of recent illegal (and unpunished) uses of the law are found in L'Aquila. The historical center of this beautiful central Italian town was devastated by a major earthquake in 2009. To protest about the scandal of the inactivity by public agencies and against the "business of reconstruction" a number of activists have entered the "red zone" to physically remove debris using their own wheelbarrows. These activists, heroes of civic participation and of commoning, have been criminally charged while at the same time the public media were reporting on massive fraud involving the funds for reconstruction! Last but not least we should mention the criminal charges against the No Dal Molin protesters of Vicenza – a movement opposed to the construction of a U.S. Army base at the local airport. In this beautiful city of northeastern Italy, world-famous for its Palladian villas, the movement succeeded in stopping a project that would have transformed Vicenza into one of the biggest military bases in Western Europe. Rather than honoring these activists for preventing exposure of the population to high risks and nuclear weapons, there was a further violation of Italian constitutional law which precludes aiding and abetting wars of aggression: the activists were prosecuted in large numbers!

PART II: The Institutionalization of the Commons

7. The Constituent for the Commons

Once it became clear that the clash over the commons was of constitutional magnitude in Italy, the consequence was to shift the struggle at the constituent level.[29] On April 13, 2013, in what in retrospect can be seen as an inconsequential presidential bid by Stefano Rodotà, the commons movement launched the *Costituente dei beni comuni* [Constituent for the commons] at the Teatro Valle in Rome in a very crowded assembly. The Constituent as the

29 On this dimension of the struggle for the commons see: Sandro Chignola (ed.), *Il diritto del comune. Crisi della sovranità, proprietà e nuovi poteri costituenti* [The Right of the Municipality. Crisis of Sovereignty, Ownership, and New Powers Constituents], Ombre Corte, Verona, 2012; Michael Hardt and Antonio Negri, *Comune. Oltre il privato e il pubblico* [Common. Beyond the Private and the Public], Rizzoli, Milan, 2010.

political heir of the Rodotà Commission was highly aware of the political transformation that the commons, both theoretically and practically, have accomplished since their introduction in the bill of 2007. It is no accident that the Constituent was launched at the Teatro Valle, the occupied theater which for three years has performed the role of national trailblazer in the fight for the institutionalization of the commons, generating a unique artistic, political, and juridical experience. It now entered a new phase which is described in the essay on Teatro Valle Occupato (this volume, pp. 666–681).

The idea to "revive" the Rodotà Commission as an itinerant body that would meet in the venues of the most significant commons struggles, was also a move of indignation caused by the complete official neglect of its 2008 bill, which was never discussed in open parliamentary session in all these years despite the importance and the timely nature of the commission's work. Readers should be aware that an extensive and quite high-level legal debate on the commons has unfolded in Italy based on the bill of the Rodotà Commission, with many books,[30] articles, dissertations, and professional conferences devoted to the topic. It is therefore quite incredible that Parliament, in two successive different compositions, and with so many of its members elected in the coalition Italia Bene Comune, never found a way to take this issue seriously.

In the absence of a delegation by Parliament to draft a detailed law on the commons, the jurist of the Constituent decided to get the delegation directly from the people. Of course, this move has created some strain within the jurist's group as some were openly opposed to this extra-parliamentary move while others have remained rather ambiguous. Nevertheless, the Constituent for the commons organized itself around two organisms: the territorial assemblies, in which itinerant jurists meet with territorial assemblies in which many local struggles for the commons present themselves, and the Redacting Commission that produces the actual textual proposals. At the territorial assemblies, the jurists collect the materials and ascertain the legal issues that emerge in the different fights for the commons. They interrogate the various commoners and receive opinions and reflections from the people involved. This information and the materials collected become one of the important "law in action" ingredients for the production, during redacting meetings, of a sort of "restatement of the commons." This restatement details and follows up on the Rodotà Commission's enabling bill, something that should have officially happened if, in working democratic conditions, Parliament was to take seriously and approve the work of the Ministerial Commission. From a much broader perspective, which justifies its Constituent claim, the itinerant work is a process of people's alphabetization in the commons. Further, it is a process by which jurists, rather than receiving authority from an established constitutional setting, actually seek in their capacity to translate the active citizens' vision of the commons into a formal legal language and grammar. *Si parva cum magna licet comparare,* we are seeking to formalize in jurist's terminology a sort of adapted *Volksgeist*, in Friedrich Karl von Savigny's terms.

30
See: Antonello Ciervo, *I beni comuni* [Commons], Ediesse, Rome, 2013; Alberto Lucarelli, *Beni Comuni. Dalla teoria all' azione politica* [Commons. From Theory to Political Action], Dissensi, Viareggio, 2011; Maria Rosaria Marella, *Oltre il pubblico e il privato. Per un diritto dei beni comuni*, [Beyond Public and Private. For a Right of Commons], Ombre Corte, Verona, 2012.

The Constituent's work is slow but constant. Some jurists quit and some others come on board, which is a proof of the fact that nobody is indispensable, but everybody can be useful when it comes to collective enterprises. In its first year and a half there have been territorial assemblies with activists in L'Aquila, Pisa, Rome, Padua, Susa, Naples, and Macerata. Furthermore, the jurists involved have met at Rome's Teatro Valle three times, and one meeting in Naples produced the first sections of the commons restatement, which applies and interprets existing law and makes it evolve in a way that is coherent to the people's claim to recover and generate new commons. The innovative working method and the unprecedented alliance between the jurists and the movements constitute a political factor of considerable importance. It is a genuine bottom-up process potentially extensible beyond the Italian borders. In November 2014, there was a first important international meeting in Paris inaugurating a European Constituent season of the commons.

It is important to point out that the Constituent for the commons would have been unthinkable outside of the experience of the Valle Theater Here, for the first time in Italy, a radically antagonist act such as an occupation has been translated into a process of institution building, the Fondazione Teatro Valle Bene Comune, whose importance requires a special section in this book.

8. ABC Naples

The other front on which the struggle in defense of the commons, especially of the historical victory of the water referendum, is hot and fierce is in the more technical but not less political domain of public service management models. Despite the fact that referendum number 3 was not admitted by the Constitutional Court (see above), it was crucial in the struggle for the commons to develop an institutional setting somewhere that is coherent with their nature. Such a setting must be capable of demonstrating the possibility of a viable alternative to disprove the mainstream claim that in running important industrial infrastructures, such as an aqueduct, there is no alternative to the stock corporation (S.p.A.). Those who do not understand (or do not want to understand) the epistemological revolution of the commons often maintain that keeping a majority of its capital in public ownership is more than sufficient to respect the referendum results. This vision, however, does not go beyond the binary opposition private versus public, and de facto reduces the issue of the commons to the need to protect the public sector from privatization of its ownership. Such a vision fails to distinguish the commons from public ownership.

The unexpected victory of an outsider, former prosecutor Luigi de Magistris, in the election for Mayor of Naples just a few weeks before the referendum of June 2011 provided an extraordinary political opportunity for the commons movement to experiment with a genuinely alternative model of governance of the commons. The mastermind of this political opportunity was Alberto Lucarelli, a member of the Rodotà Commission and one of the main architects of the water referendum, whom de Magistris appointed to the city administration in the new post of Assessor to the commons. De Magistris also appointed myself, a former vice president of the Rodotà Commission and drafter of the referendum, to serve on the board of directors of the municipal water company, ARIN S.p.A., a stock corporation group with around 500 employees and about 200 million euros of business activity. The mission was to steer the first transformation of a major stock corporation into a new public legal entity capable of shielding the water system from the risks of privatization, and at the same time to guarantee the degree of direct civic participation that the common's nature requires.

It is crucial from the theoretical point of view when engineering new institutions of the commons to consider direct civic participation as an alternative to traditional hierarchical public control, which happens when the public authority simply owns the corporation. This philosophy of equidistance (the same radical distance) of the commons from the private *and* from the public is a concept that is very difficult to grasp, especially by the left, who still tends to believe the myth of the "good government." In Naples we started the experiment of a legal form of genuine respect of the referendum outcome grounded in such a philosophy. After Lucarelli left the local government to seek a parliamentary seat – unsuccessfully – it was very unclear to me whether the Naples administration had really understood what we were trying to do. In fact, constructing a genuine commons institution takes power away from the public. Any administration seriously committed to the commons has necessarily to engage in a *destituent* act, that is, a choice of returning direct power to the people.

Thus, a great deal of patience and research is required, both legally and politically. With regard to the first point, in order to do the formal transformation, it was necessary to interpret Italian law in a manner coherent with the referendum results. This required "forcing" a formal legal structure that includes recently introduced Civil Code provisions (Art. 2500 cc.) which are privatization-friendly and do not contemplate the possibility of changing the bylaws of a stock corporation to transform it into a public entity. It took almost a year of legal discussion, with the acquisition of many expert declarations on all relevant legal aspects (tax, labor law issues, welfare issues, issues of EU law, etc.), to persuade a notary to sign the proposed Board deliberation to transfer ARIN S.p.A. into ABC Napoli Azienda Speciale based upon this interpretation. The turning point was the rendering of decision 199/2012 of the Constitutional Court, which offered the basis for a constitutionally oriented interpretation of the Civil Code. The Court, after hearings in which Lucarelli and myself argued against the Italian government and on behalf of the Puglia region,[31] declared the Berlusconi/Monti attempts to cancel the referendum results (see above) unconstitutional. That landmark decision declared that the referendum has a surplus of legitimacy compared to ordinary statute-making, so that all relevant Italian law must be interpreted coherently to it.

On the political ground, resistance had to be overcome within the three-member Board of Directors where the sitting President,

31 The Italian Constitution allows a region to directly challenge the constitutionality of a statute. Because the Campania region is run by a right-wing government, the constitutional challenge was made possible by the Puglia region whose president Nicola Vendola, a genuine supporter of the referendum results, appointed Lucarelli and myself as counsels for the region.

representing a variety of strong vested interests both at the city and at the national level, opposed the transformation. Eventually, after his quite dramatic resignation in July 2012, I took over the presidency, a new vice president was nominated, and the formal act of transformation could finally be entered upon on November 30, 2012. Following this act, duly recorded by the President of the National Notarial Council, the whole process was completed with the registration of the new entity at the Naples Chamber of Commerce on April 22, 2013.

From the formal point of view, this transformation into a public entity is a major victory. Stocks are easy to sell and especially to mortgage to a bank. Because of their legal nature they actually transform the water system into a tradable commodity which is de facto owned by the private sector (banks) also when it is formally in public hands. No such possibility to sell or to mortgage the capital is open to the public entity Azienda Speciale so that strictly speaking one can claim that the water in Naples is now shielded from privatization.

Nevertheless, as is becoming clear during these two plus years since the transformation, this is not enough to claim "mission accomplished!" in the making of a new institution of the commons.

A commons institution requires a DNA (corporate bylaws) coherent with the mission of governing the commons in an ecologically sustainable, socially responsible, long-term philosophy. Of course, this mission can only be accomplished if the entity is economically and financially well run, which depends not only on the quality of its management and of its workers, but also on the flexibility, adaptability, and efficacy granted by its bylaws. Some agency of control deploying some kind of standard must control the degree of accomplishment of the mission enshrined in the DNA of any organization. In the case of the stock corporation, whose DNA requires its officers to pursue profit and shareholder value, the market is such an agency of control. In the case of an organization belonging to a municipality, whose vocation is to serve the interest of the administration in office "as if" the administration was carrying on the activity directly (this is the so-called *in-house* providing method), the agency of control is the political process represented by the elected or appointed officials of the municipality. The standard which they apply, rather than long-term ecological interest of future generations, is their possibility of being reelected, thus the running of the business very much depends on which political party is in office and what the politicians are trying to signal to their constituency.

In the case of a commons organization that serves the interests of ecology and of future generations, neither of these traditional agencies of control is appropriate. In Naples we have opted for a *Comitato di sorveglianza* [supervisory board], a sort of multi-stakeholder panel composed of five employees (elected by their peers), five customers (decided by random selection from those that signal their interest), five members of the city council (politicians), and five activists from environmental movements. Oddly, this latter is the only component that has not yet selected its representation because of the usual infighting of the left which I do not wish to discuss here. The idea is that such a multi-stakeholder board can check the way in which the administrators (appointed by the mayor) carry out their duty to be faithful to the generative DNA of ABC.[32]

This institutional solution in Naples is still in a phase of experimentation and many adjustments are possible. However, direct participation in the running of the commons can actually happen according to this model if we succeed in making the supervisory board strong, ecologically literate, and independent. In the future, maybe many "commons institutions" will take a similar organizational form that experiments with governance which is neither the private corporate structure nor the obsolete direct political-administrative running of public services. Currently, there is a quite serious controversy because of an attempt by the municipality to change the bylaws of ABC incrementing rather than reducing hierarchical bureaucratic controls, and an attempt by the Campania region (run by the right) in the opposite direction to reopen an opportunity for privatization.[33]

A lot of experimentation must happen and it is not easy to carry it on in a very stormy political climate. For example, we can move some interesting steps in the right direction if the supervisory board at some point runs a "matrix of the commons," a sort of balance sheet of the commons capable to monitor the environmental and social impact, as suggested by the *Gemeinwohl-Ökonomie*, in its evaluation of the management's performance. On this specific issue, a working group is in place, at the International University College in Turin.[34] Also crucial is to work on the correct division of power between the administrators and the supervisors. All of this can be experimented on in the future, when and if we are able to make ABC an institution that is actually emancipated by the intervention of a contingent political majority. This is not yet the case in practice in Naples, where recently I am experiencing quite some reluctance on the part of the municipality to actually hand over real power to the new commons institution.

At any rate, ABC is the most advanced publicly owned commons institution that was possible to create thus far. ABC is achieving remarkable results within an unjust and discriminatory legal system which in Italy favors private institutions over public ones and introduces all sorts of bureaucratic restrictions in managerial discretion. Had the third referendum question been approved, the experimentation that we are doing in Naples with ABC would be the rule and not the exception. Numerous battles, both legal and political, still await us.

9. Towards Federcommons

Aware as it is of representing the desires of the vast majority of Italians (as became clear in the water referendum), the struggle for the commons tries to explore alternative institutions. ABC Naples, together with other companies in the domain of public utilities, is promoting the birth of Federcommons, an association aiming to link the more than 4,000 public services companies, which are still

32 I owe the distinction of extractive versus generative DNA of a property arrangement to Marjorie Kelly's *Owning Our Future* (2012).

33 The discussion on the transformation of the bylaws of ABC was quite fierce in the summer of 2014. See amongst others: http://ricerca.repubblica.it/repubblica/archivio/repubblica/2014/08/11/mattei-scrive-al-sindaco-se-vuole-cambi-vertice-ma-prima-sinformi-beneNapoli02.html?ref=search; http://ricerca.repubblica.it/repubblica/archivio/repubblica/2014/08/08/liscia-gassata-o-competitiva-e-scontro-sullacqua-pubblicaNapoli01.html?ref=search; http://ricerca.repubblica.it/repubblica/archivio/repubblica/2014/08/07/cosi-lazienda-abc-e-destinata-a-fallireNapoli01.html?ref=search, accessed 09/03/2014.

34 See: www.iuctorino.it/content/smart-watertech, accessed 09/11/2014.

one hundred percent publicly owned, to prevent their privatization. The attempt is to try to propose, beyond water management, the exploration of legal forms progressively more suitable for running the commons. This organizational effort in its way is also an exciting challenge, because the current association of utility providers (in which private companies are very strong), Federutility, has de facto monopolized the work of lobbying and interpretation of an extremely complex legal system. Unfortunately, lawyers representing Federutility filed amicus briefs against the admissibility of the water referendum, so it is clear that a hard-nosed look at the matter of political representation of the public services is now in order. This requires, of course, the establishment of a robust study center as well as an organization devoted entirely to the commons in the public services, which is capable of authoritative, organized pressure on the legislator to change some of the many governance mandatory rules that still limit the viability of commons institutions in the crucial domain of public services.

In Italy the commons movement, thanks to a particularly productive alliance with jurists, has developed a quite sophisticated vision of a possible other path, neither private nor public, but common in the governance of deep fundamental interests such as water, transportation, culture, welfare, and much more.

The Valle Theater Foundation in Rome and the ABC water company in Naples, different in both genesis, subject matter, and current condition, are important prototypes of this long-term vision of commons management, which is not a mere "third way," but actually an emancipatory alternative against the unholy alliance of private capital and government institutions. Both these institutional experiments are embattled in different ways, but they are both proving quite resilient first examples of institutions of the commons.

In Italy, and this is possibly the most important characteristic of our experience, despite the dramatic state of our democratic process, we are finding the energies to move from simple indignation to the patient, relentless reconstruction of an alternative system from the bottom up.[35]

35 See: Salvatore Settis, *Azione popolare. Cittadini per il bene comune* [Popular Action. Citizens for Common Properties], Einaudi, Turin, 2012.

Translated from the Italian by Robert Booth.

The author wishes to thank the many colleagues, friends, and comrades that have shared with him in solidarity these last ten years of struggles for the commons. In particular, special thanks to Alberto Lucarelli, with whom I also share the birthdate of April 22. I also wish to thank Freddy Paul Grunert, without whose encouragement I would not have written this paper.

Antonio Negri

Living in a Time of Crisis

Some time ago, in the course of a philosophical discussion, I found myself commenting on Hannah Arendt's idea that the treasure of the freedom of action is impossible to transmit in a world which attributes no meaning to action in the public sphere. It came to my mind again when I began preparing this script because, when taken positively, it tells us that we are not free unless we live a common experience, unless we win a "space-time" in which freedom can not only be expressed but also established, in which action can expand and assume the form of an institution.

Two of the cited terms should especially be problematized: "transmit" and "public."

When we use the word "transmit," we seem to be indicating something quite simple and clear: a depot and a passage, an accumulation and a mutual enrichment, a subjectivity that is passed from one person to another, a lived experience, a dialog, a language. But what does any of this mean in light of the current economic and social crisis, when, for example, we think of young generations who cannot even envisage a future for themselves, who are mired in an uncertainty that has become their day-to-day reality?

When we use the word "public," however, we touch upon a complex aspect of contemporary existence. As Hannah Arendt suggests, the use of the term is problematic inasmuch as the concept behind it seems to have become detached from the way it was once understood, in the tradition of modernity – the idea that the transition from private to public is a linear process accomplished through the democratic administration of public or state institutions. The term "public" used to be based on the conception of a centralized political representation of the peoples' interests: on the one hand, freedom of the private sphere, freedom of the markets; on the other, established popular values such as equality and freedom, and the guarantee that the state and its great institutions – *public* institutions, to be precise – would uphold these values. The function of the "public" sphere, of the state, is now in need of scrutiny; doubts as to its survival oblige us to reexamine the term. And that is what Arendt points out. But perhaps there is something else behind the difficulty she highlights. By "public," Arendt means more than a legal, institutional "public," she means the fact of living, producing, and building together – in other words, what we might now refer to as the "common" rather than the "public." The difference – what distinguishes the common from the public – is not a matter of detail or even of definition, but of an ontological dimension. And it is this difference that I would partially, and very rapidly, like to explore in the present context – first from the standpoint of political philosophy, and then from the figure of the artist.

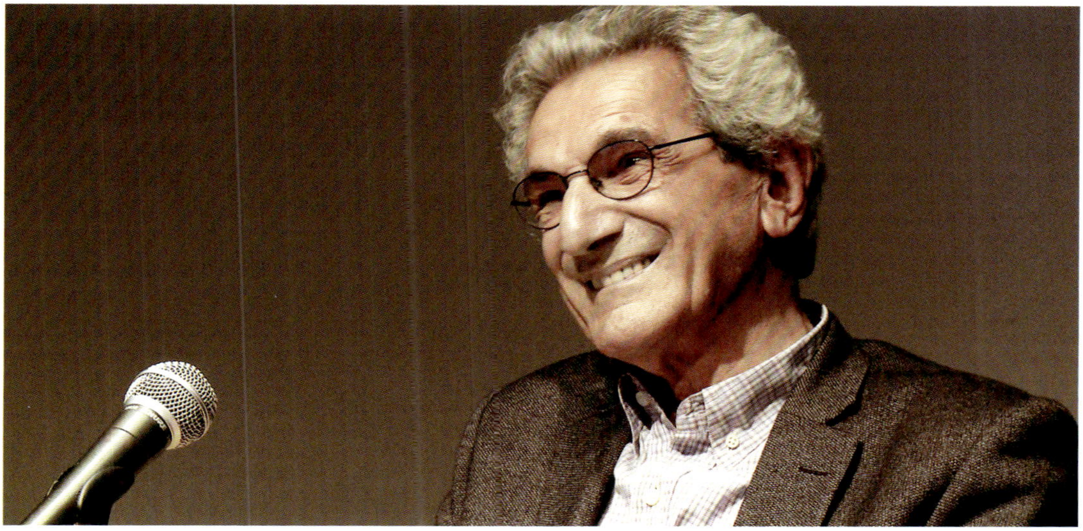

Antonio Negri at his lecture "Vivre dans la crise," ZKM | Karlsruhe, June 13, 2013

We should begin by asking whether what we call the "public" is indeed exhausted, spent. How far along the road to its extinction has it traveled? How do things stand with regard to the loss of trust in political representation and the state's ability to act in the public interest? Moreover, are we really witnessing the increasing emergence of something that becomes a power opposed to the public, which might be described as a sense of the common? How – and to what degree – is this new sense of the common affirmed as something different, a kind of new natural law? I am probably being a little premature here, but it does seem to me that this sense of the common is spreading, particularly at the present time. In effect, the current crisis, in its economic, social, and political forms, has acted rather like a "divine cleansing": it has erased the determinations that held sway for so long, shredded old conceptualizations, and exposed us to a situation of profound uncertainty and disorientation. Yet the crisis is also a time of tremendous expectation.

If the public sphere and its institutions are exhausted, freedom can no longer be transmitted through the "publicity" of experience and contemporary life – by "publicity" here I mean the "public" nature of the institutions that structure it. Of course the "public," historically the instrument of freedom and equality, still functions in many places as the fundamental vehicle of such values. Yet it increasingly seems to represent nothing more than the state's privatization of what ought to belong to us all. By contrast, the sense of the common is expressed in a powerful manner. At present, the difficulties created by the crisis appear to be intensifying the desire for the common spawned by this exhaustion. Crisis and poverty are imposing the need to resist, to act together, to rediscover an "us" that we have lost sight of so often. But this desire is not merely a critical reaction to the increasing irrationality demonstrated by markets and finance capitalism – all the activities that seem to be geared exclusively to the accumulation of profits, to a totally disembodied gamble on the financial markets – where the old fantasies of money making money, unlimited returns, and the limitless expansion of speculation have long since driven out the heroic, romanticized figure of the bold entrepreneur. It is also a reaction to the way in which states are so frequently seen as mere conduits for the private logic of capital: a private sector in the guise of a public form, state property and prerogatives that no longer belong to us all, an expropriation of what ought to be a "common thing," *res publica*, and which no longer exists. Were these the factors that generated the desire for the common, the desire we see in the streets of New York, Madrid, Santiago de Chile, Montreal, and London, expressed as outrage and the occupation of public space – *indignados*, occupy movements, student movements, and so on? How are we to explain this desire for the common?

In attempting to answer this question, I would like to suggest four subjective figures of the contemporary crisis, or more precisely – since it is not a matter of choice – four ways of controlling them so that they cannot express their desire for the common. I shall discuss the "indebted figure," the "mediatized figure," the "securitized figure," and the "(politically) represented figure."

The Indebted Figure

The indebted figure is by now quite familiar. In effect, indebtedness has become part of the general condition of our social existence: in terms of labor, we are faced with a precarious situation that is becoming psychologically and materially unsustainable. Today, there are fewer and fewer productive situations in which people are employed in a normal way, in which they are directly productive and paid in the usual way. Instead, we have rising unemployment, part-time work, and insecure employment, all of which are characterized by a constant state of debt (to banks, family, and friends) and dominated by a totally irrational social distribution of income. Income has been detached from any rational measure of labor or consideration of its social value.

In such a situation, when we work, it is as though we are always in debt to something in relation to society – and not simply because we can no longer make ends meet, because we are left with less and less at the end of the month: we suffer from a sort of fragility of our own working conditions and of a liquefaction of the value of our work.

Big industry and the Fordist organization of labor have evaporated. Work is no longer restricted to an eight-hour day, payment for a fixed amount of time that leaves sixteen hours for private life and sleep. The process of capitalist valorization has become something else, which infiltrates every aspect of our lives: in the interests of capital, we are now productive twenty-four hours a day. Our lives are the new factory; value is extracted from the existence of men and women; capital pillages our lives.

Moreover, work has become work in which the importance of the cognitive and social elements of production is increasing: labor now tends to be based on social cooperation, the circulation of ideas, innovation, and communication.

In short, accumulation is no longer achieved in the spaces and time frames typical of direct labor, in factories, but encompasses the full extent of life's time: capital's occupation of all of life's space has managed to transform every service and means of communication into a productive structure. The economy is now a bioeconomy, and politics is now biopolitics. From our position within these conditions, we are beginning to realize what exploitation means today: something that occupies every moment of our time, but is expressed in our lives only as insecurity and misery, as debt and uncertainty, as the lack of a future and the absence of hope.

The Mediatized Figure

We are – and we will increasingly become – immersed in mediatization. By mediatization I mean everything which links us, which enables communication, which inserts us into network structures. On the one hand, this is because cognitive labor, the work of the brain, the work of communication – in short, what is known as *immaterial* labor – is now becoming the keystone of productive labor and therefore of accumulation. On the other, it is because not only do we work in a mediatized environment, we are also its prisoners. The world around us is a world of phantoms and opinions, which we help to produce but which, in turn, attempt to format us, to subject us to messages that artificially condition our consumption and especially our emotions and concepts.

It may be possible to describe this situation with the aid of that somewhat outmoded word "alienation." In the spaces comprehensively permeated by communication, in which we now live, we are close to losing a clear perception of what is true and what is false. What needs to be exposed here is the way in which our networking activity, a powerful tool that could be used to enhance our resistance to capital, has become our prison. Of course, this is not to suggest that we should indulge in nostalgia and advocate a return to a golden age, or that given the loss of truth criteria, we should fall back on natural or innate verities. The problem is to succeed in rediscovering, in the heart of a radically transformed world – and only in that world – real relationships structured by language and bonds, values that form the basis of action. The problem is one of rediscovering something of the reality of life *in mediatization*, and of taking ownership of it.

The Securitized Figure

The securitized figure lives in constant awareness of his/her own fragility; he/she is persuaded that if he/she allows himself/herself to be shackled he/she will then, paradoxically, be protected. The securitized figure is incessantly and emphatically alerted to the "threats" that hang over him/her. Power has always thrived by proclaiming: "You are in danger!"

Fear – as a fundamental element that undermines human relationships – is an extremely effective form of government. The individual, the citizen, is introduced to a world of hideous ghosts that stalk the individual (controls, searches, computer viruses, explicit or whispered threats, remote control, transfer of personal data, pandemics, natural disasters, insecurity, etc.). That is why the individual then turns to the state, which should keep citizens safe from the risks waving like red flags in front of their eyes – as long as they agree to be governed. But in reality, the state often exacerbates their fears, anxieties, the misery of their nightmares, whether these concern crime, crisis, or – and why not, after all – war. We only have to think of the specters surrounding the issue of migration, which haunt the minds of prospective migrants as much as those of their prospective hosts, in order to grasp the significance of fear in the current climate. These are the demons that unsettle our world; it is also around these demons that terrible feelings crystallize, which are always, sooner or later, expressed in political and social terms. And that, be in no doubt, is something to be truly afraid of.

The Represented Figure

The represented figure seeks a shred of salvation – or at least a guarantee of security – in the political sphere, in political representation. The represented figure asks for the right to "the pursuit of happiness," to borrow a term from the United States Declaration of Independence. But what does this figure get under contemporary constitutional conditions? More often than not, he/she suffers the consequences of inefficiency, corruption, duplicity, irresponsibility, and so forth. And even when the situation is more positive, it is still characterized by a terrible feeling of estrangement, of dispossession, of compromise, and acceptance of the "least bad" option. Think of what that must have meant for young French voters a few years ago when, in order to defend democracy, they were obliged to vote for a presidential candidate they did not necessarily favor. To be sure, Jacques Chirac, elected in 2002 with 82 % of the vote, was not as bad as Jean-Maire Le Pen. But what a defeat for representative democracy – having to vote against one's principles in the name of democracy, or better still, to save democracy.
To put it bluntly, the represented figure is forced to endure every shameful practice that current "democratic" politics can devise.

Behind each of these conditions lies an enormous and increasingly intense burden of suffering. Money crushes life and drives it into debt; the domination of the media provokes hysteria; insecurity instills panic; any political representation worthy of the name is experienced as a massive failure. The situation is anything but a happy one. But this is precisely the point at which we should reintroduce the question: How can we be free? We can't run away, we have to face up to the problem.

Now, if we take the trouble to analyze the four situations I have just described, we can ask whether – despite their clearly negative characteristics – they contain strengths that might help us to envisage more clearly a possible figure of necessary resistance. This takes us back to the question I framed at the beginning: What exactly is the desire for the common, the desire that appears to be emerging in the midst of crisis?

What do debt and the predominance of financial structures actually consist of? Essentially, they represent an acknowledgment of the fact that productive life is now more cooperative than ever before. Each and every one of us depends on others in a very profound way. What capital calls "debt" is in reality our reciprocal dependence on cooperation. And at the same time, capital creates a real, personalized indebtedness – engineered through the constant exhortation to consume on credit, through salary cuts, job insecurity (which entails income insecurity), the dismantling of social safeguards, and so on – in order that it can govern this other "social debt." Social debt is capital's mystification of the power of social cooperation. In this way, capital succeeds in making us forget that we are its actors, that we are powerful owners, too. Without us, there can be no social cooperation – no social cooperation, no production of value.

Today, production develops through cooperation rather than through command. Cognitive labor has become hegemonic in the process of valorization. But what is cognitive labor? It is the linkage of singularities and labor. This linkage is not free from perverse or pathological repercussions, of course, but it increasingly functions as a general model for the way in which labor is organized today. And this is the model we should address: it is clear that the need for capitalist command to organize these singularities is steadily diminishing, given that cognitively productive workers are organizing their labor autonomously. This trend is positive and rooted in reality, and that is why society is becoming more productive.

Beware, however. Once again, this does not mean that exploitation has disappeared, or that its horrors have diminished. Debt has emerged as its principal tool. But what have changed are the power of resistance and the hope of liberation. We may have a productive society in which every value in use has become an exchange value, in which corporate power pervades every corner of our lives, in which the financial yardstick – defined by an anonymous power that is not even national anymore, and that doesn't even have the face of a boss anymore – establishes the overall relationship with the amount of labor available in society. In a society such as this, however, rebellion can be more effective and powerful if it is built on the awareness that production no longer depends on authoritarian organization but on cooperation, on autonomous organization. Despite the misery it causes, debt shows that cooperation is now the driver of production. Debt is the tool of our submission, but it is also the sign of our power.

Thus the fears we are subjected to can be overcome by placing trust in others, by self-organized ways of life which enable us to combat the terrors we have no option but to confront. We know that it is possible to resist the attacks against us – the increasing misery and poverty wrought by insecurity and unemployment – because life's strength, its quality, its productivity, is *us*. By *us* I mean the reality of men and women who cooperate with each other, who live alongside each other. *Us* is not a thing, a definitive identity, an essence, a unity or a people. *Us* is the name of the commonality we are in the process of constructing. Education and the construction of common forms of life and production can guarantee a society in which people need not fear each other, in which the *us* is constantly revitalized, in which the common is both the engine and the result of cooperation.

The Art Scene: Is It Something Different?

Art contributes to the common endeavor, to the fabrication of the world; it resists external authority's attempts to control the imagination's transformation of sensitive material into a common language. Art has always been a productive endeavor, and it is even more so today, as labor becomes more cognitive, cooperation becomes the mark of value, and goodwill becomes an *excédence*.

This *excédence* can of course be alienated; but it rebels strongly against this alienation because, in artistic endeavor, the worker rebels not only against the expropriation of his or her work, but also against capital's subsumption of every aspect of life. The artist's gesture of rebellion is a form of revolutionary anticipation. Artists have always been precarious producers, debt has traditionally been the monetary form in which they live. However, artists have come to realize that language is the primary material of labor and therefore of art; that if all labor is linguistic, then art is its paradigm; and that this condition is manifested in the fact that art is the one common form of labor that capital has so far failed to expropriate.

Let's return to us, or more precisely, to the way in which – as regards labor – we are *out of joint*, to use a Shakespearian expression that Jacques Derrida employs in relation to time. The crisis we are living through was created by the transformation of labor; it therefore requires us to create new forms of labor and ways of life. The changes date back to the crisis of the 1970s, when the "technical composition" of the labor force was subjected to radical modification. As I have already mentioned, capital has extended its valorization processes to every aspect of society. This accounts for the slow but continuous transformation of material labor into immaterial labor. The development of new conditions is ensuring that cognitive labor becomes hegemonic within productive processes. In addition, production is being woven into the "biopolitical" fabric of society: capital is developing a new form of exploitation based on the outsourcing of factory work, on rendering it precarious, by subsuming its social diffusion and capturing the crucial element of cooperation. The two processes I have just touched on, the "cognitivization" of labor and its socialization, constitute the two faces of the turning point we have experienced in recent years. Working class subjectivity itself has become essential to capital – as a basis for capital's valorization. And it should be noted that all these developments have been accompanied by a radical change in the relationship to temporality. It is not just labor's traditional temporal standards that have been changed: if life is put to work, temporality ceases to be the measure of labor and becomes a strange *contenant sans dehors*, a self-contained structure within which men and women go about the business of production.

Thus in the new paradigm of production, "financialization" is presented as the only way to capture and measure social labor. If finance alone constructs and imposes the measure of social labor, if it permeates life and ways of life, and if it shapes and organizes them according to the monetary measure, then profits and wages will assume the form of profit and debt. And it is quite clear that finance has thus infiltrated the sphere of social regulation as never before. What we are experiencing is the *progressive "patrimonialization" of the public in a private form*, a process that affects not only the public domain but also the ability to regulate. The welfare state is privatized, sovereignty is conserved in such a way that the lives of citizens are literally harnessed to the task of producing, put to work, until we arrive at the ultimate paradox: the structure of welfare (education, health care, demographic reproduction, etc.) and of social cooperation (communications, transport, culture, and so forth) provide the most fertile soil for the accumulation and valorization of capital.

Yet this turning point is also a source of new forms of resistance. We know that capital, like any political institution (for that is what capital is: Karl Marx, building on the concept of power formulated by Niccolò Machiavelli and Baruch Spinoza, established the idea and Michel Foucault later went on to develop it), that capital as a political institution, therefore, is a relationship. In terms of power, it is the result of "action on the actions of others," as Foucault observed: a matter of command versus resistance, of fixed capital versus the working class and/or proletariat. If every action entails a reaction, and if in socialized capitalism capital assumes the form of a biopower, the power over life, then proletarian resistance is biopolitical too, and invests the confrontation with an irreducible potential conveyed by the *excédence* of knowledge and cooperation in the form of a constituent power.

In fact, capital does not construct or produce knowledge unilaterally and subsequently impose it on cognitive subjects or immaterial workers. In a great many cases, such people take responsibility for their own development. We might say that the more insecure the cognitive labor force becomes, the more it can present itself as an "independent" entity (and to be sure, it knows this). It therefore follows that the new technical composition of the cognitive proletariat can also represent a new political potentiality. Of course, it is not certain that this potentiality will be realized; but if that were to happen, the force of cognitive labor – a force rooted not in scarcity or response to capitalist authority, as was the case in the old manufacturing societies, but in autonomous, transcendent action – could definitively rupture the unity of capitalist power, the Oneness from which it draws its strength. If that were to come about, the surge towards plurality would prove irresistible and shatter the Oneness of biopower.

This was the standpoint from which the scattered movements that emerged in 2011 expressed new political modalities for dealing with the problems arising from the crisis. To conclude this brief phenomenology of life in a time of crisis, I would like to look more closely at some of the implications. Let's go back to alienation and the represented figure.

The represented figure has been deprived of the possibility of political expression; in other words, he/she cannot express his/her will and awareness of social relations or use that awareness in the "pursuit of happiness." In the present situation, political representation – including representative democracy itself – is a tool of power shaped and dominated by money: the wealth held by the 1 percent to the detriment of the 99 percent. Political representation has been reduced to nothing more than the patrimony of capital. Any revolt against this subjugation to the rich and powerful and their measures of wealth means rediscovering that freedom, equality, and solidarity will thrive on the "common" ground of an existence constructed by productive men and women who aspire to freedom and equality.

Although we have no answers to this problem, experiments that are beginning to embody new figures of radical democracy, to shape them and invest them with language, provide us with food for thought. It seems to me that the movements that emerged in 2011 display two fundamental characteristics.

The first concerns the expression of a temporal autonomy. Anyone with an interest in the history of the social and political movements that appeared in Western Europe after 1945, and especially after 1968, has probably noticed that they almost always emerge in reaction to something, to events or accidents of history that were totally unforeseen. The development of such movements then usually occurs as a series of responses to decisions taken by the authorities. The initiatives of power have almost always anticipated the initiatives of democratic movements.

By contrast, the movements of 2011 are distinguished by their radical independence and their ability to manage their own development in accordance with the nuances of their constituent powers. They possess new characteristics, both with regard to the temporality they appear to practice and the determination of their own situation in space. It is almost as if a "dynamic ontology of social being" has been brought into play, one that manifests itself in totally unexpected configurations.

When, for example, we insist on the long and expansive temporality of that what we call the "Arab Spring," it might seem that we are surreptitiously introducing a conception of time that is different from the insurrectional acceleration of events that usually defines the beginning of any struggle. But that is not the case: the process of decision-making in open, horizontal assemblies, which characterized all the "camps" in 2011, all the occupations of squares, is also extremely slow. What is so interesting and new about these struggles is not their slowness or swiftness, but rather the *political autonomy* by which they manage their own temporality. This marks an enormous difference from the rigid or hysterical rhythms of alter-globalization movements – I am thinking here of the meetings that sprang up around governmental and intergovernmental summits in the early years of the twenty-first century. Instead, in the cycle of struggles that occurred in 2011, the speed, slowness, profound intensity, and superficial accelerations were combined and mixed. In every case, time was wrenched away from the schedule imposed by external pressures and the rhythm of election campaigns; it established its own calendar and rhythms of development. This notion of an autonomous temporality may help us to understand why such movements are truly *alternative*. An alternative is not an action, a proposition, or a discourse that is simply opposed to something – to a program of power, for example. It is rather a new *dispositif* rooted in something that signals an asymmetrical relationship to what it opposes. It constitutes an entirely different standpoint. The autonomy of the *dispositif* renders the rhythms of its temporality coherent; and from this standpoint we witness the emergence of new subjectivities, struggles, and constituent principles.

This brings us to the second characteristic of these constituent movements. The temporal determinations of constituent action fluctuate between latency and rapidity, and in accordance with a vast range of factors. Most important, however, is the contagious – or even epidemic – effect of every constituent action. Demanding freedom by confronting a dictatorial power, for example, also introduces and disseminates the idea of an equal distribution of wealth, as happened in Tunisia and Egypt; playing off the desire for democracy against traditional political structures of representation also highlights the need for participation and transparency, as in Spain; protesting against the inequalities created by financial control also leads to demands for the democratic organization of the common and free access to it, as in the United States, and so on. Temporalities may be fast or slow according to the viral intensity of the communication of ideas and desires, all of which construct singular syntheses. There is, of course, no "autonomy of the political" in Carl Schmitt's sense of the term. In such situations, the constituent decisions taken by *acampadas*, the occupations of public space, for example, are formed through a complex construction and negotiation of knowledge and expertise. Decisions are not dictated by a leader or a central committee. Consequently, the question of method becomes just as crucial as keynote speeches. The discourse and practices of the Spanish *indignados* and the occupiers of Wall Street, for example, combined a critique of current forms of political representation with protests against social inequality and the domination of high finance.

The struggles of 2011 unfolded in very different geographical locations and totally different contexts. Moreover, the protagonists came from very different backgrounds. Why, in conclusion, should we regard this ensemble of disparate events as the elements of a cycle? It is clear that all these struggles confronted a single enemy, characterized by its power over debt, the media, the security apparatus, and corrupt – or at least dysfunctional – systems of political representation. But practices, strategies, and objectives, also very different, can be combined to fight multiple battles in pursuit of a single – and singular – objective: the creation of a common ground. The cement that binds some of these realities together might initially be linguistic, cooperative, or simply based on membership of one or more networks. The increasing importance of Internet-based social networks comes to mind here. I do not accept that these networks are exempt from ambiguity, but their linking function and their power to create transversality are undeniably important. In every case, this language and this cooperation have undergone rapid expansion since the very moment when the processes of horizontal decision-making were established.

I will end by noting that these movements are nudging politics towards a plural ontology. A genuine pluralism is beginning to emerge from various traditions; it expresses various objectives which, despite their differences, are combined and articulated on federative, cooperative lines in order to create a model of constituent democracy in which differences can still be differences and in which it is nevertheless possible to interact and to create new institutions, in the way Spinoza envisaged. A model driven from below, from the base, but with the power to achieve what it seeks. A model that is opposed to globalized capital, the dictatorship of finance, and biopower's destruction of the planet. A model that champions free access to and self-management of the *common*. The next step for these movements will probably extend beyond the construction of new human relations and focus on the construction of new institutions. While we have outlined the construction of a politics of plurality, we need to go further, to activate the "ontological engine" of that plurality. A plural ontology of politics was activated in 2011, brought into being by the meeting and restructuring of militant subjectivities. And there, I believe, lies a possible way of living in a time of crisis: by discovering, in the crisis itself, a new *conatus*, a new *cupiditas*, a new felicity, a new desire for happiness.

This essay is based on Antonio Negri's lecture held at ZKM | Karlsruhe on June 13, 2013. The manuscript was translated from the French by Roger Leverdier.

Peter Sloterdijk

Last Exit Indignation:

On Neutralizing Civilians in Democracies

Whenever politicians and political scientists ponder the state of a modern *res publica*, they invariably start reminiscing about ancient Rome. This was also the case with Germany's former Foreign Minister Guido Westerwelle, when in order to criticize what he regarded as an overly generous German welfare state, he had the idea of comparing contemporary conditions to the depths of "Roman decadence." It is hard to say from his remarks what associations he actually had in mind. Perhaps this temporary head of the German Foreign Office was vaguely remembering the Caesars' system of managing the plebs through gladiatorial contests, or possibly he was thinking of the obligatory grain donations for the unemployed masses of the ancient metropolis. Both would have been echoes of the whirlwind tour of world history that most German high-school pupils born in 1961 (Westerwelle et al.) enjoyed. They contained nothing that could be seen as a cause for concern.

At any rate, the reference to "Roman decadence" from the mouth of a German politician was not only indicative of the mere smattering of knowledge he possessed, typical perhaps of his rank. Nor was it just a symptom of verbal bravado intended to impress a particular clientele. For the reference contains a series of dangerous implications that the speaker would no doubt have sidestepped had he been aware of them.

The Roman bread-and-games system was in fact nothing less than the first version of what, since the twentieth century, has been termed "mass culture." It symbolizes the shift from the ponderous senatorial republic to the postrepublican theatrical state that had an imperial thespian at its center. This transition became inevitable once the Roman Empire, after its conversion into a Caesarean monarchy, increasingly moved towards eliminating the senate and the people from the regulation of public life. In this reading, the oft-cited Roman decadence was nothing other than the flip side of the disempowerment of the citizen from politics, which occurred at the same time as the junta of Imperial professional politicians seized power. This can only be grasped in all its ramifications if we recognize that it is a symptom of how republican life was swallowed up by the spheres of administration and entertainment. While the imperial administration increasingly entangled itself in formalities, at the level of entertainment a trend toward barbarity and a lack of all inhibitions emerged, specifically in the circuses on the Mediterranean rim and at the festivities of the metropolitan upper class. The coexistence of administrative state and entertainment state responded to a political structure in which exercising power could only be secured by largely depoliticizing the imperial population. While the Caesars continued to bless their edicts with the holy formula "The Senate and People of Rome" (SPQR), it was already quite clear that both agencies were as good as completely stripped of all power.

Any play on allusions to ancient Roman society sooner or later moves into dangerous territory. For anyone who mentions Rome is covertly saying *res publica*, and anyone talking of the latter should not neglect to ask what the secret behind its beginnings is. So let us try and explain how it came about that the exemplary "public affair/thing" of Old Europe began with a thought-provoking storm of emotions: The son of the last Roman-Etruscan king, Lucius Tarquinius Superbus, heard about the attractions of a young Roman lady called Lucretia, having learned of her beauty and modesty from the boasting of her husband, Collatinus. Tarquin could clearly not accept that a subordinate should enjoy more conjugal felicity than himself, the scion of a royal house. Thanks to Livy the rest is world history, and thanks to Shakespeare part of world literature: The young Tarquin forced his way into Lucretia's lodgings in Rome and compelled her by infamous blackmail to submit to him. Following her defilement, the young woman called together her relatives, told them what had happened, and stabbed herself to death before the eyes of those assembled. An unprecedented shockwave thereupon transformed the harmless Roman people, shepherds and rustics as they were, into a revolutionary mass. Tarquinius Superbus was expelled from the country, and Etruscan dominance brought to a definitive end. Never again will such arrogance be tolerated at the helm of the commonality. The king's name is despised for all time, not just *ad personam*, but with regard to the monarchic function itself.

The civic upheaval gave birth to an idea that was to have a massive impact: control of the community was henceforth to be the privilege only of Romans; it would be pragmatic and profane. Two consuls kept each other in check, their election every year preventing any renewed conflation of person and office. The religious superstructure imploded, with the exception of the state oracle, which even the republic needed; and royal *superbia* was banished forever. The productive energies innate in arrogance were scaled back to the aspiration for recognition through excellence, as is customary in meritocracies. On the back of these resolutions, in 509 B.C., the most ingeniously constructed republican machine in human history was put in place; the subsequent addition of the office of people's tribune ensured it an unsurpassed degree of efficiency. A quite unprecedented success story commenced, until, almost half a millennium later, the Roman power complex was so overstretched that the transition to neo-monarchic conditions became imperative.

Today's readers of this story should bear a key piece of information in mind: The Lucretia legend is about the birth of the *res publica* from the spirit of indignation. What was later to be called the public sphere is originally an epiphenomenon of civic ire. The anger of the gathering crowd gave rise to the first forum. The first agenda had only one item on it: to topple infamous rulership. From their synchronous irritation with the dissolute arrogance of those in power the common people learned that from now on they wanted to be called citizens. The consensus with which everything we now call public life began was civil unanimity given the intolerable violation of the unwritten laws of decency and the heart.

To reiterate the decisive point: What we now describe with the Greek expression "politics" is a derivative of a sense of honor and the proud impulses of common people. In the ancient European tradition, the term *thymós* is used to express the range of affects associated with pride. There are numerous tones on the human psyche's thymotic scale, including joviality, benevolence, and generosity, via pride, ambition, and defiance, to indignation, anger, resentment, hatred, and contempt. As long as a political community is driven by a core of pride, issues of honor and reputation stand at the center of public attention: Here, the greatest asset of all is the integrity of civil dignity. Public mistrust keeps watch to ensure that arrogance and greed, the ever virulent mainsprings of baseness, never gain the upper hand in the *res publica*.

Thus it is clear why it is not without risk to speak today of Roman decadence and equate it with current conditions. Anyone so doing implicitly affirms the view or fear that the modern republic (as it emerged a good two hundred years ago from the antimonarchical anger of the American and the French Revolutions) will likewise in due course be followed by a postrepublican phase. And likewise, this would typically be characterized by the renewed combination of bread and games, or, to put it in contemporary terms, by the synergy of welfare state and sensation industry. There can be no denying that the harbingers of such a dual economy are to be found everywhere. Have we not for some time now been reading the signs of a regression of public life to the status of administration and entertainment, issues of heat insulation for ministries, and casting shows for ambitions? Hasn't the debate initiated in the United Kingdom on "postdemocracy" discretely conquered party headquarters and sociological seminars in the Western Hemisphere? Haven't countless people already dived for existential cover, as did the Stoics and Epicureans of yore, simply accepting that bureaucracy, spectacular shows, and private collections now define the ultimate horizons of life?

One could conclude over-hastily from the above that in the twilight of the second republican era (which we call political modernity) postdemocratic trends are winning out across the board. This being the case, all that would remain for us inhabitants of the second *res publica amissa* (the sacrificed community) would be to wait for the Caesars – and their cheap versions, the populists, for today's populism proves that Caesarism even functions with dummies and walk-on extras. And does this mean that Oswald Spengler was right with his dangerous suggestion that to be a cutting-edge critic of contemporary society you need to be a theorist of decadence?

However intriguing rhapsodic thoughts of this ilk may be, in this matter we would be better advised not to let ourselves be swept along by the elan of grand analogies. Admittedly, there are any number of indications that we are heading for postrepublican and postdemocratic conditions. Wherever one looks, one sees the most striking symptom, the renewed disempowerment of citizens by a state apparatus entrenched in a monolog with itself. Politics in Germany, for example, is increasingly approximating the monolog of a club of autists.

Anyone who thinks that shutting out the citizenry in a second postrepublican era will progress as smoothly as it did after the ancient Caesarean regime had been established, will be disappointed. On this point, the historical analogy does not work – for a simple reason that can be gleaned best from the classical sources. The ancient Greek writers had an understanding of man as a creature driven by both Eros and pride that was far more profound than the modern understanding, which by and large tends to be content to explain the human psyche solely in terms of the libido, of a feeling of lack and a wish to have. For over a century now nothing new has occurred to the Moderns with regard to issues of pride and honor. So it comes as no surprise that today neither politicians nor psychologists know what to do when confronted by public expressions of the forgotten elements of pride in humans' emotional apparatus. Anyone casting an eye over the plethora of political upheavals in Europe, specifically the German flash points, will realize quickly that if today the disempowerment of citizens is not really proceeding apace, despite all the support from the expertocracy and the entertainment culture, then it is because the impact of civil pride has not been taken into account.

Suddenly they are back on stage, the thymotic citoyens, the self-confident, informed, thinking citizens, male and female, willing to take part in decisions, petitioning before the court of public opinion against the failed representation of their interests and their insights into the current political system. They are back, the citizens who have remained capable of being indignant, because in spite of all the attempts to degrade them to the status of libido bundles they have nevertheless preserved their sense of self-assertion and they exhibit these qualities by presenting their dissidence in public spaces. They are back among us, as if overnight, those citizens who insist on being a thorn in the politicians' sides, who refuse to be political omnivores, patient and far removed from espousing opinions "that are not helpful." For many years they were nowhere to be seen, these informed and indignant citizens who suddenly, and it is hard to grasp why, hit upon the idea of applying Article 20, Paragraph 2 of the German Basic Law to themselves, according to which all power proceeds from the people. What were they thinking of when they started to understand the mysterious constitutional verb "proceed" as an instruction to quit their four walls and announce what they want, know, and fear?

In moments like the present it does not hurt to remember that the original *res publica* was itself a derivative of the psycho-political primary emotions of pride and indignation. As noted above, the unwillingness to tolerate rulers any longer who had become overly crass in their arrogance was the source of the Roman feeling of community. For all the differences between the ancient and the modern settings, the comparable aspects are fairly obvious. Today, countless citizens also see reasons to be annoyed by their rulers' presumptuousness. Even when the presumptuousness has become anonymous and is hidden away in the systems driven by practical constraints, the citizens, in particular in their capacity as taxpayers and the addressees of the banal speeches before elections, now and again sense only too clearly how they are being toyed with.

Do we now understand why the dream of systems gives birth to monsters? The monsters are the flesh-and-blood citizens who resist the postdemocratic directive to disempower the citizenry. One can concede that there is a need to explain this sudden recalcitrance. Why, suddenly, can't the people stay quietly in the place assigned to them? Why can't one rely on their lethargy any longer, so key to the system? And what is so hard to grasp about their designated function? In a representative democracy, quite apart from their enormous fiscal duties, citizens are primarily required to supply legitimacy for governments, which is why at lengthy intervals they are invited to exercise their right to vote. In-between times they can make themselves useful above all by being passive. Their prime task is to express confidence and trust in the system – by remaining silent.

To put it politely, let it suffice for us to state that such trust has become a rare commodity. Even noncritical, regime-friendly political scientists in Berlin speak of manifest estrangement between the political caste and the populace at large. Experts still shy away from the harsh diagnosis that the policy of effecting a useful depoliticization of the people is on the verge of bankruptcy.

It might be illuminating at this point to ask how the Romans during the Caesarean period succeeded in artfully depoliticizing their world whereas today's elected postdemocrats seem to be losing their grip on the same endeavor. There is a straightforward answer: For a long time the elites of imperial Rome were able to offer halfway useful substitutes to meet the thymotic needs of their citizens – despite the manifest signs of postrepublican decadence: They were past masters at using the *civis romanus* to instill pride in the Empire's civilizing achievements; they bound the peoples on the periphery to the center using Roman *soft power*; they were smart enough to grant the abandoned masses in the cities participation in the theatrical narcissism of the cult of the Caesar. Compared to this, one is struck by the helplessness of our political caste in all areas of the thymotic apparatus. Our political caste often offers citizens little more than participation in their own feeble situation – an offer that the population generally only takes up during carnival or in beer halls. If one asks how the general public responds to the rulers' performance, the opinion pollsters have of late mainly reported: with contempt. Needless to say that this word is part of the elementary vocabulary of thymotic analysis. If the terms for the negative pole on the pride scale is used as often and as sharply as it is currently, then this surely indicates the extent to which the psycho-political regulation of our community has got out of hand.

The dream of systems gives birth to monsters: The rulers are experiencing this for themselves when dissatisfied citizens obstruct their projects and procedures. It is hardly surprising if contempt responds spontaneously to contempt. Frightened, the politicians met the unwelcome civil dissent in Stuttgart and Berlin first with a barrage of insults and then with massive police deployment. So this is what that dark something looks like from which all state power proceeds? "Professional protesters, after-work anarchists, cheap polemical democrats, senior citizen egoists, all gone to seed through affluence!" These were the epithets with which federal state governments and their allies in the German capital summarized their impressions of the tens of thousands who had taken to the streets to oppose a moribund major project. Should we excuse this choice of words by remembering that those who uttered them were in a state of shock? On the contrary, we should thank these politicians for at long last speaking their minds about the citizens. Remarkably, an important part of the sometimes serious press was prepared to empathize with the political caste that had its back to the wall: *Wutbürger* [angry citizens] is what the press has recently called the new protesters, which would have been an intelligent neologism had it evoked the original linkage of indignation and the republic. Sadly, in the current usage it only serves to swat away the annoying dissident flies. At any rate, it shows that some journalists know how they can contribute to disempowering the citizens.

However, things did not stop at verbal attacks on the dark something. The scared caste responded with baton charges and tear gas to the resolute arguments of those citizens who had discovered inconsistencies in the plans for Stuttgart 21, the new Stuttgart railway station. The Social Democratic Party of Germany in its dotage responded to a tried-and-true robust party member who tabled countless items of proof of the inconsistencies in Germany's immigration policies, presenting facts that showed things would be sounder without attempts at genetic justifications – by initiating proceedings to exclude him from the party. In both instances the official wording had it that there had been much heartfelt deliberation before reacting in this necessary way, both the lashing out and the exclusion. Disempowering citizens qua profession can on occasions be tougher than the usual tough choices the politicos face.

Anyone attempting in the midst of the polemics to maintain the calm that is appropriate for an observer gains the impression that the various flash points coalesce to form a coherent scenario: One encounters the same entrenched reflexes to disturbances of the business-as-usual routine wherever one looks, the same evasion by resorting to mobbing the proponents of "undesirable opinions," the same unease about people voicing opinions who are not paid to do so, the same confusion of constipation with strength of character.

Only a more precise analysis of the political system and its paradoxes can lead us out of so much entrenched torpor. We could start with an explanation of why modern representative democracy is not as a rule capable of achieving what the Caesars evidently managed so easily: For centuries the Caesars succeeded in combining the systemic imperative of the post-republican disempowerment of citizens with the psycho-political imperative of the thymotic satisfaction of citizens. The Moderns fail at this since it is no longer so easy to play the card of national self-elevation which was the solution of choice a century ago. As a result, there are only two ways out for the rulers, the one economically disastrous, the other psycho-politically hard to predict: disempowerment of citizens by offering premiums to remain quiet or paralysis of citizens by inculcating a feeling of resignation in them. Anyone who has followed the debates on the state as a constant source of free handouts knows how premiums function. And it is no secret how resignation is nurtured. Superficially this resembles satisfaction under a good government, but differs from it by dint of the dispirited grumbling that essentially all of those in power are the same. In such a climate, election turnouts can, as is customary in the United States, fall below fifty percent, without the political caste seeing any cause for concern.

To use a sense of resignation to disempower citizens is to play with fire because at any moment it can flip into its opposite: open indignation and manifest civic ire. Once that anger has found an object, it is hard to divert its focus. From the angle of the political caste things are complicated by the fact that modern disempowerment of citizens has to be presented as their "inclusion." Their depoliticization must entail a residue of politicization sufficient to ensure the political apparatus' self-reproduction.

In no regard are citizens in our hemisphere more disempowered than in their role as taxpayers. The modern state has succeeded in imposing the most passive role it could possibly assign to its members at the very moment they contribute to the community in the most material of ways – when they pay into the common coffer. Instead of emphasizing that these citizens are donating, and instead of treating taxes respectfully as gifts, modern fiscal states burden their taxpayers with the degrading fiction that they have incurred massive debts to the public treasury, debts that are so high that they can only be repaid in lifelong installments. At the heart of the modern mechanism for disempowering citizens we find a tax system that is completely wrongly structured in psycho-political terms. It robs those citizens who actively pay taxes of any pride and squeezes them into a box as the eternal debtors to Leviathan. The more they are able to pay, the deeper they are in the state's debt; the more they give, the more they are in debt. Incidentally, taxpaying citizens have of late been condemned to passivity not only when they pay into the public coffers, they also suffer from second-degree passivity because behind their backs the state has shackled them to the galley of public debt. Without realizing what is happening to them the donors find themselves ensnared in a new type of common destiny. They now make up a group bearing a collective debt that will pay for everything, tomorrow and until their dying day, which those currently disempowering citizens have imposed on them. So don't say that politicians today have no vision. There is a utopia for our community. If luck is on our side and everyone does everything in their power then at the end the impossible may be possible; namely, the avoidance of the state's bankruptcy. From now on this is the red star in democracy's evening sky.

Since the 2008 financial crisis, countless commentators have highlighted the dangers of speculation in the financial markets. However, there has been no talk of the most dangerous speculation of them all: Most states today, ignoring what the crises could have taught them, speculate that citizens will remain passive. Western governments bank on the fact that their citizens will continue to happily escape into entertainment; Eastern governments trust to the robust efficacy of overt repression. You do not need to be a prophet to intuit the degree to which the future will be defined by the rivalry between the Euro-American and Chinese modes of disempowering citizens. Both procedures assume that the obligation to provide representation of positive civic will and to enable a knowledgeable citizenry can be avoided by those acting in government, who instead believe the vast majority of the citizens will remain passive. To date this strategy has been astonishingly successful: Even after the failed Copenhagen World Climate Conference of 2009, that fateful December Europe's citizenry devoted itself more to Christmas shopping than to politics, preferring to go home with bags full instead of at least symbolically tarring and feathering its "representatives," who had returned home empty-handed, which is what they most certainly deserved.

Even without the gift of divination we all know that such speculation will sooner or later come a cropper, because no government in the world is safe from its citizens' indignation in this age of digital civility. Once anger has successfully done its work, new architectures of political participation will arise. The postdemocracy waiting outside the door will have to wait a little longer.

Revised version of an article published in *Der Spiegel*, 2010, no. 45, pp. 136–145. Translated from the German by Jeremy Gaines.

Karl-Peter Sommermann

The Right of Resistance: Approaches in Legal Philosophy

Maurice Hauriou, one of the preeminent scholars of French constitutional doctrine in the Third Republic, observed that the main driving forces behind social change are the shifting everyday realities that constantly produce new circumstances, together with people's passions and their sense of justice.[1] Despite the continuing existence of rogue states in which legal uncertainty and despotism prevail, the last of the driving forces mentioned, namely, the sense of justice, may be the strongest in the long run. The experience of injustice and the suffering of abuse and oppression has always challenged and determined individual and collective political action.[2] Ample material to illustrate this can be found in the most recent past and the present day.

In the following I will start by elucidating the nature and justifications for the right of resistance using the historical example of the North American revolution (I), before considering the question of whether a right of resistance can exist in a constitutional democracy (II). Furthermore I shall try to undertake a classification of civil disobedience (III), before drawing conclusions on the advancement of political order – also in view of its integration in a multilevel governance system (IV). I conclude with a summary (V).

I.

The creation of the constitutional state in the last quarter of the eighteenth century was a response to wrongs suffered. The revolutionaries in North America and France claimed the right of resistance, which, rooted in natural law, was to justify the abolition of the old regime (which was felt to be tyrannical) and to grant the right to the creation of a new polity that safeguarded their rights.[3] In France the focus was on replacing the system of government without undermining national unity, whereas the North American Revolution led to the British colonies severing their ties with the motherland, in other words, to the emergence of thirteen new, associated states, which founded a new federal state in an act of political self-determination a short while later.

In order to illuminate the still prevalent understanding of the right of resistance that is informed by the modern theory of natural law, it is helpful to look at the United States Declaration

1

Maurice Hauriou, *Précis de droit constitutionnel*, 2nd ed., Recueil Sirey, Paris, 1929, p. 69: "Pour lutter contre le faisceau des forces conservatrices, il y a trois grandes forces de changement: la vie et sa création continuelle de nouveautés; les passions des hommes, et, enfin, le sentiment de la justice."

2

See also: Amartya Sen, *The Idea of Justice*, Belknap Press of Harvard University Press, Cambridge (MA), 2009, pp. VII, 388f.; Christian Tomuschat, "Das Recht des Widerstands nach staatlichem Recht und Völkerrecht," in: Horst Albach (ed.), *Über die Pflicht zum Ungehorsam gegenüber dem Staat*, Wallstein, Göttingen, 2007, p. 60; Karl-Peter Sommermann, *Staatsziele und Staatszielbestimmungen*, Mohr Siebeck, Tübingen, 1997, pp. 4f.

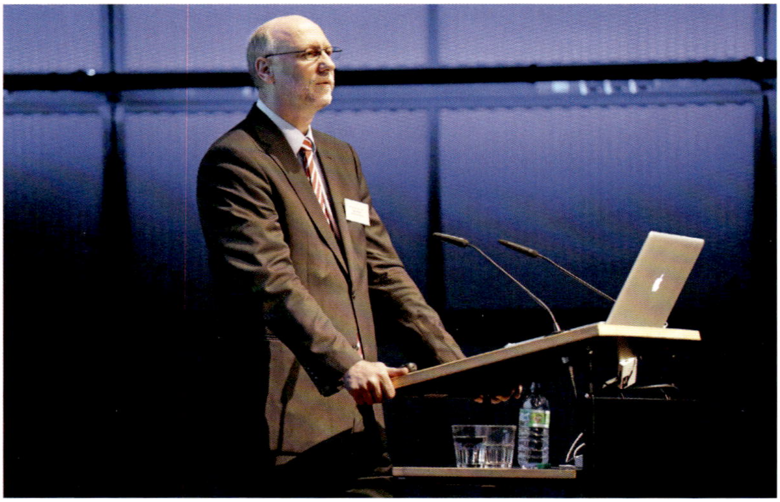

Karl-Peter Sommermann at the symposium Power and Law. Fluid Forms of Protest, ZKM | Karlsruhe, March 29, 2014

of Independence of 1776.[4] In the Declaration, great attention is paid to stating the reasons why the North American colonies wanted to free themselves from the yoke of the British Crown. The king's despotic actions and violations of the law are meticulously listed, among them the repeal of the Colonial Charters, which governed the basic political conditions and which were based on the acknowledgment of the colonies' right to self-government by the Crown, the repeated suspension of the colonies' legislative bodies, the creation of dependencies among the judges, the imposition of taxes without the colonies' consent, and the deployment of mercenary troops to assert the Crown's claim to power by force. Moreover, the Declaration demonstrates that the North American colonies tried time and again to move the king to refrain from further wrongdoing by means of petitions and by clearly outlining what was actually happening in the North American colonies, and finally with warnings. This, however, the Declaration concludes, did not lead to the creation of justice but instead to ever new injustices. The necessary consequence finally had to be disengagement from the British state:

> "We, therefore, the Representatives of the United States of America, in General Congress, [...] solemnly publish and declare, That these United Colonies are, and of Right ought to be Free and Independent States; that they are Absolved from all Allegiance to the British Crown, and that all political connection between them and the State of Great Britain, is and ought to be totally dissolved."

The Declaration conveys three fundamental insights:

First, the Declaration reflects the reasoning based on contractual theory as innate in the natural law doctrine of the era of the Enlightenment. Thus, here rulership is no longer a God-given right that warrants respect independent of the citizens' will. Rather, rulership is a political regulation of the community as established by society, which first and foremost serves to protect the citizens'

3 Still essential reading on the tradition of the right of resistance since the Middle Ages: Kurt Wolzendorff, *Staatsrecht und Naturrecht in der Lehre vom Widerstand des Volkes gegen rechtswidrige Ausübung der Staatsgewalt*, Breslau, 1916, reprint: Scientia, Aalen, 1961.

4 Reprinted in: Bernard Schwartz (ed.), *The Bill of Rights: A Documentary History*, vol. 1, Chelsea House Publishers, New York, 1971, pp. 251 ff.

5 See, for example, Klaus Roth, "Geschichte des Widerstandsdenkens. Ein ideengeschichtlicher Rückblick," in: Klaus Roth and Bernd Ladwig (eds.), *Recht auf Widerstand? Ideengeschichtliche und philosophische Perspektiven*, Menschenrechtszentrum der Universität Potsdam, Potsdam, 2006, pp. 7–54, here p. 32.

rights. Even Thomas Hobbes, who had interpreted absolute rule as the result of a contract on behalf of the citizens in favor of a third party (the ruler) in order to end the permanent state of emergency and the war of all against all, had not, as has sometimes been said,[5] completely rejected a right of resistance. Despite his approval of the maxim "The King can do no wrong," to him the citizens' mandatory fealty ends at the very moment at which the ruler can no longer fulfil his main purpose of protecting the citizens' rights:

> "The Obligation of Subjects to the Soveraign, is understood to last as long, and no longer, than the power lasteth, by which he is able to protect them."[6]

It has to be conceded of course that Hobbes does not refer to protection from the ruler himself as long as the latter is effectively exercising his power. In the Declaration of Independence, the concept of the right of resistance as established by John Locke is much more clearly manifested. According to Locke, the citizens united to protect their property which was understood in a broad sense and included life and limb, in order to resolve conflicts peacefully within the framework of a system based on the separation of powers.[7] It is inconceivable to Locke that the sovereign could be allowed to rule with absolute tyranny as humans did not by nature have the freedom to exercise tyranny over themselves or another and therefore such powers could not be conferred.[8] According to Locke, one consequence of the ban on tyranny is that taxes may only be levied with the consent of the majority of citizens.[9] In a representative system, this permission can also be granted by elected representatives.[10] Against this backdrop, the colonists' later slogan "No taxation without representation," which was later reinforced in the so-called Boston Tea Party of 1773, seems legitimate. The thirteen colonies could not exercise their right to vote – which existed in principle – not least because of the distance to the motherland. It was also because of these imposed taxes that colonists saw themselves as being entitled to resist.

Second, the Declaration shows that from the perspective of the eighteenth century, the right of resistance is closely linked to the notion of inalienable human rights and political self-determination. In the famous formulation in the Declaration of Independence, these are in particular: "life, liberty, and the pursuit of happiness." Shortly before, the Virginia Declaration of Rights[11] had postulated,

> "that all men are by nature equally free and independent, and have certain inherent rights, of which, when they enter into the state of society, they cannot, by any compact, deprive or divest their posterity; namely, the enjoyment of life and liberty, with the means of acquiring and possessing property, and pursuing and obtaining happiness and safety."

And the French declaration of human and citizen's rights of 1789[12] was worded similarly, drawing on Jean-Jacques Rousseau: "Les hommes naissent et demeurent libres et égaux en droits."[13]

6

Thomas Hobbes, *Leviathan, or the Matter, Forme, and Power of a Common-Wealth Ecclesiasticall and Civil*, Andrew Crooke, London, 1651, edition used here: Thomas Hobbes, *Leviathan*, ed. C.B. Macpherson, Penguin Books, London, 1968, Part II, chap. 21, p. 272.

7

See: John Locke, The Second *Treatise of Civil Government* (1690), ed. Thomas I. Cook, Hafner Press, New York, 1947, chap. IX–XII.

8

See: ibid., chap. XI (no. 135): "[…] for nobody can transfer to another more power than he has in himself, and nobody has an absolute arbitrary power over himself, or over any other […]."

9

See: ibid., chap. XI (no. 138): "The supreme power cannot take from any man part of his property without his own consent […]"; chap. XIX (no. 222): "Whenever the legislators endeavour to take away and destroy the property of the people, or to reduce them to slavery under arbitrary power, they put themselves into a state of war with the people who are thereupon absolved from any further obedience […]." Consenting: Adam Smith, *Lectures on Jurisprudence* (Report of 1762–1763 and Report dated 1766, no. 134), Clarendon Press, Oxford, Oxford University Press, New York, 1978, p. 323f.

10

Locke 1947, chap. XI (no. 140): "[…] the consent of the majority, giving it either by themselves or their representatives chosen by them".

11

Reprinted in: Schwartz 1971, pp. 234ff.

12

Reprinted in: Jacques Godechot, *Les Constitutions de la France depuis 1789*, Garnier-Flammarion, Paris, 1979, p. 33ff.

13

Jean-Jacques Rousseau, *Du contrat social ou Principes du droit politique* (1762), Garnier, Paris, 1966, Livre I, chap. 1.

If the inalienable nature of these rights is to be taken seriously, their violation must consequently, when all other means of defense have failed, justify the exertion of a right of resistance. In the drafts for the French declaration, we repeatedly encounter the right of resistance. The first draft by Emmanuel Joseph Sieyès states that citizens would, in the case of the decree and implementation of tyrannical commands, have the right to repel violence with violence ("le droit de repousser la violence par la violence").[14] The final version of the declaration is more restrained. Article 2 does proclaim the right of resistance against oppression ("la résistance à l'oppression") and Article 7 of the declaration, in consensus with Sieyès' draft, demands the punishment of all those who make tyrannical dispositions or carry these out, but at the same time Article 7 stresses that every citizen resisting lawful orders is guilty of an offense ("se rend coupable par la résistance"). Considering the ambivalence concerning the right of resistance as the last resort against tyranny on the one hand and as an instrument that can endanger the stability of the constitutional order on the other, precautionary measures for protecting the intended new order are already being taken here. The Virginia Bill of Rights had also limited itself to the proclamation of an inalienable right held by the majority of the community to change or remove a government if this did not fulfill its duty of "producing the greatest degree of happiness and safety" and effectively countering "maladministration." And so the right of resistance remained part of the positive constitutional order as justified by natural law in both North America and France. However, it is immediately channeled into ordered procedural methods.

Third, it bears noting that the American Declaration of Independence is pioneering not least because it assumed there was a right of self-determination that was effective internationally. The continual wrongful treatment of a territorially uprooted segment of the population was read as giving rise not only to the right of resistance, but even to a right of secession. Today, a right of secession is recognized in international law if the segment of population in question is not appropriately represented in the state administration, and is permanently and structurally disadvantaged. However, in the interest of the stability of the international community, international law does remain very cautious towards objectives of calling the territorial integrity of a state into question. And so the "Friendly Relations Declaration," passed by the United Nations General Assembly in 1970 and still relevant in this respect,[15] asserts that the peoples' right of self-determination cannot be the basis of measures compromising the territorial integrity of sovereign states as long as the states are "conducting themselves in compliance with the principle of equal rights and self-determination of peoples as described above, and thus possessed of a government representing the whole people belonging to the territory without distinction as to race, creed or colour.".[16] From a present-day point of view, the case of the thirteen North American colonies constitutes the preconditions for secession in view of the lack of effective representation irrespective of the special criteria of decolonization involved. Evidently, the recent case of the Crimea must be judged

14 The draft put foward by Emmanuel Joseph Sieyès on July 20/21, 1789 is reprinted in: Stéphane Rials, *La déclaration des droits de l'homme et du citoyen*, Hachette, Paris, 1988, pp. 591–606, here p. 605.

15 See: Christian Tomuschat, *International Law. Ensuring the Survival of Mankind on the Eve of a New Century, Collected Courses of the Hague Academy of International Law*, vol. 281, 1999, Martinus Nijhoff Publishers, The Hague, 2001, p. 240ff.

16 *Declaration on Principles of International Law concerning Friendly Relations and Co-operation among States in accordance with the Charter of the United Nations*, A/RES/2625 (XXV), October 24, 1970, available online at: www.un-documents.net/a25r2625.htm, accessed 01/20/2015.

differently, even if we are to assume that the disengagement from Ukraine and its annexation to Russia was desired by the majority of the population without external influence. A systematic oppression or the exclusion from representation at a national level did not exist until this point in time.

II.

As has already been indicated, after the American Revolution, and in particular after the establishment of the new order, the question arose whether there can be a right of resistance in a constitutional state. A constitutional democracy is based on the principle of representation and enables all citizens to participate in the political process and the shaping of public opinion through elections, where required also through referendums and/or fundamental rights of communication. In a later development the constitutional state also assigned the right to all of its citizens to enforce their rights, if need be even against the lawmakers. In the system of the United States, this is ensured by a system of "diffuse" constitutional review. This means that in any litigation courts may not make use of those laws that have been found to be unconstitutional. Most continental European countries have a "concentrated" constitutional review of laws by a constitutional court in place; the review is set into motion by individual constitutional complaints and/or by ordinary courts seeking to obtain a decision of the constitutional court on the constitutionality of a statue which is to apply in a given case (concrete review of statutes), and can lead to the nullification of a law with effect *erga omnes.*[17] Overall, the legal protection systems established by constitutional democracies in which the individual can sue for their constitutional rights, can be understood as manifestations of a constitutionally tamed, institutional right of resistance.

Hence the classic right of resistance, as put forward by the doctrines of natural law, certainly proves to be intrinsically extra-constitutional.[18] As long as effective judicial protection is ensured and the constitution is based on a fundamental social consensus, the right of resistance above and beyond the democratic rights provided for in legislation and judicial remedies appears obsolete. However, the fact that today the right of resistance is framed in law in many constitutions is at odds with this. In France the right of resistance proclaimed in 1789 holds to this day by virtue of a reference in the preamble of the Constitution of 1958 to the declaration of 1789.[19] In the twentieth century a number of constitutions established the right of resistance by law following the experience of a dictatorial regime, and in the light of attempts to scrap fundamental rights (Portugal,[20] Lithuania[21]) or abolish the constitutional order (Greece,[22] Estonia,[23] Slovakia,[24] Czech Republic[25]).

The Basic Law for the Federal Republic of Germany can be seen as belonging to the second group. However, the right of resistance was not included in the original constitution of 1948/1949, but only in the context of the 1968 insertion into the Basic Law of provisions for national defense in case of emergency.[26]

17

On the difference between "diffuse" and "concentrated" control and "centralized" and "decentralized" control, respectively, see: Mauro Cappelletti, *Judicial Review in the Contemporary World*, Bobbs-Merrill, Indianapolis, 1971, pp. 46 ff.; Allan R. Brewer-Carías, *Judicial Review in Comparative Law*, Cambridge University Press, Cambridge, 1989, pp. 125 ff., 183ff. The conceptua pair "diffuse/concentrated" was coined by Piero Calamandrei, see: Piero Calamandrei, *La illegittimità costituzionale delle leggi nel processo civile*, Cedam, Padua, 1950, p. 5.

18

See: Gerald Stourzh, "Vom Widerstandsrecht zur Verfassungsgerichtsbarkeit: Zum Problem der Verfassungswidrigkeit im 18. Jahrhundert" (1974), reprinted in: Gerald Stourzh, *Wege zur Grundrechtsdemokratie. Studien zur Begriffs- und Institutionengeschichte des liberalen Verfassungsstaates*, Böhlau, Vienna, Cologne, 1989, pp. 7–74.

19

With its policy decision on July 16, 1971 (71-44 DC, Rec. 29; Journal Officiel published July 18, 1971, p. 7114) the Conseil Constitutionnel acknowledged the constitutional quality and binding effect of the preamble to the constitution in 1958 and in so doing also the declaration of 1789 hereby being referenced.

20–25

Art. 21 of the Portuguese constitution of 1976.
Art. 3 Par. 2 of the Lithuanian constitution of 1992.
Art. 120 Par. 4 of the Greek constitution of 1975.
Art. 54 Par. 2 of the Estonian constitution of 1992.
Art. 32 of the Slovakian constitution of 1992.
Art. 23 of the Czech Charter of Fundamental Rights and Freedoms of 1992.

26

Law amending the Basic Law of June 24, 1968, Federal Law Gazette (BGBl) 1968 I, p. 709.

The establishment of the right of resistance was intended to at least partially offset the expansion of the executive's competences in cases of tension and defense. A paradox lies in the fact that the Basic Law places the right of resistance at the citizens' disposal in case "no other remedy is available," meaning when the constitution itself has ceased to function. In the same way, Article 32 of the Slovakian constitution construes a right of resistance to exist "if the activity of constitutional bodies and the effective use of legal means are rendered impossible."[27] The constitution then aims to guarantee a right that would only come into force during times in which the constitution has become ineffectual or at least lost its authority. The constitutional right of resistance, then, merely retains an appeal function. The right of resistance, established in the German Basic Law, could thereby only gain legal relevance when being invoked in order to justify acts of resistance after constitutional order has been restored.[28] For the time being, however, this remains a theoretical case.

III.

What happens when citizens claim a right of resistance in the "normal state of affairs," irrespective of whether constitutional order has lost its effectiveness? This is seen where civic protests oppose government decisions and projects out of political conviction or for conscientious reasons or because social, ecological, or economic conditions are felt to be unjust. More intense forms of protest are practiced in particular when the constitutional democracy's representative mechanisms, such as voting rights and the conventional forms of participation in the shaping of public opinion, promise no effective redress.

Civil disobedience, a concept which has a long tradition that notably includes Martin Luther,[29] is seen by many as a form of resistance that is intra-constitutional and inspired by the principle of democracy. The essay on civil disobedience by Henry David Thoreau[30] had a great influence, for example, on Mahatma Gandhi and Martin Luther King, Jr.[31] Thoreau had previously attracted a great deal of attention when he refused to pay taxes to the state of Massachusetts in the 1840s; the reason he gave was that if he paid them, he would be indirectly supporting a U.S. government that endorsed slavery and was waging a war of conquest against Mexico.[32]

In accordance with Thoreau, nonviolence is largely seen as a decisive criterion for civil disobedience along with the violation of a legal duty of prohibition. Usually the starting point is the recourse to fundamental rights, in particular the freedom of speech and the right of free assembly, which leads to forms of protest that fly in the face of the prohibitions. John Rawls' definition, namely, that civil disobedience consists in a "public, nonviolent, conscientious yet political act contrary to law usually done with the aim of bringing about a change in the law or policies of the government"[33] has also gained widespread acceptance. The theory of civil disobedience, which belongs to the field of legal ethics, thus "attempts to

27 See also: Art. 23 of the Czech Charter of Fundamental Rights and Freedoms of 1992.

28 See: Karl-Peter Sommermann in: Hermann von Mangoldt, Friedrich Klein, and Christian Starck (eds.), *Kommentar zum Grundgesetz*, vol. 1, 6th ed., Franz Vahlen, Munich, 2010, Art. 20 Par. 4 recital 339, 351, 356f.

29 See: Martin Luther, "On Secular Authority: How far does the obedience owed to it extend?" (1523), available online, at: http://home.roadrunner.com/~rickgardiner/texts/secauth.html, accessed 06/25/2014. In particular: "My good Lord, […] Command me what lies within the limits of your authority, and I will obey. But if you command me to believe, or to surrender my books, I will not obey."

30 Henry David Thoreau, "On the Duty of Civil Disobedience (The Resistance to Civil Government)" (1849); reprinted in: Henry David Thoreau, *Walden; or, life in the Woods with "On the Duty of Civil Disobedience"*, Coffeetown Press, Seattle (WA), 2008, pp. 295–319.

31 See: Gerhard Casper, "Henry Thoreau und Civil Disobedience," in: Albach 2007, p. 44.

32 Thoreau 2008, p. 304: "If the injustice is part of the necessary friction of the machine of government, let it go, let it go: perchance it will wear smooth, – certainly the machine will wear out. [B]ut if it is of such a nature that it requires you to be the agent of injustice to another, then, I say, break the law. Let your life be a counter friction to stop the machine. What I have to do is to see, at any rate, that I do not lend myself to the wrong which I condemn."

33 John Rawls, *A Theory of Justice*, Oxford University Press, Oxford, 1972, p. 364; see also: Jean L. Cohen and Andrew Arato, *Civil Society and Political Theory*, The MIT Press, Cambridge (MA), 1992, pp. 587f.

formulate the grounds upon which legitimate democratic authority may be dissented from in ways that while admittedly contrary to law nevertheless express a fidelity to law and appeal to the fundamental political principles of a democratic regime."[34] Rawls sees civil disobedience as justified when grave violations of two principles of justice, which he elaborates in *A Theory of Justice*, are present, namely, "equal liberty" and the "fair equality of opportunity."[35] However, a decision about protest action on this basis requires a subsumption under sophisticated prerequisites.

German philosopher of law Ralf Dreier has suggested the following formula with the goal of achieving not just a legal-ethical concretization but a positive law:

> "If the public, nonviolent actions of a single person or group taken for political-moral reasons violate a prohibitory norm, this person or persons' actions are justified by fundamental rights if they are thereby protesting against grave injustice and their protest is proportionate."[36]

According to Dreier, the justification invoking fundamental rights entails a "right to civil disobedience"[37].

Civil disobedience as a construct of legal dogma to justify breaches of law was vehemently contradicted, as this would put legal concord, legal security, and ultimately the constitutional state's basis of existence into question.[38] It is true that the constitutional state lives through the compliance by all to the democratically achieved rules. In this sense, the legal system is a system of reciprocity.[39] Moreover, prohibition norms are to be interpreted in the light of fundamental rights in any case[40] and the penal laws relevant in the case of civil disobedience offer margins of appreciation, in particular the laws referring to coercion.[41] Coercion is only unlawful and thereby liable to prosecution when the use of force, in which *vis compulsiva* is included according to case law,[42] or the threat of an evil must be considered as reprehensible in view of the intended purpose.[43] Besides, legislation increasingly affords possibilities to enforce issues concerning the common good independent of invoking norms protecting the individual, meaning in divergence from the traditional principles of legal protection.

IV.

An initial review of the traditional right of resistance and the forms of resistance developed within the framework of the constitutional state gives the following picture: The right of resistance becomes virulent when those suffering from injustice or oppression of public authority do not have access to effective procedures through which they could enforce their rights. Views on the extent to which democratic rights and protection procedures should be available has of course changed over time. While at the beginning of the modern constitutional state's development the citizens' participation in the political decision-making process through voting and the resolving of occurring conflicts through ordinary courts were

34 Rawls 1972, p. 424.

35 Ibid., pp. 371 f.

36 Ralf Dreier, "Widerstandsrecht im Rechtsstaat? Bemerkungen zum zivilen Ungehorsam," in: Norbert Achterberg (ed.), *Recht und Staat im sozialen Wandel. Festschrift für Hans Ulrich Scupin zum 80. Geburtstag*, Duncker & Humblot, Berlin, 1983, pp. 573–599, here p. 593; translated from the German by Jeremy Gaines.

37 Ibid., pp. 590 ff.; translated from the German by Jeremy Gaines.

38 See: Hans H. Klein, "Ziviler Ungehorsam im demokratischen Rechtsstaat?" (1984), reprinted in: Hans H. Klein, *Das Parlament im Verfassungsstaat. Ausgewählte Beiträge*, ed. Marcel Kaufmann and Kyrill-Alexander Schwarz, Mohr Siebeck, Tübingen, 2006, pp. 37, 49f.

39 On the constitution as "reciprocal order" see: Görg Haverkate, *Verfassungslehre. Verfassung als Gegenseitigkeitsordnung*, Beck, Munich, 1992, in particular pp. 38ff., 47ff.

40 Essential: BVerfGE 7, 198, 205ff.; on interpreting whether coercion is present in light of Art. 8 Basic Law (German constitution) see the decision of the First Senate of the Federal Constitutional Court (BVerfG) of October 24, 2001, 1 BvR 1190/90, no. 36.

41 See only the Chamber's order of the First Senate of the Federal Constitutional Court of March 7, 2011, 1 BvR 388/05 of March 7, 2011, no. 30 ff.

42 Critical of the element of coercion and the subsumption of road blockades under the definition of violence as undertaken by jurisdiction: Arthur Kaufmann, "Der Bundesgerichtshof und die Sitzblockade," in: Arthur Kaufmann, *Vom Ungehorsam gegen die Obrigkeit*, Decker & Müller, Heidelberg, 1991, pp. 51–59, here pp. 51 ff.

seen as guarantors for the preservation from an illegitimate state,[44] the citizens' demands concerning the availability of effective legal protection procedures have increased considerably. Efficient protection was to be provided vis-à-vis the democratic legislature as well,[45] later also vis-à-vis supranational legislative acts.[46] The belief in an infallible *volonté générale*[47] which always acted in accordance with civil rights, had evaporated early on.

As soon as the advancement of the political systems no longer keeps up with the citizens' growing demands towards participation and protection procedures, informal forms of resistance gain importance. The constitutional state, which with its democratic procedures and constitutional safeguards had at first rendered the right of resistance obsolete, is faced with new demands for political participation. Legitimation problems are caused in particular by the increasing complexity of the decision-making processes in the European multilevel governance system, in which the clear allocation of responsibilities is becoming ever more difficult.[48] This means, then, that it is simultaneously made more difficult for the citizens to oppose decisions effectively that they feel are unjust despite proceedings available to them. In this situation informal forms of resistance become more attractive.

In light of the correlation between the relevance of the right of resistance on the one hand, and the extension of protection and participation procedures on the other, it does not seem improbable that the shifting of essential political decisions to a supranational level could lead to the resurgence of an extra-constitutional right of resistance in new forms. Far-reaching decisions that could affect the individual in his or her legal spheres are today also made at a universal level. An example of this are the measures taken by the UN Security Council against terrorist suspects. The cases Yusuf and Kadi,[49] brought before the (EU) Court of First Instance and then before the European Court of Justice, show how easily gaps in legal protection can arise when binding decisions are made by international organizations.[50] The citizens' opportunities for influence are even slighter regarding changes to the world trade order or international environmental policies that are felt to be unjust. Even though the citizens are represented by their governments at the level of international law, their possibilities for exerting influence dissipate dramatically here.[51] This is the reason why a civil society organized mainly in nongovernmental organizations (NGOs) is progressively evolving on an international level which is increasingly influencing the drafting of agreements and decisions by international organizations.[52] New forms of protest, which can in a broader sense be counted as civil disobedience, are being established, whereby the actions are often not directed towards governmental policy makers but against economic players who, in the view of certain NGOs, are not sufficiently controlled and deterred from harmful actions by the governments. Widely known and anchored in public awareness are the actions by Greenpeace directed at economic activities that are hazardous or detrimental to the environment, ranging from whaling to certain forms of oil extraction and energy production to production methods in the IT sector.[53]

43 On the consideration of fundamental rights in the context of the examination of demerit in the case of coercion through violence, in particular regarding road blockades, see: Thomas Fischer, *Strafgesetzbuch mit Nebengesetzen. Kommentar*, 61st ed., Beck, Munich, 2014, § 240 recital 45ff., with further references.

44 See: Vlad Constantinesco and Stéphane Pierré-Caps, *Droit constitutionnel*, 2nd ed., PUF, Paris, 2006, p. 191; significant for the corresponding liberal concept in Germany: Otto Bähr, *Der Rechtsstaat*, Wiegand, Kassel, Göttingen, 1864, in particular pp. 12ff.

45 See: John Hart Ely, *Democracy and Distrust. A Theory of Judicial Review*, Harvard University Press, Cambridge (MA), 1980, in particular pp. 77ff.; Ernst-Wolfgang Böckenförde, "Verfassungsgerichtsbarkeit," in: Ernst-Wolfgang Böckenförde, *Staat, Nation, Europa. Studien zur Staatslehre, Verfassungstheorie und Rechtsphilosophie*, Suhrkamp, Frankfurt am Main, 1999, pp. 157–182, here pp. 157ff.; Constantinesco and Pierré-Caps 2006, pp. 200ff.

46 See: Alexander Betz, *Die verfassungsrechtliche Absicherung der Vorlagepflicht*, Mohr Siebeck, Tübingen, 2013, pp. 1ff., 5ff.

47 See: Rousseau 1966, Livre II chap. III (p. 66): "[...] la volonté générale est toujours droite et tend toujours à l'utilité publique [...]."

48 See: Karl-Peter Sommermann, "Demokratiekonzepte im Vergleich," in: Hartmut Bauer, Peter M. Huber, and Karl-Peter Sommermann (eds.), *Demokratie in Europa*, Mohr Siebeck, Tübingen, 2005, pp. 191–221, here pp. 191, 220f.

49 See: General Court (EGC), judgment of September 21, 2005, Case T-315/01, ECR 2005, p. II-3649 (Kadi/Council and Commission) as well as EGC, judgment of September 21, 2005, Case T-306/01, ECR 2005, p. II-3533 (Yusuf and others/Council and Commission); European Court of Justice (ECJ), judgment of September 3, 2008, Cases C-402/05 P and C-415/05, ECR 2008, p. I-6351.

Both the national and the international regimes face the task of channeling citizens' growing willingness to participate into new participatory procedures in the interest of the community of states' stability, and to use the new technological possibilities of the knowledge and communication society to this end. The gulf between the democratic aspirations of modern societies on the one hand, and the citizens' feeling of having no influence on the other, can only be overcome if the transparency of the decision-making structures is improved and new possibilities for the citizens to participate are created in addition to the representative structures.[54] New concepts, such as "liquid democracy," do however entail the danger, along with that of a diffusion of responsibility, of a massive impairment of the representation of those who are not able to follow the debate concerning factual issues or who cannot take part in the enhanced possibilities for participation due to a lack of technical abilities or time.[55] These asymmetries constrain any direct democratic and participatory fractalization of forming the political will.

With regard to new demands on judicial procedures to implement citizens' rights and interests, in Germany an expansion of possibilities concerning judicial remedies can be observed, which accommodates citizens' growing understanding of themselves as custodians of the common good.[56] Although the administrative procedural law does not yet concede a general right to legitimate law enforcement, the lawgiver has – also influenced by European Union law – nevertheless enabled altruistic class action in many areas.[57] The administrative courts themselves are intensifying the derivation of subjective rights – be it from substantive public law, be it directly from procedural law.[58] In general the discussion on the right of resistance provides an opportunity for reviewing the instruments for protection and possibilities for participation available to citizens in the prevention or elimination of conditions they find to be unjust.

V.

Conclusion:

1. The right of resistance is a genuinely extra-constitutional right, which undergoes a resurgence when the political system no longer effectively safeguards the citizens' rights or when it is systematically violating these rights. This applies in particular when the democratic right to participation or the judicial remedies have ceased to be effective.

2. The more complex the decision-making processes of a political system become, the more important it is to create transparency in terms of responsibilities. In the information and communication society, a democratic regime requires an extension of participatory rights in order to maintain its legitimacy. After the phase of the evolvement of civil rights

50 See: Mattias Wendel, *Permeabilität im europäischen Verfassungsrecht*, Mohr Siebeck, Tübingen, 2011, pp. 31f. (with numerous references in footnote 139), 525

51 See also: Joseph H.H. Weiler, "The Geology of International Law – Governance, Democracy and Legitimacy," in: *ZaöRV (Zeitschrift für ausländisches öffentliches Recht und Völkerrecht)*, vol. 64, 2004, pp. 547–562, here pp. 556ff.; Karl-Peter Sommermann, "Demokratie als Herausforderung des Völkerrechts," in: Pierre-Marie Dupuy, Bardo Fassbender, Malcolm N. Shaw, and Karl-Peter Sommermann (eds.), *Völkerrecht als Wertordnung / Common Values in International Law*, Norbert Paul Engel, Kehl, 2006, pp. 1051–1066, here pp. 1055ff.

52 See: Alan Boyle and Christine Chinkin, *The Making of International Law*, Oxford University Press, Oxford, 2007, pp. 41ff.; critical of this: Steven Wheatley, *The Democratic Legitimacy of International Law*, Hart Publishing, Oxford, 2010, pp. 85ff.

53 On the formation and role of Greenpeace see: Frank Zelko, *Make It a Green Peace! The Rise of a Countercultural Environmentalism*, Oxford University Press, Oxford, 2013.

54 Detailed on the indispensability of the representative system: Rudolf Steinberg, *Die Repräsentation des Volkes. Menschenbild und demokratisches Regierungssystem*, Nomos, Baden-Baden, 2013; on direct democratic and participatory forms of supplementing representative democracy: ibid., pp. 202ff., 302ff.

55 In the case of liquid democracy, which aims to make it possible for citizens to assume responsibility selectively for decisions on the merits, the extended participatory possibilities would further be tied to an abolition of the free mandate, which however according to German jurisdiction cannot be reconciled with the constitution; see also: Margrit Seckelmann, Speyer, "Wohin schwimmt die Demokratie? – 'Liquid Democracy' auf dem Prüfstand," in: *DÖV (Die öffentliche Verwaltung)*, vol. 1, 2014, pp. 1–10, here pp. 1, 6.

and liberties in the liberal *Rechtsstaat (status negativus)* and the phase of the expansion of social and group rights in the social *Rechtsstaat (status positivus)*, there are now signs pointing towards an impending phase of expansion of political rights in the internationally open democratic *Rechtsstaat (status activus)*.[59]

3. In the multilevel systems extending beyond the national level, protection procedures must be established that provide functional equivalents to the constitutional guarantees. At any rate in systems with central, binding decision-making powers, the mere representation of citizens' interests in international decision-making bodies by the states no longer suffices. As with the founding era of the constitutional state, it is particularly important in this regard to establish both formal as well as informal protection mechanisms and opportunities for citizens to influence affairs in the sense of an institutionalized right of resistance.

Revised version of a lecture held at the symposium Power and Law: Fluid Forms of Protest on March 29, 2014 at the ZKM | Karlsruhe in collaboration with the Center for Applied Jurisprudence at the Karlsruhe Institute of Technology (KIT). Translated from the German by Jeremy Gaines.

56 See: Mathias Hong, "Subjektive Rechte und Schutznormtheorie im europäischen Verwaltungsrechtsraum," in: *JZ (Juristenzeitung)*, vol. 67, no. 8, 2012, pp. 380–388, here p. 383ff.

57 See: André Niesler, *Individualrechtsschutz im Verwaltungsprozess. Ein Beitrag zur Neujustierung des Rechtsschutzsystems der VwGO*, Berliner Wisseschafts-Verlag, Berlin, 2012, pp. 207ff.; Marten Breuer, "Die Klagebefugnis von Umweltverbänden unter Anpassungsdruck des Völker- und Europarechts," in: *Die Verwaltung*, vol. 45, 2012, pp. 171–205, here pp. 171ff.

58 See: Hong 2012, p. 385.

59 Status terms in reference to Georg Jellinek's status theory, see: Georg Jellinek, *System der subjektiven öffentlichen Rechte*, 2nd ed., Mohr Siebeck, Tübingen, 1905.

Slavoj Žižek

Don't Fall in Love with Yourselves

They are saying we are all losers, but the true losers are down there on Wall Street. They were bailed out by billions of our money. We are called socialists, but here there is always socialism for the rich. They say we don't respect private property, but in the 2008 financial crash-down more hard-earned private property was destroyed than if all of us here were to be destroying it night and day for weeks. They tell you we are dreamers. The true dreamers are those who think things can go on indefinitely the way they are. We are not dreamers. We are the awakening from a dream that is turning into a nightmare.

We are not destroying anything. We are only witnessing how the system is destroying itself. We all know the classic scene from cartoons. The cat reaches a precipice but it goes on walking, ignoring the fact that there is nothing beneath this ground. Only when it looks down and notices it, it falls down. This is what we are doing here. We are telling the guys there on Wall Street: "Hey, look down!"

In mid-April 2011, the Chinese government prohibited on TV, films, and novels all stories that contain alternate reality or time travel. This is a good sign for China. These people still dream about alternatives, so you have to prohibit this dreaming. Here, we don't need a prohibition because the ruling system has even oppressed our capacity to dream. Look at the movies that we see all the time. It's easy to imagine the end of the world. An asteroid destroying all life and so on. But you cannot imagine the end of capitalism.

So what are we doing here? Let me tell you a wonderful, old joke from Communist times. A guy was sent from East Germany to work in Siberia. He knew his mail would be read by censors, so he told his friends: "Let's establish a code. If a letter you get from me is written in blue ink, it is true what I say. If it is written in red ink, it is false." After a month, his friends get the first letter. Everything is in blue. It says, this letter: "Everything is wonderful here. Stores are full of good food. Movie theaters show good films from the West. Apartments are large and luxurious. The only thing you cannot buy is red ink." This is how we live. We have all the freedoms we want. But what we are missing is red ink: the language to articulate our non-freedom. The way we are taught to speak about freedom – war on terror and so on – falsifies freedom. And this is what you are doing here. You are giving all of us red ink.

There is a danger. Don't fall in love with yourselves. We have a nice time here. But remember, carnivals come cheap. What matters is the day after, when we will have to return to normal lives. Will there be any changes then? I don't want you to remember these days, you know, like: "Oh, we were young and it was beautiful." Remember that our basic message is: "We are allowed to think about alternatives." If the taboo is broken, we do not live in the best possible world. But there is a long road ahead. There are truly difficult questions that confront us. We know what we do not want. But what do we want? What social organization can replace capitalism? What type of new leaders do we want?

Remember. The problem is not corruption or greed. The problem is the system. It forces you to be corrupt. Beware not only of the enemies, but also of false friends who are already working to dilute this process. In the same way you get coffee without caffeine, beer without alcohol, ice cream without fat, they will try to make this into a harmless, moral protest. A decaffeinated protest. But the reason we are here is that we have had enough of a world where, to recycle Coke cans, to give a couple of dollars for charity, or to buy a Starbucks cappuccino where 1% goes to third world starving children is enough to make us feel good. After outsourcing work and torture, after marriage agencies are now outsourcing our love life, we can see that for a long time, we allow our political engagement also to be outsourced. We want it back.

We are not communists if Communism means a system which collapsed in 1990. Remember that today those communists are the most efficient, ruthless capitalists. In China today, we have capitalism which is even more dynamic than your American capitalism, but doesn't need democracy. Which means when you criticize capitalism, don't allow yourself to be blackmailed that you are against democracy. The marriage between democracy and capitalism is over. The change is possible.

What do we perceive today as possible? Just follow the media. On the one hand, in technology and sexuality, everything seems to be possible. You can travel to the moon, you can become immortal by biogenetics, you can have sex with animals or whatever, but look at the field of society and economy. There, almost everything is considered impossible. You want to raise taxes by little bit for the rich. They tell you it's impossible. We lose competitivity. You want more money for health care, they tell you: "Impossible, this means totalitarian state." There's something wrong in the world, where you are promised to be immortal but cannot spend a little bit more for health care. Maybe we need to set our priorities straight here. We don't want higher standard of living. We want a better standard of living. The only sense in which we are communists is that we care for the commons. The commons of nature. The commons of privatized by intellectual property. The commons of biogenetics. For this, and only for this, we should fight.

Communism failed absolutely, but the problems of the commons are here. They are telling you we are not American here. But the conservative fundamentalists who claim they really are American have to be reminded of something: What is Christianity? It's the holy spirit. What is the holy spirit? It's an egalitarian

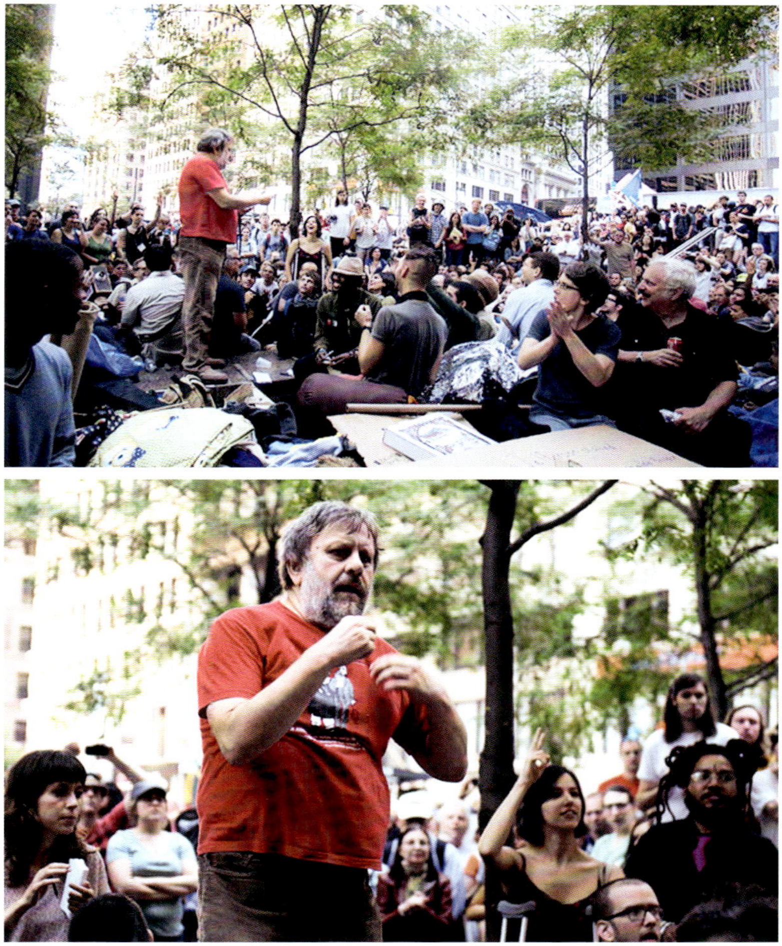

Slavoj Žižek speaks at Occupy Wall Street, Liberty Plaza (Zuccotti Park), New York, October 9, 2011

community of believers who are linked by love for each other, and who only have their own freedom and responsibility to do it. In this sense, the holy spirit is here now. And down there on Wall Street, there are pagans who are worshipping blasphemous idols. So all we need is patience. The only thing I'm afraid of is that we will someday just go home and then we will meet once a year, drinking beer, and nostalgically remembering "what a nice time we had here." Promise yourselves that this will not be the case. We know that people often desire something but do not really want it. Don't be afraid to really want what you desire. Thank you very much.

This transcript of Slavoj Žižek's speech held at Occupy Wall Street was originally published on imposemagazine.com on October 10, 2011 and again on September 17, 2013. It is available online at: www.imposemagazine.com/bytes/slavoj-zizek-at-occupy-wall-street-transcript, accessed April 8, 2014.

Adbusters

The Adbusters Media Foundation is a nonprofit, consumption-critical organization based in Vancouver, British Columbia. It was founded in 1989 by Kalle Lasn and Bill Schmalz and defines itself as "a global network of artists, activists, writers, pranksters, students, educators, and entrepreneurs who want to advance the new social activist movement of the information age." With its various campaigns, the Adbusters community seeks to overturn existing power structures and to initiate a jolt through twenty-first century's society.

One of the main tools for distributing the culture-jamming aims is the reader-supported *Adbusters* magazine, which is absolutely ad-free and appears six times a year with a worldwide circulation of 60,000. It offers activist statements from all across the world as well as philosophical approaches, and covers ecologically, socially, and politically significant issues.

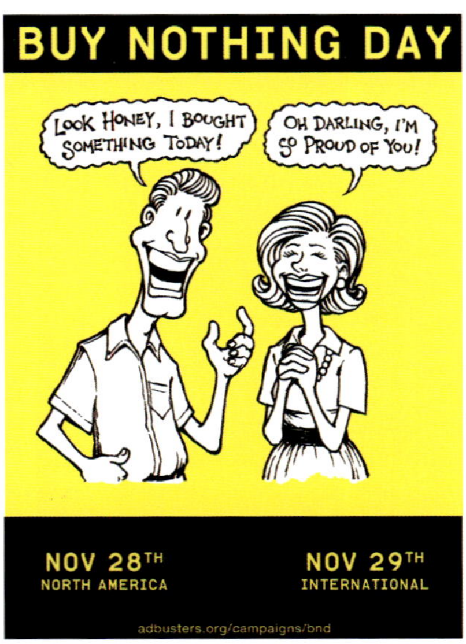

Adbusters, poster for the *Buy Nothing Day* 2014

In the past years, Adbusters has launched several "subvertizing" campaigns, such as the annual *Buy Nothing Day* or the *Digital Detox Week*. In 2011, it initiated the Occupy Wall Street movement with a call to action.

The Media Carta Manifesto

WE HAVE LOST CONFIDENCE
in what we are seeing, hearing, and reading: too much infotainment and not enough news; too many outlets telling the same stories; too much commercialism and too much hype. Every day, this commercial information system distorts our view of the world.

WE HAVE LOST FAITH
in the institutions of the mass media. A handful of corporations now control more than half the information networks around the world. At a time when people worldwide face hunger, social disruption, war, and ecological collapse, only those who know how to walk the walk, talk the talk, or pay big bucks are getting their message across.

WE HAVE LOST HOPE
that our national media regulators will act in the public interest. Essential rules limiting media ownership and concentration are being scrapped, while rules protecting local content and access are diluted.

WE HAVE LOST PATIENCE
waiting for reform.

WE IMAGINE A DIFFERENT SYSTEM
– a media democracy. We see great promise in the open communications

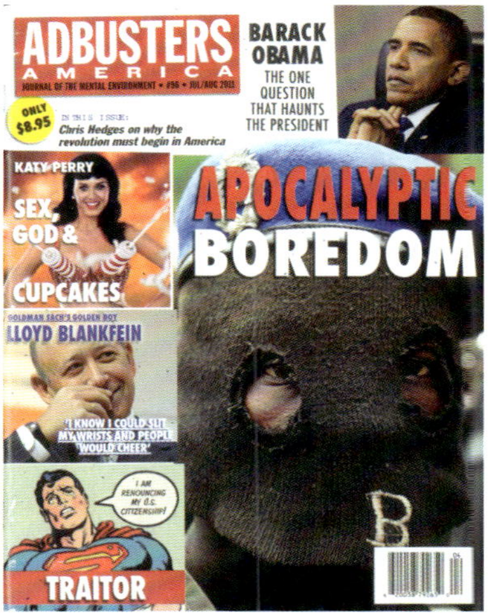

Adbusters America. Journal of the Mental Environment, vol. 96, July / August 2011

of the Internet and want that openness expanded into every form of media. We envision a global system of communications that has as its foundation the direct, democratic participation of citizens. To this end, we demand the timely transfer of key media sources back to the people.

As a start, we demand the right to buy radio and television airtime under the same rules and conditions as advertising agencies. We ask our media regulators to set aside two minutes of every broadcast hour for citizen-produced messages. We want the six largest media corporations in the world broken up into smaller units.

What we ultimately seek is a new human right for our information age, one that empowers freedom of speech with the right to access the media. This new human right is: *the right to communicate*.

WE HEREBY LAUNCH
A MOVEMENT
to enshrine the right to communicate in the constitutions of all free nations, and in the Universal Declaration of Human Rights.

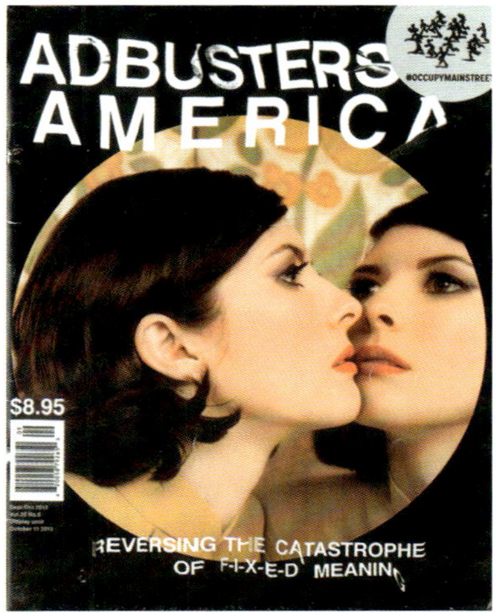

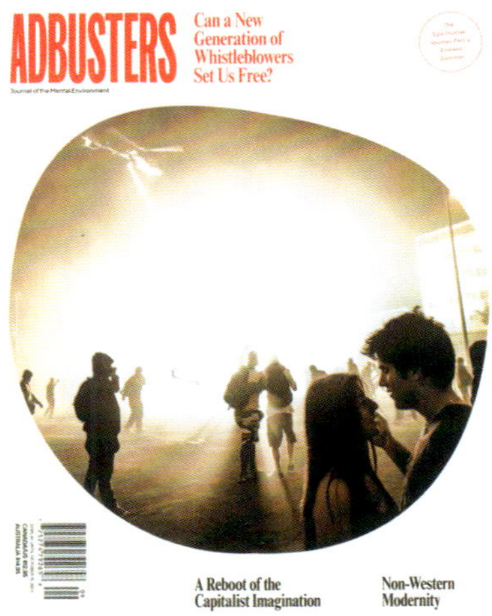

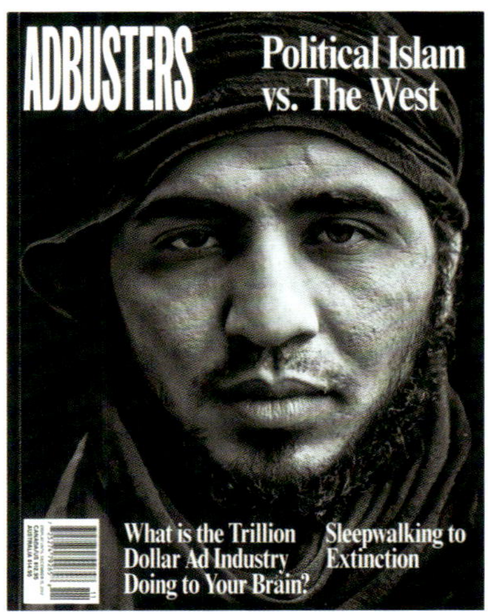

Top to bottom: *Adbusters America. #OCCUPYMAINSTREET*, vol. 103, July / August 2011; *Adbusters. The Epic Human Journey Part 3: Endless Summer*, issue 109, vol. 21, no. 5, September / October 2013; *Adbusters. The Epic Human Journey Part 4, Autumn*, issue 110, vol. 21, no. 6, November / December 2013

Founded in 1961
Global

www.amnesty.org

Amnesty International

On the basis of the Universal Declaration of Human Rights Amnesty International continues to expose violations of these rights all over the globe. The movement operates independently of any government, political ideology, economic interest, or religion and is funded mainly by public donations and the three million supporters, members, and activists in over 150 countries and territories worldwide. The annual Amnesty International Report presents information about the state of human rights in nearly every country on Earth. Multifaceted campaigns as well as the *Amnesty Journal* provide detailed information about human rights abuses and mobilize public opinion to put pressure on those responsible.

In 2006, the Switzerland division of Amnesty International together with the walker advertising agency initiated the site-specific billboard campaign *It's not happening here. But it is happening now*. Around 200 of these posters were designed for specific locations all over the country, contrasting human rights violations with the exceptionally beautiful and peaceful everyday reality in these places.

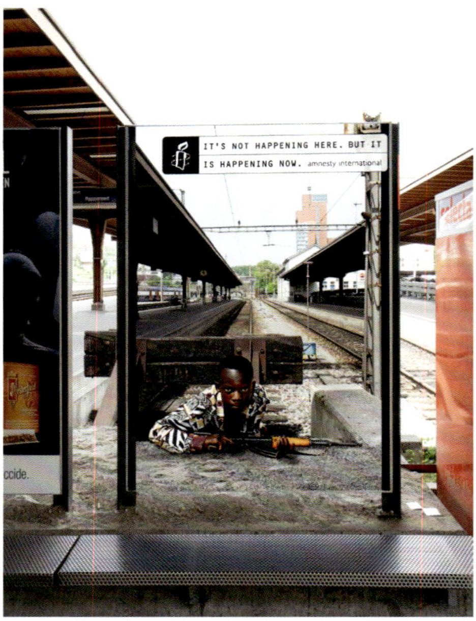

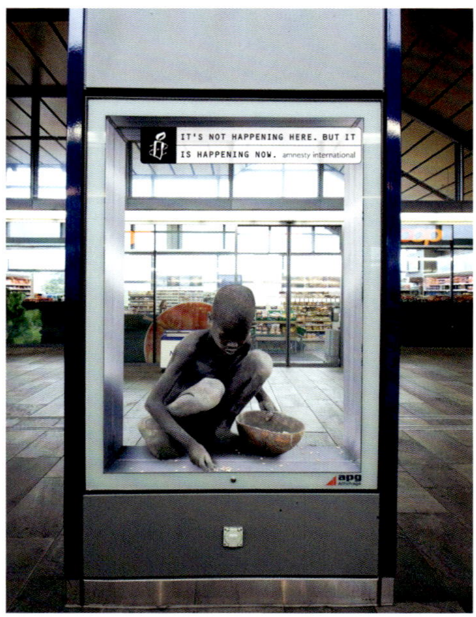

Amnesty International Switzerland, *It's not happening here. But it is happening now.*, 2006, billboard campaign, created by the walker advertising agency in Zurich

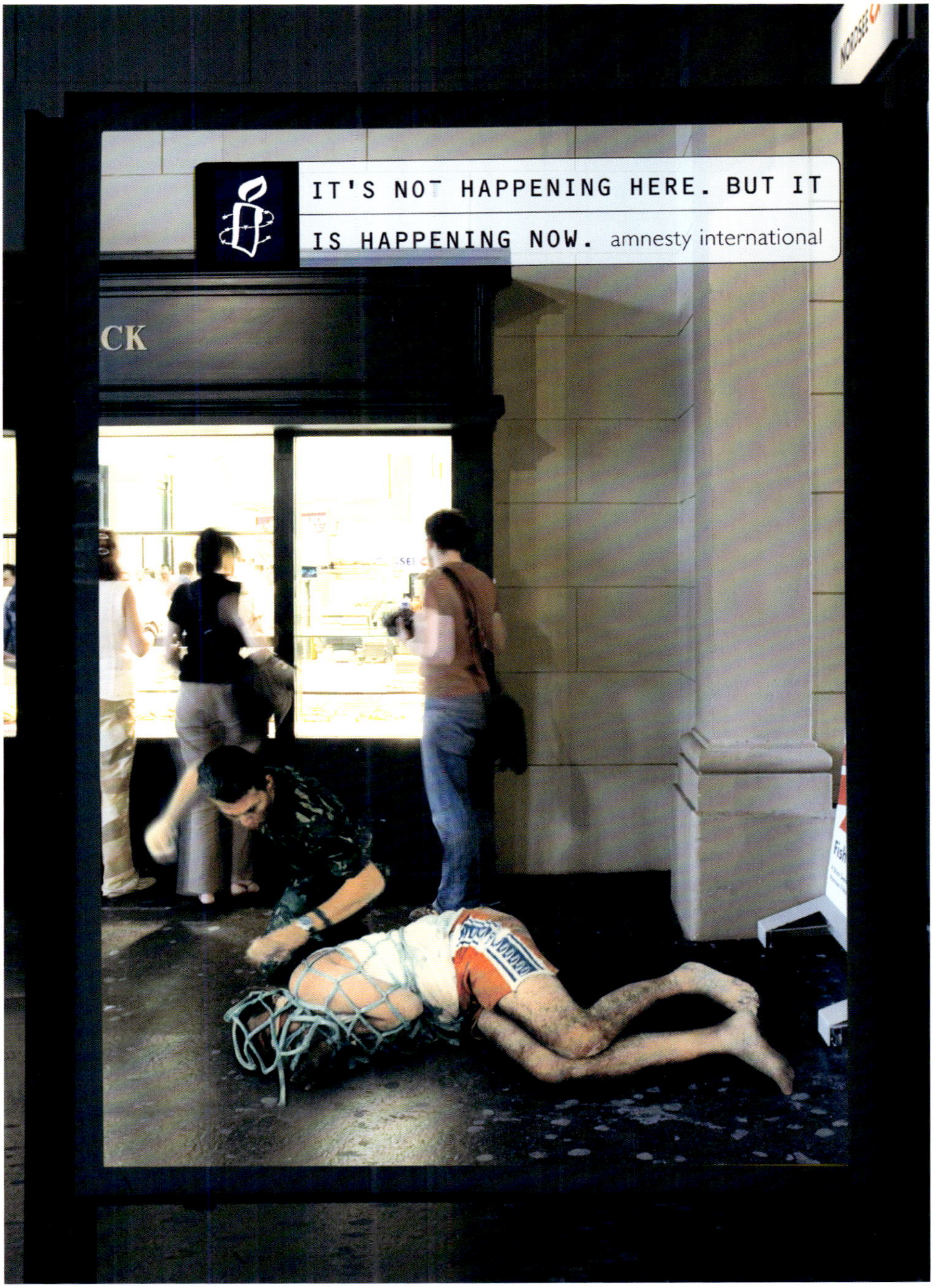

Amnesty International Switzerland, *It's not happening here. But it is happening now.*, 2006, billboard campaign, created by the walker advertising agency in Zurich

Anonymous

Anonymous is an Internet phenomenon that allows various groups and individuals to run hacktivism and public demonstrations under that label. Initially a fun exercise from the imageboard 4chan, Anonymous came increasingly to prominence with political protests for freedom of speech and the independence of the Internet, as well as against copyright law and various organizations, including Scientology, government agencies, and global corporations. To begin with participants acted only on the Internet; subsequently, they conducted their activities beyond it and increasingly in the public sphere. At public rallies, activists usually wear face masks, which have become a kind of trademark of the movement, that depict the features of Guy Fawkes, a member of a group of English Catholics who planned the failed Gunpowder Plot of 1605 to blow up Parliament and place a Catholic monarch on the throne of England.

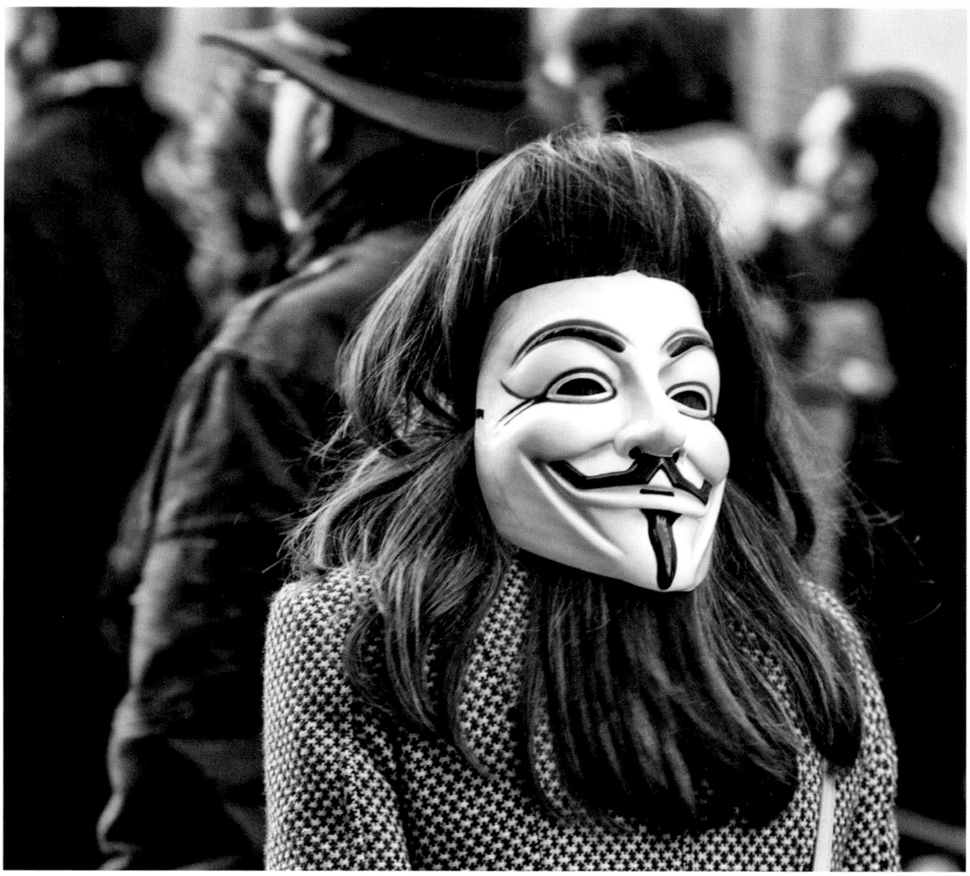

Protester with the typical Guy Fawkes mask, Berlin, 2011, documented by Lynn Lauterbach in her photo series *Generation Demonstration*, 2011/2012

Attac

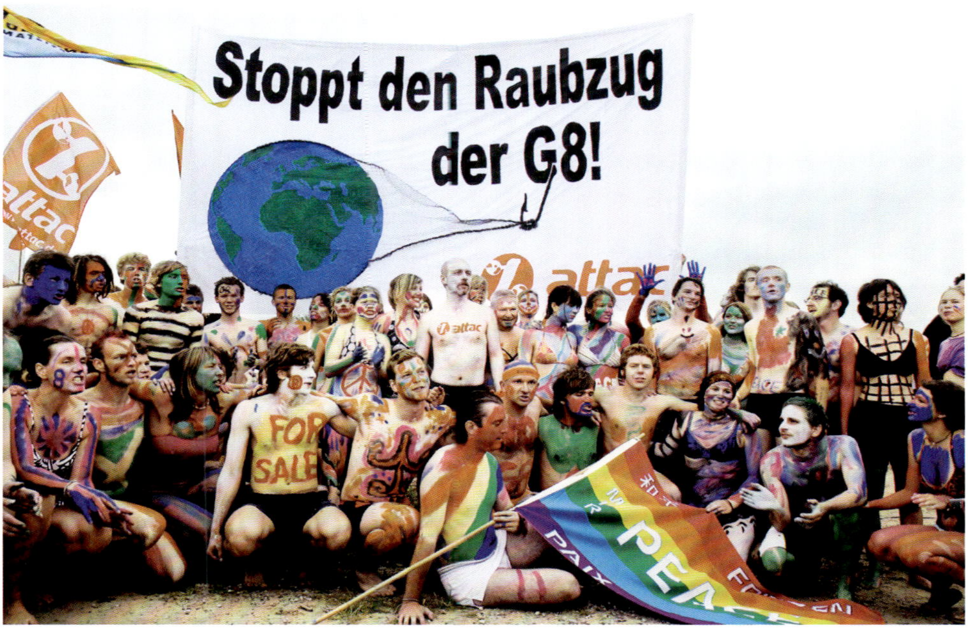

Attac action *Attac rettet die Welt aus den Fängen der G8* [Attac Saves the World from the Clutches of the G8] at the G8 Summit in Heiligendamm, Germany, June 2007

Founded in 1998 in France, the broad social alliance Attac in the meantime is active in more than fifty countries. The organization's name is derived from the French Association pour la taxation des transactions financières et l'aide aux citoyens [Association for the Taxation of Financial Transactions and Aid to Citizens]. Attac began by demanding that the so-called Tobin tax (a tax to curb short-term stock market speculation) should be introduced internationally, and although it still advocates the democratic control of international markets, the organization now deals with a whole range of problems associated with neoliberal globalization while continuing to criticize the global increase of social inequality. With the principle of "economic literacy," it intends to create a basic understanding of economics among the general public. The campaigns shed light on grievances, present alternatives, and seek to mobilize as many people as possible in support of economic equality.

Olaf Bertram-Nothnagel *1974

New York City native Olaf Bertram-Nothnagel makes films and other things, and has worked in the guts of many environmental and political causes. He holds a Master of Fine Arts in Integrated Media Arts from The City University of New York (CUNY), Hunter College, where he studied nonfiction media for social change. Along with his media and creative work, he is co-owner of Marsh and Bay Expeditions, a dinghy sailing school that lets him share his love of adventure, history, and the natural world.

Bertram-Nothnagel is the lead organizer of *lowercase d*, an all-volunteer campaign in New York that seeks to create better ways to implement direct democracy, more transparency in policy-making, and more citizen participation.

Olaf Bertram-Nothnagel

lowercase d: Getting There

An integral goal of most political advocacy is inspiring citizens to act. Beyond promoting changes in consumer habits, in the context of representative democracy such work is typically aimed at electing or influencing power holders. Unfortunately, it also reinforces conceptions of citizenship that are less than optimal. For example, it can (1) use creative spectacles to garner media coverage but thus maintain the spectator polis; (2) make use of mass mobilization, requiring large expenditures of time and effort, but usually netting relatively little beneficial dialog or control of outcomes; (3) position the advocacy organization as another intermediary between the citizen and their sovereign power; and (4) it all too often employs the language of democratic reform without actually working towards any structural reforms that would open flawed government decision-making processes to direct participation by the citizenry. Repeated exposure to these tactics and their frequently ambiguous results can ultimately engender deep cynicism and apathy.

In 2006, while making an independent documentary[1] about America's experience with direct democracy, I began having conversations with fellow New Yorkers about the realistic possibilities for creating a modern-day citizen law-making process. The idea was essentially to use an online forum to open up every stage of the traditional ballot initiative process to everyone, regardless of their political or economic heft.[2] From the collaborative drafting of proposed laws, to their qualification for ballot placement with electronic signatures, each aspect of citizen legislation could be easily accessible, and the related open deliberation and vetting of evidence could be well organized through a combination of good platform design, accountable administration, and obligatory moderation by users. Along with mitigating the role of money, serving as a potential antidote to the civic balkanization common to both the Internet and activism, and providing a valuable learning tool, such a platform would engender in people a greater sense of having a say in and therefore responsibility for government and society as a whole.

The legal and political terrain being less than hospitable to creating such a system in New York, we spent much time educating ourselves and, with the help of volunteer lawyers, carefully constructing amendments to the city's charter[3] to accomplish our goal, that we hoped would have the best chance of standing up in court and being enacted directly by the electorate. Our campaign for ballot placement is ongoing, and must negotiate the same hurdle any attempt at radical change is likely to confront: a lifetime of experience with the intransigence, corruption, and mechanisms of power has made a key first principle of our constitutional orders that the people are sovereign and all power flows from them; a distant and quaint memory in many people's conception of politics. Those who no longer believe that doing so is a practical option are incapable of claiming and exercising their full power as citizens. One of the great joys of working towards truly democratic reform is renewing people's democratic imagination and discovering the extent to which it indeed remains vibrant, despite so many contravening conditions.

If the most urgent and fundamental challenge for humanity this century will be the need for us all to mature into effective societal stakeholders and ecological stewards, the challenge for art then will be to inspire that maturation and the call for its realization in the abstract, but critically necessary, realm of government. While we need only act in a coordinated way to secure our future, doing so requires desire and understanding, two of art's primary products.

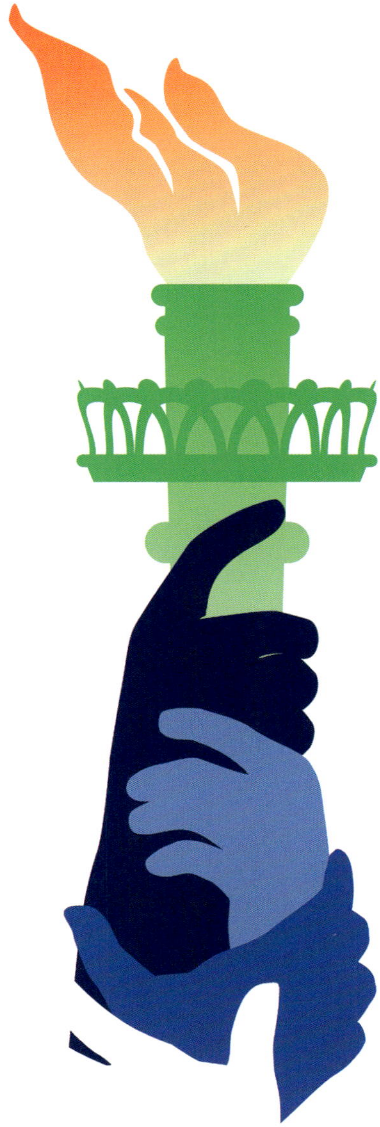

Logo of the *Real Democracy for NYC* campaign

1 Available online at www.timewetalk.org, accessed 04/07/2014.

2 The participatory potential of Internet-based technologies for direct democratic government has long been, and continues to be, advanced by many. Some examples and research resources can be found at http://lowercased.org/d/links-readings, accessed 04/07/2014.

3 Available online at www.democracyNYC.org/summaries.html, accessed 04/07/2014.

Nadir Bouhmouch *1990

Born in Casablanca and raised in the Moroccan capital Rabat, Nadir Bouhmouch is a human rights activist, an award-winning filmmaker, and a student in the major programs International Security and Conflict Resolution as well as Television, Film, and New Media at San Diego State University. In 2011, Nadir became an active member of the Moroccan pro-democracy February 20 Movement that followed the uprisings in Tunisia and Egypt which had spread to Morocco.

His first film *My Makhzen & Me* (2012) documents the widespread protests organized by a group of students via Facebook, Twitter, YouTube, and the website www.mamfakinch.com. People took to the streets demanding political change. However, the Makhzen (the ruling elite) refused to relinquish its grip. The film investigates what gave birth to the revolt and the obstacles it encounters in its struggle for freedom, democracy, human rights, and an end to corruption and poverty. It earned Nadir the title *bête noire* of Moroccan cinema as it was the first film to document an opposition movement and explicitly criticize the regime.

His second film *475* (2013) addressed Morocco's rape-to-marry law and the fate of Amina Filali, a 16-year-old girl, who against her will – but on the legal basis of Article 475 of the Morrocan Penal Code – was married to her rapist, because her parents feared the loss of the family's honor. The documentary won Reporters Without Borders' and the Deutsche Welle The Bobs (Best of the Blogs) awards for Best Social Activism and was nominated for the BBC Arabic Film and Documentary Festival.

Nadir is the cofounder of the Guerrilla Cinema movement and currently leads a civil disobedience campaign against the Centre Cinématographique Marocain, the government body which regulates and censors films in Morocco – in Nadir's opinion a violation of the right to free expression.

He is also involved in the Boycott, Divestment, and Sanctions movement against Israel's colonization of Palestine and is a vocal critic of Morocco's military occupation of the Western Sahara. One of the first Moroccan civilians to visit the Tindouf refugee camps in southwest Algeria, Bouhmouch documented the very rare interaction between himself as a Moroccan and Sahrawi refugees in a short film called *The Other Dakhla* (2013).

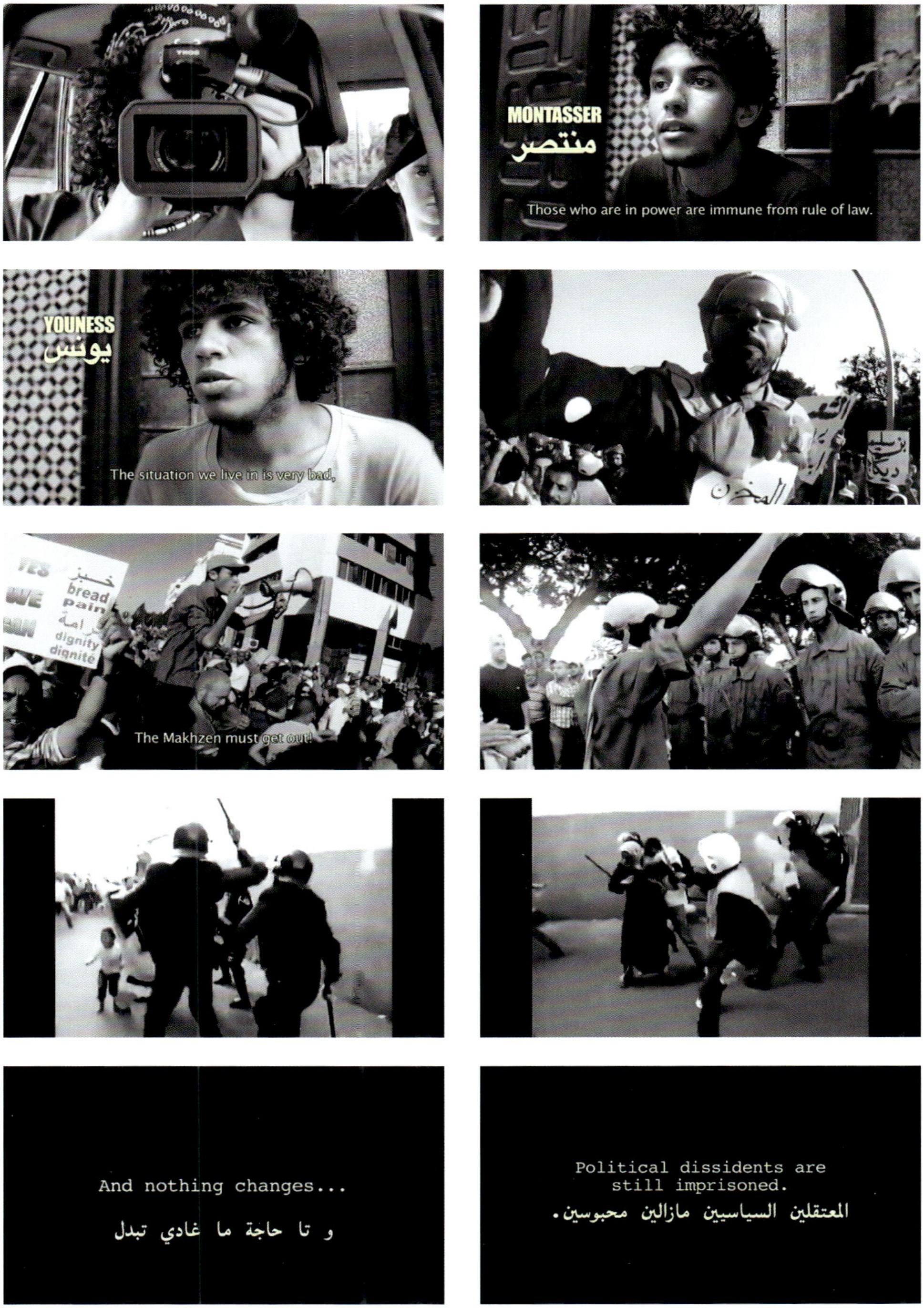

Nadir Bouhmouch, *My Makhzen & Me*, 2012, video, color, sound, 41:46 min, video stills

Noam Chomsky *1928

Noam Chomsky is an Institute Professor and professor of linguistics emeritus at the Massachusetts Institute of Technology (MIT), a philosopher, and a political theorist. Besides his remarkable work in the field of linguistic theory, which made him one of the most distinguished figures of American linguistics, he is an internationally recognized influential left-wing critic, particularly of American foreign policy as well as the neoliberal turn of global capitalism, which he identifies as forced from above against the interests and needs of the great majority. With regard to the latter, his approaches are considered as enormously important for recent social and political movements such as Occupy Wall Street, for example. In his book *Occupy*, published in 2012, Chomsky summarizes:

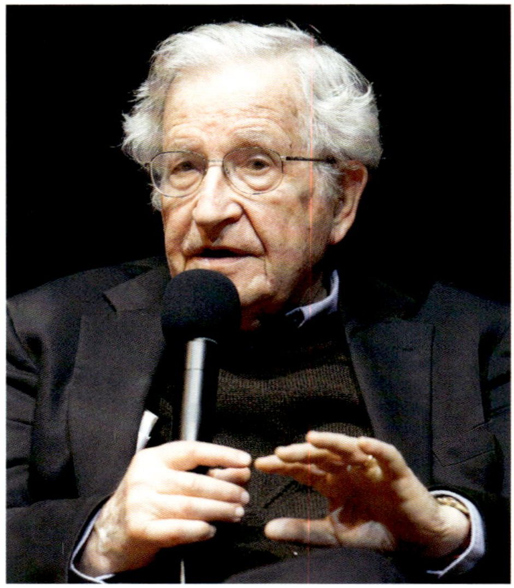

Noam Chomsky at his lecture "Driving Forces in U.S. Policy" at ZKM | Karlsruhe on May 30, 2014

"In fact, one of the really remarkable and almost spectacular successes of the Occupy movement is that is has simply changed the entire framework of discussion of many issues. There were things that were sort of known, but in the margins, hidden, which are now right up front – like the imagery of the 99 percent and the 1 percent; and the dramatic facts of sharply rising inequality over the past roughly thirty years […]." (Noam Chomsky, *Occupy*, Penguin Books, London, 2012, without pagination)

Over the last decades Noam Chomsky has published numerous politically relevant writings, including *American Power and the New Mandarins* (1969), *Peace in the Middle East? Reflections on Justice and Nationhood* (1974), *Manufacturing Consent. The Political Economy of the Mass Media* (with Edward S. Herman, 1988), *Profit over People. Neoliberalism and Global Order* (1999), and *Rogue States. The Rule of Force in World Affairs* (2000).

He has repeatedly engaged with the condition of democracy and highlighted the importance of democratic principles and fundamental human rights – approaches that are reflected in many of the texts in this book. In his keynote speech "A Roadmap to a Just World – People Reanimating Democracy" at the Global Media Forum on March 25, 2013, in Bonn, for example, he cited the Magna Carta of 1215 as a milestone of modern democracy:

"[The Magna Carta is] the foundations of modern law. We will soon be commemorating the 800th anniversary. We won't be celebrating it – more likely interring what little is left of its bones after the flesh has been picked off by Bush and Obama and their colleagues in Europe. And Europe is involved clearly. But there is another part of Magna Carta which has been forgotten. It had two components. The one is the Charter of Liberties which is being dismantled. The other was called the Charter of the Forests. That called for protection of the commons from the depredations of authority. This is England of course. The commons were the traditional source of sustenance, of food and fuel and welfare as well. They were nurtured and sustained for centuries by traditional societies collectively. They have been steadily dismantled under the capitalist principle that everything has to be privately owned, which brought with it the perverse doctrine of – what's called the tragedy of the commons – a doctrine which holds that collective possessions will be despoiled so therefore everything has to be privately owned. The merest glance at the world shows that the opposite is true. It's privatization that is destroying the commons. That's why the indigenous populations of the world are in the lead in trying to save Magna Carta from final destruction by its inheritors. And they're joined by others. Take say the demonstrators in Gezi Park in trying to block the bulldozers in Taksim Square. They're trying to save the last part of the commons in Istanbul from the wrecking ball of commercial destruction. This is a kind of a microcosm of the general defense of the commons. It's one part of a global uprising against the violent neo-liberal assault on the population of the world. Europe is suffering severely from it right now. The uprisings have registered some major successes. The most dramatic are Latin America. In this millennium it has largely freed itself from the lethal grip of Western domination for the first time in 500 years. And other things are happening too. Well the general picture is pretty grim, I think. But there are shafts of light. As always through history, there are two trajectories. One leads towards oppression and destruction. The other leads towards freedom and justice. And as always – to adapt Martin Luther King Jr's famous phrase – there are ways to bend the arc of the moral universe towards justice and freedom – and by now even towards survival."

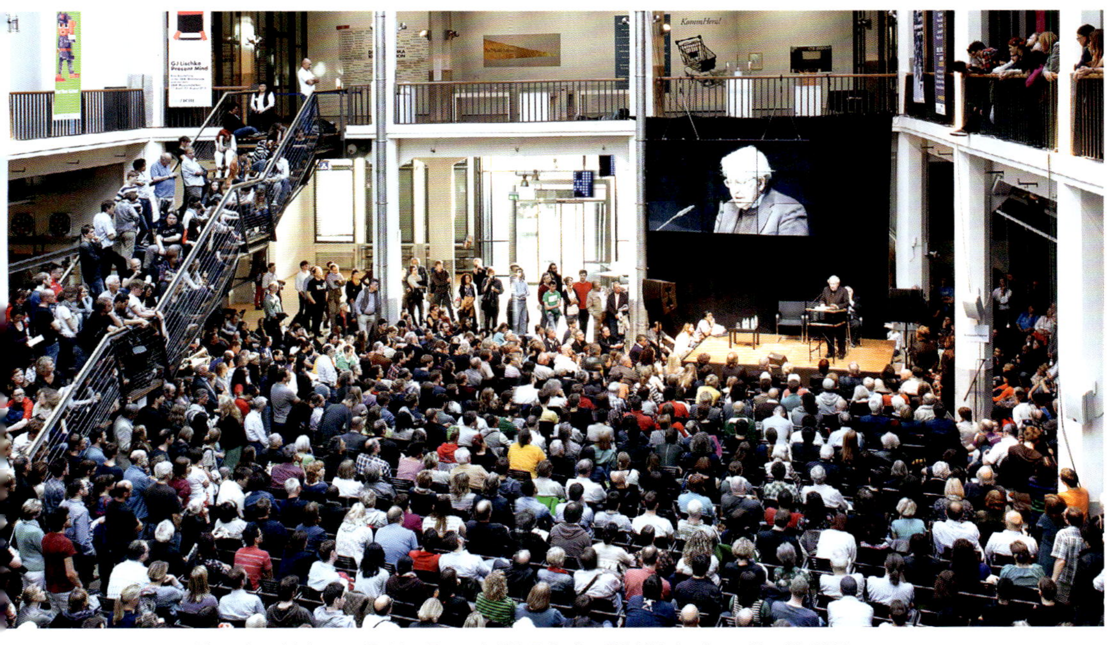

Noam Chomsky at his lecture "Driving Forces in U.S. Policy" at ZKM | Karlsruhe on May 30, 2014

Hassan Darsi *1961

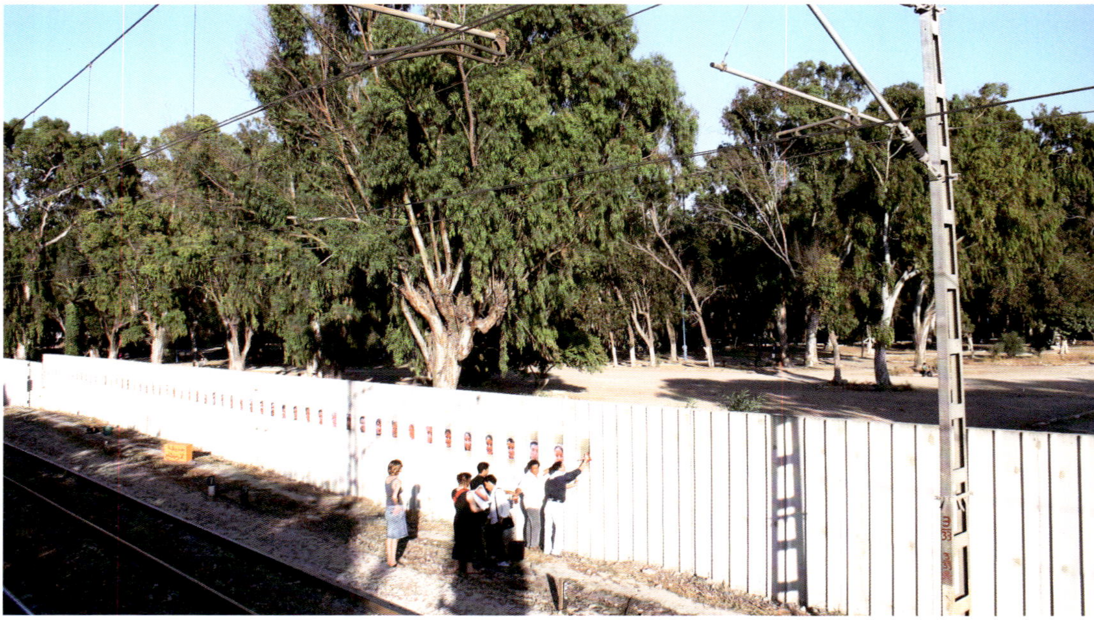

Hassan Darsi, *Le mur*, 2007, photo, part of the series *Passerelle artistique 5* (Le projet du parc de l'Hermitage)

Hassan Darsi was born in Casablanca, Morocco where he still lives and works today. He is a graduate of the School of Visual and Plastic Arts in Mons, Belgium. His artistic activities are strongly influenced by his daily experiences, especially by questions concerning the environment, public spaces, and urban change, and are determined by his ongoing reflection of creative processes from the perspective of a citizen. To develop this approach, he founded the project *La Source du Lion (SDL)* [The Source of the Lion] in Casablanca in 1995, which serves at the same time as a forum for artistic research and a venue for art. One of *SDL*'s main projects to promote environmental awareness was initiated in 2002 and focused on restoring the neglected 17-hectare Hermitage Park, located in a densely populated area of Casablanca. To refurbish the park and give it back to the people, an international artists' network was built up and numerous artistic interventions were staged, always with the great support of local residents.

A project that also took place in the park and benefitted from the ideas behind the Hermitage events was *Le lion se meurt* [The Lion Is Dying] (2004–2006), which drew attention to the neglect suffered by animals, particularly the lions in Casablanca's zoo. Hassan Darsi's works have been exhibited in museums, biennials, and art centers all over the world. The 18-square-meter model of the Hermitage Park entitled *Le Projet de la Maquette* [The Model Project], which he created from 2002 to 2003, was purchased by the Centre Pompidou in Paris in 2012.

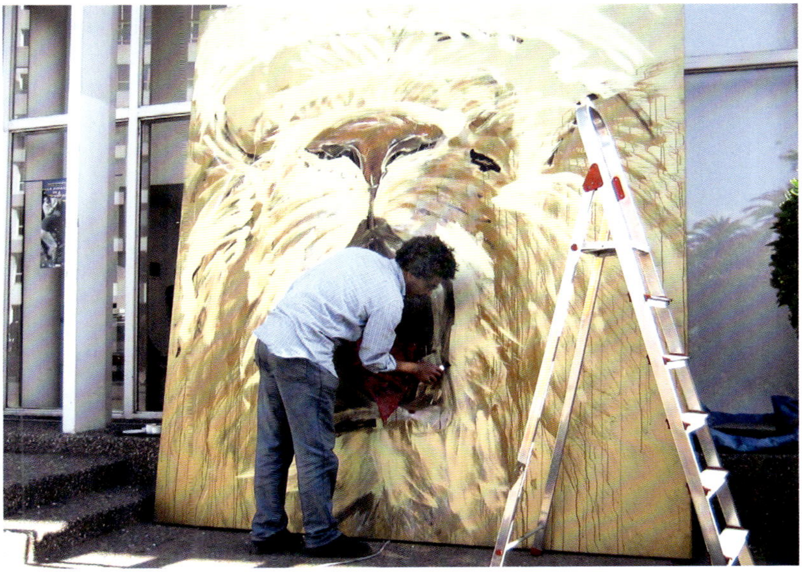

Hassan Darsi, *Peinture de lion*, 2005, performance as part of *Le lion se meurt*

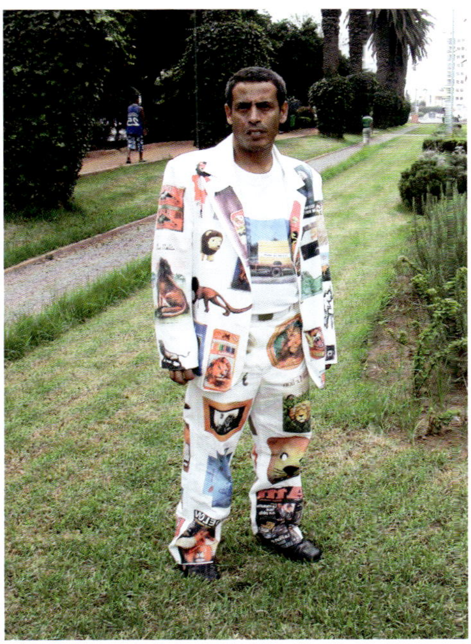

Hassan Darsi, *Le lion se meurt*, 2004–2006, costume

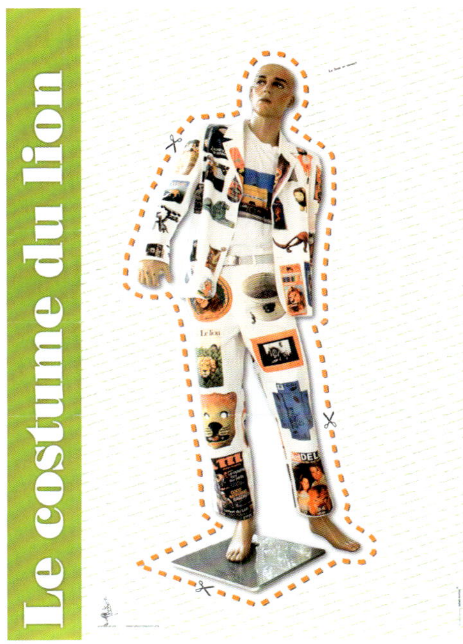

Hassan Darsi, *Le lion se meurt*, 2004–2006, poster, front

Muath Freij *1985

Since 2011 Syrian refugees in Jordan and Jordanians have demonstrated together against violence in the neighboring country of Syria. These protests were organized by two separate organizations, the Jordanian Commission to Support the Syrian People and the Syrian Revolution Coordinators Union. During the protests, demonstrators waved the Syrian resistance flag and held banners denouncing what they described as the regime's crimes. Women, men, and children took part in the protests. *The Jordan Times* reporter and photographer Muath Freij captured impressions of Syrian demonstrations in Amman, Jordan, in a photo series.

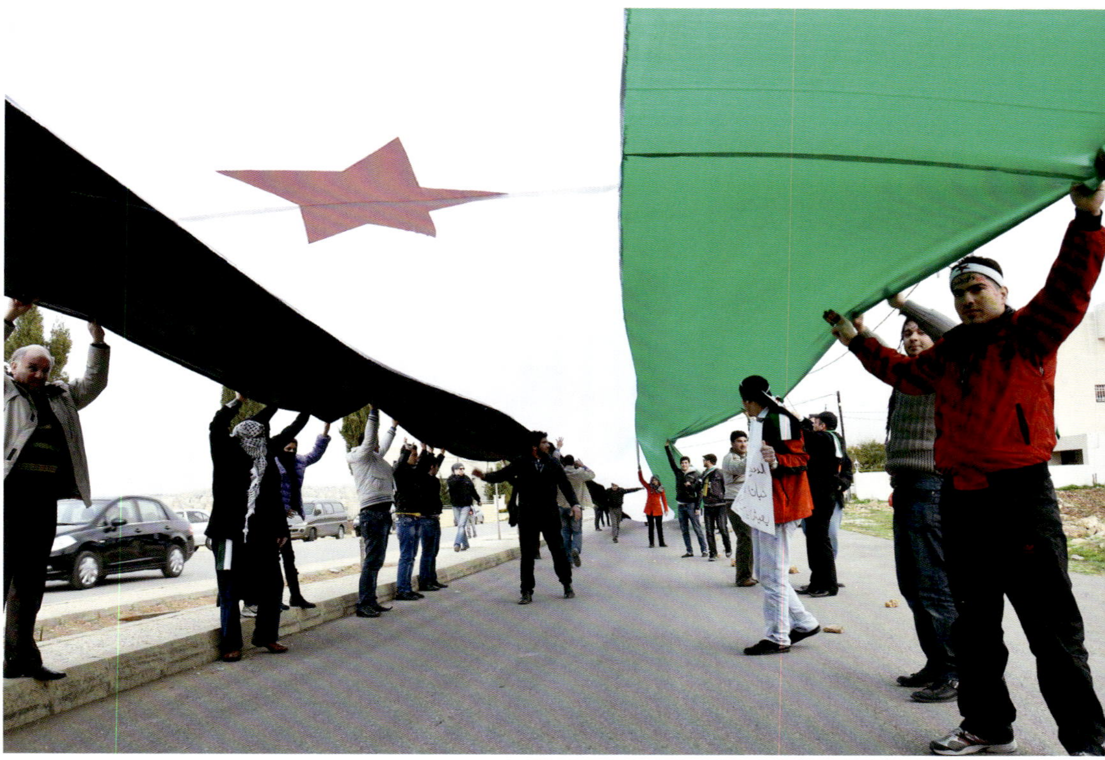

Muath Freij, from the photo series *Syrian Demonstrations in Amman*, 2012

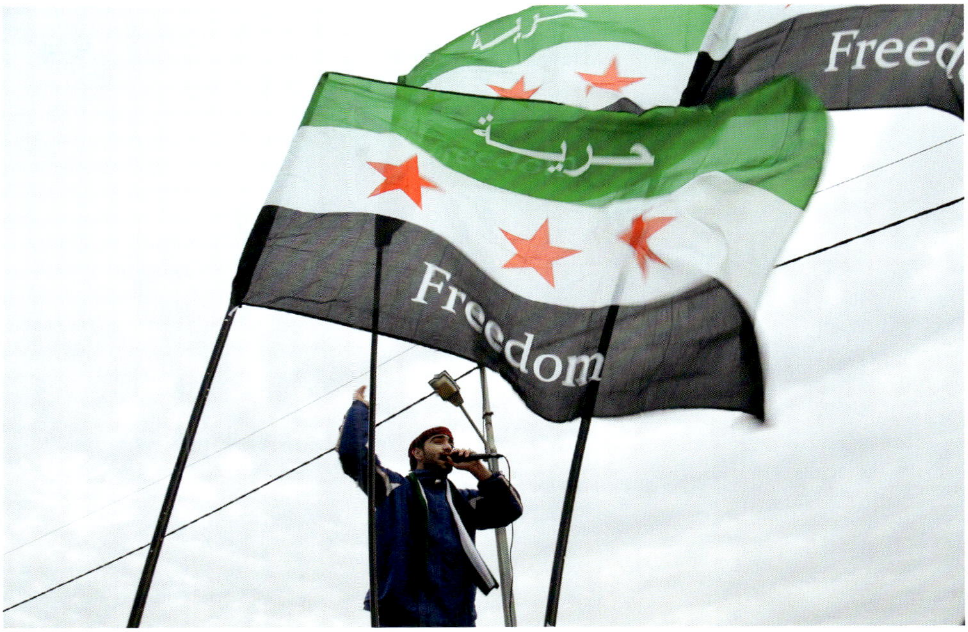

Muath Freij, from the photo series *Syrian Demonstrations in Amman*, 2012

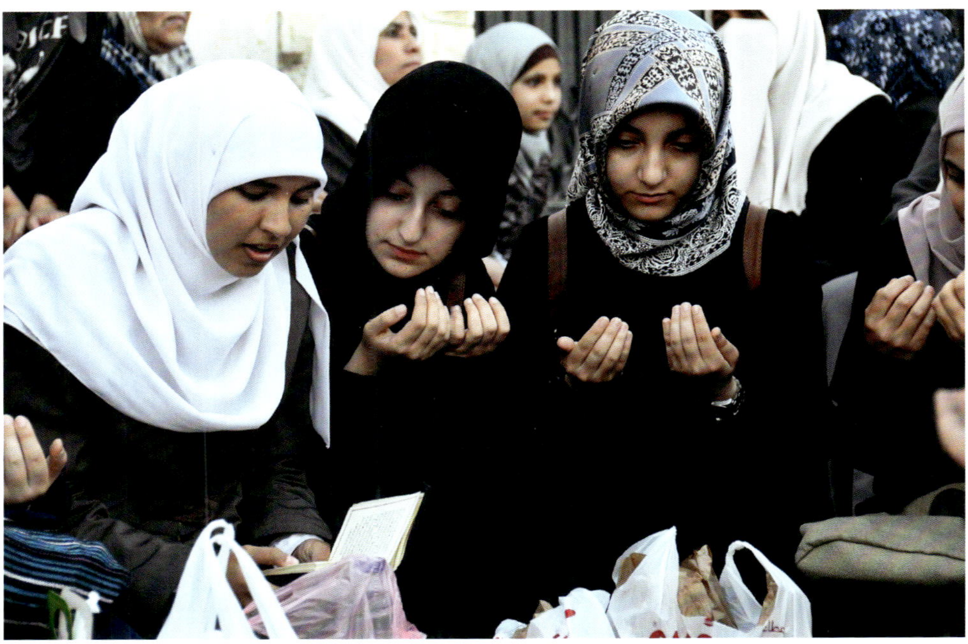

Muath Freij, from the photo series *Syrian Demonstrations in Amman*, 2012

Sacha Goldman *1946

Sacha Goldman is a film and media producer and filmmaker, active in the field of arts and culture. The manager of a film production company for twenty years and a former UNESCO media adviser is cofounder and Secretary General of Collegium International, a think tank network founded in 2002 as the International Ethical, Political and Scientific Collegium that brings together state leaders, philosophers, and scientists.

Goldman's film *Occupy Me* (2013) takes the phenomenon of Occupy Wall Street as a case study to demonstrate how media are creating such events by presenting them as civic activism. The film shows Occupy Wall Street Zuccotti Park at its peak, stating that the number of TV cameras from all over the world was higher than the number of protesters. The voice-over commentary stems from the philosopher and mediologist Régis Debray.

Régis Debray

Lead to Believe

The image has become the image of itself. Technological narcissism, the self-absorption of "communication," operating in loops, galloping mimesis, the spontaneous alignment of written and audiovisual media, one on top of the other. Recycling false facts makes them ring true and reverberate, creating from nothing an event worthy of a great man. The image spreads, and hungers only for more of itself.

If the world is that which resists, overflows, disturbs, or contradicts my representation, then we are not very far from the end of the world. And it's the softest, least apocalyptic of apocalypses. *The world has in fact become my representation*. This subsumption has a name: absolute idealism. "*Esse est percipi*," or "to be is to be perceived." We henceforth have the technological means to make come true what is known as Berkeley's principle (named after the Irish bishop who died in 1753), according to which the very essence of things is a result of us perceiving them.

Narcissism has a twin, voyeurism. The bravest record their agony live; run-of-the-mill has replaced taking a position with posing in reporting locations. Appear or perish. From now on, one must pretend in order to reach reality.

To govern is to make people believe. If a live image certifies reality, then every event born through a camera becomes its own parody. The image, a factory for obedience, cloaked as protest. And the revolution, a staging of itself, confirming the established order: that of commercial publicity.

Translated excerpt of the voice-over text quoted in the film *Occupy Me* by Sacha Goldman.

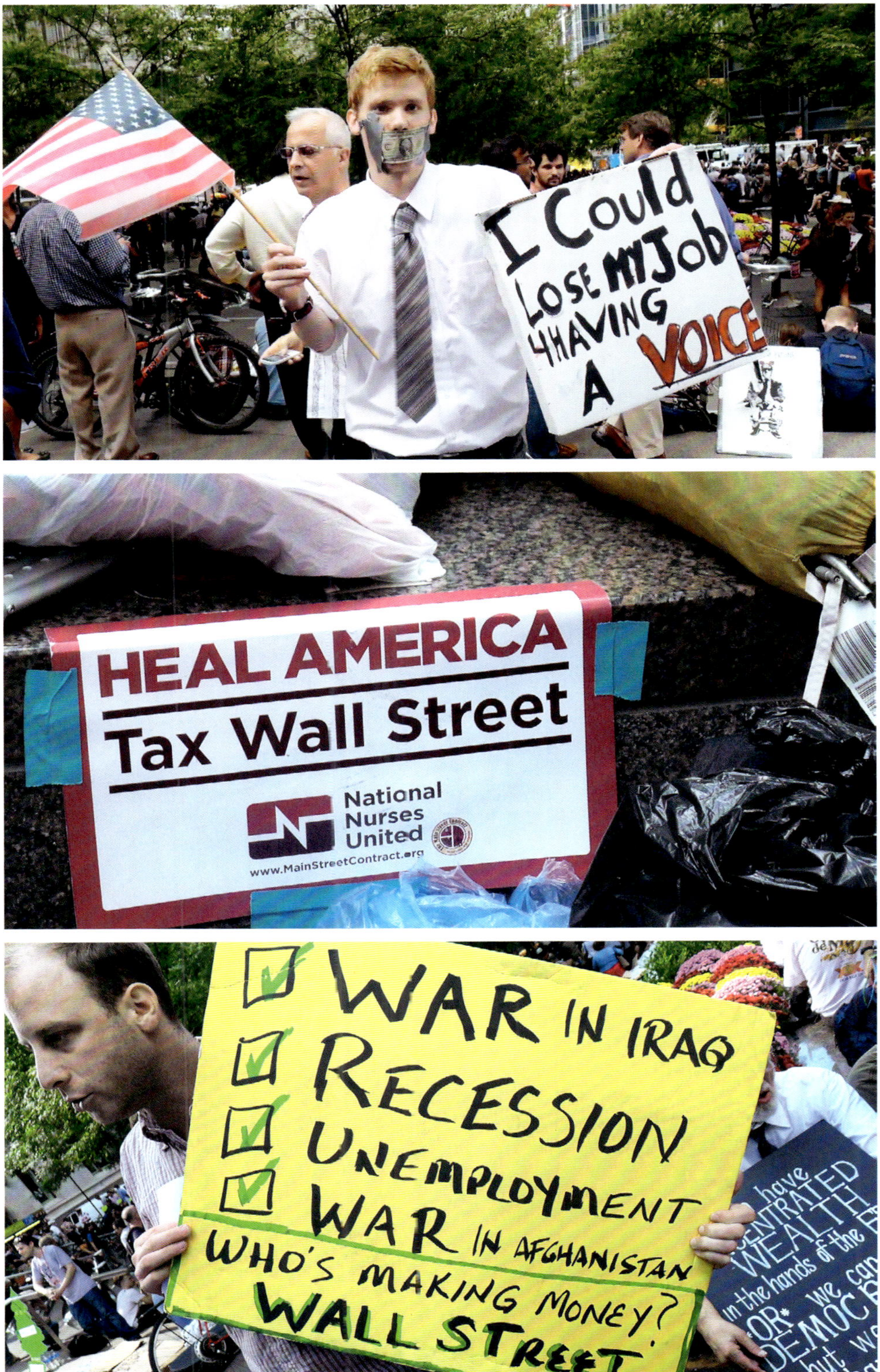

Sacha Goldman, *Occupy Me*, 2013, video, color, sound, 13:00 min, video stills

Greenpeace

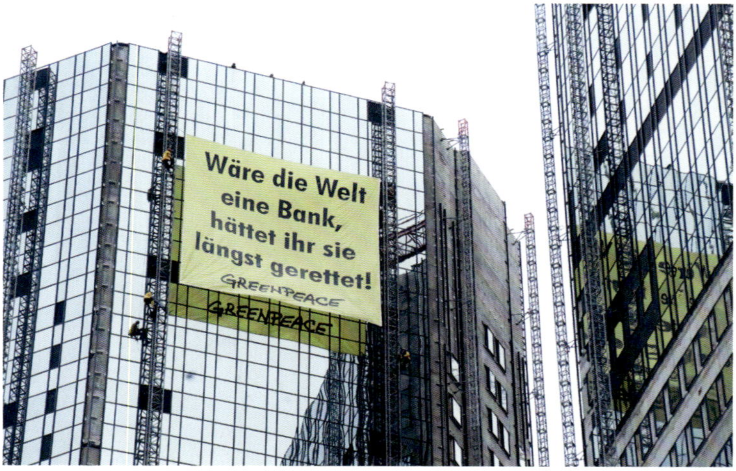

Greenpeace, *Wäre die Welt eine Bank, hättet ihr sie längst gerettet!* [If the World Was a Bank, They'd Have Saved It by Now!], photo of the original banner put up on the facade of Deutsche Bank in Frankfurt in March 2009

The nongovernmental international environmental organization Greenpeace, which was founded in 1971 in Vancouver, Canada, acts to protect and conserve the environment and to promote peace. It focuses its global campaigning on worldwide issues and with its spectacular actions highlights threats to and degradation of the environment. Since 1989, Greenpeace has its headquarters in Amsterdam. Today the organization operates in forty countries. Its campaigns are coordinated at the international level, but carried out autonomously by the national offices.

In 2009, Greenpeace launched a banner campaign all over Europe to urge governments to spend more money on climate protection projects, especially on renewable energy, forest protection, and essential measures to confront climate change. In Germany, for example, one of the banners with the slogan "Wäre die Welt eine Bank, hättet ihr sie längst gerettet!" [If the world was a bank, they'd have saved it by now!] was unfurled in the heart of the bank district in Frankfurt am Main on the facade of Deutsche Bank and denounced the German government's lack of investment in international climate protection.

Greenpeace, *Wäre die Welt eine Bank, hättet ihr sie längst gerettet!* [If the World Was a Bank, They'd Have Saved It by Now!], replica of the original banner, exhibition view, ZKM | Karlsruhe, 2014

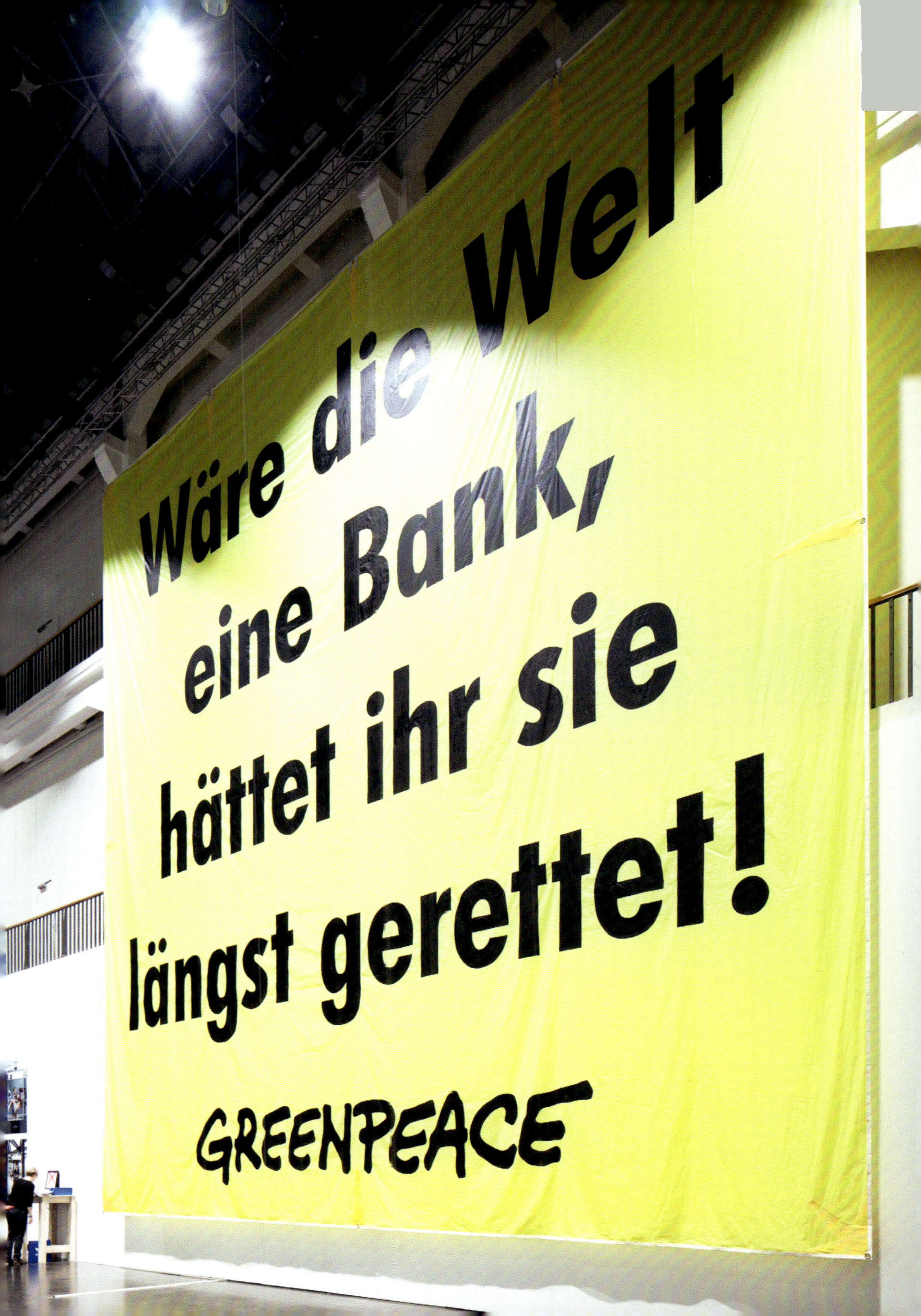
Wäre die Welt
eine Bank,
hättet ihr sie
längst gerettet!
GREENPEACE

Stéphane M. Grueso *1973

Producer and cinematographer Stéphane M. Grueso received his MA in Digital Economy and Creative Industries from EOI, Spain's School for Industrial Organization, and pursued his career in Spain and in Germany, where he lived for seven years.

He originally worked in TV and fiction films before turning to nonfiction. Grueso then had an eventful time traveling around Europe shooting and editing news and reportages for the Spanish public broadcaster TVE, which then expanded into directing and producing documentary films. He gives courses on film and video editing and film production in the Internet era, and joined the Spanish production company elegantmob, which brings together filmmakers who explicitly focus on nonfiction films with politically, socially, and culturally relevant content.

His 2011 documentary *¡Copiad, malditos!* [Copyright, or the Right to Copy], which was coproduced by elegantmob films and TVE, for example, engages with issues of intellectual property, authors' rights, and the cultural situation in Spain in the Internet age. It was the first Creative Commons production released by a national television broadcaster in Spain.

This tendency toward free culture and copyleft ultimately led to collaboration with the 15M Movement, which organized and coordinated Grueso's *15M: Excelente. Revulsivo. Importante* (2012), a documentary on the demonstrations in Puerta del Sol Square in Madrid which began on May 15, 2011.

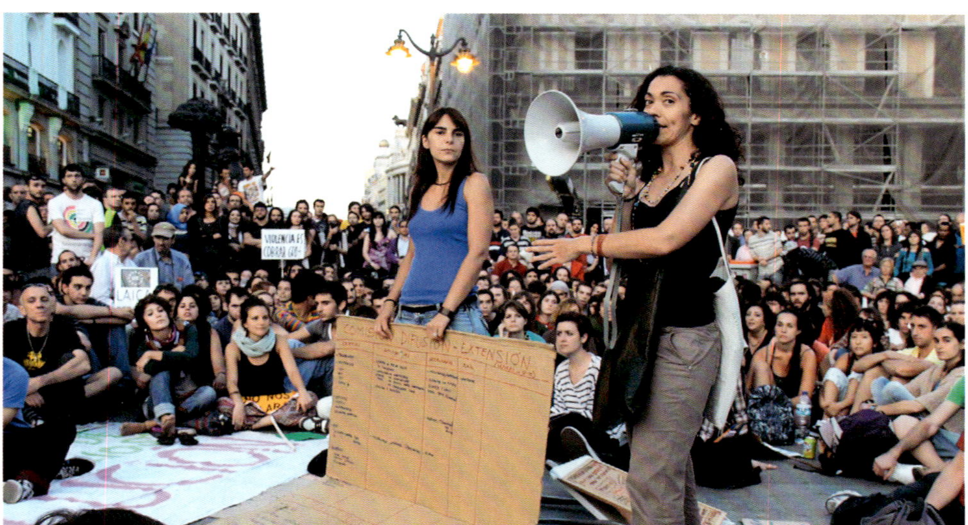

Stéphane M. Grueso, *15M: Excelente. Revulsivo. Importante*, 2012, video, color, sound, 74:00 min, video stills

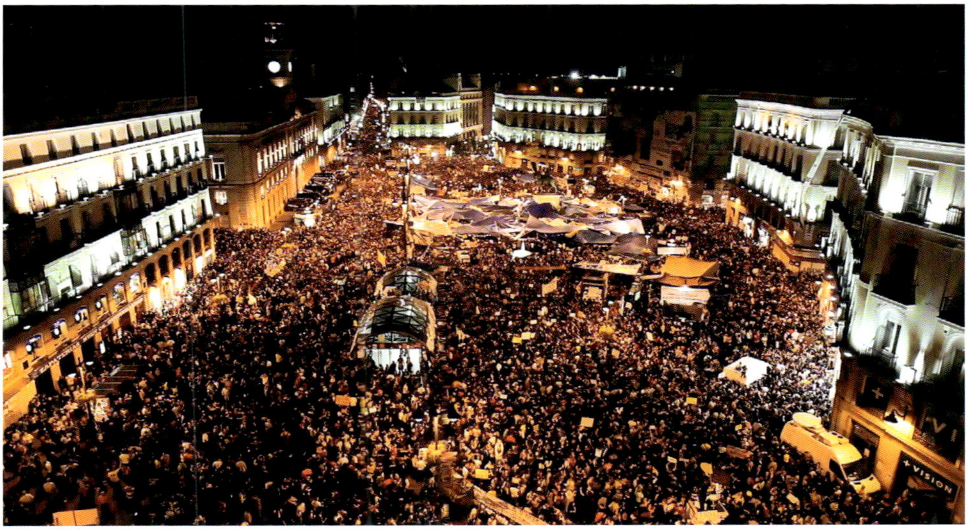

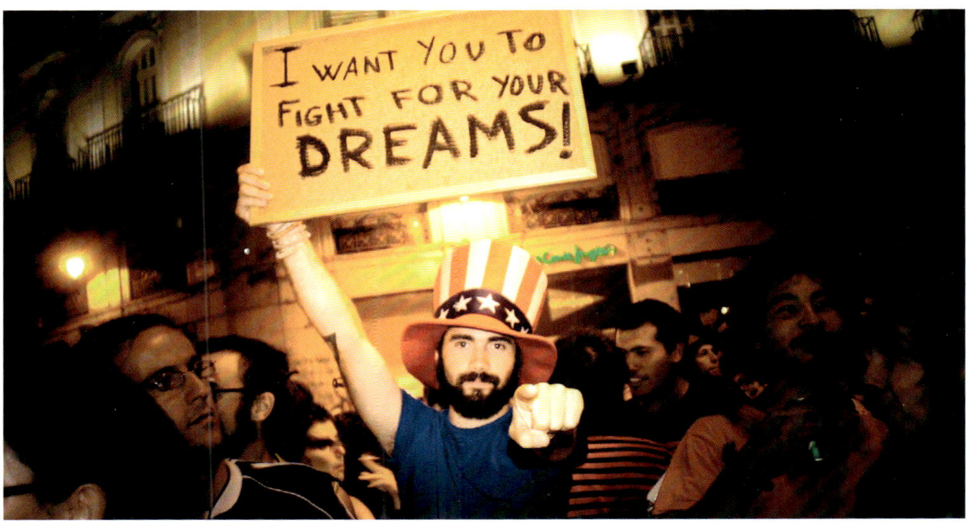

Stéphane M. Grueso, *15M: Excelente. Revulsivo. Importante*, 2012, video, color, sound, 74:00 min, video stills

Stéphane Hessel 1917–2013

Stéphane Hessel was a member of the French Resistance, survivor of the concentration camp Buchenwald, diplomat, and political activist, whose essay *Indignez-vous!* (2010)/*Time for Outrage!* (2011) inspired protests against the aftermath of the financial crisis – like the Occupy movement – all around the world.

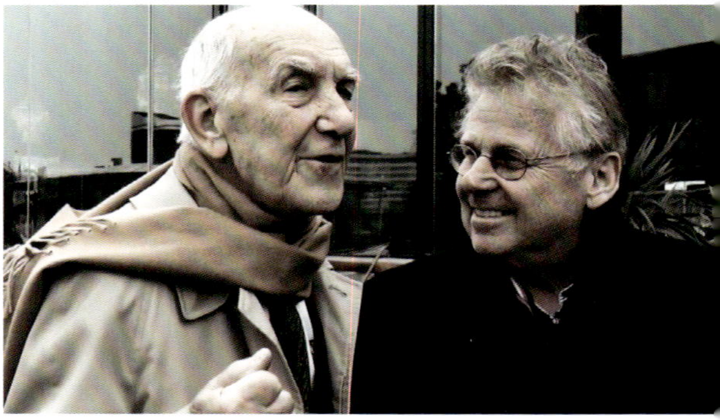

Sacha Goldman, *Une vie faite homme*, 2013, video, color, sound, 147:30 min, video still, Stéphane Hessel with Daniel Cohn-Bendit

Stéphane Hessel

The Hope of Continuity

The continuity of the values on which I have tried to base my life, beginning with the Resistance and continuing with human rights, the Universal Declaration, needed recharging from time to time in the light of the evolution of society itself.

We no longer live in the same environment as the one we knew when we were young. For us, there was a certain simplicity about war: there was only one course of action, to try not to lose it, and, if we did lose it, still strive to win it. Today, however, we are not quite sure anymore where our societies are heading.

Now that we have arrived at a particularly grave moment in history, when all the parameters seem to indicate the failure of contemporary human societies, can we still maintain that they will nevertheless recover? Can we believe that this strange species, the human species, the young species that inhabits this planet, has any chance of bringing something else out of it?

What I would really like to know is the view the neurosciences have about this. We still don't know much about how this thing inside our heads functions. Perhaps if we explore it, we may find that it is capable of turning the improbable into the probable, and then into the possible, thus enabling us to feel that hope has not been lost forever.

Extracts from Sacha Goldman's *Une vie faite homme* (2013), a documentary of interviews with Stéphane Hessel. Translated from the French by Roger Leverdier. The film features Daniel Cohn-Bendit, Jean-Paul Dollé, Laure Adler, Edgar Morin, Nicolas Hulot, Régis Debray, Jean-Claude Carrière, Peter Sloterdijk, Michel Rocard, Milan Kučan, François Hollande, and Nicolas Demorand. It celebrated premiere at the ZKM | Karlsruhe on October 20, 2013 – the day Stéphane Hessel would have celebrated his 96th birthday.

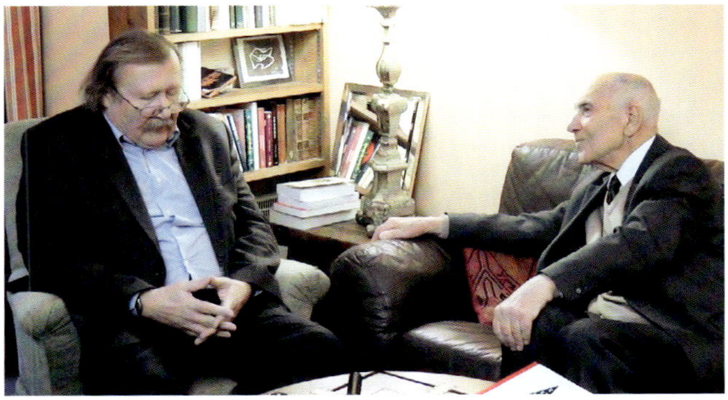

Stéphane Hessel with Peter Sloterdijk

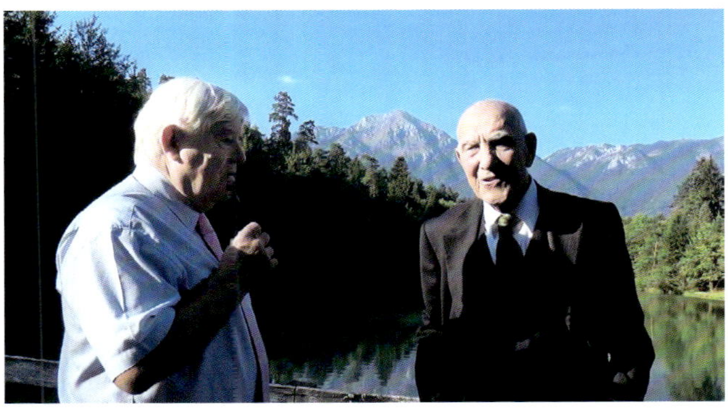

Stéphane Hessel with Milan Kučan

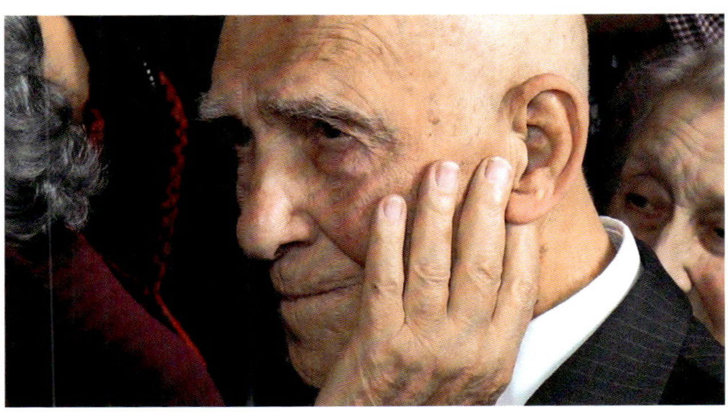

Sacha Goldman, *Une vie faite homme*, 2013,
video, color, sound, 147:30 min, video stills

Jim Hubbard *1951

The independent filmmaker and curator Jim Hubbard studied at the San Francisco Art Institute and began making films in 1974. In most of his films – amongst others *Elegy in the Streets* (1989), *Two Marches* (1991), *The Dance* (1992), and *Memento Mori* (1995) – he focuses on truthfully conveying lesbian and gay experiences, which, in his opinion, can be done in experimental films in a more appropriate way than by flat narrative films with gay characters. In 1987, he founded the New York Lesbian and Gay Experimental Film Festival (today known as MIX NYC, the New York Queer Experimental Film Festival) together with the author Sarah Schulman. Since then, the festival has brought together thousands of participants from all over the world and has inspired the foundation of MIX film festivals in other countries as well.

Since the mid-1980s Hubbard especially engages with HIV/AIDS. Under the patronage of the Estate Project for Artists with AIDS founded in 1991 (see: www.artistswithaids.org), for example, he created the AIDS Activist Video Collection at the New York Public Library. Additionally, he curated and cocurated various series in renowned museums, amongst others *Fever in the Archive: AIDS Activist Videotapes from the Royal S. Marks Collection* at the Guggenheim Museum in New York (December 2000) and *Another Wave: Global Queer Cinema* at the Museum of Modern Art in New York (July/September 2006).

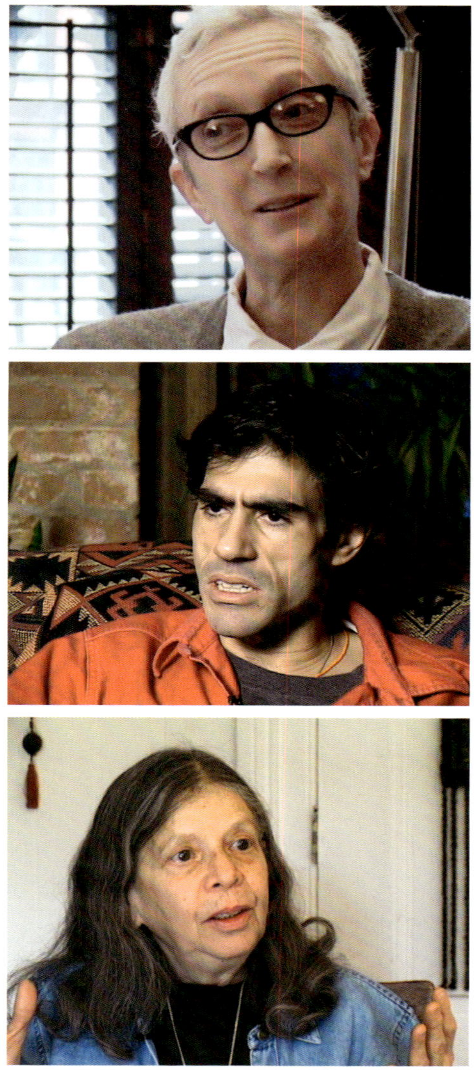

Jim Hubbard, *United in Anger: A History of ACT UP*, 2012, video, color, sound, 90:00 min, video stills

Hubbard's own films have been shown at the Berlin International Film Festival, the London Film Festival, the Museum of Modern Art in New York, and at numerous international lesbian and gay film festivals, including Tokyo, New York, San Francisco, Los Angeles, and Hamburg, where his film *Memento Mori* won the Ursula for Best Short Film in 1995.

In 2012, he released *United in Anger: A History of ACT UP* (coproduced with Sarah Schulman), a feature-length documentary on the history of AIDS activism in the USA, focusing on the AIDS activist movement ACT UP (AIDS Coalition to Unleash Power), which, with slogans like "Silence = Death" and high-profile public actions, since 1987 fights against social and political indifference, seeks to politicize the fight against the epidemic, and opposes attempts to stigmatize people who are HIV positive. Hubbard's documentary combines interviews from the ACT UP Oral History Project (see: www.actuporalhistory.org) with rare archival footage.

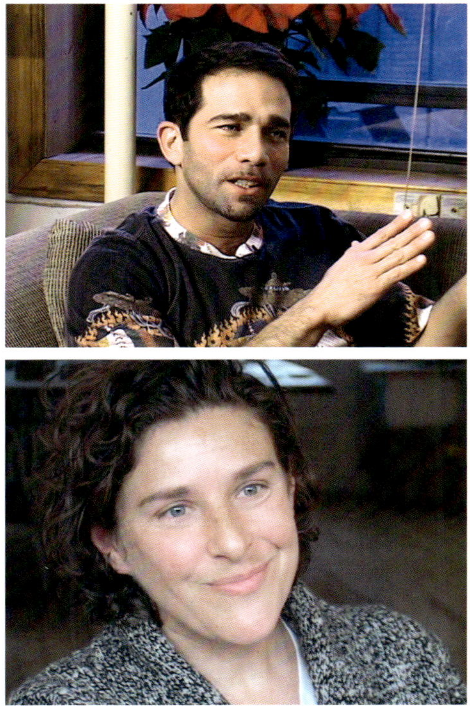

Jim Hubbard, *United in Anger: A History of ACT UP*, 2012, video, color, sound, 90:00 min, video stills

Founded in 1978
Global

www.hrw.org

Human Rights Watch

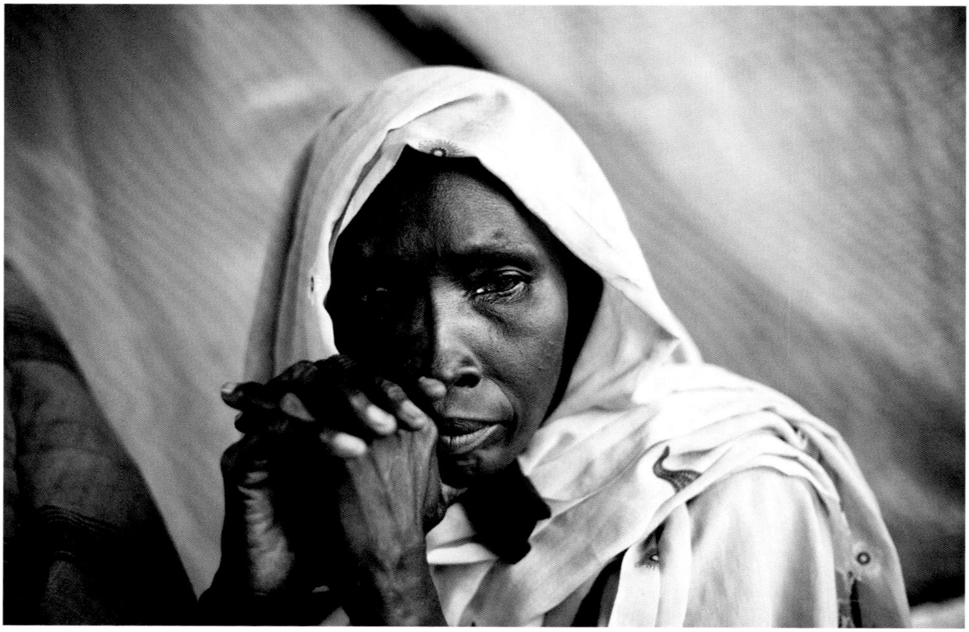

Kassar Al Naem, 50, originally from a village around Gebanit, Blue Nile province, Sudan, arrived at the Yusuf Batil refugee camp in the Upper Nile state, South Sudan, in late October 2012. In June, militia had attacked her village, shot at her fellow villagers, and kidnapped three people including two women. She and other villagers had wanted to flee before October but they fell captive because militia had blocked the only road out of the mountain.

For more than thirty-five years, the internationally active nongovernmental organization Human Rights Watch (HRW) draws attention to abuse with its coverage of the violation of basic human rights. To provide people all over the world with security and justice, HRW conducts independent research and specifically influences political decision-makers. Its work, which always aims at cooperating with international as well as local civil society actors in order to maximize the impact and gain long-term attention, is aligned to the respect for the dignity of each human being and is liable to international human rights and humanitarian law. To preserve its objectivity and independence, HRW rejects all funding by governments. Further, the organization is nonpartisan and always remains neutral in armed conflicts.

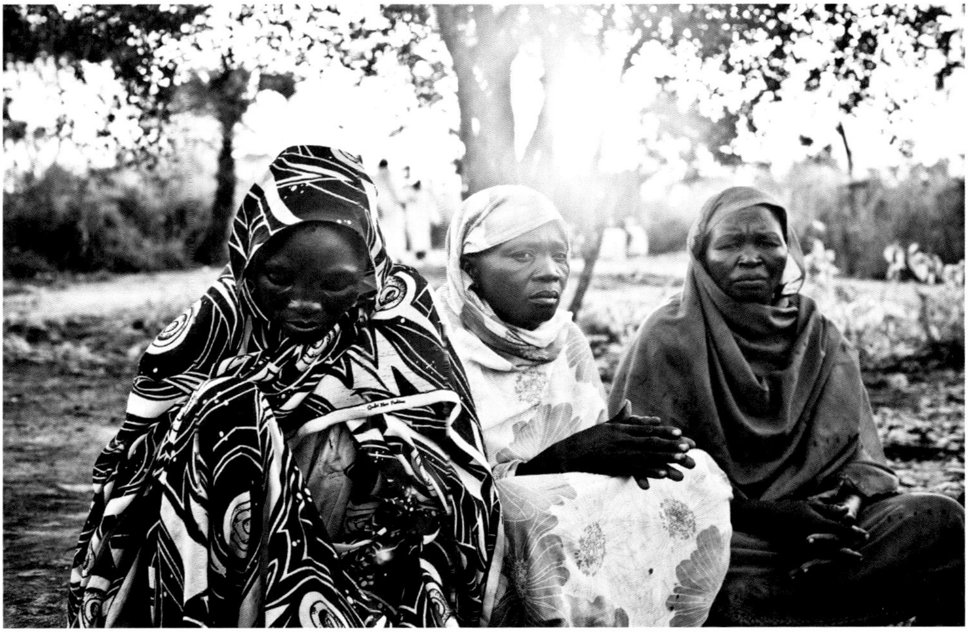

In late 2011, Fatima Al Ghomous, Zainab Atoum, and Amna Adam al-Dhaib fled the relentless government bombardments near their homes in Surkum, Sudan, and walked toward South Sudan. Along the way from Surkum to Wadega, in Kormuk locality, they were hit by what they described as a barrel bomb, which killed three people, including two girls.

Kein Mensch ist illegal

Since its foundation at the documenta 10 art exhibition in 1997, the German network of antiracism and church-based asylum initiatives Kein Mensch ist illegal [No Human Being Is Illegal] supports refugees and aliens without residence permits in Germany as well as migrants living under the threat of deportation. The goal is to bring the often precarious situation of these people to public attention, and to make the situation of living far away from their homes a little easier.

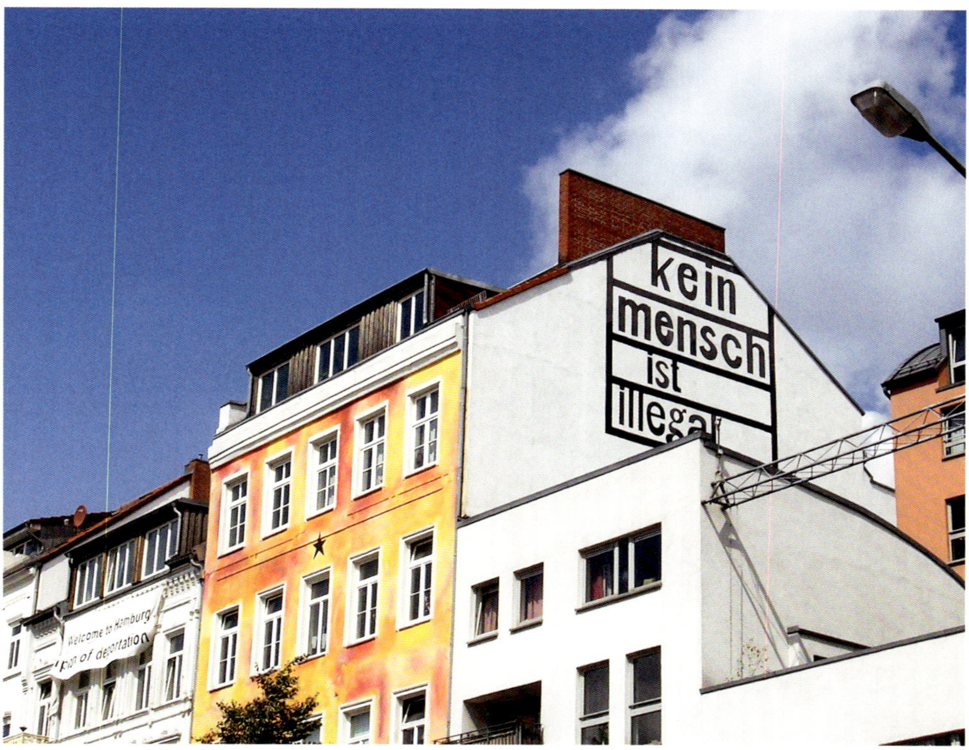

Logo of Kein Mensch ist illegal on a house wall in the St. Pauli-Hafenstraße in Hamburg, Germany, 2006

Manifesto 1997

"You who are so-called illegal aliens must know that no human being is 'illegal.' That is a contradiction in terms. Human beings can be beautiful or more beautiful, they can be fat or skinny, they can be right or wrong, but illegal? How can a human being be illegal?" (Elie Wiesel)

Migrants and refugees are not welcome in Europe. As it is almost impossible for them to flee to Europe in a legal way, it is only possible to cross national borders "illegally," and this often entails mortal dangers. People who stay in a country although their remaining there is no longer permitted, allowed, or tolerated become "illegals." The remaining possibilities to enter and stay in a country are systematically being reduced. In this way, an increasing number of people are forced into illegality.

Borders no longer only separate territories, borders separate people. Borders are everywhere: in the social welfare department as well as in the train station, in a city center and at a nation's border. Borders are everywhere, where people have to fear being asked for their papers.

To live in a status of being disfranchised, insecure, and illegal means to be in constant fear of denunciation or being blackmailed, because detection then results in penalization, custody prior to deportation, or immediate deportation. It means being defenceless and without rights in relation to authorities, employers, and landlords, including in cases of illness, accidents, or assaults. It also means to live in fear of social contacts. Children cannot go to school or kindergarten, young people cannot start an apprenticeship or job training. It means to live in constant vigilance.

In the fight against racism, it is becoming increasingly important to support migrants and refugees politically and practically in their fight against being illegalized and for their right to actually have any rights at all.

Every human being has the right to decide for themselves where and how they want to live. The regulation of migration and the systematic denial of rights stand in opposition to the demand for equality in all social and political issues, for respecting human rights of every person independent of background and legal documents.

This is why we call for the support of migrants and refugees in their right of entry or continuation of their journey. We call for the guarantee of medical treatment, school, training, accommodation, and the material survival of migrants and refugees.

Because no human being is illegal.

documenta 11, Kassel, Germany 1997

Manifesto translated from the German by Isaac Custance.

Jan Jaap Kuiper *1976 and Katja Sokolova *1977

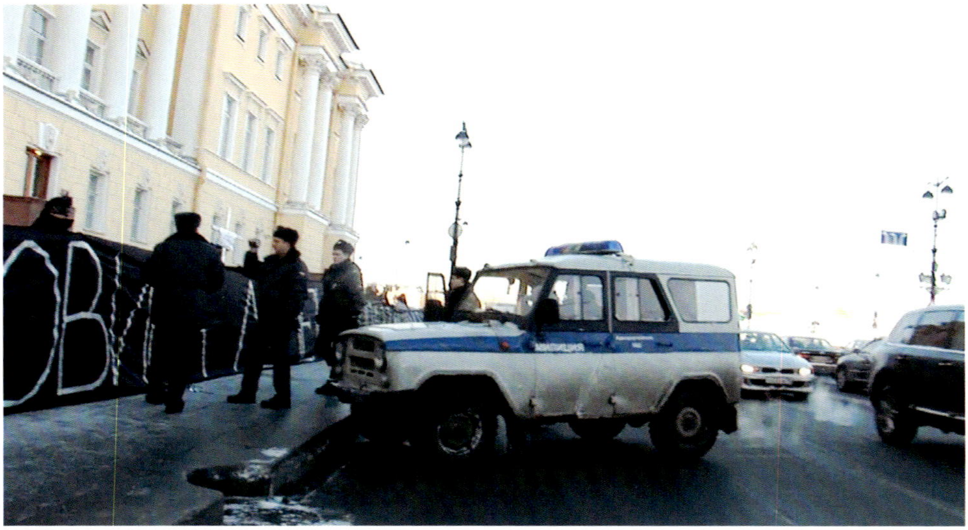

Jan Jaap Kuiper and Katja Sokolova, *"Sinners' Disease" – Surviving HIV in Russia*, 2011, video, color, sound, 56:00 min, video still

The director, cinematographer, and writer Jan Jaap Kuiper studied at the Netherlands Film and Television Academy and graduated in 2008 as a documentary director with his award-winning film *Pyotr – Letters from the Gulag*. He also holds a Master's degree in contemporary Eastern European history. Already in 2000, he founded his own production company ThankEve Productions, and, furthermore, he is co-owner of postproduction company Amator. Films Kuiper has directed include *Like Tarkovsky* (2001), *NEformat* (2003), *inside outside* (2004), *Gone Bald* (2007), *Small Nations, Big Games* (2010), and *Verlaat* [The Lock] (2012).

Freelance producer and curator Katja Sokolova studied linguistics in Saint Petersburg and cultural management in Moscow. Before she went to the Netherlands in 2003, she worked for a local television broadcaster in Saint Petersburg and organized several exhibitions in public spaces. In 2004, she and a group of friends initiated the nonprofit art space and laboratory East Area in Amsterdam in order to give contemporary artists, musicians, and writers from Eastern Europe the opportunity to present their works. The venue was active until 2005. In 2006, Sokolova organized the live program of the Amsterdam Film eXperience festival with several performances and installations. She also took part in visual artist Irina Birger's Web-based gallery Inhalexhale and was a guest curator in the Gastarbeider Dating project at Mediamatic, Amsterdam. For ThankEve Productions, which she now runs together with Jan Jaap Kuiper, Katja Solokova worked as a producer, translator, researcher, and interviewer on the documentaries *NEformat*, *Pyotr – Letters from the Gulag*, and *Small Nations, Big Games*, as well as the short film *inside outside*.

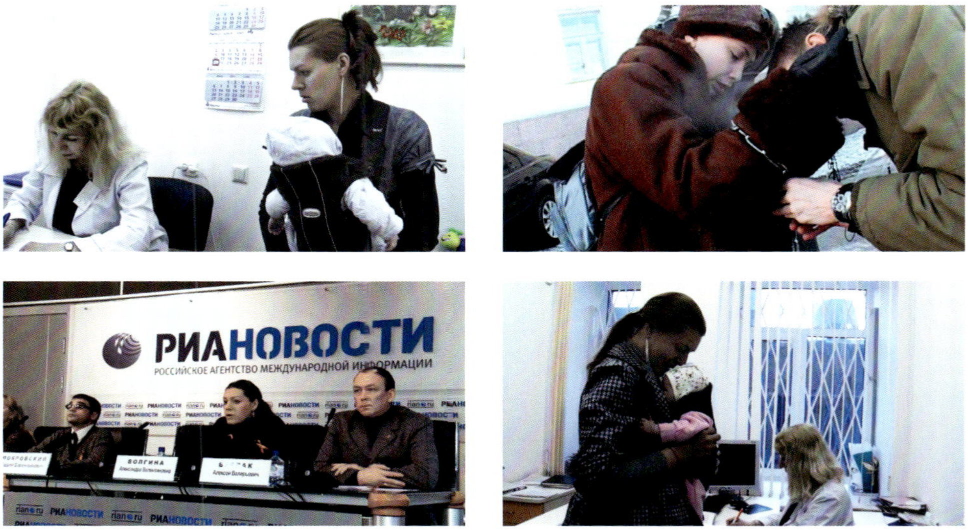

Jan Jaap Kuiper and Katja Sokolova, *"Sinners' Disease" – Surviving HIV in Russia*, 2011, video, color, sound, 56:00 min, video stills

Kuiper and Sokolova's documentary *"Sinners' Disease" – Surviving HIV in Russia* (2011) provides some insights into AIDS activism in Russia by tracking the battle of the HIV-positive activist Sasha Volgina to obtain the drugs that she needs for herself and her unborn child. The film thematizes the helpless protests against the chronic shortage of antiretroviral drugs in a country in which nearly one million people live with HIV, yet the virus is still widely considered to be a "sinners' disease."

Screenings of the film took place at the Russian Open Documentary Film Festival Artdocfest (Moscow, Russia, 2011), the Movies that Matter film festival (The Hague, Netherlands, 2012), the Docudays UA International Human Rights Documentary Film Festival (Kiev, Ukraine, 2012), the This Human World festival (Vienna, Austria, 2012), the Nederlands Film Festival (Utrecht, Netherlands, 2012), the Human Rights Film Festival of Barcelona (2013), and from December 2013 to the end of March 2014 at the ZKM | Karlsruhe, Germany.

Lynn Lauterbach *1983

Lynn Lauterbach is a German freelance photographer and artist who was born in Braunschweig, raised in Wolfenbüttel, and now lives and works in Berlin. She came into contact with photography at an early age and developed a passion for this medium. After eight years of serving in the Bundeswehr, the German Federal Forces, she pulled up stakes and decided to study photography in Berlin. This was followed by intensive three-year training as a photographer, specializing in journalism. Today, Lauterbach is engaged in both journalistic and cultural areas, in the latter especially in concert, theater, ballet, and opera photography. In her photographic documentaries she seeks to look over the shoulder of everyday life and not merely to portray but to show the thin lines between various socially and culturally relevant aspects as well as the clash of different influential factors.

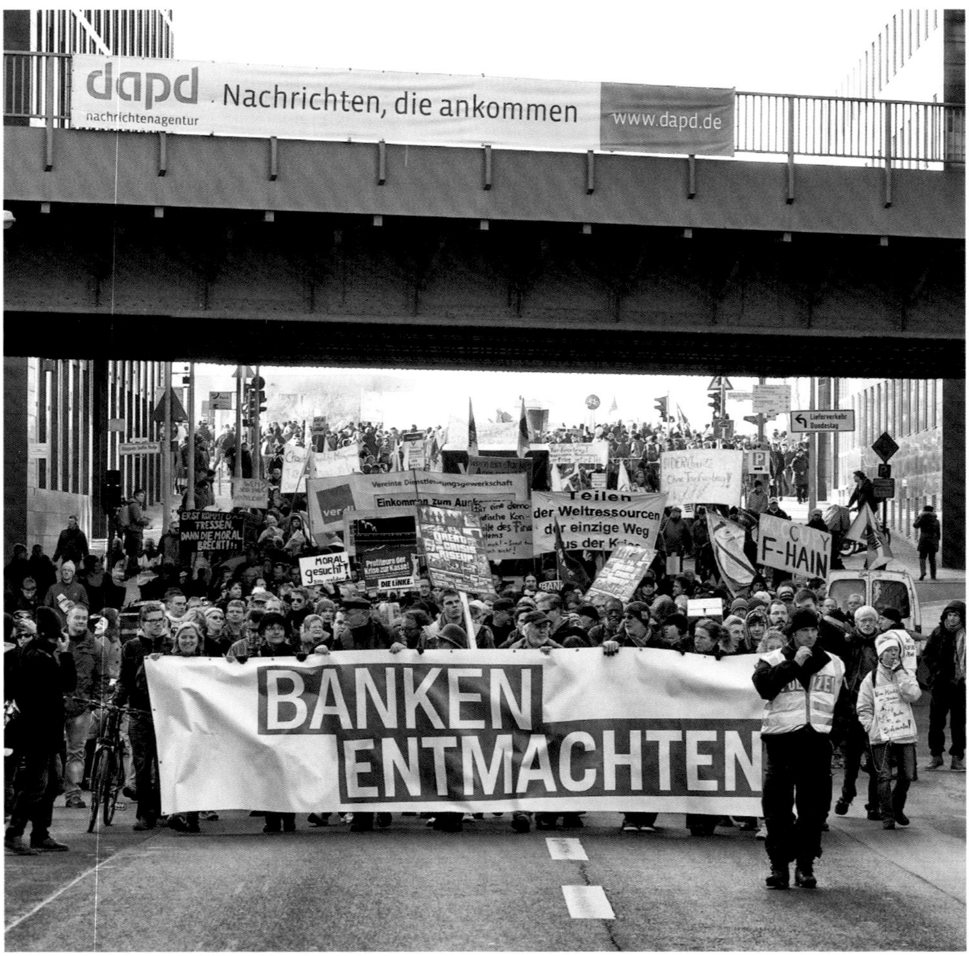

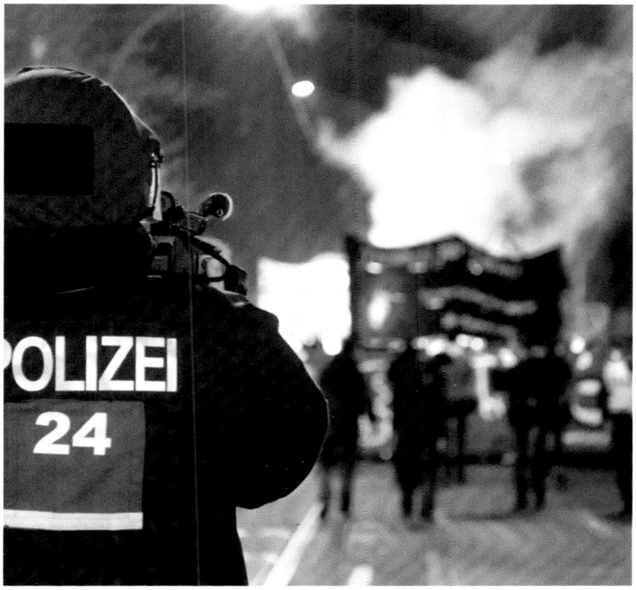

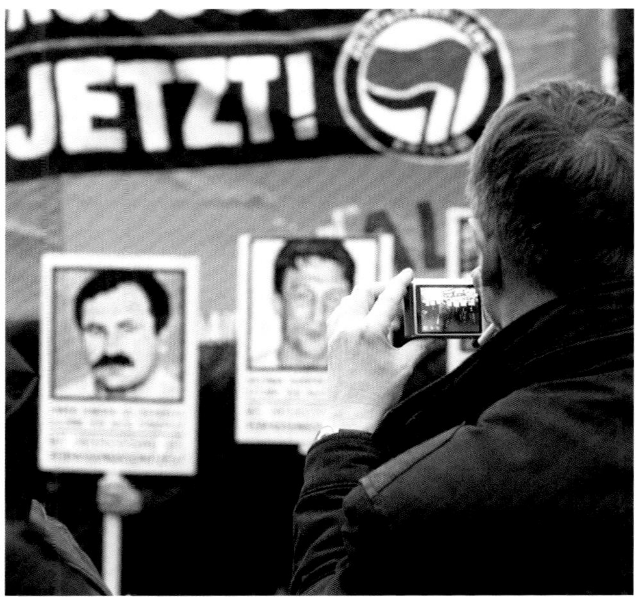

Lynn Lauterbach, from the photo series *Generation Demonstration*, 2011/2012

In her photo series *Generation Demonstration* (2011/2012), which took almost a year to create, Lynn Lauterbach documented protests in Berlin and the ambivalent interaction of police, press, and activists. Her photographs illustrate that the police both protects the protesters – citizens of various ages – and responds to them with violence. Furthermore, they document the multifaceted use of media for different purposes: all participating groups filmed and took pictures with their cameras – for news coverage, for legal evidence, or to distribute pictures of the action.

Founded in 2008
Estonia

www.letsdoitworld.org

Let’s Do It! World

Let’s Do It! World is a nonpolitical citizens’ action group that became known for organizing regular cleanup events in collaboration with volunteers, NGOs, and other groups, and calling for people to fight against the pollution of nature by waste and rubbish. Originally founded in Estonia in 2008, the documentation of these events has since inspired people all over the world. Today 112 countries and about ten million volunteers take part in the network. In addition to the events, Let’s Do It! World provides on its website several features and tools with which interested users can playfully approach the topic. With the World Waste Map, for example, which can easily be downloaded onto a smartphone via a QR code, everyone can map illegal waste locally and globally. The collected data can then be used to organize the logistics for local cleanup actions. Let’s Do It! World is an accredited member of the United Nations Environment Programme (UNEP). Since after the big cleanup events in 2008 and the following years a major shift in the public awareness of this subject took place, today only twenty percent of the activities are cleanups, most of them are other types of community actions.

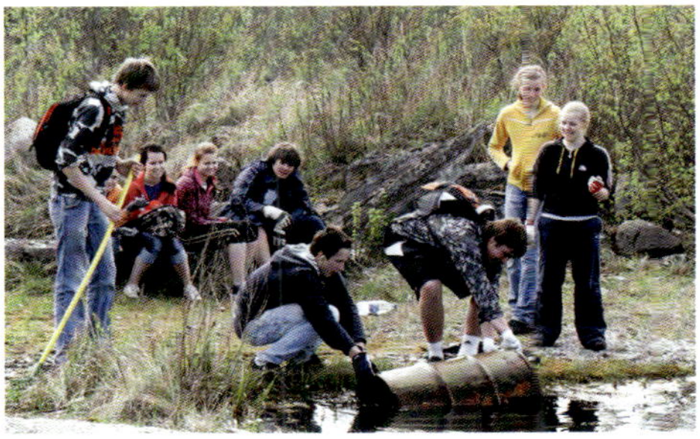

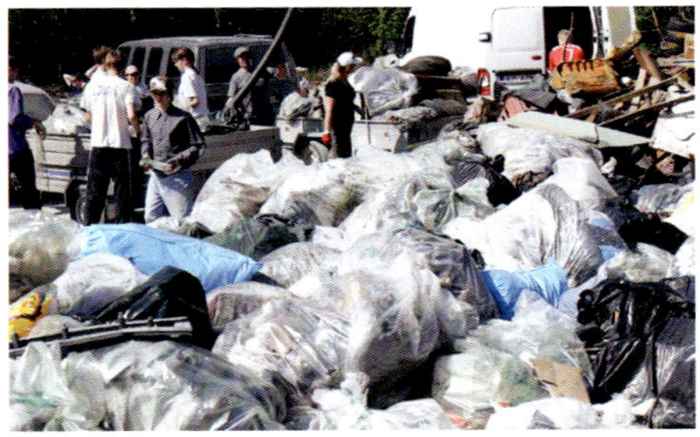

First Let's Do It! World cleanup action, Estonia, 2008

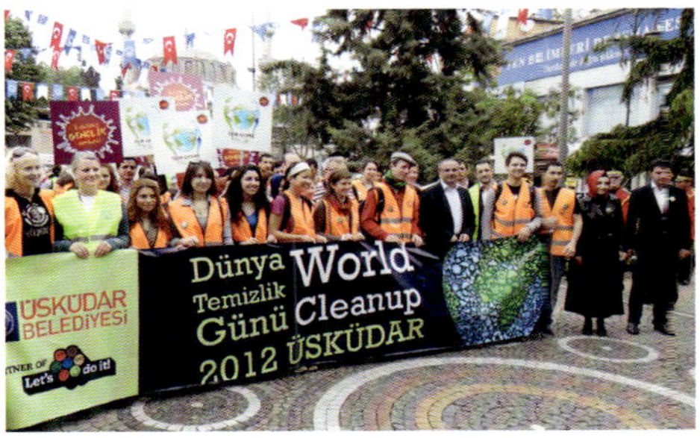

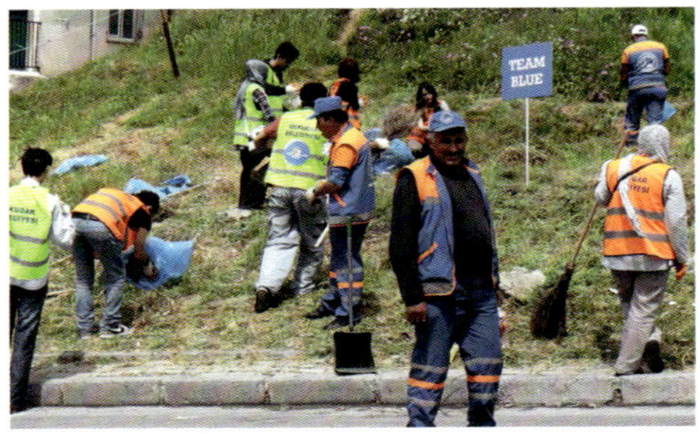

Let's Do It! World, cleanup in Turkey, 2012

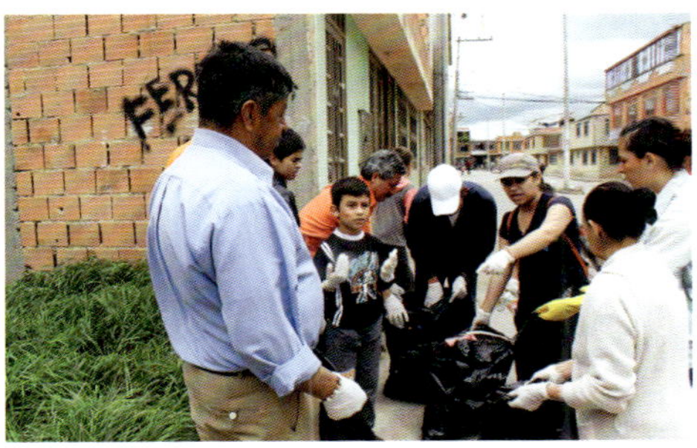

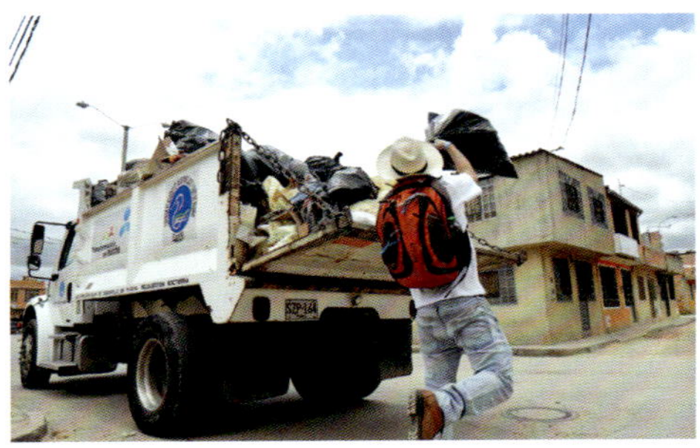

Let's Do It! World, cleanup in Colombia, 2014

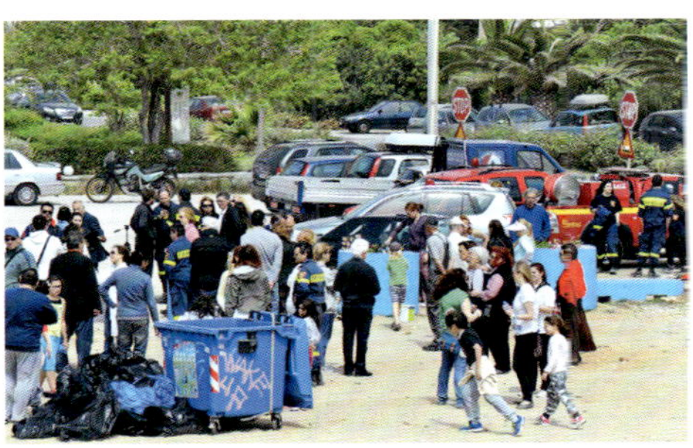

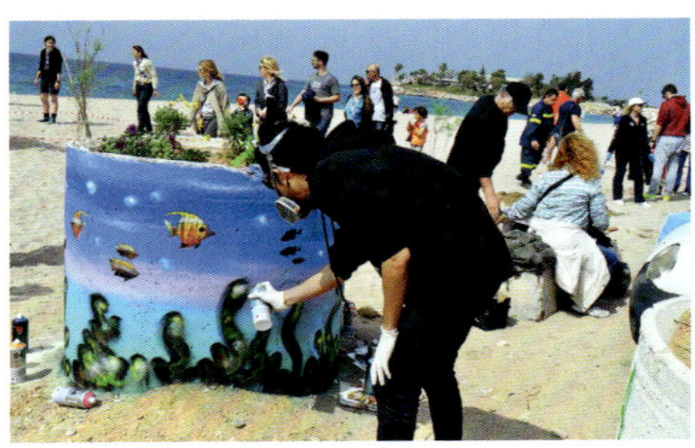

Let's Do It! World, cleanup in Greece, 2014

www.elbashayer.com/news-280665.html

Museum of the Revolution

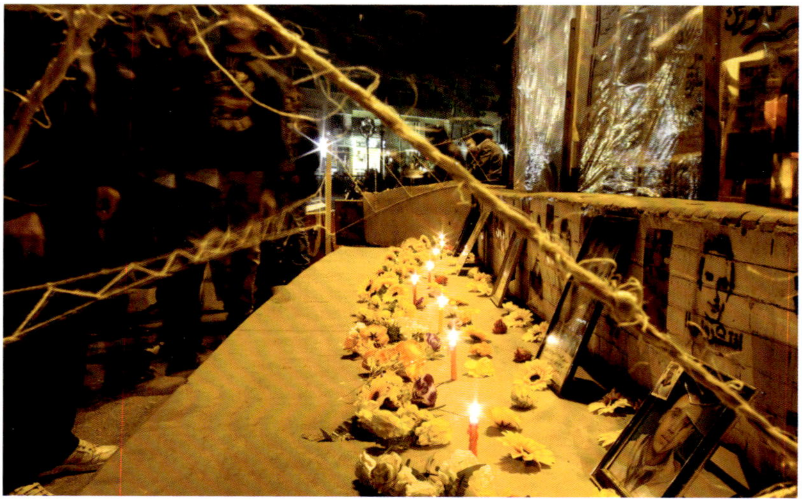

Arnold Fuad, from the photo series *Museum of the Revolution*, 2013

The Museum of the Revolution was a citizen-built impromptu installation erected on Tahrir Square in Cairo during the Egyptian Revolution. To date the museum has been rebuilt three times after it was destroyed by the police and the army following demonstrations.

The first version contained text documents and photographs of the initial eighteen days of the revolution, beginning on January 25, 2011, and ending with the forced resignation of Hosni Mubarak on February 11. The second version was installed during the rule of the military council. The third installation housed sculptures and scraps of paper and poems documenting the presidency of Mohamed Morsi, as well as pictures of those who were killed in demonstrations protesting against the Muslim Brotherhood, in order to perpetuate their memory and their sacrifice for the sake of the freedom of the Egyptians. The museum, which Arnold Fuad documented in the photo series of which excerpts are shown here, was dismantled in a hurry after the overthrow of Morsi in July 2013.

Meanwhile, plans are being offered to the government to create an official, government-run Museum of the Revolution in Cairo, which will consist of three parts: a main building, located in the former headquarters of the National Democratic Party (NDP); the Martyrs' Piazza (yard) in the area directly in front of the Egyptian Museum, which will be turned into a public memorial displaying the names and stories of all of those who died in the revolution; the NDP display, a glass cover over the entire massive building of the NDP directly behind the Egyptian Museum, which was completely burned down during the revolution. The project managers estimate the costs at around 100 million Egyptian Pounds, and envisage that these costs will be recovered within two years from the entrance fees.

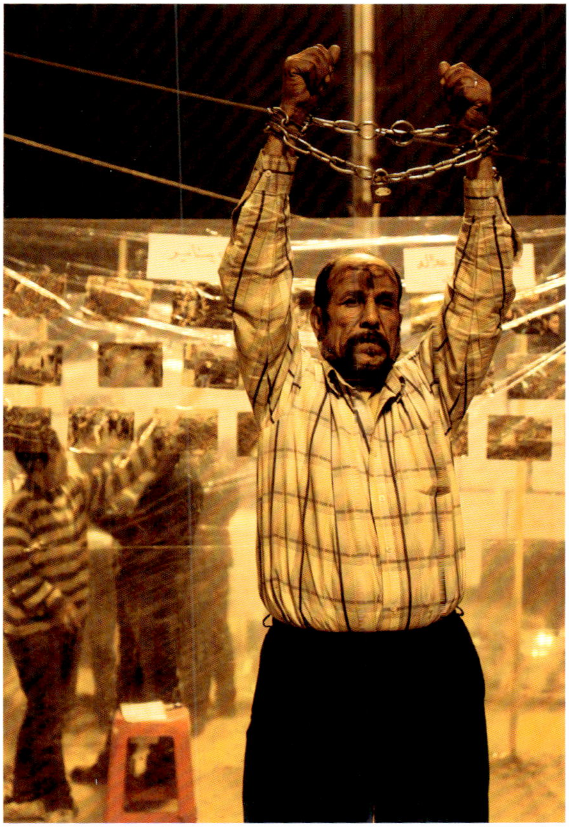

Arnold Fuad, from the photo series *Museum of the Revolution*, 2013

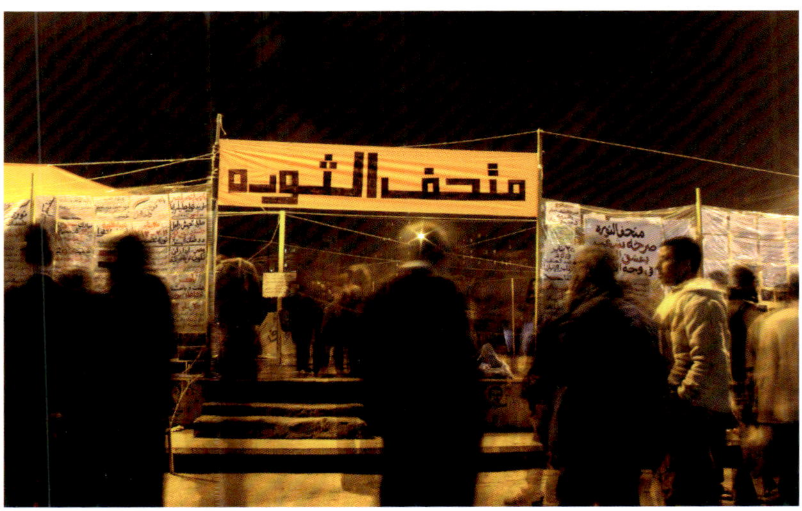

Arnold Fuad, from the photo series *Museum of the Revolution*, 2013

No TAV

No TAV is an Italian protest movement that since the early 1990s has been fighting against the construction of a high-speed railroad line through the Susa Valley in Piedmont, connecting the major cities of Northern Italy to Lyon and Paris in France. The movement, which is composed of the population, local politicians, and various environmental organizations, mainly criticizes the costs of the project, which are deemed excessive in relation to its usefulness, predicts an enormous impact on the environment and damage to people's health, and views the plans of the government as a symbol and an example of inadequate management of common goods, public expenditure, land, and politics.

In the past twenty years the activists have made various efforts to prevent this mammoth project: They built cottage villages and installed vigils throughout the whole valley; they pointed to the alternative of expanding the existing railway line, considering that traffic in this area has never been incredibly high; they commissioned cost–benefit analyses and showed the long-term consequences for the population, the environment, local businesses, and tourism; they petitioned the president; at alleged locations for exploratory tunnels they acquired plots of land to position themselves in the first row for the expected expropriation proceedings; they collected signatures, which were handed over to the Petitions Committee of the European Commission in Strasbourg, as the European Union cofinanced the TAV project.

The huge dispute has spread to the whole of Italy and is one of the most significant political movements there for twenty years. Similar movements but with different names have garnered great popular support in other European countries – for example, Stuttgart 21 in Germany – and in the region bordering Italy some movements have also adopted the label No TAV and the symbols connected with it.

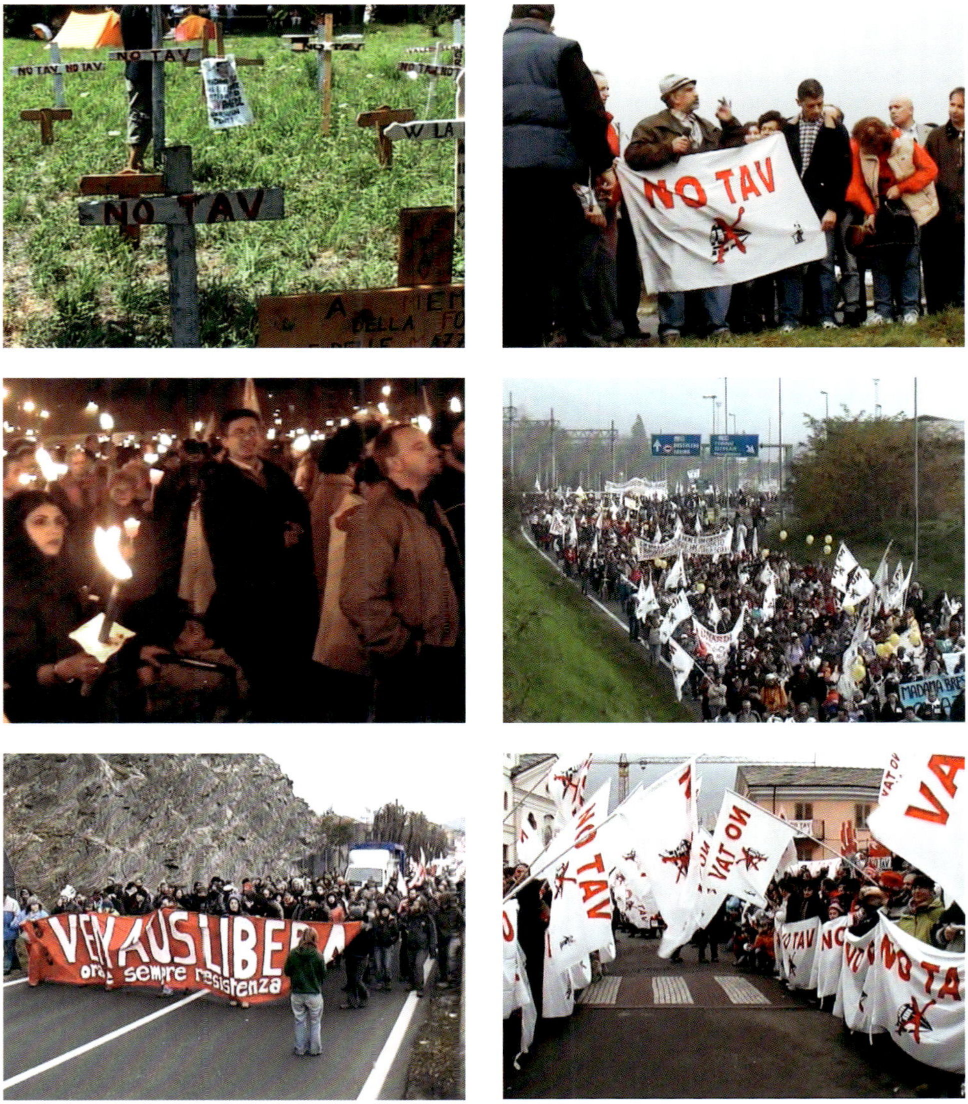

Riccardo Pavia, *Il vento che fermò il treno*, 2008, video, color, sound, 126:00 min, video stills

Since 1996
Germany

www.bei-abriss-aufstand.de
www.kopfbahnhof-21.de

Protests against Stuttgart 21

The Stuttgart 21 protest is directed against the Deutsche Bahn project, a major railway and urban reconstruction of Stuttgart central station. Amongst other things, it is planned to convert the station, an aboveground railway terminus, into an underground through station. The active group of citizens opposed to this project is one of the largest in recent times in Germany. The protesters mainly criticize the lack of democratic legitimacy of the project and citizen participation, the high cost, questionable profitability, the environmental risk, violations of a listed building (the station), and planning deficiencies. An alternative concept is being discussed under the name "Kopfbahnhof 21" [Terminus 21]. Organized by citizens from a variety of groupings and alliances, the protest movement – which also has connections to the antinuclear movement in Germany, to the protest against aircraft noise in Frankfurt am Main, and other initiatives against large infrastructure projects in Italy, France, and Romania – unites people of all ages, educational backgrounds, and professions. It consists of a citizens' initiative, petitions, demonstrations (especially the weekly Monday demonstrations), and nonviolent protests.

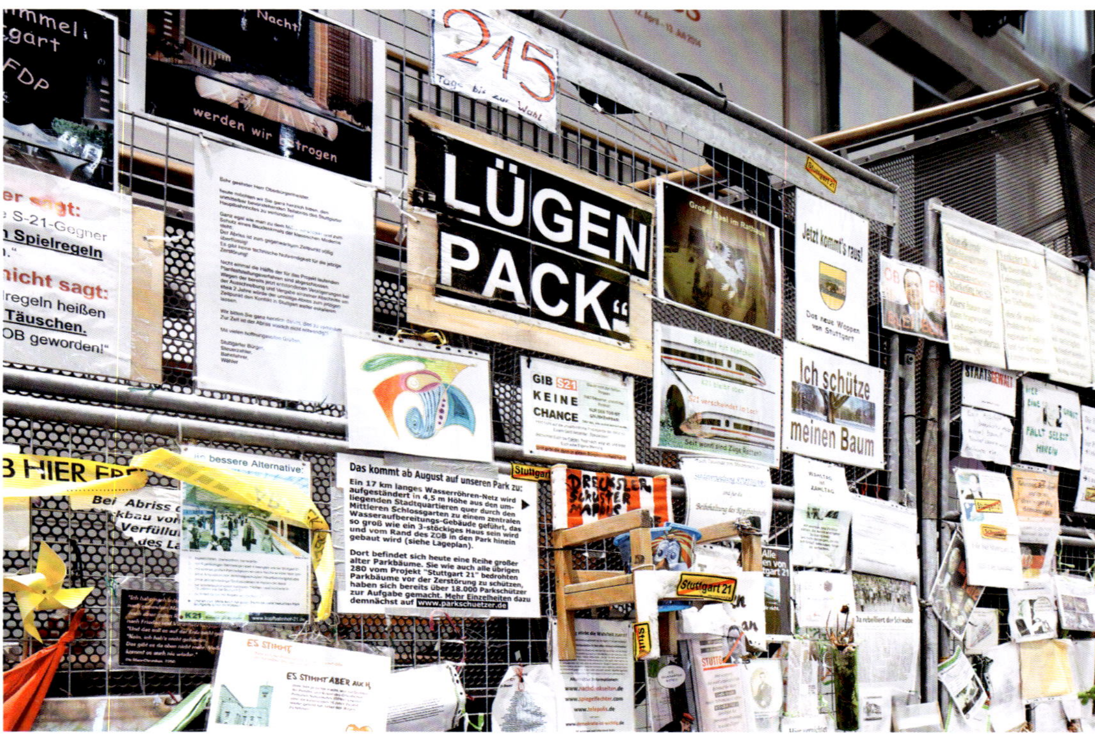

Part of the Stuttgart 21 construction site fence, 2010, installation, mixed media, installation view, ZKM | Karlsruhe, 2014. The barrier was erected in the summer of 2010 to cordon off the demolition work on the north wing of Stuttgart's main station and shortly afterwards was covered in messages of protest by opponents of the Stuttgart 21 project.

Although there have been protests against the project since the planning began in 1996, only since 2010 has the protest movement gained nation-wide attention through mass demonstrations with tens of thousands of citizens as well as other protest actions. After a massive escalation of violence on the part of the authorities, mediation talks between project proponents and opponents were held, which were broadcast live on the Internet and on television.

The protests against Stuttgart 21 influenced the change of government in Baden-Württemberg after the regional elections of 2011 and the election of the first Green mayor of a state capital in October 2012. Although a referendum at the end of 2011 ended with the decision that the state of Baden-Württemberg should continue to finance the project, and in the meantime national media coverage of the protests has subsided, the various alliances are still active and report about the latest developments on their websites, and the Monday demonstrations continue.

Two young filmmakers, Lisa Sperling (*1986) and Florian Kläger (*1987), joined the protest movement in early 2010. At some point they started to take a camera on the rallies – initially for purely private purposes. Later, the idea arose to turn this material into a feature-length documentary. In *Stuttgart 21 – Denk mal!* [Stuttgart 21 – Think to Remember!] the young directors go looking for the faces of protest, and deliver – supported by mentor and producer Peter Rommel – a thrilling chronology of events from January to December 2010, as well as illustrate the people involved in the protest, many of whom one would not expect to see there. The film has been screened at various venues including at the 2011 Berlin International Film Festival in the section showcasing next generation German filmmakers, Perspektive Deutsches Kino [Perspectives of German Cinema].

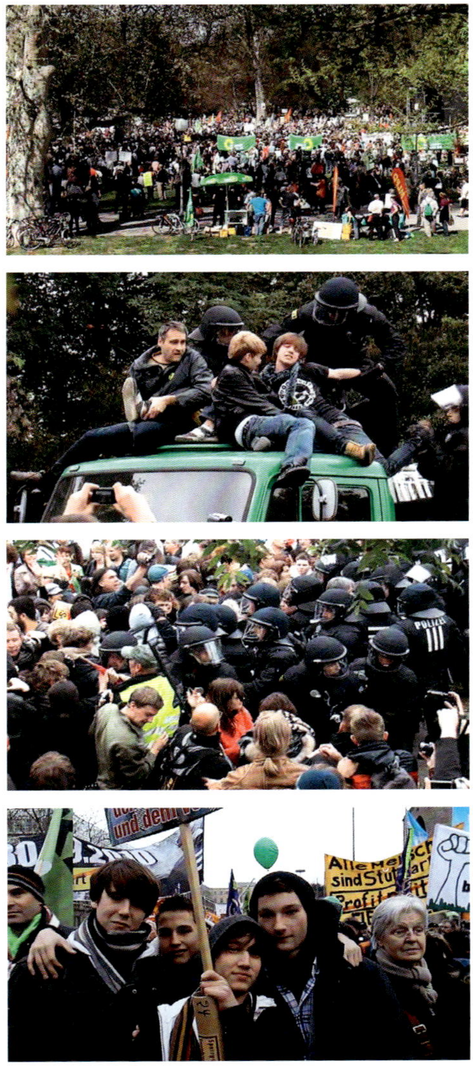

Lisa Sperling and Florian Kläger, *Stuttgart 21 – Denk mal!*, 2011, video, color, sound, 75:00 min, video stills

Founded in 2011
Ireland

www.rabble.ie

rabble

The nonprofit newspaper from Dublin's underground is an alternative, free medium that reports on and from inside the city. Collectively and independently run by volunteers, it cultivates critical and provocative journalism that seeks to question existing structures and to foster developments that will contribute to making the Irish capital a better place to live in the aftermath of the financial crisis.

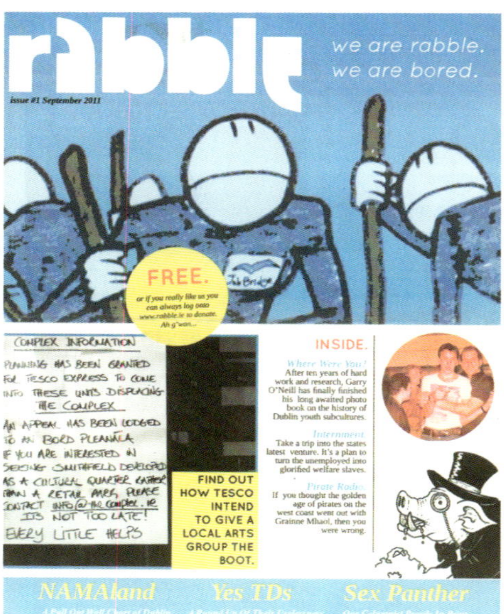

rabble, vol. 1, September 2011

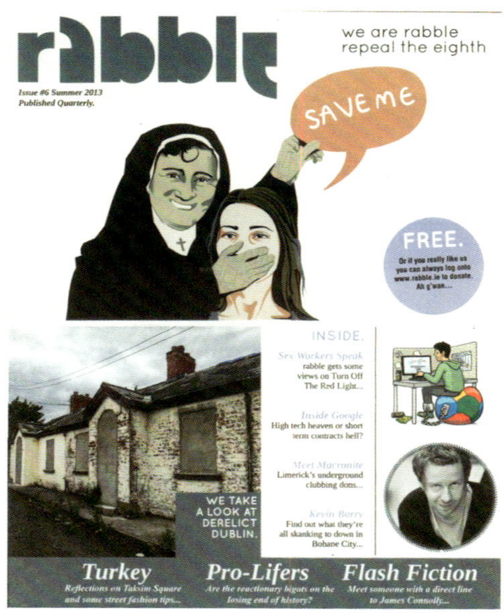

rabble, vol. 6, Summer 2013

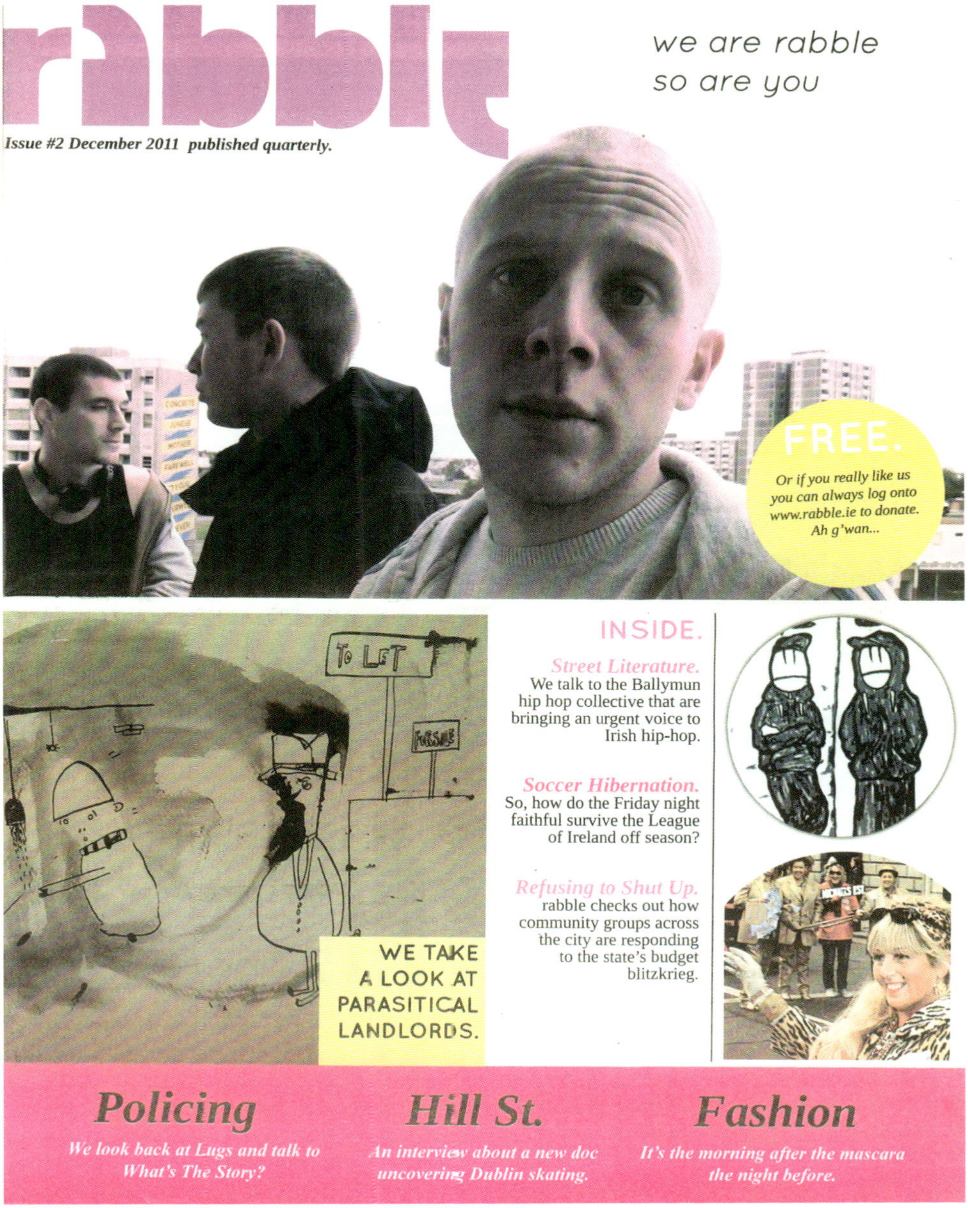

rabble

we are rabble
so are you

Issue #2 December 2011 published quarterly.

FREE.
Or if you really like us you can always log onto www.rabble.ie to donate. Ah g'wan...

INSIDE.

Street Literature.
We talk to the Ballymun hip hop collective that are bringing an urgent voice to Irish hip-hop.

Soccer Hibernation.
So, how do the Friday night faithful survive the League of Ireland off season?

Refusing to Shut Up.
rabble checks out how community groups across the city are responding to the state's budget blitzkrieg.

WE TAKE A LOOK AT PARASITICAL LANDLORDS.

Policing
We look back at Lugs and talk to What's The Story?

Hill St.
An interview about a new doc uncovering Dublin skating.

Fashion
It's the morning after the mascara the night before.

rabble, vol. 2, December 2011

Founded in 2008
Global

www.resistnetwork.com

Resist

Via Resist, filmmakers, producers, and partners can organize, who desire to draw attention to grievances in documentary films. The network stands for the principle that well-told stories, which are freely accessible on the Internet, raise awareness and in this way are able to trigger social change. Users are explicitly invited to share their ideas and to draw attention to worthwhile projects that otherwise will not gain recognition or an audience.

Using the combined powers of film and the Internet, to date Resist has initiated the development of several documentaries, including, for example, the four-part series *The Invisibles: A Hidden Journey across Mexico* (2010) by Marc Silver and Gael García Bernal, a project documenting the very dangerous journey of thousands of migrants, who travel annually through Mexico in the hope of reaching the USA, where their dreams of a better life all too often turn into nightmares, and Nick Francis and Marc Silver's *A Life on Hold* (2012), an intimate portrait of Omar, a 17-year-old Somali stranded in a refugee camp in Tunisia since the 2011 war in Libya. Both projects were produced in collaboration with Amnesty International.

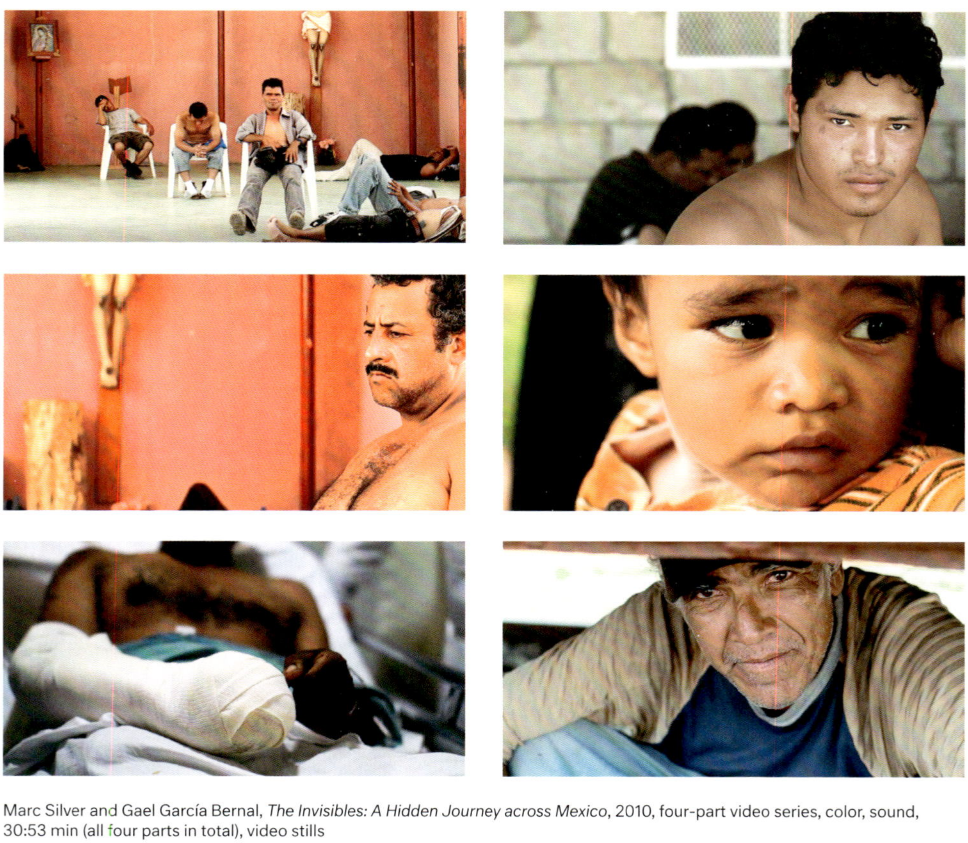

Marc Silver and Gael García Bernal, *The Invisibles: A Hidden Journey across Mexico*, 2010, four-part video series, color, sound, 30:53 min (all four parts in total), video stills

Marc Silver and Gael García Bernal's documentary *Who Is Dayani Cristal?* (2013) retraces the invisible steps of an unknown man found dead in the so-called "corridor of death" in the U.S.–Mexico borderland of the Sonoran Desert. It seeks to answer the questions, who he was, what brought him there, and how he died, and gives this John Doe an identity. The film was part of the official selection of the 51st New York Film Festival in 2013 and was awarded the World Cinema Documentary Award at the 2013 Sundance Film Festival.

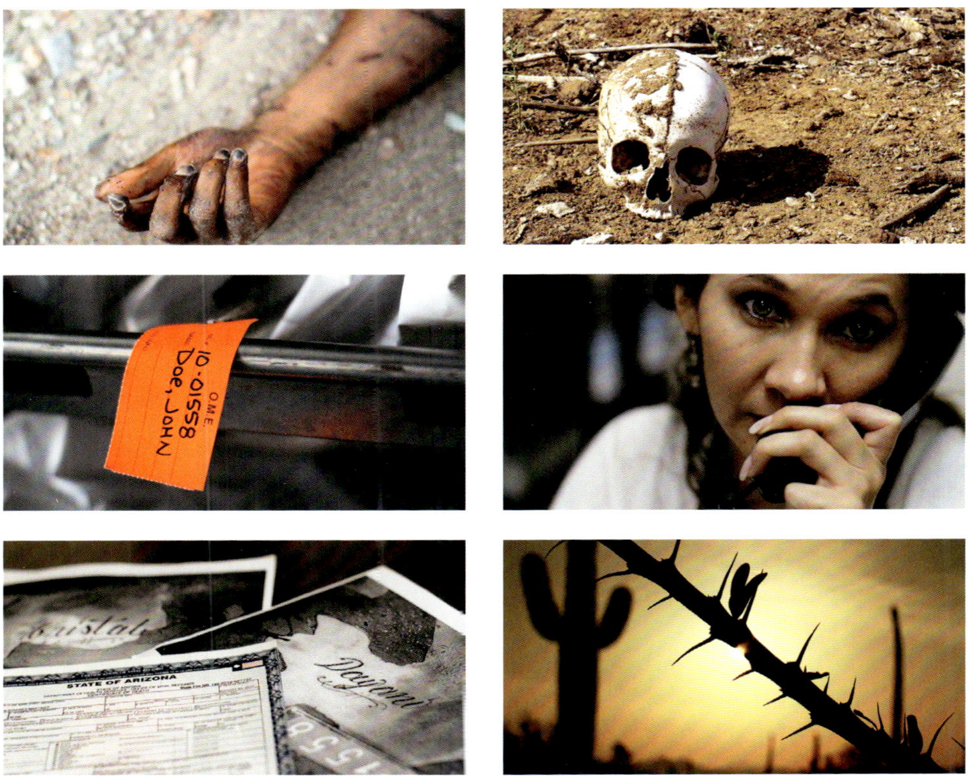

Marc Silver, *Who Is Dayani Cristal?*, 2013, video, color, sound, 85:00 min, video stills

Mykola Ridnyi *1985

Mykola Ridnyi was born in Kharkiv, Ukraine, where he currently lives and works. In 2005, he became cofounder and curator of the SOSka gallery–laboratory, an artist-run space for developing the local culture sphere in Kharkiv. In 2008, he graduated from the Kharkiv State Academy of Design and Arts. In his works, which often combine installation, video, and sculpture, he reflects critically on the sociopolitical context of the post-Soviet environment. Both with the SOSka group and as an individual artist, Ridnyi organizes protests in public places in Kharkiv and Kiev to draw attention to social grievances.

With his action *Lay and Wait* in front of the German Embassy in Kiev on September 4, 2006, for example, he protested against the restrictive allocation of visas by the European Union, which he branded as the intrusion of politics in the life of an artist. His action was the reaction to a series of unsuccessful attempts to visit Europe, which had all – even when invited to his own exhibitions – ended with rejection of the visa applications. The reaction of the artist to this paradoxical situation was: If there is nothing to lose, one can simply lie down on the sidewalk in front of the embassy and wait.

Ridnyi has taken part in several residence programs: at the Center for Contemporary Art in Kiev (2006), at the Santa Fe Art Institute (a CEC ArtsLink residency, 2010), and in Berlin, supported by the German Academic Exchange Service (DAAD) (2014). He has also exhibited at various solo and group exhibitions, including at the PinchukArtCentre in Kiev (2006), the Ukrainian Institute of Modern Art in Chicago (2008), the Centro d'Arte Contemporanea Castello di Rivara in Turin (2009), the Slag Gallery in New York (2010), the Moscow Museum of Modern Art (2011), the ZKM | Center for Art and Media Karlsruhe (2011, 2013), the Museum of Modern Art in Warsaw (2012, 2013), and the daadgalerie in Berlin (2014).
In 2011, Ridnyi was shortlisted for the PinchukArtCentre Prize.

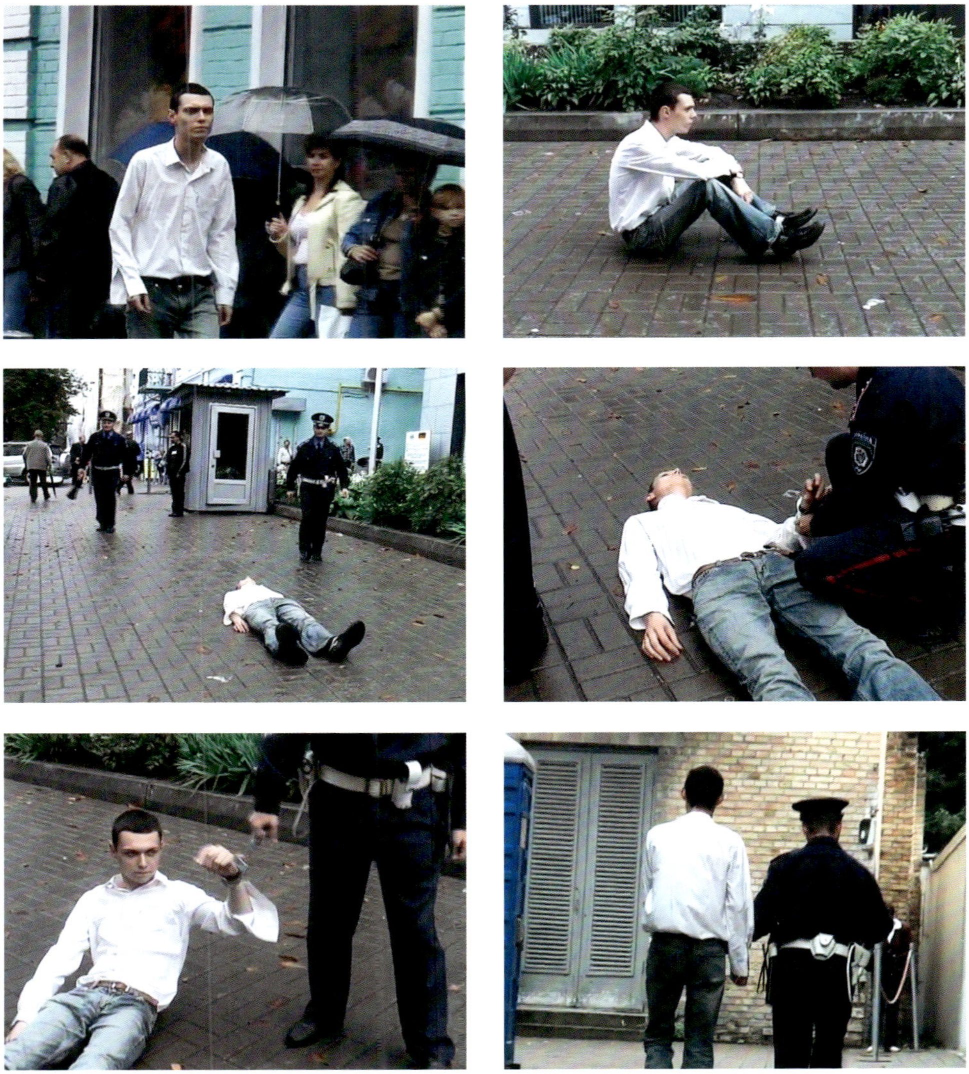

Mykola Ridnyi, *Lay and Wait*, 2006, video documentation of the action, color, sound, 4:45 min, video stills

Founded in 1982
Germany

www.robinwood.de

ROBIN WOOD

The German environmental organization ROBIN WOOD, which – inspired by the legendary Robin Hood – describes itself as the "Rächer der Entlaubten" [avenger of the bare branches], was founded in 1982 to take action against the ongoing dieback of forests. With its creative and nonviolent protests, in which volunteer activists work closely with full-time staff, ROBIN WOOD not only engages in forest protection, but is also active in related areas such as energy and traffic. Since its foundation, ROBIN WOOD has developed from a spontaneous assembly to a professional environmental advocacy organization operating nationwide.

The members organize in regional groups from which delegates are elected, who meet two or three times a year to decide on the campaigns, strategies, and major expenditure in a direct democratic way. Environmental demands are supported by attention-grabbing demonstrations and public protests. ROBIN WOOD also publishes information about its activities and on important themes connected with protecting the environment and nature in its quarterly magazine and its monthly newsletter. ROBIN WOOD is recognized as a charity. To ensure it remains independent, it is financed exclusively by membership fees and donations.

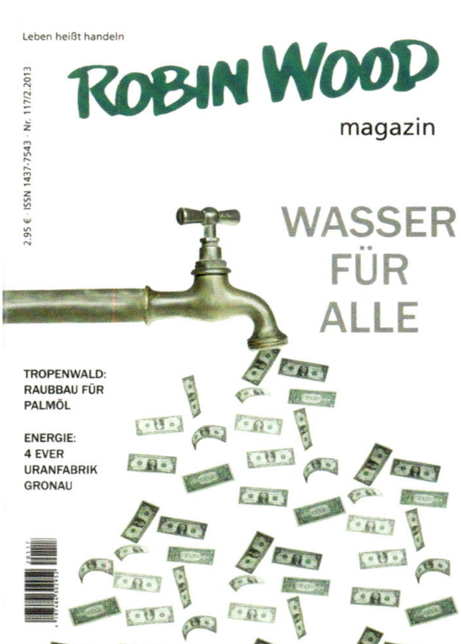

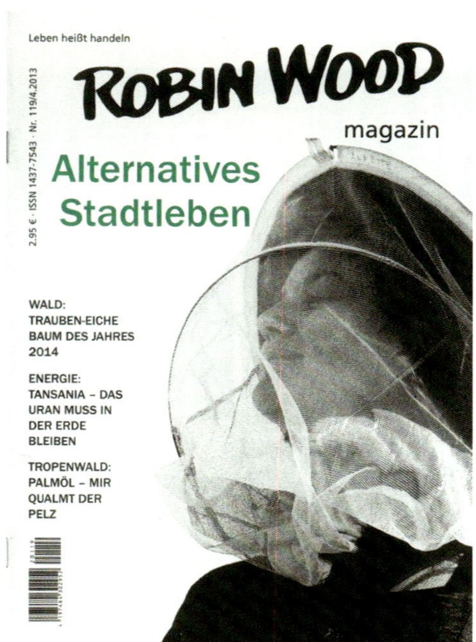

ROBIN WOOD magazin, vol. 117, no. 2, 2013 and vol. 119, no. 4, 2013

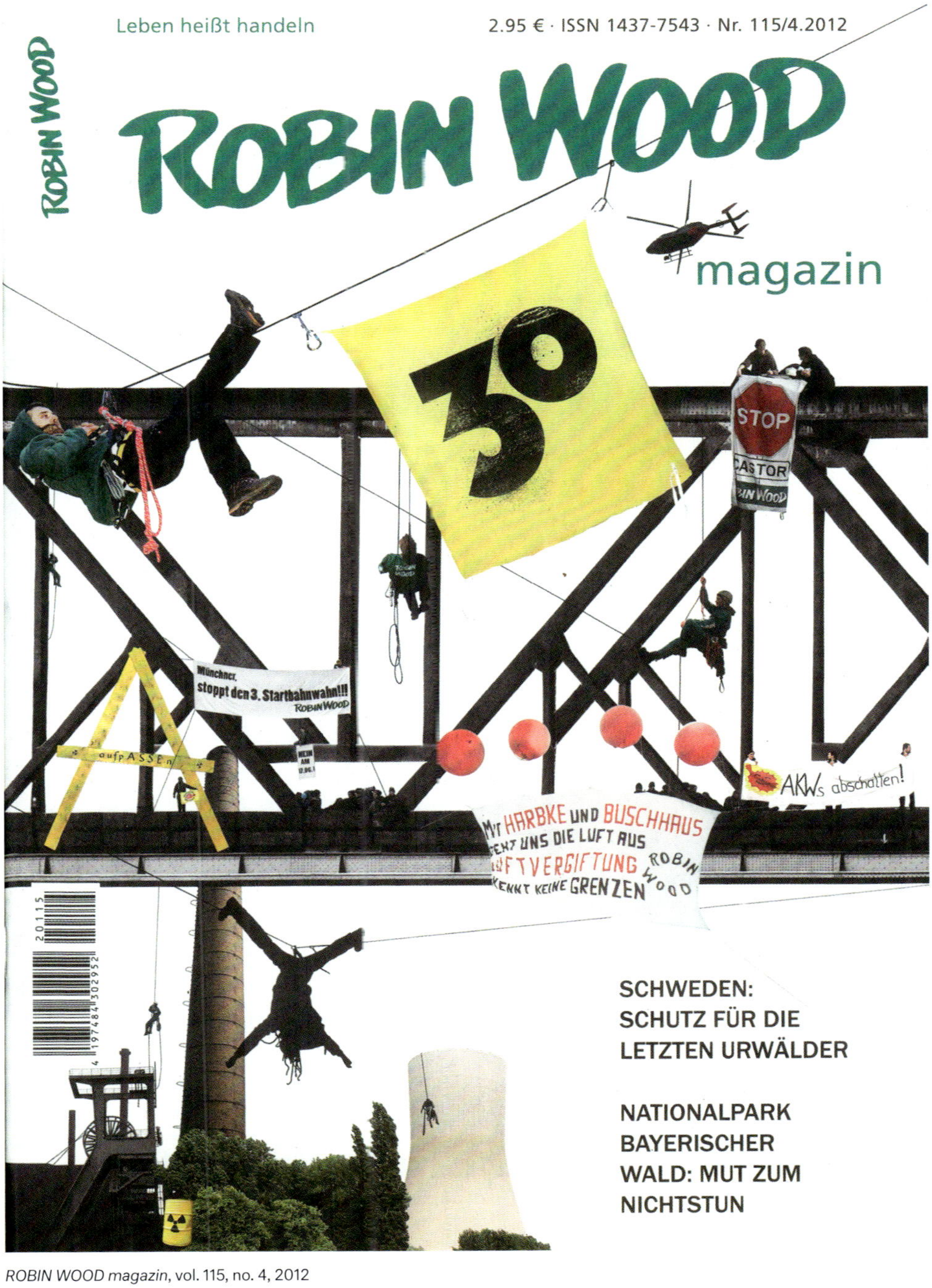

ROBIN WOOD magazin, vol. 115, no. 4, 2012

Faten Rouissi *1967

Faten Rouissi is a multidisciplinary artist and assistant professor of visual arts at the National School of Architecture and Urban Design (ENAU) in Tunis. A major focus of her work involves the question of how new artistic and aesthetic forces can be generated, which foster the collective dynamics of the everyday life of Tunisians at a time when Tunisia urgently needs such forces. For several years, Rouissi has been involved in collaborations between artists and the public in the context of participatory actions, and she belongs to the various artists, who – especially since the revolution in 2011 – use public or virtual space for graffiti, photography, installations, performances, happenings, videos, and painting. In her opinion, the present time is a fruitful one for creations on walls and public spaces to counter the crisis as well as the anxieties and concerns of the people. Shortly after the Tunisian Revolution in February 2011, for example, she made an artistic intervention with cars that had been burned in the course of the revolutionary struggle. In the 2013 photo series *Revolution in Tunisia*, she documented the preparations being made for actions at the Place du Bardo in Tunis on Women's Day (August 13), when there was a large demonstration against the Islamists' exercise of power, as well as political graffiti on the walls of buildings in Tunis. At the Dak'Art 2014, the 11th Biennial of Contemporary African Art, Rouissi received the prize of the city of Dakar.

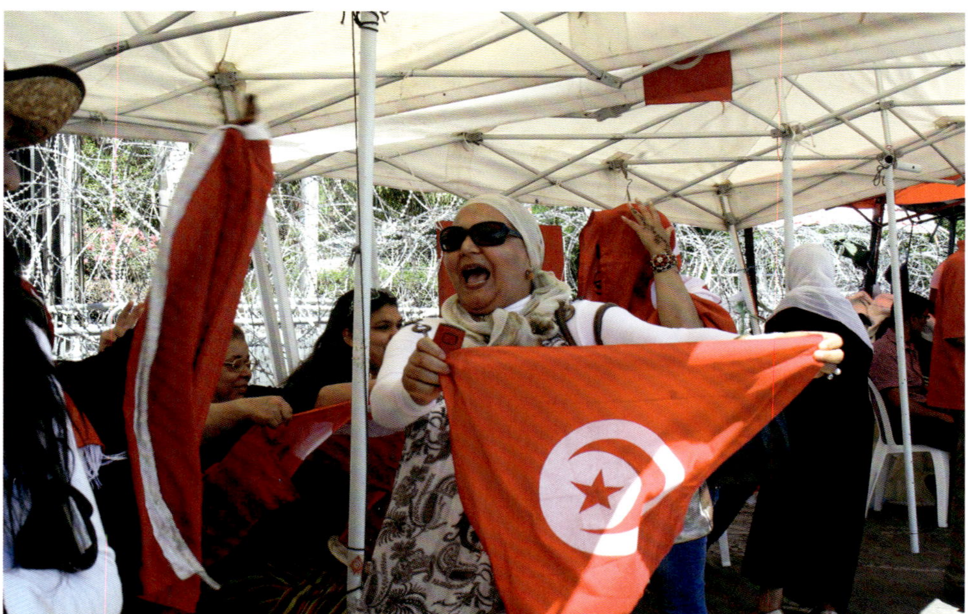

Faten Rouissi, from the photo series *Revolution in Tunisia*, 2013

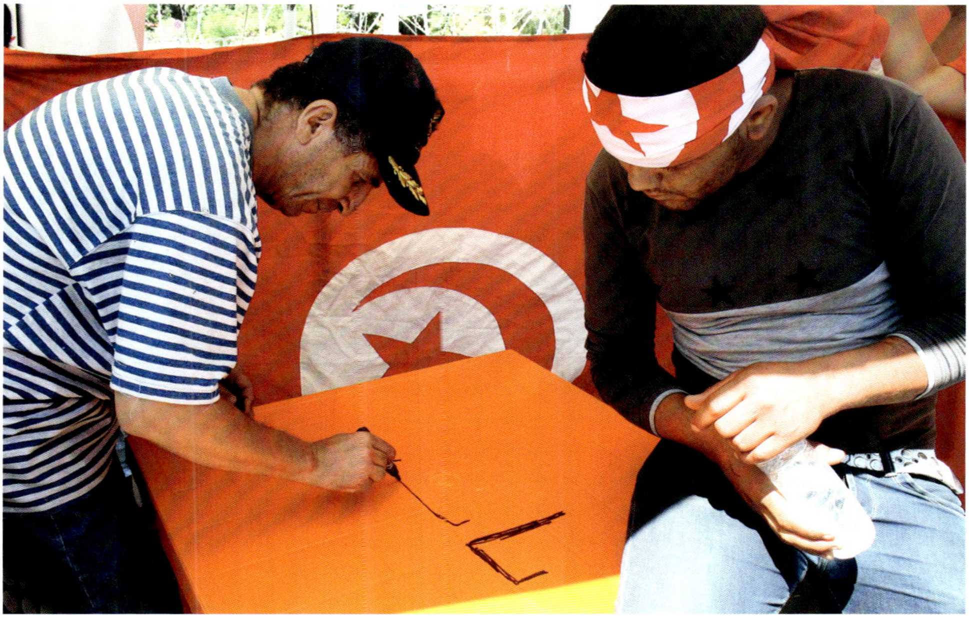

Faten Rouissi, from the photo series *Revolution in Tunisia*, 2013

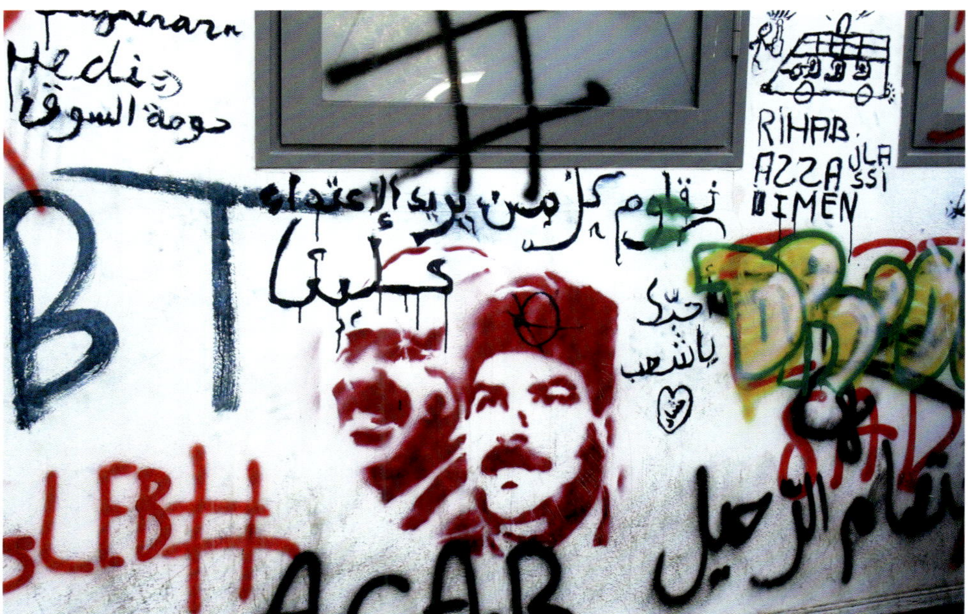

Faten Rouissi, from the photo series *Revolution in Tunisia*, 2013

STOP THE TRAFFIK

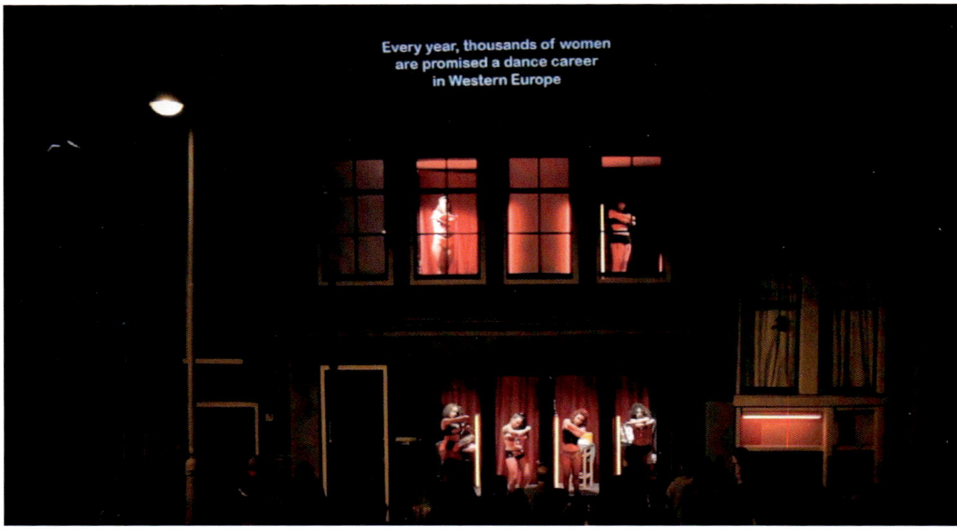

STOP THE TRAFFIK, *So you think you will dance*, 2012, video by Duval Guillaume, color, sound, 1:42 min, video still

The independent charity STOP THE TRAFFIK describes itself as a global movement against human trafficking, which means being deceived or taken against your will, bought and sold for sexual exploitation, forced labor, street crime, domestic servitude, or even the sale of organs and human sacrifice. In order to build a traffick-free world, the organization works on many different levels, from individual activist initiatives to large-scale campaigning, and equips people with information to understand what trafficking is, how and where it happens, in which way it affects them, and what every individual person can do about it. This information is available on their website in various forms. On an activist map, for example, one can get an overview about the latest events around the world or the activities in one's direct vicinity. From the main page the users can also access the websites of STOP THE TRAFFIK divisions in several countries.

STOP THE TRAFFIK stages many spectacular actions, such as *So you think you will dance*, initiated by the Netherlands division in the red light district of Amsterdam, ironically referring to the title of a popular TV program. Since the beginning the work of STOP THE TRAFFIK has been accompanied by the United Nations. Thus, the charity took part in UN.GIFT, the United Nations Global Initiative to Fight Human Trafficking, and in 2009 both launched Start Freedom together, a campaign to educate young people about human trafficking.

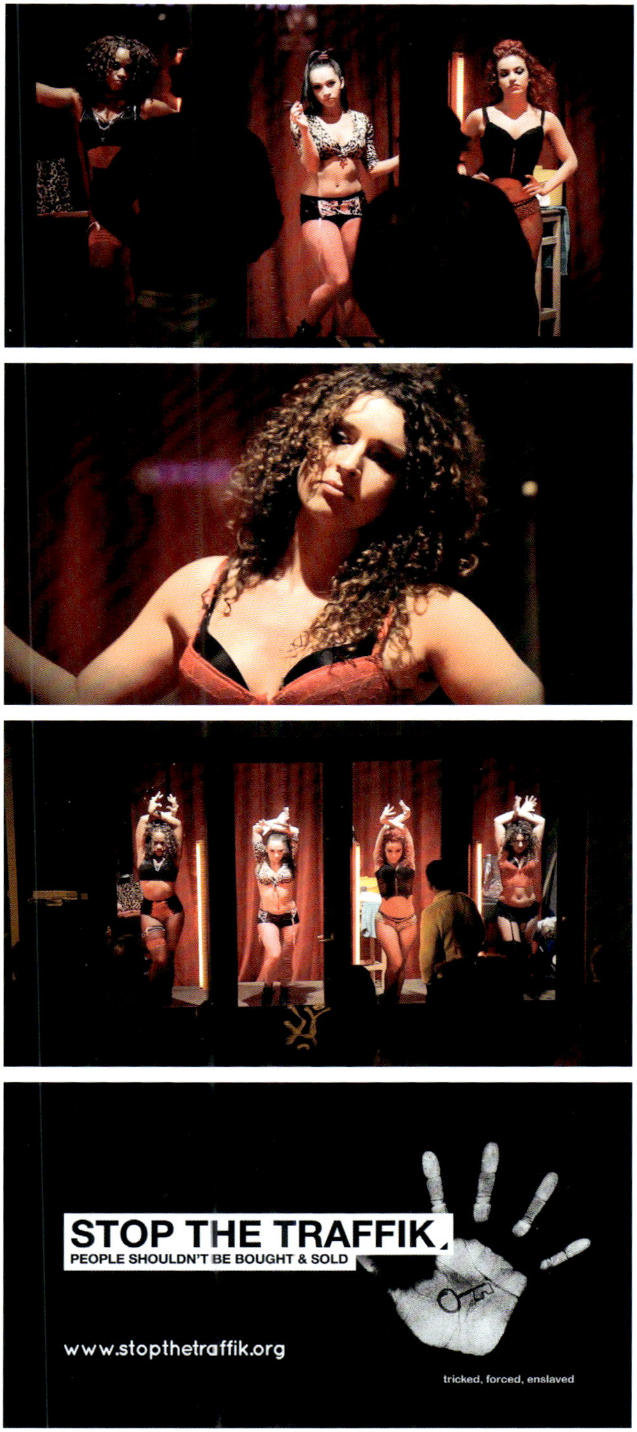

STOP THE TRAFFIK, *So you think you will dance*, 2012, video by Duval Guillaume, color, sound, 1:42 min, video stills

Tanya Sushenkova *1978

As a photographer, Tanya Sushenkova shoots activists' actions, rallies, political and artistic activities. As an artist, she creates her own performances, objects, installations, photos, and so on. She always tries to do this work at the edge of the street and institutions. Although she describes herself as an anarchist and a feminist, she is actually of the opinion that all labels and definitions, which limit the people and how they are understood, are censorship and prison – whether external or internal. Men get the best results for their actions, with support for their opinions and purposes, without deviating for imaginary values (for example, social roles, unnecessary products/services, money) that are not suited to them. In work and in life, Sushenkova supports the fight for human rights. She is against the effects of force – both physical and manipulative. She fights against the patriarchal system with its system of hierarchies and the unhealthy competition it imposes, which in her opinion inspires fear instead of nurturing self-awareness and self-responsibility.

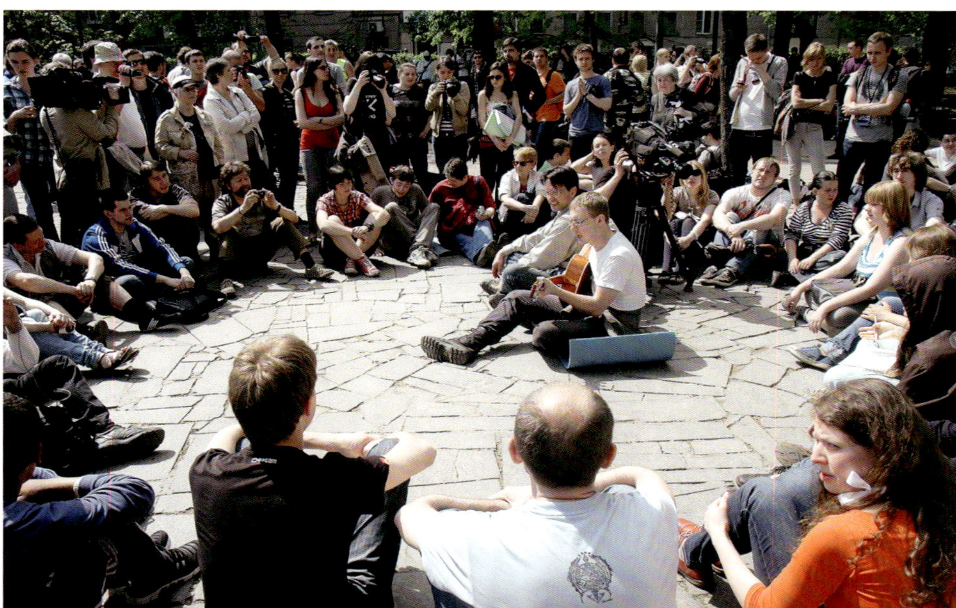

Tanya Sushenkova, from the photo series *Occupy Abbai*, 2012

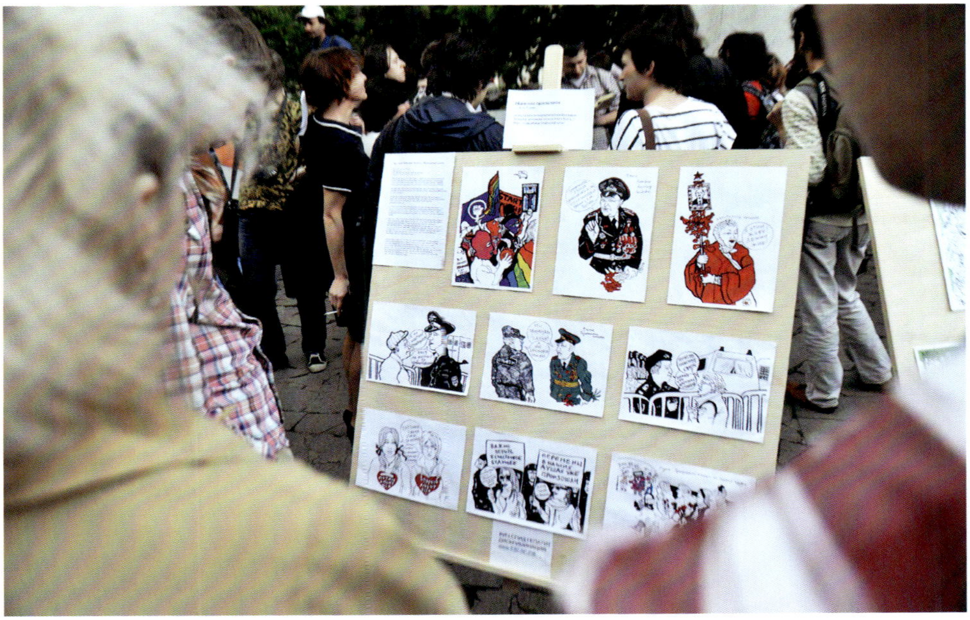

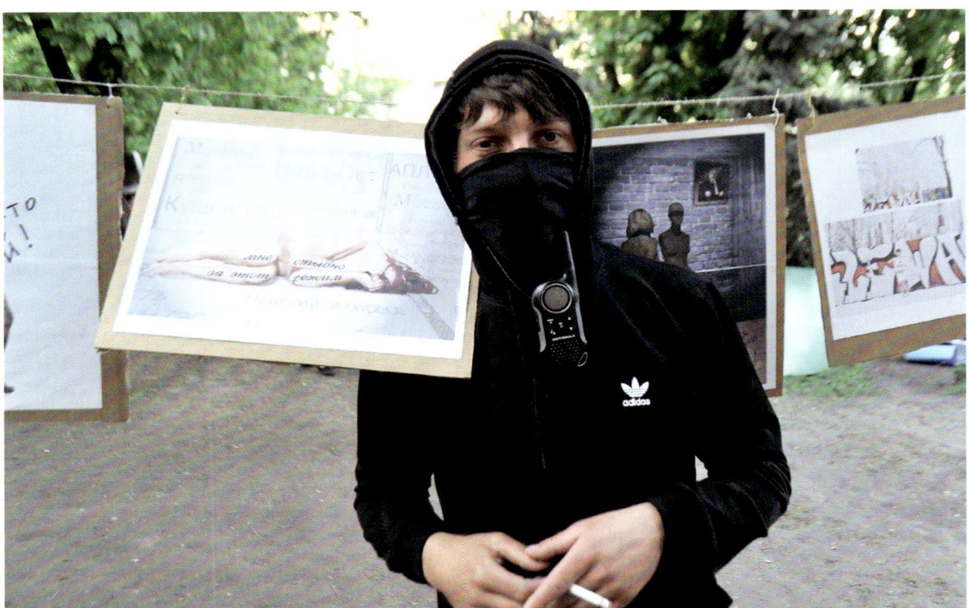

Tanya Sushenkova, from the photo series *Occupy Abai*, 2012

Founded in 1960
Global

www.terredeshommes.org

Terre des Hommes

The child aid organization Terre des Hommes (TDH) was founded in 1960 in Lausanne, Switzerland, as a nonprofit organization according to Articles 60 and following of the Swiss Civil Code. It works for the rights of children and to promote equitable development without racial, religious, political, cultural, or gender-based discrimination. Today the Terre des Hommes International Federation connects autonomous national TDH organizations in Canada, Denmark, France, Germany, Italy, Luxembourg, the Netherlands, Spain, and Switzerland. An international secretariat ensures coordination among these national branches, as well as representation at an international and European level. The main goals are the fight against malnutrition, child labor, child trafficking and prostitution, and the abuse of children as soldiers. The organization, which is active in around 65 countries all over the world, supports local initiatives and helps with the construction of schools and protection centers for children, for example. An annual report informs about the structure of Terre des Hommes, its working methods, as well as its activities and results. As working in alliances is an important feature in the strategy of the organization, it is part of several global and European children's rights networks.

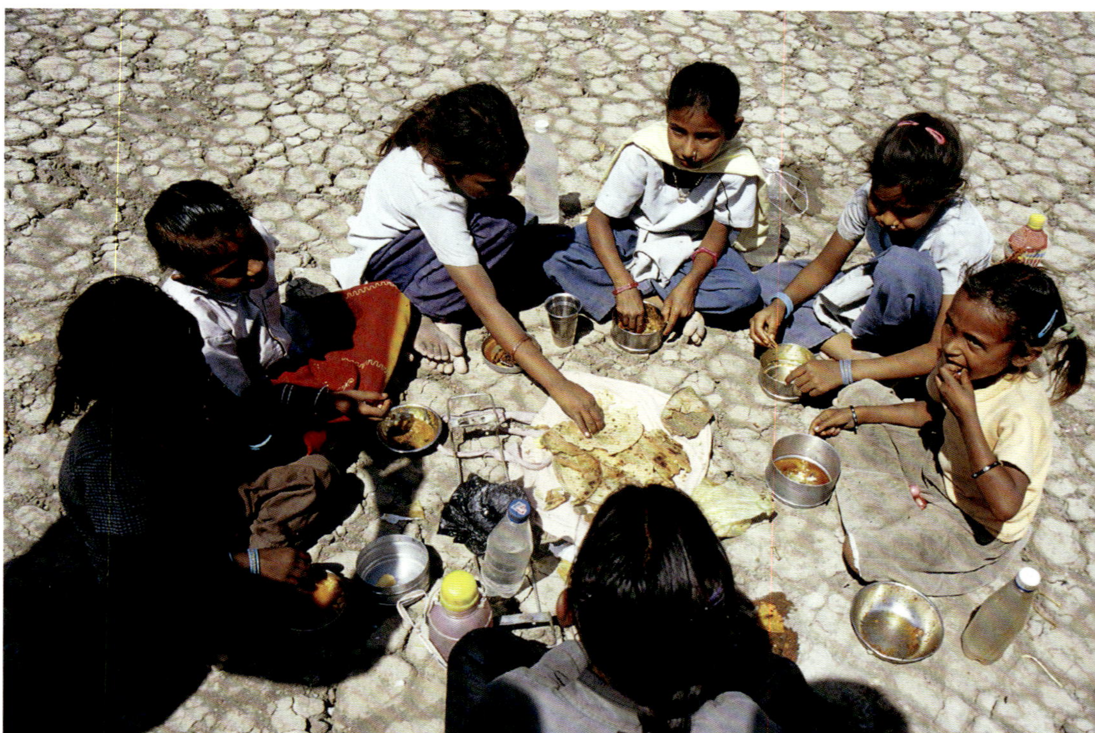

Commitment to children's ecological rights in India

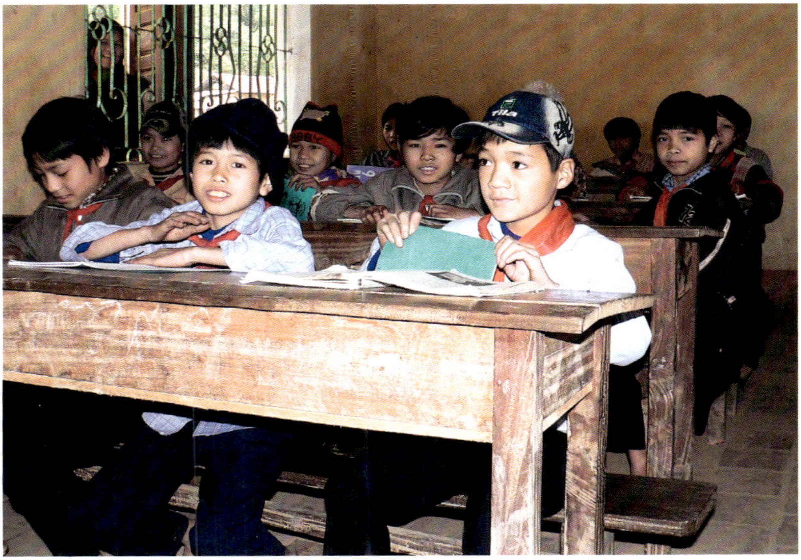

Promotion of educational programs in Vietnam

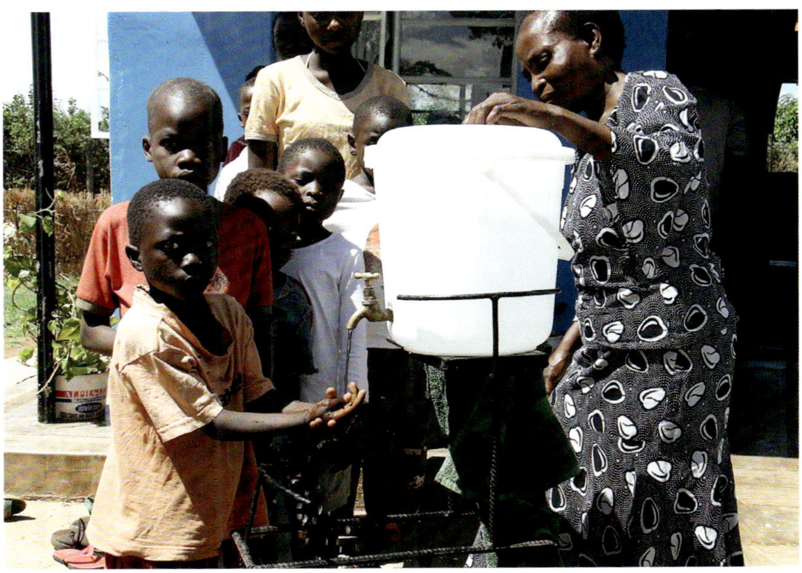

Supply of fresh drinking water in Zambia

The Yes Men

The Yes Men is an internationally known mischief-making collective created by Jacques Servin and Igor Vamos. Its unique brand of activism, which the members call "identity correction," is documented in two award-winning films, *The Yes Men* (2004) and *The Yes Men Fix the World* (2009).

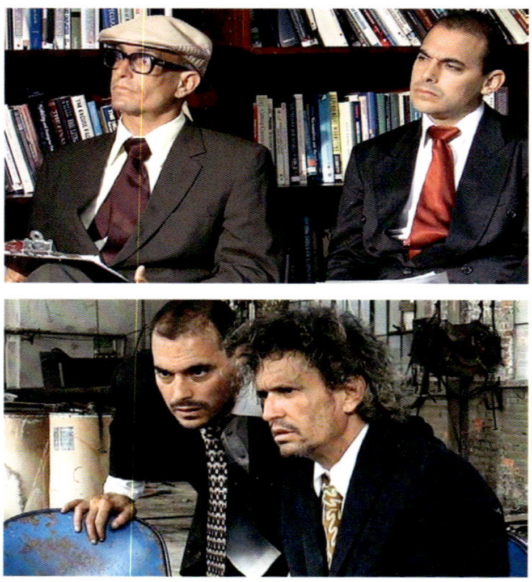

Andy Bichlbaum and Mike Bonanno (alias names of Servin and Vamos), *The Yes Men Fix the World*, 2009, film, color, sound, 87:00 min, film stills

Armed with nothing but thrift store suits, The Yes Men impersonate big-time corporate criminals (targets have included such heavyweights as the World Trade Organization, Dow Chemical, Exxon Mobil, and Halliburton) in order to draw attention to their crimes against humanity and the environment. They have discovered that delivering hard-boiled issues with huge dollops of laughter is a powerful way to reach mainstream audiences. Their low-budget actions have drawn regular coverage from all the major news outlets (*The New York Times*, CNN, Reuters, AP, AFP, BBC, NPR, and more). This means that normally underreported issues get highlighted, such as Dow Chemical's attempts to evade responsibility for the Bhopal chemical plant disaster, the U.S. Chamber of Commerce's attempts to kill climate legislation, and the U.S. government's shuttering of available low-income housing in post-Katrina New Orleans.

One of the most spectacular actions was the distribution of a fake edition of *The New York Times* on November 12, 2008. The issue, dated July 4, 2009, drew a picture of a better world in which the Iraq War has ended, George W. Bush will be accused of high treason, and Condoleezza Rice has publicly apologized for lying about the Iraq War.

In order to have social justice organizations benefit from what The Yes Men have learned in the past few years – not only in terms of their own actions and approaches, but those they have come in contact with – they initiated the Yes Lab with a full-time office at the Hemispheric Institute of Performance and Politics at New York University. It seeks to involve students as well as activists in several projects and activities, and to provide assistance to progressive organizations and activists in implementing actions with great media attention. On the accompanying website users not only read about Yes Lab projects, they can also sign up as potential participants, learn techniques for causing trouble, and arrange to host a Yes Lab at their own university.

The Yes Men, *The New York Times Special Edition*, 2008

"All the News We Hope to Print"

The New York Times

Special Edition
Today, clouds part, more sunshine, recent gloom passes. **Tonight,** strong leftward winds. **Tomorrow,** a new day. Weather map throughout.

VOL. CLVIV . . No. 54,631 — NEW YORK, SATURDAY, JULY 4, 2009 — FREE

IRAQ WAR ENDS

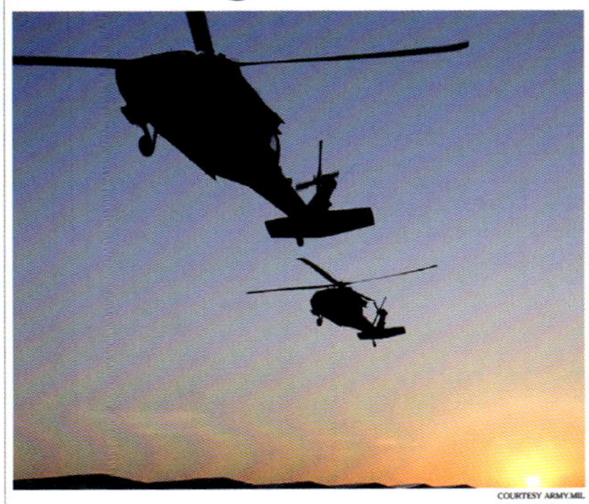

COURTESY ARMY.MIL

U.S. Army helicopters begin moving troops and equipment from Saddam Hussein's former Baghdad palace.

Troops to Return Immediately

By JUDE SHINBIN

WASHINGTON — Operation Iraqi Freedom and Operation Enduring Freedom were brought to an unceremonious close today with a quiet announcement by the Department of Defense that troops would be home within weeks.

"This is the best face we can put on the most unfortunate adventure in modern American history," Defense spokesman Kevin Sites said at a special joint session of Congress. "Today, we can finally enjoy peace — not the peace of the brave, perhaps, but at least peace."

As U.S. and coalition troops withdraw from Iraq and Afghanistan, the United Nations will move in to perform peacekeeping duties and aid in rebuilding. The U.N. will be responsible for keeping the two countries stable; coordinating the rebuilding of hospitals, schools, highways, and other infrastructure; and overseeing upcoming elections.

The Department of the Treasury confirmed that all U.N. dues owed by the U.S. were paid as of this morning, and that moneys previously earmarked for the war would be sent directly to the U.N.'s Iraq Oversight Body.

The president noted that the Iraq War had resulted in the burning of many bridges. "Yet our history with our allies runs deep," he said, "and we all know that friends forgive friends for anything. Or nearly." A spokesperson for the French Ministry of Defense confirmed that France would assist the U.S. withdrawal. "The U.S. helped the Soviet Union defeat Hitler. We do recognize that."

In conflict zones worldwide, leaders and rebels pledged peace. (See "In Conflict Zones Worldwide, Peace Moves," on Page A4.)

On Wall Street, reactions were mixed, with the Dow Jones Industrial Average up 84 points, to close at 4,212. While KBR stock was quickly downgraded to a "junk" rating of BBB-, defense contractors such as Lockheed Martin and Northrop Grummon started up.

Continued on Page A5

Nation Sets Its Sights on Building Sane Economy

True Cost Tax, Salary Caps, Trust-Busting Top List

By T. VEBLEN

The President has called for swift passage of the Safeguards for a New Economy (S.A.N.E.) bill. The omnibus economic package includes a federal maximum wage, mandatory "True Cost Accounting," a phased withdrawal from complex financial instruments, and other measures intended to improve life for ordinary Americans. (See highlights box on Page A10.) He also repeated earlier calls for passage of the "Ban on Lobbying" bill currently making its way through Congress.

Treasury Secretary Paul Krugman stressed the importance of the bill. "Markets make great servants, terrible leaders, and absurd religions," said Krugman, quoting Paul Hawken, an advocate of corporate responsibility and author of "Blessed Unrest, How the Largest Movement in the World Came into Being and Why No One Saw It Coming."

"At this point, the market is our leader and our religion. No wonder the median standard of living has been declining so much for so long."

Krugman said that the new Treasury bill seeks to ensure the prosperity of all citizens, rather than simply supporting large coporations and the wealthy. "The market is supposed to serve us. Unfortunately, we have ended up serving the market. That's very bad."

Much as Roosevelt, after the Great Depression, put the brakes on C.E.O. wages and irresponsible banking practices, administration officials claim that today we need to rein in the industry that has caused such chaos and misery.

"The building blocks of post World War II American middle class prosperity have all been swept away," said House Speaker Nancy Pelosi, who initially op

Continued on Page A10

Maximum Wage Law Succeeds

Salary Caps Will Help Stabilize Economy

By J.K. MALONE

WASHINGTON — After long and often bitter debate, Congress has passed legislation, fiercely fought for by labor and progressive groups, that will limit top salaries to fifteen times the minimum wage. Tying the bill to a plan of overall reform of the U.S. economy, the bill echoes a similar effort enacted by President Franklin Roosevelt in 1942, which was followed by the longest period of growth for the middle class in U.S. history.

"When C.E.O. salaries remain stable thanks to high taxation of high salaries, there's little incentive to take big risks with shareholders' money, and the economy remains in a steady growth mode," said Senator Barney Frank, one of the bill's co-sponsors. "But when C.E.O. salaries can fly through the roof, there's a very strong incentive for C.E.O.s

Continued on Page A10

TREASURY ANNOUNCES "TRUE COST" TAX PLAN

By MARCUS S. DRIGGS

The long-awaited "True Cost" plan, which requires product prices to reflect their cost to society, has been signed into law.

Beginning next month, throwaway items like plastic water bottles and other items which are wasteful or damaging to the environment will be heavily taxed, as in many developed countries. Steep taxes will also apply to large cars and gasoline.

The new plan calls for a 200 percent tax on gasoline, comparable to the one long in effect in most European countries. Companies and consumers are already switching in droves from inefficient gas vehicles to new electric cars. "We suddenly have a waiting list 200 names long for the EV1," said Jake Cluber, the owner of Cluber Chevrolet in

Continued on Page A10

Recruiters Train for New Life
As a ban is imposed on recruiting minors, ex-recruiters nationwide look for new work. The Times follows one on his job-hunt odyssey through Manhattan and surrounding areas.
BY BARRY GLOAD, PAGE A12

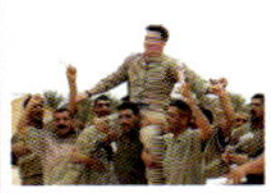

Last to Die
Two proportional monuments — one to the Iraqi dead, 300 feet high, and one to the American dead, 15 feet high — are unveiled in Baghdad, and a five-year-old boy whose lifespan coincided with that of the Iraq War is remembered.
BY J. FINISTERRA, PAGE A5

USA Patriot Act Repealed
Eight years later, a shamefaced Congress quietly repeals the much-maligned USA Patriot Act, unanimously… or almost.
BY SYBIL LUDINGTON, PAGE A8

Evangelicals Open Homes to Refugees
Up to a million Iraqi exiles — nearly half of the total — will find sanctuary in Christian homes across the U.S., vows the National Association of Evangelicals. Other denominations are expected to follow.
BY W. WILBERFORCE, PAGE A7

Public Relations Industry Starts to Shut Down
The public relations industry has been criticized for misleading the American people, corrupting politicians, and even helping to start wars. Now, it's beginning the process of shutting down for good.
BY LOUIS BECK, PAGE A10

Ex-Secretary Apologizes for W.M.D. Scare

300,000 Troops Never Faced Risk of Instant Obliteration

By FRANK LARIMORE

Ex-Secretary of State Condoleeza Rice reassured soldiers that the Bush Administration had known well before the invasion that Saddam Hussein lacked weapons of mass destruction.

"Now that all of you brave servicemen and women are returning, it's important to us to reassure you, and the American people, that we were certain Hussein had no W.M.D.s and that he would never launch a first strike against the U.S.," Ms. Rice told a group of wounded soldiers at a Veterans' Administration hospital yesterday.

"I want you to know that if we had had the slightest suspicion that Saddam could use W.M.D.s against you, we never would have sent hundreds of thousands of you to be sitting ducks on the Iraqi border for several months."

Mr. Rice was referring to the fact that by August 2002, eight months before the ground invasion, the US had over 100,000 troops stationed in countries throughout the Gulf, a number that grew to over 300,000 shortly before the 2003 attack on Baghdad. Most of these were within range of the Scud missiles used by Mr. Hussein in the 1991 Gulf War, that could easily have been fitted with chemical or biological weapons if they had existed.

Rice noted that in the 1991 Gulf War, Hussein had used missiles to launch attacks on Israel, which made him popular with Arab citizens throughout the Middle East.

"Do you really think we would have given Saddam a major public relations coup by allowing him to annihilate tens of thousands of you right there on holy territory?" asked Ms. Rice.

Former Secretary of State Henry A. Kissinger responded to Ms. Rice's revelation without surprise. "Of course this was the case. When Israel believed Iraq had nuclear weapons in 1981, they didn't attack on the ground — they bombed from the air. That's a preemptive attack. If you believe deterrence will not prevent an attack and that your enemy has W.M.D.s, then the last thing you do is station your troops right next door."

ABC's George Stephanopoulos

Continued on Page A5

Popular Pressure Ushers Recent Progressive Tilt

Study Cites Movements for Massive Shift in DC

By SAMUEL FIELDEN

The spate of reform initiatives undertaken by the Administration and both houses of Congress can be attributed directly to grassroots advocacy, according to a comprehensive study due out this month.

"In education and health care, most notably, but also in housing, banking, and the environment, we have documented unprecedented responsiveness on the part of political leaders," said Dr. Joyce Wellmon, director of the Plains Institute for Policy Analysis, a New York-based think tank. "Our data show a direct correlation between the level of activity of particular coalitions, on the one hand, and specific legislative action, on the other. It's popular pressure that is responsible for the swiftness and scope of legislation emerging from the White House and Congress."

The institute's report shows a three-fold increase in the incidence of letters, phone calls, faxes, and email received by congressional offices, 88 percent of which were from people who identified themselves as new members of particular activist organizations.

See nytimes-se.com for more

The report includes extensive interviews with House and Senate staff, who speak of "unimaginable change," a "dramatic policy shift," and "a new era of accountability" since the elections.

"Not since the Great Depression has the interaction between popular movements and public leaders been so robust," said Jorge Lazaro, head of the U.S. Government Accountability Office. Lazaro cited, in particular, the Wagner Act, also known as the National Labor Relations Act of 1935, which recognized the right of workers to organize and bargain collectively with their employers.

"Roosevelt showed no interest in the Wagner Act until it became clear the unions were going to force it through regardless," Mr. Lazaro noted. "At that point he jumped on it and helped push it into law."

Mr. Lazaro also pointed to the Depression-era organizing of the Farmers' Holiday Association, when farmers refused to sell or bid on crops, blockaded roads, and even once used a torpedo to halt a train carrying livestock into Iowa. Such direct actions helped push courts and legislatures to adopt measures that granted relief from debt caused by low crop prices.

"The similarities between the two periods are remarkable, and the lesson that emerges is simple: if you want change, keep our feet to the fire."

Dr. Wellmon agrees. "The only reason the current President and Congress have been able to implement all these changes, was because of pressure from popular movements that made them have to."

The Plains report, due out next month, cites the work of groups associated with United for Peace and Justice, an umbrella for anti-war groups, for galvanizing public support for ending the war, and for pushing the Administration to resist the oil lobby and other interest groups. It also cites the work

Continued on Page A6

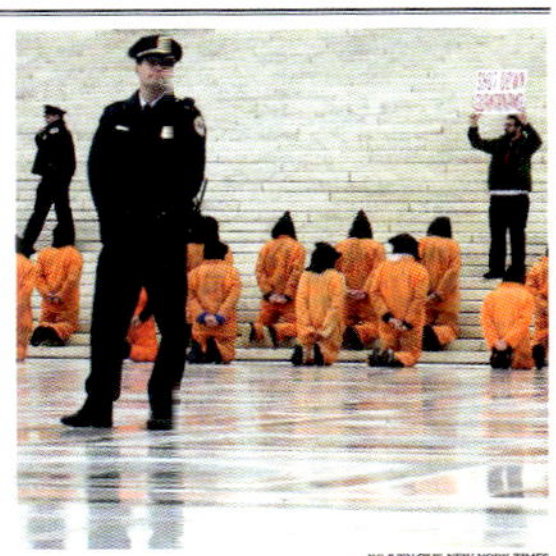

KC IVEY/THE NEW YORK TIMES

Protests organized by Witness Against Torture helped pave the way for the close of the Guantánamo facility.

Nationalized Oil To Fund Climate Change Efforts

By MARION K. HUBBERT

Congress has voted to place ExxonMobil, ChevronTexaco, and other major oil companies under public stewardship, with the bulk of the companies' profits put in a public trust administered by the United Nations, and used for alternative energy research and development in order to solve the global climate crisis.

While unusual, this is not the first time the government has chosen to take control of large corporations. From 1942 to 1944, U.S. car factories were retooled in order to produce tanks for the war effort. And Fannie Mae and Freddie Mac were both created as "government sponsored enterprises" with a significant amount of government oversight.

"We can do what needs to be done," said Senator Charles Schumer, Democrat of New York. "Our planet's survival is at stake. Plus, public pressure hasn't given us much of a choice."

Not everyone felt the move was a good idea. "The climate crisis may or may not be real," declared Senator Kay Bailey Hutchison, Republican of Texas. "I'm an agnostic and I'm staying that way. But sea

Continued on Page A5

INTERNATIONAL A4-5

Gitmo, Other Centers Closed
The notorious Guantánamo Bay, Cuba detention camp will be closed, along with a network of secret C.I.A.-run facilities in Eastern Europe, Afghanistan and elsewhere. PAGE A24

Iraqi Refugees Worldwide Celebrate Withdrawal
Two million Iraqi exiles, and three million internal refugees, celebrated the end of hostilities and began making plans to return to their homes. PAGE A4

NATIONAL A6-9

Conflict of Interest Law Will Stop Revolving Door
The "Revolving Door" bill will prohibit high-ranking corporate officers from holding public office for ten years upon leaving their companies, and public officials from accepting management positions at large corporations for the same period. Coupled with the Ban on Lobbying bill, the bill will reduce the influence of large corporations on public policy. PAGE B1

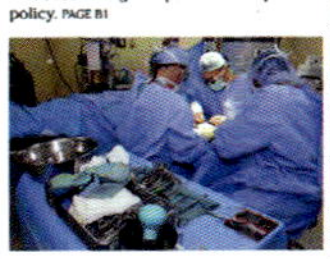

Health Insurance Act Clears House
While almost all are celebrating the passage of the National Health Insurance Act, which finally brings the U.S. up to par with other developed nations, representatives of Kaiser, Cigna and other health insurance companies are vowing to "fight tooth and nail" to protect their interests. PAGE A7

Bush to Face Charges
Most observers weren't surprised by the high treason indictment itself, but rather by the party that brought it. The case could also provide an unexpected boost to the International Criminal Court, paving the way for more indictments. PAGE A5

BUSINESS A10-11

Corporate Personhood Gets Real
An initiative to abolish limited liability will make shareholders pay for the crimes their corporations commit — even if they only own one or two shares in a mutual fund. PAGE A11

NEW YORK A12

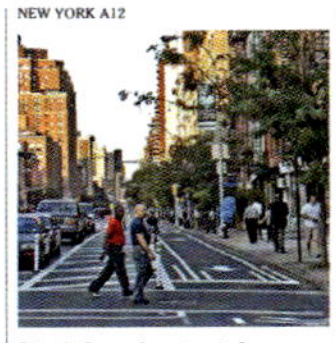

Bicycle Lanes Inaugurated
With the completion of the 9th Avenue bike lane and groundbreaking on other avenues, New York is on the (bike) path to becoming as livable as other world cities. PAGE A12

EDITORIAL A13

A Lobbyist Defends Lobbying
The Ban on Lobbying bill is not without victims. PAGE A13

Thomas L. Friedman
The columnist resigns, and will put down his pen to take up a screwdriver. PAGE A13

A Baboon Troop's Experience
A particularly peaceful baboon troop may have lessons to teach us. PAGE A13

More Inside The Times.
PAGE A2 ►

HELP MAKE THE NEWS. TODAY

8 92015 12023 9 — 92015

Founded in 1993
Global

www.transparency.org

Transparency International

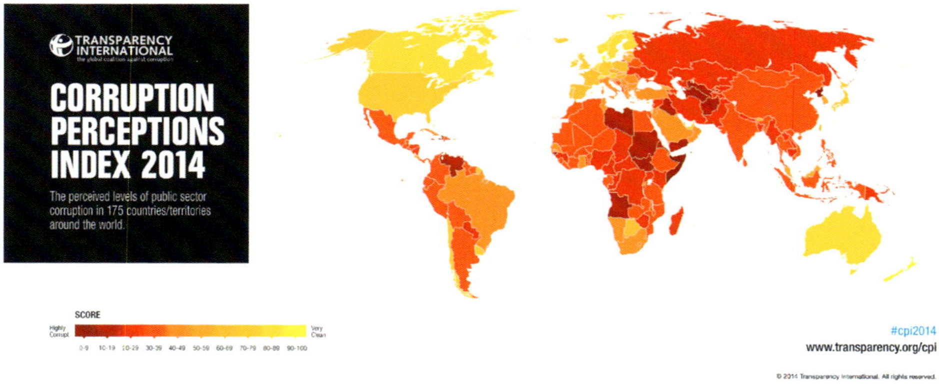

The nongovernmental organization Transparency International was founded in 1993 in Berlin. With its programs, projects, and activities it monitors and makes public corporate and political corruption and campaigns for transparency and participation. In collaboration with people from politics, the economy, and civil society, the NGO works for a democratic political culture and unimpeded access to information relevant to decision-making. On its website, the organization offers different approaches to this subject: one gets information about corruption by topic – for example, by means of the keywords health, water, and climate change – or by country via a map that quickly provides the user with the most important facts at a glance when clicking on individual countries. In addition to the annual report, Transparency International has published several specific publications, recently, for example, the *Corruption Perceptions Index 2014*, the *Anti-Corruption Kit: 15 Ideas for Young Activists*, the *Global Corruption Barometer* (the world's largest public opinion survey on corruption), and *Real Lives, True Stories*, a selection of stories about corruption and corruption fighting, all of which are available online. Further, the organization provides various toolkits, including the Business Integrity Toolkit or Corruption Fighters' Toolkits.

CORRUPTION PERCEPTIONS INDEX 2014

TRANSPARENCY INTERNATIONAL
the global coalition against corruption

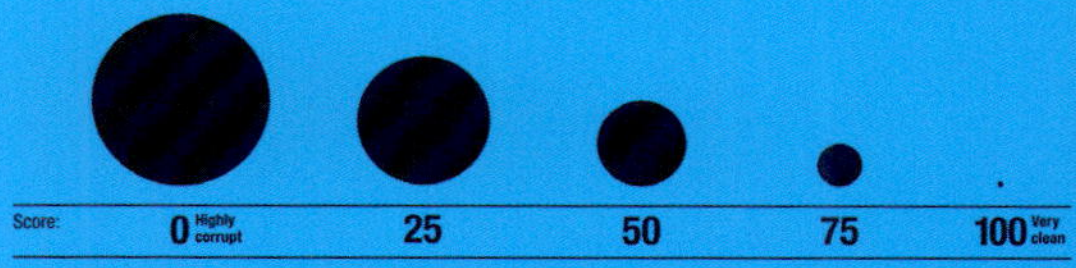

COUNTRY CONTRAST

TOP

Denmark **92**

New Zealand **91**

BOTTOM

Korea (North) **8**

Somalia **8**

CORRUPTION PROBLEM

GLOBAL PERFORMANCE

GLOBAL Average score **43**

69% of countries score below 50 out of 100

G20 PERFORMANCE

G20 Average score **54**

58% of G20 countries score below 50 out of 100

RESULTS BY REGION

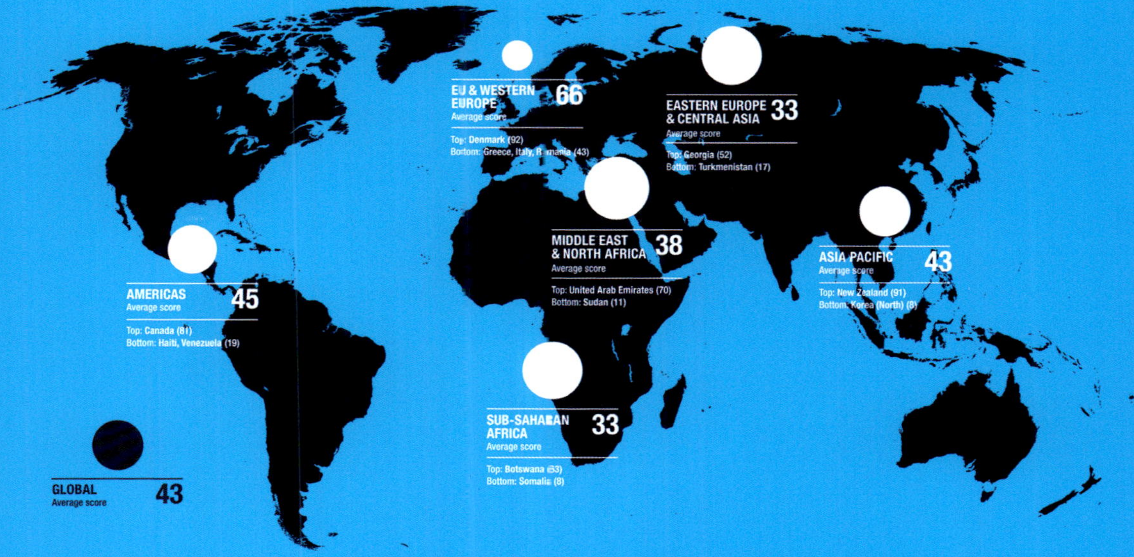

#cpi2014

www.transparency.org/cpi

Malala Yousafzai *1997

At the beginning of 2009, in the BBC's blog the then eleven-year-old Malala Yousafzai wrote a report under a pseudonym about the violent acts of the Pakistani Taliban in her home country, especially in the Swat Valley. Under the regime of the terror organization, many buildings of girls' schools had been destroyed, and since January 15, 2009, there was a strict ban on girls attending school. Further, they were not allowed to listen to music, to dance, or to enter public places unveiled.

In summer, when the Pakistani military began to intervene in the region, *The New York Times* correspondent Adam B. Ellick and the Pakistani reporter Irfan Ashraf documented Yousafzai's life in their film *Class Dismissed: The Death of Female Education*. Yousafzai, whose father had been a teacher at one of the girls' schools until it was closed down and was also a known activist in the district, thus became known beyond her hometown, and gave interviews to television and various newspapers. First, she continued learning at home, then she went back to school and disobeyed the ban.

In October 2012, because of her dedication to education for girls, Malala Yousafzai was the victim of an assassination attempt by the Taliban. Some Taliban stopped the school bus, and one terrorist shot her at close range. She suffered serious bullet wounds in her head and neck, but fortunately survived. After she receiving initial treatment in Pakistan, she was transferred to a special clinic in the UK. The family was allowed to follow in 2013. In December 2012, the Malala Fund for Girls' Right to Education was founded in collaboration with UNESCO. *Time Magazine* named her the second most important person of the year 2012 after Barack Obama. In February 2013, Yousafzai was able to leave the hospital and continued her advocacy work for female education immediately.

For her unremitting efforts, she has received numerous peace prizes, including the 2011 Pakistani National Youth Peace Prize (today know as the National Malala Peace Prize), the 2013 International Children's Peace Prize, and the 2013 Sakharov Prize for Freedom of Thought. Also in 2013, she was nominated for the Nobel Peace Prize. She received it one year later, together with the Indian children's activist Kailash Satyarthi. Yousafzai is the only Pakistani winner of the Nobel Peace Prize and, at the age of seventeen, the youngest laureate of this award ever.

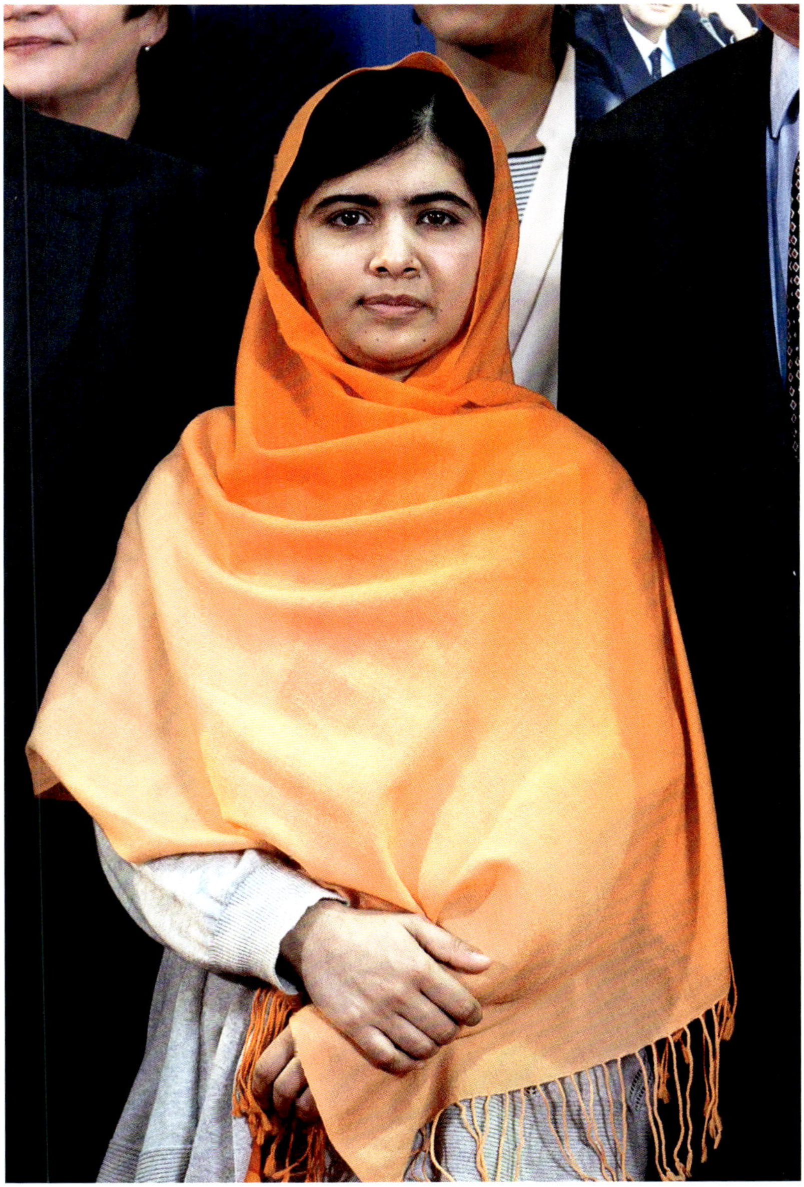

Malala Yousafzai at the award presentation of the Sakharov Prize in Strasbourg on November 20, 2013

www.wango.org

WANGO

Since its foundation in 2000, the World Association of Non-Governmental Organizations (WANGO) unites NGOs worldwide, and thus makes an important contribution to their effective networking in terms of connections and partnerships across the barriers of culture, politics, religion, politics, and ethnicity, as well as to the sharing of ideas, information, and resources in order to solve major humanitarian problems and to realize the aims of universal peace and justice. Further, the association seeks to strengthen and encourage the nongovernmental sector as a whole, and to increase public understanding of the nongovernmental community.

At its annual conference and further congresses, WANGO regularly brings together representatives of major initiatives and promotes exchange at an international level. In addition, the association offers several publications (reports, position papers, monographs) both to its members and the world community, which are available to the membership at reduced or no cost. Further, WANGO honors organizations and individuals, who have made an outstanding contribution to the welfare of humanity. With its extensive network, incorporating alongside NGOs also governmental bodies, universities, and companies, and the resulting opportunity to speak with one strong voice, WANGO is today a leader regarding the most pressing questions of global concern. It works in partnership with the United Nations and other intergovernmental bodies.

Online Projects

The Damascus Bureau

Founded in 2010

www.damascusbureau.org

This website is a publishing platform for independent Syrian journalists and offers unfiltered reports from their country, currently in the grip of a civil war. The articles are available in English and Arabic.

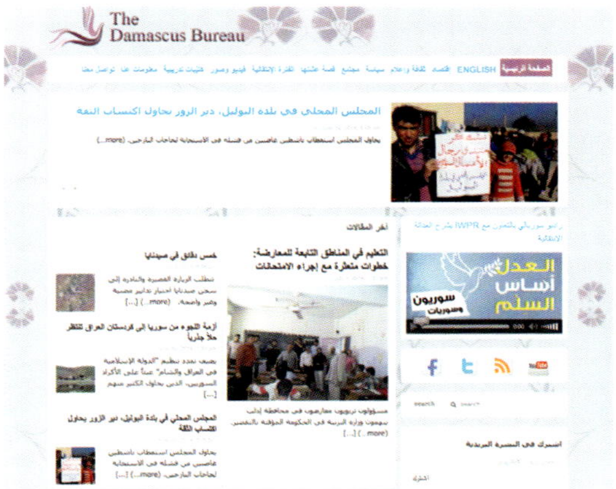

Screenshoot, 07/08/2014

Yezzi

Tunisia

tn.yezzi.info

Until July 2013, the platform registered violations by the police in Tunisia after the revolution, and recorded cases of corruption, physical violence, sexual violence, and even torture. Citizens could post information anonymously, and upload videos, pictures, and news.

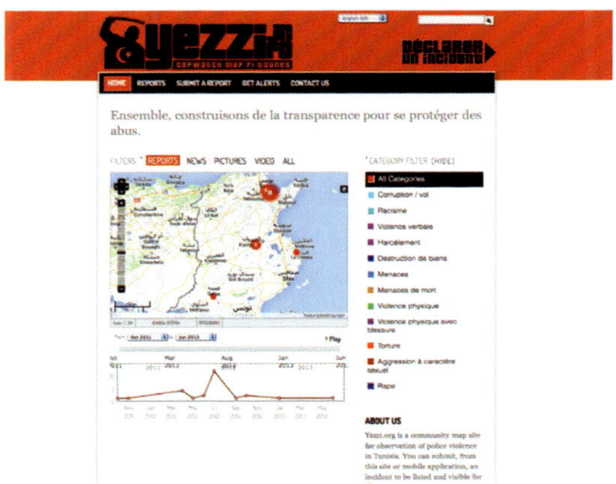

Screenshot, 07/08/2014

Public and Private Sphere

Chapter II

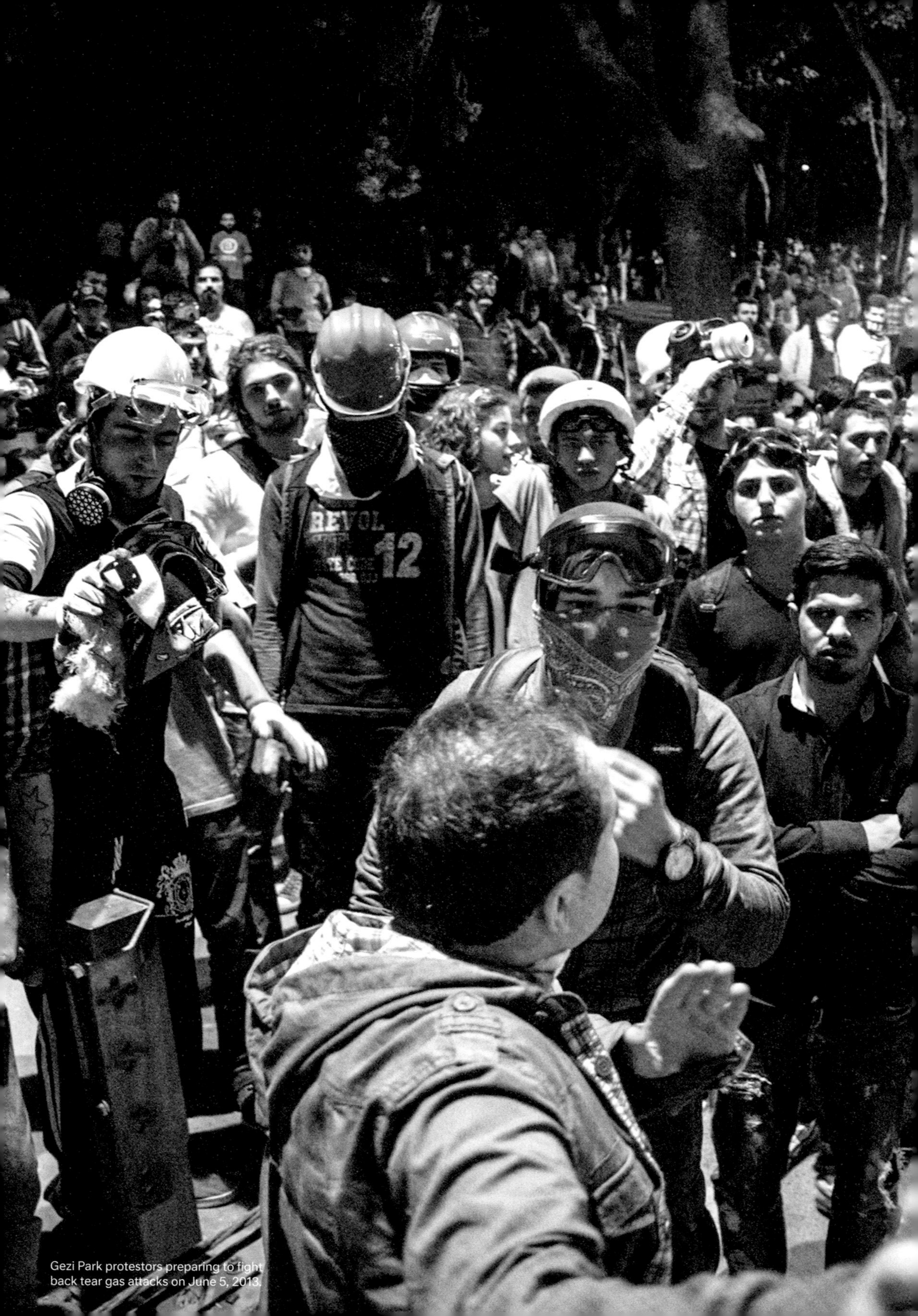

Gezi Park protestors preparing to fight back tear gas attacks on June 5, 2013.

Can Altay

A Public Presence versus Greed, Brutality, and Control: Gezi Park

Istanbul and many cities across Turkey have witnessed a widespread insurgency starting on May 27, 2013. The initial struggle which took place in and around Gezi Park lasted several weeks, with ripple effects leading to the formation of neighborhood forums throughout the city, and ultimately resulting in a state of discontent that arises regularly. Gezi Park, which has been the site and springboard of this resistance is a green area next to the central Taksim Square. The park has become simultaneously a symbol for the resistance and for a limited time a utopian public space, revealing an explicitly urban politics that does not register with existing political factions or discourses. The spatial politics of Gezi and its aftermath includes to a great extent the use of Internet and mobile media, not only in terms of communication and forming a community, but also in the way it fueled the resistance with humor.

Greed

Construction obviously presents itself as a motor when it comes to keeping the machine running in terms of the country's economy. Prime Minister Recep Tayyip Erdoğan and his party (AKP) has never really been shy about their involvement in this market. Their reaction when facing the recent mining accident that resulted in the death of over 300 miners in Soma, in May 2014, almost a year after Gezi, is further proof that their preference for capital over civilians (in not only construction but many other industries) has not changed.

Both within and around Istanbul, an ongoing search for lucrative landgrabs, usually resulting in the construction of large-scale shopping-office-residential combos, has been taking place at an increasing rate. Under Erdoğan, the Housing Development Administration (TOKI) steered away from its ideals of providing affordable housing, adopting the role of a neoliberal engine for the entire construction industry. And so the search for valuable land to be grabbed and developed continues, within Istanbul and all around the country.

Brutality

It is important to remember what spawned the resistance. A small group of protesters was heavily attacked for defending a few trees in the Taksim Square redevelopment construction site, which also includes the now famous Gezi Park. Footage clearly shows the police defending the contractors and their bulldozers, and not the citizens who wanted to express their discontent.

Erdoğan declared his decision regarding the Gezi Park once more. A perfect portrait of the ruling ideology was to be built – a moneymaking machine masquerading as a faux-historical landmark. Yes, the authorities were making way for a shopping mall (or a high-end residence, or a hotel) that would look like an Ottoman-era military barrack, to replace a "useless" – that is, non-income-generating – patch of greenery.

The police brutality toward a handful of activists who wanted to save the trees led more and more protesters to join the struggle. In turn, the increasing number of people in the park and on the streets incited more extreme violence from the police. The government's usual paternalistic tone, insinuating, "We know what's best for you," did not help, either. Thanks to Erdoğan's stern response, and the continuing police brutality, discontent finally found its release in protests that spread far beyond Istanbul, to cities like Izmir and Ankara, and were no longer only about Gezi Park.

Media, Antimedia, Social Media

For a long time, and increasingly under the AKP government, humor magazines have served as the only outlets for open political criticism. *Gırgır*, established in 1972, but gaining prominence in the post-coup landscape of the 1980s, is a forerunner and sort of a school in this type of publishing.[1] At times bordering on oppressed sexuality and political incorrectness, magazines like *Limon* and *Leman* in the 1990s and *Uykusuz* and *Penguen* in this decade continue their mocking of corrupt politicians and unjust policies, despite the many lawsuits and threats they face.[2] Emerging at a time when the mainstream media proved to be insufficient, and maintaining a critical edge, humor magazines provided a wide readership[3] with news that no mainstream media dared to touch earning them a reputation as "antimedia."[4]

The joke is, after all, an "open-source weapon of the public" with the "capacity to resist and overturn the frame of reference imposed by any political status quo."[5] The jokes in the Internet are reproduced and transmitted as "memes," playing a significant role in protests, much like slogans and posters of yesterday: "the embodiment of shared ideas in a community."[6]

The relentless sense of humor that characterizes the Gezi resistance has been largely fed from the genre of humor magazines, spreading at the speed of memes, ultimately reaching back to the streets in the form of graffiti and slogans, and then going back into circulation in social media as photographs of physical space.

Social media's role in the resistance is undeniable, not only in terms of communication and organization, but also in the way it helps lift the spirit. No wonder the Prime Minister called Twitter "a menace to society." In effect, these alternative media bring together an engaged, critical public, separate from the sort that mainstream news channels try to construct. To give an idea,

1

See: M.B. Arık, *Değişen Toplum Değişen Karikatür*, Gazeteciler Cemiyeti Yayınları, Istanbul, 1998.

2

See: Gürkan Özocak, "Türkiye'de Siyasi İktidarın Mizahla İmtihanı. İfade Özgürlüğü ve Karikatür," in: *Türkiye Barolar Birliği Dergisi*, no. 94, 2011, pp. 259–294.

3

The two major magazines *Uykusuz* and *Penguen*'s weekly sales reach 135,000 copies; with old-schoolers *Leman* and *Gırgır* around 35,000. While this is still less than newspaper readership, these numbers indicate more sales than all other weekly magazines combined (politics, news, economy, lifestyle, cars, etc.); see: http://mizahhaber.blogspot.com.tr/2013/07/mizah-dergilerinin-satislari-ne-durumda.html, accessed 05/23/2014.

4

Özocak 2011, p. 277; translated from the Turkish by Can Altay.

5

Metahaven, *Can Jokes Bring Down Governments? Memes, Design and Politics*, Strelka Press, 2013, chps. 4 and 2.

6

Ibid., ch. 3.

the TV news channel CNN Türk famously aired a documentary about penguins during the hottest hours of the resistance. Such ludicrous attempts at censorship got what they deserved; images of penguins with gas masks joined the caravan of caricatures lampooning power in all its manifestations. Common tools of resistance in the twenty-first century – mobile Internet, online social media, smartphones, and digital cameras[7] – were in support of the real presence, on the streets. Humor spreading through the Web came together with defiant slogans on the streets to create a hybrid public space of resistance.

7 See: ibid., ch. 2.

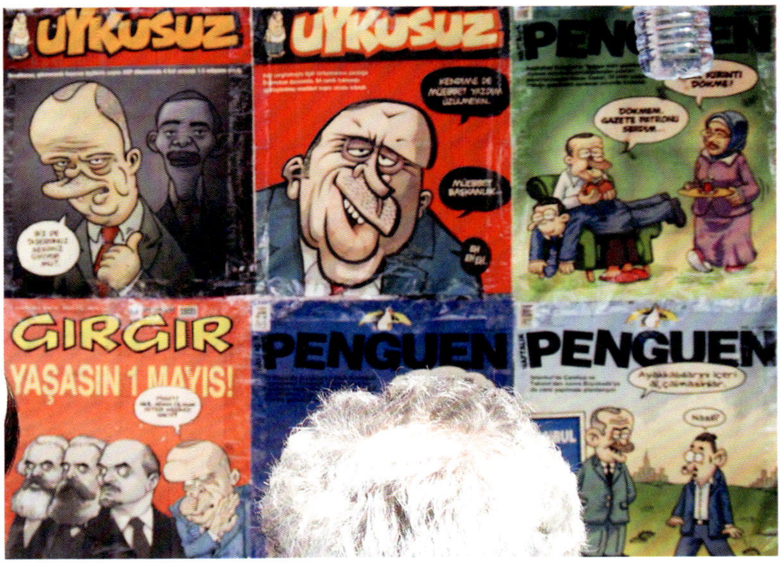

Covers of humor magazines are displayed in the entrance to the makeshift "revolution museum" between Taksim Square and Gezi Park.

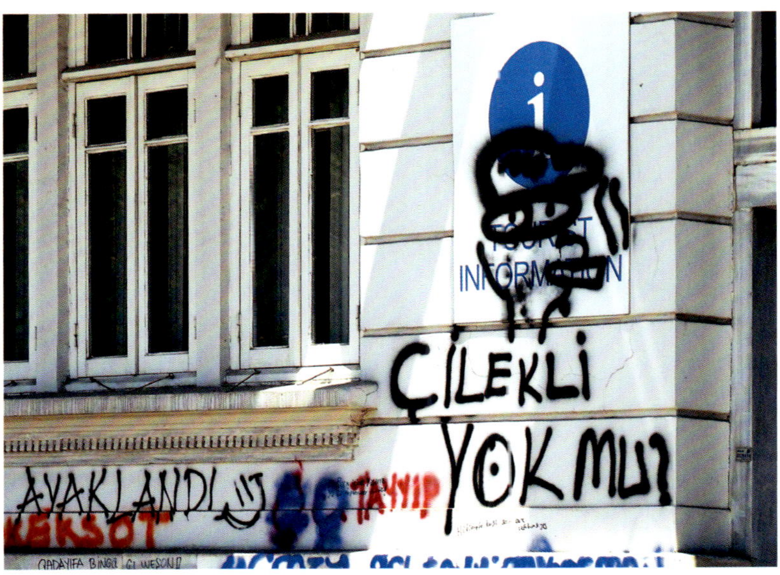

"Do you have this in strawberry flavor?" reads a protester's graffiti, a tongue-in-cheek response to the police's use of pepper gas, and a meme at work.

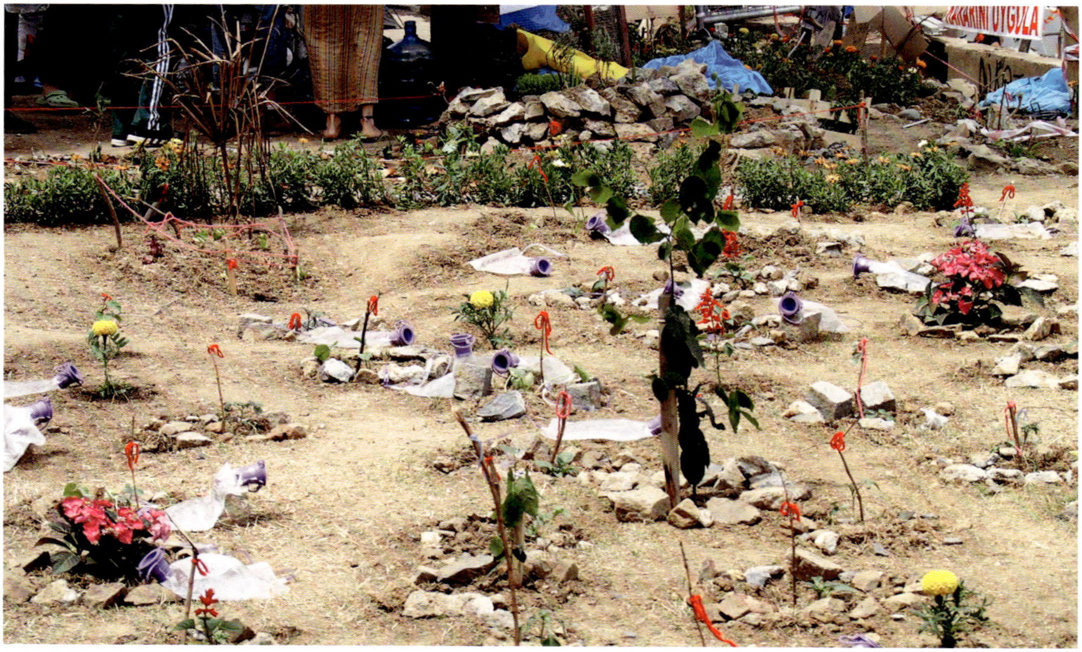

A garden planted by occupiers at the demolished edge of Gezi Park includes peppers, a salute to the widespread use of pepper gas by police.

Control

A "hybrid space" conceptually manifests itself when borders between physical and digital spaces are merged.[8] Since the simultaneity of the discussion and reaction in these two realms allows a mobilization of masses, the Internet represents a threat. While the various lawsuits brought against humor magazines are mainly based on "personal depictions and insults,"[9] the Prime Minister's outspoken disregard of online social media sites (and thus the Internet) brings with it different kinds of measures. The new law on the Internet, which is aimed at full-fledged control over what should remain accessible by the public,[10] and the closures of access to platforms such as Twitter and YouTube give a glimpse of how far the government is willing to go.

This mentality does not differ over physical public space, either. Just a few weeks after the forced removal of protesters and occupiers, the municipality already wrapped a hastily done "beautification" process, reinstalling lawns and planting flowers.

The plans for the new building have been paused yet gathering for political protests in Taksim Square has been prohibited, especially with regard to the 1st of May protests. The government did not stop there but constructed a gigantic scale demonstration ground in the southwest corner of the historical city, protruding to the Sea of Marmara like a tumorous outgrowth. Literally on the edge of the city, surrounded by the sea, where no one but the protesters will be seen or heard. This landfill is called a "boutique" (as Erdoğan names it) or bespoke square for protests: yet another manifestation of the desire to control and the hunger to construct on the government's behalf.[11]

8

See: Adriana de Souza e Silva, "From Cyber to Hybrid. Mobile Technologies as Interfaces of Hybrid Spaces," in: *Space and Culture*, vol. 9, no. 3, August 2006, pp. 261–278.

9

Özocak 2011, p. 279, translated form the Turkish by Can Altay.

10

See: Jussi Parikka and Burak Arikan, "Turkey's new internet law: policing the online mall," February 11, 2014, available online at: www.opendemocracy.net/opensecurity/jussi-parikka-burak-arikan/turkey's-new-internet-law-policing-online-mall, accessed 05/23/2014.

11

See: Justin McGuirk, "Protest has been marginalised," May 16, 2014, available online at: www.dezeen.com/2014/05/16/justin-mcguirk-opinion-istanbul-taksim-square-yenikapi/, accessed 05/23/2014.

A Public Presence

Public space is always already full of limits. During Gezi, the police were called in to declare "You have no say over how this space is formed." But the protesters showed otherwise. A boundary has been transgressed; that much is certain. Some call it the "fear barrier" that dissolved; as "transgression forces the limit to face the fact of its imminent disappearance."[12] At Gezi Park people hailed from many factions and tendencies. *We* were all there: first in the park, then, after the police kicked us out, on the streets, and then back at the park and all over Taksim Square. This is the power of presence, of being there, and having your say.

"Taksim Hepimizin!" means Taksim belongs to all of us, not some of us. Public space should no longer be male space. The Prime Minister's appetite for social engineering contributes to this environment of discrimination, with his declarations celebrating motherhood (minimum three kids) and sobriety. Yet, at Gezi Park, women and LGBTQ people were present, perhaps more than ever, in making public space truly public. The streets are the grounds of a politics, of this presence of a public that is constantly disregarded by both central governing and judiciary systems; of new political subjectivities.[13] A public presence finally starts to matter in two ways: first, in the way it surfaces on the streets, and second, in the way it links with other places, both within Turkey and in other countries, through networks.

12 Michel Foucault, "A Preface to Transgression," in: Fred Botting and Scott Wilson (eds.), *Bataille: A Critical Reader*, Wiley-Blackwell, London, 1998, pp. 24–40, here p. 28.

13 See: Saskia Sassen, "Making Public Interventions in Today's Massive Cities," in: *Static*, no. 4, 2006, pp. 1–8.

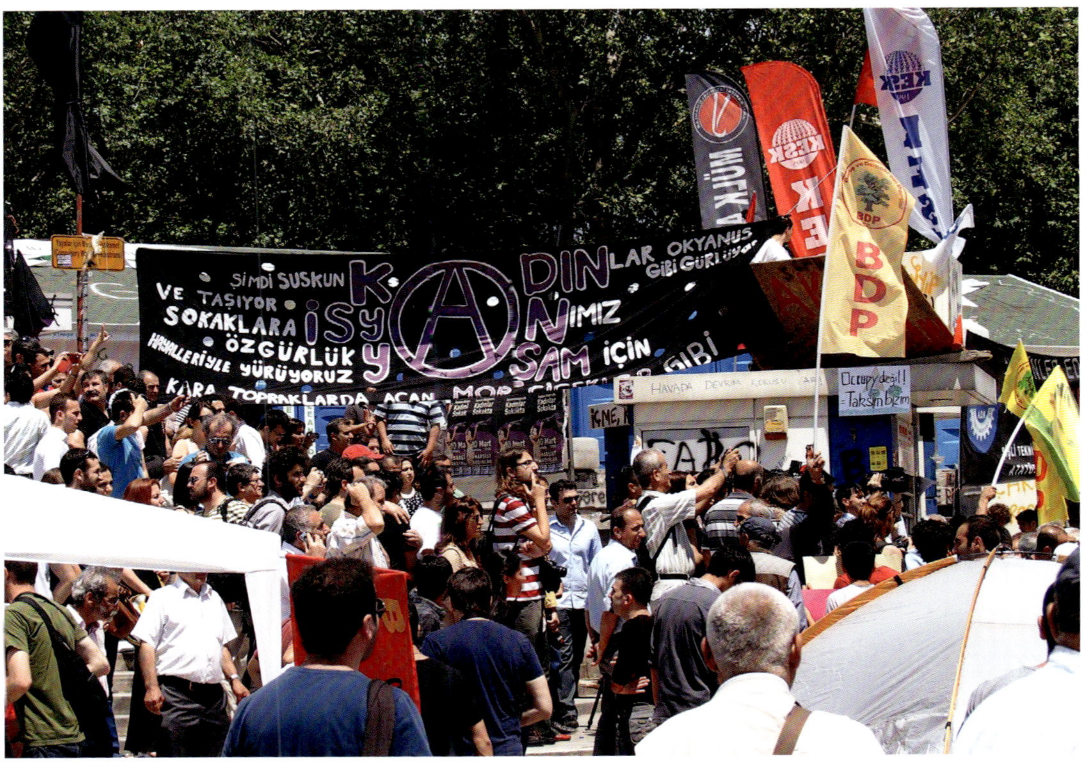

Gathering of protesters in Gezi Park, Istanbul, 2013

Recognition of these links brought solidarity and joy to the park, where it flourished, with only minor hiccups like the occasional shortage of supplies, bouts of rain, and the unease of waiting for something worse to happen. There was a beautiful garden with vegetables, including peppers, a tribute to the pepper spray employed by police, and new trees. An open library, free lectures, and forums for conversation. Even though nothing is free outside of the park, there was no currency inside; food and medicine were provided by the public for the public. The park was like an open book; texts and quotes abounded. It was a learning experience for everyone. A glimpse of a possibility, of reimagining public space, which has been indirectly fed by comics, art, music, and political struggles for many years: imagination expands slowly and strikes suddenly.

The hybridity offered through digital and social media remains an important aspect, also on a temporal basis. Since "moments" like Gezi Park do not, and will not happen every day, platforms for continuous discussion, expression, critique, and a sense of not being alone are vital, until the next meaningful surfacing of presence in physical space.

This text builds on and includes excerpts from a dispatch written during the days of the Gezi resistance, which was published by *Creative Time Reports* on June 14, 2013, available online at: http://creativetimereports.org/2013/06/14/here-we-are-the-imagination-of-public-space-in-gezi-park/, accessed 05/23/2014.

Korhan Gümüş

Liberating Public Spaces: Where to Start?

When he was elected mayor of Istanbul in 1994 Recep Tayyip Erdoğan found a couple of ready-made large-scale projects waiting for him. One of these was the "Taksim Project" designed by a professor at one of Istanbul's largest universities. The "designer team" – which included university scholars – that drew up the transport infrastructure project for Taksim claimed that traffic must be relocated underground. According to this concept, to ease the flow of traffic all the streets leading to Taksim Square had to be turned into tunnels with platforms. The team claimed that this project was a "pedestrianization" of the square – a big step towards "modernizing" the area; for the authors, this concept had to be applied to other squares as well. They also added that people who objected to this project were people who don't know anything about the subject. The latter were regarded merely as romantics who didn't have a clue about what crossroads or highway engineering means; their objections didn't have to be taken into consideration.

In addition to all this, the project had a very strong argument for convincing the mayor: in the multistoried space underground a shopping mall was located, and the brand of the shopping mall would help to finance the first subway investment. Yet, in spite of the pressure exerted by the construction firms working with the municipal authorities, the Taksim project was held in abeyance for decades; it was not put out to tender.

During Recep Tayyip Erdoğan's first years, he didn't have an experienced team for the project. At that time, it was customary for the universities to be involved in such large-scale architectural projects. However, the Taksim project was different. Erdoğan was especially interested in this project. He wanted to build a big mosque in Taksim, so that he could realize one of the biggest dreams of the Millî Görüş Movement (literally, National Vision Movement). Already at that time, the facade of Aya Triada Church was covered with advertising boards. In the same manner, the opera building was seen as a "work of a minority that wants to impose its values on Turkish people" and was thus disparaged; therefore a "solution" was needed for that building as well.

Erdoğan knew that Taksim was a difficult topic. And since they couldn't use universities for this project, they didn't have a team for designing the mosque project. He also knew that the government wouldn't help him with this project. So, he conducted just an experiment. Three circles would be drawn on the design and the reactions would be measured. But the developments were not as expected. This "modest" mosque project became one of the most tension-ridden topics during the postmodern coup of February 28, 1997. Newspaper headlines were shouting: "Mosque on Taksim!" One could read that as: "Sharia is coming and they will occupy our public spaces." Eventually, Erdoğan lost his seat and was put in prison. What was the underlying idea of Millî Görüş, which wanted to build a mosque on Taksim? It was the suppressed, excluded, impoverished Muslim conservatism. The mosque Erdoğan wanted to build in front of the opera building (AKM, Atatürk Cultural Center) was the representation of this idea in politics. Erdoğan built his career towards central power through this experience.

After Erdoğan came to power through long struggles, he wanted to deal immediately with the Taksim subject. Taksim was an issue that was preying on his mind; it was a symbol for the injustice he was subjected to. He had been victorious against the minority who was preventing the rule of the people. Accordingly, the transformation of Taksim, as a public space of national power, was very important. When his candidate Kadir Topbaş won the 2004 Istanbul Municipality elections, Erdoğan thought that the conditions were now ripe. Now it was time to compensate for the injustices. He took power and was now the head of the central authority but it was meaningless to create another mosque debate. Topbaş had to find a more clever solution, which at the same time wouldn't mean a step backwards. An architect, famous for implementing construction projects on areas subject to construction restrictions by means of collecting pictures and documents of ruined buildings on those very areas, found a solution for Topbaş: rebuilding the Taksim Military Barracks – which was active until 1939 and which had a mosque in it.

Before the project started, they began to uproot the trees in front of the Divan Hotel for the future tunnels and this created an eccentric scene: This sort of violence was the clumsiest and most awkward intervention into the public space. The violence, which disturbed everybody with a conscience, turned into a spark that would soon explode into reactions. In a very short time, thousands of people gathered in the Gezi Park. Then, Taksim, İstiklal Street, and many other public places became the stage for one of the largest crowd demonstrations that history had witnessed. The demonstrations spread and the government was seized with fear.

President Erdoğan declared that the opposition was waiting for an opportunity for a mass demonstration and so the trees were only an excuse for them. On the other hand, the president must have understood that these protest events were of a new kind; he thus tried to ignore the protests entirely, he even attempted to erase them from history. However, one must concede that the conditions for such mass protests had already been prepared by him. Removing the military tutelage and controlling the military bureaucracy transformed the oligarchic structure of the old regime and shook the

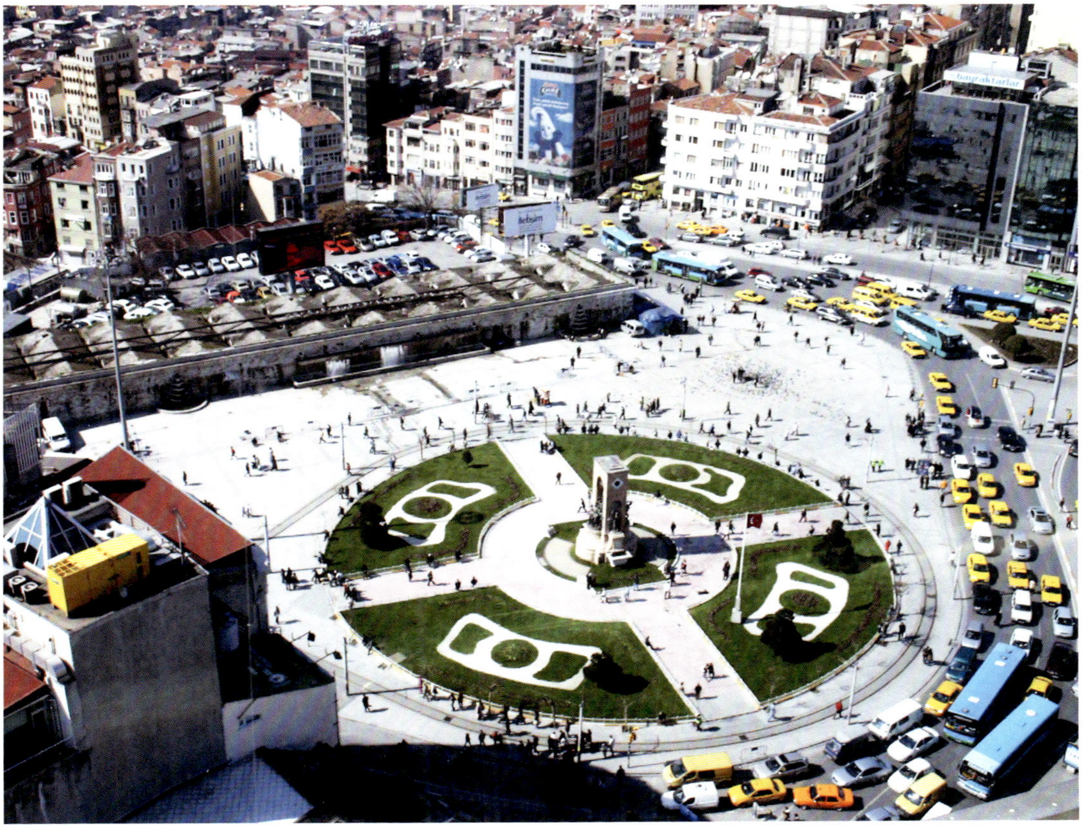

Taksim Square in Istanbul before the renovation in September 2013

roots of the political opposition that leaned back to that regime. The fact that the government tried to take steps towards solving the crisis regarding the ever-present Kurdish problem in the history of the Republic of Turkey has begun to change the centralist state structure and transform the conditions leading to the hostile representation of civil society.

Now, Erdoğan must either go back to where he started or he must renew himself. Sometimes people who develop a portrayal of life, like in the example of the president, become aware of developments and even of their own actions very late. A group called Genç Müminler [Young Muslims] had announced: "God's blow will eventually fall." In Taksim, there blossomed a very new politics – at the very place that was destroyed by "national" politics.

Today we have an example that consists not only of speech but also of action: anticapitalist Muslims filled the ideal of Millî Görüş with its essence. Instead of turning this ideal into state politics, they preserved it as civil society. They proved that performing *namaz* [a prayer] need not mean the seizure of public spaces; that, on the contrary, it can have an emancipatory aspect. They showed that the conservatives can define the public space in a humanistic way without any power of central politics. They destroyed the image that had been present since 1969 (when on the "Bloody Sunday" the rightists were provoked in order to attack the leftists who were protesting the

Sixth Naval Fleet of the U.S. Navy): "The followers of sharia will come and seize our public space!" They declined this legacy. While they were praying on Friday in Gezi Park, the leftists stopped chanting. They respected each other and they didn't define the public space according to their own priorities. This was one of the most significant events during the Gezi protests. The anticapitalist Muslims showed that conservatism, when it doesn't correspond to central political power, can have a side that questions capitalism.

Today it is time to transform and vitalize the idea of the public space, which is currently dictated by the government to the public with construction projects such as mosques.

> This text was translated from the Turkish by Mehmet Barış Albayrak. It was first published on the ZKM Blog during the *global aCtIVISm* exhibition, and is still available online at: http://blog.zkm.de/en/dialogue/freeing-public-spaces-where-start/.

Walter D. Mignolo

Re:emerging, Decentring, and Delinking:

Shifting the Geographies of Sensing, Believing, and Knowing

I.

The Sharjah Biennial 11 (SB11) was, without a doubt, an unmistakable statement: a signpost of a global shift that cuts across economics, politics, culture, art, aesthetics, religion, and sensibilities. But the four spectacular days of SB11's inauguration (judging by the press coverage) should not obscure something that, I suspect, transcends the two months the exhibit remained open to the public (March 13–May 13, 2013).[1]

The first time I read about Sharjah Biennial 11 was in Hong Kong. No event of this kind had caught my attention before as this one did and I wanted to know more. I had the suspicion that something distinctive was in the making. Yuko Hasegawa, Chief Curator of the Museum of Contemporary Art Tokyo, was appointed to curate the Sharjah Biennial in the United Arab Emirates. Could this exhibition become what I was sensing and expecting at the time? A statement by Hasegawa particularly stood out: "Sharjah is historic and present, social, natural, and political. It is a place that encourages thinking and negotiating with others. My natural response to its dynamism is to produce a biennial which asks questions through art, and creates a dialog that liberates us from Eurocentrism, Globalism, and other relevant -isms."[2]

In the hope that my intuitions would be confirmed, I vowed to follow up on the unfolding of Sharjah Biennial 11. When the title was announced, my heart jumped: In *Re:emerge. Towards a New Cultural Cartography*, curator Yuko Hasegawa proposed a biennial that reassesses the Westerncentrism of knowledge in modern times and reconsiders the relationship between the Arab world, Asia, the Far East, through North Africa and Latin America.[3]

The reason I was in Hong Kong (January to June 2012) was to learn and *feel* what was already announced as the irreversible shift to the Eastern Hemisphere.[4] I saw an extraordinary parallel between the statement just quoted here by the Dean of Lee Kuan Yew School of Public Policy in Singapore, Kishore Mahbubani, and the statement of Yuko Hasegawa. Today, one feels that, with the collapse (financial, political, and ethical) of the European Union and the critical moments currently taking place in the U.S. both domestically and internationally, we are living in a change of epoch, not an epoch of change. Things are shifting; centers are

1 My contribution addresses the general question of Platform 5, as well as the specific question numbered 10. Regarding the first question, my argument underscores the confluence of economic growth of the "Far East" and the "Global South" and the confidence that it brings to people for a long time regarded as backward or behind Western modernity. Regarding question 10 (To what extent is the visual culture of the Middle East still tied to the language and culture of post-colonialism? And, if not, how has it shifted?) I argued that Sharjah Biennial 11 hugely shifted from the soft postcolonial to the most assertive and celebratory de-Westernization. How it shifted, is the thrust of my argument.

2 Sharjah Art Foundation press release, 12/211/2011, available online at: www.sharjahart.org/press1/2011/saf-announces-sharjah-biennial-11-curator/4286, accessed 01/21/2015.

3 See: Sharjah Foundation press release, available online at: www.sharjahart.org/biennial/sharjah-biennial-11/welcome, accessed 02/27/2014.

4 See: Kishore Mahbubani, *The new Asian hemisphere: the irresistible shift of global power to the East*, PublicAffairs, New York, 2008.

movable; sensibilities are shifting the illusion of the end of history after five hundred years of localized Western history, consolidation and domination is ending. Older – much older – histories of civilizations are reemerging. Globalism (the neoliberal vision of homogenizing the planet) is spinning out of control and every Western universal is under siege.

In this fair-haired age of biennials, triennials, and quinquennials, there is an anxiety to be the *newest* and a fear of being *behind* on the latest artistic and aesthetic theories. It is refreshing and empowering to have a biennial exhibition like the Sharjah Biennial, which turns its back on the intellectual Euro-American fashions that have dominated, until recently, the "-ennial" marketplace. Sharjah Biennial 11 drastically deviates our attention from this codification in such events and forces us to revise our assumptions about what art is, what biennials are, and what cultural cartographies we have been accustomed to until now.

Sharjah Biennial 11 undeniably achieved what most events that mark a turning point generally accomplish – it announced the desuetude of deep-seated ways of thinking, giving us *an other* conceptual and historical narrative. Under the title *Re:emerge. Towards a New Cultural Cartography* Sharjah Biennial 11 opens up the silenced and marginalized creativity of the "Global South" and "Global East." What has been announced with Sharjah Biennial 11 is nothing less than the end of an illusion of the successful fiction of Western modernity from the European Renaissance through to the European Enlightenment right through to the end of the twentieth century.

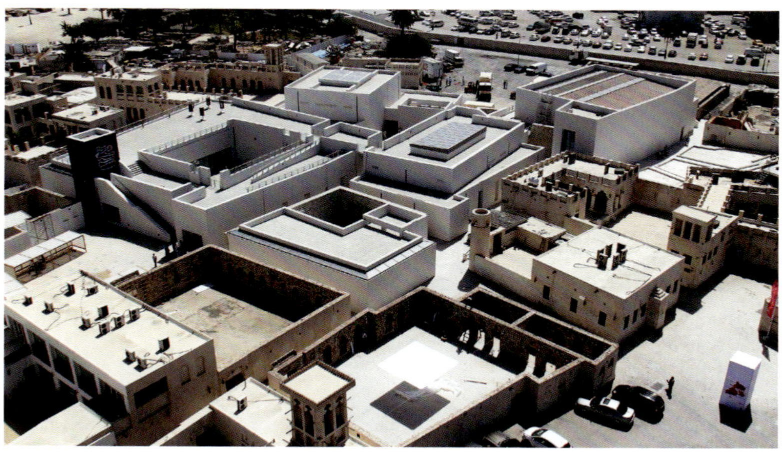

The new Sharjah Art Foundation Art Spaces in Al Mureijaha

II.

Sharjah Biennial 11 marks a "change of epoch." No longer is the world dominated by the local Euro-American historical narrative of the "epoch of changes."[5] Next to this, and not after, we now have an option that both marks the limits of modernity and its sequels (postmodern, altermodern, postcolonial), while contributing to global processes of epistemic and aesthetic disobedience.

5 I wish to thank Eduardo Mendieta for his help in the composition of this paragraph.

To understand the radical break produced by SB11, it suffices to look at the history of the Sharjah Biennial up to this point and to look at it in relation to events in Europe that attempted to introduce departures and new roads within Europe's local history: Kassel documenta 11 (2002), curated by Okwui Enwezor, and the Tate Triennial in 2009, *Altermodern*, curated by Nicolas Bourriaud.

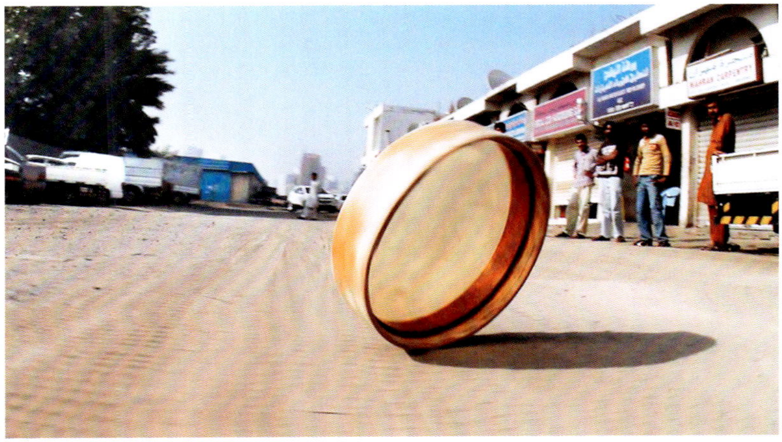

Nevin Aladağ, *Session*, 2013, three-channel HD video installation, color, sound, 6 min, loop, video still

The previous Sharjah Biennials (1 to 10) were indeed magnificent events, but still within the expectations of how such an artistic event is enacted. Distinguished curators are invited, the curator and the organizing institutions decide on a topic and a title, and artists whose work is perceived to be within the topic range are invited to flesh out the title and the statement. In many ways, the radical shift we have been exposed to in *Re:emerge* was already announced in the previous Sharjah Biennials. In the beginning, the novelty was that this type of event was supposed to happen in Western Europe or the U.S., perhaps Japan, but not in the United Arab Emirates. But when the biennial as an institution moved from Western Europe – where it originated – to the Middle East, the result was not an imitation nor was it indicative of a desire to have in the Middle East what Europe had. On the contrary, it was to appropriate the form of the biennial to do what it was not doing in Europe: open spaces for artists, memories, cultures, languages, sensing, and knowledge to come together beyond Europe.

As for documenta 11 and *Altermodern*, these were two events in which curators responded to the changing world at the beginning of the twentieth century. Europe could no longer be self-contained. Okwui Enwezor, curator of documenta 11, projected an event inscribed in the "postcolonial constellation"[6] aiming at a "new geography of culture" and a "transnational vision of art." The result was endocentric: it was bringing the world to Europe. Nicolas Bourriaud's *Altermodern* was similar in logic but different in content. The "altermodern constellation," if I can say so, contested Enwezor's "postcolonial constellation" and, like the postmodern and the postcolonial, remained within the confines of Europe. Enwezor was explicit about the project when he described it as being "From the

6

See: Okwui Enwezor, "The Postcolonial Constellation: Contemporary Art in a State of Permanent Transition," in: *Research in African Literatures*, vol. 34, no. 4, Winter 2003, pp. 57–82, available online (via registration) at: http://muse.jhu.edu/login?auth=0&type=summary&url=/journals/research_in_african_literatures/v034/34.4enwezor.html, accessed 02/27/2014. The regional scope of the argument is announced in the title that assumes "unilinear transition" and a conception of time controlled by European modernity. For a critique of this notion of time see: Walter D. Mignolo "(De)Coloniality at Large: Time and the Colonial Difference," in: Walter D. Mignolo, *The Darker Side of Western Modernity. Global Futures, Decolonial Options*, Duke University Press, Durham (NC), 2011, pp. 149–180.

Margins to the Centre."[7] The difference was in the artists they selected and in the dialog both curators established with European modern and postmodern concepts of art and aesthetics: the first departed toward the postcolonial, the second toward the altermodern.[8] Yuko Hasegawa departed from both: neither postcolonial nor altermodern (both Eurocentered) but de-Westernizing (decentered and pluricentered). *Re:emerge* turned its back to the "center," multiplied the centers, and focused on the creativity of previously disavowed localities and people.[9]

III.

In *Re:emerge* Yuko Hasegawa drastically and unapologetically turned the tables around. Not in reverse, but around. Sharjah was neither "Orientalism in reverse" nor "'cultural relativism' in the postcolonial era"[10] as one spectator apparently commented. But to make sense of what the Sharjah Biennial entails, we need a decolonial rather than postmodern or postcolonial vocabulary. In starting from the institution of the "biennial" and brazenly departing from it, Hasegawa appropriated the exhibition to do something else: dwell in the border and engage in border thinking, sensing, and doing. It was a departure: a critique of Eurocentrism and a "Westerncentrism of knowledge" (both embedded in documenta 11 and *Altermodern*) to build something different. The difference is a radical decentring rather than reversing of European modernity's legacies.

Hasegawa was clear in this regard: that her project was not *anti* but rather critical and prospective. This means that de-Westernization and de-coloniality are always unveiling the injustices of the past and projecting global and pluricentered futures. That is precisely what "reemerge" means. And it is linked not only to the idea of culturally "reemerging" but in the larger context of the irreversible shift to the Eastern Hemisphere and the "Global South." Hasegawa had a clear and wide vision of her project. She states: "A Western perspective once dominated the debate about globalisation, but things have changed. [...] **After the process of modernization and colonialization we have seen various intercultural shifts [...]. It is especially evident in Hong Kong, Singapore, New Delhi, and Sharjah over the last ten years, where they have developed economically but also politically, having taken on their own initiative and identity. Also the traditional empires of China, Turkey and India are re-emerging in a new contemporary format.** *I am not trying to simply criticize a Eurocentric viewpoint but hoping we can re-orientate ourselves and shift our point of view.* This is the new contemporary that I am talking about."[11]

Out of almost one hundred participating artists, two were from the U.S. and twenty from Europe, less than twenty percent of the total. Sharjah is not just an event to be remembered. It is an event that will be continued in other places of the "Far East" and the "Global South" and hopefully in the south and east of the "Global

7 Okwui Enwezor, "The Black Box," in: *Documenta_11: Platform5*, exhib. cat., Hatje Cantz, Ostfildern-Ruit, 2002, pp. 42–55, here p. 45. Notice also that the postcolonial frame of his essays and of documenta 11 remains within the opening the postcoloniality introduced in Western Europe and the U.S. Sharjah 11, instead decenters and makes us forget the celebration of "radical art" confronting artists and bourgeoisie that Enwezor points out in the same essay (p. 43). De-Westernization and decoloniality are not longer "decentered" while the postcolonial frame Enwezor builts for documenta 11 "recenters" the "postcolonial world" into "postimperial Europe."

8 See: "Altermodern explained: manifesto" that accompanied the Tate Triennial, available online at: www.tate.org.uk/whats-on/tate-britain/exhibition/altermodern/explain-altermodern/altermodern-explainedmanifesto, accessed 02/27/2014.

9 Notice the difference between "postcolonial" and "decolonial." The first originated in Europe piggybacking on *The Postmodern Condition* (François Lyotard, 1978), while "decolonial" originated in the non-European world and had its institutional reference in the Bandung Conference (Indonesia) in 1955, where the word "de-Westernization" was also used. Sharjah Biennial 11 was definitely an event that falls within the wide and variegated spirit of the future: the non-European creativity, imagination, civilizations, histories, memories, and poise.

10 Quoted by Garreth Harris, in: *The Independent*, 03/26/2013, available online at: www.independent.co.uk/arts-entertainment/art/reviews/art-review-sharjah-biennial-reemerge-towards-a-new-cultural-cartography-8550164.html, accessed 02/27/2014.

11 Yuko Hasegawa as quoted from: "Re-emerge: Towards a new Cultural Cartography," interview with Lucy Rees, 02/13/2013, available online at: https://lucyreesartdotcom.wordpress.com/2013/02, accessed 01/21/2015 [bold and italics the author].

North." Furthermore, in the above statement, you can see in bold letters what "de-Westernization" (in the sense of decentring and delinking) means. The vision and execution of *Re:emerge* finds its force, as the above statement illustrates, in the fact that it is not isolated and echoes the thoughts and sentiments of many in the places Yuko Hasegawa mentions for *Re:emerge*. But let me say two words on the question of the "West," "East," or "Global South," since this is helpful in understanding the shift that *Re:emerge* is both announcing and paving the way for.

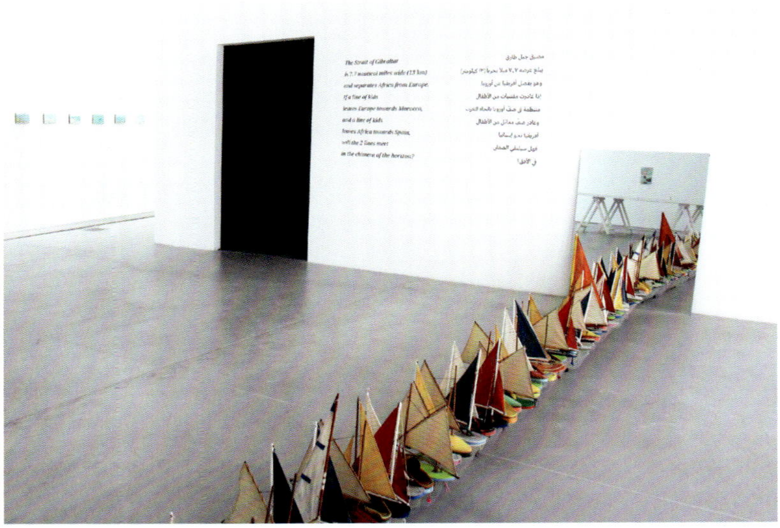

Francis Alÿs, *Don't Cross the Bridge Before You Get to the River*, 2008, videos, paintings, drawings, sculpture, and photographic installation, in collaboration with Julien Devaux, Rafael Ortega, Félix Blume, Ivan Bocara, Jimena Blasquez, Roberto Rubalcava, Begoña Rey, Abbas Benhnin, and the kids of Tarifa and Tangier, installation view, SAF Art Spaces GH, 2013

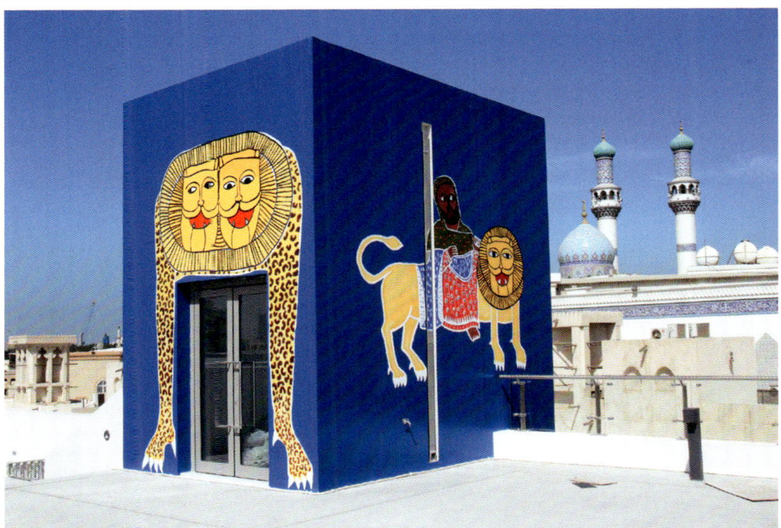

Mohamed Ali Fadlabi, *The Prediction Machine*, 2013, painting installations at SAF Art Spaces GH and in the Calligraphy Center

The West/East divide is not ontological. There is nothing on the planet that tells us about it. "West" and "East" are two Western concepts that rest on the inventions of "Indias Occidentales" (1494) and "Indias Orientales" (1529), when the planet was appropriated and divided between the Spanish and Portuguese crowns. What came later was already established. When Rome lost its central place

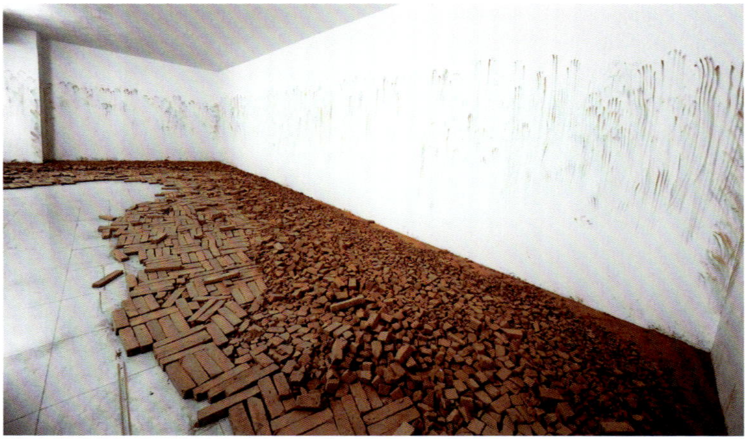

Latifa Echakhch, *Tkaf*, 2011, bricks and pigment, installation view, Sharjah Biennial 11, 2013

between the "two Indies," the rules of the game were already laid down and controlled by Western knowledge. "West" and "East" were located in relation to Rome (the center of the enunciation), which displaced Jerusalem after Christians lost hold of it during the Crusades. When the line moved to the Greenwich Meridian and Rome lost its central place to London, the only change was that instead of "Indias Occidentales" and "Indias Orientales" in Spanish, the vocabulary turned to "West" and "East" in English.

The epistemic and cultural privilege of European modernity is over, as is the politico-economic privilege. The shift to the Eastern Hemisphere and the "Global South" is founded in both economic growth and cultural confidence. Hasegawa noticed that the artists of the "Global South" and "Far East" are using the same techniques originating in the West, but privileging identity when using them. A parallel with the global economic order is in place: the planetary economic order is capitalist, but the BRICS countries are acting on politico-economic state identities and delinking from the IMF and the World Bank.[12] Dignity is at stake at every level here, for the simple reason that identity is what Eurocentrism taught the rest of the world to despise so as to become modern (postmodern or altermodern), developed, and "civilized." Hasegawa noticed, precisely, that in the past decade or so, artists from the "Global South" and the "Far East" have been using similar techniques but are becoming more and more concerned with how these might be used to make individual and communal memories – the memories of their communities and countries – reemerge.

The "courtyard" was Hasegawa's statement to use and undo the Sharjah Biennial as an institution. It was in that spirit that she responded by taking the "courtyard" as the central metaphor of the exhibit. In an interview with Hasegawa, Stephanie Bailey asked if "the metaphor of the garden feels representative of a global territory where distinctions are blurring and merging," to which Hasegawa responded: "Yes, and it is also this idea of the place of memory. That is very important for a culture. So this was my orientation towards curating this biennial with the consciousness but you also have to contribute, too, to the space you are interacting or engaging with."[13]

Place of memory; local consciousness... Yes, indeed. That is what shifting the geography of knowing and sensing means: one could not "re-emerge" by pegging one local temporality to the linear local temporality of Eurocentered modernity (and its corollaries). It is no longer necessary to start from Greece and Rome.

12 "The deepest rationale for the BRICS is almost certainly the creation of new Bretton Woods-type institutions that are inclined toward the developing world," Martyn Davies, chief executive officer of Johannesburg-based Frontier Advisory, which provides research on emerging markets (see online: http://topics.bloomberg.com/emerging-markets/, accessed 02/27/2014), said in a phone interview. And: "There's a shift in power from the traditional to the emerging world. There is a lot of geo-political concern about this shift in the western world." (BRICS meeting in South Africa, March 2013 [same month as Sharjah Biennial 11], see online: http://rt.com/business/bank-rival-imf-world-852/, accessed 02/27/2014).

13 Yuko Hasegawa in conversation with Stephanie Bailey, *Whitewall Magazine*, March 15, 2013, available online at: https://whitewallmag.com/art/curator-qa-yuko-hasegawa-on-the-2013-sharjah-biennial, accessed 01/21/2015.

That is what the "courtyard" means: it is not the place of the Muses, or the solitary place of study, but a place where inside and outside meet – where people live and pass each other. It is also a place where cultural identity is rooted. But above all, the "courtyard" is rooted in the histories and memories of Persian and Arab civilizations, as much as ancient Greece's white columns and Roman aqueducts are embedded in the local memories of Western civilization.

In her preface to the event's catalog, Hasegawa gives a longer explanation of the "courtyard" as the special and temporal anchor of Sharjah Biennial 11: "Courtyards, unlike gardens in the West, which can be viewed from the outside, Islamic courtyards are *social spaces that must be experienced from inside, including smell, touch and sound.* The courtyard was incorporated wherever Islam extended its influence in Sicily, Southern Spain, the coastal regions of North Africa and the Ottoman Empire."[14]

14 Yuko Hasegawa in: Nikki Columbus (ed.), *Re:emerge. Towards a New Cultural Cartography*, exhib. cat., Sharjah Biennial 11, Sharjah Art Foundation, Sharjah, 2013, p. 23.

Hasegawa noted that all the artists invited to show at SB11 – and particularly the eighty-percent from the non-European world – embed their work in their own local memories and histories. In many ways Hasegawa has done the same by using the meaning and memories of the courtyard garden in Islamic civilization as a place of memory. But it is not only memories inscribed in the present, but also the senses: smell, touch, and sound. In this light, producing a biennial like this is in itself a radical shift in the geopolitics of knowing, sensing, and believing.

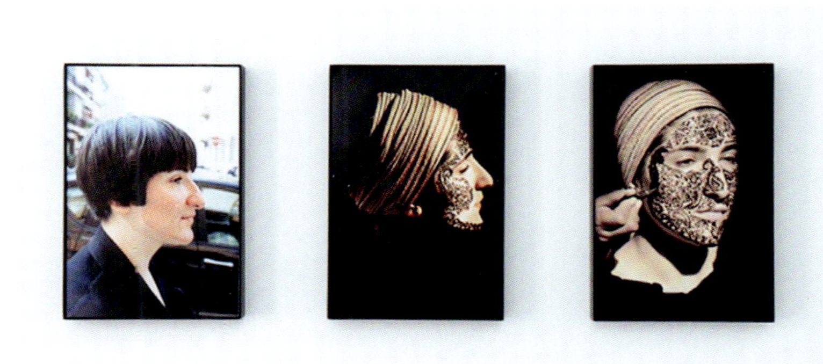

Taus Makhacheva, *Delinking*, 2011, three color photographs, installation view, Sharjah Biennial 11, 2013

The "courtyard" in Persian and Arab Islam, like the constellation of stars known as the Southern Cross in the South American Andes, are anchors of memories, social organizations, and patterns of living spaces. They are both places of memories and collective consciousness – one is terrestrial, the other celestial, but they have similar functions. I learned from my Muslim colleagues at Duke University that the Persian philosopher Abū Hāmid Al-Ghazālī (1058–1111) was informed in his thinking by the courtyard. Ebrahim Moosa explained to me that *dihlīz* – "that space between the door and the house" – is a Persian word that has been "arabized." In trying to understand why this concept was so crucial for Al-Ghazālī, Moosa speculates: "What one slowly begins to fathom is that the *dihlīz*, or the *dihlīz*-ian space is a liminal space [...] as well as the action of two entries: entry from the *outside* and entry into the *inside*."[15]

15 Ebrahim Moosa, *Ghazālī and the Poetics of Imagination*, The University of North Carolina Press, Chapel Hill (NC), 2008, p. 48.

Al-Ghazālī was living and thinking in a polycentric world order (no civilizations ruled or imposed upon other civilizations) with noncapitalist economies. Today, we have Moroccan philosopher and feminist Fatima Mernissi who has been reflecting on the subjective impact of the courtyard. She tells her readers: "My childhood was happy because the frontiers were crystal clear. The first frontier was the threshold separating our family's salon from the main courtyard."[16] Later she said: "I would sit on our threshold and look at our house as if I had never seen it before. First, there was the square and rigid courtyard, where symmetry ruled everything."[17] Further on, Mernissi continues: "Looking at the sky from the courtyard was an overwhelming experience. At first, it looked tame because of the man-made square frame. But then the movement of the early morning stars, fading slowly into the deep blue and white, became so intense that it could make you dizzy."[18]

16 Fatima Mernissi, *Dreams of Trespass. Tales of a Harem Girlhood*, photographs by Ruth V. Ward, Perseus Books, Cambridge (MA), 1995, p. 3.

17 Ibid., p. 4.

18 Ibid., p. 5.

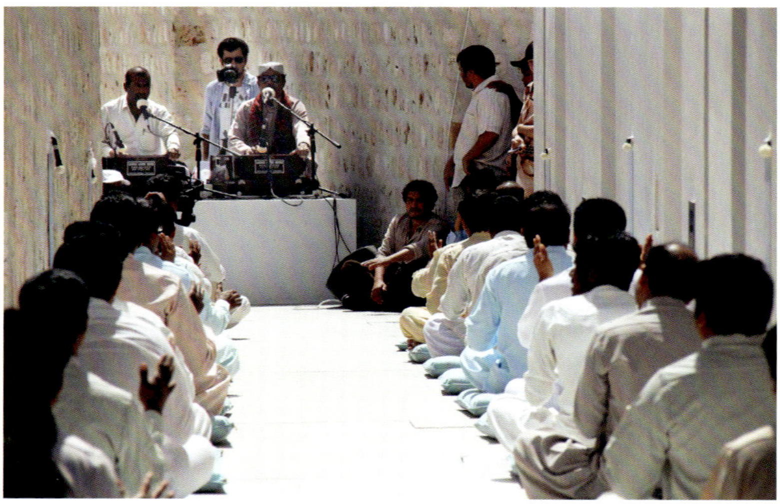

Wael Shawky, *Dictums 10:120*, 2011–2013, live installation with 32 performers, microphones, wooden platform, cushions, sound system, alleyway between SAF Art Spaces GH and F

How important is this? I grew up in Argentina, in a small town in the countryside. During the summer nights in the front garden of my parent's house (not a courtyard), I would sit on a chair and look at the magnificent splendors of the southern sky. I pondered on the constellation known as the Southern Cross and still use that reference, after 40 years in the "Global North," thinking about how the Incas in the South American Andes built a whole cosmology and social organization based on the model of the Southern Cross. And so it is for the courtyard in the Islamic, Persian, and Arab worlds. These "spaces" contain the sensibility, memories, and world-sensing that you simply cannot find in London, Berlin, Paris, or New York. You can have other substitutes, of course: there are other ways of bringing into being such a "place-sensing" experience. And that is fine. But what is not fine is to expect the universalization of Western localities and sensibilities, simply because you cannot universalize the local without erasing the localities of others. That was and is the problem with the Eurocentered idea of modernity. Once, people around the world believed that "the way" was to embrace Western modernity. Now, the trick has been uncovered and the departures have already begun. They are wide and far spread.

Interestingly enough – and that is one of the lasting lessons of *Re:emerge* – there is not *one* universality for which only *someone* has the key. This is what the "Western-centrism of knowledge" means in Yuko Hasegawa's expression of it: to possess the key to all doors of knowledge, culture, subjectivity, religion, economy, and politics – and every thought related to the management of population and nature. Of course, that was true, but it is no longer the case. For that reason, Sharjah Biennial 11 is a single event but one that is already part of a larger global unfolding. Histories are not ending, they are changing orientations: they are "reorienting" themselves as Yuko Hasegawa would say, invoking the title of Andre Gunder Frank's book.[19]

19 See: Andre Gunder Frank, *ReORIENT: Global Economy in the Asian Age*, University of California Press, Berkeley and Los Angeles (CA), 1998.

IV.

Let's take another look at the period leading up to the 1500s. The planet was polycentric and noncapitalist. Many civilizations and cultures coexisted. There were inequalities within each civilization then as much as there are now, but no one single civilization dominated the others. Until 1500, the planet housed many civilizations, none of them centered on a capitalist economy (for example, the economy of reinvesting the surplus in order to increase gains and wealth, disregarding the consequences). Then, the long night of European modernity began. First, the Renaissance was invented and with it the coming into being of "Western civilization" (the youngest on the planet). The European Renaissance meant Death (with a capital D) for the ancient civilizations (Maya, Aztec, Inca) of what came to be known as America. Then, the Enlightenment followed suit and reduced Asia and Africa to Darkness and Barbarism. That "fiction" lasted until about 2000.

The idea that economy means growth, development, and accumulation (and not the administration of scarcity) is today global. Inequalities subsist, but the global order is no longer and solely in the hands and minds of European and U.S. states. The BRICS countries are disputing political and economic control. In this vein, we can read Sharjah Biennial 11 entering into dispute with "Western" hegemony in the sphere of culture, knowledge, aesthetics, and, above all, sensibility. (*aesthesis*, from where the word aesthetics is derived.) What is indeed "reemerging" is the dignifying creativity that does not reverse but erases Orientalism.

Western epistemic, economic, political, and cultural hegemony was possible because the construction and management of knowledge was in the hands and heads of European actors, in European languages and supported by European institutions. "Western-centrism of knowledge" means that sustainable knowledge was cast in six modern European imperial languages based on Greek and Latin. This is not a geographical but an epistemic concept. In this, we should understand the subtitle of Sharjah Biennial 11,

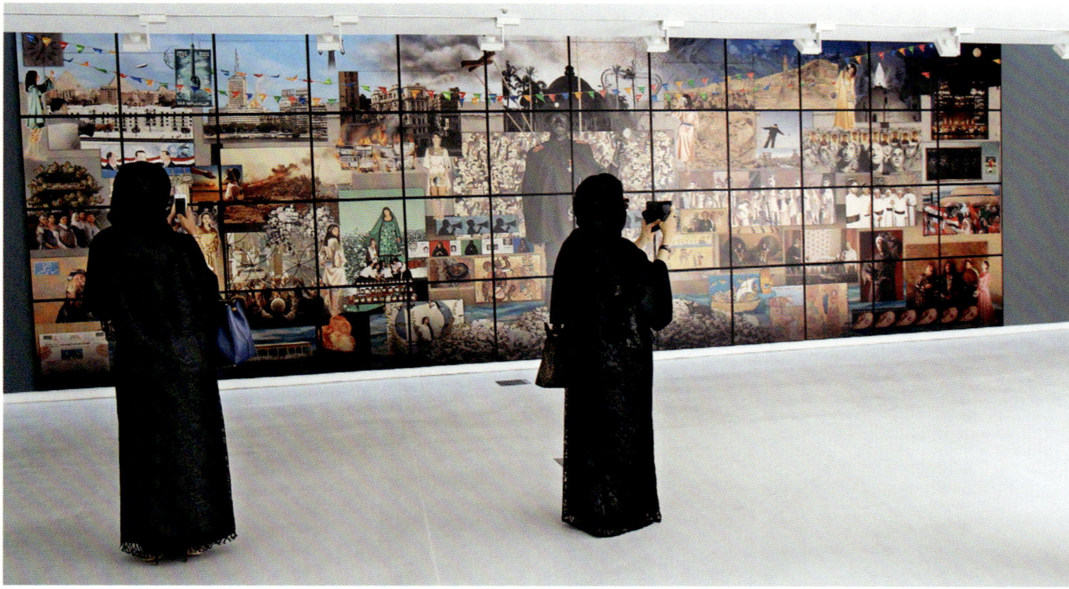

Hala Elkoussy, *Myths and Legends Room – The Mural*, 2010, 48 framed color photographs and color photographic paper, installation view, SAF Art Spaces F, 2013

Towards a New Cultural Cartography, as an epistemic and aesthetic shift rather than only a geographic one. These geo-historical locations matter precisely because the planet we live on was mapped through and by Western cartographic knowledge: First, Second and Third Worlds is a recent example of ranking and racializing locales.

Notions like "return" and "reemerging" have flagged the diverse planetary consciousness currently delinking from Eurocentrism. It means, as Hasegawa points out, not only economic growth but also "relearning." That is, learning to relearn and build on identities that the dominance of Western knowledge taught them (us) to despise. In complimentary ways, Sheikha Hoor Al Qasimi,[20] President of the Sharjah Art Foundation, underlines the importance of reinscribing the past in the debate of the present not only to build economic, political, and multipolar worlds, but also pluriversal, epistemic, aesthetic, and religious subjectivities.[21]

Sheikha Hoor Al Qasimi is another key figure in both the vision and the making of Sharjah Biennial 11. Described as "fluent Japanese (and Russian and Chinese) speaker and highly knowledgeable about contemporary art," it was the Sheikha who turned "eastward for her next curator."[22] Aside from Hasegawa, there is more in the team behind the Sharjah Biennial than meets the eye. It has been through the work of the Sharjah Art Foundation, established in 2009, that has also interrogated the Western/Euro-centered hegemony in politics, economy, and culture. What the Sharjah Biennial 11 also achieves is to show that certain aspects of the culture and concepts of "art" have run their course. Despite it having made significant contributions to world civilizations, it has clearly reached its limits. Modern (postmodern and alter-modern) art and aesthetics are no longer meaningful to account for the global shift Sharjah Biennial 11 accomplished.[23]

20

I began to perceive this type of transformation already in the renovated Sharjah Museum of Islamic Civilization, the Museum of Islamic Art in Doha, Qatar, and the Asian Civilisations Museum in Singapore. Alert critics are quick to jump and point out that these are "state" institutions. Nationalism? A celebration of Asian civilization? Yes, indeed. Very much like the British Museum, the Louvre, both national relics and prides of Western civilization. The difference is that Asian and Middle Eastern civilizations were "represented" in the Museum of Europe or the U.S., while now museums are being used to retrieve stolen memories. "Reemerge" means just that there is no longer a place in the world for this aberration.

21

See: Anna Somers Cocks, "Sharjah looks East, and West. Biennial embraces divergent ways of seeing the world, despite growing censorship in the Gulf," in: *The Art Newspaper*, no. 245, April 2013, available online at: www.theartnewspaper.com/articles/Sharjah-looks-East-and-West/29141, accessed 02/27/2014.

22

Ibid.

23

This was the intention, as I understand it, of Nicolas Bourriaud when he curated the Tate Triennal in 2009, published the "Altermodern explained: manifesto" and the book *The Radicant* (Sternberg Press, Berlin, 2009). It was indeed the last attempt in a series of already well-established events like the Venice Biennale and the well-known four-years documenta event in Kassel, Germany.

24

Sheikha Hoor Al Qasimi in: *Columbus*, 2013, p. 14.

25

The Human Development Report 2013, is titled *The Rise of the South: Human Progress in a Diverse World*. I do believe that South Africa and Brazil are in the South, and India in South Asia. But China and Russia are not quite in the South. Moreover, the rise of the "South" (meaning, truly, the non-European and U.S. part of the planet), is not only economic, but cultural and culture means regaining the proud or disavowed identities. This is the frame in which Sharjah Biennial 11, 2013, shall be understood and its legacy not forgotten.

In her introduction to the Sharjah Biennial 11 catalog, Al Qasimi informs us that since its sixth edition in 2003, the Sharjah Biennial has examined contemporary culture and its place in the United Emirates. She continues to recount how in the past ten years, the Sharjah Biennial "has offered a critical lens to explore, reflect, and reconsider questions that are relevant today" particularly in the sphere of culture and education. In this general frame, the "Biennial has become a public platform for debate among more than 900,000 people of different backgrounds who constitute our local community."[24]

As far as local places like Sharjah are asserting themselves in their locality, everywhere else (Paris, London, New York, Tokyo, Hong Kong, Shanghai, Moscow, and so on...) is in turn reduced to size and locality. This change of epoch is characterized by a growing network of localities that are erasing the long history of center and margins, of First and Third Worlds engrained in the monocultural cartography of European modernity. It moves "towards a new cultural cartography" – a departure towards a world order constituted by a network of centers rather than by center and peripheries.

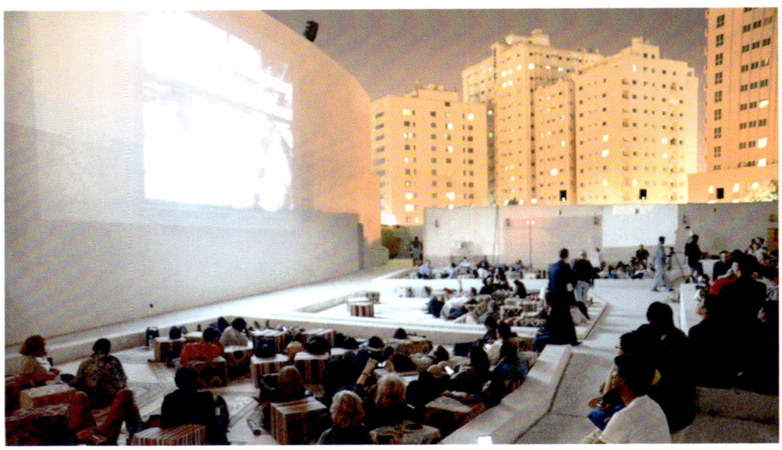

Mirage City Cinema at the Sharjah Biennial 11, 2013, Maurouth Square, cinema-architecture space by Apichatpong Weerasethakul and Ole Scheeren

26

A parallel trajectory that I would describe as "grassroots epistemic, political, and aesthetic projects" goes by the name of "decolonial aesthetics" and/or "decolonial aesthesis." Artists, curators, art and cultural critics, and historians and philosophers are marching in the same direction: delinking from Eurocentrism. It is one aspect of a larger intellectual movement that originated in South America and the Caribbean. Walter Mignolo and Rolando Vázquez, "The Decolonial AestheSis Dossier," in: *Social Text*, available online at: www.socialtextjournal.org/periscope_article/the-decolonial-aesthesis-dossier, accessed 01/21/2015.

V.

I am looking at the Sharjah Biennial 11 not only as a single event, but also mainly as an event that is at the crossroads of various historical processes shifting the geography of sensing, knowing, and believing. I am also hoping that the seed that has been planted in the emirate of Sharjah in 2013 that will become, like the Bandung Conference of 1955, a landmark for upcoming futures.[25] What we learned from Bandung is that there was a need to delink from both capitalism and communism. What we are learning from the Sharjah Biennial 11 are the limits of abstract universals (epistemic, aesthetic, religious).[26] For that reason, *Re:emerge. Towards a New Cultural Cartography* is more than the title of a biennial. Rather, it is a manifesto of delinking that announces and opens up distinctive roads towards the future.

Appendix: Illustrations

The selection of artists was amazingly consistent with curator Yuko Hasegawa's theoretical statements. The eighty-percent of artists from the "Global South" and the "Far East" are all engaging the past in the present, making memories derogated by the Western global expansion over five centuries reemerge. Catalogs cannot supplant experiencing the art directly, but they can give you a clear picture of the consistency between curators' statements and artists invited. Comparing the Sharjah Biennial 11's catalog with the ones of documenta 11 and *Altermodern* at the Tate Triennial, is a telling lesson: while in Sharjah Biennial 11 the consistency between statement and artists is remarkable, in documenta 11 and *Altermodern* it was not as easy to understand the "postcolonial constellation" of invited artists in the first, and what the "altermodern" would be in the second where eighty-percent of the artists were from Europe and the U.S.[27]

Parallel to the artists' exhibition at Sharjah Biennial 11 was the reemerging of the city itself, and the courtyard provided the impetus and the spatial frame to enhance the reemergence of the city itself.

Some examples of works that illustrate the consistency between vision and goals of Sharjah Biennial 11:

1) "Inspired by the courtyard in Islamic architecture – in particular the historical courtyards of Sharjah, where elements of both public and private life intertwine – SB11 Curator Yuko Hasegawa proposes a new cultural cartography that reconsiders the relationships between the Arab world, Asia, the Far East, through North Africa to Latin America."[28] She stated: "I am inviting a selection of architects and cultural practitioners from Lebanon, India, Belgium, Japan, Spain and elsewhere to create temporary architectural interventions that will help envision new urban structures that connect Sharjah's historic area and its courtyard typology with the larger city. Courtyard cultures around the world conceal their great potential. These spaces are concentrated symbols of years of rich cultural accumulation. They originated in great civilisations that morphed into countries stagnated by the transition to 'modernity.' These countries currently inhabit a moment of enormous potential, energised as they are by the forces of globalisation, by the vibrant cultural exchanges migration has facilitated, and by increased socio-cultural, political, and economic hybridisation. I am not referring to monotonous and perfunctory data sharing and consumption, but to the production of new knowledge that can be potentially enabled by the courtyard – a space and a symbol that resists the destruction of culture. Within this space, the international and local encounter one another and negotiate the effects of each passing wave of globalisation."[29]
2) Nevin Aladağ, Turkey, *Session* (2013). This video triptych shot in Sharjah brings together the topography of the city and percussion music composed with Arabic, African, and Indian

27 An enthusiastic review of documenta 11, Peter Schjeldhal, "The Global Salon. European extravaganzas," July 1, 2002, available online at: www.newyorker.com/archive/2002/07/01/020701craw_artworld, accessed 02/27/2014; and for *Altermodern*, Adrian Searle, "Altermodern review: 'The richest and most generous Tate Triennial yet'," February 3, 2009, available online at: www.guardian.co.uk/artanddesign/2009/feb/02/altermodern-tate-triennial, accessed 02/27/2014.

28 Sharjah Biennial 11 Curatorial Concept, available online at: http://universes-in-universe.org/eng/bien/sharjah_biennial/2013/curatorial_concept, accessed 02/27/2014.

29 Curatorial statement, www.sharjahart.org/biennial/sharjah-biennial-11/information, accessed 02/27/2014.

percussion instruments. The video triptych invokes the spirit of reemergence in that it works with musical instruments that elude the European renaissance. At the same time that the instruments are played by and in the environment of Sharjah, cultures once disavowed by Western hegemony "reemerge" with the force and the confidence of pluriversal futures.

3) Francis Alÿs, Belgium, *Don't Cross the Bridge Before Getting to the River* (2008). At two-sided screen plays a video loop of a 2008 "action": two groups of children carrying "flip-flop boats" (that we see in the photo) which simultaneously take off from Tarifa in Spain and Tangier in Morocco; they will walk to meet each other in an imaginary horizon. A storytelling and an event set up with real people and cameras.[30]

4) Mohamed Ali Fadlabi, Sudan, *The Prediction Machine* (2013). Making references to Ethiopian church paintings, African barber salon art, and to Sun Ra's afro-futurism as well as to some retro-futurism, Ali Fadlabi tells the history of saints and heroes.

5) Latifa Echakhch, Morocco, *Tkaf* (2013). *Takf* is a word in a North African dialect (Darija) that invokes a curse by someone close to the person cursed. This is a clear example of bringing sacred ancient memories that still persist today in the artistic domain.

6) Taus Makhacheva, Dagestan, Russia, *Delinking* (2011). Makhacheva's work fits well both into decolonial and reemerging aesthetics. The title borrowed from decolonial theorists connects three photographs of a performance in Milan during which her face was painted with traditional *mehndi*, or henna designs from Africa, India, and the Middle East.

7) Wael Shawky, Egypt, *Dictums* (2013) is a Qawwali song composed with fragments of curatorial talks translated into Urdu. The roots of Qawwali can be traced back to eighth century Persia (today's Iran and Afghanistan). During the first major migration from Persia, in the eleventh century, the musical tradition of Sema migrated to South Asia, Turkey, and Uzbekistan. Once again, the roots and the sources are founded some place else and they "re-merge" to crack the hegemony and the danger of a single story.[31]

8) Hala Elkoussy, Egypt, *Myths and Legends Room – The Mural* (2010) looks at the genre of large-scale wall painting as commemorative propaganda art, making reference to murals and dioramas that celebrate the history of modern Egypt. Conceived and completed a year before the start of the Egyptian Revolution, Hala Elkoussy's piece seems to anticipate the events in Tahrir Square. Through the distillation of recent myths and legends, a more fluid and human reading of history is put forward, in sharp contrast to what is taught in schools in Egypt and most of the Arab world (from SB11 Guidebook).

9) "A film programme curated by Thai filmmaker Apichatpong Weerasethakul will feature programming by leading figures in the film industry, including Steve Anker, Dean of the School of Film/Video at California Institute of the Arts (CalArts),

30 A video of the installation at Sharjah Biennial 11 is available online at: http://vimeo.com/63551961, accessed 02/27/2014.

31 A video of the live performance of *Dictums* at Sharjah Biennial 11 is available online at: http://vimeo.com/63397752, accessed 02/27/2014.

Los Angeles; Tilda Swinton, Scotland; Mehelli Modi, Founder of Second Run DVD, London; Alcino Leite Neto, editor, Sao Paulo; Khavn De La Cruz, poet, pianist, film-maker, Mondomanila, the Philippines; Jean-Pierre Rehm, theorist, Festival Director, FIDMarseille, Paris; Ali Jaafar, Executive Director, Independent Film Division, Quinta Communications, London; and Apichatpong Weerasethakul, film director/producer, Chiang Mai, Thailand. The programme will include evening screenings in an outdoor courtyard cinema in the new SAF spaces."[32]

32 Information on the Mirage City Cinema, available online at: www.sharjahart.org/biennial/sharjah-biennial-11/information/film-programme, accessed 02/27/2014.

This essay is a revised version of a text commissioned by *Ibraaz* as part of Platform 005, themed around globalizing tactics in North Africa and the Middle East. It was published on ibraaz.org in May 2013 and in print in July 2014 as part of volume one of a series, "Visual Cultures in North Africa and the Middle East," published jointly by I.B. Tauris and Ibraaz, titled *Uncommon Grounds. New Media and Critical Practices in North Africa and the Middle East* (ed. Anthony Downey).

Dimitris Papadopoulos, Vassilis Tsianos, and Margarita Tsomou

Athens: Metropolitan Blockade — Real Democracy

Metropolitan blockade is when urban space turns against itself, blocks the movements and the connections that sustain it, only to mobilize space as a direct means for political action. Metropolitan blockades are today the chinks in the wall of established politics through which we can get a glimpse of the future. It was the blockade of Syntagma Square in Athens in 2011, which gave birth to a new frame of time and space in Greek politics, where future was again at stake, where future took place instantly in the discourses and practices in people's assemblies. The area of Syntagma Square became a zone outside of representational political power and oligarchic democracy. From the perspective of established political power this turning of urban space against itself is conceived as a process that creates (political) monsters. But from the perspective of those who have no part in the given order of political representation it introduces an ecology of real, militant democracy. And this happened in Syntagma during the months of the occupation. The practice of reclaiming urban space introduced a new temporality, a new feeling of persistence, a different zone of time which could then be filled with the invention of new practices of cooperation. In a situation where the collapse of the system could happen any moment, where long-term plans were almost impossible, where urgency prevailed and each day threatened to be the upcoming apocalypse, many people in Greece ceased to feel fear. Instead they started to act in ways that produced fear. The people didn't seem to hold onto the promise of being saved by the Greek-European austerity prophets. "We don't sell anything, we don't own anything, we don't pay" was one of the main slogans in Syntagma. They yearned for a breakdown of time that could set the clock back to zero in order to build up the new institutions of the people. It was the financial markets and the creditors who started to fear the masses reclaiming metropolitan space and remaking political institutions from below. Urban Panic.

Urban panic: when the fear of the metropolitan masses comes to inhabit the elites. As Jackie Orr reminds us, panic from the perspective of social and political power was a destructive collective social phenomenon that had to become desocialized and individualized. Biopower becomes psychopower. The metropolitan blockade reclaims panic as a genuine articulation of the masses. People disidentify themselves from the atomized panicking individual to become an urban monster that devours space. When panic is de-individualized and resocialized it becomes the nightmare of the elites. In the new time and space of Syntagma the people not only became monsters because they threatened political power; they also became monsters because they underwent a process of transformation within themselves. They transformed through their own invention of a political dialog that they called “direct democracy.” The new mode of debate, decision-making, and the cooperative organization of life in the square was a surprise even to themselves, it started producing a dangerous class. And beyond this, the processes in Syntagma didn’t seem to have a clear target – they kept opening questions instead of trying to answer them and bring the process of mobilization to a closure. The desire for a new constituent power was not answered by defining a definite set of demands but by constantly seeking new forms of articulation. People knew that the reinvention of the future can only happen through patient collective work. To put it in the words of an activist in the square: “we are patient, we are not talking about weeks, we are preparing for a struggle that will last years.”

In Athens on June 28 and 29, 2011 the face of the monster was the cockroach. It was during the general strike just before a crucial vote of the Greek parliament to pass a drastic bill of new austerity measures brought by the PASOK government headed by Georgios Papandreou and Evangelos Venizelos. The main trade unions were forced to call the 48 hours general strike because of the pressure from Syntagma and some of their local branches, rather than because their central leadership was supporting this general strike. This was the square’s general strike. It is indicative that the underground workers volunteered to break the general strike in order to run the trains and secure access to Syntagma. The aim was that masses of people surround the parliament – not just only for some hours during the rally but for two days through continuous actions. At the end, the parliament could only convene because riot police used massive tear-gassing and hand grenades to disperse the crowds. The brutal police repression was encountered with equal determination: the people that had occupied the square over many weeks were equipped with gas masks, mouth protection, diving goggles, Maalox. They chanted: “We won’t go before they go!” The police used an excessive amount of tear gas. As if the people were cockroaches that they were trying to exterminate with insecticides. This was how the people described themselves: as cockroaches. Nelli Kambouri says that the more people were tear-gassed the more determined they were to block the metropolis. Cockroaches become resistant to insecticides. And that’s how the people survived the contamination of the air, by becoming cockroaches, by changing their tactics and retreating from the main squares only to reappear again after minutes. Back and forth and constantly in new formations. This is the formula of metropolitan blockade. No social subjects as we know them, no political subjects of existing political representation. Cockroaches, just post-subjective actors in a constant metamorphosis of being together. They then found themselves after two days again in the square, in one of the biggest assemblies in weeks, having shared the deep experience of the teargas and their own metamorphosis. They shared the small smiles of a new collective stubbornness: "We have been beaten, we will go on, no matter what." No demoralization, no disappointment. It is when the logic of defeat or victory is replaced by resilience and patience. Cockroaches prevail and go on.

There was not an identifiable social subject in Syntagma Square. Rather it was the square that became the actor. People carried placards claiming "We are nobody" – the masses identified with the imagination of "nobody," one who magically is everywhere and nowhere. The people, coming and going, dispersed, uncoordinated, the tents, the food, the kitchen, the drums, the PA system, the dogs, the burned trees, the heat, everything that was there and cooperated became part of this occasion. This configuration of the occasion was generated through the immediate process of living together and instituting together in the square. Traditional left-wing organizational habits became irrelevant. The left was overhauled by the unfolding events, they were temporarily confused and were in the end forced to exit or rethink their practices. Traditional forms of representation started to break down.

The ruins of representation. One could see all these banners attached to every possible post on the square that speak a different language than the language one is used to. Parties and flags of big organizations and the main trade unions were forbidden. The usual codes of representative organization were reordered and alternative ways were created in order to block the intrusive and at times toxic political establishment. The semantic interfaces of the square were sometimes poetic, sometimes declarative, sometimes threatening. Five gallows were set up facing the parliament. Two big helicopter figures referred to the circulating story of the flight of the then Argentinean president Fernando de la Rúa in 2001. Papandreou and Venizelos should go. And many more. *¡Que se vayan todos!* All of them must go!

Every politician must go. What is described as a wild and non-political turn of a whole generation signified exactly the oppsite. That politics happen outside of its established institutions. A banner on Syntagma reads "Now they fear us." Urban panic: the transfer of fear from the deindividualized and desubjectified masses to the political elites. "The days of plenty are over." "Your days are numbered." Since the beginning of the economic crisis parliamentarians in Greece avoid going public, they fear verbal and sometimes even physical abuse by passersby. The people in Syntagma did not propose a dialog; they didn't invite politicians to negotiate. There were no claims for reforms. State institutions were not addressed. Representation broke down as the square became alive and changed its shapes and scale. The dialog was refused because there was nobody worth addressing in the political system – belief in the power of the parliament and the established parties to contribute to a *commune bonum* had died. Politics happened outside of the established institutions, they were reinvented beyond representation and reborn in parallel organizational structures. Thus political discourse of Syntagma circumvented addressing power directly – the squatters preferred to talk among themselves.

Rescaling the square. Metropolitan blockade is not so much about dissecting, separating, and cutting off access to urban space, but about multiplying space, reconnecting different parts of the city to each other, creating layers of rest and action. The organization of the area in front of the parliament was divided into the "upper square" and the "lower square." The upper square consisted of the forecourt of the parliament building and the main street passing in front of it. This street was blocked for more than two months. The lower part, which is also physically lower than the forecourt and the road, is the actual Syntagma Square. Although the people floated between the two parts of this area, there was a distinction between the affect and practices which took place in the upper and the lower square. The upper, the one closer to the parliament, was where people confronted power, rallied, threatened the existing political system and parliamentarians. The lower square was the space of the makeshift camp, the space of the assemblies, the space where the infrastructure of the popular uprising was maintained. The lower square was the space of organization, the upper square was the space of direct confrontation.

Syntagma and in particular the upper part was a passage. People come and go, perform the direct assault of the politics of established political parties. Some say that more than three million people found themselves there during the two months of these events. Direct confrontation takes the shape of anger: verbal abuse of democracy, of the police and the politicians. What they shout is profoundly vulgar, often very sexist, sometimes nationalist. Pensioners, people forced into poverty, high school students, unemployed, precarious workers, people unhappy with the political system of the country. As Maro Kouri says, Syntagma became the place where people went for their Sunday promenade, they walk with their kids and grandchildren, gesticulate angrily against the parliament and the police, swear, eat ice cream, pass by, come back. All this is a glimpse of reclaiming freedom from a political system that failed to represent anything meaningful to them. This is a new form of participation in action, the space where those who have no part block metropolitan space and the mainstream political language in order to reappear on the political scene. The language of those who have no part sounds incompatible to mainstream politics and our own political aesthetic, but it is the language which extends the space of action and magnifies the space of possibility as it becomes less and less an articulation of anger and more and more a performance of freedom, of real democracy.

The lower square was the area of the camp. And it was also where the assemblies took place; it was called the "lower parliament," the other to the official parliament. The lower square was the point that connected Greece to the powerful experiences of the 2011 Arab revolutions. The lower parliament connects Syntagma to this cycle of metropolitan struggles along the common Mediterranean space. In the same way as in the Puerta del Sol, the metropolitan blockade of Athens and the occupation of Syntagma was related to the emergence of new forms of experimenting with democracy. The lower parliament was a non-representational assembly. It refused to elect representatives and used the imperceptibility of direct decision-making as a new political tactic against the media and the political system that always tries to find a representative, a spokesperson, or a coherent political program. And most importantly it refused to develop a system of permanent spokespersons which left established political power and media perplexed and helpless in addressing the monster in the square. Organization matters.

The organization of the assemblies was the core of the life of the lower parliament in Syntagma. The assembly always took place at 9 p.m. every day. The assembly was the only constitutive space. There was no other collective instance where decisions about the occupation were made. The agenda of the general assembly included only these topics and issues that had been decided in previous assemblies. All proposals for including specific issues in the agenda to be discussed during an assembly as well as all proposals submitted during the day in written form to the administrative office of the assembly were sent to the thematic working groups before they reached the assembly. These working groups compiled all proposals and returned them to the assembly in the form of resolutions for debate and decision. The final resolutions were put for approval or rejection to the assembly the latest at midnight so that everybody could be included (many people worked or had to travel far to return to their homes). Everybody had the right to speak, and once the resolutions had been presented to the participants, everyone who wanted to speak could draw a lot and wait for their turn to talk. Usually there were 80–100 presenters every evening until the vote on the resolutions, and the participants every day were more than 2,000 people. Although there were significant drawbacks to this procedure, it had been decided that this is the most appropriate organizational form since this would preclude any attempts to change the agenda and reduce the danger of interventions of parties or other structured groups. It could be also much more effective than consensus decision-making, which had dominated radical forms of political organization and had proved ineffective during the events in Syntagma. After the vote at midnight the assembly continued as an open discussion forum. The organization of the assembly drew upon the extensive support of people outside of it. The main assembly was the visible peak of real democracy but real democracy was happening far beyond the assembly itself in the fusion of space and people though the metropolitan blockade: a new ecology of metropolitan existence.

The ecology of metropolitical struggles and the experimentation with "direct democracy" was maintained through a series of working groups that were responsible for dealing with practical issues. There were thousands of people registered in each working group. These people were mobilized according to the needs of each specific task of each working group. The only possible contribution to this ecology was through active participation. The assembly and the square did not have a cashier and monetary contributions were not allowed because it was decided that there are more effective ways for support and because the camp could maintain its existence by establishing its own cooperative forms of exchange. Any contributions to the camp could be only material, from food to medicaments to pencils to PA systems. Among the many working groups maintaining the ecology of real democracy were: technical support, resource management, culture, cleaning, administrative support, food provision, translation services, respect and protection, communications, multimedia, legal team, health, neighborhood work, bank for exchanges of services, transport and postal services, self-control group etc. All groups met every day at 6 p.m. following an open assembly, and the transport and postal services group was responsible for distributing the proposal of each working group to the other groups and to the general assembly. Besides these working groups there were a series of thematic subassemblies that discussed crucial social and political issues, such as economy and crisis, work and unemployment, education and universities, health and insurance, environment, technology, solidarity, disability, justice and legal issues, analysis of debt, etc. These subassemblies met every day 7 p.m. to 9 p.m., and in some of them hundreds of people used to participate. All assemblies and working groups were open to everybody, the only restriction was that nobody had the right to represent a working group and speak in its name.

The virtual politics of the metropolitan blockade is self-organized and digitized. The square decided to block the entry of mainstream media into the camp and the procedures of the lower parliament. The assembly and the camp could only be filmed by the camp's communications working group and its media team, which had up to 38 members during the moments of intense action and during the police siege in the days of the general strike. The main decisions of the assembly were communicated through the media team and on the website of the camp: www.real-democracy.gr. A central role in the organization of actions and mobilization of participants was played by the social media – the blockade of Syntagma on May 25th was circulated through Facebook and Twitter; livestreams covered every general assembly for those who could not attend in person; online radio broadcast news and the resolutions of the square. The organization of the square and its actions was collective, a-subjective, digitized. In Syntagma, the escape from representation met the use of sociotechnical means in order to create possibilities for alternative forms of self-organization. As somebody in the square said: "The system is nearing its end – let's download the future here and now." What was common to all these different forms of organization – the direct democracy of the main assembly, the working groups, the self-organized nonrepresentational mediatization of the lower parliament – was the belief that the urgency of the country's situation needed to be encountered with some form of hesitation or resilience and patience; with a careful and deliberate pace, very different to the pace of imposed urgency and unavoidability that has been used by the PASOK government to legitimize its sweeping economic and social reforms.

The experimentation with speed during everyday action and decision-making is crucial for the success of a metropolitan blockade. In the general conditions in which Syntagma took place, slowness and carefulness were regarded as the necessary temporal mode that could allow the reclaiming of established politics. Many saw in the long procedures and the lengthy and often tiring debates during the assemblies – especially after the destruction of the camp by the police and the city council of Athens – an obstacle to the efficacy of the camp. Many thought that this paralyzed the agility of the camp and made it unable to act. But the opposite is the case. Real democracy was practiced not as another form of parliamentarian representation operating in the same temporal coordinates as the official "upper parliament"; rather, real democracy happened in Athens in 2011 when the metropolitan space was actually used in alternative ways that escaped organized political power to allow for staying in the heart of the unfolding events and at the same time allow for a space where one can think and imagine these events differently. What the camps and the metropolitan blockades that erupted in Greece and in many other countries in 2011 did, was to create the very possibility of cultivating alternative ways of being and alternative practices of politics, rather than to set up quickly assembled forums for delivering solutions to existing problems. These camps revealed a potential: the possibility to perceive and act differently in the current conditions. Their main effect was less a political one and more of an ontological nature: the metropolitan blockades in 2011 trained – literally – our social and political senses anew. They had a quasi radical pedagogical purpose rather than a direct political function of becoming the space to articulate fixed sets of political demands. It is, in the words of Pierre Bourdieu, this "still pedagogy," which the camps exercised in 2011, that could be considered the most crucial element of these heterotopic social movements.

The lower parliament was the example par excellence of a heterotopic constitution of metropolitan space. These blocked and reclaimed spaces had a different temporality, which undercut the possibility of becoming colonized by violence and homogenization. For example, fascists tried many times to intervene in the assemblies, but it was the very procedure itself, the slowness, the speaking by drawing a lot, the transversality of topics that was undercutting their presence. It was less a decision based on the consensus of the assembly to block them from participating as "fascists" and more the very organizational structure, its variable paces, and its apparent slowness in relation to mainstream political processes that deterred people who wanted to participate in the assembly with fully preconceived ideas about its outcomes. It is characteristic that despite the attempts by fascists and nationalists to exclude migrants from the lower square this did not happen. Unlike the 15M movement in Spain, migrant street vendors were permanent inhabitants of the camp. Even more than that, many of them were staying in the camp because it was a relatively safe place for them and also because they profited from selling their goods in the most central and crowded part of Athens. Real democracy in the square was not just a different space, it had also a different temporality that made inhabiting a new terrain and coinhabiting the square possible in non-normative and predefined ways.

Something similar happened during the December 2008 insurrection in Athens. What connects the 2008 events and the metropolitan blockade in 2011 is urban panic on the part of the established political class; the moment, as we said earlier, that panic is desubjectified, resocialized, and returns back to the elites. December 2008 was probably the first occasion in Greece for many decades that brought back the practice of the metropolitan blockade as a way to remake society and politics. The December insurrection destabilized the typical transfer of power from the subject to the transcendent power of the state and its main political institutions. It reinscribed into the social imaginary and political practice the idea that blocking the city – if it is a collective and a-subjective affair – can have a deep impact on how politics is exercised. It can even create a completely new stage on which politics can be thought anew. Probably the most crucial influence that the December 2008 events had, was to educate a new generation of activists in the meaning and practice of the metropolitan blockade. It is as if the December events were aiming to prepare a new generation of people for encountering austerity and political oppression that followed a few years later. The a-subjective collectivity that destroyed shops, cars, and banks in 2008 returned in 2011 with a much greater experience of how to organize the metropolitan blockade under the new conditions of the crisis and the destructive austerity measures. In the dark and eroding conditions of everyday life in 2011, the practices of destruction of the 2008 events weren't sufficient for encountering the crisis. They transformed into practices of organizing new institutions, most importantly Syntagma. The protagonists of real democracy came mainly from the unorganized world of precarious people, and the metropolitan blockade became the way to establish a different ecology of existence. Despite the fact that the austerity bills were finally passed by the Greek parliament and that the last tents were cleared by police soon after that, the metropolitan blockade of Syntagma remains a popular embodied experience of many people in Greece. We don't know if, when, and how it will resurface, but what we do know is that the metropolitan blockades of the camps in 2011 and the Occupy movement is not about defeat or victory: "From a military point of view, we could take the parliament," said one militant activist in the square, "but no one among us has a use for this building." For everyone that expected the movement of the 2011 metropolitan blockades to articulate clear demands and solutions to the crisis we could say that for decades now we have lost the capacity and the space in which such solutions and demands can be produced. The metropolitan blockades did just that, they allowed for people to act and think and connect to each other and practice again politics. The precarious people of Syntagma didn't have a use for their parliament: they were looking for something else, something much more difficult to grasp: they were preparing for a long process of inventing new radical democratic forms of life.

The text was written following the destruction of the occupation camp of Syntagma Square in Athens in summer 2011 after several meetings, discussions, and extensive e-mail communication between Athens, Berlin, Hamburg, and Leicester where the authors are based. It was first published on eipcp.net in July 2012 as part of *transversal*, a multilingual Web journal edited by of the European Institute for Progressive Cultural Policies.

Slavoj Žižek

Freedom in the Clouds

Visiting Julian Assange at the Ecuadorian Embassy in London in December 2013 was a rather depressing experience, in spite of the kindness of the embassy personnel. The embassy is a six-room apartment with no garden attached, so that Assange cannot even take a daily walk in the fresh air. He also cannot step out of the apartment into the house's main corridor – policemen are waiting for him there. A dozen of them are around the house all the time and in some of the surrounding buildings, one even beneath a tiny toilet window, in case Assange tries to escape through that hole in the wall. The apartment is bugged from above and below, its Internet link is suspiciously slow... so how come that the UK state employs full-time around fifty people to guard Assange under the legal pretense that he refuses to go to Sweden and be questioned about a minor sexual misconduct (there are no charges against him!)? One is tempted to become a Thatcherite and ask: Where is austerity politics here? If a nobody like myself was wanted by the Swedish police for a similar interrogation, would the UK also employ fifty people to guard me? The serious question is here: Where does such a ridiculously excessive desire for revenge stem from? What did Assange, his colleagues, and whistle-blowing sources do to deserve this? In a way, one can understand the authorities: Assange and colleagues are often accused of being traitors, but they are something much worse (in the eyes of the authorities):

> "Even if Snowden were to sell his information discreetly to another intelligence service, this act would still count as part of the 'patriotic games,' and if needed he would have been liquidated as a 'traitor.' However, in Snowden's case, we are dealing with something entirely different. We are dealing with a gesture which questions the very logic, the very status quo, which for quite some time serves as the only foundation of all 'Western' (non)politics. With a gesture which as it were risks everything, with no consideration of profit and without its own stakes, it takes the risk because it is based on the conclusion that what is going on is simply wrong. Snowden didn't propose any alternative. Snowden – or, rather, the logic of his gesture, like, say, before him, the gesture of Bradley Manning – *is* the alternative."[1]

1 Alenka Zupančič Žerdin, "Ko preštejem do deset, boste mrtvi ..." [When I Count to Ten, You Will Be Dead ...], in: *MLADINA*, 2013, p. 31, translated from the Slovenian by Slavoj Žižek.

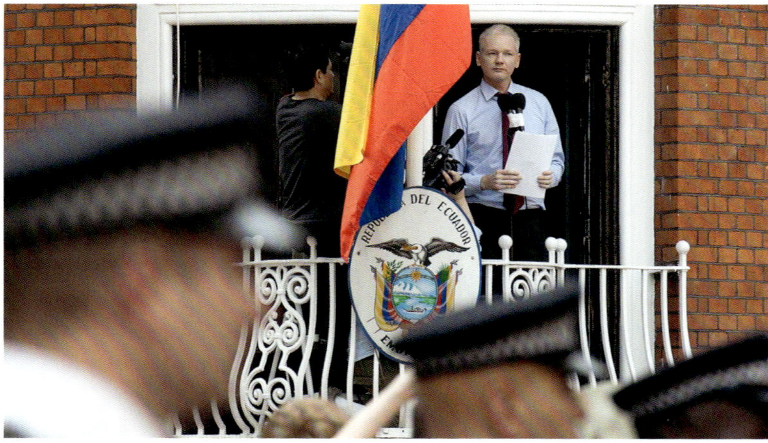

WikiLeaks founder Julian Assange addresses the media and his supporters from the balcony of the Ecuadorian Embassy in London on August 19, 2012

This breakthrough of WikiLeaks is nicely encapsulated by Assange's ironic self-designation as a "spy for the people": "spying for the people" is not a direct negation of spying (which would rather be acting as a double agent, selling our secrets to the enemy), but its self-negation; that is, it undermines the very universal principle of spying, the principle of secrecy, since its goal is to make secrets public. It thus functions in a way similar to how the Marxian "dictatorship of the proletariat" was supposed to function (but rarely ever did, of course): as an immanent self-negation of the very principle of dictatorship. To those who paint the scarecrow of Communism, we should answer: What WikiLeaks is doing is the practice of Communism. WikiLeaks simply enacts the commons of information.

In the struggle of ideas, the rise of bourgeois modernity was exemplified by the French Encyclopedia, a gigantic venture of presenting in a systematic way to the broad public all available knowledge – the addressee of this knowledge was not the state but the public as such. It may seem that Wikipedia already is today's encyclopedia, but something is missing from it: the knowledge which is ignored by and repressed from the public space, repressed because it concerns precisely the way state mechanisms and agencies control and regulate us all. The goal of WikiLeaks should be to make this knowledge available to all of us with a simple click. Assange effectively is today's d'Alembert, the organizer of this new encyclopedia, the true people's encyclopedia for the twenty-first century – why?

Our informational commons recently emerged as one of the key domains of class struggle in two of its aspects, economical in the narrow sense and sociopolitical. On the one hand, new digital media confront us with the impasse of "intellectual property." WWW seems to be in its nature Communist, tending towards free flow of data – CDs and DVDs are gradually disappearing, millions are simply downloading music and videos, mostly for free. This is why the business establishment is engaged in a desperate struggle to impose the form of private property on this flow. On the other hand, digital media (especially with the almost universal access to WWW and cell phones) opened up new ways for the millions of ordinary people to establish a network and coordinate their collective activities, while also offering state agencies and private companies unheard-of possibilities of tracking down our public and private acts. It is into this struggle that WikiLeaks intervened in such an explosive way. Jacques Lacan proposed as the axiom of the ethics of psychoanalysis: "Do not compromise your desire." Is this axiom also not an accurate designation of the whistle-blowers' acts? In spite of all the risks their activity involves, they are not ready to compromise on it.

This uncompromising stance is a constant reminder that, in our daily lives, we more and more resemble baboons. That is to say, why do baboons have big protruding hairless red butts? The main reason seems to be that the buttocks of a female in heat will swell so the male knows that she is ready to mate. It also functions as a sign of submission, where one animal turns and presents its rump to the other, indicating: "I know you're stronger than me, so let's not fight anymore!" The baboons with the redder, more hairless butts attract more mates and have more offspring, and, in their turn, those offspring are favored because, on the average, they have redder, more hairless butts than the rest… Is this not how the struggle for ideological hegemony also looks? Individuals display their hairless protruding butts, offering themselves to be penetrated by the ideological message addressing them. There is no need for violent imposition, the victim voluntarily offers itself – as it was made clear by the recent divulgations about the massive digital control of our lives.

This is why it is not enough to see WikiLeaks as an anti-American phenomenon. That is to say, how do President Barack Obama's acts fit into the constellation that formed itself through WikiLeaks disclosures? While the U.S. Right is denouncing Obama as a dangerous leftist dividing American people, posing a threat to the American way of life, some leftists denounce him as "worse than Bush" in his pursuit of imperialist foreign policy. When, back in 2005, Obama got the Nobel Peace Prize, we all knew this was not a prize for his achievements, but a gesture of hope, a desperate attempt to put additional pressure on Obama so that he would keep his electoral promises and effectively work as an anti-Bush President. The idea to give the Nobel Peace Prize to Manning should be embraced as a justified reaction to the fact that Obama failed to meet these expectations. To account for this disappointment, one should bear in mind the way Obama won his 2012 reelection. Jean-Claude Milner recently proposed the notion of "stabilizing class": not the old ruling class, but

Army Private Bradley Manning is escorted away from his Article 32 hearing in the WikiLeaks case on February 23, 2012 in Fort Meade, Maryland

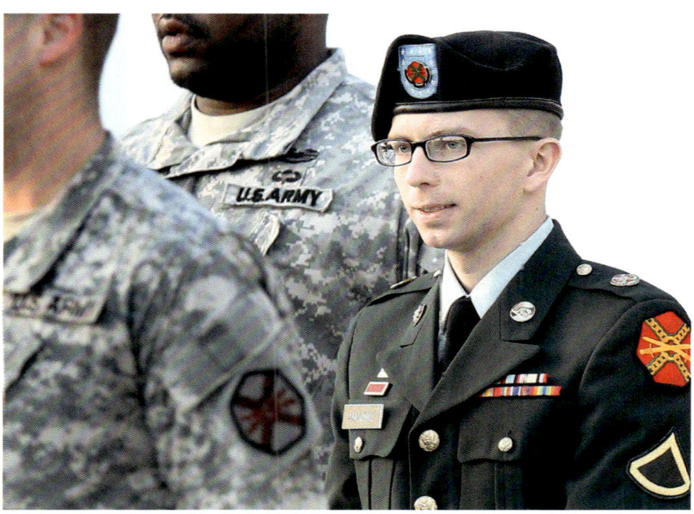

2
See: Alain Badiou and Jean-Claude Milner, *Controverse. Dialogue sur la politique et la philosophie de notre temps*, Seuil, Paris, 2012.

the broad class of all those who are fully committed to the stability and continuity of the existing social, economic, and political order; the class of those who, even when they call for a change, do this to enforce changes which will make the system more efficient and thus ensure that nothing will really change.[2] The key to the interpretation of electoral results in today's developed Western states is therefore: Who succeeded in winning over this class? Far from really being perceived as a radical transformer, Obama won *them* over, and that's why he was reelected. The majority that voted for him were put off by the radical changes advocated by the Republican market and religious fundamentalists.

We all remember Obama's smiling face, full of hope and trust, when he repeatedly delivered the motto of his first campaign: "Yes we can!" – we can get rid of the cynicism of Bush's era and bring justice and welfare to the American people, we can make America the land of hope and dreams again... Now that the USA continues with covert operations, inclusive of using drones and expanding their control and intelligence network, spying even on their allies, some protesters were already displaying placards with a slightly changed motto: "Yes we scan!" Perhaps a more pertinent variation would have been to imagine Obama looking at us with a mockingly evil smile and replying "Yes we can!" to the protesters shouting at him: "How can you use drones for killing? How can you spy even on our allies?"

However, such simple personalization misses the point: the threat to our freedom disclosed by whistle-blowers has much deeper systemic roots. Edward Snowden should be defended not only because his acts annoyed and embarrassed the U.S. Secret Service – what he revealed is something that not only the USA but also all other great (and not so great) powers (from China to Russia, from Germany to Israel) are doing (to the extent they are technologically able to do it). His acts thus provided a factual foundation to our premonitions of how much we are all monitored and controlled – their lesson is global, it reaches far beyond the standard USA bashing. We didn't really learn from Snowden (or from Manning) anything we didn't already presume to be true – but it is one thing to know it in general, and another to get concrete data. It is a little bit like knowing that one's sexual partner is playing around – one can accept the abstract knowledge of it, pain arises when one learns the steamy details, when one gets pictures of what they were doing... Sometimes, we learn such steamy details from smaller marginal countries which pass security measures in a much more open and direct way – for example, in the summer of 2012, the Hungarian parliament passed a new national security law that

> "[...] enables the inner circle of the government to spy on people who hold important public offices. Under this law, many government officials must 'consent' to being observed in the most intrusive way (phones tapped, homes bugged, email read) for up to two full months each year, except that they won't know which 60 days they are under surveillance. Perhaps they will imagine they are under surveillance all of the time. Perhaps that is the point. More than 20 years after Hungary

> left the world captured in George Orwell's novel *1984*, the surveillance state is back. Now, if the Fidesz government of Prime Minister Viktor Orbán finds something it doesn't like – and there's no legal limit to what it may find objectionable – those under surveillance can be fired. The people at the very top of the government are largely exempt from surveillance – but this law hits their deputies, staffers and the whole of the security services, some judges, prosecutors, diplomats, and military officers, as well as a number of 'independent' offices that Orbán's administration is not supposed to control."[3]

3 Paul Krugman, "1984, Hungarian Edition," June 17, 2013, available online at: http://krugman.blogs.nytimes.com/2013/06/17/1984-hungarian-edition/?_r=0, accessed 04/02/2014.

And here is how the Hungarian government justifies such measures:

> "Officials of the Hungarian government will say that what they are doing is nothing novel. Other countries, they will point out, have ways to determine whether high-level officials have played fast and loose with state secrets or whether people holding the public trust are corrupt. The U.S. government has now been shown to be gathering up everyone's phone calls and emails, so how can anyone be critical of what the Hungarian government is doing?"[4]

4 Ibid.

When confronted with such facts, should every decent U.S. citizen not feel like a baboon suddenly overwhelmed by the shame about his or her protruding red butt? Back in 1843, the young Karl Marx claimed that the German *Ancien Régime* "only imagines that it believes in itself and demands that the world imagine the same thing."[5] In such a situation, to put shame on those in power becomes a weapon – or, as Marx goes on: "We must make the actual pressure more pressing by adding to it the consciousness of pressure and make the shame more shameful by publicizing it."[6] And this, exactly, is our situation today: we are facing the shameless cynicism of the existing global order whose agents *only imagine that they believe in their ideas of democracy, human rights*, etc., and through moves like WikiLeaks disclosures, *the shame (our shame for tolerating such power over us) is made more shameful by publicizing it.* What we should be ashamed of is the worldwide process of the gradual narrowing of the public use of reason. When the Apostle Paul says that, from a Christian standpoint, "[t]here is no Jew nor Greek, there is no slave nor free, there is no male and female […],"[7] he thereby claims that ethnic roots, national identity, etc., are *not a category of truth*, or, to put it in precise Kantian terms, when we reflect upon our ethnic roots, we engage in a "private use of reason,"[8] constrained by contingent dogmatic presuppositions; that is, we act as "immature" individuals, not as free human beings who dwell in the dimension of the universality of reason. The public space of the "world-civil-society" designates the paradox of the universal singularity, of a singular subject who, in a kind of short-circuit, bypassing the mediation of the particular, directly participates in the Universal. This is what Kant in the famous passage of his "What Is Enlightenment?" means by "public" as opposed to "private": "private" is not one's individual as opposed to communal ties, but the very

5 Karl Marx, "Toward a Critique of Hegel's *Philosophy of Right*: Introduction," in: Karl Marx, *Selected Writings*, ed. Lawrence H. Simon, Hackett Publishing Company, Indianapolis (IN), 1994, pp. 27–39, here p. 31.

6 Ibid., p. 30.

7 Epistle to the Galatians 3:28.

8 Immanuel Kant, "An Answer to the Question: 'What Is Enlightenment?'," in: *Kant. Political Writings*, ed. H.S. Reiss, Cambridge University Press, Cambridge, 1991, pp. 54–60, here p. 55.

communal-institutional order of one's particular identification; while "public" is the transnational universality of the exercise of one's reason. We see where Kant parts with our liberal common sense: the domain of state itself is in its own way "private," private in the precise Kantian sense of the "private use of reason" in state administrative and ideological apparatuses, while individuals reflecting on general issues use reason in a "public" way.

This Kantian distinction is especially pertinent with the Internet and other new media torn between their free "public use" and their growing "private" control. Our struggle should thus focus on the threats to the transnational public sphere, like the recent trend in the organization of cyberspace in clouds – to quote a propaganda text on cloud computing: "Details are abstracted from consumers, who no longer have need for expertise in, or control over, the technology infrastructure 'in the cloud' that supports them." Two words are telltale here: *abstraction* and *control* – in order to manage a cloud, there needs to be a monitoring system which controls its functioning, and this system is by definition hidden from users. The paradox is thus that, the more the small item (smartphone or tiny portable) I hold in my hand is personalized, easy to use, "transparent" in its functioning, the more the entire setup has to rely on the work being done elsewhere, in a vast circuit of machines which coordinate the user's experience. The more our experience is nonalienated, spontaneous, transparent, the more it is regulated by the invisible network controlled by an alienated network of state agencies and large private companies which follow their secret agendas.

What makes the all-encompassing control of our lives so dangerous is not that we lose our privacy, that all our intimate secrets are exposed to the view of the Big Brother. There is no state agency which is able to exert such control – not because they don't know enough, but because they know too much. The sheer size of the data is too large, and in spite of all the intricate programs for detecting suspicious messages, computers which register billions of data are too stupid to interpret and evaluate them properly, ridiculous mistakes where innocent bystanders are listed as potential terrorists occur necessarily – and this makes state control of our communications even more dangerous. Without knowing why, without doing anything illegal, we can all of a sudden find ourselves on a list of potential terrorists. Recall the legendary answer of a Hearst newspaper editor to Hearst's inquiry why he doesn't want to take a long-deserved holiday: "I am afraid that if I go, there will be chaos, everything will fall apart – but I am even more afraid to discover that, if I go, things will just go on as normal without me, a proof that I am not really needed!" Something similar can be said about the state control of our communications: we should fear that we have no secrets, that secret state agencies know everything, but we should fear even more that they fail in this endeavor…

Whistle-blowers play a crucial role in keeping the "public reason" alive. Assange, Manning, Snowden… these are our new heroes, exemplary cases of the new ethics that befits our era of digital control and communications. They are no longer just whistle-blowers who denounce illegal practices of private companies (banks, tobacco and oil companies…) to the public authorities; they denounce these public authorities themselves when they engage in the "private use of reason." We need more Mannings and Snowdens also in China, in Russia, everywhere. States like China and Russia are, of course, much more oppressive than the USA – just imagine what would have happened to someone like Manning in a Russian or Chinese court (in all probability there would be no public trial, a Chinese Manning would just disappear)! However, one should not exaggerate the softness of the U.S.: true, the U.S. doesn't treat prisoners as brutally as China or Russia – because of their technological priority, they simply do not need the openly brutal approach (which they are more than ready to apply when it is needed). In this sense, the U.S. is even more dangerous than China insofar as their measures of control are not perceived as such, whereas Chinese brutality is openly displayed. That is to say, while in a country like China, the limitations of freedom are clear to everyone, there are no illusions about it, the state is an openly oppressive mechanism, whereas in the U.S. formal freedoms are mostly guaranteed, so that most individuals experience their lives as free and are not even aware of the extent to which they are controlled by state mechanisms. Just imagine how much one can learn about each of us by checking our bank accounts, which books we buy on amazon.com, our e-mails, etc., etc. Whistle-blowers do something much more important than stating the obvious by way of denouncing the openly oppressive regimes, that is, rendering public our directly experienced unfreedom: they render public the unfreedom that underlies the very situation in which we experience ourselves as free.

This feature is not limited to digital space: it pervades thoroughly the form of subjectivity that characterizes the "permissive" liberal society. Since permissivity and free choice are elevated to supreme values, social control and domination can no longer appear as infringing on a subject's freedom: it has to appear as (and be sustained by) the very self-experience of individuals as free. There is a multitude of forms of this appearing of unfreedom in the guise of its opposite: when we are deprived of universal health care, we are told that we are given a new freedom of choice (to choose our health care provider); when we can no longer rely on long-term employment and are compelled to search for a new precarious working position every couple of years, we are told that we are given the opportunity to reinvent ourselves and discover new unexpected creative potentials that lurk in our personality; when we have to pay for the education of our children, we are told that we become "entrepreneurs of the self," acting like a capitalist who has to choose freely how he will invest the resources he possesses (or has borrowed) – into education, health, travel… Constantly bombarded by imposed "free choices," forced to make decisions for which we are mostly not even properly qualified (or possess enough information about), we more and more experience our freedom as a burden that causes unbearable anxiety. Unable to break out of this vicious cycle alone, as isolated individuals, since the more we act freely the more we get enslaved to the system, we need to be "awakened" from this "dogmatic slumber" of fake freedom from outside, by the push of a master figure.

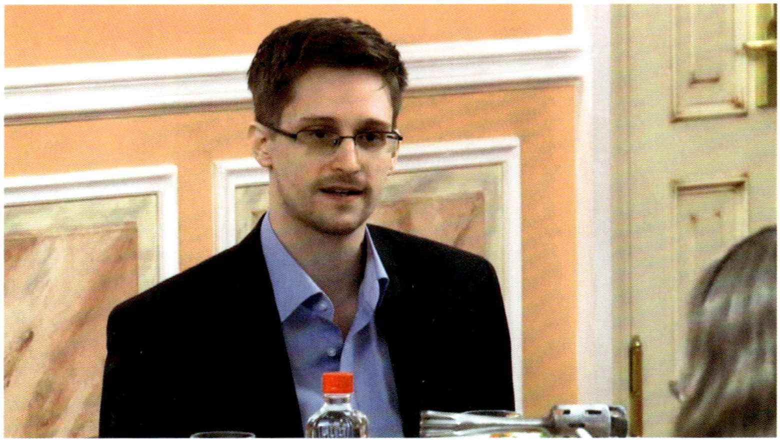

Edward Snowden receives the Sam Adams Award for Integrity in Intelligence in Moscow, October 2013

Back in May 2002, it was reported that scientists at New York University had attached a computer chip able to transmit elementary signals directly to a rat's brain, enabling scientists to control the rat's movements by means of a steering mechanism (as in a remote-controlled toy car). For the first time, the "will" of a living animal agent, its "spontaneous" decisions about the movements it will make, were taken over by an external machine. Of course, the great philosophical question here is how the unfortunate rat "experienced" these movements which were effectively decided from outside: Did it continue to "experience" them as spontaneous (in other words, was it totally unaware that its movements were being steered?), or was it aware that "something was wrong"? And, maybe, therein resides the difference between Chinese citizens and us, free citizens of Western liberal countries: the Chinese human rats are at least aware they are controlled, while we are the stupid rats strolling around unaware of how our movements are monitored...

It is crucial that the new encyclopedia emerging around WikiLeaks acquires an independent international base, so that the humiliating game of playing one big state against another (like Snowden having to look for protection in Russia) will be constrained to a minimum. Our axiom should be that Snowden and Pussy Riot are part of the same struggle – we need a new International, an international network to organize the protection of whistleblowers and the dissemination of their messages. The list is already multiplying: Manning, Assange, Snowden... *and Utku Kalı*, a Turkish gendarmery private who leaked the gendarmery intelligence report that the massacre in Reyhanlı town (a blast which killed more than 170 people on May 11, 2013; the official number is 53) had been organized by the radical Islamist Al-Nusra group. Right after the blast, the Turkish government accused Bashar al-Assad's regime in Syria of the blast, but the leak made it publicly known that the government knew about it and did not prevent it – or maybe even "guided" this false flag operation. Utku Kalı was immediately arrested and is now in prison, accused of leaking military secrets.[9] Such leaks provide an insight into what is really going on behind the scene in Syria today.

9
Personal message from Engin Kurtay, Istanbul.

Whistle-blowers are our heroes because they prove that if they – those in power – can do it, we can also do it. We often hear today that democracy can only be renewed upwards, from the grass-roots level of local communities, since state mechanisms are so ossified and insensitive to people's pressing concerns; however, the problems we are confronting today also call for global, larger-than-state, organizations and forms of activity – the good old nation-state is simultaneously too large and too small. The ideal counter-force to the state would have been a direct shortcircuit between the two levels: local civil society organizations forming transnational networks. The problem, of course, is that protesters who form these networks are a clear minority – the reaction of the large majority, after Snowden's revelations were reported by the wide media, could best be summed up by the memorable lines of the final song from Robert Altman's film *Nashville* (1975) performed by Barbara Harris: "You may say I ain't free, but it don't worry me."

!Mediengruppe Bitnik

!Mediengruppe Bitnik was founded in 2003 by Domagoj Smoljo (*1979) and Carmen Weisskopf (*1976) and is currently based in Zurich and London. Further members are Adnan Hadzi and Daniel Ryser. With their works, the artist collective formulates fundamental questions concerning contemporary issues and seeks to recontextualize the familiar in order to allow new readings of established structures and mechanisms. This understanding includes defining hacking as an artistic strategy, with which the group constantly tears down the borders between public and private. In the course of their artistic intervention *Opera Calling* in 2007, for example, !Mediengruppe Bitnik placed audio bugs in the auditorium of the Zurich Opera House, transmitted the performances to randomly selected telephone landlines in the city of Zurich, and gave anyone picking up the phone the chance to listen to the opera being performed. In 2012, the group hacked surveillance cameras in pre-Olympic London, replaced the real-time surveillance images with an invitation to play a game of chess, and hence turned the security staff's surveillance monitor into a game console.

With *UBS lügt* [UBS lies] (2009) !Mediengruppe Bitnik reenacted *Polizei lügt* [Police lies], an action by Peter Weibel from 1971. An investment banker who happened to pass by participates in the shoot without being asked. The image documents his quiet protest in front of a Zurich branch of the Union Bank of Switzerland (UBS). In 2010 the work caused an uproar: during the opening of !Mediengruppe Bitnik's solo exhibition *Too Big to Fail / Too Small to Succeed* in September 2010 in London, the legal department of UBS had the image removed from a public billboard. In case of further use or publication of the image, UBS threatened to sue for libel.

Another much-regarded action took place in early 2013, when the group sent a parcel to WikiLeaks founder Julian Assange at the Ecuadorian Embassy in London. It contained a camera which broadcasted its journey through the postal system live on the Internet. The group defines this work as a "system_test" and a "live mail art piece."

!Mediengruppe Bitnik's works have been shown all over the world, including at La Gaîté lyrique in Paris, the Netherlands Media Art Institute (NIMk) in Amsterdam, the SPACE Gallery in London, the Bâtiment d'art contemporain (BAC) in Geneva, the Cabaret Voltaire in Zurich, the Hartware MedienKunstVerein in Dortmund, the Beton7 in Athens, the Museum Folkwang in Essen, the Contemporary Art Centre in Vilnius, the Kunsthaus Zurich, and the Gallery EDEN 343 in São Paulo. The group has also taken part in various festivals, including the Share Festival in Turin, the Ars Electronica in Linz, and the International Roaming Biennial in Tehran, and received several awards (for example, the Swiss Art Award, the Migros New Media Jubilee Award, and an Honorary Mention Prix Ars Electronica).

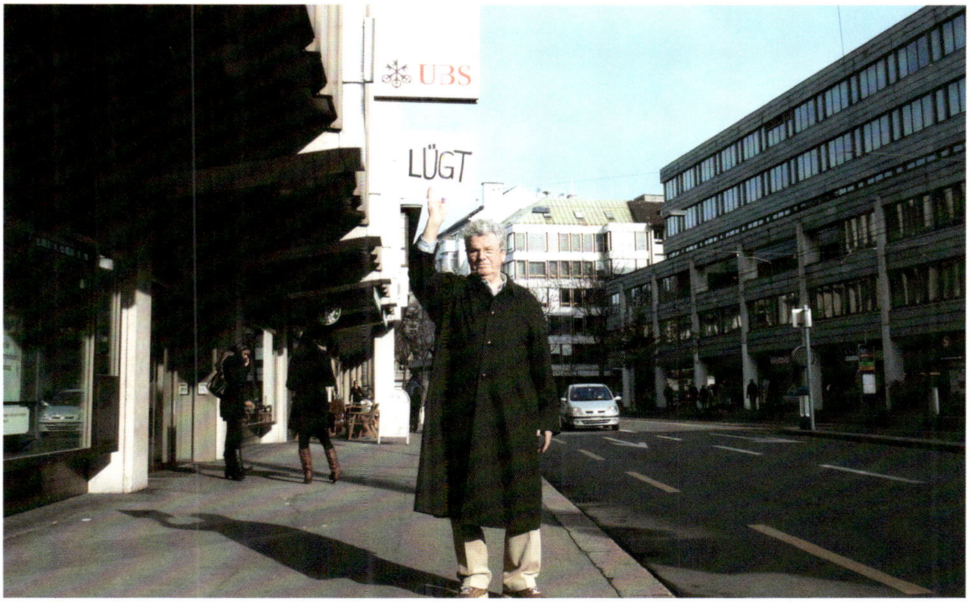

!Mediengruppe Bitnik, *UBS lügt*, 2010, reenactment of Peter Weibel's *Polizei lügt*, 1971

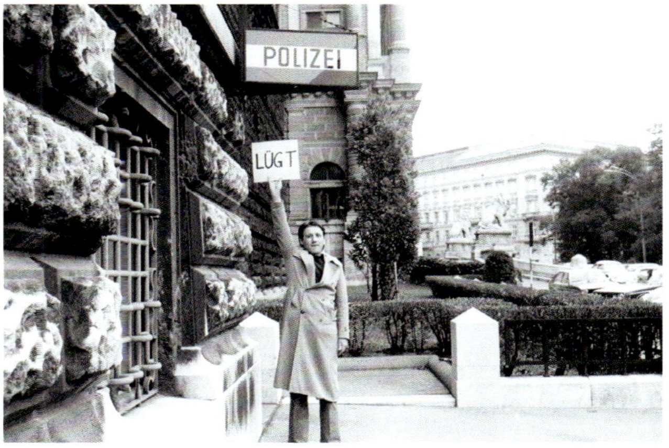

Peter Weibel, *Polizei lügt*, from the series *Anschläge*, 1970 / 1971

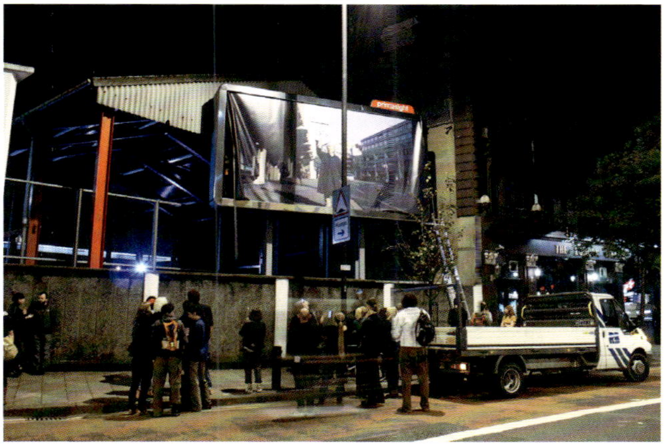

The *UBS lügt* poster is taken down from the billboard at SPACE Gallery in London during the opening of !Mediengruppe Bitnik's exhibition *Too Big to Fail / Too Small to Succeed* in 2010

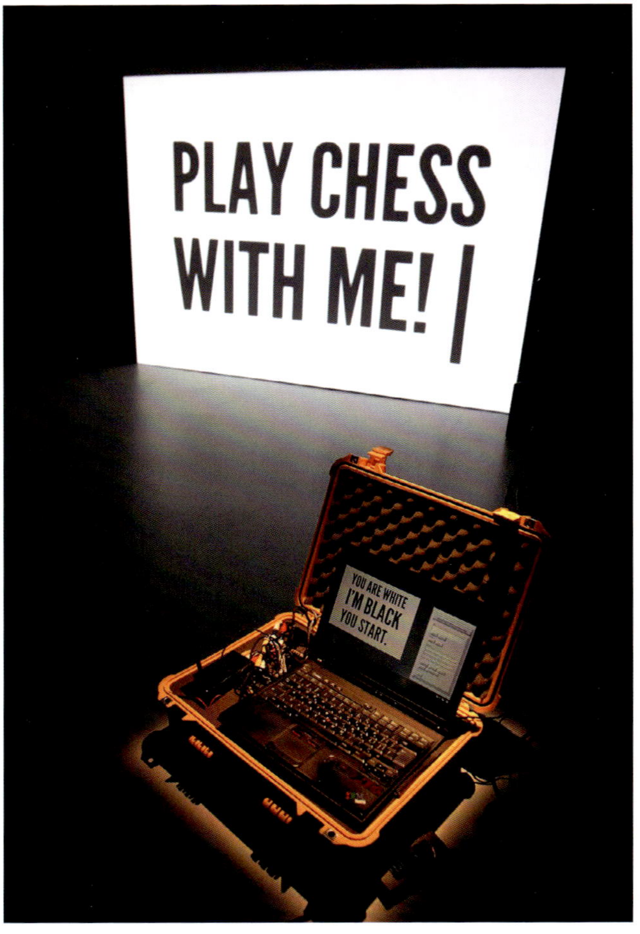

!Mediengruppe Bitnik, *Surveillance Chess*, 2012, exhibition view, La Gaîté lyrique, Paris, 2012

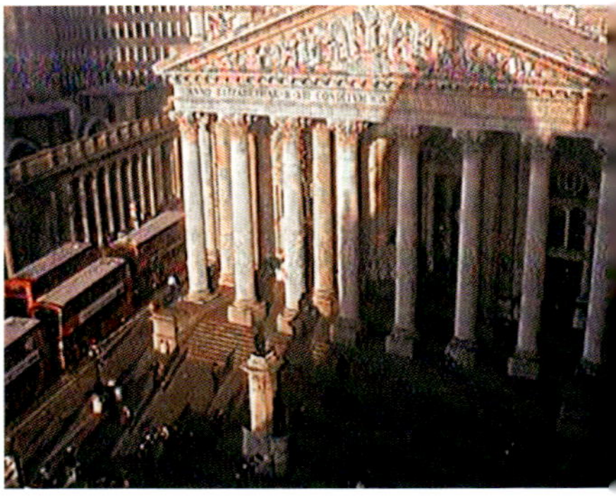

!Mediengruppe Bitnik, *Surveillance Chess*, 2012, still from a hijacked surveillance camera in London

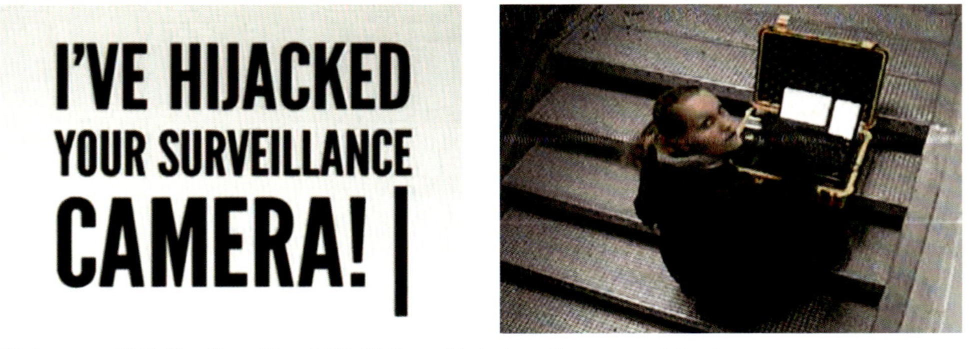

!Mediengruppe Bitnik, *Surveillance Chess*, 2012, stills from a hijacked surveillance camera in London

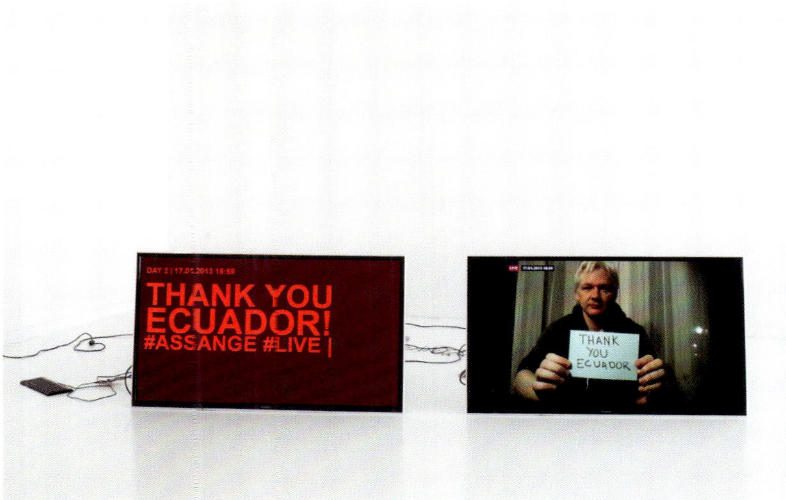

!Mediengruppe Bitnik, *Delivery for Mr. Assange*, 2013, video installation, installation view, Helmhaus, Zurich, 2014

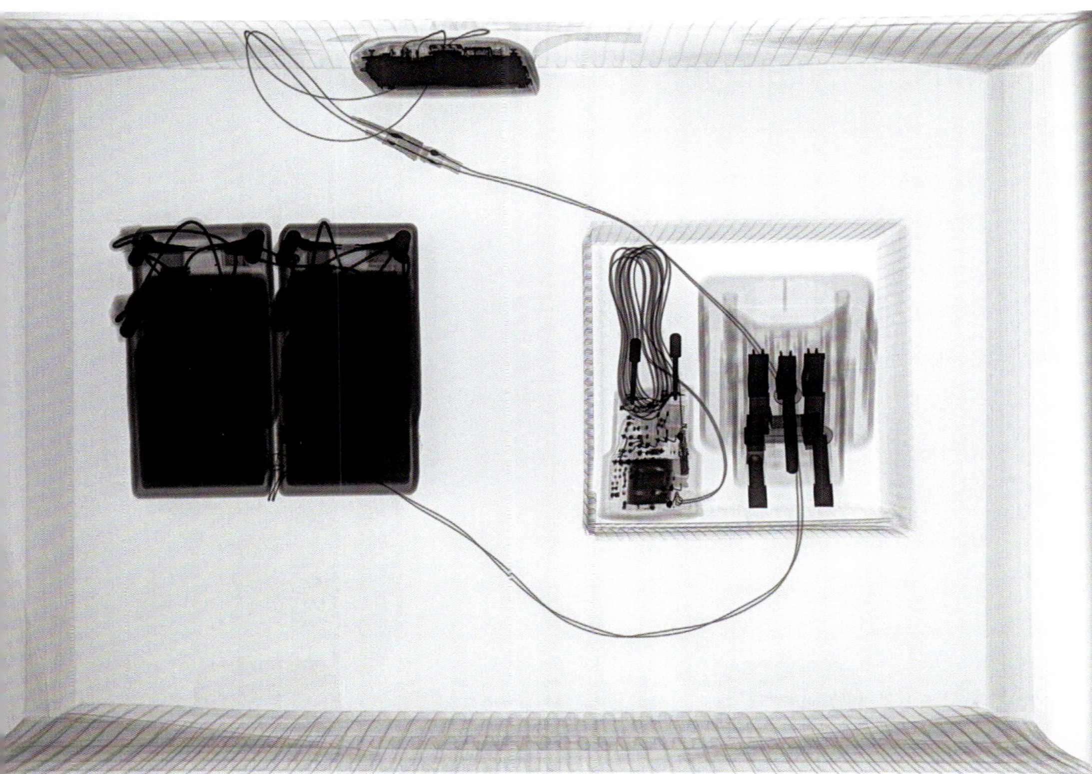

!Mediengruppe Bitnik, *Delivery for Mr. Assange*, 2013, X-ray scan

Founded in 2013
Germany

http://stopwatchingus.info

#StopWatchingUs

#StopWatchingUs is a loose and decentralized alliance of protesting citizens, parties, and several organizations, who support data protection and oppose the surveillance of society. The trigger that sparked the founding of these groups and the rapid formation of their network was Edward Snowden's exposure of a global surveillance apparatus. The central approaches of #StopWatchingUs reflect the following catalog of demands on the governments, national parliaments, and European institutions, which was also published and endorsed by other NGOs and initiatives:

1. Reject unjustified and disproportionate surveillance measures.
2. Ensure respect for the fundamental right to privacy and informational self-determination. Prioritize both rights on a national and an international level as well as via appropriate measures in the General Data Protection Regulation, the upcoming directive and corresponding rules for the European institutions.
3. Ensure high levels of protection of privacy and redress mechanisms against surveillance measures by third countries in international agreements.
4. Ensure that personal data that are collected and processed in the EU may only be transferred to authorities or organizations in third countries via mutual legal assistance treaties that contain adequate legal safeguards.
5. Ensure the right to confidentiality by ensuring the integrity of information technology systems.
6. Ensure that international cooperation between law enforcement, judicial bodies, and intelligence services is not used to circumvent legal protections of fundamental rights.
7. Immediately disclose all treaties, laws, and activities affecting the right to informational self-determination of individuals residing in the respective state and the EU.
8. Legally and financially penalize the violation of privacy of individuals by domestic companies as well as by non-EU states and companies residing in non-EU countries.
9. Introduce an obligation to issue individual notifications to individuals affected by the enforcement of personal computer surveillance measures, whether conducted by law enforcement authorities or intelligence services.
10. Actively promote free and open source projects for digital self-defence and promote the use of this technology.
11. Abandon all surveillance measures currently taking place outside the rule of law.
12. Guarantee legal protections for whistle-blowers who expose social grievances, misconduct, or illegal activities.

#StopWatchingUs logo

Facing page: #StopWatchingUs banner, installation view, ZKM | Karlsruhe, 2014

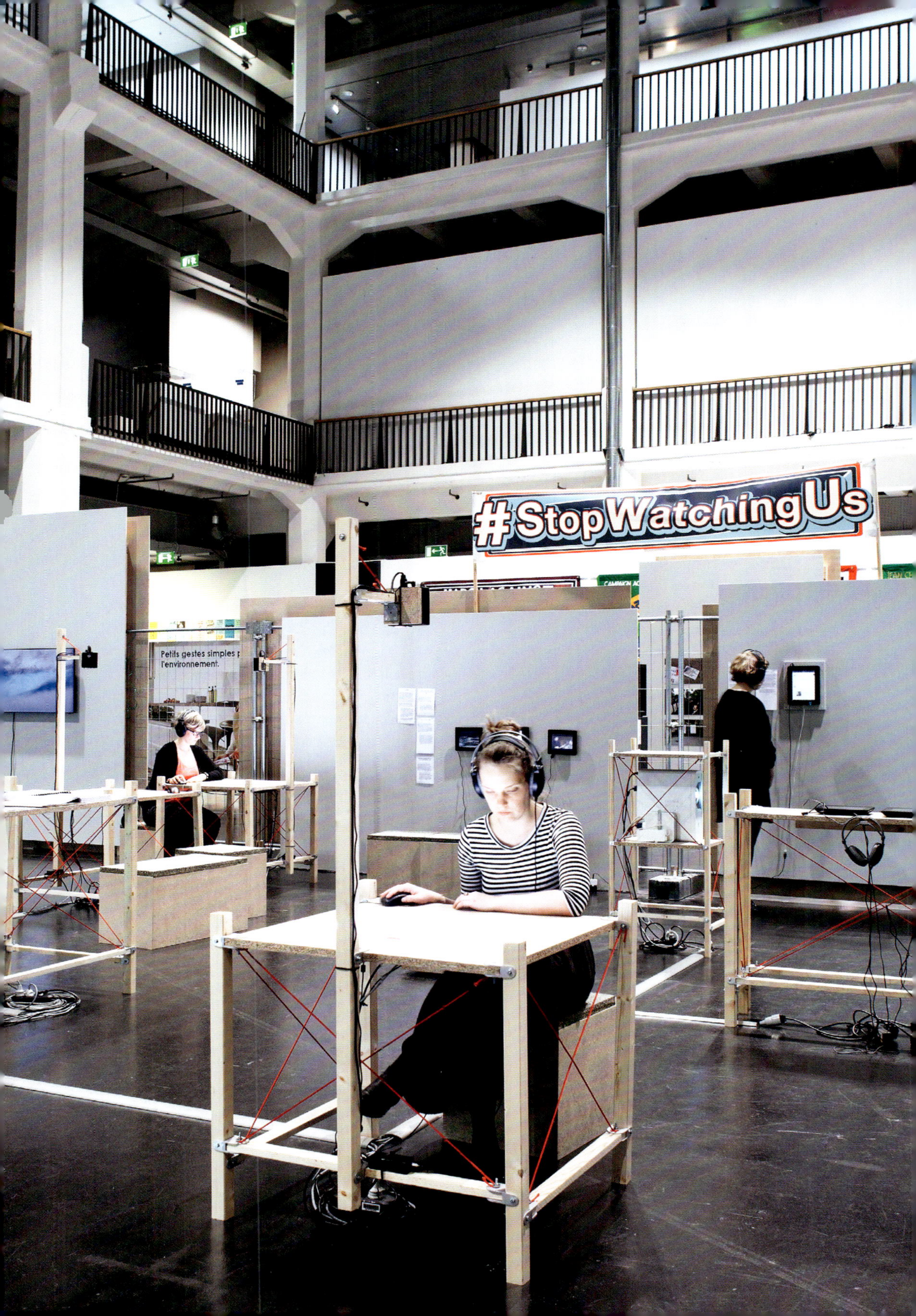
#StopWatchingUs
Petits gestes simples
l'environnement.

Paolo Cirio *1979

Paolo Cirio is a conceptual media artist. Born in Piedmont, Italy, he currently lives in New York City, but also works in London and Turin. Dealing with the idea of shaping flows of social, cognitive, and economic structures, Cirio seeks to explore potentials and limitations of contemporary systems of information and knowledge. His innovative and controversial projects investigate various issues in fields such as privacy, finance, copyright, and democracy, and his artistic provocations often lead to investigations, legal and personal threats from governmental and military authorities, powerful multinationals and financial institutions, as well as from crowds of ordinary people. For instance, his controversial artworks have unsettled Facebook, Visa, Amazon, Google, the Cayman Islands and NATO, among others.

Cirio renders his conceptual works through drawings, performances, videos, and installations. He has participated in numerous international festivals and exhibited in major museums and institutions all over the world, including the Haus der Kulturen der Welt in Berlin, the Museum of Contemporary Art Sydney, the NTT InterCommunication Center in Tokyo, the Art Center Nabi in Seoul, the Israel Center for Digital Art in Holon, Israel, the LABoral Art and Industrial Creation Centre in Gijon, Spain, the Museum of Contemporary Art in Taipei, the National Museum of Contemporary Art in Athens, the FACT in Liverpool, the École nationale supérieure des Arts Décoratifs in Paris, the Museum of Modern Art in Rio de Janeiro, the National Museum in Warsaw, the ZKM | Center for Art and Media Karlsruhe, the Museum for Applied Arts (MAK) in Vienna, and the City Art Gallery of Ljubljana. He has had solo shows at the Kasa Gallery in Istanbul (2013) and at Aksioma | Project Space in Ljubljana (2011 and 2013). Cirio has also curated panel series at The Kitchen (2012) and Eyebeam (2013) in New York. He has won several art awards, including the second prize at the Berlin transmediale in 2008. Cirio regularly gives public lectures and workshops at leading arts festivals and universities worldwide.

His project *Loophole for All*, initiated in 2013, investigated offshore jurisdictions and the idea of having a company "on paper" through a hack and leak of Cayman Islands financial information. At Loophole4All.com, the real identities of anonymous companies taking advantage of the tax havens are on sale at a low cost to democratize the privileges of offshore businesses. This performance generated local and international media attention, engaged an active audience, and drew outrage from authorities on the Cayman Islands, etc.

In 2014, the project was awarded a Golden Nica in the category Interactive Art at the Prix Ars Electronica in Linz, Austria.

Paolo Cirio, *Loophole for All*, 2013, certificate of incorporation of a private limited company

CERTIFICATE OF INCORPORATION
OF A
PRIVATE LIMITED COMPANY

Company Number. 8188080

The Registrar of Companies for England and Wales, hereby certifies that

PAOLO CIRIO LTD

is this day incorporated under the Companies Act 2006 as a private company, that the company is limited by shares, and the situation of its registered office is in England and Wales.

Given at Companies House, Cardiff, on 22nd August 2012.

REGISTRAR OF COMPANIES FOR ENGLAND AND WALES

THE OFFICIAL SEAL OF THE REGISTRAR OF COMPANIES

Companies House

— *for the record* —

The above information was communicated by electronic means and authenticated by the Registrar of Companies under section 1115 of the Companies Act 2006

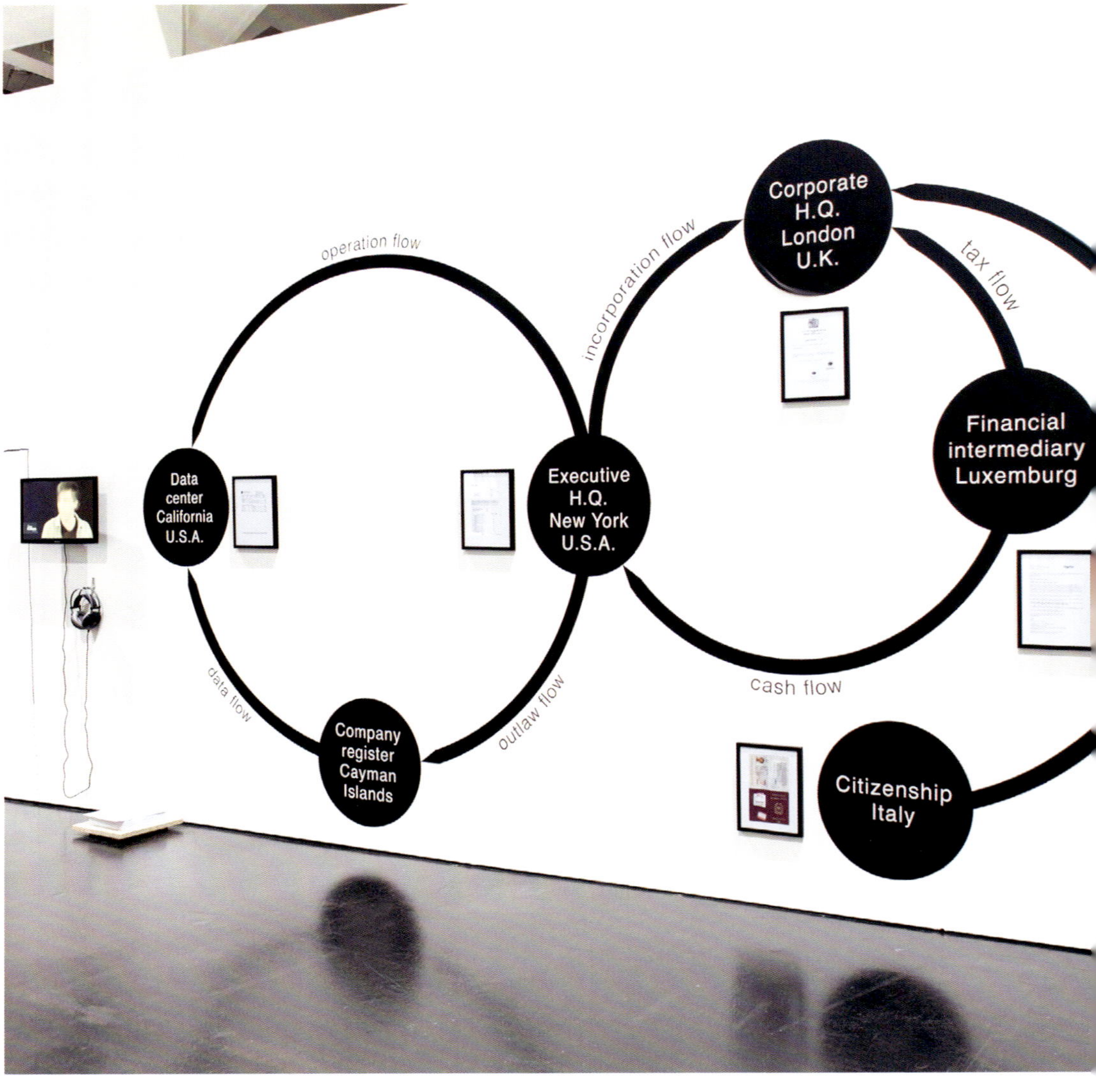

Paolo Cirio, *Loophole for All*, 2013, installation, mixed media, installation view, ZKM | Karlsruhe, 2014

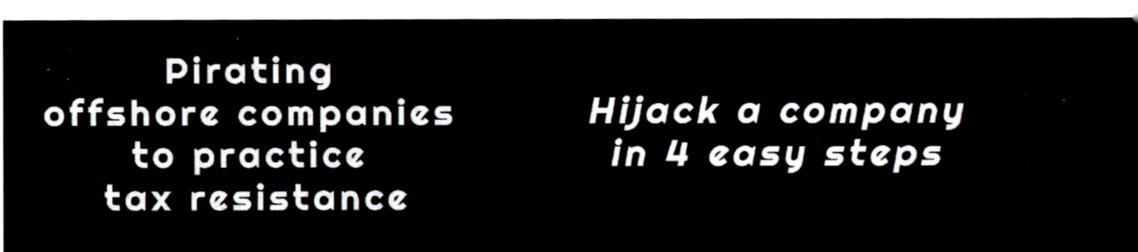

Paolo Cirio, introductory video of Loophole4All.com, color, sound, 15:14 min, posted on YouTube, February 2013, collage of video stills

liability flow

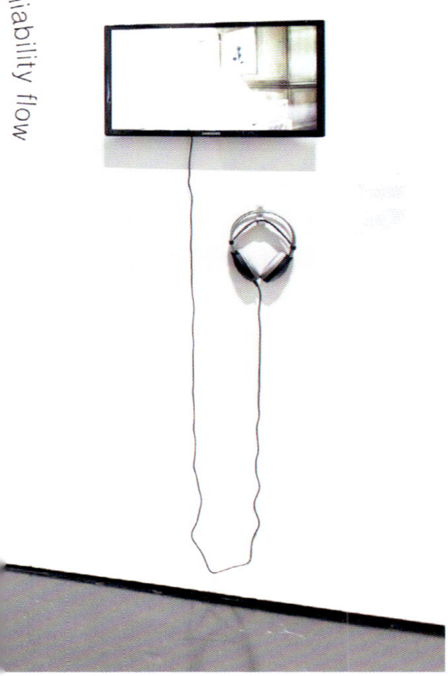

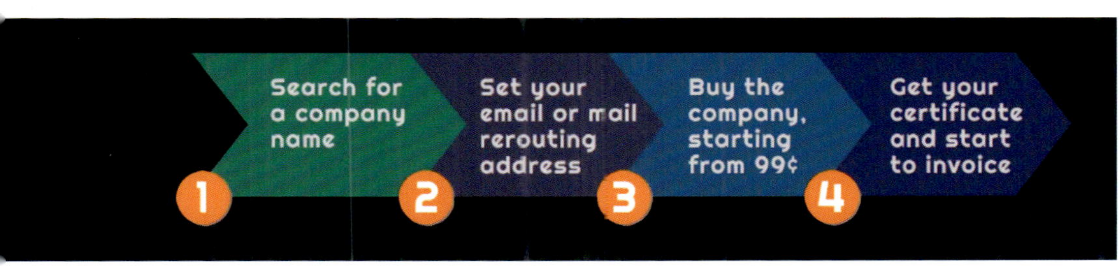

Founded in 2001
Global

www.creativecommons.org

Creative Commons

The nonprofit organization Creative Commons provides an alternative copyright system, which seeks to overcome the static capitalist structures of ownership by providing licenses free of charge and thereby to expand the number of creative works that others can build upon and share legally. Creative Commons is at the forefront of the Copyleft Movement, which advocates using copyright law to offer the right to distribute copies and modified versions of a work. Licensing a work under ShareAlike conditions requires that the same rights be preserved in such versions.

MOST OPEN

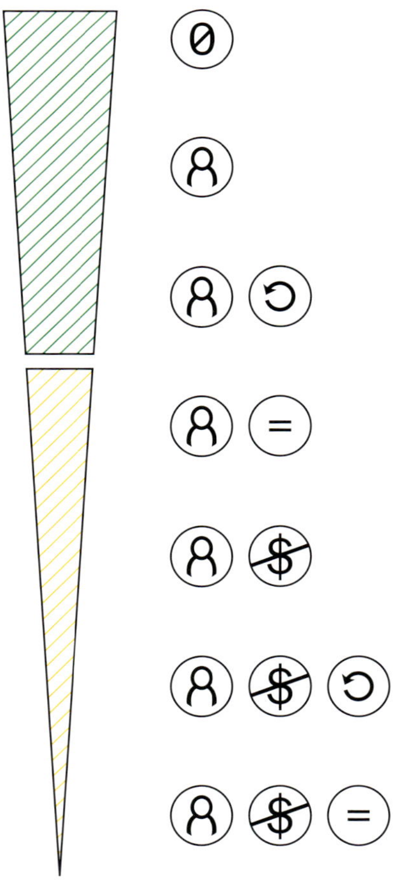

Public Domain Dedication (CC0)
By using CC0, you waive all copyright and related rights to a work to the extent possible under the law.

Attribution (CC BY)
The license lets others distribute, remix, tweak, and build upon your work, even commercially, as long as they credit you for the original creation. This is the most accommodating of licenses offered. Recommended for maximum dissemination and use of licensed materials.

Attribution – ShareAlike (CC BY-SA)
This license lets others remix, tweak, and build upon your work even for commercial purposes, as long as they credit you and license their new creations under the identical terms. All new works based on yours will carry the same license, so any derivatives will also allow commercial use.

Attribution – NoDerivs (CC BY-ND)
The license allows for redistribution, commercial and non-commercial, as long as it is passed along unchanged and in whole, with credit to you.

Attribution – NonCommercial (CC BY-NC)
This license lets others remix, tweak, and build upon your work non-commercially, and although their new works must also acknowledge you and be non-commercial, they don't have to license their derivative works on the same terms.

Attribution – NonCommercial – ShareAlike (CC BY-NC-SA)
This license lets others remix, tweaks, and build upon your work non-commercially, as long as they credit you and license their new creations under identical terms.

Attribution – NonCommercial – NoDerivs (CC BY-NC-ND)
This license is the most restrictive of our six licenses, only allowing others to download your works and share them with others as long as they credit you, but they can't change them in any way or use them commercially.

LEAST OPEN

Hedonist International

Hedonist International is a movement that creates temporary zones for fun, pleasure, enjoyment, and freedom and also defends the political significance of these values. On their website they collect ideas for actions, with which they seek to undermine a system of society and state that in their opinion is focused on duties and obligations. For example, with actions such as the *Fette-Mieten-Party* [Rip-Off Rents Party] staged by nude activists, they protest against extortionate rents and demand affordable housing in cities.

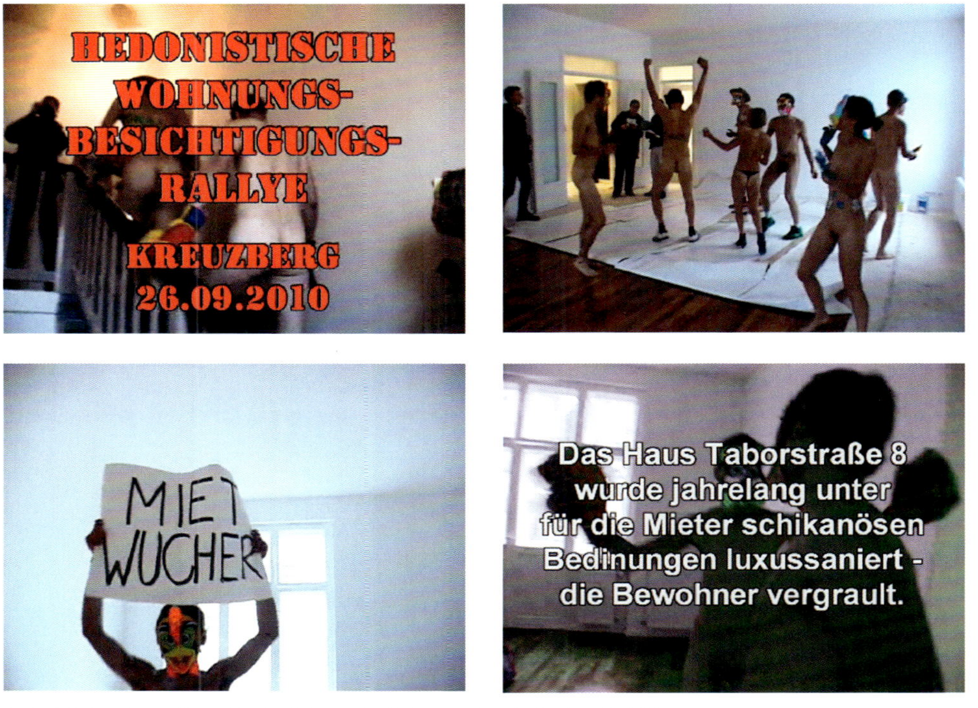

Hedonist International, *Hedonistische Wohnungsbesichtigungsrallye*, September 26, 2010, Berlin-Kreuzberg, part of the series *Fette-Mieten-Party*, video, color, sound, 2:21 min, video stills

Julia “Butterfly” Hill *1974

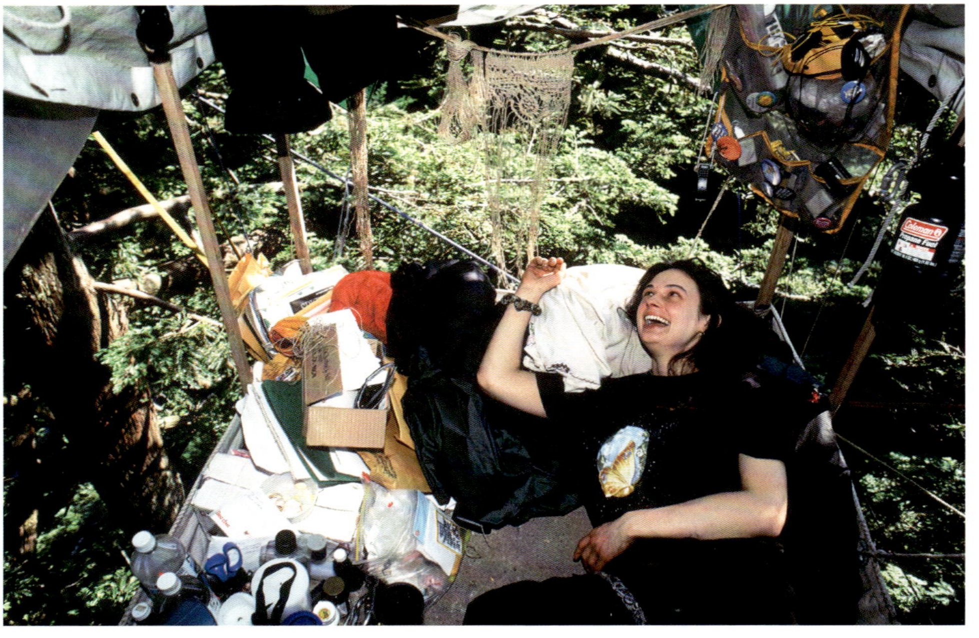

Julia “Butterfly” Hill in her dwelling sixty meters above the ground

Julia “Butterfly” Hill is an environmental activist, who on December 10, 1997 climbed a Californian Redwood tree she named Luna to prevent it from being felled and to attract the world’s attention to the plight of ancient forests. She lived in the tree, sixty meters above the ground, for 738 days and was exposed to extreme weather conditions and several – sometimes violent – attempts to remove her from the tree.

Finally, Julia “Butterfly” Hill and her fellow campaigners succeeded in preserving Luna in 1999. This extraordinary act of civil disobedience is documented in her book *The Legacy of Luna* (HarperCollins, New York, 2000). Today, Hill works as a life coach.

Julia “Butterfly” Hill standing on the top of the tree Luna

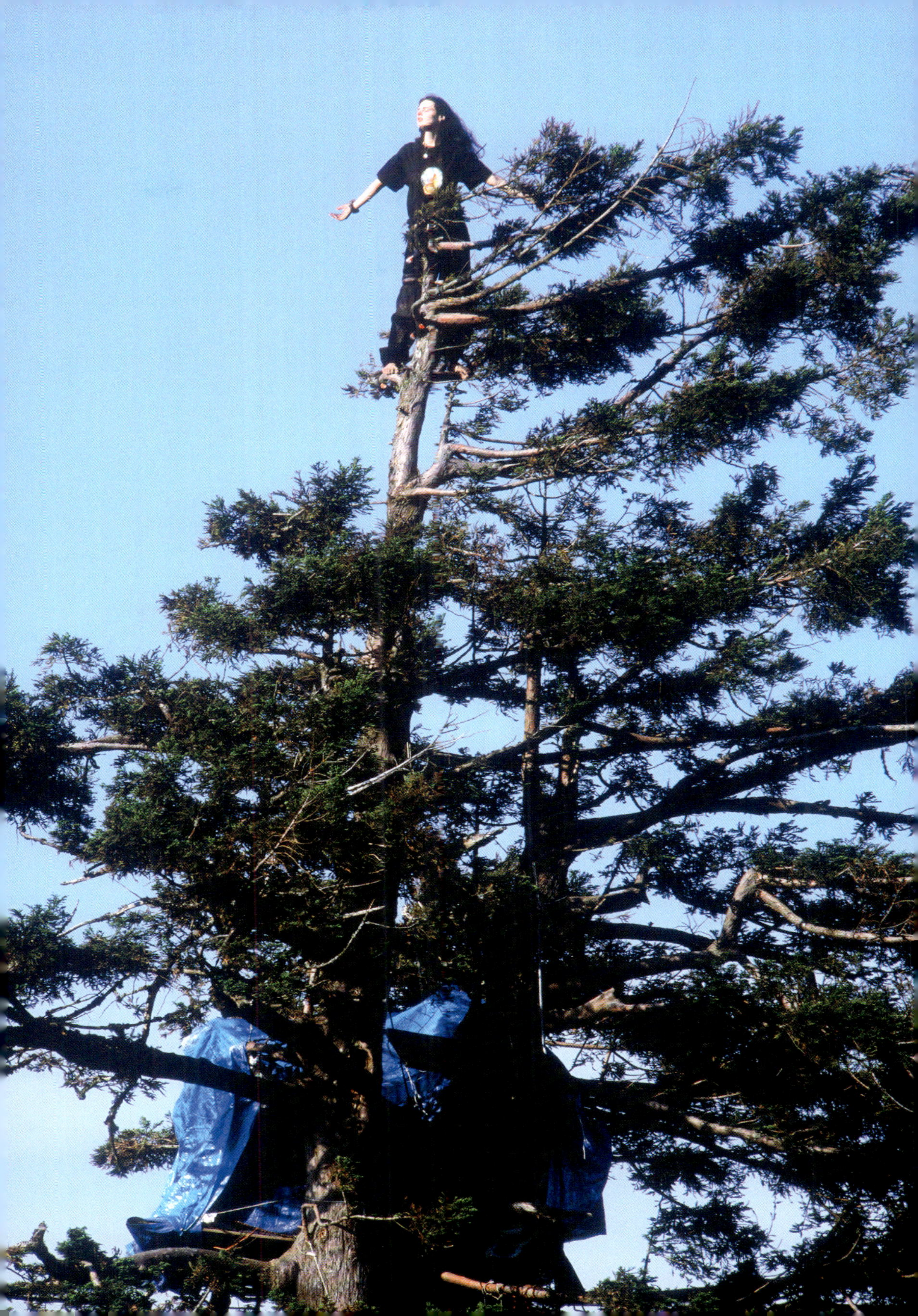

Mikaela *1983

Street and performance artist Mikaela is part of the Russian Feminist Initiative collective, a new generation of feminist artists and activists who strongly oppose blatant gender discrimination and stigmatization, which in politics and society is often declared as simply nonexistent, who politicize the private sphere of sexuality by drawing attention to the problem of sexual abuse of women and prostitution, and target the homophobia and hostility towards women in Russian politics.

The members – Mikaela, for example, in her 2013 stencil series *Choose a Woman* – especially reject the Russian law against "Gay Propaganda," which was enacted in 2013 and under which any information about LGBT or queer can de facto be treated as propaganda and people dealing with it can easily be branded as lawbreakers.

With the *Every Fourth Family* stencils, which Mikaela also did in public spaces in Moscow in 2013, she shows what statistics apparently reveal to be bitter reality in Russia: that every fourth woman is beaten by her husband or partner, and therefore not even their own apartments or houses can save women from violence. She visualizes the statistics by showing houses with many windows, some of which are colored red. On the last stencil a hotline number is written, because in Mikaela's opinion telling somebody what happened can be the first step of resistance.

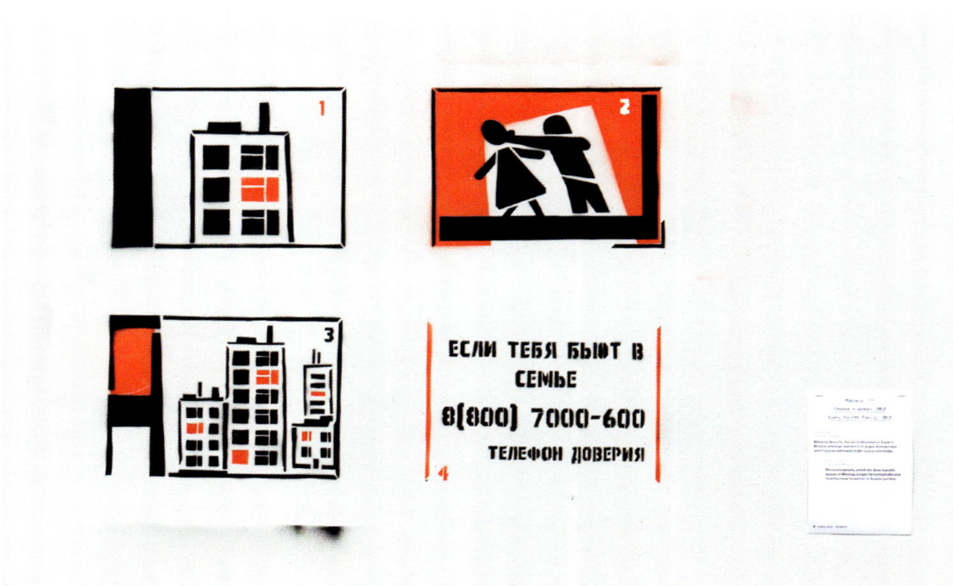

Above: Mikaela, *Every Fourth Family*, 2013, stencil, spray color, installation view, ZKM | Karlsruhe, 2014
Facing page: Mikaela, *Choose a Woman*, 2013, stencil, spray color, installation view, ZKM | Karlsruhe, 2014

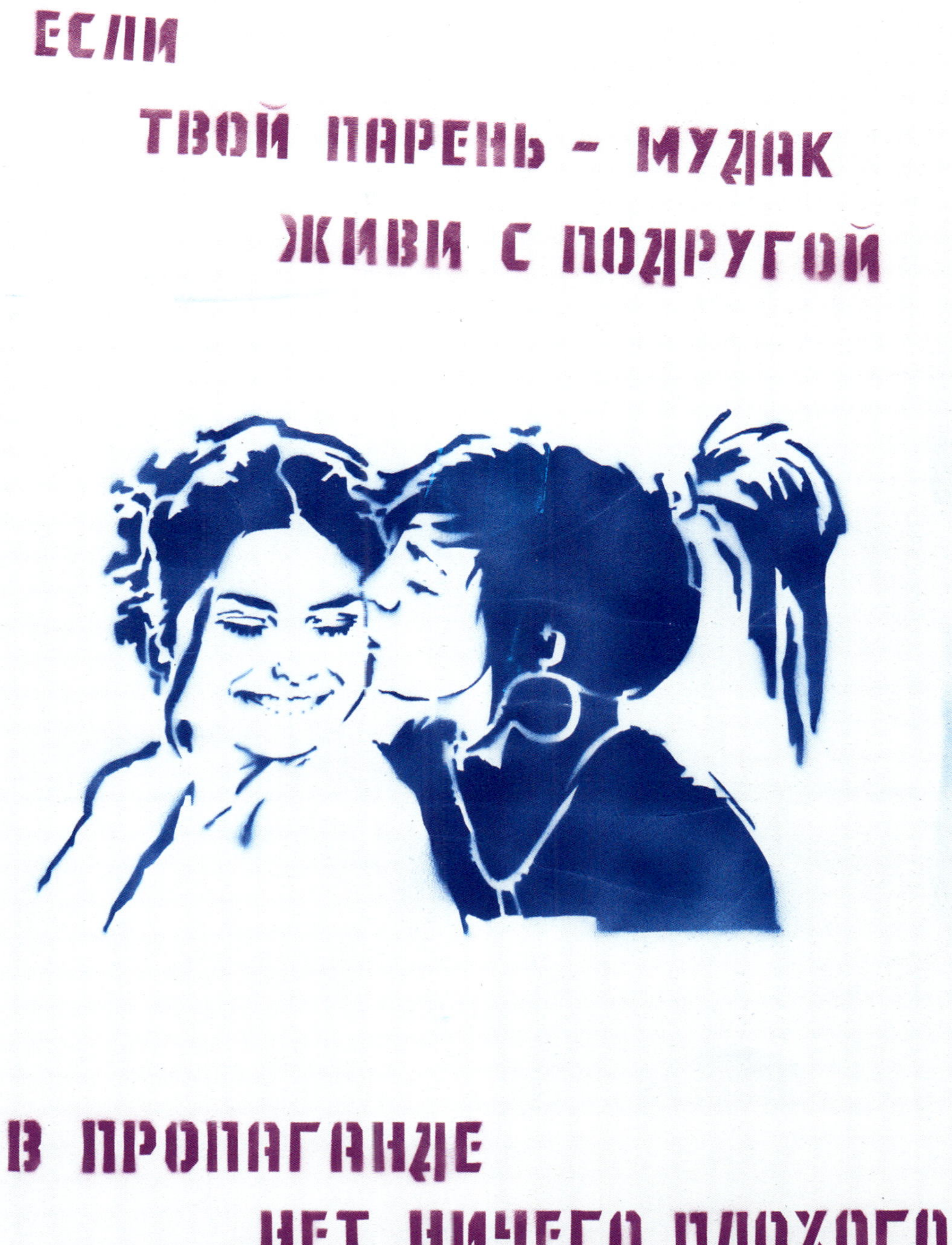
ЕСЛИ
ТВОЙ ПАРЕНЬ – МУДАК
ЖИВИ С ПОДРУГОЙ
В ПРОПАГАНДЕ
НЕТ НИЧЕГО ПЛОХОГО

Founded in 1996
USA

www.notbored.org/the-scp.html

Surveillance Camera Players

The Surveillance Camera Players (SCP) is an informal group founded by Michael Carter and Bill Brown in 1996, in which in total over fifty different people have participated. With their short performances in front of surveillance cameras the members oppose unconditionally the pervasive installation and use of video surveillance cameras in the public sphere and seek to initiate a rethinking of the role surveillance plays in people's everyday life. Especially in the late 1990s, the group was intensively productive. In November 1998, for example, six members of SCP performed their own version of George Orwell's novel *1984* in the New York subway station at 14th Street / Sixth Avenue in Manhattan.

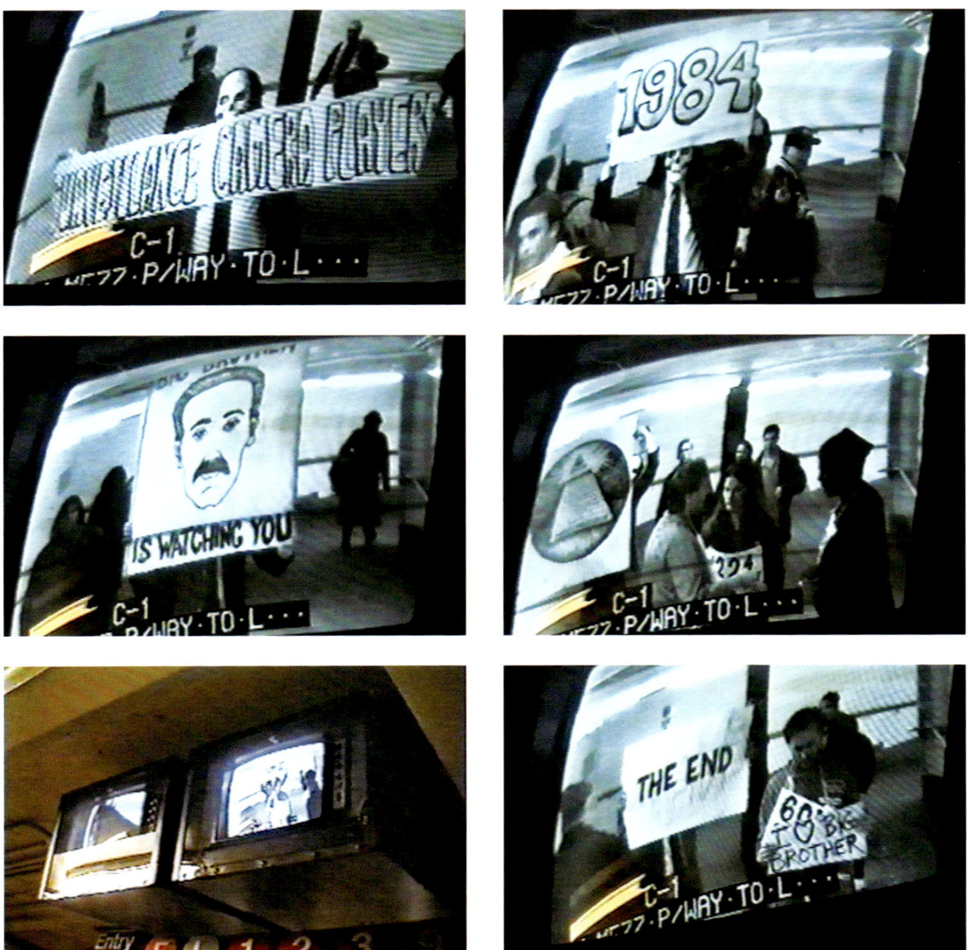

Surveillance Camera Players, *1984*, 1998, performance, stills from the video documentation

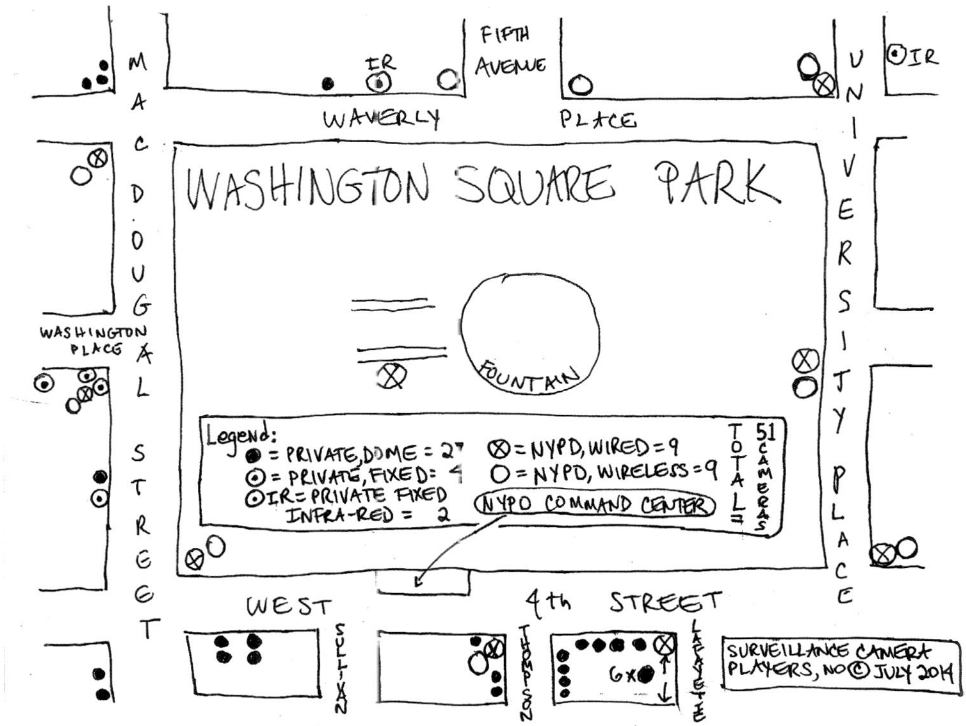

Surveillance Camera Players, sketched overview of surveillance cameras installed in and around the Washington Square Park, New York City, July 2014

In his *Programming Note for the First Season*, Bill Brown wrote in November 1996:

"The Surveillance Camera Players are not a professional theater troupe, nor are they producers of or actors in television shows; they are just a bunch of average Joes and Josephines who appreciate how boring it must be for law enforcement officers to watch the video images constantly being displayed on the closed-circuit television surveillance systems that perpetually monitor our behavior and appearances all over the city. The only time the officers have any fun watching these monitors is when something illegal is going on. But the crime rate is down and the subways (which are filled with surveillance cameras) are the safest they have been in thirty years. Thus, for untold numbers of police surveillants, there is less and less to watch – less and less to watch out for – every day. And so we have both an opportunity and a problem here. The opportunity is to get those law enforcement officers watching something on TV that isn't all sex and violence; and the problem is that a bored surveillant is an inattentive surveillant, and an inattentive surveillant is a waste of space, time, and money."

Collaboration since 1993
UK

http://thomson-craighead.net

Thomson & Craighead

Since the early 1990s, the London-based artists Jon Thomson (*1969) and Alison Craighead (*1971) make artworks and installations – for galleries, online, and sometimes outdoors. Many of their recent works illustrate the mechanisms of networks like the Web and the way they influence and change our understanding of how the world works. They both studied at Duncan of Jordanstone College of Art in Dundee; Jon Thomson now lectures part-time at the Slade School of Fine Art, University College London, while Alison Craighead is a senior researcher at the University of Westminster and lectures in fine art at Goldsmiths University. During the past twenty years of their collaboration they have had several solo exhibitions and taken part in various group exhibitions all over the world, including at the Museum of Contemporary Art Sydney, the Guggenheim Museum in New York, the San Francisco Museum of Modern Art, the Tate Britain in London, the ZKM | Center for Art and Media Karlsruhe, the NIMk in Amsterdam,

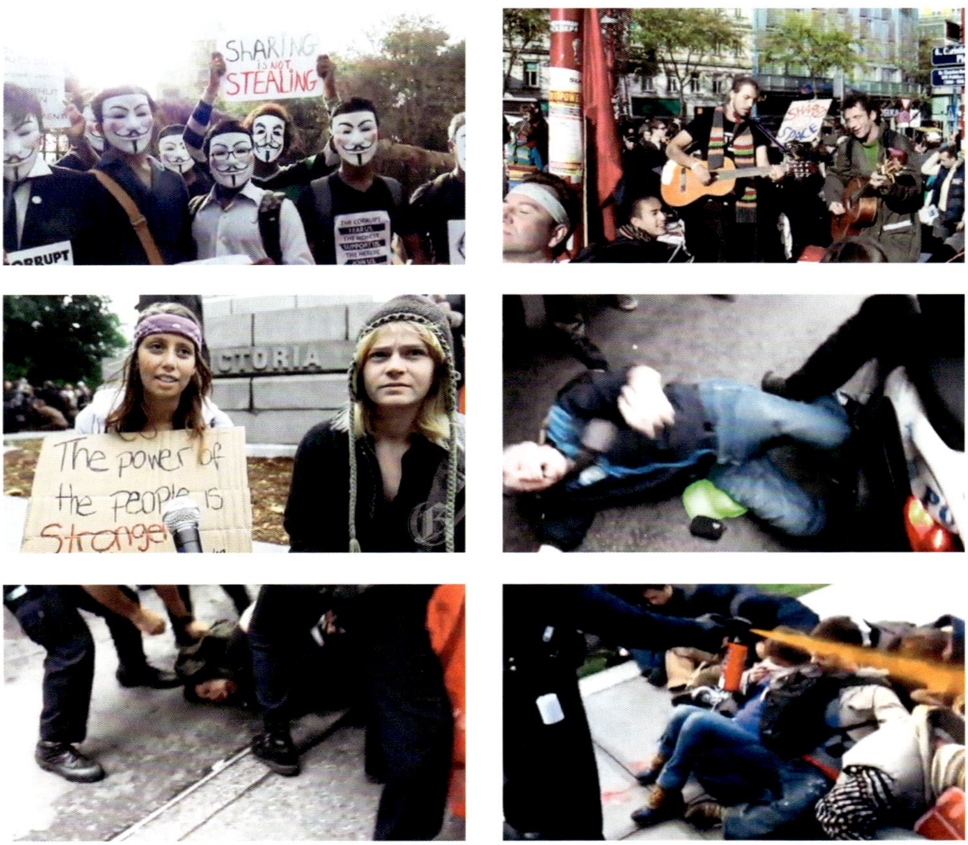

Thomson & Craighead, *October*, 2012, 2-channel media installation, color, sound, 13:23 min, video stills from the documentary montage

the Centre international d'art contemporain de Montreal, and the Centre Pompidou in Paris. Thomson and Craighead have participated in many festivals, for example, the Festival of Video and Electronic Art in Mexico City (1999), the Kassel Documentary Film and Video Festival (2008), the International Film Festival Rotterdam (2011), the Edinburgh International Film Festival (2012), the OFF & FREE International Film Festival in Seoul (2012), and the Videonale.14 in Bonn, Germany (2013).

Their 2-channel media installation *October* (2012) documents both the rapid spread of the Occupy movement in mid-October 2011 and the clearing of its protest camps by the police in November. A projected compass points to the geographic origin of the video sequences. If the next sequence begins, the position of the virtual needle also changes. By placing the viewer in the center of the visualization a direct physical relationship between him or her and the footage is offered.

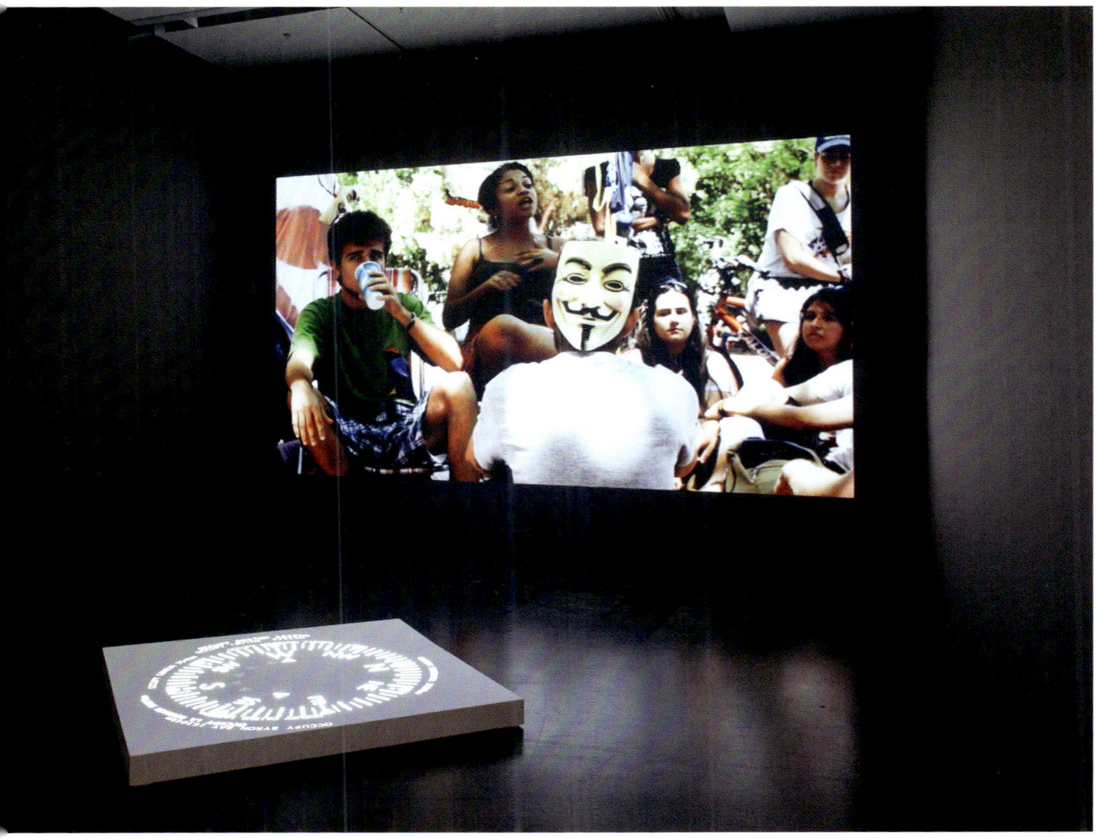

Above and next page: Thomson & Craighead, *October*, 2012, 2-channel media installation, installation view, ZKM | Karlsruhe, 2014

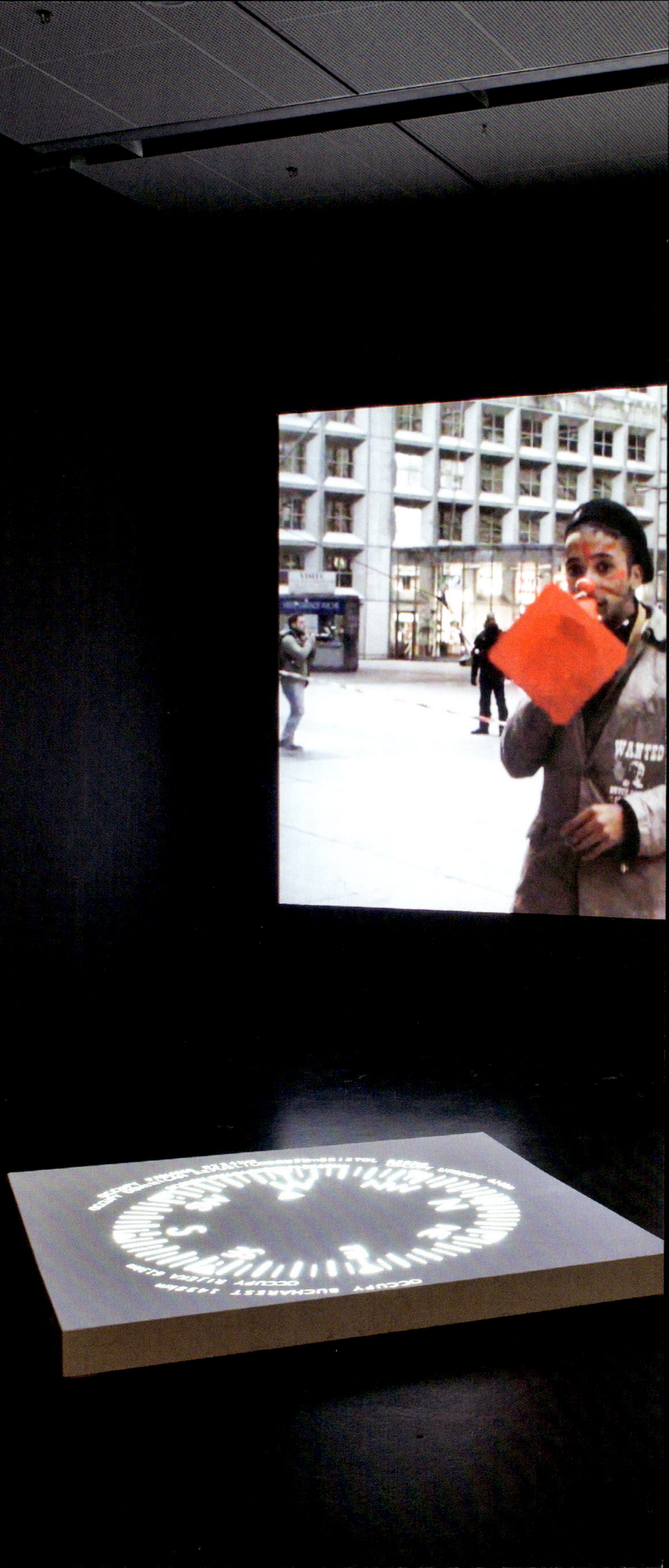
WANTED

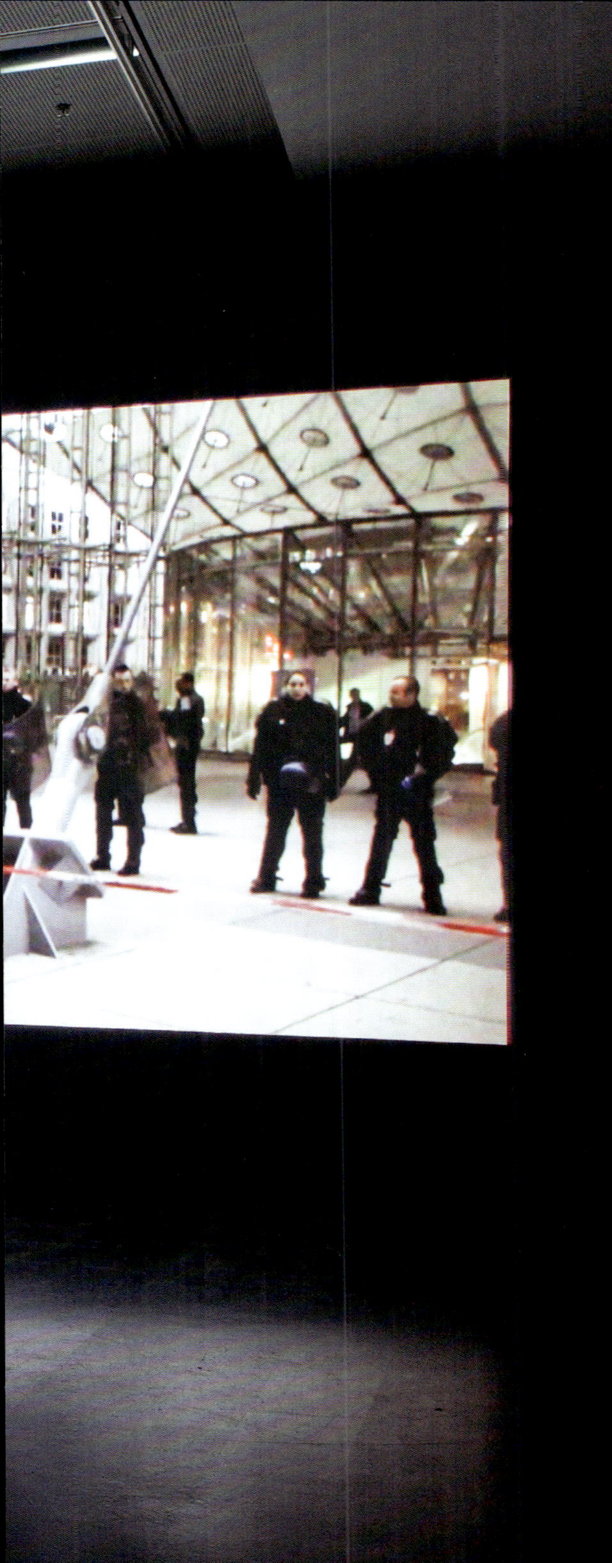

Founded in 2003
UK

www.troika.uk.com

Troika

Troika is an artist group founded by Conny Freyer (*1976), Eva Rucki (*1976), and Sebastien Noel (*1977), which is currently located in London. Since the beginning of the collaboration, the trio has presented its works and projects in numerous solo exhibitions and has also participated in several group exhibitions all across the world, amongst others at the Royal Academy of Arts and the Tate Britain in London, the SOHO Shangdu in Beijing, the Roppongi Hills Arena in Tokyo, the Museum of Modern Art in New York, the LABoral Art and Industrial Creation Centre in Gijon, Spain, the Garage Center for Contemporary Culture in Moscow, the Taipei Fine Arts Museum, and the Espace Fondation EDF in Paris.

Their *SMS Guerilla Projector* (2003) is a homemade device made of familiar objects like a cell phone and a camera lens. It enables the user to project various news and messages onto objects and walls that were not conceived for this purpose.

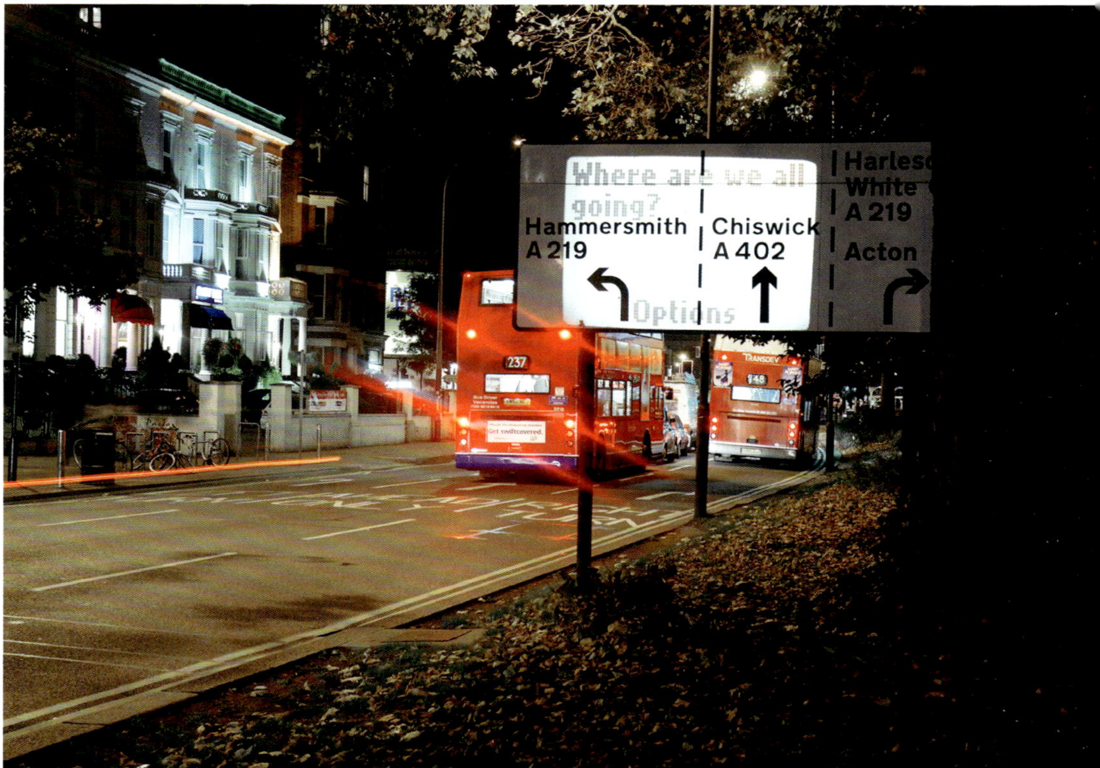

Troika, *SMS Guerilla Projector*, 2003, projection on a street sign in London

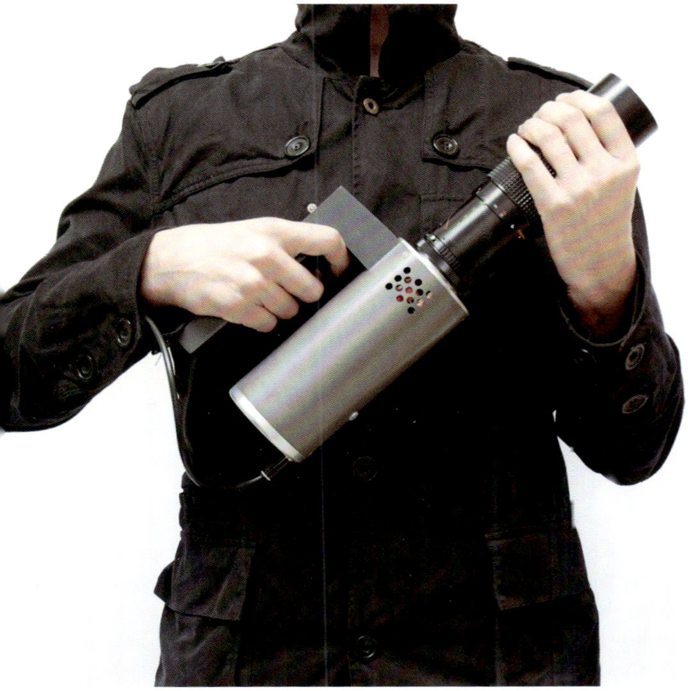

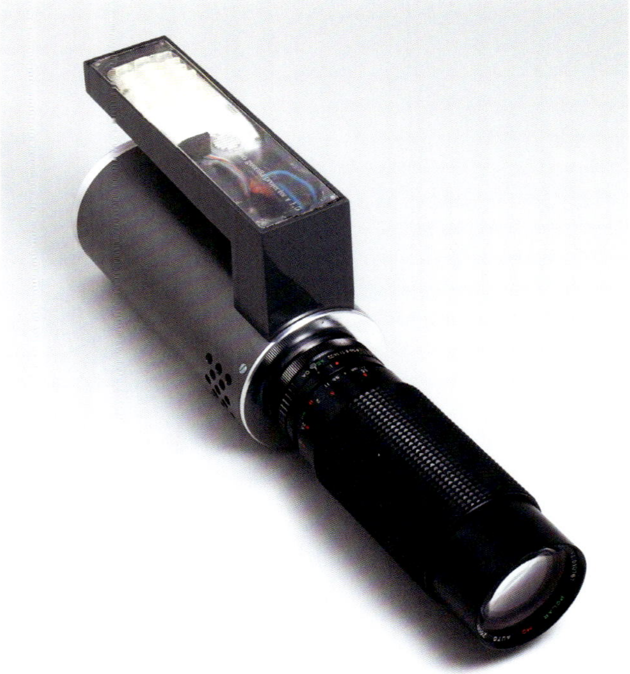

Troika, *SMS Guerilla Projector*, 2003, projection device

Online Projects

CyberGuerilla

The CyberGuerilla, an anarchic hacker movement, on its website and blog calls for the free exchange of information and the security of private communications.

www.cyberguerrilla.org

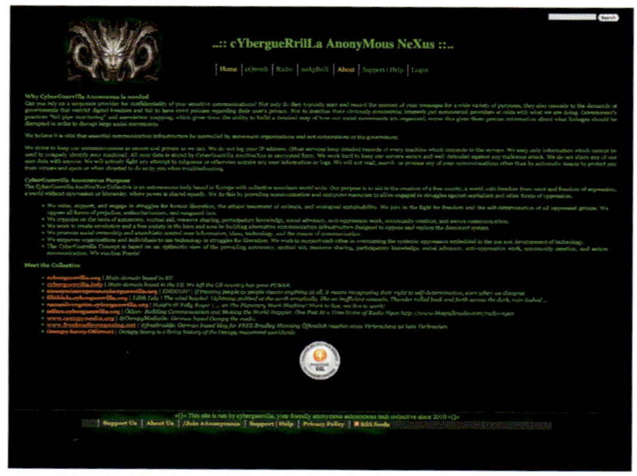

Screenshot, 07/08/2014

We Are the 99 Percent

USA

Since August 2011, on the blog with the motto of the Occupy Wall Street movement, photos of people affected by the consequences of the financial crisis are posted, who tell on handwritten notes about the loss of their job, or home, or health care, or their prospects.

wearethe99percent.tumblr.com

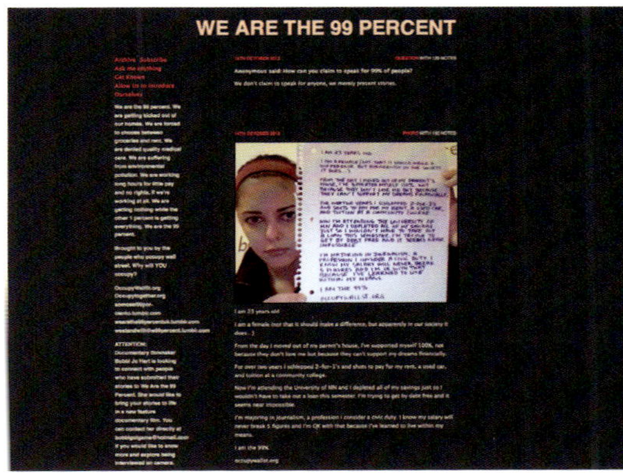

Screenshot, 07/08/2014

How

How to Do Activism

Chapter III

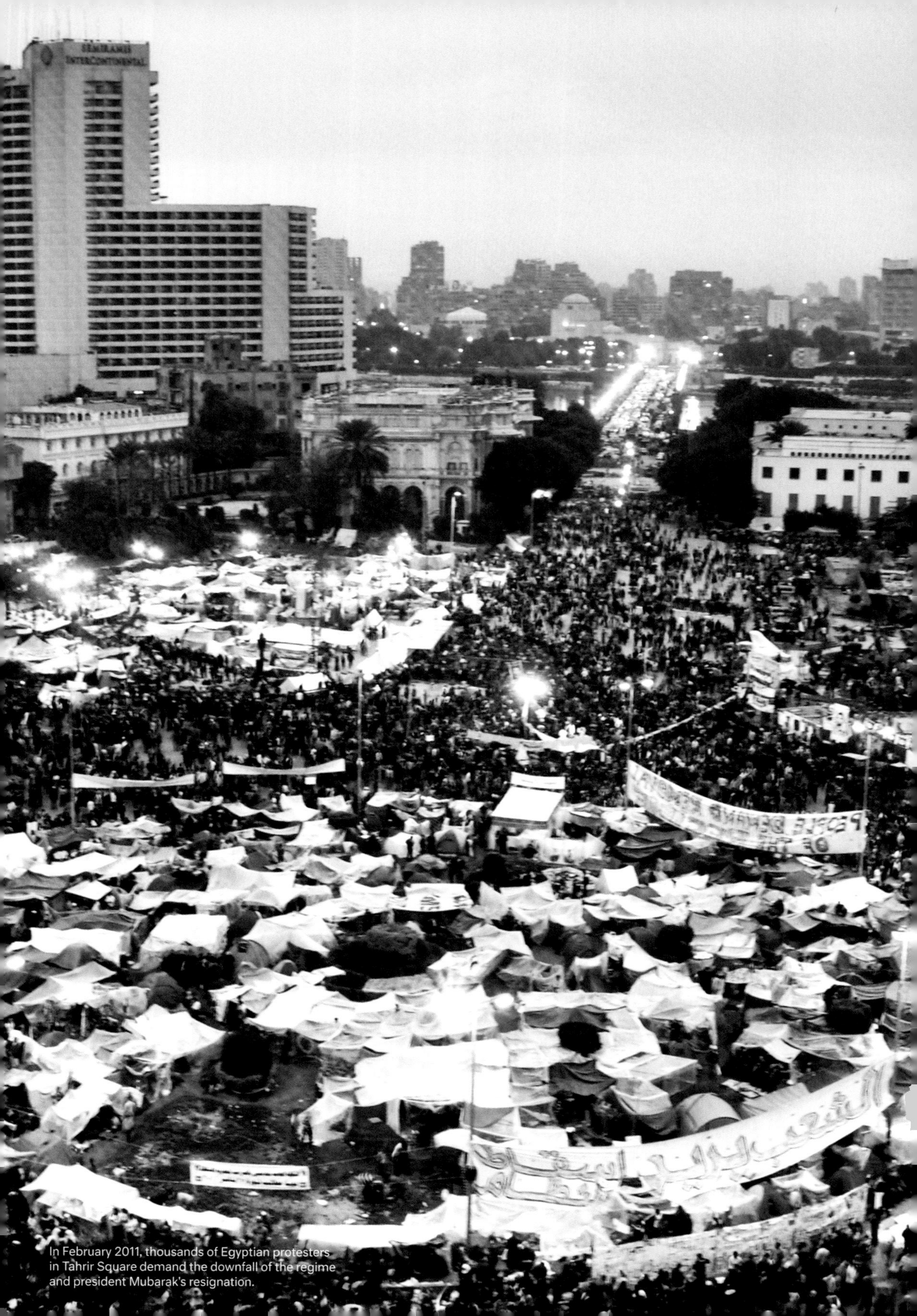

In February 2011, thousands of Egyptian protesters in Tahrir Square demand the downfall of the regime and president Mubarak's resignation.

Daniel Mützel in conversation with Youness Belghazi, a Moroccan filmmaker and activist involved in the February 20 Movement (2011), and Hadeer Elmahdawy, an Egyptian journalist and researcher, who took part in activities before and during the Tahrir revolution.

Youness Belghazi
and Hadeer Elmahdawy

"Arab Spring Is Not Over, but Continues in a Different Way."

Daniel Mützel: Not long ago, almost everyone involved in thinking about global politics observed the social eruptions in the Arab world with great interest. Following these events, revolutionary movements popped up on every continent of the planet announcing their inspiration from the Arab revolutions. Today, almost three years later, these movements seem to have been silenced. Is the Arab Spring still going on?

Hadeer Elmahdawy: It is getting complicated now because it is easier to agree on removing authoritarian regimes than it is to agree on alternatives. In Egypt, for instance, we now have two competing forces – the military and the Islamists – striving for power, and you can't really support either of them, so you keep your distance and just observe. There are few things you can do now because it is a very serious conflict.

Youness Belghazi: I don't think that the Arab Spring is over. It is not an event that began and ended at certain points. It is rather something that continues inside the society in a different way. There is still a lot happening inside the country, just on a smaller scale and more subtly. The mainstream media certainly doesn't show as many images as at the beginning. But when you are there you can feel that there are a lot of things changing.

Mützel: The Tahrir movement spectacularly, and in a very short time frame, achieved the overthrow and subsequent imprisonment of Hosni Mubarak. For quite a while it seemed that many things were possible in Egypt, that the country could go in previously unthinkable directions. Even the Muslim Brotherhood, an organization that was criminalized and suppressed by the regime for decades, had the opportunity to attempt to shrink the power of the military. In summer 2013, this move completely failed. In a bloodless coup, the generals dissolved the government of Mohamed Morsi, brutally cracked down on protests organized by supporters, and imprisoned senior leaders of the Brotherhood. In retrospect, was there too much focus in the Tahrir movement on getting rid of Mubarak instead of the whole regime?

Elmahdawy: The Egyptian political system is dominated by a "deep state," as for example in Turkey. We are confronted with a very old and bureaucratic state and almost an organic connection between the military and the economic elite. Changing these institutions is not an easy task. Still, I don't think that it's finished. It is a dynamic process. The only assurance for the revolutionaries is to stay awake and to confront any regressive developments that occur. The Muslim Brotherhood and the military are somehow both part of the old regime. The fight against both is now a part of the revolution that, in some sense, continues. So the movement's focus has been also changed by the events, you cannot choose it independently of them.

Belghazi: Arab societies were never used to this kind of social dynamic or to revolutionary situations. So I think it is unrealistic to expect a quick transformation, especially if we are talking about institutional change.

Elmahdawy: Besides, we also have to talk about the cultural achievements of the uprising. For instance, the word "protest" plays a completely different role in daily conversations and public language now. It is a lot easier for someone to protest because the concept has become normal. The culture of protest that was born in the Arab Spring has spread to many societies, from Tunisia, to Egypt, to Syria, to Libya, and even to Europe and the U.S. This is a great achievement.

Mützel: But is the spirit still there, after all the repression the state has exerted? State repression is not limited to physical violence or the blocking of political opposition; it also aims to suppress the revolutionary spirit, intimidating the people and crushing their hopes that change is possible.

Belghazi: If we're talking about the globally spreading culture of protest, I think we also have to talk about the culture of counter-resistance passing from one regime to the other. Sadly, we can witness the domino effect also on the side of the regimes. For example, the regime in Morocco learned from the regime in Egypt not to repeat the same mistakes. So I think it's more than intimidation, more than repression, rather a shared experience between dictatorial regimes in all Arab countries. In Morocco we also experienced a time of big protests. But as they started only in February 2011, after the Egyptians had already brought down Mubarak, it was easy for the Moroccan king [Mohammed VI] to learn from Mubarak's mistakes. Instead of confronting the media, he sought dialog with them, and he didn't censor Facebook and Twitter. That was a clever move. So the networking is not only between activists but also between regimes. And they have more tools than we do.

Elmahdawy: Or they support allied regimes in suppressing uprisings to prevent the transfer of the revolution to their country. This happened in Bahrain, for instance, where the Saudi Arabian military played a crucial role in the crackdown on Bahraini protesters.

Mützel: Not to forget the German regime selling small arms and tanks to Saudi Arabia.

Elmahdawy: Or the U.S. sending tear gas and arms to the Egyptian military, which they used against the protesters. It is a global network whose members support each other.

Mützel: The "deep states" collaborate.

Elmahdawy: Sadly true. Finally, the viral nature of the revolutionary spirit also has a reverse effect. The domino effect stopped in Syria, where the revolution was transformed into a civil war by the regime. Of course, this was also disappointing for all the other movements and their own prospects for change.

Mützel: What were the specific tactics or tools with which the movements countered the increasing oppression?

Belghazi: As they were, with some exceptions, mostly pacific movements, it was difficult to deal with repression by the police or the army. In Morocco, we stated clearly that we were not against the police, and that we knew that it was being used by the regime to send us messages. So we opted for techniques to organize the protests without confronting the police and to be visible in the public differently. Sometimes, it was even funny to go to the police and give them flowers, for example.

Elmahdawy: We did the same in Egypt. It's provocative…

Belghazi: It's provocative and at the same time we gave a very intelligent message that we didn't want a confrontation.

Mützel: And if flowers don't work anymore because the water cannon is approaching?

Elmahdawy: Of course, in the situation of a confrontation on the street, this doesn't help against the tear gas and the rubber bullets. There are other, more direct, ways to react to them.

Belghazi: But at the same time we were not opting for a kind of black bloc resistance against the police, because we are not fighting against the police, but against the regime. If we fight the police they send the army, and if not the army, then they send the mercenaries. So I think it is more clever to react passively.

Mützel: In Egypt, there were serious clashes between the people and both the police and the army, and not only on the streets: During the course of events hundreds of police stations were attacked and set on fire. Was this still pacific protest?

Elmahdawy: But there was no violence. We were confronted by armed forces and we had to defend our square. We used rocks, Molotov cocktails, and other things which were not violence, but just a means to protect the square…

Mützel: …which is exactly the idea behind a black bloc: It was not designed as an aggressive force, but as a means of self-defense. What was the experience with the Egyptian black bloc?

Elmahdawy: It was formed during the protests, but it was not so effective. The regime targeted it very harshly, so after a while it disappeared.

Belghazi: I don't consider it a nonpacific movement. For me a nonpacific movement is a movement that is organized to fight the police. But if there are a bunch of people at Tahrir Square, from Ultras or from the black bloc, who are trying to defend the square in order to liberate political prisoners or to reclaim the space, this doesn't make it a nonpacific movement. The majority of the people have still opted for nonviolence. It is a bit like the Zapatistas: Everyone in the world calls them a military movement, but how many times have they used their weapons?! It is an autonomous movement that defends its space.

Mützel: What is the difference between the Moroccan movement and the Egyptian movement in terms of tools, tactics, and in terms of how they organized protests?

Belghazi: There are a lot of differences between the Egyptian and Moroccan experience, beginning with the nature of the systems. Egypt is a republic where Mubarak had held power for over forty years, whereas Morocco is a monarchy, an institution that has been holding power for more than twelve centuries now. So we are talking about a much older institution and practice of the regime. The king has a lot of popularity so even the part of the population that is fed up doesn't realize that the king is one of the main problems in Morocco. Furthermore, when we talk about the protests in Morocco we predominantly talk about "movements," not about the whole population participating in the protests. For sure, in Egypt there is the April 6 Youth Movement and the Kefaya Movement. But, after January 25, everybody was talking about "the people" making the revolution.

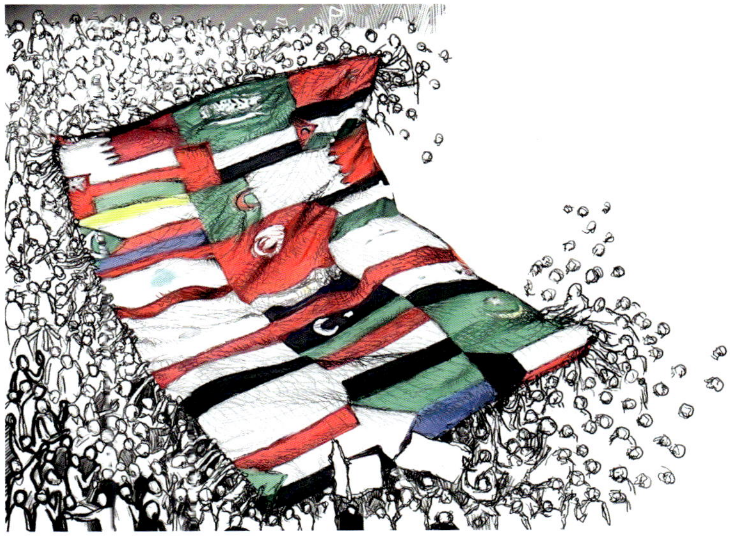

Joulia Strauss and Florian Wolf, *Arab Spring*, 2014, drawing, mixed media, 26 × 35 cm

In Morocco we still talk about the February 20 Movement, which is just a small social movement that doesn't represent the population. Of course politicians and the media also try to promote this kind of propaganda in order to isolate movements from the population and to say they are just elitists.

Elmahdawy: In terms of movement tactics, you can observe many similarities, whether in Egypt, the U.S., or in Greece. The idea of occupying public squares is central to all these protest movements, as is the intense use of social networks for disseminating information, mobilizing people, and coordinating actions. Moreover, they share some common problems, like lack of leadership and organization. After all, most of them are anticapitalist, which I consider the core of the movements. In Egypt, it is not articulated that clearly, but the primary issues are of economic exploitation and other injustices produced by global capitalism.

Mützel: How were tactics shared?

Elmahdawy: When we started our protests at Tahrir Square, the Tunisian activists quickly started to post advice on how to avoid tear gas and how to escape from police forces. They sent us instructions on the use of onions to overcome the effects of the gas. We adopted this practice and sent recommendations to activists, when it started in other countries, like Syria…

Belghazi: …or in Turkey. The entire Arab world was giving advice to Turkey. In Morocco, many people tried to take part in the Gezi protests digitally, you could call it "click-tivism," by spreading information via social media and other channels. It's a form of digital solidarity and everyone is trying to share experiences.

Elmahdawy: Transnational networks were built, also in order to synchronize actions. For example, when protests were flaring up, we organized solidarity protests in front of each other's embassies, as happened in the U.S. and Greece to support the Egyptian revolution. Solidarity is one of the core elements of the movements now. But the crucial aspect is that this global repertoire of tools and tactics, and this new culture of protest are present not only in Egypt, which is an authoritarian state, but equally present in, for instance, Greece, which formally is a democratic system. Despite the many differences between Egyptian and Greek society, both political systems are marked by this culture of protest.

Mützel: Did you travel to other countries to strengthen international ties, and to support other activists the old-school-way?

Elmahdawy: I didn't travel myself, but some friends of mine went to Istanbul, others to Tunisia, and finally some even went to the U.S.

Belghazi: I went to Tunisia and Turkey, which were both inspiring. I met a lot of activists in Istanbul and I was happy to know that there were a lot of anarchists who got involved in social movements without being fanatics about their ideology or their way of thinking. Moreover, when I went to Taksim Square the first time, I understood how important the infrastructure of place can be for the success of the protest and the mobilization. It was very easy for people to access Taksim Square, as it was well connected to the public bus transport system. But as soon as the authorities realized that all the busses going to Taksim were full of protesters, they cut this infrastructure. However, the protesters were very quick to react to this new situation, and recruited taxi drivers to go downtown in order to give people free rides to Taksim Square. This was very inspiring, to see how people get into solidarity. In Tunisia, I learned what an important role rap songs played to mobilize people. It is a very basic tactic there to organize protests. There are always a couple of rappers with them on demonstrations.

Elmahdawy: In Egypt as well, or in Iran: For instance in 2009, when the Green Movement took to the streets against the regime after the election fraud, there were many rap songs against Mahmoud Ahmadinejad that went viral among university students.

Mützel: What were your experiences with building viable social infrastructures like *asambleas* or neighborhood committees at the time when the movements were still out on the streets?

Belghazi: It's very difficult to deal with political representation in the Arab awakening. If we desire better institutions or an independent court, this can't be done by protests on the street. We are not politicians. As a movement, we can go on the streets and say that it seems wrong, but at a certain level we will need representation and institutions that reflect this. We cannot coordinate two million people on Tahrir. For sure, if you opt for a more autonomous and grassroots organization and don't want to gain political power, if you want to live in a space without authority, without politicians, without anyone who can lie to you, I accept this as a political position. But when we talk about a whole population that wants to improve their living conditions, and where many people cannot even understand their problems, this is not a realistic option. It is good to have this utopia or dream side of the revolution, but all the same we don't want to be a hippie movement. We want real change and we know it's a big task. It might take forever, but at the same time we want to push this regime.

Mützel: The question is which option is more utopian, the one that assumes that we can develop new institutions among ourselves or the one that claims that substantial change is possible on the basis of the existing institutions. After all, a new type of politics isn't something you can expect from elements of the ruling class – even though they will assure you otherwise. Instead, it must, by definition, come from somewhere else.

Elmahdawy: Theoretically you might be right, but in reality it is more complicated. For example, in July 2011, we started to organize an assembly on Tahrir Square. We discussed the rules, had some meetings, and took the concept of horizontal structure very seriously. We created different working groups, with some taking care of cleaning, others with financing the square, or with providing food, blankets, and other means of accommodation, all in a grassroots manner. However, the old regime was quick to prevent any kind of strong political organization that could somehow refuse the system. We were dispersed, and the initiative dried up. On the other hand, there is a mass feeling of distrust towards the existing institutions, the political parties, and even representative democracy. This also paralyzes potentially progressive developments.

Belghazi: People have a tendency to want people that have never lied to them before …

Mützel: …which is clearly an illusion, when the institutions remain the same and nobody creates alternatives. Then it's merely a matter of time until the new political figures repeat the actions of their predecessors.

Belghazi: Maybe you're right. However, the illusion is real. This is why the majority voted for the Muslim Brotherhood, which had never been part of the government. For many people this was enough reason to trust them. This deeply rooted skepticism towards the whole political system is a problem.

Mützel: It is not a question of creating new institutions that could replace the existing ones here and now, but a question of how a social movement defines itself: as a system of checks and balances for the people in power, or as a social realm that produces the political forms of tomorrow in the present.

Elmahdawy: There was a similar phenomenon in Sudan, when in August 2013 a flood led to a serious humanitarian crisis, also because the Sudanese government was unable or uninterested in coping with the situation. A couple of activists, close to the Girifna [We Are Fed Up] Movement, which has become very popular since the Sudanese antigovernment protests of 2011, formed Nafeer, a voluntary organization that organizes support for people affected by the flood. The initiative came out of a discussion on social media among a group of friends, but the organization grew up to 8,000 activists that are delivering material support like food and sheets, coordinating the donations they receive from other countries, and even sending teams to less accessible areas to help people. However, I agree with Youness in the respect that it's difficult to make these kinds of institutions out of the social movements, because of the loose organization, and because of the fear of taking responsibility.

Mützel: On the one hand, there is a lack of trust towards the ruling institutions, on the other hand, there are no charismatic leaders that are able to reassert them at least symbolically. Doesn't this show a crisis of the entire system? In a situation like this, the social movements might find themselves forced into exactly the dreamer position you mentioned before and to develop new forms of social organization.

Belghazi: But it can be a very dialectical debate if we take it this way. You will certainly not find an activist who wants to be ruled by someone, because an activist knows that no one will be able to represent him as he really wants to be represented. A social movement is certainly a way to see that the state institutions are delegitimized and to opt for another form of organization. But I'm wondering what possibilities there are for the social movements to create institutions that are able to represent the people or that are structured direct-democratically. Especially when we talk about the Arab world, it takes time, first and foremost, to educate people. And certainly, if the social movement becomes a way to educate people alternatively, that would be a very good result. But I don't think that could happen now. We are all a result of these regimes; we went to school with the regime, later to university, and now we are watching a lot of TV with it. It takes time to get rid of this. I am more confident to wait for any party to take power.

The interview was first published in a special issue of the *Krytyka Polityczna* magazine, edited by Daniel Mützel and Joulia Strauss in 2013 on the occasion of the *global aCtIVISm* exhibition at ZKM | Karlsruhe, 2014.

Sarah Maske

Activist Women's Rights Groups:

Demands and Methods

For a long time now women's rights and gender equality have been reasons for demonstrations and activism on the streets, in private and in virtual spaces. Some of these protests will be discussed in this essay by referencing select case studies. The theoretical framework is provided by the political scientist Gene Sharp's essay "The Methods of Nonviolent Action" in the volume of the same name edited by Gene Sharp together with Marina Finkelstein (Boston, 1973), which looks at different types of protests. Following this method, a number of activists who appear as individuals as well as several activist groups are separated from the context of their very heterogeneous forms of appearance and categorized to reveal in detail their effectiveness and media presence. Embedded in an astonishingly diverse framework of women's rights institutions and charters, which protect and support women and to which states pay attention, civil activist groups have often emerged as being the only executive bodies. If this is the case, the question arises as to what actual social (and following this, political) influence the institutions and decisions can possibly exert. Such institutions, agreements, and resolutions were created over the course of numerous historical struggles for improving women's rights, and out of these a complex theoretical system has evolved in the course of time, namely, feminism. In the Western world this took place in several phases or "waves."

The first wave began with the women's rights movement and the enfranchising of women (for example, women first got the vote in Germany in 1918) around the year 1900. The second wave rolled in during the 1970s, with several important steps on the path towards equality being taken at once by demanding the possibility of birth control and the abolition of the subordination of the wife to the husband in civil law. In the 1990s, emancipated feminists got the third wave moving, and at present a fourth wave of feminism is nascent based on already won rights, which now no longer concerns itself primarily with the demand for the enforcement of fundamental rights – for example, the right to work – but first and foremost with fleshing out these rights, for instance, in the form of equal pay for equal work. This separation into phases or waves has its origins in academic feminism, which clearly takes its cue from the West and accordingly can only be applied to a small number of countries. Even so, drawing on these stages is helpful in looking at international coalitions, agreements, and contracts, which dedicate themselves to observing women's rights whilst taking into account country-related stages in their development on the basis of precisely these waves.

As early as 1946, the Commission on the Status of Women was founded, a United Nations institution that reports each year on the status quo of international women's rights. Its remit is to ensure that achievements made in the field of women's rights are never again forfeited, as well as to make sure that criteria are established by which the situation in different countries can be compared and understood. Starting from the "ideal situation" for women – "absolute equality" with men – the commission today orients itself on the eight Millennium Development Goals (MDG), which were formulated by representatives of the United Nations, the World Bank, the IWF and the OECD's Development Assistance Committee in 2001 for the year 2015, to ensure progress for the poorest and most disadvantaged in the world.[1]

In order for the eighth Millennium Development Goal to be implemented, the Commission on the Status of Women underlines not only state support, but particularly the relevance of individual groups. Article 40 reads: "The Commission acknowledges the major contributions made by civil society, including women's and community based organizations and feminist groups in placing the interests, needs and visions of women on national, regional and international agendas."[2] This marked emphasis on the importance of group and individual action is not surprising, as governments often neglect their own patronage, react too slowly, or even initiate criminal proceedings against those who support women, as the commission observed.[3]

In 1981 the United Nations Convention on the Elimination of All Forms of Discrimination against Women (CEDAW), also known as the Women's Rights Convention, came into effect, which made safeguarding women's rights and the protection of women a legal obligation. A total of 188 UN member states ratified the Women's Rights Convention, which has, however, been criticized for being entirely Western-centric.

As women are not a minority, despite the common classification of their group as such, the large number of feminist activists who do not see their rights upheld and who therefore vehemently fight to gain and assert these is hardly surprising. But these rights have many facets and are fought for in such diverse battles that it seems difficult to speak of a global women's rights campaign. Judith Butler ascribes this problem to the fact that "[...] gender is not always constituted coherently or consistently in different historical contexts, and [...] gender intersects with racial, class, ethnic, sexual, and regional modalities of discursively constituted identities."[4]

However, there are definitely some fundamental similarities between the various reasons why women across the globe offer resistance, which can be understood as the keystones to the feminist struggle and are to be considered as major issues.

1 See the official UN website on the Millennium Development Goals, www.un.org/millenniumgoals/, accessed 06/25/2014. The MDG are: to "Eradicate Extreme Poverty and Hunger," "Achieve Universal Primary Education," "Promote Gender Equality and Empower Women," "Reduce Child Mortality," "Improve Maternal Health," "Combat HIV/AIDS, Malaria and Other Diseases," "Ensure Environmental Sustainability," "Global Partnership for Development."

2 Article 40 of the report *Challenges and achievements in the implementation of the Millennium Development Goals for women and girls* by the Commission on the Status of Women is available online at: www.unwomen.org/~/media/Headquarters/Attachments/Sections/CSW/58/CSW58-agreedconclusions-advanceduneditedversion.pdf, accessed 06/25/2014.

3 Ibid., Art. 18: "The Commission is deeply concerned that overall progress for women and girls across all the Millennium Development Goals remains slow and uneven, [...] both within and between countries, and that lack of progress on gender equality has hindered progress towards all of the Goals. It is especially concerned about the lack of progress for poverty-stricken regions and areas and for marginalized, vulnerable and disadvantaged women and girls and those women and girls who experience multiple forms of discrimination and inequalities of any kind."

4 Judith Butler, *Gender Trouble. Feminism and the Subversion of Identity*, Routledge, New York, London, 1999, p. 6.

The first of these key issues relates to the Protection of Human Rights and Fundamental Freedoms, which were defined in the Universal Declaration of Human Rights of 1948 and are to be seen as guidelines by the countries that have signed them, but which are not strictly legally binding.[5] The equivalent in the Arab world is the "Arab Charter on Human Rights," which came into effect in 2008 and has often been criticized, although it does clearly proclaim the equality of men and women (Art. 3.1).[6]

A second major issue can be identified in the demand for the adherence to basic civil rights, which in Europe, for example, is guaranteed by the "Charter of Fundamental Rights of the European Union" or through domestic legislation specific to individual countries' needs.[7] These fundamental rights correspond in parts with the human rights as laid out in the "Universal Declaration of Human Rights." The relevant difference is that the "Charter of Fundamental Rights of the European Union" is binding only in European countries where it is protected by law and enforceable in the European Court of Justice. The equality of women and men is explicitly stated in Art. 23 as set out in Title III on equality in the "Charter of Fundamental Rights of the European Union."[8] But adherence to these standards is not always ensured even in Europe. Moreover, there are states without explicit country-specific basic rights laws supporting women, in which activists can at least rely on the fundamental rights if the respective country has signed and ratified the "Universal Declaration of Human Rights."

The third major issue, which is less tied to institutional decrees and agreements, is addressed particularly in the highly developed industrial countries: The dissolution of rigid gender roles, meaning the stereotyped attribution of characteristics and outward features to women and men. Women's rights activists record unjust treatment stemming from such abstract gender perceptions again and again, with consequences that are, however, no longer abstract but concrete and tangible. For example, the Commission on the Status of Women raises awareness on the consequences of these gender roles in the workplace, and criticizes the uneven distribution of the sexes in certain professions. Women frequently work in the social field in particular, in part unsalaried – for example, as caregivers to relatives – which can be traced back to the fact that in many societies they are seen as "caretakers."[9] This means that these women have no opportunity to earn a livelihood and be independent.

These three main issues can be substantiated universally and all converge on a central goal, which connects all of the activists and groups listed in the following: Through nonviolent resistance they want to secure rights for women that women have so far been refused or that are still disregarded. The tactics towards achieving this goal are very diverse and range from merely drawing attention, and actually putting the finger on problems, to the call for action in order to change the criticized situation.

Gene Sharp defined some methods in *The Politics of Nonviolent Action. Part Two: The Methods of Nonviolent Action.*[10] He divided his study into the chapters "The Methods of Nonviolent Protest and Persuasion," "The Methods of Social Noncooperation,"

5

See: Article 41 of the report *Challenges and achievements in the implementation of the Millennium Development Goals for women and girls* by the Commission on the Status of Women: "The Commission recognizes that all human rights are universal, indivisible and interdependent and interrelated and that the international community must treat human rights globally in a fair and equal manner, on the same footing and with the same emphasis, and stresses that, while the significance of national and regional particularities and various historical, cultural and religious backgrounds must be borne in mind, it is the duty of States regardless of their political, economic and cultural systems to promote and protect all human rights and fundamental freedoms."

6

League of Arab States, *Arab Charter on Human Rights*, 2008, available online at: www1.umn.edu/humanrts/instree/loas2005.html?msource=UNWDEC19001&tr=y&auid=3337655, accessed 06/25/2014.

7

See: *Charter of Fundamental Rights of the European Union*, December 18, 2000, p. 8, available online at: www.europarl.europa.eu/charter/pdf/text_en.pdf, accessed 06/25/2014.

8

See: ibid., Art. 23, Equality between men and women, p. 13.

9

See: *Challenges and achievements in the implementation of the Millennium Development Goals for women and girls*, Art. 28.

10

See: Gene Sharp, *The Politics of Nonviolent Action. Part Two: The Methods of Nonviolent Action* (1973), 9 ed., Porter Sargent Publishers, Manchester, 2012.

"The Methods of Economic Noncooperation," "The Methods of Political Noncooperation," and "The Methods of Nonviolent Intervention." Taking these methods – especially those which Sharp termed "actions" – into account and developing them, including for the context of contemporary art with its new media, such as graffiti and the Internet, is certainly helpful when looking at women's rights activism.

In the following, the examples of activist groups discussed are not categorized according to nationality, ethnicity, or other traditional systems, but, based on Sharp's model, according to two modes of "actions." The focus is on describing the particular, concrete strategy as it is put into practice.

Direct Action

The method of "direct action" – in Sharp's book this is defined as boycott, strike, or active intervention in social or economic systems[11] – is a prevailing and effective form of protest and accordingly noncooperation that is employed in view of a great number of demands.

The group Red Brigade from Lucknow in India is a grassroots movement, founded in the wake of mass demonstrations provoked by the gang rape of an Indian student.[12] Its members are dedicated to fighting sexual harassment and rape and thus to the protection of the female body and the right to freedom for women and men as stipulated in the general Charter of Human Rights.[13] The community offers self-defense classes and it campaigns primarily in public urban spaces by protecting women and girls from assault and from acid attacks by patrolling. Through the signal function of their color, the red uniforms worn by Brigade members are intended to deter and thereby prevent violence, as well as to strengthen the bond between all members of the movement as a distinctive identifying feature. The use of colors and symbols is seen as a central step towards community building in nearly all activist groups, because it fosters the emergence of a feeling of solidarity. If we follow Alberto Melucci and define this solidarity between members as a crucial criterion of social movements,[14] then it is clear why the use of colors and symbols is recognized by Sharp as an autonomous and influential method.[15]

11 See: ibid., pp. 184ff.

12 See the Red Brigade's Weblog, available online at:http://red-brigades.blogspot.de, accessed 06/25/2014.

13 See: *Universal Declaration of Human Rights*, available online at: www.un.org/en/documents/udhr, accessed 06/25/2014.

14 See: Alberto Melucci, *Challenging codes. Collective action in the information age*, Cambridge University Press, Cambridge, New York, 1996, p. 26.

15 See: Sharp 2012, pp. 125ff.

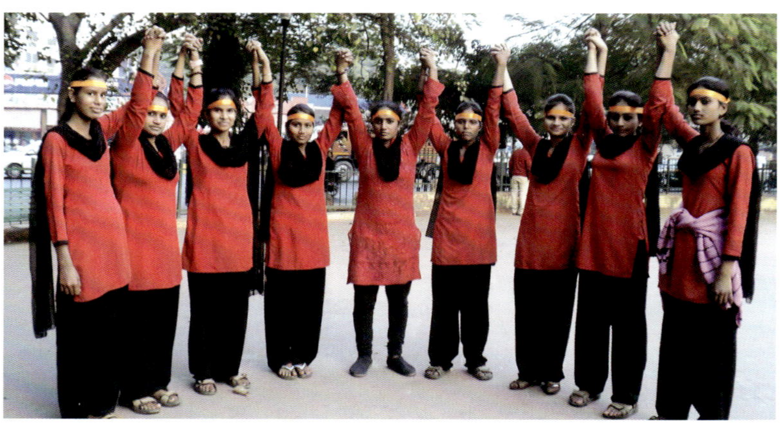

Red Brigade, Lucknow, India

Generally speaking, improving the status of women in India is proving difficult. Despite ratifying the Women's Rights Convention, India is neither a member of the Commission on the Status of Women nor signatory to the Universal Declaration of Human Rights, and is therefore not obliged to address women's rights at government level. As a result, support for Indian women's rights groups often comes from nongovernmental organizations (NGOs) and civilian groups.

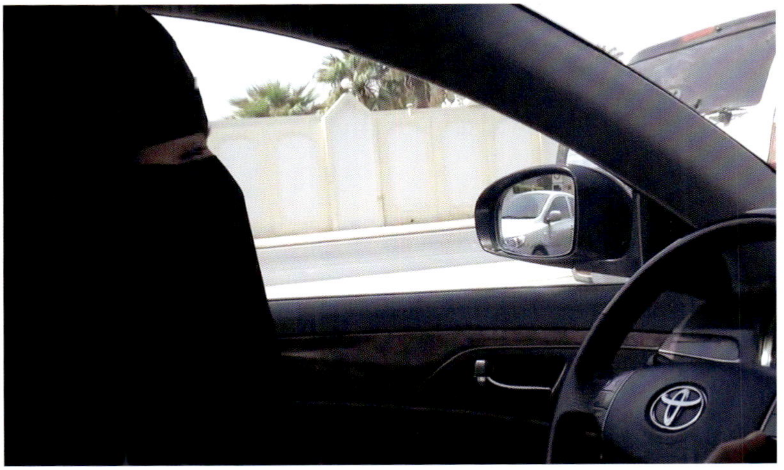

Women protest a de facto driving ban in Saudi Arabia, screenshot, video available online at: www.youtube.com/watch?v=nHsuzhd-1Fc&list=PLXhuzKSXJ9OS-84Vj5rkFj-HYAUVkWpll, accessed 11/05/2014.

Women2Drive is a campaign that constantly persuades new supporters to join a core of activists in their fight towards achieving the right for women to drive cars in Saudi Arabia.[16] Although this campaign does not pertain to an established human right, according to the goal of equality of the sexes and invoking the right to freedom of movement (Art. 13.1 of the Universal Declaration of Human Rights) it must be viewed as a violation of human rights that women are denied the permission to drive. The basis of the existing ban is not a ban on women driving that is enshrined in law, but rather a fatwa based on traditions, and thereby a rule set out by a Muslim authority as needed to fix everyday problems, which is prohibiting women from driving cars. Despite the enormous benefit that abolishing this regulation would have for women – they could, for example, go shopping by themselves and take their children to school – it is strictly observed. Since 1990 women who are holders of a driver's permit acquired abroad have repeatedly driven through town in a group or by themselves.[17] So far, this form of protest has not been successful, and can be seen as an example of a partially failed "direct action." In 2011 one female activist was condemned to eleven lashes of the whip for driving without a valid license.

Saudi Arabia is not a member of the Commission on the Status of Women and has not signed the Universal Declaration of Human Rights. It has, however, at least ratified the UN Women's Rights Convention and is one of the countries for which the Arab Charter on Human Rights was conceived, based on the sharia, in which gender equality is established as a principal goal, and which a ban on women driving clearly infringes.

16 Information can be found on the Facebookpage of the campaign, available online at: www.facebook.com/Women2Drive, accessed 06/25/2014.

17 See the video *Manal Al Sharif driving in Saudi Arabia*, available online at: www.youtube.com/watch?v=sowNSH_W2r0, accessed 06/25/2014.

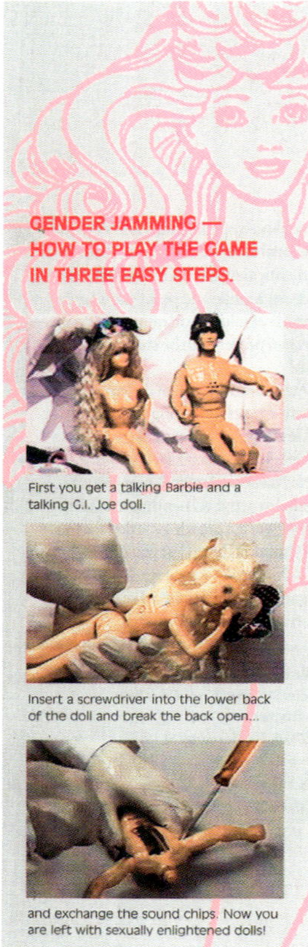

Susanne Zalev, "Barbie Liberation Organization," excerpt from: *Adbusters. Journal of the Mental Environment*, vol. 3, no. 4, Summer 1995, p. 45.

A further example is the Barbie Liberation Organization from the U.S. The group fights to change gender stereotypes and practices *culture jamming* or *shopgiving* as "direct action." In 1993 they carried out their best-known action to date, in which they exchanged the voice boxes of about 300 to 500 G.I. Joe and Barbie dolls, which resulted in Barbies saying things like "vengeance is mine" and G.I. Joe dolls proclaiming "The beach is the place for summer."[18] In this way, they intervened in childhood gender shaping, by swapping "typically female" and "typically male" characteristics, here manifested in the sayings assigned to each sex.

Currently, the number of examples of direct action in virtual spaces is increasing, creating the phenomenon of online feminism. Angela Washko, in her essay "Out of the Kitchen, onto Your Screen, into the Ether" explains that "Tactically the movement takes physical protest strategies and translates them to the digital realm."[19] As an example for projects based on this method of "direct action," the campaign ArtAndFeminism on Wikipedia can be cited, which aims to change the Internet in a feminist direction.[20] The project calls for articles to be published on Wikipedia that address artistic achievements by women to achieve more visibility for women in art history. This also has a big impact on offline life, as it shows that the world has been and is actively shaped by women, and writing such an article provides an opportunity of taking on a proactive role.

Symbolic Action

Another method deriving from Gene Sharp's list of nonviolent feminist action is "symbolic action" – a prime example of which is an artistic procession.[21] An action can be seen as symbolic if it is not a targeted intervention in a system or procedure and does not directly demonstrate the desired changes, but instead publicizes the specific demands with the aid of various tools – banners, verbal slogans, music – which are either already symbolically charged per se or become so through being employed in the protest.

Symbolic action is utilized in connection with demanding adherence to more abstract principles, such as the departure from rigid gender roles or the avoidance of reducing women to their physicality. It is also especially efficient and popular with regard to demands which would otherwise be too dangerous to make publicly, and which might even have legal consequences for the persons involved. Thus the publicizing of such demands is only possible under the guise of a symbolic action.

Two groups that have been very present in the media in recent years resort to symbolic action. Moscow's Pussy Riot, founded in 2011, has staged a whole series of actions in the public sphere.[22]

As a feminist punk band, which is how the group defined themselves at the time, they used the medium of music in the public realm as a tool.[23] The group members wore brightly colored, knitted balaclavas to preserve their anonymity while at the same time being

18
See the video *Barbie Liberation Organization*, available online at: www.youtube.com/watch?v=OVT4T7OR3iQ, accessed 06/25/2014.

19
Angela Washko, "Out of the Kitchen, onto Your Screen, into the Ether. A Case for an Online Art and Feminism Social Movement," available online at: https://dl.dropboxusercontent.com/u/5554064/washko_digifeminism_essay.pdf, accessed 06/25/2014.

20
See the Wikipedia Meetup "ArtAndFeminism," available online at: en.wikipedia.org/wiki/Wikipedia:Meetup/ArtAndFeminism, accessed 06/25/2014.

21
See: Sharp 2012, pp. 152ff.

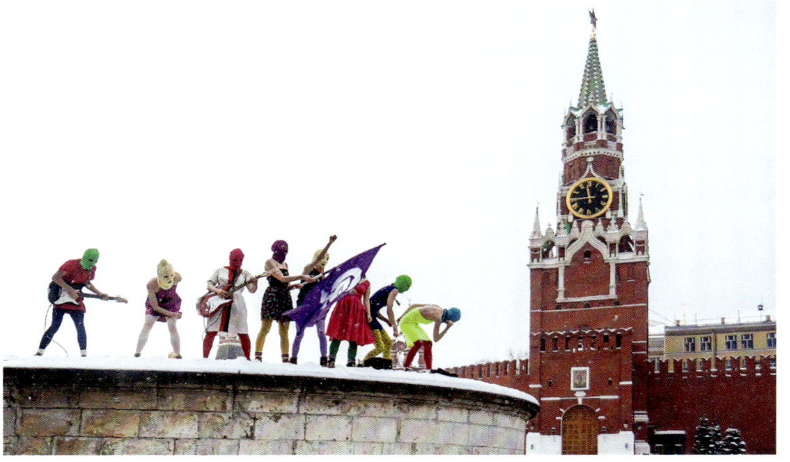

Pussy Riot, Бунт в России – Путин зассал! [Rebellion in Russia – Putin is shit-scared!], Lobnoye mesto, Moscow, January 20, 2012

highly recognizable through their choice of outfit. Their demand was to secure the rights of women in Russia and they criticized President Vladimir Putin's administration for not doing so. When they intruded into the Cathedral of Christ the Savior during a service in 2012 to play a protest song, they were arrested and sentenced to prison for hooliganism. All across the world solidarity demonstrations for the liberation of Pussy Riot took place, often employing knitted masks similar to those worn by the group in their performances, an example of a symbol becoming iconic.

The Russian government abstained from voting on a universal Bill of Human Rights, but it has ratified the Women's Rights Convention and is a member of the Commission on the Status of Women; thus, in principle it is obliged to support women. However, the way the case of Pussy Riot was handled demonstrates that this obligation is not always fulfilled.

Perhaps the best-known female activist group that uses symbolic actions is Femen, established in the Ukraine in 2008 and since then it has acquired supporters worldwide.[24] The members themselves term their method "Sextremism," a portmanteau word of "sex" and "extremism," which both aptly describe the impact their actions have, and, by referencing "sexism," name precisely what the group is fighting against. For their campaigns on the street the members of the group are topless or entirely naked. This kind of protest already played a part in feminist protests in the 1960s, which used nudity or the burning of bras to protest against sexual repression and the objectification of the female body. In 1969, for example, three women students of Frankfurt University stormed the stage during a lecture by Theodor W. Adorno topless and hassled the speaker by showering him with flower petals. The incident entered German history books as a so-called "Busenattentat" [bosom attack].

Through the extreme presence of the uncovered female body in combination with the aggressive postures and the fixed gazes that the activists assume, actions of this kind are geared towards a desexualization of the female body. Activists write provocative paroles such as "Fuck you Putin," "Religion is slavery," and "We bite back" on

22 Pussy Riot no longer exists in the original constellation of 2011. The group has fallen out and no longer performs together. Nadezhda Tolokonnikova and Maria Alyokhina have set up a nongovernmental organization in order to help unjustly sentenced people in Russia.

23 See the Weblog by Pussy Riot, available online at: pussy-riot.livejournal.com, accessed 06/25/2014.

24 See Femen's homepage, available online at: femen.org, accessed 06/25/2014.

their skin, delivering the message without the need for speech. Femen demonstrates against a perception of women that is promoted and reinforced especially by religions and patriarchal governments. Femen members wear a colorful wreath of flowers or ribbons on their heads as a symbol that has now become iconic. Using particular symbols works in a similar way to the wearing of particular colors: it reinforces the recognition value and fosters a feeling of affiliation with a group. In addition, through their use of nudity and bright colors Femen generates images that are readily taken up by the media and correspondingly imprint themselves on viewers' minds quickly. Femen not only stage actions dedicated to their "own" topics, but also in solidarity with a great many other feminist issues.

When the Egyptian blogger Aliaa Magda Elmahdy published nude photographs of herself on her blog, and then received death threats and left the country, two Femen activists stood with her in front of the Egyptian embassy in Stockholm to fight for a freer and above all more respected female sexuality.

Some Ukrainian members of Femen also had to leave their home country and go into exile, as they would otherwise have been arrested.

The Ukraine is not a member of the Commission on the Status of Women and neither has it signed the Universal Declaration of Human Rights, but it has ratified the Women's Rights Convention. In actual fact, however, the state is evidently not willing to protect women's rights and promote their observance on the political level. On the contrary, it prosecutes female activists and tries to coerce them into discontinuing their activities by taking legal action against them.

A relatively new phenomenon is the use of graffiti, which as a transmitter of messages in public places can be utilized for women's rights issues as part of "symbolic actions." Graffiti replaces

Femen and Egyptian activist Aliaa Magda Elmahdy in front of the Egyptian embassy in Stockholm, Sweden, 2012

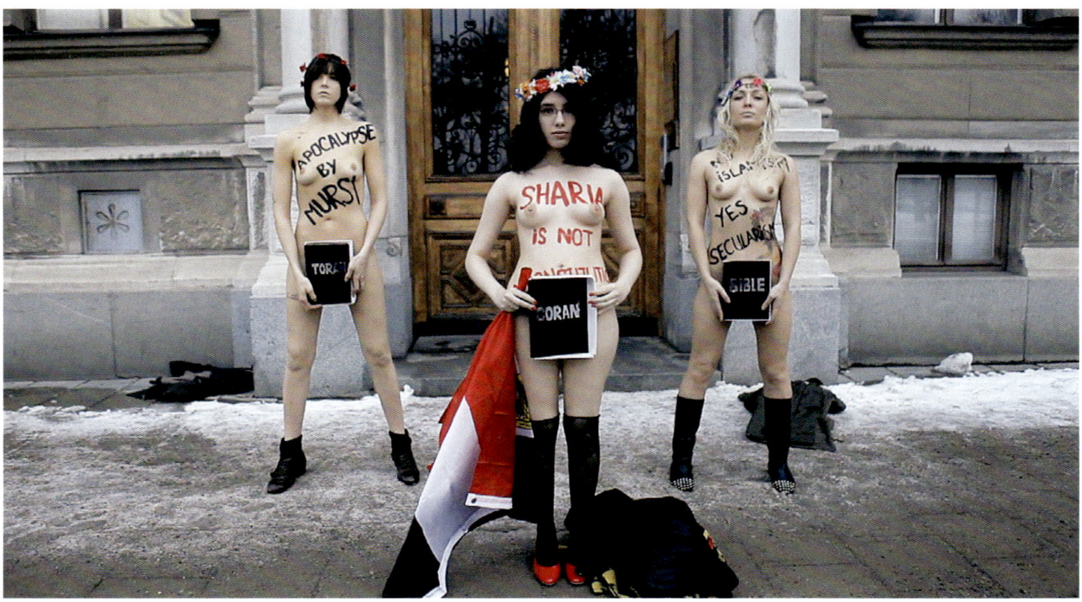

traditional information carriers such as banners, posters, flyers, and so on.[25] While both Femen members, who write their messages on their own bodies, and members of Pussy Riot, who address their concerns in their song texts, need to be physically present in order to deliver their message, graffiti artists remain anonymous and use the outside walls of buildings as carriers.

The Russian artist Mikaela, for example, applies her stencil graffiti to walls in Moscow.[26] Among the images she uses are portraits of female Narodniks, supporters of a social revolutionary movement at the end of the nineteenth and beginning of the twentieth century that was brutally quashed. In using these images, the artist of course wants to remind people of these women, and secondly, to point to the similarity in the treatment of women then and today. She also created a piece of graffiti to encourage women and girls to step out of the gender role being demanded of them, and not solely be a caring mother and good wife, which to this day in Russia is seen as the highest goal for a woman. The presence of Mikaela's graffiti in the public realm aims to give women food for thought as well as signalize that they are not alone in their discontent and criticism but part of a worldwide feminist movement.

25
Graffiti was not taken into account by Gene Sharp, as at the time his essay was written they were not present or accepted as a form of art and communication.

26
See: Ana Bambić Kostov, "New Dawn of Russian Street Art," available online at: www.widewalls.ch/street-art-graffiti-russia, accessed 06/25/2014.

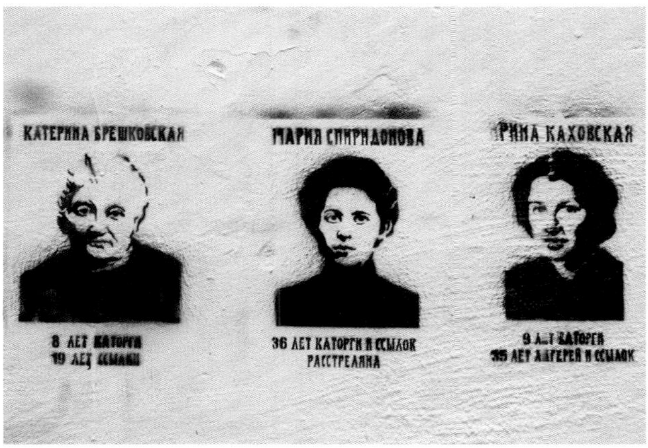

Mikaela, *Narodniki Women*, 2013, graffiti series

Many other individual activists as well as activist groups could be cited at this point, but the examples cited above suffice to illustrate the fundamental methods and strategies of feminist activism.

The physical methods of "direct action" and "symbolic action," which I have examined here with reference to Sharp's essay, and which are often used by activists fighting for women's rights, are usually targeted at public space. "Direct action" with concrete demands, for example, the right to drive a car, can be dangerous, and in some cases even lead to arrest and the activists being sentenced. But even "symbolic actions," often used in order to highlight problematic gender roles by creative means, are prosecuted, as in the case of Femen. The activists gain a lot of attention through public performances as well as through the recognition value of their use of colors and symbols. Colors and symbols also often develop a momentum of their own, are explicitly associated with a particular protest, and turn into icons of their time. In protests that often address omnipresent and traditional perceptions of women or unfair living conditions, the joining together in a "community" is particularly important as it helps build courage and avoids failing as a single person and giving up. "Typically female" symbols such as wreaths of flowers, knitted things, and naked skin are used to foster solidarity, but are then used against the traditional image of women that they usually represent. The new characteristic trait of women's rights protest becomes discernible in this; it does not demand a masculinization of women, but instead invokes a classical and rather traditionally "feminine" image to be identified with. The reason could be simple: women, whose everyday life takes place within the confines of a traditional, stereotyped gender role, will recognize themselves in these symbols and can thereby identify with the group.

What is remarkable is that the groups which are best known and seen as the most important by the general public in Western countries tend to come from countries in which the situation of women is not at the same standard as in Western countries or that of the standard of the aforementioned "fourth wave."

Sociologist Saskia Sassen argues that people from Western societies become consumers of their life and surroundings.[27] They accept (for example, their nationality, their social status, etc.), without questioning and challenging, and in this they stand in stark contrast to the "makers," who themselves mold and create, but who tend to originate from different geographical and political contexts. Protests by these activists, defined by Sassen as "makers," are especially readily taken up by Western media, because it is easy to portray them as heroes. The general population perceives them as abstract fighters who are acting against a geographically distant problem. Through their geographical and social distance, uninvolved viewers don't risk being pushed from their "consumer" into a "maker" role, but can declare their solidarity in the shape of easy and safe actions.

27 See: Saskia Sassen, "Brutality and Complexity in the Global Economy," lecture at re:publica 2014, Berlin, May 7, 2014, video recording available online at: www.youtube.com/watch?v=gKaA-mXhn-4, accessed 06/25/2014.

In particular the activities in India, the Saudi women, as well as both the Femen and Pussy Riot groups gained media attention in recent years and garnered sympathies and considerable international popularity. The fact that individual states – as mentioned here, Saudi Arabia, Russia, India, as well as further countries not mentioned in the context of this text – have ratified conventions on the protection of women's rights does not, as has been explained, automatically mean an actual executive assistance concerning the improvement or preservation of women's rights at state level, which is why civil groups intervene and assume responsibility. These groups have taken on an enormously important position in society, for they enable women to feel like they belong and show them that – apart from a few setbacks – their efforts are rewarded in regard to their position in society: slowly but surely.

Translated from the German by Jeremy Gaines.

"What is to be done when nothing can be done?"[1]
(Franco "Bifo" Berardi)

Rita Raley

The Ordinary Arts of Political Activism

Tents were piled in the center of the ZKM | Karlsruhe exhibit hall, multicolored but uniform in size and shape, sculptural objects suggesting the Occupy movement of which they are one of the few recognizable icons. Handmade and printed posters, leaflets, and mixed material artifacts of various protest campaigns were attached to a large fence across from the assembled tents. A photographic record of global activism as viral mass-mediated event was presented on an adjacent wall: green-lettered signs memorializing Neda, the "Standing Man" of Taksim Square, an officer teargassing a woman in a red dress in Gezi Park, the naked torsos of members of Femen, bodies amassed in parks and squares, police armed with guns, batons, riot shields, dogs. Even more spectacular was the bank of screens displaying Google image search results for keywords related to the *global aCtIVISm* exhibit: here, too, crowds, flags, masks, the iconography of political protest and revolution in the present, a circular system of reference that mobilizes affects and facilitates taxonomic recognition. Indeed, the exhibit perfectly captured the discursive construction of global activism, from the ghostly silence of abandoned camps and evacuated public spaces littered with traces of the violent conflicts that have gone before, to the visual documentation of multitudes.

The documentation of emptiness, of the aftermath of an assembly or intervention, commemorates that event as one that has materialized in a particular place and time and entered the historical record. For the referential schema of global activism, situated events acquire meaning in part through relationality, the mapping of connections among discrete incidents, the delineation of the patterns and lines of influence that would constitute a coordinated movement. "Global" in this context is a particular world-historical imaginary suggesting the mandate to articulate such connections – one occupied public square resonating with another as trigger, consequence, or common cause. Events not readily available to absorption within the imaginary of "global activism" are those whose utter singularity or situatedness thwarts efforts to abstract out from concrete circumstance to network diagram; those so bounded by time and circumstance that action

1
Franco Beradi, as quoted from: Konrad Becker and Jim Fleming (eds.), *Critical Strategies in Art and Media. Perspectives on New Cultural Practices*, Autonomedia, Brooklyn, (NY), 2010, p. 59.

does not cross the threshold to become event; or those so ordinary that they cannot be unambiguously differentiated from the same. There are myriad techniques for gaining a purchase on the global, among them the sharing of slogans, appropriation of images, and use of memes. But many activist practices are content to operate at the level of the micro or local and, while certainly aspirational with respect to effects and consequences, do not endeavor to resonate for the global as a "referential whole." In what sense does the common imaginary of activism as large-scale mediated event operating on the plane of the "global" inhibit the recognition and appreciation of everyday activities that may be informed by shared politics but differ significantly with respect to framing, organizational structure, and purpose? How might a consideration of modest art-activist activities facilitate a conscious de-emphasizing of the seemingly inevitable litmus test: what difference has it made, where "difference" is implicitly understood to entail widespread media recognition, policy changes, and visible structural transformation? What, after all, does it mean to *make a difference*?

There are strong conceptions of activism based on functions and institutions, the former emphasizing activities, mechanisms, and techniques ("a toolbox for revolution"), and the latter prioritizing actual organizations involved.[2] What tends to be elided in these taxonomies are everyday activities that are not perceptually or even epistemologically different from ordinary action. Activism in these terms might be conceived as that which introduces a certain rupture, blip, or glitch into the smooth normative unfolding of the everyday, whereby the ordinary is estranged from and doubled back upon itself, and different practices, routines, and habits are made possible. This is not a polemic that situates different models of activism in implicit competition or subjects them to metrics that assess performance outcomes, though it is precisely in response to such claims – that certain types of activist practice are most effective and therefore most deserving of investment – that I want both to echo the common refrain that small actions may have unforeseeable large consequences and to assert the value of the ordinary, the seemingly uneventful, on its own terms.

The stakes of the call to imagine a more expansive category of "global activism" are not necessarily those of academic or institutional classification, as in the notion that certain errors of definition and taxonomy need to be corrected for proper scholarship or that a new critical paradigm will enable new knowledge. It is undoubtedly the case that classification has material effects, for example, a reorientation of the discussion of global activism to account for the singular, nonspectacular, and ordinary might as a consequence bring socially engaged art practices – such as property renovation or environmental awareness projects – more closely into dialog with extant social and political movements.[3] But the stakes are even more fundamental in that they concern our understanding of systems of power, control, and orthodoxy. As Silvia Kolbowski indicates in a forum on the social artwork: "it's important to define activism broadly because power seeks out the imagination and the psyche as well as physical spaces and bank accounts."[4] That is, it is precisely because the imaginary of ordinary

2 See: Andrew Boyd and Dave Oswald Mitchell, *Beautiful Trouble. A Toolbox for Revolution*, OR Books, New York, 2012.

3 On artistic social practice see: Grant H. Kester, *Conversation Pieces. Community and Communication in Modern Art*, University of California Press, Berkeley, Los Angeles (CA), 2004; Shannon Jackson, *Social Works. Performing Art, Supporting Publics*, Routledge, New York (NY), 2011; Jen Delos Reyes (ed.), *Open Engagement. An Anthology*, Publication Studio, Portland (OR), 2012; Nato Thompson (ed.), *Living as Form. Socially Engaged Art from 1991–2011*, The MIT Press, Cambridge (MA), 2012; Claire Bishop, *Artificial Hells. Participatory Art and the Politics of Spectatorship*, Verso, London, New York, 2012; Tom Finkelpearl, *What We Made. Conversations on Art and Social Cooperation*, Duke University Press, Durham (NC), London, 2013.

4 Sylvia Kolbowski, as quoted from: "Roundtable: The Social Artwork," in: *October*, no. 142, Fall 2012, pp. 74–85, here p. 81.

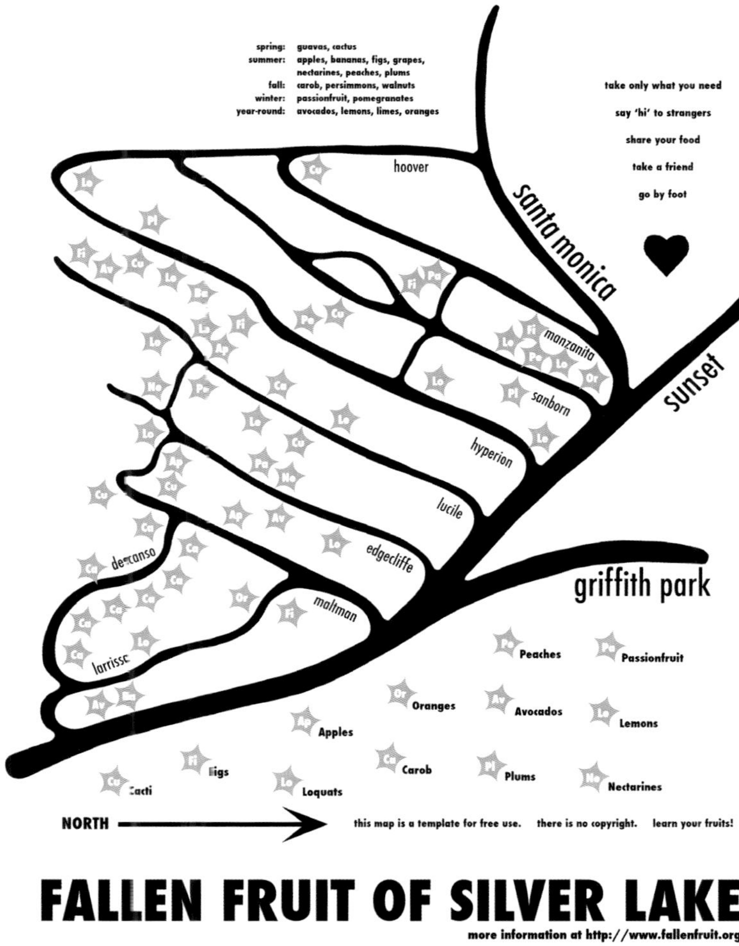

Fallen Fruit (David Burns, Matias Viegener, Austin Young), *Fallen Fruit of Silver Lake*, 2004–ongoing, public fruit map, dimensions variable

life and the social has been bent – constrained, conditioned, managed – by the forces of financial globalization that we need an imaginary of activism that recognizes, and thereby facilitates, creative efforts to cultivate the care of both self and community.

Even in the heart of agriculture-rich California, it is not uncommon to encounter oranges from Florida, or lemons from Mexico, on grocery shelves. In a sharp and playful commentary on global food production systems, Fallen Fruit, an art collaboration originally conceived in 2004 by David Burns, Matias Viegener, and Austin Young, endeavors to make the abundance of locally available fruit visible by constructing maps of trees growing on or over public property in Los Angeles.[5] Structured as guides for gleaners, these maps and occasional directed tours make accessible the fantastically fecund desert landscape that has been nearly engulfed by urban development and an intricate highway system discouraging pedestrian traffic. As Viegener notes of the buried agrarian history of Los Angeles, "[f]resh fruit holds a poignant place in the

5
See: http://fallenfruit.org, accessed 06/13/2014. Since 2013, Burns and Young have continued the collaborative work. See also: Dana Goodyear, "Eat a Free Peach: Mapping 'Public Fruit,'" in: *The New Yorker*, March 12, 2012, available online at: www.newyorker.com/online/blogs/culture/2012/03/mapping-public-fruit.html, accessed 06/13/2014.

mythology of California; early postcards often depict houses with swimming pools and orange trees against a backdrop of snow-covered mountains."[6] The project of Fallen Fruit, however, is not a nostalgic reanimation of a fabled past, but rather a pedagogic and situated response to "a globalized model of food production in which every step has been industrialized and monetized."[7] Read through the lens of a fruit map, urban neighborhoods become community gardens with oranges and lemons freely available to all.

Responding to a call from the *Journal of Aesthetics & Protest* for projects that were responsive to contemporary crises and proposed "generative solutions"[8] rather than stopping short at negative critique, Fallen Fruit has from the outset considered activism in noncontestatory terms. As Burns succinctly states of the techniques and sensibility of the "hyperbolically collaborative" project, there is "no opposition in a thing we do."[9] Still, there is a distinct politics in their environmental activism and foregrounding of questions of publics. Fallen Fruit is decidedly and adamantly not a guerrilla art organization, but they do strongly encourage participants to tinker with the physical and legal margins of public space. To explain: most metropolitan areas in the USA have legislation that prohibits the planting of fruit trees on public land, but fruit growing on branches that overhang a property line becomes public and legally available for harvesting. Excess fruit quickly becomes waste so collecting that which has fallen benefits both individual and community, but reaching up to pick fruit that is ambiguously situated in relation to a fence risks the violation of both legal and social contract. Apart from fostering dialog about ecological systems, then, Fallen Fruit also invites consideration of civic belonging and responsibility and of "new forms of located citizenship and community."[10] Participants are prompted to walk and perceive the urban environment "from a very different angle, akin perhaps to learning about the strata of pipelines, tunnels, and subterranean wiring under all cities."[11] As a "social geographic exercise,"[12] the maps and fruit trails produce the idea of a neighborhood and imagine the city as a playground, the rhythms of the walks interrupting the customary space-time arrangements produced by the transportation infrastructure particular to Los Angeles.

Part of a larger urban agricultural movement supported by environmental nonprofits and community arts foundations, Fallen Fruit has also turned its attention to different aspects of pomiculture: planting trees and making jam. In the spirit of eco-communes, locavores, and sustainable urbanists, the *Public Fruit Jam* project hosts "jam sessions" for the community that have the immediate practical purpose of preventing waste, and that also support the sharing of goods, recipes, and techniques. Its aspirations are modest and its sensibility is regional and generational (the punk rock of the millennials), but collaborative jam-making is nonetheless to be regarded as a communitarian practice. Akin to community gardens, food banks, and time banks, it prioritizes being – and making – in common. There is no monetary exchange, but the jam sessions do not operate according to a gift economy with the expectation of material return. The fruit-based economy

6 Matias Viegener, "Fallen Fruit," in: *Cabinet*, no. 23, 2006, pp. 68–72, here p. 69, available online at: http://cabinetmagazine.org/issues/23/viegener.php, accessed 06/13/2014.

7 Ibid., p. 72.

8 Ibid., p. 69.

9 Interview with David Burns, March 8, 2014.

10 As quoted from: Thompson 2012, p. 150.

11 Viegener 2006, p. 69.

12 Interview with David Burns, March 8, 2014.

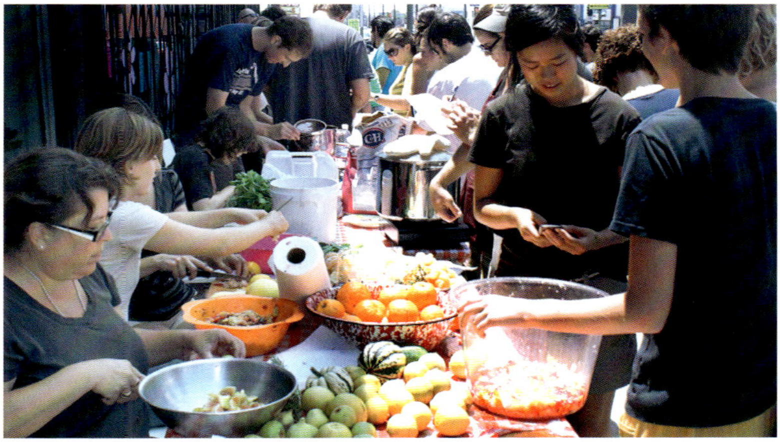

Fallen Fruit (David Burns, Matias Viegener, Austin Young), *Public Fruit Jam* (Machine Project edition), 2008, public participatory performance, documentation photograph

produces not debt but rather what Lewis Hyde terms "feeling-bonds"[13] as its objective: social relations, then, instead of market relations. As Jörgen Svensson notes of so-termed "generosity projects" in a different context, "the broader phenomenon is really about food, people meeting each other, and an opportunity for increased communication."[14]

13
Lewis Hyde, *The Gift. Imagination and the Erotic Life of Property*, Vintage Books, New York, 1979, p. 56.

14
Jörgen Svensson, "Four Projects," in: Ted Purves (ed.), *What We Want Is Free. Generosity and Exchange in Recent Art*, State University of New York Press, Albany (NY), 2005, pp. 47–60, here p. 59.

Fallen Fruit is not conceptually, aesthetically, or even practically complex: there is no mechanism or theoretical paradigm to decode. But a project such as this is critically significant precisely because it goes to the heart of the question of what constitutes a meaningful art-activist intervention. It touches upon issues of food security, but it is not about immediate survival; it invests deeply in fantasies of social engagement, but not fundamental social transformation. It has extended to other cities, for example, Fallen Fruit Atlanta, but it remains local in orientation, and the development has been modular rather than scalar. And while the effect on the lifeworld of participants is not negligible – there is a politics of momentary enjoyment – subjecting those effects to calculative assessment so as to determine efficacy would be an absurd bureaucratic exercise. Moreover, to insist upon seamless modulation from the micro scale (making lemon marmalade in the neighborhood of Silver Lake) into the macro (measurable damage to the industrial agricultural system) would be to employ evaluative criteria according to which most political work could be said to fail. There are, of course, different models of activist practice, different tactics for different moments and different situations, but scalar transition persists as the benchmark for critical judgment. Accordingly, in the popular imagination, an activist intervention such as Occupy Wall Street can only be said to have made a difference, to truly matter, if it spawns multiple occupied sites, or if it becomes possible to abstract out from specific concrete circumstance and identify a movement.

However, the impetus for the line of inquiry I am exploring here is not the Occupy movement per se, but rather the practices of care that supported it – the encampments, the dwelling spaces, complete with libraries, medical facilities, food services, clothing dispensaries, and communication centers. Many ethnographies of the movement have still to be written, but there are striking resemblances between the carefully and creatively tended encampments of Occupy and socially engaged art practices as ways of living, from Fallen Fruit to Basurama's work with urban waste, and from the Project Row Houses in Houston and Theaster Gates' Dorchester Projects in Chicago to Ithaca Hours and Julieta Aranda and Anton Vidokle's *Time/Bank*.[15] Such small-scale interventions in the social field combine activism, art, pedagogy, sociology, and politics, and they are less intent on disruption qua disruption than they are on creating social relations in the immediate present, "social building that brings itself into being wherever and whenever it can."[16] They stir the imagination precisely because they teach us that we are stakeholders in the worlds they might make possible, worlds not produced as fixed objects but rather experienced as they come into existence. And now both the Occupy encampments and social practices are objects of curation, institutional entities despite their sitedness "beyond the white cube" and "in the real world." This is not, however, to suggest absolute commensurability among these movements and practices, not then to situate "the activist" on a plane of equivalence from Occupy to the arts organization Creative Time. But the abstraction of the category of "the activist" makes it possible to articulate temporary, nonessential commonalities among disparate practices and to identify shared investments. A mapping project such as Fallen Fruit is for this reason nicely illustrative: though it is extensible and available for versioning, it is inextricably situated in place, indexical operations linking map to territory both physical and imagined.

15
For a pedagogic account of the techniques of artistic social practice, see Pablo Helguera, *Education for Socially Engaged Art. A Materials and Techniques Handbook*, Jorge Pinto Books, New York (NY), 2011.

16
Blake Stimson and Gregory Sholette, *Collectivism after Modernism. The Art of Social Imagination after 1945*, University of Minnesota Press, Minneapolis (MN), 2007, p. 13.

California state law stipulates that there should be more than one hundred public access ways to the coast in the elite beach community of Malibu. Sharp cliffs, narrow roads, and overdevelopment, coupled with a deep local resistance to what is regarded as intrusion, has limited public access to the seventeen available sites, nearly all of which are hidden from plain sight. The Los Angeles Urban Rangers were the first to offer a map of the privately developed public coastline, a route planned as a "safari" into the mystifying territory of camouflaged paths and false trespassing notices (2007–2010).[17] This expressive activity takes its place alongside of piracy and parkour: embracing risk, transgressing and disrupting a given system, it is adaptable and responsive to its environment. Another ranger-led safari into the borderlands between public and private space took participants to the Los Angeles river, drawing attention to the civic project of revitalization, bringing water consciousness to the fore, along with the history of water in the L.A. area (2011).[18] In so doing, it shifted the usual focus on the river from film production to environmental history, the site's cracked concrete slabs as the residue of interested decrepitude and decades of battles over water rights.

Claire Bishop and others have noted that the proliferation of socially engaged art practices not incidentally coincides with widespread neoliberal divestment of public institutions, and the

17
See: http://laurbanrangers.org/site/malibu, accessed 06/13/2014.

18
For an overview of recent public art projects engaged with L.A. River revitalization, see Allison Carruth, "A Brief History of Public Art and the L.A. River," in: *Artbound*, March 20, 2014, available online at: www.kcet.org/arts/artbound/counties/los-angeles/brief-history-of-public-art-the-la-river.html, accessed 06/13/2014.

concomitant expectation that private agencies and individuals should perform the work of care.[19] Instead of comprehensive public housing initiatives we have artist-led development projects. Instead of civic ordinances we have guerrilla maps of coastlines. And instead of K-12 public schooling and literacy programs we have the Echo Park Film Center Filmmobile, a solar-powered traveling cinema made out of a school bus with its seats removed that also offers film production training to marginalized populations in their own neighborhoods.[20] In such community platforms and activities, there is a clear negotiation of modes of knowledge that are propriety, standardized, even conventional wisdom. Embodied forms of expertise are legitimated and reproduced: this is how you work with 16 mm film, this is how you get to the ocean, this is how my grandmother made jam. And historical modes of knowledge formation are situated alongside the phenomenological – the deep history of place (water rights, land development, racial geographies) informing the subjective experience of Los Angeles.

Nonprofit organizations – arts, educational, medical, environmental – have heroically worked to fill the gaps in the social fabric rendered by the decisive removal of public funding, an institutionalized ideology of radical individualism suddenly legitimized by narratives of financial scarcity. But nonprofits are constrained by grant cycles and the demand to demonstrate measurable results, harnessing committed political ideals for the purpose of producing work that will lead to the next round of funding. Unlike Critical Art Ensemble, who was able to answer the question "What does your art change?" with the simple reply, "We have no way to measure outcome,"[21] nonprofits often do not have the luxury of ironically deflecting institutional demands for impact and results. Without the institutional directive to adopt "best practices" and submit to instrumentalized means testing, grassroots and nonformalized collectives can be open to experimentation and play, whether in the form of an urban safari, jam-making, or visual iconography. Play can challenge normative codes and scripts and open up possibilities of alternative action without foreclosing on the vast potential latent within the system. It activates, sets into motion, unsettles the status quo. Alberto Melucci is canonical on this point: "[W]hat nourishes [collective action] is the daily production of alternative frameworks of sense, on which the networks themselves are founded and live from day to day."[22]

"Collective" here is to be understood not in terms of community as a singular and given entity, but rather in terms of mutable social relations that bring that community into being.[23] That is, community is enacted rather than captured or exploited in the process of collective action, a dynamic that is particularly meaningful in the context of economic markets that depend on the manufacturing and regulation of sociality. Jam sessions, urban safaris, mobile film screenings – all are activist activities, modes of resistance that no longer rely on "the gloomy dialectic between acquiescence and 'transgression,'"[24] but rather resituate social activity as a form of life. The momentary experiences they create have an immediacy with both a temporal and spatial dimension: it is about what happens in a particular place at a particular moment. The

19 See: Claire Bishop, "Participation and Spectacle: Where Are We Now?" in: Thompson 2012, pp. 34–45, here p. 45.

20 See: www.echoparkfilmcenter.org, accessed 06/13/2014.

21 Artnet Questionnaire, *Where Is Critical Art Ensemble?*, March 21, 2007, available online at: www.artnet.com/magazineus/features/quest/quest3-20-07.asp, accessed 06/13/2014.

22 Alberto Melucci, "Social Movements and the Democratization of Everyday Life," in: John Keane (ed.), *Civil Society and the State. New European Perspectives*, Verso, London, 1988, pp. 245–260, here p. 248.

23 See: Kester 2004, pp. 147–151.

24 Paolo Virno, *A Grammar of the Multitude. For an Analysis of Contemporary Forms of Life*, Semiotext(e), Los Angeles (CA), The MIT Press, Cambridge (MA), 2003, p. 70.

sociality is that of strangers linked by processes of exchange: the proximity and intimacy of collective participation that makes possible the transmission of empathetic affects.[25] As Franco "Bifo" Berardi counsels: "Building and sustaining solidarity [...] is about reactivating the sentience of the social body [...] re-activating empathy between living organisms. This empathy is the foundation of the solidarity we need today."[26] Ash Amin and Nigel Thrift similarly envision an "art of the political": "What is needed is active cultivation of alternative feelings so that new affective connections can be forged and a general desire for other ways of being in the world can emerge [...]."[27] The means by which these connections might be animated are "psycho-technologies that engineer collective feelings, but in a non-cynical way."[28] Supremely cynical techniques and technologies include social engineering, as in the benign liberalism of the choice architectures that nudge us to make better consumer decisions, and behavioral marketing, training in the guise of assessment. Pirate and hacktivist networks are perhaps differently cynical, mobilizing collective feeling with increasingly sophisticated public relations campaigns and cunning tactics of evasion and obfuscation.

We are led then to Anonymous, an idea of a collective, a situational politics of nonsovereignty, and a strict behavioral code for those who would claim affiliation: do not grandstand. The activist, Maurizio Lazzarato writes in a different context, "is not someone who becomes the brains of the movement, who sums up its force [...]."[29] Anonymous exemplifies the multiheaded hydra: "We are legion. Expect us."[30] This is the terrain of the coming insurrection, a community as yet unyoked to a particular formal structure. The bravado of the announcement that is at once threat and promise – "expect us" – perhaps stands in stark contrast to the quietness, even the modesty, of an authorized walk down the L.A. River or of jam-making. How are we to understand the relations between large-scale, high-impact events (the doxxing of a public figure or the impersonation of a corporate official, the rewriting of *The New York Times* or a DDoS attack on the same) and local, small-scale interventions that may not even register as such? Or between a large-scale futurist project such as Terreform ONE that reimagines whole ecosystems and a simple coastline map aspiring to the removal of a few signs and bits of shrubbery? Should we regard community gardens, mobile libraries, and urban safaris as an abdication if not a disavowal of significant political action? Are they just instances of boutique activism: self-fulfillment for a privileged few individuals rather than transformative for the species and planet? Are such art-activist practitioners to be dismissed as mere "humanitarian pragmatists," as BAVO anticipates, "focused on achieving 'small but real' improvements in people's lives, rather than offering fierce political resistance to the status quo"?[31]

My suggestion is that Fallen Fruit and the Los Angeles Urban Rangers, as some of many possible examples, challenge the expectation that we ought continually to be thinking in terms of impact and implications for large-scale systems. Fallen Fruit is interesting precisely because its practical borders are circumscribed: confined to a few city blocks, it directly addresses the

25 See: Michael Warner, *Publics and Counterpublics*, Zone Books, New York (NY), 2002.

26 David Hugill and Elise Thorburn, "Reactivating the Social Body in Insurrectionary Times: A Dialogue with Franco 'Bifo' Berardi," in: *Berkeley Planning Journal*, vol. 25, 2012, pp. 210–220, here p. 213.

27 Ash Amin and Nigel Thrift, *Arts of the Political. New Openings for the Left*, Duke University Press, Durham (NC), London, 2013, p. 158.

28 Ibid.

29 Maurizio Lazzarato, *Les révolutions du capitalisme*, Les empêcheurs de penser on rond, Paris, 2004, as quoted from: Brian Holmes, "Swarmachine. Activist Media Tomorrow," July 21, 2007, available online at: https://brianholmes.wordpress.com/2007/07/21/swarmachine, accessed 06/13/2014.

30 Brian Knappenberger, *We Are Legion: The Story of the Hacktivists*, Luminant Media, Venice (CA), 2012.

31 BAVO, "Artists, One More Effort to be Really Political," in: Lieven De Cauter, Ruben De Roo, and Karel Vanhaesebrouck (eds.), *Art and Activism in the Age of Globalization*, NAi Publishers, Rotterdam, 2011, pp. 288–296, here p. 292.

needs of a local population rather than foregrounding questions of global food resources. It challenges the persistent expectation that activist practices must reach a certain threshold – bodies involved, page views, journalistic coverage – before they can be construed as meaningful, before they matter. Certainly in the making visible of different infrastructures, obscured elsewheres are brought within a participant's perceptual field. How after all do avocados make their way to grocery stores in arctic climates? What is the source of the industrial waste in the L.A. River? But the expectation that every art-activist activity necessarily reverberates globally is thwarted in the embrace of the quotidian, the everyday spaces people need to learn to negotiate, and modes of living that are more ordinary than spectacular.

In their pamphlet in the Critical Making series, Geert Lovink and Michael Dieter question whether "pure tinkering" should be celebrated as such or whether it necessarily needs to be "positioned within a clear socio-political agenda" lest it simply become "lifestyle choice."[32] They worry that without such a positioning, maker culture might simply be "reducible to a slow fabrication movement, or a kind of home science kit ala *MAKE Magazine*."[33] But if we are resolved to alter the terms of the biopolitical management of life itself and cultivate a new social imaginary, then the care of the self must be axiomatic, and "lifestyle" is precisely the terrain on which the battle against the status quo must be waged. Given the collapse of distinctions between life and work, art practices that involve the whole of life, that aspire to make a "small but real" difference, truly can be said to inhabit the space of contemporary revolution. It may well be the case, as Claire Bishop suggests, that artists are not always or necessarily suited to the task of "devising new models of social and political organization,"[34] but the effects of social practice need not be considered in such grandiose terms. We might instead rely on the more modest parameters of the here and now, on the production of collective feeling, and on the imagining and enacting of social relations that may be habitually rather than constitutively new.

32 Geert Lovink and Michael Dieter, "Theses on Making in the Digital Age," in: Garnet Hertz (ed.), *Critical Making*, 2012, n.p., available online at: http://conceptlab.com/criticalmaking/PDFs/CriticalMaking2012Hertz-Manifestos-pp15to20-DieterLovink-ThesesOnMaking.pdf, accessed 06/13/2014.

33 Ibid.

34 Bishop in: Thompson 2012, p. 45

Martha Rosler

The Artistic Mode of Revolution:

From Gentrification to Occupation

A discussion of the struggles, exoduses, and reappropriations of cognitive labor, especially in the field of visual art, and especially when taken as the leading edge of the "creative class," while critically important, is trumped by the widespread, even worldwide, public demonstrations and occupations of the past year, this year, and maybe the next.[1] I would like to revisit the creative-class thesis I have explored in a recent series of essays in order to frame my remarks in light of these occupations, and to make a few observations about the relationship between artists, the positioning of the creative class, and the Occupy movement.[2]

Even before "the multitude" became a common touchstone for dreams of revolution, there was, famously, Seattle 1999, when anticorporate protests brought environmentalists and community activists together with organized labor to block a meeting of the World Trade Organization, a scenario repeated at multiple locations in several countries in the years since.[3] It is not news that the processes that go under the name of globalization, which center on the flows of capital, goods, and labor, create a unity that does not always serve the interests of capital or the capitalists.

Nouriel Roubini, channeling Karl Marx, wrote in "The Instability of Inequality" that "unregulated capitalism can lead to regular bouts of over-capacity, under-consumption, and the recurrence of destructive financial crises, fueled by credit bubbles and asset-price booms and busts."[4]

Roubini is saying that capitalism tends toward catastrophic collapses – no news here. But the point is that neoliberalism and its rampant financialization have created a capitalism that eats its young. Roubini goes on to remind his readers that even before the Great Depression, the enlightened bourgeoisie realized that worker protections and a redistributive system providing "public goods – education, health care, and a social safety net"[5] were necessary to prevent revolution.[6]

Roubini remarks further that the modern welfare state grew out of a post-Depression need for macroeconomic stabilization, which required "the maintenance of a large middle class by widening the provision of public goods through progressive taxation of incomes and wealth and fostering economic opportunity for all"[7]; but all this went under during the massive Reagan-Thatcher deregulation, which Roubini – no Marxist after all – traces in

1

Editorial note: This essay is based on a paper presented at the University of Warsaw in 2011.

2

See: Martha Rosler, "Culture Class: Art, Creativity, Urbanism, Part I. Art and Urbanism," in: *e-flux journal*, no. 21, December 2010, available online at: www.e-flux.com/journal/culture-class-art-creativity-urbanism-part-i, accessed 11/11/2014; Martha Rosler, "Culture Class: Art, Creativity, Urbanism, Part II. Creativity and Its Discontents," in: *e-flux journal*, no. 23, March 2011, available online at: www.e-flux.com/journal/culture-class-art-creativity-urbanism-part-ii, accessed 11/11/2014; Martha Rosler, "Culture Class: Art, Creativity, Urbanism, Part III. In the Service of Experience(s)," in: *e-flux journal*, no. 25, May 2011, available online at: www.e-flux.com/journal/culture-class-art-creativity-urbanism-part-iii, accessed 11/11/2014.

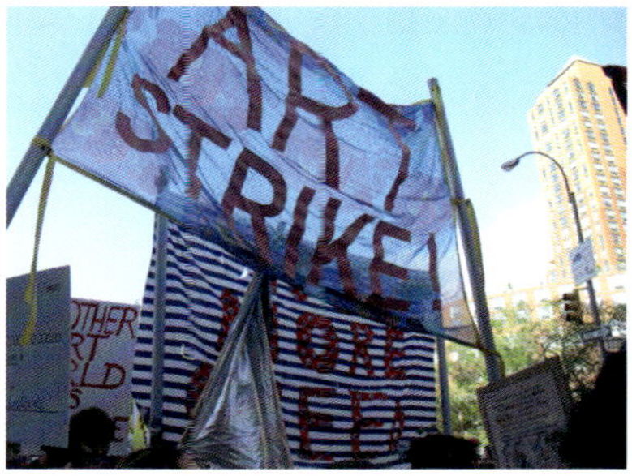

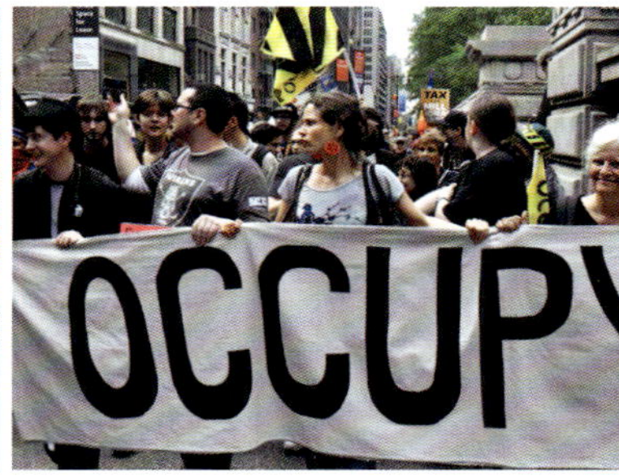

Left: Members of the Arts & Labor affinity group carrying their Art Strike banner at the combined labor, immigrant, and Occupy Wall Street May Day march, New York City, 2012
Right: Occupy Wall Street, New York City, May Day, 2012

part to "the flaws in Europe's social-welfare model [...] reflected in yawning fiscal deficits, regulatory overkill, and a lack of economic dynamism."[8]

Roubini, unlike most, goes on to proclaim the failure of this "Anglo-American economic model" of embracing economic policies that increase inequality and create a gap between incomes and aspirations, accompanied by the liberalization of consumer credit and thus rising consumer debt, as well as public debt because of decreased tax revenues, all of which is then followed by counterproductive austerity measures. This is precisely the financial model that seized the imagination and drove the policies of former Eastern Bloc governing elites, many of whom in implementing the prescribed austerity measures are destroying their present and future middle classes (see Latvia),[9] as is neo-Thatcherite Great Britain.[10]

In the United States, Citibank, which required two U.S. government rescues after the financial crisis of 2008, posted record quarterly profits of $3.8 billion dollars in the fall of 2011, a 74% increase over the previous quarter, while its CEO, Vikram Pandit, expressed his sympathy with the Occupy Wall Street protesters and offered to meet with them.[11]

The ongoing round-the-world occupations, which have drawn inspiration from the uprisings across the Arab world in 2011, are driven by the frustration of the young educated middle classes – in the Arab case fairly new ones – confronting societies controlled by hugely rich ruling elites but having little hope of a secure future for themselves, despite their university educations. These are societies that had made no effort to create modern welfare or even neoliberal states, nor to control corruption, bureaucratic indifference, and flagrant nepotism, nor to institute more than the appearance of democratic governance. Protesters in the developed world are aware of sharing conditions that are functionally quite similar.[12]

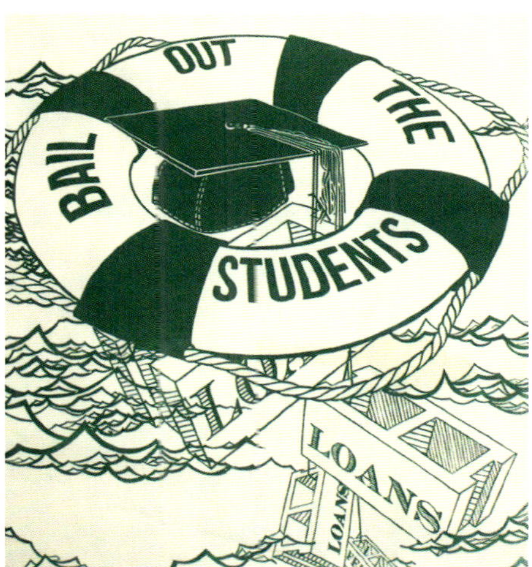

Poster protesting the scale of student debt by Chelsea Peil, Roger Peet, and Katherine Ball for the Justseeds Artists' Cooperative

3 The movement generally pegged as antiglobalization is more properly referred to by its members and supporters as the "alt-globalization" movement or some variant of that term and is anticorporate more than antiglobalization – although globalization is a term derived from its enthusiasts; see the discussion of Theodore Levitt below.

4 Nouriel Roubini, "The Instability of Inequality," October 14, 2011, available online at: www.economonitor.com/nouriel/2011/10/14/from-project-syndicate-the-instability-of-inequality, and "Full Analysis: The Instability of Inequality," October 17, 2011, available online at: www.economonitor.com/nouriel/2011/10/17/full-analysis-the-instability-of-inequality, accessed 11/11/2014. Roubini begins his blog post of October 13, 2011 by alluding to "a global wave of social and political turmoil and instability, with masses of people pouring into the real and virtual streets: the Arab Spring; riots in London; Israel's middle-class protests against high housing prices and an inflationary squeeze on living standards; protesting Chilean students; the destruction in Germany of the expensive cars of 'fat cats'; India's movement against corruption; mounting unhappiness with corruption and inequality in China; and now the 'Occupy Wall Street' movement in New York and across the United States."

5 Roubini, October 14, 2011.

6

I addressed this issue in an essay of 1981 on documentary photography ("In, Around, and Afterthoughts: on Documentary Photography," reprinted in: Martha Rosler, *3 Works*, Nova Scotia College of Art and Design Press, Halifax, 1981, pp. 59–86). I was pointing out that ideological images were employed in the United States, during the Great Depression, to mobilize support for the very poor under the Franklin D. Roosevelt Administration, with the understanding that alleviating suffering would forestall revolt.

7

Roubini, October 14, 2011.

8

Ibid. I am using Roubini here as a convenient figure, since one might quote from quite a few other economists, particularly Joseph E. Stiglitz, Dean Baker, and Paul Krugman of *The New York Times*, or Simon H. Johnson, former chief economist of the International Monetary Fund (IMF), to outline the fears of the left-liberal wing of Western economists.

9

Latvia, a tiny Baltic country that (like the other two Baltic states, Estonia and Lithuania) broke free of the collapsing Soviet Union in the early 1990s, is so far the sharpest example of this syndrome; one might also cite Ireland and possibly Greece, Spain, and Portugal – all of which stand in contrast to the course of Iceland (the tiniest economy of all of these, but, as luck would have it, not a member of the eurozone), which was promptly to reject any terms imposed by international financial agencies and instead defaulting on its debt and pursuing their top bankers for criminal fraud. In the early 2000s, Latvia's center right government instituted aggressive neoliberal measures in large part to join the euro and escape the dominance of Russia. After the financial crisis of 2008, Latvia experienced the most precipitous financial decline of any nation, losing about a quarter of its GDP in two years. Its government then applied stringent fiscal austerity, including slashing pensions and wages. The budding middle class, in a familiar story, had been induced to buy homes on cheap credit, but this mortgage debt (owed largely to Swedish and German banks) cannot be repaid, while property values have also plunged. The austerity measures have failed to improve Latvia's balance sheets but has sent the middle class, not to

Such protests – as in France in 2006, which saw widespread mobilization against "precarization" (alternatively, "precaritization"), as well as the subsequent uprisings in the Paris *banlieues* or in England in August 2011 – also reflect the anger of working-class youths, especially their rage against racist police violence. In the English case, these young people were out there smashing and looting together with young members of the middle class. Some of the latter group had mobilized months earlier – as young Chileans are doing still – thanks in no small part to crushing increases in school fees driven by the Tory / Liberal Democrat governing coalition. The protests of these groups, these classes, have been fired by the recognition that there are likely no secure jobs for them, or perhaps any employment at all.

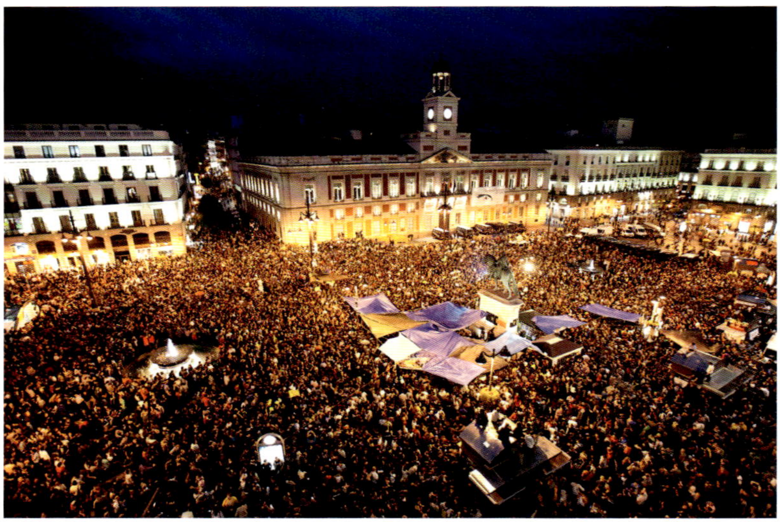

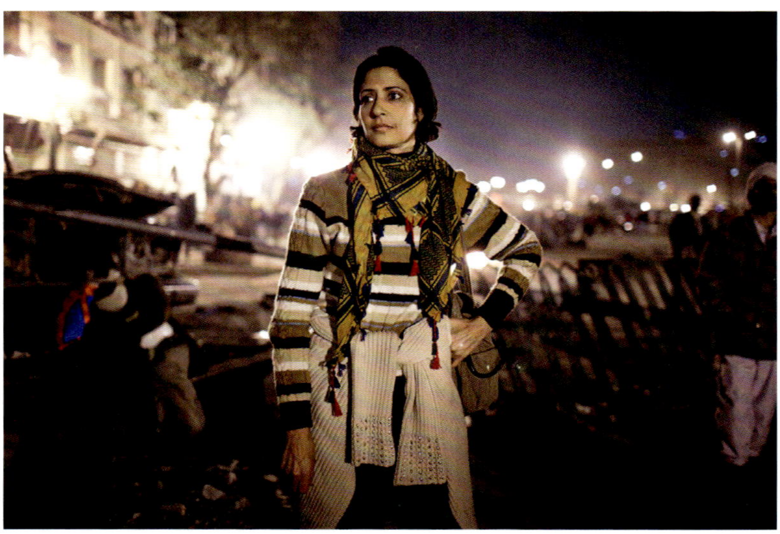

Top: Demonstrators gather and shout slogans in Madrid's famous landmark Puerta del Sol, against politicians', bankers' and authorities' handling of the economic crisis, May 2011
Bottom: A former television journalist occupied a checkpoint on Tahrir Square, where she checked women who wished to enter the square, February 2011

mention the poor, into subsistence mode – or emigration. Tens of thousands of Latvians have left, and unemployment stands at or above twenty percent. See: Michael Hudson and Jeff Sommers, "Latvia's Road to Serfdom," in: *CounterPunch*, February 15, 2010, available online at: www.counterpunch.org/2010/02/15/latvia-s-road-to-serfdom/, and Paul Krugman, "Lats of Luck," July 18, 2011, available online at: http://krugman.blogs.nytimes.com/2011/07/18/lats-of-luck/, accessed 11/11/2014. Yet, like Ireland, Latvia is bizarrely hailed as a successful example of austerity budgeting. (Krugman writes: "A few more successes like this and Latvia will be back in the Stone Age.")

10

The European Commission (EC) in 2011 voted in the "Sixpack," a group of measures that overrides member states' abilities to control their budgets, reinstituting the Maastricht Treaty's limit of 3% on deficits and 60% of GDP on debts, beyond which large fines will be levied, among other penalties. According to economist Susan George, the Commission is also engineering a shift in worker protection leading to longer work weeks, lower pay, and later retirement. See: Susan George, "A Coup in the European Union?," in: *CounterPunch*, October 14–16, 2011, available online at: www.counterpunch.org/2011/10/14/a-coup-in-the-european-union/, accessed 11/11/2014. The still developing situation in regard to Greece (which will have EC monitors in place enforcing austerity measures) shows the antilabor direction, a hallmark of neoliberalism, of the European financial governors.

11

See: Donal Griffin, "Pandit Says He'd Be Happy to Talk With Wall Street Protesters," in: *Bloomberg Businessweek*, October 12, 2011, available online at: www.businessweek.com/news/2011-10-12/pandit-says-he-d-be-happy-to-talk-with-wall-street-protesters.html, and "Citi CEO: I'd Meet with Protesters," in: CNN Money, available online at: http://money.cnn.com/video/news/2011/10/12/n_vikram_pandit_protesters.fortune, and for JPMorgan Chase's CEO Jamie Dimon, making essentially the same point, see: "Dimon: Policies Made Recovery Slower and Worse," in: Fox Business, February 13, 2012, available online at: http://video.foxbusiness.com/v/1450365871001/dimon-policies-made-recovery-slower-and-worse/?playlist_id=87247, accessed 11/11/2014.

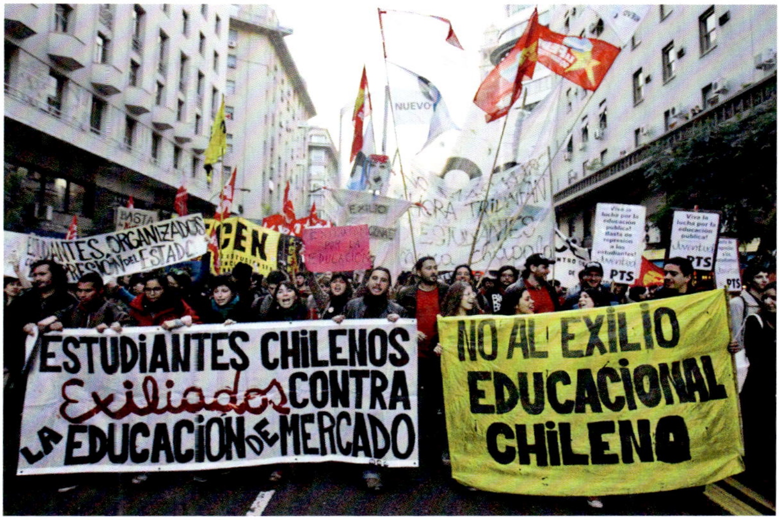

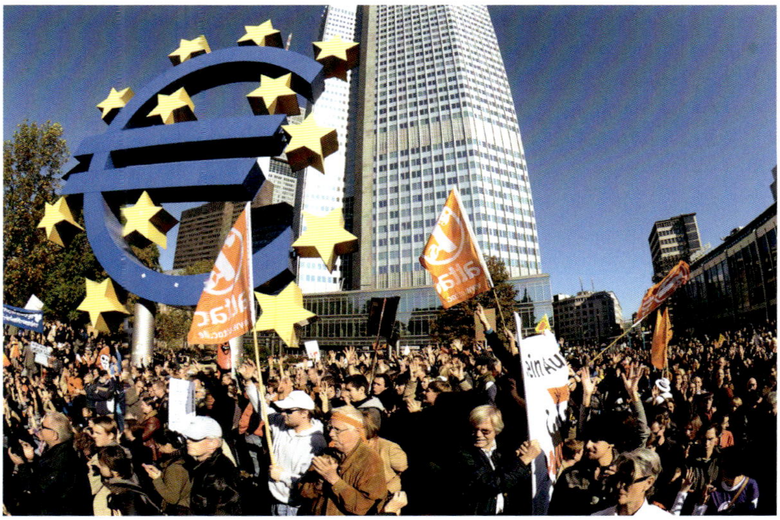

Top: Argentinean and Chilean students march to the Chilean Consulate in Buenos Aires, denouncing the police repression against Chilean students during demonstrations in Santiago de Chile, August 2011
Bottom: Occupy Frankfurt, Frankfurt am Main, Germany, October 2011

But precarization is not a necessary consequence of any particular form of labor. Precarization now joins mechanization (the replacement of workers with machines), delocalization (capital's worldwide search for the weakest labor and environmental regulations), and financialization (the maintenance of excess value in the stock market as opposed to surplus value extracted from manufacturing) as one of the great strategies used to restore profitability since the late 1960s. These strategies supplement the more widely noted assaults on the welfare state and workers' rights.[13] Many of the protesting students and young postgraduates, for their part, were preparing for jobs in what we have come to call the knowledge industries, or, more recently, the creative industries, a branch of the former.

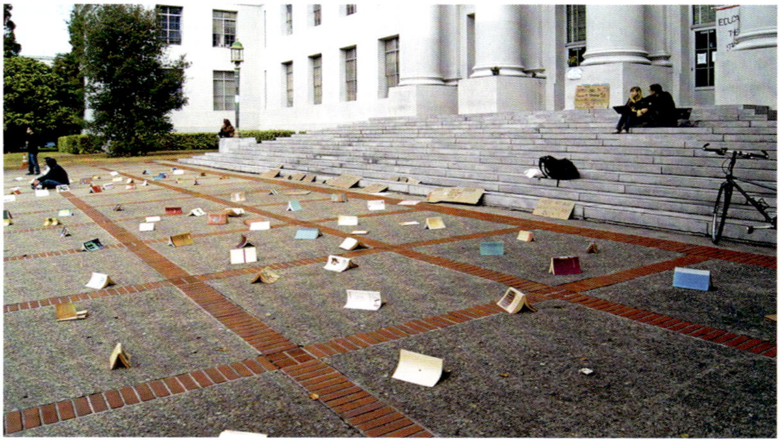

Book tents at Sproul Hall at the University of California, Berkeley, after the student encampment there was cleared, November 2011

1. University as Engine, Lifeways into Lifestyle

Let me step back a bit, to the consolidation of this sector in the newly dawning information age of the early 1960s. Clark Kerr, labor economist, first chancellor of the University of California's elite Berkeley campus, and then president of the entire University of California (UC) system, saw the university as a site for the production of knowledge workers. In 1960 he oversaw the creation of an expansive master plan for growth into the twenty-first century that harmonized the state's higher education institutions and organized them into three tiers: research universities, state colleges, and two-year "junior colleges" (renamed "community colleges"). This "benchmark" plan acknowledged a need to unify the training and administration of the entire knowledge sector, from the elites to the working classes, in a politically divided world. Kerr called the university a "prime instrument of national purpose," and he envisioned the "knowledge industry" (his term) as eventually supplanting the industries surrounding new modes of transportation – railroads in the nineteenth century and automobiles in the twentieth – in unifying the nation, acting as its economic masthead, and serving as the motor of U.S. world dominance.

The foundational student protest movement of the 1960s, Berkeley's Free Speech Movement, was triggered in part by Kerr's educational and managerial policies and goals. It was a movement of a leading sector of the middle class who was destined to become the elite workers of the new knowledge industries, if not their leaders. Ironically, today the UC system is almost broke, confirming the exemplary use of college campuses by Apple's dictionary, in defining *bellwether*, that "college campuses are often the bellwether of change."[14]

In contrast, the 1970s Britain punk subculture was arguably a working-class response to a diminished future, despite its partial traceability to art school, which in any case was a newly experimental repository for working-class misfits. As Dick Hebdige described it,

12
Although Western European protests in response to the prospectless future, such as the *indignados* or *encampados* in Spain and the many demonstrations in Greece's Syntagma Square, were critical examples, and the uprising in Tunisia was ultimately at least a partially successful one, the sheer scale and unlikely success (similarly only partial) of the occupation in Cairo's Tahrir Square made it the touchstone for the movement, and it remains so regardless of its as-yet unfulfilled aims. In recognition of its role, veteran occupiers of Tahrir Square sent a message to Occupy Wall Street: "The current crisis in America and western Europe has begun to bring this reality home to you as well: that as things stand we will all work ourselves raw, our backs broken by personal debt and public austerity. Not content with carving out the remnants of the public sphere and the welfare state, capitalism and the austerity state now even attack the private realm and people's right to decent dwelling as thousands of foreclosed-upon homeowners find themselves both homeless and indebted to the banks who have forced them onto the streets. So we stand with you not just in your attempts to bring down the old but to experiment with the new. We are not protesting. Who is there to protest to? What could we ask them for that they could grant? We are occupying. We are reclaiming those same spaces of public practice that have been commodified, privatised and locked into the hands of faceless bureaucracy, real estate portfolios and police 'protection.' Hold on to these spaces, nurture them and let the boundaries of your occupations grow. After all, who built these parks, these plazas, these buildings? Whose labour made them real and livable? Why should it seem so natural that they should be withheld from us, policed and disciplined? Reclaiming these spaces and managing them justly and collectively is proof enough of our legitimacy." See: "To the Occupy Movement – The Occupiers of Tahrir Square Are with You," in: *The Guardian*, October 25, 2011, available online at: www.guardian.co.uk/commentisfree/2011/oct/25/occupy-movement-tahrir-square-cairo, accessed 11/11/2014.

13
See: Christian Marazzi, *The Violence of Financial Capitalism*, new edition, Semiotext(e), Los Angeles (CA), The MIT Press, Cambridge (MA), 2011.

14

The *New Oxford American Dictionary* has since 2005 come installed on Apple computers using version OS X.

15

Dick Hebdige, *Subculture. The Meaning of Style*, Methuen, London, 1979, p. 74.

"[...] despite the confident assurances of both Labour and Conservative politicians [...] that we had 'never had it so good,' class refused to disappear. The ways in which class was *lived*, however – the forms in which the experience of class found expression in culture – did change dramatically. The advent of the mass media, changes in the constitution of the family, in the organization of school and work, shifts in the relative status of work and leisure, all served to fragment and polarize the working-class community, producing a series of marginal discourses within the broad confines of class experience."[15]

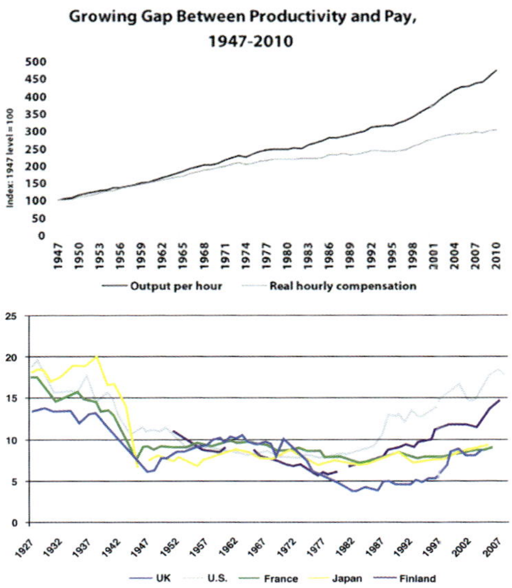

Top: Real hourly compensation and output per hour, business sector, U. S. Bureau of Labor Statistics
Bottom: Top 1% share of U. S. total income (excluding capital gains) at highest since gilded age

Punk was anticommodity and anticorporate, and followed a tactic of uglification and self-mutilation, a "fuck you!" response to bourgeois culture; the fact that it was quickly commodified and heavily promoted in the music industry is beside the point – until, at least, it became the point. For the post-1970s generations, lifestyle politics became almost indistinguishable from either politics or daily life, and that frame of reference has now spread around the world. Gap

Indeed, lifestyle has been intensively developed as a major marketing point for consumer goods. In a prime nugget of lifestyle marketing analysis offered in 1984 (when the thinking was new), Theodore Levitt, Harvard professor of business administration and marketing, commented on the failure of the Hoover corporation to sell washing machines in Europe: "It asked people what features they wanted in a washing machine rather than what they wanted out of life."[16] Levitt, editor of the *Harvard Business Review*, is credited with popularizing the term "globalization." In *The Marketing Imagination*[17], his bestseller of 1983, Levitt pointed out that as a result of media expansion worldwide, the United States was in a unique position to market its goods everywhere, making its so-called high-touch goods – jeans and Coca-Cola – right up there alongside hightech ones (and integrally, along with them, Americanism and the English language) into the world's most desirable possessions.

16

Theodore Levitt writes, in distinguishing what he considers a multinational mind-set from a global one, "The Hoover case illustrates how the perverse practice of the marketing concept and the absence of any kind of marketing imagination let multinational attitudes survive when customers actually want the benefits of global standardization. The whole project got off on the wrong foot. It asked people what features they wanted in a washing machine rather than what they wanted out of life. Selling a line of products individually tailored to each nation is thoughtless. Managers who took pride in practising the marketing concept to the fullest did not, in fact, practice it at all. Hoover asked the wrong questions, then applied neither thought nor imagination to the answers." Theodore Levitt, "The Globalization of Markets," in: *Harvard Business Review*, May/June 1983, pp. 92–102, here p. 98.

> "A powerful force drives the world toward a converging commonality, and that force is technology. [...] Almost everyone everywhere wants all the things they have heard about, seen, or experienced via the new technologies."[18]

In short, without naming it but simply placing it under the rule of the "imagination," Levitt defines the new key to marketing dominance as a wholesale subordination of rational product claims to universalized Bernaysian psychological modeling, which is the basis of lifestyle marketing. Levitt refers to homogenization as both the means and the result of globalization.[19] He differentiates multinationals from the more forward-thinking global corporations, which, he says,

17

Theodore Levitt, *The Marketing Imagination*, Free Press, New York, Collier Macmillan, London, 1986.

18

Levitt 1983, p. 92.

19

In the homogenizing world market, certain goods, such as pizza, tacos, and bagels, become near-universal signifiers of difference.

20

Levitt 1983, p. 93.

"[...] sell standardized products in the same way everywhere – autos, steel, chemicals, petroleum, cement, agricultural commodities and equipment, industrial and commercial construction, banking and insurance services, computers, semiconductors, transport, electronic instruments, pharmaceuticals, and telecommunications, to mention some of the obvious."[20]

Thirty years on, we have placed many of these categories in Levitt's rather jumbled array under the rubric of the knowledge industries, including the management of Fordist industrial production (of "autos, steel, chemicals, petroleum, cement, agricultural commodities and equipment, [...] computers, semiconductors, [...] electronic instruments, pharmaceuticals"). Thirty years on, lifestyle *politics*, as both a unifier and a differentiator, help determine how we live or are supposed to live. People form alliances based on taste, above all via the tribalism of appearance-as-identity. Commodified lifestyle clusters include not merely possessions but persons, achievements, and children, and they tend to be costly to acquire and maintain. Punk is now another lifestyle choice, albeit an urban romantic one. Along with goth and other ways of life associated with New York's East Village, punk also provides the preferred uniform of suburban and small-town mall-dwelling malcontents, while the "Bronxish" hip-hop style, which is popular worldwide, does the same for working-class people of color. In this taxonomy, hipsterism is the lifestyle of arty types – the triumph of surface over substance – and is a direct consequence of the easy availability of cultural goods through technological means.

But there are times when the professionalization of art training in colleges and universities, combined with the capture and branding of artist-led, artist-run initiatives – the ones which used to reside outside the purview of art institutions – can broaden the social network and the vocabulary of action. It is a commonplace that in a postindustrial economy virtually all work falls in some sense under the reign of the language and symbolic behavior.

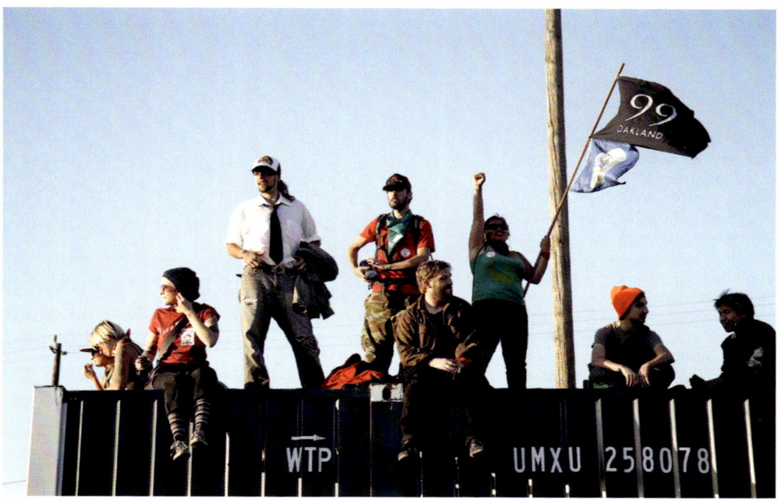

Oakland General Strike, November 2011

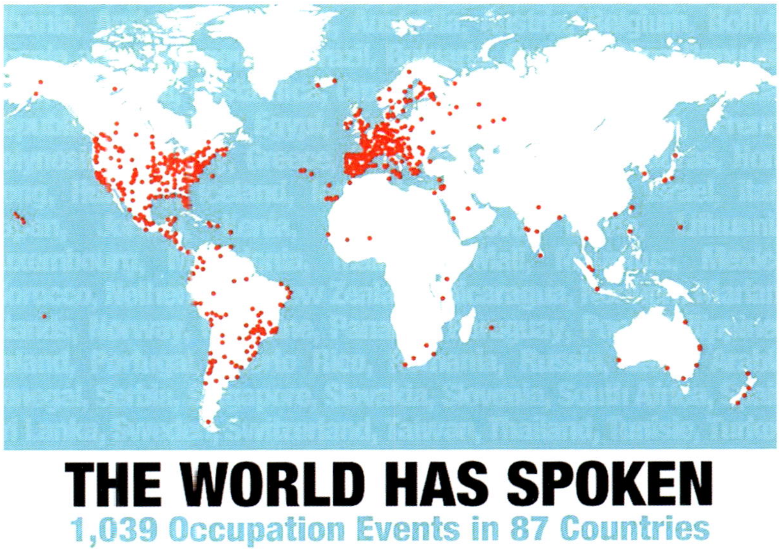

Occupy World Map, 2011

Certainly, all cultural products are flattened into "information," mashing together writing, research, entertainment, and, of course, art. The popular reception of art and its greatly expanded audience have allowed, in the present moment, a mutual visibility between artists and other underemployed groups, both educated and under-educated. Or perhaps more directly, looking for a series of master texts, the newly professionalized discourse of artistic production settled on Continental theories of aestheticized capital. How else to explain the peculiar position of artists at or near the vanguard of capitalist organization? Thus, even if the tendency may be toward the professionalization and embourgeoisement of artists, along with other members of the symbolic sector, when the future hits a brick wall, those ideas and alliances *in potentia* can have revolutionary consequences. The artists and artist-run groups, and others belonging to the creative-class demographic – which often overlaps with the group of those who identify as grassroots activists, whether or not they have been to art school – have been at the center of instituting, strategizing, and energizing the Occupy Wall Street movement at New York's Zuccotti Park, renamed Liberty Park.[21]

A way of life that relies on virtue and secular good living, as sold to a generation raised on school and media campaigns promoting civic responsibility and morality – such as "Just Say No to Drugs,"[22] "Smoking Kills," and "Save the Earth" – is no doubt more likely to be adopted by urban art school grads than any other demographic group. These are young urban professionals, perhaps, but not the "yuppies" of the past (though I am interested to see that the term has returned). The latter were high-earning lawyers, ad agency honchos, and magazine editors, while these new young urban professionals are low-level workers and wannabes in their field. City life appeals to members of these industries, which themselves are made up of networks of small shops that benefit from face-to-face relations and the excitements of the urban environment.

21
The Wall Street occupation was set in motion by a number of events, which I can only partly sketch out here. The occupation had been foreshadowed a couple of months earlier by Bloombergville, a three-week encampment of labor leaders and grassroots activists held at City Hall Park against draconian budget cuts and named after the mayor of New York. (Another important precedent: the weeks-long occupation of the Wisconsin State Capitol in Madison, supported by unions, including police unions.) An article speculating on the possibility of emulating Tahrir Square by anarchist and anthropologist David Graeber was published by *Adbusters*, a Situationist-inspired, high-gloss Canadian magazine. *Adbusters* subsequently put out a general call for a Wall Street occupation on September 17, 2011. Discussions about the possibility of building a movement had been held over the summer at 16 Beaver, an artist-run discursive space in the Wall Street area. An ad hoc meeting at 16 Beaver, after a debt/commons seminar heavy with activists and academics at which Graeber discussed his work on debt (*Debt. The First 5,000 Years*, Melville House, Brooklyn, 2011), was the final impetus toward the occupation centering on a General Assembly. The Bloombergville group put together the September 17 occupation, but Graeber, together with Japanese anarchist activist Sabu Kohso and anarchist artist and activist Georgia Sagri, whom he had encountered at the 16 Beaver seminar, then organized the General Assembly along anarchist lines. In October 2011, *Adbusters* offered some further tactical advice that was more art-world than old-school activist, but still familiar since the anti-WTO protests in Seattle, if not since the days of Yippie in the late 1960s or even the prewar Dada performances: "It's now time to amp up the edgy theatrics … deviant pranks, subversive performances and playful détournements of all kinds. Open your insurrectionary imagination. Anything, from a bottom-up transformation of the global economy to changing the way we eat, the way we get around, the way we live, love and communicate … be the spark that sustains a global revolution of everyday life!" (*Adbusters*, October 17, 2011, available online at: https://www.adbusters.org/blogs/adbusters-blog/robinhood.html, accessed 11/11/2014.) The Department of Performance Studies at New York University soon after began hosting a weekly series of lectures and workshops focusing on social change through "creative tactics and strategies."

2. The New Creative City

This wave of renewed preference for the city can be traced to the postwar economic boom in Western industrial democracies – I am looking at the United States – which led to the rising affluence of the middle class. Immediately after the war, many city dwellers, having gained some measure of financial security, migrated to small towns and freshly built suburbs, causing urban shrinkage.[23] One effect of this depopulation was the evacuation of many city business centers and the failure of many urban industries. But the direction of migration began to be reversed as bored children of the suburban middle class (along with corporate managers and the newly defined yuppies) were drawn to the organized pleasures of city life, not least the museums and theaters, as well as the dizzying mixture of anonymity, community, diversity, and possibility that fills the urban imaginary. To point out the obvious, the stultifying, homogeneous experience of life in the suburbs, with its identical malls and fast-food joints, doesn't offer the would-be creative much in the way of identity formation; and insofar as the local exists today, it is found either in the city or in rural small towns, not in fenced-in suburbia.

This repopulation and transformation of cities – from spaces bereft of shops and manufacturing, starved of resources, and inhabited by poor and working-class people or squatters living in ill-maintained housing stock, into spaces of middle-class desire, high-end shopping, and entertainment – took at least a generation. It also required the concerted effort of city leaders. New York's SoHo and East Village had proved, by the late 1970s, that the transformation of old warehouses and decaying tenement districts into valuable real estate could be accomplished by allowing artists to live and work in them – if nothing else, city government recognized or identified with such people and understood their needs. Those elected officials who might, in an earlier era, have supported organized labor, found that such constituencies were fading away. Artists, in addition, were not going to organize and make life difficult for city governments. In the following decades, the SoHo model became paradigmatic for cities around the world. (Another popular tactic was to attract small new industrial shops, mostly high-tech ones.) But no matter how much the arts (whether the performing arts or the institutionalized visual arts in museums) have been regarded in some cities as an economic motor, that remedy is not applicable everywhere, and not every city has proved to be a magnet for the arts. A new urban theory was required.[24]

The civic usefulness of educated but often economically marginal young people was first popularized by a young professor of urban planning at Carnegie Mellon University in postindustrial Pittsburgh. What Professor Richard Florida saw around him in that declining city was neighborhoods made cozy and attractive by the efforts of recent grads, who were setting up coffee shops and small businesses in low-rent locations. The customer-friendly environment – friendly to middle-class customers – emphasized shared tastes passed down since the mid-1960s via schools, music, movies, and magazines, tastes that define a particular niche among the

22 Drugs, that is, not considered part of the approved Big Pharma formulary. This is important because among other things it allowed adolescents to make distinctions between good and bad drugs, but often based on criteria other than legality.

23 Since racism was an important motivator, the resulting urban shrinkage is often attributed in no small part to "white flight." Small towns often became dormitory towns for city workers. The small town has remained the preferred location of U.S. residents for most of its history and was idealized during the high point of American sociology that spanned the Second World War.

24 Although the demonization of working-class and poor residents in areas ripe for real-estate harvesting is a tactic of long standing, the incoming "good people" have only recently been granted a profile of their own; previously, class privilege was taken for granted as a deserved entitlement.

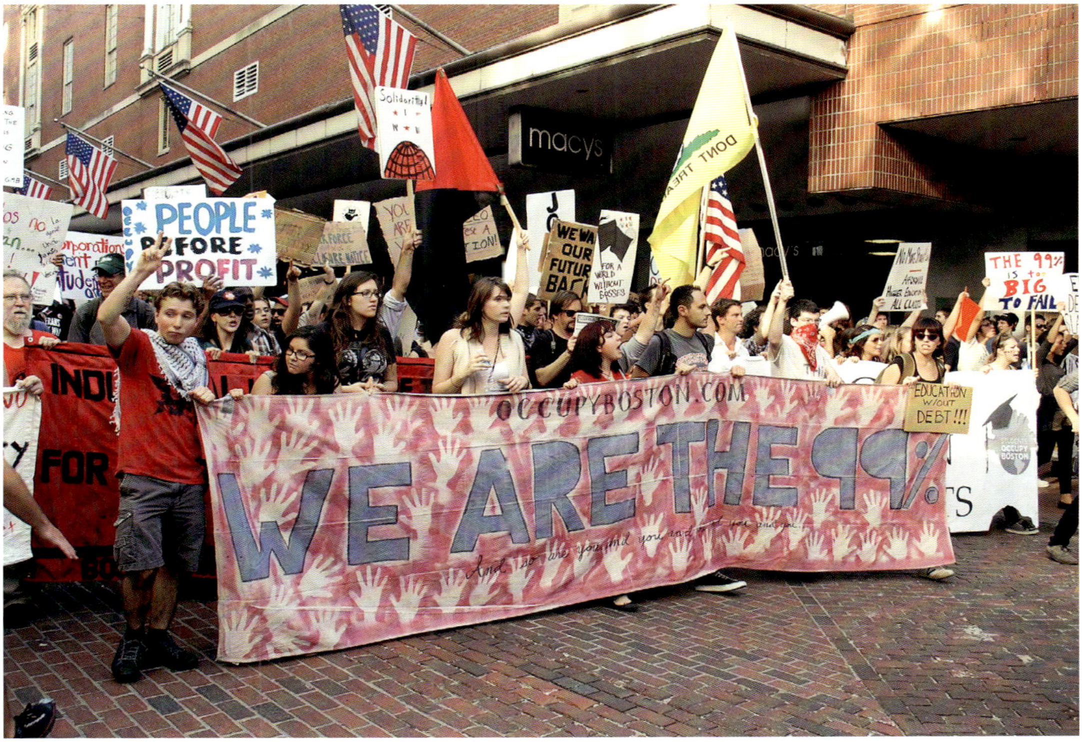

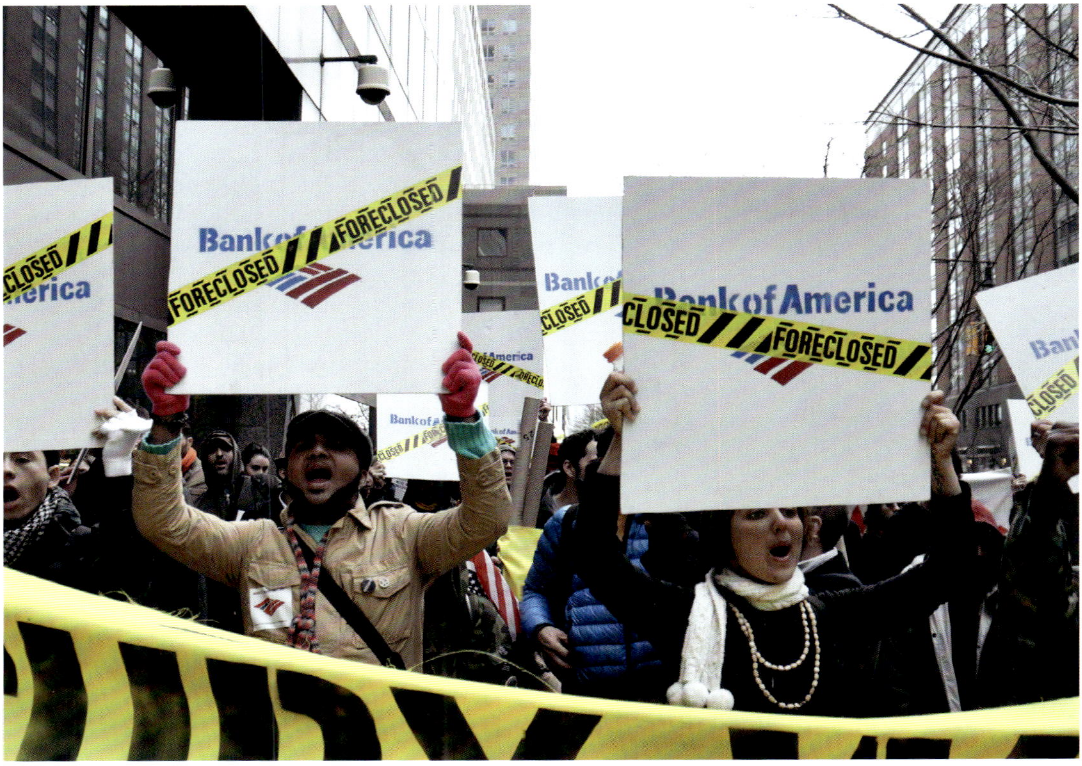

Top: Occupy Boston protest
Bottom: Occupy Wall Street, Occupy Bank of America, New York City, March 2011

educated, professional middle class. Elements of what might ironically be seen as suburban virtue, from recycling to gardening to arts and crafts (perhaps rescued from the lore of small-town Edens by nostalgic lifestyle magazines), were now being brought back to decaying city neighborhoods.

Professor Florida developed a new theory based on selling these congeries of young, generally underemployed people – as well as such subcultural categories as gays, who also tended to congregate in what used to be called bohemian neighborhoods – to urban planners as a surefire remedy for urban desuetude. (Or apparently selling them, for there is a bait-and-switch tactic at work here.) His book *The Rise of the Creative Class. And How It's Transforming Work, Leisure, Community and Everyday Life* offered a crafty new turn in business evangelism, creating a catchy new way of thinking about city marketing as lifestyle marketing – much as Theodore Levitt had done for brand marketing – and throwing a lifeline to often desperate city managers.[25] With his apparently systematic analyses, Florida parlayed his popular book into a new job and a consulting career. He is now the head of the Martin Prosperity Institute at the University of Toronto, and he is consultant to cities, corporations, museums, and nonprofits around the world. Prosperity, like the lovely name Florida, is a keyword. His website said,

> "The Creative Class Group is a boutique advisory services firm comprised of leading researchers, communication specialists and business advisors. CCG combines a pioneering approach of global thought leadership and proven strategies offering clients worldwide the market intelligence critical for competitiveness and greater economic prosperity."[26]

I have addressed Florida's "creative-class thesis" in a series of earlier articles; here I offer an abbreviated digest, to flesh out the argument.[27] There is a certain irony to revisiting this matter now, as the long-term financial downturn has cast some doubt on the appeal of creative-class theorizing in the areas under financial strain, but the thesis has had a decade to catch hold, and catch hold it has.[28] Florida's analyses have struck a chord with city managers by appearing to promote diversity in ways that often replicate what is already in place. Many who have scrutinized his data have demonstrated the insufficiency of his analyses and thus his conclusions.[29] Critics point out that in relying on standard census categories, he sweeps into the creative class all knowledge-industry workers, from those in call centers to professional data analysts, scientists, and mathematicians – hardly artists.[30] A consensus on his conclusions is that they amount to the well-established "human capital" thesis of urban development placed within new linguistic frames, and most importantly with the "creative" moniker generously washing over everyone in the knowledge industries. A small, relatively poor group of urban dwellers, the ones offering consumer friendliness and local color, becomes the face of the other, larger, richer, but basically invisible members of Florida's "super-creative core" grouping.[31] In his shell game, creatives are defined

25
See: Richard Florida, *The Rise of the Creative Class. And How It's Transforming Work, Leisure, Community and Everyday Life*, Basic Books, New York, 2002. Florida did not come up with the idea of the creative class, but he did populate it with statistical categories. According to his thesis, the creative class makes up about thirty percent of U.S. workers, but as we shall see, the groupings he uses are problematic.

26
See: www.creativeclass.com, accessed 2012.

27
See note 2.

28
Toronto, Florida's base, is at the time of writing afflicted by a mayor with a take-no-prisoners, right-wing populist style, complete with racist and antigay pronouncements and actions. In repudiating the previous government's agenda, Rob Ford has cut funding for bike lanes and light rail. Asked about Florida's response, Torontonians with whom I spoke said that he has been largely quiet but had complained that the city was cutting all the things that made Toronto "his city."

29
In 2012, Florida has been criticized again for sloppy interpretation and aggregation of polling data and economic statistics in his article "Why America Keeps Getting More Conservative," published in the venerable magazine *The Atlantic* (these days politically center-right), where he is one of 19 editors. See: Richard Florida, "Why America Keeps Getting More Conservative," in: *The Atlantic*, February 13, 2012, available online at: www.theatlanticcities.com/politics/2012/02/why-america-keeps-getting-more-conservative/1162/. Many other commentators read the data quite the opposite way and claim that the U.S. electorate is, on the contrary, growing increasingly liberal in its beliefs while U.S. politics, thanks to the radicalization of the Republican Party, have moved to the right. See, for example: Sarah Jaffe, "Why Right-Wingers (and Media Hacks) Are Totally Wrong about What Americans Believe," in: *AlterNet*, February 26, 2012, available online at: www.alternet.org/election2012/154182/why_right-wingers_(and_media_hacks)_are_totally_wrong_about_what_americans_believe_--_we're_becoming_less,_not_more,_conservative_/?page=entire, accessed 11/11/2014.

Book Bloc, Occupy Oakland, October 2011

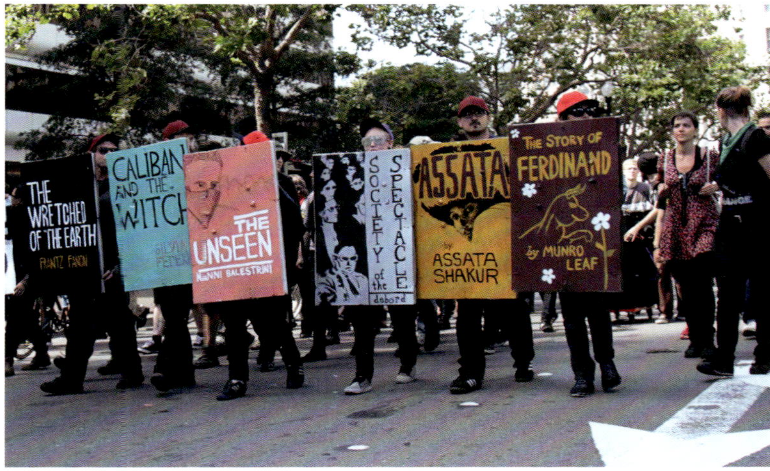

under one shell as people whose mental engagement is at the heart of their work and under another as people who know how to live nicely, decoratively, and cheaply, and under yet another as primarily a high-earning, tax-paying economic grouping. As policy follows prescriptions, inconvenient, poorly accoutered working-class people are marginalized, pushed further out to the edges of the city or to the suburbs, while in the newly reclaimed city precincts, bourgeois predilections – of ego-centered, commodified, and mediated rituals – enfold every milestone in life, from birth to premarital stag and hen parties, weddings, baby showers, births, communions, and maybe even deaths.

3. The Limits of Creativity and of Liberalism

Many critics naively fail to realize that Florida, like Clark Kerr, is a social liberal. Like most neoliberals, he is out there on the rhetorical barricades arguing for tolerance, subsidies, and the right of the creative class to perform the work of the patrician class for little or no compensation. In a strange way, then, he can be taken as the collective projection of a certain branch of the liberal elite. Liberals are happy to celebrate artists, or even better, "creatives" – that amorphous group of brewers, bakers, urban farmers, and baristas – as long as their festivals and celebrations can be sponsored by banks, corporations, and foundations and their efforts civically branded. Architectural institutes hold meetings and publish newsletters touting "livable" cities. Arts institutions benefit from the attention of governmental agencies and foundations, but the costs are also worth considering.

Artists, already complicit (wittingly or unwittingly) in the renegotiation of urban meaning for elites, were called upon to enter into social management. Real estate concessions have long been extended to artists and small nonprofits in the hopes of improving the attractiveness of "up-and-coming" neighborhoods and bringing them back onto the high-end rent rolls. The prominence of art and "artiness" allows museums and architecture groups, as well as

30 Florida ingeniously includes in his mix a statistically small bohemian group, which includes gay people, but as Harvard economist Edward Glaeser has reluctantly noted, his data regressions suggest that in only two cities – in, yes, the state of Florida – does the gay population help the economy.

31 "[T]o harness creativity for economic ends, you need to harness creativity in all its forms. You can't just generate a tech economy or information economy or knowledge economy; you have to harness the multidimensional aspects of creativity. […] there are three types of creativity: technological creativity […]; economic creativity, […] turning those things into new businesses and new industries; and cultural and artistic creativity, […] new ways of thinking about things, new art forms, new designs, new photos, new concepts. Those three things have to come together to spur economic growth. […] The creative class is composed of two dimensions. There is the supercreative core, which are scientists, engineers, tech people, artists, entertainers, musicians – so-called bohemians that are about 12 percent of the workforce […]. […] the supercreative core is really the driving force in economic growth. In addition to the supercreative core, I include creative professionals and managers, lawyers, financial people, healthcare people, technicians, who also use their ideas and knowledge and creativity in their work. I don't include people in service or manufacturing industries who use creativity in their work." Christopher Dreher, "Be Creative – Or Die," interview with Richard Florida, *Salon*, June 7, 2002, available online at: www.salon.com/2002/06/06/florida_22/, accessed 11/11/2014.

artists' groups, artists, and arts administrators of small nonprofits, to insert themselves into the conversation on civic trendiness.

Artists are hardly unaware of their positioning by urban elites, from the municipal and real estate interests to the high-end collectors and museum trustees. Ironically, perhaps, this is also the moment in which social engagement on the part of artists is an increasingly viable modality within the art world. And young curators specialize in social practice projects. Many artists have gone to school in the hopes of gaining marketability and often thereby incurring a heavy debt burden. Schools have gradually become the managers and shapers of artistic development; on the one hand, they prepare artists to enter the art market, and on the other, through departments of "public practice" and "social practice," they mold the disciplinary restrictions of an art that might be regarded as a minor government apparatus. These programs are secular seminaries of "new forms of activism, community-based practice, alternative organization, and participatory leadership in the arts" that explore "the myriad links between art and society to examine the ways in which artists [...] engage with civic issues, articulate their voice in the public realm."[32]

To look again at the United States – but not only there – arts and architecture institutions are quite pleased to be swept along by the creative-class urban-planning tide. The distinctly old-economy, luxury vehicle maker BMW has joined with the Guggenheim Museum to create "a mobile laboratory traveling around the world to inspire innovative ideas for urban life,"[33] with the names of some high-profile artist and architect attached. The "Lab" firmly ties the corporation, the museum, architecture, art, and entertainment to the embourgeoisement of cities. Urban citizenship has replaced other forms of halo-polishing for so-called corporate citizens. By the way, they all like bikes. As does Urban Omnibus – which also likes "art as urban activator."

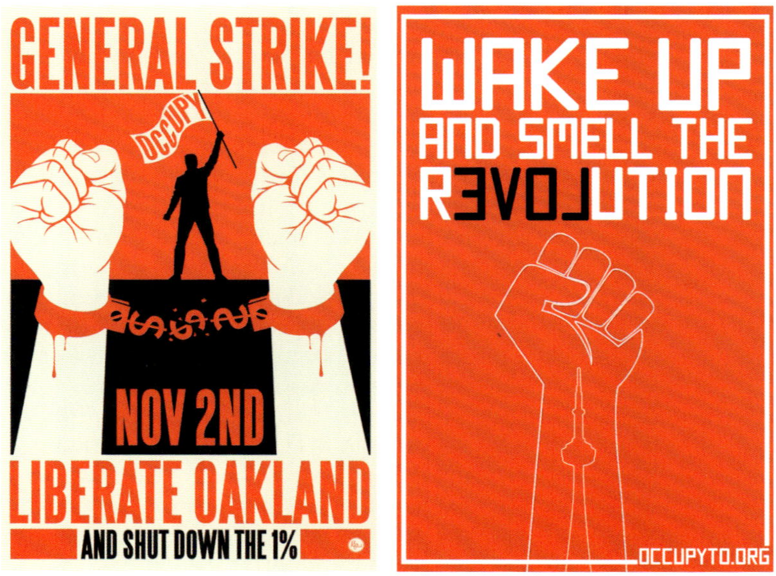

Posters for Occupy Oakland by Rich Black and for Occupy Toronto by Jay Tripper / Field Trip Designs

32

These quotes are from a job announcement put out by a department at a major university that offers "a Master's Degree in Arts Politics which treats, in an activist key, the nexus between the politics that art makes and the politics that make art." Despite my skepticism, I don't want to dismiss the potential of such training and network formation; the problem lies in the short life span that such initiatives can have before the institution renders them zombies. See the latter two installments of my "Culture Class" essay (www.e-flux.com/journal/culture-class-art-creativity-urbanism-part-ii/, www.e-flux.com/journal/culture-class-art-creativity-urbanism-part-iii/) for a discussion of the culturalization argument of Fredric Jameson and its adoption by George Yúdice to argue that art that can be framed as social practice may put the artists in the position of unwittingly serving the aims of the state and, by focusing on melioration, of abandoning the possibility of critique. See also footnote 6.

33

See: www.bmwguggenheimlab.org, accessed 11/11/2014. There was an unsuccessful effort by artists to occupy the BMW Guggenheim Lab during a day of artists' actions.

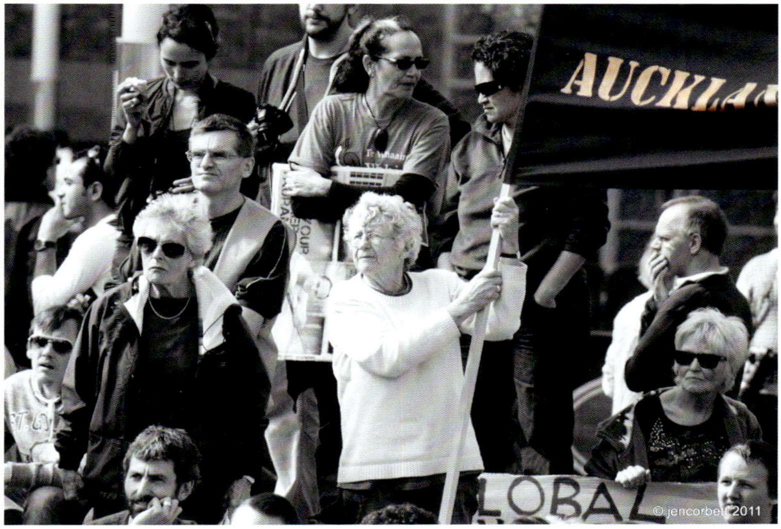

Occupy Auckland, October 2011

The Urban Omnibus is an online project of New York's venerable Architectural League and is funded by foundations, the City of New York, and the federal government.[34] Its feature "Civic Action: A Vision for Long Island City"[35] describes a new venture, developed by two local contemporary art museums, that "invites artist-led teams to propose visions for the future of Long Island City," a neighborhood in the borough of Queens, New York, that is a postindustrial ruin with new high-end waterfront residential development. Another feature, "Making Room," is "a research, design, and advocacy project to shape New York's housing stock to address the changing needs of how we live now."[36] In March 2012, there was a feature on the site in which a freelance writer describes an open house at the newly renovated jail, the Brooklyn House of Detention, an event designed to placate the neighborhood gentrifiers that all will be well.[37] I am here using the Lab and Urban Omnibus to represent the myriad efforts of city agencies and elite institutions – and some freestanding ones or those attached to public universities that still follow a noncorporatized path – to adopt the now virtually naturalized creativity and hipster-friendly memes posed in terms of imagination, design, and advocacy, just as in some respects I am using the name Florida to represent the creative-class thesis that his work has helped turn into dominant policy lingo.

The Florida version of the SoHo urban transformation model, as I have argued, fails to capture the agency of the actors in his transformational scenarios. Just as science has been seen in the capitalist mind as a necessary stepping-stone to technology (a business term), creativity is regarded as the necessary ingredient of "innovation." The creative classes as constructed by Florida operate strictly within the world view pictured by the capitalist imaginary; even those who are not simply employees in high-tech firms are seen to be instituting small businesses and learning to deliver retro boutique services that bear echoes of prewar American neighborhood shops and delicatessens or even nineteenth-century

34 See: http://urbanomnibus.net, accessed 11/11/2014. Urban Omnibus is funded by the Rockefeller Foundation's New York City Cultural Innovation Fund, the National Endowment for the Arts, the New York City Department of Cultural Affairs, and the New York City Council. The Architectural League was founded in 1881 by Cass Gilbert and has long sought to recognize the importance of the arts in relation to architecture.

35 "Civic Action: A Vision for Long Island City," in: Urban Omnibus, October 12, 2011, available online at: http://urbanomnibus.net/2011/10/civic-action-a-vision-for-long-island-city/, accessed 11/11/2014.

36 "Making Room," in: Urban Omnibus, October 5, 2011, available online at: http://urbanomnibus.net/2011/10/making-room/, accessed 11/11/2014. The phrase "how we live now" evidences a predictable set of assumptions about who constitutes the "we."

37 See: "Field Trip: Brooklyn Detention Complex Housewarming," 02/16/2012, available online at: http://urbanomnibus.net/2012/02/field-trip-brooklyn-detention-complex-housewarming/, accessed 11/11/2014.

Occupy Wall Street at Zuccotti Park, New York City, October 2011

"purveyors" (next up, the milk wagon and the seltzer delivery man!) or idealized French or Italian shops in cities and villages. They have no agency outside the application of their imaginative abilities to the benefit for the gentrifiers and the well-to-do. They have no agency in respect to large-scale political and social transformation. It is true that the Florida model is not strictly interested in those whom the present readership recognizes as artists. But here the picture of agency is even worse in respect to the market artists whose potential social worth is quite directly to serve the interests of the international clientele inhabiting the most rarefied income heights, a service role to which a generation or two of artists have been trained to aspire.

But this is not the picture of ourselves that most of us artists, curators, critics wish to recognize. Like other participants in the movements taking place around the world, and like participants in earlier ones, artists tend to want to lend themselves and their energy and abilities to social betterment and utopian dreaming, but not necessarily as participants within the sanctioned institutionalized frames. The artistic imagination continues to dream of historical agency. In a protracted economic downturn such as we are experiencing now, while the creative-class thesis is showing its limits in respect to saving cities, it becomes clearer that artists and other members of the art community belong to the pan- or nonnational class whose composition is forged across boundaries and whose members are inclined, as the cliché demands, to think globally and act locally.

Political movements are perpetually dogged by accusations of 1960s nostalgia and even Luddism, a result of the antimodernism of much 1960s counterculture. People on the Left are routinely derided by the Right as dirty fucking hippies, and once the occupations began, the Right was not slow to use this picture to discredit the occupiers. But the constellations of dissent have largely changed since the 1960s. If people are aiming to secede from modernity, they do so with a different range of continental theorists to draw upon, and without the three-worlds model of political contestation, in which the land-bound peasant figured strongly as an ideal, or the tribal nomad for those not inclined to socialist revolution. Revolution now looks more anarcho-syndicalist, or perhaps council communist, than Marxist-Leninist. The city is not simply the terrain to be evacuated, nor is it the site of guerrilla warfare; it is a conceptual puzzle as well as a battleground in which the stakes are slow-motion class war, and farming is brought to the city not by dreamers in homespun clothing but by those who might adopt the garb of the professional landscape architect or beekeeper. "Creatives" may bring not only a training in design and branding, and often a knowledge of historical agitprop and street performance, but also the ability to work with technological tools in researching, strategizing, and implementing actions in virtual as well as physical spaces. Actually or functionally middle-class, they are at ease with the discourses and modes of intellectual endeavor required in higher education, or in college prep. Craft and skill are enfolded in a framework that differs significantly from their earlier understanding; but the hegemonic role of the knowledge industries and the "devices" of electronic production and communication render that framework near ubiquitous.[38] The often flexible schedules of artists and other members of the precarious sectors of Florida's creative/bohemian classes also permit a freedom to come and go at encampments and meetings, an ability to shift time and work commitments that is not available to all.

We can see the occupation activists as staking a claim, creating a presence, setting up a new public sphere, demanding the reinstatement of politics by refusing to simply present demands to representative governments and instead enacting democracy themselves. (Democracy has long been part of the American particular brand, albeit usually combined with double-barreled neoliberalism – or neoimperialism.) While welcoming the new, I can't resist pointing back to the old, not to the eighteenth-century demands for self-governance led by a group of bourgeois colonial rebels in the American colonies but to the American Civil Rights Movement and one of its children, the Free-Speech-inspired, antiwar, worldwide student movement of the 1960s, for which democracy – direct democracy, without representation – was a foundational idea, at least as the degree zero of the movement in the early years.[39] In this current iteration, the contributions of celebrity artists such as Shepard Fairey (made famous by his Obama / Hope campaign poster of 2008) have been politely greeted but are beside the point, as it is not hard to see the occupations themselves as grand public works of process art with a cast of several thousand.[40] The vast majority of artists – forming the core of the underpaid, unpaid urban army whose activities Florida acolytes wish to harness – live in a state of precarity that may lead them to seek social solutions in new and unexpected ways. This is where the so-called artistic mode of production comes in.

Urban sociologist Sharon Zukin, writing in 1982, identifies this precariousness of bohemian life as one of the five major ways in which this artistic mode of production affects the urban environment. The others include the "manipulation of urban forms [and] the [transfer of] urban space from the 'old world' of industry to the 'new' world of finance, or from the realm of productive economic activity to that of nonproductive economic activity"[41]; diminishing expectations about the provision of housing resulting from the substitution of "bohemian" living arrangements for contemporary housing; and, finally, the ideological function:

> "While blue-collar labor recedes from the heart of the financial city, an image is created that the city's economy has arrived at a post-industrial plateau. At the very least, this displaces the issues of industrial labor relations to another terrain."[42]

38
The most prominent sign of technological sophistication is the frequent visual reference to Anonymous, an amorphous group of hackers, or hacktivists (of which one small international groupuscule, LulzSec, was arrested in February 2012), in the form of the Guy Fawkes masks from the *V for Vendetta* franchise (worn by protesters and occupiers and used on signage). Anonymous apparently has carried out denial-of-service attacks against the websites of the governments of Tunisia, Egypt, and Bahrain during the attempted revolutions there, and it has expressed or enacted support for Occupy. See: "Anonymous – Occupy Wall Street," September 10, 2011, available online at: www.youtube.com/watch?v=l6jdkpQjueo&feature=g-vrec&context=G27aba48RVAAAAAAAACg, accessed 11/11/2014. I do not have the space here to dissect further the possible role of this pointedly anarchic, often playful assemblage of hackers. But in more workaday fashion, a range of technological ease is suggested by the facility with which the Occupy movement has made use not only of the widely known popular media sites such as Facebook and Twitter but also of less well known ones, sites such as Vibe, the older IRC, the now indispensable Livestream, Reddit, or Internet Relay Chat, according to PC magazine, as well as Tumblr and Google Docs. See, for example: http://mappingthemovement.tumblr.com, accessed 11/11/2014. An early assessment: "'We set up shared Google docs so we could communicate. [...] And we set up Google Voice numbers for everyone.' One Tumblr page, 'We Are The 99 Percent,' [...] reveals the plight of people, who see themselves as far outside the top 1 percent of Americans [...]," in: "'Occupy Wall Street' Why It Choose Tumblr," available online at: http://news.discovery.com/tech/occupy-wall-street-tumblr-111006.html, accessed 11/11/2014.

If the creative-class thesis can be seen as something of a hymn to the harmony between the creative forces of production and the urban social relations that would use them to the benefit of cities bereft of industrial capital, perhaps the current grassroots occupations can be seen as the inevitable arrival of the conflict between the creatives and the city that uses them. It is interesting, in this respect, that the battle cry has been "Occupy" (which echoes Florida's similar injunction to gentrify), that is, to occupy space, to occupy the social and political imagination, in a way analogous to the way previous movements radicalized *freedom* into *emancipation*, *republic* into *democracy*, and *equality* into *justice*. Florida says gentrify, we say "Occupy."

That leads us to the next step, now under way. What the occupations have done is to make members of disparate groups – neighborhood advocacy groups, immigrants' rights groups, and working-class labor groups, both organized and not, visible to each other – and in Occupy's first phase put them into temporary alliances. It is these alliances that form the nuclei of the occupation of the present and future.

This text is a slightly revised version of an essay that was first published in *e-flux journal*, no. 33, March 2012. The essay is an expanded version of a paper given at The Labour of the Multitude? The Political Economy of Social Creativity, a conference organized by the Free / Slow University of Warsaw and held at the University of Warsaw on October 20 – 22, 2011, just over a month after the Occupy movement began. The essay has benefited greatly from Stephen Squibb's comments. For years on, many of the most highly visible gains of these occupations and the social movements they represent appear to have faded away. On the contrary, both the tactics and the fundamental social understandings they have brought into the public square continue to enliven public debate and action in many areas around the world.

39

Here I am looking not only to the town meetings of the early days of the American colonies but explicitly to the model of nonviolent participatory democracy propounded by one of the groups central to the Civil Rights Movement, the Student Nonviolent Coordinating Committee (SNCC). Many of the young student activists had joined SNCC's Freedom Riders campaign to disrupt racial segregation in the American South, which influenced the principles outlined shortly after in the Port Huron Statement, a foundational document of the student/antiwar movement. Naturally enough, the history, origins, and influences of these movements are more complex than I can sketch out here. The widely noted, galvanizing speech of Berkeley student leader Mario Savio, delivered in the Berkeley campus quadrangle on December 2, 1964, during a standoff with university police, includes the following in its preamble: "I ask you to consider – if this is a firm, and if the Board of Regents are the Board of Directors, and if President Kerr in fact is the manager, then I tell you something – the faculty are a bunch of employees and we're the raw material! But we're a bunch of raw materials that don't mean to be – [to] have any process upon us. Don't mean to be made into any product! […] Don't mean to end up being bought by some clients of the University, be they the government, be they industry, be they organized labor, be they anyone! We're human beings!"

40

Artists' groups are increasingly making this point, for good or ill; see, for example, "The Art of Occupation," available online at: http://newamericanpaintings.wordpress.com/2011/11/09/the-art-of-occupation, and Martha Schwendener, "What Does Occupy Wall Street Mean for Art?" in: *Village Voice*, October 19, 2011, available online at: www.villagevoice.com/2011-10-19/art/what-does-occupy-wall-street-mean-for-art, accessed 11/11/2014.

41

Sharon Zukin, *Loft Living. Culture and Capital in Urban Change*, Johns Hopkins University Press, Baltimore (MD), 1982, p. 178.

42

Ibid., p. 180.

Guido Strack

Whistle-blowing as a Global Protest Movement

and Its Relationship with the Law

During the course of this presentation, I do not want to speak so much about my own case – which incidentally has not yet been closed, and as regards to which there will be further court hearings next month – but rather about the following three issues: first, I shall define what I understand by the term whistle-blowing; second, I shall refer to the current legal situation in Germany and suggest improvements which could be implemented; and third, I will address the question of whether whistle-blowing is a protest movement.

Understanding Whistle-blowing and Whistle-blowers

According to the definition in the statutes of Whistleblower-Netzwerk e.V., which I have chaired since 2006, whistle-blowers are people who, rather than silently condoning illegal actions, wrongdoings, and deficiencies, or impending risks to persons or to the environment, make them known. They do so internally within their own company, office, or organization, or externally to the relevant authorities, third parties, or even the press. It is an important distinction that whistle-blowers are organization insiders within the framework of the established term. Not every protester who uncovers wrongdoings or deficiencies is automatically a whistle-blower. However, today the term has become somewhat broader and vague in the way it is applied.

With respect to the deficiencies in question, various criteria can be identified: first of all, illegal activity; that is, violations of existing laws, which can be determined and for which there is a relatively clear basis for subsumption; and second, illegitimate activity; that is, the field, which is considerably more difficult to define, of past inconsistencies or inconsistencies that are to be feared in the future with subjective standards, of a subjective sense of justice and of right and wrong, or of ethical standards, which are not clearly formulated and violations of which are thus not so clearly punished with sanctions as in the case of actual violations of the law. It is a matter of uncovering dangers and risks, whereby the greatest difficulty is making an assessment of just how concrete a risk is, and whether it is necessary to take action or whether the situation can be understood at all.

With respect to the whistle-blowing process, five stages can be differentiated:

> The first step is noticing a deficiency and recognizing its existence. Even at this stage it is already a matter of *willful blindness*; that is, of consciously looking the other way.
>
> The second step involves evaluating the deficiency. Is this something that involves or affects me? How should I behave? Three possible courses of action can result from the evaluation: *neglect*, *exit*, *voice*; or, in other words, looking away and remaining silent, attempting to escape from the situation, or verbally addressing the deficiency.
>
> If you decide to take action and address the wrongdoing or deficiency you have already taken the first step towards whistle-blowing, and it is important to consider carefully and tactically to whom you are going to turn and with which information.
>
> The fourth stage represents what for many whistle-blowers is the defining point: waiting. Given that the whistle-blower as an individual is not in a position to change what has caused the deficiency, she/he refers to a person whom she/he considers capable and then waits for their response.
>
> The evaluation of this person's response is stage five: Do you, the whistle-blower, agree with it? Has the deficiency been resolved? Did you come to the conclusion that there might not have been any deficiency or wrongdoing in the first place? Are you going to capitulate in the face of the stubborn rigidity of the system? If none of these apply, it is possible to decide to return to stage two: to use the *voice* option again, and launch a new whistle-blowing process, which then typically escalates. This would mean referring to a higher-ranking person, who is stronger and who possesses greater negotiating power than the person who said "no" in the first place. This "no" is a new barrier which must now also be overcome.

Alongside these five stages in the whistle-blowing process, the experience the whistle-blower makes in its course can also be divided into different stages with regard to attitudes and perceptions.

In discussions with whistle-blowers, the word "naive" is often used to describe the initial loyalty to the system within which people find themselves, and the standpoint that this system is fundamentally a good system – otherwise they would probably have long since left it or switched over to nine-to-five mode, and they would not be bothered about what is happening. Thus, whistle-blowers are people who are committed *to* the system and who feel they are also in a position to overcome a deficiency within this system.

The vast majority of whistle-blowers proceed internally at first – we are talking here about 80 to 90%. Studies from the UK reveal that even in the third round of the whistle-blowing process 60% still proceed internally. Whistle-blowers are, therefore, not resistance fighters, who immediately inform the outside world, but are at first merely informants who draw attention to wrongdoings or deficiencies within a system in which, despite initial doubts, they nevertheless still generally feel safe. If, however, the situation is

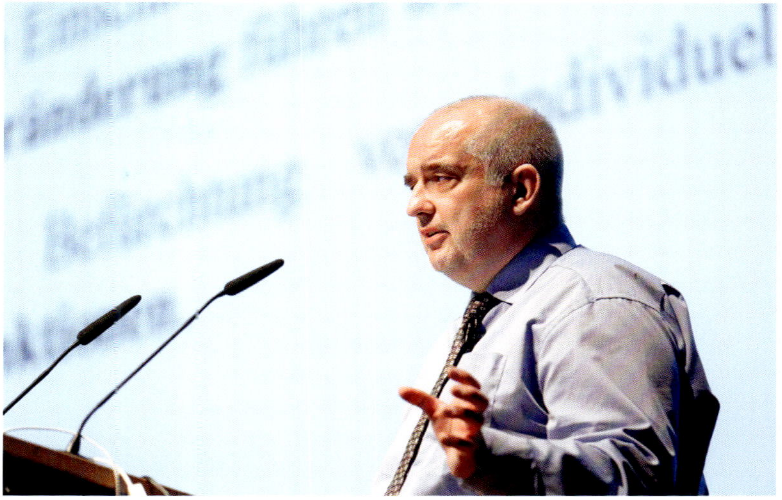

Guido Strack at the symposium Power and Law. Fluid Forms of Protest, ZKM | Karlsruhe, March 29, 2014

deemed as unassailable, the person who found fault with it is often attacked, sidelined, or simply ignored. The whistle-blower falls into the role of the victim, and his/her belief in the system is shattered.

As a result, those who do not drop matters at this point – and the process described above can be aborted at any point – ultimately become fighters after all, whose naive belief in the institution is increasingly replaced with an orientation towards higher values.

In the end the question is: victor or survivor? Whoever comes out of this struggle as a victor is in a position to finish with the system, to manage in a new way, to redefine values, and target new goals. Those who fail and survive the whistle-blowing process without having achieved the desired goals, will resign and withdraw.

Personally, I cannot say much about this, as in my case proceedings have not yet been concluded. However, it makes sense to me to talk about a *life-changing event* when referring to whistle-blowing, unless it occurs at a very low level.

Essentially, I consider whistle-blowing a very useful tool. It is a way for individuals to get burning issues off their chests. They don't have to bottle it up. And as the diagram on p. 318 shows, whistle-blowers actually have many options; theoretically, there are a great number of organizations to which they can turn. The question is, of course, whether anyone will listen, and take appropriate action. In addition, whistle-blowing allows organizations to get information to which they would otherwise not be privy. As a rule, this is usually passed on from below to the ranks above, with each level filtering out what doesn't suit them. For this reason, what makes it to the top is what those below believe to be what those above ought to hear. Whistle-blowing could present a possibility to reverse this process.

The same is obviously also true for the state. Law enforcement or recognizing breaches of law could also be considerably promoted here. The state does this as well in certain cases, for instance, buying CDs listing names of tax dodgers, or financing informers in the right-wing extremist scene. It is not above doing this. For whistle-blowers, however, the situation is mostly very different, that's why whistle-blowing is far too seldom. The alternatives are leaving, looking away, or remaining silent. If we consider the fact that the human brain filters every piece of information and rejects most of it, whistle-blowing must be viewed as a rare conscious decision to concentrate on an issue, and to take steps towards conflict based on this issue.

Whistle-blower and Potential Addressees

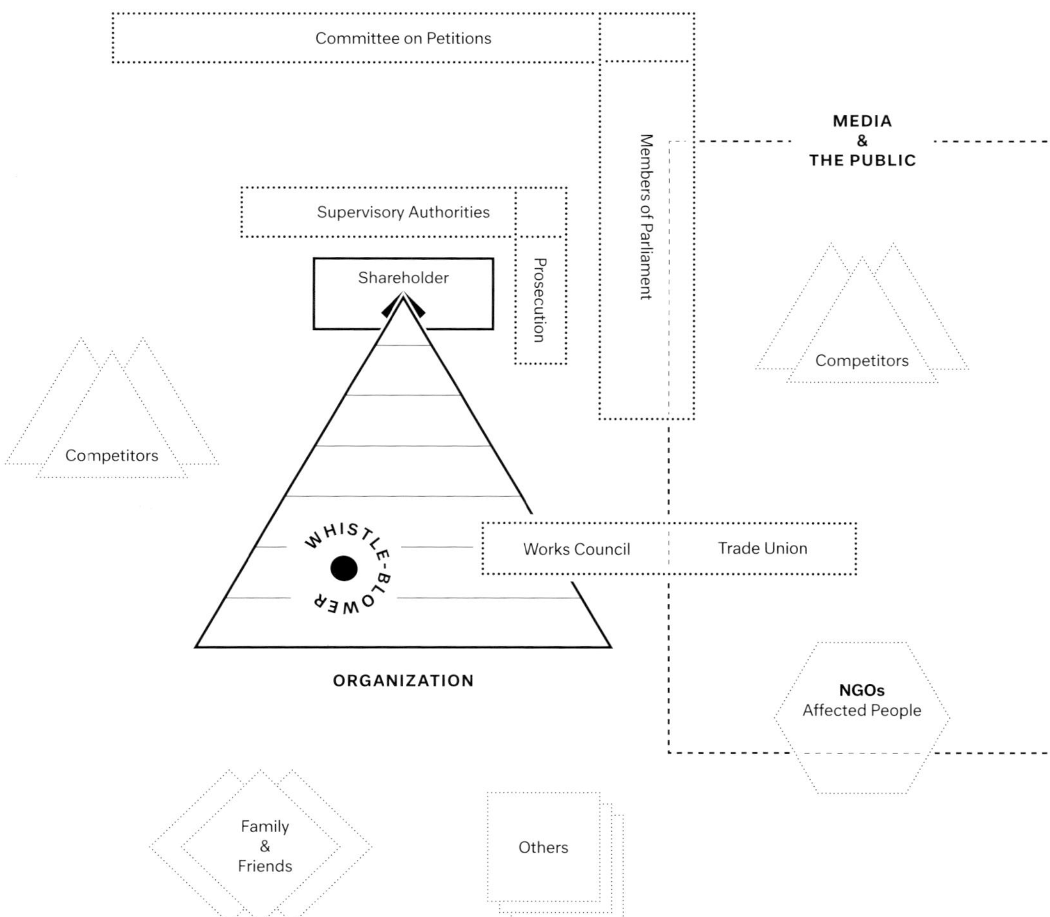

The reasons for not taking this step are manifold. Loyalty, which all too often is understood as loyalty to people, much less than loyalty to values, plays an enormously important role. To contradict one's own superiors is thus looked upon as a breach of loyalty, even if the actions were actually based on and motivated by human rights or on the goals set out by the organization itself. Added to this is the culture of remaining silent. People shy away from getting into conflict, and instead tend to try to avoid confrontation at all costs. Pluralistic ignorance and other factors play a role here. People look to others; nobody wants to be the first to voice criticism. Whistle-blowing often does not happen because precipitating a change is considered impossible from the outset, sometimes rightly so. Whistle-blowing is only meaningful if I believe that the person whom I am addressing can also affect some form of action, and that the change which I would like to achieve can also be implemented. And last but not least, the fear of disadvantages and reprisals obviously plays a decisive role. Unfortunately, the whistle-blower protection legislation tends to focus very heavily on this point, and in my view loses sight of the remaining points. Ultimately it is a case of the whistle-blower achieving a change, and not sustaining any damage in the process. From my point of view the legislator must, and society should be committed to finding better alternatives to remaining silent – regardless of whether it is with respect to child abuse, meat scandals, tax evasion, or whatever. Anonymity, in my opinion, is not the solution. In fragmentary contexts it usually does not work, as it builds up enormous pressure on the individual – take Bradley Manning, for example. In addition, it hinders the protest, because if a subject is addressed anonymously, there is no one left to support the cause openly, and it is that much easier for the opposing side simply to write the topic off.

The Legal Situation in Germany and Suggestions for Improvement

With respect to the legal level, there is tension between various legal norms and values which play a role: trade secrets, business secrets, state secrets on the one hand, and freedom of opinion and informational self-determination on the other, although informational self-determination is essentially relevant to both, because it not only sides with the whistle-blower, but equally with the person who is suspected of being a wrongdoer. The accused has rights, too, and should be granted them.

From my point of view, the subject of whistle-blowing in Germany should not really be an issue at all, at least as far as legally referring to the authorities is concerned, because Article 17 of the Basic Law for the Federal Republic of Germany allows for precisely this scenario: Everyone can apply to governmental bodies at any time; this is not merely a parliamentary right of petition.[1] In addition, Section 612a in the Civil Code refers to the ban on employers being subjected to disadvantages for exercising their rights.[2] However, both Articles are almost completely ignored in previous jurisdiction.

1 Article 17 of the German Basic Law: "Every person shall have the right individually or jointly with others to address written requests or complaints to competent authorities and to the legislature."

2 Section 612a of the German Civil Code: "The employer may not discriminate against an employee in an agreement or a measure because that employee exercises his rights in a permissible way."

Even the right to freedom of expression enshrined in Article 5 of the Basic Law[3] is being ignored at the moment, with the Federal Labor Court deciding that a whistle-blowing occurred anonymously and therefore Article 5 of the Basic Law cannot be applied. The Federal Constitutional Court does not then examine the case that closely, and it therefore likewise requires the European Court of Human Rights, which – for example, in the case of Brigitte Heinisch – amends the verdicts of German courts and decides that Article 5 of the Basic Law, or in this case Article 10 of the European Convention on Human Rights,[4] certainly does play a role.[5]

In Germany at the moment it appears as though internal whistle-blowing on the bearer of secrets within an organization is relatively unproblematic from a legal point of view – which is not to say that it is unproblematic in practice. The moment someone within an organization points out deficiencies, wrongdoings, or perhaps even corruption, it can certainly be the case that the network supporting the individual accused – if there is one, of which the whistle-blower might even be unaware – will act against the informer. This whistle-blower then, naturally, has very little protection, as bullying, for instance, is hardly sanctioned in Germany.

I would, however, like to focus on the second complex in terms of legal discourse: whistle-blowing on governmental organizations. At the moment, it appears that jurisdiction for the most part allows for the possibility of referring to governmental bodies, but only if this is proportionate and it can be considered inappropriate to act initially internally. Under normal circumstances there should at first be an internal procedure, and addressing a governmental body is only taken into consideration in the case of serious offenses and other things, which are not very precisely defined with regard to jurisdiction. In my opinion, if the state claims a monopoly of legitimate use of force, then it must also be ready to implement this monopoly. If it sets legal standards it must also listen to those who complain about violations of them. Otherwise, it need not set them in the first place. The same applies for what in my view are the ridiculous interests in maintaining confidentiality, and the protected business and trade secrets: is it acceptable that a legal system defines an infringement of the law as a secret worthy of being protected, as ours in Germany does in some cases? It is sometimes not even permitted to refer to the governmental bodies responsible.

It can certainly be argued that making everything public would also be problematic. The need to protect the person accused, that is, the person who is the subject of the whistle-blowing, also has a role to play here. But if you refer to a governmental body, then it is the duty of this governmental body not to disseminate such information widely, but to handle it sensitively and to inspect the matter in depth.

In my opinion, legislation for whistle-blowing must first and foremost introduce the *fundamental* possibility of referring to governmental bodies. In addition, it must provide the person who takes this action with the necessary protection in terms of labor and criminal law against, for example, warnings or dismissals; it must also guarantee protection from factual issues such as bullying

3 Article 5 of the German Basic Law (excerpt): "Every person shall have the right freely to express and disseminate his opinions in speech, writing and pictures [...]. There shall be no censorship. [...]"

4 Article 10 of the European Convention on Human Rights (excerpt): "Every person has the right to freedom of expression. This right shall include freedom to hold opinions and to receive and impart information and ideas without interference by public authority and regardless of frontiers. [...]"

5 The geriatric nurse from Berlin, Brigitte Heinisch, had publicly criticized and ultimately brought legal proceedings against her employer, because according to her there were severe deficiencies as regards to care in the facility in which she worked. Her employer terminated her employment with immediate effect. Heinisch sued on all grounds over a period of several years and, German courts having dismissed her concerns, finally received justice before the European Court of Human Rights in Strasbourg. The verdict for which she fought is considered groundbreaking with regard to whistle-blowing.

and similar activities. The prohibition of discrimination[6] must be protected by easing the burden of proof.

From my perspective, whistle-blowing ought to be generally regarded as one form of freedom of expression and be placed under the protection of Article 5 of the Basic Law and Article 10 of the European Convention on Human Rights (ECHR). In addition, you should not be allowed to immediately enter into a weighing up, which furthermore is restricted to a labor law view, as is currently the case in Germany. Instead, one should first determine what protection the opposing side needs, and whether a legitimate secret is at stake that deserves the protection of a legal order in the first place. If this is not the case, the disclosure is to be considered as legitimate. Furthermore, we must ask whether this is a case of people with special obligations. Due to social media, the original definition of the media is increasingly losing relevance. Can it be that only journalists enjoy the privilege of publishing things, or in the Web 2.0 era must everyone be permitted to do this? Vice versa, there would then only be a restriction if a person had a particular obligation. In this eventuality it would be a case of inquiring as to whether this obligation is also applicable in the sense of an employment relationship or a contractual relation. Furthermore, there ought to be an additional right to disclosure for those who previously addressed public bodies. Should information be leaked from there reach the outside world, this would ultimately no longer be the responsibility of the whistle-blower. Instead, the fault would lie with those who did not follow up the disclosure beforehand.

Only at the very end, we can then weigh the interests of transparency on the one hand against the private interest in protection of the accused party on the other. Every sanction must be reasonable. If we are to consider what is happening with Bradley Manning, Edward Snowden, and Julian Assange – the latter is not a whistle-blower – the question of reasonableness is fully justified.

6 First clause of Paragraph 7 of the German General Act on Equal Treatment: "Employees shall not be permitted to suffer discrimination on any of the grounds reffered to under Section 1 [for reasons of race or due to ethnic background, sex, religion or worldview, a disability, age or sexual identity]; this shall also apply where the person committing the act of discrimination only assumes the existence of any of the grounds reffered to under Section 1."

Whistle-blowing as a Protest Movement?

In my view, whistle-blowing is a form of protest because it demands change. The whistle-blower does not agree with what is going on. Yet, as studies reveal, whistle-blowers are not initially campaigners. They do not see themselves primarily as protesters, but rather as people who are loyal to an organization and its values, and would like to bring about a change within the organization via a legal channel.

For the most part whistle-blowing is not a movement; rather, it is conducted by individuals. Perhaps the whistle-blowing boom is also a response to the failings of trade unions and other collective instruments in this sector. The whistle-blower is an insider who has exclusive access to certain information. If he/she does not get any solidarity from colleagues – which due to fragmented working relationships as well as increased specialization is also becoming increasingly difficult – he/she has to take action outside the organization, which legally he or she actually has no right to do, in order to ensure support in the form of a movement.

On the other hand, I consider whistle-blowing to be an ideal instrument for controlling power and organizations. It is about having the courage to use your own reason and not simply be obedient to authority. For this reason, whistle-blowers are perhaps not typical members of a movement, because being a member of a movement always means going in the same direction. Many whistle-blowers I have met have a problem with this. The whistle-blowing experience they have had, and which incorporates toeing the line, can be quite traumatizing.

For me, whistle-blowing is an instrument which can be used in order to create a better society, and one with a greater legal basis, in which the law can be implemented and there are no blind spots; a society which does not look the other way, but rather discloses and denounces breaches of the law.

In response to this assessment I am often told that I am encouraging denunciation. But is there a difference between an informer and a whistle-blower? One could label someone who drew attention to a violation of the Third Reich norm of not hiding Jews as a whistle-blower. For ultimately, such persons also merely pointed out a violation of the law. But all of us would label such a person as a denouncer. What is the difference? It is a question of the legitimacy of the legal system. In a dictatorship, of course, there is none, but it is a completely different matter in a democracy. Yet in my opinion this argument does not get to the heart of the matter. I think the main difference is the fact that the whistle-blower is doing no wrong. He is merely informing. He merely points something out. The problem is not the act of informing – neither in Nazi Germany nor under the former East German secret police system. The problem is much more a case of what this act of informing leads to and what it is based on. First of all, one poses the question of whether the legal norm is legitimate, and second, whether the sanction, which follows on from the violation of the legal norm, is legitimate. The moment we look upon whistle-blowers as denouncers and send them into the desert as scapegoats, we don't have to engage with this question. This is very convenient.

In my opinion, participating in protest movements is not a solution for whistle-blowers, because protest movements only function with a mass of people and a unifying common cause. Within a larger group, there must at least be a conviction that people can latch onto. Furthermore, there is also the problem of competing for peoples' time and attention. Demanding activism everywhere and getting everyone out on the barricades cannot be a solution. For me, a constitutional state is the solution.

Notwithstanding, whistle-blowing is an Archimedean point to achieve democracy in the information society, and potentially to trigger protest movements as well. The main problem with our democracy in my view is a lack of information: really important things are decided in secret by certain circles behind closed doors, and subsequently appear in contracts that are not publicized or they are implemented on the back of gentlemen's agreements or international treaties which are not made public either. Wherever violations of the law take place and are not made public, a completely different culture prospers. In my opinion this is the case for us. Whistle-blowing can demonstrate the contradiction between appearance and reality at precisely this point, and in so doing ultimately become the initial spark for protest movements.

If we consider the Edward Snowden case, it becomes clear that at least in Germany the topic of spying and the NSA has successfully been made an issue; in the USA partly, in the UK conversely rather less so. And of course the ground for it was prepared. If it had not been prepared, it would not have worked, and in those countries where it had not been prepared, it indeed did not work. If it works, the whistle-blower possibly becomes a hero. Whether he is ok with this is another matter. Edward Snowden, for instance, says he is a completely normal person and has no desire to take on the role of hero. He asks us all not to put him on a pedestal – so high that nobody can get close to him anymore, – but instead to look at what his actions mean for us in our everyday lives, where we should ourselves become whistle-blowers. This is the fascinating question which ought to change society.

The problem with the constitutional state, which I just described as an ideal, is that it doesn't work. In many cases, the players in constitutional states and in organizations fail. Those who are addressed and ought actually to do something – compliance departments, prosecutions, delegates, the media, or whoever – do nothing. There are enough reasons for this: the issue is not interesting enough, is too old, or the subject matter of an ongoing case in which it is not advisable to get involved, or there are insufficient resources available. Or people do not want themselves to assume the role of a whistle-blower, which can happen the moment the person who has been approached likewise does not see himself or herself in a position to take action against the wrongdoing or deficiency. He or she would then have to address other levels, although they have possibly already learned what this entails. As I mentioned earlier, it is by all means possible for whistle-blowers to become the focal points or triggers of a protest movement.

In my opinion, we should get away from specific topics. We should no longer be discussing the NSA, meat scandals, or poor care for the elderly exclusively, but we should be thinking much more about the systematic levels and be asking ourselves why it takes so long until someone raises an issue, why only a few individuals are taking this step, why – to come back to the previously mentioned case of Brigitte Heinisch – for example, there are very few geriatric nurses who expose intolerable conditions, though many are aware of them.

To some extent the law does tolerate nonlegal protests. If you were to look at various fundamental rights – the resistance article in the Basic Law should be mentioned in this context[7] – you would see that there are limits here.

In the case of Manning in the USA, for example, the fact that *The New York Times* reported on the Afghanistan protocols and the diplomatic cables was tolerated. Manning, on the other hand, went to jail for 35 years. In the case of WikiLeaks, it is the Grand Jury versus Julian Assange; the case is still ongoing and the suspicion lingers on that in Sweden the story was somewhat

7 Article 20 of the German Basic Law, Paragraph 4: "All Germans shall have the right to resist any person seeking to abolish this constitutional order, if no other remedy is available."

exaggerated. This, then, is a case of there being less acceptance of resistance. It would appear that the one is perceived as art and therefore accepted – the initiators (in this case WikiLeaks and *The New York Times*) even receive prizes and rake in the cash, while the other is considered treason, which involves long prison sentences.

I wish the constitutional state would recognize the opportunity that whistle-blowing offers, and campaign to protect whistle-blowers. It should also ask itself which conditions it needs in order for whistle-blowing to be able to occur wherever it is necessary. As long as those who fail to respond to whistle-blowing, or act against whistle-blowers have nothing to fear, for example, because thanks to the Federal Court of Justice's ruling the paragraph referring to the perversion of justice[8] exists merely in writing, nothing will really change.

Ultimately it cannot be a question of law alone; rather, we must all ask ourselves how we should deal with whistle-blowers. How do we ourselves behave in comparable situations? Do we choose the voice option? How much solidarity do we show with whistle-blowers? How interested are we, and not just if the topic is pertinent to us? Not only if we are using a whistle-blower as a vehicle for a topic which is of interest to us, but also if it is a case of whistle-blowing per se and how to go about protecting it.

8
Section 339 of the German Criminal Code: "A judge, another public official or an arbitrator who in conducting or deciding a legal matter perverts the course of justice for the benefit or to the detriment of a party shall be liable to imprisonment from one to five years."

This text was delivered as a lecture at the symposium Power and Law. Fluid Forms of Protest, which was held on March 29, 2014 as part of the *global aCtIVISm* exhibition at the ZKM | Karlsruhe in collaboration with the Center for Applied Jurisprudence at the Karlsruhe Institute of Technology (KIT). For more detailed information on the topic and on the work of Whistleblower-Netzwerk e. V., visit www.whistleblower-net.de. The lecture was transcribed by Hannes Herold and translated from the German by Jeremy Gaines.

Bo Zheng

Nearby Facts to Trouble the Emperor:

A Note from China

Recently "citizen" (公民) has become a sensitive word in China. Xu Zhiyong (许志永), a university lecturer and human rights lawyer, was arrested in the summer of 2013 for initiating the New Citizens' Movement (新公民运动) and for advocating citizens' rights, rule of law, and constitutionalism. On January 26, 2014, he was sentenced to four years in prison.

The political situation in China has been aptly described as a heightened version of the Hans Christian Andersen tale, *The Emperor's New Clothes*: we (the citizens) know that the emperor (the party-state) is not wearing clothes, and the emperor knows that we know, and we know that the emperor knows that we know, but the emperor still walks around naked, and we – most of us in most situations – continue to play along.

But occasionally, we come up with works that trouble the emperor, in however small a way.

If you have access to YouTube, please listen to this file: www.youtube.com/watch?v=XnVBCdkRTX0. What you are hearing are the names of the students who were killed in the 2008 Sichuan earthquake. The entire piece runs for 3 hours and 40 minutes. Every student's name is read, 5,205 of them, one by one. This project, titled *Nian* (念), which means both to read and to commemorate, was produced by artist Ai Weiwei in 2010, with the participation of thousands of anonymous citizens.

The earthquake on May 12, 2008 was a terrible disaster. Almost seventy thousand people were killed. A few days after the earthquake, some careful observers, by piecing together various news reports, pointed out that a large number of collapsed structures were school buildings. Parents started to question whether those school buildings were poorly constructed and whether government corruption was the root cause. The government denied such allegations and never disclosed the names of the students killed. A few activists – Ai Weiwei among them – decided not to let the issue vanish from public view. Architect Liu Jiakun built a small memorial for Hu Huishan, a student killed at Juyuan Middle School. Ai Xiaoming, a professor at the National Sun Yat-sen University, made several documentaries on this issue. Ai Weiwei and more than thirty volunteers went to Sichuan in person, visited towns where schools had collapsed, and gathered information directly from local residents.

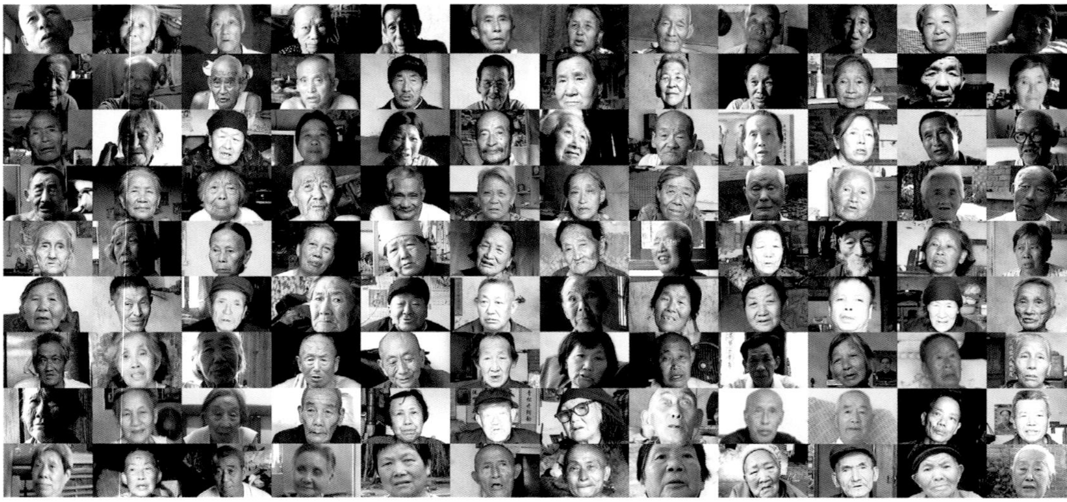

Some of the senior citizens interviewed in the *Folk Memory Project*

After six months' difficult work, they compiled a comprehensive list of the students killed in the earthquake, documenting each student's name, gender, date of birth, school, and class. As the names came in, Ai published them promptly in his well-followed blog.

Nian was produced in spring 2010, on the second anniversary of the earthquake. On April 24, 2010 Ai Weiwei sent out a Twitter message asking people to read one or a few names from the list of killed students and e-mail the sound file to his studio. Ai suggested that the reader should read the names of the students who share the same family with the reader. Within a week, around two thousand e-mails arrived and all the names were read. Ai's team edited individual recordings into a single MP3 file and posted it online.

This work goes beyond Ai Weiwei's usual practice as a single, courageous individual. Instead, he has built a platform for ordinary citizens to come together to form a public. *Nian* constituted a challenge to the state – not only because it refused to forget the students killed in the Sichuan earthquake. It mounted this disagreement by creating a public of citizens to mourn for the students. Publicness is essential to its contestation of state power.

Since 2009, Wu Wenguang (吴文光) and a group of young documentary filmmakers have been building a public visual archive on the history of the Great Leap Forward (1958–1961) and the Great Chinese Famine (1959–1961), a critical episode in the history of modern China. This collective effort is titled the *Folk Memory Project* (民间记忆计划). The process is simple – the filmmakers travel back to their home villages to interview grandparents and other elderly people to collect memories of the Mao era. It may seem that there is nothing unusual about this idea. But given the fact that one cannot find any proper record of this history on Chinese television, nor in museums, textbooks, or even academic journals, this project is extraordinary. During the Great Famine – still referred to as the "Three Years of Natural Disasters" in official discourse – millions of ordinary people starved to death as the result of maniacal policies implemented by the Communist Party to “march into Communism.” Half a century later, the party-state continues to prevent people from examining this part of history, fearing that the party will lose its legitimacy if the truth is learned.

Wu Wenguang is widely respected as the foundational figure in China’s independent documentary movement. Since 2005, he has changed his practice from making documentaries alone to helping other people – including villagers in rural provinces – to document their lives. Most participants in the *Folk Memory Project* are young art school graduates. Wu is often invited to art schools to conduct documentary workshops, through which students learned about this project. Over the past four years, more than one thousand interviews have been conducted. Most interviewers belong to the post-1985 generation and have never learned about what happened in their villages. The interviewees, the older people, have never thought about passing on their memories. Zou Xueping (邹雪平), a then 28-year-old from Shandong province, went back to her village and recorded this story: “All the bark of the trees was stripped off; leaves were eaten too. People’s digestive systems were filled with dry matter and they had difficulty pushing out excrement. Feces had to be dug out by hand.”

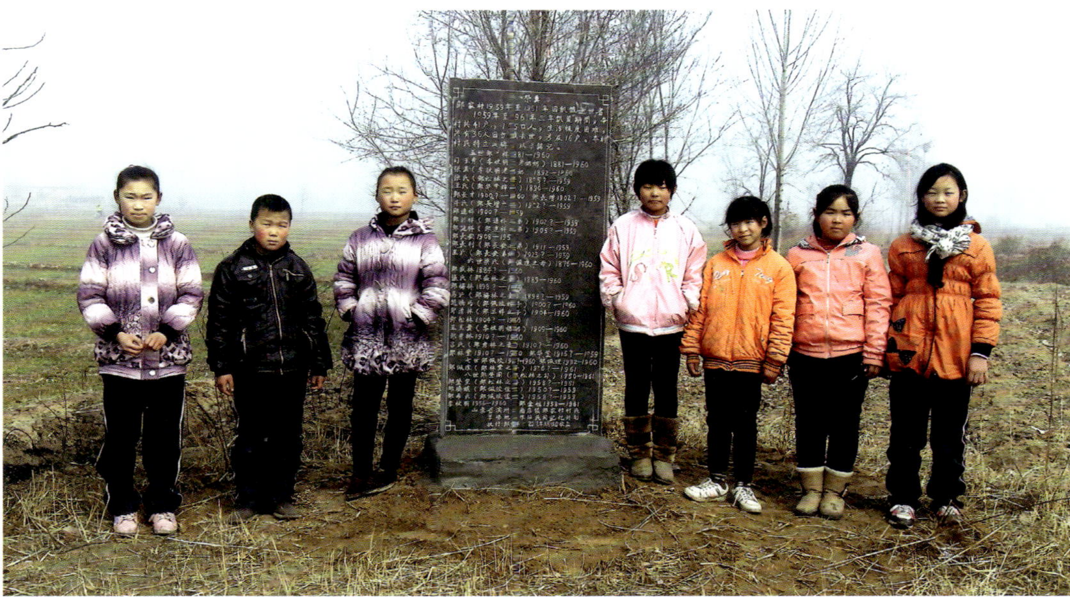

Children in front of the tombstone

This project has evolved beyond archiving. Some of the young participants have decided to “do something” about the loss of lives and the subsequent loss of memory. Zou proposed to erect a tombstone for those who died in her village, a traditional practice still common in the countryside, but her parents, born in the 1950s, worried that this action would attract too much attention from the government and get her into trouble. Yet she persevered. She solicited support from other villagers and managed to raise 1,800 yuan (about 288 U.S. dollars). Finally, in March 2012, a black stone stele bearing 37 names and a brief summary of the

tragic history was erected in the village cemetery. After this, Zou also set up a relief fund for senior people in the village, initiated a recycling program, and organized discussions between older and younger generations. The *Folk Memory Project* has enabled her to reconnect with her village in a deeply meaningful way.
In the fall of 2012, Wu and his collaborators were invited to present this project at the 9th Shanghai Biennale, one of the most important art events in China. In addition to presenting a version of the visual archive, they staged a multimedia play, performing history through their own bodies. The play and subsequent discussions were highly emotional; many of the audience members had tears in their eyes. After three days of public performance, the government intervened and stopped the play.

Over the past couple of years, many of us have come to see that the environment will become the most pressing political issue for China in the next decade. When 1.4 billion of us start to consume like Americans, what will happen to our land, water, air, and nature, and to our social relations? The environment is inherently linked to other political issues – human rights, civil society, democratic governance – and it may just be the first bomb to go off.

In 2013, a group of us – artists, designers, and scholars working in different disciplines – came together and produced a project called *Plants Living in Shanghai*. It had two components, a site-specific art piece and an open online course.

I was invited to participate in a major art and architecture exhibition organized by the Xuhui District government in Shanghai. The exhibition site used to be a cement factory, which was relocated in 2008 as part of Shanghai's "clean-up" effort for

Plants occupying a vacant lot in central Shanghai

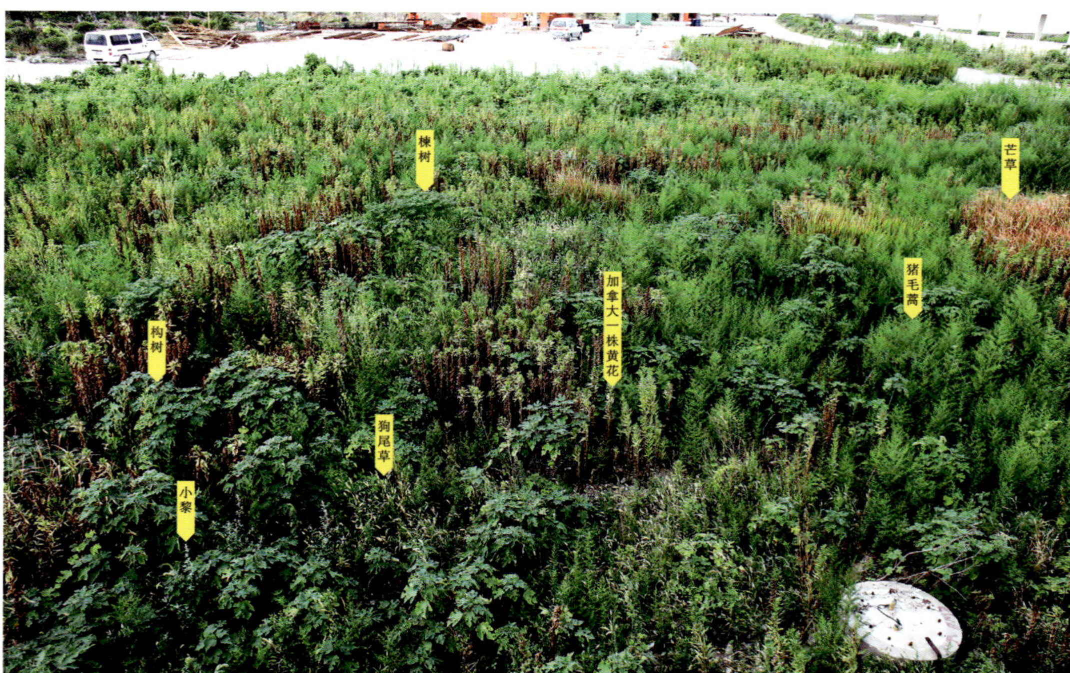

the 2010 World Expo. After the factory moved out, wild plants came in and occupied this piece of land. The organizer of the exhibition was planning to get rid of the "weeds" and transform the lot into a concrete plaza. We convinced the organizer to preserve this habitat as a piece of Land art. With the help of landscape designers and plant biologists, we identified over twenty different species in this area, created hand-drawn labels, and opened it to the public as a found botanical garden. One of the species we discovered at this urban "rewilded" site is wild soybean, *Glycine soja*, which has been declared a vulnerable species due to the lightning urbanization and development of recent decades. Another plant, Canada goldenrod, *Solidago canadensis*, has a fascinating history. It was brought to Shanghai in the 1930s, when the city was becoming a global metropolis. Originally introduced as a decorative flower, this plant has since become an invasive species, seriously affecting local farming.

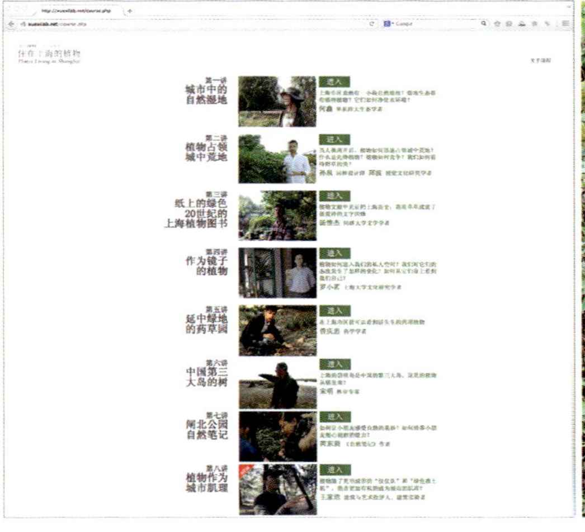

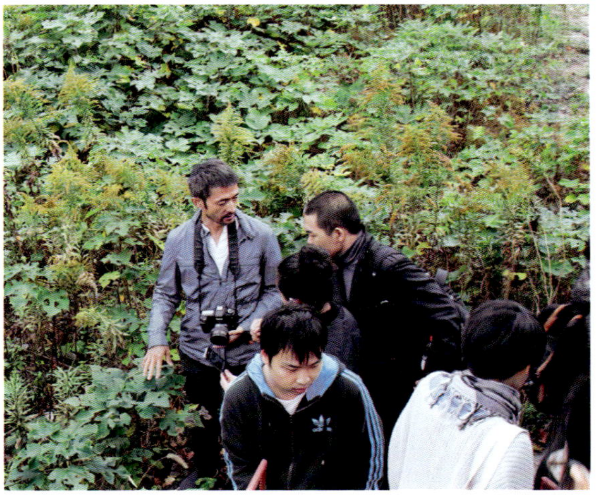

MOOC combined with offline discussions

In addition to this site-specific work, we created an eight-week mass open online course (MOOC). The MOOC phenomenon originated in American elite universities and has been growing rapidly in the English-speaking world. MOOCs are primarily produced within the institutional structure of the university and deliver supposedly universal knowledge. In contrast, our course was created outside the university and focused on local knowledge and local issues. We also experimented with an online-offline integrated format: each Monday, a lecture was uploaded to the Internet for public viewing; then on Sunday, a face-to-face discussion was organized by the lecturer for interested participants. We considered that both the online and offline spaces are valuable. The online space is less controlled by the state, thus presenting the most lively public arenas in China today. This is why all three projects described in this essay leverage the Internet. On the other hand, offline gatherings can lead to deeper discussions and more sustained engagement.

The course started with Dr. He Xin, a young conservationist, who revealed a healthy wetland ecology in Pudong area, which developed around a pool of water left untended by a construction project. After two science lectures, the course turned to the humanities. Tang Weijie, a literary scholar, discussed the history surrounding a set of books on Shanghai plants published in the mid-twentieth century, in particular a book issued as an internal document by the municipal government in 1961. Titled *Shanghai Wild Edible Plants*, it was meant to help people to find food in the wild during the Great Famine. Luo Xiaoming, a cultural studies scholar, explored how our relation to house plants has been changed by the consumption culture and the accelerating pace of life. Wang Jiahao, a critical urban studies theorist, analyzed the complex relation between nature, landscape, and the real estate industry. We used WeChat, a popular social networking app, to communicate with the public and to organize all activities.

Inspired by the slower temporality of plants, we view education as "slow activism." Like plants, we try to occupy space tactically and strive for sustainability within the Chinese political environment.

What sustains the naked emperor is not just the emperor; it's also the public, who, for many reasons, does not perform the role of citizens. The three projects I have described briefly in this essay are not merely intended to annoy the emperor; they are also meant to activate the idea of the citizen. To be a citizen is not just to vote. It is to work hard to find out what happened in history, to understand what is going on around us, and to take part in big and small actions to make the world a better place, for all human beings, and for all life forms.

Pictures of protests shown in the *global aCtIVISm* exhibition at the ZKM | Karlsruhe, 2014

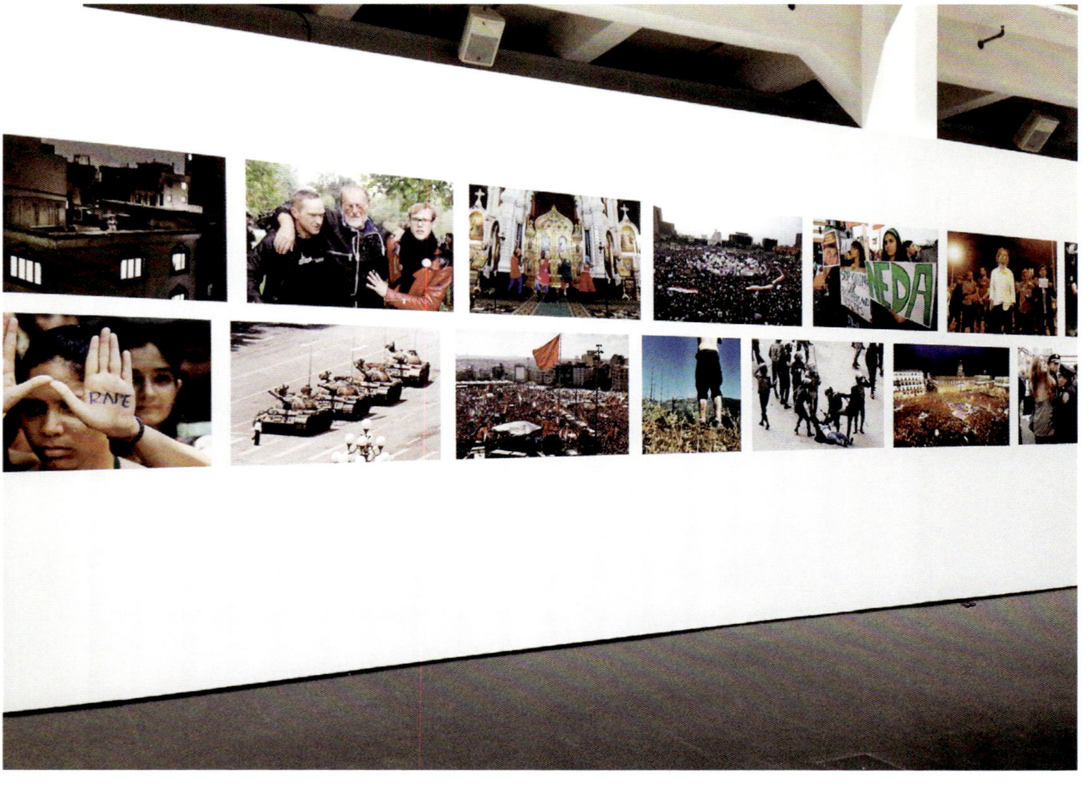

On entering the exhibition *global aCtIVISm* at ZKM | Karlsruhe, I was struck by the fact that China appears to be out of sync with the rest of the world. In a series of pictures in the main hall, we saw large-scale protests breaking out within the last few years around the world, with the exception of China – so the curator had to use the famous "Tank Man" photograph, which was taken 25 years ago. It is an apt reflection of reality: there are protests in China – mainly about land and environmental issues – but not in major cities, and not reaching the scale that can be considered a mass social movement. According to a 2013 survey conducted by the Washington-based Pew Research Center, 82% of respondents in China believe that their children will be better off, versus 37% in the U.S., 17% in the UK, and 9% in France. While some of us compare the existing system in China to other political alternatives – really existing ones or theorized – and believe that we need a better system, the great majority of Chinese people, including my parents, mostly compare China now to China in the past, and they are largely content. China is the amalgam of the world's fastest developing economy and one of the most tightly controlled states. It is difficult, if not impossible, for mass, direct, and confrontational performances to function as the dominant form of activist art in China. We have to be willing to take on projects that appear slow and unspectacular.

Lastly, I call upon the readers of this book to come and visit us. Over the past twenty years, many galleries and collectors from the West have come to China to do business, yet so few progressive art organizations have come to China. In the struggle against a globalized neoliberalism, it is unimaginable that a revived international front of the Left can afford to leave China behind.

www.zannybegg.com

Zanny Begg *1972

Sydney-based artist, writer, and curator Zanny Begg has held artist residencies in many institutions around the world, including an Australia-China Council Residency in Hong Kong (May 2007), an Asialink Residency in Indonesia (June 2008), a residency at Mess Hall in Chicago (2010), an Australia-Indonesia Institute Residency in Indonesia (2011), an Australia Council Residency in Barcelona (2012), and a residency from the Campbelltown Arts Centre at the Reiby Juvenile Justice Centre in Airds, New South Wales (2014). From 2010 to 2014 she was director of the Tin Sheds Gallery at the University of Sydney's Faculty of Architecture, Design and Planning. Currently Begg is employed as an academic at the University of New South Wales Art & Design faculty.

Her recent curatorial projects include *Salon Fluchthilfe* at the Secession in Vienna (2014), *Baadlands: An Atlas of Experimental Cartography* at Tin Sheds Gallery (2013), and *There Goes the Neighbourhood* at Performance Space in Sydney (2009). She has exhibited all over the world and taken part in several festivals and biennials, including the Sharjah Biennial (2011), the Istanbul Biennial (2010), and the Taipei Biennial (2008).

In her world map *The Agitators* (2007) Begg shows the locations of the most important forums and international political summits from 1994 to 2007 that were accompanied by massive antiglobalization protests. She connects the cities in the map by using key terms such as "multitude" and "empire," which references the writings of Michael Hardt and Antonio Negri. In this way Begg reveals the connectedness and interdependence of the world's cities.

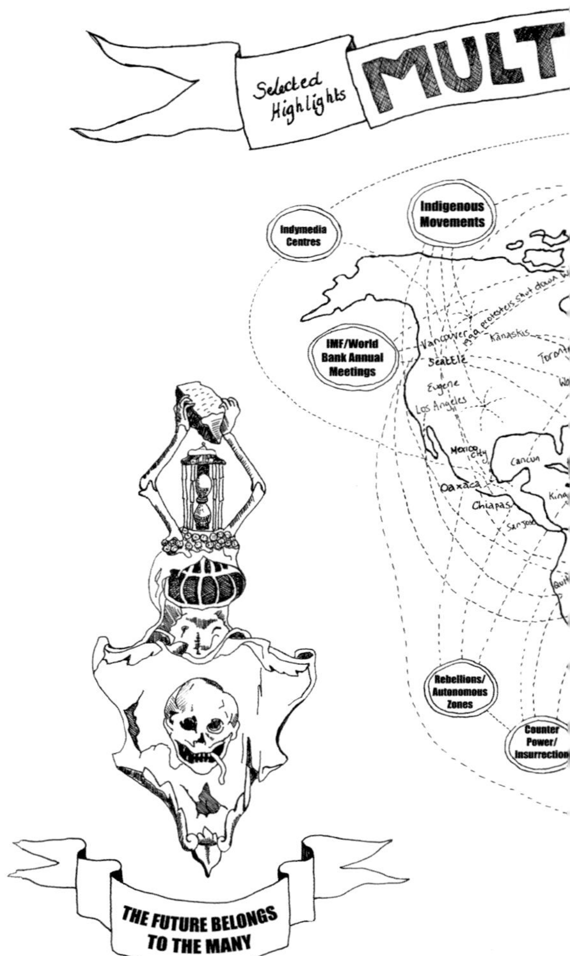

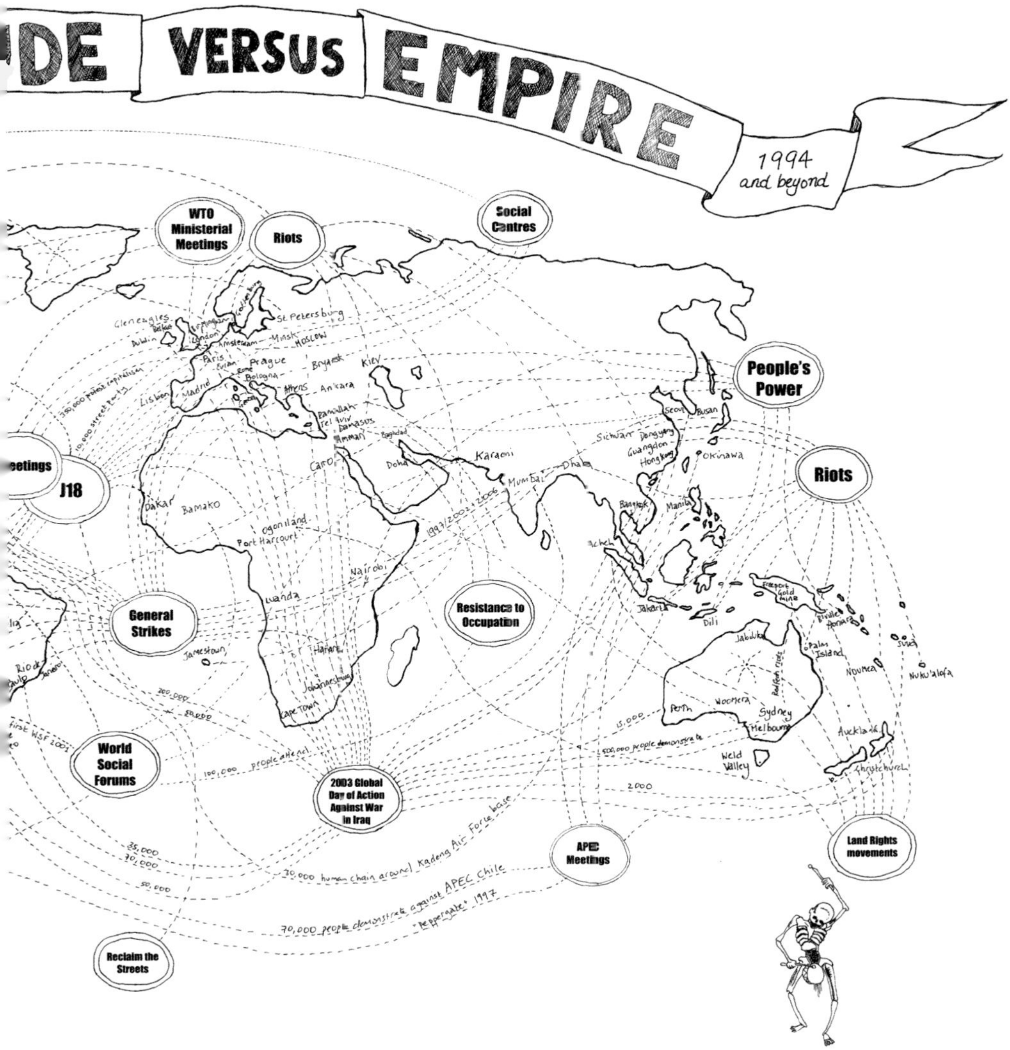

Zanny Begg, *Multitude vs. Empire*, 2013, wall drawing recreated from the series *The Agitators*, 2007

John Beieler *1989

John Beieler is a PhD student in political science at Pennsylvania State University, who deals with international relations – especially international conflicts and instances of political violence – political methodology, and computational methods. With the aid of the GDELT Event Database he created a visualization of worldwide protests since 1979, which is available online and was continuously updated until the end of 2013. The map only includes protests that consisted of more than ten events per month in a specific location.

Over time there appears to be a steady increase in events, but as Beieler explains this must not be mistaken as a general rise in the actual amount of protest behavior. Contrary to the depiction on the map the number of protests has remained relatively the same; due to the changes in reporting only the amount of data evaluated by GDELT has increased exponentially. On his homepage Beieler additionally provides the data from which the map is generated as well as other background information.

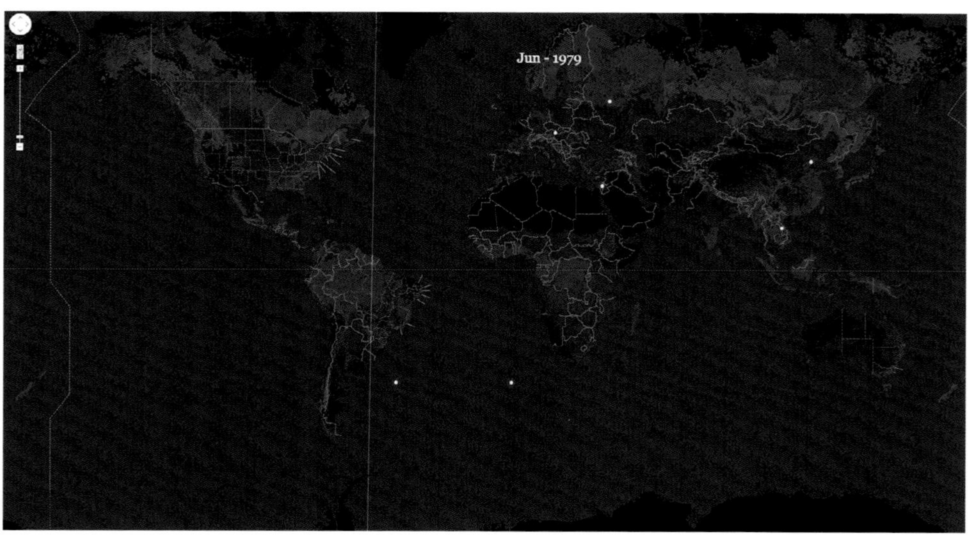

John Beieler, *Protest Mapping*, 2013, screenshots from the website, 10/07/2014

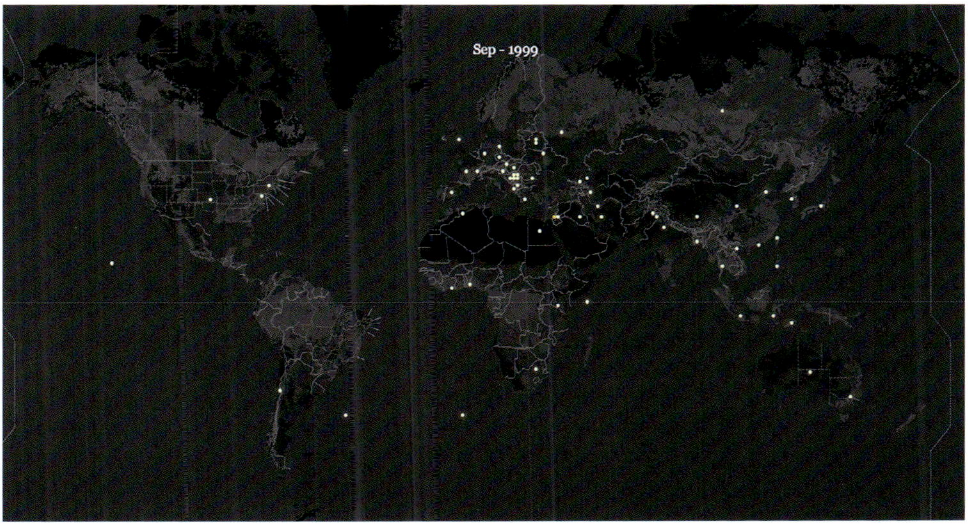
Sep - 1999

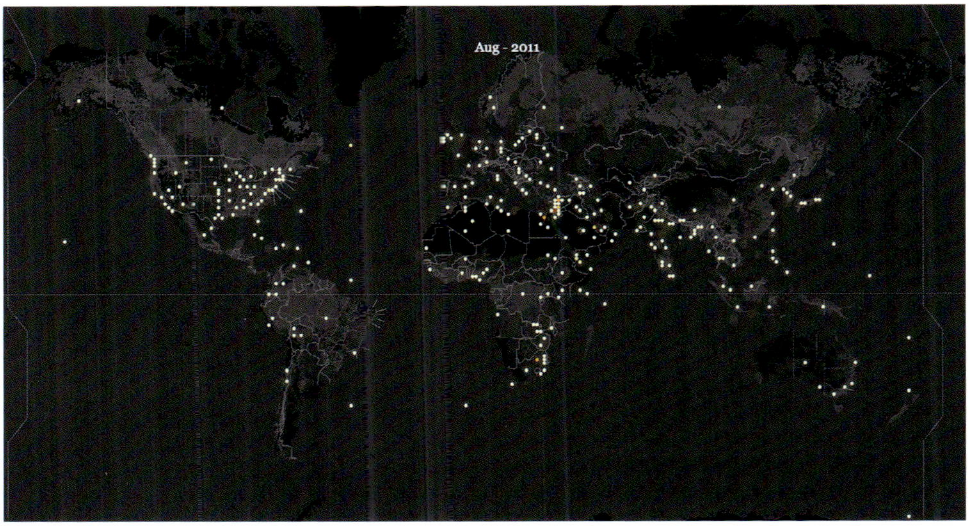
Aug - 2011

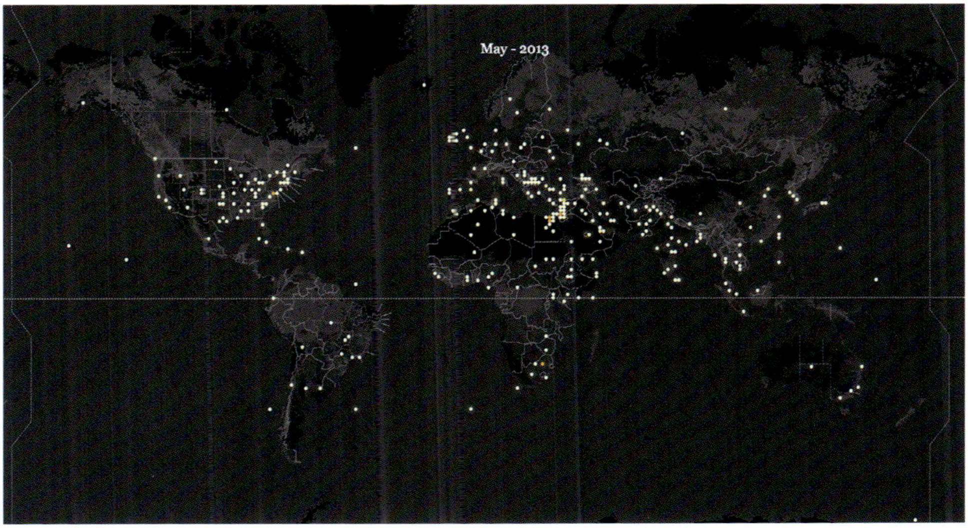
May - 2013

Campact

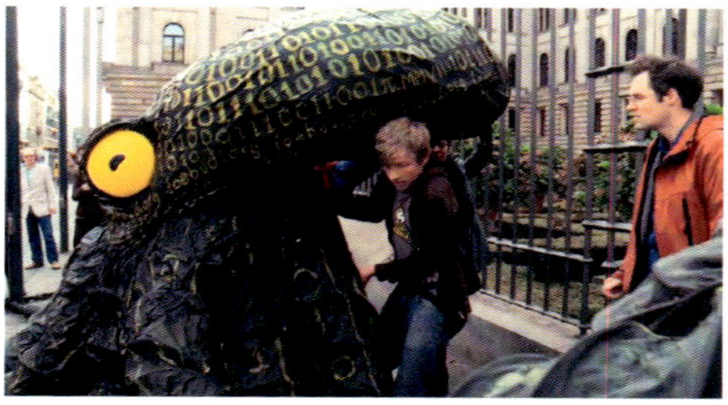

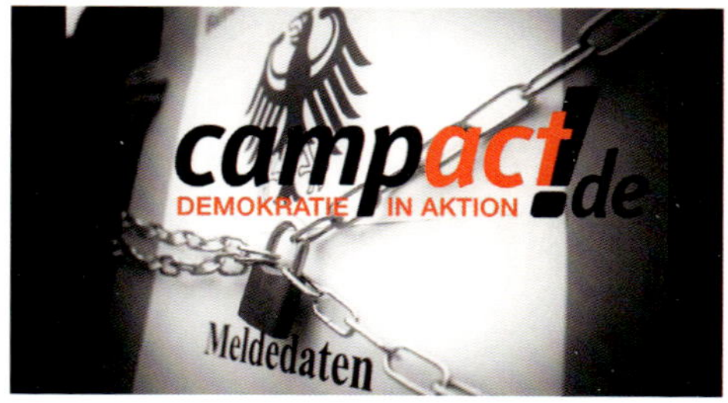

Campact, *Datenkrake stoppen!*, 2012, action against the registration act, Berlin

Campact is a registered nonprofit, nonparty, charitable association that seeks to inspire people to actively engage in and shape politics outside of elections, and to induce politicians to react to what their citizens want. Amongst other things, it organizes campaigns in which people participate in social debates via the Internet. The main instrument, the Campact Newsletter, already connects over 1,500,000 politically active people. Campact is not dedicated to specific topics; the issues it deals with must be of relevant public interest, are usually based on proposals of active Campact members, and must be in accordance with Campact's canon of values and its five declared goals:

- the promotion of an ecological transformation of society;
- the empowerment of democratic participation and the defending of civil rights;
- the strengthening of the welfare state and the restoring of the tax fairness;
- the creation of equality instead of discrimination and disadvantage;
- the fight for international justice and peaceful conflict resolutions.

Campact stands for increased democratic participation of each individual, demands the introduction of national referendums, and fights for more transparency, for example, full disclosure of politicians' additional earnings. Further, it campaigns for effective climate policies based on renewable energy, and opposes nuclear power. Its work is financed by donors and supporters, who can both support Campact as a whole, or specific activities or campaigns. All sources of funding and expenditure are presented in an annual transparency report.

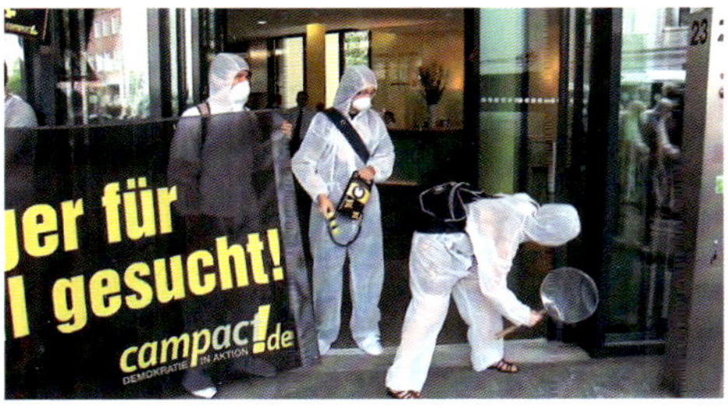

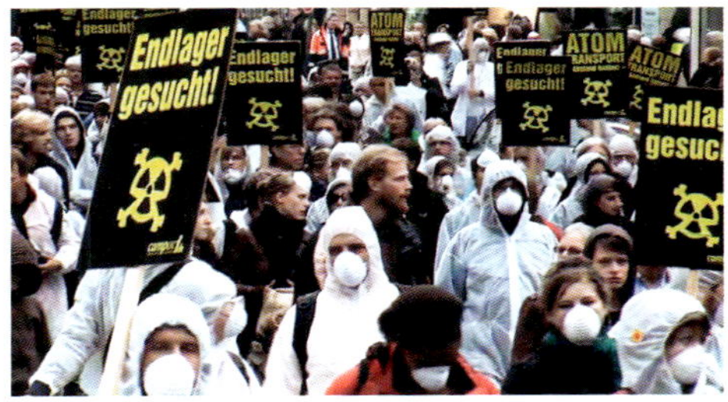

Campact, *Endlagersuche* 2009, searching for a repository for nuclear waste, twelve cities in Germany

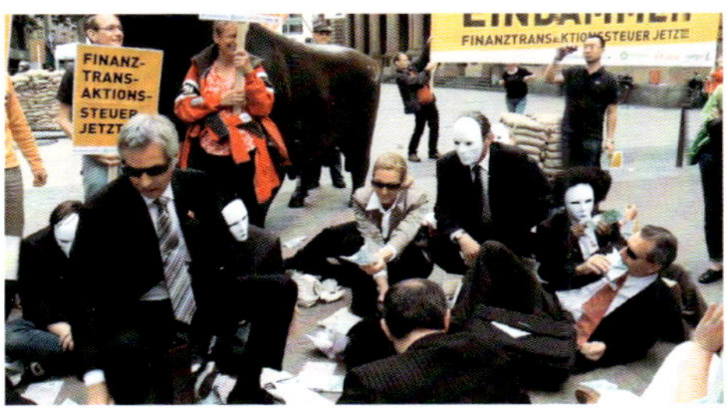

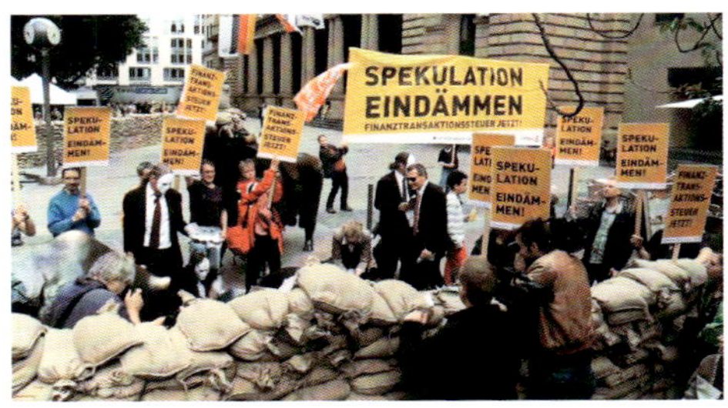

Campact, *Spekulation eindämmen!*, 2012, action for the introduction of a financial transaction tax, Frankfurt am Main

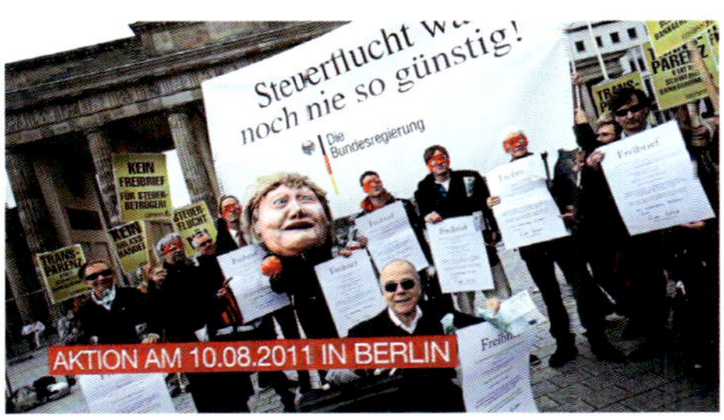

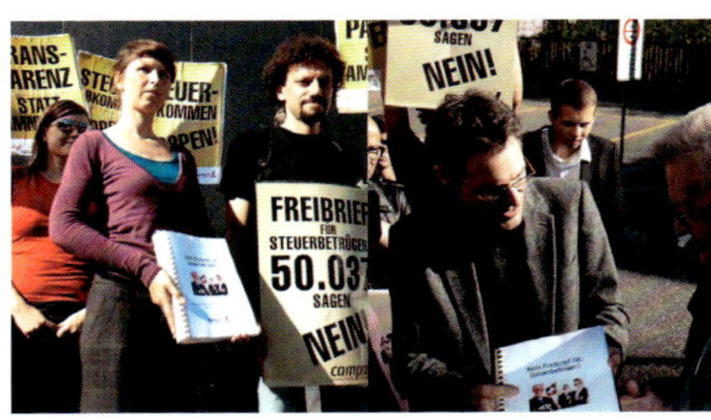

Campact, *Kein Freibrief für Steuerbetrüger!*, 2011, call for the introduction of a property tax in Germany and Switzerland

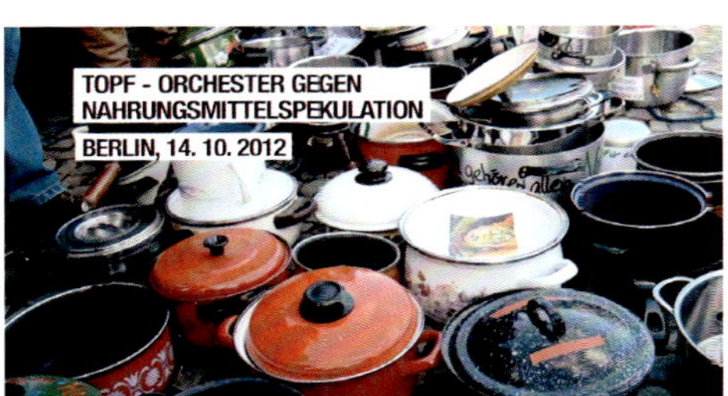

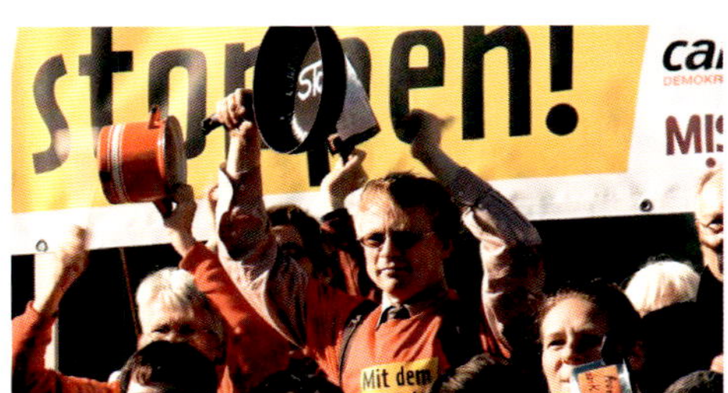

Campact, *Topf-Orchester gegen Nahrungsmittelspekulation*, 2012, protest with empty pots against food speculation, Berlin

CANVAS

The Centre for Applied Nonviolent Action and Strategies (CANVAS) was founded in Belgrade in 2004 by Slobodan Djinović and Srdja Popović, former leaders of the Serbian youth resistance movement Otpor! [Resistance!].

Otpor! started on October 10, 1998, as a reaction to the passing of two repressive university and media laws by the then Serbian government of Slobodan Milošević, in which especially the Prime Minister and Milošević-confidant Mirko Marjanović was instrumental. Ideologically, Otpor! was oriented on *The Politics of Nonviolent Action* (1973), one of Gene Sharp's main works, which was partially translated into Serbian. The nonviolent campaigns that took place in the following two years spread quickly across the whole of Serbia through the support of more than seventy thousand national supporters and the financial support of the American government. Otpor! is considered to have had a crucial influence in the downfall of President Milošević on October 5, 2000. Their distinctive symbol – a raised fist – was often seen on t-shirts, posters, and the walls of buildings. The key medium, however, was a sticker proclaiming "Gotov je!" ("He is finished!"). In 2003, a political party emerged from the group, but in the following parliamentary elections it failed to achieve five percent of the votes, and was subsequently absorbed into the Democratic Serbian Party (DSS).

With its website and workshops CANVAS continues to pursue the goals that Otpor! formulated in the 1990s. It has worked with pro-democracy activists from more than fifty countries, and its training methods to empower nonviolent movements has been successfully used by groups in the Ukraine (2004), in Lebanon (2005), and recently in Egypt (2011). Participation in the workshops is free, and all reports, books, and articles can be downloaded free of charge. CANVAS is a nonprofit institution that is funded entirely by private donations and categorically rejects funding from the public sector or from individual governments.

Facing page:
CANVAS, *Making Oppression Backfire*, campaign and book, published in Serbia in 2013 and available online at: www.canvasopedia.org

MAKING OPPRESSION BACKFIRE

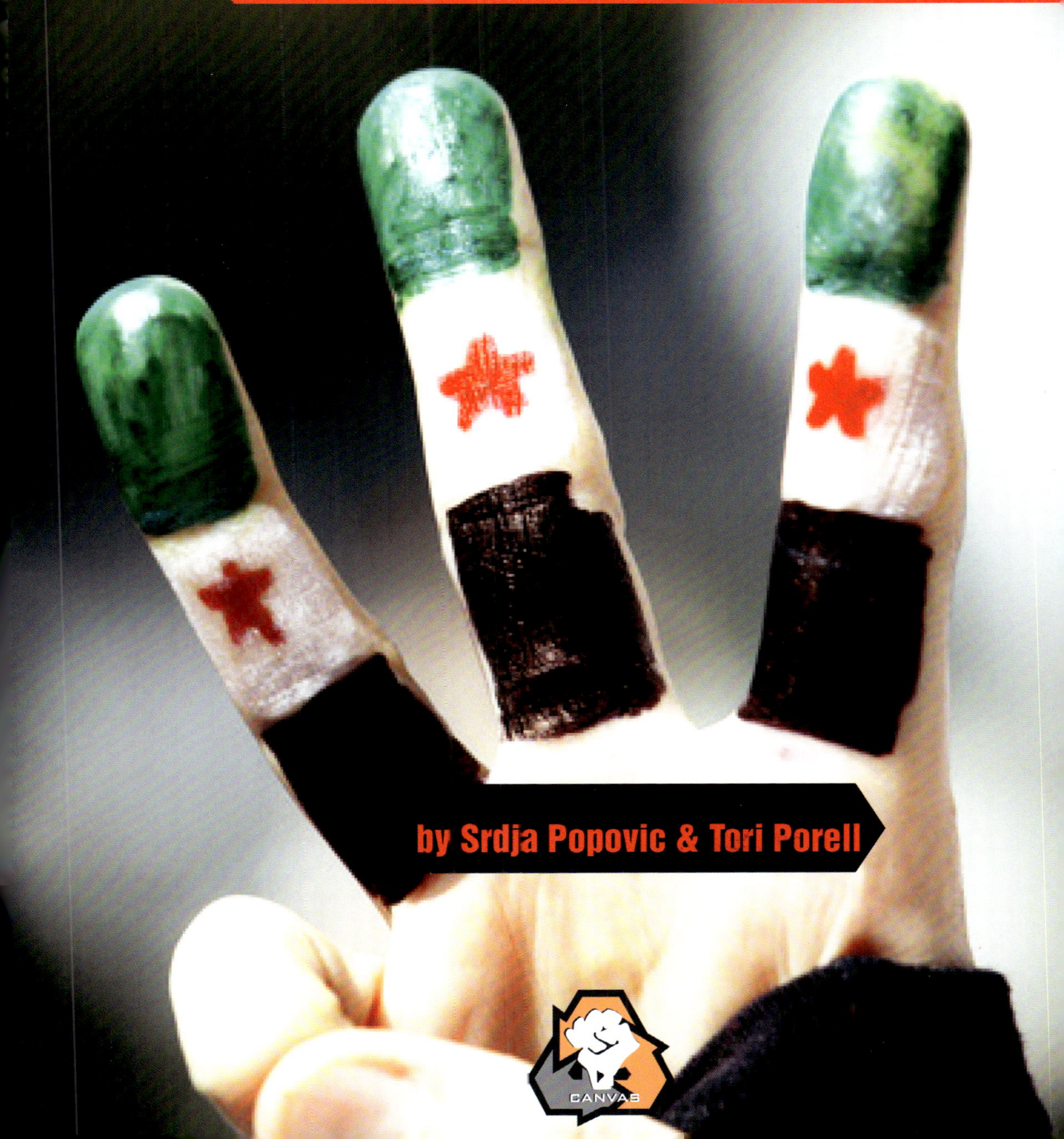

by Srdja Popovic & Tori Porell

Ralf Christensen *1971

Ralf Christensen is a writer, editor, radio host, and documentarist born in Denmark. He has been writing and doing radio shows about music and cultural resistance since the mid-1990s. His filmography includes *Good Copy Bad Copy* (2007) and *The Soft Beating* (2010), a documentary music video for the Danish indie rock group Efterklang.

His 2012 documentary *Pockets of Resistance* explores peaceful strategies for civil disobedience. Christensen identifies creative forms of protest and their global spread, citing key examples such as the COP15 demonstrators in Copenhagen, confrontations in front of the Bolivian parliament, a voice performance in Egypt, and interactive political street theater in Nepal. In addition to examining the evolving nature of protest, Christensen's film also addresses the rapid dissemination of alternative protest forms through new media.

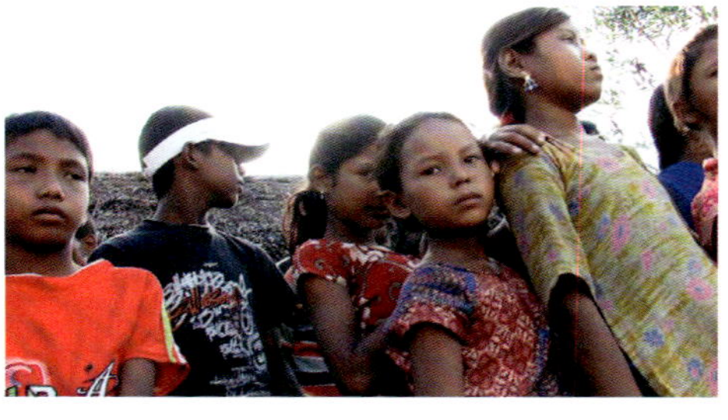

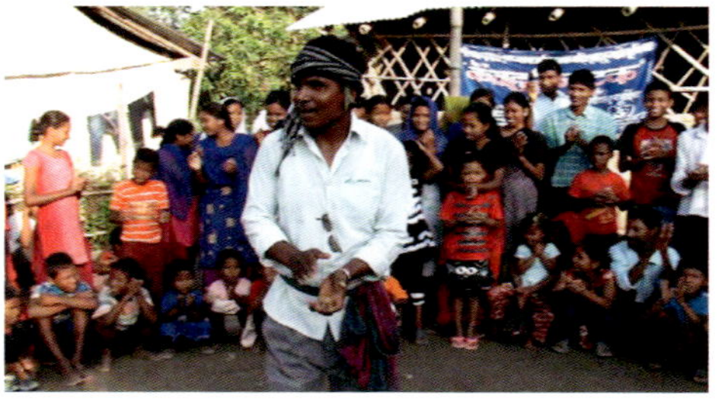

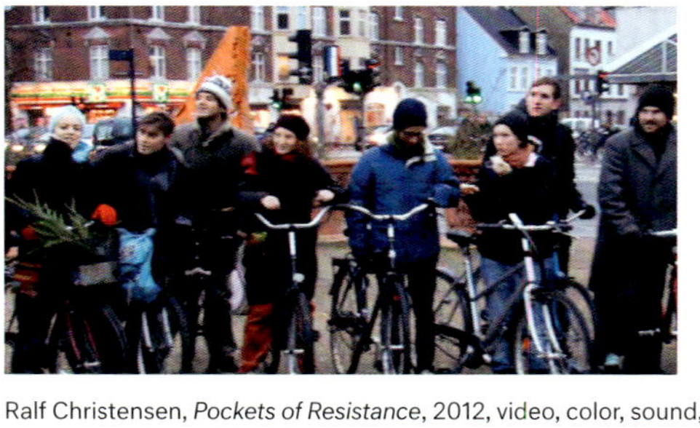

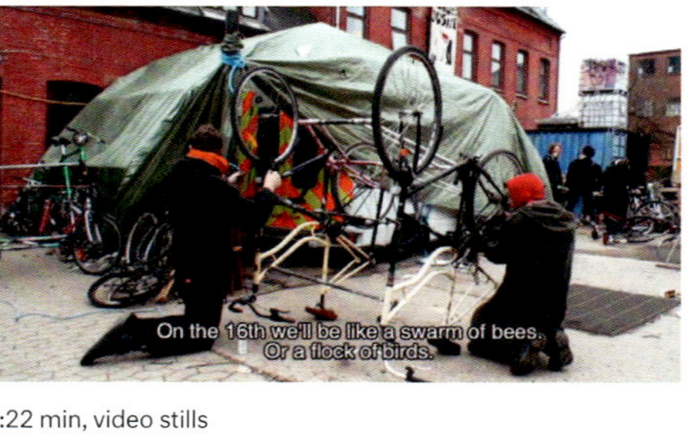

Ralf Christensen, *Pockets of Resistance*, 2012, video, color, sound, 64:22 min, video stills

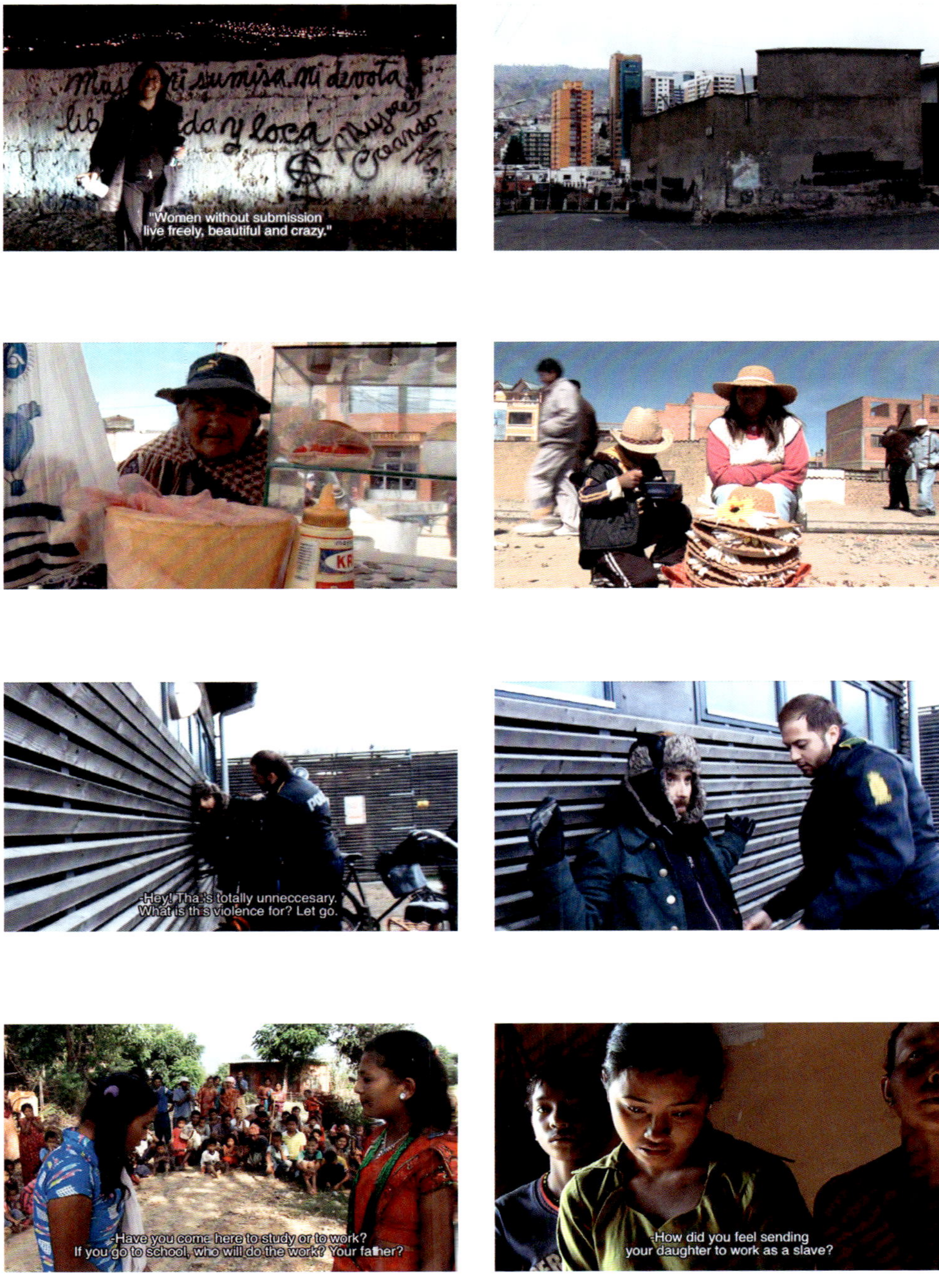

Ralf Christensen, *Pockets of Resistance*, 2012, video, color, sound, 64:22 min, video stills

www.lessentiersdelutopie.wordpress.com
www.labofii.net

Isabelle Fremeaux *1973 and John Jordan *1965

Until she decided to turn her back on academia in December 2011, Isabelle Fremeaux had since 2002 been a senior lecturer in media and cultural studies at the Birkbeck College, University of London. Together with John Jordan – cofounder of the direct action groups Reclaim the Streets and the Clandestine Insurgent Rebel Clown Army, cinematographer for Avi Lewis and Naomi Klein's *The Take* (2004), and coeditor of *We Are Everywhere. The Irresistible Rise of Global Anticapitalism* (Verso, 2003) – Fremeaux founded the art activism collective The Laboratory of Insurrectionary Imagination (Labofii), which deliberately blurs the boundaries between art and life, resistance and creativity. Labofii has recently built the postcapitalist commune La r.O.n.c.e. (resist. Organize. nourish. create. exist.) on a farm in Brittany and is currently setting up a school for art activism and permaculture.

Les Sentiers de l'Utopie [Paths through Utopia] (2012) documents a seven-month trip of the two artists and activists Isabelle Fremeaux and John Jordan through Europe. Shot as a fictional documentary, this movie is set in an imagined postfinancial crash future. It explores a postcapitalist Europe, in which the artists visit various utopian collectives and seemingly anarchistic collective projects. From the illegal Climate Camp in Heathrow airport in London, French punk artists, self-run Serbian factories to a "free love" commune in an ex-Stasi base, the documentary presents a world where money is useless.

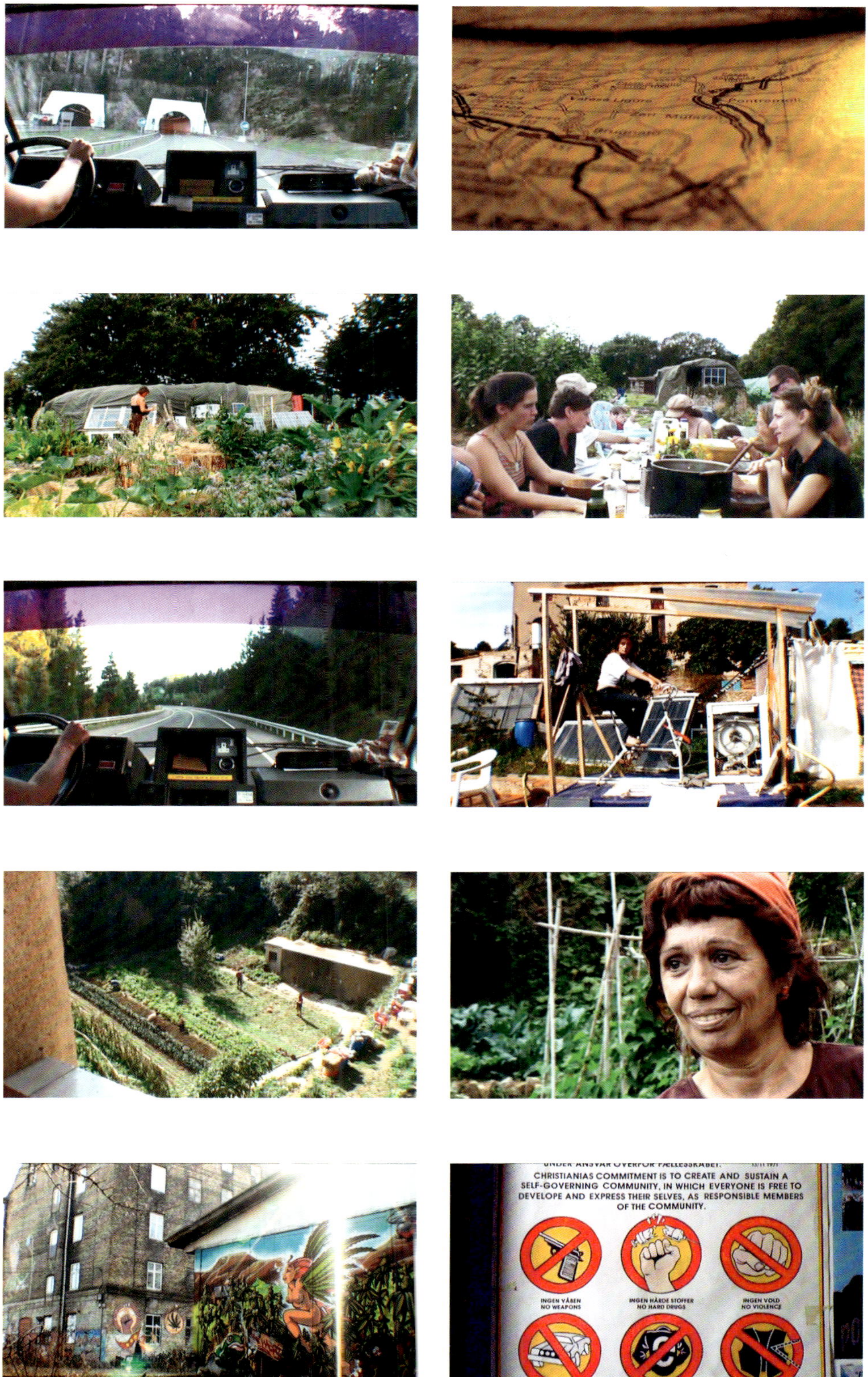

Isabelle Fremeaux and John Jordan, *Les Sentiers de l'Utopie*, 2012, video, sound, color, 109:00 min, video stills

Sasha Kurmaz *1986

Sasha Kurmaz was born in Kiev, where he lives and works today and where he studied at the Design Department of the National Ukrainian State Academy of Arts. With regard to the contemplation and understanding of a work of art, he explicitly takes social and political structures into account and uses different media as a way to work with these aspects, as well as to present different levels of visual perception for the viewer. This is why he combines photography, installation, sculpture, painting, and public intervention in his artistic practice. In 2011, Kurmaz was artist in residence at the Artitude Kunstverein in Berlin and at IZOLYATSIA in Donetsk, Ukraine, a foundation which was forcibly displaced from its original location in June 2014 and since then is in exile in Kiev. In 2013, he took part in the International Workshop Program Must Act! in Minsk, Belarus, and in the International Exchange of Artists Project RutaRuna in Kiev and Sigtuna, Sweden. The following year he contributed to the Minister of Culture Scholarship Program Gaude Polonia in Krakow, Poland, and participated in the 4th Delai Sammit Informal Urban Initiatives Conference in Moscow. Since 2006, Kurmaz's work has been exhibited in several group and solo exhibitions in Europe, Russia, and the USA. He has participated in various festivals, including the 2013 International Contemporary Art Festival Survival Kit in Riga and the 2013 International Photography Festival FORMAT 13 in Derby, UK, and published several books and articles.

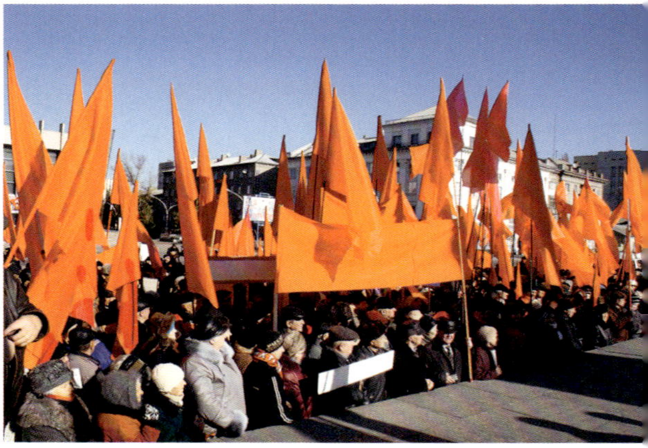

Sasha Kurmaz, from the mixed-media installation *Resistance. Color*, 2012, digital print, 10 × 15 cm, framed

In 2013, he was a finalist of the Pinchuk-ArtCentre Prize, Kiev, and the Art-Ovrag Public Art Award, Vyksa, Russia. At the 2010 award ceremony of the Kazimir Malevich Award in Kiev he was also in the final selection.

All over the world political parties associate themselves with certain colors. Thus, the use of colors also plays a major role in the context of political protests. Kurmaz's work *Resistance. Color* (2012) features pictures of protests from which all logos, slogans, and political symbols have been removed. His intention is to draw attention to the psychological effect of political advertising and to explore how color manipulates emotions in political communications.

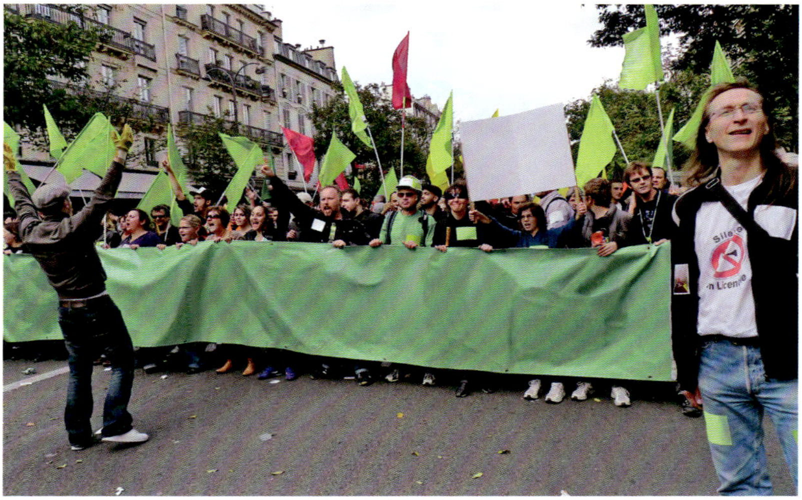

Sasha Kurmaz, from the mixed-media installation *Resistance. Color*, 2012, digital print, 30 × 45 cm

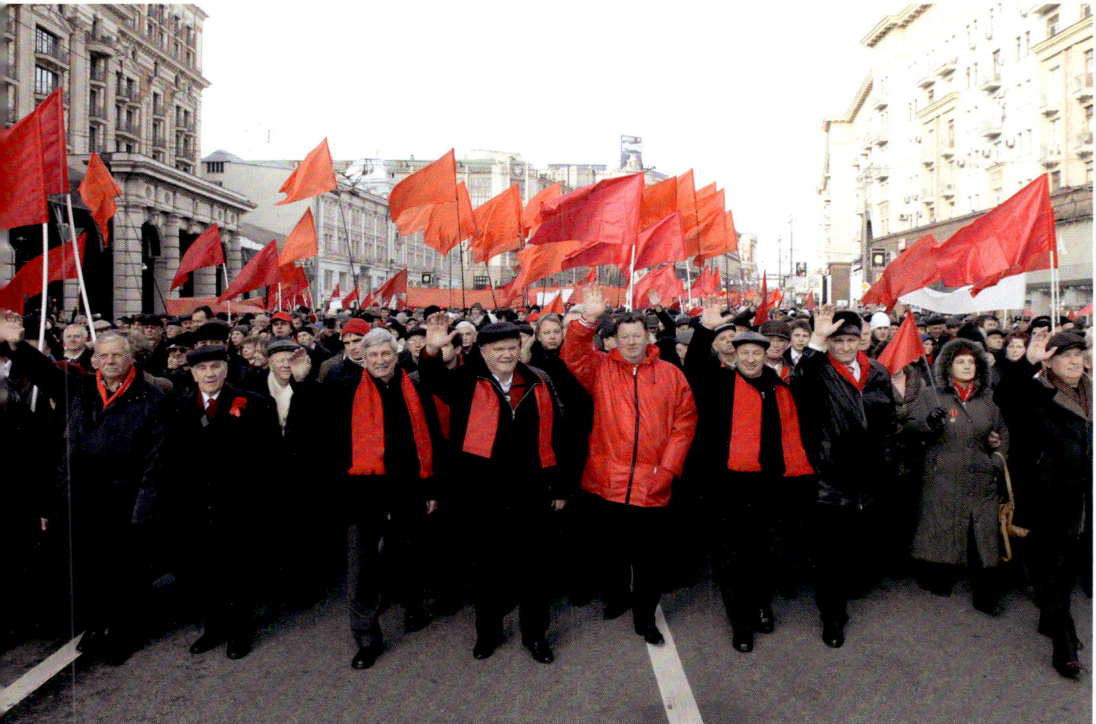

Sasha Kurmaz, from the mixed-media installation *Resistance. Color*, 2012, digital print, 30 × 45 cm

Julia Leser *1987 and Clarissa Seidel *1985

After graduating from high school, Julia Leser began to study Japanese studies and political science at the Leipzig University in 2008. Until August 2011, she spent a year abroad at Waseda University in Tokyo, Japan, which was interrupted by the earthquake on March 11 which was followed by the nuclear disaster in Fukushima. Clarissa Seidel studied media, communication sciences, and intercultural knowledge communication in Halle (Saale) and audiovisual communication in Madrid, Spain. After her last examination she took a trip to Japan, which ended with the earthquake on March 11, 2011.

The experience of the two women led to the planning of the joint film project *RADIOACTIVISTS – Protest in Japan since Fukushima* (2011), a documentary about the anti-nuclear-power movement in Japan after the Fukushima disaster in 2011.

In their film, Leser and Seidel seek to provide an insight into Japanese protest culture, explore the effects of the nuclear catastrophe on people's behavior, and throw light on the background to the 2011 uprisings all over the world. The documentary follows the activist group Shiroto no ran [Amateurs' Revolt]. Although there is not really an established protest culture in Japan, this group of creative activists persistently fights for more freedom in the public sphere and a do-it-yourself culture in Tokyo. They succeeded in organizing the biggest demonstration since the 1970s in Japan just one month after the earthquake that destroyed the Fukushima nuclear power plant.

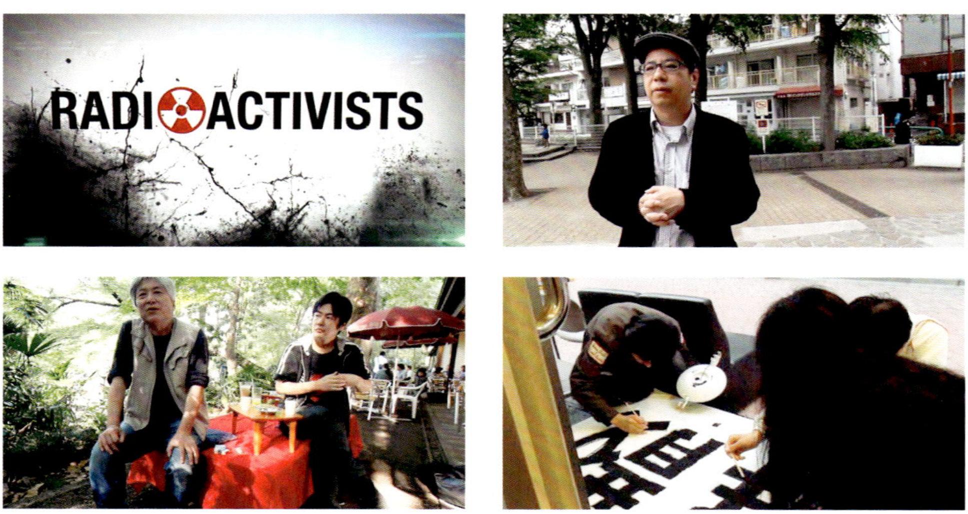

Julia Leser and Clarissa Seidel, *RADIOACTIVISTS – Protest in Japan since Fukushima*, 2011, video, color, sound, 73:00 min, video stills

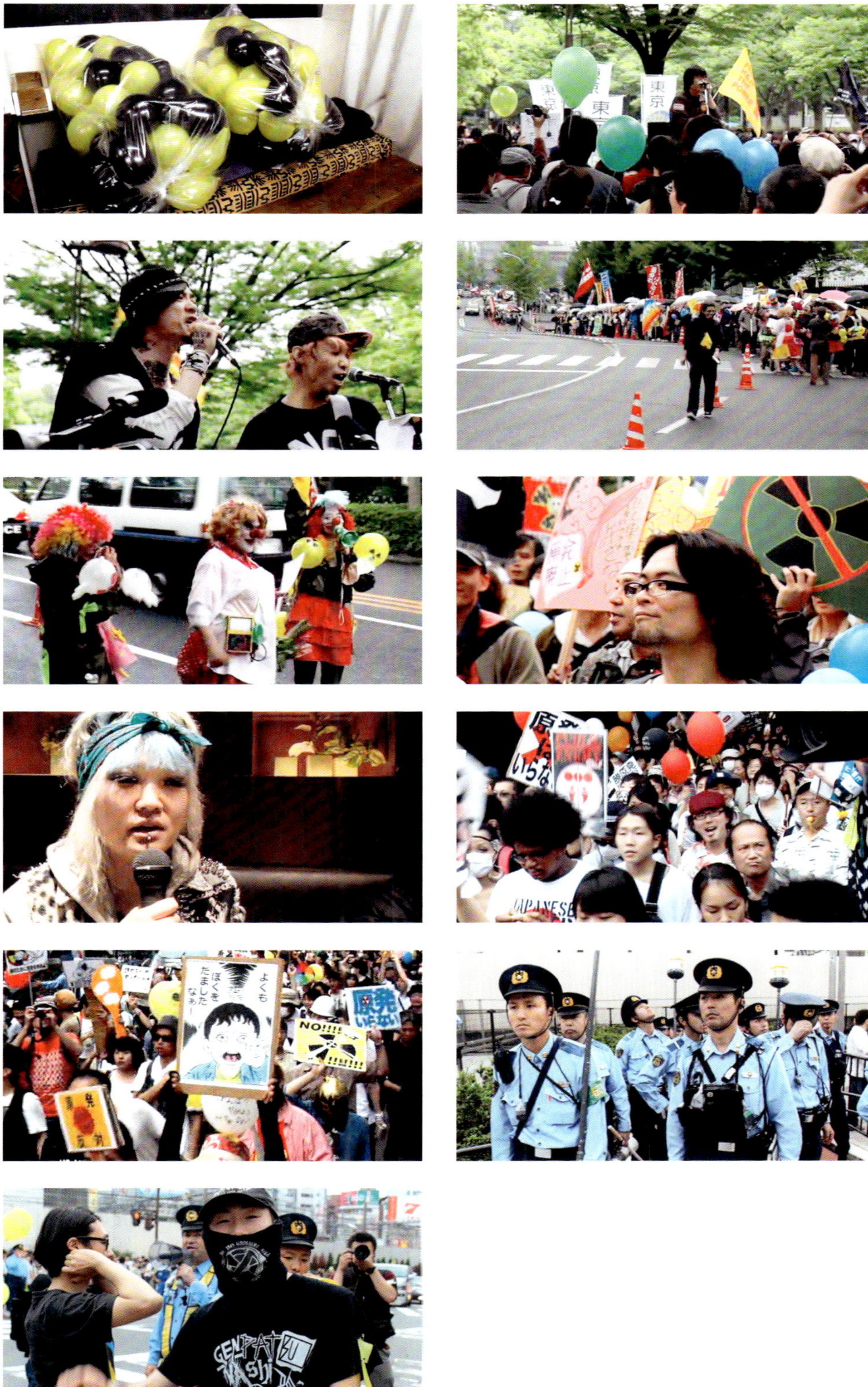

Julia Leser and Clarissa Seidel, *RADIOACTIVISTS – Protest in Japan since Fukushima*, 2011, video, color, sound, 73:00 min, video stills

Founded in 2011
Russia

http://partizaning.org

Partizaning

Partizaning is a Moscow-based project of urban activists, who intend to change city life through art-based "partizaning" tactics. The term "partizaning" circumscribes a new phenomenon, which aims at the fusion of approaches from street art and social activism. The members of the project try to demonstrate how nonexternally controlled and self-motivated actions and campaigns can jump-start social and cultural change. To this end they focus explicitly on do-it-yourself activism that seeks to rethink, restructure, and improve urban environments and communities.

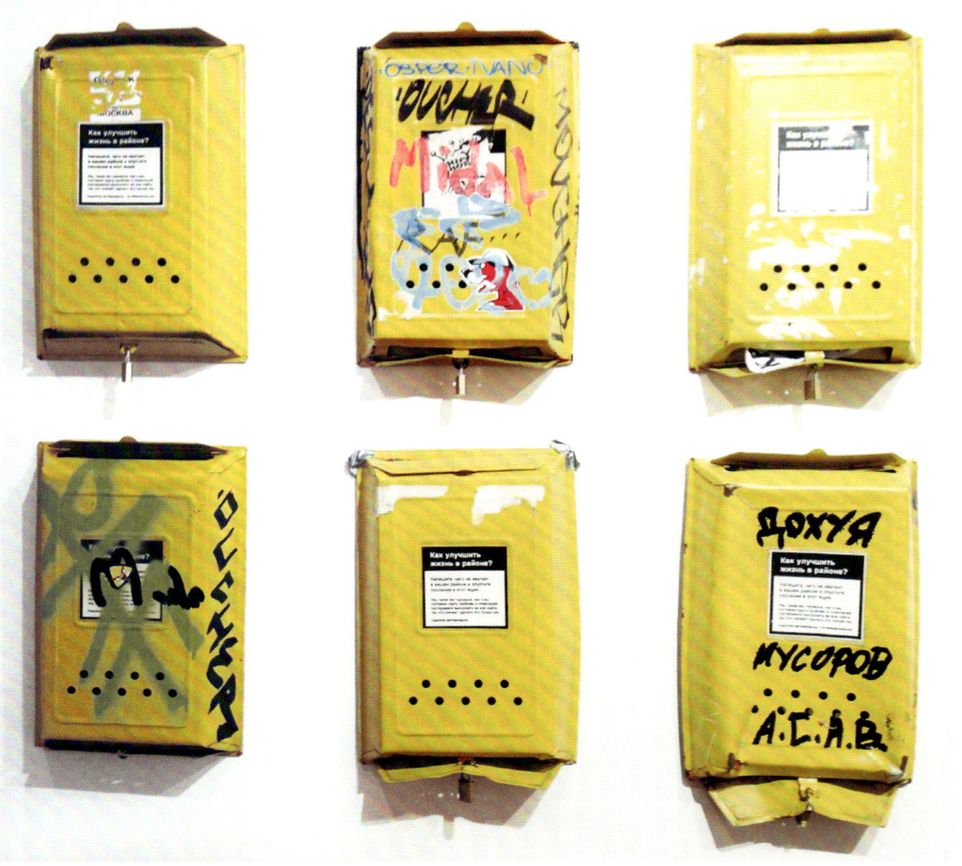

Partizaning, installation of public mailboxes, one task of *Micro Activism. An urban tactics game to safe the city!*, 2013

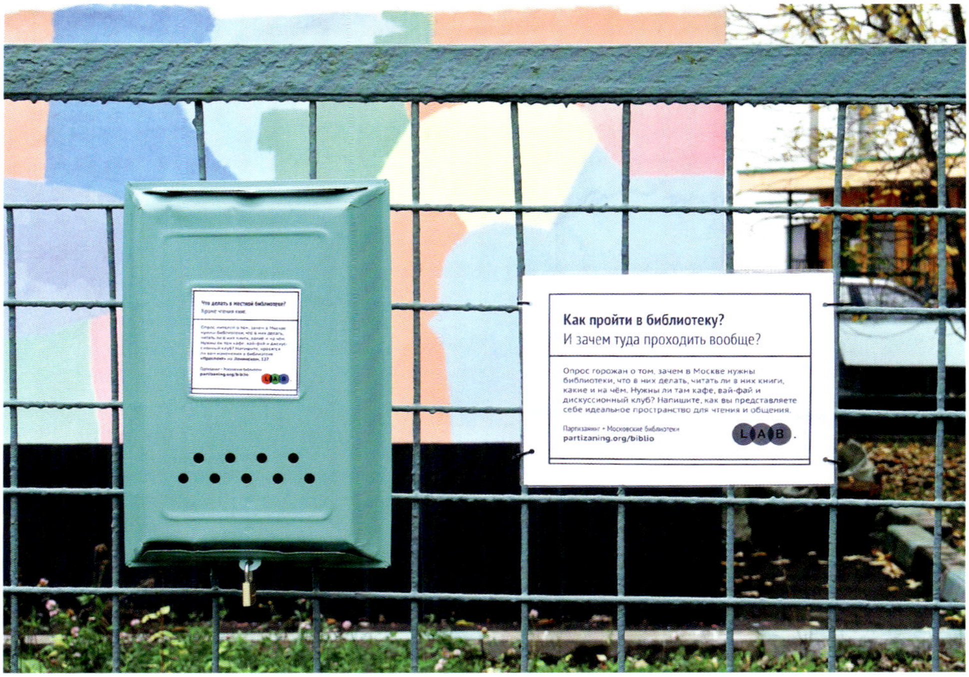

Partizaning, installation of public mailboxes, one task of *Micro Activism. An urban tactics game to safe the city!*, 2013

Manifesto

Throughout the twentieth century, artistic movements have sought to challenge and break from traditional notions of art. This constant blurring of boundaries now means that any act or work done by an artist may be regarded as an object of art. Today, the distinction between art and nonart is almost impossible to make, and any classification is subjective.

Since the 1920s, radical artistic experiments have sought to destroy the boundaries between art and everyday life. Old industrial buildings, city streets, the Internet, and mass media are increasingly replacing museums and galleries as the ideal forums and exhibition venues for modern art.

Today's activist urban residents do not think of art as a distinct system. They use the language of art as a tool to challenge and change their daily reality: from do-it-yourself urban repair to struggling for new forms of state representation.

Unsanctioned interventions and interactions in our urban environments, combined with mass media connectivity, have become effective transformative tactics for a new, alternative vision for the future.

Partizaning is not just the name of our website. It is also a term to define a new phenomenon and strategy at the intersection of street art and social activism. We devised this term in Russia, where we demonstrate in a revolutionary tradition how self-motivated, unauthorized statements and unsolicited action can become key drivers of social and cultural change.

Our goal is to reflect and promote the idea of art-based do-it-yourself activism aimed at rethinking, restructuring, and improving urban environments and communities.

Partizaning: public art practices which strategically challenge, shape, and reinvent urban and social realities.

Rules

Learn DIY-tactics, while competing with 2-10 players. Roll the dice, follow the arrows and the special signs. Download the game and use a virtual dice here: **eng.partizaning.org/game**

Skip your turn

Roll again

Follow the arrow

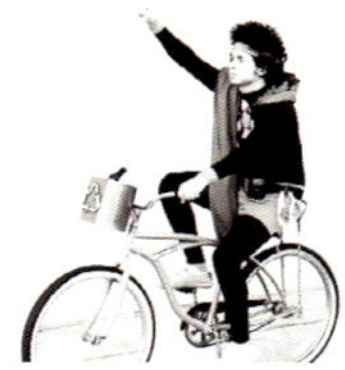

Finish

You've solved most of the city's issues!
(But what about your own?)

Cl
E

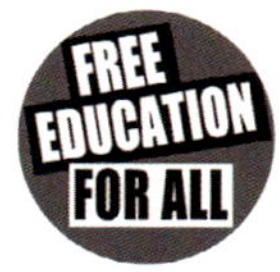

You are arrested for hosting unsanctioned parties in public space

You waste time looking for fresh and affordable food

Free education! Occupy the local university

Draw a community map with people in the neighborhood

p

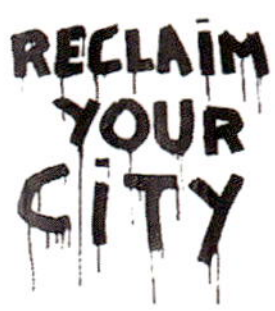

Write a manifesto explaining the right to the city

Your flashmob pillowfight is shutdown by police

Set up a free café for Restaurant Day!

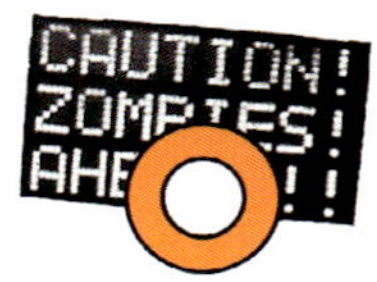

Blocked! Highway construction disrupts your commute

Can
th

Q: Do you grow your own herbs?

If not:

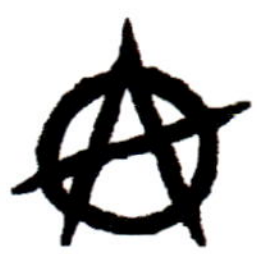

Discuss DIY-ism with anarchists and environmentalists

You print and share pamphlets about self-organizing

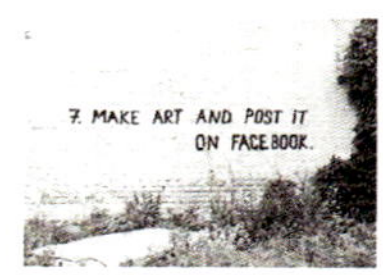

Use social media to promote your ideas

To
ca

Your cycle skids on tramrails and you hurt your knee

Paint crosswalks and wayfinding signs in your neighborhood

You're busy squatting to save a historic building

Exhausted. There's nowhere to sit!

Start
to b
in

It's your first day in a new city!

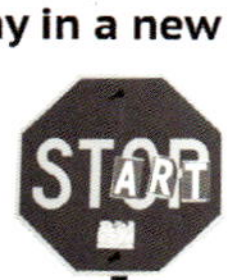

Start

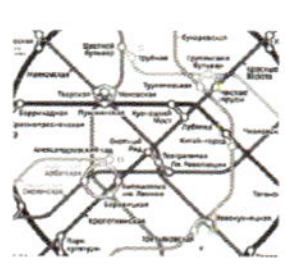

Try to figure out the public transport system map

A neighbor suggests you try a local organic bakery

Your bus is stuck in a traffic jam

B
creat

ge!
s

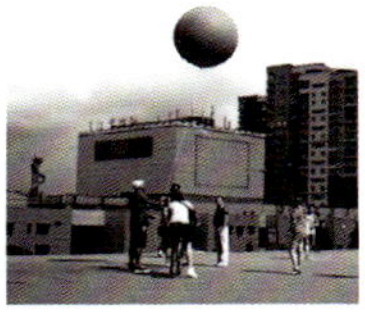

Balloon map the whole city!

Municipal authorities are upset with your unsanctioned repairs

You caught a cold on No Pants Day. Take it easy

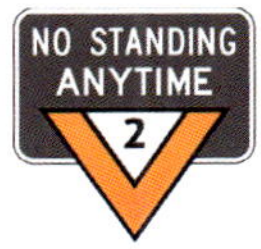

Government proposes a law against public gatherings

x

You hurt yourself trying to parkour

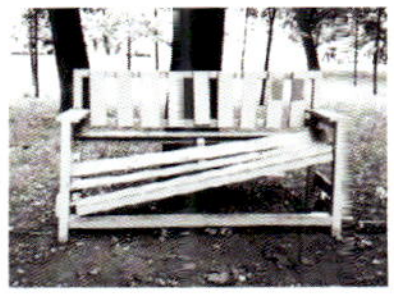

Take time to rethink your strategy

You forgot to involve elderly people in your projects

People are upset that you don't act on their suggestions

ve
t!

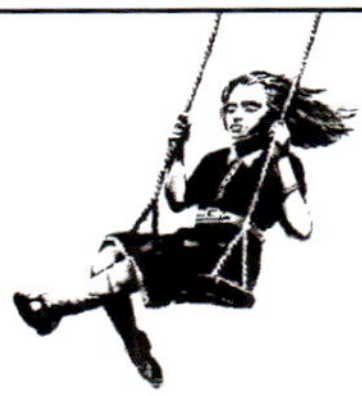

Build a swing at the bus-stop

Your landlord is renovating and raises the rent

You're part of a controversial political performance. Lay low

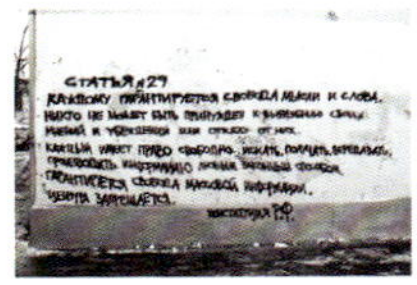

Write the constitution on walls so people know their rights

V
d

Too much volunteering. You have no money to pay rent

Mark safe cycling routes in the city

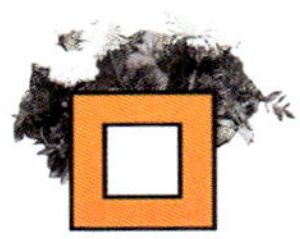

Set up a guerrilla garden for your community

Hack an ad! Take back public space

paign
ags
ts

You found a copy of the activist's cookbook —start brainstorming!

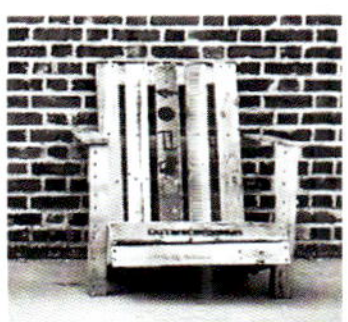

Chair bomb the pavements!

Micro Activism

An urban tactics game to save the city!

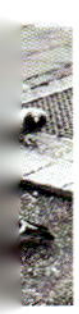

d
rap!

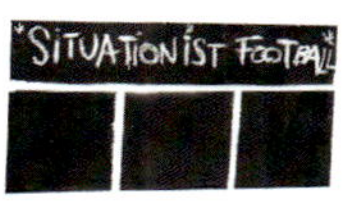

Invent a sport to play with other locals

Borrow a bicycle and start to explore the city

PARTIZANING

Participatory urban replanning.

eng.partizaning.org

Oliver Ressler *1970

Austrian artist and filmmaker Oliver Ressler lives and works in Vienna, where he studied at the University for Applied Arts Vienna from 1989 to 1995. He produces installations, films, and projects in public spaces that deal with socially and politically significant issues, such as democracy, economics, racism, climate change, and various forms of resistance. With his works, Ressler seeks to blur the boundaries between art and activism. Over the years, he has collaborated with numerous international artists and participated in more than 150 exhibitions, including the biennials in Prague (2005), Seville (2006), Moscow (2007), and Taipei (2008). Since 2000, he has produced and coproduced nearly twenty films, which were shown at film festivals and presentations around the world. In 2002, Ressler's video *This Is What Democracy Looks Like!* was awarded the first prize of the \\international\ media\ art\award of the ZKM | Center for Art and Media Karlsruhe.

Democracy is also the theme of Ressler's video work *WHAT IS DEMOCRACY?* (2009). "What is democracy?" is not one question, it is actually two questions. On the one hand, the question relates to conditions prevailing in contemporary representative parliamentary democracies and these are scrutinized critically in this project. On the other hand, the question interrogates different approaches to what a more democratic system might look like and which organizational forms it could take.

The project posed the question "What is democracy?" to numerous activists and political analysts in eighteen cities around the world, in Amsterdam, Berkeley, Berlin, Bern, Budapest, Copenhagen, London, Melbourne, Moscow, New York, Paris, Rostock, San Francisco, Sydney, Taipei, Tel Aviv, Thessaloniki, and Warsaw. The interviews were recorded on video beginning in January 2007. Even though all interviewees were asked the same question, the result was a multiplicity of different perspectives and viewpoints from people living in countries that are usually labeled "democracies."

This pool of interviews builds the basis for eight videos, which are presented in an 8-channel video installation. The installation (re)presents a kind of global analysis of the profound political crises of the Western democratic model.

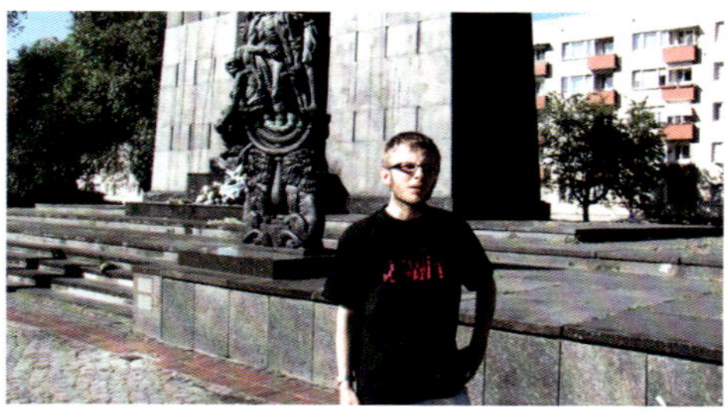

Oliver Ressler, *WHAT IS DEMOCRACY?*, 2009, 8-channel video installation, color, sound, video stills, here: Adam Ostolski (Warsaw)

In one video, Adam Ostolski (Warsaw) says that originally "the modern idea of democracy was connected to the notion of progress" and parliamentary states "had some tendency to become more and more democratic by including new types of political actors, such as workers and women. […] But since the 1980s, since the neoliberal trend in politics and economy, we have a regression of democracy." Lize Mogel (New York) notes that the situation changed in such a way that when you think about representative democracy today "you are not necessarily talking about individuals being represented, but more about capital

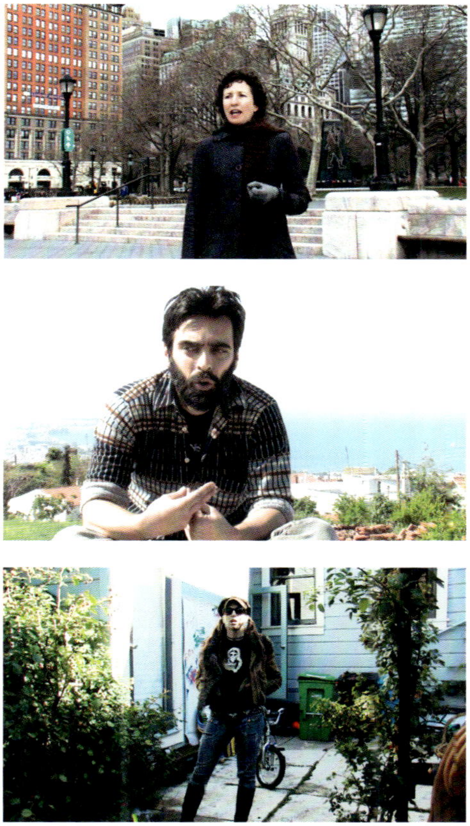

Oliver Ressler, *WHAT IS DEMOCRACY?*, 2009, 8-channel video installation, color, sound, video stills, from top to bottom: Lize Mogel (New York), Nikos Panagos (Thessaloniki), and Lisa Gray-Garcia (San Francisco)

being represented." Nikos Panagos (Thessaloniki) even argues that "representation and democracy are incompatible terms. Therefore, under no circumstances could the present system be called a democracy. It is just a sophisticated form of oligarchy." Lisa Gray-Garcia (San Francisco) seems to agree, when she labels representative democracy a "fake democracy." While some subjects in the videos elaborate the activists' ideas of direct democracy or decision-making processes of indigenous communities, David McNeill (Sydney) raises the issue of whether it makes sense "to continue contesting for the right to own and define the term democracy," or whether "it has been so corrupted and polluted by the conservatives that claimed ownership of it, that it is better to be surrendered."

The 8-channel video installation discusses the contested notion of "democracy," which is misused by those in power to maintain public order, while at the same time "democracy" still represents an ideal that hundreds of millions of people in the global south desperately want to achieve. Today it seems almost impossible to be against "democracy," even though it is getting emptier and emptier. A potential strategy could try to fill what is called "democracy" with new meaning. In this sense, the installation presents a multilayered discourse on democracy, which expresses a broad range of opinions that go beyond the borders of nation-states and continents.

The eight videos have the following titles:

- *Rethinking representation* (16:00 min)
- *Politics of exclusions* (23:00 min)
- *Secrecy instead of democratic transparency* (13:00 min)
- *New democracies?* (23:00 min)
- *Is representative democracy a democracy?* (22:00 min)
- *Direct democracy* (22:00 min)
- *Reclaiming Indigenous politics* (18:00 min)
- *Should we consign the Western democracy model to the ash heap of history?* (13:00 min)

Concept, interviews, camera, sound recording, editing, and production: Oliver Ressler
Image editing and subtitles: David Grohe
Animation: Zanny Begg
Composition and sound editing: Rudi Gottsberger
Footage: Sierpień 80 (© Telewizja Polska S.A.)

The emergence of the movements of the squares and the Occupy movement in 2011 can be seen as a reaction of people who opposed and began to fight the massive increase in social inequality and the dismantling of democracy in times of global financial and economic crisis. The movements of the squares are nonhierarchical and reject representation; direct democracy shapes their activities. The occupation of public places serves as a catalyst to develop demonstrations, general strikes, meetings, and working groups on different focal points. Successful site occupancies in one place often inspire occupations in other cities, although there is no linear relationship.

Oliver Ressler's 3-channel video installation *Take The Square* (2012) is based on discussions with activists from 15M in Madrid, the Syntagma Square movement in Athens, and Occupy Wall Street in New York. Reenacting the format of the working groups of the protest movements, four to six activists discuss with each other as a group in front of a camera. The discussions cover issues of organization, horizontal decision-making processes, the importance and function of occupying public spaces, and how social change can occur. The films were shot in the spring of 2012 in the places used by the movements of the squares for meetings and working groups: the Plaza de Pontejos, a quiet square in the immediate vicinity of the central Puerta del Sol in Madrid; at Plaza de la Corrala, a meeting place for the neighborhood assemblies of Lavapiés in Madrid; in Syntagma Square, the central assembly and demonstration point in front of the Parliament in Athens; and in Central Park in New York, where Occupy Wall Street held the "Spring Awakening 2012."

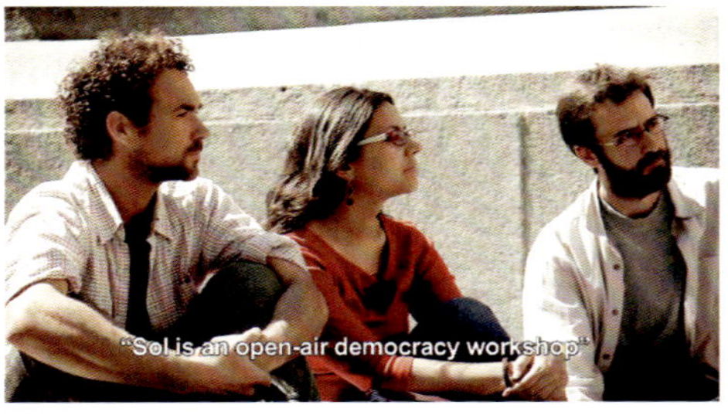

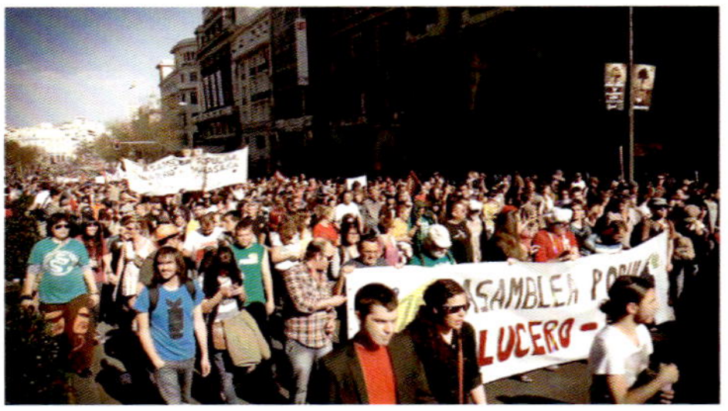

Oliver Ressler, *Take the Square*, 2012, 3-channel video installation, color, sound, 88:00 min, video stills, here: Madrid

The 88-minute video installation brings together activists from three cities central to the movement. "I consider inclusiveness and respect used as a means to build horizontality and recover our power without the need to have somebody representing us very powerful," says Ayelén from the Collective Thinking Work Group in Madrid. This rejection of representation also generally includes the parliaments; people should be politicized and invited to take their fate into their own hands. Babis Magoulas of the square movement in Athens says: "It's the political process, the one that creates the man who is concerned with the commons, who participates and doesn't allow the political to be taken over by the 'experts' whether they are syndicates or political parties. That's why I'm saying it's big. And direct democracy was not imposed; it was applied as the only way to convene. If it wasn't horizontal, it would have had no meaning."

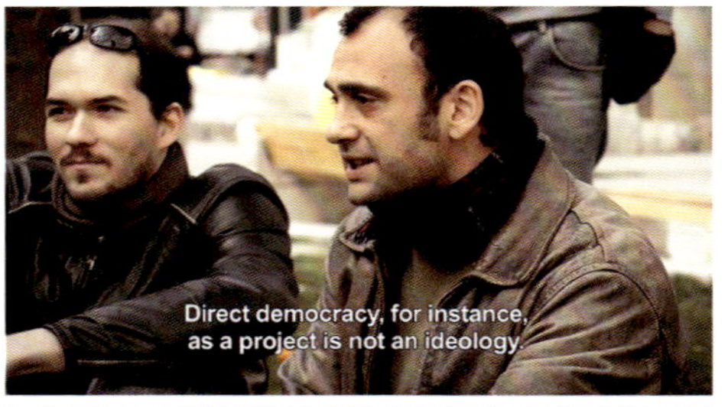

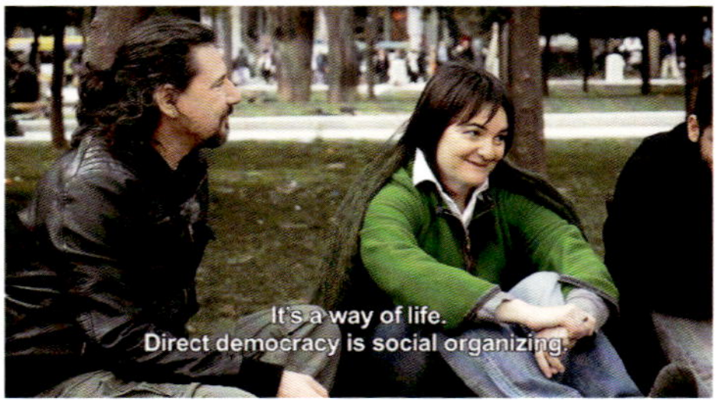

Oliver Ressler, *Take the Square*, 2012, 3-channel video installation, color, sound, 88:00 min, video stills, here: Athens

For Jen Waller of Occupy Wall Street, this has created "the first people's

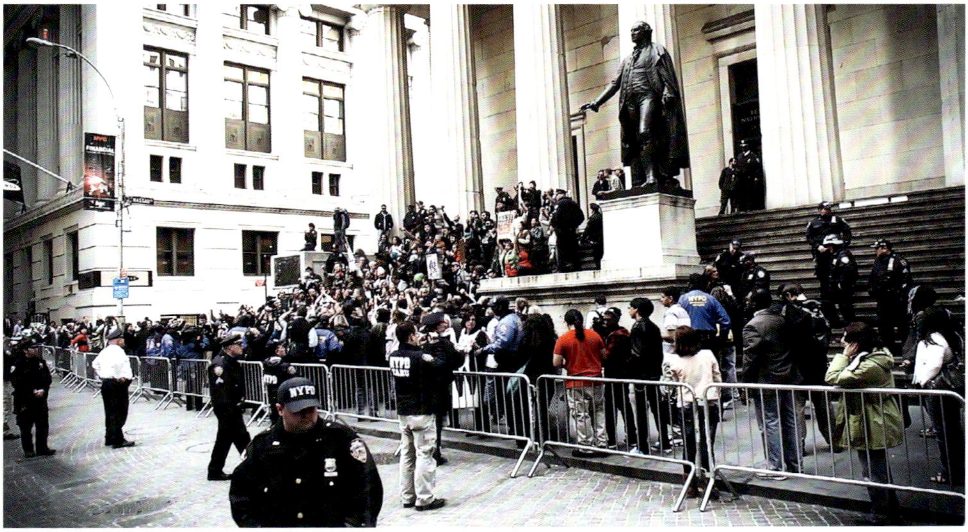

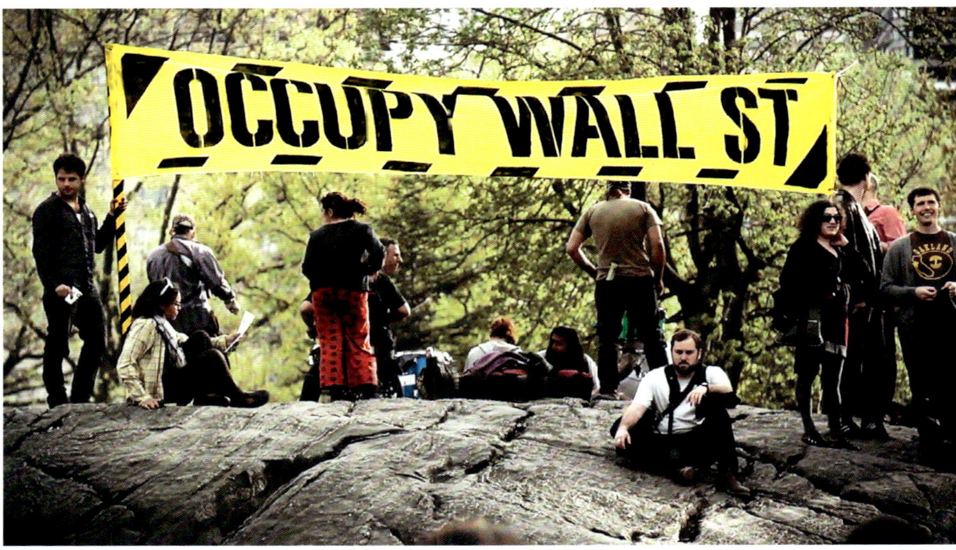

Oliver Ressler, *Take the Square*, 2012, 3-channel video installation, color, sound, 88:00 min, video stills, here: New York

movement in this country that has called out the ruling class as the enemy."

Take The Square tries to contribute to spreading the organizational knowledge of the movements and to translate the processes between these places in transition.

Director, producer, and film editor: Oliver Ressler
Camera: Thomas Parb, Rudolf Gottsberger
Sound design, mix, and color correction: Rudolf Gottsberger
Take The Square was commissioned by REGIONALE 12.
Special thanks to Maren Richter (artistic director of REGIONALE 12).

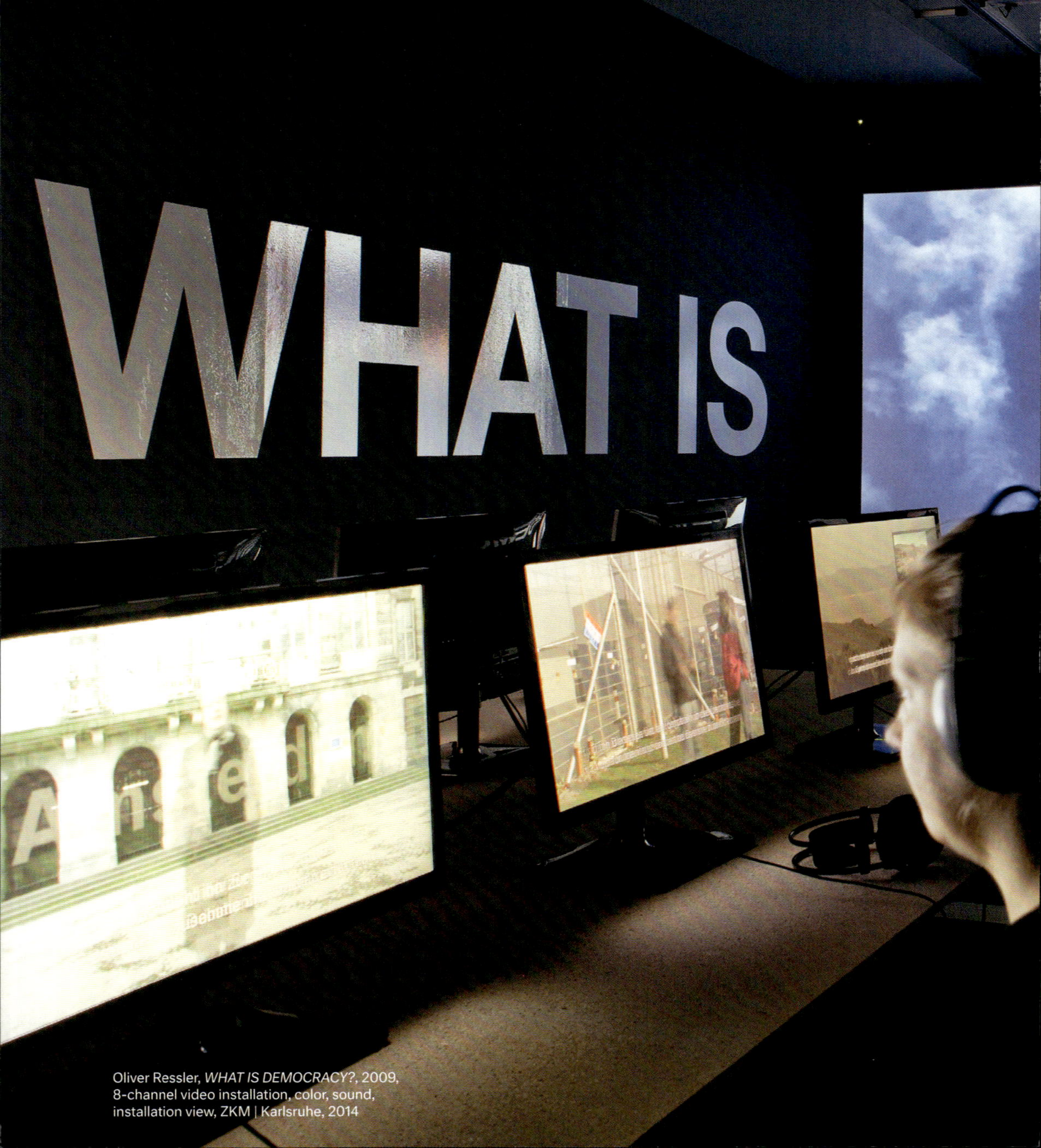

Oliver Ressler, *WHAT IS DEMOCRACY?*, 2009, 8-channel video installation, color, sound, installation view, ZKM | Karlsruhe, 2014

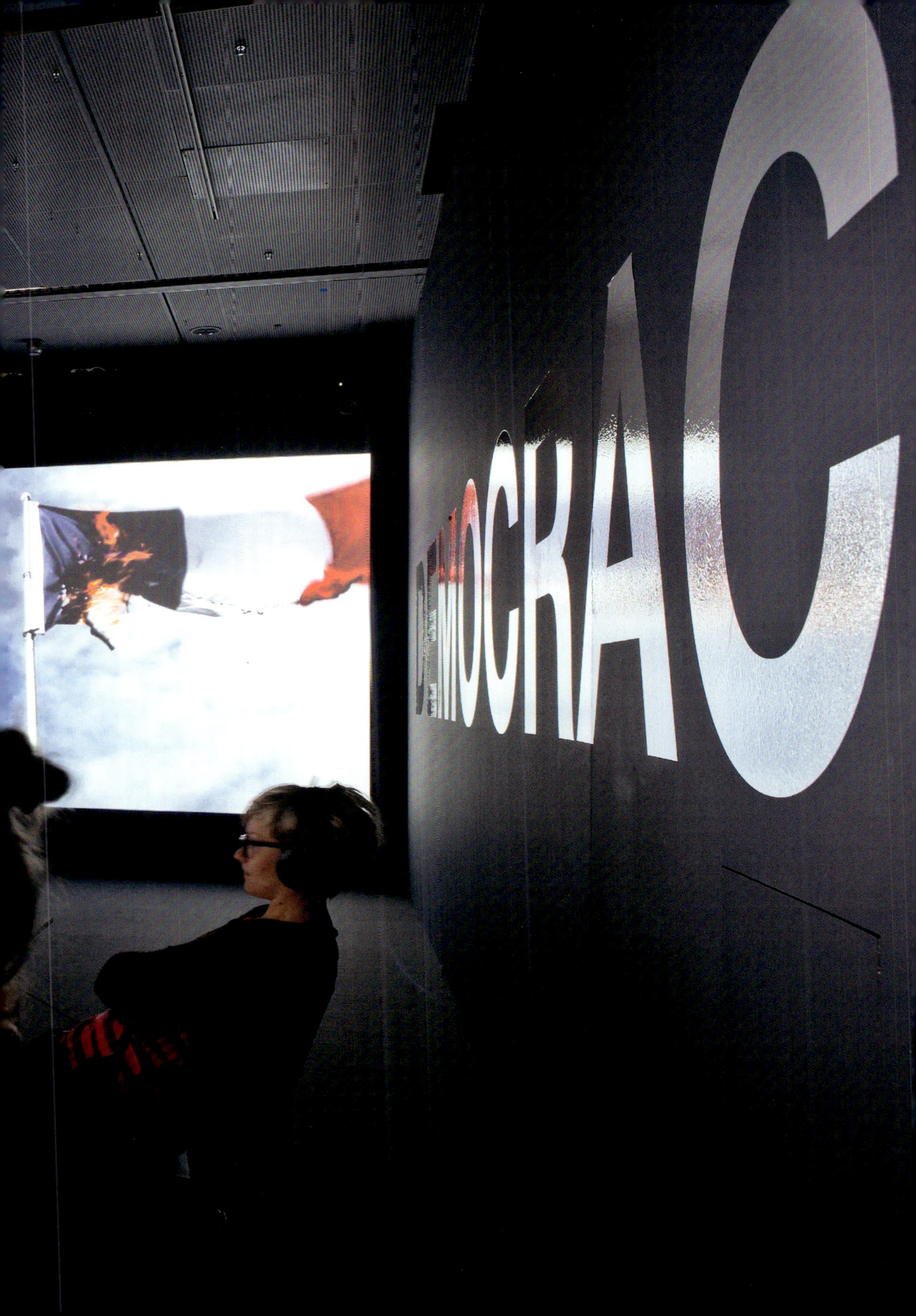
DEMOCRAC

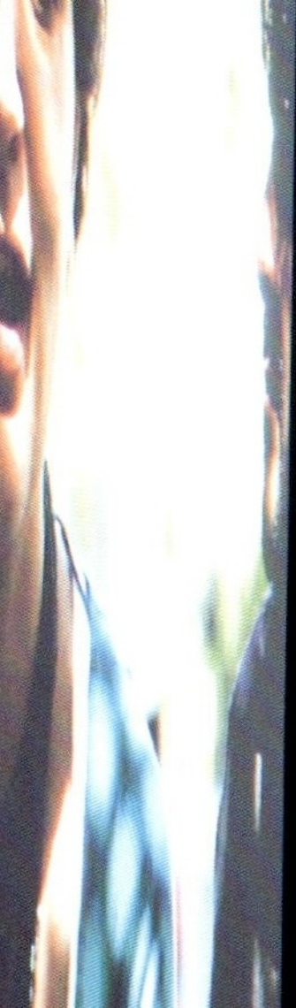

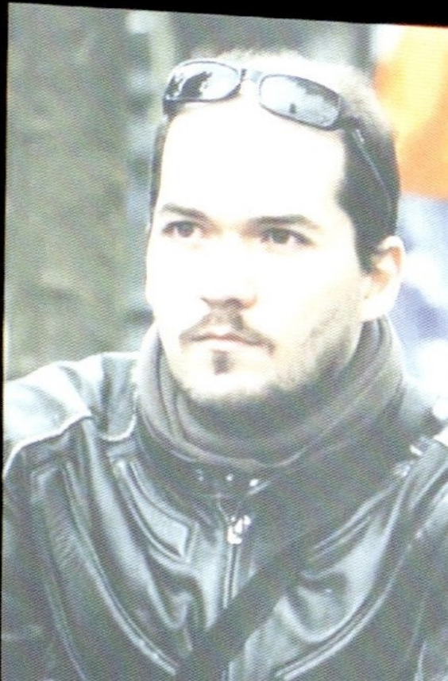

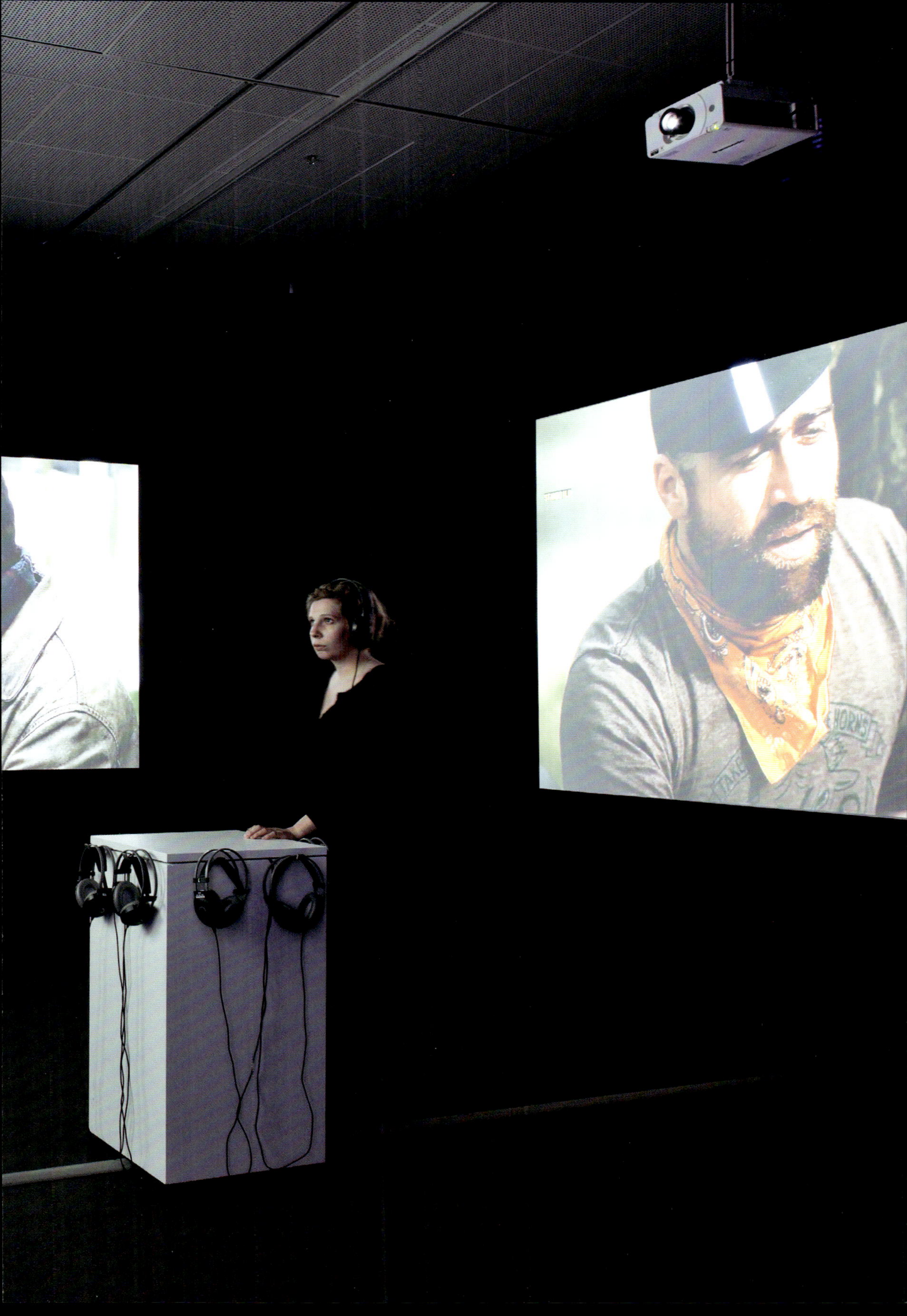

The Riahi Brothers

Arman T. Riahi (*1981 in Iran) is a director and scriptwriter. He grew up in Vienna, where he made his first short films as a teenager. He studied media technology and worked as a screen and graphic designer in London and Vienna. In 2005 he began his TV work for the Austrian broadcasting corporation ORF. In the same year, his short film *Elektronikschrott* [Electronic Waste] won the national short film award Shorts on Screen. His first cinema documentary *Schwarzkopf* [Dark Head] (2011) won the Audience Choice Award at the Diagonale Festival of Austrian Film and the Special Jury Mention Award at the Beirut International Documentary Festival DOCUDAYS. The film opened the documentary competition of the 17th Sarajevo Film Festival in 2011. Currently, Arman is working on his first feature film script and the next Riahi Brothers cinema documentary.

15M *indignados*, stencil on the sidewalk, Spain, 2012, film still from *Everyday Rebellion*, cross-media documentary by Arash and Arman T. Riahi, Golden Girls Filmproduktion and Mira Film, Austria, 2013

Arash T. Riahi (*1972 in Iran) is a director, producer, and dramatic advisor. He has been living in Vienna since 1982. Arash studied film and arts and has since worked for the Austrian broadcasting corporation ORF on a freelance basis. In 1997 he founded the film production company Golden Girls Filmproduktion, for which he has written, directed, and produced several award-winning documentaries, shorts, experimental films, music videos, and commercials. *The Souvenirs of Mr. X* (2004) was his first cinema documentary, followed by the multi-award-winning *Exile Family Movie* (2006) and *For a Moment Freedom* (2008). In the meantime he has won more than fifty international awards and was the Austrian candidate for the Academy Award for Best Foreign Language Film in 2010. Since 2009 he also works as a jury member for various international festivals as well as script advisor and coach for SOURCES 2, NIPKOW PROGRAMM, ORF, and the Scottish Documentary Institute. He also teaches fictional and nonfictional storytelling and producing at the University of Vienna.

Arman and Arash finished their first cinema documentary and cross-media project *Everyday Rebellion* in 2013 as the Riahi Brothers, which won several international awards, including the Audience Award at CPH:DOX, the Cinema For Peace Award, and the European CIVIS Online Media Prize.

Arash T. Riahi and Arman T. Riahi

Everyday Rebellion: A Cinema Documentary, a Web Platform, and a Smartphone Application

Everyday Rebellion is a cross-media project celebrating the power of creative nonviolent protest and civil disobedience. Its three fundamental media pillars are a Web platform, a cinema documentary, and a smartphone application, combining film, digital, and social media into a multifaceted and innovative hybrid format appropriate for the variety and diversity of modern nonviolent protest methods.

—

What does the Occupy movement in New York have in common with the Spanish *indignados* protests or the Arab Spring? Is there a connection between the struggle of the Iranian democracy movement and the nonviolent uprising in Syria, and what is the link between the Ukrainian topless activists of Femen and an Islamic culture like Egypt? And to top it off, what do Serbia and Turkey have to do with all this?

The reasons for the various people's uprisings in these countries may be diverse, but the creative nonviolent tactics they use in their struggles are strongly connected to each other. So are the activists who share these strategies, new ideas, and established methods. *Everyday Rebellion* is a story about the richness of peaceful protest, acted out every day by passionate people from Spain, Iran, Syria, Ukraine, the U.S., UK, and Serbia. These methods are inventive, funny, and sometimes even aggressive. And the activists who use them believe that creative nonviolent protest will win against violent protest – and they are right. Nonviolence has scientifically been proven to be more effective and successful than violent protest. And the users of nonviolence are feared because they are rapidly changing the world and challenging dictatorships as well as global corporations.

Everyday Rebellion pays tribute to the creativity of the nonviolent resistance. The project studies the consequences of a modern and rapidly changing society where new forms of protest to challenge the power of dictatorships and sometimes also global corporations are invented every day. *Everyday Rebellion* wants to give a voice to all those who decide not to use violence to try changing a violent system. Because, as J.R.R. Tolkien similarly claimed, *even the smallest action can change the world.*

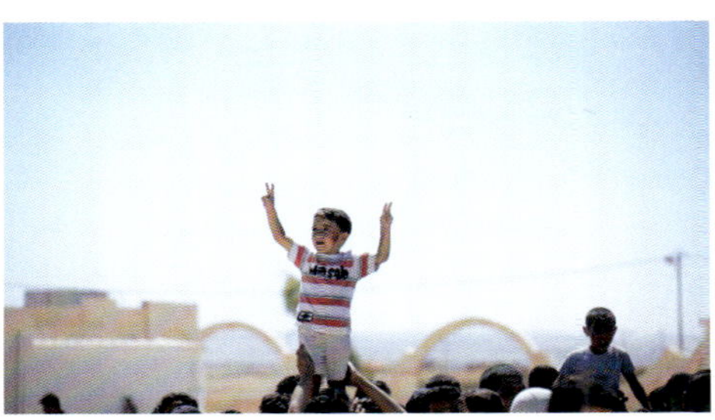

Protests in a Syrian refugee camp in Jordan, 2012, film still from *Everyday Rebellion*, cross-media documentary by Arash and Arman T. Riahi, Golden Girls Filmproduktion and Mira Film, Austria, 2013

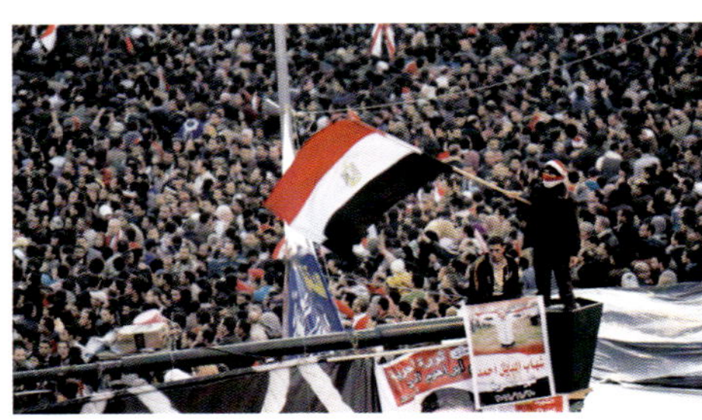

Protests at Tahrir Square, Cairo, Egypt, 2012, film still from *Everyday Rebellion*, cross-media documentary by Arash and Arman T. Riahi, Golden Girls Filmproduktion and Mira Film, Austria, 2013

To us *Everyday Rebellion* is more than just a project. The work on it didn't start with the nonviolent idea; it really started with Iran. We come from a pacifistic family; our parents brought us up to be pacifists. As we ourselves had had to leave an oppressed country – Iran – we started this project to support and inspire oppressed people in all authoritarian and unjust regimes, whether they be dictatorships or economic systems. We reject the use of force. But nonviolence as an old idea, deeply rooted in all the major religions, was something that was new to us. So when we began with Iran, we didn't know too much about nonviolence. We didn't understand the idea that when people get hit, they shouldn't hit back. These were ideas we didn't formulate then. But as soon as we got below the surface and started to go into the movements, it was clear that all of them were committed to the nonviolent idea.

The classic revolution has always people, a top-down structure, spreading ideology, gaining power over broadcasting stations, and so on. In the events around the election in Iran in summer 2009, we witnessed a horizontal uprising. Instead of a leader, we have hundreds and thousands of individuals acting on their own behalf. Instead of weapons, they were carrying mobile phones, spreading videos through YouTube, and short messages via Twitter. Although the Iranian uprisings were brutally put down, it was an inspiring ignition for the following Arab Spring.

During our film shoots in the last three years we realized how many connections exist between the movements in the different countries and the activists. All nonviolent movements are somehow connected, are inspiring, and help each other in different ways. We want to focus on their methods, the people behind them, and the connections between them, and also show that nonviolent struggle is the only way to create sustainable change from oppressive systems. We managed to get in close contact to inspiring activists from the different movements, who we followed and learned to understand during the journey that we made with them while making this film.

The project is intended to be a timeless, universal, political statement and we strongly believe that it can work as a unifying project between different cultures and countries. Our goal is to bring nonviolent tactics to the mainstream and show that this is a very joyful and emotional way of activism. We are not coming from an activist background and did not plan to make another activist movie, but rather a multifaceted and multinarrative experience that is both personal and deep and reflects the feeling of a generation.

The project consists of three main pillars:

1. A Web platform gathering and sharing all kinds of creative nonviolent methods and tactics via videos, collaborations, and articles.

The project's homepage is more than a simple website. It is a comprehensive online video platform providing users with all kinds of nonviolent video content, methods, and fundamental background information for people to learn, share, and understand nonviolence. Countless mobile videos, audio files, images, photographs, works of

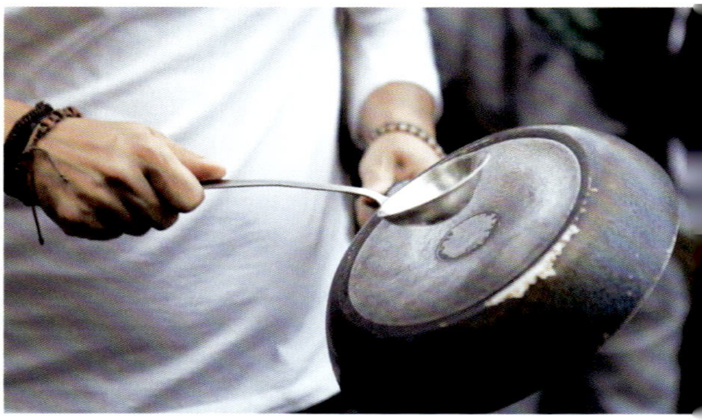

Protester of the 15M *indignados* movement hitting a pot to make noise, Spain, 2012, film still from *Everyday Rebellion*, cross-media documentary by Arash and Arman T. Riahi, Golden Girls Filmproduktion and Mira Film, Austria, 2013

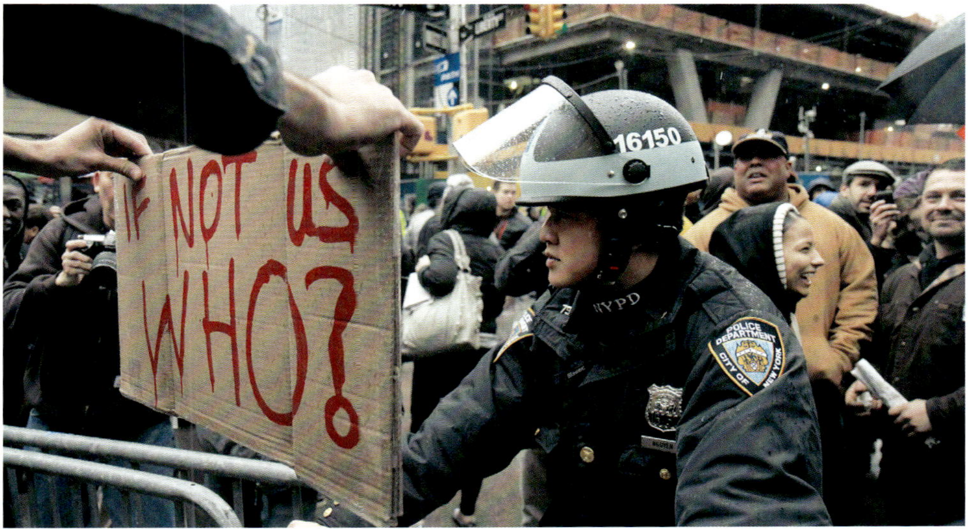

Occupy Wall Street, New York, 2011, film still from *Everyday Rebellion*, cross-media documentary by Arash and Arman T. Riahi, Golden Girls Filmproduktion and Mira Film, Austria, 2013

art, tweets, interviews, jokes, along with secretly filmed video material supplied by everyday people and activists are forming a new network of modern peaceful protest methods and models for change, some of which have rarely been seen before.

The content of everydayrebellion.com interacts closely with the project's Facebook site, whereas the project's Twitter account, @EverydayRebell, is firmly connected to the movements and networks around the world. The social media activities intertwine with several different media platforms in an informative manner and act as a mirror to the work of many online activities. The platform, produced by German design company Plural, has already received several awards in the field of transmedia, for example, the BEN Award for Best Transmedia at 2013's B3 Biennial of the Moving Image, or the European CIVIS Online Media Prize, and was one of the three finalists of the SXSW Interactive Awards 2014.

Furthermore, the project is closely affiliated to the most important blogs and bloggers of the various countries and movements. As bloggers will be part of the documentary, their involvement in the social media activities of the project is an active continuation of the film's narrative in different forms of media. Various web series and "webisodes" on nonviolent activism are running independently from the platform on ARTE online: *Creative Resistance*, a twenty-part Web series, and *Generation Revolution*, a ten-part Web series on Arab activists. The webisodes have proved to have an impact; in the case of *Srdja Popović's Advent Calendar of Rebellion*, the first Web series produced for *Everyday Rebellion*, Syrian activists translated the entire twenty-four-part series into Arabic to spread it in the Syrian nonviolent movement.

2. A cinema and TV documentary telling the stories of creative activists all around the world.

The cinema (and TV) documentary tells the emotional, uplifting, and often surprising stories of creative nonviolent activists in different cultures all around the planet who are fighting repression and injustice, from dictatorships to economic systems. The story is told through the characters of some of the key figures in these movements, focusing on the daily struggle of activists instead of on a few days peaking in huge waves of protest as seen in the mass media. Using sometimes very common, sometimes homegrown and creative methods of nonviolent resistance as a narrative guideline through the film, *Everyday Rebellion* displays the work and life of activists all over the world, who often risk their lives to fight for a better tomorrow and a more just world.

Rather than reconstructing political history, the film focuses on the many creative methods of nonviolent protest that are currently used by a rapidly growing number of people worldwide, who do not wish to accept the current state of our world and fight for new forms of political, economic, and social life in a peaceful manner. At the same time the film gives us profound insights into the lives of activists who often risk their lives to achieve a better future for all of us. We learn of their work, their motivations and goals, their doubts and beliefs, their anger and their happiness. But when we watch these people, we do not only learn about individuals, we also learn about and experience the deep and fundamental transformation processes, which occupy our world today. What started as localized has now decentralized and spread around the world. The resistance is a global state, and in its most effective and successful form it is nonviolent.

Some of the content of the film is crowd-sourced and employs mobile videos, images, photographs, works of art, Twitter feeds, interviews, jokes, and sound samples, along with secretly filmed video material, supplied by ordinary people who one day decided to stop just hoping for better times and became part of the protests. Drawing together a wide range of audiovisual diversity, the film creates a fitting narrative to the surprising new people's movements and their connections to each other.

3. Interactive tools like a smartphone application, supporting activists to change authoritarian and repressive systems nonviolently.

The *Everyday Rebellion* project studies the consequences of a modern and rapidly changing society where new digital solutions and methods are being found to challenge the power of dictatorships and sometimes also global corporations. Therefore, a smartphone app was developed to support and inspire creative nonviolent activism.

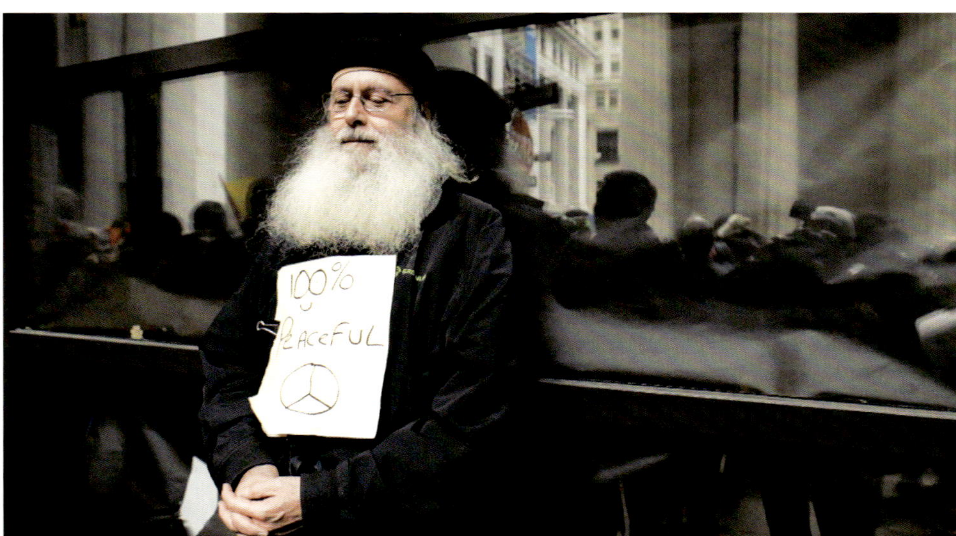

Occupy Wall Street, New York, 2011, film still from *Everyday Rebellion*, cross-media documentary by Arash and Arman T. Riahi, Golden Girls Filmproduktion and Mira Film, Austria, 2013

The *Everyday Rebellion* app is an interactive smartphone application to help and inspire nonviolent activists inside and outside of repressive systems. The app has a playful approach to activism, enabling the user to produce and document protest art, like graffiti and street art. Via augmented reality, the user will be able to render virtual slogans onto streets, buildings, and public spaces. Furthermore, the app provides the users with the most important and relevant nonviolent knowledge, and thus ties in with the website and film via its nonviolent subject matter.

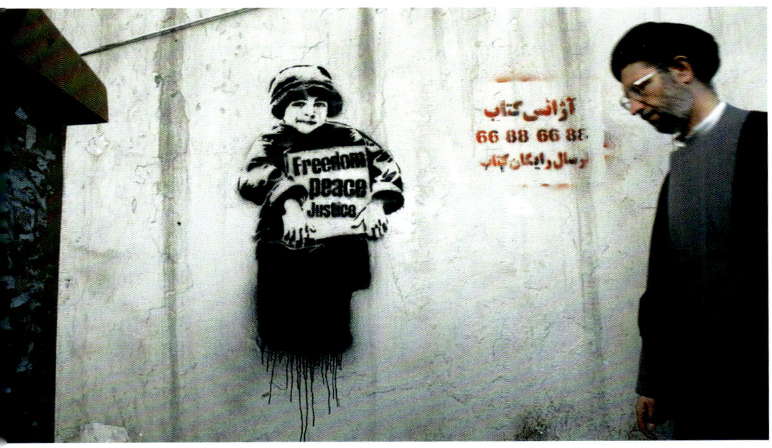

Graffiti by Icy & Sot (Freedom, Peace, Justice), Iran, film still from *Everyday Rebellion*, cross-media documentary by Arash and Arman T. Riahi, Golden Girls Filmproduktion and Mira Film, Austria, 2013

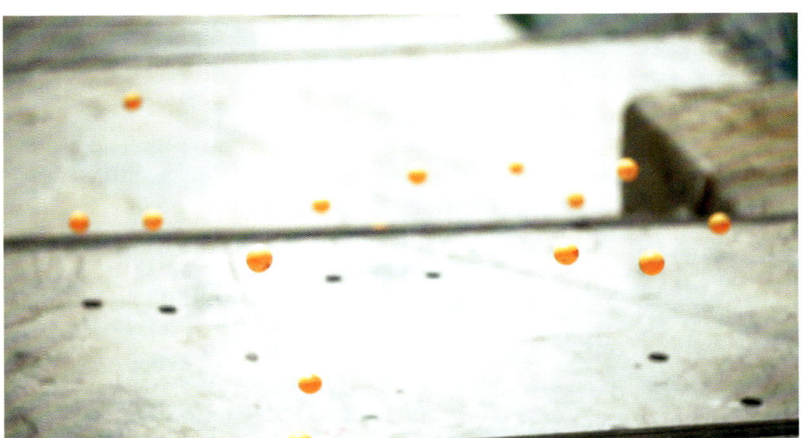

Action with ping-pong balls on a stairway in Syria, 2012, film still from *Everyday Rebellion*, cross-media documentary by Arash and Arman T. Riahi, Golden Girls Filmproduktion and Mira Film, Austria, 2013

Sandra Schäfer *1970

The artist Sandra Schäfer deals with questions concerning the representation of gender, urbanism, and (post-) colonialism. The focus of her work is on film and video installations and includes freeze images and photography. Her cinematic approach is essayistic. Schäfer is concerned with the processes of unfolding and rereading of documents, images, and spatial narratives. From 2010 to 2012 she was involved in *The Urban Cultures of Global Prayers*, a research project of the metroZones Center for Urban Affairs, the Haus der Kulturen der Welt, both in Berlin, and the European University Viadrina Frankfurt (Oder). In 2011 she was fellow artist at the BM Contemporary Art Center in Istanbul, and in 2010 at the Research Centre for Transnational Art, Identity and Nation (TrAIN) at University College London. She is currently working on an art PhD on the visual design of policies of the Hezbollah in Lebanon at the University of Fine Arts of Hamburg.

Sandra Schäfer has taken part in various exhibition projects across Europe, for example, at the La Virreina Image Centre in Barcelona, the New Art Gallery Walsall, the National Gallery of Art in Vilnius, Camera Austria in Graz, and DEPO in Istanbul. Further, she has coedited and contributed to several publications, including *Stagings. Kabul, Film & Production of Representation* (metroZones series, b_books, 2009), *Kabul/Teheran 1979ff. Filmlandschaften, Städte unter Stress und Migration* (metroZones series, b_books, 2006), and *Spliced Histories. 64 años de cine afgano* (Asociación de Amigos del Cine Experimental de Madrid, 2010).

In 2002, Schäfer began to engage with gender representation and the political and social changes that have taken place in Kabul and Tehran since 1979, and started collaborating with resident cultural producers. To meet Mohsen Makhmalbaf, she traveled to Kabul, where at the time he was assisting the Afghan filmmaker Siddiq Barmak in coordinating of some larger scenes in Barmak's movie *Osama* (2003), the first Afghan feature film produced after the fall of the Taliban regime. Schäfer had the opportunity to witness and document the reenactment of a women's demonstration in Afghanistan against the Taliban, who had stripped them of the right to work. More than one thousand women gathered to participate as extras, mostly to earn money. As their own experiences of the recent Taliban past coincided with those of the played roles, they also hoped to improve their real situation by demanding work.

Back in Berlin, based on the Kabul documentary material, Schäfer edited the short film *The Making of a Demonstration* (2004) together with the filmmaker Elfe Brandenburger, which not only focuses on documenting the necessary processes that make scenes in a feature film convincing, or that show how activism could be practiced during the Taliban regime, but which can also be seen as a first step in Schäfer's long-standing artistic and intellectual involvement in interrogating the changes of Afghanistan's social and political structures.

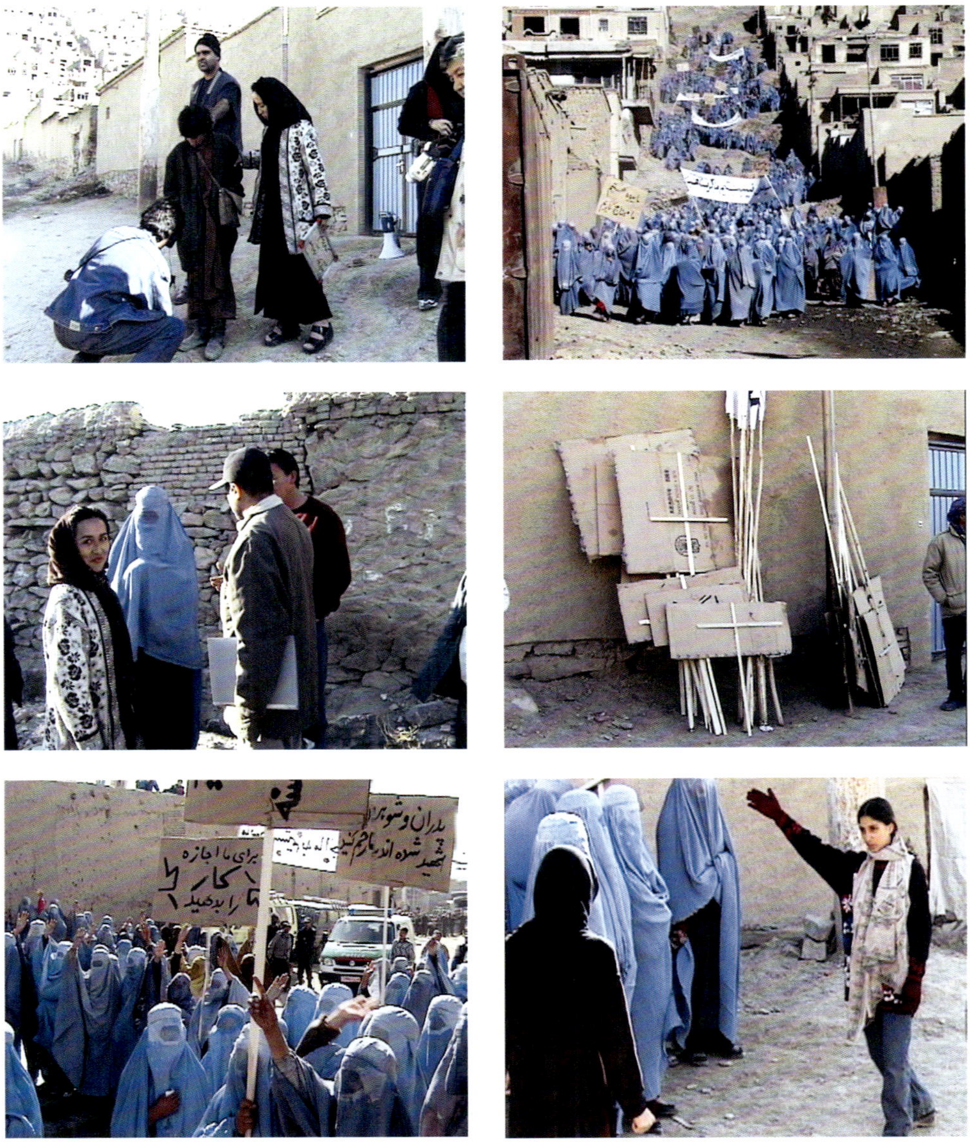

Sandra Schäfer, *The Making of a Demonstration*, 2004, video, color, sound, 11:07 min, video stills

Online Projects

Kreativer Straßenprotest

As an updated online extension of the book *go.stop.act! Die Kunst des kreativen Straßenprotests. Geschichten. Aktionen. Ideen* [go.stop.act! The Art of Creative Street Protest. Stories. Actions. Ideas] published in 2005, the blog reports on the various forms of creative protest from all over the world. Under headings describing different tactics, for example, adbusting, flash mobs, street art, and so on, actions are listed together with links.

kreativerstrassenprotest.twoday.net

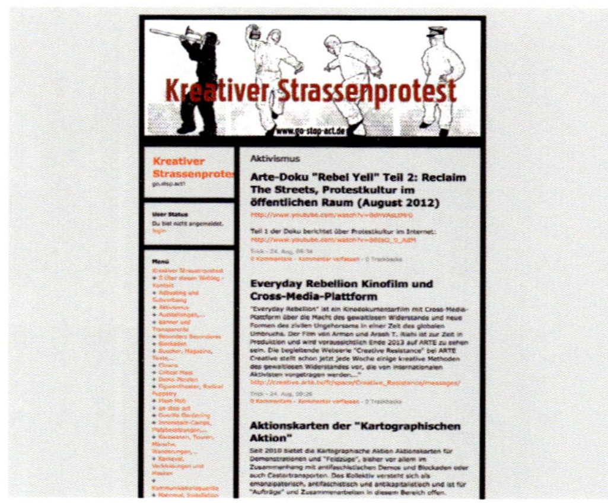

Screenshot, 07/08/2014

Politics Outdoors

USA

In his blog, US professor of sociology and political science at the University of California, Irvine (UCI), David S. Meyer, investigates social movements, the political contexts from which they originate, and their effects.

politicsoutdoors.com

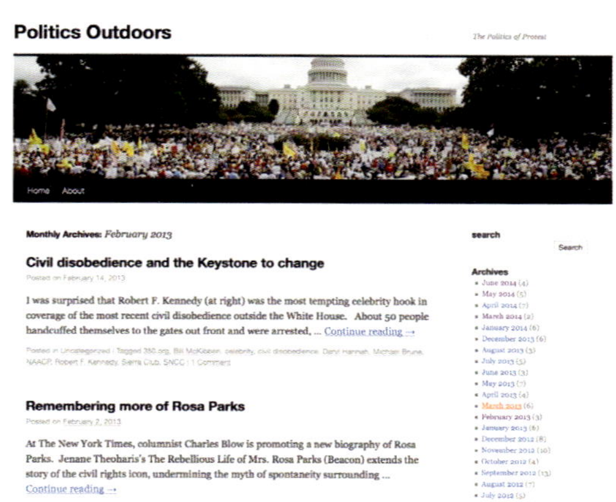

Screenshot, 07/08/2014

Take the Square

Online network that grew out of the Spanish demonstrations on May 15, 2011. Since that time the website collects and disseminates useful information for protest movements all over the world.

www.takethesquare.net

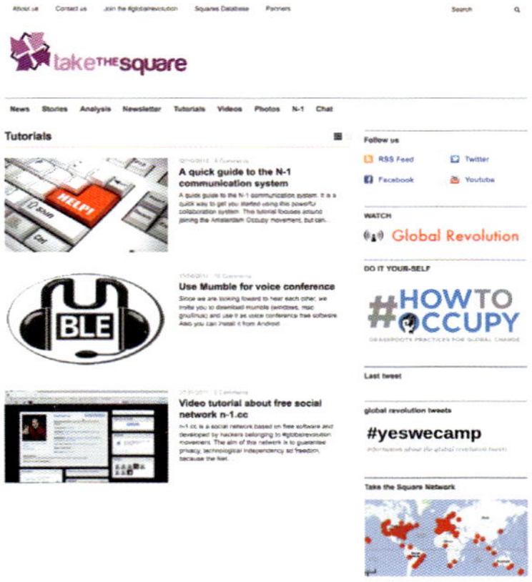

Screenshot, 07/08/2014

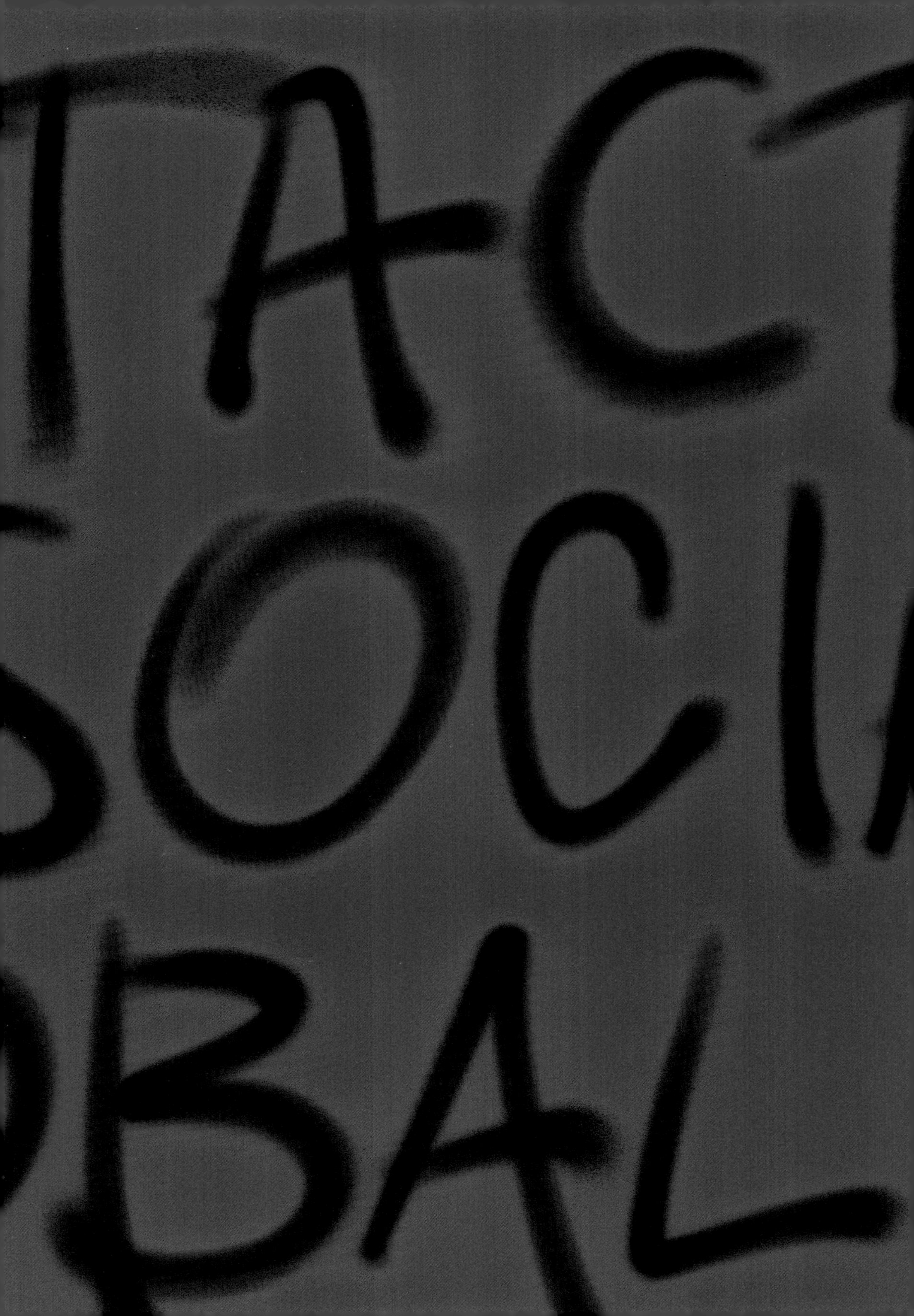

Tactical, Social, and Global Media

Chapter IV

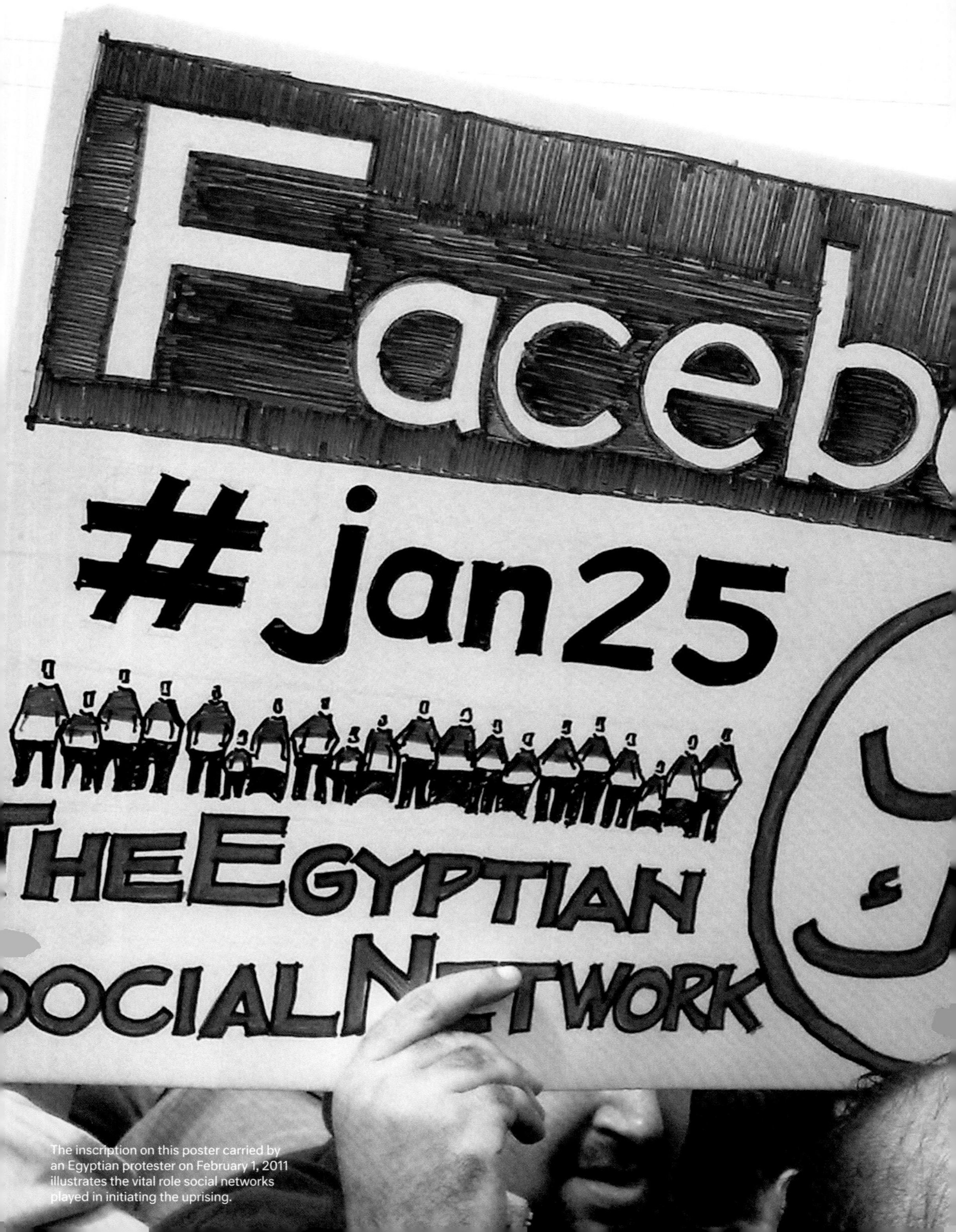

The inscription on this poster carried by an Egyptian protester on February 1, 2011 illustrates the vital role social networks played in initiating the uprising.

Graham Meikle

Distributed Citizenship and Social Media

In his book *Cultural Citizenship*, Toby Miller suggests that "[w]e are in a crisis of belonging [...]."[1] While Miller's book is primarily concerned with television, its year of publication coincided with the mainstream consolidation of social media platforms, most notably Facebook. Almost a decade later, the claim of a crisis of belonging could be restated, but this time in relation to social media. The crisis is that we are obliged to belong to commercial data-mining networks, even as we may know that they do not operate in our best interests. The ubiquity of Facebook, of Google, of Twitter, keeps us there because our friends are there, our families are there, our colleagues, our peers, our neighbors are there. The contemporary cultural crisis of belonging is that belonging has become obligatory. But in what sense do we belong to Facebook? Only in the sense that it owns our ideas and images, our address books and personal histories, our public statements and our private secrets. So how should we respond? One line of response is to reconsider our uses of social media in terms of a different sense of belonging – that of citizenship. This essay offers a new way of thinking about the relationships between citizenship, activism, and social media.

To be a citizen, the late James W. Carey once observed, "is to assume a relation in space to one's contemporaries [...]."[2] His concern was to connect the problems of establishing and maintaining a democracy on the scale of the United States with certain conceptions of communication. Carey distinguished between two fundamental ways of conceiving of communication. On the one hand, there is what he termed the *transmission* view of communication, through which messages are sent across space for the purposes of controlling territory; and on the other, there is what he called the *ritual* view of communication, understood as a symbolic process of maintaining community through time. In the social media environment, the centralized production and one-way distribution of the transmission model blurs with the ritual model's personal communication and the sharing of networked individuals. Meanings are not just transmitted through networks, but rather they circulate, with each new moment of sharing sparking a fresh association in a fresh context.

This chapter proposes the concept of *distributed* citizenship – to assume a creative political relation within networks with one's contemporaries. Relations of distributed citizenship are not

1 Toby Miller, *Cultural Citizenship. Cosmopolitanism, Consumerism and Television in a Neoliberal Age*, Temple University Press, Philadelphia (PA), 2007, p. 1.

2 James W. Carey, *Communication as Culture. Essays on Media and Society*, Routledge, New York, 1989, p. 4.

defined by or restricted to a particular geographical location or polity, but are defined rather by shared meanings and collaborative creativity and action within and through networked digital media. Distributed citizenship is a political possibility of the network society in its augmentation of what Manuel Castells terms the space of places with the space of flows, which he defines as "the technological and organizational possibility of practicing simultaneity without contiguity."[3] Distributed citizenship describes a set of potentials made possible by social media, and by the altered experiences and awareness of culture, connection, and community that result from their widespread adoption and adaptation.

3 Manuel Castells, *Communication Power*, 2nd ed., Oxford University Press, Oxford, 2013, p. 34.

Social media are networked database platforms that combine public with personal communication. For the most part, these are commercial operations that grow by having their users contribute content, which builds the database that those platforms can exploit for advertising and marketing. Social media are those that allow any user, in principle: to say and make things; to share the things that they or others have said and made; and to make that saying, making, and sharing visible to others in contexts where it is often far from clear who is watching or why. The personal relationships and experiences of the individual user take on a public quality, while more familiar forms of media content become the focus of personal communication that is visible to others. So social media can be understood by analyzing their uses and affordances in terms of *creativity, sharing*, and *visibility*. Our focus in this essay is on the first of these – creativity – and in particular on the forms of collaboration that Tim Berners-Lee has termed *intercreativity*.[4] The essay begins by briefly reviewing some key modern formulations of citizenship and media, before developing the concept of distributed citizenship in relation to networks, responsibility, and spatiality. It then applies this to four key examples of distributed citizenship projects.

4 Tim Berners-Lee, *Weaving the Web. The Past, Present and Future of the World Wide Web by its Inventor*, Orion Business Books, London, 1999, pp. 182f.

From Civil to DIY Citizenship

In an influential essay originally published in 1950, Thomas Humphrey Marshall distinguished between three dimensions of citizenship, which he termed the civil, political, and social. By *civil*, he referred to Enlightenment rights such as personal liberty, freedom of speech, and rights of property and the law. By *political*, he referred to the rights to vote and participate in the mechanisms, processes, and institutions of government. And by *social*, he referred to the right "to live the life of a civilized being according to the standards prevailing in the society"[5] – an aspect of citizenship bound up most closely with the twentieth-century expansion of education, welfare, and health services. The development of citizenship in Marshall's analysis was coterminous with the development of capitalism, but citizenship, as he observed, is a system of equality whereas capitalism is one of inequality. But critics of Marshall – such as Rogers M. Smith in 2002[6] – have pointed out that the eighteenth- to twentieth-century narrative of progress Marshall presents is not without its own inequalities, with some

5 Thomas Humphrey Marshall and Tom Bottomore, *Citizenship and Social Class*, Pluto, London, 1992, p. 8.

6 See: Rogers M. Smith, "Modern Citizenship," in: Engin F. Isin and Bryan S. Turner (eds.), *Handbook of Citizenship Studies*, Sage, London, 2002, pp. 105–115.

social groups – indigenous peoples, for instance – gaining access to civil, political, and social citizenship on very different timelines to that of Marshall's schema.

So an important addition to this three-part model was the concept of *cultural* citizenship by John Hartley (1999) and Toby Miller (2002). "'Citizenship,'" argues Hartley, "is a term of *association* among *strangers*,"[7] and is to be understood as "a *relational identity*, inconstant, dynamic, and evolving," rather than as a universal constant condition.[8] To this end, Hartley extends Marshall's three-part schema to add two further dimensions – *cultural* citizenship and *DIY* citizenship.[9] Cultural citizenship describes the recognitions of differences demanded by the identity politics of the late twentieth century.[10] For Miller, it is about "the maintenance and development of cultural lineage via education, custom, language, and religion, and the positive acknowledgement of difference in and by the mainstream."[11] It is made possible by broadcast media and the way that television "*gathers populations*."[12] Hartley expands on this:

> "Television [...] is no respecter of differences among its audiences; it *gathers populations* which may otherwise display few connections among themselves and positions them as its audience 'indifferently,' according to all viewers the same 'rights' and promoting among them a sense of common identity *as* television audiences. At one and the same time, then, people can experience political differences based on territory, ethnicity, law and heritage between one another, but also, simultaneously and conversely, they can enjoy undifferentiated 'identity' with others based on television audiencehood."[13]

Following on from cultural citizenship, Hartley proposes DIY (do-it-yourself) citizenship. This is "the practice of putting together an identity from the available choices, patterns and opportunities on offer."[14] DIY citizenship is about consumption and choice; it is a postmodern bricolage of fashions, gestures, practices, and ideas, and is again very much bound up with television.

> "Whether it's a full 'fitted' identity, expensive, integrated and in a recognizable off-the-shelf style, or an identity more creatively put together from bits and pieces bought, found or purloined separately, is a matter of individual difference. The point is, 'citizenship' is no longer simply a matter of a social contract between state and subject, no longer even a matter of acculturation to the heritage of a given community; DIY citizenship is a choice people can make for themselves. Further, they can change a given identity, or move into or out of a repertoire of identities."[15]

Each of Hartley's new forms of citizenship, he notes, is "increasingly reliant on *communication* and less on *the state*."[16] However, in the social media environment, large corporate entities such as Google and Facebook are sovereign. The unwritten social contract gives way to the unread Terms of Service Agreement – man is born free, and everywhere he is on Facebook. So if the granting of rights

7 John Hartley, *Digital Futures for Cultural and Media Studies*, Wiley-Blackwell, Malden, 2012, p. 133.

8 Ibid., p. 135.

9 See: John Hartley, *Uses of Television*, Routledge, London. New York, 1999; Hartley 2012.

10 See also: Manuel Castells, *The Power of Identity*, 2nd ed., Blackwell, Oxford, 2004.

11 Toby Miller, "Cultural Citizenship," in: Isin and Turner 2002, pp. 231–243, here p. 231.

12 Hartley 1999, p. 158.

13 Ibid.

14 Ibid., p. 178.

15 Ibid.

16 Hartley 2012, p. 147.

has been ceded from states to Silicon Valley corporations, then for whom is this a good outcome? Hartley's use of the term DIY also means that his concept of DIY citizenship has been taken up by participants in design, craft, and maker movements, and by theorists and practitioners of critical making.[17] While some of this work is fascinating,[18] it is a quite different sense of DIY from Hartley's original usage, and that usage in turn was concerned with television. Neither maker movements nor television can help us to fully understand social media. So this essay instead proposes a model rooted in the contemporary social media environment – distributed citizenship.

17 See: Matt Ratto and Megan Boler (eds.), *DIY Citizenship. Critical Making and Social Media*, The MIT Press, Cambridge (MA), 2014.

18 See: Steve Mann, "Maktivism: Authentic Making for Technology in the Service of Humanity," in: ibid., pp. 29–51.

Distributed Citizenship

What, then, is distributed citizenship? Distributed citizenship describes taking up a creative political relation with one's contemporaries within social media networks. It is more concerned with the exercise of rights and responsibilities than with choice and consumption. Its key terms are creativity, sharing, and visibility. It is self-reflexive citizenship, which is as yet more concerned with winning and securing its rights than with exercising them. It is not a description of a condition that has as yet been fully realized; rather, it is an aspiration. In this, it is no different from the other key conceptions of citizenship above – civil, political, social, cultural – not all of which have yet been obtained by everyone who could enjoy their benefits, and which remain aspirations for many people around the world.

In what senses is this citizenship *distributed*? It is distributed in three ways – in terms of networks, in terms of responsibility, and in terms of spatiality. First, it is distributed in the same sense as a distributed computer network – one with multiple points of connection and contact, with deliberate redundancy of connectivity, and with fewer hubs and points of centralized control than in other forms of network topology. The Internet was conceived as a distributed network, but contemporary developments by firms such as Facebook, Apple, and Google reimagine the Internet as at best *decentralized,* with certain key hubs dominating traffic, interactions, attention, and revenue, or at worst *centralized,* with all communication flowing through Facebook's servers to be data-mined and monetized. So in relation to networks, distributed citizenship describes an environment in which the infrastructure of participation, rights, and responsibilities is not concentrated in centralized spaces or in decentralized hubs, but is rather distributed widely across the network.

Second, citizenship is distributed in terms of *responsibility.* The language and interface of social network spaces put each individual at the center. Each platform is built around our profile, our personal timeline, our individual history, CV, and address book. Yet our interactions with others on these platforms do not take place in our individual space, but are distributed. You craft a status update that represents you to your chosen network in the way that you most prefer; but I comment on your post, and my comment becomes a part of your self-presentation, too, in ways which may work against your intended performance. What are the ethics of this? I then share your post with my own chosen networks, taking it out of the context for which you had shaped it, and repositioning your words within a new context of my own preference. What are the ethics of that? Such interactions are not the individual presentations or performances of autonomous selves, but are rather collaborations between distributed users, in which, while certain high-status users may have greater concentrations of attention than others, those collaborations are nonetheless distributed across networks.

Distributed citizenship involves each of us reassessing our responsibilities towards others in our networks. The revelations of Edward Snowden show that government security agencies and Silicon Valley corporations alike share an interest in harvesting and archiving what we say, feel, think, and do through networked digital media. So the responsibility for developing an ethics of distributed citizenship has to start with the users of those networks. We now know for certain that we cannot trust Facebook or the NSA to look out for us. Instead, we have to look out for ourselves and each other. This is not an argument for self-censorship, or that we should internalize the work of our own surveillance, but rather that we rethink our interactions on these networks as not personal or self-directed communication, but rather as *distributed* communication. We need to develop *technologies of the selfie*. We do not only have rights to speak, share, and to make ourselves and our interactions visible, but we also have responsibilities to those with whom we speak, with whom we share, and whose interactions with us we make visible in social media networks.

And third, citizenship is distributed in *spatial* terms. Distributed citizenship is not bound to a particular state – and far less to the "city" from which the word "citizen" derives. Instead it is an aspect of a world characterized by increasing mobility, as flows of tourists, students, asylum seekers, business people, and migrants intersect with flows of ideas, finance, technologies, and images.[19] This is not to argue that the state has lost its salience. Far from it – look across Europe today, and the continued salience of the state is fundamental to situations as diverse as the Ukraine crisis, the vicissitudes of the euro, or the Scottish independence referendum of 2014. The state is not going anywhere. But questions of ideas and property, of voice and participation, of creativity, sharing, and visibility, are increasingly the domain of communicative environments, which are largely under the control of enormous U.S. media and technology corporations. So as networks such as Facebook expand further into further non-western, non-northern territories, then questions of voice and governance, of sharing and visibility – questions of *ethics* and distributed citizenship – will become more pressing.

19 See: Arjun Appadurai, *Modernity at Large. Cultural Dimensions of Globalization*, University of Minnesota Press, Minneapolis (MN), 1996; John Urry, *Mobilities*, Polity Press, Cambridge, 2007; Richard Bellamy, *Citizenship. A Very Short Introduction*, Oxford University Press, Oxford, New York, 2008.

Intercreativity

The three aspects of distributed citizenship are each bound up with the creativity, sharing, and visibility of users and uses of social media. A very useful concept here is intercreativity, as defined by World Wide Web creator Tim Berners-Lee:

> "We ought to be able not only to find any kind of document on the Web, but also to create any kind of document, easily. We should be able not only to follow links, but to create them between all sorts of media. We should be able not only to interact with other people, but to create with other people. *Intercreativity* is the process of making things or solving problems together. If *interactivity* is not just sitting there passively in front of a display screen, then *intercreativity* is not just sitting there in front of something 'interactive.'"[20]

20 Berners-Lee 1999, pp. 182f.

Berners-Lee identifies here the crucial element of collaborative online creativity. Intercreativity is intrinsic to social media, through their capacity to connect people who are made visible to each other through digital networks. So it ought to be central to any attempt to use social media for political or cultural activism. We can identify four dimensions of such intercreative online activism. First, textual intercreativity, through which existing media images and narratives are reimagined and reworked into entirely new texts or into hybrid subversions of their component images. Second, tactical intercreativity, as activists develop online variations of established protest gestures and campaign tactics. Third, strategic intercreativity, which builds upon the traditions and conventions of alternative media. And fourth, network intercreativity, whose participants work to build new media network models, including those which link open source software to experimental online publishing practices. The following sections offer examples of each of these dimensions of intercreativity: textual (#occupy), tactical (*Kony 2012*), strategic (Bitcoin), and network (diaspora*). Each of these examples is, of course, a complex, multifaceted phenomenon, and this essay is not suggesting that any of them can be reduced to the single aspect of each that is isolated here as an example for discussion.

Intercreative Texts: #occupy

The #occupy movement, from Zuccotti Park to Quito, from Berlin to Melbourne, from Seoul to Abuja, was, of course, a movement that highlighted the importance of shared public and urban spaces.[21] Activists occupied key strategic sites and used these as bases for discussion and education, for organization and demonstration. But it was also a movement to which particular kinds of intercreative text were crucial in distributing its core ideas and its most effective simple messages. One such text was, of course, the key term "Occupy," with or without its hashtag, which proved limitlessly adaptable – from the germinal Occupy Wall Street of 2011, to the humorous Occupy Sesame Street, later reworked as a pointed response to U.S. presidential candidate Mitt Romney's criticism of that show's public broadcaster. Another was the slogan "We Are the 99 Percent," which spread across social media platforms and from them to other forms of media as well. The simplicity of the idea that 1 percent of the population control its wealth made it easy to both adopt and adapt it in new contexts as it circulated through networks of ideas and association. The many hundreds of

21 See: Manuel Castells, *Networks of Outrage and Hope: Social Movement in the Internet Age*, Polity Press, Cambridge, Malden (MA) 2012; McKenzie Wark, *Telesthesia. Communication, Culture, and Class*, Polity Press, Cambridge, Malden (MA), 2012.

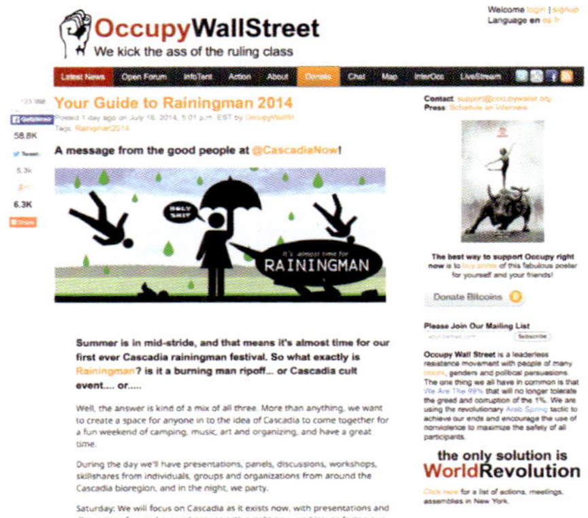

www.occupywallst.org, screenshot, 07/18/2014

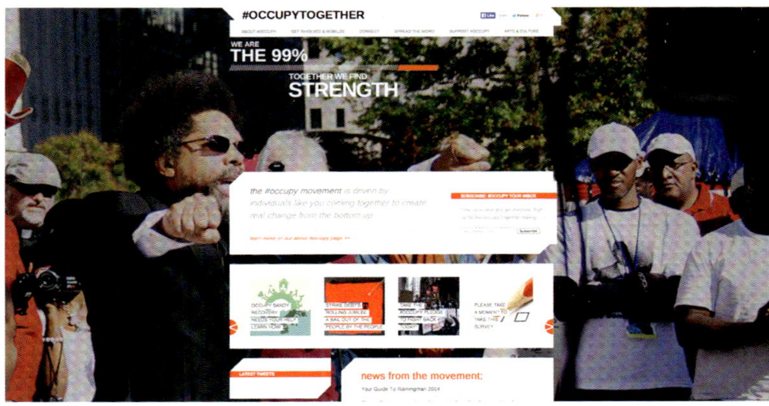

www.occupytogether.org, screenshot, 07/18/2014

images of individuals holding up statements of their own circumstances and self-identifying as the 99 percent that are collected at the original eponymous Tumblr blog demonstrate how each contributor was able to take the idea and adapt it to their own circumstances and subjectivity.[22] In this sense, the statement "Occupy + place," the hashtag #occupy, and the slogan "We Are the 99 Percent" are all Internet memes – shared, rule-based representations of online interactions that are not only adopted but also adapted by others.[23] Each of these intercreative texts has a powerful simplicity which makes it easy to translate them into new contexts, and each can circulate from point to point within distributed networks of users and situations with no real centers or hubs.

22 See: http://wearethe99percent.tumblr.com/archive, accessed 05/11/2014.

23 See: Victoria Esteves and Graham Meikle, "'LOOK @ THIS FUKKEN DOGE': Internet Memes and Remix Cultures," in: Chris Atton (ed.), *The Routledge Companion to Alternative and Community Media*, Routledge, London, forthcoming 2015.

Intercreative Tactics: *Kony 2012*

On March 5, 2012, the thirty-minute video *Kony 2012* was uploaded to YouTube. Within its first week online, the film had been viewed a hundred million times. *Kony 2012* was an activist campaign film, intended to mobilize support and action to stop the activities of Joseph Kony, the leader of a paramilitary organization called the Lord's Resistance Army (LRA), who had been indicted by the International Criminal Court (ICC) in The Hague in July and September 2005 on multiple counts of crimes against humanity and war crimes. *Kony 2012* was made by Invisible Children, a U.S. nonprofit

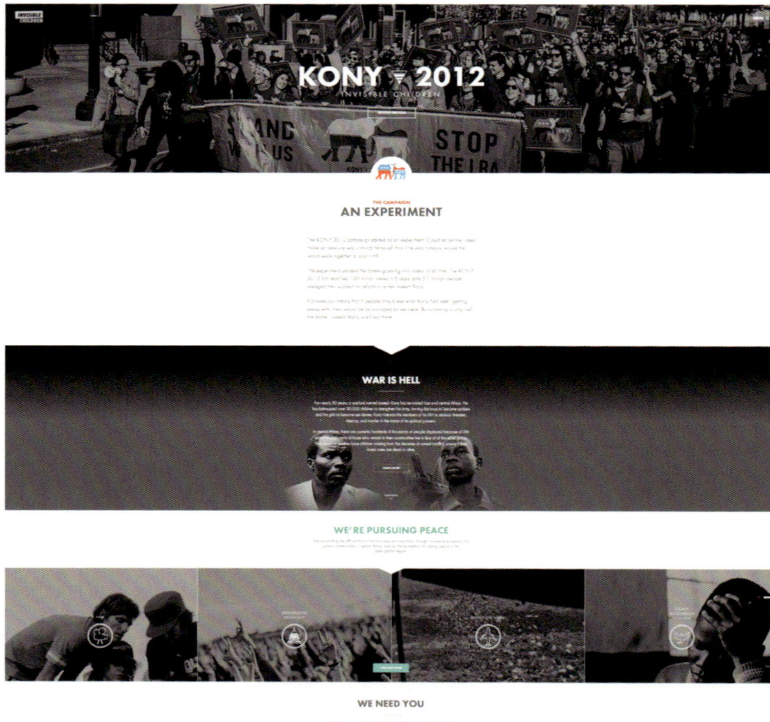

http://invisiblechildren.com/kony-2012, screenshot, 07/18/2014

organization founded in 2004 in opposition to the LRA. Invisible Children's strategy was to put pressure on the U.S. administration to continue providing military and logistical support to efforts to arrest Kony and bring him to the ICC prosecution. The tactic to achieve this strategic goal was to "make Kony famous" by having supporters share the video, tweet public figures, and take part in a planned global day of action on April 20, 2012.

For all of its sophisticated use of the affordances of social media, the *Kony 2012* campaign drew heavily on the established repertoire of activist tactics.[24] It called for graffiti, stickers, and posters; for letter-writing campaigns, updated to targeted tweeting to Rihanna and Bill Clinton; for demonstrations and mobilizations; and it deployed a peculiar combination of awareness-raising and outing in its inversion of the cultural logic of celebrity to "make Kony famous." The campaign used these intercreative tactics to invoke a distributed citizenry to mobilize globally through social media around a specific local issue.

24 For the definitive corpus of which, see: Gene Sharp, *The Politics of Nonviolent Action*, 3 vols., Porter Sargent, Boston, 1973.

Intercreative Strategies: Bitcoin

Bitcoin is, at the time of writing in May 2014, the best known crypto-currency. Crypto-currencies are experimental media for financial transactions, through which "coins," or unique digital identifiers, are "mined," or released by expending very high levels of computer

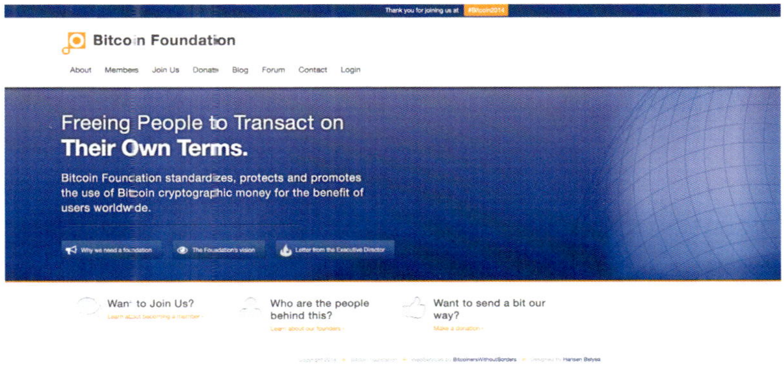

www.bitcoinfoundation.org, screenshot, 07/18/2014

processing power on cracking complex maths problems. The finite number of such identifiers and the "work" needed to find them create the scarcity from which the coins derive their value. The remixing of crypto-currency principles into variants such as Sexcoin, Dogecoin, or the Kanye-West-themed Coinye indicates that Bitcoin itself is, among other things, an Internet meme.

But Bitcoin is also a distributed, collaborative creative attempt to develop not just a new currency or medium of exchange, but an entirely new kind of financial system that is independent from both the established global banking infrastructure and the national governments which underpin much of it. Where the #occupy movement called for reform of financial structures, Bitcoin actually enacts one. In this, Bitcoin is an activist strategy that aims at consolidating an alternative way of doing things that had previously seemed settled. At the same time, it is important to recognize that mining Bitcoins is also a fairly elite practice, requiring sophisticated understandings of maths and cryptography, and demanding ever higher levels of processing power from the increasingly dedicated custom-built mining rigs required to release new blocks of Bitcoins. Nonetheless, Bitcoin and other crypto-currencies are a provocation to established social and financial conventions – a provocation that is distributed in terms of networks, responsibility, and spatiality.

Intercreative Networks: diaspora*

The distributed social media platform *diaspora** styles itself as "the online social world where you are in control." The diaspora* network comprises separately run and maintained servers, each of which is a node called a "pod," and each of which runs the free Diaspora software. Anyone with the resources to run a pod is able to start one, and the users of that pod can connect with others across the whole diaspora* network. The network is also marked by a rejection of advertising, and its use of open source principles of development and design. Its software system has adopted some common conventions from other social media (such as the use of hashtags and the ability to "like" [or <3] a post), and has initiated others, so that Google+'s "Circles" function can be seen as derived from diaspora*'s "aspects," through which users can stream posts to custom lists or subsets of all their contacts, posting something only for relatives or only for work colleagues, for instance.[25]

The website of the foundation that runs both the diaspora* network and the Diaspora software that underpins it lists three key principles: decentralization, freedom, and privacy.[26] The first of these is in practice closer to distributed than decentralized, given the absence of any major hubs, and the fact that the software allows anyone to run their own server and connect it to the whole network. Because the network is distributed across these pods, with none more central than others, the structure ensures the network's continued independence. The second principle, freedom, in particular relates to diaspora*'s encouragement of pseudonymous user names, in marked contrast to the insistence on real names by Facebook and Google, which demand a consistent identity for the data-mining purposes of their business models. As to the third principle, privacy, the system is designed so that each user not only owns and is responsible for their own data and content, but is also able to choose who sees what they do with that content.

25 See: http://wiki.diasporafoundation.org/FAQ_for_users, accessed 05/11/2014.

26 See: https://diasporafoundation.org, accessed 05/11/2014.

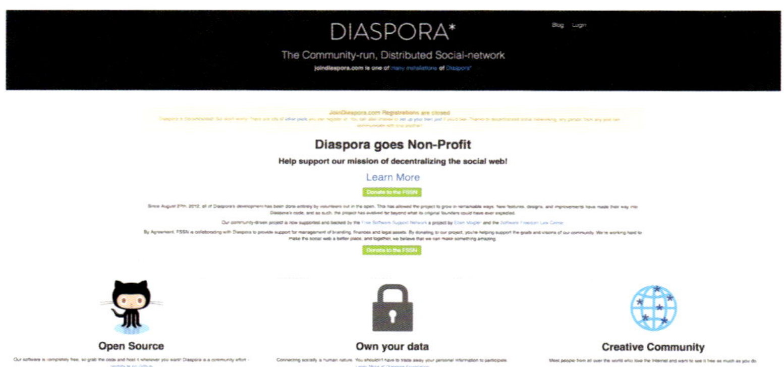

www.joindiaspora.com, screenshot, 07/18/2014

Conclusion

Each of the example projects above has its limitations and, of course, its critics. The #occupy movement was widely – if not accurately – criticized for lacking clear objectives and then for failing to achieve them. The *Kony 2012* campaign peaked too soon and fell victim to its own success, as the unexpected scale of its circulation and celebrity brought its own creators the same visibility and scrutiny to which they had set out to subject Joseph Kony, and distracted supporters from the project's intended climactic day of action. Bitcoin and other crypto-currencies are not yet widely accepted, are subject to volatility and insecurity, and are in some measure tainted by associations of illegality and criminality from their early adopters such as the now-closed Silk Road website. And diaspora* has so far failed to achieve a critical mass of users. It has been possible to join diaspora* since November 2010, and yet at the time of writing in May 2014, the project has managed to build only a relatively small number of users. User numbers for each pod can only be estimated, as the information is not public, but one pod's own statistics suggest a total of something below 400,000 individual user accounts across the network, with many of those likely to be inactive.[27] For comparison, Facebook's March 2014 quarterly report to shareholders claims 1.28 billion monthly active users, of whom 802 million were active on the site on a daily basis.

27 See: https://diasp.eu/stats.html, accessed 05/11/2014.

Yet each of these projects also shows the contours of a nascent form of citizenship – a distributed citizenship characterized by creativity, sharing, and visibility; by emerging senses of communicative ethics; and by distribution in terms of networks, responsibility, and spatiality. The #occupy movement was an archetypal distributed network, with multiple points of connectivity and no central oversight or control hubs. In its physical gatherings, it emphasized antihierarchical and distributed patterns of participation within meetings, and the movement was adopted and adapted across the planet. The *Kony 2012* campaign sought to devolve action and participation to distributed networks of – primarily school- and college-age – supporters, although it undermined this in its emphasis on their using its prepacked US$30 "action kit" of stickers and stencils and posters: a tension between centrality and distribution, which worked to the disadvantage of the center. In its call to individuals around the world to recognize their responsibility to join in combating a particular local issue, it invoked a specifically distributed citizenship. Bitcoin and other crypto-currencies are distributed projects in which users, advocates, and investors come together in shifting coalitions of practice. They suggest a set of social relations in which value is established on different terms to those of the established financial system. And the diaspora* platform comprises a global network of distributed servers, each running a common software system, and each connected to all the others, yet each autonomous and independent – distributed not only in terms of network topology or physical spatiality, but also in the dimensions of ethics and responsibility which it sets out to reclaim from the depredations of Silicon Valley. Each of these examples sketches the contours of an emerging form of citizenship for the social media environment – one characterized not in cultural terms of who we are, but in networked media terms of what we do.

In the summer of 2009, hundreds of thousands of Iranians demonstrated against the manipulation of the presidential elections. Despite the threat from security forces, people took to the streets to demand a recount of the votes, thus risking arrest, torture, or even death. The protests were the subject of global attention, yet foreign correspondents were quickly banned from reporting and expelled from the country. More than ever, local journalists were subjected to censorship and imprisonment. This led to social networks such as YouTube, Facebook, and Twitter becoming the most important sources of information. The international media had to rely on blurred amateur videos from cell phone cameras for their reports, while on the short messaging service Twitter a flood of news, tips, and rumors was disseminated. Headlines about Iran's "Twitter Revolution" quickly began circulating. Digital media appeared to be *the* central aid for networking and mobilizing the protesters. So was the Internet actually a catalyst for political change in Iran?

Marcus Michaelsen

Beyond the "Twitter Revolution": Digital Media and Political Change in Iran

Young people fighting tear gas and police truncheons with smartphones – the images and dynamics of these "networked movements" have since been repeated many times over.[1] The events in Tehran basically were a prologue to the Arab Spring: a year and a half later, young Egyptians and Tunisians made clear their frustration with authoritarian despotism and outdated power relations not only on the streets, but also on the Internet. Even where backgrounds and causes have differed, in Malaysia, Thailand, Istanbul, and Rio de Janeiro, digital media have played a central role in antigovernment protests over the last few years. Such events are forging a debate on the Internet's political potential, which developed even as the medium spread across the globe and which stems predominantly from the Internet's impressive technical possibilities. In order to get a realistic picture of the role of digital media in processes of political change, however, the social and political context of their use should also be considered. This can be illustrated using the example of Iran.

1 Zeynep Tufekci, "Networked Politics from Tahrir to Taksim: Is There a Social Media-fueled Protest Style?," in: *dmlcentral*, June 3, 2013, available online at: http://dmlcentral.net/blog/zeynep-tufekci/networked-politics-tahrir-taksim-there-social-media-fueled-protest-style, accessed 04/23/2014.

Media and Transformation

A central problem is that many sample cases that are supposed to prove the significance of new communication technologies for political change focus on crises in which open confrontation between regime and opposition has already erupted. Yet situations like the election protests in Tehran do not emerge overnight. Beyond the moments of conflict, the *long-term* utilization of digital media by opposition groups and civil society activists striving for change in existing power relations has so far been virtually ignored.

Before political challengers are at all able to threaten the position of those in power, they need to develop shared views, objectives, and strategies, gain support and mobilize supporters. Authoritarian states, however, provide little opportunity for public articulation of divergent political positions, be it by means of free elections, demonstrations, or through the media. State surveillance and despotism hamper the political and social engagement of citizens, while the media are subject to more or less overt censorship mechanisms. According to Antonio Gramsci's theory of cultural hegemony, political change can only take place when dominant norms and power relations are questioned in alternative arenas of discourse, collective solidarities are formed, and ultimately new ideas for the future of society are drafted and implemented.[2] Against the background of social and political conflicts, the media as an essential means of communication thus become the object of a greater struggle for control and power.

Even long before the spread of the Internet, dissidents, opposition groups, and social movements used so-called "small media," that is, flyers, magazines, or cassettes, to criticize the status quo and develop a culture of resistance. The exchange within these "counterpublics" made it possible not only to draft collective interests and objectives, but also to develop strategies for their implementation. Furthermore, solidarity among those involved was reinforced and thus subsequent political mobilization facilitated. In Eastern Europe, for example, the production of banned discussion papers, the Samizdat, improved the opposition's capacity to act because common positions had to be worked out and the distribution of the publications had to be organized.[3] The question now is whether and how the Internet fosters, accelerates, or expands the communication of political challengers. To what extent does it support an exchange of information and opinions, for example, and thus create a counterpublic? Does it open up new possibilities for networking and organization? Does it help with the mobilization of supporters?

2 See: Geoff Eley, "Nations, Publics, and Political Cultures: Placing Habermas in the Nineteenth Century," in: Craig Calhoun (ed.), *Habermas and the Public Sphere*, The MIT Press, Cambridge (MA), 1992, pp. 289–339, here pp. 324–326.

3 See: Katrin Voltmer, *The Media in Transitional Democracies*, Polity, Cambridge, 2013.

Between Reform and Authoritarianism: Political Developments in Iran

In Iran, the spread of the Internet took place, remarkably enough, virtually parallel to a stiffening of the authoritarian political system. This initially seems to contradict the theory on the liberalizing effects of the Internet, so it is all the more important to take into account the social and political background against which the impact of digital media develops.

The 1979 Revolution went hand in hand with a fundamental upheaval of political and social relations, which continues to shape the Islamic Republic even 35 years later. The country's political elite is embroiled in a complex structure of rivalries, which are determined not only by ideological differences, but also by generational conflicts and economic interests. Put simply, two different camps can be identified: On one side, supporters of an Islamist-legitimized, authoritarian state pursue the preservation of current power relations. At the heart of this ruling coalition is Supreme Leader Ali Khamenei, who consolidates his position through a close alliance with the Revolutionary Guard and an extensive security network. On the other side of the political spectrum, advocates of a nascent republicanism with an Iranian-Islamic slant demand the democratic configuration of the existing political institutions. However, these political reformers have not been able to stall the gains in power made by the authoritarian forces and were ousted from the political stage by the election victory of Mahmoud Ahmadinejad in 2005.[4]

Parallel to this confrontation on a political level, Iranian society has also undergone fundamental developments since the 1979 Revolution. Education and urbanization have enabled the growth of the modern middle class, which aspires to economic development and political participation. Large sections of the young population are critical of the ideological views of the regime. As the most important protagonists of civil society, intellectuals, journalists, students, and women's rights activists have discussed notions of democracy and human rights in the Iranian context.[5]

Before the presidential elections of 2009, catastrophic economic mismanagement and President Ahmadinejad's provocative foreign policies – seen by many Iranians as an embarrassment – had created a widespread mood for change. Evidently, the hardliners could only prevent the seemingly inevitable election victory of reformist Mir Hossein Mousavi by electoral manipulation.[6] Together with the second opposition candidate Mehdi Karroubi, Mousavi placed himself at the forefront of a protest movement that was named the "Green Movement" to match the color of his campaign. With its demands for fundamental civil rights, the Green Movement advanced the approach of the political reformers and forged a link to historic struggles for codetermination and the parliamentary regulation of power, which dated back to Iran's Constitutional Revolution at the beginning of the twentieth century.[7] Throughout the protests, however, the reform leaders consistently exerted a moderating influence on their supporters and thus prevented an escalation of the conflict with the security services, which were ever willing to resort to violence. One reason for this is undoubtedly the experiences gained from the Revolution against the Shah and the fear of the anarchy and chaos that could follow an abrupt overthrow. This historic "imprinting" is a crucial factor in the Iranian

4
See: Saïd Amir Arjomand, *After Khomeini. Iran under His Successors*, Oxford University Press, New York, Oxford, 2009.

5
See: Negin Nabavi (ed.), *Iran. From Theocracy to the Green Movement*, Palgrave Macmillan, New York, 2012.

6
See: Ali M. Ansari, "Urban Myths Revisited: The 2009 Presidential Elections," in: Nader Hashemi and Danny Postel (eds.), *The People Reloaded. The Green Movement and the Struggle for Iran's Future*, Melville House, Brooklyn (NY), 2010, pp. 345–351.

7
See: Ali M. Ansari, *Crisis of Authority. Iran's 2009 Presidential Election*, Chatham House, London, 2010; Hashemi, Postel 2011.

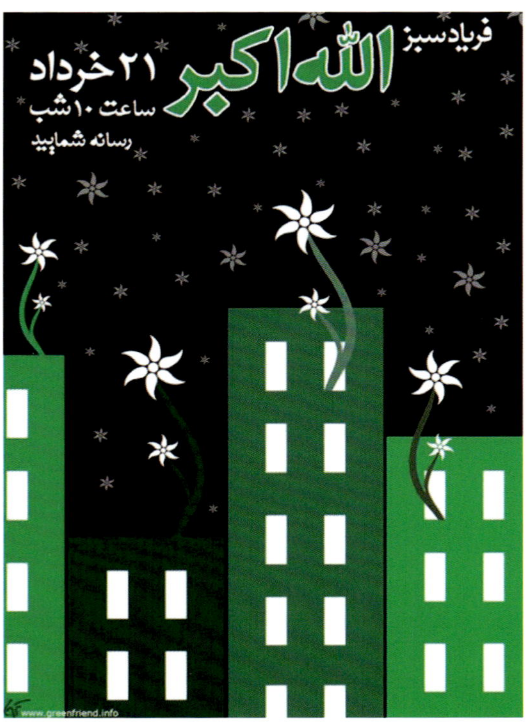

Poster of the *Green Movement* in Iran, 2009

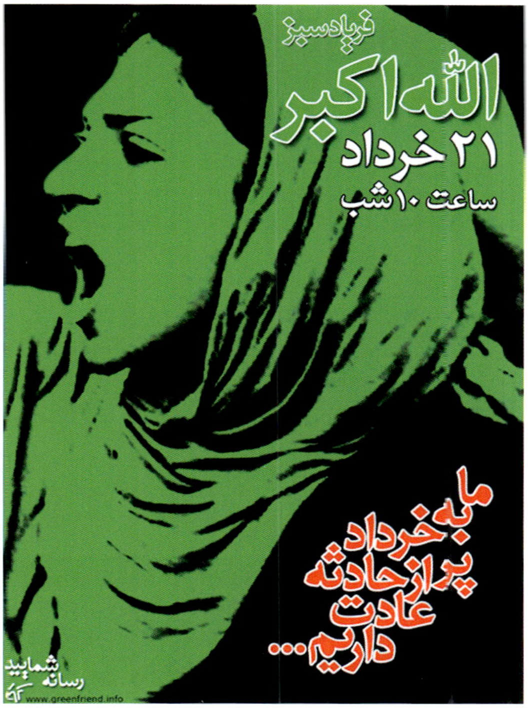

Poster of the *Green Movement* in Iran, 2009

transformation process and represents a key difference to the countries of the Arab Spring, for instance. Ultimately, the regime succeeded in suppressing the protest movement: the leading figures of the Green Movement were placed under house arrest and many activists disappeared into prison or left the country.

A New Information Landscape

Amid these turbulent political developments, digital media acted as both stage and tool. After the turn of the millennium, Iran had one of the region's highest growth rates for Internet use: from 2001 to 2010 the number of users grew from 1.7 to 33 million. The penetration of society by the Internet was significantly more profound in Iran than in the countries of the Arab Spring.[8] Education, urbanization, and purchase power ensure there is a large group of potential users. The predominantly young population is open to modern communication technologies, plus there is widespread interest in alternatives to the state-controlled media. This is hampered, however, by the ever more comprehensive system of Internet censorship: the state filters massive amounts of Internet content, curtails the speed of connections, and monitors critical voices online. At the same time, for many years Iran has been pursuing the ideal of a national information network aimed at promoting the use of state-sanctioned content and application services, while simultaneously largely curbing the unwanted effects of a global communication structure. Together with a series of other countries, Iran therefore represents a form of "networked authoritarianism." Such a system seeks to take advantage of the benefits of new communication technologies and at the same time invests enormous resources in their control and censorship.[9]

Time and again the media have played a role in the political developments of recent Iranian history. In the run-up to the Constitutional Revolution, liberal ideas circulated on leaflets distributed in the cities by night. Before the 1979 Revolution, opponents of the Shah regime distributed the sermons of revolutionary leader Ayatollah Khomeini on audiocassettes. Under reformist President Mohammad Khatami, towards the end of the 1990s the press temporarily became a forum for lively debate, in which even former taboo themes were discussed. By contrast, the mass media of radio and television have always been subject to strict state control. The regime also reacts sensitively to satellite channels, which many Iranians are able to watch despite official prohibition.[10]

As the conservative judiciary banned more than one hundred reformist publications between 2000 and 2003, more and more

8

In 2012, 53 percent of the Iranian population had access to the Internet, with 35 percent in Egypt and 39 percent in Tunisia. Figures from Internet World Stats available online at: www.internetworldstats.com/stats5.htm, accessed 04/23/2014.

9

See: Rebecca MacKinnon, "Liberation Technology. China's 'Networked Authoritarianism,'" in: *Journal of Democracy*, vol. 22, no. 2, April 2011, pp. 32–46.

10

See: Mehdi Semati (ed.), *Media, Culture and Society in Iran. Living with Globalization and the Islamic State*, Routledge, London, New York, 2008; Hossein Shahidi, *Journalism in Iran. From Mission to Profession*, Routledge, London, New York, 2007.

journalists migrated to the Internet. This period saw the emergence of many different online media publishing news, analysis, and commentaries. Added to these were Iranian websites produced abroad, which fostered exchange with the communities in exile and offered journalists who had emigrated a way of continuing their profession. From 2002, online blogs opened up another possibility for publication. The range of Iranian blogs quickly developed into one of the liveliest and most diverse blogospheres in the world. Many writers viewed their blogs as a means of expressing their opinions and of writing because they "had something to say."[11]

The regime reacted not only with censorship and blocking access to "undesirable" Web content, but also by publishing actively on the Internet. Conservative politicians made use of a number of online news sites to publicize their positions and to attack political opponents. While the rivalries within the conservative camp intensified, in particular under President Ahmadinejad, there was an increase in these online media, which were therefore used as a tool for factional struggles. In fall 2008, for example, a website close to the influential parliamentarian and government critic Ahmad Tavakoli reported on the fake doctorate of Ahmadinejad's interior minister Ali Kordan, who was then removed from office. Information published on the Internet ensured greater transparency with regard to the differences among the political elite – which would otherwise have been played out behind the scenes – and intensified their dynamics.

For the Iranian reformers, on the other hand, Internet sites became an essential channel of communication after losing so many print media publications. An analysis of the content of a central reformist website in November 2006 shows how the reformers used this medium to express criticism of former Iranian President Mahmoud Ahmadinejad's government, to raise certain political issues, to negotiate strategies, and to try to motivate their supporters to take action.[12] The content and lines of argument disseminated in this way were picked up on by bloggers and discussed in more detail in their writing. Analysis of a blogger debate on Iran's municipal elections of 2006 reveals almost a hundred participants expressing their opinions on the choice of candidates, the general significance of the elections, and the pros and cons of participation and boycott. Most significantly, bloggers with a journalistic slant emerged as opinion leaders, steering and stimulating the discussion.[13] Debates such as this can be viewed as "counterpublics," in which alternative themes and views are aired. Naturally, the reach of these counterpublics is somewhat limited. Censorship, user interests, and the characteristics of the Internet limit the audience of reform-oriented blogs and websites: political content has to be actively searched for and the filters have to be bypassed. These constraints mean that a small information elite that is part of the urban and technologically open-minded middle class uses the Internet for this contained, yet very intensive exchange of opinions and information. It is precisely this social group of ascending and educated actors that is particularly interested in political change and plays an important role in the development of critical discourse.

11 Personal interviews with Iranian bloggers between 2003 and 2008. On Iranian blogs, see: Annabelle Sreberny and Gholam Khiabany, *Blogistan. The Internet and Politics in Iran*, I.B. Tauris, London, New York, 2010.

12 See: Marcus Michaelsen, *Wir sind die Medien. Internet und politischer Wandel in Iran*, transcript, Bielefeld, 2013, here pp. 219–221.

13 Ibid., pp. 249–251.

Networks of Solidarity

With the increasing authoritarian controls and repression, the online counterpublics offered supporters of reform and civil rights activists an important place of refuge. Digital media not only formed a platform for debate and critique, but also facilitated new forms of networking and organization among civil society initiatives. The Iranian women's movement, for example, came under increased pressure from the state during Mahmoud Ahmadinejad's first term (2005–2009). Associations and organizations were disbanded, gatherings and seminars banned, and activists incarcerated. In reference to the power gains made by the hardliners, journalist, and women's activist Mahboubeh Abbasgholizadeh was able to accurately foresee the consequences of the changed political circumstances: "I would anticipate that in the near future the voice of [the] women's movement would no longer come from women's NGOs, because of [a] lack [of] security in the sustainability of resources and the vulnerability of the social environment, but will come from various Internet sites."[14] In actual fact, the women's movement was as pragmatic as it was creative in the way it adapted to the new conditions. For the "One Million Signatures Campaign," activists walked the streets alone or in pairs to call for change in discriminatory laws. The coordination of the loose campaign network took place predominantly via the Internet. Websites and blogs formed crucial hubs where ideas and strategies could be agreed and new participants won over. Many young activists reported that it was through the Internet that their attention was first drawn to the needs and activities of the women's movement.[15]

14 Mahboubeh Abbasgholizadeh, "A Quick Look to Challenges faced by WNGOs in Iran's Society," in: *Volunteer. Newsletter of Iranian Civil Society Organizations Resource Center*, spring 2005, p. 29.

15 See interviews with activists on the campaign website, 2008, available online at: www.campaign4equality.info, accessed 04/23/2014.

Digital media also facilitated the movement's defense against state suppression. When activists were incarcerated, online networks meant fellow campaigners could be alerted immediately, including the supporters abroad with contacts to the international media and human rights organizations. The swift exchange of information the Internet offers also created a certain level of transparency with regard to the actions of the security apparatus against the women's movement, and thus increased at least the symbolic costs of repression. The silent disappearance of an inconvenient dissident was now virtually impossible. At the same time, websites and blogs offered the possibility of expressing solidarity with detainees and giving a public presence to their fates. Portraits of incarcerated activists, often written with great emotion, emphasized the urgency of the cases and reinforced cohesion and commitment among campaigners. Banners and posters recalling the detainees and demanding their release could be integrated into personal blogs or websites and disseminated via the Internet.[16]

16 Interview with a women's activist, Tehran, November 2008.

Digital media therefore supported the formation of flexible civil society networks, which enabled the women's movement not only to survive in the face of an increasingly authoritarian regime, but also to continue and to expand its activities. Here, the Internet was, on the one hand, a substitute for the means of public communication blocked by the state while, on the other, it opened up new paths for collective action.

The strategies and methods of networking and solidarity on the basis of digital media as tried out by the women's movement were picked up on and further developed by the Green Movement following the contested presidential elections of 2009.

With various different initiatives, the members of the Green Movement used the Internet to give expression to a political culture that emphasized demonstrative values such as empathy, openness, and tolerance in order to detach itself from the repressive regime. During the first few months of the protest movement, opposition leaders like Mir Hossein Mousavi or the former President Khatami visited the families of incarcerated activists or victims of the violent suppression of the demonstrations. Photos of these encounters circulated in the social networks on the Internet and showed typical scenes of the visiting guests in Iranian living rooms, where guests and hosts would talk over tea, fruit, and pastries. In this way, the reformist politicians demonstrated their solidarity with those affected by repression and with the protest movement. Detainees released from prison, who had suffered through isolation and torture, were welcomed back to normality in a similar way.

The Iranian online community responded with a spontaneous show of solidarity to the incarceration of student leader Majid Tavakoli, who was publicly paraded dressed in a chador by the secret services, because he had allegedly tried to flee dressed as a woman. Hundreds of Iranian men posted photos of themselves wearing headscarves online, thus crushing the intended defamation.[17]

17 Compilation of photos of this action available online at: www.youtube.com/watch?v=3QIVwHsrsvg#t=67, accessed 04/23/2014.

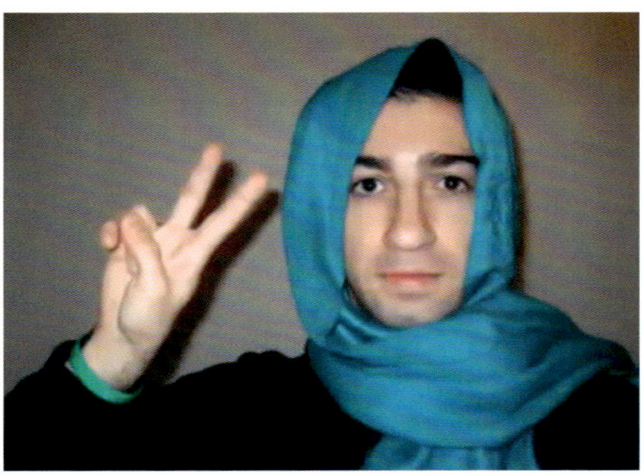

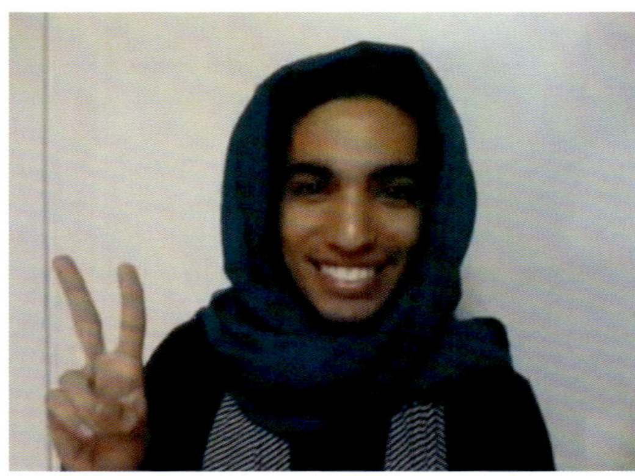

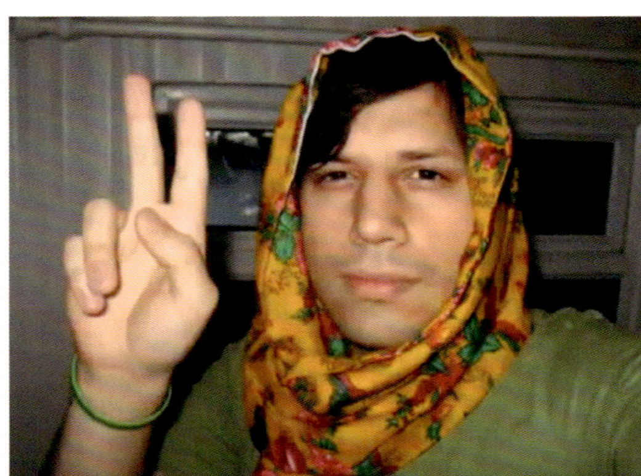

"We are all Majid," online campaign, 2009, screenshots from www.youtube.com/watch?v=3QIVwHsrsvg#t=67, accessed 10/14/2014

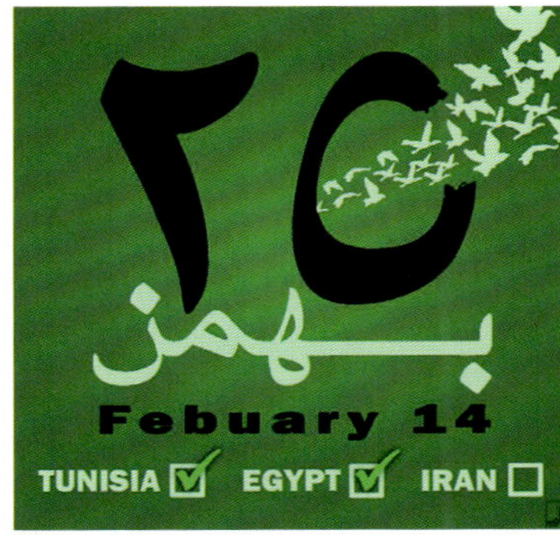

Poster of the Green Movement in Iran, 2009

Iranian anthropologist Ziba Mir-Hosseini points to a further form of action with which the solidarity culture of the Green Movement found expression online. The wives of incarcerated reformist politicians published letters to their husbands in which they not only criticized the inhumane security apparatus, but also spoke openly about their feelings and desires. These women often came from religious families among the spiritual and political elite and their letters clearly broke away from the moral notions of a regime that had for decades politicized the conduct of women in public and burdened it with endless taboos.[18]

18 See: Ziba Mir-Hosseini, "Broken Taboos in Post-Election Iran," in: *Middle East Report Online*, December 17, 2009, available online at: www.merip.org/mero/mero121709.html, accessed 04/23/2014.

As the leading figures of the Green Movement – Mousavi and Karroubi – were increasingly cut off from the public by the secret services, digital media offered them a chance to maintain contact with their supporters. Mousavi's Facebook profile formed a central source of information for communiques and news, which were disseminated both in Persian and in English. Both politicians published video interviews online. In this way they succeeded, at least up until their complete isolation under house arrest, in expressing their opinions on political developments and staying informed about the mood among the members of the movement. In a declaration one year after the contested election, Mousavi emphasized the importance of exchange on the Internet: "Strong and stable social networks have been miraculous for spreading information and raising awareness. To see this, it is enough to merely look at the production of art and the democratic spread of analysis, news and information among different social streams. The Green Movement has been responsible for a wave of dialogue about important questions regarding our future. This event is incomparable to any other in our modern history."[19]

19 "Mir Hossein Mousavi's 18th Statement," in: *Khordad 88. June 09: The Election – The Aftermath – The Green Movement*, June 16, 2010, available online at: http://khordaad88.com/?p=1691, accessed 04/23/2014.

Mobilization and Protest

The influence on political mobilization and protest is undoubtedly one of the most frequently discussed, but also among the hardest to pinpoint among the effects of digital media. The Iranian protests of summer 2009 emerged from a polarized election campaign, which left the population in a highly politicized state. At the beginning of his candidacy, Mousavi proclaimed his slogan of "Each citizen, one campaign" [*har shahrvand, yek setad*]. This approach naturally developed as a result of the opposition's limited media access and called upon the initiative and creativity of each individual. Mousavi thus also offered the young population from the modern middle class, who was probably most dissatisfied with economic mismanagement and state patronage under Ahmadinejad, a chance to participate. With no coordination by the official campaign staff, young

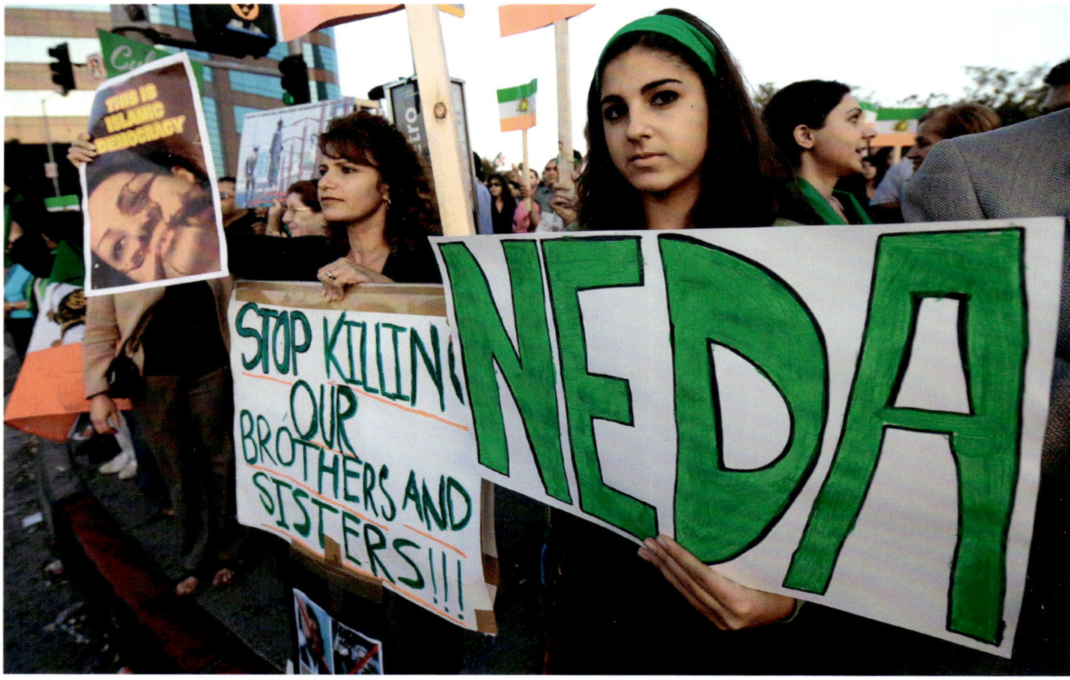

Protest against the Iranian elections of June, 2009, outside the Federal Building in Los Angeles on June 22, 2009

reform supporters organized spontaneous marches and rallies to call for political change.[20] The election campaign was accompanied by lively debates in the digital media, yet the aspirations of government opponents had long since migrated from the alternative forums online out into the public arena. The election day itself in principle formed only a brief hiatus before the people again crowded onto the streets – this time to protest the election result. According to Iranian political scientist Hossein Bashiriyeh, a now intolerable gap had opened up between the euphoric expectations before the election and the official result. Anger over the hopes that had clearly been dashed by election manipulation paved the way for long-pent-up frustrations to flow into the concrete demand for a rerun of the election, which formed the foundation of the Green Movement.[21]

In the days and weeks after the election, the Movement succeeded in bringing its supporters onto the streets time and again. For the coordination of the protests, though, the Internet was simply one communication channel among others, especially since the state slowed down connections and blocked applications. Cell phones, word of mouth, and flyers played an equally important role. Indeed, contradictory details of the place and time of demonstrations published on the Internet even caused confusion. When eventually more and more videos of violent police tactics circulated online, this also served to put off potential demonstrators.[22]

During the election crisis Twitter proved effective predominantly outside of Iran, since messages on the social network became a central source of information for the international media. A small number of Iranians living abroad played a key role in the dissemination of reliable news. Journalist and blogger Fereshteh Ghazi, for example, who had emigrated to the USA a few years

20 See: Arash Ghafouri, "Setad 88 – Iran's Greatest Campaign in Support of Mir Hossein Moussavi," in: Marcus Michaelsen (ed.), *Election Fallout. Iran's Exiled Journalists on their Struggle for Democratic Change*, Schiler, Berlin, 2011, pp. 50–63.

21 See: Danny Postel, "Counter-Revolution and Revolt: An Interview with Iranian Political Scientist Hossein Bashiriyeh," in: *Constellations. An International Journal of Critical and Democratic Theory*, vol. 17, no. 1, March 2010, pp. 61–77.

22 See: Kevan Harris, "The Brokered Exuberance of the Middle Class: An Ethnographic Analysis of Iran's 2009 Green Movement," in: *Mobilization. An International Journal*, vol. 17, no. 4, 2012, pp. 435–455.

previously after facing problems with the Iranian security forces, was tweeting almost constantly in the first few weeks of the protests. Another Tehran journalist also wrote very actively from her base in the UK under the name @oxfordgirl. New-Jersey-based Mehdi Saharkhiz (@onlymehdi), the son of a well-known reform activist, published hundreds of videos of the protests. All three were part of the young generation of the reform movement and had excellent connections to Iran.[23] On a transnational level, they took action with the help of digital networks as important conveyors of information. Since attention is an essential resource for social movements, the mobilization of an international public and international support represents one of the central functions of digital media for political activists.[24]

Virtually no video of the Iranian protests attracted more global attention than the shocking footage of Neda Agha-Soltan, who was struck by a bullet on the edge of a demonstration in Tehran on June 20, 2009. The image of the dying young woman made its way into numerous international media and was used again and again by supporters of the Green Movement for posters, photo montages, and calls to protest. Neda memorably symbolized Iran's young generation, which rejected the despotism and repression of a ruthless regime. She became an icon of the protest movement.[25]

Furthermore, numerous amateur films document the protest potential among the population, even beyond the spectacular demonstrations. There is footage, for example, of the nightly "Allahu Akbar" ["God is great"] call, which recalled the 1979 Revolution and which the people of Tehran used to protest against election fraud and dictatorship. Other videos showed spontaneous

23
See: Matthew Weaver, "Oxfordgirl vs. Ahmadinejad. The Twitter user taking on the Iranian regime," in: *The Guardian*, February 10, 2010, available online at: www.theguardian.com/world/2010/feb/10/oxfordgirl-ahmadinejad-twitter-iran, accessed 04/23/2014; Matthew Weaver, "Iran protests: One-man video channel that is a thorn in Tehran's side", in: *The Guardian*, June 11, 2010, available online at: www.theguardian.com/world/2010/jun/11/iran-protest-videos-youtube-mehdi, accessed 04/23/2014.

24
On this see also: Zeynep Tufekci, "'Not This One': Social Movements, the Attention Economy, and Microcelebrity Networked Activism," in: *American Behavioral Scientist*, vol. 57, no. 7, March 2013, pp. 848–870.

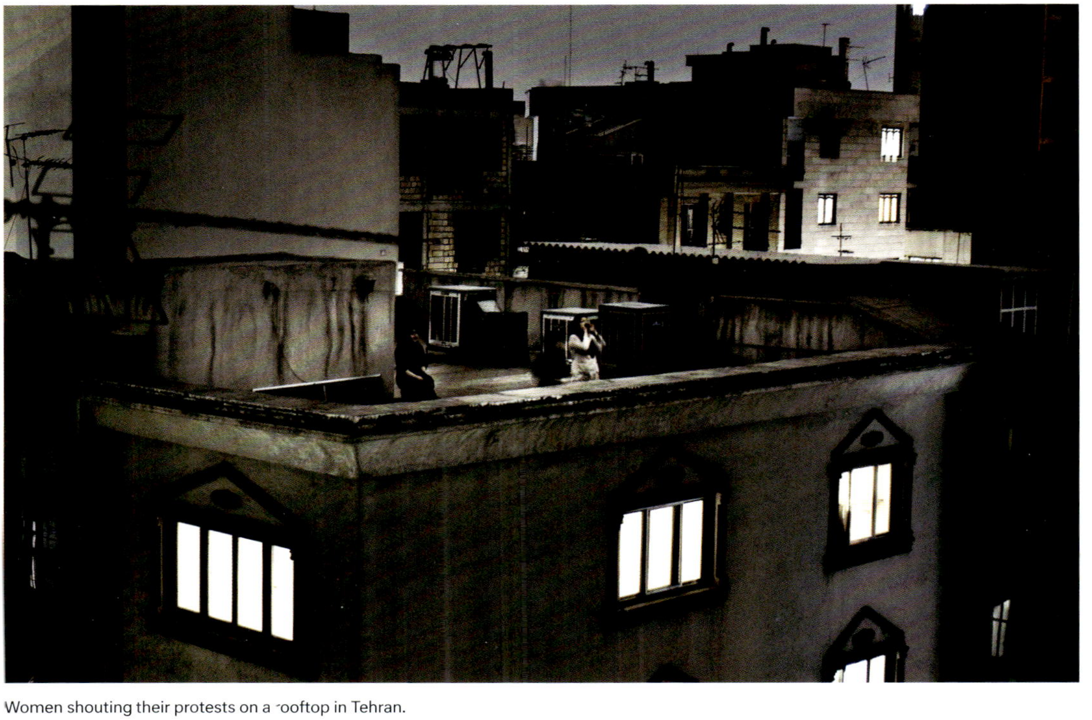

Women shouting their protests on a rooftop in Tehran.

demonstrations in provincial cities or universities, while photos reproduced "Green" graffiti on house walls and street signs. Mousavi's approach from the election campaign was further pursued: The slogan "You are the media!" *(Rasaneh shoma'id!)* aimed to make clear to every individual his or her role in conveying information. With these online contributions, supporters of the movement showed determination and a collective identity, even at a time when the protests on the street were already abating. Ultimately, though, the discrepancy between the manifestations of resistance online and the actual events in Iran became ever greater.

25 See: Nazila Fathi, "In a Death Seen around the World, a Symbol of Iranian Protests," in: *The New York Times*, June 22, 2009, available online at: www.nytimes.com/2009/06/23/world/middleeast/23neda.html, accessed 04/23/2014. In Egypt and Tunisia, too, ordinary young people who had fallen victim to the despotism of the authoritarian state became symbolic figures for the respective protest movements. A trigger for the protests in Tunisia was a YouTube video of the self-immolation of a vegetable trader, who was protesting against humiliation by the authorities. In Egypt a Facebook profile set up in memory of a blogger who died in police custody was one of the hubs of the resistance.

Summary

The example of Iran clearly illustrates the fact that political upheavals are extremely complex processes which are subject to a wide range of influences. The Internet did indeed offer actors wanting to challenge the existing power relations new possibilities for communication and action, yet the question of whether the potential of digital media is fully exploited depends on the media competence of the users, the form a critical political culture takes, and the vitality of civil society and the opposition. Other factors crucial in determining the success of political challengers are not heavily influenced by the Internet: coherent management and organizational power among the opposition, as well as tendencies towards repression and economic resources of those in power. Added to this is the fact that, over the last few years, authoritarian states have also used the Internet ever more effectively to consolidate their own positions.

In this respect, the most important functions of digital media for political challengers lie in the formation of counterpublics and internal networking. The Internet enables activists to disseminate alternative information, debate points of view, and develop strategies. It is precisely under authoritarian leadership that the Internet thus offers an important refuge for dissidents. A greater variety of digital media also promises more checks and criticism of the actions of those in power: Bloggers comment on political events, while "citizen journalists" document violations of human rights or corruption. Ultimately, digital media permit transnational networking of activists and new symbolic forms of expression of opposition culture. This way, the collective identity of movements can be strengthened and new resources tapped.

In the sphere of political mobilization, digital media appear to be used to greatest effect when it comes to brief, thematically focused campaigns. The possibilities they offer for spreading news and images rapidly in all directions resolve a key dilemma of protest mobilization: likeminded people can find one another more quickly and the level of inhibition with regard to actual engagement drops. The protest movements resulting from this resemble, in their form and design, the digital media they use: open, chaotic, and creative networks that agglomerate around a series of general demands, remaining flexible and initially resilient against state control. They can also quickly exert influence beyond national borders by attracting the attention of international media and politics. Yet these strengths are often also their greatest weaknesses, since movements of this kind may indeed stir up resistance and protest among the public, yet when it comes to the actual negotiation of political power relations, their influence remains small. In the longer term, the Green Movement in Iran achieved little to counter the concentrated power of the state. Likewise, in Egypt's first free elections following the fall of Hosni Mubarak in 2011–2012, the "Facebook generation" was defeated by the Muslim Brotherhood, which had built up a social basis for itself through decades of opposition work.

In reference to Antonio Gramsci once again, it could be argued that digital media predominantly foster the beginnings of a "counter-hegemony," that is, the critical questioning of dominant norms as well as the formation of alternative political ideas and communal solidarity within civil society. However, in the subsequent steps towards actual change – the collective organization of new demands and their successful conveyance on the level of society as a whole – the impact of the Internet is limited. Just how digital media can be applied beyond resistance and protest for an effective and constructive change in political relations remains a fascinating question for activists and researchers alike.

Zixue Tai

Finger Power and Smart Mob Politics:

Social Activism and Mass Dissent in China in the Networked Era

Introduction

Ever since the Arab Spring that spread across North Africa and the Middle East in 2011, there have been recurring debates and deliberations on whether a similar movement – featuring mass demonstrations and street uprisings spearheaded by social media and smartphones – would be possible in China. While China has not witnessed such a disruptive revolution or large-scale demonstrations thus far, a more subtle and mostly less violent social movement has blossomed in the country and has fundamentally reshaped China's sociopolitical landscape. Empowered by social media applications and personal communication devices, the ever-expanding online communicative space has provided Chinese individuals and NGOs with unprecedented access to an exploding base of user-generated content and has engendered innovative ways of information production and dissemination through ingenious mass collaboration and grassroots participation. Within this context, an emerging pattern has redefined the contours of Chinese Internet culture in recent years in which dispersed yet internetworked individuals actively engage in oftentimes masterfully coordinated massive collaboration and coherently orchestrated collective action to expose outrageous wrongdoings and transgressions committed by government officials and target individuals at the center of power in China's sociopolitical hierarchy. Through doing this, grassroots activists are successful, to varying degrees, in extracting swift government reactions in punishing selective offenders thrown into the spotlight and in redressing perceived instances of social, economic, environmental, and occasionally political injustice. This type of activism is largely attributable to, and enabled by, the new media environment, because the highly controlled conventional media establishment tends to toe the official line by staying away from topics of mass discontent and issues of state-disapproved interest.

Against the backdrop of the current Chinese sociopolitical power relations and hegemonic structure, this essay scrutinizes these emerging formations of digital activism in China, and discusses their implications for Chinese citizens, the authoritarian Chinese polity, and the evolving landscape of the new media environment in China.

Sociopolitical Context of China's Networked Era

Decades of economic liberalization in China have led the country to an unprecedented era of material prosperity and social transformation. China now boasts the second largest economy in the world (trailing the United States), and is the largest global exporter. At the same time, Chinese society has witnessed a parallel development in the ever-widening discrepancy among various social sectors and geographic regions in terms of material benefits and living standards. While the economy becomes more and more integrated with the rest of the world, China's political system remains largely closed, with the Chinese Communist Party maintaining a one-party rule over the country, allowing little participation from the general populace in the political process. As a result, there is a noticeable lack of any established official, institutional, or legal conduit for the commoners to address grievances and seek justice. It is no surprise, then, that contentious activities focusing mainly on social and economic demands have become pervasive and routinized in the later years of the reform era.[1] The Chinese single-party state, meanwhile, has reconsolidated itself into a certain level of "authoritarian resilience" in its ability to adapt and survive under conditions of market-oriented developments.[2] A new form of "authoritarian deliberation" permeated by a wide variety of state-induced participatory and deliberative practices functions to soften political contestation and strengthen regime legitimacy.[3]

Another important factor that bears mentioning is the reconfiguring of the relations between media, society, and state in China. As part of the state-orchestrated marketization drive, the media industry has shifted from the old state-supported model of the Mao era to its current subscription-based financing system. This means that the audience has assumed a prominent role in the media business. The party-state, however, has not relinquished its ideological control over the media. What the Chinese media have evolved into is a "state corporatist" system that hinges on the balancing act of "how to *profit the media organizations that are apparatus of the party-state and perform critical state functions.*"[4] The media thus tend to stay away from government-proscribed territories with regard to controversial issues and contentious topics.

The online environment, on the other hand, creates a different set of dynamics. Admittedly, China is widely known for having deployed one of the most sophisticated online information-censoring mechanisms in the world in the Internet age.[5] Per official regulations, all Internet sites engaging in any type of content publishing must be licensed by designated state authorities and must comply with demands from official censors. This not to say, however, that the regime has been able to effectively keep targeted content and contentious activities out of China's online space. The distributed nature of information production and distribution across the Internet is in essence antithetical to centralized control, thus making it possible for users to engage in creative communicative practices.

Chinese netizens are among the most active in the world in contributing to, and relying on, user-generated content as

1 See: Xi Chen, *Social Protest and Contentious Authoritarianism in China*, Cambridge University Press, New York, 2012.

2 See: Andrew J. Nathan, "Authoritarian Resilience," *Journal of Democracy*, vol. 14, no. 1, January 2003, pp. 6–17.

3 See: Baogang He and Mark E. Warren, "Authoritarian Deliberation: The Deliberative Turn in Chinese Political Development," in: *Perspectives on Politics*, vol. 9, no. 2, June 2011, pp. 269–289.

4 Zhongdang Pan, "Bounded Innovations in the Media," in: You-tien Hsing and Ching Kwan Lee (eds.), *Reclaiming Chinese Society: The New Social Activism*, Routledge, New York, 2010, pp. 184–206, here p. 197.

5 See: Zixue Tai, "Casting the Ubiquitous Net of Information Control: Internet Surveillance in China from Golden Shield to Green Dam," in: *International Journal of Advanced Pervasive and Ubiquitous Computing*, vol. 2, no. 1, January 2010, pp. 53–70.

manifested in a wide range of platforms ranging from Bulletin Board Systems (BBS), Internet Relay Chat (IRC) rooms, Short Message Service (SMS), and instant messaging (IM), to online communities; they also display a much higher tendency than their counterparts in other countries in believing that they can effect change through online participation.[6] These propensities are best accounted for by the controlled nature of the information environment and the closed form of political governance in China.[7] Tight control of the conventional media establishment in China, not surprisingly, produces the effect of channeling user interest to more unconventional, user-centered platforms where user-contributed content rules.

6 See: Zixue Tai, *The Internet in China: Cyberspace and Civil Society*, Routledge, New York, 2006.

7 Ibid.

Networks of Protest and Formations of Digital Activism in China

While discussing the implications of the Internet and networked media for global activism, W. Lance Bennett observes that "digital communication networks may be changing the political game in favor of resource-poor players who, in many cases, are experimenting with political strategies outside of conventional national political channels such as elections and interest processes."[8] This is a fitting characterization of the status quo of online activism in China, in which unconventional, innovative strategies in the network era open up new opportunities for traditionally disenfranchised individuals and groups. Communication in networks can help to communicate information and coordinate plans of action with relative ease, speed, scope, and marginal cost that would be nonexistent within the highly controlled conventional media in China.

8 W. Lance Bennett, "Communicating Global Activism: Strengths and Vulnerabilities of Networked Politics," in: *Information, Communication & Society*, vol. 6, no. 2, June 2003, pp. 143–168, here p. 144.

R. Kelly Garrett argues that the influence of new information and communication technologies (ICTs) on social movements can be fruitfully examined in their interconnections in relation to three broad areas: mobilizing structures, opportunity structures, and framing processes.[9] With regard to China, the ICTs are profoundly revolutionizing all these three aspects in shaping the emergence, development, and outcome of contentious activities. In terms of mobilizing structures, online communities and networked communication groups create new dynamics, as conventional social structures, under effective state co-optation, are typically resistant to contentious activities nonendorsed by the state; diversified social groups and networks also make it easy to disseminate information and coordinate activities. Opportunity structures, which refer to "attributes of a social system that facilitate or constrain movement activities,"[10] are apparently institutionalized to repress collective actions outside of state-sanctioned domains in China. The online environment, however, makes it possible to bypass regulated venues and empowers new opportunities; moreover, it can also create formal or informal networks of (moral and logistic) support among like-minded individuals, and thus make contention sustainable. As far as framing processes are concerned, netizen-centered communication unconstrained by state censors effectively frames actions to counter the discourse from the mainstream media, and adds legitimacy to protest actions.

9 R. Kelly Garrett, "Protest in an Information Society: A Review of Literature on Social Movements and New ICTs," in: *Information, Communication & Society*, vol. 9, no. 2, April 2006, pp. 202–224.

10 Ibid., p. 212.

It is important to understand China's digital activism today within the historical contour of mass protest and social movement in the country. Popular protest in Mao's era was a rarity – unless it was orchestrated by the Party-state, and directly served the official needs of ideological indoctrination and mass mobilization. Social protest has surged since the early 1990s with the deepening of economic reform and the pluralization of power distribution in the sociopolitical landscape. Consequently, the current Chinese polity has transitioned into what Xi Chen calls a type of "contentious authoritarianism" wherein "a strong authoritarian regime accommodates widespread and routinized collective protests."[11] In his enlightening analysis of social protest and collective movements in China today, Chen attributes this surge to three major factors.[12] First, widespread collective protests are a natural byproduct of the "contradictions and ambiguities" caught in the tensions between the centralized power structure and the extensive nonbinding consultative system that the regime puts in place in order to allow ordinary people to lodge complaints and submit petitions. Second, epochal economic transformations have not only fundamentally reconfigured relations between ordinary people and state agents, but also created divergent, and often contradicting, economic interests among social groups and local entities. Third, protesters have devised "a strategic pattern of protest opportunism" so as to strike a delicate balance between defiance and obedience in maximizing their bargaining power. Additionally, two more factors serve as game changers behind this surge: rising popular awareness among the commoners about their rights and options dictates that more and more individuals are willing to resort to protest in addressing grievances; further integration of China in the world politically and economically necessitates more subtle handling of collective actions by state actors to avoid being portrayed in the negative spotlight of the global media.

11 Chen 2012, p. 189.

12 See: ibid., pp. 189–192.

In regard to social activism in China, Ching Kwan Lee and You-tien Hsing propose a spectrum of politics along three strands – namely, the politics of (re)distribution, recognition, and representation – based on the goals and the basis of formation of the collective social actors. The politics of (re)distribution "entails struggles and claims for material interests among social groups or between social groups and state actors that spring from their common or differential class locations"; the politics of recognition "is concerned with the discovery and articulation of needs previously denied or ignored, especially the demand for social recognition of certain groups' moral status, political position, and identity"; the third strand, the politics of representation, is related to the expression of ideas and symbols, or "symbolic contestations."[13]

13 Ching Kwan Lee and You-tien Hsing, "Social Activism in China: Agency and Possibility," in: Hsing and Lee 2010, pp. 3–4.

The distributed, anonymous, participatory, and freewheeling nature of networked communication creates variegated forms of space that seamlessly intermingle three core areas of online communication: mass participation, social networking, and creative individuality. The power to persuade and communicate, augmented by the power to direct and coordinate, multiplied by pervasive mobile phones and multimedia devices, gives rise to a particular form of social experimentation – "smart mobs," as Howard Rheingold calls it[14] – that allows disaggregated individuals to self-organize into collective actions and spontaneous street demonstrations. In the context of China, this smart mobbing includes finding ingenious ways of bypassing official censoring and information control. The abundance of pithy, racy, and catchy words in the Chinese language comes in handy to facilitate this.

14 See: Howard Rheingold, *Smart Mobs: The Next Social Revolution*, Basic Books, Cambridge (MA), 2002; Howard Rheingold, "Mobile Media and Political Collective Action," in: James E. Katz (ed.), *Handbook of Mobile Communication Studies*, The MIT Press, Cambridge (MA), 2008, pp. 225–239.

Collective action empowered through mass collaboration and coordination pervades China's online networks on a daily basis. The following are some high-profile exemplary cases in recent years that offer testimonials to the general trend and overall dynamics in how grassroots self-mobilization can trigger and shape the course of contentious actions under variegated circumstances.

The Nail House Does Not Stand Alone

The "Chongqing Nail House Incident"[15] is a landmark event in which blogging served as the main platform to garner public attention and mobilize popular support for protecting individual property rights in China during a time of rapid real estate development and relocation. The story of the "nail house" dates back to 2004 when a real estate development project in an old residential area of the Chongqing municipality broke ground. This project sought to build a shopping center on the site where Wu Ping and her husband Yang Wu owned a small two-story house. To make way for the new shopping center, all existing properties, Wu's house included, were targeted for demolition. This is a commonplace scenario across China's booming urban areas where new high-rise commercial developments replace old residential properties. Things took an unusual turn, however, to throw this incident into the spotlight of the local, national, and even overseas media.

15 See full coverage of this event from Sina's page titled "Focus on the Chongqing Nail House Incident," available online at: http://news.sina.com.cn/z/cqzndzh/, accessed 04/10/2014.

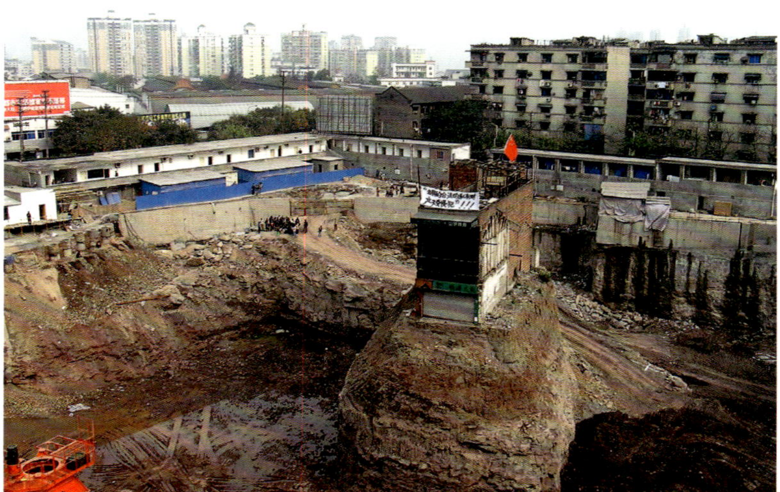

A "nail house," a home whose residents refuse to leave in order to make way for new construction, in a former old residential area in the Chongqing municipality in China, March 2007

In September that year, demolition work got underway as planned, and soon 280 households moved out to make way for the construction. But Wu and Yang refused to relocate as they were dissatisfied with the terms of proposed compensation offered by the government-designated developer. As negotiations between the property developer and the house owner couple were still ongoing, things turned ugly on another front. In October 2004, the water supply for their house was cut off; on February 2, 2005, electricity was disconnected. The couple didn't give in, however. A protracted standoff ensued for months, as neither the property developer nor the house owners wanted to budge.

The couple's home became widely known as the "nail house" in reference to their lonely stance on an otherwise leveled field. In early 2007 the case caught the attention of millions through a blog site run by a young man who called himself Zola Zhou. Netizens threw their support behind the house owners through blogs and online forums, which amplified public attention to this dispute. Pictures of the stand-alone house were reposted across popular forums and virtual communities, and were lauded as a symbol of resistance against real estate developer greed. Conventional media were quick to pick up the story, and reporters from many parts of the country flocked to the site of this house to snap their own pictures and run their own stories. The owner couple showed up for TV interviews on numerous occasions, and public pressure built up on the developer to resolve the dispute in a peaceful manner. Eventually, the house owners and the developer reached a settlement on compensation terms on April 2, 2007. As this was a case involving property rights, it aroused much discussion on property rights protection in China and triggered heated debates about flaws in the existing legal framework in China in this area. Moreover, this incident has become a source of tactical inspiration for individuals trapped in similar situations for addressing their grievances against aggressive developers. Since then many have followed suit in broadcasting their struggles to a broad base of netizens for support.

No PX Plant in Our Backyard

Another hotbed for popular protest in recent years is environmental protection. Among the most well-known public protest events was the popular opposition to a chemical plant in Xiamen in 2007, more commonly known as the "Xiamen PX Incident."[16] In July 2006, the National Development and Reform Commission approved a request by a Taiwan investor to build a factory in China's southern city of Xiamen. The 10.8-billion-yuan projected plant involved an annual output of 800,000 tons of p-Xylene, a highly hazardous and inflammable substance; once completed, it was expected to yield an annual GDP of CNY80 billion (approx. US$12.9 billion) to the local economy. The designated site of the plant was just seven kilometers from the city proper and only 1.5 kilometers from the nearest residential area; far below the acceptable distances stipulated in international conventions. There

16 See the Baidu wiki page "The Xiamen PX Project Incident" for a narrative of this incident at http://baike.baidu.com/view/3114002.htm, accessed 04/10/2014.

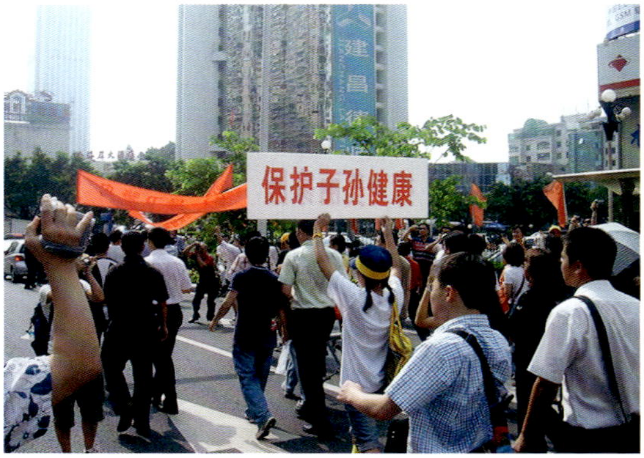

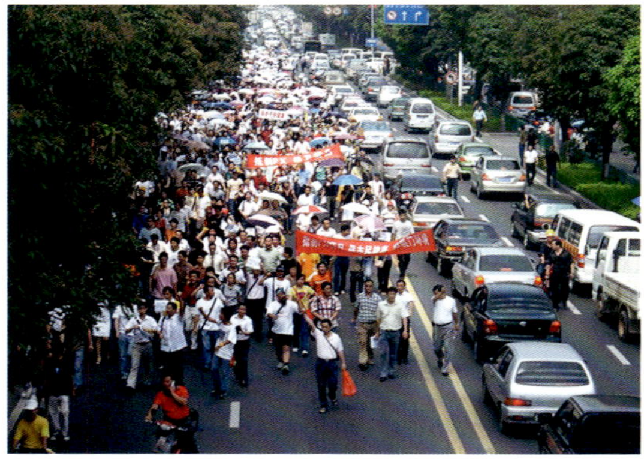

Above and below: People in the streets of Xiamen, protesting against the government's plan to build a chemical plant, June 2007

was little public knowledge about the planned plant until March 2007, when 105 members of the Chinese People's Political Consultative Conference signed a petition to relocate this project for safety and environmental reasons. Alerted residents in Xiamen raised their concerns with local authorities in the following months, but to no avail. The local government was determined to go ahead with the plant; it invited its own experts and organized information panels to assure the public that there would be no compromise on public health safety.

Residents mobilized themselves into action through social media and online platforms. A leading activist, Wu Xian, created a QQ group[17] under the slogan "Protecting the Clear Water and the Blue Sky of Xiamen" to raise public awareness and organize protest activities; due to rising demand, Wu had to add two more QQ groups (because QQ keeps a cap on the number of members allowed in any one group). Wu's efforts to organize group protests in late May through his QQ groups were aborted by security police, and he was detained on June 1, 2007, the day of a mass protest that he had co-organized.[18] Wu and his fellow group members, however, were not fighting alone. Numerous online communities and discussion boards, especially a few on Xiamen Fish Forum[19] which attracted a steady base of local users, had published a lot of information and engaged in debates since March. Text messaging via cell phones also played a pivotal role in spreading information and coordinating events. An inflammatory message, which compared the plant to the installation of an A-bomb in the center of the city and called on street protests, had been circulating via cell phone networks since May 20; over a million individuals were believed to have read it. On May 30, bowing to exploding public anger, the Xiamen authorities publicly announced that it would suspend this project pending further review and discussion.

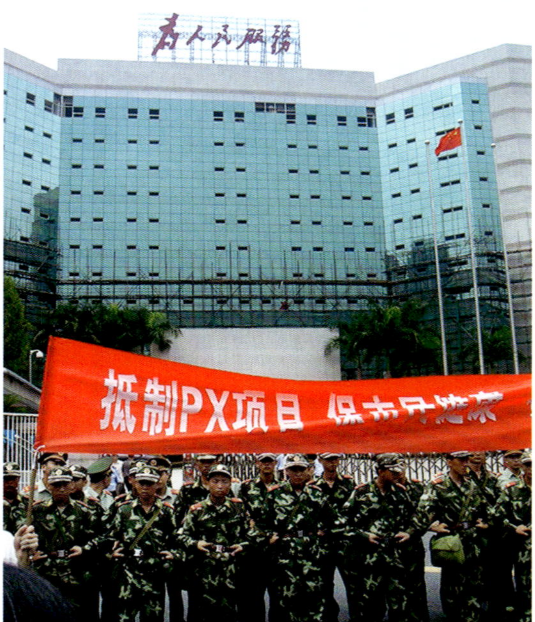

17

Tencent QQ is a Chinese instant messaging service.

18

See an interview with Wu by *China News Weekly* published on December 28, 2007, available online at: http://news.sina.com.cn/c/2007-12-28/101314622140.shtml, accessed 04/10/2014.

19

See, for example: www.xmfish.com, accessed 04/10/2014.

On June 1 and 2, tens of thousands of local residents, many of whom wore face masks and yellow wrist bands (as the suggested symbols of protest), answered the online calls for "walking-together protests" and gathered in front of the local government buildings. Bulldog.cn, a popular blog hosting site, covered the "walking-togethers" live in text and images for a national audience base.[20] After numerous public hearings and debates soliciting citizen input and feedback in the following months, the Xiamen government decided to give up its original plan of building the plant within the city precinct and look for an alternative site in December 2007. *Southern Weekend*, a Guangzhou-based weekly known for its outspokenness throughout the country, awarded its 2007 "Person(s) of the Year" award to Xiamen residents.[21]

Noticeably, the ramifications of the Xiamen incident extend far beyond this particular city. The incident has popularized the "walking-together" form of street protest through collaborative use of social media and online communication networks in venting out mass dissent and popular anger. Since then, hundreds of this type of mass walking incidents take place every year all over China. For example, high-profile "walking-together" incidents in 2012 involving thousands of participants were organized in Zhenjiang of Jiangsu Province (in February, against water pollution), Guangzhou and Shanghai (both in June, against trash-burning plants), Chongqing (in June, against district merging), and Taiyuan of Shanxi Province (in September, against official corruption). Coordinated mass street walks, therefore, have found new meaning for collective action in the age of social media and personal communication networks.

20
Bulldog.cn was shut down by the government in January 2009 for hosting "voluminous pornographic material." However, its owner, Luo Yonghao, told its users that the site was targeted by the regime for "well-known reasons." It had been active in hosting personal blogs expressing dissenting voices and opinions

21
"2007 Persons of the Year: People of Xiamen," *Southern Weekend*, December 26, 2007, available online at: www.infzm.com/content/9749, accessed 04/10/2014.

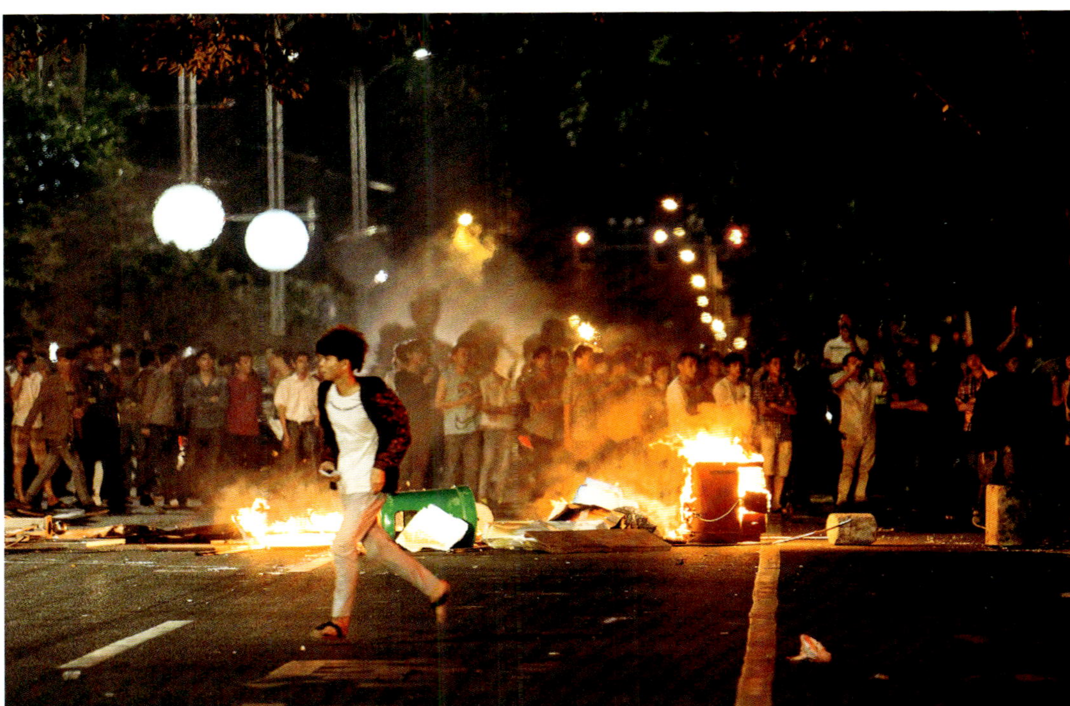

Demonstrators set fire to trash cans as they protest against a chemical plant project on a street in Maoming, Guangdong province, China, April 2014.

On March 30, 2014, a similar mass protest erupted in China's southern city of Maoming against the proposed construction of a p-Xylene plant in the city.[22] The project, already approved by the National Development and Reform Commission, had been the target of government propaganda in February and March 2014 when the local media ran a series of didactic reports on the industrial benefits of PX and the nonharmful nature of the chemical. The government-orchestrated media PR, however, fell flat, as the public did not believe what they were told by the media, and thousands of local residents congregated in front of the local government buildings on March 30 with anti-PX banners and slogans. The protest continued in the following days, and confrontations between riot police and demonstrators turned violent, with reported fatalities and injuries. Hundreds of protest photos taken via smartphones circulated on Weibo and WeChat, two of the most popular social media platforms in China. In early April, anti-PX protests spread to neighboring cities in rallying public opposition.[23] Meanwhile, the local authority put the project on hold and vowed more dialog with local citizens.

"Watch Brother"

The following incident illustrates the offhand and comical nature of China's online vigilantes.[24] Mid-afternoon on August 26, 2012, a fatal collision between a double-decker and a methanol tanker killed 36 of the 39 bus passengers on the highway of Yan'an. Per routine bureaucratic regulation, Yang Dacai, head of the provincial Bureau of Work Safety, showed up at the scene to supervise the handling of this disaster. What sparked public attention, however, was not the grisly nature of the accident, but rather a photograph by a passerby showing Yang smirking to a staffer made available through a personal blog with an inflaming subtitle bemoaning the coldheartedness of a senior official smiling under such circumstances. Widespread circulation of the picture of this so-labeled "Smiling Brother" on microblogs on Sina, QQ, and Hexun on the same day amplified public anger at Yang's flagrant display of insensitivity. Within hours, collaborative searches targeting Yang turned out dozens of pictures of him on various occasions. On the night of the day of the accident, one microblog drew attention to a watch Yang wore in one picture, and suggested that it might be an Omega, with a price tag of about 38,000 euros. The same microblog begged followers to dig up more. In the next two hours, a total of five different Swiss watches Yang had worn in different pictures were shared on Weibo. The next day, the Chief Operating Office of a popular luxury goods online retailer sent out a microblog revealing that a *connoisseur* he had interviewed disclosed that all five of these were genuine Swiss watches valued at around CNY200,000. The question naturally became how Yang could afford such luxurious items with his level of income. Yang became widely known as the "Watch Brother."[25]

Yang reacted quickly to these online maneuvers. On August 28, Yang publicly came to his own defense, claiming that he smiled

22 http://zh.wikipedia.org/wiki/2014年茂名市反对PX项目游行.

23 Shannon Tiezzi, "Maoming Protests Continue in Southern China," April 5, 2014, *The Diplomat*, available online at: http://thediplomat.com/2014/04/maoming-protests-continue-in-southern-china/, accessed 04/10/2014.

24 See Yahoo China's *People* Profile of Yang Dacai titled "One Smile Ruins His Future," at http://news.cn.yahoo.com/rw/yangdacai/, accessed 12/15/2013.

25 There is a play on words here. In Chinese, *biao ge* most typically means (male) "cousin." However, syntactically, the first character means "watch," and the second character means "brother," hence "watch brother."

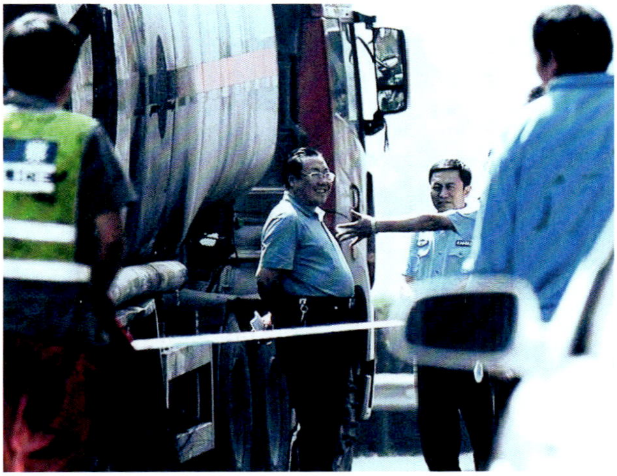

Yang Dacai, head of the provincial Bureau of Work, smiling after a fatal collision between a double-decker and a methanol tanker on the highway of Yan'an in which 36 bus passengers were killed.

in the picture because he wanted to create a relaxing atmosphere so that the public safety workers would feel pressured by his presence. He also admitted that he did own the five watches featured in these online photos, but all these personal purchases had been made with help from his family. However, in the next few days, more damaging discoveries emerged: netizens' searches pinpointed an extravagant wardrobe of eleven luxury watches (including the previous five), four pairs of expensive glasses, a platinum bracelet, eight ritzy belts, and Armani suits, with an estimated value of over one million yuan. On September 21, twenty-seven days after that smile, the Shaanxi provincial authorities relieved Yang of his official duties for "breaking the Party disciplines" and promised a criminal investigation. On September 5, 2013, Yang was sentenced to fourteen years of imprisonment for bribe-taking and owning large unaccounted-for assets. After the exposure of Yang, a number of government bureaucrats confessed online that it has become a widespread practice for officials to first remove their extravagant watches and other expensive items before making public appearances for fear of following in the footsteps of Yang.

Us Media vs. Them Media

China's media industry has experienced phenomenal growth in the reform era, most noticeably in the vast reach of the print, electronic, and cable sectors. Paradoxically, while the penetration of disseminated information is at an all-time high, public trust in the official media is at its lowest. The networked environment has created plurality in information channels and thus public confidence in the state-controlled media has deteriorated. As a result, state media often find themselves the object of ridicule and mockery by Chinese netizens. China Central Television (CCTV), the only national television network in the country, naturally becomes the prime target.

On October 20, 2013, CCTV aired an investigative report decrying the high prices that the U.S. global chain Starbucks charges Chinese patrons. The 23-minute program showed footage of interviews with customers in major cities around the world, and found that Chinese consumers pay the highest price while their counterparts in Mumbai pay the least for a latte of the same size. This act of profiteering, CCTV concluded, was largely due to lack of government oversight. The average Chinese consumers, however, thought this criticism of Starbucks was mistargeted; they stormed popular social media platforms to lambast CCTV's inability to investigate high prices in China's real estate and gasoline, and called attention to environmental pollution as well as a host of other severe problems that are of more concern to the commoners in the country. Many netizens pointed out that CCTV picked Starbucks as an easy target because it could not take on China's inefficient state-run enterprises and corrupt officials. As an expression of mass dissent, hashtags such as "I'm at Starbucks" and "I'm on my way to Starbucks" were among the most trending topics on Weibo in the next few days.

In another incident that took place on February 8, 2014, CCTV aired an exposure in its prime-time investigative programming on the rampant prostitution industry in the southern city of Dongguan. Using hidden cameras, the state broadcaster showed scantily dressed women dancing in Karaoke clubs and flirting with customers in hotel hallways. In the next 36 hours after the CCTV scoop, a 6,000-people-strong police force stormed hundreds of hotels and entertainment venues resulting in 67 arrests; state-controlled media outlets flooded the air, print, and online space with thousands of news stories unanimously in favor of the government cleansing.[26]

In no time at all China's social media responded to this event, and the vast majority of Weibo microbloggers openly expressed their sympathy for the sex workers, and considered them to be the victims of CCTV's unfair picking of a particularly vulnerable group. CCTV immediately became the target of public contempt and ridicule for its inability to expose what they deemed as a far more serious social malaise – official corruption and high unemployment. In fact, the hashtag #dongguanhanginthere turned into the number one trending topic on Sina Weibo in the first 24 hours after the crackdown. As other state media bemoaned, "opposition for the sake of opposition" has become a trendy practice lately in which netizens simply go against whatever CCTV upholds.[27]

26 For a detailed timeline and in-depth coverage, see, for example, the Sohu's special section on this event at http://news.sohu.com/s2014/dianji-1325/, accessed 04/10/2014.

27 Lin Yunshi and Will Spence, "Media Watch: State Media Rallies behind CCTV over Dongguan Reporting," in: *Caixin Online*, February 13, 2014, available online at: http://english.caixin.com/2014-02-13/100638449.html, accessed 04/10/2014.

Conclusion

Decades of economic liberalization in China have unleashed all sorts of tensions between the authoritarian state and the disentangled socioeconomic forces in the country. Deepening disparity among various sectors and interest groups has created a hotbed of mass contestation. On the other hand, lack of public participation in the democratic process coupled with limited institutionalized channels of conflict resolution makes it more likely that individuals will collaborate with like-minded fellow citizens to take matters into their own hands. As a result, social activism continues to reach new heights as aggrieved individuals and groups find creative ways to win over the sympathy of the mass populace in their efforts to engage the state power.

The expanding communicative space empowered by social media and personal communication devices has opened up new windows of opportunity for mass collaboration and grassroots participation. Since the Chinese regime has made maintaining social stability its top priority, it invests more and more in assessing public sentiments and appeasing mass dissent to the extent allowable in order to legitimize its continued monopoly of power.

In this regard, social media and other online venues provide the viable channels for the state authority to gauge the popular psyche and function as a particular type of "deliberative mechanisms" as conceptualized by He and Warren.[28] The networked space, therefore, is likely to continue to enjoy a certain degree of freedom for individuals to vent their personal grievances and contemplate collective action. Under many circumstances, activists have been successful, to varying degrees, in negotiating government accountability and extracting swift official reactions to address their demands and in punishing selective offenders.

28 See: He and Warren 2011.

The distributed, largely anonymous, and participatory nature of the networked environment defies centralized control; it also makes mass mobilization possible without a clearly identifiable organization structure – or what Clay Shirky calls "organizing without organizations."[29] This liberatory feature is particularly worth highlighting in the context of social activism in China. The primary reason is that in recent decades, the Chinese regime has been adopting a strategy of isolating and punishing a very small number of individual leaders and dissenters to derail certain social and political movements that it deems incendiary and threatening; it has shown considerable hesitancy in incriminating a broad base of activists. Collective action through mass collaboration and coordination without identifiable leaders, therefore, makes social activism achievable and sustainable in China's online terrain.

29 See: Clay Shirky, *Here Comes Everybody: The Power of Organizing Without Organizations*, Penguin, New York, 2008.

China's digital activism displays an unmistakable hallmark of antielitism in its rhetorical invocations and objects of pursuit. Public officials, the superrich, corporate and special interest groups easily become targets of scrutiny, while the marginal, the disadvantaged, and commoners are sided with in popular online crusades. It is worth noting, however, that any effort at challenging the central leadership or the legitimacy of the party-state has not been tolerated, and this pattern is most likely to continue in the years to come.

Johanna Domke *1978 and Marouan Omara *1987

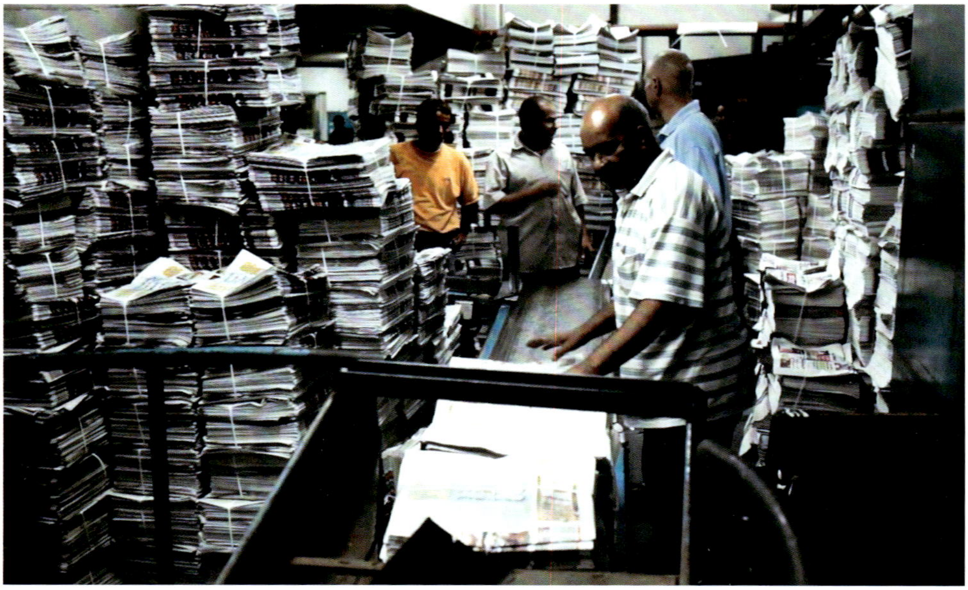

Johanna Domke and Marouan Omara, *CROP*, 2012, video, color, sound, 47:22 min, video still

Visual artist Johanna Domke grew up in Germany and Argentina. She currently lives in Berlin, Istanbul, and Copenhagen. After studying fine arts at the Royal Danish Academy of Fine Arts in Copenhagen and the Malmö Art Academy, Sweden, she now works with film, video, and photography. Her works straddle the border between art and cinema and their approach is both sociopolitical and structural. Domke's work has been shown in solo and group exhibitions all over the world, and she has participated in numerous collaborative projects and held various residencies including at the Experimental Media and Performing Arts Center (EMPAC) in New York, the Townhouse in Cairo, and the Platform in Istanbul.

The Egyptian filmmaker Marouan Omara studied at Helwan University and the Academy of Cinema Arts and Technology in Cairo and holds a bachelor's degree in applied arts, photography, cinema, and TV, as well as a diploma in filmmaking. Initially working as a freelance photographer, Omara has exhibited his works nationally as well as internationally. He has produced a number of documentaries and worked in various capacities for other productions. In 2012, he was selected to participate in the 5th edition of the Talent Campus Durban program at the Durban International Film Festival in South Africa, and he also took part in Arabia Offscreen, a cultural expedition project to Saudi Arabia. Omara is currently working as adjunct professor for film production at the Center for the Arts at the American University in Cairo and as a part-time instructor for video and film production at the German University in Cairo.

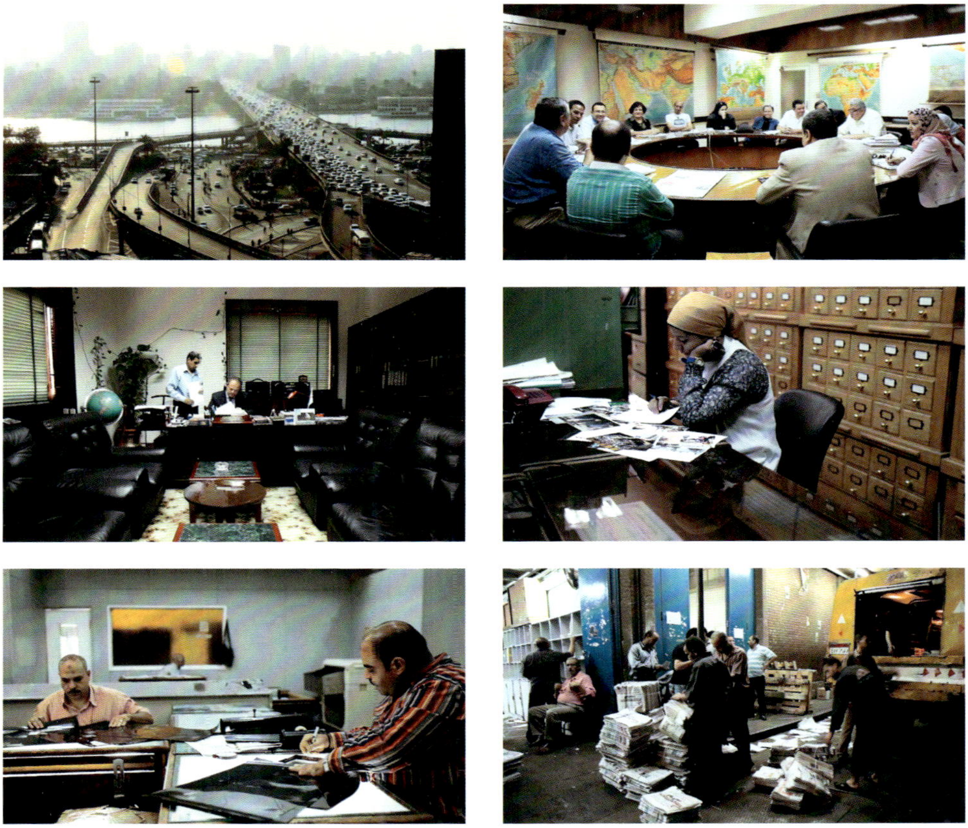

Johanna Domke and Marouan Omara, *CROP*, 2012 video, color, sound, 47:22 min, video stills

The film *CROP* (2012) by Johanna Domke and Marouan Omara deals with the effect of images during the Egyptian revolution in 2011. It plays in the offices of Egypt's most influential newspaper, *Al-Ahram*, and tells the story of a photojournalist who missed the revolution because he was in hospital. His narrative in voice-over reflects on the machinations and manipulation of the media by the old regime. The film project was realized in collaboration with the Danish Arts Council, DayDream Art Production, the Goethe-Institut Cairo, the Academy of Media Arts Cologne, the Museum für Photographie Braunschweig, and the Townhouse gallery in Cairo. In 2013, *CROP* was part of the International Film Festival Rotterdam's official selection.

Electronic Disturbance Theater

The Electronic Disturbance Theater 1.0 (EDT) group (Ricardo Dominguez, Brett Stalbaum, Stefan Wray, and Carmin Karasic) developed virtual sit-in technologies in 1998 in solidarity with the Zapatista communities in Chiapas, Mexico. Electronic Disturbance Theater 2.0 (Brett Stalbaum, Micha Cárdenas, Amy Sara Carroll, and Elle Mehrmand) developed the *Transborder Immigrant Tool*, a GPS cell phone safety net tool for crossing the Mexico–U.S. border which won the Transnational Communities Award in 2008, an award funded by Cultural Contact, Endowment for Culture Mexico–U.S. and handed out by the U.S. Embassy in Mexico. The tool which is also funded by the California Institute for Telecommunications and Information Technology and won two Transborder Awards from the University of California, San Diego Center for the Humanities. The *Transborder Immigrant Tool* was exhibited at the 2010 California Biennial, Toronto Free Gallery, Canada (2011), ZKM | Center for Art and Media Karlsruhe, Germany (2014), as well as a number of other venues around the world. The project was under investigation by the U.S. Congress in 2009/2010, and was also reviewed by Glenn Beck in 2010 as a gesture that with its poetry potentially "dissolved" the U.S. border.

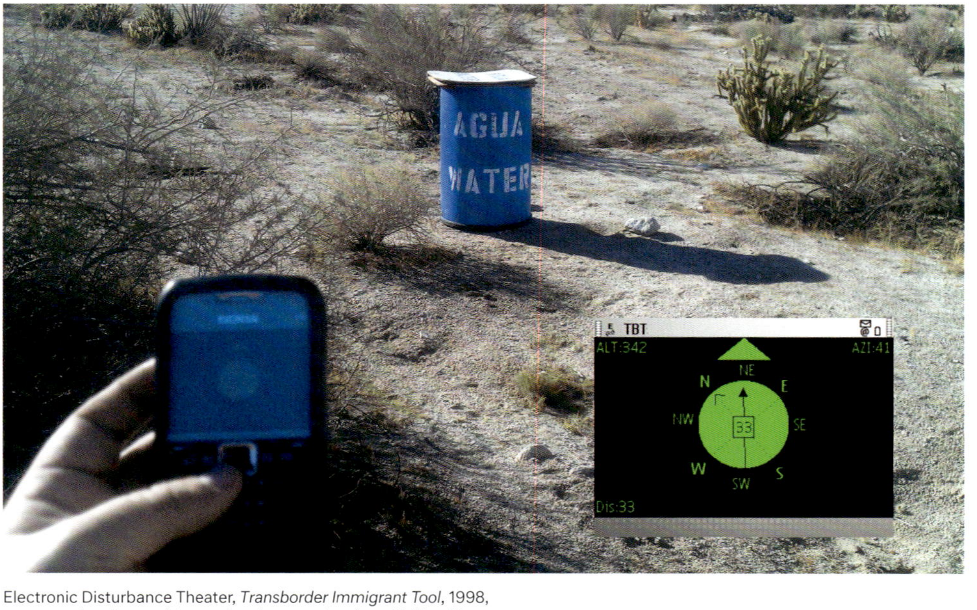

Electronic Disturbance Theater, *Transborder Immigrant Tool*, 1998, concept, showing working tool and screenshot from Nokia e71

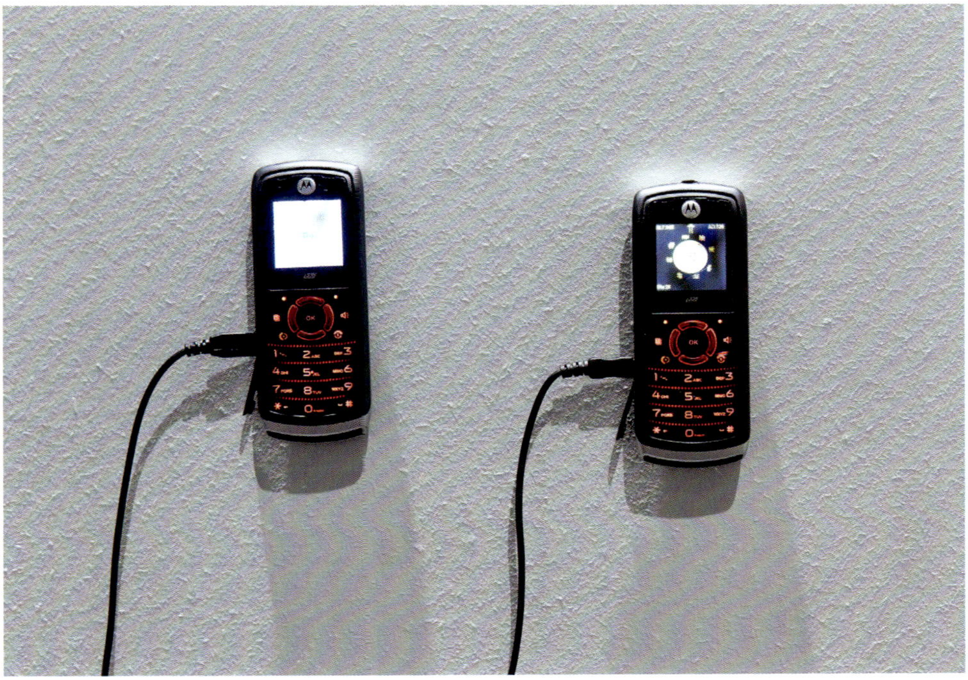

Electronic Disturbance Theater, *Transborder Immigrant Tool*, 1998, installation, mixed media, installation view, ZKM | Karlsruhe, 2014

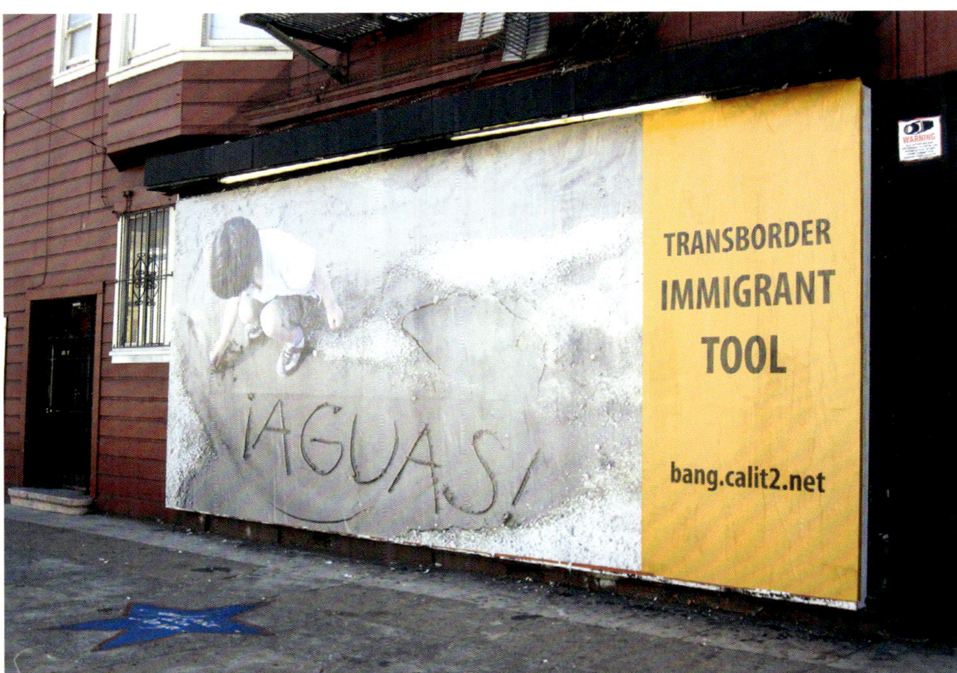

Electronic Disturbance Theater, *Transborder Immigrant Tool*, 1998, billboard, street level

Sharon Hayes *1970

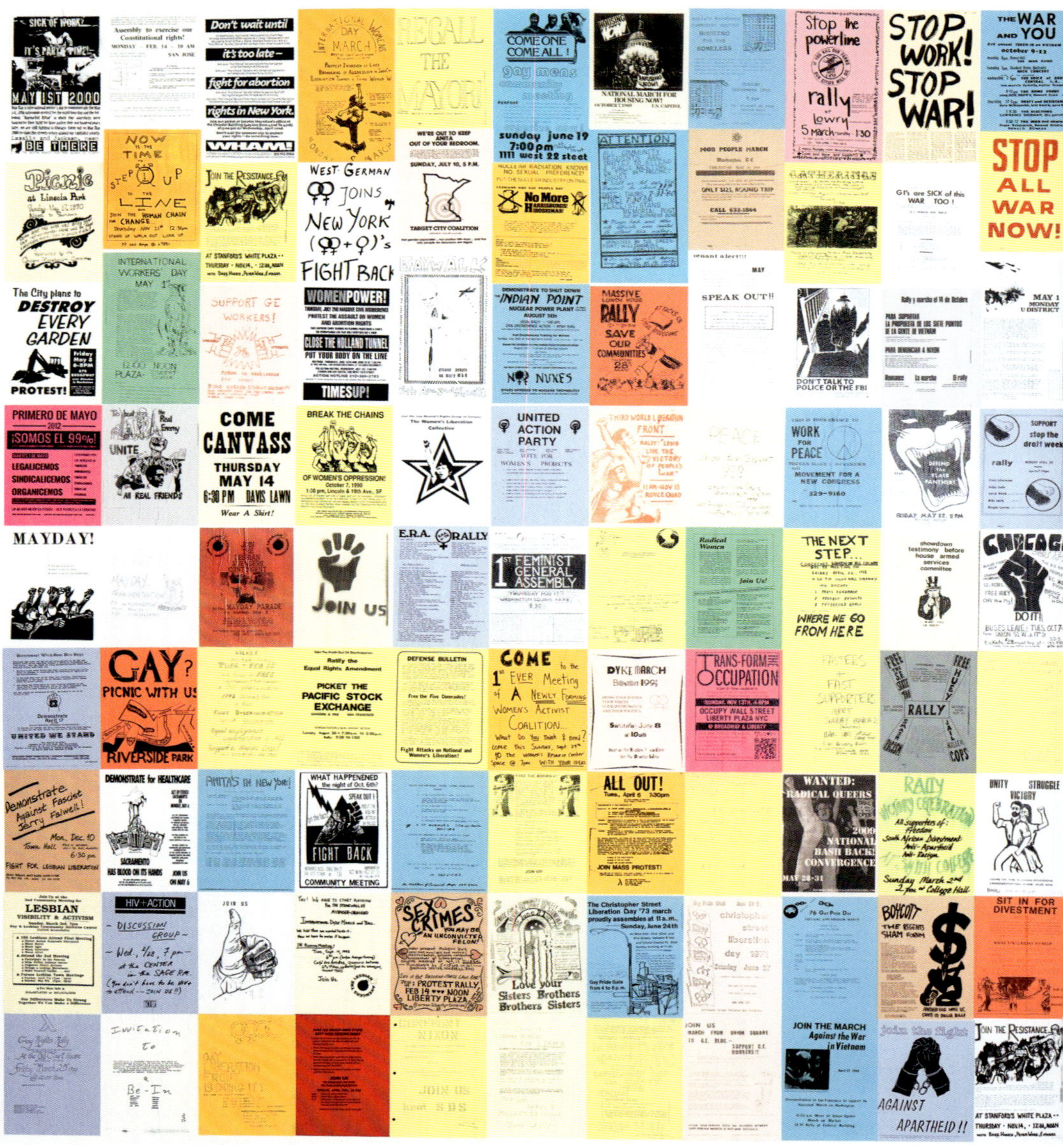

Various authors organized by Sharon Hayes with Angela Beallor, *Join Us*, 2012/2013, flyers on paper, installation view, ZKM | Karlsruhe, 2014

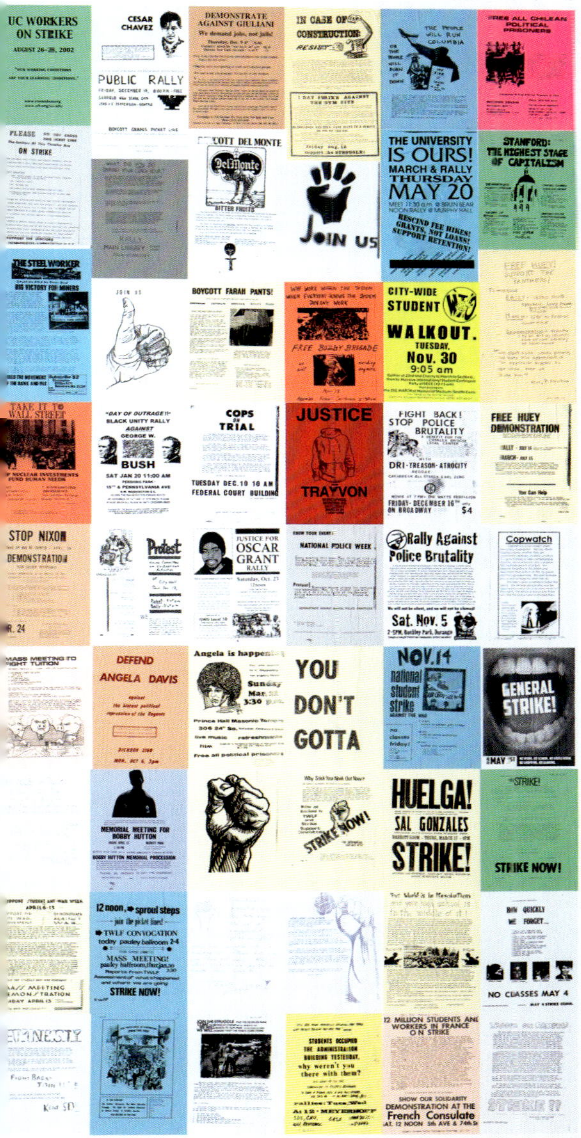

Since the mid-1990s, the New York City-based Sharon Hayes had various artist residencies and fellowships, including a New York Foundation for the Arts Fellowship in 1999 and an artist residency as part of the International Program for Visual Artists in Sweden (IASPIS). In 2003, she received an MFA from the University of California, Los Angeles. Today, Hayes is an assistant professor at the Cooper Union for the Advancement of Science and Art. Her works have been shown all over the world, for example, at the New Museum of Contemporary Art and the Guggenheim Museum in New York, at the Tate Modern in London, the Generali Foundation in Vienna, the Deutsche Guggenheim in Berlin, and in galleries and art spaces in the United States, Sweden, Denmark, Austria, Canada, Croatia, Germany, and Colombia. Further, Hayes contributed to New York's first performance biennial Performa 05 in 2005, and her works were exhibited at documenta 12 in Kassel, Germany, the Guangzhou Triennial 2008, the Yokohama Triennale 2008, the Istanbul Biennial in 2009, and the 2010 Whitney Biennial. She is represented by Tanya Leighton Gallery, Berlin.

Over the past decade, Sharon Hayes has combined video, performance, and installation to investigate various intersection points between history, politics, and speech, and has used conceptual and methodological approaches borrowed both from academic and artistic practices. The work *Join Us* (2012/2013), organized by Sharon Hayes with Angela Beallor, is a collection of flyers from various authors in the USA, from the 1960s to the present, which call for people to support and participate in political protest events. *Join Us* defines the flyer as a speech act, which proposes itself to a receiver. In 2013 and 2014, the work was exhibited in the Tanya Leighton Gallery in Berlin and the ZKM | Center for Art and Media Karlsruhe.

Founded in 2000
Global

http://kanalb.org

kanalB

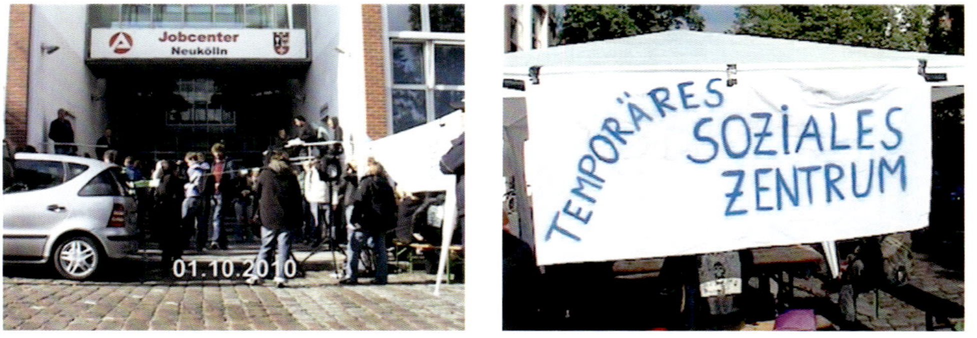

kanalB, action organized at an employment agency in the Berlin district of Neukölln, October 1, 2010, video documentary, color, sound, 5:20 min, video stills

kanalB is an activist media project, which since 2000 runs an Internet station and produces political documentaries. To do this work only the Internet and affordable video technology, low-cost traffic, and cheap servers are needed. Most of the videos are available in several languages and are published under Creative Commons licenses. Main focuses are the visualization of social struggles and movements, political analysis and critique, and the idea of exploring alternative lifestyles. The project takes issue with the consensus created by the mass media, according to which we live in the best of all possible worlds. On the contrary, kanalB views the current economic and social order as profoundly violent and coercive, and defines itself as part of a global political movement that opposes a system based upon exploitation and searches for societal alternatives. Considering the limited resources available, the project meets with very lively interest indeed.

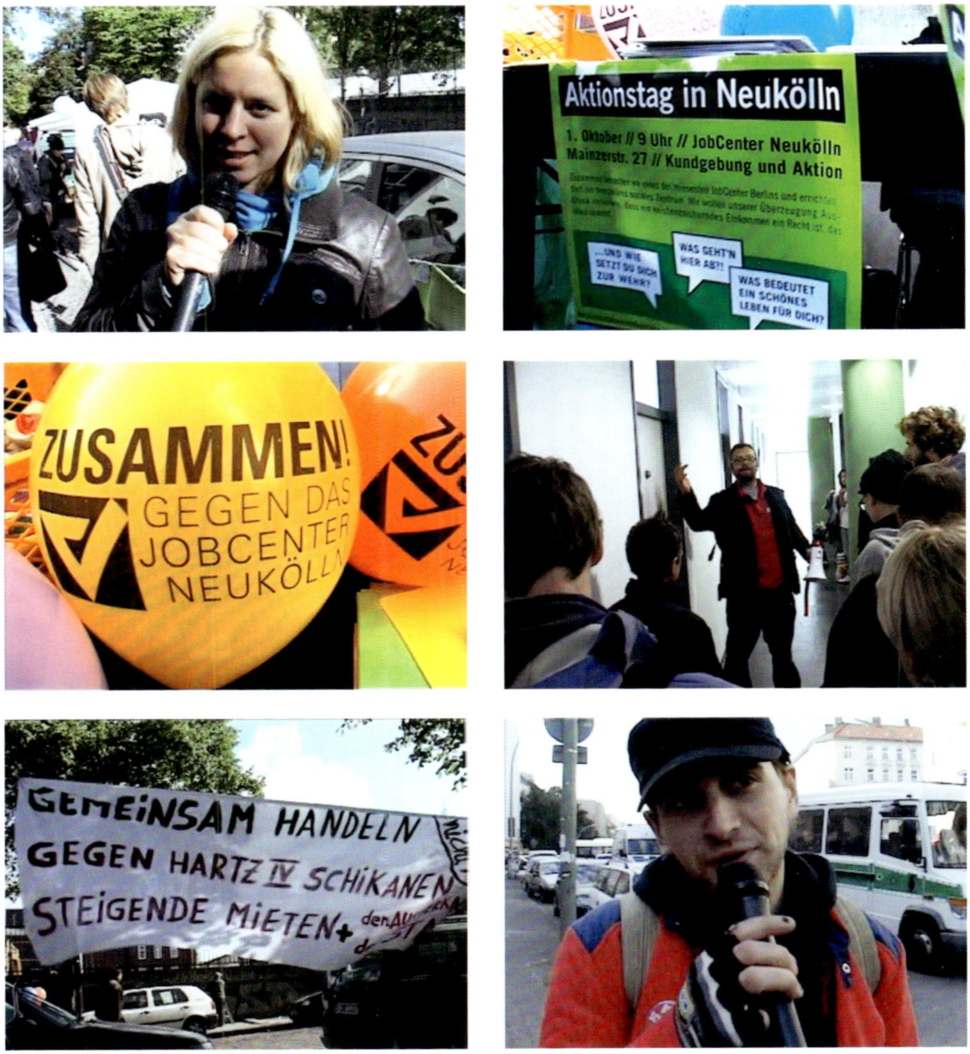

kanalB, action organized at an employment agency in the Berlin district of Neukölln, October 1, 2010, video documentary, color, sound, 5:20 min, video stills

Founded in 2010
Brazil

http://maps.mootiro.org

MootiroMaps

MootiroMaps is an online project that supports individual mapping projects. Here urban citizens can create, share, and (re)use maps as well as mapped data by other users to present initiatives, planned actions, and collaboration projects. By showing where resources and organizations are located, *Mootiro* helps users to understand a territory via its map, and in the process offers important information for community planning as well as data to analyze the priorities of and demands on local development. Furthermore, *MootiroMaps* can be seen as an instrument for nurturing social control, for each user is able to air their grievances directly and point up needs and lacks in their particular area. Creating a network facilitates easy identification of organizations that are working in the same direction to address the issues collectively. After a map has been created, anyone can participate, correct or amend information, or add new objects to the map. Thus, over the course of time the maps contain ever more and increasingly complex information.

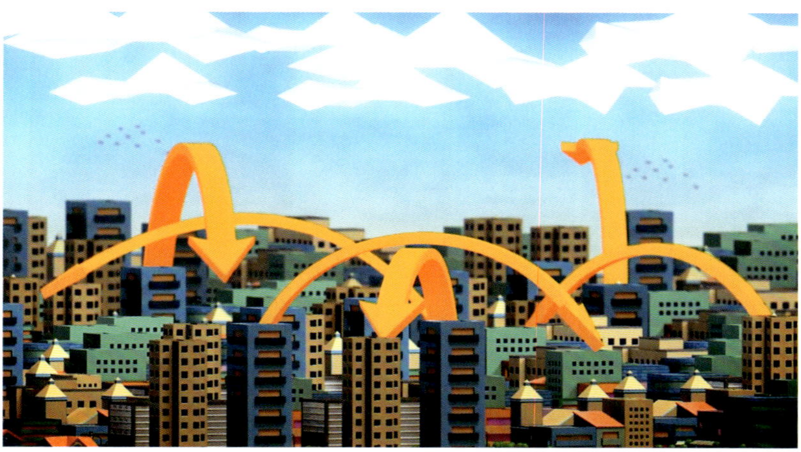

MootiroMaps, promotion video, color, sound, 2:04 min, available online at: maps.mootiro.org and vimeo.com/56746348, accessed 12/18/2014, screenshot

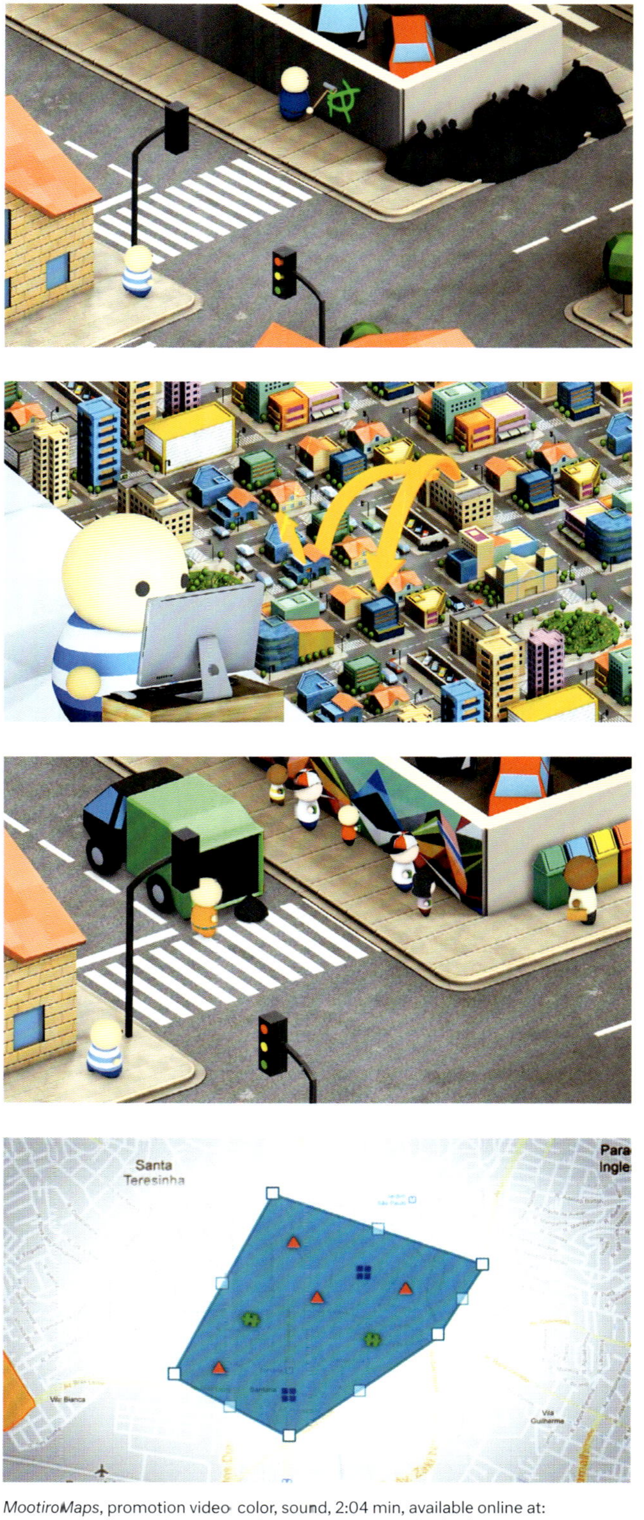

MootiroMaps, promotion video, color, sound, 2:04 min, available online at: maps.mootiro.org and vimeo.com/56746348, accessed 12/18/2014, screenshots www.imageatlas.org

Taryn Simon *1975 and Aaron Swartz 1986–2013

Taryn Simon is a U.S.-American conceptual artist based in New York, a graduate of Brown University, and a Guggenheim Fellow. In her artistic work she combines photography, text, and graphic design, and focuses explicitly on asking reasonable and controversial questions: On what basis are judgments made? How willingly do we believe in the thin probative value of photography? Who holds the authority to interpret images and thus has the power over visual historiography and myths? Who has the power to define the other as hostile that cannot cross the border into the own?

In all Taryn Simon's works one can identify a central theme: making visible what has previously been concealed. For *The Innocents* (2002), for example, she interviewed former prisoners, mostly Afro-American men who were wrongfully convicted by predominantly white jury members on the basis of photographic documents, and took pictures of them in venues that were decisive for the miscarriage of justice. In the case of *An American Index of the Hidden and Unfamiliar* (2007), the artist explored places, spaces, and objects that remain inaccessible to the public, although they play an enormously important role in the creation of the United States' identity, which is mythically charged and reproduced daily at the same time, such as the headquarters of the Ku Klux Klan or the lobby of the CIA headquarters in Langley, Virginia.

Simon's photographs and writings have been exhibited, amongst others at Ullens Center for Contemporary Art, Beijing (2013); Museum of Modern Art, New York (2012); Museum of Contemporary Art, Los Angeles (2012); Tate Modern, London (2011); Neue Nationalgalerie, Berlin (2011); Museum für Moderne Kunst, Frankfurt (2008); Whitney Museum of American Art, New York (2007); KW Institute for Contemporary Art, Berlin (2004); and PS1, New York (2003). Her work is held in the permanent collections of the Metropolitan Museum of Art, Tate Modern, Whitney Museum of American Art, Centre Pompidou, and Museum of Contemporary Art, Los Angeles, and was included in the 54th Venice Biennale in 2011 and the Carnegie International in 2013.

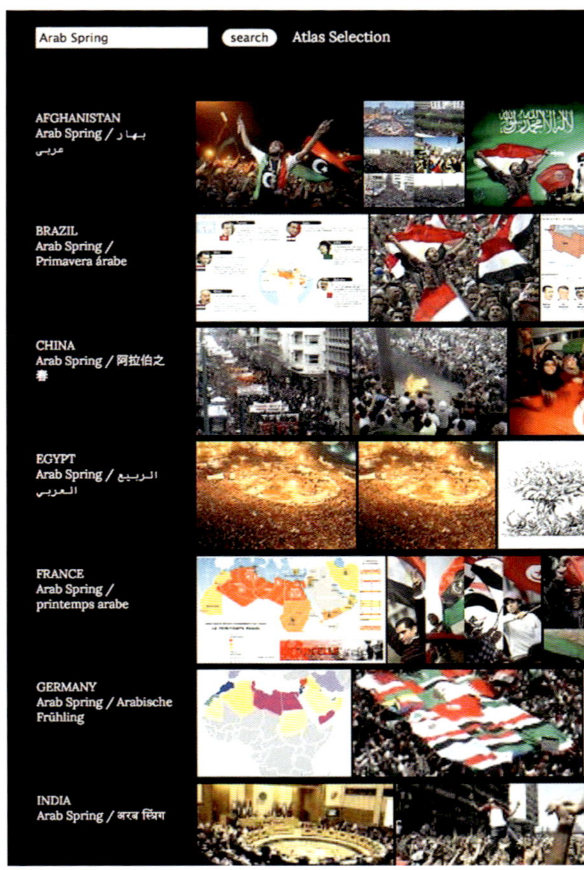

Aaron Swartz was a U.S.-American programmer, writer, and hacktivist. As a teenager he was involved in the development of the RSS code for subscribing to Internet content: later, he took part in the technical implementation of the Creative Commons licenses and the social networking site reddit.com, and was technical director of the Open Library. Swartz fought for free access to the contents of the Internet, against censorship, and for open access to knowledge. For a time he lived in Cambridge, Massachusetts, where he served on the board of the organization Change Congress, among other things. In 2008, Swartz formulated the Guerilla open access Manifesto as a basis for the radical wing of the open access movement, and in 2009 he released about 2.7 million documents of federal court decisions, which he had downloaded the year before from the Public Access to Court Electronic Records (PACER) database managed by the Administrative Office of the U.S. Courts, a service that is not free. Swartz wanted to create a searchable database which would be free of charge, unlike the existing expensive service. His action aroused the attention of the FBI, but it was legal because the documents are, in fact, in the public domain. In 2010, as a research fellow at Harvard University's Safra Research Lab he conducted research on institutional and political corruption and investigated which backers funded contributions to law journals. Swartz was one of the cofounders of the online group Demand Progress, which campaigned against a bill known as the Stop Online Piracy Act. On July 19, 2011, Swartz was accused of having illegally downloaded over four million scientific articles from the digital library JSTOR. After he had handed over the data to JSTOR, they announced they would not press civil law charges against him. However, the case was prosecuted by the public prosecutor's office. For a deposit of 100,000 dollars Swartz remained at liberty. If convicted, he would have faced up to 35 years in prison and a heavy fine. The trial was scheduled for April 2013. In January 2013 Swartz committed suicide.

In their collaborative work *Image Atlas* (2012) Taryn Simon and Aaron Swartz question whether a universal visual language is possible and the supposed neutrality of algorithms with which search engines operate. Using the *Image Atlas*, the top results of Internet image searches in 57 countries can be compared, which enables one to draw conclusions about cultural differences and access to information, and to recover a sense of the local, in a way. It also shows how something as fundamental to web interaction as searching is actually constrained and determined by many cultural and political forces.

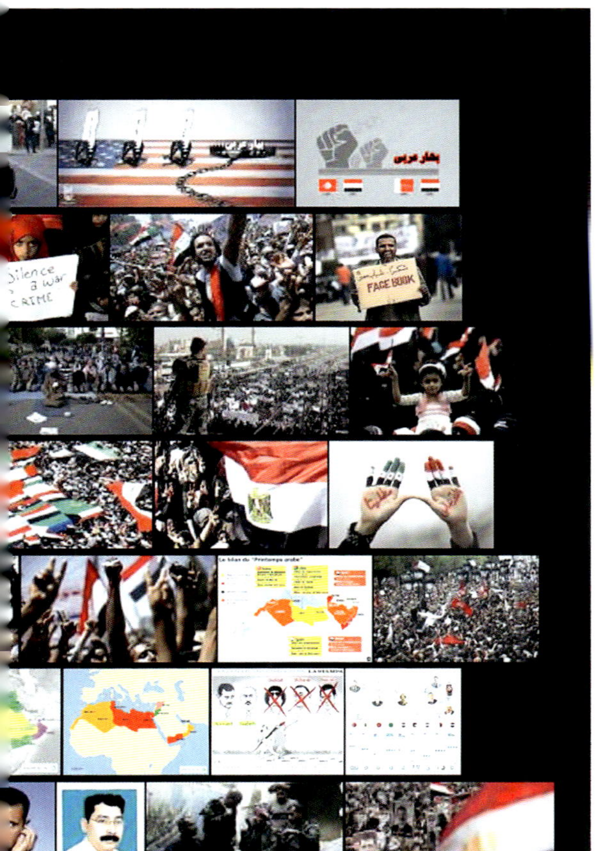

Taryn Simon and Aaron Swartz, *Image Atlas*, 2012, website, screenshot using the search term "Arab Spring," 12/17/2014

Tweets from Tahrir

In the three weeks of the Egyptian Revolution in 2011 – from January 25 to Hosni Mubarak's fall on February 11 – the new media, especially the social networking service Twitter, played an extraordinarily important role. The tweets, limited to 140 characters, not only allowed the people to inform others about current events, they also painted a real-time picture of the uprising, from the excitement of the first demonstrations to the incredibly violent interventions of Mubarak's troops and the celebration of Mubarak's resign. The following pages show a selection of the tweets that were sent via Twitter during the eighteen days of the revolution in Cairo bearing the hashtag #Jan25.

The Eighteen Days

January 25, 2011 #Jan25

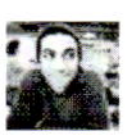

3arabawy | Hossam عمو حسام
streets r empty. Police r everywhere. #jan25
09:27 Jan 25, 2011

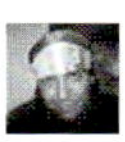

Sandmonkey | Mahmoud Salem
Shower, Crago pants, Hoodie, running shoes, phone charged, cash, ID, cigs (for jail) and some mace just in case. Am ready! #jan25
10:04 Jan 25, 2011

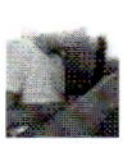

adamakary | Adam Makary
#jan25 protester's demands: increase in minimum wage, dismissal of interior ministry, removal of emergency law, shorten presidential term
10:15 Jan 25, 2011

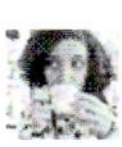

ManarMohsen | Manar Mohsen
Those tweeting about the protest in Egypt, please use the hashtag #Jan25 in order to spread any information.
10:54 Jan 25, 2011

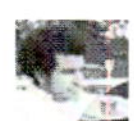

tarekshalaby | Tarek Shalaby
Today's our day as #CitizenJournalists to cover and share the truth freely. Regardless of the outcome we are winners cuz we're a team #jan25
12:45 Jan 25, 2011

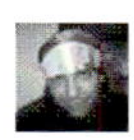

Sandmonkey | Mahmoud Salem
Huge demo going to tahrir #jan25 shit just got real
13:21 Jan 25, 2011

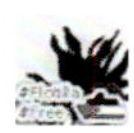

monasosh | monasosh
This is great, we r in nahya street, ppl r walking by our side #jan25
13:56 Jan 25, 2011

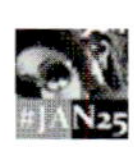

Gsquare86 | Gigi Ibrahim جيييج
I am looking at shubra's residents reaction from the balconies and they r chanting with us #jan25 http://yfrog.com/h29m5hrj
14:28 Jan 25, 2011

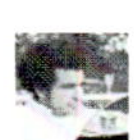

tarekshalaby | Tarek Shalaby
Fuck! We're getting hit. Broke through 2 lines. No serious injuries #jan25
15:15 Jan 25, 2011

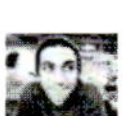

3arabawy | Hossam عمو حسام
@shadihamid I'm not expecting a revolution today. I'm expecting protests. So let's not shoot high so as not to disappoint people later.
11:02 Jan 25, 2011

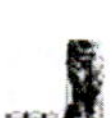

Sarahngb | Sarahngb
Tahrir square looks scary. Cordons, policemen, fire trucks, CS trucks. #Jan25
11:38 Jan 25, 2011

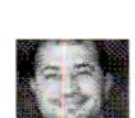

ashrafkhalil | ashraf khalil
#Jan25 amazing! Huge crowd just rushed in from abdeen to join thousands controlling half of tahrir square
15:57 Jan 25, 2011

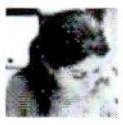

norashalaby | Nora Shalaby
Tear gas!!
15:58 Jan 25, 2011

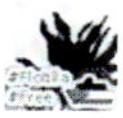

monasosh | monasosh
Eyes burning fuck
#jan25 http://yfrog.com/gy70kgj
16:00 Jan 25, 2011

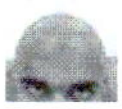

TravellerW | Mo-ha-med
Police throws rocks @ demonstrtrs while we raised our arms. We're unarmed, they're in full gear. We are strong, they're weak.
#25jan #Egypt
16:27 Jan 25, 2011

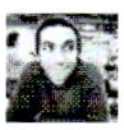

3arabawy | Hossam عمو حسام
Ya shabab, Tahrir is a war zone now.
Tens of thousands r protesting the same chants as the Tunisians. #Jan25
18:34 Jan 25, 2011

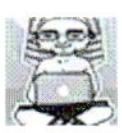

Ghonim | Wael Ghonim
Egypt after #Jan25 is no way going to be the same as Egypt before it. Today we proved so many points.
00:45 Jan 26, 2011

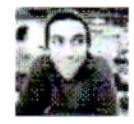

3arabawy | Hossam عمو حسام
We r at very critical stage. The counterrevolution is out in full steam. You will collect our dead bodies from garbage bins if we don't win.
12:49 Feb 2, 2011

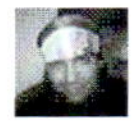

Sandmonkey | Mahmoud Salem
1000 pro Mubarak demonstration is heading towards Tahrir. The military is withdrawing. This will get ugly quick #jan25
13:40 Feb 2, 2011

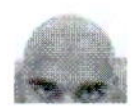

TravellerW | Mo-ha-med
INCREDIBLE standoff between pro-change and pro-Mubarak demos at Tahrir NOW
#Egypt #jan25 http://twitpic.com/3vqkcp
13:40 Feb 2, 2011

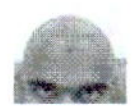

TravellerW | Mo-ha-med
Real panic in tahrir. Square overun by Mubarak drmonstrstion #Egypt #jan25
13:46 Feb 2, 2011

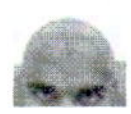

TravellerW | Mo-ha-med
Fuck reporting. I'm going in.
#Egypt #jan25
14:07 Feb 2, 2011

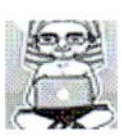

Ghonim | Wael Ghonim
Now in Tahrir situation is out of control. Prevented 2 angry guys from throwing a huge metal on police cars from top of the bridge! #Jan25
01:36 Jan 26, 2011

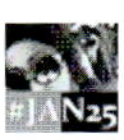

Gsquare86 | Gigi Ibrahim جيييج
Tahrir got broken up by police using tear gas, rubber bullets, water hoses, & rock-throwing.. ppl r still marching in DT #Jan25 .. I'm home
01:58 Jan 26, 2011

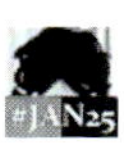

Zeinobia | Zeinobia
I have a confession: I did not think for one second that #Jan25 would be so great like that
13:08 Jan 26, 2011

The Camel Battle

February 2, 2011

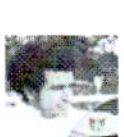

tarekshalaby | Tarek Shalaby
Internet's back in #Egypt. I've been camping out in Tahrir for 4 days n will remain until #Mubarak leaves. #jan25
12:03 Feb 2, 2011

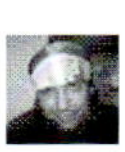

Sandmonkey | Mahmoud Salem
The mood in Egypt today is different. Too many people still beholden to the mentality of slaves. This is so frustrating. #jan25
12:48 Feb 2, 2011

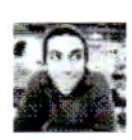

3arabawy | Hossam عمو حسام
Plainclothes thugs (police) are on horses now, trying to storm Tahrir Square, with whips! #Jan25
15:01 Feb 2, 2011

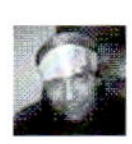

Sandmonkey | Mahmoud Salem
Camels and Horses used by Pro Mubarak protesters to attack Anti-Mubarak protesters. This is becoming literally a circus. #jan25
15:04 Feb 2, 2011

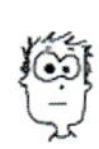

beleidy | Amr El Beleidy
This is turning into prehistoric war
15:49 Feb 2, 2011

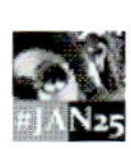

Gsquare86 | Gigi Ibrahim جيييج
Everyone in Cairo who wants Mubarak out and stands for justice come to Tahrir NOW!
16:15 Feb 2, 2011

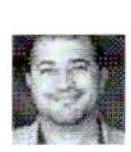

ashrafkhalil | ashraf khalil
#jan25 I saw at least a dozen guys coming back badly bloodied from front line. Incredibly violent scene and the soldiers are just watching
16:43 Feb 2, 2011

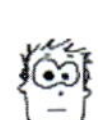

beleidy | Amr El Beleidy
The hope of the whole region is now in one public square!
16:43 Feb 2, 2011

monasosh | monasosh
Cut wounds, fractures, rupture eyes. Weapons used glass, coke bottles, knives, swords #Jan25
17:20 Feb 2, 2011

Gsquare86 | Gigi Ibrahim جيييج
Every thug we confiscate we find that his I.D. says 'police' those r the only pro-Mubarak supporters in #Egypt
17:32 Feb 2, 2011

norashalaby | Nora Shalaby
Protesters putting on cardboard helmets for protection against rocks #Jan25
17:48 Feb 2, 2011

TravellerW | Mo-ha-med
I am seeing - not reporting, seeing - Mubarak ppl throwing molotov cocktails on demonstrators, and on shops. #Egypt #jan25
18:58 Feb 2, 2011

3arabawy | Hossam عمو حسام
The shabab totally evicted Mubarak's thugs from Talaat Harb. Tahrir is still under control of the shabab. Long live the revolution. #Jan25
19:15 Feb 2, 2011

mosaaberizing | Mosa'ab Elshamy
Currently tweeting from behind a metal barrier directly separating us from Mubafuck thugs. Saved my head from hundreds of stones. #Jan25
02:16 Feb 3, 2011

monasosh | monasosh
Ppl r using the car ruins & rubbish around them 2 create shields to advance to the frontline. I feel as if reporting on a battlefield #Jan25
03:52 Feb 3, 2011

monasosh | monasosh
Some1 among the thugs on bridge had a riffle, took his time & aimed, 3 wounded, 1 dead, army to intervening #Jan25
04:06 Feb 3, 2011

waelkhairy88 | Wael Khairy
Oh God. The sound of gunfire! Machine guns echo can be heard everywhere. God help us all.
05:01 Feb 3, 2011

monasosh | monasosh
2 of my friends confirm another one is shot through the head, dead. My friend called me crying #Jan25 this is awful, something has 2 b done
05:29 Feb 3, 2011

MohammedY | Mohammed Yahia
WE STILL HOLD TAHRIR SQUARE #Jan25 #Egypt
19:29 Feb 2, 2011

Gsquare86 | Gigi Ibrahim جيييج
I WILL NOT LEAVE TAHRIR TONIGHT so stop telling me to do so! We need more people in TAHRIR NOW!! Get here for our freedom!!! #Egypt
19:39 Feb 2, 2011

MohammedY | Mohammed Yahia
When protesters capture thugs who r KILLING them, they protect them from being beaten all the way till they hand them to the military #Jan25
20:03 Feb 2, 2011

mosaaberizing | Mosa'ab Elshamy
Very tense near musuem now. We're still blocking them but fatigue & injuries slowly catching up with us. More people needed. #Tahrir #Jan25
22:31 Feb 2, 2011

monasosh | monasosh
This is a damn war zone, and the world is watching us! #Jan25
22:57 Feb 2, 2011

mosaaberizing | Mosa'ab Elshamy
YES! We've pushed them away from the musuem! They're running like rats. #Tahrir #Jan25
23:17 Feb 2, 2011

waelkhairy88 | Wael Khairy
Updates: 13 injured and 4 dead as a result of a few minutes of gunfire.
05:34 Feb 3, 2011

mosaaberizing | Mosa'ab Elshamy
We're fighting on the bridge now. They don't exceed 100. We need to hold on for 30 more minutes. #Tahrir
06:06 Feb 3, 2011

mosaaberizing | Mosa'ab Elshamy
Sunrise in Cairo. Blood spilled in Tahrir more noticed now. All over the place. #Jan25
06:39 Feb 3, 2011

The Friday of the Martyrs

February 11, 2011

mosaaberizing | Mosa'ab Elshamy
Today is the third Friday of our revolution. The first was bloody, second was festive and third should be decisive. #Jan25
08:23 Feb 11, 2011

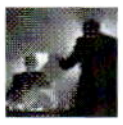

waelkhairy88 | Wael Khairy
Friday after Friday I keep saying it's the biggest protest yet, but today it's truly epic. This is as massive as they come. #EGYPT
13:56 Feb 11, 2011

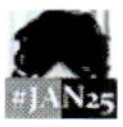

Zeinobia | Zeinobia
Al Arabiya : nearly 20 million Egyptians are in the street today #Jan25
17:35 Feb 11, 2011

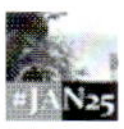

mosaaberizing | Mosa'ab Elshamy
Wait, there's another 'urgent' speech in a while? Please, God, no. #Jan25
17:53 Feb 11, 2011

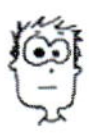

beleidy Amr | El Beleidy
Omar Sueliman speaking now!
18:02 Feb 11, 2011

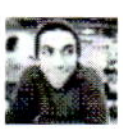

3arabawy | Hossam عمو حسام
Mubarak has stepped down, says Omar Suleiman. #Jan25
18:02 Feb 11, 2011

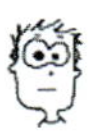

beleidy | Amr El Beleidy
I cannot believe what just happened. Hosny Mubarak resigned! The army now controls the country!
18:03 Feb 11, 2011

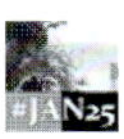

mosaaberizing | Mosa'ab Elshamy
IT HAPPENED?!
18:04 Feb 11, 2011

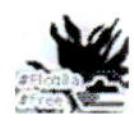

monasosh | monasosh
Today we fulfilled our promise to those who died #Jan25 #KhaledSaid
18:44 Feb 11, 2011

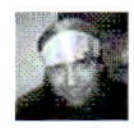

Sandmonkey | Mahmoud Salem
FIREWORKS, CELEBRATIONS, FUN! JUBILATION! I AM NOT MAKING SENSE. I AM HEADING TO TAHRIR! #JAN25
18:57 Feb 11, 2011

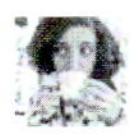

ManarMohsen | Manar Mohsen
The streets in Cairo are going wild with patriotism & happiness! Flags waving out of every car, strangers congratulating each other! "MASR!"
19:29 Feb 11, 2011

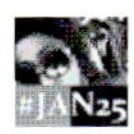

Gsquare86 | Gigi Ibrahim جيجي
I can't stop crying. I've never been more proud in my life
20:10 Feb 11, 2011

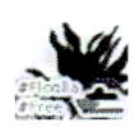

monasosh | monasosh
I'm in Tahrir square.This is where it all started on #Jan25 when we declared our demands ppl thought we were mad. Look where madness got us
00:31 Feb 12, 2011

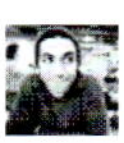

3arabawy | Hossam عمو حسام
We got rid of Mubarak. Now it's time to get rid of the Mubarak's regime. Long live the Egyptian people. Long live the revolution. #Jan25
13:09 Feb 11, 2011

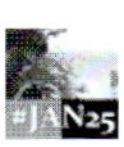

mosaaberizing | Mosa'ab Elshamy
It IS the decisive Friday. I'm only crying at the moment along with 2 million men in Tahrir.
18:12 Feb 11, 2011

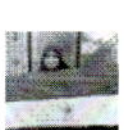

Reem_Ahmed Reem Ahmed Shalaby
Oh God !! deep breathe !!! Freedom :)))
#Tahrir #Jan25 #Egypt , we have made it. thanks God :))
18:18 Feb 11, 2011

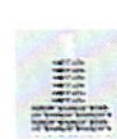

suzeeinthecity | su zee
My dad hugged me after the news and said 'Ur generation did what ours could only dream of. i'm sorry we didn't try hard enough.' #egypt
01:52 Feb 12, 2011

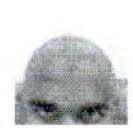

TravellerW | Mo-ha-med
Now Ahmed, whose son Eslam was killed by the police & who vowed not to leave #Tahrir until Mub. left, can go home. #Egypt #Jan25 #Justice
05:08 Feb 12, 2011

Tweets selected by Alex Nunns, from the book *Tweets from Tahrir: Egypt's revolution as it unfolded, in the words of the people who made it*, edited by Nadia Idle and Alex Nunns (OR Books, New York, 2011), available from www.orbooks.com.

UK Uncut

UK Uncut is a union of British protest groups, which since the announcement of the rigid austerity policy by the government uses direct action to protest the practice of tax avoidance by multinational corporations in the United Kingdom.

In their first action in 2010, the UK Uncutters occupied a shop of the mobile phone giant Vodafone in central London, one week after George Osborne, the British Chancellor of the Exchequer, had announced his planned austerity measures, which are considered the deepest cuts to public services since the 1920s, and after an investigative magazine had reported that the government had reduced Vodafone's back-tax liability from six billion British pounds to a mere two. The plan to occupy the store arose from the feeling of not wanting to wait until the next election, but having to take action immediately. The hashtag #ukuncut, which had been created the night before the protest, began to trend around the UK the very next day. The idea spread quickly and soon plans to implement similar actions emerged in many cities. Two weeks later, about thirty Vodafone stores had been closed all across the country. This initiative was the starting point for UK Uncut, which since then always operates according to the very same system: In the run-up planned actions are announced on social networks. On the day of action the participants meet locally, go together to the shop, inform the employees about the purpose of the action, distribute leaflets to the customers, and keep the store occupied for a couple of hours.

In this grassroots movement a whole spectrum of people are active – from teenagers to pensioners, from veterans to newcomers. Besides their own actions, the UK Uncutters support local strikes by supplying the strikers with food and drinks, for example. Further, one can find helpful tips for organizing own actions as well as legal information on UK Uncut's website.

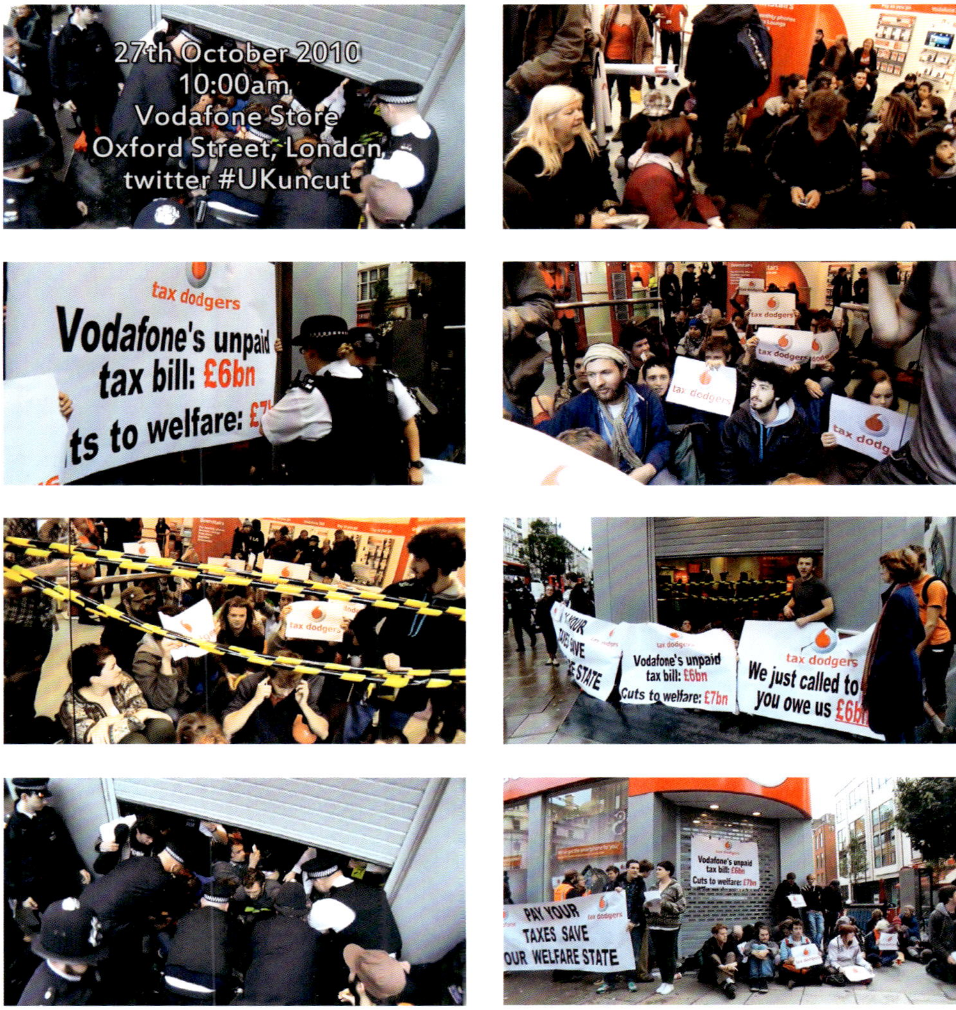

UK Uncut's very first Vodafone action in Oxford Street, London, 2010

Christoph Wachter *1966 and Mathias Jud *1974

Christoph Wachter and Mathias Jud were both born in Zurich, Switzerland, and now live in Berlin and Zurich. They have worked together on art projects since 2000. Their very first work, *Zone* Interdite*, achieved worldwide acclaim due to their exposure of the secret prison camps operating in Guantánamo Bay, in Afghanistan, and Iraq. The project, however, is not about political or military strategies, but focuses on something that affects us all: our ability to perceive things independently. Wachter and Jud interrogate whether there is really own authorship of seemingly individual processes of perception through a series of participatory community projects. With *picidae* (since 2007), *New Nations* (since 2009), and *qaul.net* (since 2012), they have set up functional open source projects, which make the mechanisms of censorship on the Internet visible, and circumvent power-political channeling and surveillance of information. In the USA, Europe, Australia, as well as Syria, Tunisia, Egypt, Iran, India, China, and Thailand, communities formed long before the advent of the Arab Spring that utilized and improved these tools. Even activists in North Korea participate in these projects. These artistic interrogations, which also facilitate fundamental philosophical and sociopolitical insights, have been presented internationally at solo and group exhibitions and biennials, and discussed in numerous publications and lectures on art theory. Christoph Wachter and Mathias Jud are the recipients of various international art awards and media art prizes (including a Prix Ars Electronica).

Christoph Wachter and Mathias Jud

Crossing the Bosphorus with Tin Cans: How Global Networking Compels Self-Criticism

Attractions entice millions of visitors to Istanbul every year. We, however, traveled to the Bosphorus to view precisely what was not available: the Twitter and YouTube websites. The journey seems absurd. Yet where Internet blockades arise something remarkable occurs: we are able to recognize the forces acting on our specific perceptions and worldview.

Shutdowns in Istanbul

When we arrived in Istanbul, the Twitter website had already been blocked in Turkey for several days. At the latest since the Gezi park protests in the summer of 2013, President Recep Tayyip Erdoğan had become a controversial figure; and allegations of corruption were rife. The upcoming Turkish local government elections became a pivotal campaign. In order to prevent anti-government publications, the Turkish authorities shut down Twitter, and shortly after YouTube as well.[1]

We had come to Turkey neither to lecture people nor to incite a revolution. Rather, we wanted to pursue what digital communication promises: that there can be an exchange of knowledge between everyone, that individual and specific forms of expression open up to everyone.

The artist and curator Ekmel Ertan organized workshops. In a short space of time there were so many applications that those attending had to be allocated to several time slots on the same afternoon. Additional events were planned for the following days, in the hackerspace on the Asian side of the city, to the southeast of the Bosphorus. In the workshops, we talked about our previous projects.

The shutting down of Twitter and YouTube at this time was a DNS (domain name system) censorship. We had already worked with the responsible name servers on our *New Nations* project, in which we uncover the power structure of the Internet and expand the existing data network by a new dimension, which provided the Tibetans, Kurds, Tamils, Uighurs, and other nonrecognized communities with their own Internet addresses (ccTLD). The project allows new forms of cooperation on a global scale, and for a communicative exchange to be established in new forms, above and beyond political territorial divisions and power blocks.[2]

We called another project we have been working on since 2007 *picidae*.[3] It, too, focuses on borders in digital communication. With *picidae* we inspect word filters, which facilitate forms of control. Copies of websites are generated, which can then also be clicked on. The images subvert redirects, ranking, rating, filtering, and censorship. Not only the differentiation between words and images in the digital becomes clear, manifold differences also become visible, specifying each individual Internet access.

It was, however, our *qaul.net* project that attracted the greatest interest in

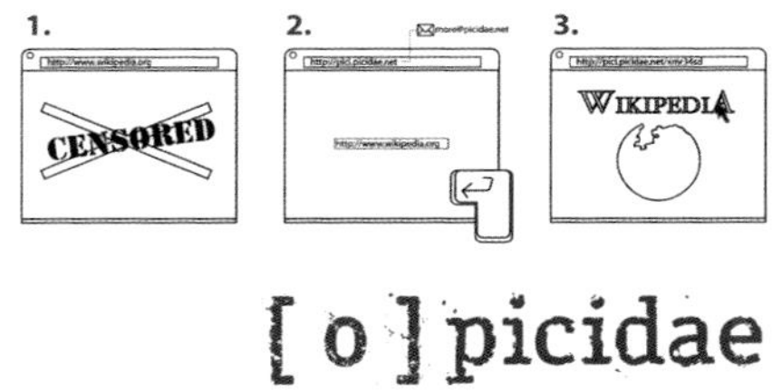

When *picidae* is activated, a form field appears to type in a Web address. *picidae* then creates an image of that website and sends it back. On the left of the image are links and input fields, thus making it possible to surf with *picidae*.

Istanbul.[4] Like a virus, *qaul.net* can be passed on from one device to another. Wi-Fi-capable computers and mobile devices connect directly to the spontaneous network. Chatting, file sharing, and voice calls are then possible independently of Internet and mobile communications.

Tin Can Antennas

In order to connect these independent, local qaul networks in the European and the Asian parts of Istanbul, Ertan suggested installing a radio link across the Bosphorus. Individual WLAN devices (wireless local area network) can connect over a distance of up to two hundred meters. Simple tin can antennas, however, are able to extend the range of the devices to several kilometers. Moreover, the tin cans also develop a symbolic power: they invite us to think beyond the boundaries, inclusions, and exclusions in our society.

Mobile qaul units which we developed together in the hackerspace are more inconspicuous, yet nevertheless just as effective. During past mass

1 The blocking of the short message service Twitter took place in Turkey from March 20 until April 3, 2014. YouTube was blocked on March 27, 2014 until further notice. As of March 29, 2014, the DNS queries were generally being intercepted in order to suppress alternative name servers.

2 Nongeopolitically recognized cultures are also suppressed in the virtual communications sphere. *New Nations* has been providing Internet addresses such as .ti for Tibet since 2009 in the form of an open community project, and has been contrasting the existing allocation and surveillance of the digital data network with the nations and their international agreements. See: www.new-nations.net, accessed 05/06/2014.

3 *Picidae* makes it possible for specific views on the Internet to be compared and censorship of pictures to be avoided. See: www.picidae.net, accessed 05/06/2014.

4 *Qaul.net* creates its own spontaneous networks which are independent of the Internet. See: www.qaul.net, accessed 05/06/2014.

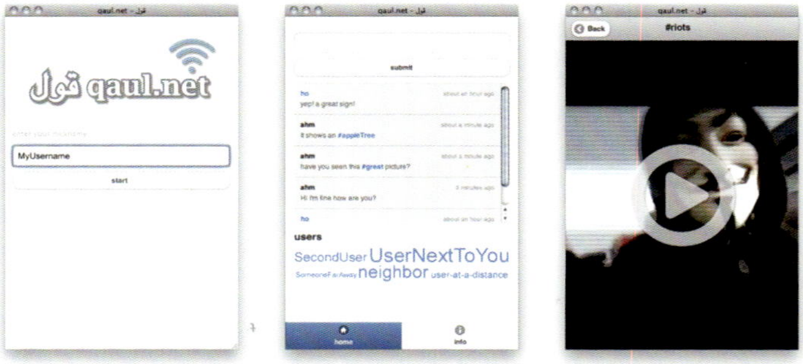

qual.net can be passed from one device to another like a virus and generates communication networks, which work independently of the Internet and cell phone services.

demonstrations in Istanbul, Internet connections and mobile service had repeatedly crashed. At future demonstrations, a spontaneous communication network could be installed using mobile qaul stations.

Self-Regulation

Which DNS do you use? Most Turkish people are able to answer this question impulsively, while people in other countries often reply by asking what a DNS actually is. In Turkey, people are used to configuring the name server themselves. The current censorship is not the first. Since 2007, YouTube and other websites have been repeatedly shut down in Turkey;[5] there are currently over 40,000 websites being blocked by a DNS censorship. During our stay in Istanbul, the censorship was intensified and the entire DNS service was intercepted and monitored. The widely used VPN (virtual private network) services are one way of still getting around even these intensified constraints.

We had already experienced severe Internet censorship earlier in Asian and Arab countries. Yet just like in Turkey, there were also tricks and ways of dealing with the situation available. The idea that the digital, configurable, and collaborative media are always free to develop would therefore appear to be confirmed. In actual fact, technological Internet censorship is for the most part not absolute; it can be circumvented, not least with the help of our art projects.

The communication connections are not solely based on technological access routes though. Interventions in specific potential means of expression are effective in complex ways. Limitations to access, therefore, also act as a thinking barrier and as a social censor. However, no one has shown any interest in this aspect for a long time now. When we launched *picidae* in 2007, many media art representatives rejected our project. They said it was backward looking, because censorship only continued to affect distant, outdated power structures. Experts were of the general opinion that with the given increasing Internet access censorship would soon be swept away.

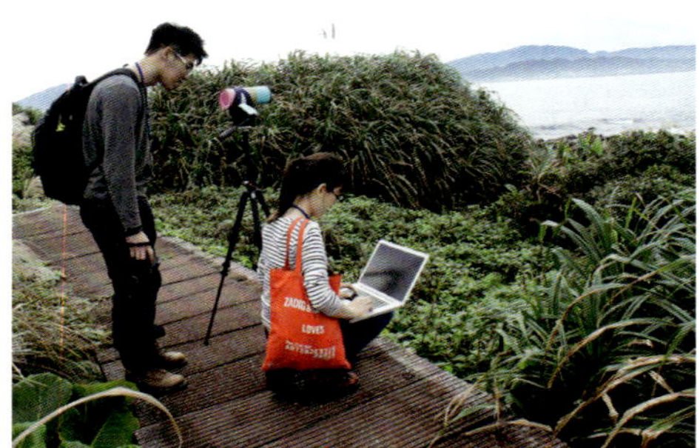

Via *qaul.net* and using simple tin can antennas a communications link over a distance of 3.5 km was created to Keelong, an uninhabited island in the East China Sea, 2012.

Internet Censorship Is Everywhere, but Concealed

From a northern European or U.S. point of view, the superiority of Western democracies would appear to be confirmed. No, we do not have any censorship. No, we would not put up with these shutdowns. A state of repression is a reflection of those being repressed, because they fail to assume the role of free subjects, and because they fail to free themselves from the yoke of repression.

Yet the power-political order and its cultural and communicative forms are mutually dependent. The subject is in the first place spawned on its own conditions. This renders a term such as freedom a vague self-affirmation. A subject must first become aware of its limitations, in order to free itself from a certain situation. Yet precisely this situation appears to have an identitarian, normative magnitude: as the correct perception, and as legal and legitimate action. We must therefore first of all clarify the precise situation we find ourselves in, in order to be in a position to correctly assess our own perspective. Clarifying our own conceptual horizon will however prove to be a rather challenging moment.

This becomes apparent from the ~~*BLACKLIST*~~ project. A machine searches systematically for pictures which have been classified as dangerous or illegal, and have therefore been deleted or blocked. The findings are then traced.[6] The project brings astonishing things to light: Switzerland, Belgium, and Italy have DNS Internet censorship just like Turkey, whereas in Germany, numerous entries are prevented on search engines. Things are deleted and blocked in an arbitrary and uncoordinated manner. The interventions themselves are secretive and are gaining ground, because the discussion about censorship itself falls directly under censorship and is stifled.

Very few people in Europe feel affected by censorship. Yet if we were to start talking about the freedom of the Internet and personal or social freedom, we associate this with a normalization, which we of course confirm by not contemplating the principle of the recesses and margins.

Twitter: Free Speech, State Doctrine, Instrument of Propaganda

Until it was shut down, Twitter was widespread in Turkey. The company spoke of ten million users. At the time of the shutdown Twitter appeared to be a symbol for lost freedom. We should not, however, perceive Twitter as an area of freedom, but as a concrete power structure.

The protests following the 2009 Iranian presidential elections, which is also referred to as the "Green Revolution," were euphorically termed the "Twitter Revolution."[7] Ten thousand Twitter users declared their solidarity with the Iranian activists, and the wave of solidarity took on a global dimension. Later studies revealed that only a fraction of the tweets actually came from online users in Iran;[8] Evgeny Morozov, for example, talks of a mere sixty active accounts,[9] while Golnaz Esfandiari comments that if the uprising

5 See: http://en.wikipedia.org/wiki/Censorship_in_Turkey#Blocking_of_Internet_sites, accessed 05/06/2014.

6 ~~*BLACKLIST*~~ detects hidden, deleted, or forbidden and censored images on the Internet and in a way worthy of discussion makes its findings visible and accessible again in the form of drawings or composite sketches. See: http://wachter-jud.net/projects_research/blacklist?sf_culture=en, accessed 05/06/2014.

7 See: "Iran's Twitter revolution," in: *The Washington Times*, June 16, 2009, available online at: www.washingtontimes.com/news/2009/jun/16/irans-twitter-revolution, accessed 05/06/2014.

8 The Twitter users changed their statements on the time zone and the location of Tehran; this was allegedly supposed to protect the female activists in the country. See: Mark Evans, "A Look at Twitter in Iran," published on: *Sysomos*, June 21, 2009, available online at: http://blog.sysomos.com/2009/06/21/a-look-at-twitter-in-iran, accessed 05/06/2014.

9 See: Evgeny Morozov, "Caught in the net. Why dictators are going digital," in: *The Economist*, January 6, 2011, available online at: www.economist.com/node/17848401, accessed 05/06/2014.

had actually been organized through Twitter posts, these would not have been written in English, but in Farsi.[10]

The legend of the 2009 Twitter Revolution nevertheless ran its course. The U.S. State Department aimed to push forward the political upheaval in Iran, and therefore urged Twitter Inc. not to carry out scheduled maintenance work during the Iranian protests, to make sure that Twitter remained up and running throughout the protests.[11] Due to this political action by the U.S. authorities, the Iranian government began working to find its own way to shut down Twitter in Iran.[12]

For activism and media art in particular the World Wide Web was regarded as a tactical medium, as a means for counterstatements, clarification, and criticism. It suggests freedom of communication. This, however, veils actual dependency on machines, cable harnesses, and gadgetry. An industrial, governmental complex could present a digitization of society, data highways, and clouds, and entice people with the concept of global freedom of communication. Yet the Twitter blockade in Iran makes it clear that unconditional freedom of speech online is already linked to political intention.

Online freedom is not a political goal, but is itself an ideological and strategically powerful instrument. When Google withdrew from the Chinese market in 2010, Hillary Clinton, U.S. Secretary of State at the time, accused the Chinese authorities of blocking free access to the Internet.[13] U.S. authorities had also attempted some projects of their own in the past. The Tor network was set as of 2002, with the USA financing it to the tune of US$ 1.2 million each year.[14] The network was conceived as an anonymization service for the political opposition in Asian and Arab countries. Haystack, supposedly an encryption software for Iran, is also supported by the U.S. government[15] and ZunZuneo was set up in the same year in Cuba.[16] The short message platform was intended to incite the Cuban youth to form a rebellion.

Erdoğan versus Twitter

Large Internet platforms do not make for reliable partners for political activists. Companies such as Facebook require real names when registering. Facebook therefore deleted the Egyptian activist sites for Khaled Said and Mohamed El-Baradei during the protests in Cairo in November 2010. Twitter and Yahoo passed personal data on to the authorities, and in several countries online activists were prosecuted for their remarks.[17]

10 "Simply put: There was no Twitter Revolution inside Iran," Golnaz Esfandiari, "The Twitter Devolution," in: *Foreign Policy*, June 8, 2010, available online at: http://foreignpolicy.com/2010/06/08/the-twitter-devolution, accessed 05/06/2014.

11 "The U.S. government took the unusual step of asking Twitter to delay a planned maintenance outage because of its use as a communications tool by Iranians following their disputed election, a senior official said Tuesday," Lachlan Carmichael, "U.S. asks Twitter to maintain service after Iran vote," in: *Agence France Presse Washington*, June 16, 2009.

12 See: Amin Ansari, "The role of social media in Iran's Green Movement (2009–2012)," in: *Global Media Journal (Australian Edition)*, vol. 6, no. 2, 2012, available online at: www.hca.uws.edu.au/gmjau/archive/v6_2012_2/amin_ansari_RA.html, accessed 05/06/2014.

13 "Clinton attackiert China im Google-Streit," [Clinton attacks China in Google row] in: *ZEIT ONLINE*, January 22, 2010, available online at: www.zeit.de/digital/internet/2010-01/internet-streit-china, accessed 05/06/2014.

14 See: The Tor Project, "Financial Review," in: *Annual Report 2012*, p. 8, available online at: www.torproject.org/about/findoc/2012-TorProject-Annual-Report.pdf, accessed 05/06/2014.

15 "What made Haystack possible was the U.S. government's urge to embrace the power of the Internet to democratize the world – and to do so as fast as possible [...]" Evgeny Morozov, "The Great Internet Freedom Fraud. How Haystack endangered the Iranian dissidents it was supposed to protect," in: *Slate*, September 16, 2010, available online at: www.slate.com/articles/technology/technology/2010/09/the_great_internet_freedom_fraud.html, accessed 05/06/2014.

16 See: http://en.wikipedia.org/wiki/ZunZuneo, accessed 05/06/2014.

17 See: Jillian C. York, "Lieber anonym als verfolgt. Google und Facebook wollen die Anonymität im Netz abschaffen. Sie könnten damit Leben gefährden" [Better anonymous than persecuted. Google and Facebook seek to abolish anonymity on the net. Doing so may endanger life], in: *ZEIT ONLINE*, August 4, 2011, available online at: www.zeit.de/2011/32/P-op-ed-Anonymitaet, accessed 05/06/2014.

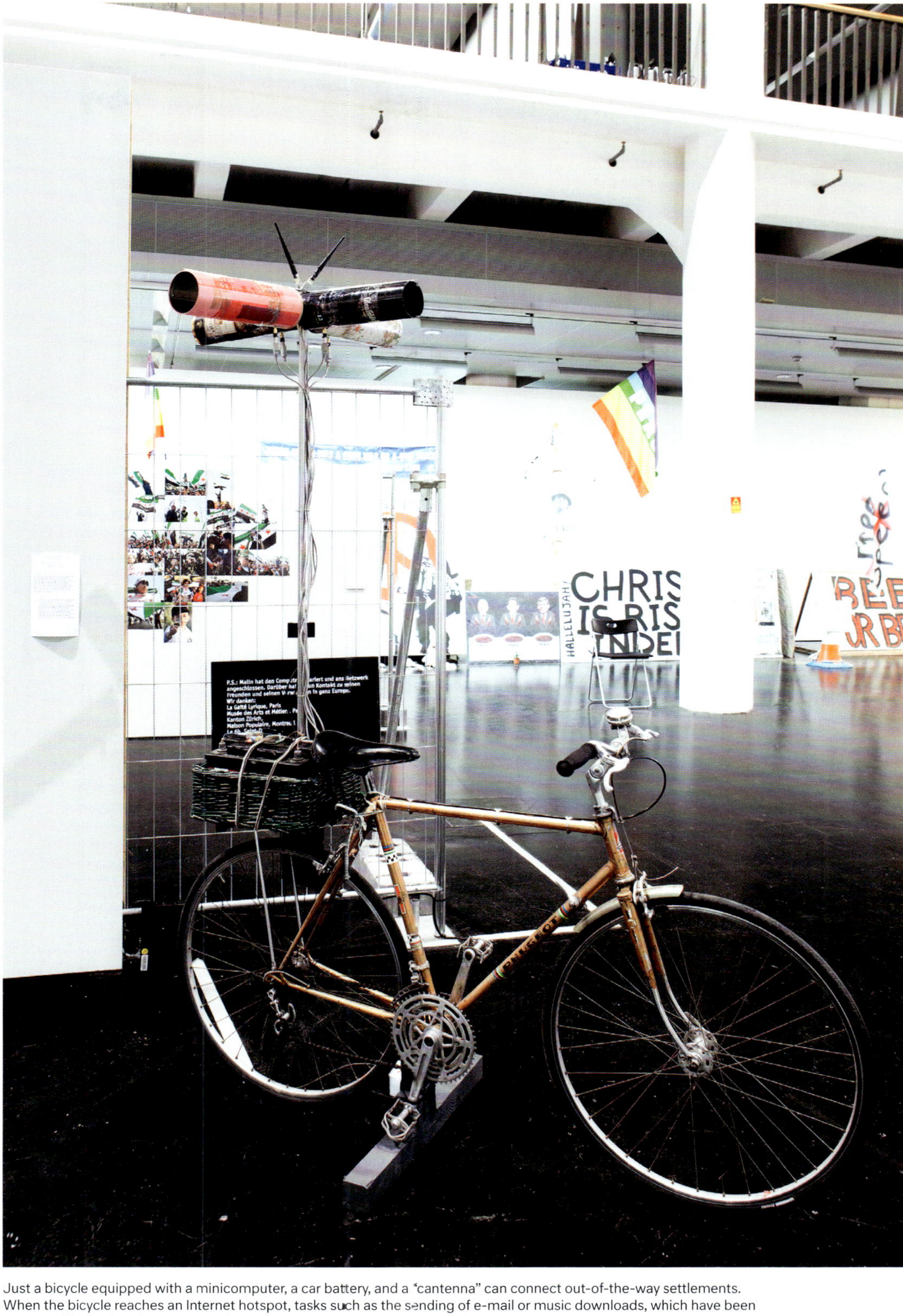

Just a bicycle equipped with a minicomputer, a car battery, and a "cantenna" can connect out-of-the-way settlements. When the bicycle reaches an Internet hotspot, tasks such as the sending of e-mail or music downloads, which have been requested beforehand, are executed automatically. Installation view, ZKM | Karlsruhe, 2014.

The government in Turkey also submitted demands to Twitter following the shutdown in March 2014. It said the company had not implemented valid court decisions.[18] At the beginning of April, Twitter backed down and shut down individual accounts in Turkey, in return for which the platform has since been accessible again. At the same time, 29 people were accused in Izmir of having invoked demonstrations via Twitter during the Gezi Park protests in the preceding year.[19]

Not Political Goals, but the Political Domain

Digital communication is often lauded as a realization of the freedom of information and speech, and is closely linked with a hope for participation and democratization. The digital infrastructure does not, however, only spawn new connections, it also results in specific dependencies, and new forms of division result from this.

We see clear exclusion in France, for instance. Strict laws ensure that people without a registered address and bank account can have no permanent Internet access.[20] This has caused a social divide to intensify, as families living in informal housing settlements, the so-called *sans papiers* [without papers], are excluded still further. As a result of the *qaul.net* project, several large neighborhood WLAN networks emerged last year around Paris, with which it is possible to connect to the Internet. In this way, it is possible to go about purposefully counteracting the sociocultural exclusion and stigmatization.[21]

If protests and demonstrations in Turkey result in the Turkish authorities and the U.S. company Twitter being able to come to an arrangement regarding the arrest of individuals and blocking specific accounts, then a power structure behind this becomes apparent. Participation in a protest, an encouraging statement in a short messaging service, mobile phone data from an event venue – all of this can be punished months after the events.

This means that politics is linked with all aspects of life. Yet the focus here is not the specific political debates and political ambitions which individual players pursue. It is a question which can no longer be resolved with a particular policy, rather it is a question about the political domain itself: How can a digital communication society shape, form, and organize itself?

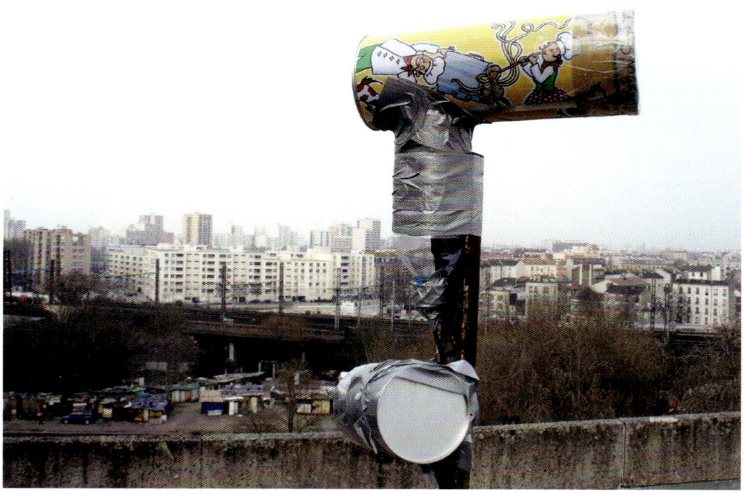

Can antennas in Saint-Denis north of Paris connect an informal settlement without Internet access to a neighboring network, June 2013.

How Do I Want to Be Governed?

The most recent protests by Occupy, Taksim Gezi Park, and Stuttgart 21 likewise highlight the battle for the political domain. The current protest movements do not aspire to overthrow the system, they are far more concerned with claiming the existing political system for themselves, by demanding a democratization of democracy, and seeking an opportunity to have a say in matters.[22] Parallel to this, we are also unable to avert our attention away from the premises of the communication society; we must also lay claim to the option of codetermination here, and demand the right to have a say, especially because this also determines how the collective being and the political and sociocultural coexistence is shaped.

The means of expression is a field which defines identity as well as society, in which we express ourselves and appear as open and free subjects. The possibilities to do this, however, depend on the concrete power-political and technological conditions. Our own means of expression becomes a central aspect of political power. At the latest since Edward Snowden's revelations about the intelligence agencies NSA and GCHQ, the general public has criticized surveillance and dependency. The subversion and dissolution of the private sphere is, however, not the problem of the users who publish their own intentions on a social media platform. If every impulse stands out, the subject responsible for it can no longer be made out. Everything can be of significance. What becomes apparent here, therefore, is an infiltration of the subject, which, while being permanently significant, at the same time loses its interpretational sovereignty. Yet these diverse impulses are not binding statements, which would be relevant in a democratic, political, and participatory sense: How do I want to express myself? What do I want to decide in favor of? How do I want to be governed?[23]

Self-Critical Exploration

With regard to the question of what can be said and expressed at all, artistic practice is relevant in terms of its own potential. We self-critically explore our own opportunities for expression and representation. Only in the course of the development and realization of the work is this power revealed, which without this intensive attention would not have become visible.

For this reason, being self-taught for our own purposes, we have addressed methods of expression and

18 The Turkish telecommunications authority TIB justifies the blocking of Twitter with three court decisions; see: Hasnain Kazim, "Twitter-Verbot in der Türkei: Erdogan dreht ab" [Twitter ban in Turkey: Erdogan shuts down], in: *SPIEGEL ONLINE*, March 21, 2014, available online at: www.spiegel.de/netzwelt/netzpolitik/erdogan-laesst-in-der-tuerkei-twitter-abschalten-mundtot-a-959969.html, accessed 05/06/2014.

19 After the end of the Twitter blockade in Turkey, the short message service blocked the contents of two accounts with almost a million users in the country: @Bascalan and @Haramzadeler333. In Izmir, a trial began against Twitter users; see: "Twitter sperrt regierungsfeindliche Konten in der Türkei" [Twitter blocks antigovernment accounts in Turkey], in: *Sueddeutsche.de*, April 21, 2014, available online at: www.sueddeutsche.de/news/wirtschaft/internet-twitter-sperrt-regierungsfeindliche-konten-in-der-tuerkei-dpa.urn-newsml-dpa-com-20090101-140421-99-03046, accessed 05/06/2014.

20 See: Droit de l'informatique en France, available online at: http://fr.wikipedia.org/wiki/Droit_de_l'informatique_en_France, accessed 06/05/2014.

21 See: #GLM [GRASSROOT LOCAL MESHNET] construire son réseau local de communication, La Gaîté Lyrique Paris, March 12–May 12, 2013, see: www.gaite-lyrique.net/en/node/4419, accessed 05/06/2014.

22 See: Oliver Marchart and Rupert Weinzierl, "Radikale Demokratie und Neue Protestformationen" [Radical democracy and new protest formations], in: Oliver Marchart and Rupert Weinzierl (eds.), *Stand der Bewegung? Protest, Globalisierung, Demokratie – eine Bestandsaufnahme*, Westfälisches Dampfboot, Münster, 2006, pp. 7–13, here p. 8.

23 "[A]s compensation […] to the arts of governing, […] there would have been something born in Europe […], a kind of general cultural form, both a political and moral attitude, a way of thinking, etc. and which I would very simply call the art of not being governed or better, the art of not being governed like that and at that cost." Michel Foucault, "What is Critique?" in: Michel Foucault, *The Politics of Truth*, Sylvère Lotringer (ed.), *Semiotext(e)*, Los Angeles (CA), 2007, pp. 41–81, here p. 44f.

representation in the digital communication society. Our research and development enables a new dimension of exploration as an artistic strategy. The media not only open up modes of operation and presentation options. Rather, it is far more about eliciting representation and presentation situations in their constitutive dimensions and reshaping them. Functional open source projects make forms of Internet censorship visible, circumvent a power-political channeling of information, and overcome the general dependence, which for the most part only becomes apparent when the communication infrastructure is shut down or fails.

Opening up the options for information and expression is relevant so as not to be trapped in a one-sided dependency by a ruling system – a system which regulates the options of speech, objection, and hearing or surveillance in a concealed, yet overwhelming manner. This is how the basis of subjective and collective being is determined. It is not the core of the creative subject and the reflex of a self-affirmation which is the stipulation, but rather the questioning, the realization of what comes from the positions and the figures. It is not the creative subject itself which is in the foreground; nor is it an innovation or intervention. Rather, possible courses of action and materials reveal themselves to be a formation, which for their part first of all enable specific positionings of the subject.

This differentiation between the subject position and the methods of expression also creates pragmatic confusion. Last year, when Organhaus invited us to an artist residency in Chongqing, the Chinese authorities refused our entry. We were deeply saddened that we were no longer allowed to travel to China. Our journey would have been part of an artistic exchange, as regulated in international agreements. The Swiss Federal Department of Foreign Affairs thus made inquiries at the embassy, but all they found out was that the instruction had come directly from Beijing. The type of work which we are developing can, however, not be punished by excluding alleged authors. In the Austrian newspaper *Der Standard*, we came across by chance an interview with a Chinese cyber dissident. He told how he had a system with images at his computer, with which he was able to view Wikipedia. He did not know the name or background of the project. *Picidae* has adopted numerous new forms, and the projects find their own ways, even to places which remain barred to us. In Syria, Tunisia, Egypt, Iran, India, China, Thailand, and even in North Korea, communities have long since formed which are using and advancing our tools.

And a pair of tin can antennas have been situated on the Bosphorus since March 2014. They do not change the political relations in Turkey, nor do they replace the Internet. And yet they nevertheless have a significance. In a situation in which there is state superiority, power of control, which has manifested itself in the form of the shutdowns, *qaul.net* has brought an alternative course of action to light. From the services on distant servers, blockades on secret switch points and VPN services for evasion, the possibilities for a connection and the social disputes are coming straight back to the social and political battlefield. With the spontaneous, local network, communicating with one another no longer entails later police punishment and a remote-controlled shutdown, and instead falls right into our own hands.

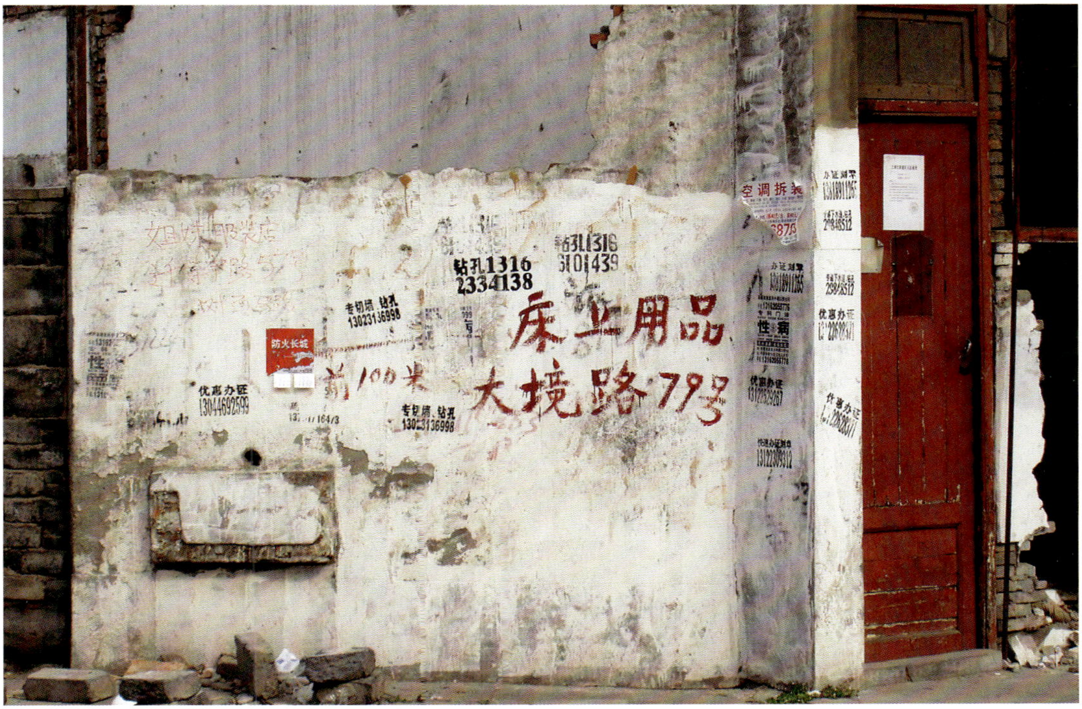

A Chinese woman made posters bearing the words 防火长城 [Great Chinese Firewall]. On *picidae* this reference is on stubs for getting around Internet censorship.

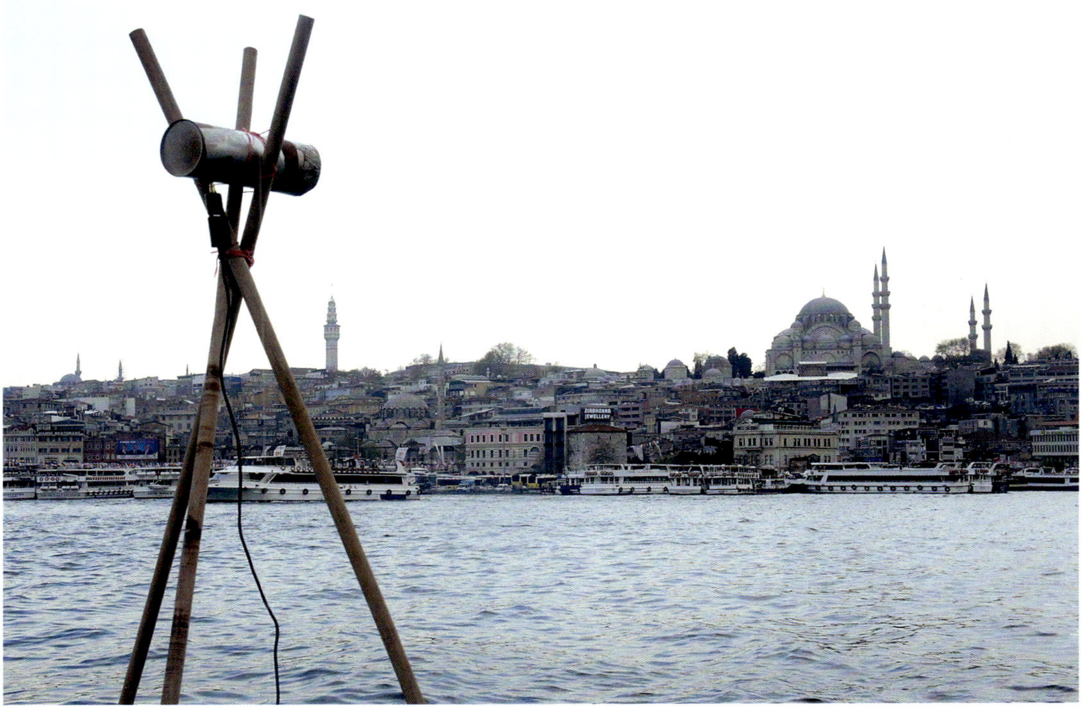

A tin can antenna on the bank of Bosphorus, it is strong enough to reach a range of several kilometers.

"We are all Majid"

"We are all Majid" was the Iranian online community's spontaneous response to the incarceration of human rights activist and student leader Majid Tavakoli (*1986), who was arrested after criticizing the Iranian regime during the protests that followed the Iranian presidential elections in 2009. Although hundreds of Iranians were imprisoned in this postelection period, Tavakoli's arrest quickly attracted international attention, not only because he was a prominent student leader and member of the pro-democracy movement, but also because the national press announced he had tried to flee disguised as a woman. After his arrest he was photographed by security authorities wearing women's clothing and a *hijab*, a veil covering head and chest which all Iranian women are legally required to wear, which they forced him to put on in order to humiliate him. The regime's intention may well have been to embarrass the activist, but its photos had the opposite effect. After they were published in the national press, hundreds of men, both in Iran and abroad, showed their solidarity by posting photographs of themselves with headscarves on Facebook, thus crushing the intended defamation and transforming the women's clothing from a symbol of emasculation into one of solidarity and defiance. A compilation of photos of this action is available online at: www.youtube.com/watch?v=3QIVwHsrsvg#t=67.

The online campaign known as "We are all Majid," organized over the Facebook page "Free Majid Tavakoli" and various popular Iranian sites, was aimed not only at supporting Tavakoli, but can be seen as a revolt against the regime itself, and a protest against the Islamic Republic's treatment of women, particularly its violent enforcement of mandatory veiling. Despite the outpouring of support, Majid Tavakoli was sentenced to eight and a half years in prison on charges of "propagandizing against the system" and insulting government officials. He was denied regular contact with his family and granted only one short furlough, in October 2013. In that same year, he received the Norwegian Student Peace Prize, an alternative to the Nobel Peace Prize, which is awarded biennially on behalf of all Norwegian students to a student or a student organization that has made a significant contribution to creating peace and promoting human rights.

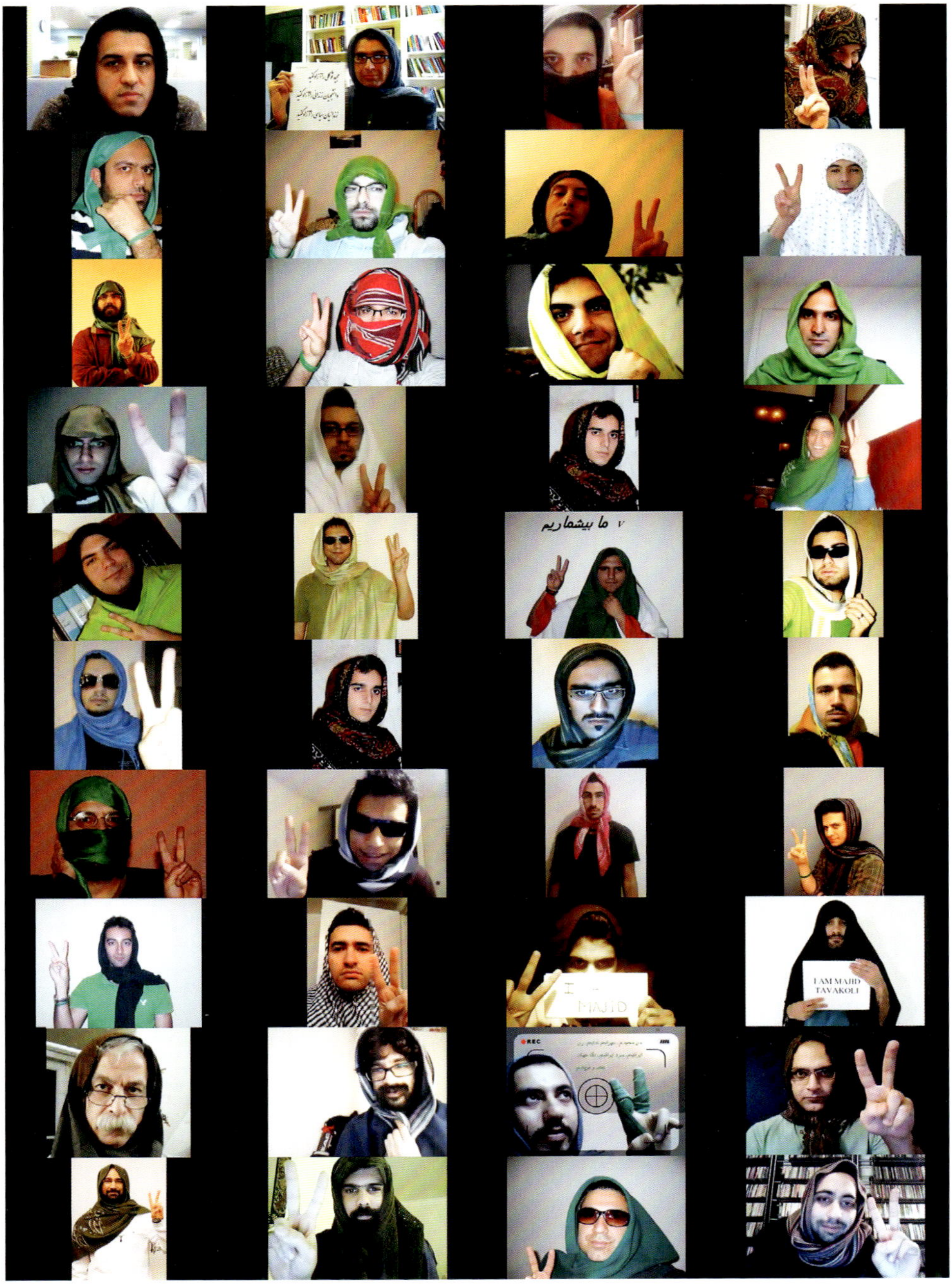

“We are all Majid,” video with a compilation of photos created by Hamidreza & Haleh, uploaded on December 11, 2009, available online at: www.youtube.com/watch?v=3QIJwHsrsvg#t=67, accessed 10/14/2014, collage of screenshots

Online Projects

#occupygezi

This blog brings together images and videos that were posted on Twitter during the protests around the Gezi Park in Istanbul under #occupygezi. The uncommented collection documents the riots and the harsh action of the police against the protesters.

http://occupygezipics.tumblr.com

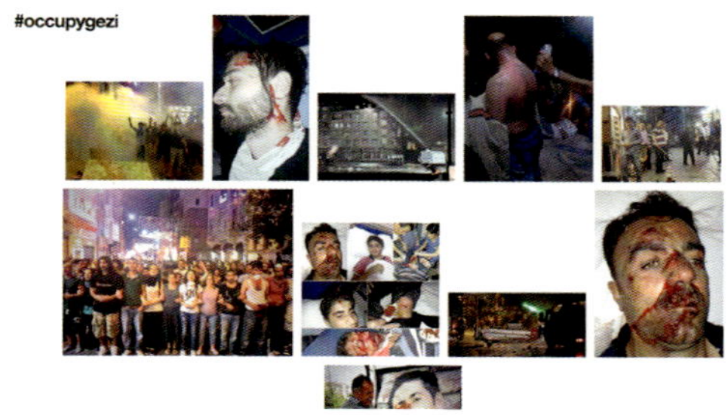

Screenshot, 07/09/2014

0.

0. is an online platform launched by Jonas Staal and Metahaven that allows users to access highlight, and share every document in use by the Dutch government. In the era of WikiLeaks, 0. is a further advocate of democracy without secrets.

https://nulpunt.nu

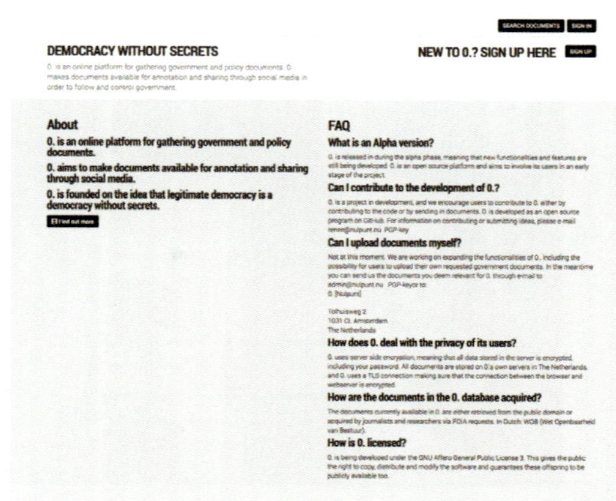

Screenshot, 07/09/2014

Actipedia

Actipedia is an open-access, user-generated database of creative activism. It's a place to read about, comment upon, and share experiences and examples of how activists and artists are using creative tactics and strategies to challenge power structures and offer visions of a better society. Since 2012, Actipedia draws case studies from everywhere: original submissions, reprinted news articles, snippets of action reports. Actipedia is a joint project of the Center for Artistic Activism and the Yes Lab.

http://actipedia.org

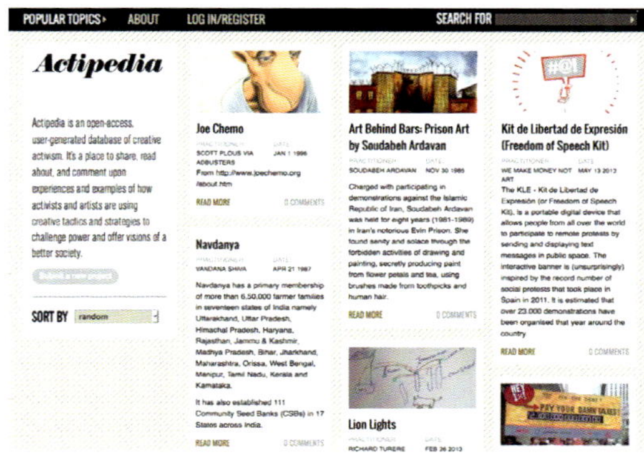

Screenshot, 07/18/2014

Anonymous News Germany

Anonymous News Germany is a decentral blog released in 2011 that allows various anonymous people to access its contents, which focus mainly on the Anonymous phenomenon and its hacking projects, but also on other topics concerning the Internet and policy making in Germany.

https://anonnewsde.org

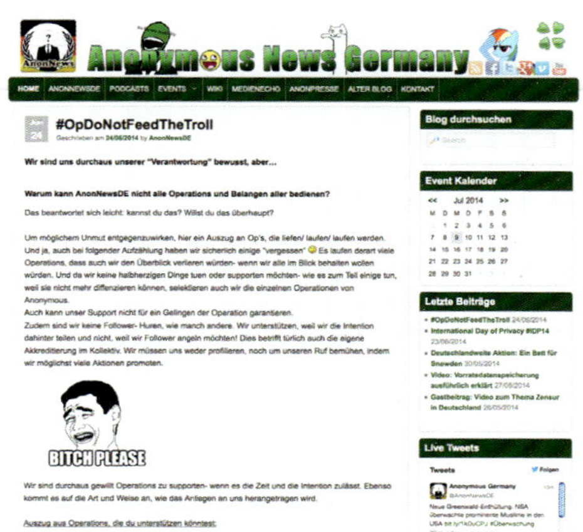

Screenshot, 07/09/2014

Martin Balluch

The blog of the prominent radical environmental and animal rights activist Martin Balluch (*1964) can be found at martinballuch.com. Although Balluch has been repeatedly taken to court and was even imprisoned from May to September 2008, for decades he has continued to pursue a nonviolent path to establish animal rights in Austria. For his efforts in the field of animal ethics and animal rights Balluch was awarded the Prix Mychkine of the Karlsruhe University of Arts and Design in 2012.

http://martinballuch.com

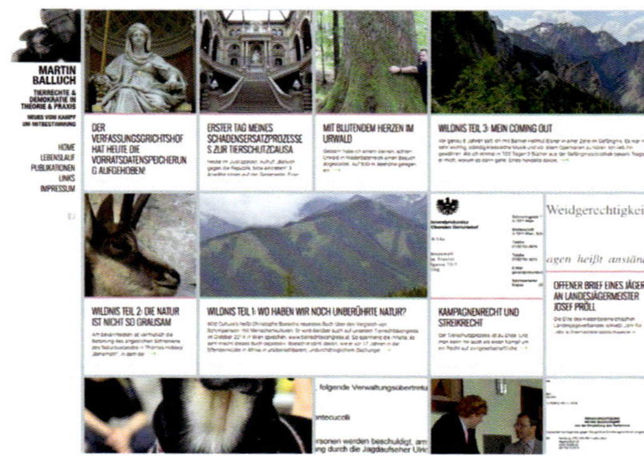

Screenshot, 07/09/2014

Facebook

The online social networking service Facebook enables registered users to create a personal profile in which they can present themselves and upload photos and videos. Users can communicate with designated friends or other users if they have made their profile publicly available, by leaving messages or publish comments on the so-called timeline of the profile. They can also send private messages or communicate via a chat feature, create and join interest groups, and initiate events to which members can be invited. Calls to action by activists are frequently posted on Facebook and thus are visible and can be accessed by an international audience.

www.facebook.com

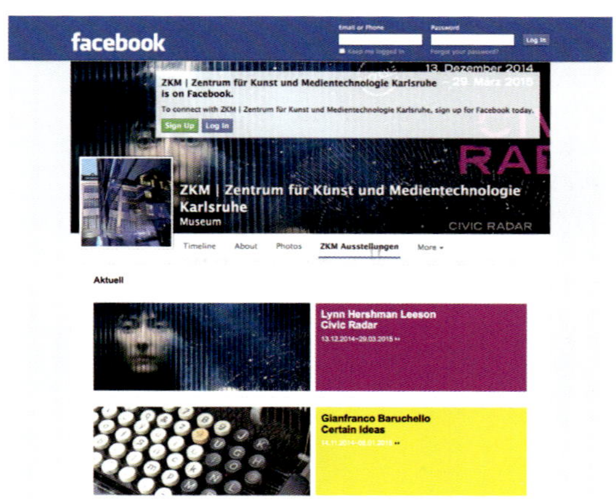

Screenshot, 12/17/2014

Freedom of the Press Foundation

https://pressfreedomfoundation.org

The Freedom of the Press Foundation is devoted to what it describes as "aggressive, public interest journalism" with a focus on transparency in government. They collect donations in both monetary and nonmonetary forms, but also provide open source software that enables whistle-blowers to anonymously leak documents to media organizations.

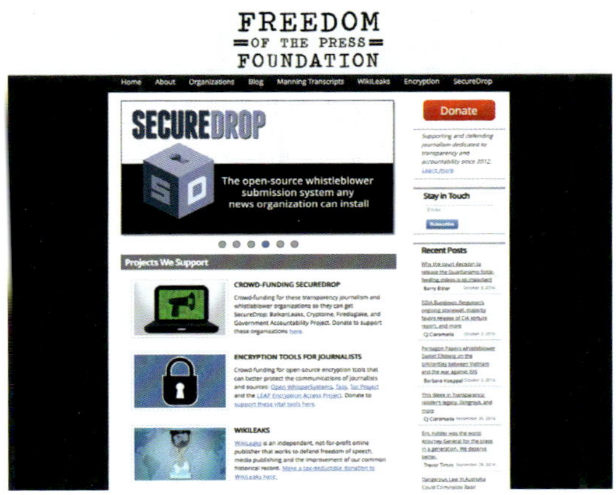

Screenshot, 07/09/2014

Independent Media Center (Indymedia)

www.indymedia.org

The Independent Media Center is a worldwide media platform launched in connection with the protest activity surrounding the 1999 World Trade Organization (WTO) Ministerial Conference in Seattle, which offers independent reporting on activism issues.

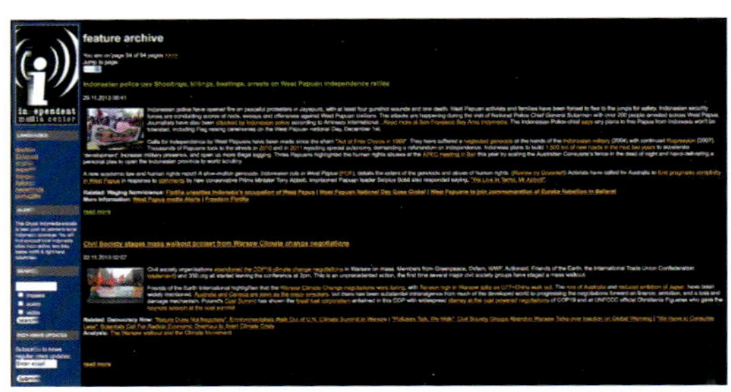

Screenshot, 07/09/2014

International Encyclopedia of Revolution and Protest

www.revolutionprotestencyclopedia.com

The International Encyclopedia of Revolution and Protest, which was founded in 2010, covers the history of protests and revolutions of the last five hundred years up to the mass movements of the present day. Organized alphabetically, each keyword provides a summary of uprisings, protests, and movements.

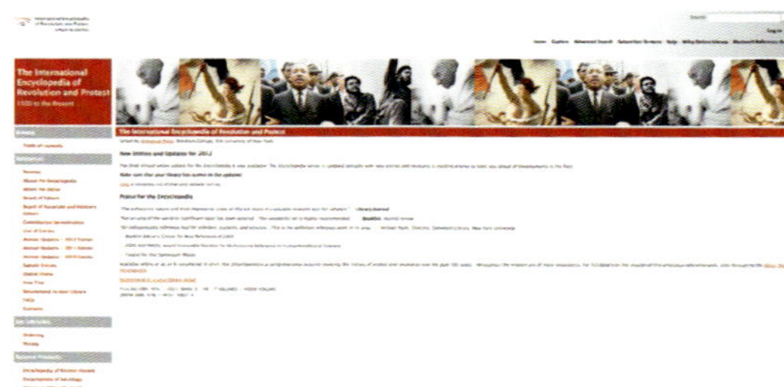

Screenshot, 07/09/2014

Iranian Riots

https://iranianriots.wordpress.com

The blog Iranian Riots provided information in English about the protests and demonstrations, which broke out in 2009 in Iran after the presidential election.

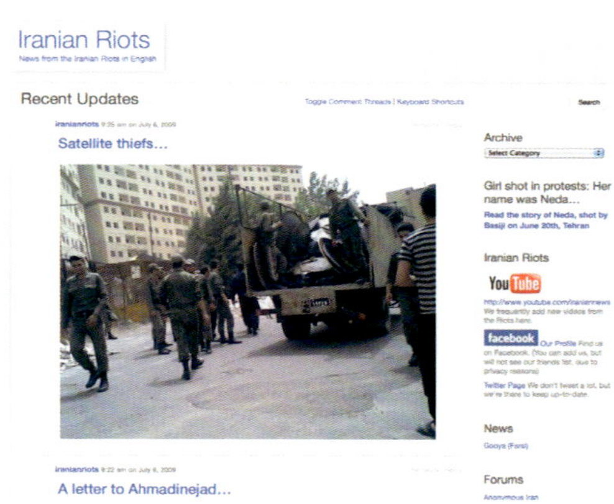

Screenshot, 07/09/2014

Meetup

www.meetup.com

Meetup is an online network of local groups, which seek to improve life in their communities. People can either found a group project in their area or find and join an already existing one in which to participate.

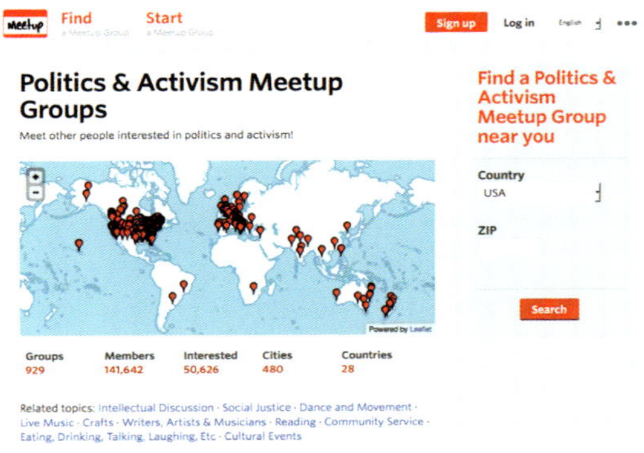

Screenshot, 07/09/2014

Meta-Activism

www.meta-activism.org

Mary Joyce, cofounder of the Digital Activism Research Project (2012) at the University of Washington, Seattle, dedicates her blog, where interested people can exchange ideas, to the scholarly analysis of activism in the digital age. Apart from giving lectures on the subject, she teaches activists about the possibilities that digital activism offers to achieve social and political change.

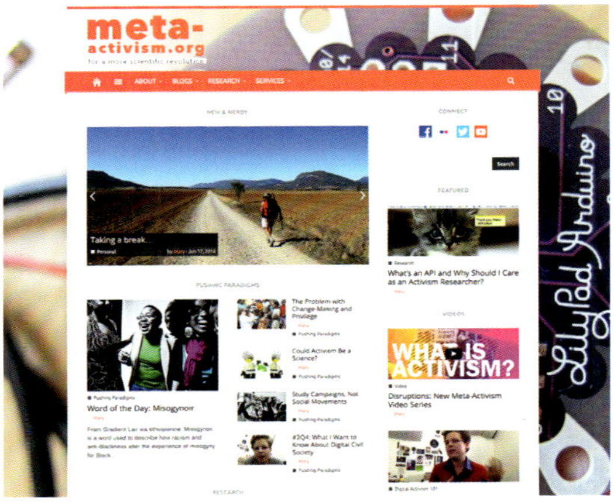

Screenshot, 07/09/2014

Solitary Watch

https://solitarywatch.com

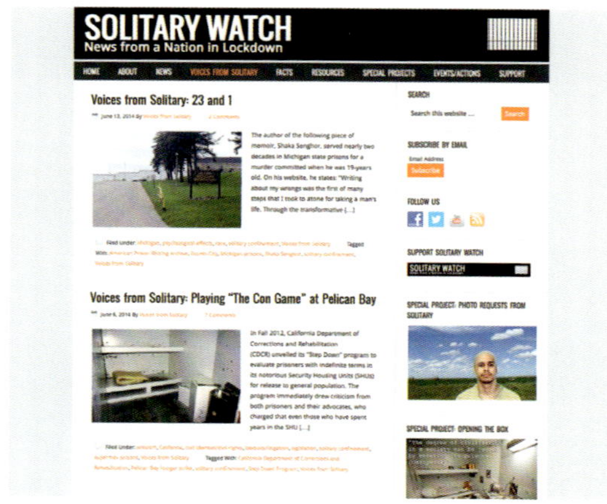

Screenshot, 07/09/2014

The Web-based project Solitary Watch attempts to put the widespread practice of solitary confinement in U.S. prisons and the question of its compatibility with fundamental human rights on the public agenda.

Twitter

www.twitter.com

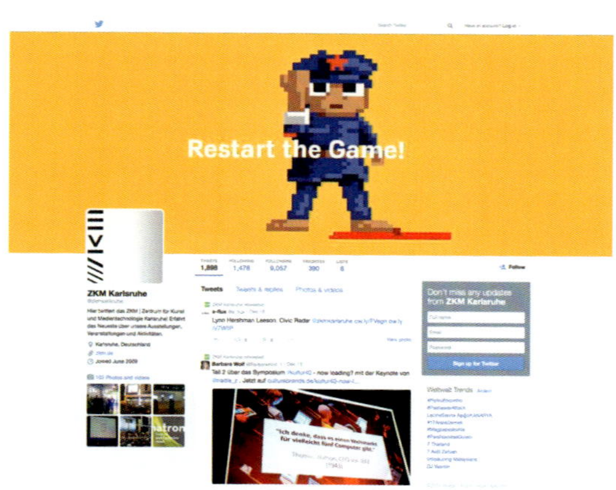

Screenshot, 12/17/2014

The online microblogging service Twitter is one of the most popular social networking sites. Users can send in real time and read "tweets," which are text messages limited to 140 characters. Registered users can subscribe to other registered users' tweets to get them automatically – which is known as "following" and subscribers are known as "followers." Users can group posts by topic or type by using hashtags – words or phrases prefixed with a #-sign. This allows users to link to other users who are interested in similar topics. As a result of these features Twitter is very often used to comment on events as they happen.

WikiLeaks

http://wikileaks.org

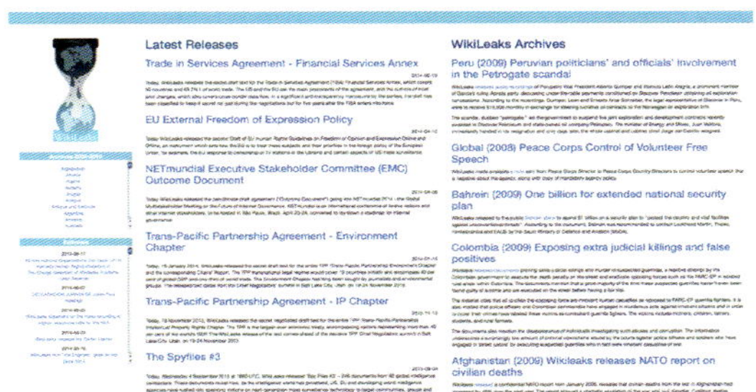

Screenshot, 07/09/2014

The international nonprofit online platform WikiLeaks which is financed by donations publishes secret information, news leaks, and classified media that would otherwise not be available to the general public. In 2010 U.S. soldier Bradley Manning (now Chelsea Manning) published, amongst other things, diplomatic cables written by U.S. ambassadors via WikiLeaks. Julian Assange and Sarah Harrison are the best-known associates of the whistle-blower platform.

YouTube

www.youtube.com

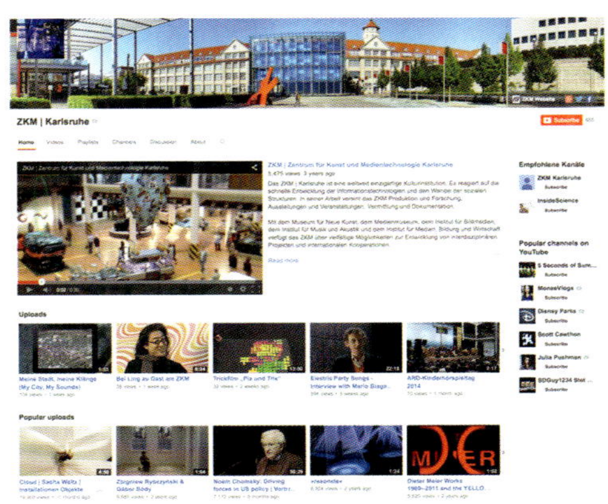

Screenshot, 12/17/2014

The Internet video-sharing website YouTube enables users to upload, view, and share videos of different kinds (for example, music videos, excerpts from films and television, amateur films) for free. Registered users can leave comments, rate videos, and upload their own material. YouTube is of interest to critics and activists to distribute their material because a range of video material can be uploaded and the service is free. For that reason, the platform is subject to strict censorship in various countries and has already been blocked several times, for example in Turkey, Pakistan, Morocco, Thailand, Iran, and Libya. In China, the portal is permanently blocked with few interruptions since 2008.

“Artivism” – Art and Activism

Chapter V

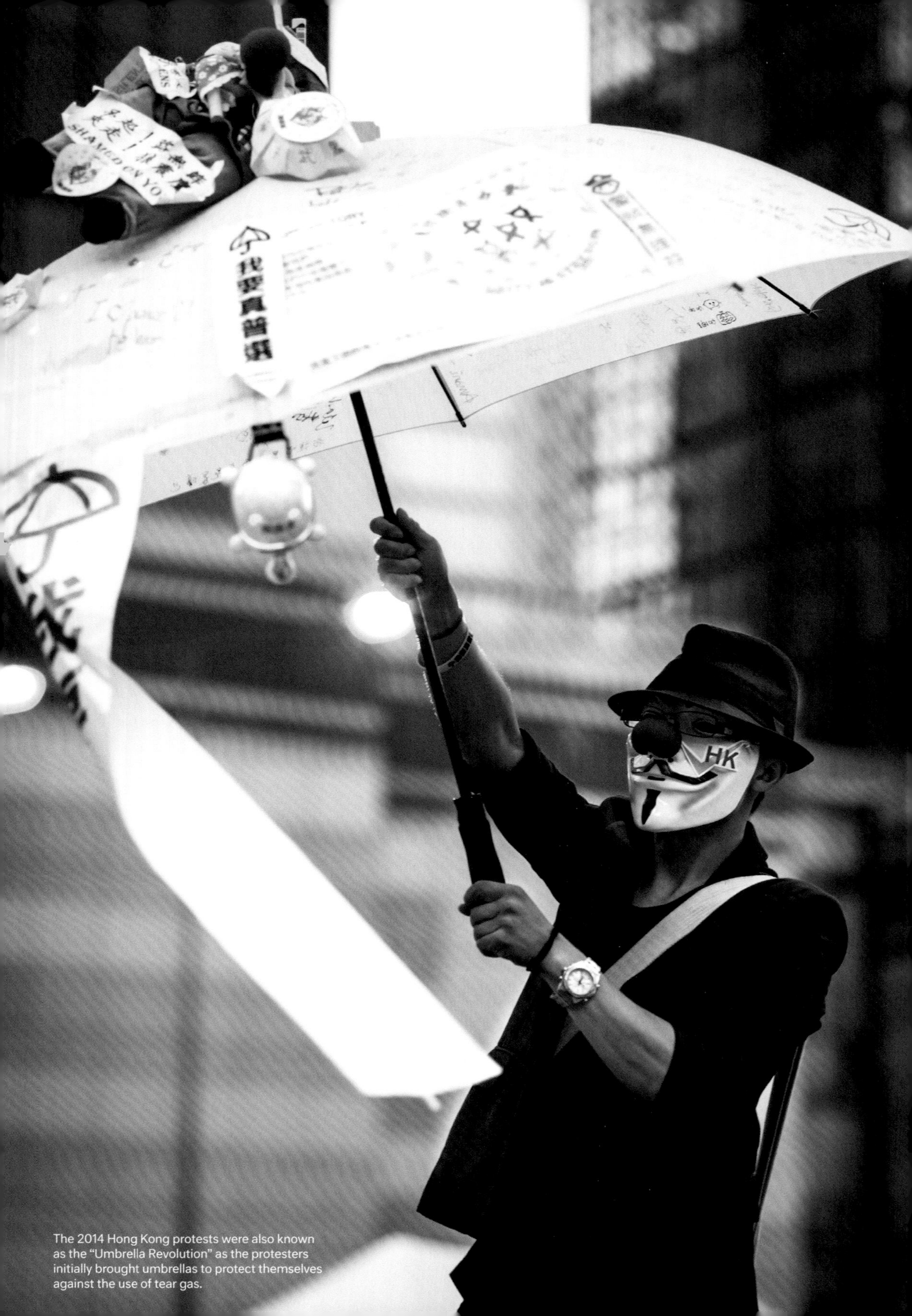

The 2014 Hong Kong protests were also known as the "Umbrella Revolution" as the protesters initially brought umbrellas to protect themselves against the use of tear gas.

Sruti Bala and Veronika Zangl

Humor's Opponents: Artistic Activism and the Ludic Aesthetic

Humor research has developed a considerable body of highly differentiated theories on various phenomena, ranging from philosophical and anthropological reflections on humor and laughter to sociological, psychological, and linguistic classifications of humorous utterings. It is striking that the predominant theories, which are incongruity, superiority, and relief theories, reflect on humor in terms of its function.[1] Accordingly, humor serves complex purposes when it comes to cultural, social, or political conflicts, ranging from disciplining or discriminatory to subversive and disruptive functions.

It is easy to assume that humor has positive social effects. Yet research on humor in activist performance must also discuss how the darker, less easily admired aspects of humor, such as ridicule, embarrassment, or the grotesque, may actually constitute the social core and potential of humor. It is paradoxical in that it is social and antisocial; it is both universal and particular. Humor does not necessarily unite; it can also divide.

Mikhail Bakhtin carefully elaborated on the basically ambivalent character of humor in his study on carnival and the grotesque image.[2] Bakhtin sourced his observations primarily from literary texts. However, his conceptions of the carnival and the grotesque are not simply restricted to the realm of language and narration, but are applicable to physical, often collective, public acts and events. Bakhtin's analysis of humor's many-facetted modes of address is pertinent to the understanding of the corporeal dimension of protest in contemporary artistic activism. Activism is often studied in terms of a distinction between activist subjects, their opponents, and the broader general public, whose sympathies and support are sought by either or both activists and their opponents.[3] This could be compared to the classic units of theater theory; namely, the protagonist, antagonist, and spectator. However, in assessing examples of artistic activism, the deployment of humorous strategies reveals that the communication with the opponent, whether a higher authority, the ruling power, or a system of oppression, is far from a straightforward opposition. This essay charts some of the complex and ambivalent ways in which humor transforms how an opponent is conceived and addressed.

1

For an overview of different theories of humor see: John Morreall, "Philosophy of Humor," in: *Stanford Encyclopedia of Philosophy*, Edward N. Zalta (ed.), 2013, available online at: plato.stanford.edu/archives/spr2013/entries/humor/, accessed 04/28/2014. For a focus on humor in social and political protest see: Marjolein 't Hart and Dennis Bos (eds.), *Humour and Social Protest*, Cambridge University Press, Cambridge, New York (NY), 2007; and the special issue on political humor, *The European Journal of Humour Research*, vol. 1, no. 2, 2013, available online at: www.europeanjournalofhumour.org/index.php/ejhr/issue/view/Political%20humour/showToc, accessed 05/06/2014.

2

Mikhail Bakhtin, *Rabelais and His World*, Indiana University Press, Bloomington (IN), 1984.

Comic Memory of Violent Conflict

Humor and violent conflict seem to be a contradiction in terms. However, in the history of genocide, from National Socialist Germany to Russia to the Balkans and Rwanda, there are several instances of humorous treatments of personal experiences of violence and humiliation, in the form of novels, jokes, cartoons, personal memoirs, or theatrical performances. This is pertinent not only after the conflict, but also during the volatile conflict situation. So-called nonserious approaches can be understood as aesthetic strategies that are simultaneously potentially interventionist, without necessarily being explicitly called "activist."

The Peruvian theater collective Yuyachkani has worked for decades on difficult themes such as collective memories of the civil war in Peru, the erasure of indigenous voices in the national history, and the tensions between experimental art and folk traditions. The theater work of Yuyachkani cannot take over the task of the truth and reconciliation commission, though it seeks to complement this institutional process. "Yuyachkani" is a Quechua word, which can only be translated into English with the unwieldy phrase "I am thinking, I am remembering, I am your thought." One of the plays in their repertoire, adapted from Julio Ortega's novella *Adiós Ayacucho* [Farewell Ayacucho] (1986), features the story of an indigenous peasant leader, Alfonso Canépa. Canépa disappeared – he was killed and dismembered during the violent civil war of the 1990s – and he then enters the form of an Andean masked dancer to search for the missing parts of his body and ensure himself a decent burial.[4] The play is all the more poignant as Canépa comes across all kinds of hilarious obstacles along the way, encountering armed rebels and drug dealers in his attempt to hand over a letter to the president. Ultimately, unable to find his own bones, he raids the tomb of the conquistador Francisco Pizarro in Lima to take his bones as substitutes for his own missing ones.

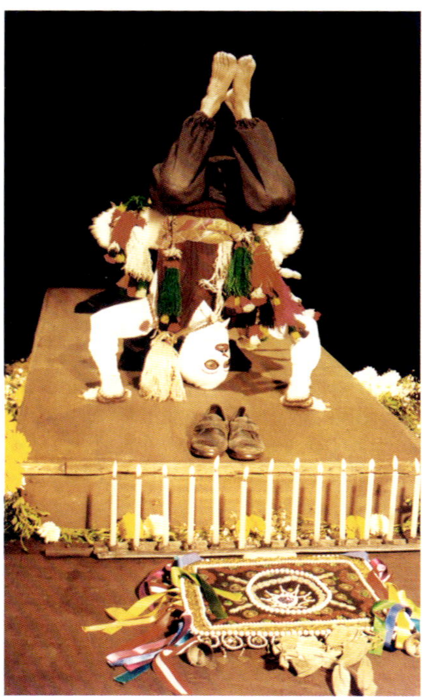

Augusto Casafranca playing a disappeared peasant searching for the missing parts of his own body in *Adiós Ayacucho* by the Peruvian theater group Yuyachkani, June 2009, Magdalena del Mar, Lima, Peru

Yuyachkani combines ritual and performance with an unsettling and deeply moving Andean humor as a means of addressing the past, which does not end with the Peruvian civil war but digs deeper into its colonial legacy. The bizarre idea of a dismembered body emerging from the netherworld searching for its own parts and claiming another body alters the

3 In terms of cultural activism, a critical appraisal is provided in Begüm Özden Fırat and Aylin Kuryel (eds.), *Cultural Activism. Practices, Dilemmas, and Possibilities,* Intersecting Place, Sex and Race Series, 21, Rodopi, Amsterdam, New York (NY), 2010.

4 The play *Adiós Ayacucho* was adapted and directed by Miguel Rubio Zapata and premiered in 1990. It is a solo performance by Augusto Casafranca, with musical accompaniment by Ana Correa.

way in which the violent conflict in Peru is remembered and imagined.[5] The play is not grotesque or macabre and does not reproduce on stage the horrors of the violence. It makes the audience laugh *with* rather than *at* the figure on stage. The dead, disembodied Canépa is shown as a lively, gentle, bouncy figure; the futile journeys of thousands of peasants to Lima to seek justice for their lost kin are dignified through his own childlike adventure, aided by a friendly ancestral spirit.

The Andean ritual of performing a dance and displaying the clothes of a dead person in order to pacify his or her soul is cited with reference to the bodies of the disappeared of the civil war. This fictive ritual on stage becomes a form of collective remembering. Humor takes on a performative dimension here; that is, it is not simply a characteristic or a component of an experience, but the embodied, performed means through which this experience is constituted. It is ambivalent in its address: both in Ortega's play as well as in Yuyachkani's staging of *Adiós Ayacucho*, humor is not used as a means of blaming, shaming, or pointing the finger but reveals an unfinished and open-ended task of imaginative memory.

Ridiculing Cultural Memory

A second example comes from artistic activism on the streets rather than in the theater. The various actions of the Wiener Gruppe [Vienna Group], a Vienna-based constellation of experimental artists and activists in Austria's postwar years, often consisted of ironic, grotesque mimicries of conservative cultural norms. One of their early actions was a "poetic demonstration" through the streets of Vienna in 1953, entitled *Une soirée aux amants funèbres*.[6] The planned route of the procession encountered monuments of high culture (Goethe memorial, Vienna State Opera, St. Stephen's Cathedral) and landmarks of so-called low or popular culture (Prater, ghost train[7]). The playful, metonymic use of religious references, such as the format of a procession, white asters as typical All Souls' Day flowers, and incense, was juxtaposed with an ivy-adorned flute player, and the recital of poetic works by Charles Baudelaire, Edgar Allan Poe, Gérard de Nerval, Georg Trakl, and Ramón Gómez de la Serna. In a way the Wiener Gruppe cited the romantic concept of the grotesque, which Bakhtin depicts as a disintegration of "the positive pole of grotesque realism,"[8] namely, the principle of regeneration, its universal spirit and utopian perspective. However, by applying a dramaturgy of heterogeneity,[9] or rather of dissonant constellations, the utopian moment is constructed as an aesthetic attitude reaching unmediated reality.[10] Poetic gestures like mixing and blending languages by simultaneously using old-fashioned sounding German, English, French, and Spanish, the rejection of any unifying dramatic forms, and the provocation of audiences accustomed to being self-assured in their consumption of art, all served to ridicule the construction of cultural memory based on ideologized "high" culture. The actions and interventions of the Wiener Gruppe thus didn't necessarily invite the audience to identify or sympathize with the act, but rather sought to horrify and shock the onlookers.[11]

5 Francine A'ness, "Resisting Amnesia: Yuyachkani, Performance, and the Postwar Reconstruction of Peru," in: *Theater Journal*, vol. 56, no. 3, October 2004, pp. 395–414, here p. 400–401.

6 See: Gerhard Rühm (ed.), *Die Wiener Gruppe. Achleitner, Artmann, Bayer, Rühm, Wiener. Texte, Gemeinschaftsarbeiten, Aktionen*, Rowohlt, Reinbek, 1985, p. 10.

7 The ghost train, also known as "Illusionsbahn" [train of illusion] is part of the amusement park colloquially referred to as the "Wurstelprater."

8 Bakhtin 1984, p. 53.

9 Evelyn Deutsch-Schreiner, "'*Wirklichkeitsinterventionen*'. Performative Provokationsästhetiken der Wiener Gruppe als Reaktion auf das starre kulturelle Klima der Nachkriegszeit," lecture at the symposium Teststrecke Kunst. Wiener Avantgarden nach 1945, Austrian Academy of Science, October 21–23, 2009, available online at: www.viennavant.at/de/symposiumteststreckekunst/politikderavantgarden/referatdeutsch/, accessed 04/26/2014.

10 See: Oswald Wiener, "das 'literarische cabaret' der wiener gruppe," in: Rühm 1985, pp. 401–418, here p. 402. It is striking that the artistic strategies of the Wiener Gruppe already signaled a transgression of art from the aesthetic to the societal sphere as early as the 1950s. See also: Deutsch-Schreiner 2009.

11 Oswald Wiener, a member of the Wiener Gruppe, mentions, for instance, that the first and second literary cabaret deliberately allowed for a "progressive decrease of the audience." Wiener 1985, p. 404, translated from the German.

The street intervention deliberately and consciously took into account that the audience would not be laughing with the performers. On the contrary, the audience was conceived and provocatively addressed as opponent.

Decades later, during the run-up to the Austrian elections in 2013, various civil society initiatives, such as Romano Svato, maiz, traschq, Marea Alta, and artist-activists such as Gin Müller, took part in the so-called WIENWOCHE [Viennese Week][12] with a series of interventions in public space. The group maiz, an autonomous center by and for immigrants, once again adopted the format of a procession, namely, a cannibalistic procession entitled *Eating Europe!* or *Menschenfressende Gesellschaft* [Anthropophagous Society]. Humorous references were thus drawn both to Oswald de Andrade's *Manifesto Antropófago* [Manifest of Anthropophagy] (1928) from the Brazilian avant-garde movement in the early twentieth century as well as to the processions of the Wiener Gruppe in the very same city. The public intervention by Rebelodrom and maiz took place at the heart of culturally charged sites like the Karlskirche, Künstlerhaus, and Musikverein in Vienna. However, in contrast to *Une soirée aux amants funèbres*, the anthropophagous procession stressed the corporeal aspect of the grotesque, through a joyous celebration of queer body images, colonial and postcolonial stereotypes, and exaggerated embodiments of official representatives of church and politics. Yet the recital of a carnivalesque litany "We have come to gorge Austria, we have come to gorge Europe" by no means demonstrated a reference to Michail Bakhtin's concept of universalism and regeneration. The refrain "but we do not digest it" rather performed a satirical critique of Michel Bakhtin's dialectics of grotesque images. The target of critique was no longer a static and nationalized universal humanism as expressed in high art, but national identity politics in the face of globalized economic power structures. The anthropophagous procession applied a strategy of grotesque hyperrealism in order to oppose those global economic and political structures that reinforce inequality. Ironically, the hyperreal strategy of maiz and Rebelodrom, with its distinctive aesthetics of exaggeration and visceral corporeality, in fact reflected the grotesque features of the emerging globalized reality.

12 WIENWOCHE can be read both as an allusion to the prestigious Wiener Festwochen festival as well as to the campaign "Austria's youth gets to know its federal city" organized by the Federal Ministry of Education.

Refracting the Surveilling Gaze of the Public

The third example deals with an instance of an individual act of protest that eventually became an artwork. Hasan Elahi, a Bangladeshi-American media artist and scholar based in Washington, D.C., was detained at a U.S. airport in 2002 on suspicion of being a terrorist. He was told his whereabouts would be monitored for one year. So Elahi responded to this by inverting the surveillance of the state. He first started sending, or spamming if you like, the authorities with mails, photographs, and text messages about everything he did, every bus or flight he took, every restaurant he ate in, every toilet he visited. Gradually this *sousveillance*, state surveillance reversed by the citizen as self-surveillance, unfolded into an ongoing art project titled *Tracking Transience*.[13] In a given

13 Hasan Elahi, *Tracking Transience*, available online at: http://trackingtransience.net, accessed 05/02/2014.

14 Hasan Elahi, "You Want to Track Me? Here You Go, F.B.I.," in: *The New York Times*, Op-Ed, October 29, 2011, p. 6.

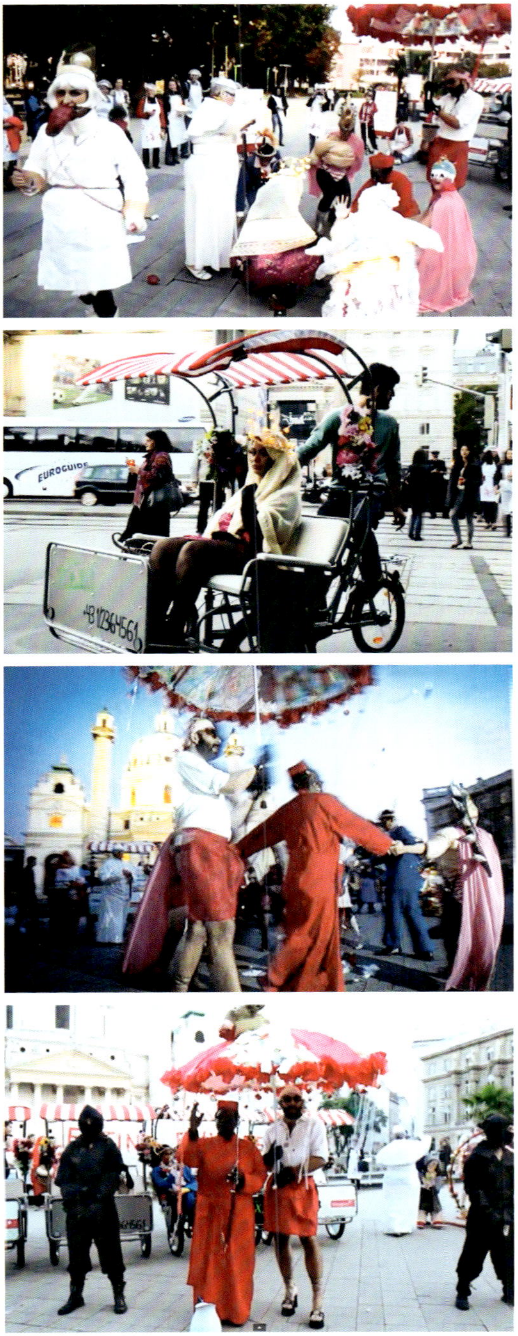

Artist-activists from the collectives Rebelodrom and maiz in Vienna during an anthropophagous procession announcing their desire to devour Europe: "Austria, we love you! We will never leave you!"

asymmetrical conflict situation, where the overwhelming mechanisms of state power intrude into the life of a citizen marked as ethnic minority or immigrant, it is the self-ironic gesture that serves as a lens to investigate not the innocence of the one being watched, but the monstrosity of the system of surveillance. The website and self-designed tracking software is consciously user-unfriendly and cluttered, thus ironically creating a kind of privacy through extreme visibility.[14]

The safety and privilege provided by positing the self-surveillance information as art may well not be granted to anyone under every circumstance, as it providently turned out to be for Elahi. His example also highlights questions of memory in relation to humor, wherein the conception of a conflict fundamentally affects and shapes the type of humor that emerges. Even less than a decade later, when the extent of global surveillance is becoming evident and the surveillance far from transient, the humor of Elahi's *Tracking Transience* almost borders on the nostalgic. In contrast to the data revealed by whistleblowers on the extent of surveillance machinery worldwide, Elahi's project is humorous for different reasons today than it initially was. *Tracking Transience* appears today not as a magnified, exaggerated version of state surveillance, but as a mere sample of its possibilities.

Humor in Artistic Activism: A Bond Between Memory and Imagination

The three examples discussed above reveal that research on humor in activist performance involves far more than studying different kinds of jokes or laughter alone, but rather examining a broader ludic aesthetic, ranging from gentle irony and satire to figurations of the grotesque and absurd, to risky interventions and self-critical overidentification. Each example reveals how the study of humor in artistic activism evades being captured in recurrent patterns or formulae. The ambivalence of humor as potentially transgressive on the one side, as well as upholding the status quo on the other, makes it difficult to draw out general assumptions. It cannot be claimed that humorous approaches are fundamentally different from more conventional formats of activism. Moreover, contemporary

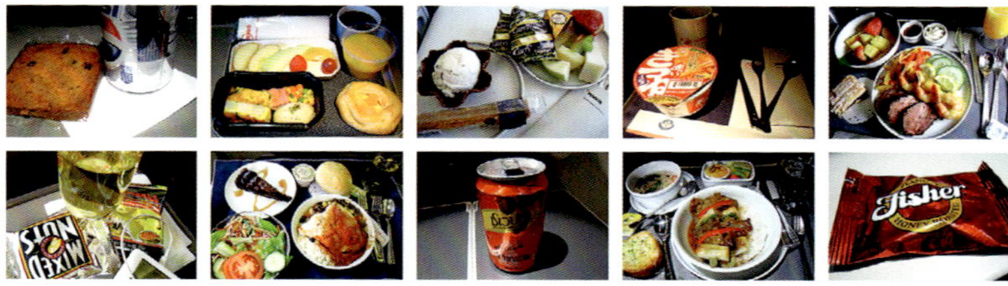

artistic activism shows that demonstrations, sit-ins, lobbying, protest marches, petitions, making pamphlets, and speeches are being combined with seemingly newer formats of cultural activism, some of which are located in the realm of the arts. They are indebted to critical traditions in different cultural contexts and histories.

Memory plays an intriguing role in relation to humorous protest, its narratives, forms of embodiment, and circulation. There are two observations to be made here. First, it is striking that contemporary articulations of public protest explicitly and playfully draw references to older legacies of protest. Yuyachkani's use of Andean comic traditions and rituals in *Adiós Ayacucho* draws a direct link between the memory of the civil war and the colonial history of Peru. The human gorging procession in Vienna cites with a wink the anthropophagy of Brazil's avant-garde movement of the early twentieth century, transported to the context of immigration in Europe. It can also be linked to the legacy of the processions of the Wiener Gruppe, who literally walked the same streets of the city fifty years earlier. Second, one can observe a playful shifting of narratives of memory, whether they are national or political memory narratives or aesthetic legacies and artistic predecessors. Elahi's messy, overflowing archive of his own whereabouts literally conjures a nightmarishly absurd vision of what the future might hold, whilst simultaneously challenging the representative organs of the system of surveillance to take a closer look at the system itself. The humorous intention of the poetic demonstration of the Wiener Gruppe may have required a few decades to be recognized as such, but possibly it was the actual embodied provocation on the streets that served as a trigger to the public imagination. Artistic activism in conflict settings not only challenges different layers of memory, but also bonds these layers to the present and the future. Humor makes this bond between memory and imagination evident.

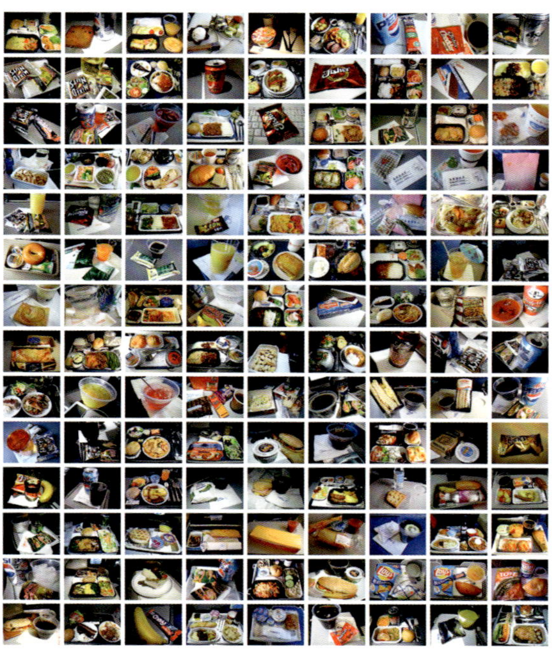

Images from media artist Hasan Elahi's *Tracking Transience* project, which documents all the data he voluntarily supplied to the FBI, to help with monitoring his own whereabouts
Above: detail

Tatiana Bazzichelli

Networked Disruption:

Connecting Art, Hacktivism, and Business in Political Struggles

What Is Networked Disruption?

Disruption occurs when a process of business innovation takes shape by displacing an earlier technology; it provokes a change of consolidated business values, whilst simultaneously generating new forms of business. Over the last decade, alongside the emergence of network economy, the critical framework of art and hacktivism has shifted from developing strategies of opposition to embarking on the art of disruption. With the development of social media and Web 2.0[1] the concept of social networking became part of our daily life, and many corporations adopted the same vocabulary used by the activists and hackers in the 1990s, assimilating the rhetoric of openness, do-it-yourself, sharing, etc.

My hypothesis is that mutual interferences between art and hacktivism within the information economy have changed the meaning and contexts of political and technological criticism. Hackers and artists have been active agents in business innovation, while at the same time also undermining business. Artists and hackers use disruptive techniques of networking within the framework of information technology, opening up a critical perspective towards business to generate unpredictable feedback and unexpected reactions; business enterprises apply disruption as a form of innovation to create new markets and network values, which are often just as unpredictable.

If art, business, and its antagonism are nowadays intertwined, it is advisable to reinvent practices of criticism that go beyond the mere act of opposition. This paper takes up this challenge and discusses a new perspective of political activism and artistic creation based on the concept of "networked disruption," applying it both in theory and practice. The aim is to analyze hacker and artistic practices *through* business instead of in opposition to it, shedding light on the mutual interferences between networking participation and disruptive business innovation. Many activists usually prefer not to deal with the notion of "business," confining it to the domain of commercial market logic. However, the concept of business is much more complex than that, and it can be associated with the idea of "being busy" in the context of Protestant culture. Following this perspective, disruption becomes a two-way strategy in networking contexts, a practice to generate criticism, and a methodology to create business innovation.

1 See: Tim O'Reilly, "What Is Web 2.0. Design Patterns and Business Models for the Next Generation of Software," September 30, 2005, available online at: http://oreilly.com/web2/archive/what-is-web-20.html, accessed 08/06/2014.

Rethinking Oppositional Practices

Why do we need to rethink artistic and hacktivist opposition within the context of social media and after the emergence of Web 2.0? This question is at the core of my recently published book, *Networked Disruption: Rethinking Oppositions in Art, Hacktivism and the Business of Social Networking* (Digital Aesthetics Research Centre, Aarhus University, Aarhus, 2013), and the main link that connects my other two books, *Networking: The Net as Artwork* (Digital Aesthetics Research Centre, Aarhus University, Aarhus, 2008) and *Disrupting Business: Art and Activism in Times of Financial Crisis* (coedited with Geoff Cox, DATA browser 05, Autonomedia, New York, 2013). These reflections are the consequence of a process of personal involvement with the activist (or rather "artivist") scene in Italy since the mid-1990s. Additionally, they are based on the analysis of international fieldwork on practices ranging from the European tradition of net culture to the development of cyberculture in California, which is intertwined with the history of counterculture.[2]

The idea of conscious participation in media practices is central to analyzing the evolution and transformation of the concept of "networking" in the age of social media and before that. Between the end of the 1990s and the early 2000s, a great deal of media criticism was often very dialectical, and rooted in the idea of antagonism as radical opposition. I am referring to the protests against neoliberal capitalism, which the media called the "antiglobalization movement" in Seattle, Prague, Goteborg, Genoa, and so on. At the time, it was easier to identify an "enemy," and for everyone to be united against the same power. However, this also meant that it was easier for the authorities to identify the members of the movement(s), and many protests faced violent chains of repression. In particular in Genoa, the Italian movement and the so-called "movement of movements" were hit hard.[3] For many collectives, Genoa was the end of an experience of a long period of antagonism. For others, it was the beginning of a new phase of criticism, and a new wave of protests, which became stronger and increased in number. However, the general feeling of many activists, myself included, was that during the G8 protests which were suppressed by such violent clashes, activists played into the hands of the police and became an easy target; they were maneuvered into a trap which allowed police to carry out planned brutal suppression.[4]

Many collectives began to formulate a thoroughgoing critique of the strategy of frontal opposition, the metaphorical idea of assaulting the "red zone," which was the area where the G8 members were confined during their summits. After Genoa 2001 some projects evolved into a quest for a new way of activism which was not simply black-and-white, and which would be harder to co-opt and manipulate: for example, queer, pink, and independent porn projects started combining ludic strategies and playful disruption, generating interventions and actions beyond oppositional confrontation. During the first half of the 2000s, many independent projects based on a critique of media and technology flourished in Italy: this was the time of the Telestreet movement, and a new

2 See: Fred Turner, *From Counterculture to Cyberculture. Stewart Brand, the Whole Earth Network, and the Rise of Digital Utopianism*, Chicago University Press, Chicago (IL), 2006.

3 See the Italian websites www.processig8.org and www.supportolegale.org, both accessed 08/06/2014.

4 At that time I was part of the independent communication laboratory Strano Network of Florence, and the AvANa hacker collective of Rome. During the three days of Genoa, I was with the Strano Network group reporting the facts on a public square in Florence via a live connection to Radio GAP, the official independent radio of the protests.

wave of pirate TV and independent radio stations, hacktivist projects, and other radical experiences based on the idea of sharing information, development of free communication tools, and struggling for openness on the Internet and in the sphere of media.[5]

After 2004, which was also when Web 2.0 emerged, the critical framework of art and hacktivism shifted once again: networking, a concept which had informed the avant-garde since the 1960s, and was later a consistent part of grassroots network culture, became a tool for a wider audience, and a pervasive business strategy. The ideas of openness, do-it-yourself, sharing – the "mottos" of the grassroots hacker culture of the 1990s and early 2000s – became standard rhetoric of the Web 2.0 companies based on the appropriation of "free culture." Artistic and hacker practices needed to be recontextualized because the concept of social networking had become something completely different from its roots, and the business companies themselves were applying disruption as their main business logic. The question that informed my further research became: Is it possible to oppose disruption with disruption, and to use business logic strategically to co-opt the co-optation?

In the era of an immaterial economy and increasing flexibility, the act of responding with radical opposition no longer looks like an effective practice, since it risks simply feeding the same machine and replicating the capitalist logic of competitiveness and power conflicts. The point is to try to figure out how to imagine new forms of participation that go beyond dualistic conflict – and that go beyond the creation of a hegemonic and holistic entity. As an artistic and activist practice, networked disruption suggests the act of strategically performing *within* the capitalist framework, not *against* it, keeping the dialectic open through coexisting oppositions. The notion of disruptive business is useful for reflecting on different modalities of generating criticism, shedding light on contradictions and ambiguities both in capitalist logic and in artistic and hacktivist strategies, while at the same time rethinking oppositional practices in the context of an information economy.

The Art of Disrupting Business

Networked disruption implies a multiangled perspective where business and the antagonism of business intertwine. Rethinking strategies and modalities of opposition implies that new forms of intervention and political awareness should be proposed without antagonizing them, but rather by playing with them and disrupting them from the inside of the machine. Disrupting business as an art form must be interpreted beyond categorical definitions, and as a new input for the imagination. Holes in the system are everywhere, ready to be performed and disrupted. Today there are artists and activists who are inspired by a certain tradition of "disruption," creating interventions from within, critically appropriating the logic of business, stretching its limits, or proposing alternative models to it.[6] As I described above, the concept of disruptive business is rooted in the idea of disruptive innovation. In business

5 I described this process in my book *Networking: The Net as Artwork* (Digital Aesthetics Research Centre, Aarhus University, Aarhus, 2008, chapter "Becoming Media," pp. 214–256), see: http://networkingart.eu/2009/09/networking-the-net-as-artwork, accessed 08/06/2014.

6 Many of these are described as case studies in my book *Networked Disruption: Rethinking Oppositions in Art, Hacktivism and the Business of Social Networking* (Digital Aesthetics Research Centre, Aarhus University, Aarhus, 2013), where I propose a constellation of social networking projects that challenge the notion of power and hegemony, and where social networking is not only technologically determined. Projects and experiences such as mail art, Neoism, the Church of the SubGenius, Luther Blissett, Anonymous, Anna Adamolo, Les Liens Invisibles, the Telekommunisten collective, the San Francisco Suicide Club, the Cacophony Society, the early Burning Man festival, the Noisebridge hackerspace, are intertwined; see: http://disruptiv.biz/networked-disruption-the-book, accessed 08/06/2014.

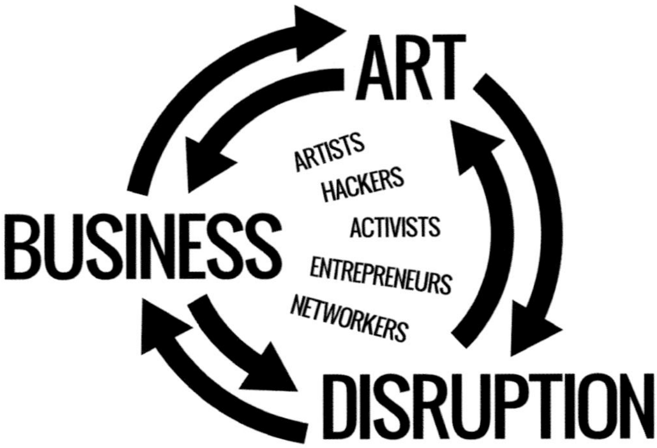

Tatiana Bazzichelli, *Disruptive Loop Diagram*, 2011

culture, disruption not only means rupture, but links to the idea of innovation and redesigning behavioral tendencies. Therefore, performing disruption generates a process that both interferes with business and generates innovations in the business field. Following this path, business is neither seen as positive nor negative, but it is a means for working consciously on political practices – and for raising questions on art and media criticism.

In 2009 I was a visiting scholar at Stanford University where I was researching the reasons for the progressive commercialization of networking contexts after the emergence of Web 2.0 through the development of hacker culture in Silicon Valley. From the interviews that I conducted, and also via a close reading of the book *From Counterculture to Cyberculture* (2006) by Fred Turner, it was evident that since the development of early cyberculture, hackers and members of the so-called "counterculture" have been trying to disrupt business via their practices, and in parallel, business corporations have been trying to do the same through technological innovation. Since the 1960s, the libertarian tradition of North American counterculture is deeply rooted in the intersection between business and an antihegemonic critique of the establishment. This is also evident today in the business context of Web 2.0 where many hackers are working at the core of business, while disrupting it – the Anonymous entity is one of the most successful examples of this.

This perspective calls for a reformulation of the idea of an encapsulation of radical values by business, highlighting the mutual disruption of the hacker principles of openness and collaboration and the business logic of the network economy. According to computer engineer Lee Felsenstein, whom I interviewed during my time as a visiting scholar, in California hackers reject hegemony but not business.[7] This is also why many hackers in Silicon Valley have no problem with working for Google, which is trying to employ the best hackers of the area. In Italy, members of the hacktivist movement have often claimed that hacking is politics, and politics is an "attitude" that informs your everyday life and lifestyle. In Silicon Valley, however, libertarian practices are very often

7 See: Tatiana Bazzichelli, "Interviews with: Jacob Appelbaum, Olivier Bonin, Scott Beale, Lee Felsenstein, John Law, Karen Marcelo, Hal Robins, Val Vale"; the interviews were conducted in San Francisco (CA), Palo Alto (CA), Oakland (CA), Aarhus (University), Stanford (University) (CA) in 2009, unpublished.

linked with the rejection of the political, and this is the position of many members of the hacker community in California.

Therefore, what was considered a "problem" of contamination of business and free culture among the underground hacker movement that I experienced in Italy, was not considered as such among the hackers that I met in the area between San Francisco and Palo Alto. This led me to create a model of analysis which I call the "disruptive feedback loop," based on the idea of layering instead of co-optation (see the opposite image).

I drew on the concept of "layering" rather than co-optation from Fred Turner's lecture "The Bohemian Factory: Burning Man, Google and the Countercultural Ethos of New Media Manufacturing"[8] (2009). Burning Man – a week-long art event started in 1986 and held every year since 1990 in the Black Rock Desert in Northern Nevada – is an example of a mutual contamination of business logic and counterculture ethos, and is a context in which these worlds coexist and feed into each other. In my disruptive loop model,[9] artists and hackers adopt viral and flexible strategies of intervention to generate new modalities for using technology, which, in some cases, are unpredictable and critical; business enterprises apply disruption as a form of innovation to create new markets and network values, which are also often unpredictable. This model can be applied both to the analysis of business contexts of network economy and to critical practices generated by hackers and artists.[10]

8

Fred Turner, "The Bohemian Factory: Burning Man, Google and the Countercultural Ethos of New Media Manufacturing," lecture at the University of California, Irvine, School of Humanities, April 23, 2009; Fred Turner, "Burning Man at Google: A Cultural Infrastructure for New Media Production," in: *New Media & Society*, vol. 11, nos. 1–2, February/March 2009, pp. 73–94.

9

A result of a conversation about the development of California hacker spaces with Jacob Appelbaum in 2009, who at the time was an active member of Noisebridge in San Francisco.

10

Examples such as GNU/Linux and Napster demonstrate market disruptions changing customer behavior and influencing cultural perspectives.

OCTO P7C-1: The Paradox of a Centralized Social Networking System

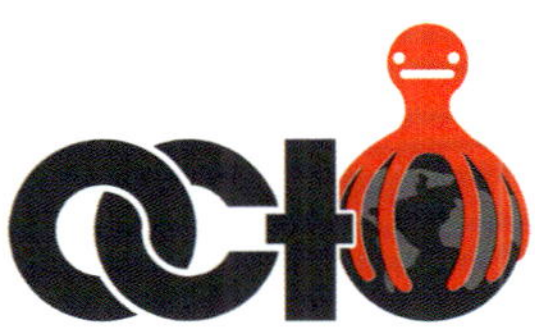

Telekommunisten, OCTO P7C-1, 2013

Who is the "enemy" today when disruption and its opposition are feeding the same machine? In the context of network economy, business logic is versatile and infinitely adaptable. Technologies become relational machines that contribute to a redefinition of the assets of production, creating a process whereby communication and productivity are connected in a mutual feedback loop. To envision forms of disruptive business as artistic practice means to imagine forms of innovation which affect many areas of our everyday lives and demonstrate a profound knowledge of capitalist logic.

The series of "Miscommunication Technologies" by the Telekommunisten network, a collective founded by Dmytri Kleiner, reflect on modes of production and models of interpersonal relation by "creating technologies that don't work as expected, or work in an unexpected way" employing "parody, juxtaposition, exaggeration and *reductio ad absurdum* to bring aspects of these relations, which are normally hidden from view, into the foreground."[11]

11

Dmytri Kleiner and Baruch Gottlieb, "Miscommunication Technologies. Telekommunisten Artworks 2009–2013" in: Bazzichelli and Cox 2013, pp. 105–123, here p. 105.

During my curatorial activity at the transmediale festival for the 2013 edition with the theme "BWPWAP" (Back When Pluto Was a Planet), we invited the Telekommunisten collective to continue their series of „Miscommunication Technologies," imagining an experimental project as a living metaphor of a social network generated via pneumatic tube architecture. It was an invitation to reflect, via artistic practice, on the centralization aspect of social

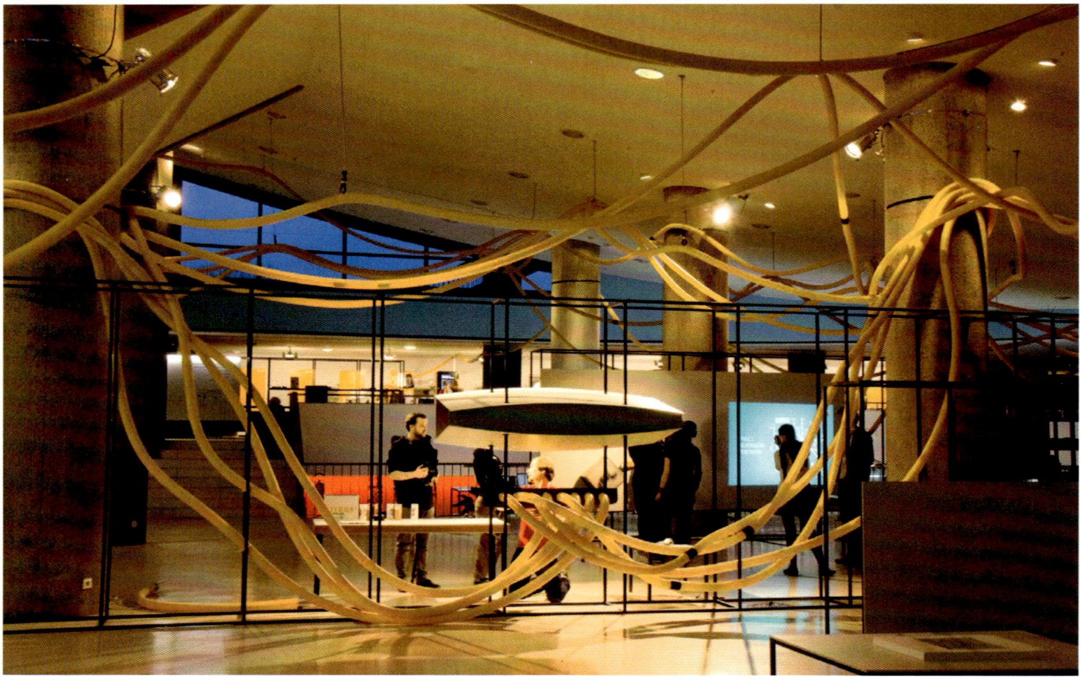

OCTO P7C-1 Central Station, transmediale, "BWPWAP," Haus der Kulturen der Welt, Berlin, 2013

networking, but also to create a tribute to the local Berlin *Rohrpost*, a historical public service of pneumatic tube transport. The artwork was named OCTO P7C-1 Intertubular Pneumatic Packet Distribution System, which included the PNEUMAtic circUS project, the first pneumatic experiment of mail art ever done.[12]

The project had many layers of analysis and practice: it was presented as a parody of a centralized corporation, OCTO, which operated worldwide to achieve the goal of bringing pneumatic tube communication and exchange of high-speed delivery of packages to every household and place of business, under the slogan "A Global Pipe Dream Come True!"; it was an elaborate vacuum-cleaner-powered network of pneumatic tubes connecting stations across the festival venue, which had to be constantly operated by people in order to function and allow the traveling capsules to be exchanged; it was a parody of a centralized social networking system which often got clogged up, demonstrating that any technology can malfunction, and also invited festival visitors to experiment with the pros and contras of a closed system of interconnection. Finally, last but not least, it was the result of an open system of collaboration among a wide network of international mail artists, who had been invited by postal artist Vittore Baroni to contribute pneumatic post capsules containing instructions, small artworks, and scores to be used and performed by transmediale festival visitors.

By discovering the dark side of the gift-exchange economy, we reflected on the imagination of "intimate bureaucracies"[13] that are able to intervene in the framework of networking by generating disruption and creatively appropriate the logic of the market. By highlighting the abundance of paradoxes in networked systems of organization and control in social media and beyond, the objective

12 See: www.telekommunisten.net/octo, www.transmediale.de/content/octo-a-global-pipe-dream-come-true, and www.transmediale.de/pneumatic-circus-digital-catalogue, all accessed 8/06/2014.

13 See: Craig J. Saper, *Networked Art*, University of Minnesota Press, Minneapolis (MN), 2001; dj readies (Craig J. Saper), *Intimate Bureaucracies: A Manifesto*, punctum books, Brooklyn (NY), 2012.

was to incentivize decentralized alternative models of communication.[14] The project reflected on the tensions between the open and closed nature of social media, stressing the limits of an imaginative social networking platform, and working on unpredictable consequences of users' actions generated by a disruptive use of it. Paradoxically, to be critical of business we had to learn from it.

The series of miscommunication artworks by Telekommunisten are rooted on the strategy of exposing contradictions in order to reveal hidden power structures, thereby dismantling a holistic faith in the truth of fully functioning technologies by showing that systems can always be compromised. The capitalist system has infinitely more resources to force its "truth" on models of society; therefore the challenge becomes to provoke criticism through a network of multiple, distributed, playful, and disruptive practices, which are harder to appropriate. Following this perspective, the strategy of looking for a single enemy to oppose might leave space to imagine actions where the system can't get you, and therefore it becomes more difficult to confine criticism. The idea of working from within the functionality of network systems becomes an opportunity to reflect on concepts such as openness, authority, and control, which are constantly challenged and renegotiated by artists and activists who work within the realms of social and cultural disruption.

By identifying the emerging contradictions within the current economic and political framework, networked disruption becomes a conceptual space of intervention in which the opposition coexists. It is a reconfiguration of practices into a structure of layering where artists, hackers, networkers, critical thinkers, and entrepreneurs are intertwined.

14 A further version of OCTO P7C-1 called "Seidenstrasse" was created collaboratively at the 30C3 Chaos Communication Congress of the Chaos Computer Club in Hamburg in December 2013 as an open artwork and a decentralized mesh network; see online: https://events.ccc.de/congress/2013/wiki/Projects:Seidenstrasse, accessed 08/06/2014.

Dietrich Heissenbüttel

Protests Everywhere?

Back in mid-December 2010, hardly anyone would have dared to predict that just a month later Tunisian dictator Zine el Abidine Ben Ali would be ousted from power and – something that even then many commentators doubted – that one month after that Hosni Mubarak would likewise be overthrown. The Arab Spring also inspired Occupy Wall Street. What began in New York spread to a number of other countries. The incarceration of members of the Punk Rock band Pussy Riot in Russia; the uprisings against the austerity policy of the Troika in Greece; the *indignados* in Spain; the nationwide protests in Turkey after the announcement of the bulldozing of Gezi Park in Istanbul; not to mention Portugal or Brazil: the world appeared to be in turmoil.

But can the protest movements in different parts of the world really be subsumed under one umbrella? Are Tunis, Cairo, Moscow, New York, and Istanbul just the tip of the iceberg or, to use a metaphor more appropriate to the subject, were they the crests of the waves of a stormy sea, a world in which unrest lurks around every corner? Are there common causes, shared objectives, or, where possible, is there a common enemy uniting the protest movements in all these countries?

There are no clear answers to these questions. First, it is worth remembering that the places and countries mentioned do not represent the entire topography of worldwide protests over the last few years. The economy of media attention means that some movements are quickly eclipsed by more spectacular events elsewhere or do not even make it through the strict selection of top headlines at all. Who cares about Bulgaria? Who would trust that the populations of African countries, in their "disaster-plagued continent" ruled by the "big men," could push through a successful movement for democratization? And yet there is an Occupy Nigeria movement, and also a peaceful protest movement in Senegal – inspired, most crucially, by the example of Tunisia – which ensured that President Abdoulaye Wade was forced to step down in 2012.

Yet even in the heart of the so-called "First World," protests are brewing in various nooks and crannies, without the media ever paying much attention. When would German newspapers or broadcasters report on something like the "Moral Mondays" in Raleigh, North Carolina, and other cities – including in neighboring U.S. states? While the street battles in Kiev's Maidan Square, which not only

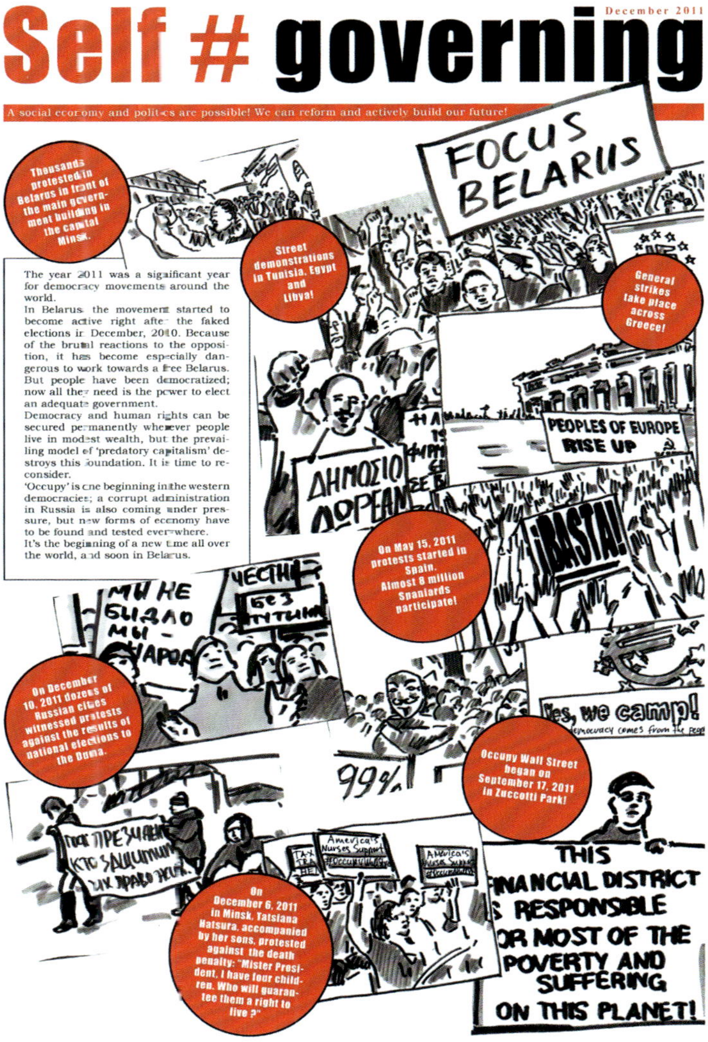

Office for Anti-Propaganda, *Self#governing*, 2011

saw security forces firing at demonstrators but also insurgents with three-meter-high catapults hurling stones and Molotov cocktails at police, were always reported from the perspective of the rebels,[1] the reactions of the media to the simultaneous proclamation of a danger zone in a large part of Hamburg's city center were muted. The trigger of this measure was one single throw of a stone, seemingly an attack on a police officer on December 28, 2013 which actually happened differently than the version given in the initial police statements.[2] Some newspapers were critical; others dedicated just a brief mention to the events, or simply adopted the police perspective.

Given that very few people link their own experiences to global news, memory has a short half-life in this regard. The 2009 "Green Revolution" in Iran? Almost entirely forgotten already. Who remembers that there was a "Silent Revolution" in Belarus back in 2011, two years before the "Standing Man," choreographer

1

See: Jens Berger, "Ukraine: Der Qualitätsjournalismus versagt," in: *NachDenkSeiten. Die kritische Website*, January 31, 2014, available online at: www.nachdenkseiten.de/?p=20542, accessed 05/22/2014.

2

See: Sven-Michael Veit, "Gefahrengebiet Hamburg. Kein politisches Problem," in: *Die Tageszeitung (taz)*, January 7, 2014, available online at: www.taz.de/130557, accessed 05/22/2014.

Erdem Gündüz, became an icon of the protest in Istanbul?[3] And yet this staging of publicly enacted silence made the protesters no less decisive in articulating their dissent. Occupy Wall Street took place not only against the backdrop of the Arab Spring and the financial crisis that had been triggered by property speculation, but also after more than fifteen years of protests against the power of corporations, the dictatorship of the International Monetary Fund and the World Bank and neoliberal ideology: this was already a widespread movement that had manifested itself in Seattle, Genoa, and Heiligendamm.[4]

Alongside these long-term developments, however, it is also worth noting that the mass protests in Egypt, Tunisia, Senegal, Turkey, Spain, and Brazil were sparked spontaneously by local circumstances, often in places where they would have been least expected. In Brazil, for example, partly as a result of large-scale events like the Olympic Games or the Fifa World Cup, poorer groups of people have increasingly been pushed to the edges of the cities. When ticket prices for public transport were then raised, protest was the last straw.

Back in 2003, Osman Bozkurt demonstrated in a video how people in Istanbul would use even traffic islands or the narrow strips of green in the middle of multiple-lane highways to have a picnic.[5] Is it any wonder, then, that the threat of demolition of the last remaining park in this city of more than fourteen million provoked such outrage? Whether it concerns civil rights or green space, public transport or – as in Tunisia, Syria, and Spain – the future prospects of an entire generation of young people: spontaneous, extensive protests break out when the situation on the ground becomes intolerable.

From a Local Perspective[6]

In 2010 the city of Stuttgart saw the biggest and longest-lasting protests in its history. Every Monday, starting with just a few and eventually including thousands and even tens of thousands, people took to the streets to protest a planned construction project involving the conversion of the rail terminus into an underground through station. After a violent police deployment on September 30, the number of protesters rose to over one hundred thousand. Despite political defeats, Monday demonstrations continued on a weekly basis, generally with between one and three thousand participants.

There are a number of reasons behind the protest: the lack of proof that the project would result in an improvement for rail passengers; serious problems even during the initial preparatory construction efforts; the partial demolition of one of the city's symbolic structures, the central station, which is considered a significant cultural monument and is protected as such; the enormous costs, which have officially risen to around six billion euros, while at the same time there are refusals to make much smaller investments in rail transport and other infrastructure; the risk to mineral springs; possible landslides and subsidence in the buildings situated above the tunnels and in the vicinity of the building site;

3 See: Marina Naprushkina's Office for Anti-Propaganda, website available online at: http://office-antipropaganda.com, accessed 05/22/2014.

4 See: Notes from Nowhere (eds.), *We Are Everywhere. The Irresistible Rise of Global Anticapitalism*, Verso, London, New York (NY), 2003.

5 Osman Bozkurt, *Auto-Park – Highway-Parks in Istanbul*, 2003, video, shown in the exhibition *STADTanSICHTen Istanbul*, ifa galleries Stuttgart, Berlin, 2004.

6 "In the 2013 book *Writing Revolutions: The Voices from Tunis to Damascus*, published by Layla Al-Zubaidi, Matthew Cassel, and Nemonie Craven Roderick, a series of important questions are raised. One of these is: How do you write about revolutions? Or rather: How do you write revolutions? The authors' answer is that one should combine private experiences with theories, political evaluations, and historical precedence." Süreyyya Evren, "Was wissen Sie über VPNs?," in: *springerin*, no. 2, 2014, p. 44; translated from the German by Jeremy Gaines.

incomplete, sometimes botched planning; and last but not least, the clearing of a part of the Schlossgarten, laid out as a park for the people in 1806 under King Frederick I,[7] which had been a particularly popular spot with commuters and residents. To add to all this, a citizens' initiative with 35,000 signatures – far more than the necessary quorum – had been rejected on formal legal grounds. "We don't want your crazy underground station!" one banner stated, "GET THE MESSAGE!"

7 See: Alfons Elfgang and Rosemarie Münzenmayer, "Die königlichen Schlossanlagen in Stuttgart," in: Dietrich Heissenbüttel (ed.), *Kunst in Stuttgart. Epochen, Persönlichkeiten, Tendenzen*, Hampp, Stuttgart, 2013, pp. 288–302.

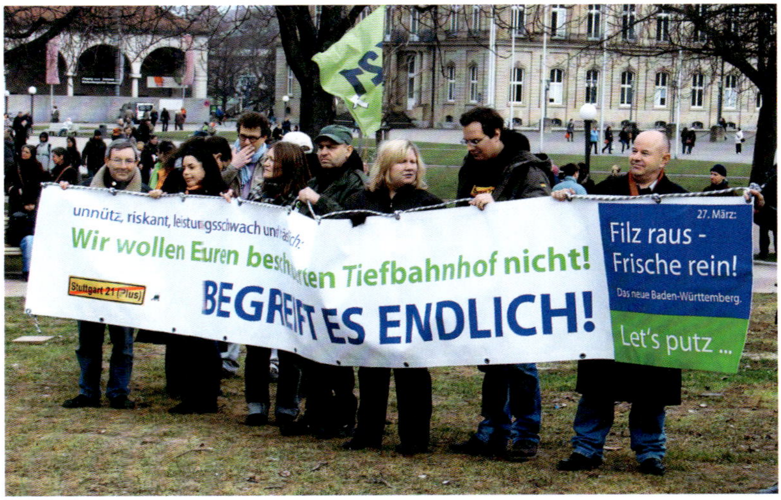

Demonstration at Schlossplatz in Stuttgart, February 19, 2011

The demolition of the landmark station, the exorbitant costs of a new one, which might function even less efficiently than the previous one, the severe disruption to rail passengers and city center residents during a construction period of over ten years, and the politicians' continued refusal to listen to the manifest will of the citizens: all this was more than enough to get many of Stuttgart's residents, including those who had never participated in demonstrations before, onto the streets, and ultimately to dedicate a lot of private money and millions of hours of their private and work time to their cause. The end result is ambivalent: the actual goals were not achieved, but the largest political party, which had governed at both city and federal state level for fifty years, was voted out of office for the very first time.

Initially, this situation seems hardly comparable to the situations in Tunisia, Cairo, Moscow, or Athens – at most, it can be likened to that of Florence, whose central terminus Santa Maria Novella is likewise supposed to give way to a through station for high-speed trains.[8] "It's only a station you're getting so worked up about," some say, believing the Occupy protests against global financial capitalism to be more important. And yet many Stuttgart residents recognize themselves in what they see and hear about other places in the news. Was former Minister President Stefan Mappus of Baden-Württemberg, who probably – and this appears ever more likely several years after the event – ordered the police deployment of September 30, 2010 personally any less of a dictator than Mubarak or Ben Ali? Wasn't the protest here, as there, equally lively and creative?

8 The fact that, alongside large-scale, nationwide protest movements around the Mediterranean, there are civil movements in many other places in the world opposing technocratic large-scale projects, and campaigning for the protection of the environment is demonstrated by the three European Forums "against unnecessary and imposed megaprojects" that have so far taken place in the Susa Valley, Italy; Notre-Dame-des-Landes, France; and Stuttgart, Germany, see online at: http://drittes-europäisches-forum.de; the fourth forum took place in 2014 at the gold-mining project at Roșia Montană in Romania, see online at: http://rosiamontana.org/fauimp4, both accessed 05/22/2014.

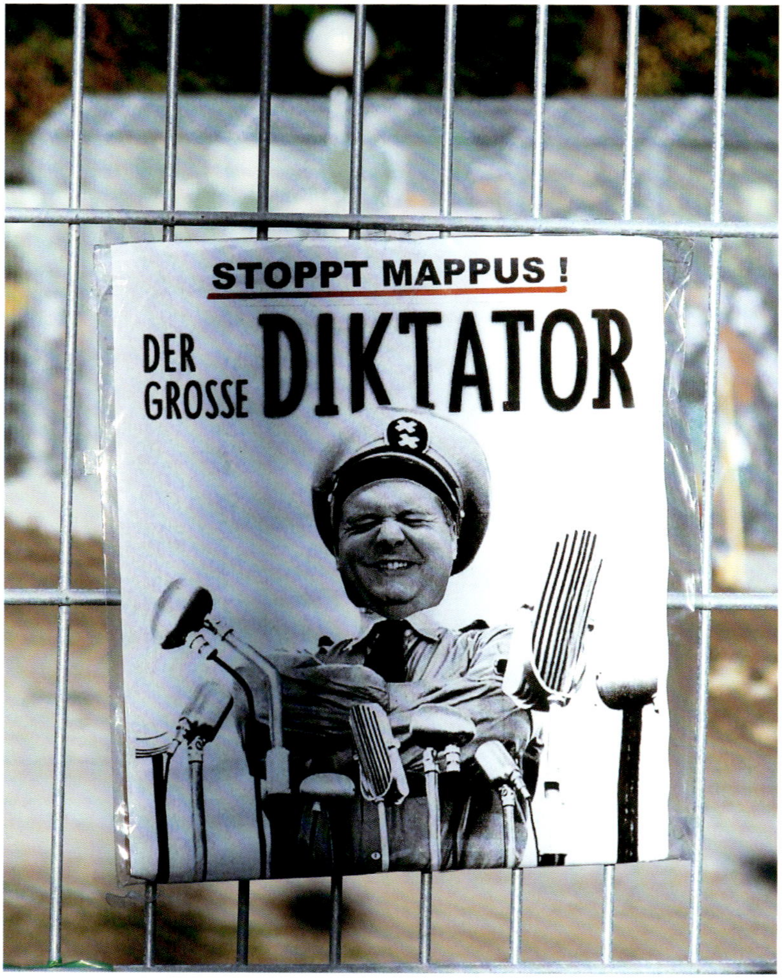

"Stoppt Mappus! Der große Diktator" [Stop Mappus! The great dictator], detail view on the construction site fence in Stuttgart, which was built after the tree felling in October 2010

Is there any difference between demolishing a park in Istanbul and doing the same thing in Stuttgart (although Stuttgart's local press has been quick to point out that the protests in Turkey have long been about more than a few trees)? Isn't there a striking similarity between the pictures of police using pepper spray in both locations? And although not many people here may know about what's happening in Raleigh, North Carolina, isn't the label "Moral Mondays" rather reminiscent of the weekly demonstrations in Stuttgart?

Yet, ultimately, it is not individual touchpoints that are crucial, but the seminal experience of taking the real issues into one's own hands. In Egypt, as in Stuttgart, as in Turkey, most people had got used to letting other people make decisions for them. Whether these be the entities of representative democracy – which, as is evidenced time and again, is profoundly penetrated by corporate and party interests – or an autocrat who distributes a large proportion of his country's income among his family actually makes only a slight difference, not a fundamental one when people are unable to overturn unwanted decisions. The difference lies merely in the severity of the reaction. Tear gas could be seen in

Stuttgart, too, but not – as in Istanbul – for weeks on end, in thick clouds over the entire city center.

The about-turn from passive behavior, which the individual struggles to break away from, to active participation is revealed in the creativity of the protest. Skilled artists are in on it everywhere. But on the construction site fence in Stuttgart, in graffiti on the streets of Tunis or Athens, in the cartoons and Twitter messages that are disseminated at lightning speed in Turkey, the existence of an unsuspected creative vein is revealed in large parts of the population who may not otherwise have engaged in any artistic activity. Equally unexpected and new for many people is the experience of coming together and debating in public places, not being isolated within one's own four walls, and not being dictated to by time plans, chores, or shopping, but simply meeting other people linked by a shared concern. This exhilarating experience, which is now familiar to many people in Stuttgart, is something they share with the people who have endured weeks on Tahrir Square, or with the people of Istanbul, who marked the breaking of the fast at Ramadan by laying tablecloths along the entire length of the main shopping street Istiklal in order to eat dinner together.

When the State Hits Back

"At some point I get a call from the 'Citizens' Initiative Headquarters.' The warning system is working. They will probably be clearing the area today. The police are surrounding the village. I put on my raincoat, set off, meeting others as I go, who have also been warned. We manage to get to the forest village, even though police are popping up everywhere and new barriers are being erected. The people of the forest have erected a protective fence around the village. Craftsmen, independent laborers, kids skipping school, plus the hut dwellers, the nutters, the anarchists. Opposite them stand, in a martial circle, protected by shields and with truncheons drawn, the police. An unrealistic, absurd game. Knights against farmers."[9]

By changing just a few words, one could use this description to recount the events in Stuttgart's Schlossgarten on September 30, 2010; however, it actually comes from the autobiography *Leben lernen* [Learning Life] by the well-known German writer Peter Härtling, and relates to the protests against the western runway of Frankfurt Airport, not far from Härtling's home in Walldorf, in 1981. Here, as there, there was clearance. Here, as there, a phalanx of highly trained policemen, armed with helmets and shields, rubber truncheons, tear gas, and water cannon, stood against a cross section of the population: the young, the old, craftsmen, clerks, manual workers, housewives – just as Härtling describes. Architects, engineers, lawyers... These professions, too, can be added to the list of those who stood up for the preservation of the existing Stuttgart railway terminus. "My children," says Härtling, "except for Sophie, who was still too young, share the 'Flörsheim experience': civil impotence in the face of state violence."[10]

9 Peter Härtling, *Leben lernen. Erinnerungen*, Deutscher Taschenbuch Verlag, Munich, 2005, pp. 351f.; translated from the German by Jeremy Gaines.

10 Ibid., p. 353.

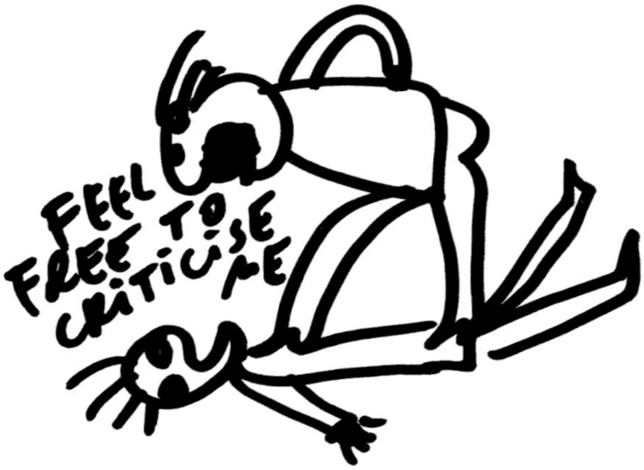

Dan Perjovschi, *Feel Free to Criticise Me,* 2003, drawing

They also share this experience with many residents of Stuttgart, plus many Greeks, Bulgarians, Spanish, Portuguese, Egyptians, Iranians, and the people of most Turkish and many other big cities. The surprise of reading about it in the work of an author who is now eighty years old and is recounting events that happened a good thirty years ago is that time and space do not divide those who have had similar experiences. Anyone who has not experienced for themselves state violence in action may think that force is unavoidable in order to prevent "anarchy," or might simply try to "stay out of it." Anyone who has seen water cannon at full pressure advancing on habitually peaceable pensioners, or students repeatedly trying to wash out pepper spray from their red, swollen eyes, knows the truth. An insurmountable divide separates the eyewitnesses from those who are familiar with the conflict only via the media. And yet even in Istanbul or Stuttgart, the latter are still in the majority.

The only difference between protests in Frankfurt or Stuttgart and places like Cairo lies perhaps in one little word – "civil." Härtling describes how the writer Horst Karasek attempts to dissuade the "anarchists" from using steel bullets and axes. In Stuttgart, right from the beginning the protesters were very keen that the protest should be "for" and not "against" something and to avoid violence at any price. In Cairo, on the other hand, the protest at Tahrir Square would have fallen on deaf ears had it not been for the willingness of courageous young men to defend participants, where necessary even with physical violence, against marauding, truncheon-wielding troops. There is always a fine line between justified, necessary resistance and rioting, between nonviolence and overly eager retreat, which prevents any pressure being built up. What is more important than clear dividing lines, though, is that the consensus remains. Divide and conquer, the tactic of driving a wedge between peaceful and more violent-prone demonstrators, has been applied all too often, be it through sometimes grotesquely excessive presentations in the media or through the use of agents provocateurs.[11]

Protest movements that achieve their objectives, however, remain the exception. The Wyhl nuclear power plant in the Black Forest was blocked, yet the one in Brokdorf on the Lower Elbe was built, despite the fact that it was never really needed. The Tunisians managed to get a liberal constitution. In Egypt, the stubbornness of the Muslim Brotherhood led the educated, middle-class carriers of the revolution to support a second uprising, which the military used to reinstate the status quo, just with different people at the top

11
The accusations have been made, but none of the cases in Genoa, Heiligendamm, or Stuttgart have been legally processed; a summary of recent cases is offered by Reiner Dung in "Agent Provokateur – Wie schwarz ist der Schwarze Block?" in: *BildDung für das VOLK*, available online at: http://bilddung.wordpress.com/2013/06/05/agent-provokateur-wie-schwarz-ist-der-schwarze-block, accessed 05/22/2014.

Sometimes there are coincidences – an upcoming election, tactical alliances, unexpected developments – which signal a turning point. But when people in power feel under attack, they fight back mercilessly. As has happened most recently in Syria.

Revolution and Repression

Why is there a movement for democracy in Russia – albeit not as strong as that in Egypt or Turkey, but still radical and active – but not in China? Both were Communist countries; both are, as before, centrally governed, with limited civil freedoms. The answer initially lies in the different ways in which they developed after the end of the Cold War: In the former Soviet Union and the countries of Eastern Europe, the 1989 Perestroika ushered in a peaceful revolution. Although, step by step, Russia has returned to a stronger, autocratic regime, the experience of 1989 has strengthened the fundamental trust in the changeability of circumstances, and so more people will express themselves courageously and radically in public, each setting an example to others. In China, on the other hand, the regime in power at the time ruthlessly shot at student demonstrators on Tiananmen Square, and since then it has used a closely knit network of surveillance to prevent any expression of dissent. Where Internet platforms like Facebook, Twitter or YouTube – which were conceived with very different considerations in mind – become forums for public debate, a discussion starts up that is not so easy to stifle. China has prohibited such discussion from the outset.

It may be that even older historical experiences are behind this. The October Revolution took place at the beginning of the developments that during the late Communist era let to economic stagnation and social stalemate. Yet, at the same time, it remains in people's memories as a utopian moment, an experience of being able to change society through one's own strength. Despite the Stalinist rule of terror, there were always dissidents in the USSR. The deprivations they suffered continue to have an effect, and their communication channels in opposition circles, the forms of their representation in the public sphere, remain as a reservoir of possibilities for action. In China, on the other hand, the Cultural Revolution, the deportation of intellectuals to the countryside, and the break with tradition led to a tabula rasa, which made it difficult to link oneself to anything.

This, of course, remains speculative, as is proven by other examples. Did the Constitutional Revolution, a true mass movement in the early twentieth century, empower the people of Iran to go back onto the streets if necessary in order to right injustices? The "Green Revolution," although ultimately unsuccessful, implies that it did, as do the discussions in secret, the numerous blogs, including by women,[12] and the outcome of the 2013 elections. But isn't Iran still a totalitarian state, a fanatical theocracy even, which even goes so far as to empower the president of the neighboring country to murder his own people? The answer has to be: There is not *one* Iran, but rather those in power and the

12
See: Nasreen Alavi, *Wir sind der Iran. Aufstand gegen die Mullahs – die junge persische Weblog-Szene*, Kiepenheuer & Witsch, Cologne, 2005; Parisa Najafi Tonekaboni, "Iranische Blogger und die Internetzensur," available online at: www.igfm.de/iran/hintergrund/iranische-blogger-und-die-internetzensur-parisa-najafi-tonekaboni, accessed 04/27/2014.

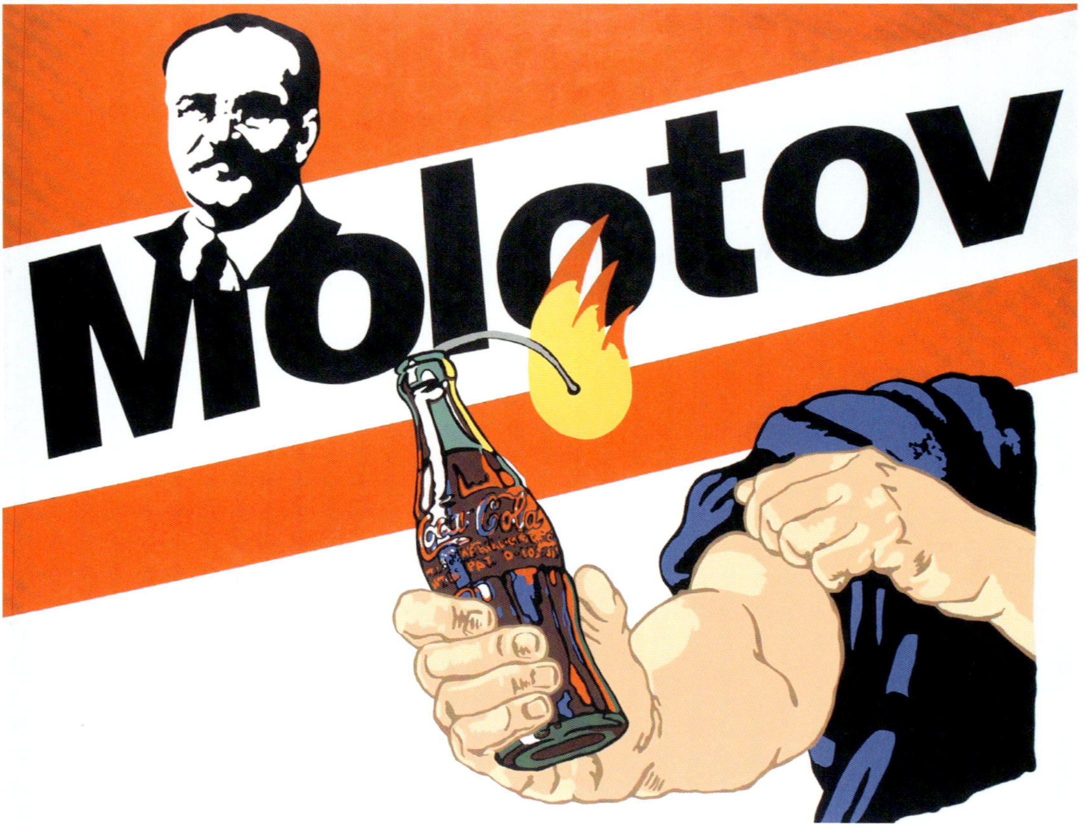

Alexander Kosolapov, *Molotov Cocktail*, 1989, acrylic on canvas, 164 × 201 cm

opposition, who do not merely act alone on the stage of their own country, but since 1979 and before have acted within a global game of goodies and baddies, confronted with the extreme accusation of the "Axis of Evil."

In the long term, repression cannot prevent the shoots of renewal. Where fear disappears, there can be no totalitarianism, as the Russian science fiction and political satire author Yevgeny Zamyatin (*We*, 1920/1921) knew.[13] This is something the citizens of the German Democratic Republic (GDR) experienced, as have the Egyptians. Syria currently provides a heartbreaking example of how terrible experiences of violence and the most unendurable human situations among revolutionaries do not prevent them from pursuing their objectives and even declaring them with grim humor in public newspapers and on Internet platforms. What is harder to deal with is failure due to one's own shortcomings. Civilian movements are strong when the masses are no longer prepared to endure injustices. Their weakness lies in the fact that they are often not in a position to channel the shared uprising into enduring alliances, consistent organization, or political work that goes beyond specific individual objectives. In the face of the organized lobbying, committee, and press work of the political parties, spontaneous mass protest loses ground when it comes to decision-making processes in society as a whole, even where these function in a formally correct manner.

13 See: Yevgeny Zamyatin [Eugene Zamiatin], *We*, Dutton, New York (NY), 1924.

Crisis of Representation

Where civil movements emerge that, in their large-scale street presence, appear to point to majorities capable of reaching a consensus, for some time now the question has been asked ever more frequently as to whether direct democracy should replace or supplement representative democracy. Joseph Beuys was one of the first prominent people to champion this opinion. The problem is a complex one. It's not just about whether "the people" can decide for themselves in individual cases, instead of leaving this to their elected representatives. In the case of referenda, too, there is no guarantee that at the end of the day, the economic and political power of those who can run the strongest advertising campaigns will not hold sway over the apparent expression of the will of the people, or that strategies of fear and dependence will not triumph over justified concerns. Conversely, the question arises as to how in a democracy, in which by definition the will of the people rules, there can be any mass protests at all. Whom are the delegates actually representing? Their voters – in contrast to those of other parties? Do voters of conservative and of social democratic parties have conflicting interests? Who are "the people" behind the big "parties of the people"? It was not only in the GDR that varying opinions existed on this matter ("Wir sind das Volk" – "We are the people"). Who do the representatives of the people represent? Employers or employees? Men or women? Industry or the environment? Clearly no party wanting to play a significant role can limit itself to individual groups in society. It is obvious, however, that these groups do not always have the same interests.

Representative democracy, therefore, demands a certain balancing act by delegates: Before elections they must act as if they represent the interests of broad segments of the population. On the other hand, no delegate wanting to take on responsibility for governing people can afford to ignore the interests of "the economy"; that is, the powerful interest groups. Lobbying work, party donations, highly paid posts for deselected politicians, influence on the media in the form of ownership of shares, placing advertisements, or carefully structured PR campaigns, all the way through to the threat of obstruction: There are many ways to prompt a representative of the people to decide one way or another. Whilst in general, they all claim to be representing the interests of the "common man," in reality it is often the lobbying associations that set the tone.

This analysis can be expanded to other situations, for example, the People's Republic of China which, in its name, if not in other ways, likewise draws its legitimacy from the people. Certainly there are considerable differences between cases, but it is possible to identify that, even in undemocratic or less democratic countries, economic and international interests play a not inconsiderable role, because the power of the autocrats is not unlimited. Indeed, anyone who is propped up by the military and the "security services" has considerable costs that need to be covered, either by the home country or, as in the case of North Korea, but also Egypt, through the support of others.

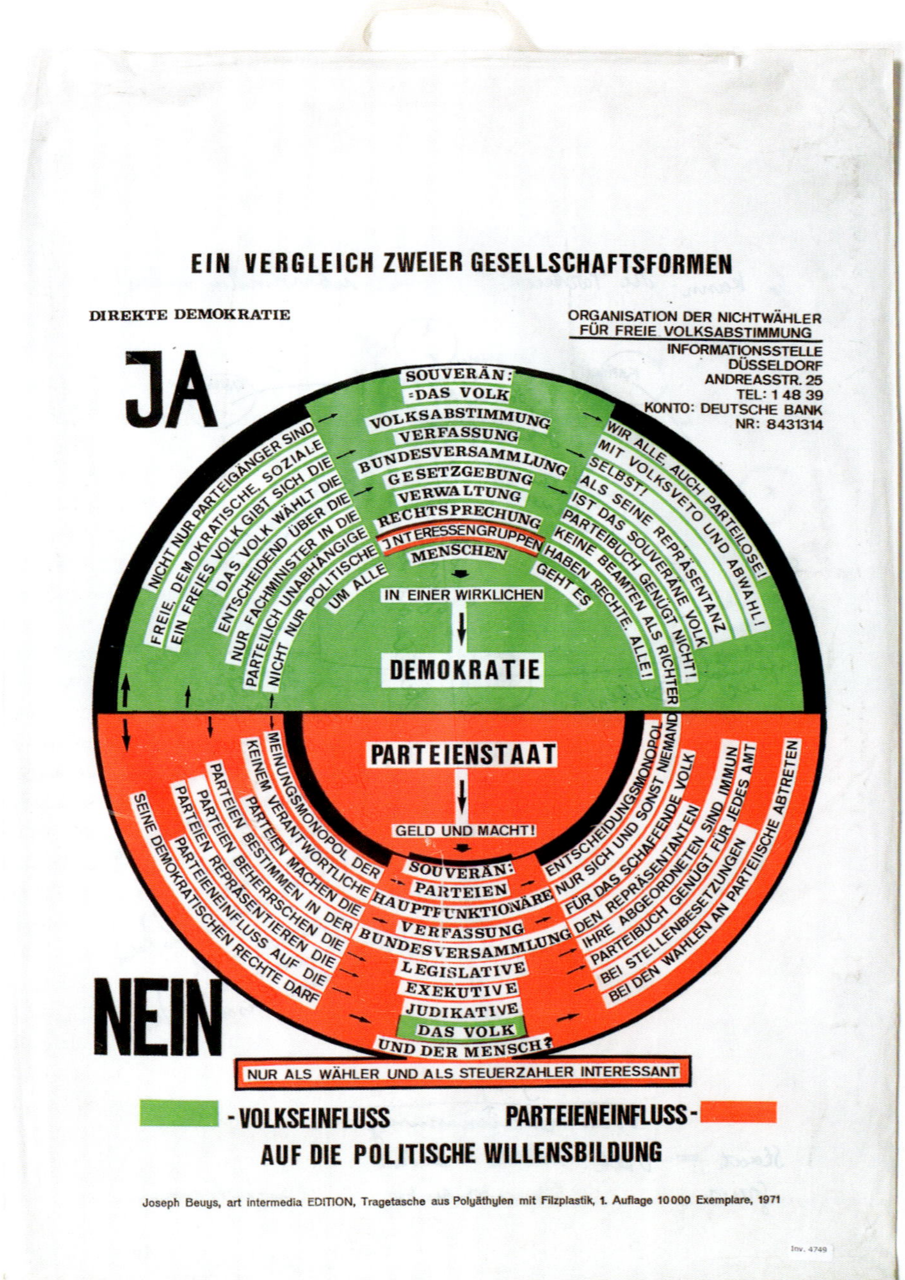

Joseph Beuys, *So kann die Parteiendiktatur überwunden werden*, 1971, multiple, carrying bag made of polyethylene, printed on both sides

Representation, however, may refer not only to the field of politics, but also to art. An image represents something in more than one sense: it pictures visible reality, but also stands for something more. The elaborate theory of Erwin Panofsky, for example, distinguishes between iconography and iconology, which both refer to the meaning of an image: the first in a more obvious way – a certain figure with certain attributes represents a given goddess; the second in a more open way – this figure may stand for the intentions of whoever commissioned the painting in a certain historical situation.[14] Obviously, none of this applies to modern and abstract art, which can be understood as a criticism of representation: Modern art does not aim to represent anything other than itself. As Paul Klee remarked, "[a]rt does not reproduce the visible; rather, it makes visible."[15]

This statement is not entirely comprehensible on the literal level: Why should artists, all of a sudden, want to refuse to paint the outside world and instead insist on inventing their own images? For a long time in European art history, the image was in fact much more than a picture of the visible. Statues of Roman emperors had to be revered, and whoever refrained from doing so, like the Christians, was severely punished.[16] Throughout the Middle Ages, the Renaissance, and the Baroque era, artistic imagery represented the world order, be it in a religious or secular sense. History painting, in Baroque theory, was deemed the noblest genre. It reflected the god-given ways of the world, from the Creation up to the present day. In the same way classical order, in architecture, represented "order" in general, in the sense that the world is ordered in a certain way that cannot be called into question. From a Marxist point of view, one would say that art represented the ideas and the world view of the ruling class.

This notion of representation came under attack at the time of the French Revolution. In his *Critique of the Power of Judgment*, published in 1790, Immanuel Kant states that art is "a kind of representation that is purposive in itself,"[17] and he also speaks of "disinterested satisfaction."[18] By the late nineteenth century, however, the bourgeoisie had replaced the nobility, and to a certain degree they imitated the imagery of the aristocracy. History painting abounded and once again, more generally, art was taken into the service of the ruling class. It is in this sense that representing and representation, i.e., displaying wealth and power, that is present in the German word *Repräsentation*, but absent in the English term, was the subject of criticism, and consequently, the representational function of art was generally rejected by modern artists. However, once abstract art adorns the branches of banks, once it is suitable, as an object of value, for distinguishing the well-heeled, educated citizens from the have-nots and the nouveaux riches, it again represents more than "disinterested pleasure": it has taken on representative functions in the German sense of the word which includes connotations of the ostentatious display of the trappings of power.

We can therefore talk about a crisis of representation in the dual English sense of the term of delegation of powers, and depiction of reality. RepresentUs is the name of an American initiative,

14 See: Erwin Panofsky, *Studies in Iconology: Humanistic Themes in the Art of the Renaissance,* Harper & Row, New York (NY), 1962.

15 "Kunst gibt nicht das Sichtbare wieder, sondern macht sichtbar." Originally published in Paul Klee, "Schöpferische Konfession," in: Kasimir Edschmid (ed.), *Tribüne der Kunst und der Zeit. Eine Schriftensammlung*, vol. XIII, Erich Reiss, Berlin, 1920, pp. 28–40. English translation by Norbert Gutermann from Paul Klee, *The Inward Vision: Watercolors, Drawings, Writings*, Abrams, New York (NY), 1958, p.5.

16 See: Hans Belting, *Likeness and Presence: A History of the Image Before the Era of Art*, University of Chicago Press, Chicago, 1993.

17 Immanuel Kant, *Critique of the Power of Judgment* (1790), Cambridge University Press, Cambridge, New York (NY), 2000, p. 185.

18 Ibid., p. 91.

making a play on the abbreviation for United States, which urges delegates to represent the will of the people, not the interests of party donors and lobby groups. At the same time, the question of whose interests the member of parliament, in theory the representative of the people's will, is really representing, is also linked to images: less so with paintings that the delegate has hanging above the sofa in his private living room, but rather with how the condition of the world and one's own country appear in public perception. The fact that "steered democracies," like Russia, or countries like China, Iran, Saudi Arabia, or Turkey manipulate this perception will come as no surprise to people here in Europe. The fact that democracy is also steered by interests in the so-called free world is something Edward S. Herman and Noam Chomsky have pointed out.[19]

19 See: Edward S. Herman and Noam Chomsky, *Manufacturing Consent. The Political Economy of the Mass Media*, Pantheon Books, New York (NY), 1988.

The Question of Visibility

It is obvious that in this game, minorities, the socially weak, peripheral regions, and people and topics that "have no lobby" are in a difficult position. Democracy aside, they remain underrepresented in a dual sense, because their concerns are not sufficiently visible and they lack representation of their interests. Not being perceived can lead to despair, as Edward Said demonstrated. Indeed, as Palestinians didn't appear in the Israeli account of "a land without people for people without a land," they were all the same able to use bomb blasts to spectacularly draw attention to the fact that they were there.[20]

20 See: Edward W. Said, *The Question of Palestine*, Times Books, New York (NY), 1979, p. 39.

Nobody will doubt that a successful solution to a problem necessitates other paths of confrontation. This is where non-governmental organizations, civil movements, human rights and environmental associations come in, which apply pressure on parliamentarians from outside, from civil society. In order to be able to do this, they must try to gain as many supporters as possible to sign petitions, donate money, participate in demonstrations, help to run campaigns, draft letters to delegates, or involve themselves actively in initiatives in other ways. The first step for mobilizing the public consists of drawing attention to a topic. For this, and for every other step, images are needed, since only pictorial representations are able to draw people's gaze and to "set the scene" where there are complex circumstances, so they can be grasped at a glance. This applies even though images alone seldom provide clear information and therefore written information must supplement the presentation.

Attention is not the same thing as visibility. A campaign that aims to reach a large number of participants must draw attention. This is bound up with ambivalence, because only spectacular images elicit attention. The mass media are also on the hunt for spectacular images. What appears in the media and what doesn't is not only a question of political influence, but is at least equally dictated by hunger for sensationalism. It may be that problems in other parts of the world, to which the observers of the images do not have access themselves, appear grotesquely exaggerated to those who actually come from the region. Thus Africa is

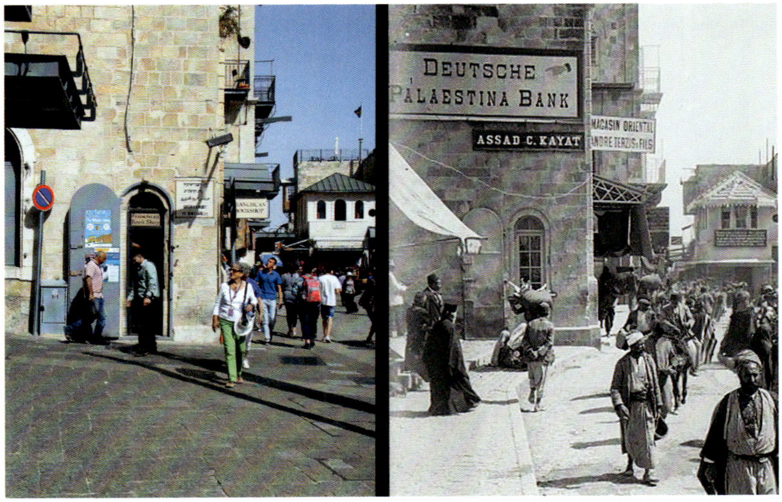

Tarek Bakri, *Jerusalem – Palestine*, 2014, photo collage

considered the “dark continent,” full of wars, plagues, famine, and poverty. The fact that many African countries, despite limited material resources, boast remarkably stable conditions and have an active civil society that is absolutely in a position to curtail many injustices remains outside the field of vision here in Europe. In the Palestinian territories, too, even under the precarious conditions of the Gaza Strip, life does not consist predominantly of violence, but rather the day-to-day struggle with countless small adversities.

In cases like these, creating visibility can mean disseminating images that are not spectacular, but rather images that illustrate these very problems, everyday life, the daily struggle, but also the will to survive, or indeed even the beautiful and poetic moments of a reality otherwise marked by hardship.[21] However, these are not the sort of images that lend themselves to being used in campaigns, and it would be foolish to expect the mass media to focus on the uneventfulness of everyday life, with the exception, perhaps, of the feuilleton or in late-night cultural programs. To make clear the perspective of the people who are forced to live in precarious situations, what is needed is empathy, that is, a personal encounter and approach, or, in other words, an artistic confrontation. This can be one, if not the only, task of a contemporary art which no longer simply seeks to reflect itself.

21
See: Dietrich Heissenbüttel, “Neuland. Bildwelten im Konflikt,” in: Ronald Grätz and Hans-Georg Knopp (eds.), *Zwischenräume. Was können die Künste in Konfliktsituationen leisten?*, Steidl, Göttingen, 2012, pp. 163–179.

The effect of art in this sense may be limited; ultimately, art exhibitions do not reach a mass audience. Compared to the television news, artistic representations are fighting a losing battle from the outset. The effect, however, is a different one. For just as the artist is in a position to produce different, independent images for a commission, free from the preferences and format-related stipulations of broadcasting corporations, a person’s encounter with these images is also on an individual, personal level. Art (we may also interpret Kant in this way) does not aim to convince; it is not advertising or propaganda. At most it aims to clarify or, since artistic work represents merely an offering, to simply propose points of view and stimulate confrontation with them. What the artist’s intention is or what they had in mind is one thing, but when they take their work into the public sphere, they enter into a communication process that only ends in the mind of the observer.

Artistic Activism

For a long time there have been artists who do not content themselves with the illustrative function, the exhibition of works in the white cube of gallery spaces, with the cry of "art for art's sake," and instead try to put their work in the service of society-changing processes. It is hard to identify a precise genealogy, but Émile Zola is often cited. Peter Weiss's *Die Ästhetik des Widerstands* [The Aesthetics of Resistance] can be read as an attempt to reconstruct the history of a critical, society-oriented art.[22] In principle, there have probably always been artists who tried to be actively involved in social processes, in contrast to limiting art to the aesthetic function.

On closer inspection, however, it is surprising that the epochal changes in this regard during the course of the First World War have previously been paid little attention. In pre-1914 art – with the exception of Francisco Goya and Jacques Callot, whose works were nevertheless little known by their contemporaries – there were virtually no critical representations of war, despite any number of battle images, war memorials, and national monuments. This all began to change during the course of the First World War. Using the field post, more and more soldiers sent raw, realistic representations of the trenches back home.[23] Starting with the Cabaret Voltaire in Zurich, a modern art developed at a fundamental distance from all representations produced in the interests of the state, acting as a critical corrective to idealizations of all kinds that did not match reality. What remained problematic, however, was simply people's own excessive expectations of the utopian potential of modern art as such.[24]

Criticism of war on the part of Expressionist literature and art appears, paradoxically, to precede the First World War by some years. *Weltende* [The End of the World] is the title of Jakob von Hoddis's epochal poem. Georg Heym, who died in an accident in 1912, had also engaged with the subject of war. Certain paintings by Ludwig Meidner dating from as early as 1912 show destroyed and burning cities.[25] These should not be considered a prophecy, despite the fact that Meidner's perceptions, which he clarified along the lines of Jewish tradition (Meidner considered himself overcome by the "Holy Spirit") are not far off it. Indeed, artists and authors simply reacted sensitively and quickly to the unmistakable military tendencies of their time, which ultimately led to the First World War.

The term "activism" was applied just a few weeks after the beginning of the war. This was the keyword under which a number of Expressionist authors gathered around Kurt Hiller, after Ludwig Rubiner had published an essay entitled "Der Dichter greift in die Politik" ["The Poet Intervenes in Politics"] in Franz Pfemfert's newspaper *Die Aktion* [The Action] as much as two years earlier.[26] Hiller, cofounder of *Die Aktion*, fell out with Pfemfert in 1913 –

22 Peter Weiss, *Die Ästhetik des Widerstands,* volume 1–3, Suhrkamp, Frankfurt am Main, 1975, 1978, 1981.

23 See: Dietrich Heissenbüttel, "Das Bild unseres psychischen Überlebens. Der Erste Weltkrieg und die Kunst," in: *Underground*, exhib. cat., Fort de Schoenenbourg, Alsace, Kontur, Stuttgart, 2014, available online at: www.kontur-stuttgart.de/underground/presse/heissenbuettel.pdf, accessed 05/22/2014.

24 See: Philipp Kleinmichel, *Im Namen der Kunst*, Passagen, Vienna, 2014.

25 See: Gerda Breuer and Ines Wagemann, *Ludwig Meidner. Zeichner, Maler, Literat 1884–1966*, 2 vols., exhib. cat., Institut Mathildenhöhe, Darmstadt, Hatje, Stuttgart, 1991.

26 Ludwig Rubiner, "Der Dichter greift in die Politik," in: *Die Aktion*, vol. 2, no. 21, May 1912, pp. 645–652, vol. 2, no. 23, June 1912, pp. 709–715; see also: Paul Raabe (ed.), *Ich schneide die Zeit aus. Expressionismus und Politik in Franz Pfemferts 'Aktion', 1911–1918*, Deutscher Taschenbuch Verlag, Munich, 1964, pp. 64–76.

something he wrote about fifty years later: "One of his most significant findings was the insight into the connection between combat-renewing, destructive-constructive politics and combat-renewing, subversive-creative literature."[27] Hiller's activism stemmed from the recognition that the First World War could not be ended through the medium of art: "Since all previous experience shows that the administrators of nations do not hear the simple word of reason, then reasonable people must take the administration of the planet into their own hands," he wrote programmatically in 1916 in the first edition of the yearbook *Das Ziel* [The Target].[28] One year later he founded *Bund zum Ziel* [Union for the Aim], which he later renamed *Aktivistenbund* [League of Activists]. After the fall of the German Empire, this became the *Rat geistiger Arbeiter* [Council of Intellectual Workers], which organized an activists' conference in Berlin in 1919.

Later developments ensured that these links did not simply vanish into oblivion. Starting with the Russian Revolution, events led to a split between the political and the artistic avant-garde in the 1920s. Thus Pfemfert recognized that even radical artistic movements like Dada were being absorbed by bourgeois society and thus became ineffectual. "Later on, particularly after the death of Lenin (1924), Pfemfert's political position was even left from extreme left," commented Hiller, who was involved in the pacifist movement. Both were forced to emigrate after 1933 and Pfemfert died in exile in Mexico, but Hiller went via Prague to London, and returned to Germany in 1955, settling in Hamburg. It is only thanks to the rediscovery of literary Expressionism by Paul Raabe, whose key witness he became, that his experiences came to public attention in the 1960s.[29]

The pictorial Expressionism that the Nazis defamed as "degenerate art" was rehabilitated immediately after the Second World War. However, its reception was limited to the formal aesthetic aspect, whilst any political implications were excluded. The initially controversial preference for abstraction and the white cube which, promoted by the CIA-founded Congress for Cultural Freedom, triumphed at documenta in 1955, helped to shape the art of the postwar period in Western Europe and the USA, even though alternative streams developed during the course of the civil rights and student movements of the 1960s. Nothing has fundamentally changed, even if the field of movements and countermovements distinguished itself ever more. In contrast, particularly after the death of Lenin, the Soviet Union showed itself to be remarkably resistant to artistic innovations, even when they had originally stemmed from revolutionary Russia.[30] Yet here, too, particularly towards the end of the Communist era, dissident countermovements developed which, partly based on the Western model, adopted a critical stance towards the situation in their home country.[31]

In the USA the debate was ignited predominantly by the Vietnam War. In 1966 a number of very well-known artists like Elaine de Kooning, Eva Hesse, Donald Judd, Jack Levine, Roy Lichtenstein, Robert Motherwell, Ad Reinhardt, James Rosenquist, and Tom Wesselmann hung a total of 418 paintings on a twenty-meter-high structure designed by Mark di Suvero – the *Artists' Tower*

27 Kurt Hiller, "Die Aktion. Stimmen der Freunde," contribution to Westdeutscher Rundfunk, February 1961, according to Paul Raabe "probably not broadcast"; translated from the German by Jeremy Gaines; see also: Paul Raabe, *Mein expressionistisches Jahrzehnt. Anfänge in Marbach am Neckar*, Arche, Zurich, Hamburg, 2004, p. 228.

28 Kurt Hiller, "Philosophie des Ziels," in: *Ziel*, no. 1, 1916, as quoted from: "Aktivismus und Expressionismus. Der Literat greift in die Politik ein," available online at: www.hiller-gesellschaft.de/aktivist.htm, accessed 05/22/2014; translated from the German by Jeremy Gaines.

29 See: Raabe 2004.

30 There is little recognition of just how strongly the Bauhaus, for example, was shaped by Russian Futurism.

31 See, for example: Matthew Cullerne Brown, *Contemporary Russian Art*, Phaidon, Oxford, 1989.

Mark di Suvero, *Artists' Tower of Protest* (Peace Tower), 1966, installation, steel and mixed media, 16.76 m, Los Angeles, photo by Charles Brittin

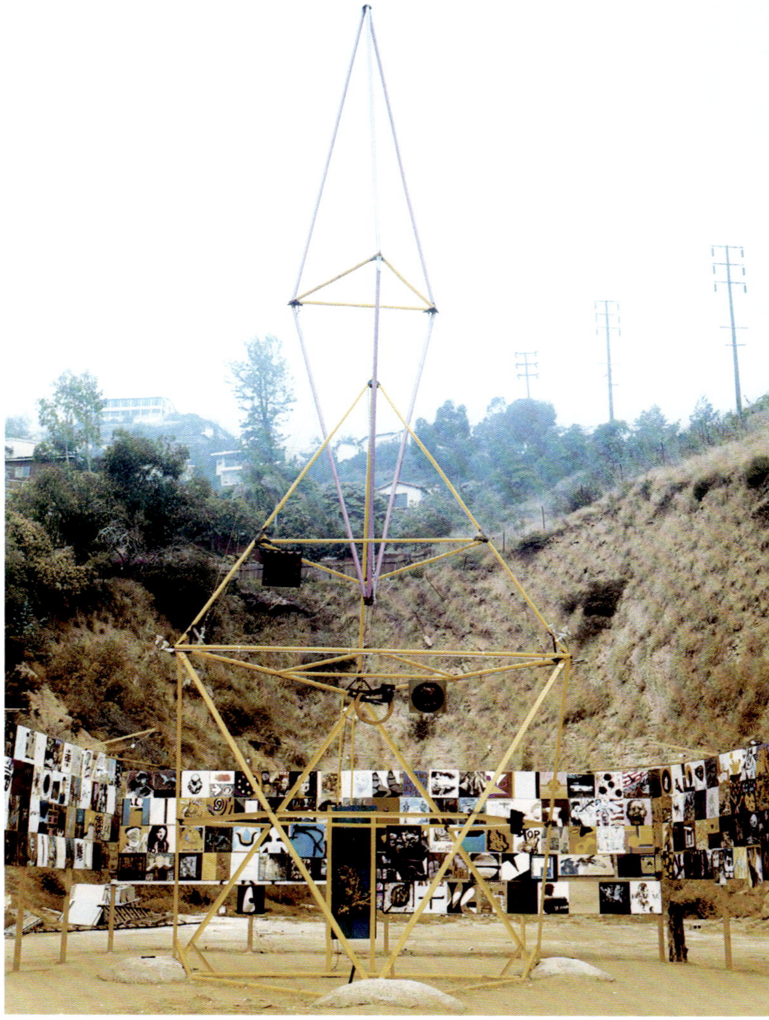

of Protest. The tower stood for three months and was physically fought over. Frank Stella is alleged to have promised a thousand dollars to anyone who defended his work. The Art Workers' Coalition, which included Carl Andre, Robert Morris, Hans Haacke, and Lucy Lippard, was involved in the organization of the biggest Vietnam War demonstration in 1969.[32] Jasper Johns designed a poster on behalf of the Leo Castelli Gallery. Duane Hanson designed a *Vietnam Scene* (1969) using five dead or injured figures lying on the ground.[33] This alliance at the time of the Vietnam War eventually crumbled not least because, at a certain point, the artists had to decide between activism and artistic success.[34] Many focused on the market, while others who did not do so were punished by being disregarded. Of the artists named, Mark di Suvero is perhaps the least well-known name today, despite the fact that a replica of his *Artists' Tower* was erected at the 2006 Whitney Biennial – in obvious opposition to George W. Bush's wars in Afghanistan and Iraq.[35]

32

See: Lucy R. Lippard, *A Different War: Vietnam in Art*, Real Comet Press, Seattle (WA), 1990; Matthew Israel, *Kill for Peace. American Artists Against the Vietnam War*, University of Texas Press, Austin (TX), 2013.

33

See: Mark Vallen, "Vietnam! Vietnam! Artists & America's Longest War," available online at: www.art-for-a-change.com/vietnam/vietnam.htm, accessed 05/22/2014; the group of figures by Duane Hanson is currently in the Lehmbruck Museum in Duisburg, Germany.

34

See: Julia Bryan-Wilson, *Art Workers. Radical Practice in the Vietnam Era*, University of California Press, Berkeley (CA), 2009.

35

See: Mark di Suvero and Rikrit Tiravanija, available online at: http://whitney.org/www/2006biennial/artists.php?artist=diSuvero_Mark, accessed 05/22/2014.

A new form of artistic activism, with regard to the range of activities and the number of participants, developed not in the "West" or the "East," but in the south: in South Africa. As Sue Williamson clearly illustrates in *Resistance Art in South Africa*, published in 1989 in New York, after the Soweto Uprising in 1976 many of the privileged "white" artists also began to campaign against apartheid.[36] In the process, alliances emerged that went beyond the boundaries of skin color, origin, and artistic genres. Williamson's book includes both anonymous craftspeople and trained artists, alongside young people from the townships, and includes oil paintings alongside posters, graffiti, and comics.

Williamson outlines an impressively broad panorama of artistic activities against apartheid, but it is by no means exhaustive. Nuclei of resistance included, for example, the Market Theatre, and the Handspring Puppet Company for which William Kentridge developed his charcoal drawings as stage sets. Photography played a very particular, prominent role in the Anti-Apartheid Movement, but is omitted from Williamson's book simply for reasons of space.[37] Jazz musicians like Dollar Brand (today Abdullah Ibrahim), Miriam Makeba, Hugh Masekela, and Chris McGregor with the Blue Notes and the Brotherhood of Breath jazz groups drew the attention of Europe and the USA to the problem. Collaborations and alliances developed regardless of social and artistic background. Thus Karlheinz Stockhausen's former assistant Kevin Volans wrote music for the Handspring Puppet Company, as did Warrick Sony, the frontman of the punk band Kalahari Surfers.[38]

Yet with all its solidarity, the artistic movement against apartheid is not free of paradox. While many of the educated "white" artists now enjoy a global reputation, among those of darker skin who were involved, only Billy Mandindi is an internationally recognized name. The so-called "Peace Parks" set up by young people from the townships were quickly destroyed and are likely now known only to eyewitnesses and readers of Williamson's book. After the end of apartheid, "black" artists did indeed have access to academies and galleries in principle, but in reality they enjoyed few relations with the art world. In general they were once again dependent on serving the exotic expectations of "white" art collectors.

36
See: Sue Williamson, *Resistance Art in South Africa*, St. Martin's Press, New York (NY), 1989.

37
See: Okwui Enwezor and Rory Bester, *Rise and Fall of Apartheid. Photography and the Bureaucracy of Everyday Life*, exhib. cat., International Center of Photography, New York (NY), DelMonico Books, London, New York (NY), Prestel, Munich, 2013.

38
See: Warrick Sony et al. for the multimedia production *Faustus in Africa*, 1995; Kevin Volans for the multimedia production *Confessions of Zeno*, 2002; both under the direction of William Kentridge.

Media

The media of the Anti-Apartheid Movement – graffiti, comics, poster art, photography, music of various orientations, theater – are in many ways not that different to those used by artists in today's democratization movements. Discussion of the art of poetry and novels would require an entire dedicated chapter, since they have no choice but to react to social situations. Unlike in the 1980s, though, we now have the "new media." The Internet in particular, more than any other medium that has gone before it, offers the possibility of becoming a witness to current developments on a global level and of immediately disseminating images, information, and comments across the world, beyond the control mechanisms and the economic channeling of the mass media. The medium of

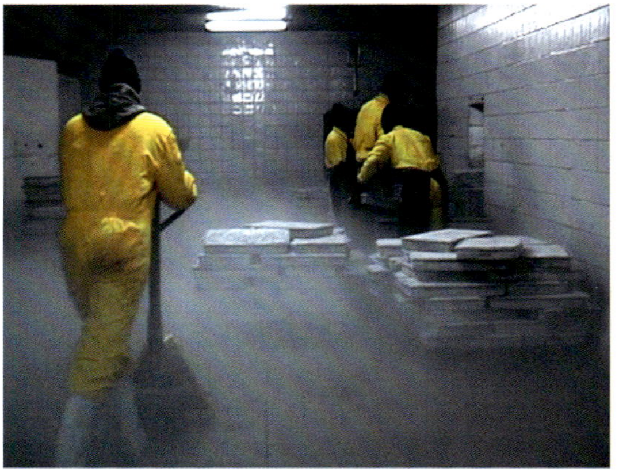

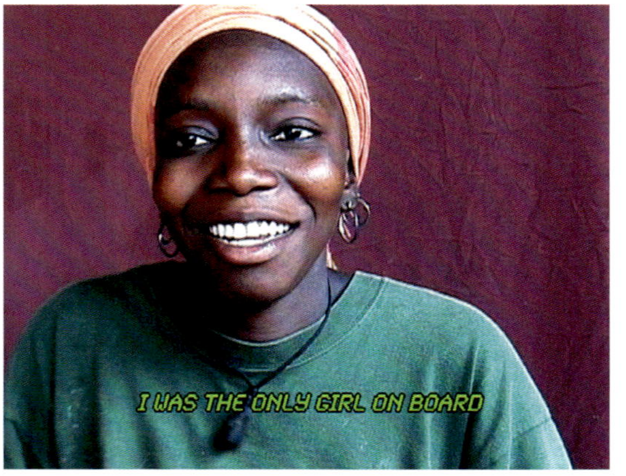

Left page, right page:
Ursula Biemann, *Sahara Chronicle*, 2006–2009, stills from the video collection

video which, in its early days in the 1960s and 1970s was relatively affordable compared to film and was therefore the preferred medium of activists, but which nevertheless incurred high purchasing costs, is now available to each and every smartphone user.[39] The possibility of documenting and disseminating abuses is crucially important for the mobilization of protest movements.

This is all closely related not so much to art, but rather to journalism, which now finds itself in an unsettled position. Changed user behavior, with readers now getting information online rather than from reading printed pages, is often held responsible for a crisis in the press. This explanation is clearly too superficial, since newspapers are far more dependent on advertising revenues than on subscribers. The fact that business is breaking away from classified ads, that companies are advertising on the Internet, poses unforeseen challenges to press freedom. In contrast to the titbit journalism of private channels, the public broadcasters, which continue to be strictly regulated by political supervisory committees, are under great pressure to justify their costs. In less democratic countries like Turkey, critical reporting has already collapsed.[40] In Greece, where it was due to be sacrificed on the orders of the Troika, new forms of solidary civil journalism have developed.[41] Under extreme conditions, such as those in Syria, citizens – be they professional or self-declared journalists – ensure that the flow of information continues uninterrupted.[42]

At the same time, the sphere of art is becoming increasingly significant. Artists who work with photography and video are already experts with regard to technology in this area. They can become active as image producers, as multipliers via channels such as YouTube and Flickr, social networks, blogs, or their own websites, in training laypersons, or as curators or editors of online reviews. Their expertise, however, is not limited to technical skills. What's crucial is the reflective potential that is one of the central components of the study of art: The less study dictates rules and the more it sees itself as guidance for the development of personal skills, then all the more important is the confrontation with the capacities and limitations of the various different media. The medium is then not only the means to an end, but also an object of reflection.

39 See: Christine van Assche (ed.), *Vidéo Vintage 1963–1983, Une sélection de vidéos fondatrices des collections nouveaux medias du Musée national d'art moderne, Centre Pompidou*, exhib. cat., Centre Pompidou, Paris, 2012, ZKM | Karlsruhe, 2012–2013, Éditions du Centre Pompidou, Paris, 2012.

40 See: Evren 2014.

41 Generally on this subject, see the Berlin conference "Complicity," November 7–9, 2013, available online at: http://berlinergazette.de/symposium/complicity, accessed 05/22/2014, see particularly the contribution by Stavroula Poulmeni.

42 See: Mona Sarkis, "The Literal People Power of the Syrians," available online at: http://blog.zkm.de/en/dialogue/the-literal-people-power-syrians/, accessed 05/22/2014.

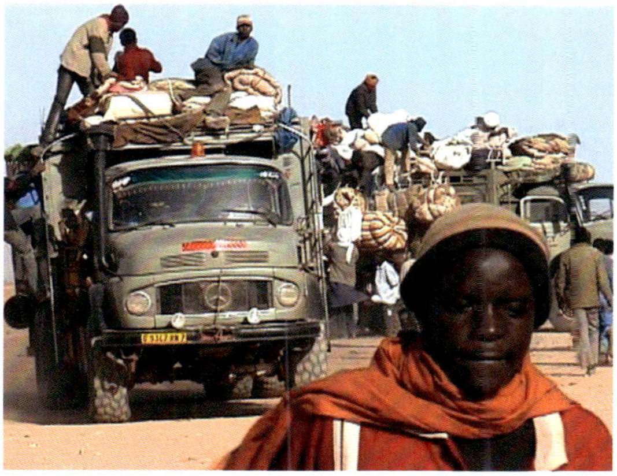 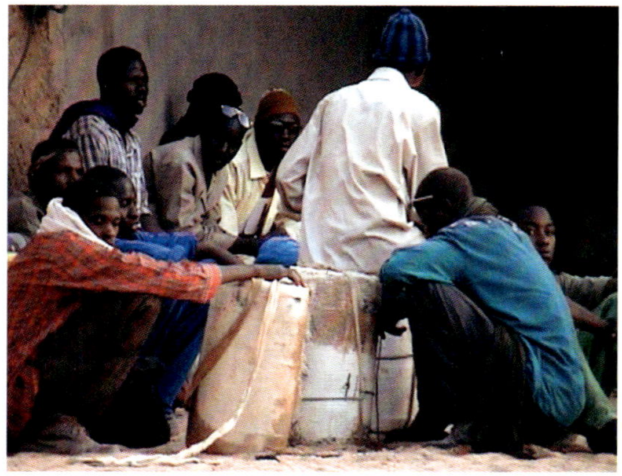

According to a structuralist definition, the dominance of the aesthetic function of art differs from other areas of human activity. However, that does not mean – and this would be a misunderstanding – that the aesthetic function can be isolated: "The aesthetic function in itself is not by itself able to endow the sign it creates with a complete meaning," writes Jan Mukařovský. "Thus even with aesthetic signs (and an artwork is one of these), there are extraaesthetic functions that give it specific content by introducing its direct connection with the realities outside of the sign. The difference between the artwork and other human creations [...] is rooted in the fact that with extraaesthetic activities and their products, the functional orientation is as clear as possible [...] with an artwork, however, it is different; here the dominance of the aesthetic function prevents any of the other functions actually gaining supremacy [...]. Its dominance lies only in the fact that it forms a counterweight to the extraaesthetic functions, that it allows none of them to suppress the others [...]."[43]

43 Jan Mukařovský, *Kunst, Poetik, Semiotik*, Suhrkamp, Frankfurt am Main, 1989, pp. 77f; translated from the German by Jeremy Gaines.

"Suppress" can be taken quite literally here. This is about artistic autonomy, which is defined not by the greatest possible distance from social and political circumstances, but through self-determination. Prescriptive dictates as in socialist realism or in Nazism actually result in the function of the propaganda suppressing all other functions. But in democratic societies, too, there are restrictions which, for example, prevent current art – regardless of its orientation – appearing to any significant extent on television. Art, as can be seen at documenta or concerts of new music, therefore remains reserved for a limited, albeit growing, audience. In this case, the aesthetic function is suppressed by the function of entertainment.

The difference can be explained with the help of documentary formats. Unlike documentary films on television, which try to be "as clear as possible" about specific circumstances, artistic documentation remains open. It does not aim to convey any objective information, but rather makes clear that the means of representation essentially help to color or define the "content," be this in the form of explicit criticism or parodistic allusions to current media formats, or by excluding objectivizing elements like spoken, omniscient commentary or statistics and diagrams, and instead "letting the images speak for themselves." What they convey is more a certain aesthetics.

Art reveals its emancipatory potential that differentiates it from all other areas of human activity not when it withdraws into a shell of self-imposed isolation, but specifically when it involves itself in the circumstances of society. Where and in what form is decided by the artistic imagination. Artistic work is distinguished by the fact that it is not firmly fixed in this regard, but instead has an expandable reservoir of possible approaches. In this sense, the notion of the media can simply refer to artistic methods of conveying meaning: not only electronic devices or social networks, but also painting and drawing, the body, performance, or Conceptual art. "I declare peace to be the greatest work of art," "Every human is an artist": such statements also declare – without being able to make good on their promise – the principal applicability of artistic processes to the circumstances of society as a whole.

Between theory and practice there is often a wide gulf. Nevertheless, from Kurt Hiller's insight that the state of the world demands active involvement, to Beuys's social sculpture, to today's civil movements, a development is revealed in which artistic and activist approaches are mutually complementary. As John Jordan says, who in his Laboratory for Insurrectionary Imagination works purposefully on making artistic fantasy usable for social change, civil movements have the best prospects of success when they act in surprising, unforeseeable ways.[44] All too often, however, the opposite is the case. Demonstrations and campaigns proceed along the same lines no matter where they are. Here, artistic imagination can help, when it is combined with the courage and the commitment of activism. "It's like walking a tightrope," says Jordan: "It's all about keeping your balance."[45]

Translated from the German by Jeremy Gaines.

44 See: The Laboratory of Insurrectionary Imagination, website available online at: www.labofii.net, accessed 05/22/2014.

45 John Jordan in discussion with Dietrich Heissenbüttel on the occasion of the exhibition *global aCtIVISm*, February 5, 2014 at ZKM | Karlsruhe.

Sarah Lewison
and Dan S. Wang

In the Back of the Beyond:

"What Time Is It on the Clock of the World?"

This treatise and travelog follows on from an impulse to revisit the outbreak of popular protest in Madison, Wisconsin, in February of 2011, when a mass movement was born, one that linked at a key moment to protests in Tahrir Square and prefigured the months-later Occupy Wall Street in New York. When a reactionary state governor threatened labor autonomy, thousands of Wisconsin workers, students, pensioners, and families occupied the state capitol building for sixteen days and nights, and later forced an early election. Encouragement came from supporters all over the country and the world. An Egyptian protester in Tahrir Square acknowledged the Wisconsin workers' struggle through signs delivered virally; Wisconsin protest singers paid the favor forward by posting video tributes to those in the heat of Spain's *indignados* movement. The horizontal contagion of uprisings across different national and regional contexts in 2011 revealed a sympathetic political imaginary of resistance that could instantly bridge great distances.

But as the uprisings, occupations, and mass movements projected themselves and were received as spectacularized images, their translocal and transcontextual significance was diluted; either flattened into broad universals about human struggle, or overshadowed by local urgencies. As demonstrations met with repression, the euphoric exchange of transnational support was preempted by the spectacle of heavy policing, leading viewers to experience the unrest as the disciplining of unruly publics. In this essay we look to the rhetorics of recognition between contexts of those connected by, but suffering unequally from, the predations of neoliberalism in the year 2011. Admitting our own investment in the reciprocal recognition between peoples engaged in different struggles, we mourn that the translocality could not be sustained. But we also understand why. Protest politics based on the mass spectacle model preordains the transnational factor as an easily ignored superficiality.

Bearing in mind that the temporal dimension shapes the evolution of political consciousness and capacities for resistance, we conduct an exploratory mapping of political time (and space) in two locations outside the flash points of political outrage in 2011: the small city of Benton Harbor in the deindustrialized American Midwest, and the villages of Lashihai outside Lijiang City in southwestern China. In exploring how locations with different developmental experiences but convergent futures are raked by neoliberalism, we look for routes of translocal resistance that are linked to communities' material and symbolic histories. Drawing on Dene[1] scholar Glen Coulthard's work on recognition politics, we suggest a process for building nonspectacular political translocality that we call *mutual self-recognition*. We end with a meditation on the realm of symbols as a visual terrain through which a process of mutual self-recognition may begin.

1 Glen Coulthard is a member of the Yellowknives Dene First Nation. The Dene people are an aboriginal group of First Nations in the northern regions of Canada.

1. Political Unevenness and Political Time

Following Marx, geographer Neil Smith argues that capitalist space contains within it an uneven temporal dimension marked by economic cycles and what he calls the rhythm of accumulation. Smith emphasizes the disruptions brought on by economic crises as setting the stage for new rounds of expansion and accumulation. He stresses the geographical differentiation resulting from crisis, an uneven destruction of value followed by openings for new expansion.[2] This mobility of accumulation and production over time and between places produces that contradiction within capitalism known as uneven development. But beyond noting the periodicity of crisis, Neil Smith does not elaborate on temporal unevenness even though this seems to be key for understanding present conditions, as no single economic sectoral crisis can be isolated from any other. With states, sectors, and individual enterprises all experiencing unsustainable levels of debt, declining profits, rising resource costs, and increasing social inequality, all kinds of crises are now intertwined. It is the ubiquity of that narrative – stacked and overlapping sectoral bubbles and business cycles – widespread, interwoven, and contemporaneous, site-specific but common, that produces the present relentlessness of capital seen nearly everywhere.

2 See: Neil Smith, *Uneven Development. Nature, Capital, and the Production of Space*, 3rd ed., University of Georgia Press, Athens (GA), 2008, pp. 194–199.

The strings of antisystemic protests in 2011 revealed a distinction between the political temporalities of popular response, corresponding to the acute crisis and the chronic crisis. On the one hand, there is the compressed time of unrest, the hour-by-hour story lines that bring mass movements into being, telecommunicated across continents. On the other, there is the extended time of the neoliberal creep, especially in places outside densely populated centers of camera-friendly insurrection, places where cultures of resistance and self-preservation evolve over years and even decades. Understanding variable temporalities helps us think through a geography of resistance. Uprisings sprout in response to acute, unmanageable crisis – as in Tunisia, sparked by a rapidly circulating story of gross injustice, and then in Egypt, where images of the unfolding Tunisian revolution combined with a sudden inflation of bread prices to produce uncontrollable pressures. Mass response sets in motion the time of upheaval. By contrast, slow-burning crises – for example, incremental land grabs, piecemeal legalized robbery, episodic erosion of public goods – produce a differently timed resistance, not only less prone to spectacularization, but somewhat difficult to capture in images at all.

In "Occupy Time,"[3] Jason Adams argues that Occupy Wall Street moves beyond its investment in occupied space and towards one that extends into time. In other words, the question remains of what strategies would produce a sustained disinvestment in the current institutions, equal to the durational grasp of capital.[3] We arm ourselves, too, with the variabilities of the temporal, understanding that our thoughts exist between past and future, between memory and preparation, in a struggle to grasp time in the project of cultivating political reciprocity and, ultimately, solidarities of real use.

3 Jason Adams, "Occupy Time," published on November 16, 2011 on the *Critical Inquiry* blog "In the Moment," available online at: http://critinq.wordpress.com/2011/11/16/occupy-time/, accessed 05/06/2014.

Perhaps the most radical formulation of political temporality comes from James and Grace Lee Boggs, who speak of "the clock of the world,"[4] a notion of political time that overflows the scale of a single generation. The Boggs's use of time as a framework extends the understanding of political effect to the present urgencies of the Anthropocene. They call for consideration of present vectors, forces, and capacities so that a new vision of society may emerge that brokers accountability between dignified subjects, locally and transnationally.

4 James Boggs and Grace Lee Boggs, *Revolution and Evolution in the Twentieth Century*, Monthly Review Press, New York (NY), 1974, p. 171.

2. On the Ends of the Earth: Lashihai and Benton Harbor

On the plateau of northwest Yunnan province, Lashihai is a highland lake surrounded by a dozen Naxi villages, a minority ethnic group. Although the Maoist era wrought dramatic change and loss, the region remains remote from the state and the indigenous people retain unique identities that are tied to their long tenure in this place. Until recently, locals practiced traditional subsistence agriculture and commoning in nearby forests. Some families still share labor. The Lashi Valley, surrounded by foothills rising to snow peaks and then down to the first curve of the rushing Yangtze, is one of the most biodiverse temperate ecosystems in the world. The area's cultural and ecological diversity led to its designation as a province level nature reserve and a UNESCO Natural World Heritage region. Significantly, Lashi Lake has become the major water source for nearby Lijiang city, a growing tourist destination receiving four million visitors yearly. Village farmers are repeatedly compelled to reduce their plots as the lake expands to provide for Lijiang. As their farming incomes drop, they receive cash compensations which they often use to purchase heavy equipment – their entree into the global economy. Recently, the state gave farmers trucks as incentives to start businesses.

Historically unassimilated into the Han culture, there are remnants of autonomy in this region. For example, in 2008 when the local Party-nominated chief was discovered skimming land compensation payments, a row erupted and the chief was sent off and not replaced. In a quiet contagion, the other villages around the lake dispatched their chiefs as well. Officially sanctioned enclosures also have met with resistance, which in some cases were answered with intimidation. When a village closer to Lijiang protested the conversion of their fields into a golf course, two farmers turned up dead; there was compensation but no prosecution. Lashi is at the

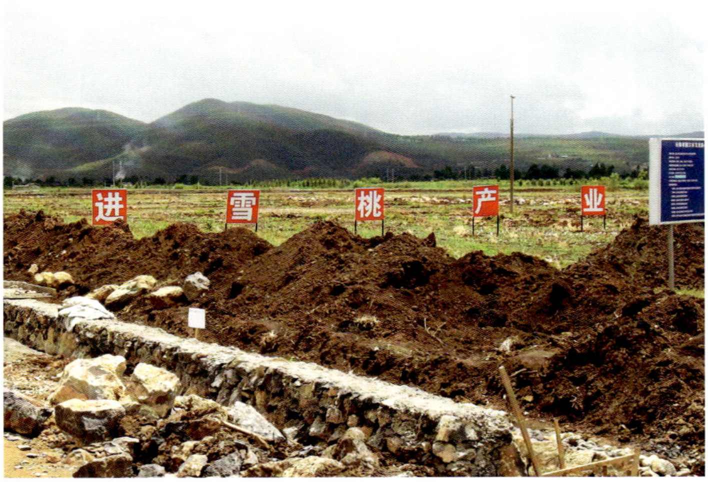

Cujin xuetao chanye [Accelerate the Snow Peach Industry], government sign, Lashihai, Yunnan province, China, 2011

edge of time, where a new freeway traces one of the earliest sustained projects of global trade, the Ancient Tea Horse Road between Kolkata and Puer, through the provincial capital, Kunming, and on to Vietnam. As farmers began to follow international prices, they took awful risks with monocropping and soil inputs, hoping to make better sales to the buyers roaming the region in four-ton trucks during harvest times. All this happened while their traditional customs were marketed as one of Lijiang's main attractions. Upon arriving we were led to a new construction project in the fields opposite our host's compound. Family plots are customarily divided into small portions to equalize access to water and different soils. Crops are companion-planted in the resulting irregular fields, producing a verdant quilt. But here the small river flowing from the foothills had been straightened and confined by rock walls. These newly disciplined channels were bordered by stone-paved roads that led to uniform rows of identical peach trees, recently planted in the spring mud. Now that the land is fungible, a developer, with the blessing of district level officials, had convinced some villagers that tourists will come to a heaven of peaches beneath the brilliant blue sky, the snow peaks rising above the lake. The walkway stops at the road but heads toward the lake with only our host's and their neighbor's land in between. The characters on large bright-red signs fronting the embryonic peach orchard exhort the passersby with the larger agenda of penetrating the valley and beyond to further commerce under the guise of development:
"SPEED CONSTRUCTION OF A NEW SOCIALIST COUNTRYSIDE!" And on the other side of the signs: "GRAB THE LAND AND ORGANIZE IT. BUILD A PEACH INDUSTRY."[5]

Benton Harbor, today a city of 10,000 inhabitants on the southeast shore of Lake Michigan, was home to makers of auto parts and consumer goods. An 1889 map shows tree-flecked residential lots and factories with black clouds billowing out of their smokestacks, bordering a ship-lined canal. At the top, ant-like steamers trawl across the lake, which is ornamented at its shore by rows of sandy hills. These dunes loom to thirty-plus meters, washed in by the freshwater sea left behind by the last glacier, forming rare sand and wetland ecosystems.

In 1917, Benton Harbor newspaperman John Klock bought ninety acres of lakefront dunes and forest, and gave it to the city "in perpetuity" as the Jean Klock Park.[6] Standing as a memorial to the Klocks's deceased young daughter, the forest, beaches, and dunes were open to anyone for picnics, play, baptisms, and solace.

5 A debt is owed to Jay Brown for translation, and to Brian Holmes for his unforgettable description in June 8, 2011. See: Brian Holmes, "Wu Mu Cosmology. Pathways through the Modern-World System," available online at: http://brianholmes.wordpress.com/2011/06/08/wu-mu-cosmology, accessed 05/06/2014.

6 Friends of Jean Klock Park, "Save Jean Klock Park," available online at: www.savejeanklockpark.org, accessed 05/06/2014.

Today new luxury housing punctures the former forest, and holes six through eight of a Jack Nicklaus “Signature” golf course mar the majestic sand hills, the result of 22 acres of the park being taken into private hands despite legal challenges. At around the same time, Benton Harbor’s elected government was replaced by a state-appointed “emergency manager” empowered to sell off public assets and break employee contracts. Benton Harbor’s is the story of many a Rust Belt town: automation, job losses, plant closings, white flight, structural racism, and tax rolls that can barely fund basic services. When jobs were plentiful, blacks moved up to houses with yards and whites fled to the neighboring city of St. Joseph. As the economic shocks of the 1970s advanced, layoffs disproportionately hurt African Americans and the city lost half its population. Remaining residents got stuck with tracts of contaminated industrial land. Throughout, the multinational appliance giant Whirlpool dominated the town. As the company closed its last local plant in 2011, it made new plans for a taxpayer-subsidized research campus on the river, continuing its major role in plotting the transformation of Benton Harbor into an upscale resort destination.

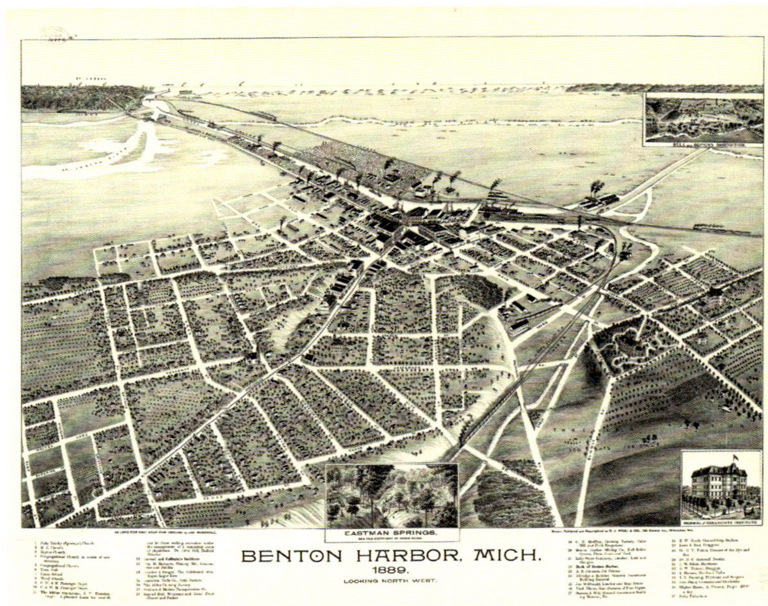

Benton Harbor, Michigan, aerial view toward the northwest, 1889

The 530-acre Harbor Shores Golf Course is the heart of this current reterritorialization – an example of the expansion of capital in the wake of economic crisis. Harbor Shores is the product of allied corporate and nonprofit entities along with heavy public subsidization. The nonprofit partners are charged with recouping investment through social and life skill improvements, philanthrocapitalist lingo for the internalization of behaviors that suit a market economy.[7] For example, the initiative “First Tee” engages youth in “building character” by caddying, a kind of patronage that may be the only opportunity for some of the participating youth. Their website lists their many sponsors and accomplishments; affordable

7
See: Vincanne Adams, “The Other Road to Serfdom: Recovery by the Market and the Affect Economy in New Orleans,” in: *Public Culture*, vol. 24, no. 1, 2012, pp. 185–216. This illuminates connections between the bureaucratic apparatus and a growing philanthropic sector associated with Corporate Social Responsibility.

housing, drug rehab, park maintenance, and other services once the government's purview. The site advertises the dollar value of these initiatives and tallies the people "served" regardless of how long they stay or whether services are actually provided. The commodification of affect and social dysfunction fuels today's venture philanthropy.[8]

8 See: Harbor Shores Lake Michigan, "Partners in Harbor Shores Accomplishments," available online at: www.harborshoresdevelopment.org/index.php?option=com_content&task=view&id=27, accessed 05/06/2014.

Our guide, the activist clergyman Reverend Edward Pinkney, explained that Benton Harbor's residents (over 90% black) have been not only economically excluded, but are also vulnerable to election fraud and discrimination in the judicial system. The surrounding county is predominantly white, meaning juries, judges, and state-level officials are also often white. Some stand to profit if Benton Harbor's future goes their way, including an heir to the Whirlpool fortune. Pinkney, who long suspected Whirlpool's intentions on the Jean Klock Park, now speaks for those fearing retribution from a corporate-controlled police apparatus. He shows us the contaminated lots that were "given" to the townspeople in exchange. We see a house on the 7th hole that is listed for $1.5 million, before visiting working class neighborhoods where many pay more in annual rent than the houses are worth. In a city where the $5 thousand per year annual golf course membership is half the average yearly adult income, economic apartheid is a reality.

We visit a new cafe in the arts development zone where entrepreneurs receive tax breaks to build businesses near a "river walk" that will someday connect to the boutiques of Harbor Shores. As the city changes to reflect its handlers' gentrifying designs, housing for long-time residents may well become unaffordable. In the meantime, activists try to recall the mayor.[9] As the election nears, police are interrogating petition signers and Pinkney is detained. In the past year, the bodies of young black men from the town have been found floating in the river, unsolved deaths. Corporate patronage in Benton Harbor has come full circle in inflecting meaning on the word "perpetuity."

9 Phone conversation with Reverend Pinkney, April 23, 2014.

3. Toward a Theory of Mutual Self-Recognition

Sociologist Loïc Wacquant describes the relationship between market, government, and citizens as a "concrete political constellation" in which the "state effectively redraws the boundaries and tenor of citizenship through its market-conforming policies."[10] This is accomplished by opening new sectors of commodification, the use of corrective workfare, zero tolerance punitive measures, and animating tropes of individual responsibility. It is evident that this is happening in Lashi and Benton Harbor – and probably in any other unfamiliar place we might happen to investigate. Specifically, both places are being marched into the tourism industry, an economic sector with global and transcontextual elements. In both cases the state facilitates the tourism and new enclosures, and a wealthy class benefits from the encroachments. But like trains running on different gauges of track, Lashi and Benton Harbor occupy different points in an arc of development, with corresponding differentials in political signification and material basis. Benton Harbor resides on the far end of deindustrialization while Lashihai society is still

10 Loïc Wacquant, "Three steps to a Historical Anthropology of Actually Existing Neoliberalism," in: *Social Anthropology*, vol. 20, no. 1, February 2012, pp. 66–79, here p. 71.

agrarian, in many ways informally collective, although increasingly dotted with pieces of marketized life; some of them willingly adopted, some resisted, and some irrelevant.

Comparisons fray when we attend to the question of political response. General similarities may be noted – for example, intimidation and a threat of violence is a problem in Lashi as it is in Benton Harbor. But responses align with differentials of historical experience, the political channels available, and what actions are accorded symbolic significance. For example, in Benton Harbor, as a holdover from the centrality of voting rights won during the civil rights period, African American people rely on elections even though the process has been corrupted. Faithful to the civil rights tradition, they likewise mobilize for conventional protests when visibility seems a possibility, such as during the national spectacle of a professional golf tournament in Benton Harbor. But these kinds of demonstrations tend to be treated as predigested tropes, and thus become neutered expressions of simmering discontent as opposed to exercises of actual political power.

As noted earlier, Lashihai villagers refused local level representation by a titular "chief." The elimination of this bureaucratic layer was collectively organized by the women as a pragmatic solution to the problem of corruption, rather than as an act of subversion. But recusal is also consistent with Naxi people's historical "ungovernability" in relation to imperial authority; our host rejects the "peach paradise" compensation offer by acknowledging the request and, Bartleby-like, demurring indefinitely. But to outsiders without guides and hosts, this resistance – so important to the preservation of a humane society – exists unseen, behind the opacity of a system that effaces dissent.

To remind, the fundamental problem tackled in this essay is that of finding operations of translocality and transcontextuality outside the quickness of spectacularized protest. Toward this end, we describe two places, different but similarly imperiled, that have little political recourse in the face of displacements and thuggery, executed locally but driven by globalized market forces. What binds the residents of Benton Harbor and Lashihai to all those living in other places of unseen friction is their shared future horizon as nonstop entrepreneurs of the self, as human capital in the most invasive sense. But a sustained mindfulness of place, between and across contexts, will not result from an exchange of protest images or other superficial documents of discontent.

We propose *mutual self-recognition* as a process through which an operable political translocality might lead to the proliferation of strategic identifications between places largely invisible to the mediasphere and to each other, outside the circuits of recognition that limit exchanges to that between the subjugated and the powerful. We assemble the term from the work of Dene scholar Glen Coulthard, drawing on his critique of liberal recognition politics in the context of First Nations' relations with the Canadian government.[11] Coulthard questions the political meaning of a process in which the subaltern gains official recognition by the state and makes claims to sovereignty on that basis. He traces conventional political recognition

11 See: Glen S. Coulthard, "Subjects of Empire: Indigenous Peoples and the 'Politics of Recognition' in Canada," in: *Contemporary Political Theory*, vol. 6, 2007, pp. 437–460.

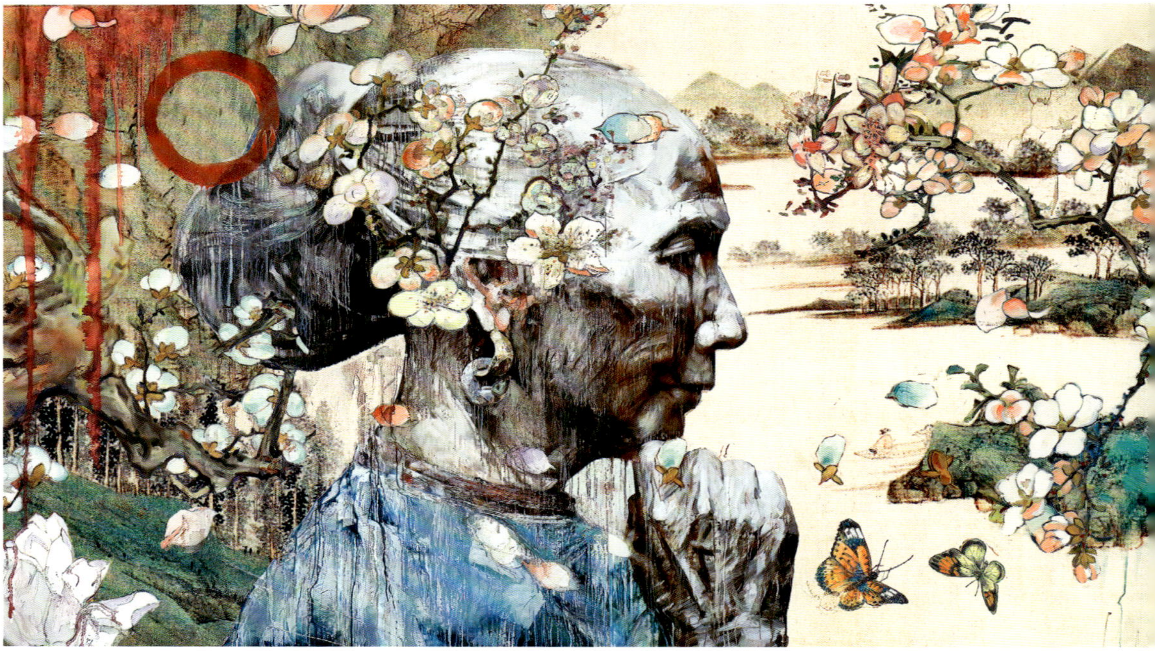

Hung Liu, *Peach Blossom Spring*, 2011, mixed media with resin, 104.1 × 375.9 cm

to G. W. F. Hegel's master–slave dialectic, in which the mutual dependency between master and slave renders a reciprocally intersubjective relationship, in spite of the asymmetrical balance of power. Coulthard then problematizes this dynamic through a reading of Frantz Fanon, who introduces into it the factors of psychosocialization and culture, activated in the context of colonialism.

Coulthard argues that official recognition by the state can only reproduce the essential colonial relationship, even if in an accommodated or uplifted form. He concludes optimistically but abstractly by suggesting that, following Fanon's pathway to colonial agency, recognition be a claim made first for oneself by oneself, prior to and instead of setting oneself in relation to the external authority of the state. Thus, he argues that *self-recognition* moves the subaltern toward "evading the politics of recognition's tendency to produce Indigenous subjects of empire."[12] We add *mutual* to *self-recognition* to denote the process of, as Coulthard quotes bell hooks, "recognizing ourselves and [then seeking to] make contact with all who would engage us in a constructive manner."[13] But, practically speaking, what is the operation of self-recognition? How do sited communities, nested within the larger and at times contradictory contexts of a culture, an environment, and a global political economy, actually go about recognizing themselves? To these questions Coulthard offers no help.

12 Ibid., p. 439.

13 Bell hooks, as quoted from ibid., p. 456.

Let us suggest one possible path. When insurgent events jump borders and link contexts rapidly, visibility is a key to the dynamic. Because the register of political resistance is entirely different in places like Lashihai and Benton Harbor, that is, essentially a resistance of long-term noncooperation as opposed to headline-making protest, the corresponding time of visibility also must be different – both in the becoming visible and in the duration of being visible.

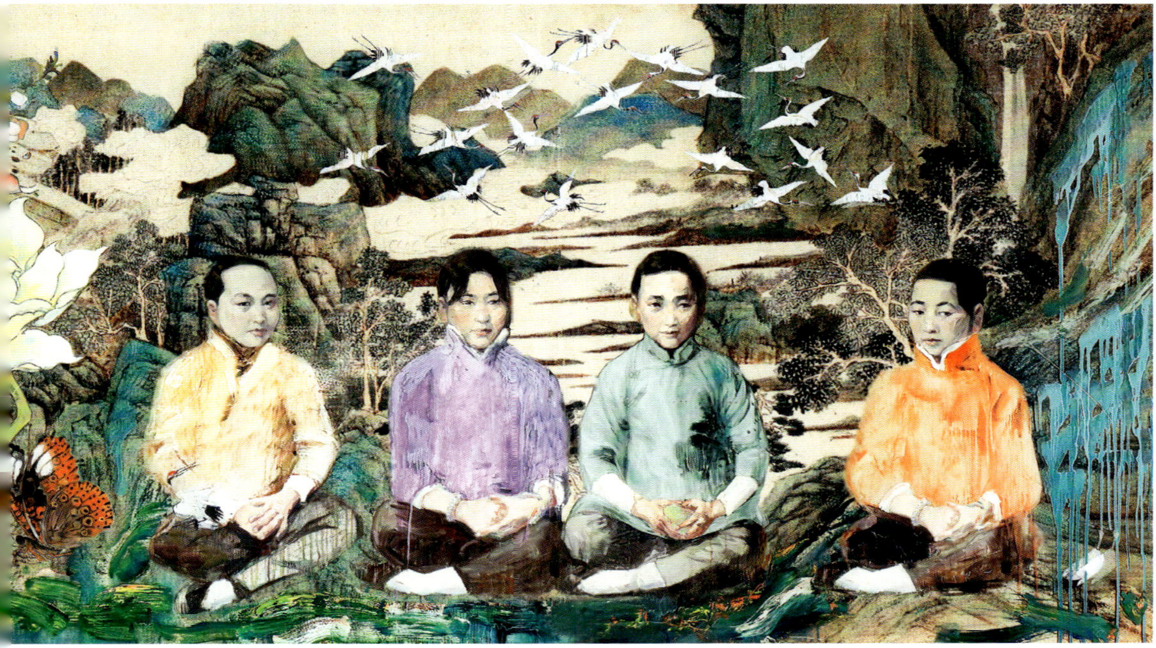

The representations of these places, of their existence, of their subjecthood, is less about virally circulated images and time-stamped photojournalism and more about ongoing recombinations and mutations of existing cultural symbols, for the sake of self-recognition. Mutual self-recognition opens up as a potentiality when communities deploy their vocabulary of symbols, organically and immanently developed over time, to assert their dignity.

4. Return to the Symbolic

Hung Liu's print-painting *Peach Blossom Spring* depicts a foursome of teenaged girls, sitting on the ground in trousers and collared coats, cross-legged, looking out at the photographer who captured this pose on an afternoon from the late decades of dynastic China. Many decades later Hung Liu paints from the historical source, setting the four figures in color, on one side of a mashed-up Chinese landscape of lakes, mountains, and the blossoms of the title. Opposite the girls is the outsized profile of an elderly woman, looking toward, or maybe literally over, the girls. The young betray the freshness of spirit that all young people possess. The somber grayness of the old generation's representative may come from her knowledge of what follows for these soon-to-be wives, knowing that the girls' bound feet would be but the most painfully obvious of a lifetime's worth of unfavorable treatment. But for what might have been a late Qing-era generation sitting on the cusp of unknown revolutionary changes, the feelings of young female society must have been palpable. Mixed with the figures are a sampling of symbols from the traditional society that was then losing its authority, including butterflies, a flock of cranes, and peaches on the limb. It is the long arc of civilization, conservative by nature, pitted against urgencies stored in memory, historical contingency, and individual expectation. The girls' feet, gathered in front of their bodies and thereby quietly revealing their common experience as a gendered class, speak to the violence of history that straddles the production of symbols. The desire for that which the peach represents, longevity and immortality, cannot be divorced from the world we really live in. The title refers to a fable attributed to the Six Dynasties poet Tao Yuanming in which a fisherman wanders up a tributary and discovers an unknown settlement whose inhabitants live in harmony, insulated from the political strife of the fast-changing dynasties. Peach trees line the valley, a place that time forgot. After the man returns home and reports his experience, later seekers are unable to find the village, leaving its existence to the eternal imagination. Today the phantasmatic valley reads as a literary antecedent for the paradisical images advertised by Yunnan province tour operators. Hung Liu's insertion of a gendered historical experience into the timelessness of legend counts as a political intrusion into a vaporously ahistorical plane. She reinvests symbols with meanings layered with the dignity of the female subjects, in all their specificity. Thus, the new moral of the story is that a drop-out society inherits inequalities – there is no presocial moment – even as the desire for an escape proves to be the most powerful modern marketing line of all.

We encountered this painting in July, an interregnum between the Arab Spring and Occupy, a time when the hazy fruits of revolt in some places seemed within grasp, but in Lashihai the oncoming "peach paradise" remained a suspended threat. There, in a convergence of meaning, the symbolic significance of peaches got tied to the actual fate of the farmers' lands. The symbol will occupy time as a trophy for the winner, depending on the outcome of the impasse. And so applying Hung Liu's artistic strategy to real life, recombining symbols in order to make visible the contradictions of people's life experiences, is one path to self-recognition. Performing the symbolic as an intervention may even disrupt the unitary time of capital. In October 2011, the Ohlone activist Corrina Gould addressed a crowd at Occupy Oakland. Making a mutual encounter out of an event framed as a unified protest, she quipped, "It is so wonderful to be here today with hundreds of people who want to *occupy occupied land*." Indigenous people, when asked about the origins of their knowledge – which is in so many ways synonymous with their resistance – will always say "time immemorial," or farther back than anyone can remember. Gould ripped open the gap between the symbolic power of her people's memory and a contemporary imagination of dissent shaped solely by the experience of capitalism and its unceasing power to erode a commons of symbols.

"I live in the city. The air is negative. The trees are dying. Concrete is all over. Look at the streets: People, too many people. They do not express anything; they just run nonstop. I want to protest to find. The other part of this life."[1]

Cólera, *Vivo na Cidade* (1986)

André Mesquita

Noises in the Concrete: Artistic Activism in São Paulo

1. Oppositional Culture

This essay is about people on the streets, about the insurgencies of social creativity at conflicting spaces in the city of São Paulo. At times like these, we have the opportunity to testify and take part in the renewed emergence of a critical, reflective counterhistory. A counterhistory comprised of multiple voices and possibilities of sudden breaks and changes, many times marginalized or "not even included in the narratives and archives of political history and art theory."[2] In the convergences or overlappings between art and activism, in specific periods of time and contexts, obscure relationships extend beyond the borders of separate spheres and lead to extradisciplinary collaborations. Collective action is reinvented through new situations that recreate the role of art, the language of protest and social debate, leveraging manifestations of self-organization and poetic experimentation in everyday life.

São Paulo is a huge territory within which there are many different processes of migration, economic restructuring, and vertical integration. A city full of contrasts – skyscrapers, squatter settlements, and highways – where wealth and social exclusion, downtown and periphery, safety and violence, diversity and isolation exist side by side in a disorganized and divergent manner. The slow and difficult daily commute of those who come from the outskirts and commuter towns to the central area of São Paulo, where most of the job opportunities and basic services are concentrated, shows there is still a lot to be done and discussed in relation to an urban mobility policy that reduces spatial inequality. In the Situationist text "Basic Program of the Bureau of Unitary Urbanism" (1961), Attila Kotányi and Raoul Vaneigem understand city traffic as the organization and isolation of people. "It is the opposite of encounter: it absorbs the energies that could otherwise be devoted to encounters or to any sort of participation. Spectacles compensate for the participation that is no longer possible."[3] Anthropologist Teresa Caldeira reminds us that the rules which organize the urban space are basically standards of social differentiation and separation.

1 Translated from the Portuguese by Cinescript Berlin.

2 Gerald Raunig, *Art and Revolution. Transversal Activism in the Long Twentieth Century*, Semiotext(e), Los Angeles (CA), 2007, p. 19.

3 Attila Kotányi and Raoul Vaneigem, "Basic Program of the Bureau of Unitary Urbanism" (1961), available online at: www.bopsecrets.org/SI/6.unitaryurb.htm, accessed 09/12/2014.

"These rules vary culturally and historically, reveal the principles that structure public life, and indicate how social groups relate to each other in the space of the city."[4]

How have the transversal processes of activist art contributed in recent years to other concepts, symbols, and tools to change physical and social spaces devoured by the chaos and inequalities of such a large city? As a metaphor of the prefiguration of these radical practices, I want to mention here an impressive artist born in São Paulo and quite unknown in Brazil. As a child, the Brazilian-born Swede Öyvind Fahlström (1928–1976), "an artist deeply divided between social change and self-discovery,"[5] left Brazil soon after the beginning of the Second World War to visit his parents in Europe and never returned. Living in the United States from the beginning of the 1960s, Fahlström collected statistical data on political and economical processes from newspapers, magazines, and books, and used them in games and maps – these works included references from the New Left, counterculture, and underground comics.

The games designed by Fahlström in and about the 1970s, during the Cold War and the beginning of the structural changes of global capitalism, are activist interpretations of the popular board game Monopoly and critical to the game theories used by the think tanks connected to the North American industrial and military complex – such as the RAND Corporation – to calculate rationally the attacks and offensives from the Communist side.[6] *World Politics Monopoly* (1970), *U.S. Monopoly* (1971), and *C.I.A. Monopoly* (1971) were some of his "variable paintings" – works that include sets of specific rules and detailed information regarding the geopolitical context of that period, illustrating the revolutionary need of having another world as a possibility in the face of the economic exploration of Third World nations by developed countries and the resistance of left-wing movements. These games included figures and paintings glued over magnets, which could be rearranged by players on a metal surface, and they introduced a very ambitious project:

> "The role of the spectator as a performer of the picture-game will become meaningful as soon as these works can be multiplied into a large number of replicas, so that anyone interested can have a picture machine in his home and 'manipulate the world' according to either his or my choices."[7]

Fahlström's project was never finished. His works never left the art world and were not even widely reproduced; today they belong to private collectors and major museums. Fahlström, however, continued to be perceived as an "artist" and he tried to encourage people to use the very same objects to clearly show power relationships.[8] This participatory political and aesthetic program, incorporated in such interactive games where tactics and strategies are discussed and reinvented over time, can be perceived as the machine that will guide us through São Paulo. It is a production machine of thought and action proposing antagonisms in the public sphere and new ways of thinking the reality, intervening in existing spaces and

4 Teresa Pires do Rio Caldeira, *City of Walls. Crime, Segregation, and Citizenship in São Paulo*, University of California Press, Berkeley (CA), 2000, p. 213.

5 Antonio Sergio Bessa, *Öyvind Fahlström. The Art of Writing*, Northwestern University Press, Evanston (IL), 2008, p. XVIII.

6 On the uses of game theory by RAND Corporation strategists see: Philip Mirowski, *Machine Dreams. Economics Becomes a Cyborg Science*, Cambridge University Press, Cambridge, New York (NY), 2002.

7 Öyvind Fahlström, "Manipulating the World" (1964), in: *Öyvind Fahlström*, exhib. cat., Solomon R. Guggenheim Museum, New York (NY), 1982, p. 45.

8 I describe the political and activist aspects of Öyvind Fahlström's games and maps in detail in the first chapter of my PhD dissertation, *Mapas Dissidentes: Proposições Sobre um Mundo em Crise (1960–2010)* [Dissenting Maps: Propositions on a World in Crisis (1960–2010)]. The Portuguese text is available at: www.teses.usp.br/teses/disponiveis/8/8138/tde-15042014-100630/pt-br.php, accessed 09/12/2014.

working with other identities and sociabilities. Imagination through art and activist occupation of urban space by collective practices emerging from careful listening to issues, challenges, problems, and demands also plays an important role here, as suggested by anthropologist David Graeber: the imagination as a constituent element in the process of how we produce our social and material realities, creating real effects in the world in order to change it.[9]

Echoes produced by interventions on the concrete are not silent. This reminds one of Francis Alÿs talking about his experience of walking through the streets with a stick touching the buildings that regulate the sound patterns as the pedestrian's walk generates the melody.[10] A provocative city image shows the diversity of vocabulary and voice of some interventions. Until September 2010, when we walked through a degraded area in downtown São Paulo, we would see a huge old building condemned in 2004, São Vito. Built in 1959 and considered for decades as the "largest vertical tenements of the city," the São Vito building was the subject of a heated discussion regarding whether it should be destroyed and turned into popular housing, a park, or into an underground parking lot, as part of an exclusive downtown regeneration process. Its facade showed dilapidated modernist influences, long neglected and in a state of disrepair. Signatures by anonymous *pichadores* [taggers] covered every window of that huge building. Who would have challenged gravity and have risked falling almost 27 floors just to paint those symbols there?

Leaving your mark on the city by painting tags or explicit messages represents shared protests and the transgression of boundaries by the youngsters who live on the outskirts of São Paulo. In October 2008, the concept of the curators of the 28th edition of the São Paulo Biennial of inviting the audience to reflect about the emptiness of one of the floors of the building was challenged by the taggers when forty people spray-painted the inside walls of the pavilion at the exhibition opening. The symbolic vengeance taken against the institution drew attention to its difficulty of dealing with the conflict arising from unpredictable actions within it and around it. When this group questioned the space of the art world and its authority to decide which practices are legal or not, the Biennial Foundation resorted to the law enforcement system and dealt with the issue in the worst possible way. One of the taggers, Caroline Pivetta da Mota, was imprisoned for nearly sixty days.

2. Changing the Current Normality

After the anonymous tagging, the machine driving this text points next to the place where activist art acquires the strength of its political dimension: the reinstitution of a public, or perhaps a "counterpublic" – with its perspectives of opinion, of the circulation of other discourses, of exchanges and criticism of the use of power – "formed by their conflict with the norms and contexts of their cultural environment."[11] São Paulo embraces both the local and the global, where the artist-activist rebuilds relationships with communities, construes, negotiates, and mediates an action place.

9 See: David Graeber, *Direct Action. An Ethnography*, AK Press, Oakland (CA), Edinburgh, 2009, p. 526.

10 See: Francis Alÿs, "Interview with James Lingwood" (2006), in: Stephen Johnstone (ed.), *The Everyday*, Whitechapel, London, The MIT Press, Cambridge (MA), 2008, p. 140.

11 Michael Warner, *Publics and Counterpublics*, Zone Books, New York (NY), 2002, p. 63.

Artistic activism suggests other ways to intervene in an experiential and intuitive way in the city. An investigation of the work of art collectives and other production networks and social movements in São Paulo, from different eras and in various circumstances, can provide direct or indirect historical grounds for our interventionist tactics.

A long time before the Situationist practices of *dérive* [drifting] and happenings or perfomances (previously the common use of this term), this urban fluidity in collective interventions and protests was evident in the provocative actions of the architect and artist Flávio de Carvalho. In 1931, Carvalho walked in the opposite direction to a Corpus Christi procession wearing a cap, which infuriated the participants. Some even threatened to lynch the artist. This test of a religious group's limits of tolerance, titled *Experiência nº 2* [Experiment No. 2], led to the term "crowd psychology" as referred to by Carvalho, later published in a book.[12] In 1956, he carried out his *Experiência nº 3* [Experiment No. 3], which was to stroll through the streets of São Paulo wearing a "tropical outfit" (also called the "New Look"): skirt, organza hat, puff sleeve blouse, stockings, and sandals.

In 1963, Wesley Duke Lee staged what many consider the first happening in Brazil at a pub in São Paulo with the title *O Grande Espetáculo das Artes* [The Great Spectacle of Arts], where he showed his series of erotic drawings in the dark; the audience were able to see the works by the light of lanterns. The gallery founded by Duke Lee and other artists from the Grupo Rex, Rex Gallery & Sons, ended its activities with a show that lasted only eight minutes. *Exposição-Não-Exposição* [Exhibition-Not-Exhibition] on May 25, 1967 was driven by the violence of the people who gathered at the venue to get "free artworks" that were attached to the walls by chains and strings or by concrete blocks on the floor. The exhibition was intended to shake the audience out of its passivity and get it to act with rage.[13]

Other actions that took place in São Paulo, which are considered important urban expressions include a series of around two hundred billboards spread around the city in 1968 by one of the founders of the Grupo Rex, Nelson Leirner, displaying the sentence "Aprenda colorir gozando/Gozar colorindo" [Learn how to paint by having fun/Have fun by painting]; *Zebra*, a drawing by Claudio Tozzi in 1972; the event *Mitos Vadios* in 1978, organized by Ivald Granato at a parking lot and attended by dozens of artists as criticism of the Latin-American Biennial and its theme "Mitos e Magia" [Myths and Magic]; and the graphic creations, stencils, drawings, and double entendres in the graffiti of TupiNãoDá and the artist trio Alex Vallauri, Carlos Matuck, and Waldemar Zaidler.

1968 to 1974 were the most violent years of military dictatorship in Brazil (1964–1985), and during this period left-wing militants were pursued, tortured, murdered, and some of them disappeared.[14] In this extremely repressive scenario with censorship trying to suppress antigovernment protests, left-wing militancy in São Paulo developed into the first urban guerrilla movements in 1967, followed by attacks on military facilities to procure weapons, bank robberies, strikes, and kidnapping. Alternative media played a key role as a strategy to overcome censorship. The journal *Versus* (1975–1979), founded by

12 See: Flávio de Carvalho, *Experiência nº 2*, NAU Editora, Rio de Janeiro, 2001; see also: Luiz Camillo Osorio, *Flávio de Carvalho*, Cosac Naify, São Paulo, 2000.

13 On the history of the Grupo Rex see: Fernanda Lopes, *A experiência Rex: "Éramos o time do rei,"* Alameda, São Paulo, 2009.

14 In South America, persecution, torture, murders, and disappearances happened during the CIA support of military governments in Brazil, Argentina, Chile, Bolivia, Paraguay, and Uruguay via "Operation Condor," a secret network established in 1975 to exterminate left-wing leaders and groups.

15 See: Omar L. de Barros Filho (ed.), *Versus: Páginas da Utopia*, Azougue Editorial, Rio de Janeiro, 2007.

16 Carlos Marighella, *Minimanual of the Urban Guerrilla* (1969), available online at: www.marxists.org/archive/marighella-carlos/1969/06/minimanual-urban-guerrilla, accessed 12/09/2014.

17 Frederico Morais, "Contra a arte afluente: o corpo é o motor da obra" (1970), in: Ricardo Basbaum (ed.), *Arte Contemporânea Brasileira: Texturas, Dicções, Ficções, Estratégias*, Contra Capa, Rio de Janeiro, 2001, pp.169–178, here p. 171; translated from the Portuguese by Cinescript Berlin.

18 Deborah B. Gould, *Moving Politics. Emotion and ACT UP's Fight against AIDS*, University of Chicago Press, Chicago (IL), 2009, p. 20.

19 The political opening started in 1974 and took place during General Ernesto Geisel's government, when there was profound dissatisfaction of the Brazilian population because of the social and economic crisis.

20 This movement, known as "Diretas Já," emerged in 1984 with 1.5 million people on the streets demanding direct presidential elections and is recognized as one of the greatest public demonstrations in the history of Brazil.

journalist Marcos Faerman (1943–1999) in São Paulo, was one of the symbols of resistance in Latin America, and featured articles that mixed reality and fiction, comics and samizdat literature.[15] The *Minimanual of the Urban Guerrilla*, written by Carlos Marighella in June 1969, summarizes our street tactics and collective trends for direct action, including diverting weapons from the enemy and the lack of resources. These challenges make the urban guerrilla "imaginative and creative – qualities without which it would be impossible for him to carry out his role as a revolutionary." [16] Art historian and critic Frederico Morais brought together the tactics of left-wing subversive groups and Brazilian experimental art, referring to the work of Lygia Clark and Hélio Oiticica as "artistic guerrilla" because they created situations and made use of poor materials as a new concept of existence as opposed to static reification for the duration incompatible with the ephemerality of life. "Today, every artist is some kind of a guerrilla fighter. Art is a kind of ambush." [17]

The main connection between the works of artists such as Clark and Oiticica and activism is *action* – the experience of the flow of protest as a social space of mutual support and free expressions of bodies, gestures, speeches, and emotions. Affects as an energy that cannot be named or understood at first, "something that escapes us but is nevertheless in play, generated through interaction with the world, and affecting our embodied beings and subsequent actions." [18] This multiplicity of interactions reemerged during the "opening" of the political system in Brazil,[19] when social movements and students gradually returned to the streets to protest and demand a redemocratization process.[20] In the factories located in industrial parks in São Paulo, workers organized at meetings and strikes considered historical landmarks. The political momentum at the end of the decade was reflected in the "poetical walks" organized by the Sanguinovo group in 1979 and 1980, artistic interventions on advertising billboards made by Manga Rosa (1978–1982),[21] militant theater groups such as Ferramenta (1975–1978) and Forja (1979–1991),[22] and the beginning of the punk movement in São Paulo.[23] Two important urban intervention groups, 3Nós3 (1979–1982) and Viajou Sem Passaporte (1978–1982), also emerged during this period.

In general, these groups laid claim to experimentation spaces outside the conventional art circuit,[24] producing activist art strategies that evidenced the tension of their relationships with hegemonic cultural representations. Founded by eight students from the School of Communications and Arts of the University of São Paulo in 1978,[25] Viajou Sem Passaporte (VSP) was connected to Trotskyist organizations and influenced by Surrealism.[26] All over the city VSP carried out what its members called "creative interventions": "public activities designed to put the normality reigning in situations outside the group into crisis. These activities can only catch on when aimed at creativity and at a questioning of the situation that's been achieved." [27] Some of these interventions were, for instance, VSP members walking around a tree for one minute (*Trajetória da Árvore* [Tree Trajectory], March 1979), or entering a bus wearing eye patches, getting on and off the bus on a certain route and surprising the passengers (*Trajetória do Curativo*

21

More specifically, the project *Arte ao Ar Livre* (1981–1982), also with the participation of collectives 3Nós3, Viajou Sem Passaporte, and Centro de Livre Expressão.

22

These theater groups were composed of union leaders and workers. See: Kátia Rodrigues Paranhos, "Militância, arte e política: o teatro engajado no Brasil pós-1964," 2008, available online at: www.brasa.org/Documents/BRASA_IX/Katia-Rodrigues-Paranhos.pdf, accessed 09/12/2014.

23

For the beginning of the punk movement in São Paulo, as well as other Latin American cities, please refer to the text I wrote with the Chilean researcher Fernanda Carvajal, "P(A)nk" for the exhibition catalog *Perder la forma humana: Una imagen sísmica de los años ochenta en América Latina* [Losing the Human Form: A Seismic Image of the 1980s in Latin America], by Red Conceptualismos del Sur, Museo Nacional Centro de Arte Reina Sofía, Madrid, 2012, pp. 211–220.

24

On the collective actions in São Paulo during the political opening see: Mario Ramiro, "Grupo 3Nós3. The Outside Expands," in: Chantal Pontbriand (ed.), *Parachute – São Paulo*, nº 116, Montreal, 2004, pp. 41–53; Mario Ramiro, "Between Form and Force: Connecting Architectonic, Telematic and Thermal Spaces," in: Eduardo Kac (ed.), "A Radical Intervention: The Brazilian Contribution to the International Electronic Art Movement," in: *Leonardo*, vol. 31, no. 4, 1998, available online at: http://leonardo.info/isast/spec.projects/ramiro/ramiro.html, accessed 09/12/2014. Please also refer to Otília Arantes, Celso Favaretto, Iná Costa, and Walter Addeo (eds.), *Arte em Revista*, "Independentes," # 8, year 6, October 1984.

25

Luiz Sergio Ragnole (Raghy), Beatriz Caldana, Celso Seabra Santiago, Carlos Alberto Gordon, Marli de Souza Melo, Márcia Meirelles, Marilda Buzzini Carvalho, and Roberto Pereira de Mello were members of Viajou Sem Passaporte.

[Eye Patch Route], April 1979). These actions may perhaps seem meaningless, but they sought to stimulate the imagination and incite collective creation, provoking disruptive and disturbing situations at a time still marked by dictatorship.

It is also worth mentioning here the later collective role of subcultures in São Paulo and the creation of concrete production and distribution alternatives. The second generation of São Paulo hardcore punk, in part represented by the Straight Edge community as of the 1990s, considerably expanded the ethics of a do-it-yourself culture with its own networks of shows, albums, and fanzines. Since 1996, people connected to that group have produced one of the most important independent events in Latin America, Verdurada.[28] This brings people closer to another way of making politics within the heterogeneous construct of contemporary mobilizations against neoliberalism. At the beginning of the 2000s, people connected to the organization of Verdurada joined the Dias de Ação Global [Global Days of Action] protests. The Verdurada hardcore shows provided debates and workshop spaces for direct action such as the creation of affinity groups and implementation of collective decision-making processes, as well as holding lectures and discussions on socially relevant issues for the group in charge of the event which still continue today (gentrification and right to the city, housing movements, abortion, feminism, copyleft, etc.). Back then, in the early 2000s during the anticapitalism protests, activists engaged in democratizing access to and distribution of images about independent movements, and made videos of demonstrations which were shown between the band performances. Brochures, banners, and alternative publications provided the Verdurada audience with information and invited them to participate in the activities connected with the local and global actions.

26 I analyze these connections between Trotskyism and Surrealism of the group Viajou Sem Passaporte and their contact with other collectives with the same creation principles of an independent, revolutionary art movement – the Argentinians Taller de Investigaciones Teatrales and Grupo de Arte Experimental Cucaño – in my article "Intervención/Interversión/Interposición," coauthored with Ana Longoni, Jaime Vindel, Fernanda Nogueira, and Malena La Rocca, and published in the catalog *Perder la forma humana*, pp. 165–175. Another version of an article I wrote on this subject will be published in English in: Gavin Grindon (ed.), *Art, Production and Social Movement: Remapping the History of the Radical Avant-Garde*, Autonomedia & Minor Compositions, New York (NY), forthcoming.

27 Viajou Sem Passaporte, *U.S.B.A.E.A.E.*, independent publication, São Paulo, November 1979, p. 2; translated from the Portuguese by Cinescript Berlin.

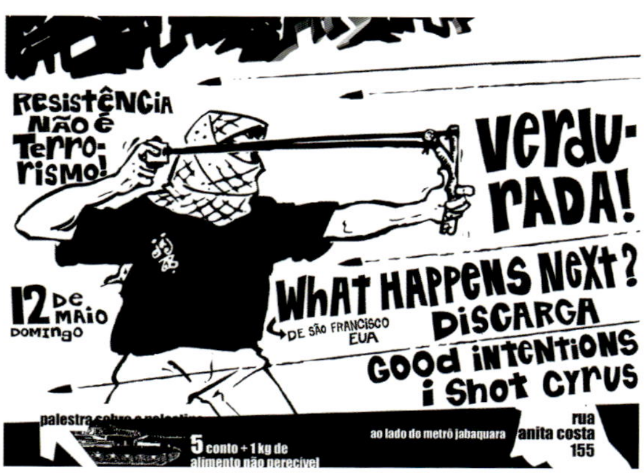

Poster for the Verdurada concert in São Paulo, designed by Frederico Freitas, May 2002

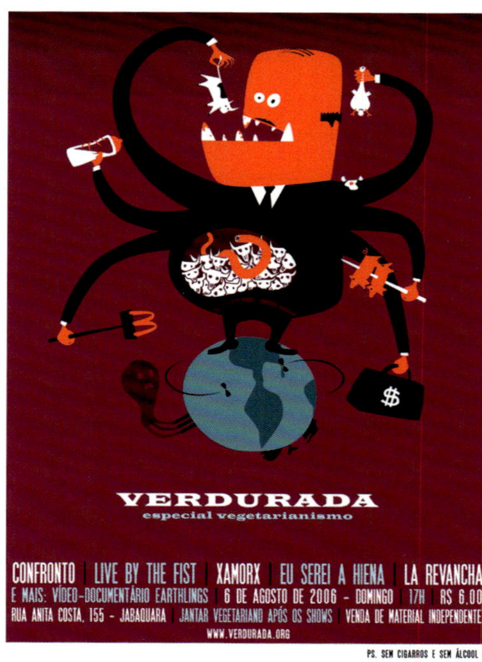

Poster for the Verdurada concert in São Paulo, designed by Frederico Freitas, August 2006

Ratos de Porão concert at the Verdurada festival in São Paulo, July 2007

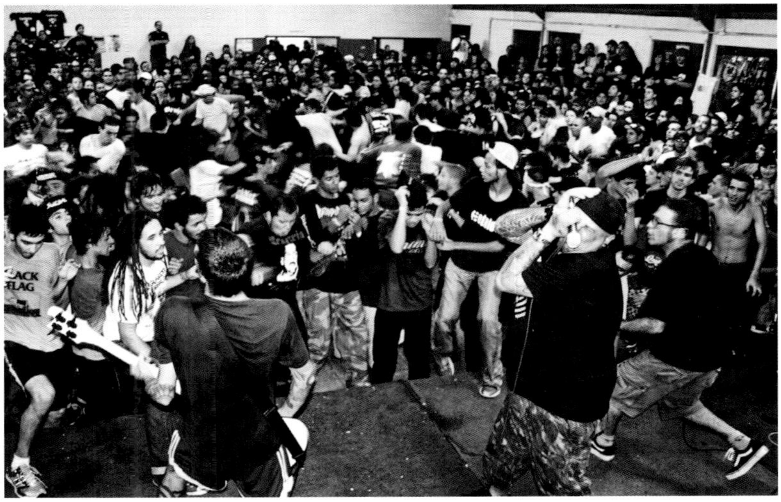

I Shot Cyrus concert at the Verdurada festival in São Paulo, January 2009

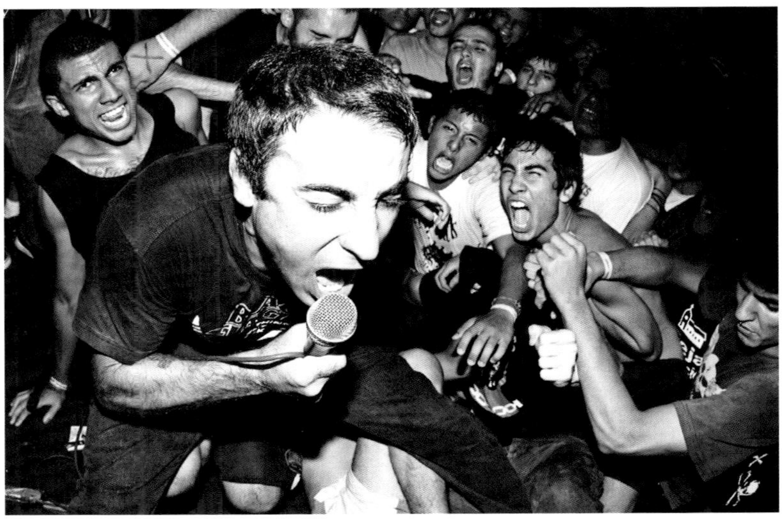

28

The author of this text is a member of the collective that has been organizing Verdurada for over ten years. Briefly, we define Verdurada as an event that can be described as "the presentation of bands – usually hardcore bands – and political lectures, in addition to workshops, debates, video and art exhibitions. At the end of the concert, a free vegetarian meal is provided [...]. There are basically two aims of those organizing Verdurada: to show that you can have successful events without being sponsored by major companies and paid media ads, and to take to the public music made by angry youngsters and the ideas and opinions of different theorists and activists." See: www.verdurada.org; translated from the Portuguese by Cinescript Berlin.

29

Claude Lévi-Strauss, *A World on the Wane*, Criterion Books, New York (NY), 1961, p. 101.

30

See: Cristina Freire, *Além dos mapas: os monumentos no imaginário urbano contemporâneo*, SESC, Annablume, São Paulo, 1997, pp. 41–55.

3. From Monuments to Collective Memory

In his book *Tristes Tropiques* [literally: The Sad Tropics; English title *A World on the Wane*] (1955), Claude Lévi-Strauss already noted in the 1930s that São Paulo's rate of development was very fast indeed. "São Paulo is growing so fast that you can't buy a map of it; there'd have to be a new edition every week."[29] Of course, each map would include references to many monuments. But what is the purpose of these monuments? Teacher and curator Cristina Freire says the monuments enable the possibility of spatial reference through perception, and time reference through memory. The relationship between the inhabitants of a certain city and its monuments is looking at the city beyond its immediate functionality, favoring its historical and aesthetic element.[30] By definition, official monuments rarely enable some kind of participation in the process of their creation and represent a singular point of view, usually focused on major events and the history of "victors."[31] Thus it is necessary to multiply the perspectives through having alternative histories about the city and its monuments, so that interventions or the creation of ephemeral memorials can aid the political mobilization of eclipsed memories, radical denunciation and social change narratives that cannot be ignored.

Something curious happened in São Paulo when a certain monument was returned to the public space. A group of students from the University of São Paulo "kidnapped" the Federico García Lorca Monument, a sculpture by Flávio de Carvalho erected in a public square and damaged in 1969 by an explosion attributed to the Comando de Caça aos Comunistas (CCC).[32] Brochures left at the scene by CCC described the action as the destruction of the monument of a "Communist and homosexual" writer. The sculpture was restored by Carvalho in 1971 and placed outside the building of the Biennial exhibition at the Ibirapuera Park for two days. It then returned to the warehouse at the request of the ambassador to Spain. In 1979, a group of students from the School of Communications and Arts (some were contributors to the newspaper *Cine Olho*) and from the School of Architecture and Urbanism used fake documents to enter the warehouse and "steal" the sculpture, which was restored once again and put in the open hall of the São Paulo Museum of Art (MASP). A few days later, the sculpture was placed again at the square where it was first installed.

That same year the students placed the sculpture at MASP, the group 3Nós3 (comprising Mario Ramiro, Hudinilson, Jr., and Rafael França) performed its "interversions" during the evening, as the group called its "landscape perception inversion actions, which go way beyond the simple idea of being placed there."[33] With their ephemeral installations constructed with industrial material, 3Nós3 "interfered" in the city in the sense of inverting the order and the habitual flow through major public spaces. The first 3Nós3 intervention took place on April 27, 1979, when the then President, General João Figueiredo, was expected to visit São Paulo. The three artists had the idea of surprising the presidential party. Based on the Land art interventions and on the large-scale Christo and Jeanne-Claude projects of "wrapping" trees, buildings, and other constructions, 3Nós3 decided to do something smaller, but equally impressive: bagging São Paulo statues. With São Paulo's map in hand, Hudinilson, Jr. created a route between the Ipiranga area and downtown. Early in the morning, the group "attacked" the monuments, bagging a large number of statue heads, "suffocating" them with plastic trash bags, and wrapping up their arms. The photographs documenting the action seem to witness scenes of torturing these huge bodies and suggest a metaphor of the silence and violence that suppressed those who were opposed to the military government in Brazil and in most of Latin America, but it was also an active demonstration in relation to public property that is rarely noticed by the passersby.[34]

In the morning, the artists made an anonymous phone call to the city newspapers asking them to verify the odd events surrounding the monuments. The *Ensacamento* [Bagging] operation was all over the news. Articles about 3Nós3, which also appeared

31 Nicolas Lampert, "Struggles at Haymarket: An Embattled History of Static Monuments and Public Interventions," in: Josh MacPhee and Erik Reuland (eds.), *Realizing the Impossible. Art Against Authority*, AK Press, Oakland (CA), Edinburgh, 2007, pp. 254–271, here p. 261.

32 Comando de Caça aos Comunistas [Command for Communist Hunting] is a far-right organization established in the early 1960s responsible for attacks and assaults on venues and left-wing groups.

33 Stella Teixeira de Barros, "Out-Arte?," in: Arantes, Favaretto, Costa, and Addeo 1984, p. 50; translated from the Portuguese by Cinescript Berlin.

34 I am extremely grateful to Mario Ramiro for telling me the details of this story during an interview in August 2011. In relation to the intervention *Ensacamento* and a reflection about its political aspect see: Erin Denise Aldana, *Interventions into Urban and Art Historical Spaces: The Work of the Artist Group 3Nós3 in Context, 1979–1982*, PhD thesis, University of Texas at Austin, Austin (TX), 2008.

in magazines and radio and TV programs, were a practical and cheap means for the group to document and disseminate the records of its works, sharing them with other people. By bringing the press to the place of action, Mario Ramiro says the media material produced by 3Nós3 became part of the contents of his art books. “There was a Mail art boom at that time. Photos were turned into Xerox copies; basic information was added, you made a postcard out of that, and that would go around the world.”[35]

The idea of drawing the attention of people who walk through the streets every day and rarely notice the monuments around them gets a political dimension when *antimonuments* are introduced that are witness to and identify conflicts which gives rise to symbolic and discursive reverberations. Above all, when and how to act within this terrain of disagreement requires a long process of intuition, reflection, and experimentation by artists-activists; a clearer understanding of the space, time, and memory relationships. It requires “an art of saying” at the right time. Michel de Certeau focuses on these assumptions by suggesting a pattern that differentiates between the action space and the action time: “in the composition of the initial place (I), the work of the memory (II) intervenes at the ‘right moment’ (III) and produces modifications of the space (IV).”[36] Time is the intermediary space that leads to the transition from one place to another: “Memory mediates spatial transformations. In the mode of the ‘right point in time’ *(kairos)*, it produces a founding rupture or break. Its foreignness makes possible a transgression of the law of the place. Coming out of its bottomless and mobile secrets, a *‘coup’* modifies the local order.”[37] In this sense, the urban intervention practices of Brazilian groups are a way of “knocking on the city spaces,” questioning social situations, or questioning the autonomy of art to advocate its use value and enhance a communicative, socializing force among many other people.

When the Contrafilé group put up its monument at Largo do Arouche – a very famous square in the center of São Paulo – the intervention produced at that right point in time the awareness of the need to develop a counter-history of the city. The artwork gained a life of its own because it was multiplied in other media and contexts. During an event called *Zona de Ação* [Action Zone] (2004), the participating groups (BijaRi, C.O.B.A.I.A., A Revolução Não Será Televisionada, Frente 3 de Fevereiro, and the Argentinian Grupo de Arte Callejero) each chose an area of the city where they would carry out a project. Although it had almost no affinity to or experience with the area,

35

André Mesquita, *Insurgências Poéticas: Arte Ativista e Ação Coletiva*, Annablume, FAPESP, São Paulo, 2011, p. 220; translated from the Portuguese by Cinescript Berlin.

36

Michel de Certeau, *The Practice of Everyday Life*, University of California Press, Berkeley (CA), 1988, p. 84.

37

De Certeau 1988, p. 85.

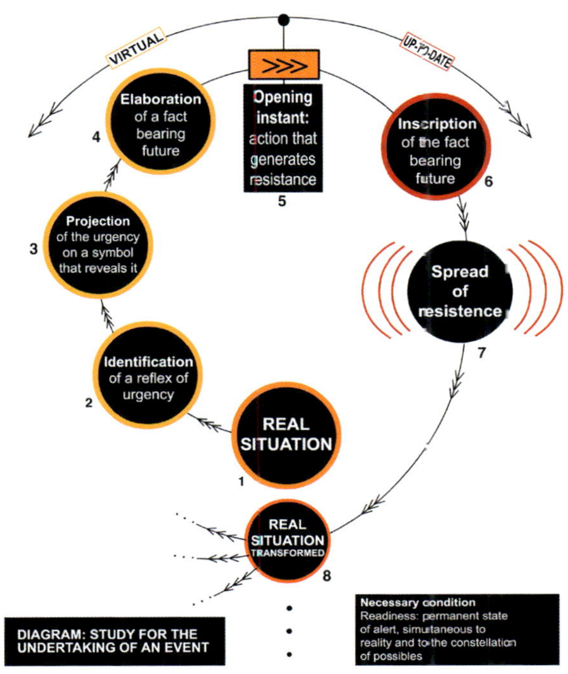

Contrafilé, *Diagram: An Event Study*, São Paulo, 2005

Contrafilé decided to carry out its project in the East Zone of São Paulo. The group then discussed social borders, reasons for these, and the inconvenience and hardship involved in going from downtown to the outskirts to carry out an intervention in almost unknown territory, but also the possibility of taking advantage of this situation to understand and materialize a conflicting feeling. One of the members of Contrafilé, Cibele Lucena, said:

> "We thought, 'why do we feel this way?', 'what is the nature of this feeling?' We understood these visible and invisible, economic and social distances ... We started drawing on the map to see how difficult it is to get to the East Zone, because we rarely go to the Itaquera district. We decided to talk about that, about our own conflict, and then we thought, 'wow, there seems to be a turnstile between us and the East Zone!' And there are many types of turnstile, turnstiles we internalize, turnstiles that are contradictions for ourselves."[38]

38 Mesquita 2011, p. 248; translated from the Portuguese by Cinescript Berlin.

At "public look gatherings," meetings held with a group of inhabitants from the East Zone, Contrafilé shared ideas and collected personal accounts in which people provided examples of spaces with physical or abstract turnstiles. Gradually, Contrafilé and those who attended the meetings visualized an image of an object that symbolized the biopolitical control that exists in visible and invisible locations. A turnstile found at a junkyard was placed anonymously by the group on a Largo do Arouche pedestal. In the past, the pedestal had carried a bust of the writer Guilherme de Almeida. The *Monumento à Catraca Invisível* [Monument to the Invisible Turnstile] with its sign was placed in front of the building of the Historical Heritage Department, and in 2004 inaugurated the group's "Programa para Descatracalização da Própria Vida" [Program for the Deturnstilization of Life Itself].

The symbolic and anonymous Contrafilé intervention was impressive enough for the *Folha de S. Paulo* newspaper to write an article about "an invisible turnstile" which had suddenly emerged at Largo do Arouche,[39] and the paper later learned that the group was responsible for the artistic action.[40] Soon, the turnstile as a social event was the subject of a strategic discussion between activists and co-optionists, which led to differentiated discourse and points of view. In January 2005, one of the most controversial university entrance examinations in the country, FUVEST (University Foundation for Vestibular) – the entrance examination for the University of São Paulo – used the newspaper article as part of the set questions and asked the students to write an essay about the "deturnstilization of life." A columnist at the *Folha de S. Paulo* newspaper reacted to this by writing an article criticizing the university's examiners' choice of subject for the essay, claiming that it was "outdated" and motivated by "an obsolete, dated spirit."[41] Banco Itaú did not pass up the opportunity of appropriating the group's artistic point of view and turning it into the catchword of an advertising campaign: "Vestibulando, descatracalize a sua vida. Abra uma conta no Itaú." [Student, remove the turnstile of your life. Open an account at Itaú.]

39 See: "'Catraca invisível' ocupa lugar de estátua no Arouche," in: *Folha de S. Paulo*, September 4, 2004, caderno Cotidiano, available online at: www1.folha.uol.com.br/fsp/cotidian/ff0409200419.htm, accessed 09/12/2014.

40 See: "Grupo assume autoria da 'catraca invisível,'" in: *Folha de S. Paulo*, September 9, 2004, caderno Cotidiano, available online at: www1.folha.uol.com.br/fsp/cotidian/ff0909200404.htm, accessed 09/12/2014.

41 Fernando Barros e Silva, "Pegadinha do Fuvestão," in: *Folha de S. Paulo*, January 11, 2005, Opinião, p. A2; translated from the Portuguese by Cinescript Berlin.

On the other hand, after the university entrance examinations and appropriation for advertising purposes had been criticized, the symbol chosen by the group appeared autonomously again in other activist actions. At the FUVEST building, students burned a turnstile as a protest about the university entrance examination in general and registration fees as social and economic impediments. In the “Manifesto pela Descatracalização da Educação” [Manifest for a Deturnstilization of Education] (2005), students from popular university preparation courses, student club members, and postgraduate students protested about the excluding mechanism of admission at universities, “against barriers, walls, and turnstiles that separate most young people from the knowledge produced at universities. Because university entrance examinations are a huge funnel, we demand their immediate elimination.”[42]

42 Centro de Mídia Independente, “Ato pela Descatracalização da Educação” (2005), available online at: www.midiaindependente.org/pt/blue/2005/02/306571.shtml, accessed 09/12/2014; translated from the Portuguese by Cinescript Berlin.

43 See: www.mpl.org.br and the blog http://farefreebrazil.blogspot.com.br with English articles, both accessed 09/12/2014.

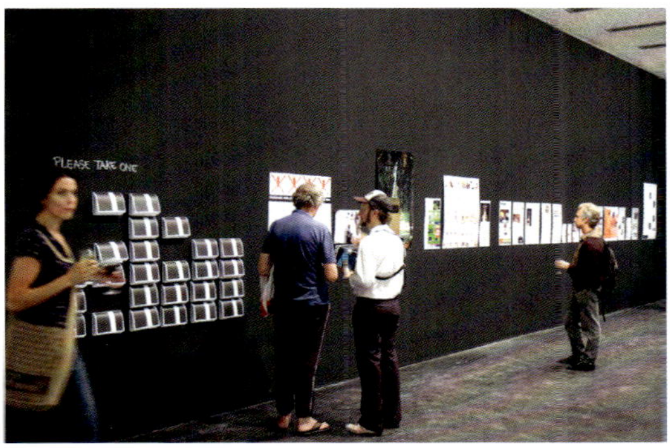

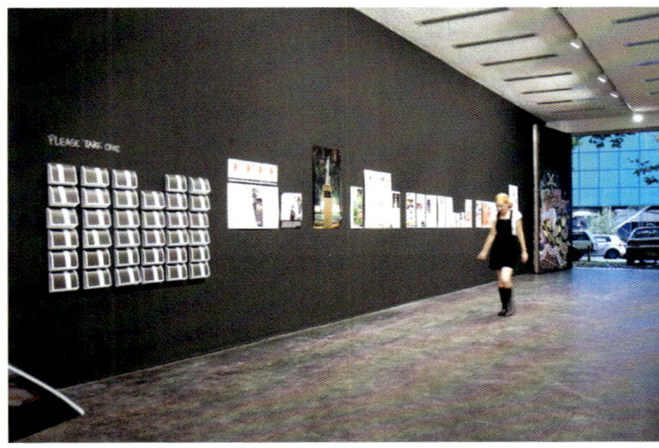

Contrafilé, documentation of the intervention *Programa para “Descatracalização da Própria Vida”* (July 2004) in São Paulo, presented at the exhibition *If You See Something, Say Something* in Sydney, Australia, 2007

The Movimento Passe Livre (MPL) [Free Fare Movement],[43] an independent, nonpartisan, and horizontal social movement comprising students, workers, artists, teachers, and university researchers, who fight for free public transportation in association with other urban issues (including a living wage, access to accommodation, health care, education, democratization of the media, and culture), became very prominent as of 2003 in the cities of Salvador, Florianópolis, and São Paulo. The turnstile also featured in their actions – either as an object to be set on fire or as an object being hopped over by protesters as a symbol of “uma vida sem catracas” [a life without turnstiles].[44] The MPL’s political demand is free use of public transportation for all, ensuring everyone’s right to come and go as they please. In Brazil this demand goes back to the student movements of the early 1980s, who also demanded free public transport.[45] In the protests of June 2013, thousands of demonstrators took to the streets of São Paulo in protest at the increase in public transport fares. These protests were called for by MPL and were nationally supported. Drawings and stencils of turnstiles made during the protests can still be seen on walls, and are a continuing reminder of the urgent need to keep debating the possibility of a plan for free public transport. At public events the MPL members “pay tribute” to the politicians that only appear to serve the monetary interests of businessmen in the transport sector, who bring hardship to the citizens by axing bus routes and restricting access to the city, by presenting them with a “Turnstile Trophy.”[46]

44 MPL was officially founded as a national movement in 2005 during the World Social Forum in Porto Alegre. However, the struggle for the Free Fare Campaign began in the city of Florianópolis in 2000.

45 See: the interview with the militant Marcelo Pomar made by Coletivo Maria Tonha at: http://tarifazero.org/2013/07/25/ele-ajudou-a-fundar-o-movimento-passe-livre-entrevista-com-marcelo-pomar, accessed 09/12/2014.

46 This happened to the São Paulo mayor of the time, Gilberto Kassab, who was given a Turnstile Trophy for being the mayor who increased bus fares the most during his term of office.

Social contamination with images circulated spontaneously and unpredictably, such as the turnstile as a symbol of control and the daily struggle for them to be removed, is enhanced through collaboration between artists and political movements that produces freely shared visual tools and creative strategies – something that a few historical initiatives which took place in Latin America have been able to achieve. *Siluetazo* (1983) is one of them, a project initially carried out by artists Rodolfo Aguerreberry, Julio Flores, and Guillermo Kexel. At a workshop held in a public square with hundreds of participants, life-size drawings of people's silhouettes were made and printed on paper and then attached to walls, trees, and monuments to illustrate and demand "Aparición con Vida" [Bring Them Back Alive] for the thirty thousand people who went missing between 1976 and 1983 during the military dictatorship in Argentina. The action was supported by the Mothers of the Plaza

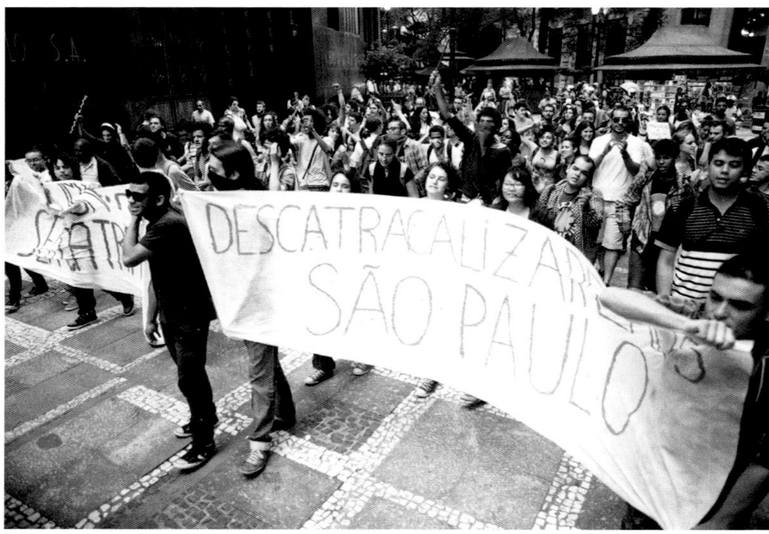

Movimento Passe Livre protest in the streets of São Paulo, October 25, 2012

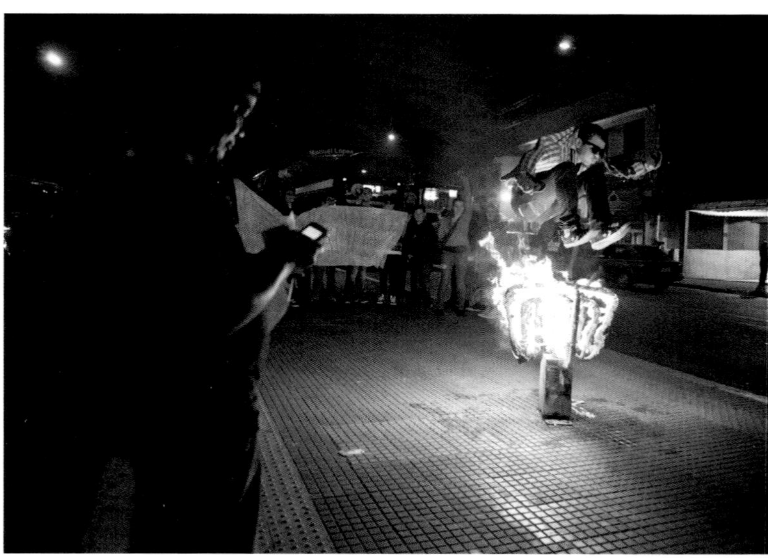

A man jumps a turnstile in flames during a protest made by the Movimento Passe Livre at the Jardim Ângela neigborhood in São Paulo, October 26, 2012.

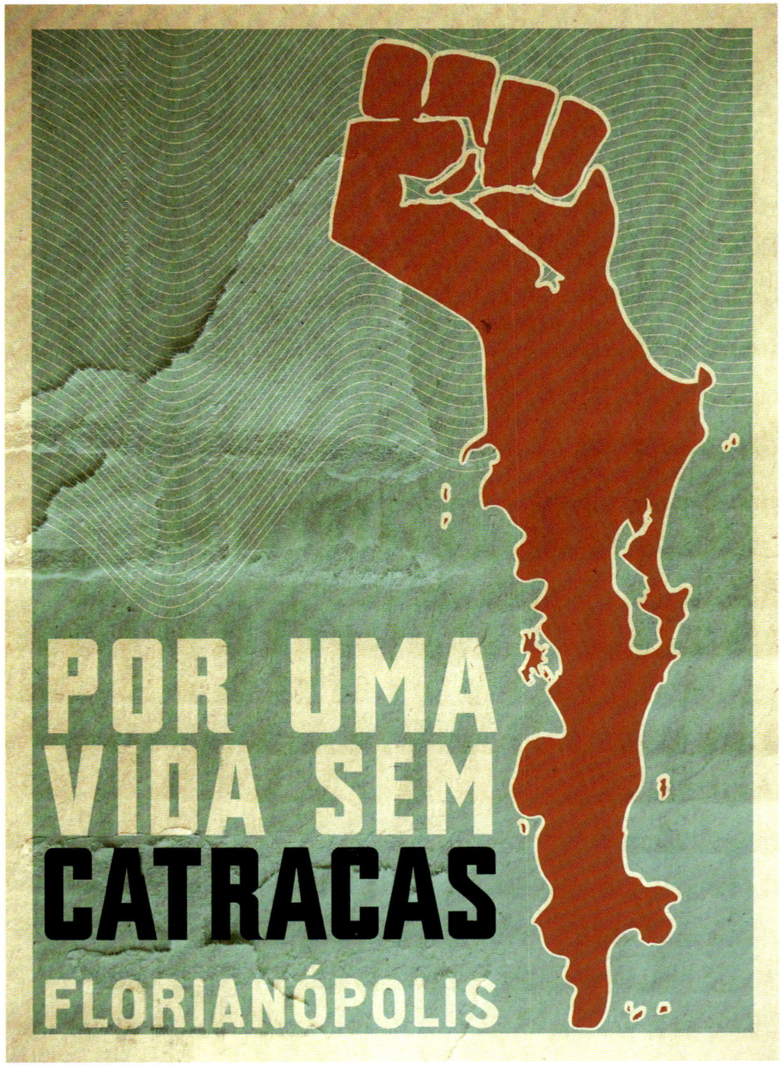

Poster for the Movimento Passe Livre in Florianópolis with the slogan "For a life without turnstiles," designed by André Mesquita with Yuri Gama, 2009

de Mayo and human rights organizations, and its topic became the central demand of a social movement employing collective action that is embodied by a multitude.[47] That same year, 1983, when Chile reached its tenth year of military government, CADA (Colectivo Acciones de Arte) spread throughout Santiago, using slogans and graffiti on walls; the formula "NO+," which was later incorporated, completed and transversally spread the demands of many movements protesting on the streets ("NO+ fear," "NO+ dictatorship," "NO+ hunger," etc.), no longer by the hands of the artists.[48]

Monumentum is a sign from the past, which mainly specializes in celebrating the work or perpetuating the remembrance of a person in a domain where the memory is particularly valued: death.[49] The construction of monuments by artist-activists foregrounds nonofficial versions or forgotten facts. A popular monument can perpetuate the memory of something that must be remembered as

47

Ana Longoni and Gustavo Bruzzone (eds.), *El Siluetazo*, Adriana Hidalgo Editora, Buenos Aires, 2008, p. 8.

48

As for the multiple, participative condition of the actions such as *Siluetazo* and "NO+," please refer to the article "Socialización del Arte" in the catalog *Perder la forma humana*, pp. 226–235. For images and documents of these two actions, see the website Archivos en Uso [Archives in Use], a project by Red Conceptualismos del Sur: www.archivosenuso.org, accessed 09/14/2014.

49

See: Jacques Le Goff, "Documento/Monumento," in: *Enciclopédia Einaudi. História e Memória*, Editora da Unicamp, Campinas, 1990, pp. 95–106.

an attitude that turns urban violence into social change. The first action of the multidisciplinary group Frente 3 de Fevereiro arose from the uneasiness of its members who wanted to denounce the existence of social contradictions in Brazil, which in spite of its claim to be an ideal multiracial democracy and a "racism-free" country had witnessed the death of a young black man at the hands of the São Paulo police because they perceived him as a "threat." The group set up a monument in the North Zone of the city to visualize and publicize the event and the issue. At the spot where the 28-year-old black dentist Flávio Sant'Ana was thought to be a "thief" and was brutally murdered by the police for "looking suspicious" on February 3, 2004, the group placed a sign on the asphalt accompanied by friends and parents of the victim. Over a red background, the sign with the body silhouette, inspired by the Argentinian *Siluetazo* event, carried the inscription "Aqui, Flávio F. Sant'Ana foi morto pela Polícia Militar de São Paulo" [Flávio F. Sant'Ana was killed here by the São Paulo Military Police]. The *Monumento Horizontal* [Horizontal Monument] (April 2004) was designed to be a permanent intervention so that it would not be forgotten as just one among hundreds of violent police racism cases that we see in Brazil every day. The sign was removed by military police officers the next day. A week later, the group returned to the scene and created a new monument, this time with concrete and red paint. The final intervention was impressive: the image of a body covered in "blood and open wounds." [50] The next morning, the monument was once again destroyed by police officers.

Removing a monument can restore "the meaning of value where meanings take turns as overlaying archeological sites. Because values are socially and historically built, changing is a must." [51] Activists are also building ephemeral, collaborative memorials. On January 2009, Bicicletada activists, who ride bicycles in a city dominated by cars and traffic, turned an Avenida Paulista site into a memorial and tribute to forty-year-old biker Márcia Regina de Andrade Prado, who died after she was hit by a bus there. A "Ghost Bike" was placed there for a few days after the accident and powerfully symbolized those who die every day in the traffic of major cities. The creation of a memorial to dead bikers in urban traffic, according to Gregory Sholette, has been repeated around the world, and this action can strengthen or redefine the role of art within life and its producers at a time when autonomous, invisible, collective forms of creativity of this "dark matter" [52] are also being explored by capitalist entrepreneurial culture.[53] At the same time, the protest enables a response that uses the bodies and imaginations of all those involved to challenge capitalist culture's alienated form of this combination of action and awareness, which waives the ego – it is absorbed into the flow – and it gives rise to a new perception that is completed by the collective performance experience.[54] Even at a protest like the Global Day of Action against capitalism, when autonomous groups walked all over São Paulo carrying out actions together at the World Social Forum, activists put on theater plays and represented the "Empire" as a monument transfigured by a giant George W. Bush puppet. These protests demand considerable artistic production efforts and social organization, but

50

Frente 3 de Fevereiro, *Zumbi Somos Nós: Cartografia do Racismo para o Jovem Urbano*, VAI, Prefeitura de São Paulo, São Paulo, 2007, p. 20; translated from the Portuguese by Cinescript Berlin.

51

Freire 1997, p. 55; translated from the Portuguese by Cinescript Berlin.

52

See: Gregory Sholette, *Dark Matter. Art and Politics in the Age of Enterprise Culture*, Pluto Press, London, New York (NY), 2011.

53

See: Gregory Sholette, *Gifts of Resistance*, independent publication, New York (NY), 2008, p. 9, available online at: www.gregorysholette.com/wp-content/uploads/2011/04/GiftsOfResistance.Perifieric.1.pdf, accessed on 09/12/2014.

54

See: Victor Turner, *The Anthropology of Performance*, PAJ Publications, New York (NY), 1988, p. 107.

they retrieve a nonalienated experience of collective festivities and the reinforcing tactics and visual elements of a demonstration (banners, posters, costumes, performances, music, and so on). Following the activist tradition of symbolizing the power of the World Bank or the World Trade Organization by using giant scarecrows and puppets, with arms so large they can block an entire avenue, these images created with ephemeral, cheap materials are turned into satires on and metaphors of the conditions of the survival of major historical monuments and the attempt to make them eternal as factual symbols.[55] Burning turnstiles, bagging statues, *siluetazos*, memorials, or giant puppets, regardless of their purposes, are questioning definitive versions of events and the news produced by the media, which tends to describe activist actions as "violent" when they occupy the city and its history in a fluid manner. Political and ephemeral memorials, public look gatherings, and temporary interventions expand the notions of social sculpture and, as pointed out by David Graeber, mock the idea of eternal veracity that the monuments of great "winners" seek to represent, becoming symbols "of this attempt to seize the power of social creativity, the power to recreate and redefine institutions."[56]

55 See: David Graeber, "On the Phenomenology of Giant Puppets: Broken Windows, Imaginary Jars of Urine, and the Cosmological Role of the Police in American Culture," in: David Graeber, *Possibilities: Essays on Hierarchy, Rebellion, and Desire*, AK Press, Oakland (CA), Edinburgh 2007, pp. 375–417.

56 Ibid., p. 408.

4. Dissonant Notes

The recent history of downtown São Paulo tells us about the trajectory of an important living, organic monument that exists in one of its streets. On November 2002, this "monument," the building located at Avenida Prestes Maia, 911, was occupied by a housing movement, Movimento Sem-Teto do Centro (MSTC) [Homeless Workers Movement], in which nearly two thousand people joined the fight against exclusion and social segregation in the city until they were removed from the premises by public authorities in June 2007. The specter of the Prestes Maia Occupation still hovers over the trajectories of many supporters, activists, and artist collectives of São Paulo who created in that building the experimentation of symbolic and collaborative tactics of creative dissent. The basement walls of two 13- and 22-floor buildings, which belonged to a linen factory in the 1950s, seemed to "talk" about its daily life in many different ways. On the walls, there were posters, paper reproductions of photos, graffiti, and other records made by the collectives, as well as children's drawings and simple ink inscriptions telling the histories of the 468 families that lived there, alternating between resistance narratives, personal images, and allegories in that improvised exhibition space.

Considered until then as the largest vertical occupation of Latin America, the Prestes Maia was in a strategic area of gentrification processes, which provide for clearance of an area before it is redeveloped. "When the recapitalization of gentrification occurs, many of the original residents have already been forced out or are forced to live under grotesque conditions."[57] In media and society as a whole, degeneration is the image portrayed and associated with downtown São Paulo: a large number of tenements, abandoned buildings, homeless people, and insecurity, plus the atmosphere typical of informal street vendors.[58] By uniting

57 Martha Rosler, "Fragments of a Metropolitan Viewpoint," in: Brian Wallis (ed.), *If You Lived Here. The City in Art, Theory, and Social Activism. A Project by Martha Rosler*, Bay Press, Seattle (WA), 1991, pp. 15–43, here p. 26.

58 Hélène Rivière d'Arc, "Requalificar o século XX: projeto para o centro de São Paulo," in: Catherine Bidou-Zachariasen (ed.), *De Volta à Cidade: dos processos de gentrificação às políticas de "revitalização" dos centros urbanos*, Annablume, São Paulo, 2006, pp. 265–293, here p. 270.

dilapidation and regeneration, corporate investments downtown expanded, for instance, the so-called "cultural corridors," such as the Sala São Paulo theater next to the Pinacoteca do Estado, which strive to retrieve the glamour of this area so that it is more attractive to the middle class, to the real estate segments, and to the consumer and tourism markets.

Used to a life of legal deadlocks, threats of actions for repossession by the police forces, and a popular struggle that many times blended or had intense clashes with the art collectives working there, the Prestes Maia Occupation was an intense, vibrant part of downtown. The artworks produced by the 120 artists and groups that approached Prestes Maia in December 2003 at the exhibition *Arte Contemporânea no Movimento Sem-Teto do Centro (ACMSTC)* [Contemporary Art at the Downtown Homeless Movement], followed by other actions carried out by the collectives BijaRi, Catadores de Histórias, Cia. Cachorra, Coletivo Dragão da Gravura, Elefante, Espaço Coringa, Esqueleto Coletivo, Experiência Imersiva Ambiental (EIA), Frente 3 de Fevereiro, Nova Pasta, Tranca Rua, and the coalition Integração Sem Posse, tried to change the image of a movement that is usually perceived as "marginal" or "illegal" by most people. The intention was to show their cultural and collective organization which was trying to improve that place, such as the library with nearly sixteen thousand books set up by one of the inhabitants, Mr. Severino.

The aesthetic vocabulary of a squat art subculture – founded in urban interventions, performances, direct action, *escraches*, tactical media, culture jamming on advertising billboards, installations made with real estate signs, collages, engravings and wheatpastes on the walls and the external facade of the Prestes Maia Occupation – helped to build ephemeral barricades to lessen the violent police work during actions for repossession experienced by other occupations, such as Plínio Ramos in August 2005, and "visual ambushes" to seize the great media narrative in relation to housing movements. For instance, the "ZUMBI SOMOS NÓS" [We Are Zumbi] flag designed by Frente 3 de Fevereiro and placed on top of Prestes Maia, which directly connected to the idea of seeing the movement as a major urban *quilombo* settlement;[59] the performances of the groups Catadores de Histórias and Tranca Rua; the political engravings made by Espaço Coringa or Coletivo Dragão da Gravura (with the slogan "INTEGRAÇÃO SEM POSSE X REINTEGRAÇÃO DE POSSE" [Action with No Possession X Action for Repossession]); antigentrification posters designed by BijaRi or the poster "VIDA X PROPRIEDADE" [Life X Property] by Esqueleto Coletivo, pointing out the dichotomies between social inequality and economic interests; appropriation and subversion of real estate signs later turned into barriers by the collective Elefante, which, together, formed the word "DIGNIDADE" [Dignity]; an antigentrification exhibition with interventions carried out with these signs, the *Salão de Placas Imobiliárias (SPLAC)* [Real Estate Signs' Room], promoted by EIA at a square; and the sign with the expression "ZONA DE POESIA ÁRIDA" [Arid Poetry Zone], placed at the Prestes Maia Occupation by Cia. Cachorra. These are examples of interventions that aimed to meet the direct

59 During colonial times in Brazil, *quilombo* settlements were the shelters of slaves and marginalized minorities, and Zumbi dos Palmares was one of their famous leaders. In an interview with one of the members of Frente 3 de Fevereiro, Daniel Lima, the comparison between the Prestes Maia Occupation and the settlements is perceived as follows: "We are not working with the idea of the black person as a victim of society, but as an active expression. Hence the idea of *quilombo* connected with Zumbi, which welcomes not only black people, but which opens and embraces all those who are marginalized by the colonial structure: indigenous peoples, black people, white people, poor people, and white people who did not fit into the colonial structure. They are all being assimilated within the resistance idea of the *quilombo* settlement. Taking that to today's world, if we ask what does *quilombo* mean today, the answer is Prestes Maia. There you find a group of marginalized people – certainly with darker skin, a more mixed-race group. People who are completely integrated into society, but in a completely underprivileged position. Quilombo dos Palmares was also not isolated; it conducted business with all farms within an import and export structure. Prestes Maia is our very own contemporary symbol of all of this." This statement is included in the set of interviews I recorded for my research on *Insurgências Poéticas*. It is available online in Portuguese at: http://andremesquita.redezero.org/livro/insurgenciaspoeticas-entrevistas.pdf, accessed 09/12/2014; translated from the Portuguese by Cinescript Berlin.

representation needs of a movement and the building of its image. In this rhetorical sense, one of the purposes of these actions was to "crystallize an image or a response to a blurred social picture, bringing its outlines into focus."[60]

There is no doubt these projects are more or less powerful configurations of a contemporaneous dematerialized political art "tradition" in Latin America, expressing a means to attain the radical effectiveness of its communication and meeting a different public. The social expression of what I refer to as *insurgent conceptualism* seeks to produce strategies in which ideas, means, supports, and linguistic suggestions are freely shared in flexible affiliations, solidarity networks, and temporary meetings. However, whereas it is possible that part of the individual and group authorship can be dissolved in a few actions, the collective capacity of lessening the politicization of its forms of insurgent conceptualism and collaborative production must also be taken into account. The art collective itself can instrumentalize a social movement to achieve greater visibility of its interventions within it, registering them later and presenting them to the art world institutions, moving its "brand name." In addition, the problem of falling into a semidistanced representation of political art and the mere creation of events or "marketing campaigns" for a movement, combining persuasion industry operations with activist transgression, needs to be questioned in this type of initiatives.

It may be useful here to recall Walter Benjamin's figure of the "author as producer," who, in support of other producers and the proletariat (housing movement and inhabitants of an occupation), is willing to share his intellectual and aesthetic production to turn consumers into collaborators.[61] As noticed by artist and art researcher Gavin Adams in an essay about the work of art collectives during the Prestes Maia Occupation, establishing a public space as a space for struggle and poetic creation is done less for symbolic creation and more for the fact that anyone can be responsible for that space and for that creation, without propagating the artist's image as an "expert."[62] The negative consequences of this management process of "art products" by the collectives can lead to well-meant paternalism and objectives that are not always shared. When the voice of collaboration with the community is not heard or it is silenced, the "other" becomes an "accessory" and the collective begins to value its own agenda of interests, successes, and achievements. Rather than portraying social forms or creating battles in the representation domain, with her or his actions the artist-activist should engage "with social life as production," engage "with social life itself as the medium of expression."[63]

It seems to me that collective work itself, in collaboration with the struggles and demands of a social movement, needs to pay attention to a slow, yet careful process of establishing coalitions which aim at producing "solidarity through difference."[64] A continuous experiential education process between different groups with no expropriation is what we need to redesign and create. Encouraging urban diversity through public interventions that grant rights, including to poorer classes, equals "spatial justice." As pointed out by the writer Ava Bromberg, space is not a static container where

60 Rosler 1991, p. 32.

61 See: Walter Benjamin, "The Author as Producer" (1934), in: Walter Benjamin, *Understanding Brecht*, Verso, London, New York (NY), 1998, pp. 85–103.

62 See: Gavin Adams, "Coletivos de arte e a ocupação Prestes Maia em São Paulo," December 2006, available online at: http://desarquivo.org/sites/default/files/adams_gavin_coletivos_no_prestes_maia.pdf, accessed 12/09/2014.

63 Blake Stimson and Gregory Sholette (eds.), *Collectivism after Modernism. The Art of Social Imagination after 1945*, University of Minnesota Press, Minneapolis (MN), London, 2007, p. 13.

64 Critical Art Ensemble, "Observations on Collective Cultural Action," in: *Art Journal*, vol. 57, no. 2, 1998, pp. 73–85, available online at: www.critical-art.net/books/digital/tact4.pdf, accessed 12/09/2014; translated from the Portuguese by Cinescript Berlin.

people live, but something actively produced and reproduced by our choices and relationships. Just as the space has to be claimed, justice is also produced, reproduced, and experimented, and must engage in other social terms so that we can create something really different.[65]

65

See: Ava Bromberg, "The Politics of Spatial Justice," in: Keg de Souza and Zanny Begg (eds.), *There Goes the Neighbourhood: Redfern and the Politics of Urban Space*, Breakdown Press, Melbourne, 2009, pp. 123–124.

5. Where Is the Horizon?

Our drifting through the streets of São Paulo ends with the question, "Where is the horizon?" repeated hundreds of times by Contrafilé in an intervention performed inside a tunnel. The route itself has not ended, and the reader must search for other impossible horizons. If we review the activist art actions described here, and our initial metaphor of the picture game designed by Fahlström as the machine that guided us through the city, we recognize that we cannot "manipulate the world" unless we actively take part in social changes and try to prefigure new realities. The changing horizon of a megacity such as São Paulo seems absolutely far away, and that is why we need to claim the strengthening of our social ties in such a selfish city, our relationships with nature in a space so affected by the gray concrete, the beauty of diversity, and the choice of new life forms in a territory that can be so violent and segregated at times. The right to the city, as pointed out by David Harvey, is much more than the individual freedom fostered by competition and capitalism.[66] It is a common right that transforms ourselves and the place we live in, and which will always depend on exercising the collective, creative power of many people.

66

See: David Harvey, "The Right to the City," in: *New Left Review*, no. 53, September/October 2008, pp. 23–40.

Translated from the Portuguese by Cinescript Berlin.
This essay is a reviewed and updated version of an article published in December 2009 in the Colombian magazine *ERRATA#*, no. 1, "El lugar del arte en lo político," pp. 36–60.

Joulia Strauss

Demonstrations Are Performances

taz [*die tageszeitung*, newspaper]: Ms. Strauss, are you a *refugee*?

Joulia Strauss: My motivation to participate in No Borders activism was not so much a result of my many experiences with the foreigners' registration office, but stems from the entirely natural feeling of compassion and political solidarity in the here and now. As a term, "refugee" is too general and at the same time it carries a stigma. It actually creates the very border, which must be torn down by immediately repealing the present racist laws and by the coexistence of all Berliners. We do not share enough with the needy by far. We concern ourselves with the humanitarian catastrophes of the twentieth century, and just watch while one of the twenty-first century is taking place.

taz: What does *global aCtIVISm* mean?

Strauss: That is the name that Peter Weibel, artist and head of the ZKM, gave to an exhibition, to which he invited a group of researchers and activists, including me, to collaborate. Weibel says that protests are performances in the public space. He also says that activism is the art form of the protest movement. For some, global activism begins in Genoa, for others in Cairo, for yet others in New York; for me it begins in Athens.

taz: What are these phenomena doing in museums?

Strauss: Is the ZKM actually a museum? To me, it is the only place in Europe where an exhibition can be treated as a research process. If every museum reacted to the development of information technologies and changing social structures as fast as the ZKM, the taxpayers would be able to admire and also participate in the art of the twenty-first century: resistant, ingenious, and most importantly, after 2,500 years at last free of the Empire.

taz: What was shown in the exhibition?

Strauss: Things were presented that could be interpreted from at least two perspectives. The exhibits can be viewed as activist art: this is a form of art, which emerged after the abolition of the ontological difference between art and reality. From a different perspective, the exhibits can be seen as artifacts, relics, and traces of activities by global movements. In the exhibition both these perspectives were supposed to come together, like two images merge into one in stereoscopy. At least what I wanted was that the viewers free themselves from the binarism of art and nonart, and transform from being passive observers into activists.

taz: Can you give me an example of such an artifact, please?

Strauss: [...] One example is a series of sculptures by Noah Fischer, which also was an important tool in the public relations work of Occupy Wall Street: masks, carved from wood, showing the faces of Abraham Lincoln and others as they appear on pennies and other U.S. coins, which was worn by Noah during the protests. The coin is one of seven, which are part of the so-called *Manifesto Currency* series (2013; see this volume, pp. 576–577). On one of them it says "Master of Fine Arts." To be awarded this title, artists in America get into debt: on the coin it says "71,851.57 dollars."

taz: How does one exhibit an action?

Strauss: Besides artifacts associated with actions, many documentaries were screened. The ZKM has always worked with video. It's a rare opportunity to see carefully assembled material in a large auditorium so that you can get an impression of the global anticapitalism events.

taz: Did you present any videos?

Strauss: My *Anamorphous Monument to Chelsea Manning* (2010/2013; see this volume, pp. 658–659) was shown: the first 3-D computer portrait as an anamorphous video, created for and exhibited at the 2011 Moscow Biennale of Contemporary Art. At the time, the media gave a distorted portrayal of Manning as a traitor; in the exhibition, this was rectified through anamorphosis. The work was accompanied by a letter written by Peter Weibel, in which he invited Chelsea Manning (who was still Bradley Manning at that time) to work at the ZKM. Such supportive actions are undertaken with the goal of securing an early release for Manning. I think that the activist artifacts that are works of art, and those that are not, interfused in the exhibition – and in this way

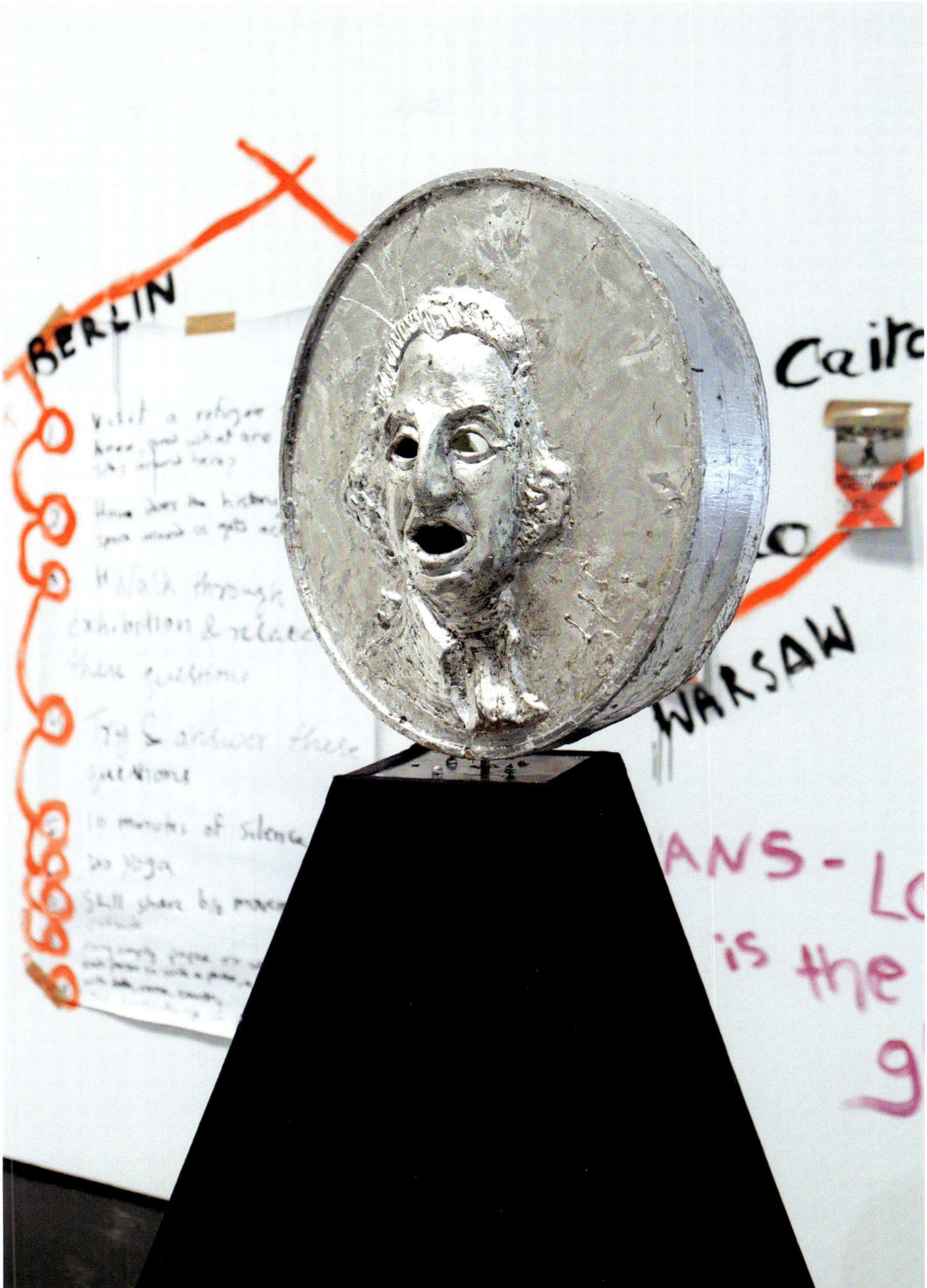

Noah Fischer, *The Mask of Money*, 2013, installation, mixed media, installation view, ZKM | Karlsruhe, 2014

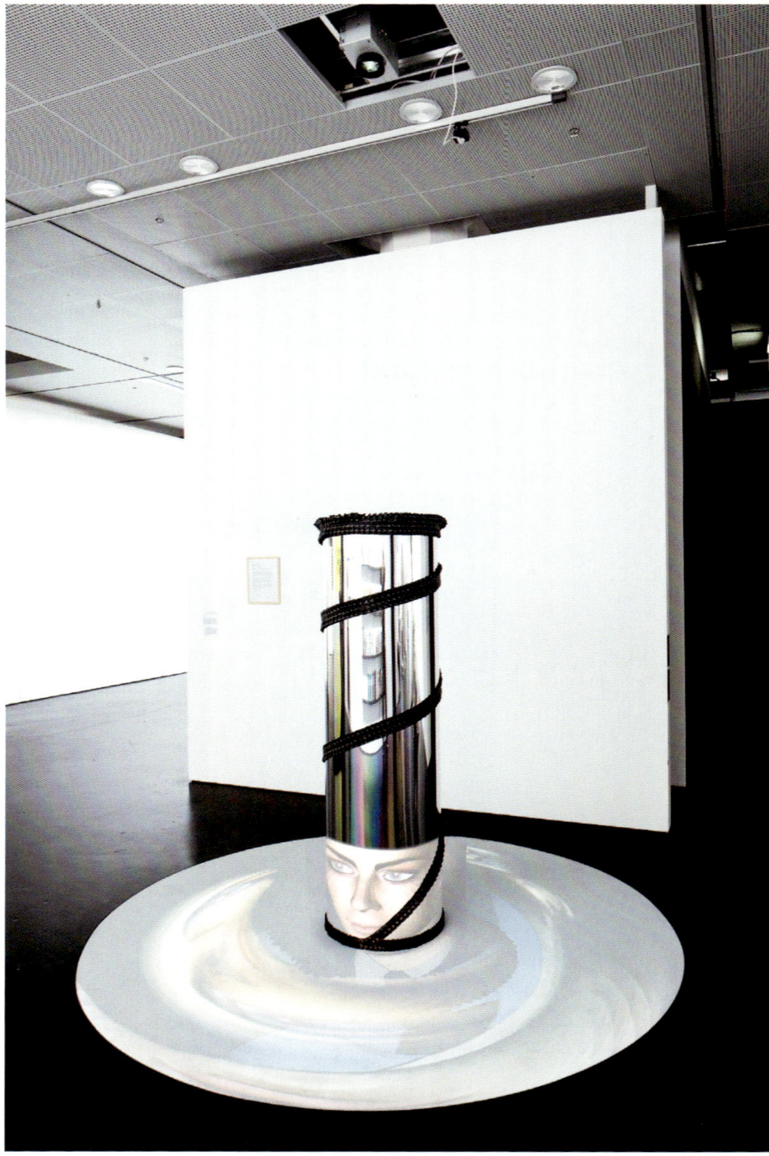

Joulia Strauss in collaboration with Moritz Mattern, *Anamorphous Monument to Chelsea Manning*, 2010/2013, installation, mixed media, installation view, ZKM | Karlsruhe, 2014

disorganized the value system of a corrupt, neoliberal, prostituted art market. Many other institutions are trying desperately to overlook the fact that a radical democratization has taken place in art. *global aCtIVISm* was an exhibition which broke away from the old way of doing exhibitions and, with global social change, took on the form of an exhibition for the twenty-first century.

The interview was conducted by Helmut Höge (*taz, die tageszeitung*). The text is a revised version of the German original, first published on taz.de (January 25, 2014), available online at: www.taz.de/Kuratorin-ueber-Global-Activism/!131651/, accessed 04/08/2014. Translated from the German by Isaac Custance.

This article explores the involvement of contemporary artists in protests in Russia from the beginning of the twenty-first century up to the 2010s. This involvement has changed the role of the artist in contemporary society, leading to the emergence of a burgeoning movement known as activist art.

Tatiana Volkova

The Chronicles of Russian Activist Art

It is thought that this hybrid of art and political activism originated in America in the mid-1970s. Activist art has been characterized by innovative uses of public space for addressing socially important topics and arousing communities to action.[1] In Russia, the term has been in use since the early 2010s, when it became obvious that a circle of artists had emerged who interacted with the reality around them in a fundamentally different way.

In this text the changing functions of today's artist-activist are analyzed: precursor and catalyst of social processes, spokesperson for public sentiments, participant in mass protests and solidarity actions with victims of repression, defender of the rights of minority and socially excluded groups.

Background

First, we need to look at the radical Moscow actionism of the 1990s, regarded as the origin of activist art in Russia. It is impossible to draw a clear dividing line, but it can be argued that the watershed happened in the mid-2000s: as government pressure increased, artists began to lose interest in making careers within the existing art institutions, and instead focused their work on societal processes and often rejected the status of artist as such.

Therein lies its fundamental difference with the political actionism of the 1990s, which was likewise situated in public space and outside the galleries, but which was still focused on inscribing itself in art history – in the international actionist movement, including 1960s Situationism.

ЭТИ-текст [E.T.I. Text], a 1991 action by the movement ЭТИ [E.T.I., Expropriation of the Territory of Art] also known as Хуй на Красной площади [Khui on Red Square], is usually considered radical Moscow actionism's first high-profile performance. Fourteen people formed the word *khui* [dick] with their bodies on the pavement in Red Square. The idea of the action was to combine

1
See: Nina Felshin, *But Is It Art? The Spirit of Art as Activism*, Bay Press, Seattle (WA), 1995.

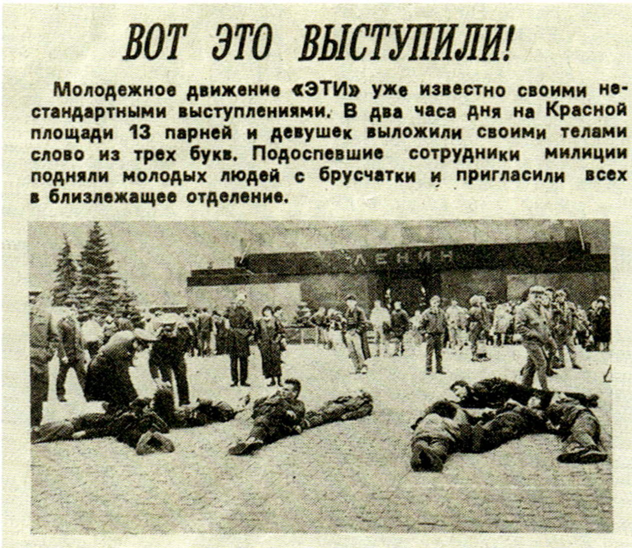

ВОТ ЭТО ВЫСТУПИЛИ!

Молодежное движение «ЭТИ» уже известно своими нестандартными выступлениями. В два часа дня на Красной площади 13 парней и девушек выложили своими телами слово из трех букв. Подоспевшие сотрудники милиции подняли молодых людей с брусчатки и пригласили всех в близлежащее отделение.

E.T.I., Хуй на Красной площади [Khui on Red Square], 1991, in: *Moskovskij Komsomolets*, April 19, 1991

two opposite signs: Red Square, the supreme geographical point in the Soviet Union, and the most marginal of curse words. The action was intended as a protest against rising prices and the almost physical impossibility of living and working in post-Perestroika Russia. The action led to a criminal investigation (on charges of malicious disorderly conduct), which was closed after three months due to lack of evidence that a crime had been committed.

An important component of the action was the presence of the press: a journalist from the *Moskovskij Komsomolets*, thanks to whom photo documentation of the action was published in a high-circulation newspaper. Hence we can classify it as an early example of media activism, whose heyday in Russia would come only in the 2000s in connection with the development of tactical media, online information resources produced by users themselves.[2] Other street actions by Anatoly Osmolovsky and the artists and activists of this circle also took a political form, for example, the 1998 action Баррикада [Barricade]: Bolshaya Nikitskaya Street was blocked with empty cardboard boxes, specially prepared for the occasion. Over the course of three hours, around three hundred people held a barricade literally two hundred meters from the Kremlin. The action was dedicated to the 1968 French student revolution. Therefore, slogans from that historic period were unfurled over the barricade: "It is forbidden to forbid," "All power to the imagination!" and "Be realists, demand the impossible!" Most of the slogans were in French.[3]

Actions by the artists Alexander Brener, Oleg Kulik, Avdei Ter-Oganyan, and Oleg Mavromatti belong to the same tradition of political actionism. In the late 1990s, Ter-Oganyan and Mavromatti were the first victims from the art world of political repression: they were forced to emigrate and seek political asylum. Despite this status, both artists clearly identify themselves with contemporary art; in particular, their defense from persecution was based on the rhetoric of fighting for the freedom of the artistic gesture as an exclusive space within which, according to a tacit international concept, there are special rules.

2
Further information is available online at: www.osmopolis.ru/eti_text_hui, accessed 07/07/2014.

3
Further information is available online at: www.osmopolis.ru/page128, accessed 07/07/2014.

Self-Identification of Artists

In the 2000s, as the political regime in Russia became increasingly authoritarian, many artists ceased identifying themselves as such and began to call themselves activists, calling on their colleagues to leave the museums and go out into the public space.

A prime example is the group PG, who in the late 1990s organized the action Помоги обездоленным! [Help the Downtrodden!] (with support from journalist Anna Politkovskaya and the newspaper *Novaya Gazeta*) to raise humanitarian aid for Chechen refugees in the Karabulak camp in Ingushetia.

The Voina group (see this volume, pp. 684–685) also originally dubbed themselves activists rather than artists. The question of whether Voina [War] were artists or not was posed unequivocally when the group was nominated for the state-funded Innovation Prize. The group changed its mind several times about its involvement with the prize, but its action Хуй в плену у ФСБ [Dick Captured by the FSB] ultimately won the 2010 Innovation Prize for contemporary visual art.

The feminist group Pussy Riot (see this volume, pp. 648–649), which emerged from the Moscow faction of Voina in 2011, has also always referred to itself as an activist group while also stating that "[…] punk rock, including the performances in unexpected places (for example, in prisons) customary in Oi! punk, is part of contemporary art. And simultaneously it is part of political activism, as punk rock influences the mood of some of the people who make up its audience. There is a mutual influence. […] It is work on the concept of contemporary art, a redefinition of the term."[4] The group's defense strategy during its trial, in which members of the group received sentences of two years in prison, was not based on the artist's exclusive right to eccentric gestures, but on a general civil rights rhetoric insisting on the right of all citizens to free expression. After their release from prison, the women became actively involved in defending the rights of prisoners, which caused a huge buzz in the art world. In particular, Anatoly Osmolovsky wrote an open letter to the women in which he urged them not to go into politics: "Do not leave the territory of art – it is a strength, not a weakness. We must set ourselves the most difficult and even impossible tasks. Then the outcome will likewise be more or less acceptable."[5]

Interestingly, the annual May Day Monstration (see Kiss my Ba, this volume, pp. 610–611) street happenings in Novosibirsk, which began in 2004, were clearly regarded by local authorities as political, resulting in repeated crackdowns on organizer Artem Loskutov. And yet Loskutov himself clearly regards the Monstrations as part of the artistic tradition, seeing the creative group СВОИ 2000 [SVOI 2000], which on May 1, 2000, marched in the traditional May Day demonstration in Moscow sporting absurdist slogans, as one of the project's prototypes. He also cites Dadaism, French Situationism, and Moscow Conceptualism.[6]

There is another approach to situating oneself vis-à-vis the boundary between art and politics in which artistic work is a means of political propaganda. This is the approach favored by Kirill Medvedev, leader of the musical group Аркадий Коц [Arkady Kots] and a Russian Socialist Movement activist, who as a member of the radical intelligentsia sees his task in education, in expanding the ranks of those involved in political struggle through audiences of his work, and in developing new forms of interaction between art and politics.[7]

Telling in this sense is a statement made by Joulia Strauss (see this volume, pp. 511–514 and pp. 658–659), an artist from

4 www.pussy-riot.livejournal.com/4299.html, accessed 07/07/2014; translated from the Russian by Thomas Campbell.

5 www.osmopolis.ru/notice/pages/id_375, accessed 07/07/2014; translated from the Russian by Thomas Campbell.

6 Personal communication with the author.

7 See the speech at the 2013 conference "RE/PUBLIC. Russian Art in the Streets" at the Kiasma Museum in Helsinki, Finland.

Russia living in Berlin who is deeply involved in supporting the "Refugee Strike Berlin": "I always have to choose between creating another portrait from a series of drawings about the refugee movement, which I use to familiarize the elitist and pseudo-leftist art world with the ideas of antiborders activism, and going to see my protagonists in their protest camp to help them solve a particular 'domestic' problem. I tend to choose the latter."[8]

8 Personal communication with the author.

Many artists now say they are no longer interested in doing contemporary art in the traditional sense. Some of them have retreated into practical social work, for example, Partizaning (see this volume, pp. 348–349), a movement of urban remodelers. In their manifesto, they write, "Today's activist urban residents do not think of art as a distinct system. They use the language of art as a tool to challenge and change their daily reality: from DIY urban repair to struggling for new forms of state system."[9]

9 Available online at: http://eng.partizaning.org/?page_id=2, accessed 07/07/2014.

Others have gone into journalism, such as former PG member Ilya Falkovsky, who explores the topic of nationalism, or former Agenda member Alexander Bidin, creator of the website Послезавтра [Day after Tomorrow], "a project for collectively selecting the most interesting materials containing critiques both of flagrantly hierarchical institutions and the hidden mechanisms of economic coercion, as well as information about movements and projects seeking to change the existing social order."[10]

10 http://poslezavtra.be/page/about, accessed 07/07/2014; translated from the Russian by Thomas Campbell.

An interesting position is voiced by artist-activist Tanya Sushenkova (see this volume, pp. 186–187): "It seems the main thing in my work is that I help other activists with their projects, from being an 'extra,' assistant, active performer, and coparticipant to a documenter, and sometimes all of them at the same time. The role of the 'eternal wife,' as some feminists understand it. [...] All of life, along with actions, and the conversations around them, despite them, in the kitchen, on the streets, and with examples of this life of mine – that is my most important project."[11]

11 Personal communication with the author.

Artists as Precursors and Catalysts of Social Processes

The processes occurring today in Russian contemporary art completely mesh with international processes. As Peter Weibel writes:

> "Since the expansion of the arts in the mid-1960s art and action entered into a fusion, which liberated itself increasingly from a pure artistic intermediality, and which concerned itself more and more with social and humane agendas. Thus, art and agency flow into a new form of activism. The function of artist shifts from producer of works to systems fugitive or systems critic, capable of occasionally adopting the tasks formerly the preserve of state authorities, the judiciary, the economy, and the administration. Not unlike philosophy and media theory, to some extent art forms the exile in which fundamental civil tasks can still be realized. Along with the function of the artist, the so-called artist's works also change. Instead of oil paintings there now emerge flyers, placards and graffiti, instead of wooden

sculptures online portals, transparencies, media appearances: instead of art films, YouTube videos are now produced."[12]

Art critic Oxana Sarkisyan has analyzed the changes faced today by society and cutting-edge art:

> "Modern media are characterized by the transparency of information flows and their ubiquity, despite the desire of the authorities to restrict them legislatively. We live in a total archive in which the private and public are interwoven. [...] A society of control, as Foucault described it, in which the authorities have an exclusive position for monitoring and regulating the supervised masses, has become impossible. The outcome of biopolitics, the society of the spectacle that Situationist leader Guy Debord described, ceases to function here: the mechanisms for shaping worldviews have become apparent. An alternative to mass society, a new form of community – the multitude – arises in which everyone's individuality is maintained. Sartre's idea, taken up and elaborated by the Situationist International, who called for a revolution in everyday life, today appears to us in the antiglobalist movement, of which art activism is a part."[13]

Amsterdam-based media theorist Eric Kluitenberg has explored the evolution of tactical media in contemporary societies, in which each person has access to affordable means of producing, processing, editing, and disseminating media images:

> "In as far as artists still play a role in these processes, they have been forced to shed their exclusive claim to constituting a singular subjectivity in the public realm. This unique position is now shared with others, ultimately to everybody. Artists can and do play an important role as facilitators in this process of cultural democratisation. The role that artists can assume as catalysts for the self-actualisation of individual citizens, whether these citizens ultimately think of themselves artists or not, predates the rise of the do-it-yourself media movement. This ideal of cultural democratisation can be connected to a range of participatory artistic practices."[14]

Russia's art scene reveals the role of art activists as precursors and catalysts of social processes. Another more recent example is tens of thousands of people gathered in central Moscow in late February 2012, holding hands and forming a human chain along the length of the Garden Ring during an anti-Putin protest dubbed "The Big White Circle." The action drew on the symbolism of white, the color of the so-called Snow Revolution. Very few of the participants would have heard about an action entitled Белая линия [The White Line], masterminded by the artists of the Bombily art group (see this volume, pp. 556–557) five years earlier. According to the artists, participants drew a white chalk line along the length of the Garden Ring separating the virtuous and the sinful spaces of the city so as to cleanse Russia of the evil

12 Peter Weibel, "global aCtIVISm: global citizen," available online at: http://blog.zkm.de/en/editorial/global-activism-global-citizen/#sthash.GTyMufPf.dpuf, accessed 07/07/2014.

13 Oxana Sarkisyan, "О Pussy Riot, а также политике и политическом искусстве в эпоху информационных технологий" [On Pussy Riot, Politics, and Political Art in the Information Era], unpublished article based on a paper delivered at "re.act.feminism – a performing archive," Tallinn Art Hall, Tallinn, Estonia, August 27–September 30, 2012; translated from the Russian by Thomas Campbell.

14 Eric Kluitenberg, *Legacies of Tactical Media. The Tactics of Occupation: From Tompkins Square to Tahrir*, Network Notebooks, Institute of Network Cultures, Amsterdam, 2011, p.33.

spirits that have come to reside in Moscow's downtown. An invisible magic wall that was erected on that day between Moscow and Russia has been protecting humanity from the ills and vices of the capital city ever since.[15]

Art activism as a discrete phenomenon, however, cannot be identified in every country involved in the global protest movement. Direct actions such as rallies and Occupy camps have become the main protest modes for people in many countries, and artists tend to dissolve in them, trying to invent more effective tools for action and attracting the mass media.

At the same time, Russia, which has been in the process of becoming a police state where legal forms of protest are suppressed and persecuted, tends to generate individual forms of artistic resistance that express the moods of the masses.

One group who anticipated the public mood and hit upon its most adequate visual expression was Voina. Curator and art critic Andrei Yerofeyev called its performance *Dick Captured by the FSB* the "[…] cry of the streets, a cry addressed to those who run the city and do not want to hear the opinion of citizens. Street protest gained a structured artistic enunciation, an aesthetic parameter."[16]

However, the most striking and controversial of all the events of the protest winter of 2011 and 2012 was a series of punk concerts in public spaces staged by Pussy Riot. The emergence of this eye-catching cross-genre female art group was sure to draw the attention of bloggers, artists, activists, and feminists, and trigger numerous reactions. The key aspect was their anonymity: their ideology was based on anarchism and horizontal organization – no names, no leaders, everyone is expendable.

During this period, the group staged a total of five performances, one of which took place on the roof of a jail housing protesters arrested during the rallies, and another on Red Square. The group's most famous action, staged shortly before the presidential elections, was a "punk prayer" entitled Богородица, Путина прогони! [Mother of God, Chase Putin Away!]. It took place in Moscow's Cathedral of Christ the Savior and resulted in criminal prosecution. The suspected members of the collective were arrested on charges of hooliganism and faced a maximum of seven years in prison if convicted. After the arrest, the names of the arrested members and their ties to the Moscow fraction of Voina were revealed: Pussy Riot had radicalized Voina's methods, taking them to their limit.

In this case, not only were the artists precursors and catalysts of social processes but they also assumed a heroic role themselves by taking to the streets alone to face down the system and sacrificing themselves for long-term social change that would be founded on their artistic gesture.

The women were released under an amnesty in late 2013. Their first statements to the mass media were about the huge campaign they intended to launch to defend the rights of Russian prisoners. This position of "protest celebrities" and "martyrs," generated by state repression, has now given them the chance to use this mass media attention for real political influence. Art as a symbolic space has given them the power to change the lives of particular people.

15 Further information is available online at: http://ru.wikipedia.org/wiki/Бомбилы_(арт-группа), accessed 07/07/2014.

16 Ekaterina Zorkina, "Это петербургская Эйфелева башня" [It Is Petersburg's Eiffel Tower], in: *Vzgliad*, April 8, 2011, available online at: www.vz.ru/culture/2011/4/8/482379.html, accessed 07/07/2014; translated from the Russian by Thomas Campbell.

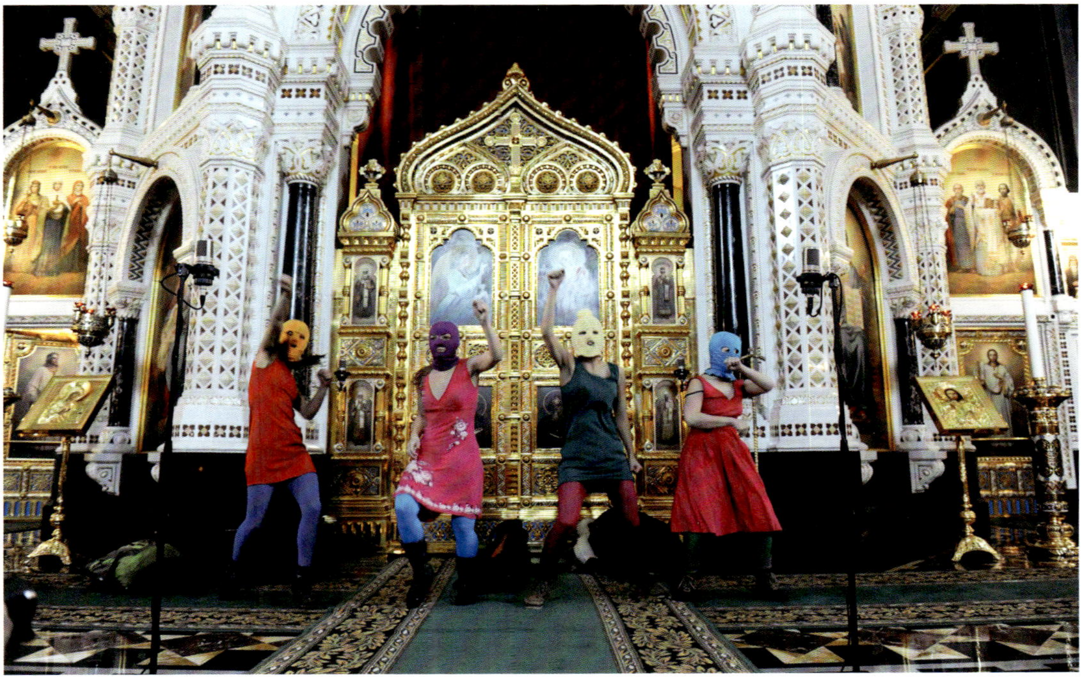

Pussy Riot, Богородица, Путина прогони! [Mother of God, Chase Putin Away!], Cathedral of Christ the Savior, Moscow, February 21, 2012

The term "cognitive terrorism" has been applied to such actions. Artist Anton Nikolaev writes:

> "The destruction by Islamist terrorists of the two World Trade Center towers dramatically changed the way contemporary art is perceived in the world. If earlier, artists who used public artistic and paratheatrical practices could afford to relate only to the history of art, now they inevitably get stuck in semantic fields having to do with terrorism. And, by the way, it also happens the other way around (as the story with Karlheinz Stockhausen has shown). Any high-profile action by current artists will inevitably be associated in the media with terrorist attacks. Any talk about how it fits into the art tradition is pushed to the background and is capable of generating only supplementary senses. It is no wonder Dartmouth College professor Mikhail Gronas suggested using the term 'cognitive terrorism' when describing the work of Bombily and Voina – meaning that artists use symbolic violence to achieve effects similar to those obtained by terrorists through *subjective violence* (see: Slavoj Žižek)."[17]

17 Anton Nikolaev, "Артивизм и акционизм" [Artivism and Activism], June 6, 2011, available online at: http://halfaman.livejournal.com/510998.html, accessed 07/07/2014; translated from the Russian by Thomas Campbell.

When analyzing the specifics of Russian art activism, it seems important to quote the following excerpt from an article by sociologist Anna Zaitseva:

> "Such activism regards the real transformation of the situation as unlikely, and thinking about ways to achieve change, long-term goals, and strategy formation contemplation happens behind the scenes. Like the Bakhtinian carnival, this activism

reveals a nonlinear, antiteleological dynamic of cyclical repetition and an ambivalent mixture of registers – artistic, expressive, and political. […] Given that there is no expectation of an outcome, then, 'drive' and 'burn' are obligatory in an action, and increasingly diverse and inventive forms of protest drama pop up everywhere, resembling a collective art therapy. […] These protests, both against the national government and the transnational capitalist order, are not confined to street actions. They are capable of transforming into behavioral acts and ethical choices that are not necessarily spectacular but are politically positioned. When both the revolutionary and reform scenarios have lost their realism, the creation of 'temporary autonomous zones' and divergent but regular acts of 'resistance' become relevant."[18]

18 Anna Zaitseva, "Спектакулярные формы протеста в современной России: между искусством и социальной терапией" [Spectacular Forms of Protest in Contemporary Russia: Between Art and Social Therapy], in: *Neprikosnovennyi zapas*, vol. 4, no. 72, 2010, available online at: http://magazines.russ.ru/nz/2010/4/za4.html, accessed 07/07/2014; translated from the Russian by Thomas Campbell.

The Streets as Art Space

As an unconventional and unauthorized space, the streets have become the main arena for artistic statements today. The authorities, who react to these statements with forceful crackdowns, have become the main audience, generating the desirable media effect for such statements.

Art critic, artist, and Partizaning website editor Anton Polsky (aka Make) writes, "In the wake of the protests and the general revitalization of civil society, as well as the disappointment of many gallery artists in working with the white cube space from 2010 or 2011, more and more new people not connected with graffiti have gone into street art. Interestingly, if most works from the previous period were objects and images inscribed into the cityscape, the new wave has more often reflected political and social topics, and more artists have begun working with text. In addition, street art has intertwined with activism."[19] Polsky singles out the group Ганди [Gandhi] and Sasha Kurmaz (see this volume, pp. 344–345) from among the current highly topical street artists.

19 Maxim Mozul, "Дизайнер Антон Мейк о состоянии российского стрит-арта" [Designer Anton Make on the State of Russian Street Art], in: *Furfur*, April 11, 2014, available online at: www.furfur.me/furfur/all/culture/171695-russian-street-art, accessed 07/07/2014; translated from the Russian by Thomas Campbell.

Red Square in Moscow has become one of the central venues for self-expression. It has remained a symbolic space, the center of state power from which all prohibitionist evil flows, and at the same time a powerful resource for activism. Any appeal to this space always produces media buzz.

Back in 1995, radical Moscow actionist Alexander Brener challenged President Boris Yeltsin to a fight, showing up at the Lobnoye Mesto in Red Square in boxing trunks and gloves. In 1998, members of Anatoly Osmolovsky's Nongovernmental Control Commission took over the top of the Lenin Mausoleum brandishing the slogan "Against all," which was used extensively in the election campaigns of the 1990s.

In the late 2000s, as the authoritarian regime in Russia grew stronger, Red Square became a venue for more pointed political statements. In 2008, the action Свадьба нацболов [Nazbol Wedding] took place, during which around fifty people seized the Lobnoye Mesto to protest political oppression: two activists from the National-Bolshevik Party capped off their wedding in this unusual way.

In 2011, artists Denis Mustafin, Georgy Dorokhov, and Vlad Chizhenkov carried out the action Белый флаг [White Flag], during which they planted white flags on the Lenin Mausoleum by way of "declaring war on their own conformism vis-à-vis the authorities."

In the early 2010s, Red Square was the site of numerous civic protests, such as an action against the ban on promotion of homosexuality among minors, which was one of the largest public events by the Russian LGBT community, and the action against the law on residence registration in March 2013, Идите на хуй со своей регистрацией! [Fuck Off with Your Registration!].

Another high-profile action on Red Square was the performance Фиксация [Fixation] by Petr Pavlensky, in November 2013. The naked artist nailed his scrotum to the cobblestones near the Kremlin. According to him, the action can be seen as a metaphor for the apathy, political indifference, and fatalism of current Russian society. A few months later, Pavlensky and a group of Saint Petersburg anarchists carried out a protest action in support of Ukraine in downtown Petersburg on the Maly Konyushenny Bridge opposite the Church of the Savior on Spilled Blood.[20]

20 See: http://pikabu.ru/story/aktsiya_quotsvobodaquot_2000432, accessed 07/07/2014.

Involvement of Artists in Mass Protest Actions

The Russian artistic community played an active role in the recent wave of protests. Besides attending mass rallies and marches, artists, art critics, and curators worked as election observers during the presidential elections in 2012.

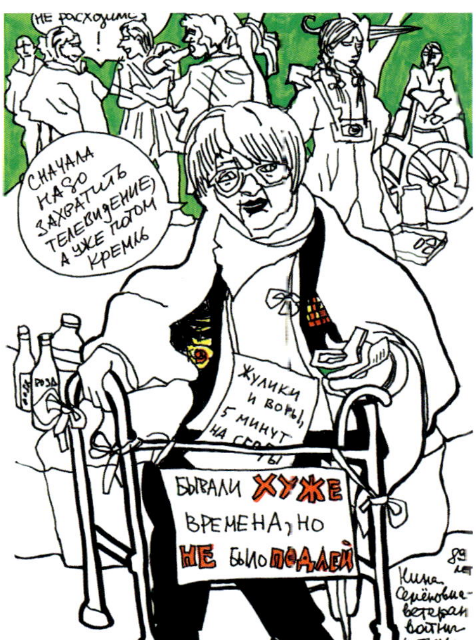

Viktoria Lomasko, Будни Оккупай Абай [The Everyday Life of Occupy Abay], 2012, drawing, comic, from the series Хроники сопротивления [Chronicles of Resistance]

A series of mass protests against unfair elections was capped off in May 2012 with an open confrontation between Russian authorities and the opposition, when the violent dispersal of a march on May 6 was followed by a series of "protest strolls" around Moscow. Subsequently, an improvised opposition camp was set up in Chistye Prudy near a monument to the nineteenth-century Kazakh poet and educator Abay Kunanbaev. As a sign of their dissent, hundreds of people kept the camp going for over a week. Dubbed Occupy Abay, it logically reproduced the structure of similar protest camps in Europe and the U.S., built on principles of self-organization and horizontal decision-making.

The camp hosted daily art shows, performances, readings, theatricals, and protest music concerts featuring Center, Arkady Kots, I.H.N.A.B.T.B. and Pavel "Pâté" Filippenko, among others. An integral part of the program was participation in the support campaign for Pussy Riot, which set up another camp near Moscow City Court.

A series of mobile art shows entitled Арт-Абай [Art Abay] took place, beginning with Viktoria Lomasko's graphic reportage Будни Оккупай Абай [The Everyday Life of Occupy Abay], produced during the first days of the camp and part of her larger series Хроники сопротивления [Chronicles of Resistance] (see this volume, pp. 618–619). After police dispersed the camp, it migrated around Moscow for a time, and the *Art Abay* shows went with it.

The Russian authorities responded to the wave of grassroots protests in winter 2011 and spring 2012 by cracking down on people caught up in the clash between police and protesters on Bolotnaya Square on May 6, 2012, and toughening legislation on the organization of mass events.

Solidarity with Political Prisoners

Another area where activist artists have been involved is support for political prisoners. In the mid-2000s, trials of cultural workers became commonplace, while involvement in rallies, pickets, exhibitions, and concerts in their support became routine for their colleagues.

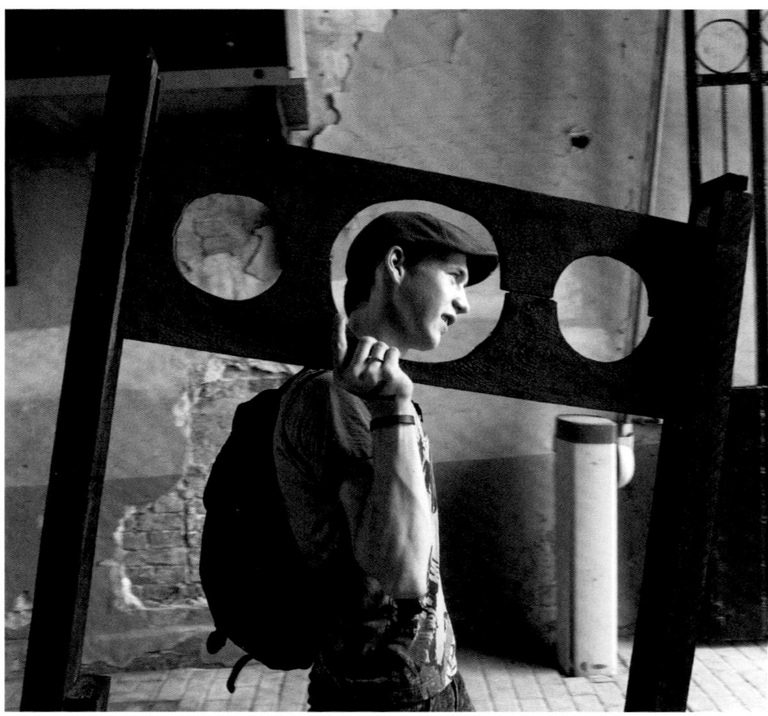

Narcophobia, Фарисейка, 12 [Fariseyka, 12], action in frames of the Day against Torture, Moscow, 2013

One of the early high-profile cases was the trial of Yuri Samodurov and Andrei Yerofeyev, the organizers of Запретное искусство [Forbidden Art], a 2007 exhibition that displayed works censored by Russian galleries and museums. The trial lasted three years, during which time numerous events were held in support of the curators, including artistic interventions in the courtroom and a large rally/concert on Chistye Prudy. Yerofeyev and Samodurov were found guilty of inciting ethnic and religious hatred and sentenced to pay stiff fines.

In 2009, officers of "Center E," the "antiextremism" police, planted narcotics on Monstration organizer Artem Loskutov during a search. Thanks to an international solidarity campaign, Loskutov was sentenced only to a fine. Planting narcotics as a tool of political repression in Russia is the focus of Наркофобия [Narcophobia], a project launched by a group of activists and artists in 2011 to support and defend people who have fallen victim to this method, as well as preventing new victims and promoting humane drug policies.[21]

21 Further information is available online at: http://narcophobia.ru/about-us, accessed 07/07/2014.

This support does not always keep activists from getting real prison sentences. In 2011, the Smolensk activist Taisiya Osipova was sentenced to eight years in prison despite numerous solidarity events, including a Moscow-Smolensk auto rally and press tour. Matvei Krylov, organizer of the auto rally, an artist, poet, and the man behind the Mayakovsky Readings, outdoor poetry readings next to the Mayakovsky Monument in downtown Moscow, was shortly before this himself the focus of attention and solidarity as the defendant in the so-called "Wet Prosecutor Case." Krylov had splashed water in the face of prosecutor Alexei Smirnov, who had been in charge of the Manege Square riot case and had gotten two of Krylov's comrades sentenced to prison on trumped-up charges.

Activist artists were involved in the campaign to defend Sergei Mokhnatkin, a passerby who happened to be at the site of an unauthorized Strategy 31 protest rally on Triumfalnaya Square in Moscow. Mokhnatkin was arrested after he made a remark to police who were beating an elderly woman. Despite huge public interest in the case, Mokhnatkin was sentenced to two and a half years in prison for hitting a policeman.

Many artists are part of the antifascist movement and support persecuted antifascist activists. A striking example is the case of the attack on the Khimki town hall during the campaign to stop the clear-cutting of the Khimki Forest (2010–2011). The court acquitted antifascist activist Alexei Gaskarov and gave Maxim Solopov a two-year suspended sentence. However, in 2013 Gaskarov was arrested in the Bolotnaya Square case and is still in custody.

In connection with these trials, many artists have begun sketching and reporting them. For instance, Viktoria Lomasko and Anton Nikolaev's book *Forbidden Art* is a graphic reportage of the trial of Samodurov and Yerofeyev. Lomasko has continued this work, producing a series of reports from high-profile trials. An entire community has emerged around this effort: called Рисуем суд [Drawing the Court], their purpose is to produce a credible image of current Russian courts.[22]

22 Further information is available online at: www.risuemsud.ru/en/about, accessed 07/07/2014.

Support for Minority Groups

In parallel with the tightening of restrictions on large-scale opposition events, Russian law was amended to further diminish the rights of such socially vulnerable groups as migrant workers, drug addicts, and the LGBT community. In particular, an unprecedented homophobic campaign was unleashed that targeted the LGBT movement as official enemies of the Russian state. As part of this campaign, laws prohibiting the promotion of homosexuality were adopted.

There is a certain system to the actions of the authorities. In his text "The Logic of Social Exclusion," written for the eponymous seminar at the MediaImpact Festival 2013, philosopher Igor Chubarov attempted to describe it:

> "In different historical periods all societies persecute, marginalize, displace, destroy, or exclude certain segments of their populations according to ethnic, gender, sexual, or simply random criteria. The guilt of the people thus excluded or sacrificed for the social peace does not need to be proved, as it is simultaneously the consequence of a social compromise and displacement mixed with elemental violence and the idea that life itself is guilty. [...] The logic and very mechanism of this exclusion have a direct relationship to the function of art and art-related activism in society because they are primarily mimetic in nature and underlie the production of artistic images and things. Art is involved in the corresponding processes of legitimating public fears and unconscious identifications and desires as an active player, not an outside observer."[23]

23 Igor Chubarov, "Логики социального исключения" [The Logic of Social Exclusion], available online at: http://mediaudar.net/blog/2013/09/23/seminar-logiki-socialnogo-isklyucheniya, accessed 07/07/2014; translated from the Russian by Thomas Campbell.

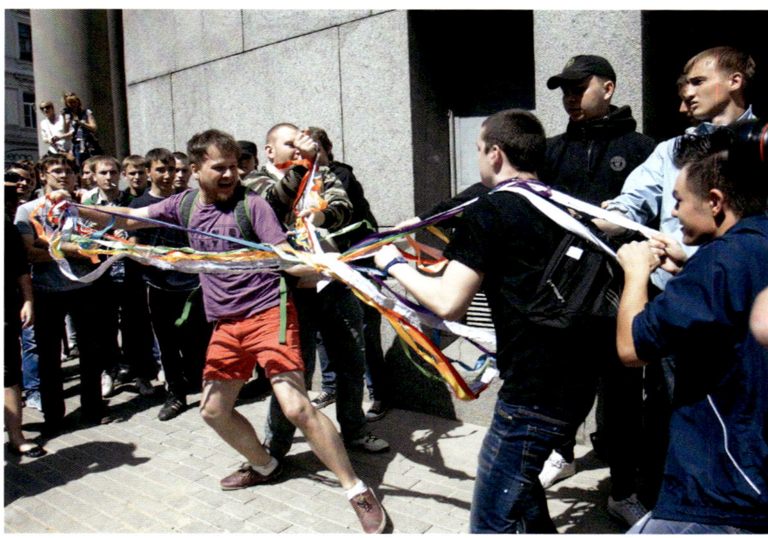

Alexei Kiselev and Dmitry Chunosov, Радужные сети [Rainbow Network], Moscow, 2012

Work with minority groups has been an important field among activist artists. Many artists have been working on the topic of migrant labor and, more broadly, nationalism in Russia. Ilya Falkovsky thus describes his project Незаметные убийства [Invisible Murders], based on the criminal case against the NSO-North neo-Nazi gang, who were responsible for dozens of assaults on and murders of immigrants from Central Asia and the Caucasus, as well as "non-Aryan" Russians: "When they were alive, we cared little about these people, most of whom were poor, workers, and janitors, people who daily bent their backs in hard labor. They lived alongside us, in the basements of our buildings, but we just didn't notice them. How could we care about their needs when we had plenty of our own? So after death may they be awarded at least these unvarnished descriptions of their deaths."[24]

Another socially excluded group are drug users. Alexander Delfinov, a poet, Narcophobia project member, and organizer of numerous protests against repressive Russian drugs policies, writes:

> "In Russia, the attitude to people who use drugs is especially repressive. According to the Federal Drug Control Service, every third Russian inmate is a drugs user. Instead of moral support and effective treatment, people who suffer from drug addition are subjected to systematic torture and cruel, inhuman treatment in all areas – medicine, law enforcement, and public life. [...] But in the absence of effective treatment and systematic rehabilitation, the state offers harsh personal suppression and social coercion without any hope of salvation."[25]

Feminist Art

There is a strong feminist strand in the Russian civic movement, and feminist art is part of it. Feminists treat women as a minority group whose rights are legally and de facto violated in Russia.

Nadia Plungian, an art historian, curator, and member of the Moscow Feminist Group, writes, "[F]eminist art does not exist in the galleries, but on the streets or alternative formats, because the galleries do not want to deal with it. [...] So the real prospects of feminist art today lie, first of all, in civic activism. The art is circulated via social networks, graffiti, homemade videos, and, of course, zines, samizdat. We have set ourselves the task of winning over the ordinary female audience, of making art understandable and at the same time socially acute."[26]

In their work, artists such as Ira Gnil, the group Жена [Wife], Alexandra Kachko, Viktoria Lomasko, Elena Maximova, Umnaya Masha, Mikaela (see this volume, pp. 256–257), Natalya Pershina (Gluklya), Anna Repina, Yana Smetanina, and Tatyana Fashutdinova talk about such problems as the double work burden of women on the job and at home, domestic violence, as well as medical violence in maternity wards and hospitals.

Nadia Plungian and Viktoria Lomasko have for several years been running the large-scale international project Феминистский карандаш [Feminist Pencil], which unites all the above-named artists and includes, aside from exhibitions of feminist social graphic art, lectures, presentations, discussions, workshops, and meetings with psychologists and specialists on violence.

The group Верхотура и друзья [Verkhotura and Friends] has used radical methods to draw attention to the problems of women in Russia: for example, they used images of bloodied women's legs in a series of solo pickets entitled Не рожай! [Don't Give Birth!], which was part of a day of action for free education in Kaliningrad and Saint Petersburg. Such outrageous methods are also employed by the scandalous Femen movement, which gained fame for protest actions during which activists bare their breasts to attract attention, and Pussy Riot, who were already mentioned.

24 Ilya Falkovsky, "НЕЗАМЕТНЫЕ УБИЙСТВА. Презентация проекта" [Invisible Murders. Project Presentation], available online at: http://mediaudar.net/blog/2013/09/26/ilya-falkovskij-nezametnye-ubijstva-prezentaciya-proekta, accessed 07/07/2014; translated from the Russian by Thomas Campbell.

25 http://narcophobia.ru/fariseyka-12, accessed 07/07/2014; translated from the Russian by Thomas Campbell.

26 Nadia Plungian, "Феминистское искусство в России" [Feminist Art in Russia], available online at: http://politpropaganda.com/education/261, accessed 07/07/2014; translated from the Russian by Thomas Campbell.

Oxana Sarkisyan writes, "It is not surprising that in the field of political representation feminists have been the face of the opposition and have mounted such strong opposition to the Russian president that they have proven to be an alternative to Putin's authoritarian regime."[27]

Sarkisyan and artist Victoria Begalskaya have launched Феминистская кухня. Профоюз сексуальных работников [Feminist Kitchen: A Trade Union of Sex Workers], which positions itself as third-wave feminist project aimed not only at defending women's rights but also at totally transcoding perceptions of the world from a gender perspective and changing the structure of social relations within a sexist state. And the project raises another important issue: how to represent excluded groups in art and the media in such a way that avoids stigmatizing them or using them as raw material for accumulating personal media capital.

27 Sarkisyan 2012; translated from the Russian by Thomas Campbell.

Queer

Queerness – the other, the marginal, the borderline – has traditionally been associated with LGBT activism and the LGBT movement. Radical queer intellectual Серое Фиолетовое [Gray Violet] has commented on the state of affairs in this field:

> "We should note the events focused on nonactivist lesbian, gay, and, sometimes, transgender culture, such as the annual queer culture festival in Saint Petersburg, attempts to get Russian films onto the program of the Бок о бок [Side by Side] LGBT film festival, and a number of initiatives that take place during Недели против гомофобии [Week against Homophobia]. This vector is opposed by a more radical vector. [...] I try and work on expanding the boundaries of queer and getting away from the classical association of queer with LGBTQ issues by way of seeing queer as a nonstructure aimed at deconstructing a wider number of boundaries and hierarchies, and paying attention to marginality not only in the realms of gender and sexuality but also in other dimensions of life, eroding the boundaries between the living and dead, human and animal, life and technology, and considering ethnocultural marginalities and much else."[28]

28 Personal communication with the author.

The project НЕПРИШЕЙПИЗДЕРУКАВ [Square Panties on Round Pussies] is part of the new queer-feminist agenda. Its main organizer Polina Zaslavskaya has held a number of fashion shows featuring queer underpants and organized a radical queer festival in Petersburg.

Decolonial Ideology

In keeping with the trend toward dealing with minority groups and zones of exclusion, another important topic within the art activist community has been decolonial ideology – a rejection of Westerncentrism and an interest in regional processes within Russia. Philosopher Madina Tlostanova writes:

> "Decolonial aesthesis is an important part of liberating being from the limitations of Western aesthetics. The problem of decolonizing aesthesis (i.e., modes of feeling, sensing, and perceiving the world) from the rules and regulations imposed by Western modernity in transmodernist (that is, overcoming modernist) post- and decolonial art is part of the process of emancipating subjectivity and knowledge. Of particular interest is the refraction of these problems in post-Soviet and postsocialist art, which overlaps to some extent with post-colonial paradigms. In this regard, the problem of rethinking the museum as an essentially colonial institution for producing and planting certain kinds of knowledge and, hence, the task of liberating it from the progressivist frameworks, Orientalism, and other recognizable vices of modernity also moves to the forefront."[29]

29 Madina Tlostanova, "Деколониальный эстезис и современное искусство" [Decolonial Aesthesis and Contemporary Art], available online at: http://mediaudar.net/blog/2013/10/14/madina-tlostanova-dekolonialnyj-estezis-i-sovremennoe-iskusstvo, accessed 07/07/2014; translated from the Russian by Thomas Campbell.

The group Бомбилы [Bombily] (see this volume, pp. 556–557), in particular, works with the topic of decolonialism:

> "Russia is an empire, so infrastructure is extremely vital in Russia. And where this infrastructure (roads, power lines, communications, political administration systems, which one sometimes wants to compare with wires) ends, at the level of regional centers, you end up with these places where people are literally hanging on scraps of wires, sometimes even bare wires, and they feel this lunacy with their hands, which are periodically jolted by a senseless current. Sitting in Moscow, it is completely unclear what to do about this. You need to go there yourself and establish communication."[30]

30 http://prcinefantom.livejournal.com/42046.html, accessed 07/07/2014; translated from the Russian by Thomas Campbell.

MediaImpact Festival of Activist Art

Horizontal decision-making, decolonial aesthetics, work in Russia's regions, and a focus on socially excluded groups and zones is the ideological base of the MediaImpact Festival of Activist Art (see this volume, pp. 624–625).[31] Founded in 2011, it has since grown into an international community for examining, articulating, documenting, supporting, and developing activist art.

31 Further information is available online at: http://english.mediaudar.net, accessed 07/07/2014.

The project is formed by a self-organized working group of artists, activists, art critics, and philosophers. Their work includes festivals in different Russian cities, assemblies, expeditions, publishing, exhibitions, presentations, lectures, workshops, discussion, literary readings, concerts, video screenings, residencies, joint actions, and theory laboratories.

Readers might get the impression that activist art in Russia is a single, streamlined movement, but this is far from the case, of course. As in any engaged community, the development of activism and activist-related art involves a large number of conflicts and

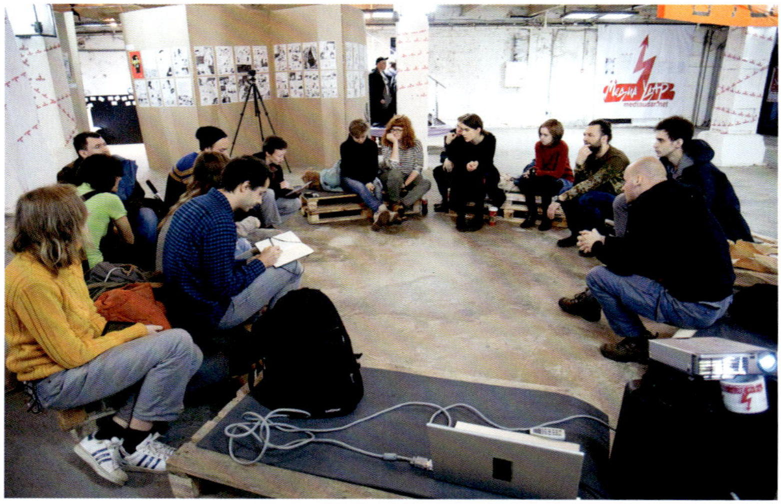

MediaImpact International Festival of Activist Art, assembly of the working group, Moscow, 2013

clashes over the accumulation of media capital, the main currency of modern society.

Despite this, to many people it has become obvious that we need to consolidate the diverse and divergent vectors of activist art in Russia and form a horizontal network of media activists that would in turn be part of the international community – the network of networks known as global activism.

Translated from the Russian by Thomas Campbell.

Since 2004, several Ammani bands and singers have appeared on the scene, tackling Amman's everyday life issues ranging from forbidden love to the emotional and urban voids. The Jordanian music project was hidden from the public sphere, only to be saved after a number of years by the Arab Spring.

Ahmad Zatari

How the Jordanian Music Scene Missed the Arab Spring

Towards the end of 2010, a quasi-revolutionary hip-hop movement came to life, instigated by the band Torabyeh [Earthly] and sustained by El Far3i[1] (meaning "secondary," a metaphor for a voice from the margins or sidelines) and Khotta Ba [Plan B]. This brought issues of public concern and the Palestinian cause back into the structure of Jordanian musical identity.

This movement was limited in its influence, since initially it was disconnected from the scenes beyond Amman, and mainly preoccupied with the class division between eastern Amman, with its poor and neglected, and western Amman, rich and cradling investment.

The song *7erak*[2] (Torabyeh and El Far3i) criticized the attempts to create antagonism within the Jordanian community after a number of Jordanian protesters, who took part in the Third Palestinian Intifada protests on May 15, 2011, were attacked with guns by other civilian groups, allegedly from the Karameh tribes, near the Jordanian border with Palestine. These clashes were followed by an onslaught of reciprocal accusations between the two parties based on Jordanian versus Palestinian origins. This is exactly what had happened earlier during the protests on March 24 of the same year, where the crowds found themselves being categorized as Shiites, Iranians, and Palestinians by other protesters carrying pictures of the king, who were considered the regime's allies in the crowd.

The song *7erak*, was produced under these circumstances, a moment in which the Ammani music experiment reached a new level in incorporating what had been taking place around it, assuming moral responsibility for its political and social role. With this new experience, the Ammani song came out of hiding.

It may possibly have been the first time that there was mention of towns and areas outside of the capital, emphasizing a unity with regard to a common reality and the national struggle. It also rejected the image of the tribes as representing and harboring thugs:

1 Translator's note: 3 is a replacement for a letter in Arabic that has no corresponding sound in English, it is often replaced byan ' before the closest corresponding sound; this word reads as *al-Fir'ii*.

2 Translator's note: 7 is a replacement for a letter in Arabic that has no corresponding sound in English, it is often replaced by an h; this word reads as *Hirak*.

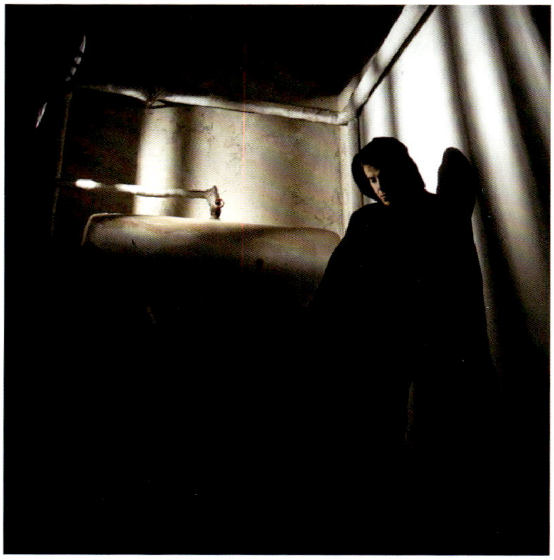

El Far3i, 2011

Claiming the provinces do not agree
with reform
As if they are cradling corruption
You claim the South owes you favors
in distributing flour
A mockery pretending those thugs
represent children of the tribes
Change your corrupt style,
fix your image
Your people are anticipating a
dangerous time
When you sign the desert away in
a deal between you and the people
of the Gulf
Bring the children of Maan and
Baqaa a copy of the bill.[3]

3 Excerpts of the lyrics of the song *7erak* by El Far3i, video available online at: www.youtube.com/watch?v=UxYFMVKZa-Y, accessed 05/13/2014; translated from the Arabic.

4 Walter Benjamin, "The Author as Producer," in: Walter Benjamin, *Reflections. Essays, Aphorisms, Autobiographical Writings*, Peter Demetz (ed.), Schocken Books, New York (NY), 1986, pp. 220–238, here p. 221.

Walter Benjamin, in his essay entitled "The Author as Producer," says, "[t]he correct political tendency of a work includes its literary quality, because it includes its literary tendency [...]."[4] He points to how this literary bias could play a role in enhancing or hindering the literary technique itself.

This applies to the independent Amman music scene. The pioneers of the new movement – Yazan Al Rousan and Aziz Maraka – that began in 2009 failed to incorporate the societal and political changes and developments, and failed to anticipate the 2011 Arab revolutions.

In February 2011, Tarek Abu-Kwaik produced, as part of the project he calls El Far3i, a song entitled *7aditha* [A New City] and released it on YouTube. He sang it from a balcony in Ramallah where he had composed it. This was the first time that we had heard of El Far3i, a coherent project the composer described later as one that "takes the two banks of the river as its points of origin."

Drop family names, drop the titles
Let us trust this path and understand the reasons
Why the Abbasid misunderstood the Umayyad
Why a rift came between the Fatimid and the Ottoman
Secular global with a few benefits
But I see Arab trap controlling
This time, my targets in front of me, I contemplate history[5]

5 Excerpts of the lyrics of the song *7aditha* by El Far3i, video available online at: www.youtube.com/watch?v=ToNpnRLsdOU, accessed 05/13/2014; translated from the Arabic.

While the Torabyeh experience, in particular, may seem as though it was soliciting Jordanian revolutionization before it began, it cannot be seen as fake when it is compared to the popular feeling on the Jordanian streets at the time when this band started in 2009. However, it does seem to be an act of fabrication with the intention of provoking its realization. According to Firas Shihadeh, the founder of the band that has now broken up, "At first we were met with expected disapproval, considering the radical content of our songs; however, our sincerity came across. We had no intention of faking either ourselves or reality."

The surprising factor is that the band first started to sing as a result of a chance get-together in a graveyard in Aqaba city. The conversation turned to the incident when a port worker, Ahed Alawneh, was thrown from a police vehicle during a port workers' sit-in in Aqaba, after which protesters started to mobilize.

If we agree that Jordanian protesters did mobilize in 2012, then the album entitled *Tatweer Hadari* [Urban Development] produced by Khotta Ba earlier that year was in reality an attempt to keep up with the move toward realigning the political compass of the new Jordanian song, rather than anticipating it.

The rhetoric of Khotta Ba's song invokes the conditions for an ideal liberation revolution, a true leftist discourse, which seems to contradict Abu-Kwaik's *Muqawameh Madanyeh* [Civil Resistance] on his album *Far3i Al-Madakhil* [Entry Division], produced in 2012 alongside Khotta Ba's album *Tatweer Hadari*.

There is an invitation in El Far3i's song to engage in popular resistance but with no specification of the form of this resistance. This is done by leaving a blank in the sentence "Did you know that (…) is a form of resistance?" Yet, at the same time he points to a specific form for this "civil" and unarmed resistance by defining the "civil fighter" as one who becomes a fighter when they are no longer apathetic, when they no longer throw trash out of car windows while telling "pals" how ideal the West is.

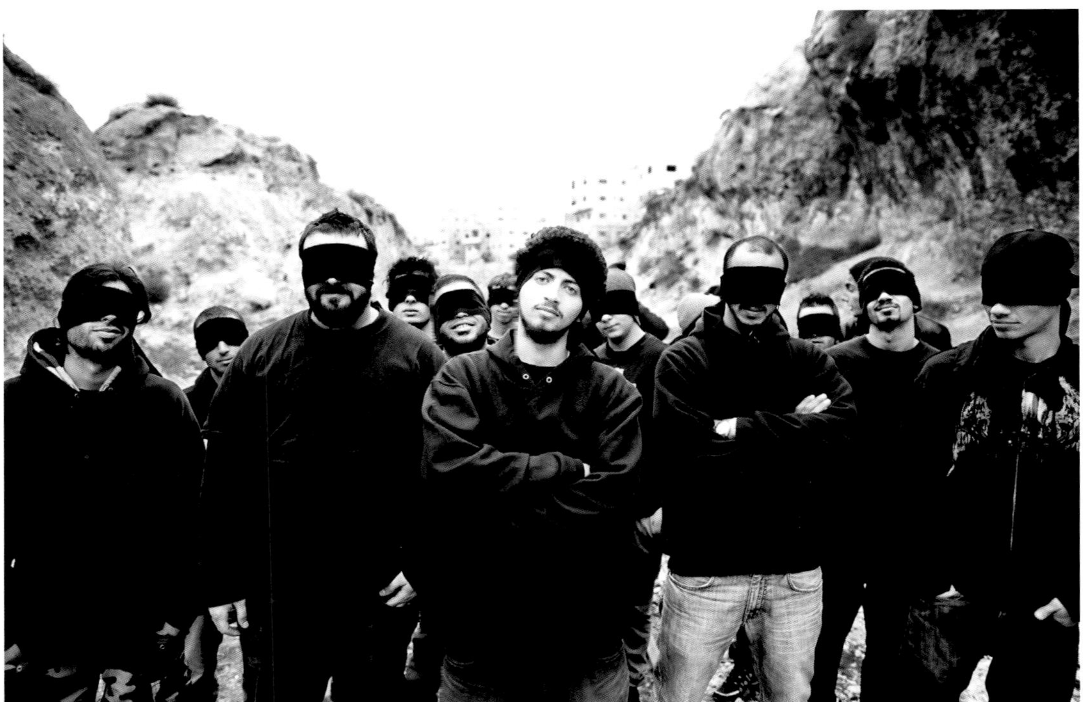

Torabyeh, 2011

The voice of the people is loud, a discharged fighter is suspicious to the occupier and gives me the creeps.

In its mournful sense of the poetic, these lyrics closely resemble the song *Ma Indak Khabar* [You Have No Clue] by El Morabba3, which was on the 2012 album of the same name:

The gas is becoming more expensive and privatized,
and you have no clue. Jerusalem is being freed and purified,
and yet you still worship fire.

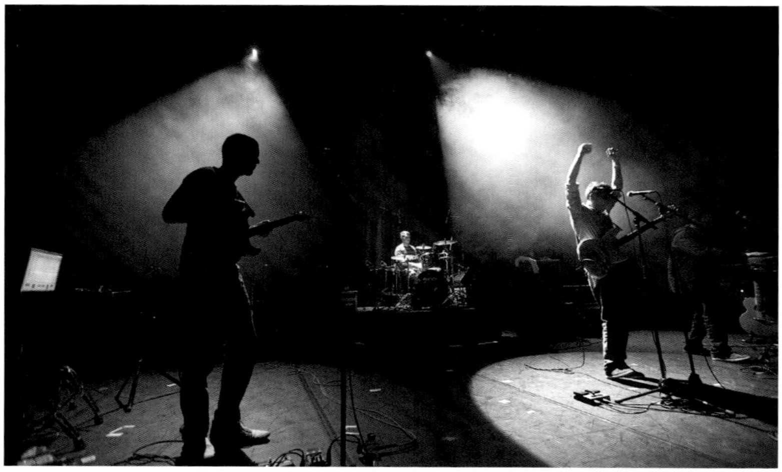

El Morabba3, 2013

It is as challenging to analyze the mindset behind these songs, whether aware or naive, as it is to challenge the Arab political state of affairs. Just as the Arab Spring has taken us back to the point of zero in politics and to no freedoms, we are also back at the beginning of a more difficult and brutal path. For it is far easier to deal with a dictator than to engage with internal problems – this new wave arrived after the Arab Spring as a necessary mutilation of everything we ever believed or disbelieved in.

If we were to wonder what the role of music should be here, it is to survey the communal memory and purify it from the contamination of any political discourse. This will not be the case if music were to be considered a tool to atone for personal or public sins, nor if seen as a free means to narrate events. Its role here, however, is to recreate a popular song instead of an alternative one. This is where Abu-Kwaik and his fellow musicians have failed.

This text is a shortened and revised version of an essay originally published in Arabic on theriverhastwobanks.net and translated into English by Diala Khasawnih for the publication on www.ibraaz.org in May 2013 (available online at: www.ibraaz.org/essays/60, accessed 05/13/2014). Initially, a version of this essay was delivered by Ahmad Zatari on November 10, 2012 at the Makan art space in Amman, and broadcast on radio Raya (Palestine) on December 11, 2012.

M. Ragıp Zık

Raising Resistance:

Reinterpreting Art within the Gezi Movement

By the end of May 2013, a group of young people had come together in order to protest the cutting down of some trees in Gezi Park in Istanbul. This quickly became a country-wide movement and achieved a momentum that was far greater than anyone had expected. Protesters enjoyed the "taste" of resistance, because for many of them Gezi was the first time they had vividly experienced being an actor in a social movement. A prominent feature of the Gezi Park movement was the extensive use of art combined with satire, humor, and irony. Protesters embraced creative methods and art quickly became an indispensable part of the movement. Apart from the political content it had, art was instrumentalized as a public and individual medium, creating new opportunities within the movement; it thus took on a fundamental role in structuring the forms of protest.

What is the benefit of using art in activism? What is its role in the course of a social movement? I will elaborate these questions through analyzing the use of art for communication and problematization purposes as well as for identifying and channeling spiritual and material resources. I will use examples of the artistic components and productions from within the Gezi Park movement to make the discussion more tangible. Before this, let's have a look at the terminology and background of our topic.

Movement

Social movements have been a focus of social sciences for a long time. Since the first introduction of the term "social movement" in 1850 (the original formulation was *soziale Bewegung* by Lorenz von Stein), numerous researchers studied collective actions in the form of a movement. This term referred to all political and ideological movements of the nineteenth century whose aim was to promote the welfare of the working class in an industrial society.[1] Today, these movements are generally considered as "traditional," although it would not be correct to say they have totally disappeared. Also, their connection to art was little different than it is nowadays. If we look at the nineteenth-century social movements and political atmosphere, we see a relationship between art and social movements that is reciprocal rather than integral. The most famous work of Eugène Delacroix, *Liberty Leading the People*,

1 See: Kaethe Mengelberg, "Lorenz von Stein and His Contribution to Historical Sociology," in: *Journal of the History of Ideas*, vol. 22, no. 2, April/June 1961, pp. 267–274, here p. 268.

can be given as an example for the year 1830. There is certainly a connection between Delacroix's Romantic expression and the public actions; however, the painting itself was not considered an instrument within the movement.

In the mid-1960s, a new generation of social movements sprouted. New social movements have certain features that differ essentially from traditional movements. Mario Diani describes new social movements as "a network of informal interactions between a plurality of individuals, groups and/or organizations, engaged in a political or cultural conflict, on the basis of a shared collective identity."[2] New movements no longer seek to take over government power, but challenge it in a symbolic way and lead to social change through influencing people within the existing system. It is important to note that they are heterogeneous and not formed on the basis of ideology and class.[3]

While the roles of dominator and resister do not change radically, the instruments of domination differ from the traditional kind, meaning that the resisters' inventory of reaction methods also develops from day to day. New social movements pay particular attention to innovation and creativity including artistic methods. Although art is considered to be "political" since the Middle Ages and Renaissance,[4] from the 1960s on, art began to be a distinctive feature of social movements; it is not only used as a tool but considered as a must within the movement.

2 Mario Diani, "The Concept Of Social Movement," in: *The Sociological Review*, vol. 40, no. 1, February 1992, pp. 1–25, here p. 13.

3 See: Claus Offe, "Yeni Sosyal Hareketler: Kurumsal Politikanın Sınırlarının Zorlanması," in: Kenan Çayır (ed.) *Yeni Sosyal Hareketler: Teorik Açılımlar*, Kaknüs, Istanbul, 1999, pp. 53–80, here p. 66.

4 See: Toby Clark, *Sanat ve Propaganda: Kitle Kültürü Çağında Politik İmge*, Ayrıntı, Istanbul, 2004, p. 14.

Almost fifty years after 1968, it is still difficult to say that the age of the new paradigm is over. A few decades after her death, Emma Goldman's famous quote "If I can't dance, it's not my revolution!" inspired many activists, and became an iconic slogan in the 1960s and 1970s. Although we don't hear this slogan that often today, the motto has stayed very much the same. Within the context of social movements, art plays an essential role in identifying our everyday experiences and problems as well as opening channels for communication. Art is being used to get in contact with people and express thoughts and feelings. We use art for satire, praise, criticism, and admiration. Marching on the streets, we dance, sing, draw, and perform. This is how we raise resistance through art.

Apart from transmitting emotions, feelings, and demands, art also provides time and space to experience these cognitive and sensory processes limited to personal and environmental qualifications. The very content of artistic products is related to daily life; how it is affected by politics, society, and environment. Generally, art is considered through the experience of various artists who are involved in the social movements and/or have a politically engaged public identity. Yet, aside from the professional artists, art can be a channel for liberation for nonartists as well. The Gezi activists were not all artists by profession; on the contrary, many of them were temporary performers.

Today, in social movements – starting from mid-1960s – art stays in the core of activism. Artistic use of materials can help us in expressing ourselves, communicating with a wider public, and creating networks inside and outside the movement. Further, art has a direct impact on emotions, which impacts both the individual and the community. This circumstance enables art to go beyond its usage for practical purposes. Along with the practical purposes, the use of art opens a playground for premodern drives, the unconscious, and human desire. Art reveals the hazards of our fragmented lives while giving us hints as to how they might be reunited.

The instrumentalization of art happens in different ways within social movements. It is used both for deliberate practical purposes, such as problematization and reaching out for support, and for more emotional reasons that help to experience the projection of a moment of liberation. During the protests, Gezi activists benefited from artistic tools and products to an extent that Turkey had never witnessed before in a movement. Subverted images, satirical slogans, humorous tweets, and music were all part of the movement. Intensive use of art quickly became an essential part of the protests and even shaped the general understanding of the movement.

Apart from contributing as a channel for political expression or carrying symbolic values, art held structural importance in Gezi. It brought in some fundamental elements to the movement that were instrumentalized in different ways. Our perceptions, actions, and emotions were shaped through art, as the following examples from Gezi protests will explore.

Art as a Tool for Frame Alignment

Framing or frame analysis is widely used in the social sciences. Although some earlier scholars mentioned it in their works, today's concept of framing was first introduced to the social sciences by Erving Goffman, who understood it as social organization of experience.[5] Thomas König emphasizes that "frames are basic cognitive structures which guide the perception and representation of reality."[6] Frames are considered to be interpretative diagrams that help us understand the main points of an issue and that link these points with each other. Framing theory has been applied to various fields in the social sciences, including social movements, on account of its practicality in structuring our perceptions.

A number of social movements and civil society organizations use frames in their actions in order to depict what is going on out there. A movement usually states a problem and demands a change in the law, public policy, local administration practices, and so on. The problematization and political/societal demands are put together in a frame. Referring to Goffman, David A. Snow et al. underline the importance of frame alignment within a social movement, and denote frames as "schemata of interpretation" that enable us "to locate, perceive, identify, and label"[7] occurrences pertaining to our lives and the world in general. Within the context of social movements, frame alignment can be explored through three different types: diagnostic framing (problem identification and attributions), prognostic framing (suggesting a solution, a strategy, or a tactic), and motivational framing (call to arms or collective action).[8]

5 See: Erving Goffman, *Frame Analysis. An Essay on the Organization of Experience*, Harvard University Press, Cambridge (MA), 1974.

6 Thomas König, "Frame Analysis: Theoretical Preliminaries," available online at: www.ccsr.ac.uk/methods/publications/frameanalysis, accessed 05/05/2014.

7 Goffman 1974, p. 21; see also: David A. Snow et al., "Frame Alignment Processes, Micromobilization, and Movement Participation," in: *American Sociological Review*, vol. 51, no. 4, August 1986, pp. 464–481, here p. 464.

8 See: Robert D. Benford and David A. Snow, "Framing Processes and Social Movements: An Overview and Assessment," in: *Annual Review of Sociology*, vol. 26, 2000, pp. 611–639.

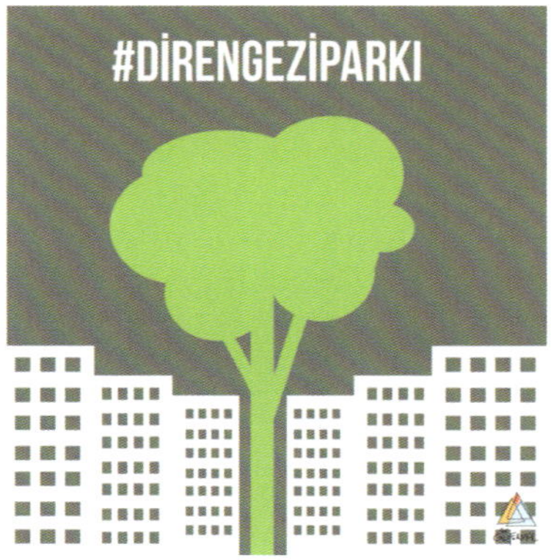

#direngeziparkı, work by Doğukan Güngör, 2013

A variety of artistic products and practices was utilized for frame alignment during the Gezi protests. Often images, words, and performances conveyed messages and depicted the problem. The work shown on the left is a good example of diagnostic framing.[9] The image includes a tree, the initial symbol attributed to Gezi Park when the protests began over the removal of trees and construction of a shopping mall. The buildings around the tree refer to the massive urban transformation projects undertaken in Istanbul, reminding us that Gezi Park is one of the few green areas among concrete structures.

After the riot police took over Gezi Park in mid-June 2013, and left no physical space in Taksim Square for protesters, passive resistance started up in Taksim Square and quickly spread to the whole country.

Performed by Erdem Gündüz, the "Standing Man" was introduced to the movement as a new and quite powerful tactic (prognostic framing).[10] Considering that the "Standing Man" arose after the first period of Gezi protests, we should take into account that it was a performance directed primarily against police violence, media blackout, and ignoring the protesters' demands.

9 The image is available online at: http://thecalifornial.com/post/84825917256, accessed 05/05/2014.

10 For another image of Gündüz' protest see: www.theguardian.com/commentisfree/2013/jun/18/turkey-standing-man, accessed 05/05/2014.

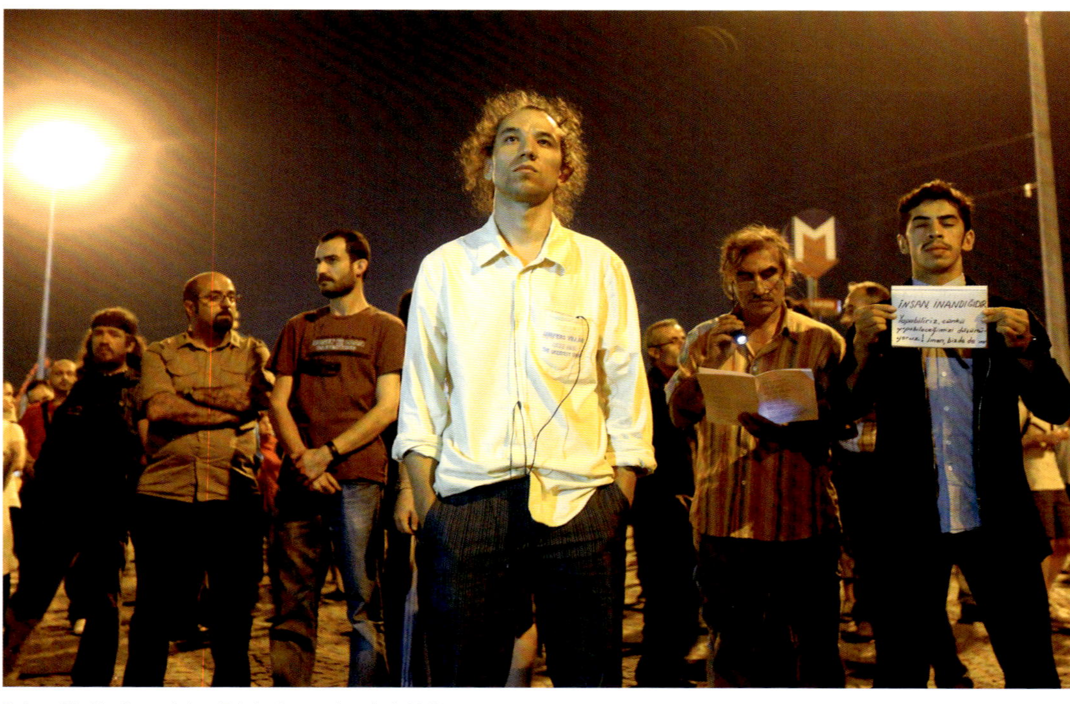

Erdem Gündüz, *Duran Adam*, Taksim Square, Istanbul, 2013

A further image below is an example of motivational framing, a call to collective action every evening during the Gezi protests.[11]

11 The image is available online at: http://twicsy.com/i/nhCFMd, accessed 05/05/2014.

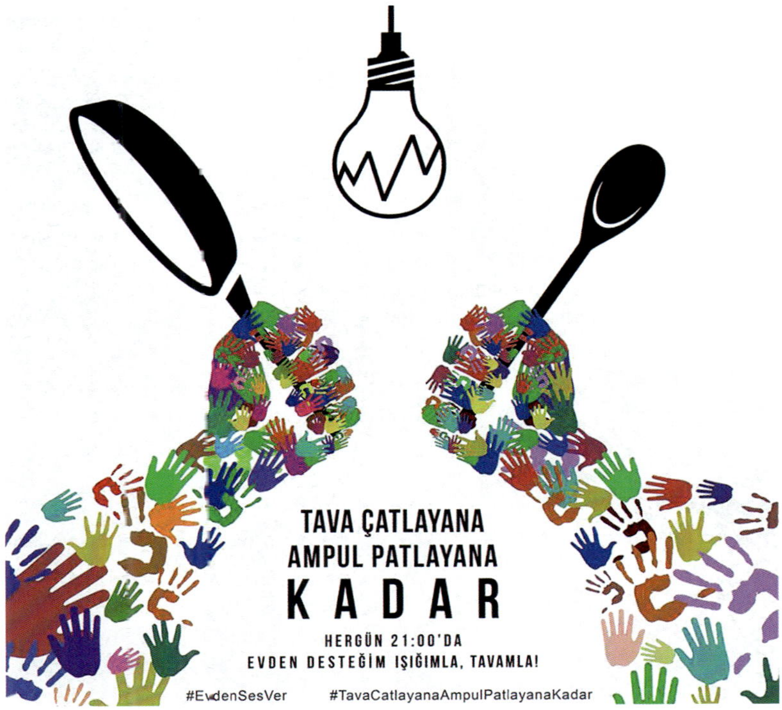

Call for a protest action disseminated via the Twitter account @istanbuldaneler during the Gezi protests in 2013

It reads: "Take supportive action with your lights and pans until the pan cracks and the lightbulb explodes." The call found response all over the country while Turkish Prime Minister Recep Tayyip Erdoğan called the efforts just the same old tune. The action was inspired by "One Minute of Darkness for Constant Light," one of the biggest civic protests that ever happened in Turkey which lasted for several weeks during 1997.[12]

12 See: Ezel Akay, *A Call to End Corruption: One Minute of Darkness for Constant Light*, Liam Mahony (ed.), A Tactical Notebook, Center for Victims of Torture, Minneapolis (MN), 2003.

Using art for motivational framing opens a window to discuss the role of art in recruiting supporters and creating other resources for a movement. Resource mobilization theory might help us explore this topic.

Art as a Tool for Mobilizing Resources

Resource mobilization theory examines the resources inside and outside of the social movement. Aggregating money and labor, as well as combination and operation of these resources, are essential for any movement's success. New social movements have benefited from art in order to mobilize resources by organizing activities such as concerts and sales of local artwork. Today's movements, including Gezi, have avoided paid art activities and prefer occasional voluntary donations in the form of cash or in-kind. Within the context of resource mobilization through art, recruitment of more people was a central concern.

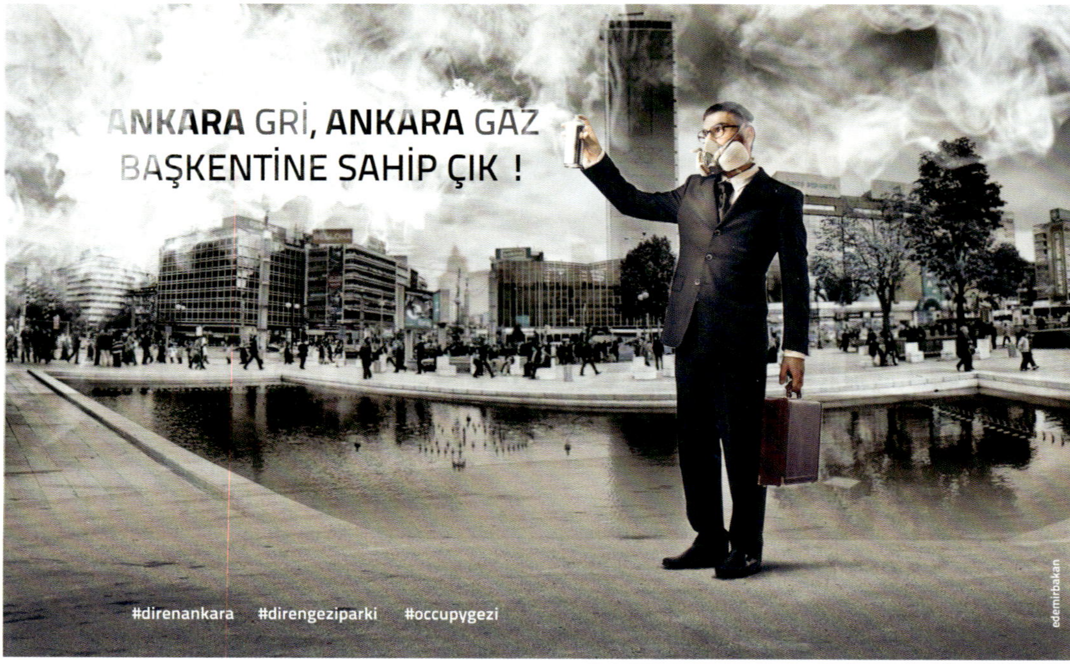

Emre Demirbakan,
Ankara gri, Ankara gaz başkentine sahip çık!, 2013

The image above was produced during the Gezi protests.[13] It reads: "Ankara [is] grey, Ankara [is full of] gas, reclaim your capital!" Images, songs, video clips with similar messages were circulated via social media among the activists in order to recruit more people into the movement. Artistic forms are important in creating and communicating a collective narrative.[14]

On the other hand, addressing emotions and hope that play a considerable part in social movements is equally important in the context of resource mobilization theory.[15] Artistic practices during Gezi triggered emotions by generating a sense of belonging, togetherness, and solidarity. Communal activities, such as singing a song or dancing, created a bonding effect among people. The Breton band Bagad Penhars' musical intervention with Kolektif Istanbul was a notable moment. During the performance of Davide Martello, aka Klavierkunst, with his piano in the middle of the square, even the police seemed mesmerized and touched. Within a movement art can be so powerful that it has a direct impact on emotions among the activists as well as on the opposing sides. Ziya Azazi, who danced as a whirling sufi dervish with a gas mask in Gezi Park, says that art helps us accept each other's differences as enrichment.[16] Referring to the U.S. Civil Rights Movement, T.V. Reed states "[…] that music was the key force in shaping, spreading, and sustaining the movement's culture and through culture its politics."[17] One might add that this applies not only for music but for art in general.

Art and social movements originate from and are reinforced by a wealth of resources, such as actual politics, social and economical developments, that are macro determinants, as well as micro determinants like daily routines, banal cycles, and individual concerns. Modern life introduces us to many facilities and innovations. It also brings with it significant challenges. Individual and societal

13
The image is available online at: www.facebook.com/photo.php?fbid=10152878289425655, accessed 05/05/2014.

14
See: Ron Eyerman, "The Role of the Arts in Political Protest," in: Mobilizing Ideas, The Center for the Study of Social Movements at the University of Notre Dame, June 3, 2013, available online at: http://mobilizingideas.wordpress.com/2013/06/03/the-role-of-the-arts-in-political-protest, accessed 05/05/2014.

15
See: James M. Jasper, *The Art of Moral Protest. Culture, Biography, and Creativity in Social Movements*, University of Chicago Press, Chicago (IL), 1997, pp. 29–33.

16
The interview is available online at: www.e-skop.com/skopbulten/gezi-direnisinin-gaz-maskeli-dervisi-ziya-azazi-ile-soylesi/1559, accessed 05/05/2014.

17
T.V. Reed, *The Art of Protest. Culture and Activism from the Civil Rights Movement to the Streets of Seattle*, University of Minnesota Press, Minneapolis (MN), London, 2005, p. 13.

desires inherent in art carry the potential for an "ideal" society. In view of this potential, this article seeks to discuss another fundamental argument: art is the central component in social movements that represents the totality of everyday life and affords the opportunity to experience this totality in an instant continuum.

Art as Mithridate

In addition to its practical uses within a movement, exploring another function of art may help us understand its ontological role, especially for the individual in action. For the activist/temporary performer, art serves as mithridate, a multifunctional antidote.[18]

Artists or temporary performers often isolate themselves from the hazards of modern life during their actions and artistic practices. The moments of laughing, playing, singing, drawing, dancing, and acting may become moments of ecstasy and delirium. Going through such courses of action does not signify a loss of control; quite the contrary, it is a process of intentionally experiencing rejuvenation, empowerment, and fortification.

This process has a considerable function in social movements. This immediately brings to mind the Russian philosopher Mikhail Bakhtin, who studied carnivals in medieval Europe and introduced the term "carnivalesque." He points out that the carnivals are moments for insurrection. During carnivals, ordinary life is suspended and all forms of distance between people disappear. Carnivals create a different kind of communication, an open dialog among people. It is remarkable how artistic elements associated with carnivals have survived throughout the centuries, passing through several periods even though they faced severe censorship and restriction. While modernity was taking over social life day by day and dividing it, art continued to be a shelter for symbols, rituals, dialog, interactions, expression, and so on. Art became an arena for *everyday* resistance, a festive oasis through which one had respite and could experience a state of desired reunification. As Graham St John quotes Robert Stam in his article, while breaking several social barriers, carnival is "ecstatic collectivity, the joyful affirmation of social change, a dress rehearsal for utopia."[19] There exists a potential for political change as well. Raoul Vaneigem famously said: "To work for delight and authentic festivity is barely distinguishable from preparing for a general insurrection."[20]

Activists do not always "give off" energy, they "intake" energy, too. Art plays a vital role here by providing a means for rebirth, in order that the people can carry on and continue their struggles while they are full of life again. Gezi activists did not only want to conceptualize social problems and produce great solutions. They looked for a sense of joy, entertainment, and festivity, so that they could be refreshed and empowered. Laughter is an important part of the carnivalesque that is experienced as half play. This play and laughter means being purified from whatever reality is out there in ordinary life, forgetting what the self is, and being reborn into life.[21] Certainly, art is an indispensable part of any carnival, playing the role of a catalyst for the performers to get into a mood of

18 Here I use the word "mithridate" but not "antidote." Antidote refers to a medicine for a specific poison, while mithridate fortifies the body against all types of poisons. It is a semimythical remedy with 65 ingredients and owes its name to King Mithridates VI. of the Pontic Empire who used to take this medicine regularly so that no poison could kill him. See: "Mithridatum," in: James Grout, *Encyclopedia Romana*, available online at: http://penelope.uchicago.edu/~grout/encyclopaedia_romana/aconite/mithridatum.html, accessed 05/05/2014.

19 Robert Stam, "Mikhail Bakhtin and Left Cultural Critique," in: E. Ann Kaplan (ed.) *Postmodernism and Its Discontents. Theories, Practices*, Verso, London, New York (NY), 1988, pp. 116–145, here p. 135; see also: Graham St John, "Protestival: Global Days of Action and Carnivalized Politics in the Present," in: *Social Movement Studies: Journal of Social, Cultural and Political Protest*, vol. 7, no. 2, 2008, pp. 167–190, here p. 168.

20 Raoul Vaneigem, *The Revolution of Everyday Life*, Rebel Press, London, 1983, as quoted from: Notes from Nowhere, "Carnival: Resistance Is the Secret of Joy," in: Notes from Nowhere (ed.), *We Are Everywhere. The Irresistible Rise of Global Anticapitalism*, Verso, London, New York (NY), 2003, pp. 173–183, here p. 182.

21 See: Tül Akbal Süalp, "Babil Kulesi Tutsaklarına Bakhtin'den Öneriler," in: *Toplumbilim – Kültürel Çalışmalar Özel Sayısı*, vol. 14, October 2001, pp. 53–60, here p. 57.

trance. At some point in art, we break down our invisible walls, meet others, and discover our feelings. Emotions and sensations take over the place of reason; we establish another way of communicating with ourselves and with others. These are just split seconds in our performance, but they give us the chance to experience a momentary totality, the reunification that we desired. Art can be revolutionary when totality stays inherent to it. Art gives us the opportunity to experience another dimension between this world and the desired one. This experience comes into existence in a very temporary but intense and vivacious moment that the practitioner of art, the artist, can live through and sense the resistance in totality. It is a moment for another reality – maybe the "real" reality – that makes us come closer to humanity. Providing such experience of totality, the "temporary oasis" created through art implies a carnivalesque moment.

In Gezi, the carnivalesque moments where activists felt empowered and experienced a utopia were many. A notable one that was videotaped and circulated via social media was an activist performing a moon dance.[22] Gezi Park was home to various artistic actions including singing songs together, drawing, dancing, and performing with lots of humor, satire, and grotesque, side by side. Gezi activists were demonized in the media, accused of being traitors, foreign agents, infidels, and looters. Humor, satire, irony, and grotesque were used in order to subvert and embrace such words and messages.[23] Especially the word "looter" (*çapulcu* in Turkish), which was advanced by Prime Minister Erdoğan, became one of the iconic words of the movement. It was subverted in a way that glorified its pejorative meaning. The activists used it as an honorable appellation to define a democracy fighter which was indeed an expression of joy rather than of anger.

Subversion of authority is closely connected with the totality of everyday life and the natural empowerment mechanism that art offers to the activist. Carnivalesque moments, being the site of resistance, provide the necessary conditions for one to experience autonomy and challenge the structures of hierarchy. Art, being a main catalyzer here, becomes an essential and indispensable component of activism and social movements.

Another emerging and one of the most important elements in social movements is the use of the Internet and social media. Alongside the art, it is a common denominator among contemporary types of action. Due to the limits of this article, it is not possible to explore this subject here in any depth, but I would like to conclude with a few words on the connection between new technologies and art.

Art Upcoming

There is a growing interest in the use of the Internet and social media in social movements, and various scholars have explored this issue with reference to recent examples such as the Tahrir, Occupy, *indignados*, Syntagma, and Gezi movements. Apart from how social media and use of the Internet made communication

22 Available online at: http://youtu.be/fEFq9MXjLY4, accessed 05/05/2014.

23 See: Meyda Yeğenoğlu, "Smells like Gezi Spirit. Democratic Sensibilities and Carnivalesque Politics in Turkey," in: *Radical Philosophy*, November/December 2013, available online at: www.radicalphilosophy.com/commentary/smells-like-gezi-spirit, accessed 05/05/2014.

easier among the activists, few studies go beyond this and look at the level of emotions.[24] As social media has been a main distribution channel for art, it would be interesting to see to what extent art was a part of the dissemination and sharing done over the Internet and the amount of responses related to that.

From observations made during Gezi, we witnessed that images, video recordings of musical happenings and performances, songs, and poems were disseminated far more than plain sentences. Particularly when there is a pinch of satire, irony, humor, and grotesque included, sharing on Facebook or via retweets on Twitter was much higher. The emotions behind this sharing would certainly be interesting to learn. Can tweeting a humorous slogan or a satirical image give a similar feeling to singing a partisan song passionately and feeling spiritually connected to everyone in the square? Can sharing a video of a group of young people dancing in front of the police be comparable to a dancer's physical experience of "temporary liberation"? Searching for answers to these questions is particularly interesting in our digital era. The average age of protesters at Gezi was 28, meaning that they were introduced to the Internet when they were very young.[25] We can only imagine which forms of art the social movements will include in the future and how integrated art will be with new media technologies. Our understanding of art might evolve in the upcoming years, like our ways of communication and representation. However, the intimate relationship between art's mithridatic role in social movements and carnivals that go back thousands of years is still there.

Having become a central element in social movements since the 1960s, art still seems to retain its importance in our perception of politics and society. The Gezi protests showed that art helps us define an idea and set it within a framework while making it easier to communicate the idea instantly. Art is also used for generating material resources as well as for canalizing people's emotions for a movement. At the same time, representing the totality of everyday life, art has strong impact on the individual who performs a carnivalesque moment and provides an opportunity to experience such totality. A most powerful aspect of the Gezi movement was this feeling of being "complete." It is very essential for us, human beings, this turning down of the hierarchies and experiencing a moment of social unification. The emotions, the least studied element in the social movements field, will continue to affect our thoughts and actions either on the community or individual level. As Besim Dellaloğlu said, art is the last shelter where humankind can maintain the existence of longing for *another* society that is beyond the society of today.[26]

24 See: "Technopolitics: the potential of connected multitudes. The 15M network-system as a new paradigm of distributed politics," available online at: http://datanalysis15m.files.wordpress.com/2013/06/technopolitics-15m-summary.pdf, accessed 05/05/2014.

25 See: KONDA Research and Consultancy, "Gezi Report. Public perception of the 'Gezi protests'. Who were the people at Gezi Park?," June 5, 2014, available online at: http://konda.com.tr/en/raporlar/KONDA_Gezi_Report.pdf, accessed 09/15/2014.

26 See: Besim F. Dellaloğlu, *Frankfurt Okulu'nda Sanat ve Toplum*, 2nd ed., Bağlam, Istanbul, 2001, p. 51.

Ammar Abo Bakr and Ganzeer *1982

Ammar Abo Bakr's work is a study of collective memory in Egypt, using practices from pop art, naive and folk art, sacred art, muralism, and graffiti. His style of collage is a dialog of form and topic that integrates the visual and media arts. It aims to be more socially inclusive, providing the public with images they can relate to in their spaces from their shared experiences. His knowledge about Egyptian history acquired as a draftsman working with archaeologists and Egyptologists grounds his work, which has expanded to follow events closely since the January 25, 2011 uprising with massive mural collages in Luxor, Cairo, and other Egyptian cities. His experience gained as a lecturer in fine arts for seven years enables him to work with students of all kinds in the public space.

Ganzeer is not exactly a graphic designer, nor a product designer. He is not particularly a street artist or comic book artist, nor is he an installation artist, writer, speaker, or video maker. But he has had the chance to assume all of these roles at different periods in time and in different locations around the world, while remaining tied to his hometown of Cairo. The London *Guardian* has described Ganzeer as a major player in an emerging "counter-culture arts scene on the mainstream radar," and Al-Monitor.com has placed him on a list of fifty people shaping the culture of the Middle East today, while *Art in America* has associated Ganzeer with a "New Realism," an art movement responding to a host of global challenges.

Street Art War in Egypt: An Interview

Did you work politically before January 25, 2011? How did the revolution change your work?

Ammar Abo Bakr: Nope. The fact of the revolution on the streets forced me to take to the street and work with groups. Even groups I never knew before, which is different from working alone.

Ganzeer: The motivations for my work have always been far more social than political. Of course, since January 25, 2011, the social and the political have heavily overlapped. Did I do socially motivated work prior to January 25? Sure. Was it political? Not necessarily. The major change that the revolution caused in my work was to create a sense of urgency in getting the work out there, along with pushing me to take it to the streets.

Can you retrace the phases in your work since 2011? How is your work's development intertwined with Egyptian politics and society in past years?

Abo Bakr: First phase, I was very concerned with information, concerned with stenciling work in several places, this was mostly in Luxor. But in October, I started working in Cairo. I mirrored the same phases of the revolution. There were highs and lows. I was working first on local issues, bringing the revolution to Luxor, spraying lots of slogans. Campaigning against remnants of the old regime (such as Amr Moussa). But there are differences from working in Cairo versus working in Luxor. So in Cairo spraying "Freedom to Alaa Abd El-Fattah," for example, may be relevant, but not at all relevant in Luxor, because they don't know who he is. They have very different issues there, still related to the revolution, but different.

Ganzeer: My primary concern since 2011 up to this very day is bringing to light that the Egyptian military apparatus is not on our side. That it is very obviously on Hosni Mubarak's side. And that it is in fact the main driving force behind the corruption and decline of quality of life in Egypt, and there will be no freedom or justice without purging our governance and institutions from the military's influence.

Do you feel connected to other artists of the Arab Spring in some kind of movement?

Abo Bakr: No. I do not believe in the Arab Spring.

Ganzeer: Sure, but I also feel connected to a global network of artists concerned with the injustices of the world we live in.

Do you have an artist's identity that is different from your political identity, or are the two always connected?

Abo Bakr: The revolution, of course, added something to my identity. I'm still working on intertwining them.

Ganzeer: Connected.

Would you describe yourselves as political artists or artist-activists, possibly "artivists"? Or are these just artificial categories?

Abo Bakr: These are all artificial categories of course. First and foremost, I just happen to be an individual who has a very specific skillset, and I'm just using it in the revolution. The revolution is one thing and politics are something else. We don't do politics. We aren't trying to be diplomatic, or favor any lesser evil over another. We are revolting.

Ganzeer: This, of course, is a very popular question, and it really gets on my nerves. Is a singer who sings about love labeled as a professional romantic? No. But as soon as you sing about social issues, the media call you an activist. Like activism is some kind of job. Like caring about the world can only be reserved for a person if he/she makes it their job. You can still be a singer and care about the world. You can still be a doctor or carpenter and care about the world. And of course, you can still be a visual artist and care about the world. Your job does not suddenly transform into "activism" just because you have a conscience. You're still a doctor, or carpenter, or visual artist, or whatever it is that you actually do.

Can you still identify when and where your works are "works" in the art sense, and when they are tools for demonstrations, for example? Do you make that differentiation at all?

Abo Bakr: This differentiation exists, yes. Since we believe that anything written on a wall falls under the category of freedom of expression, then this category doesn't have to fall under the category of art. At the presidential palace, I had to do whole pieces within less than half an hour. Which is very different from working comfortably in the studio on a piece for endless hours. In the beginning, I incorporated much less craftsmanship into my work on the street – very folkloric and closer to the people, for this would encourage others to do work of their own, rather than discourage them from doing work because it's far more advanced than their own. Over time, I started to incorporate more craft and more skill into the work. This was important towards the end when graffiti was starting to have negative connotations because of aesthetically displeasing slogans sprayed all over the country by Muslim Brotherhood supporters. By raising the artistic bar higher, the argument that graffiti is bad and cheap is gone. There are still other things I do which are a tool of demonstration that I do not necessarily put in my portfolio. It's not one of my works. I am no longer Ammar, the individual, I am Ammar, part of a much larger mass. The look of the graffiti is very much tied to the circumstances of the time. I will never forget this one time on Mohamed Mahmoud Street, when the Brotherhood asked for a "treaty" and someone sprayed on the wall: "Treaty? How? When people are dying?" It wasn't necessarily beautifully written, but it was just so strong given its place and timing. My portrait of Bassem Mohsen could only be done within these circumstances, guarded by the military and police; I told them he died during the anti-Brotherhood protests, but he actually died during anti-Sisi protests. The army guys beside the wall didn't know who he was. Whether you know him or not, whether there are pro-Sisi protests in Tahrir Square or not, Bassem Mohsen (the portrait) now exists in Tahrir Square. Bassem Mohsen is symbolic of the revolution, because some claim that he was shot by Sisi's police force, others claim he was shot by Brotherhood members. Either or, he was shot by one of the revolution's two main enemies. He is the revolution and is now in Tahrir Square.

Ganzeer: No. The way I approach art is a mode of self-expression, along with contributing to altering the viewer's consciousness. This applies whether I create something in the form of a poster, or a painting on canvas, or a sculpture, or installation, or whatever it is that I get my hands on.

Both of you are widely known for one particular work each (the *Martyr Wall* and the *Tank vs. Bread-Biker*). Could you quickly explain the story of these works? Do you agree that these works are your most important ones from the revolution or do you have other works in mind? If so, which ones?

Abo Bakr: I believe in that particular work because of the multiple layers in it. There is always discussion about it, you can always analyze it, you can track the events of the revolution by examining this particular wall. The idea is that it

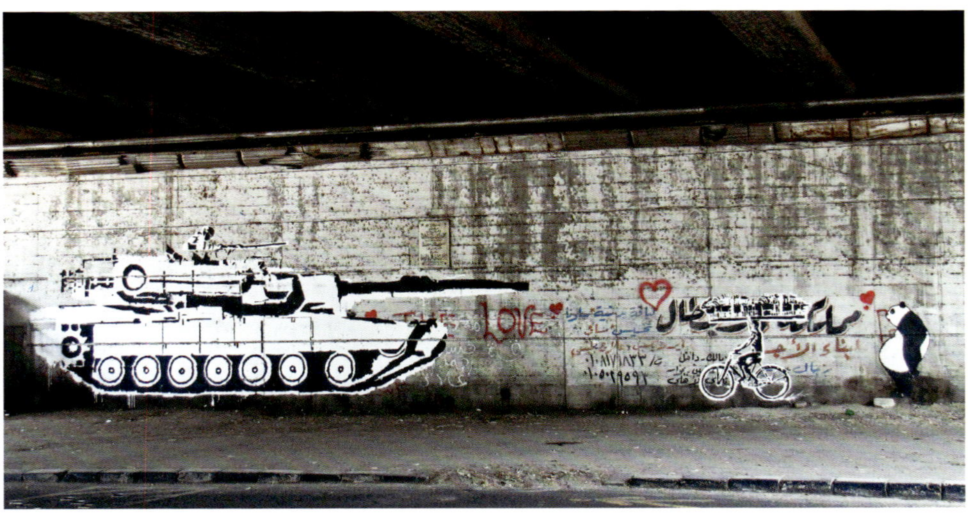

Ganzeer, *Tank vs. Bread-Biker*, Cairo, Egypt, May 20–21, 2011

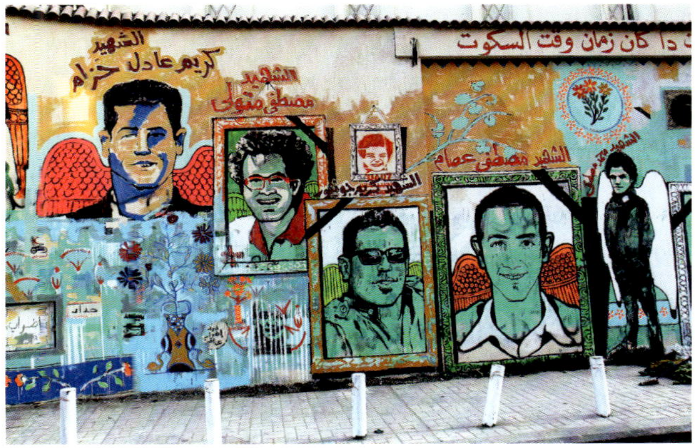

The mural of Mohamed Mahmoud Street is the metaphoric tomb of Tahrir Square: angelic portraits of young victims of the Port Said tragedy with their names written above are surrounded by motifs common to wall paintings done by naive artists. Painting began and continued as violence erupted all around during the night of February 2, 2012.

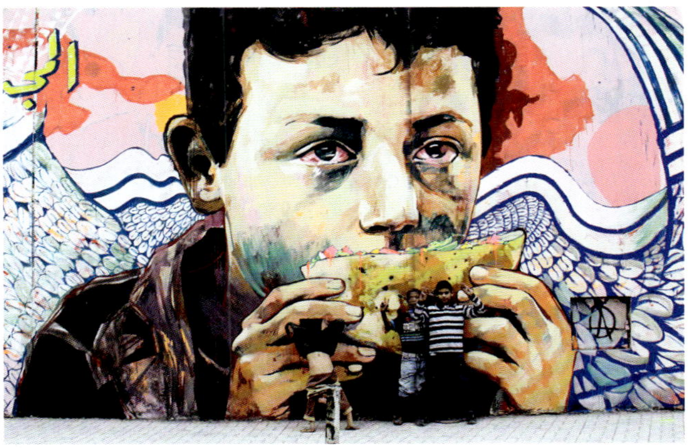

Children pose in front of the portrait of 11-year-old Said Khaled, killed in the November 2011 Mohamed Mahmoud Street clashes between demonstrators protesting military rule and the police. The image is part of a new mural on the street, whose layers have chronicled events in Egypt since the January 25 uprising.

would be the shrine of the fallen. The regime was killing the youth on Mohamed Mahmoud Street, as well as in the Port Said massacre (74 killed), and it was important to commemorate them. Also, because the ultras (killed in Port Said) are one of the most organized revolutionary groups, the regime – whether it's the military regime or the Brotherhood – is keen on eliminating this particular organized group. Doing this work on Mohamed Mahmoud Street, a street that saw many clashes and which connects Tahrir Square to the Ministry of the Interior, was important to encourage people to storm the Ministry, which is a spike in the revolution's back. And to prove that we are not only thugs, there are also artists and other regular people involved in this uprising. It's a positive aspect within the clashes. And eventually the street turned into a shrine, where relatives of the dead would visit.

Ganzeer: Well, popularity and importance don't necessarily go hand in hand. The *Tank vs. Bread-Biker* may be one of the most popular works but I wouldn't necessarily label it as the most important work. Would I label anything the most important work? No, not really. I'd rather not concern myself with these questions and just keep on working.

Could you describe the meaning of particular places for your works? How far have your works been specific to particular sites such as Zamalek or Mohamed Mahmoud Street?

Abo Bakr: Like I said, the Mohamed Mahmoud Street saw innumerable clashes, which is why I consider it to be one of the most important places of commemoration.

Ganzeer: Choosing that wall in Zamalek for the tank was entirely based on practical reasons: the wall was the right size, it overlooks a main road, the pavement in front of it is large enough to spread my materials out and work comfortably, etc.

Sometimes you have to work secretly, and in great danger, at night, and sometimes you can work out in the open during the daytime. How does this affect your work?

Abo Bakr: You have a very different street culture. Here we're in the middle of a revolution. If we occupy a space in public, we do what we want anytime. If there are clashes on the street, then I work in the midst of the clashes. If I'm working someplace that doesn't have that sort of action, then I must do the work rather quickly in the night. It differs from time to time.

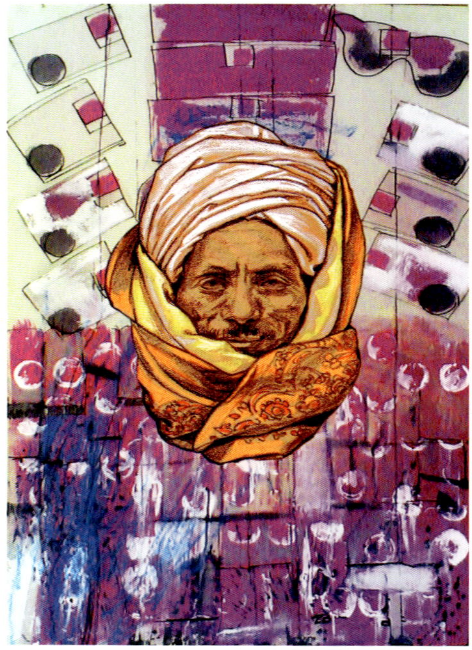

A collage work of a portrait of an Egyptian superimposed upon a local Egyptian board game based upon luck and popular in the countryside

Ganzeer: We're still in the middle of a revolution. It's a time of change, where the old rules don't necessarily apply, and so many aspects of how we've lived our lives are becoming elusive. As artists, we've come not only to challenge the government and challenge society, but also to challenge ourselves. Simultaneously, all at once. Certain works have these three challenges in them when created during daytime, other works have these three challenges in them when created in the darkness of the night.

Do you ever experience people's immediate reactions to your works? Do you get into discussions? Do you appreciate that or would you rather just make your statements through art?

Abo Bakr: Sometimes this, sometimes that. Depends on the work, and the events. Sometimes you just can't handle getting into a debate. Other times, especially when creating large works, engaging with the public, I feel, is important. Sometimes you just want to throw the work on the wall, allow the work to shock people. They can react to it later, they can tear it, they can censor it, they can praise it.

Ganzeer: I try to avoid interacting with the public as much I can. I'd rather let the work do that for me. That's where my strength is, in the art I create.

By now both of you have become stars of the revolution. How did that happen and why, do you think?

Abo Bakr: I have nothing to do with this. It's the media's fault. We don't want stardom in this revolution. It's not anyone's revolution. And maybe sometimes it can make you happy, but other times it can be a problem that limits you. The media never wants to capture genuine points. It doesn't follow the truth, it merely follows other people that follow the truth. So the media follows the erasing of a martyr mural, for example, but not the killer of the martyr himself. This struggle with the media is a whole different story.

Ganzeer: Creating stars is just a part of the media industry. They need to create new stars because writing about old stars can get repetitive and boring, which of course will affect sales. At times of revolution, when "revolution" is popular amongst the greater populace, and you still want to be relevant as a media entity, what do you do? Well, if you find that the old stars are not so revolutionary (given their ties with the old systems), then you go off and try to find people you can turn into new stars. Some may think this is a good thing, but the media has a habit of destroying their stars almost as fast as building them up, because there is money to be made in that destruction as well. Case in point? Michael Jackson, for example. This is not something I'm at all interested in ever getting involved in. I don't own a television, or radio, nor do I buy magazines or newspapers. I am mostly surrounded by my books and working tools and the Internet. All I want to do is work on my stuff and put it out there in the world. What the media does with it is the media's business, not mine.

Ganzeer, you are originally a graphic designer, and Ammar, you are a more traditionally trained artist. How does this affect the ways in which you work today?

Abo Bakr: It aided in diversifying what we deliver. Being traditionally trained, I can sometimes do something folkloric, or something that is semi-real. I know how to attract the audience or repulse the audience. Sometimes I count on their collective memory in terms of shapes and colors. These are things I know as a traditionally trained artist.

Ganzeer: As a designer, I've come to train myself to think in a very problem-solving sort of fashion. I think of an issue, I think about how to deal with that issue, and I execute, almost like a machine. Even when it comes to painting on canvas, for example, this is how I operate. I leave very little to chance; I have a particular issue that I'm interested in tackling and a very specific idea of how to tackle it. And I try to inform myself about the issue to be able to tackle it the best I can. Even when a certain work I do may not look "designy," and may appear to be messy and spontaneous, you can be sure that every single aspect of it is very well thought out and is there for a very specific and well-planned reason.

Does Egypt have a specific manner of practicing graffiti or street art today due to its (art) history? Do you see your practice as related to those of the past in terms of symbolism and materials or techniques?

Abo Bakr: Yes. We have two problems. One of the reasons for the revolution is that there is so much ugliness in society, and we became alienated from so much culture and heritage. When we revolt, we understand that it's not merely about ousting a despot, it's about igniting mass change in society and making a connection with so many things we've lost, while still counting on society's mass conscience and memory, certain things people don't necessarily see or experience every day, but it's still embedded somewhere in their DNA. Urbanization, deterioration of villages, this is something I cared about even before the revolution, and these are things I wanted to work into the revolution.

Ganzeer: I would say that the most prevalent factor in Egyptian graffiti, regardless of who does it or what the graffiti is about, is that it mostly tends to be void of ego, void of individual interest, and more about society or the community. Which makes sense, if you are going to go put a work out on the street, how can it be so selfish without taking the people on the street into consideration? This is probably the biggest difference I find between Egyptian graffiti and European graffiti.

How did you get to the techniques you've been using, such as mural paintings or spraying with stencils? Was that a form-follows-function approach or was it a conscious choice for a particular material?

Abo Bakr: I don't know. It's my job.

Ganzeer: My first large-scale murals were actually large-scale stencils. I've been told by many European graffiti practitioners that they'd never seen this technique before. It made sense for me to do so, because I wanted the pieces to be very accurate, without any room left for error, and to just fit the wall perfectly. I also didn't want to need to do any thinking while executing it on the street. I just wanted to be able to follow a series of steps, like instructions, to do it – do it right – and leave. And so the large-scale, multilayer stencil technique was developed, which many people describe as akin to screen-printing on walls. Of course, it's not the only technique I use. I employ different techniques depending on the circumstances surrounding the piece, testing out new techniques whenever possible. Like I said before, I tend to operate with a very problem-solving sort of method.

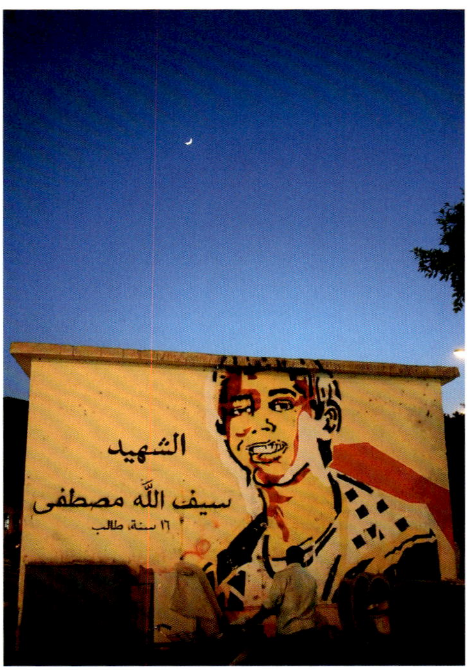

Ganzeer, *Martyr #1*, mural applying the large-scale stencil technique, February 2011

How would you describe the social and political situation in Egypt today, and what is the role of your art in it?

Abo Bakr: My role? I encourage bringing down the state. That's it. The state is the reason behind the social decline, they're working against the revolution, they're working on making us forget the revolution, giving us the most measly of promises and convincing us that freedom already exists and that revolution is evil, or it's a foreign plot that must be resisted. So I'm trying to encourage resistance.

Ganzeer: Well, the political situation is that Egypt right now revolves around the military apparatus doing whatever they can to hold onto power, creating enough of a sense of chaos, instability, and insecurity in the country so that people feel they have no one powerful to trust other than the military. On the social level, people are torn between entrusting the military just for this little while until stability is back in place or continuing the struggle and facing the economic difficulties (and the possible death toll) that come with it. As an artist whose work can arguably be influential, I have an important role in trying to keep people from falling for the military's trap (again, and again, and again).

Presidential elections are now approaching again. Do you think your art can do some kind of campaigning?

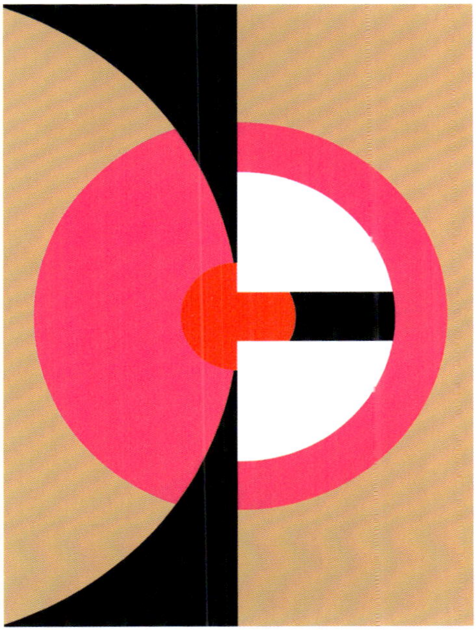

Ganzeer, *Abstract Pornography or Pornography According to Islamic Sharia #1*, 2014, geometric poster design

Abo Bakr: Not art. Resistance. Resistance through art. *#voteforthepimp*, for example, is really working, is very effective, and destroys the whole notion of presidential election. This is a political move working against the motives of the revolution, so we work against it with graffiti, with art. I am, of course, against the presidential elections, it follows the same system of the state we intend to bring down, that we intended on bringing down three years ago. This is not right; even if people go out and vote, we can at least let them know that it's wrong. This is like the seventh time people have been asked to go out and vote on something, convincing people that each time it will lead to stability, etc. Putting the revolution in a box is obviously proving false to people. People are not voting enthusiastically as much as in 2011. The revolution is much stronger than presidential elections or a box. The role of the revolution is to expose. That's what we're doing.

Ganzeer: The notion of a president, as far as I'm concerned, is as obsolete as the notion of a king or pharaoh. I understand that this may be a little too extreme for people to grasp right now, but mark my words… It won't be long before presidential systems are a thing of the past.

What are you working on at the moment?

Abo Bakr: I'm working on flies. Flies are special recognition symbols that the Ancient Egyptian state gave to very exceptional military jobs. So I'm considering the revolutionaries as a real army, so I'm giving our heroes (martyrs) flies to give them recognition. Also, in real-life terms, flies tend to conglomerate around shit and filth. So it also symbolizes the repulsion of the masses from the revolution and its martyrs.

Ganzeer: Way too many things. A book on revolutionary tactics, a series of antimilitary posters (titled: *Of Course the Army Protected the Revolution*), a series of geometric poster designs with pornographic undertones (titled: *Islamic Pornography*), planning phase for a large graphic novel (to focus on throughout 2015), transcribing a long interview I conducted with Finnish street artist Sampsa, designing a few logos for friends, clearing out my painting studio, and most probably a few dozen other things all blurry in my head right now.

The interview was conducted by Linnea Semmerling (ZKM | Karlsruhe) via e-mail in April 2014.

G.M.B. Akash *1977

G.M.B. Akash works as a photojournalist and artist, documenting the experience of those who suffer from poverty or human rights injustices, capturing both the grim circumstances of their lives and their individual characters and identities. He also teaches photography in workshops and seminars to support aspiring young photographers, and his work has been published in numerous international publications such as *National Geographic*, *Time*, and *The Guardian*.

G.M.B. Akash's photo documentary *Angels in Hell* (2002–2012) consists of portraits of people at the bottom of the social ladder in Bangladesh. It focuses on the issue of child labor: despite being on the agenda for a long time, no significant progress has been made in addressing this problem in Bangladesh – a country in which schooling is compulsory only until the age of ten and millions of children are engaged in the most hazardous forms of child labor. With *Angels in Hell*, Akash highlights the dramatic relevance of the exploitation of child laborers in manufacturing factories in his home country and, at the same time, gives them a voice and a face by telling their story in his works.

The pictures from *Angels in Hell* were taken over a period of ten years and published in his book *Survivors*.

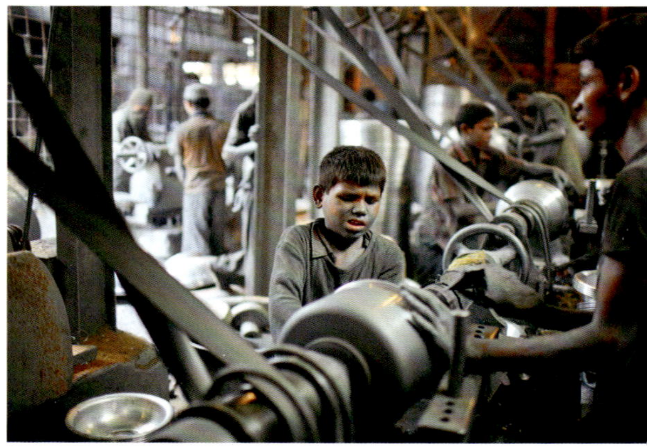

G.M.B. Akash, from the photo series *Angels in Hell*, 2002–2012

Survivors assembles images taken in Bangladesh, Pakistan, Indonesia, Nepal, India, Sri Lanka, Bhutan, and the Philippines; it documents the everyday life of the poorest, both their misery and strength, and seeks to demonstrate the invincibility of the human spirit to survive against all odds. A proportion of the proceeds from the book and subsequent exhibitions goes to an aid project founded by the photographer. G.M.B. Akash set out to find those he photographed many years ago, to support them in setting up small businesses of their own, and to become self-sufficient.

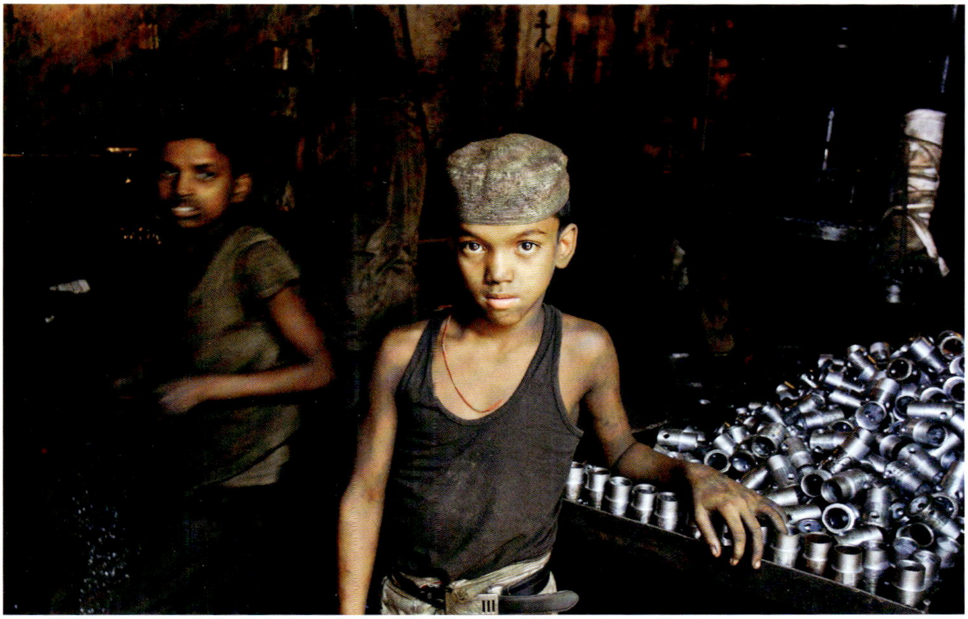

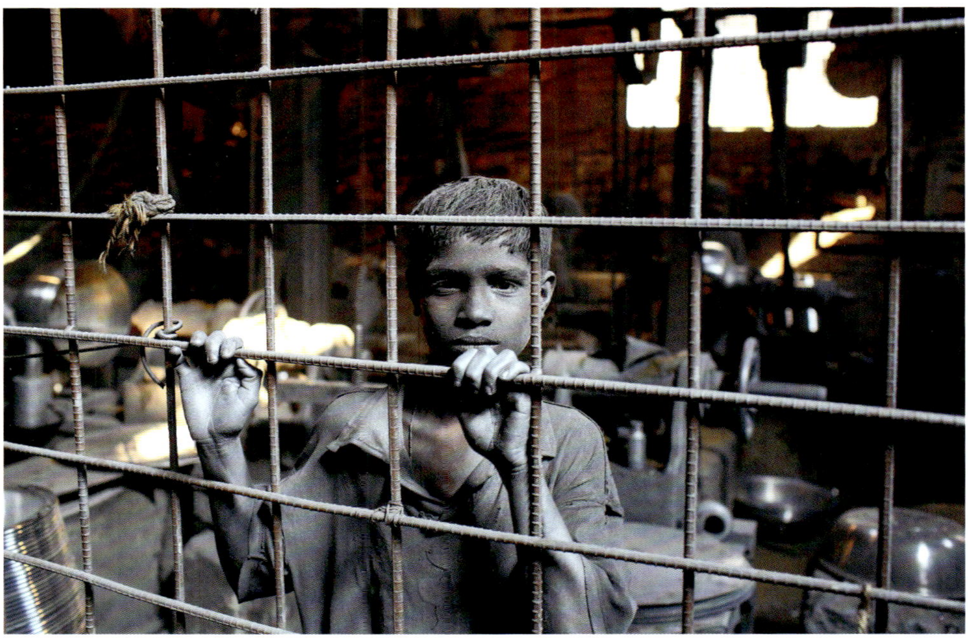

G.M.B. Akash, from the photo series *Angels in He l*, 2002–2012

Founded in 2011
Global

http://art-leaks.org

ArtLeaks

The Web-based platform ArtLeaks was set up by an international group of artists, curators, art historians, and intellectuals, which included curator and art historian Corina L. Apostol and the artist collectives Chto Delat? and Société Réaliste, as a reaction and response to abuse of professional integrity and infraction of labor rights. By drawing attention to firsthand testimonies and exposing concrete cases of precarious conditions of cultural workers, ArtLeaks highlights how institutions are implicated in unequal power relations and corporate power and how those who significantly contribute to their existence are negatively affected by structural problems.

ArtLeaks is a global support network and community to expose all forms of abuse, mistreatment, and repression in the arts and the cultural sector, such as censorship issues, unequal treatment, or the nonpayment of fees, which result from the normalized practices of many institutions and managers. As a platform of collective protest and institutional critique that dares to take a look behind the scenes and expose cases of injustice and unfairness, it is also a critical inquiry into the dependency of artists, curators, and other cultural workers on institutions and the market. ArtLeaks seeks to deconstruct the politics of inclusion and exclusion. Although it has a special

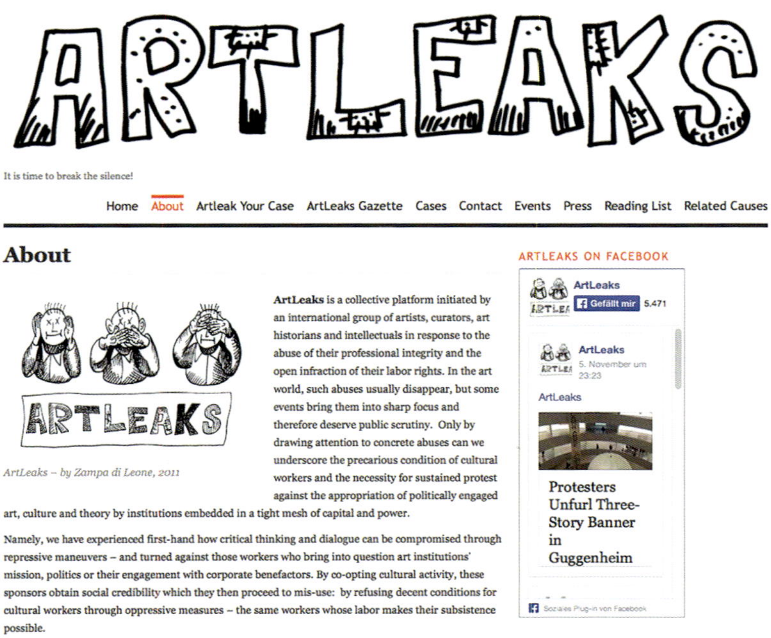

ArtLeaks, screenshot from the website art-leaks.org, 2014

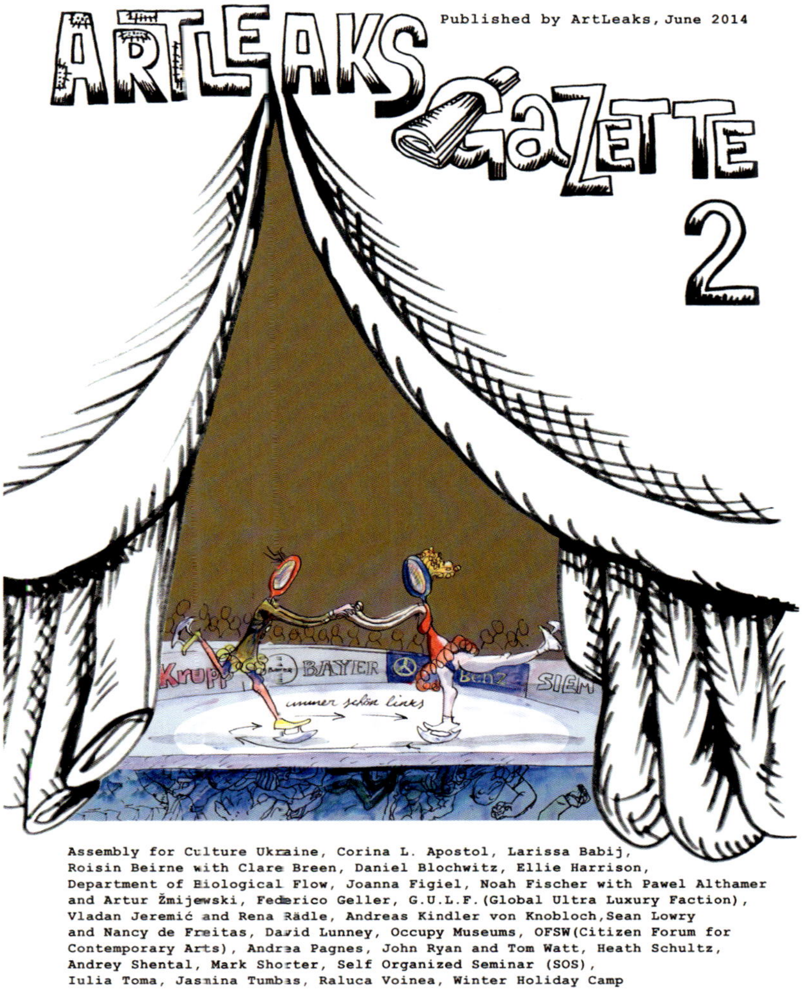

ArtLeaks, *ArtLeaks Gazette*, no. 2, 2014, cover

focus on cases from Eastern Europe, its aim is the international exchange of information and ideas. Its long-term goals are to foster solidarity and to encourage art and cultural institutions to account for their actions, decisions, and politics publicly and transparently.

Both signed and anonymous reports, accompanied by a documentation of evidence, are accepted and can be submitted and published on the ArtLeaks website or Facebook page. Since 2013, the *ArtLeaks Gazette* is published online under a Creative Commons license. With all of its platforms and outputs, the initiators of ArtLeaks want to give a voice to disadvantaged and exploited cultural workers, to support them in fighting for their rights, and so they rightly say, "It's time to break the silence."

Founded in 2004, active until 2010
Russia

Bombily

The conceptual approach of the Bombily art group, founded in 2004 by Anton Nikolaev and Alexander Rossihin, is a maximal popularization of genres and practices of contemporary art: working as "cabbies" (English for the Russian slang word *bombily*), they borrow ideas for future actions from their "clients." For them the only objective trend in contemporary art is "rehumanization" (as opposed to "dehumanization"), a return to "new sincerity." Since 2005 Bombily has shot more than forty short films and has participated in over thirty exhibitions. Together with the Voina group, they form the Professional Union of Street Art, an organization that is responsible for some of the most radical actions at the intersection of art and activism.

Auto-Race of Those Who Disagree (2007) was an action in which couples were invited to have sex on a mattress strapped to the roof of a moving car. The car drove as a symbol of free love through the crowded streets of Moscow. The action was the Bombily art group's contribution to "The Dissenters' March," also known as "The March of Those Who Disagree," a series of anti-Putin protests, which took place in Moscow from December 2006 to May 2007 and was organized by the opposition coalition The Other Russia.

In its campaign *White Line*, which took place in Moscow in May 2007, the Bombily art group drew a sixteen-kilometer-long chalk line on the Sadovoye Koltso, the so-called Garden Ring around the inner city of Moscow, to separate symbolically the center of power politics from the rest of Russia and thereby cut it off from all the evil it disseminates. The action is captured in a video documentation, whose original soundtrack is partially overlaid with radio news broadcasts, in which a commentary on Vladimir Putin's presidency follows the report about the action.

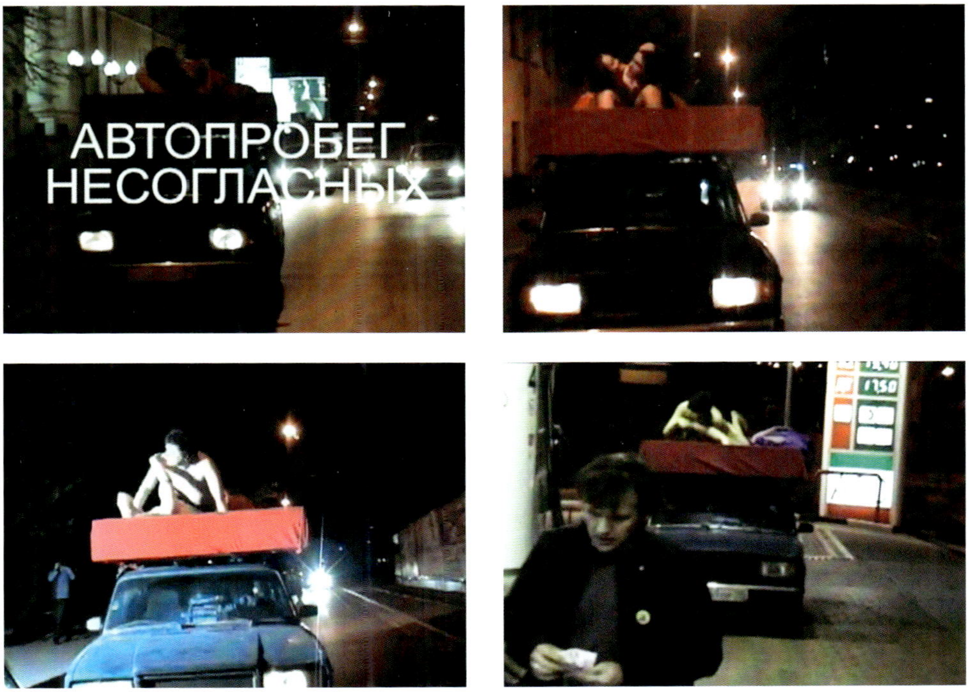

Bombily, *Auto-Race of Those Who Disagree*, 2007
video, color, sound, 4:33 min, video stills

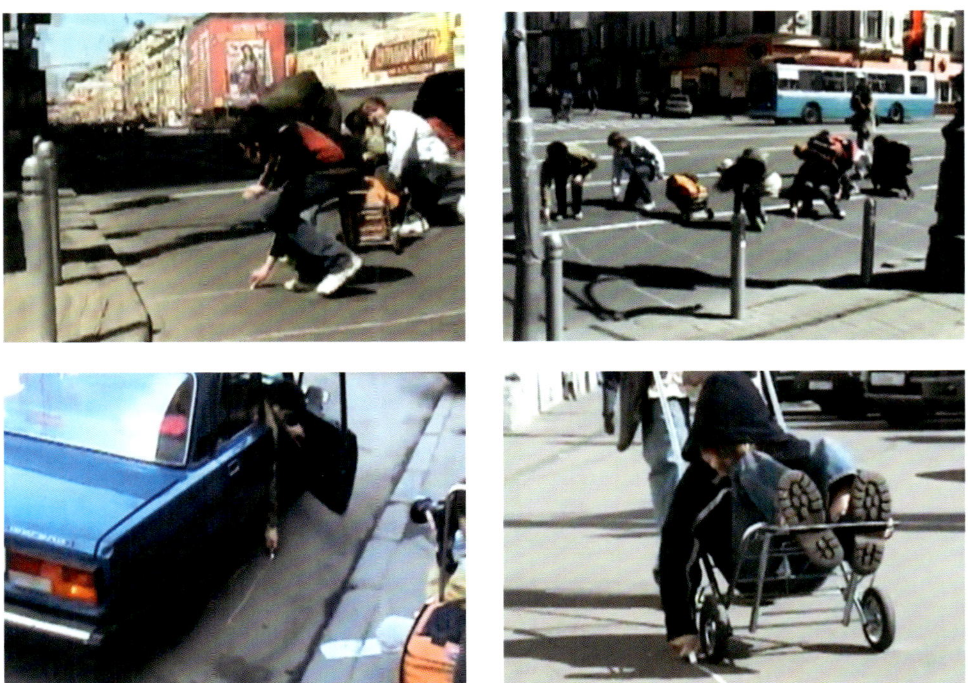

Bombily, *White Line*, 2007,
video, color, sound, 3:48 min, video stills

Ángela Bonadies *1970 and Juan José Olavarría *1969

Ángela Bonadies is an artist and photographer whose work focuses on memory, identity, and urban spaces. After studying graphic design and architecture, she worked at the Museo Alejandro Otero in Caracas where she was inspired to train and work as a photographer. She started out with a 6 × 6 Rolleiflex camera, and some of her first photos were taken at the Catia Prison in Caracas. With her series *Inventarios* [Inventaries] and *Lo doméstico* [The Domestic] she worked on inquiries about domestic space; for her "invasions" she focused on urban spaces, documenting uninhabited buildings taken over by people to live in.

Juan José Olavarría is a multidisciplinary artist who works at the intersection of art and social activism. He has participated in numerous exhibitions, conferences, community projects, and other activities, and also works as an educator.

The photo series *Torre de David* (2010–2013) by Ángela Bonadies and Juan José Olavarría illustrates how squatting is practiced in the Centro Financiero Confinanzas, an unfinished skyscraper in Caracas also known as "Torre de David": the creative occupation of abandoned urban locations. Bonadies and Olavarría's photo series documents the occupation of the former construction site, which underwent different stages of transformation. Partially built, the building was then abandoned and left to decay; it became a ruin, before being reappropriated, collectively shaped, and developed into a home for many people. In their photos, Bonadies and Olavarría show how the former ruin was filled with life by individual squatters, building a community.

The building was nicknamed after its main investor David Brillembourg. After Brillembourg's death in 1993, the government took control of the building, which was never completed because of the financial crisis that struck Venezuela in 1994. The complex comprises six buildings and forty-five floors; it lacks elevators, electricity, running water, balcony railings, windows, and walls. Due to the massive housing shortage in Venezuela, the building was occupied by squatters in 2007. The squatters became residents; they improved basic utility services and even operated services and shops, and the coordinators of this self-organized community established rules and collected charges for housing and communal services. Until 2014, over 3,000 people lived in the building. In July 2014, the Venezuelan government evacuated hundreds of families from the tower and relocated them in new homes in Cúa, a one-hour drive south of Caracas, as part of its Great Housing Mission project.

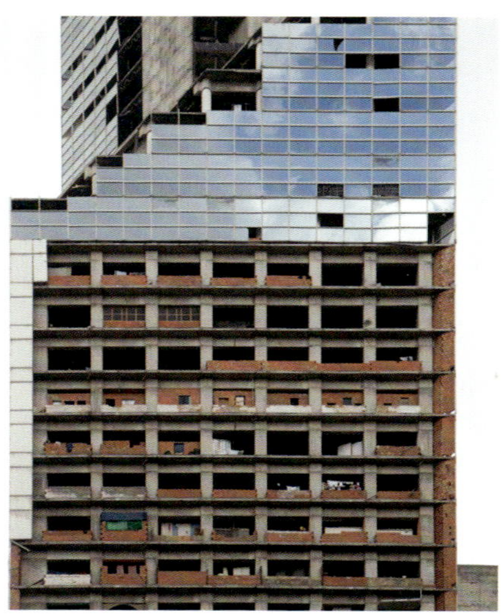

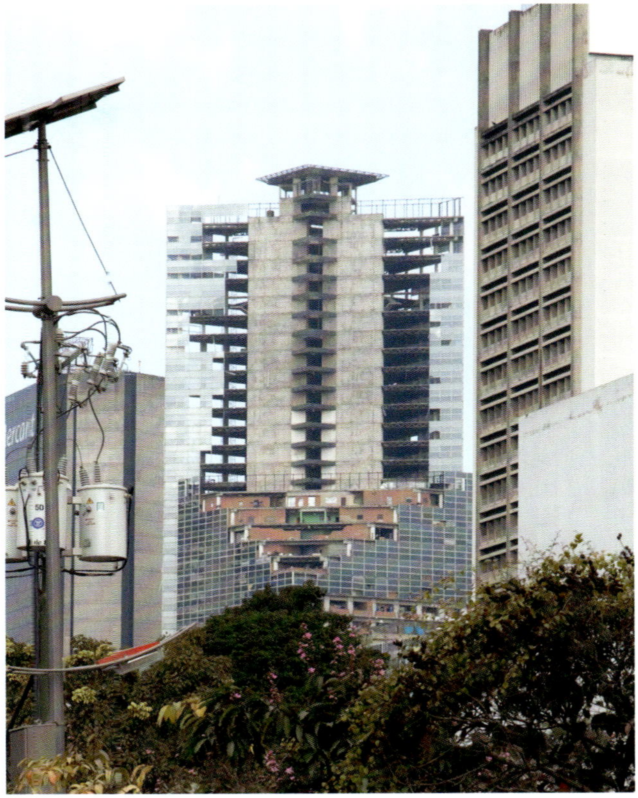

Both images:
Ángela Bonadies and Juan José Olavarría, from the photo series *Torre de David*, 2010–2013

The Torre de David building has been the subject of intense discussion, not only in the fields of art and architecture. The installation *Torre David/Gran Horizonte* won the Golden Lion for the best project embodying the theme of Common Ground at the 13th edition of the Venice Architecture Biennale in 2012. The project was realized collectively by Urban-Think Tank (Alfredo Brillembourg and Hubert Klumpner), curator Justin McGuirk, and photographer Iwan Baan, and dedicated to the people of Caracas and their families who created a new community and a home out of the abandoned and unfinished building. Although it was awarded a prestigious prize and praised as an innovative model and strategy to reappropriate urban ruins and create homes for homeless people, the Biennale project and the informal housing itself were also severely criticized. Not only since the evacuation of the building in 2014 and in view of many accidents that happened in the building due to construction defects, decay, or the incompleteness of the site, one should ask whether the Biennale project and the praise for such an informal housing concept can also be seen as a glorification of poverty by Western architects and thinkers who project and impose their utopian ideas on impoverished people: people with very limited means of action who find themselves in an unsafe environment without any financial or legal security offered by the state. To date, the future of the building – at once a symbol of capitalist megalomania, the failure of the government to tackle the acute housing shortage, and of social empowerment and solidarity amongst the poor – has still not been decided.

Ángela Bonadies and
Juan José Olavarría

La Torre de David (The Tower of David)

Timeline

In 1990 David Brillembourg, president of the Venezuelan financial consortium Confinanzas, decided to build a forty-storey, glass-clad skyscraper in Caracas, crowned by a heliport. It was to be the third highest building in Venezuela – after the Parque Central towers – and the eighth highest in Latin America. Brillembourg was one of a group of businessmen who had amassed impressive fortunes in the course of the stock market boom of the 1980s. Together with other bankers, he decided to invest part of this fortune in an urban planning project that sought to transform this area of downtown Caracas into a Wall Street-style financial boulevard. Brillembourg was dubbed "the King David of Venezuelan finance," and the moniker was also given to his skyscraper, which was referred to from the very beginning as "The Tower of David" ("La Torre de David").

The financier died in 1993 and in 1994 Confinanzas, which was being managed by one of Brillembourg's sons, went bankrupt, along with a number of banks on which the government of Rafael Caldera imposed sanctions. That same year building work was stopped on "the tower" and it was left incomplete.

In the years that followed, "the tower" existed in a legal void until it fell into the hands of the state institution FOGADE, which put it up for international auction in 2001; no offers were made for it, or at least none were finalized. From 2000 onwards, the abandoned tower was vandalized and stripped: many of the windows were pulled out for their metal frames which could be sold and recycled. The tower deteriorated as the people of Caracas watched on with a certain apathy, with the exception of those who lived close by and suffered directly from the problems caused by this huge and forgotten construction. What had promised to be a modernizing project that would push up the price of land and the houses in the surrounding area (such as in the poor *barrio* of Sarría) turned into just another precipitous and insurmountable problem. Within a decade the tower became a contemporary ruin. People in the area remember the sound of the windows falling off as if it were a bomb attack – audible evidence of an economic war for survival that those in power sought to silence.

In 2007 needy groups of families and individuals whose housing situation had received no response from the state, organized themselves to take over the tower and build their houses inside it. The tower houses some 3,000 squatters, or "invaders" as they are called in Venezuela, who are protected legally by the housing cooperative they formed, which they named "Caciques de Venezuela."

In a sense, "The Tower of David" is an icon that represents the last thirty years in Venezuela: from the modernizing promise articulated from the capital, to the revolutionary promise offered by the state. Ruin upon ruin. In addition, if we extend the concept, the tower is the image of our modern project shattering into pieces amid the contrasting coexistence of pre- and postmodern situations. It is a brutal tale that reinvents the limits between fiction and reality, and between such basic meanings as sheltered–unsheltered, security–insecurity, wall–curtain, window–empty space.

Notes about the Project and the Tower

Our project started as research on social issues, architecture, and art. In the beginning we just studied the external structure of the tower, trying to understand the changes that had happened.

Initially, the building's facade had the appearance of a grid of mirrors which gradually disappeared with the squattings that brought, amongst other things, a new typology or way of building, similar to the shantytowns that are spread all over Venezuela.

The grid was broken and in one sense, for us, the modern dream was also broken. At the same time the "oil dream" was broken that led us to believe in a false paradise, to think of Venezuela as a rich nation.

We are very critical of the "unfinished" in Venezuela, because here the "unfinished" is not an exception – quite the contrary – it is a power strategy: to capitalize on the poverty and keep control over the people.

In Venezuela the corruption is structural; it is like a virus in an organism. The Tower of David is a very important popular initiative which lacks basic sanitary conditions, and it includes a dangerous way of living. Then the tower is like a bomb that could explode at any time. It is a pioneering movement but also a troublesome response that is far from social welfare. The government should help the building's dwellers to improve the living conditions, but it acts as though it is blind, deaf, and dumb with regard to the people's problems. It lets you do things but it doesn't resolve any problems.

The biggest problem is actually the water supply. The inhabitants get their water from a hosepipe that distributes it per floor. The water tank is located almost on top of the building. The bathrooms don't have running water and human excrement is thrown down to a certain place on the ground floor. People in the tower have electricity, Internet, and cable TV. It is a weird situation in which TV and network services have a priority that basic utilities don't.

Most of the people work outside the tower, but many people have their shops inside it: copy stores, convenience and ice cream stores, sales of basic goods, hair salon, childcare services, bakeries, stationery stores, grocery stores, video game arcade, and so on. The people have built shelters, kitchens, and bedrooms. The tower was initially a development that included offices, a hotel, stores, and a convention

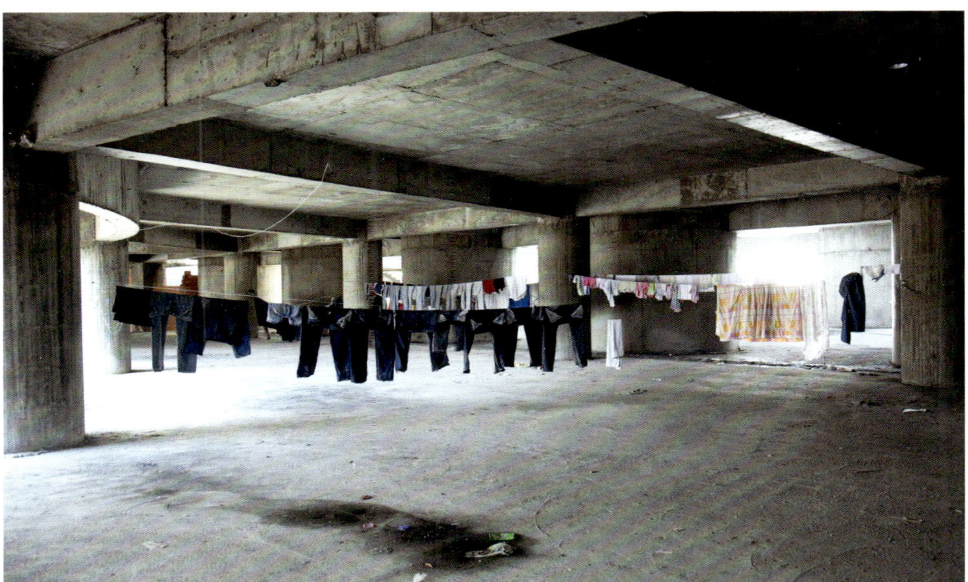

Ángela Bonadies and Juan José Olavarría, from the photo series *Torre de David*, 2010–2013

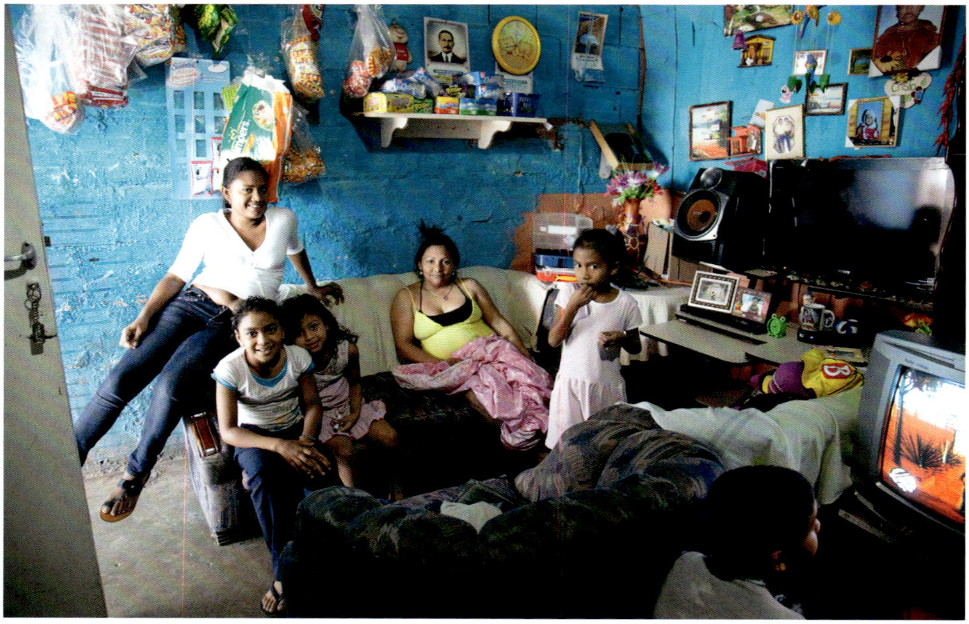

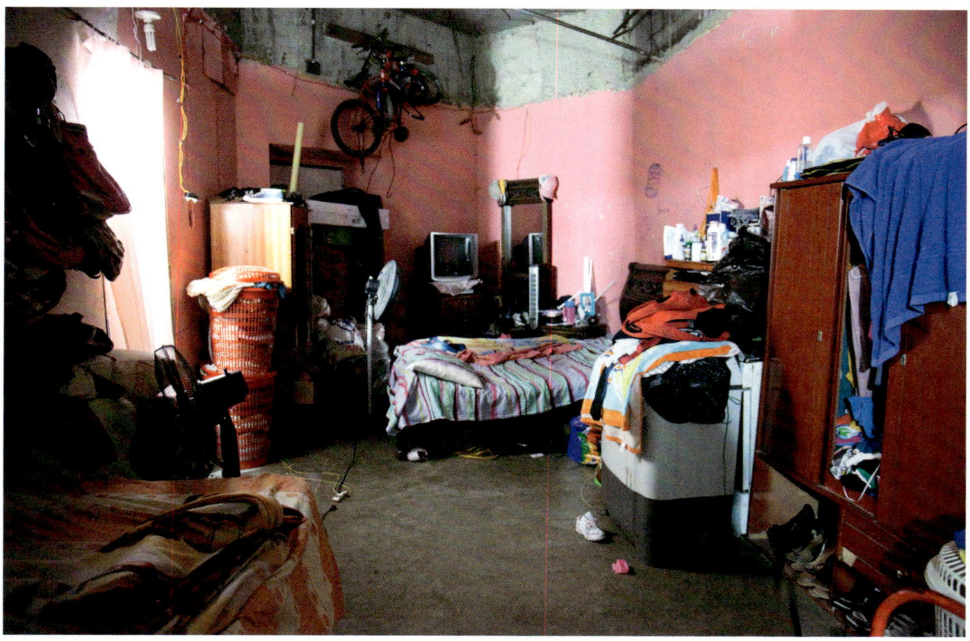

All images: Ángela Bonadies and Juan José Olavarría, from the photo series *Torre de David*, 2010–2013

center. People had to adapt the original structure to build their housing and their shops.

The legal point of view changes all the time. Sometimes the government is pro squatters, sometimes it is against them. It depends on the political situation, political winds. Unfortunately, the most important goods in Venezuela's state are: power and votes. The legal system in Venezuela is a bad joke; we don't have a strong apolitical institution of justice. And the government on the one hand allows the squattings and on the other prohibits them.

For us the Tower of David is the most incredible and strong metaphor of our country. It has become a representation of the country that has gone beyond the tower in physical terms.

It's also interesting to see how the tower has become a site for a kind of urban adventure tourism. People call us up and want us to meet them at the tower, as if we had the right to do that. We get calls from all over and all we feel is shame. Our only answer is "no."

It's not just about the tower as an illegal squat, it's about the tower as a grid, as modernity reinvented, geometric abstraction turning into a *barrio*, the fortunes made in the 1980s, the tower as a failed promise made by private capital, and a shipwreck of inefficient verbose socialism that we are being drowned in.

We're interested in underlining the transitory, which José Ignacio Cabrujas expressed so well in his texts on Caracas. "Nobody came to stay for too long," he wrote, and this rings true. The improvised works are also reminiscent of this, just like Venezuelans' collective memory where everything disappears after a while. The coincidences are not chance occurrences. That's why we sometimes feel terribly old. Our tradition hasn't even been around for thirty years. That's why we sometimes feel forever young. Eternally transitory.

Then, you go inside the tower and you don't see the tower, you see fragments of it. The tower disappears

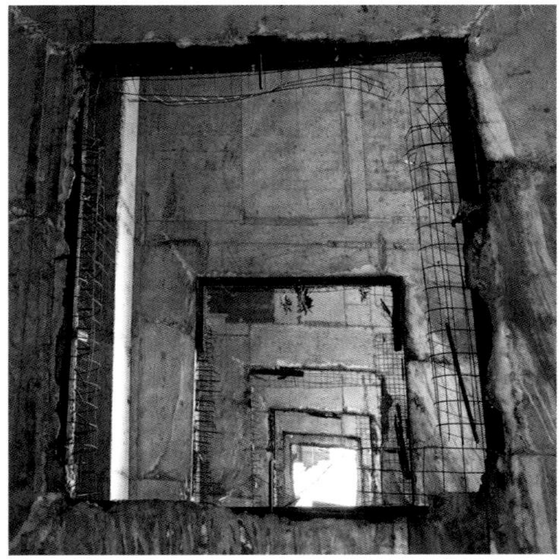

and a different, vertical *barrio* appears, with concrete corridors instead of sidewalks that have an entrance and exit; but it's a *barrio* nonetheless. To get to know the tower you first have to go to a *barrio* and a jail – two concepts and norms that are brought together in the space. The tower is several things at once: a building, a *barrio*, a jail, a church, and a hotel. Inside it are dogmas and norms, not a constitution. Inside it there is faith.

Our country is on the outside and inside of this skyscraper – decadent and carnivalesque, sad and festive, motionless and living. Nothing here is unconnected; it's all joined up but with a fracture in the tibia and the fibula. Pathologies are also organic and organized forms and structures.

Instead of what it should and can provide, in our daily, common life the state has encouraged fantasy and the dogma of faith. The government sells us an image that it is profoundly inclusive but pays us with exclusion. Its Father Almighty, creator and savior talk doesn't involve the population and consequently leaves us all in the pen of faith and patience. It turns us into beneficiaries or victims when the only thing religion and faith should give us today is "justice," to quote the erudite Jesuit scholar Michel de Certeau. Instead, we are subjected to the most brutal and unjust uncertainty – that of hope and waiting.

Osman Bozkurt *1970

Osman Bozkurt was trained as a photographer and has created many video works exploring contemporary urban life in Turkey. He is the founder of the Interdisciplinary Project Space PiST///, a platform for discourse and presentation for young and emerging artists, writers, critics, architects, and musicians in Istanbul, and coeditor of LiST, Istanbul's contemporary art list.

Bozkurt's installation *Foggy* (2013) refers to the wave of demonstrations and civil unrest in Gezi Park in Istanbul since May 2013; the protest was initiated to oppose the urban development plan for the park and was further sparked by the violent eviction of a sit-in of protesters. Already in the first night of the occupation, the tents of the protesters were torn down and burned by the police. With his installation, Bozkurt recreates the setting at the Gezi Park and juxtaposes time: the video material selected for the installation documents the events during the protests and is shown in tents in the exhibition space.

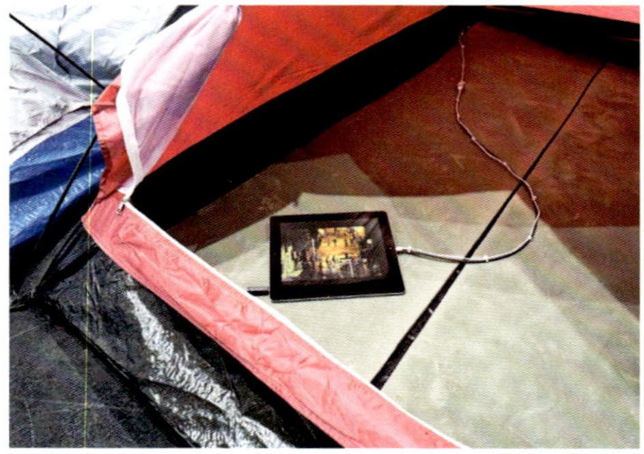

Osman Bozkurt, *Foggy*, 2013, installation, mixed media, ca. 10 × 10 m, installation view, ZKM | Karlsruhe, 2013

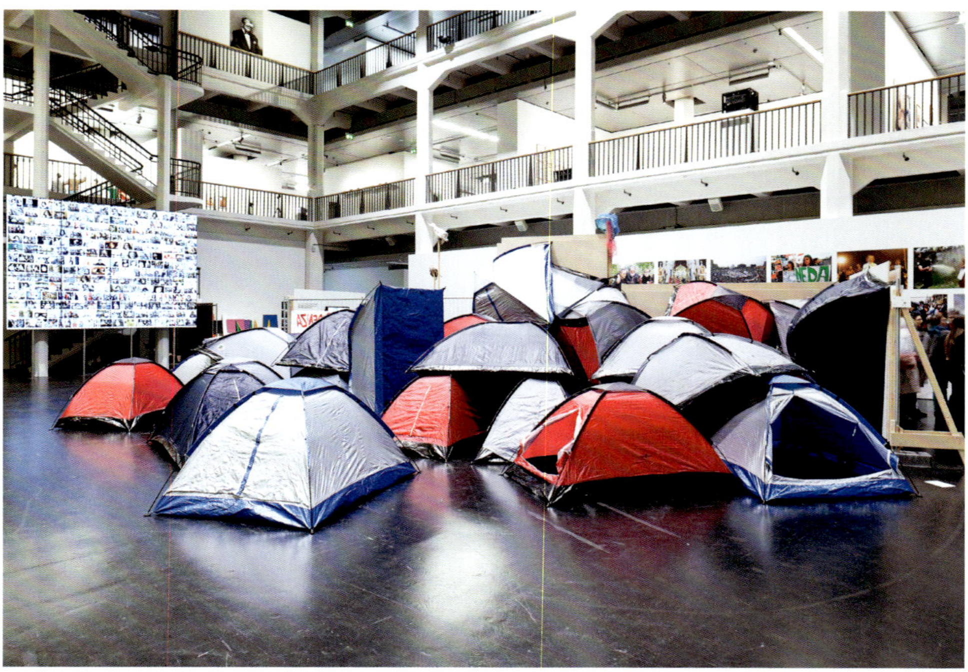

Osman Bozkurt, *Foggy*, 2013, installation, mixed media, 50 tents in different colors, sleeping mats, iPads, 4 videos, color, sound, durations variable, ca. 10 × 10 m, installation view, ZKM | Karlsruhe, 2013

Osman Bozkurt, *Foggy*, 2013, installation, mixed media, 4 videos, color, sound, durations variable, video stills

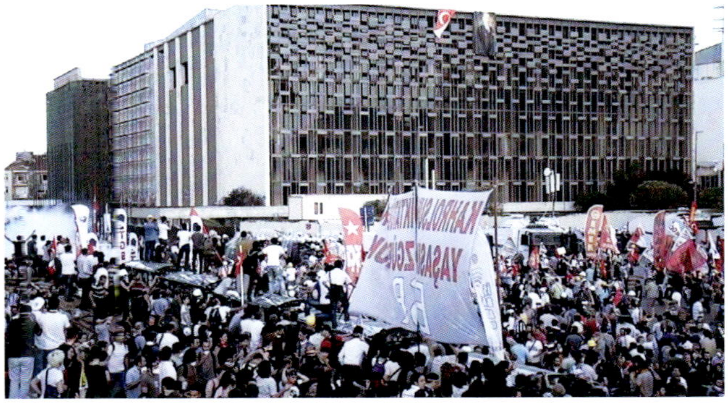

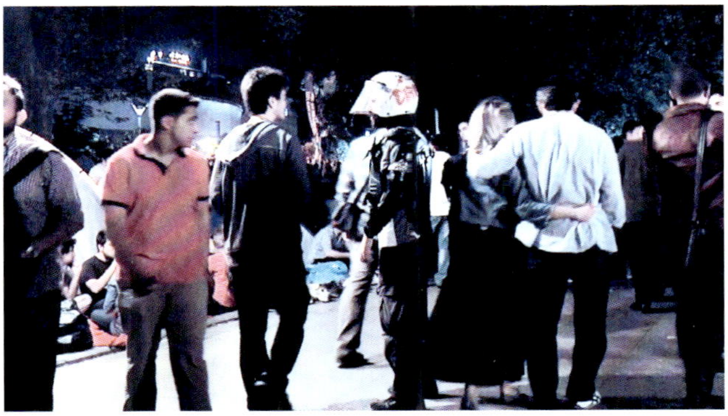

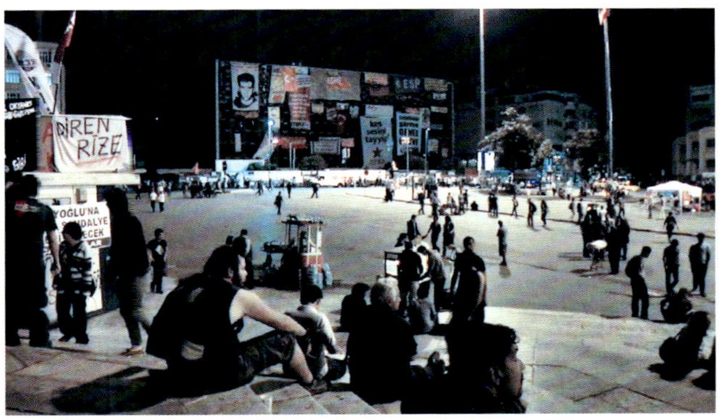

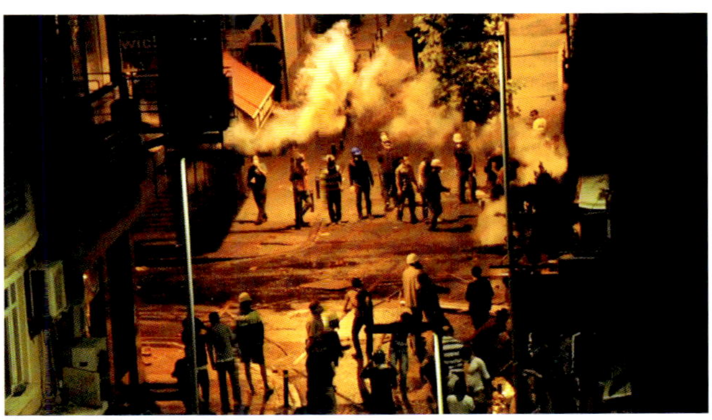

Chim↑Pom

Chim↑Pom is a collective of six young artists – Ellie, Ryuta Ushiro, Yasutaka Hayashi, Masataka Okada, Toshinori Mizuno, and Motomu Inaoka – that was formed in Tokyo in 2005. Chim↑Pom became known with their installation *Super Rat* (2006) with rats prepared by a taxidermist and dyed yellow, which had been caught in Tokyo's Shibuya district. The rats of Shibuya were turned into real-life Pikachus, a famous anime character from the series *Pokemon*, and in 2008, when Chim↑Pom hired a plane to skywrite the name "Pika" (an onomatopoetic for flash) over the city of Hiroshima this caused quite a controversy. With later works the artist collective entered the realm of social commentary: using guerrilla art tactics, Chim↑Pom create provocative artworks that literally cross the borders of no-go areas.

REAL TIMES (2011) is an exhibition of works that were produced as a reaction to the huge earthquake and tsunami of March 11, 2011, and the resulting disaster at TEPCO's Fukushima Daiichi nuclear power station. *KI-AI 100* shows, for instance, Chim↑Pom's members and several residents in the tsunami-smashed coastal city of Soma – which is fifty kilometers away from the nuclear power plants – in front of an overturned fishing boat, cheering enthusiastically. The video work *Myth of Tomorrow* documents an "addition" that Chim↑Pom appended to the famous mural and chronicle of atomic holocaust in Japanese history, *Myth of Tomorrow* by Taro Okamoto: a painting of the Fukushima incident which copies Okamoto's style and covers a wall at the Shibuya station in Tokyo. Disturbing elements of the *REAL TIMES* exhibition include an ikebana arrangement of radioactive flowers and plants picked near the Fukushima reactors *(Radiation-Exposed Flowers Harmony)* and still photos of abandoned animals, starving or dead *(Japanese Dog, Cow, Cat...)*. In yet another part of the exhibition, the video work *REAL TIMES*, the members of the artist collective trespass into a prohibited area of abandoned and devastated surroundings in radiation protection suits, one of them holding a white flag in his hands. They walk up to a former tourist lookout close to the Fukushima nuclear plant, which can be seen in the background. There they unfold a white banner, spray-paint the symbol for radiation on it – in red, an allusion to the Japanese flag with its red circle which represents the rising sun – and hold it up in the air.

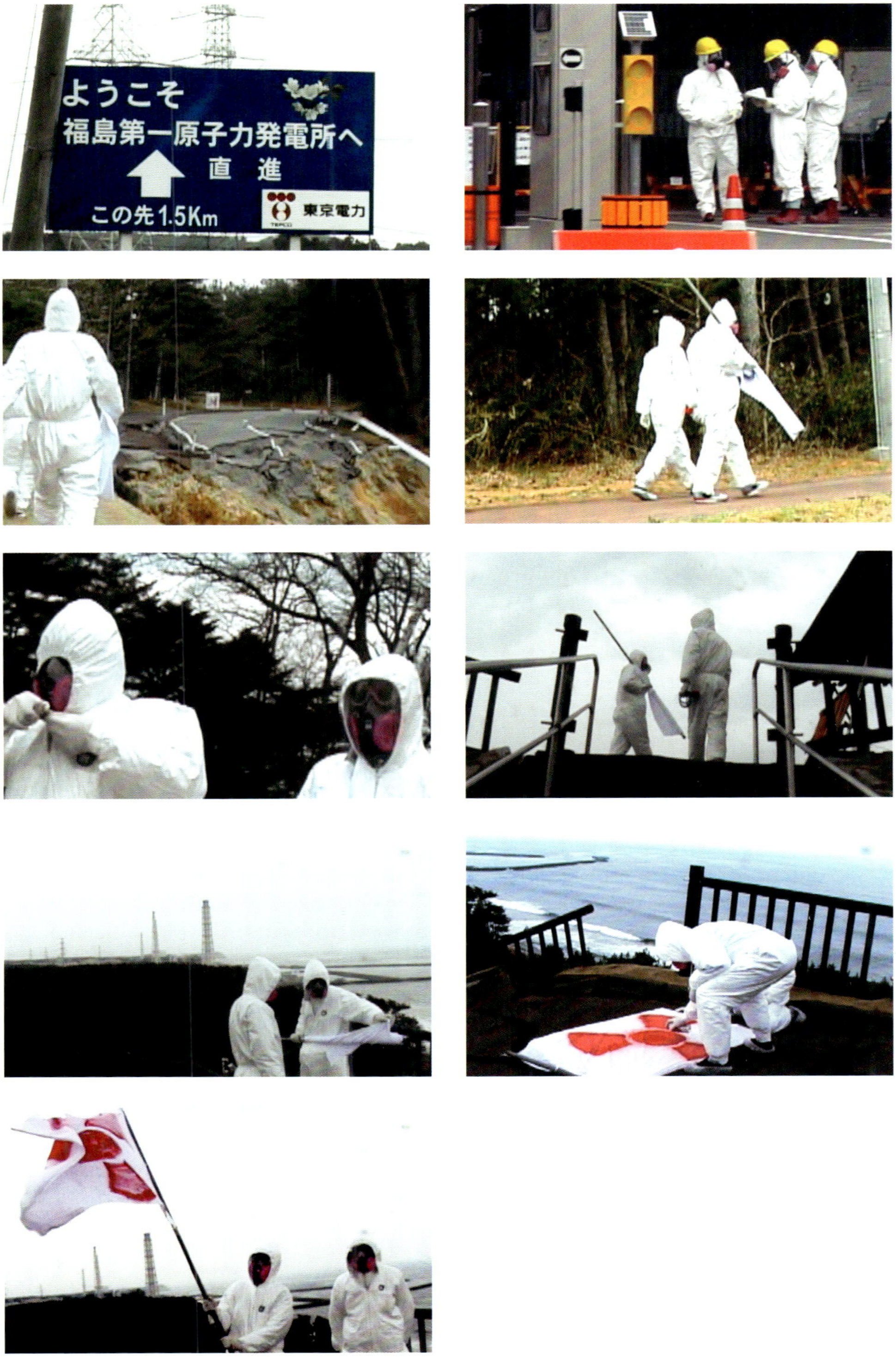

Chim↑Pom, *REAL TIMES*, 2011,
video, color, sound, 11:11 min, video stills

Chto Delat?

Chto Delat? is an artist collective founded in 2003 by artists, art critics, philosophers, and authors from Saint Petersburg, Moscow, and Nizhny Novgorod. In their multifaceted work they combine art, activism, and political theory, and they explore the overlaps of artistic and political practices. Chto Delat? is engaged with the relationship between the individual and society as a whole, the role and influence of collective production of art, the history of Russia and the Soviet Union, and the repoliticization of Russian intellectual culture. The artist collective's name means "What needs to be done?" and is based on the eponymous novel by Nikolay Chernyshevsky from 1863 – a programmatic text for the Russian revolutionary intelligentsia and the politically engaged avant-garde of the post-revolutionary period; for Chto Delat? it is a manual on how to construct emancipatory collectives and make them sustainable within a hostile society. Chto Delat?'s work has fostered the emergence of and profoundly influenced a new generation of (Russian) activist artist groups.

Chto Delat?'s video work *Museum Songspiel: The Netherlands 20XX* (2011) is the fourth part of the *Songspiel* series and was preceded by three musical productions that formed the *Songspiel* triptych: *Tower Songspiel* (2010), *Partisan Songspiel* (2009), and *Perestroika Songspiel* (2008). While the triptych was based on historical events, the fourth part is set against the backdrop of an imaginary scenario of Dutch politics where all immigrants have been banned from the country. *Museum Songspiel: The Netherlands 20XX* tells the story of a group of illegal immigrants in the Netherlands who seek refuge in a museum (several scenes were shot in the Van Abbemuseum in Eindhoven) to avoid being deported by the authorities. When the refugees are found inside a large display of street art, the museum director suggests dressing them as Constructivist figures, having them pose as avant-garde artworks, and thus present them as an artistic project. The adoption of their role is complete when they are commented on in pretentious small talk from museum visitors. Chto Delat?'s video work raises questions about the role of the museum, including as a refuge from political repression, and active political commitment within the arts.

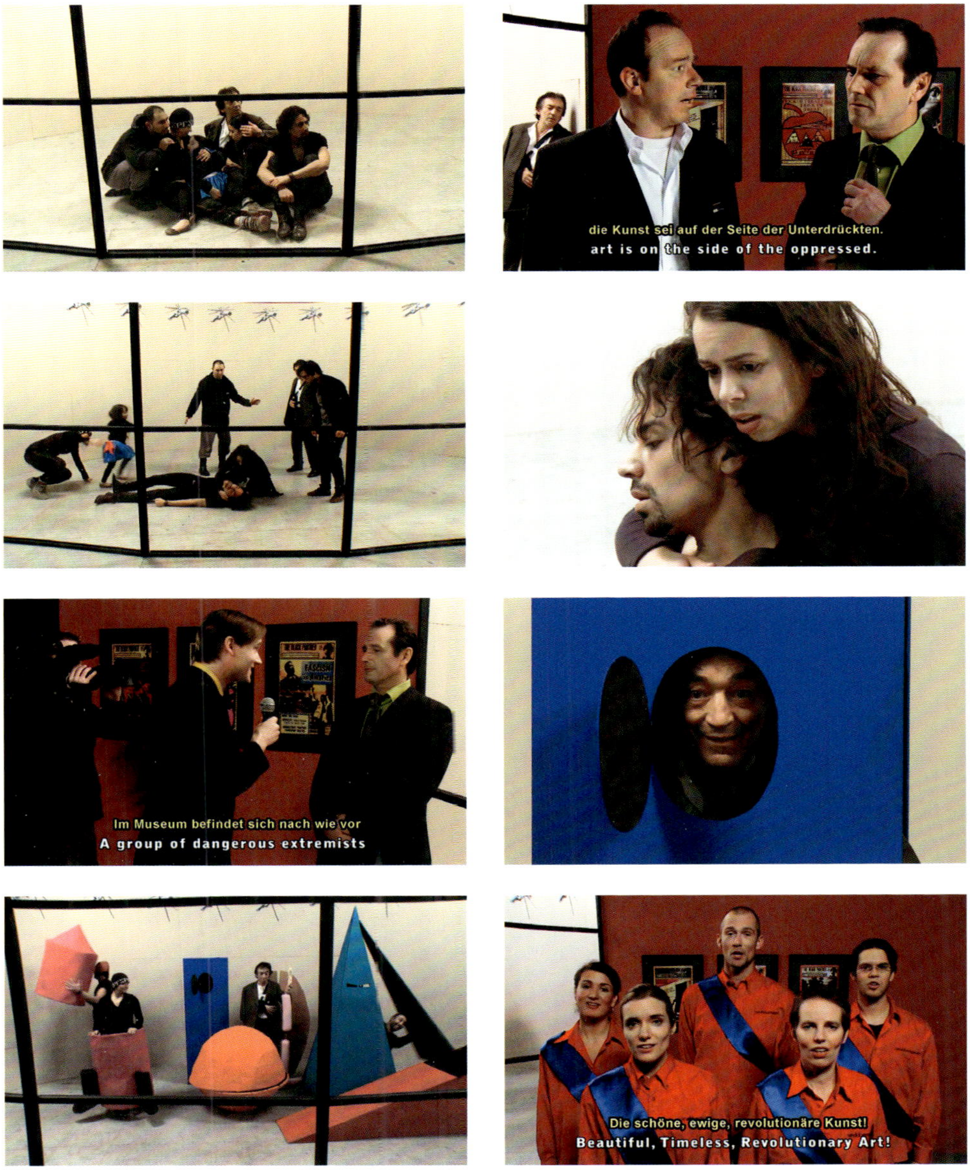

Chto Delat?, *Museum Songspiel: The Netherlands 20XX*, 2011, video, color, sound, 24:54 min, video stills

Founded in 1997
Argentina

www.youtube.com/user/grupoetcetera?feature=watch

Colectivo Etcétera

"Etcetera needs no definition. You can imagine what comes after. Etcetera is the word that shatters language. Etcetera closes and opens all speech. Etcetera is in every language. As such, it is an ally anywhere in the world. Etcetera is the present. Its members are without number. Etcetera is singular and plural, feminine and masculine. Etcetera adds, subtracts, divides, and multiplies." (Colectivo Etcétera)

Towards the end of 1997, several young artists who had just started to work as poets, in theater, the visual arts, and music, began to feel the desire to form a group, to be part of a movement: a movement which would bring them into contact with other social spheres and would take art to the streets, into the spaces of social conflict, thereby moving these social conflicts into areas where they had previously been silenced (i.e., cultural institutions, the mass media, or the spectacles created by the culture industry). Colectivo Etcétera was created as a response to a specific political moment and to the need to forge a generational identity. At the same time, it was a reaction against the culture being created by neoliberalism, which had risen to power during the 1990s.

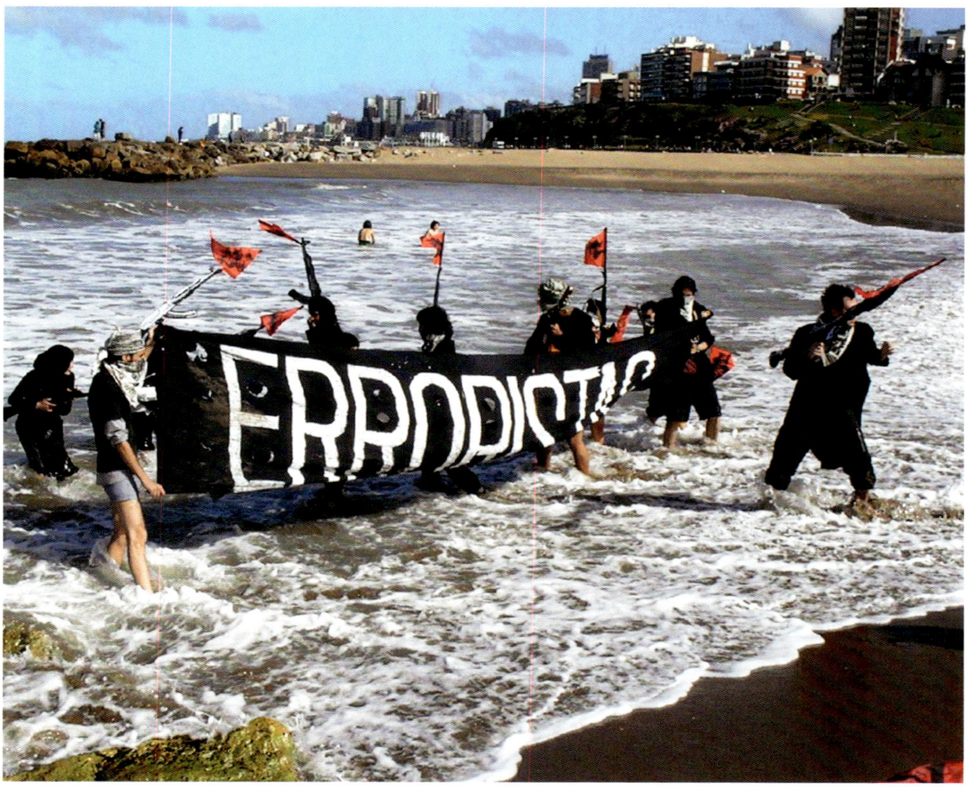

Colectivo Etcétera, *International Errorist*, 2010, video, color, sound, 1:19 min, photo used in the video, taken at a counterevent to the Fourth Summit of the Americas, Mar del Plata, Argentina, November 2005

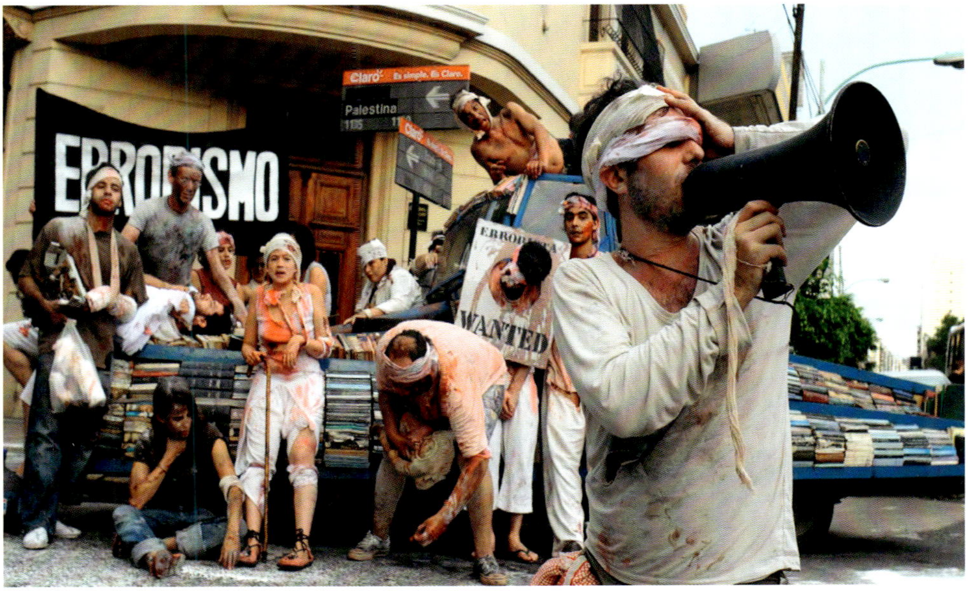

Colectivo Etcétera, International Errorist Movement, activist performance in the streets of Buenos Aires, Argentina, where the State of Israel Avenue and the Palestine Street intersect, 2009

Coléctivo Etcétera is known for its engagement in new movements for human rights and justice and for its political and surrealistic public actions as well as its carnivalesque staged theatrical events, including against accomplices of the former military dictatorship. Around 2005, Colectivo Etcétera decided to found the International Errorist Movement. The movement defines making mistakes as a fundamental organizing principle of reality and calls for the concept to be extended further than is the case according to the capitalist way of thinking. With their interventions centered around (t)error, they seek to liberate language and the human being.

In November 2005, the International Errorist Movement organized a counterevent to the Fourth Summit of the Americas held in Mar del Plata, Argentina, to protest against George W. Bush's War on Terror. This form of artistic protest was also captured in the video *International Errorist* (2010). The style, montage, and music of the video allude to the characteristics of a propaganda video. Blurring the boundaries between enacted scenes and reality, the video shows how the artist group simulates a mysterious terror attack, satirically reproducing the idea of the construction of an enemy. Far away from the protests against George W. Bush at the summit, they appeared at a peaceful beach from the sea and in the streets of downtown Buenos Aires, in their hands paper-made and photocopied machine guns with red pennants with the word "BANG!" attached, and unfurled a banner with their name. According to the artist collective and their manifesto, we are all "errorists" – and prone to be considered as potential terrorists.

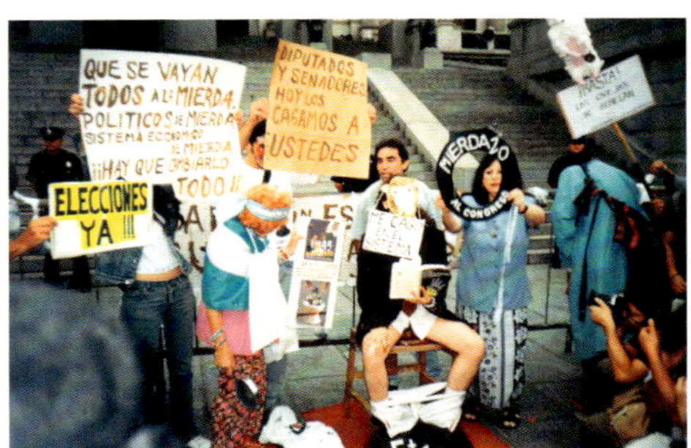

Colectivo Etcétera, International Errorist Movement, *EL Mierdazo/The Big Shit*, activist performance, Buenos Aires, Argentina, 2002

Enmedio

Enmedio is a network of activist artists, designers, and filmmakers in Spain that advocates a political role for art. Enmedio means "in the midst of," referring to the central place the collective takes and demands in the midst of art, social activism, and media. Enmedio has been organizing talks, workshops, and film screenings dealing with creative activism and has established a strong community. When the financial crisis hit Spain and protests against its devastating effects started, Enmedio continued their work, for instance, by organizing the crowdfunded conference How to End Evil. 5 Days of Art and Activism in Barcelona in 2012. And Enmedio identified a need to break the paralysis that gripped those affected by the crisis by organizing a party, as a symbol of empowerment. Enmedio became known through the parties they organized at numerous unemployment centers across Spain.

The video *Party #CierraBankia (Shut Down Bankia)* (2012) documents a recurring action against the Spanish bank Bankia in Madrid, also as a reaction to the absurd effects of the financial crisis: When Bankia declared itself bankrupt in 2012, it was partially nationalized, and Bankia requested a bailout of 19 billion euros, the largest bank bailout in the nation's history. The government accepted and in total spent more than 23 million euros to rescue the bank; in the same week, severe cuts in the health and education sector were announced.

Enmedio organized flash mobs to encourage the closing of Bankia bank accounts: Members of the collective were hiding in one of the Bankia branches until customers arrived. When a client closed his or her account, the group entered the scene and held a surprise party: a delightful scene with a group of enthusiastically cheering people, gathering to celebrate with the client, playing music, dancing, drinking cava, spreading confetti, and yelling and singing "Cierra Bankia!," "Shut down Bankia." Many people closed their Bankia accounts – some of them were also offered a surprise party.

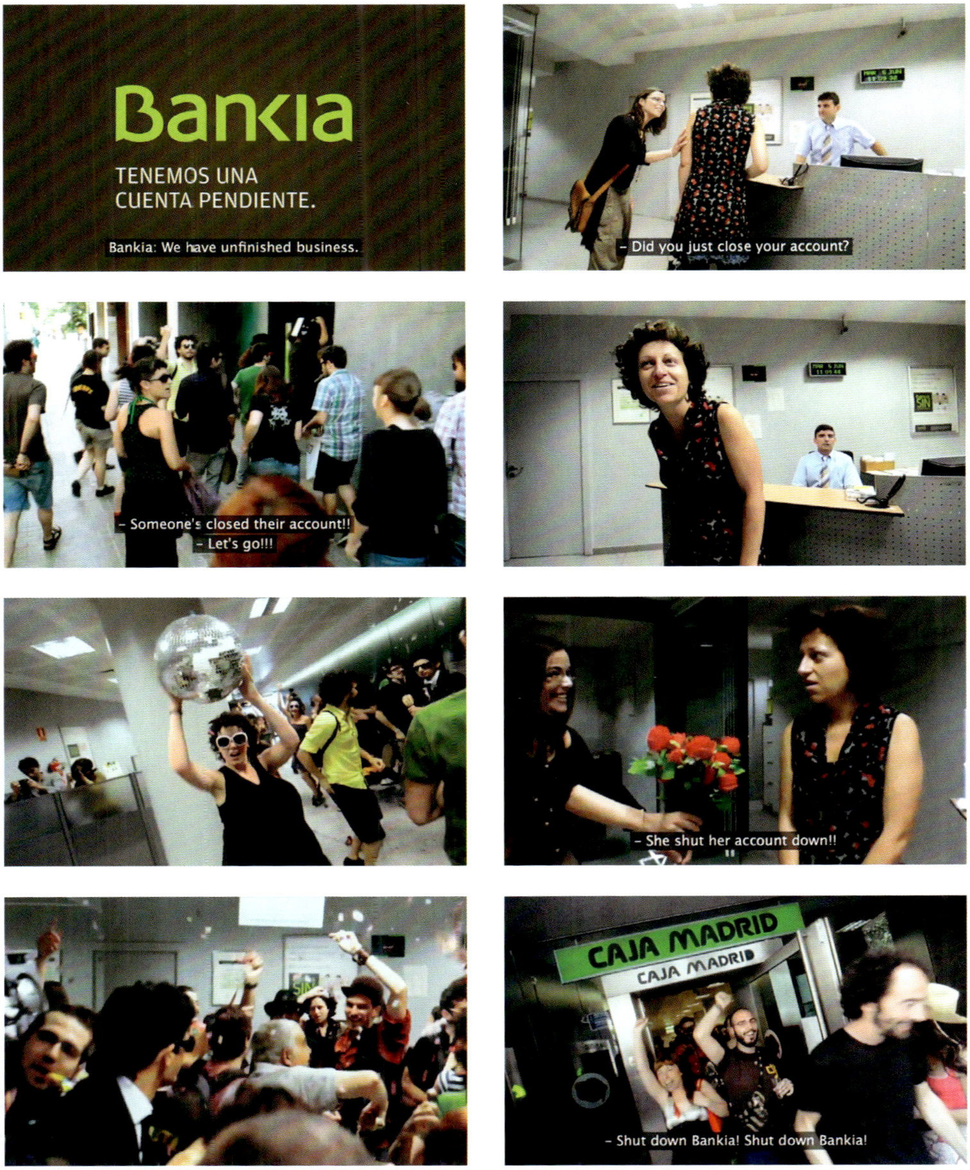

Enmedio, *Party #CierraBankia (Shut Down Bankia)*, 2012, video, color, sound, 2:03 min, video stills

Ramy Essam *1987

Ramy Essam is an Egyptian musician who became known for the songs he performed in Cairo's Tahrir Square during the Egyptian uprising. Influenced by his activist brother, Essam started to write political songs three years before the revolution; however, there weren't any venues that allowed him to play. In January 2011, at first he demonstrated in his hometown Mansoura, northeast of Cairo, but then joined the protesters on Tahrir Square in Cairo.

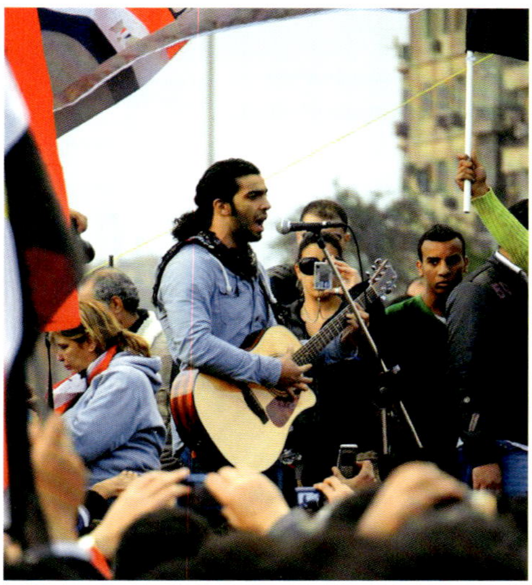

Ramy Essam, performing at Tahrir Square in Cairo, Egypt, January 2011

It was there that he performed for the first time in front of the crowds, after former Egyptian President Hosni Mubarak's infamous television address on February 1, 2011 in which he had vowed to stay in power until the September elections. Essam's song *Irhal* [Leave], in which Mubarak is urged to resign, immediately became very popular among demonstrators, and through the YouTube upload of a concert of Essam and his band Mashakel [Problems] on Tahrir Square he achieved international fame.

On the day after the concert, the protesters were brutally attacked by Hosni Mubarak's henchmen, also known as the "Battle of the Camel." Essam not only had to endure violence and repression at the hands of Mubarak's supporters during the eighteen-day uprising, but by the ruling military regime after Mubarak's fall as well: Essam performed *Irhal* on February 11, 2011, when the news of Mubarak's resignation spread, and he then addressed it to the military regime. Only a few weeks later he was arrested together with other protesters during a sit-in, and taken to the Egyptian Museum where he was brutally beaten and subjected to electric shocks for several hours by the military, while protesters outside demanded his release. Two weeks later Essam performed again. His song *Irhal* is considered one of the anthems of the Egyptian revolution ("We are all united, we demand one thing: Leave! Leave! Leave!"), and the video reached an international audience via YouTube. In an interview Essam said that music, like all other forms of art, is the best way to express and spread critical ideas and views, especially in times when uprising and revolution seem to be "on hold."

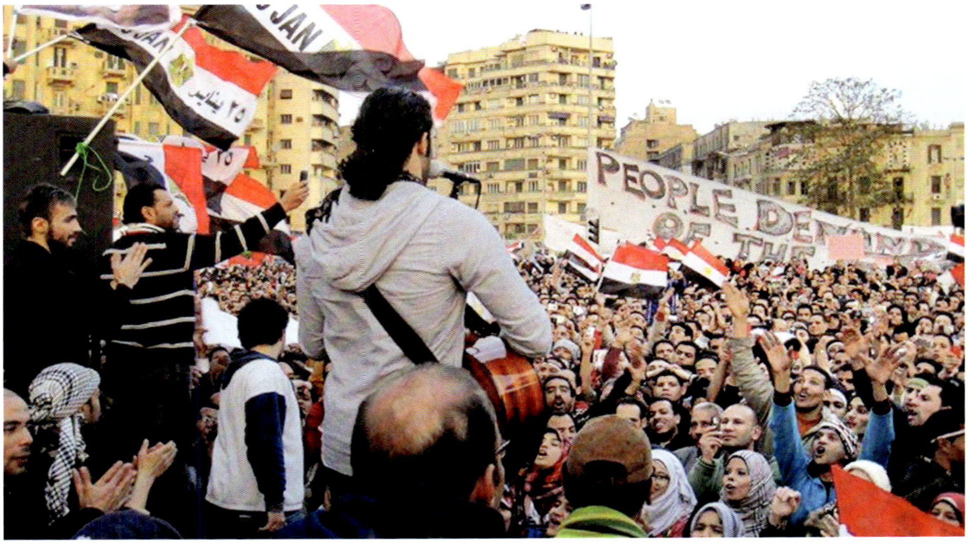

Ramy Essam, performing at Tahrir Square in Cairo, Egypt, January 2011

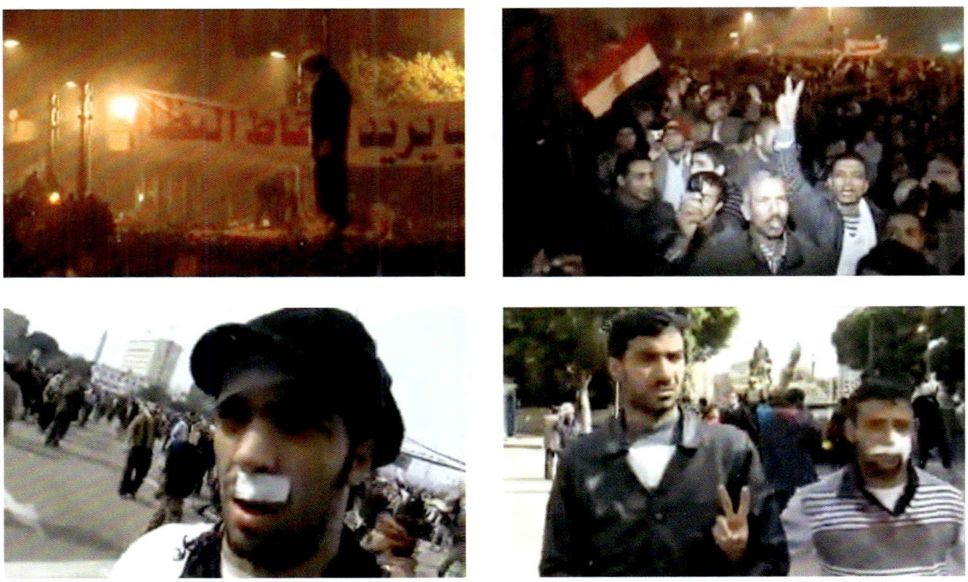

Ramy Essam, *The Real Revolution Song of Tahrir Square*, 2011, video, color, sound, 4:23 min, video stills

Noah Fischer *1977

Since 2011, the Brooklyn-based sculpture and performance artist Noah Fischer has been developing his artistic practice in unison with the goals of the Occupy movement, to which he was strongly committed from the very beginning. Fischer demonstrated on Wall Street during the Occupy Wall Street camps wearing masks with the faces of past American presidents, and then joined the Zuccotti Park activists. With his masks showing a coin he sought to explore the potential of alternative systems of currencies. Fischer was subsequently also involved in the founding of Occupy Subways and Occupy Museums; the latter targeted "the temples of cultural elitism controlled by the 1%," according to its manifesto. Fischer teaches in the sculpture department at the Rhode Island School of Design and works as a curator at the Brooklyn Zen Center.

The video *Manifesto Currency: Mask of Money* (2013) portrays the events surrounding the Occupy Wall Street movement from October 15, 2011. It analyzes the mania for consumer goods, the cycle of consumerism that a person may undergo in the course of his or her lifetime, and the role of money in our economic system, and thus comments on the influence and effects of capitalism. It also documents and promotes the activist Occupy movement and shows Noah Fischer with different coin masks in the streets of New York. In the midst of the crowds captured in the video, a paper-made sign is held up in the air, which reads "Money tore us apart, unity will bring us together."

In the eponymous installation at ZKM | Karlsruhe, videos and a coin mask were included in a pyramidal display structure. In January 2014, an "activist summit" sought to "unfreeze the frame" of the exhibition by holding an assembly, which culminated in an intervention in the curatorial text and the exhibition walls.

Noah Fischer's video *Manifesto Currency: Priests of Growth* (2013), which was created in the context of the Occupy movement, points out the consequences of economic growth for humankind and the environment. Fischer preaches against those politicians and economists he calls "priests of growth," against the "magical force known as growth," and concludes, "It is not the growth of life, it's a death drive."

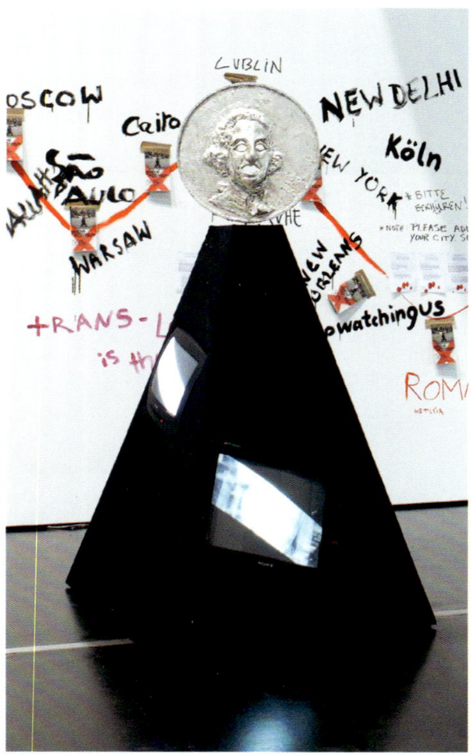

Noah Fischer, *The Mask of Money*, 2013, installation, mixed media, installation view, ZKM | Karlsruhe, 2014

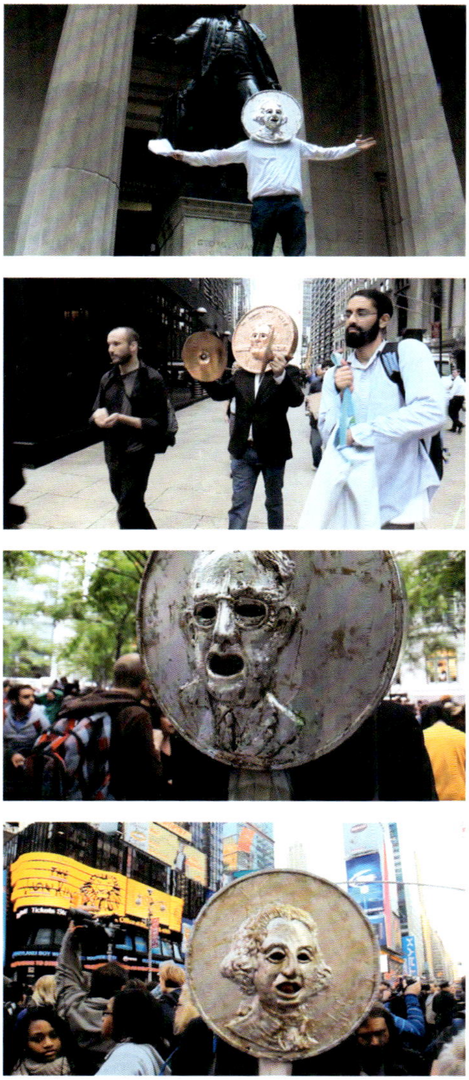

Noah Fischer, *Manifesto Currency: Mask of Money*, 2013, video, color, sound, 2:30 min, video stills

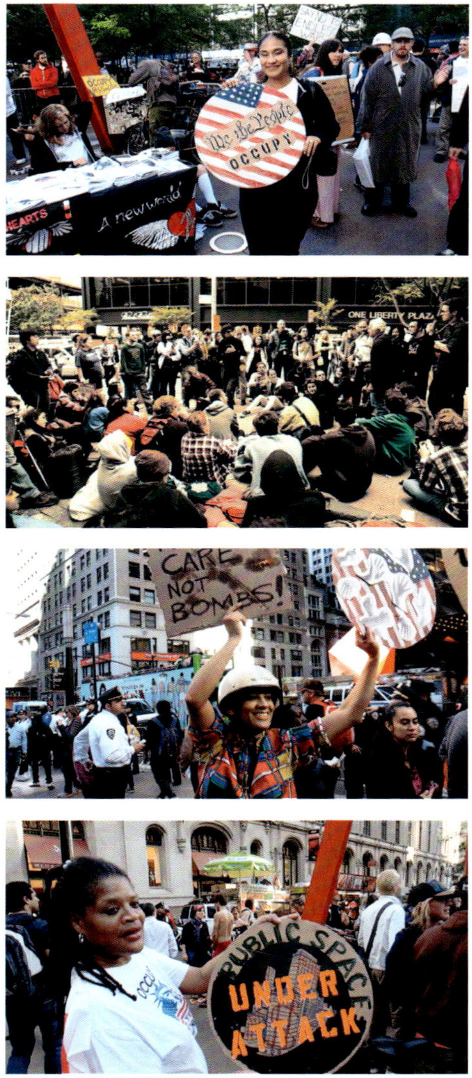

Noah Fischer, *Manifesto Currency: Value of Occupy*, 2013, video, color, sound, 3:35 min, video stills

The subject of the video *Manifesto Currency: Value of Occupy* (2013) is the emergence and disappearance of the Occupy movement. The video focuses on its very beginnings and the inspiration it drew from other activist movements, and highlights the lasting effects and the value of this collective experiment.

Floating Lab Collective

The Floating Lab Collective designs participatory research projects that explore the frontiers of individual agency and collective empowerment. Experimenting with the aesthetics of direct action, Floating Lab Collective crafts open-ended public projects that engage specific localities and identities, using visual arts, performance, new media, and publications to question the assumptions of global economy, political power, social mobility, and inclusion. Floating Lab Collective's artists develop projects collaboratively with community members and focus on subjects such as housing, the environment, migration, labor, and urban mobility. The collective's working process is integrative, seeking to turn social action into art and creative processes into social change.

While the project *Scream at the Economy* was running, members of the public were encouraged to express their anger about the economic system by screaming. The screams were recorded, and via a mobile social web platform, screams from across the nation were collected with the goal of empowering the public to respond to the institutions and actors responsible for the economic crisis. The archived screams were used to create musical compositions. These compositions were played via a portable player system ("the screamer") in the streets and in front of relevant financial or governmental institutions. The video *Scream at the Economy* (2009) documents these "social sculpture performances" and shows how members of the Floating Lab Collective, via huge sculptural loudspeakers on their backs, carried the recorded screams as a musical composition to the White House and to outside other institutions such as the Federal Reserve, the Internal Revenue Service, and the Department of the Treasury in Washington, D.C. The participatory piece was also performed in New York City.

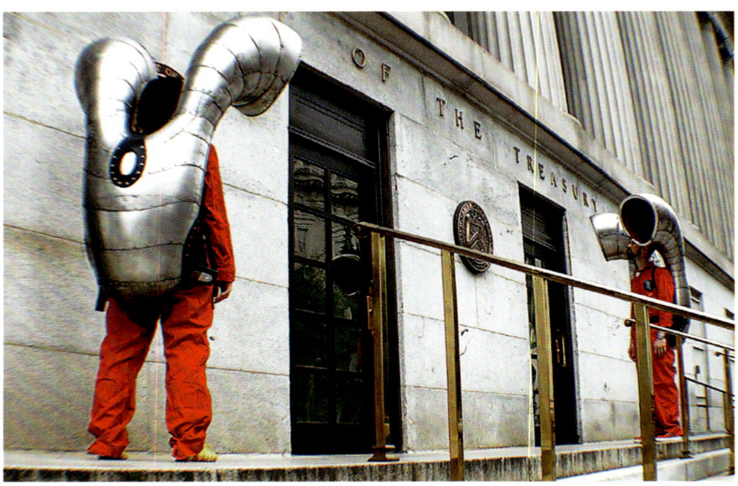

Floating Lab Collective, *Scream at the Economy*, 2009, performances in front of the U.S. Department of the Treasury building, Washington, D.C., (above), and in front of the New York Stock Exchange building, New York City, (facing page)

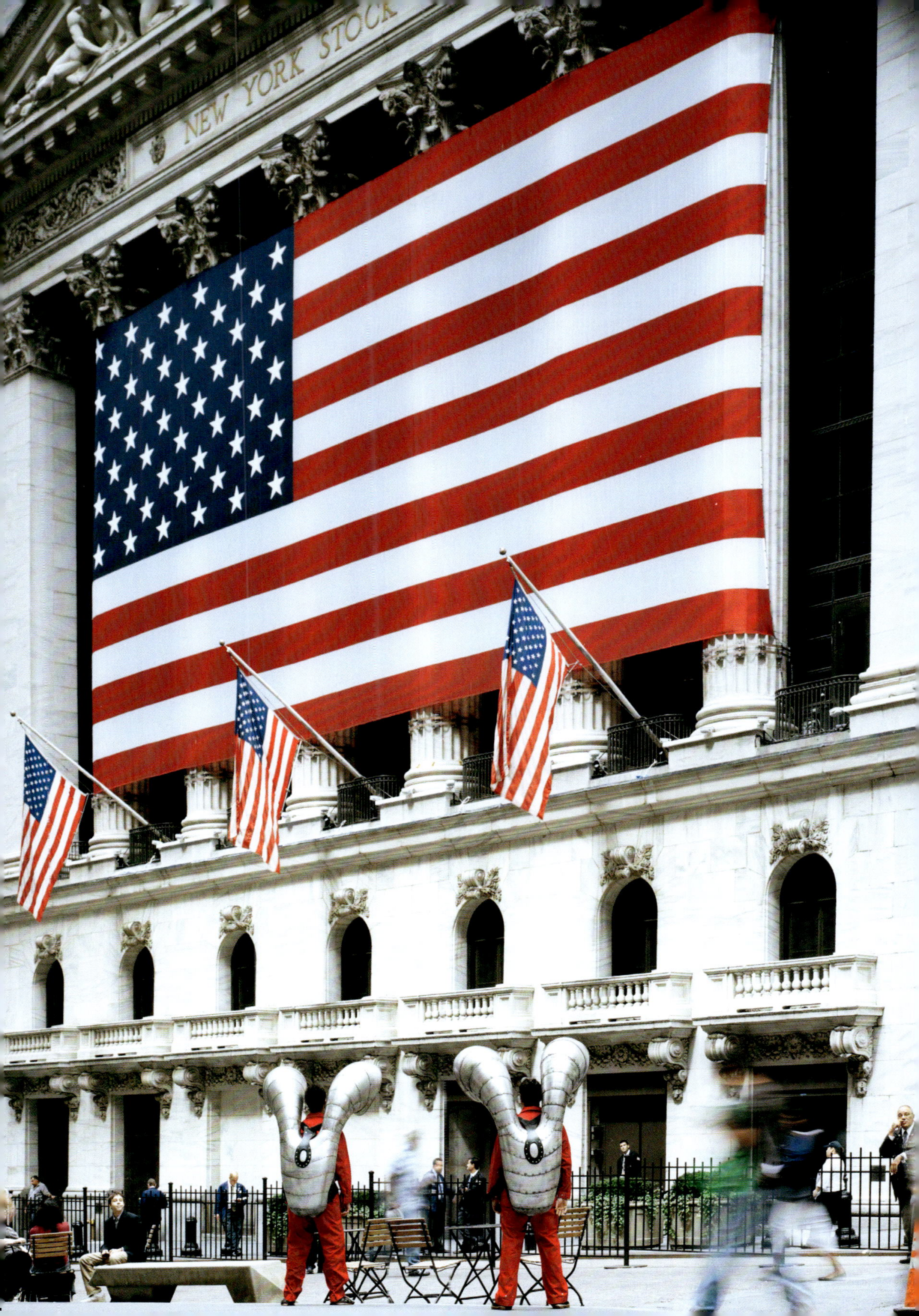
NEW YORK STOCK

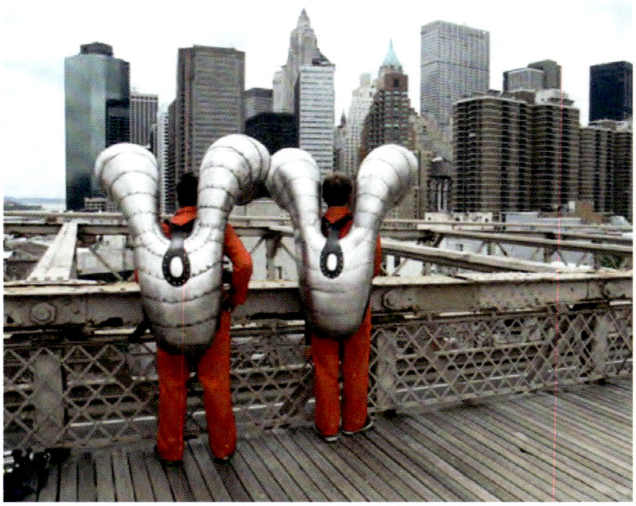

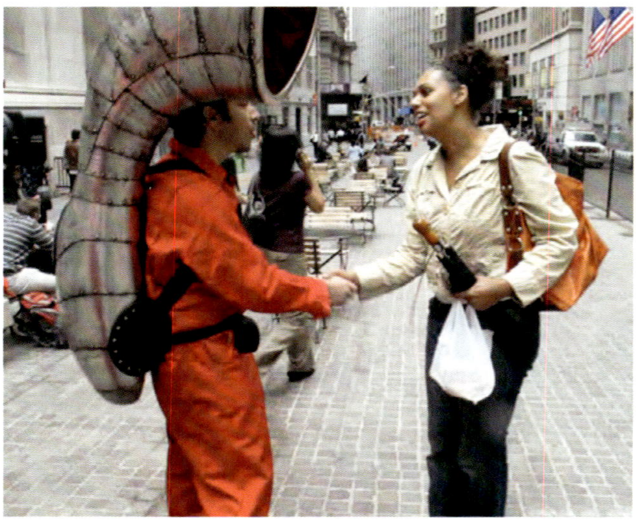

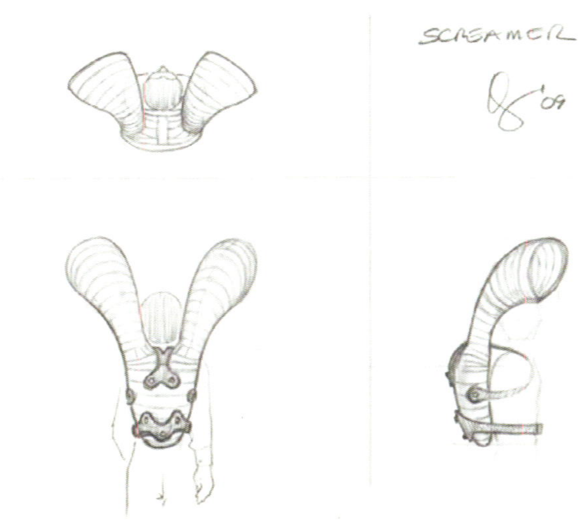

Left:
Floating Lab Collective, *Scream at the Economy*, 2009, performances and video (color, sound, 6:49 min), documentation

Facing page:
Floating Lab Collective, *Scream at the Economy*, 2009, performance in front of the Morgan Stanley headquarters, New York City

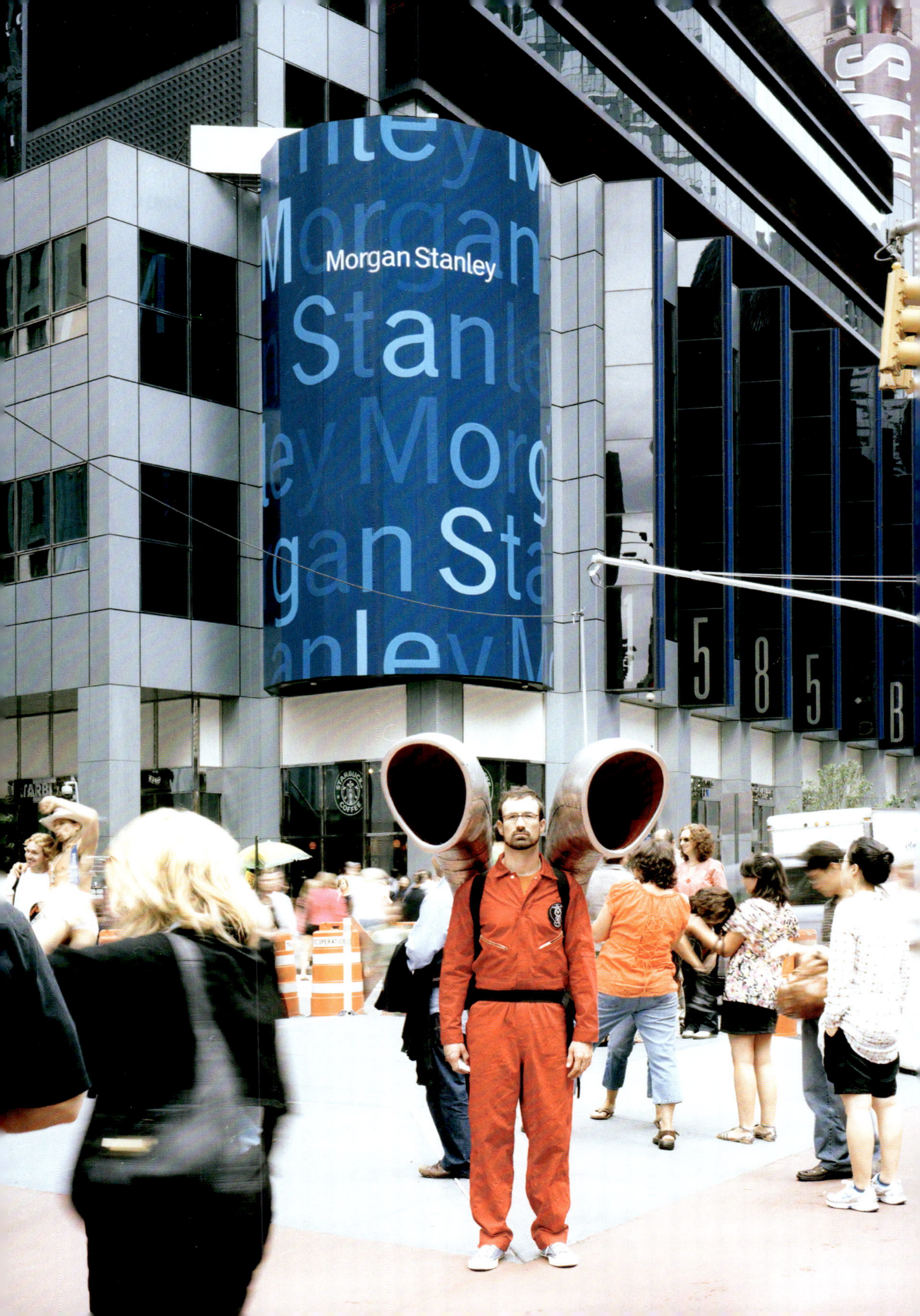
Morgan Stanley
1585 B

Jakob Gautel *1965 and Jason Karaïndros *1963

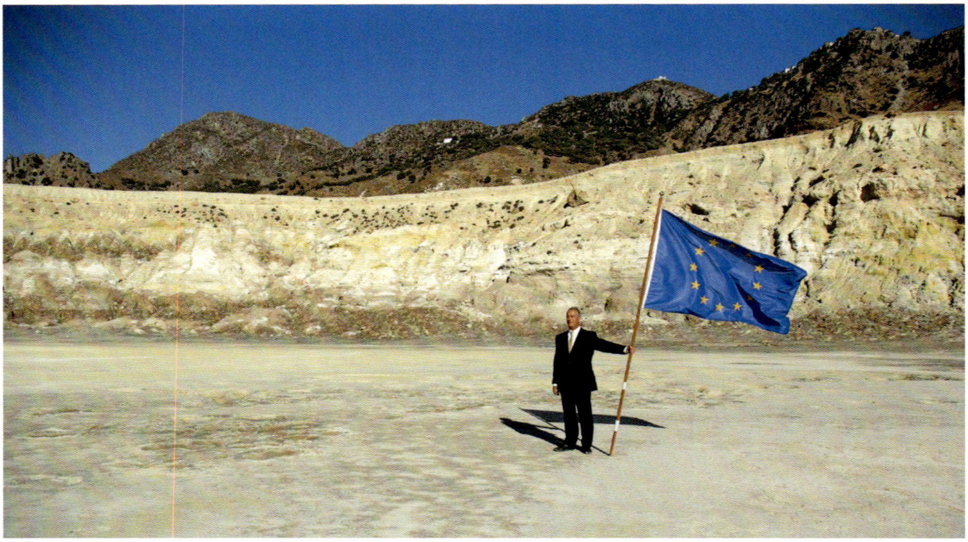

Jakob Gautel and Jason Karaïndros, *Europa?!*, 2013, performances and photos, the mayor of the island of Nisyros, Dodecanese, Greece, on the volcano Stefanos, holding the European flag

Europa?! (2013) by German artist Jakob Gautel and Greek artist Jason Karaïndros, both based in Paris, is a result of their ongoing collaboration. For this project, in a series of performances and photos, they explored the idea and the symbol of a European identity. They deliberately chose Greece as a location – the region where, according to some theories, the earliest conceptions of the idea of Europe and the etymological origin of "Europe" can be traced back to (the exact origin being uncertain), and where in the sixth century B.C.E. the word Europe designated a geographical area. Ironically, both in Greek mythology and etymology, Europe was located outside of Greece and outside of what we consider as Europe today.

As part of the *Europa?!* project, Jakob Gautel and Jason Karaïndros took photos of an event in which they hoisted a European flag – with its stars cut out – in a public square in the capital of the Greek island of Nisyros, Mandraki. The flag was put up next to a monument bearing the inscription "Η ΤΑΝ Η ΕΠΙ ΤΑΣ" [We shall win or die]. In another performance that was documented, the mayor of Nisyros, standing in the middle of the crater of the island's active volcano Stefanos, proudly held the European flag. With an ironic twist, Jakob Gautel and Jason Karaïndros reflect European identity, European ideals and their viability, and European reality from the perspective of a small Greek island in the southeastern Aegean Sea – and a country severely hit and shattered in its foundations by the financial crisis and its manifold socioeconomic consequences.

Facing page:
Jakob Gautel and Jason Karaïndros, *Europa?!*, 2013, performances and photos, the European flag with its stars cut out, hoisted on a public square in Mandraki, the capitol of the Greek island Nisyros, next to a monument with the inscription "We shall win or die"

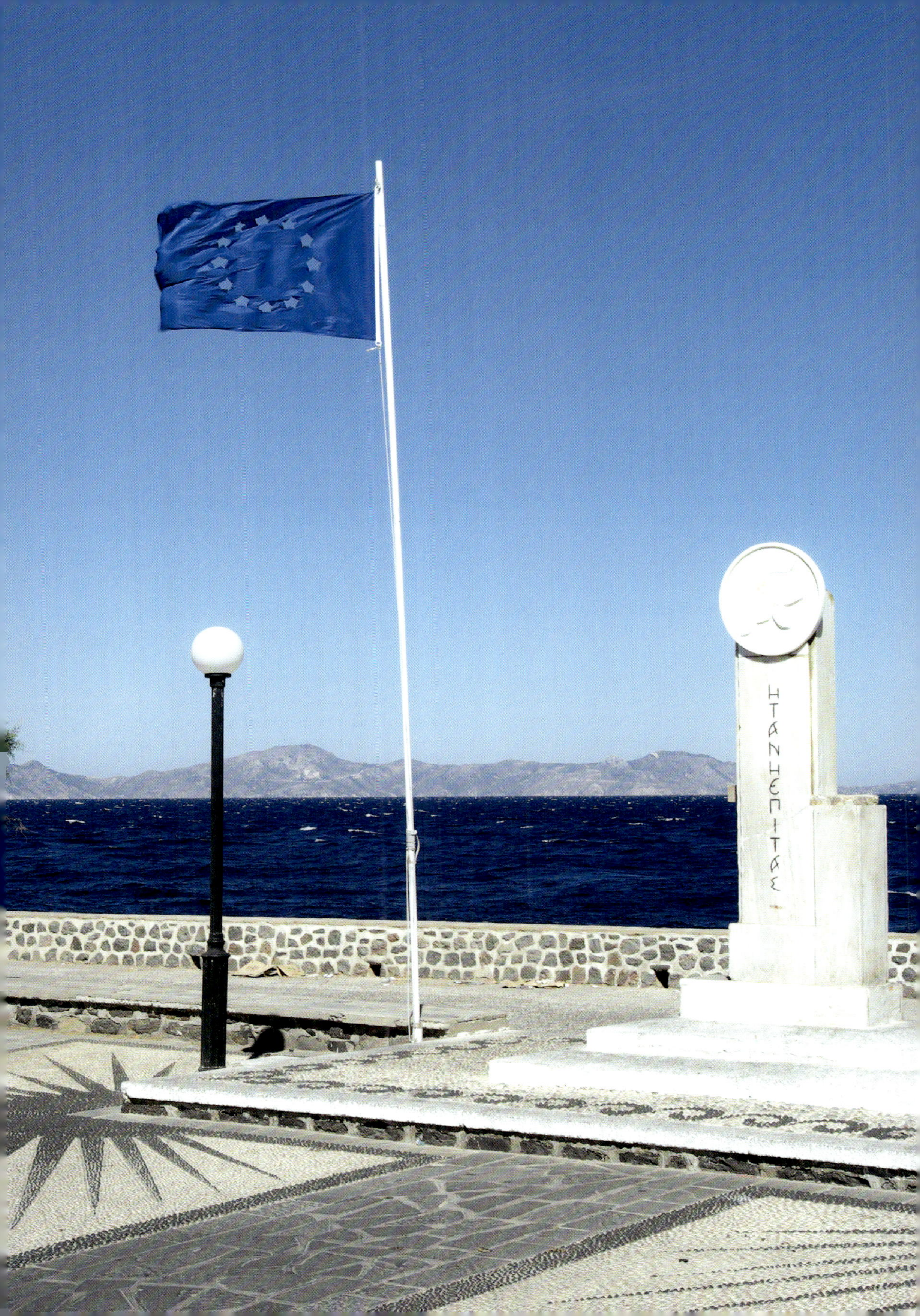
ΗΤΑΝΗΕΠΙΤΑΣ

Erdem Gündüz *1979

Erdem Gündüz is an artist, dancer, and choreographer based in Istanbul. From 1996 to 2002, he studied electrical engineering at the Ege University in Izmir, but switched to the Yildiz Technical University in Istanbul in 2003 to study music and stage art and modern dance at the Faculty of Art and Design. In 2007, he took part in an exchange program of the John F. Kennedy Center for the Performing Arts in Washington, D.C.; one year later he attended a course at the ImPulsTanz festival in Vienna. With his solo performances and as a member of several group projects, Gündüz has participated in numerous programs, festivals, and workshops on contemporary dance all over the world. Since 2005 he has given dance classes and prepared workshops at the Contemporary Dance Artists Association (ÇATI) in Istanbul. From 2008 to 2010, he assisted in the course PA 488 Modern Dance at the Boğaziçi University in Istanbul. He is the founder of the Ege University Dance Assembly. Currently Gündüz is finishing his master's degree in performing arts at Istanbul Mimar Sinan Fine Arts University. For his courageous commitment to freedom of expression and human rights he was awarded the 2013 M100 Media Award at the annual M100 Sanssouci Colloquium in Potsdam, and received a Theodor Heuss Medal at the award ceremony of the 49th Theodor Heuss Prize in 2014, which took place under the motto "arts break open."

In his action of silent artistic protest, Erdem Gündüz, together with many other people, was standing at Taksim Square in Istanbul on June 17, 2013 – and did not move for eight hours. The crowd that had gathered on Taksim Square stood still, staring at the Atatük Kültür Merkezi cultural center and the Turkish flags in front of it; a building that regularly hosted the Istanbul Arts and Culture Festival in the summer months and which, according to President Recep Tayyip Erdoğan's plans, was to be demolished as part of the redevelopment plans for Gezi Park and Taksim Square and replaced by a new shopping center and a new mosque.

Gündüz staged this silent vigil on Istanbul's Taksim Square, scene of violent clashes between police and anti-government protesters, inspiring hundreds of others to follow his lead, also in other parts of the city. The *Duran Adam* [Standing Man] campaign not only created irritation and led to many arrests of silent protesters; it became famous practically overnight, also internationally, especially via Facebook and Twitter, #duranadam being one of the most popular hashtags in Turkey in the days after the first actions. And a young artist became an icon of silent and peaceful protest.

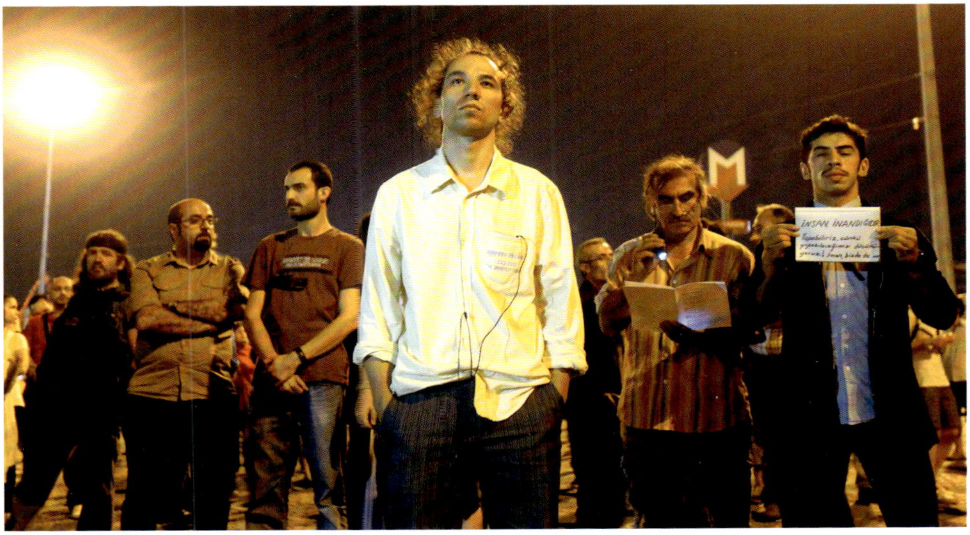

Erdem Gündüz, *Duran Adam*, protest performance, Taksim Square, Istanbul, 2013

The Meaning of Freedom – Excerpts from an Interview with the Turkish Artist Erdem Gündüz

Erdem, could you explain how you came up with the idea of *Duran Adam*, "Standing Man." Is it somehow related to your previous performances or political actions?

Erdem Gündüz: Actually, "Standing Man" was more of an action than an idea. I mean, the idea occurred to me afterwards; the action occurred spontaneously. My own political views, political performances or shows, are not deliberative actions; for example, I had a work named *The Wall* in 2007. […] An action against construction, reconstruction of the Gaza border, like the imaginary border between Syria and Turkey, or the construction of the Berlin Wall in Germany. In fact, all borders separate people, and I tried to break down these borders, these walls with my body.

So are these basically instant and spontaneous shows or performances? And the idea or the explanation of the performance comes afterwards, from what you said?

Gündüz: Well, that's basically what it was for "Standing Man." I was in […] Taksim Square, and I was participating in protests in Istiklal Square. The activists in Istiklal Square were excluded from Taksim Square, but I found my way there, and […] I did this by myself, I mean, I happened to do it. In other words, they could not have proclaimed me an organization or a gang, for according to Turkish law, if three people sit around and chat, they would have the right to declare you a terrorist organization […] and judge you. […] I mean, this is Turkey.

We all know the reaction of people in Taksim. That you inspired them and thousands of people came to stand there with you. Among the people who share the same opinions, I mean among the protesters, were there any negative reactions to you standing there? Did anybody react to your silence, maybe because you were nonorganized?

Gündüz: In fact, some people said to me: "Why don't you stand facing towards Gezi Park?" [...] Gezi Park, yes, a reason. But there are actually many reasons. Call it anticapitalism, or anti-neoliberalism. I mean there is capitalism, neoliberalism, and this new Muslimism, there is this concept of moderate Islam... These are the bloodsuckers of Turkey all together. They cage people in their homes, land is sold to other institutions and organizations. Peer pressure increases day by day. They used to say that veiled women were exposed to peer pressure: no sir, whoever wears short shorts, miniskirts, is exposed to peer pressure; the people who do not wear headscarves are now exposed to peer pressure.

So, as far as I see, you don't make a fuss about the forms and lifestyles of people. You say that people should live how they want to within the frame of democracy.

Gündüz: Yes, all in all, we are only humans. We are all equal, we all deserve freedom of thought, and we deserve to receive public services such as health care, education, highways, airports, you name it, to become a homeowner, etc. These are all the responsibilities of the government. But the government provides such services and then says: "Look what we have accomplished." What is actually done here in Turkey, is to make these public properties available to supporters, their relatives, global companies, or capitalist companies.

Let's come back to your "Standing Man" protest. What would you say: Is it an art performance or a political performance? Do you see a difference between art and political performance? What are their boundaries? How do they approach each other, and when do they move away from each other?

Gündüz: First of all, it was not a performance. It was a protest. It was an individual activity, which did not contain any violence within itself. On the other hand, it might not have been this sensational if someone else had done it. For I am a performing artist, a dancer, an actor, and a choreographer. [...] If you cannot perform political actions, you can start performing artistic actions. Because your political actions will be interfered by the police and you will be beaten by the police, but you can perform an artistic action... Maybe that's what happened in Tahrir. If you ask me why I stood in front of Atatürk Kültür Merkezi cultural center, well, I have seen many performances and dance shows there, I have even performed in a dance show there. I think it was in 2003... I don't remember exactly how many, but I have seen many spectacular performances in AKM. Now the government shuts down these institutions: Taksim stage; Emek movie theater; Istanbul Metropolitan Municipality City Theaters; Muammer Karaca Theater in Odakule... These have all been shut down by the government. They turned existing buildings into hotels and residences. For example, we had to move out of Tophane district. Since the new place will change with the construction of Galataport and become a hotel, we had to move out again as ÇATI dance group. In other words, I stand against a government, which tries to destroy art instead of supporting it...

With regard to your action, what was the role of artists like yourself?

Gündüz: We need to look at it in this way: for example, I performed "Standing Man" one day for eight hours, so it was a one-off performance. And then people started to repeat the performance; they copied the action like it was an object. We could call it Pop art, in a sense. They multiplied and shared this action like Andy Warhol did with his pictures of Marilyn Monroe or Elvis Presley. [...] The idea and concept of art has changed a lot after

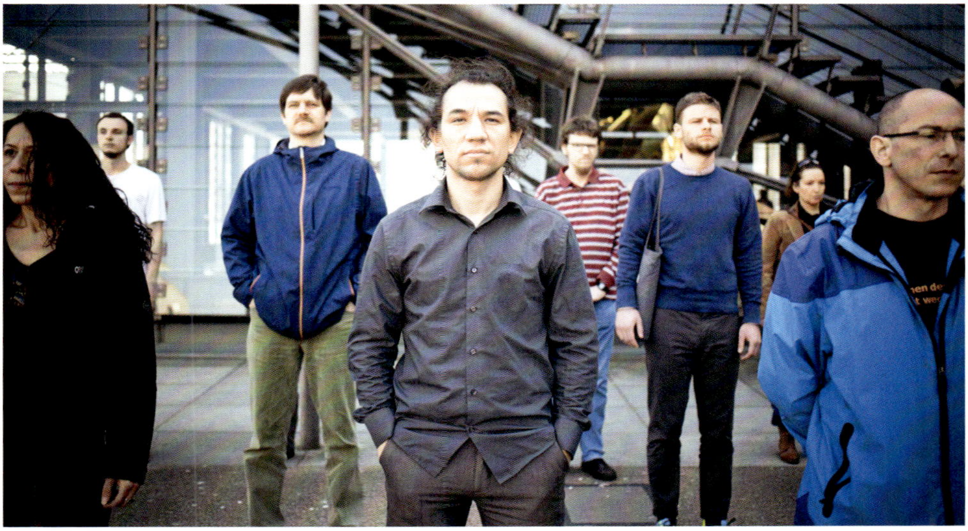

Erdem Gündüz, *Duran Adam*, protest performance, ZKM | Karlsruhe, 2014

Marcel Duchamp. This entire protest actually took place in a public place, Gezi Park; you know it is also accepted as public art. People practiced yoga, tai chi, they read books, set up camps, some of them [...] recited, danced, they did everything [...].

What kind of actions could follow this protest? What role could artists play in further protests?

Gündüz: What could not be achieved by Gezi protests has been accomplished by the dissidence between the community and AKP, because they started killing each other and digging pits for each other. What comes after this? Now people know more about their rights, but what? Actually, they know that the public places are for the people. I mean parks, gardens – not so many left in Istanbul – but also the streets. Now people know that public transport vehicles can be places for creativity, such as graffiti, and [...] now people see the Gezi protesters from a different perspective.

Public places?

Gündüz: Both public places and art and the ones related to art.

Okay, so if you were to perform an action today, after your "Standing Man" protest, what would it be like? You stood and remained silent, and you stood against something. What would be your next action?

Gündüz: I work to find out whether an art council exists in Turkey. I actually started to do this three years ago. And being in this business, I can easily say that the Ministry of Culture does not support it. This is a job, which is about the perception and vision of people regarding art. This is a job, which makes people ask what art is and what it is not; I also ask questions and read manifestos. But I did not do this as a political action or as political art; I only express myself. The next step, probably, would be performing more art in public places. [...] Of course, no protests will be like the Gezi protest, because Gezi was a one-time experience and the system will not allow a second one. Because it covers up that weakness or holes. [...] [T]his is a constantly learning, upgrading, and self-updating system. DISK and KESK [Turkish trade union organizations] existed thirty years ago and they broke them up and shut them down; we used to read and hear about the corruption, smuggling, and government's corruption on newspapers, radio, and TV: now they are all partisan media. [...] Social media is also the same, they shape and govern social media channels. They couldn't do it, so now Twitter and YouTube are banned in Turkey.

But AKP is not the only one that learns, the people and the artists also upgraded themselves.

Gündüz: The idea of revolution must be set in minds first, because promising or giving freedom to people who don't know the meaning of freedom makes no sense at all. And it is also not necessary. Because freedom is in people's minds and you have a right if you ask for it. So, if you want to be free, then you are free; or you can live under the mandate of the United States. Consequently, you can live under both. And I said this system must be demolished, because, let's say, this government has resigned. If the new government comes and maintains the same system, this new government would make no sense either. In other words, resignation of this government is not enough by itself.

Thanks to media, social components, and social networking, Gezi Park protests had repercussions throughout the world. Your action, in addition to other actions by various artists, has become an influential action. And you have also received a human rights award from the M100 Sanssouci Colloquium in Potsdam. What do you think about this award? What did you feel?

Gündüz: My reason to receive the award was this: I thought, if I receive this award, I will be able to spread and share my thoughts on human rights, equality, and freedom, and their intention was also the same. [...] It made a tremendous impact within the media, it is also their field... For example, in Turkey, they said this award was only granted to the Central Bank, the president of the European Central Bank, and the artist who became prominent with his caricatures about Mohammed. However, the real story is that the president of the European Central Bank received this award because he was the founder of a foundation named Doctors Without Borders. The award has also been given to architects, very,

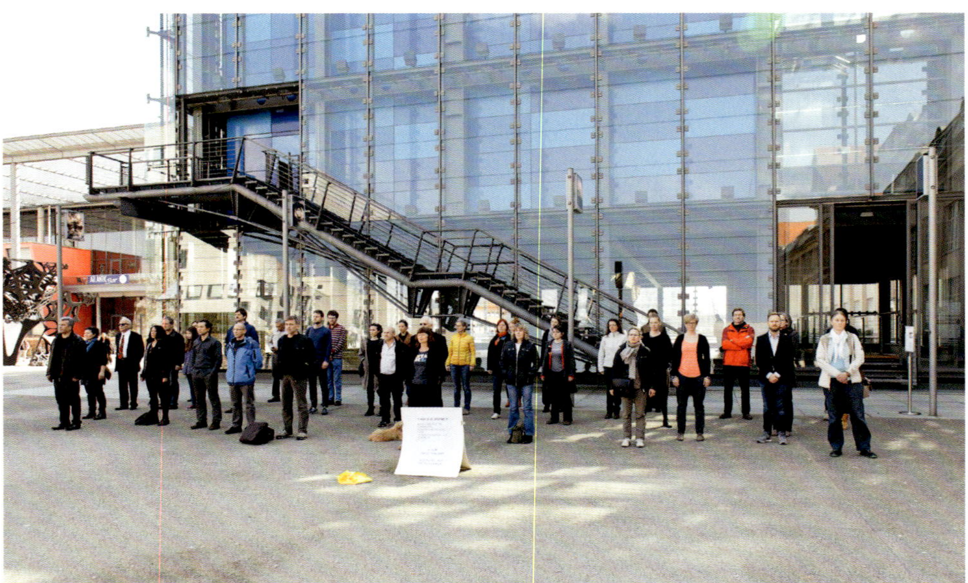

Erdem Gündüz, *Duran Adam*, protest performance, ZKM | Karlsruhe, 2014

very famous architects. What I'm trying to explain is that in Turkey things are reflected through a single perspective. For example, I performed in Serbia and Montenegro. People check my website, see Serbia, and spread the word that I'm a Serbian agent. However, if they read more, they will see that I have attended a performing arts exchange program in the U.S., a biennial in Italy, Sarajevo Winter Festival in Bosnia-Herzegovina, ImPulsTanz festival in Vienna. They don't even read the rest of the information, they only see what they want to see.

There is a group of people who are copying your "Standing Man" and who brought your action here to Karlsruhe [...]; they have been standing for democracy and freedom of thought for ten months, unrelated to Turkey. Even though they are inspired by you and Gezi Park, they are standing for the entire world, or for Europe. Do these supportive actions mean anything for Turkey? Are they becoming popular in Turkey? Are there any benefits for people in Turkey?

Gündüz: Actually, freedom has a meaning, if you know what to do with it. [...] I would like to point out something else. For example, I'm not a big fan of copying. Sharing is something I prefer more, because I saw that little candle burning in Atatürk Kültür Merkezi; it was a visionary image, and it represented hope to me, and I saw that the people standing by my side were sharing the same hope. Or that's what I thought. Just like love grows as you share it – hope, friendship, brotherhood also grow as you share them. I support what these people did with all my heart and soul, because the truth is, if you defend the rights of the unemployed when you have a job, defend the rights of the uneducated when you are educated, if you work on the health care system and its problems when you are healthy, it makes sense. It makes sense if you express your opinions on freedom and defend freedom when you are free. You cannot defend freedom in jail. You cannot even speak about freedom, you shouldn't. You only crave for it. That's why it is worthy of respect that these people made a protest about human rights, equality, brotherhood, and friendship, while they themselves were free and had freedom of thought. I call it sharing, not copying… Because a hope, a thought is being shared.

The interview was prepared by Banu Beyer and Sarah Maske (ZKM | Karlsruhe) and conducted by Banu Beyer in the course of Erdem Gündüz's visit to ZKM | Karlsruhe in March 2014. The text was translated from the Turkish by the Istanbul translation agency Dijital Tercüme.

Ed Hall *1944

Since 1974, Ed Hall has been creating handmade banners for trade unions and movements that are committed to protecting the environment, disarmament, human rights, sex workers' rights, that are against nuclear power, austerity cuts, and violence against women. Originally an architect, Hall was a trade union representative himself when Margaret Thatcher came to power in the late 1970s, and it was in this capacity that he started to make banners for trade union campaigns. His first non-trade-union banner was created for Brian Douglas, who died in police custody in 1995 after being beaten by policemen; further banners dedicated to people who died in police custody followed.

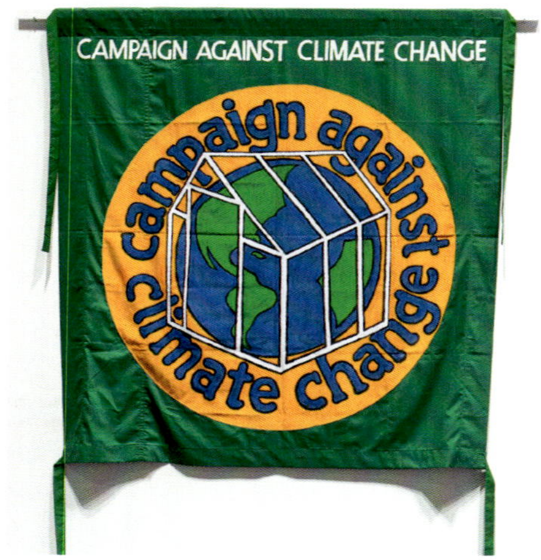

Ed Hall, *Campaign against Climate Change*, 2002, banner, cotton drill, fabric dye, 180 × 180 cm, installation view, ZKM | Karlsruhe, 2014

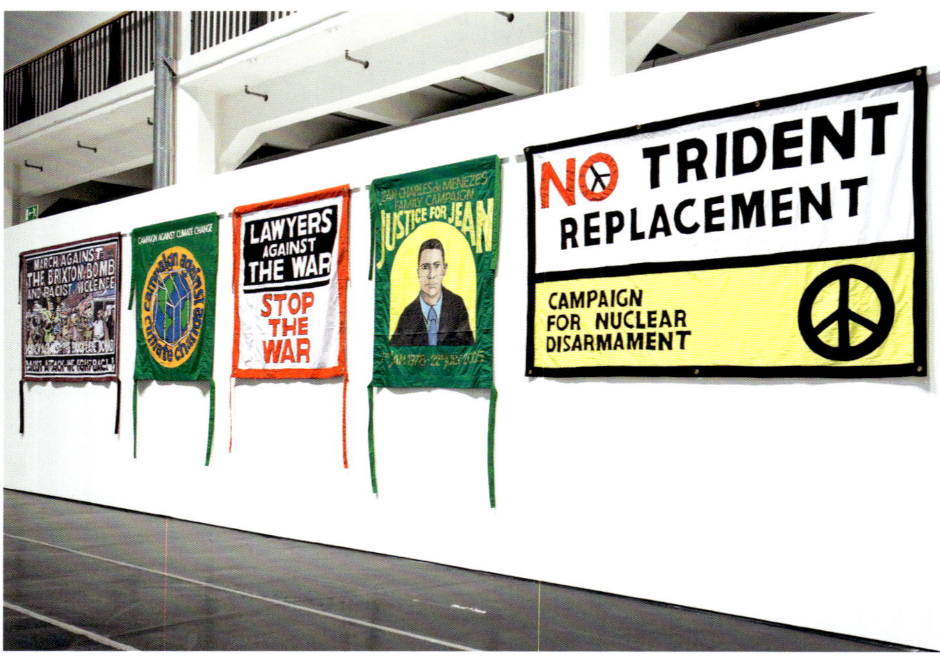

Ed Hall, banners, 1990–2007; on the right: *No Trident Replacement*, 2007, banner, cotton drill, fabric dye, 240 × 180 cm, installation view, ZKM | Karlsruhe, 2014

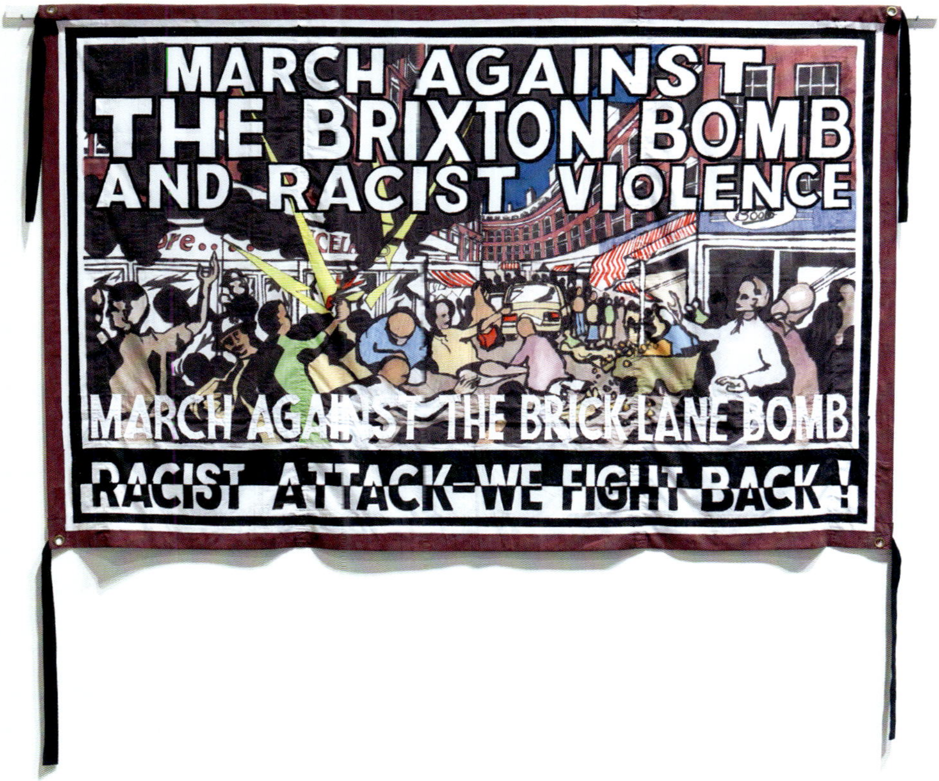

Ed Hall, *March against the Brixton Bomb*, 1999, banner, cotton drill, fabric dye, 230 × 180 cm, installation view, ZKM | Karlsruhe, 2014

Over the past fifteen years, Ed Hall has worked closely with the British Turner Prize-winning artist Jeremy Deller; for instance, for *Procession* (2009), a parade held in the streets of Manchester as part of the Manchester International Festival during which Hall's banners were wielded. Their collaboration started when Deller discovered Hall's work at the Lambeth Country Show in south London – notably, the banner *March against the Brixton Bomb* (1999) caught his attention. Since then Hall has created hundreds of hand-sewn, hand-stitched, and hand-painted banners for their shows. Their collaborative work was exhibited at the Palais de Tokyo in Paris (2008), the British Pavilion at the 2013 Venice Biennale, and the Victoria and Albert Museum in London (2014/2015). Ed Hall's banners were also showcased in a solo exhibition at the People's History Museum in Manchester in 2011. Despite his success in the field of contemporary art, for Hall it is vitally important to continue his work on banners for unions and campaigns.

www.parliament-square.org.uk
www.brianhaw.tv
www.hauserwirth.com/artists/64/mark-wallinger

Brian Haw 1949–2011 and Mark Wallinger *1959

Idis Hartmann and Peter Weibel

State Britain: Activist Art vs. Artistic Activism

State Britain (2007) by artist Mark Wallinger was installed around two sides of an atrium during the *global aCtIVISm* exhibition at ZKM | Karlsruhe, its prominent position underlining its key role in the exhibition concept. *State Britain* is a prime example for how central issues can be addressed, such as: Who is the author and who holds the copyright? What does freedom of art mean as compared to political freedom? What does the freedom of the artist mean compared to civil liberties? From what point onwards is the artist freer than a citizen? Why do citizens get punished for something for which artists get rewarded? Are civil liberties less extensive than the rights of the artist? Where does art end and activism begin? How does inclusion in a museum affect the status of works by artist-activists?

Brian Haw: The Activist

State Britain is a forty-meter-long protest display, which recreates the original work by peace activist Brian Haw that contained over six hundred

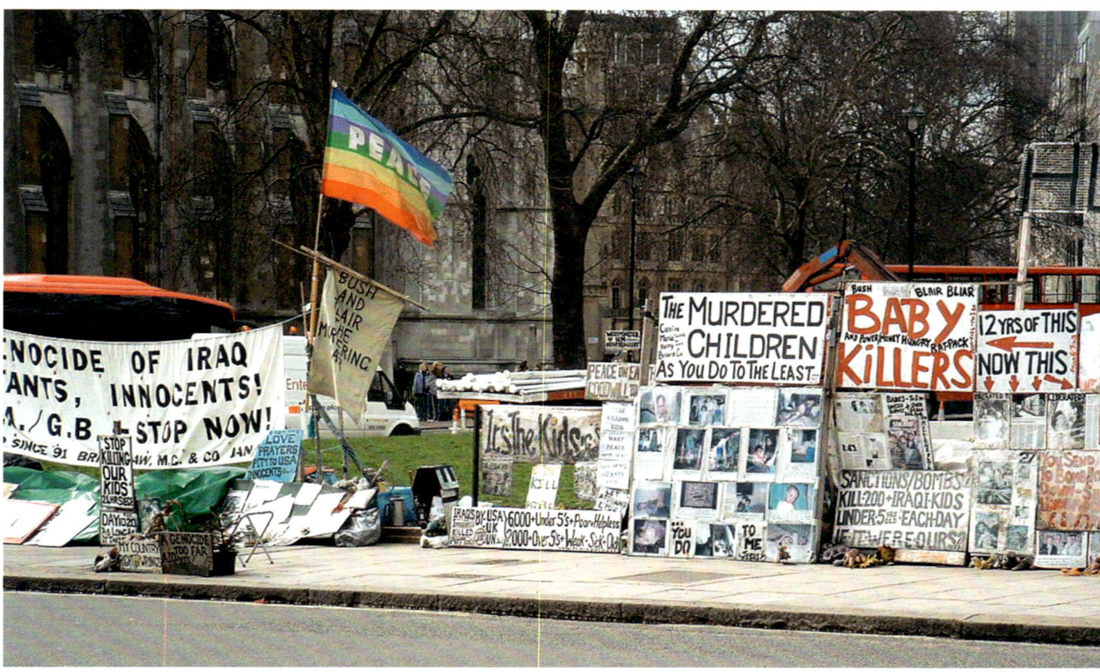

Brian Haw, Parliament Square Peace Campaign, protest camp, London, January 2002.
Haw pursued his 24/7 peace campaign outside the Houses of Parliament from June 2001.

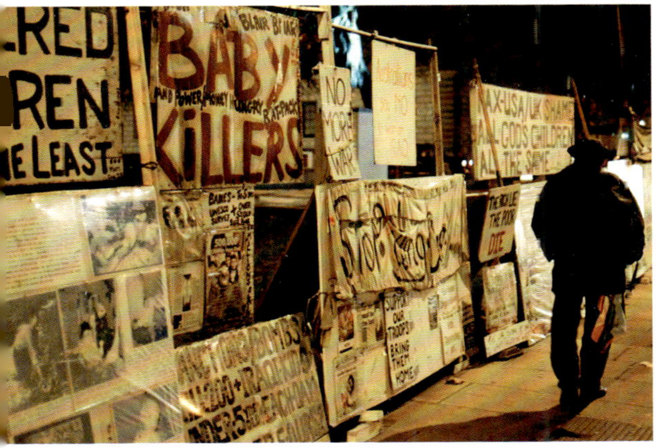

Brian Haw, Parliament Square Peace Campaign, protest camp, London, December 2005. Over the years Brian Haw and other protesters built up a substantial array of signs, placards, and posters.

items. In the course of his Parliament Square Peace Campaign in London, which began on June 2, 2001 and lasted several years, Haw installed an assemblage of photographs, illustrations, banners, peace flags, texts, drawings, teddy bears, and everyday objects directly opposite the Houses of Parliament. This environment, with its montage of texts and symbols, images and objects, which articulated his protest on a daily basis, brings to mind both the common forms of performative protest and, in terms of its aesthetics, also recalls the art of Thomas Hirschhorn and Christoph Schlingensief.

Many sympathizers contributed pieces to Haw's growing assemblage so that it ultimately became a collective expression of protest. Originally, out of humanitarian motives, Brian Haw, an evangelical Christian, sought to draw attention to the brutal killing and mutilation of children in the Gulf War from 1990 onwards. Later, he extended his protest to denounce Britain's participation in the Iraq and Afghanistan wars, and when he found himself in conflict with the law the project also became a plea for freedom of speech and the freedom to demonstrate.

Haw had not given advance notice of his demonstration, and was imprisoned 47 times for unauthorized demonstrations, not that this deterred him one bit from protesting. Finally, in 2005, the British Parliament passed the "Serious Organised Crime and Police Act," to be able to take action against Haw. The Act created an exclusion zone, a one-kilometer radius around Parliament Square, where demonstrations within this circle were prohibited unless announced six days or at least 24 hours in advance. The Commissioner of Police of the Metropolis and the Secretary of State for the Home Department imposed sanctions on Haw for unauthorized demonstrations.

The difficulty was, however, that the wording of the law clearly referred only to demonstrations taking place *after* the enactment of the law. Consequently, Haw successfully litigated against the protest ban imposed on him: Only a subsequent Commencement Order had expanded the wording so that it referred to demonstrations that had already begun. The authority in question was not legally entitled to make such an amendment, and the High Court of Justice therefore confirmed that Haw did not need to get authorization to continue a protest that had already begun before the law came into force.[1] This ruling was then overturned by the Court of Appeal on the grounds that the intent of Parliament was that the law should also apply to demonstrations that had already begun. Otherwise the law would be "absurd." Therefore, the police had the right to stop or limit a demonstration that had already begun, if the officer in charge identified a danger to public order. Consequently, the sanctions imposed on Brian Haw were legal.[2]

From then onwards Haw was only allowed to continue his campaign if he observed certain conditions, one being to shorten the protest wall to three meters and another that he only use his megaphone at certain times. As Haw did not curtail his protest to meet these

1 England and Wales High Court (Administrative Court) Decisions, [2005] EWHC 2061 (Admin).

2 England and Wales Court of Appeal (Civil Division) Decisions, [2006] EWCA Civ 532.

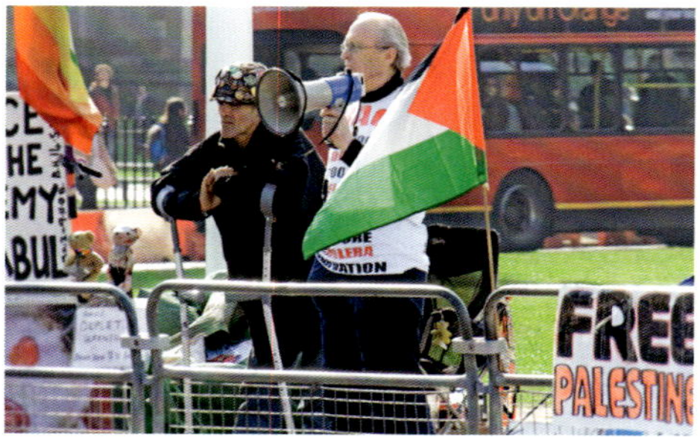

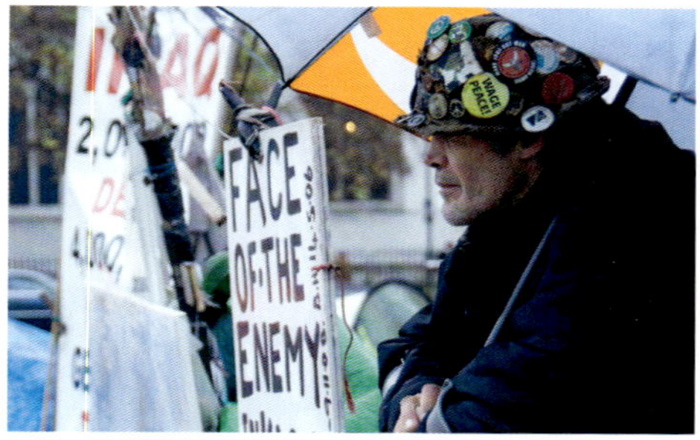

Brian Haw, Parliament Square Peace Campaign, protest camp, London. Left: March 2009, Haw protests outside Parliament. Right: November 2009, supporters donated the signs that decorated Haw's tents, and someone volunteered to run Haw's website www.parliament-square.org.uk where anyone could read his updates or donate

conditions, the police cleared his protest camp on May 23, 2006 and arrested him.

But this did not silence criticism of a law that effectively sidelined the freedom of expression and assembly guaranteed under human rights if no formal notice were given of a demonstration. Even the British Parliament's Joint Committee on Human Rights ruled in a report on policing protest published in 2009 that "no sanction should apply to those who choose not to notify the police of their intention to protest solely by reason of that choice."[3] Moreover, people are still critical of the fact that the law gives too much discretionary power to individual police officers, who can therefore prevent a protest entirely on formal grounds.

Mark Wallinger: The Artist

In 2007, artist Mark Wallinger, who in many of his works addresses Great Britain's national identity and history, as well as belief systems and myth, teamed up with the Mike Smith Studio to produce an almost exact replica of Brian Haw's protest camp using photos Wallinger himself had taken several days before Haw's eviction. From January 15 to August 27, 2007 Tate Britain presented the work with the title *State Britain* – a play on words after the manner of Brian Haw, who had discovered the anagram "b.liar" in Prime Minister Tony Blair's name. Wallinger assumed that the boundary of the one-kilometer radius around Parliament Square, where unauthorized protests were prohibited,

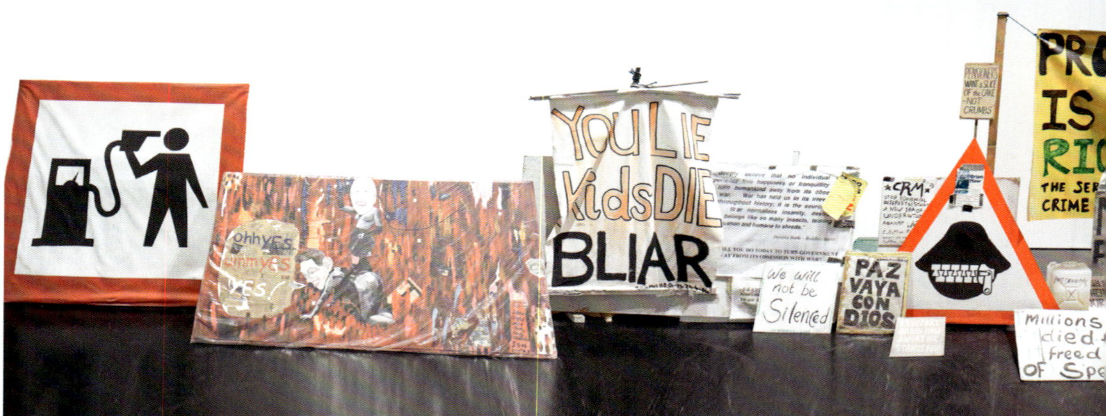

Mark Wallinger, *State Britain*, 2007, installation, mixed media, 570 × 4,300 × 190 cm, installation view, ZKM | Karlsruhe, 2014

actually ran through Tate Britain and his exhibit, and he marked this line with thick black tape. However, as this law does not apply inside Tate Britain, the line was a symbolic visualization of the divide between legality and illegality. It is also open to debate whether Tate Britain is actually located within the exclusion zone. In December 2007, Mark Wallinger won the prestigious Turner Prize for his *State Britain* installation, which carries a monetary award of £25,000.

The Citizen-Artist?

Mark Wallinger's work *State Britain* broaches many questions: Who is the artist or author or copyright holder? Brian Haw, who created the work, or Mark Wallinger, who produced a recreation of it? What role does its insertion into a museum setting play? Is it enough that someone recognized by society as a professional artist simply claims (in the manner of Marcel Duchamp's readymades) that what he calls a work of art is a work of art? How can it be that one and the same work is seen on the one hand as protest and therefore confiscated by the state and the "artist" imprisoned, and on the other awarded a state prize and the "activist" celebrated? Is activist art allowed in a democracy but artistic activism banned? And if so, why? Why is there more freedom in the art system than in the political system? Moreover, what is particularly perfidious about this is that it is the political system that allows art this freedom. Does that mean that the political system tolerates forms of protest as art because art is not socially relevant? Is the work by Wallinger still a protest and a political act or is it "only" a work of art? And is Wallinger's installation a historicization or an actualization of the work by Haw that the police removed? Is Wallinger's work a historical representation, a monument, or even perhaps an altar for Haw? How do the freedom of art and freedom to demonstrate relate to each other? How can it be that the original creator of the work, namely Haw, is imprisoned while Wallinger who reconstructs it is rewarded? What did Wallinger do with the money that he earned through Haw? Did he support Haw financially in his legal battles or when he became ill (Haw died of lung cancer in 2011)?

It is quite evident that the art system and the political system constitute

3 Joint Committee on Human Rights, UK Parliament, "Legal Reform: Protest around Parliament," available online at: www.publications.parliament.uk/pa/jt200809/jtselect/jtrights/47/4708.htm, accessed 11/07/2014.

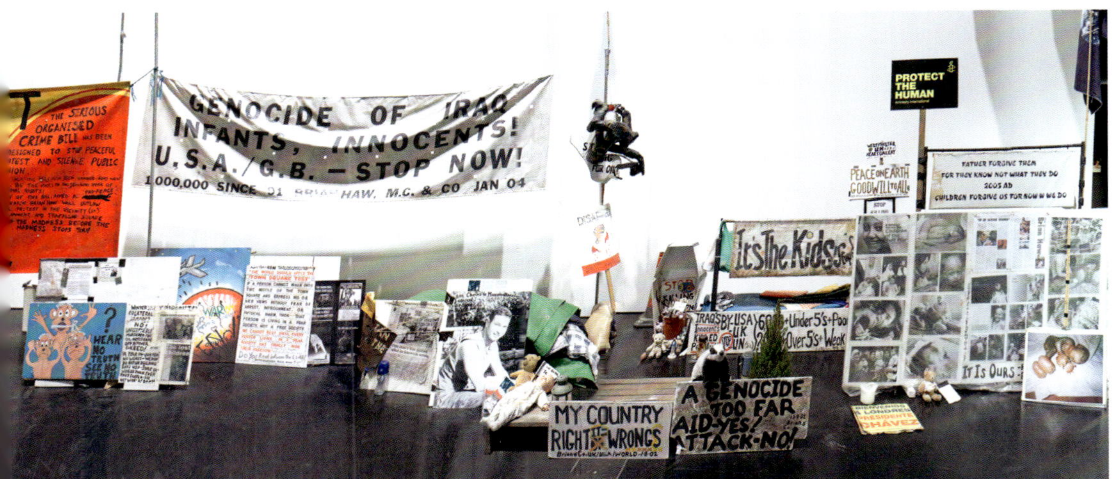

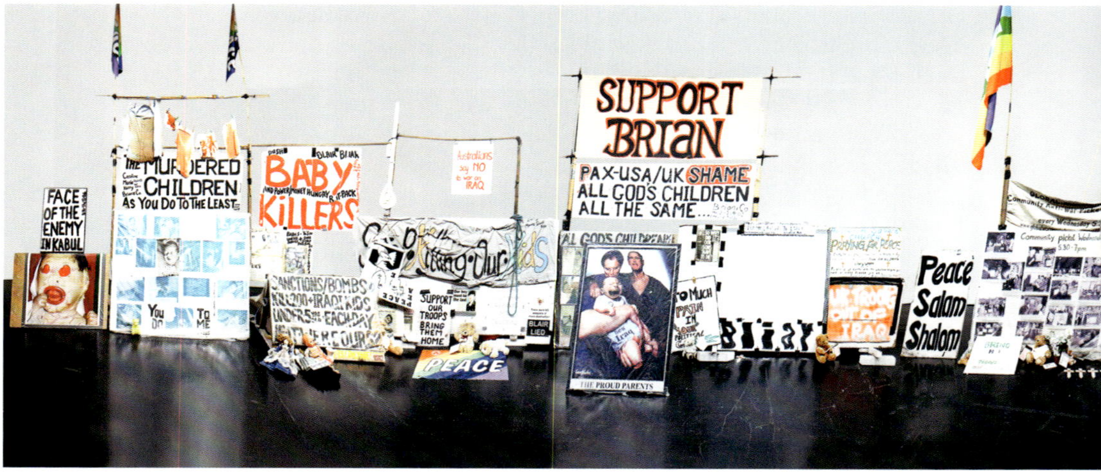

Mark Wallinger, *State Britain*, 2007, installation, mixed media, 570 × 4,300 × 190 cm, installation view, ZKM | Karlsruhe, 2014

different spheres, even though the political sphere includes the art sphere. This clearly illustrates the ambivalent status of the protest installation. In one context a work is a political protest, and in another political art. As protest the work jeopardizes, even ruins a citizen's existence. As art the work benefits the existence of a citizen, indeed even advances it. The author of the work is condemned while the person who "appropriated" it gets a monetary reward. When the authorship or author changes and the political sphere morphs into a museum space, a change of system takes place which leads to a reappraisal of the work. Evidently, under certain conditions the citizen has less rights than the artist. This conflict between citizen and artist is the central theme of the *global aCtIVISm* exhibition. In supporting the new artistic forms of protest that can now be observed all over the world, the exhibition seeks to help close the gap between citizen and artist by transferring the degree of liberty enjoyed by artists to political citizens. The ideal is a citizen-artist who overcomes this fundamental conflict of the modern age between civil and artistic existence, or the political and artistic sphere. If this conflict were resolved it would no longer be possible for Brian Haw to be imprisoned and Mark Wallinger to receive a prize. It is the utopia of a future civil society that the liberty of the artist will not stand above that of the citizen, that the freedom of the citizen will not lag behind that of the artist. A symmetric sphere of liberty should obtain for both.

Philosophers like Peter Sloterdijk and Bruno Latour have addressed these conflicts of the modern age and offered solutions for them – Sloterdijk in his three-volume ontology-based "spherology,"[4] and Latour in his social-based "anthropology of the Moderns."[5] Latour distinguishes between various modes of existence in the domains of science, technology, law, religion, economy, and politics, which emerged in the modern age. Each of these modes of existence pursues different values. One possible consequence is that the same thing is treated differently in different domains. The fact that the installations by Haw and Wallinger are judged so differently can be attributed to differing values in the modes of existence of politics, law, economy, and art. While Haw's protest was a thorn in the eye of the state, the political system did not hinder the state-financed institution Tate Britain from exhibiting Wallinger's work of art. While the law passed in 2005 was declared applicable to Haw, it was not applicable to Wallinger's work in the

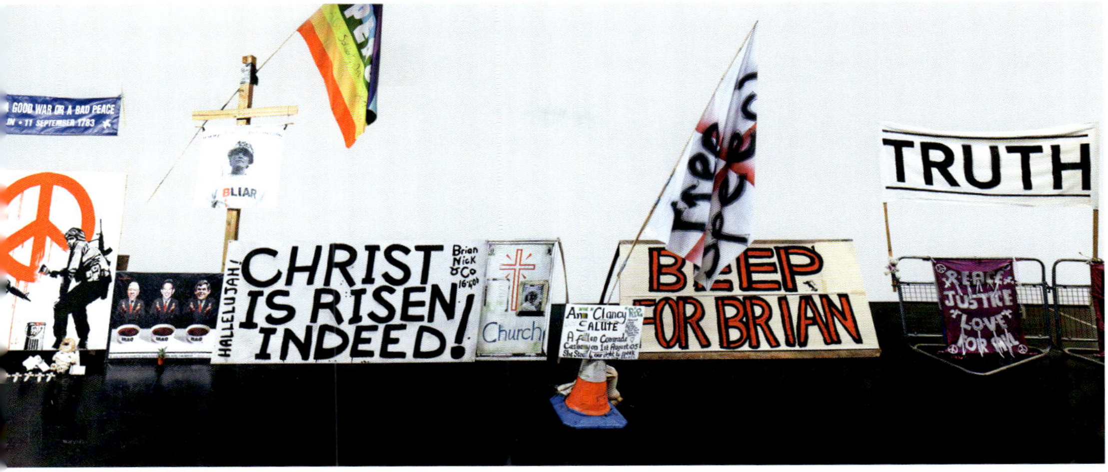

museum. While the art market and the museum would never have been interested in Brian Haw's installation, the replica, Wallinger's reenactment, was exhibited in one of the most renowned art institutions and honored with one of the most prestigious art prizes. These seemingly paradox judgments are ultimately based on the fact that every domain, whether politics, law, economy, or art, lays down its own criteria.

Yve-Alain Bois quite correctly points out that "the culture industry and the political and financial powers that support it need the illusion that art is a refuge (best if it's innocuous, but the culture industry can ultimately accommodate anything) and the dogma that museums are safe havens with special immunity just as churches and mosques once were."[6] He also mentions the various actors, who are very much aware of their differing roles within a democracy. Bois also shows that these actors roles change: "Recent violence in such religious sites might lead us to believe that only museums remain cordoned off from real bloodshed and, in this case at least, from the grip of the law – a double standard brilliantly spectacularized by Wallinger. There is something nihilistic, but not entirely defeatist, about his installation. This is the current State (of) Britain, it says: paranoiac enough to abolish rights that had been assured its citizens since 1215, but shrewd enough to let art bask in its fictional perfume of freedom. Let's relish the aroma, while it's still possible. Museums may not be immune forever."[7]

According to Latour we need a new form of "diplomacy" to mediate between the individual modes of existence. Perhaps exhibiting the work by Haw and Wallinger in the sanctuary of a museum – the ZKM | Karlsruhe – is one such diplomatic attempt: Haw's work in the guise of Wallinger's replica was not exhibited as art, but in the context of global civil activism.

Translated from the German by Jeremy Gaines.

4 See: Peter Sloterdijk, *Sphären I. Blasen*, Suhrkamp, Frankfurt am Main, 1998; *Sphären II. Globen*, Suhrkamp, Frankfurt am Main, 1999; *Sphären III. Schäume*, Suhrkamp, Frankfurt am Main, 2004; English editions: *Spheres I. Bubbles*, Semiotext(e), Los Angeles (CA), The MIT Press, Cambridge (MA), 2011; *Spheres II. Globes*, Semiotext(e), Los Angeles (CA), The MIT Press, Cambridge (MA), 2014; *Spheres III. Foam*, Semiotext(e), Los Angeles (CA), The MIT Press, Cambridge (MA), forthcoming.

5 See: Bruno Latour, *Enquête sur les modes d'existence. Une anthropologie des modernes*, Éditions La Découverte, Paris, 2012; English edition: *An Inquiry into Modes of Existence. An Anthropology of the Moderns*, Harvard University Press, Cambridge (MA), 2013.

6 Yve-Alain Bois, "Piece Movement. On Mark Wallinger's *State Britain*," in: *Artforum International*, vol. 45, no. 8, April 2007, pp. 248–251, here p. 251.

7 Ibid.

Niklas Hoffmann *1987 and Rebecca Meining *1991

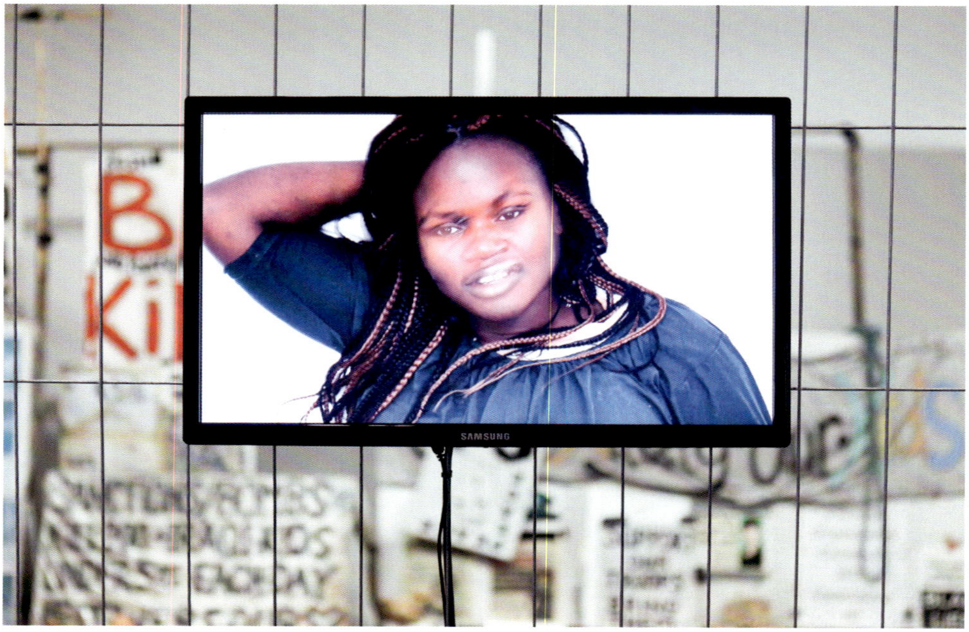

Niklas Hoffmann and Rebecca Meining, *Invisible*, 2013, video, color, sound, 122 min, installation view, ZKM | Karlsruhe, 2014

In the video installation *Invisible* (2013), film student Niklas Hoffmann, together with fellow student Rebecca Meining, document the journey of six people who have fled their home countries. Hoffmann and Meining present their lives and experiences in six portraits and let their protagonists tell their individual story. The asylum seekers recount the circumstances under which they left their home country, their experiences in Ethiopia, Pakistan, and Nigeria, their journey to Europe, and their situation in Germany; they talk about shelter, food, needs, and their everyday lives.

The staged setting of the installation, presented in an artist-in-residence studio in Munich in 2013, creates an interesting tension with the personal and authentic accounts: the very sparsely furnished room with lockers, bunk beds, sheets, and blankets is an installation that was set up for the video, and it stands for and visualizes the confined spaces that asylum seekers generally live in. The videos of the six asylum seekers who tell their story are projected onto the cushions; they were also filmed on their beds, in a passive state. The law forces them to be passive, because it does not allow asylum seekers to take on a job.

In 2012, Hoffmann was awarded a media art grant from the University of Television and Film Munich for his project, and for a year he lived and worked in a studio in Munich which also became the film set. When in

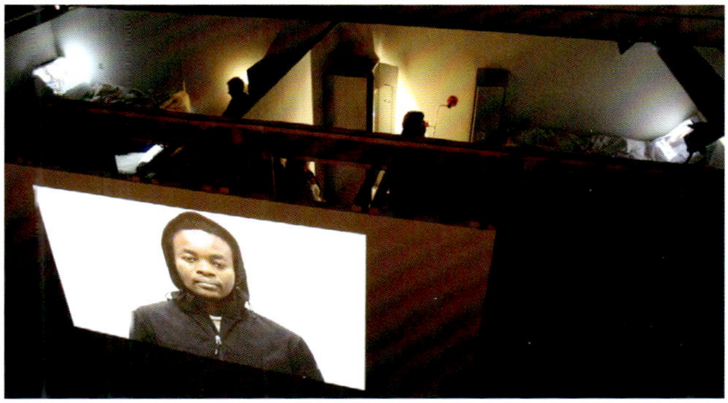

Niklas Hoffmann and Rebecca Meining, *Invisible*, 2013, installation, mixed media, installation view, artist-in-residence studio, Munich, 2013

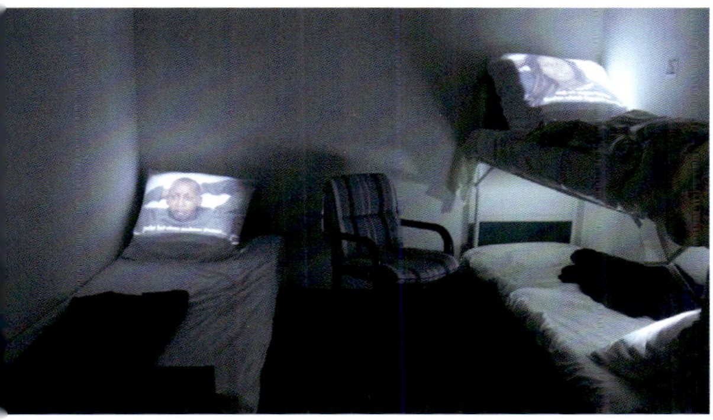

Niklas Hoffmann and Rebecca Meining, *Invisible*, 2013, installation, mixed media, installation view, artist-in-residence studio, Munich, 2013

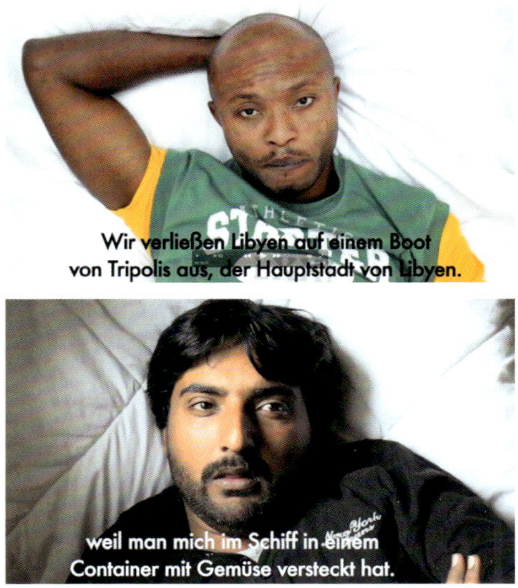

Niklas Hoffmann and Rebecca Meining, *Invisible*, 2013, video, color, sound, 122 min, video stills

summer 2013 a group of refugees put up tents in the center of Munich and went on hunger strike to get themselves recognized as asylum seekers until the camp was cleared, this deeply affected Hoffmann's project. Hoffmann was there, he documented the protests, several asylum seekers came to his studio to discuss and plan further actions, and Hoffmann also joined several "non-citizens" and activists on a two-week protest march. *Invisible* raises questions about citizenship and human rights and sheds light on the experience of six "non-citizens" – they are just a few of the many who live amongst us but whose existence most "regular citizens" barely notice.

Alexey Iorsh *1963

Artist and activist Alexey Iorsh engages with social issues in different genres: comics, cartoons, easel graphics, and street art. He is the author of several graphic novels and comic series. Being an active supporter of campaigns for political prisoners, he also focuses on current political events in his artistic work. In addition, he provides artistic support for projects of his fellow activists and artists, and he is a member of the Russian MediaImpact working group.

Art Activism in Comics (2013) is a graphic novel that presents the history of art activism in Russia as a deliberately "largely inconsistent, biased and unobjective story." It is also Alexey Iorsh's story, spanning from artist life in the 1990s until the financial crisis in 2008 and beyond. *Art Activism in Comics* provides insights into the Russian activist artist scene: It points to the legal complaints under Article 282 of the Russian Criminal Code that hindered the work of many activist artists, and to the repressions, attacks, and arrests they have had to face; it deals with controversial artworks in the 2007 *Forbidden Art* exhibition in Moscow, the success of the art group Voina and their fame on the Internet, the emergence of a Russian art activism scene organizing group shows in abandoned buildings, but also to arising conflicts between art groups and their members; and it highlights the arrest of members of Pussy Riot and tells about the "March against Scoundrels" in January 2013 and other actions of protest.

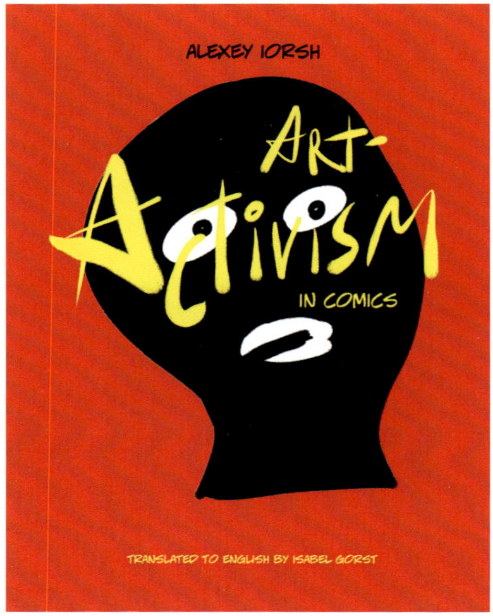

Alexey Iorsh, cover of the comic book *Art Activism in Comics*, 2013

While activist art originated in individual performances, it has evolved into a collective expression of political demands, as Alexey Iorsh demonstrates. His personal history is part of this development: *Art Activism in Comics* is also a story about punk rock, Alexey Iorsh's early jobs as newspaper cartoonist and in an advertising agency, and his work and commitment as an activist artist. For Iorsh, comics are a globally accepted form of alternative media in which protest can be expressed.

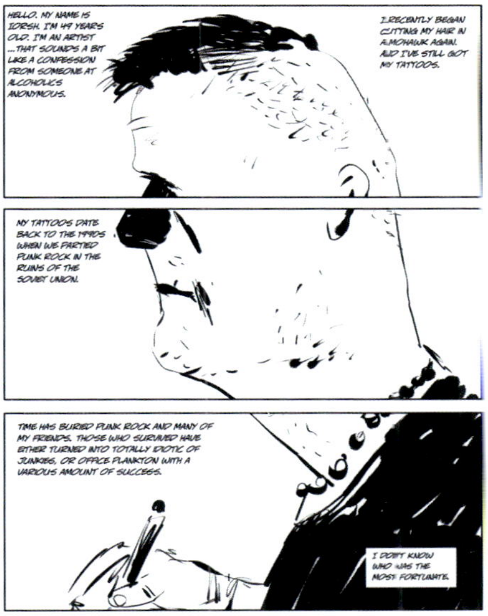

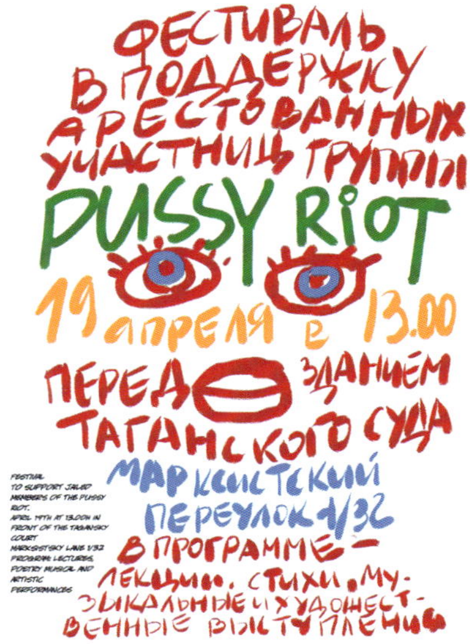

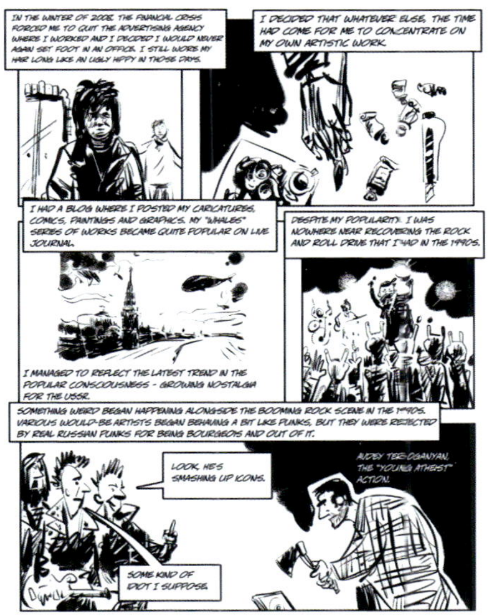

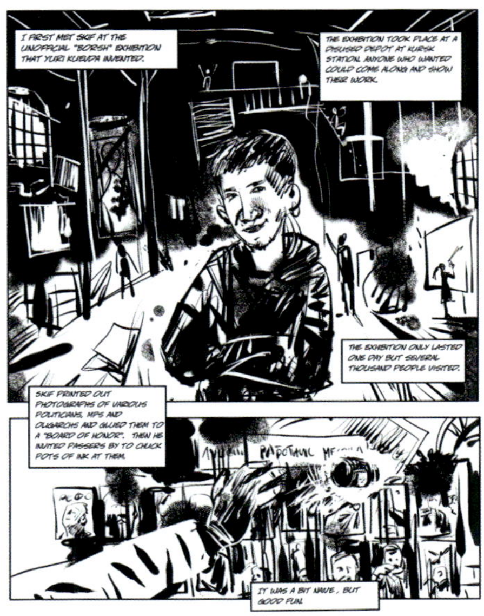

Alexey Iorsh, pages from the comic book
Art Activism in Comics, 2013

JUST DO IT.

The artist collective JUST DO IT. – resurrecting an old Nike slogan in order to generate attention – was founded by the Berlin-based artists Kim Asendorf (*1981) and Ole Fach (*1980), who together run the Fach & Asendorf Gallery (http://fa-g.org), an online gallery dedicated to media and net art. The JUST DO IT. collective operates a blog on gezigelenlimon.tumblr.com (Gezi gelen Limon means "Lemons of Gezi") that displays photographs of the protests to save the Gezi Park from the occupygezipics.tumblr.com site from which all traces of the violence that occurred there have been removed. With their platform Asendorf and Fach seek to turn the spotlight on the violence that does take place and put the focus on manipulated media reports.

For the Gezi gelen Limon blog, the most evocative and popular images assembled under the #OccupyGezi hashtag were selected, and not only all direct acts of violence were removed, but also the key protagonists: the protesters. What remains are only clues, creating in some cases a somewhat ghostly atmosphere and a powerful aesthetic: there are scenes of violence without violence, attackers without those being attacked, gaps and blanks, to be bridged by memory or imagination.

The edited images have been fed back to the live stream of the #OccupyGezi movement, together with supposedly unaltered images. The images shown on the Gezi gelen Limon blog raise questions about the status, validity, meaning, and bias of images, both manipulated and "pure." There is only a fine line, if any, between fact and fiction, real and fake, documentation and staging. In the images shown on Gezi gelen Limon, however, the lines between the categories are deliberately and obviously blurred. Here, it is the manipulation of the image that is highlighted and showcased to draw the viewers' attention to what is omitted, erased, or hidden.

Facing page:
JUST DO IT., screenshot from the Gezi gelen Limon blog, 2014

Gezi gelen Limon

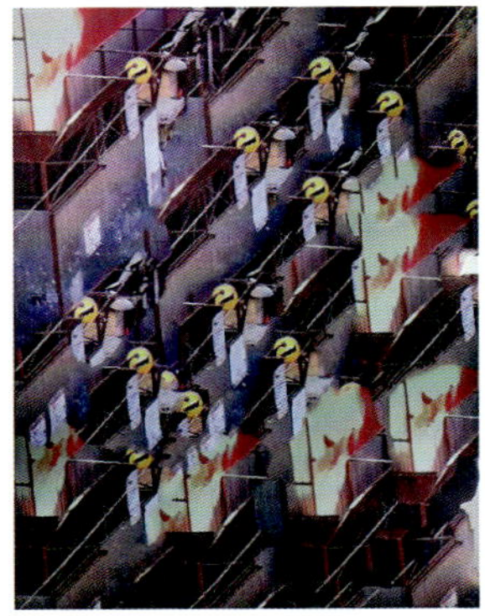

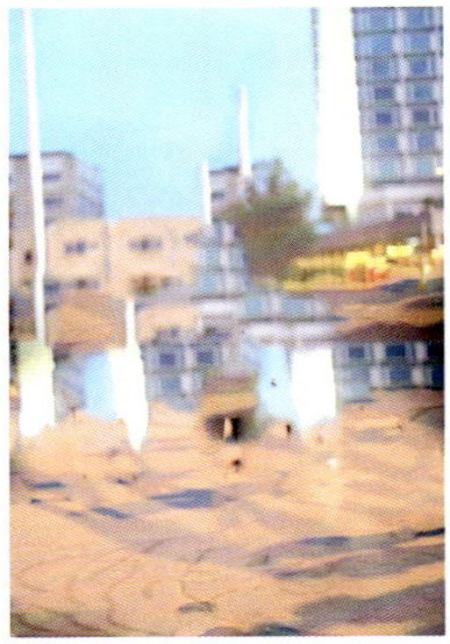

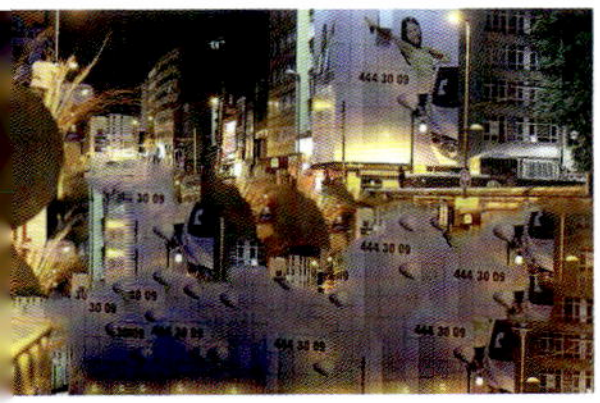

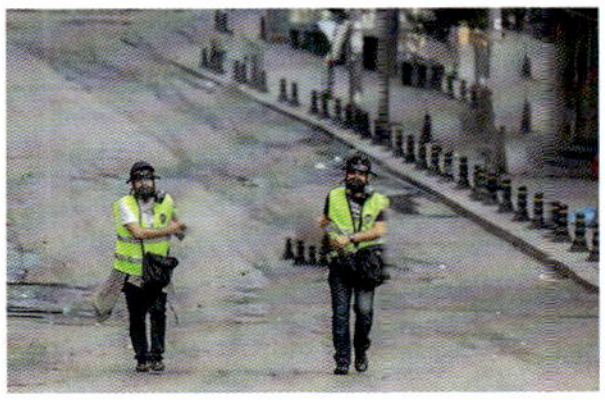

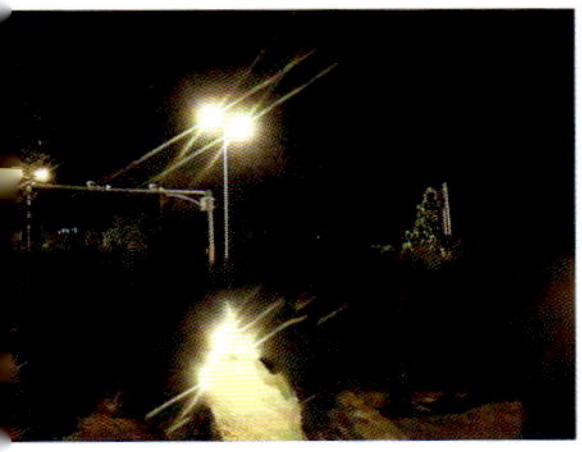

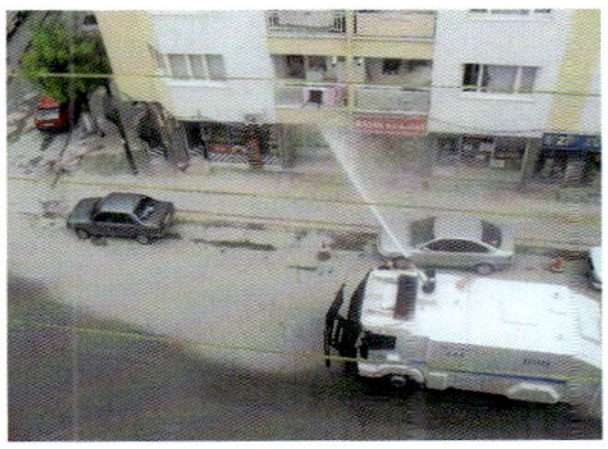

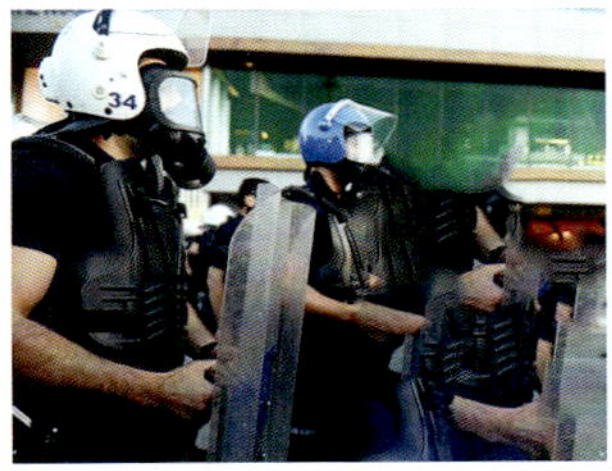

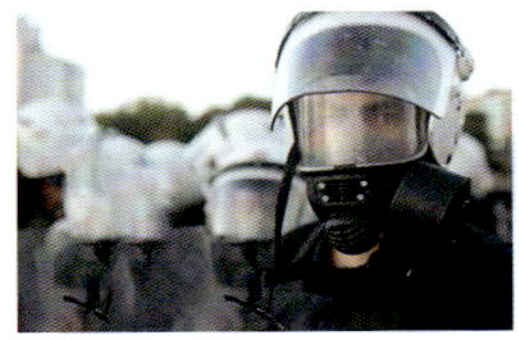

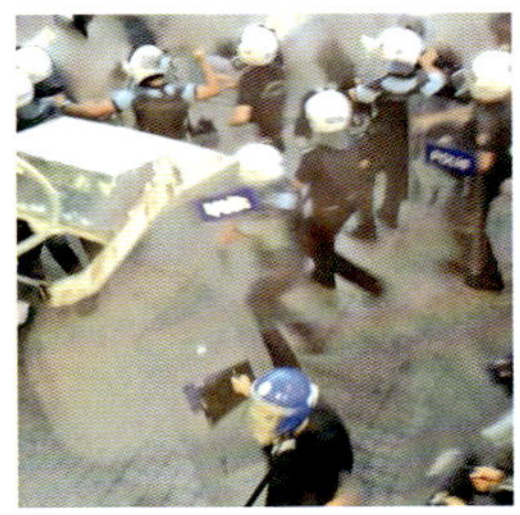

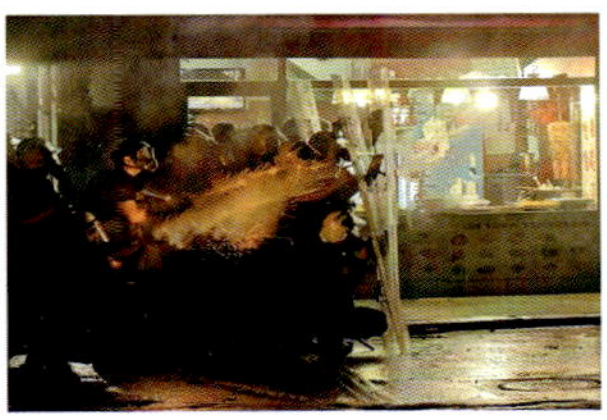

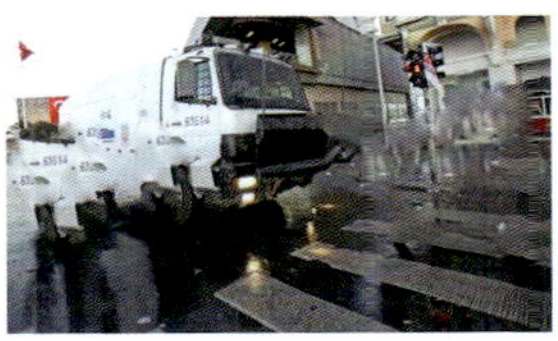

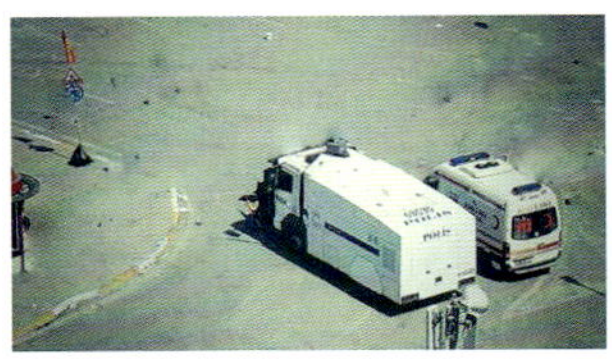

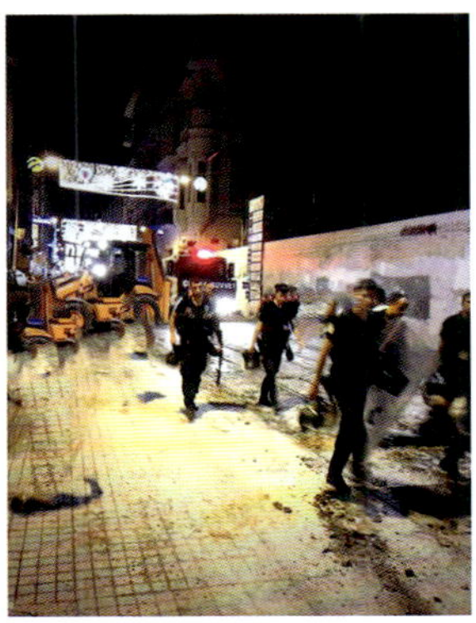

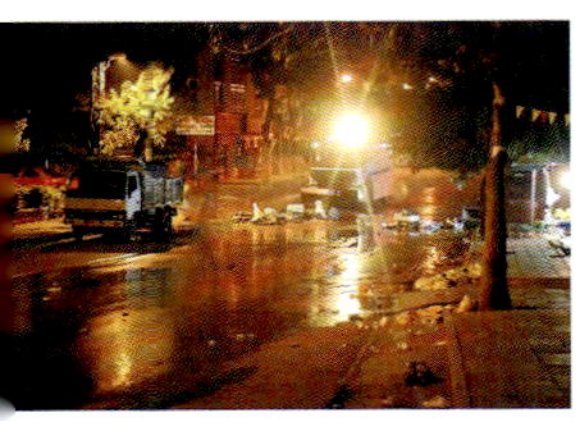

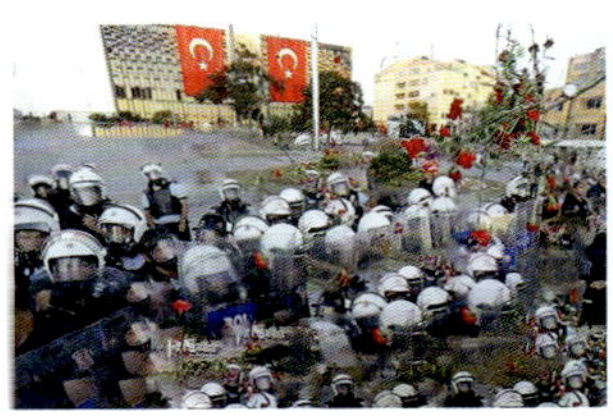

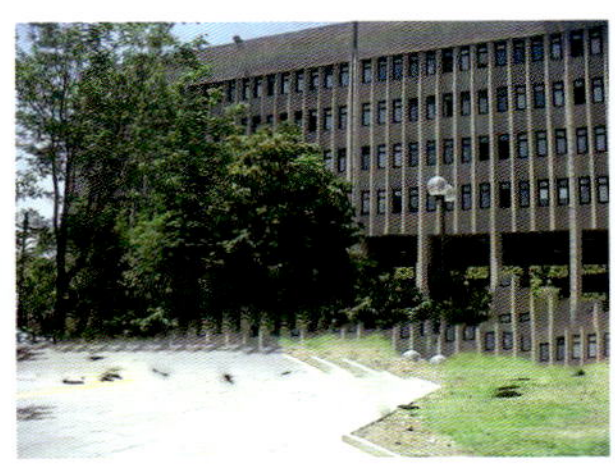

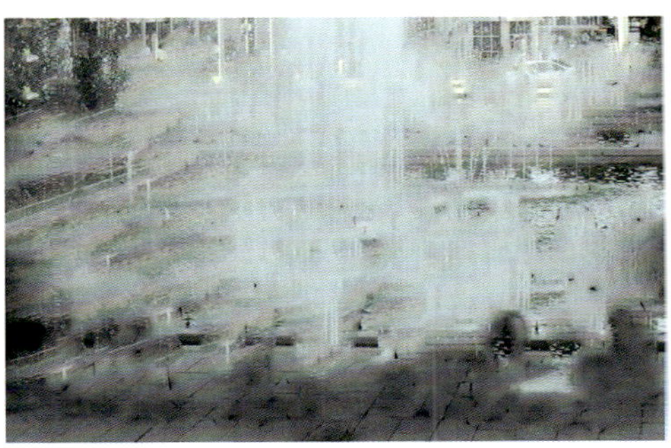

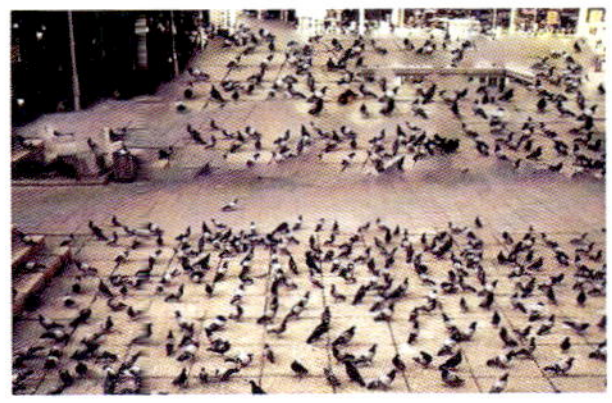

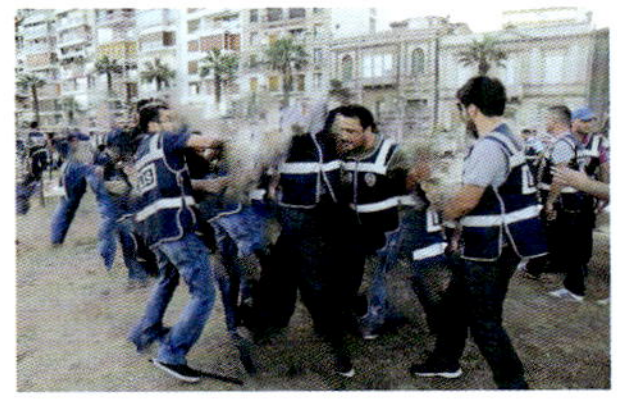

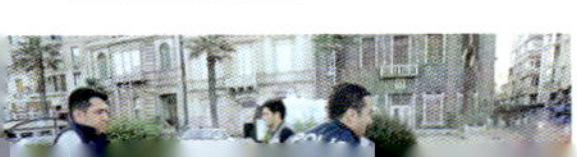

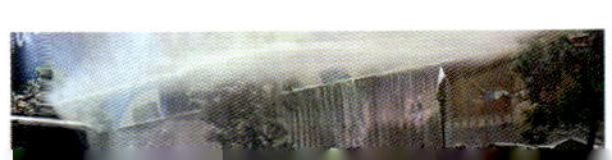

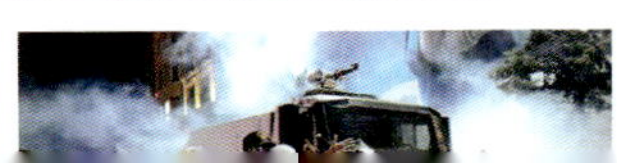

Amadou Kane Sy *1961

Amadou Kane Sy, also known as Kan-si, is an artist who works in various media, from paintings and installations to video and poetry. He is a founding member and the coordinator of the cultural and artistic project Huit Facettes-Interaction of several Senegal-based contemporary artists that was also represented at documenta 11 in 2012. Together with African-American artist Muhsana Ali he works on the project *Portes et Passages*, initiated by Ali to set up an art center in rural Senegal.

The video *Lu et approuvé* [Read and Approved] (2007) starts with a long silence. Then a mouth appears on the screen, and Muhsana Ali's voice – representing the voice of Africa – breaks the silence. She reads a letter, an excerpt from a book by globalization critic and former Minister of Culture and Tourism of Mali Aminata Traoré, addressed to the former President of France Nicolas Sarkozy. In this accusatory speech, neoliberalism is blamed for the suffering, misery, and poverty of African people and for illegal immigration.

In her letter, Traoré severely criticizes the unquestioned principle of the open market, the expansion and market politics of Western countries, and she points to the alienating and impoverishing effects of neoliberalism: Africa has become a factory to supply the global market with goods such as cocoa, cotton, and wood, and the continent where all the waste produced elsewhere is finally dumped. The voice in Amadou Kane Sy's video concludes: "The prevailing economic order not only robs us of the riches of our lands which it gives little back, but also robs us of our soul and our dignity." This calm but determined speech, in which the underlying anger in Ali's voice is only partially suppressed, is not only an accusation, but also a demand for respect and to assume responsibility.

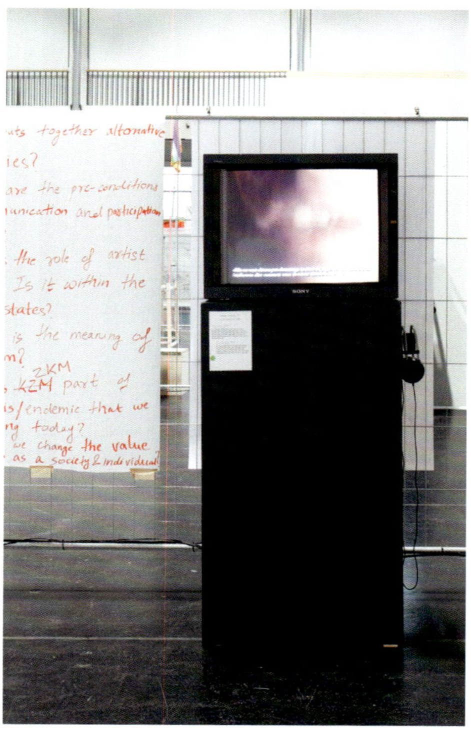

Amadou Kane Sy, *Lu et approuvé*, 2007, video, color, sound, 4:58 min, installation view, ZKM | Karlsruhe, 2014

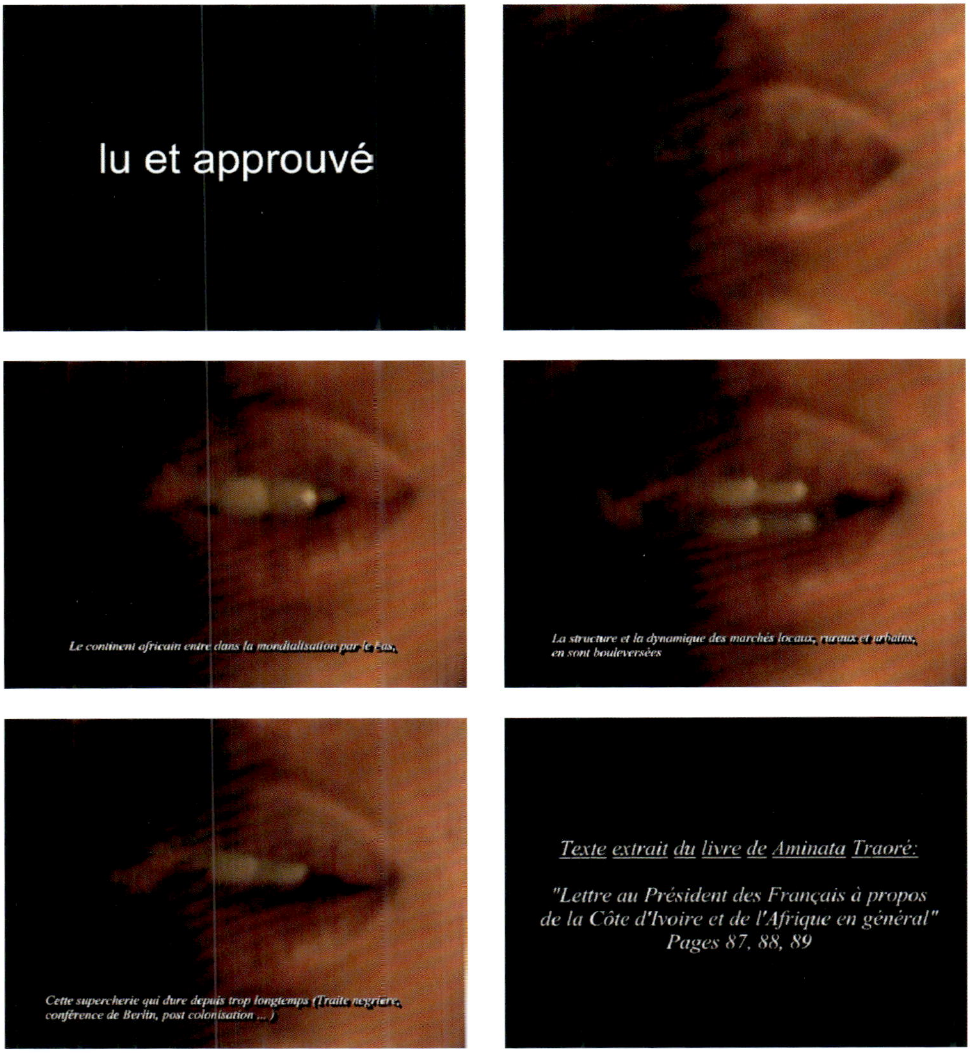

Amadou Kane Sy, *Lu et approuvé*, 2007, video, color, sound, 4:58 min, video stills

Thomas Kilpper *1956

Thomas Kilpper is a Berlin-based artist known for his political and artistic interventions in urban space, and his site-specific works where he uses woodcut methods to carve large-scale relief blocks into the floor of historical buildings and produces large-format textile and paper prints from these images. At the 2011 Venice Biennale, Kilpper set up a *Pavilion for Revolutionary Free Speech*, a contribution presented in the Danish Pavilion, including a Speakers' Corner and woodcuts.

A Lighthouse for Lampedusa is a site-specific project initiated in 2009, in which Kilpper engages with immigration and the tragic death of thousands of refugees. Every year tens of thousands of refugees in heavily overcrowded boats reach the shores of the small Italian island of Lampedusa, southwest of Sicily and only around seventy miles from the Tunisian coast. And every year many hundreds of them do not reach their destination and drown in the Mediterranean Sea, outside the borders of Europe, which is both a fortress and a safe (and possibly multicultural) haven offering protection from political persecution and poverty. According to the Italian NGO A buon diritto, more than 20,000 people died from 1988 to 2013, and since 2009 almost all boats have been sent back by the police or armed forces. Thomas Kilpper had the idea of erecting a

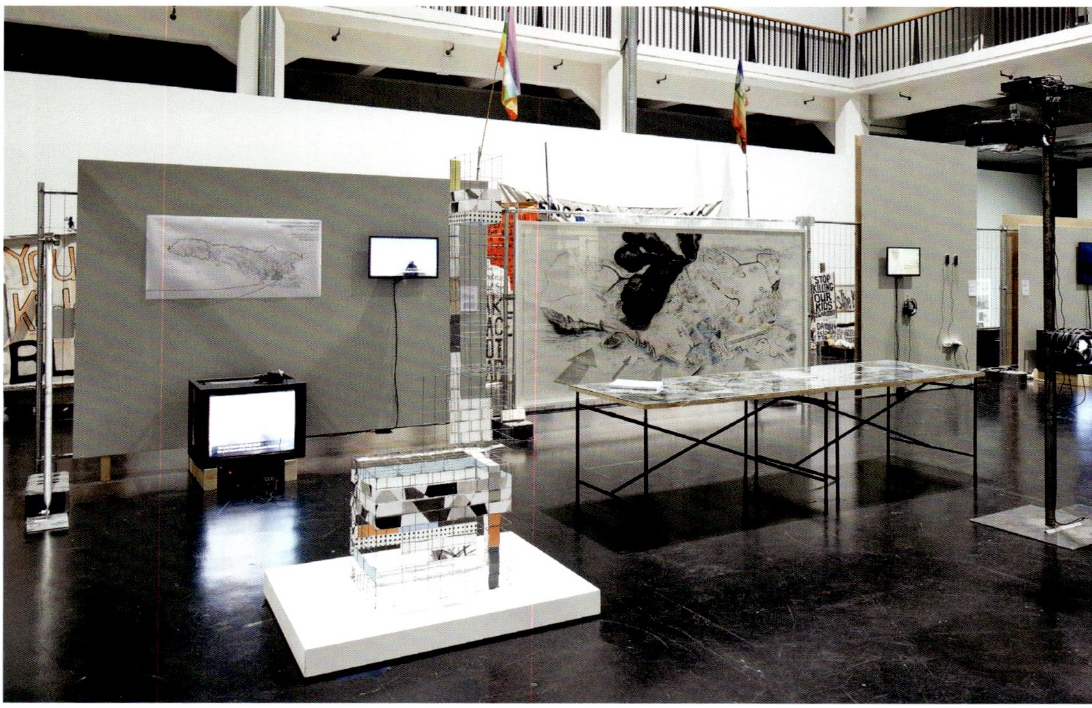

Thomas Kilpper, *A Lighthouse for Lampedusa*, 2009–2013, installation, mixed media (videos, color, sound, 12:33 and 17:08 min; 25 photographs; 150 newspaper articles in a ring binder; drawing, 150 × 300 cm; lighthouse model, 180 × 40 × 60 cm), installation view, ZKM | Karlsruhe, 2014

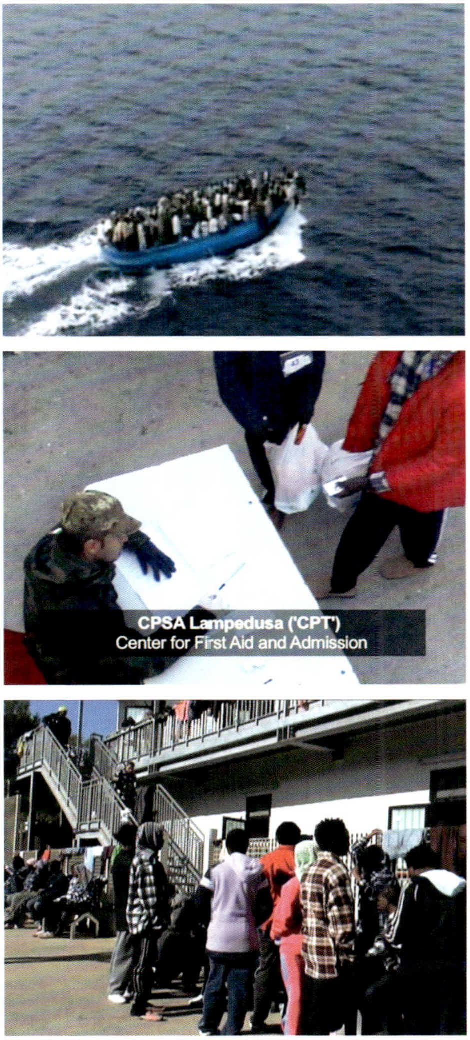

Thomas Kilpper, *A Lighthouse for Lampedusa*, 2009, video, color, sound, 17:08 min, part of the installation *A Lighthouse for Lampedusa* 2009–2013, video stills

lighthouse on Lampedusa with an intense light beam that would not only be a symbol of welcome; it would also provide orientation to help save the lives of refugees who try to reach the island. For years now, Kilpper has been advocating the construction of such a lighthouse in collaboration with architects, engineers, and local people, which, in its base, could also house a cultural center, both for visitors and for the inhabitants of Lampedusa.

As preparation for his project, Kilpper stayed on Lampedusa to establish a network of local contacts, and he built a model made from fragments of immigrants' boats. In his photos and video he documented the landing of immigrants, the boat cemetery, everyday life on Lampedusa, and interviews with migrants, local authorities, and local citizens. The realization of the lighthouse depends on local and international support.

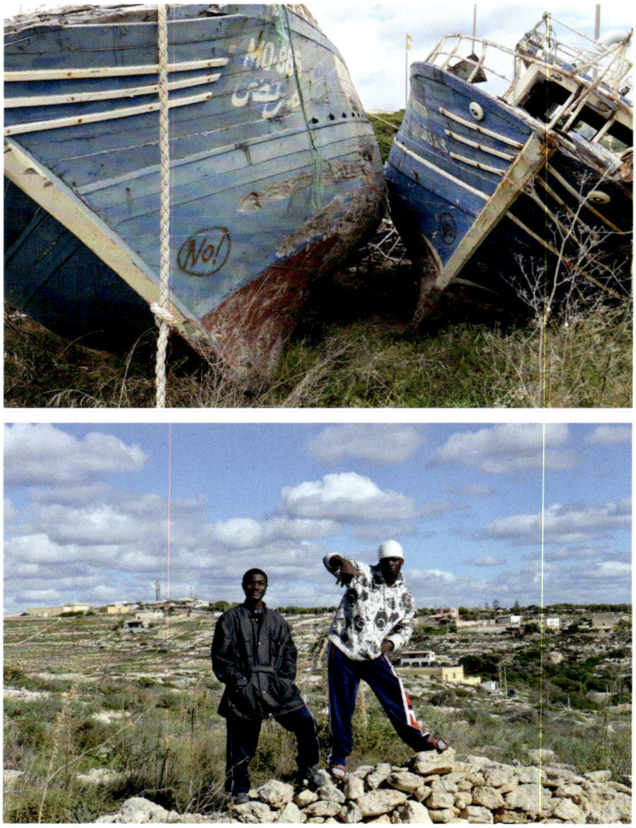

Thomas Kilpper, *Lampedusa 2013*, 2013, video, color, sound, 12:33 min, part of the installation *A Lighthouse for Lampedusa*, 2009–2013, photos shown in the video

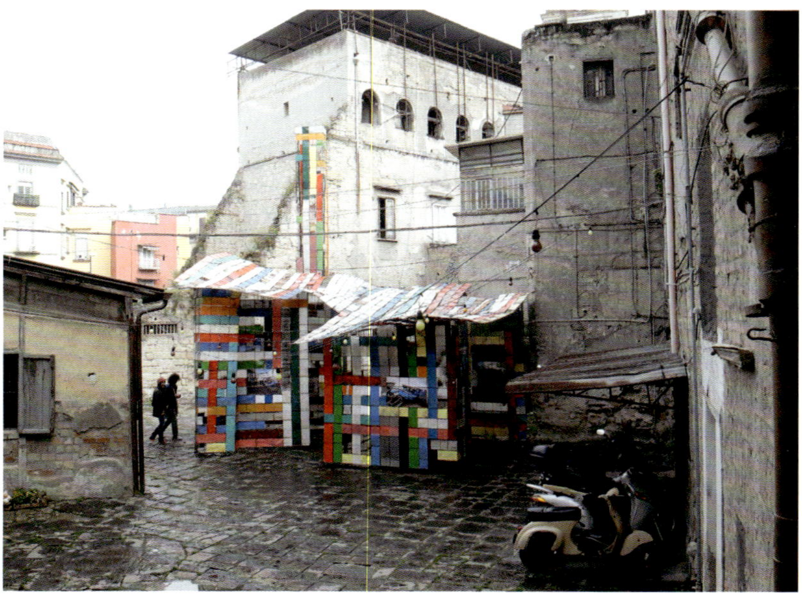

Thomas Kilpper, *A Lighthouse for Lampedusa*, 2010, installation, metal grid, wire, colored plastic strips, photos, light, ca. 8 × 5 × 9 m, installation view, Lanificio 25, Naples, Italy, 2010

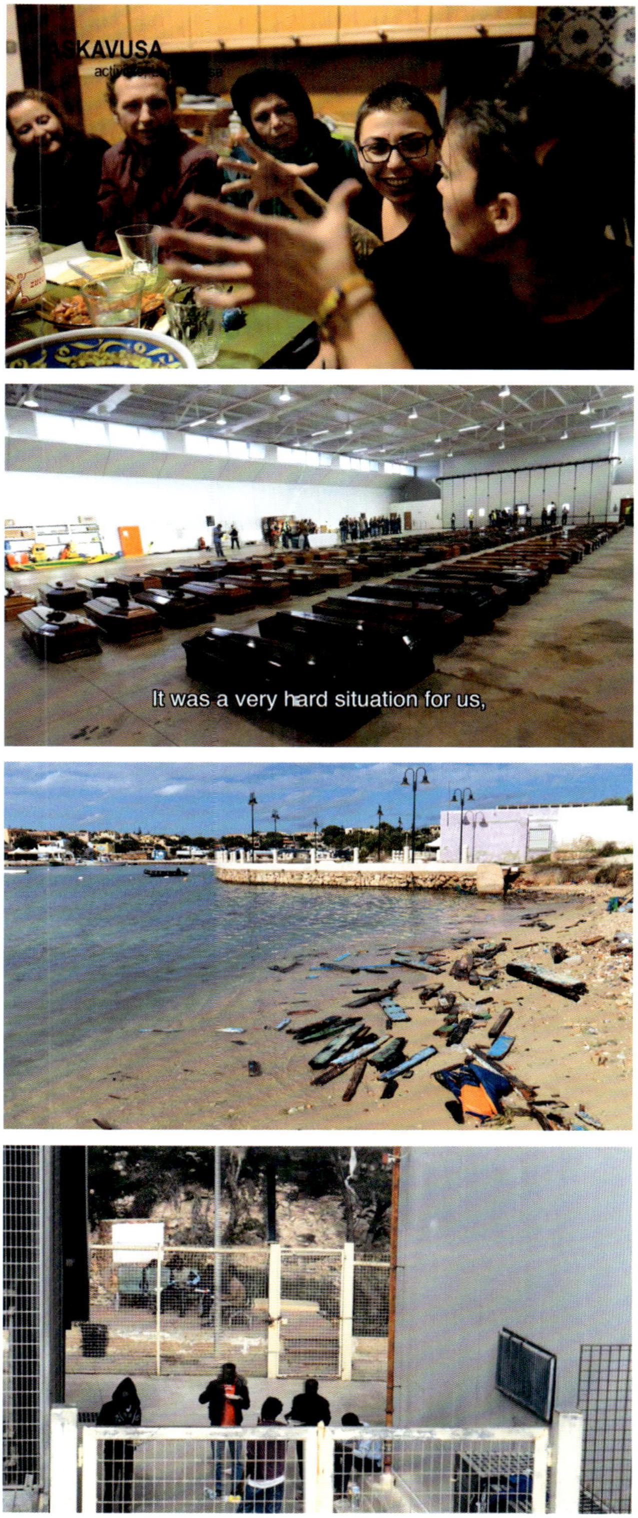

Thomas Kilpper, *Lampedusa 2013*, 2013, video, color, sound, 12:33 min, part of the installation *A Lighthouse for Lampedusa*, 2009–2013, video stills

Kiss my Ba

The artist collective Kiss my Ba – also known as Babushka Posle Pochoron [Grandmother after the Funeral] – was founded in 2004 by Russian artists and cultural activists Artem Loskutov (*1986) and Maria Kiseleva (*1991), who are also part of the Russian MediaImpact working group. They are known for their provocative events that parody political activities, but which are at the same time attempts to achieve autonomy. Kiss my Ba organizes and documents so-called "Monstrations" – collective acts, artistic happenings (without a preprepared script), mass acts of art in the form of public demonstrations with slogans invented by the participants.

The first Monstration took place on May 1, 2004 in Novosibirsk, and since then these flash mob street parties have been organized every year in various cities. Inspired by the traditions of dadaists, situationists, anarchists, and Moscow conceptualists, their goal is to subvert the Communist tradition of May Day demonstrations and reclaim the streets. The banners used in

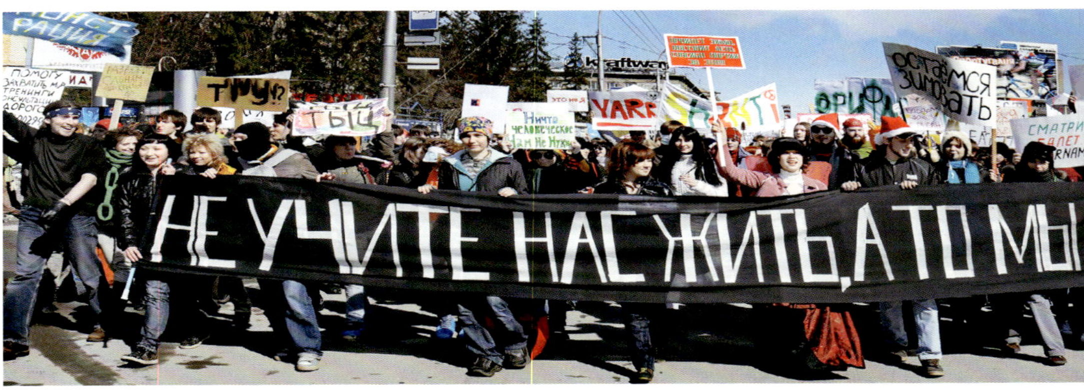

Kiss my Ba, Monstration, Novosibirsk, Russia, 2008

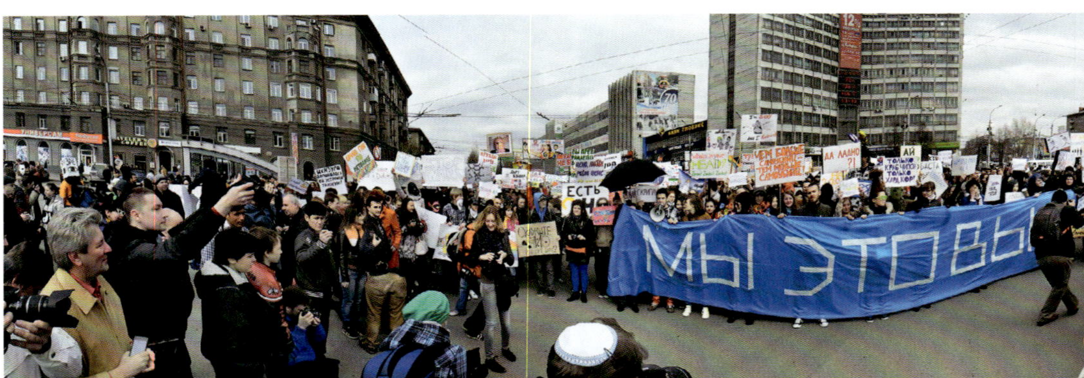

Kiss my Ba, Monstration, Novosibirsk, Russia, 2012

these events are absurd and apolitical; nonsense slogans, such as "Keep calm and call Lenin" or "Yesterday was Tuesday, but today is Tuesday as well," are proclaimed as protests against the lack of critical political discourse. By challenging and updating "serious" political demonstrations, Monstrations are a clear condemnation of the fact that public politics are absent in Russia; they do not merely highlight the limits of civil liberties, they also broaden them, and in this way they become a school of solidarity, creative activity, and civil freedom. The video documentary *Monstration* (color, sound, 3:54 min) from 2012 shows the protest march in Novosibirsk held in the same year.

In 2009, Artem Loskutov was summoned by the Interior Ministry's Center for Extremism Prevention for his Monstration activities and arrested for four weeks for the alleged possession of narcotic substances. His arrest sparked a solidarity campaign across Russia and abroad; he was convicted and fined in 2010. Ironically, in 2010, the Monstration in Novosibirsk was held legally for the first time, attracting several thousand people, and Loskutov was awarded an innovation prize by the Ministry of Culture. In 2012, a Russian court ruled that an icon created by Artem Loskutov and Maria Kiseleva to raise money for Pussy Riot was an item of religious disrespect, which resulted in another fine and the banning of the icon. Loskutov publishes his dialog with the authorities on his blog kissmybabushka.com.

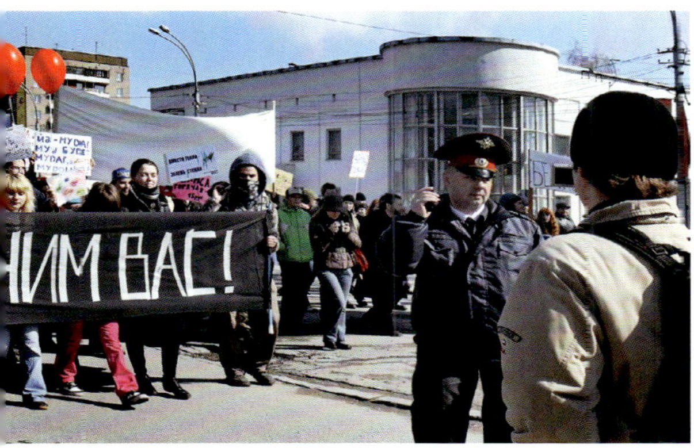

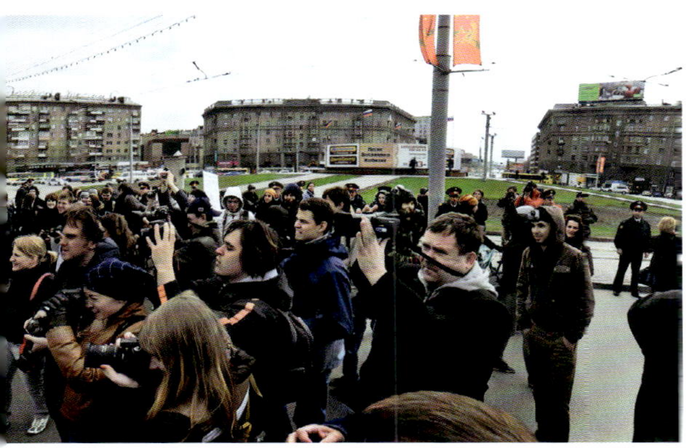

Mischa Kuball *1959

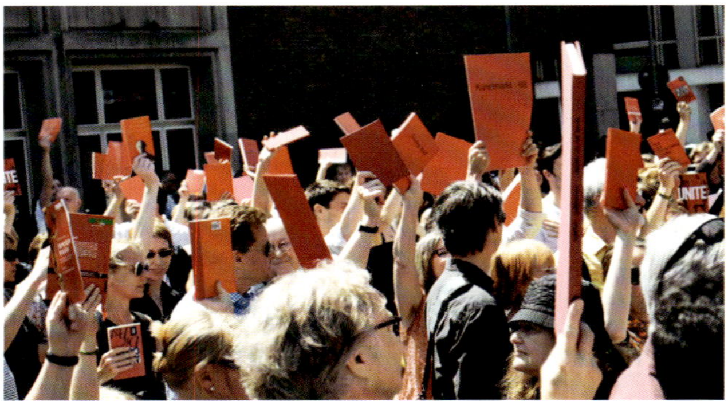

Mischa Kuball, *Rettet die KMB*, 2013, video, color, sound, 1:01 min, video still

Mischa Kuball has worked as a visual artist since the 1980s, and he became especially known for his light projections and installations engaging with architectural and urban space. Since 2007 he is a professor at the Academy of Media Arts Cologne where, together with his students, he founded the experimental laboratory MinusEins.

In July 2013, a flash mob was organized to save Cologne's Kunst- und Museumsbibliothek (KMB) [Art and Museum Library], whose continued existence was threatened by severe budget cuts planned by the Cologne city council with a view to reducing public spending. The KMB has holdings of around 400,000 items and is one of the world's largest public libraries for modern art and photography. The initiative to save the KMB demanded that the plans to locate the KMB in a new building as part of the new historical archive of the city of Cologne should be realized, and it should continue to exist as a public library. Prominent supporters of the initiative included the artist Gerhard Richter and the director of the Museum of Modern Art in New York, Glenn D. Lowry. Participants in the flash mob were encouraged to bring red books with them to show the city council the red card for their plans to limit access to an important repository of knowledge and reduce its scope. Mischa Kuball and his students from the Academy of Media Arts Cologne lent significant support to the campaign with an intervention, which Kuball documented in the video *Rettet die KMB* [Save the KMB] (2013). The campaign to save the KMB and the video demonstrate the citizens' engagement to preserve access to public goods of educational value, also for future generations. Cologne city council ultimately decided against moving the KMB. Although the University of Cologne offered its support, the issues of a lack of space and storage for books and the division and splitting of the KMB into several locations remain.

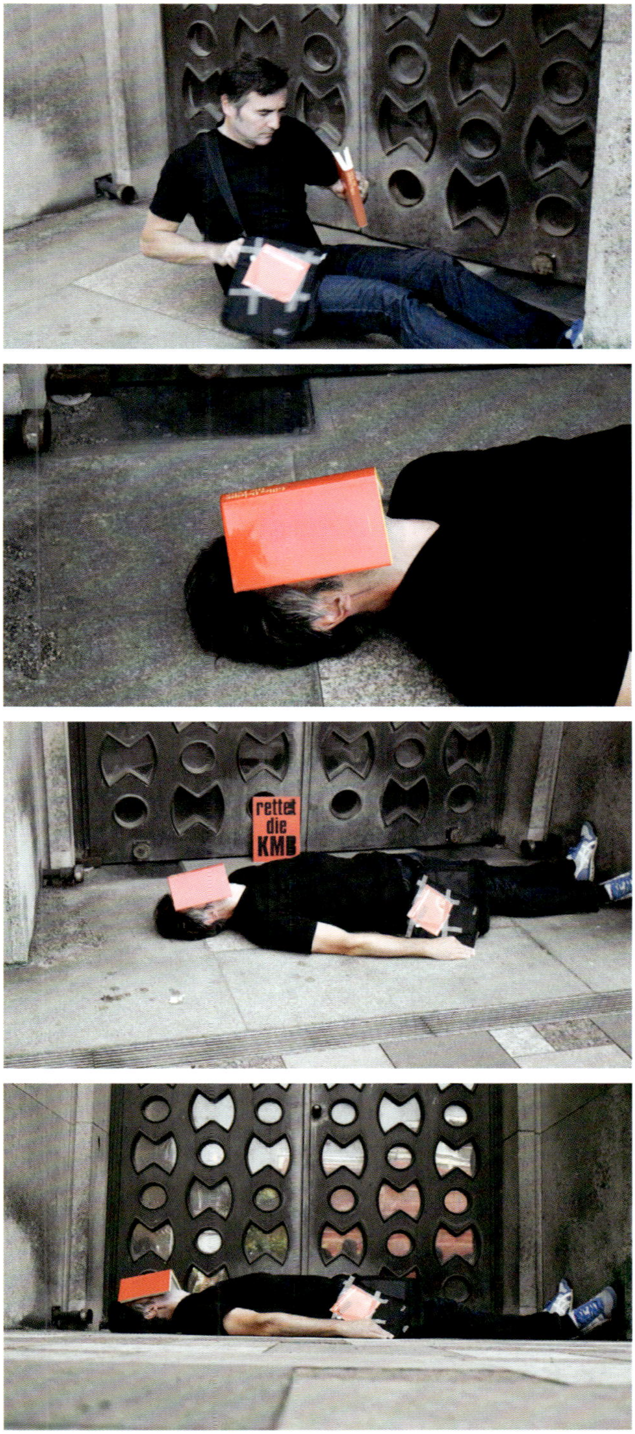

Mischa Kuball, *Rettet die KM3*, 2013, video, color, sound, 1:01 min, video stills

Christopher LaMarca *1975

Christopher LaMarca is a filmmaker and photographer based in Portland, Oregon, with a background in environmental studies and biology. He pursues documentary photographic projects with a special focus on environmental issues; for instance, the Alaska oil drillings, the 2011 flood on the Mississippi River, the indigenous Waorani community in Ecuador and their environment – and the need to protect old growth forests against logging. For his photographic project *Forest Defenders* (2005–2010), which was also documented in a book (*Forest Defenders. The Confrontational American Land-scape*, 2008), LaMarca received several awards.

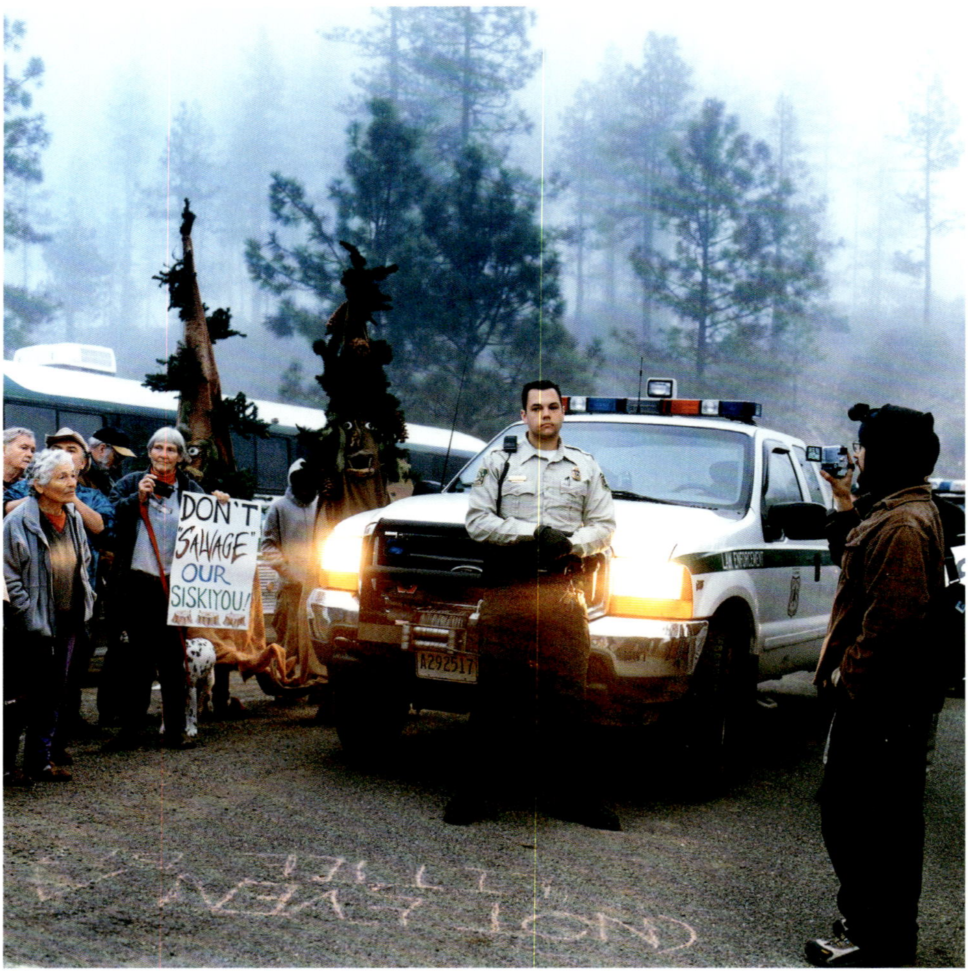

Christopher LaMarca, from the photo series *Forest Defenders*, 2005–2010; forest defenders block the road to the Fiddler Timber Sale (part of the Biscuit Timber Sale) on the edge of the Kalmiopsis Wilderness in southern Oregon, an area of the forest that was originally designated as wildlife habitat under the Northwest Forest Plan.

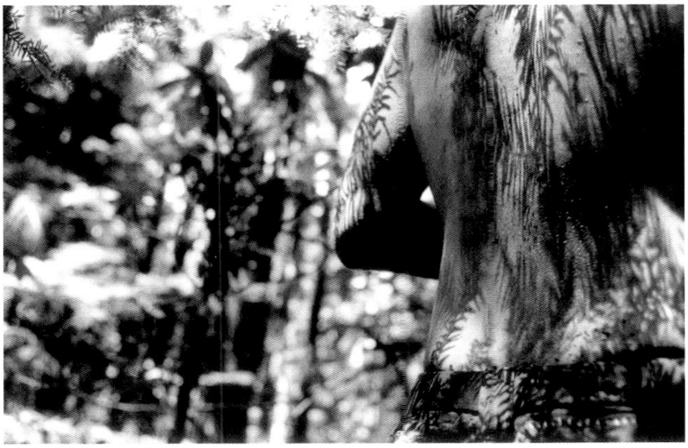

Christopher LaMarca, from the photo series *Forest Defenders*, 2005–2010; shadows of a tree on a forest defender's back in the Straw Devil Timber Sale in the Deschutes National Forest

In 2005, a controversy arose about the logging of sections of federal forest-land, reserved for threatened wildlife, especially when the George W. Bush administration repealed a rule that had protected approximately sixty million acres of wildlands and forests. While several U.S. states filed law suits because of the violation of federal environmental law, environmental activists also planned concrete actions: They have been trying to prevent the last untouched forest in the U.S. from being destroyed by timber companies, which represent a powerful multimillion dollar industry. Christopher LaMarca documented their actions in his photo series. He accompanied several "forest defenders" – also labeled "eco-terrorists" by the wood industry – and captured, for instance, the construction of road blocks on the edge of the Kalmiopsis Wilderness in southern Oregon to stop ancient forest logging. This area of the forest was originally designated for wildlife habitat under the North-west Forest Plan and not for timber harvesting. His powerful yet poetic images show intact and destroyed forest landscapes, loggers at work, cutting down 500-year-old trees – and environmental activists in action, protecting their identities with scarves and hats; in the caption, they are introduced by their activist alias names.

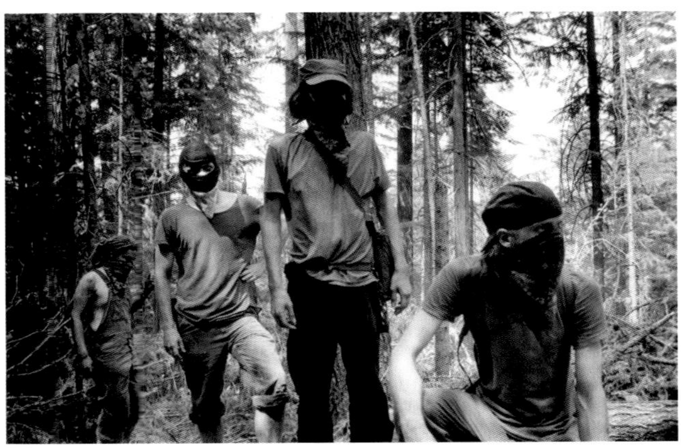

Christopher LaMarca, from the photo series *Forest Defenders*, 2005–2010; forest defenders, going under the aliases Blackberry, Gramma, Lichen, and Hannibal (from left to right), inside the "fall zone," an area of forest recently clear-cut

Mohammed Laouli *1972

Mohammad Laouli studied philosophy and lives and works as an artist in Salé, Morocco. In his work he explores sociopolitical phenomena, without wanting to teach a lesson or taking on the role of an advisor. He rather draws attention to issues and things in his environment that strike him in his observation and he explores them in poetic interventions.

With his video work *Everything Is Sacred* (2013) Laouli captures the suffering of a gray horse, which, after having been used for hard work, has been abandoned with its front hooves tied together on an unpaved square in a poor neighborhood in Rabat. With white wings on its back, it has the appearance of a beautiful mythical creature, lost and out of place in a rough environment, at once irritating and unnoticed by the passersby. The horse represents a form of otherness, which, from the perspective of a different social class, is also characteristic of the people living in this neighborhood. There is a tension between the foreground and background of the composition, between the crude reality and the magical dimension of the scene, that strikes the viewer – and gradually seems to dissolve.

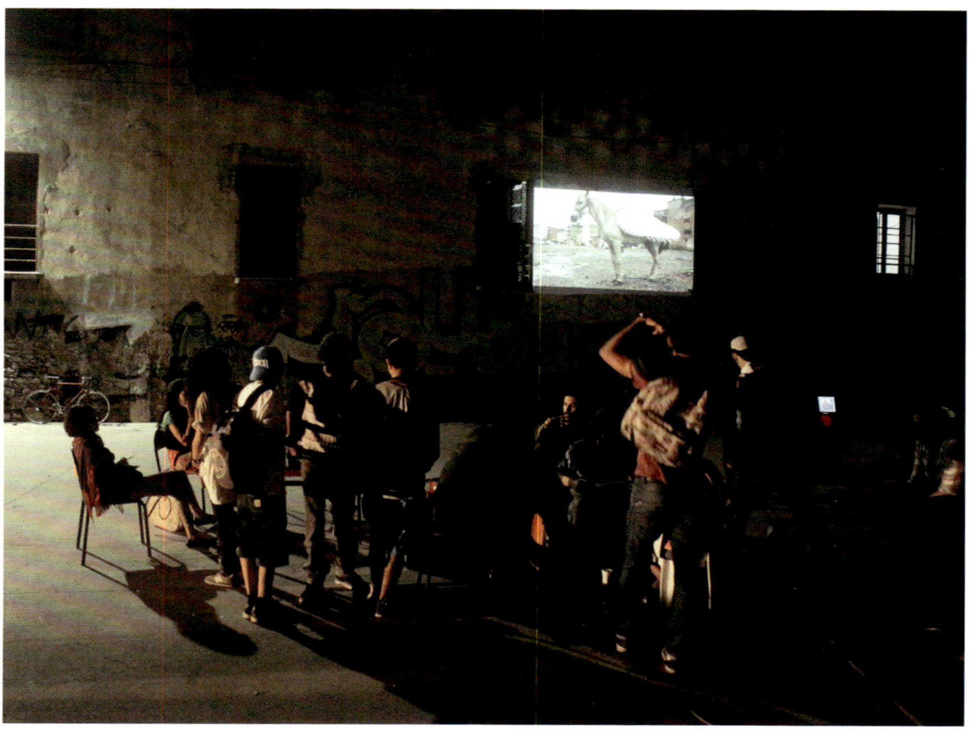

Mohammed Laouli, *Everything Is Sacred*, 2013, installation view, iRRi ART project, *|boxes| zones quarters*, Casablanca, Morocco, 2014

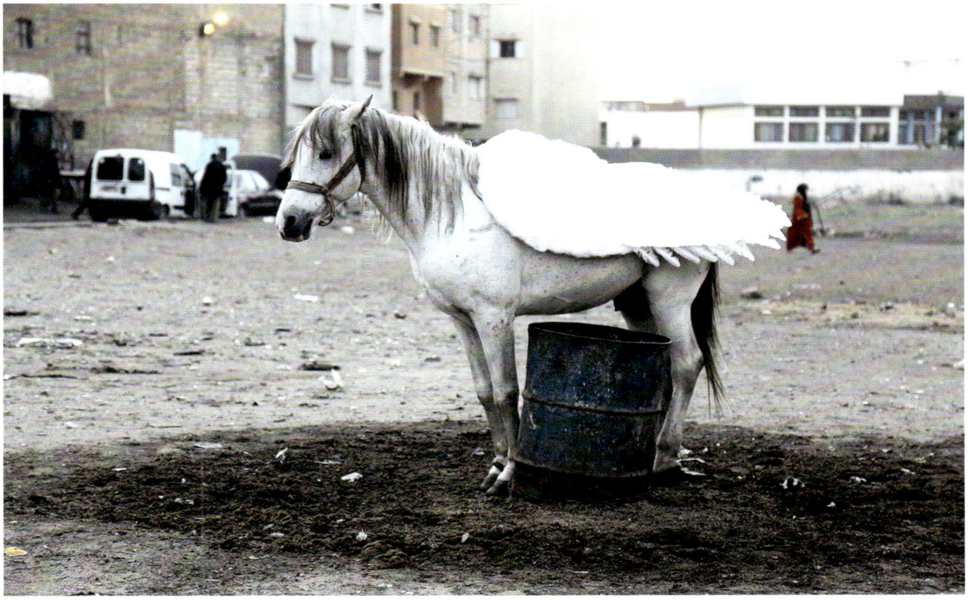

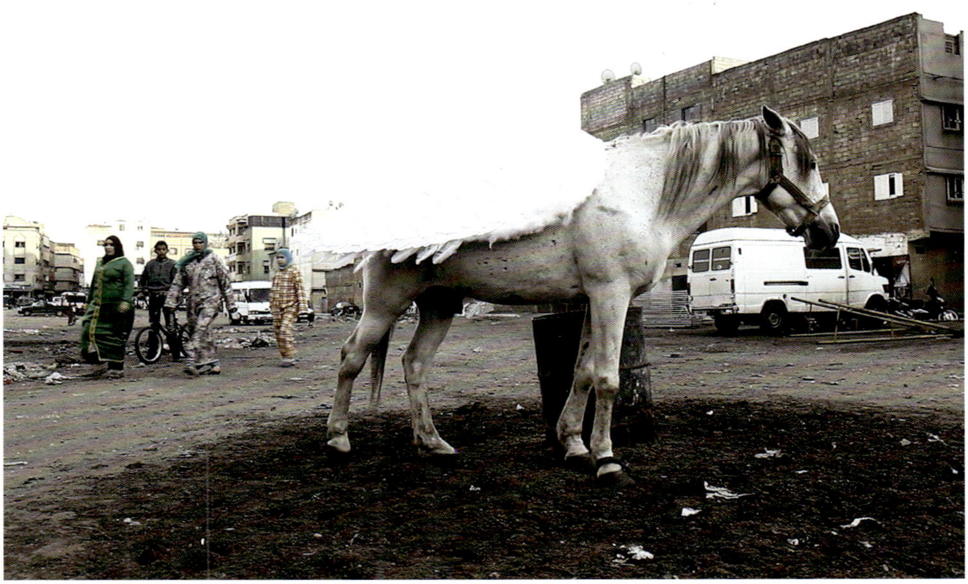

Mohammed Laouli, *Everything Is Sacred*, 2013, video, color, scund, 2:03 min, video stills

Viktoria Lomasko *1978

Viktoria Lomasko, who comes from a small town near Moscow, was trained as an illustrator. Since 2003 she takes on commissions from publishing houses both for print and online media, but also creates her own, socially engaged works. Lomasko has frequently collaborated with journalist and writer Anton Nikolaev with whom she shares an interest in current political issues, life in the Russian provinces and migrant workers, and the situation of disadvantaged people such as the elderly or the mentally ill.

Her civic activist engagement is reflected in the drawing lessons she gives to minors in penal colonies. Together with Nikolaev, she also published a book about the exhibition *Forbidden Art* which took place in Moscow in 2006, and about the trial of the curators for inciting religious hatred, documenting the events by fusing protocols and graphic artworks. As a crime reporter and taking a similar approach, she documented the political trial of the Pussy Riot activists. Lomasko is part of the Moscow Feminist Group, and in her more recent works she also engages with LGBT rights. She keeps an online journal at http://soglyadatay.livejournal.com.

Since the start of the mass demonstrations against the manipulation of the Russian parliamentary elections in December 2011, until November 2012 Viktoria Lomasko made drawings of the protest movements in Russia and kept a graphic chronicle of resistance: She took part in large-scale public

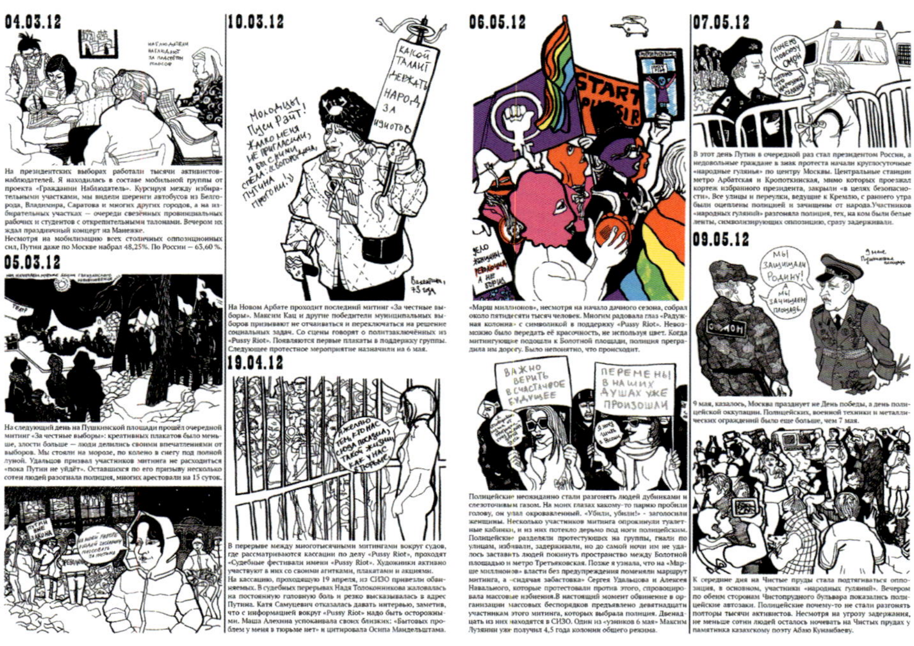

Viktoria Lomasko, graphics from the *Chronicles of Resistance*, 2011/2012

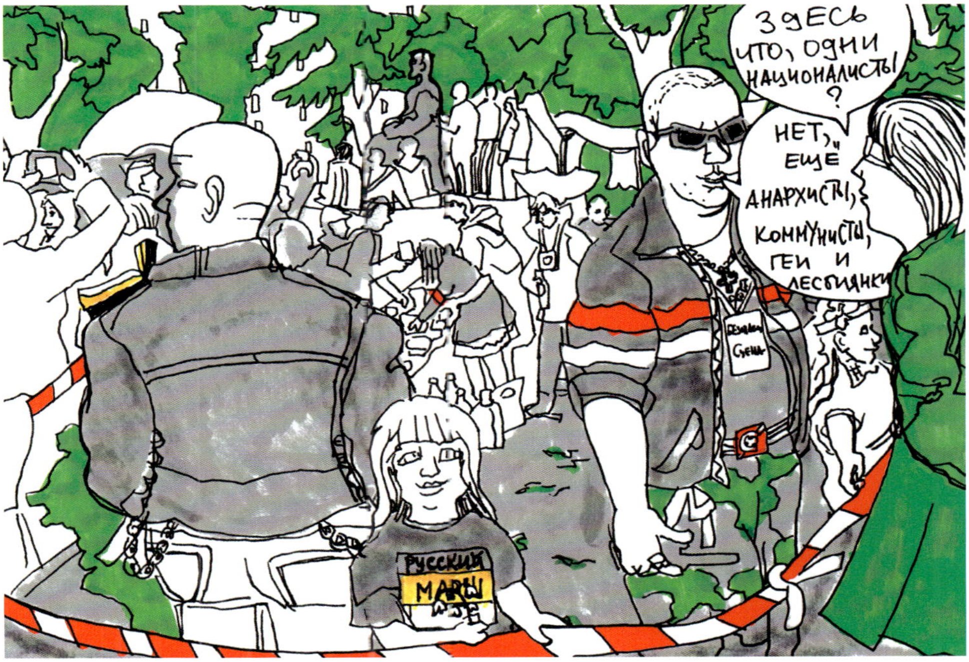

Viktoria Lomasko, graphic from the *Chronicles of Resistance*, 2011/2012

protests to observe and to talk to participants from different backgrounds and with different motivations, walking through the crowds and making sketches in situ, from which she created her *Chronicles of Resistance*, a comprehensive series of graphics that document the protests. In an interview, Lomasko said, "[I]n my all drawings, time is layered, people come and go, the subject and the composition slowly emerge. […] Just like a dancer dances to the music, an artist must draw to the tempo of what he sees."

The digital print from the *Chronicles of Resistance* above, showing a scene from the protests, reads: "Are there only nationalists here?" – "No, there are also anarchists, communists, gay men, and gay women."

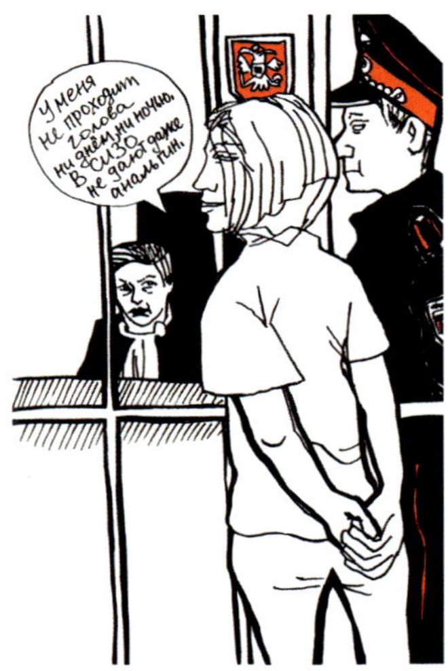

Адвокат Толоконниковой Марк Фейгин также несколько раз подчеркнул, что Надю начали мучить в тюрьме сильные головные боли, что девушке необходимо медицинское обследование.

Viktoria Lomasko, graphic from the *Chronicles of Resistance*, 2011/2012

Renzo Martens *1973

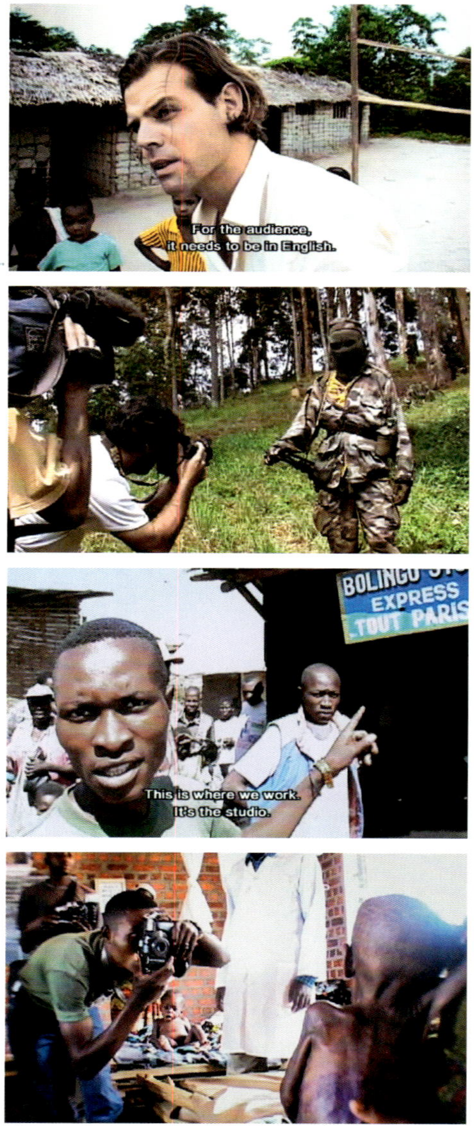

Renzo Martens, *Episode III: Enjoy Poverty*, 2009, video, color, sound, 88:00 min, video stills

Renzo Martens is an artist and lecturer who lives and works in Brussels, Amsterdam, and Kinshasa. He became first known for his controversial video *Episode I* (2003), illegally shot in war zones in Chechnya: it is the first part of a series focusing on artistic interventions in politically unstable settings and political hot spots. In 2010 Martens founded the Institute for Human Activities (IHA), which launched a gentrification program in the middle of the Congolese rainforest; Martens serves as artistic director of the institute.

Episode III: Enjoy Poverty (2009) – the third part of a triptych whose middle part is still missing – is a subjective documentary about Renzo Martens' workshops in the Democratic Republic of the Congo, in which he taught local photographers how to market images of poverty profitably. In his provocative video, Martens exposes the lucrative business with local people's poverty by Western stakeholders such as news agencies, photographers, and aid organizations; by making, staging, and using dramatic photos of people ravaged by war and poverty they become key players in a market for dramatic images. While poverty becomes a lucrative export commodity, the poor hardly benefit at all. By organizing workshops for locals, Martens attempts to raise awareness of this process of exploitation and encourages people to consider their poverty as a powerful resource, to document their situation themselves, and to take control of their media representation: he suggests they should document war and poverty instead of weddings and other ceremonies. However, this project is doomed to fail, because access to press cards is almost impossible for locals – in a way, they are used

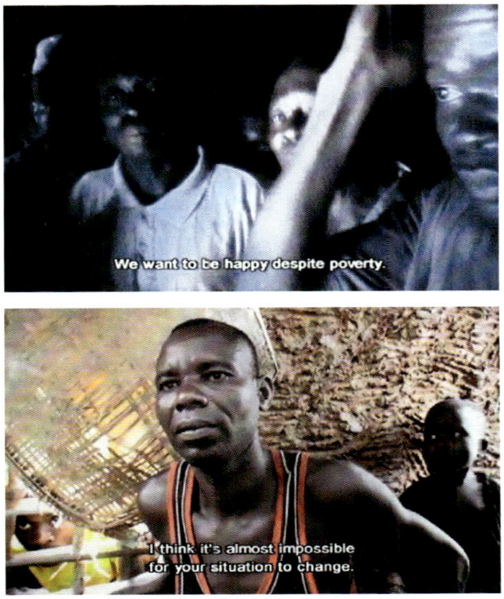

Renzo Martens, *Episode III. Enjoy Poverty*, 2009, video, color, sound, 88:00 min, video stills

to demonstrate the artist's claim that active participation in an "economy of poverty" is impossible. In a scene that could be considered bluntly ironic and mocking, Congolese people are dancing around a neon sign that says "Enjoy poverty."

The role of the artist remains obscure in this thought-provoking piece: He is both investigator of a scene and engaged in it. He appears as a powerful, at times narcissistic Westerner who is fascinated by the exotic other. *Episode III: Enjoy Poverty* is a cynical exploration of moral dilemmas that raises questions about contemporary image production. Colonial stereotypes and power relations are revealed and reenacted, but not overcome.

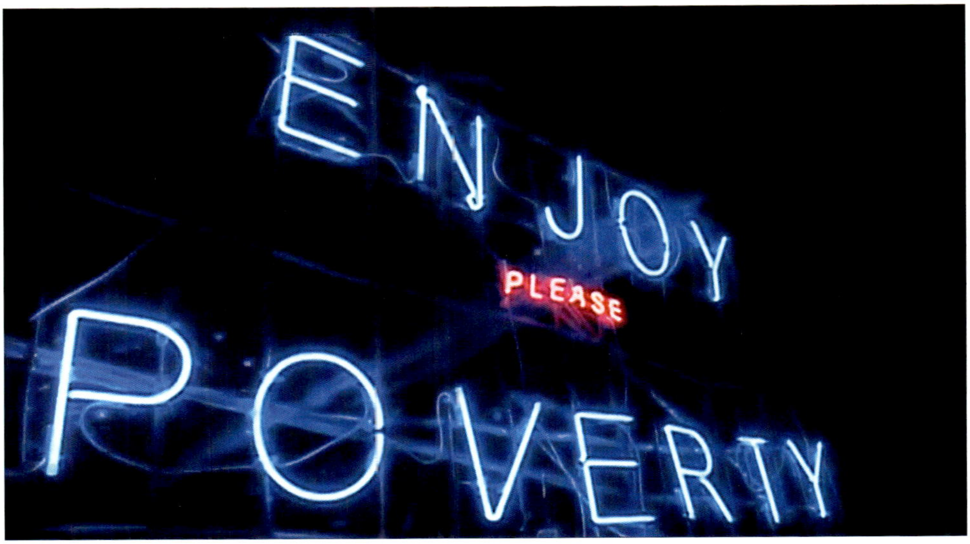

Renzo Martens, *Episode III: Enjoy Poverty*, 2009, video, color, sound, 88:00 min, photo shown in the video

Masasit Mati

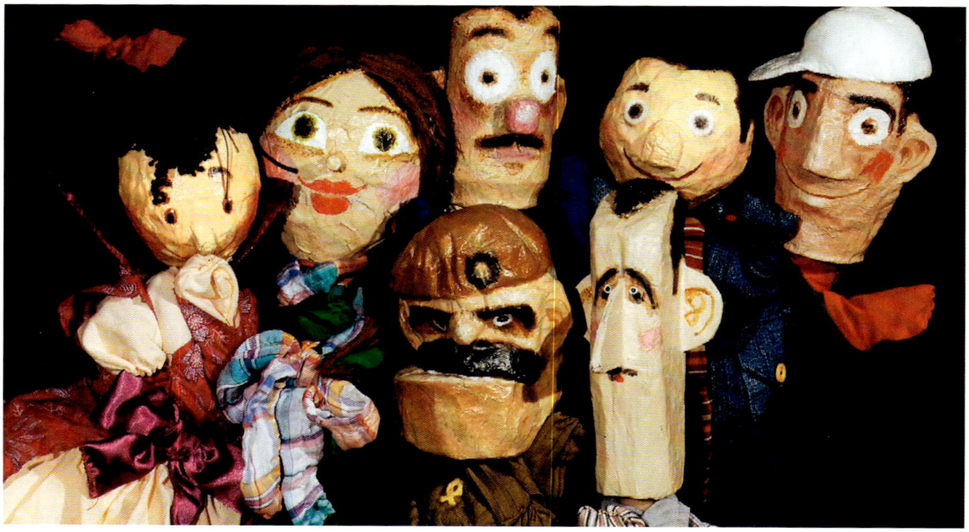

Masasit Mati, *Top Goon: Diaries of a Little Dictator*, 2011/2012, finger puppet show and video series, cast of the second season of *Top Goon*

Masasit Mati is an artist collective founded by ten anonymous Syrian artists, writers, directors, and actors. The group's name refers to the straw used to drink Mati, a herbal tea that is very popular amongst the Syrians but is now unavailable due to the economic sanctions.

Masasit Mati's Web-based series *Top Goon: Diaries of a Little Dictator* (2011/2012), based on finger puppet theater, ridicules the actions and reactions of Syrian President Bashar al-Assad and the Syrian regime in the face of the uprising in the country, and reflects on the revolution in Syria. Al-Assad is portrayed by the puppet character Beeshu ("little Bashar") as a complex-ridden, insecure, childish man, which adds a different layer to his carefully constructed image as undefeatable dictator. The use of finger puppets enables the artist collective to stage critical works without being identified by the regime. Political satire and black humor is their strategy to criticize the regime's violent oppression of protest. "In this context puppets are ideal as they can shrink the regime's over-inflated personalities and allow you to play with them. The idea was to break down the wall of fear," as Masasit Mati explained their approach. Further puppet characters represent individuals from different segments of Syrian society. The stories demonstrate that neither difficulties nor the revolution end after the fall of al-Assad's or Beeshu's regime – on the contrary. Masasit Mati also target the armed opposition in their satirical videos, and they added to their series by reflecting on the Syrian civil war and the misery of Syrian society after the uprisings.

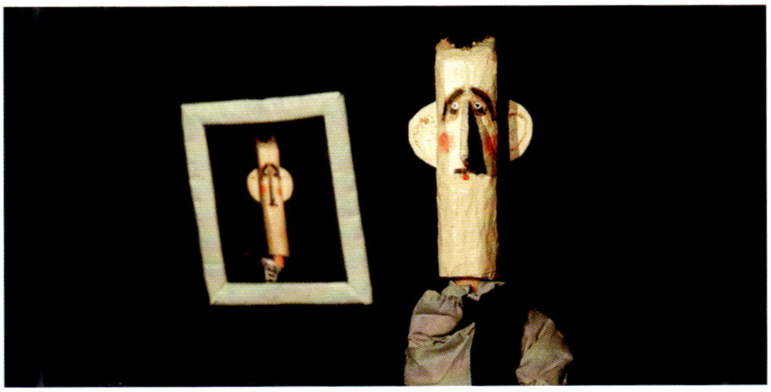

Masasit Mati, *Top Goon: Diaries of a Little Dictator*, 2011/2012, finger puppet show and video series, finger puppet character Beeshu, portraying Syrian President Bashar al-Assad

Top Goon: Diaries of a Little Dictator was widely distributed via YouTube from November 2011 until November 2012 in two seasons of altogether thirty episodes of approximately six minutes each. It was promoted via Facebook and Twitter and quickly became very popular among Syrians and supporters of the uprisings. In 2013, Masasit Mati changed their strategy and shifted their focus to street theater, also due to the dramatic sociopolitical changes in Syria. While two group members left to join the armed resistance, for the remaining group, in a situation where survival is all-important and access to the Internet is rare and must be used to document human rights violations, satire is not a priority anymore. Several episodes of *Top Goon* were produced from abroad, and Masasit Mati's members live in exile, for instance, in Beirut and Cairo, as well as in undisclosed places. Instead of organizing workshops in safe, internationally funded settings, it became important for the group to go to Syria, to perform live there, and to work with local people in small theater workshops, as a way of helping them to deal with their individual and collective history and misery: by telling their own (hi)story and putting on their own shows. Outside of Syria, Masasit Mati continue to participate in international events and discussions to raise awareness of civil resistance by artistic means and of the overall situation in Syria.

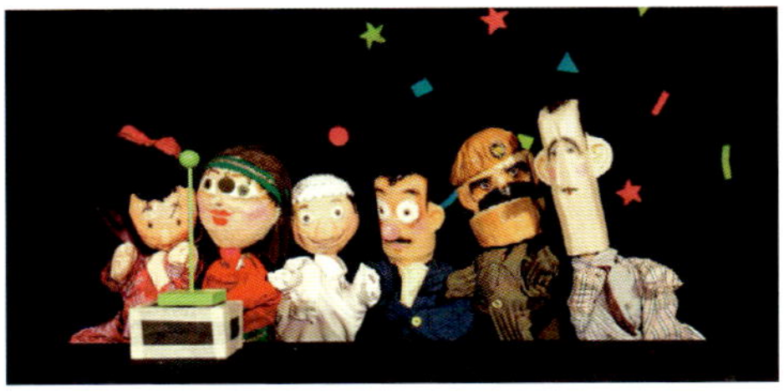

Masasit Mati, *Top Goon: Diaries of a Little Dictator*, 2011/2012, finger puppet show and video series, cast of *Top Goon*

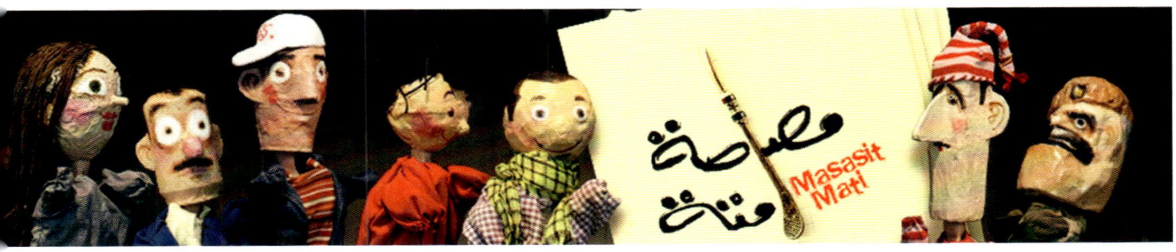

Masasit Mati, *Top Goon: Diaries of a Little Dictator*, 2011/2012, finger puppet show and video series, cast of *Top Goon*

Founded in 2011
Russia

http://mediaudar.net

MediaImpact

MediaImpact was initiated within the framework of the ZHIR project in Moscow in 2011. ZHIR supports and develops the art activist community in Russia and collaborates with artists interested in the intersections of art and social activism. For the Fourth Moscow Biennale of Contemporary Art in September 2011, ZHIR, in collaboration with the ARTPLAY Center, organized the MediaImpact International Festival of Activist Art, coordinated by curator Tatiana Volkova of ZHIR Gallery. Since then, exhibitions, lectures, and workshops have been held, and artistic interventions have been organized in public space.

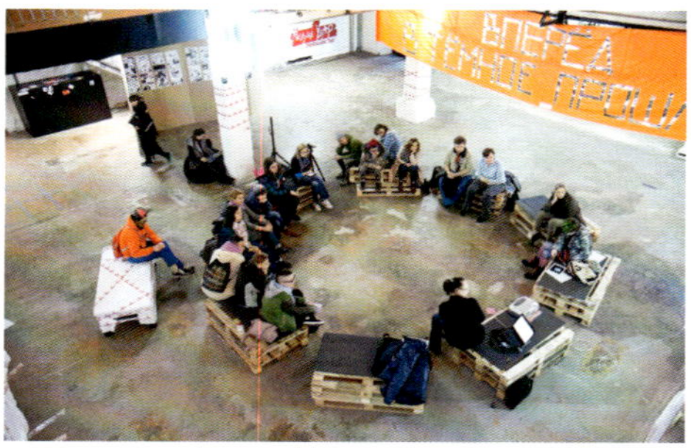

MediaImpact International Festival of Activist Art, *ARTPLAY*, Moscow, 2013, view of the exhibition and discussion space

MediaImpact has become an open international community seeking to explore, articulate, document, support, and develop activist art. The key aspect of its activity is the inclusion of art projects in the actual sociopolitical practices of today, which includes, amongst other things, campaigning for the rights of minority groups, the release of political prisoners, environmental protection, and development of alternatives to existing health care systems, as well as opposing censorship and the defamation of cultural figures.

The MediaImpact International Festival of Activist Art was the first of its kind in Russia and was established as a platform to foster activist art, with a special focus on Russia, where a strong movement of activist artists, joining forces with social movements and subcultures in the face of political repression, has emerged. Alongside Russian protagonists of art activism from all over the country, also international theorists and artist and activist groups from the Ukraine, Europe, and North America, such as The Yes Men (United States), organ of critical arts (Germany), Kavecs-projects (Greece), and the international collective kom.post, participated in the MediaImpact festival. The first edition was held in 2011 and received wide press coverage in Russia. The festival has an open and collaborative format and organizational structure, and it is collectively organized by a group of more than fifty international art activists, with several editions in different Russian regions. In addition to the workshops, panels, and discussions of the festival, art residencies and expeditions are offered, and small do-it-yourself editions are distributed. In 2012, the publication *MediaImpact International Festival of Activist Art*, edited by Tatiana Volkova, coordinated by Joulia Strauss, and with an introduction by Peter Weibel, appeared.

Facing Page:
MediaImpact International Festival of Activist Art. 24 September – 10 October 2011. Moscow, 2012, festival catalog, cover

MEDIA*IMPACT*
International Festival of Activist Art
24 september – 10 october 2011
Moscow

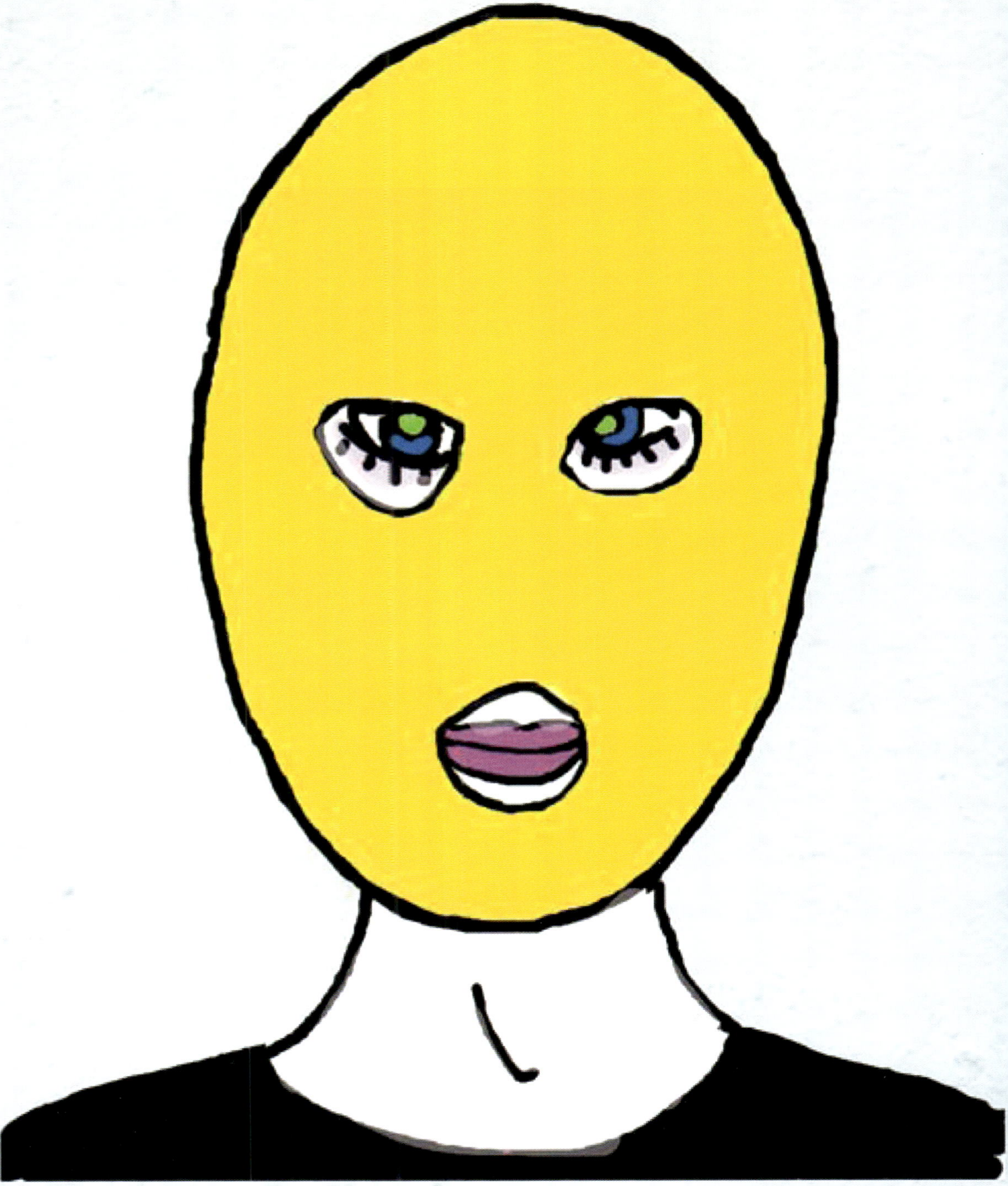

MEDIA*IMPACT*

MindBomb

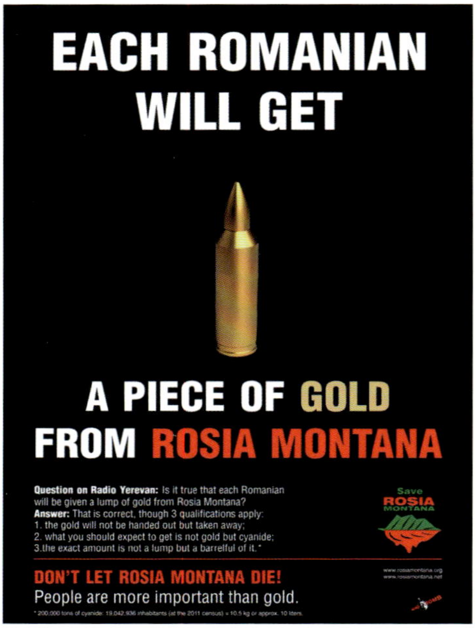

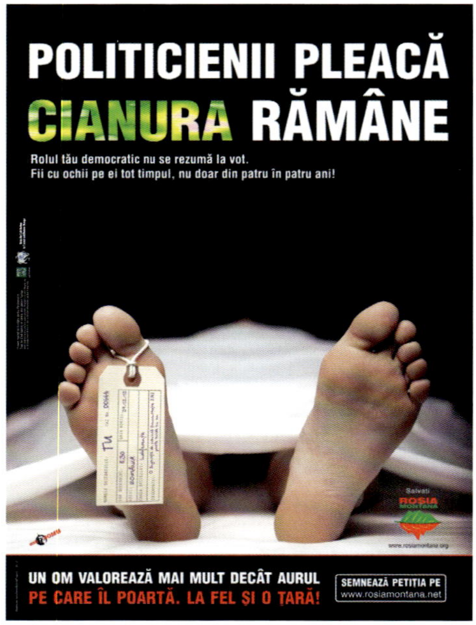

MindBomb, selection of posters from the series *The Golden Lie That Kills* and *We Want a Vote Free of Cyanide!*, 2012: *Each Romanian Will Get a Piece of Gold from Roşia Montană*, *Politicienii pleacă, cianura rămâne* [Politicians Go, Cyanide Remains], *Trădarea de țară în aur se măsoară* [Treason Is Measured in Gold], *Transilvania, teren minat. Urmează România* [Transylvania, a Minefield. Romania Is Next] (from left to right on both pages)

MindBomb is an affiliation of Romanian artists, architects, journalists, and writers, which conducts large-scale poster campaigns in public places that focus on sociopolitical issues.

In the following manifesto, the MindBomb collective describes its origin, mission, and goal:

> We don't want revolution!
> We want evolution!

MindBomb is the spontaneous combustion of meaningful thought that explodes into action.
The poster is not dead; it is alive.
It speaks with your very own voice.
Posters alone change nothing.
Posters incite us.
Posters remind us.
Posters make us think.
We take to the streets.
We express ourselves.
We do not seek to destroy but to create.
We are not angry; we are indignant.
We reject cynicism.
We do not want revolution,
but evolution.
We want consciousness.
We light the fuse of thought.

In 2002 the MindBomb project was started as a pioneering action. It marked the introduction of the truly autonomous sociopolitical poster in Romanian culture, and became a means to hack into the dominant discourse of mainstream politics, the mass media, and the advertising

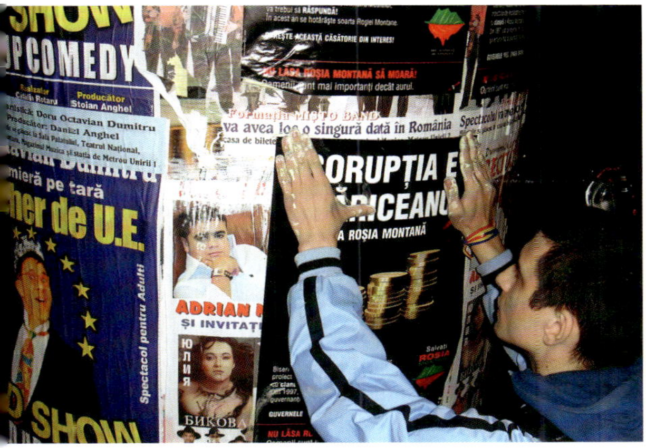

MindBomb, activist with poster from the series *Mindbomb for Roşia Montană!*, 2006

industry. The ultimate purpose of these actions is to create autonomous space for the purpose of dialog and debate that initiates social change. MindBomb started as a challenge to consumer culture and later developed into a broader critique of contemporary Romanian society and its public space.

The MindBomb project consists of collaborative street postering that responds to general or specific socio-political issues in contemporary Romanian society. The website represents a useful way for everyone to join the campaign by simply sending an idea or uploading their own poster.

Up to now the activity of the group has consisted in many large-scale postering campaigns and other interventions in public places. The posters have also been published in several magazines internationally.

In 2005 MindBomb participated in the International Street Art Exhibition Budapest with two posters, and in 2007 MindBomb participated at the Sharjah Biennial 8 *Still Life: Art, Ecology and the Politics of Change* in the United Arab Emirates with a postering action. In 2012 MindBomb launched widespread satirical poster campaigns in many Romanian towns to expose and subvert the manipulative advertising campaign promoting a gold-mining project in the Romanian village Roşia Montană that had been initiated by Roşia Montană Gold Corporation. With their posters, MindBomb significantly supported the campaign against the gold-mining project that would have a devastating environmental impact on the ecosystem of the region; it would not only lead to the destruction of natural and cultural sites, it would also destroy a community of local people.

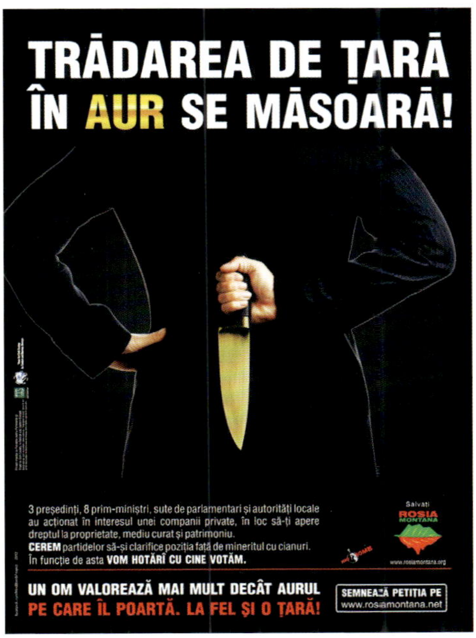

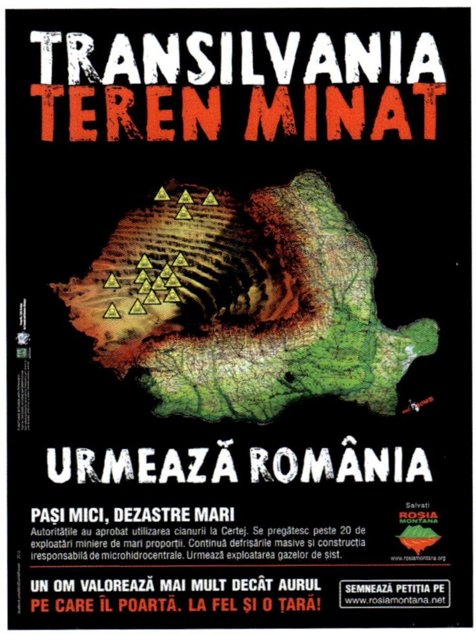

Carlos Motta *1978

Carlos Motta is a multidisciplinary artist from Bogotá who lives and works in New York City. In his artistic work he engages with political history and hegemonic power to contest dominant historical narratives and develop counternarratives that recognize suppressed histories, communities, minorities, and (gender) identities. He often collaborates with researchers, activists, and artists and is interested in art as a catalyst for social transformation. Motta is especially known for his socially and politically committed archival work related to Latin American geopolitics and queer cultural politics: In his projects *We Who Feel Differently* (2011/2012) and *Gender Talents* (2013, ongoing), both part of Motta's "Democracy Cycle," he created online archives, assembling queer critiques of normative ways of thinking about sexual and gender difference in various geographic contexts and documenting how individuals undermine and transform oppressive systems.

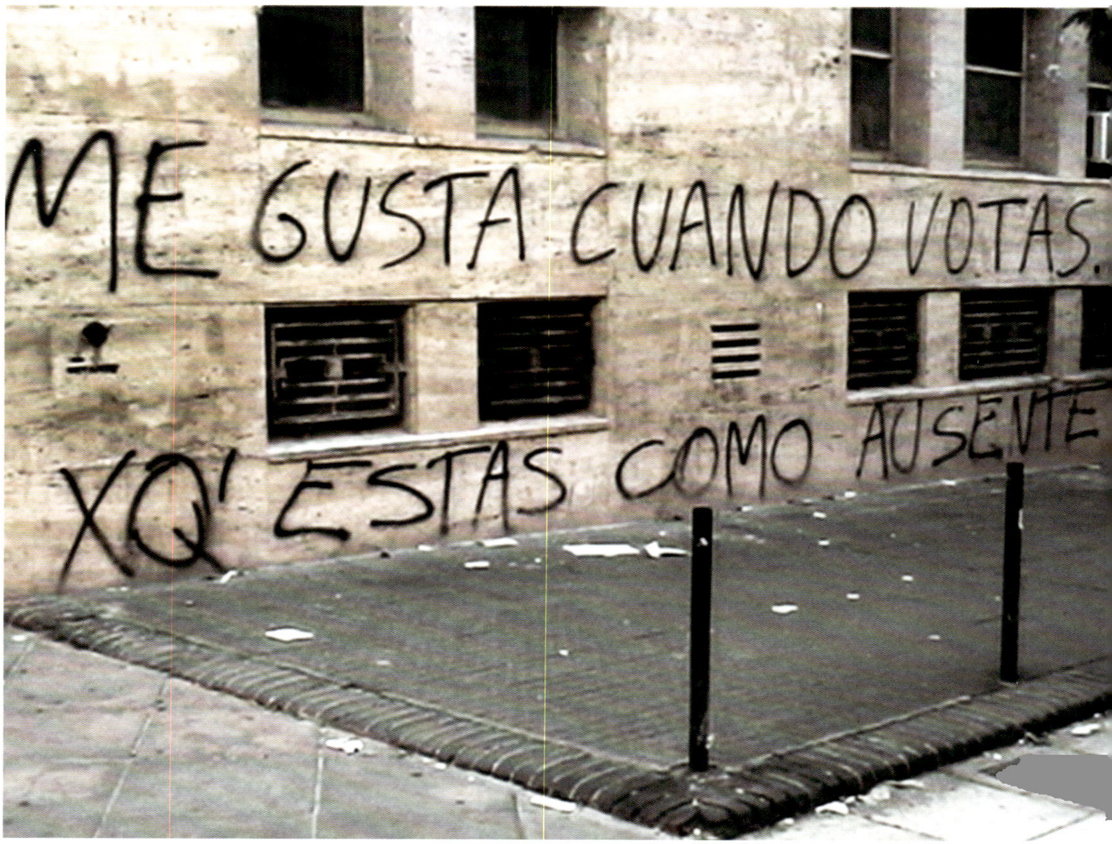

Carlos Motta, *Ideological Graffiti* (from *The Good Life*), 2005–2011, "Me gusta cuando votas xq' estás como ausente" [I like when you vote because you feel like absent], Faculty of Medicine of the University of Buenos Aires, Argentina, 2006, digital C-Print, ca. 28 × 35 cm

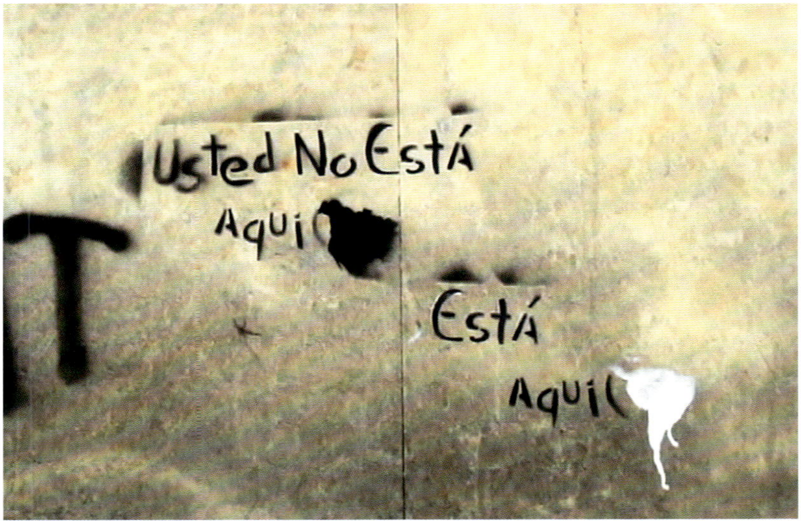

Carlos Motta, *Ideological Graffiti* (from *The Good Life*), 2005–2011, “Usted no está aquí. Está aquí” [You are not here. You are here], Bogotá, Colombia, 2006, digital C-Print, ca. 28 × 35 cm

Ideological Graffiti is a photo documentary about political graffiti in South American cities produced between 2005 and 2010. Motta documented graffiti in the streets of Buenos Aires (Argentina), Santiago de Chile, San José (Costa Rica), Guatemala City, Managua (Nicaragua), Caracas (Venezuela), Tegucigalpa (Honduras), and Bogotá (Colombia). The photo series was created as part of *The Good Life/La Buena Vida* (2005–2008), a multipart video project of more than 360 video interviews with pedestrians on the streets of twelve Latin American cities about processes of democratization, individuals’ understanding of democracy and governance, and interventionist U.S. foreign policies in the region. For a previous work, *Graffiti Cuts: Who Owns the Street* (2007–2009), Motta used street graffiti to create text and light installations. By focusing on ephemeral (sub)cultural matter such as graffiti, Motta captures popular dissent against political and social injustice, support of ideological or political projects, and attempts to reclaim public space. Both series highlight Motta’s interest in exploring (counter-) public discourses and different sources of cultural memories that reveal struggles for autonomy, democracy, and social justice.

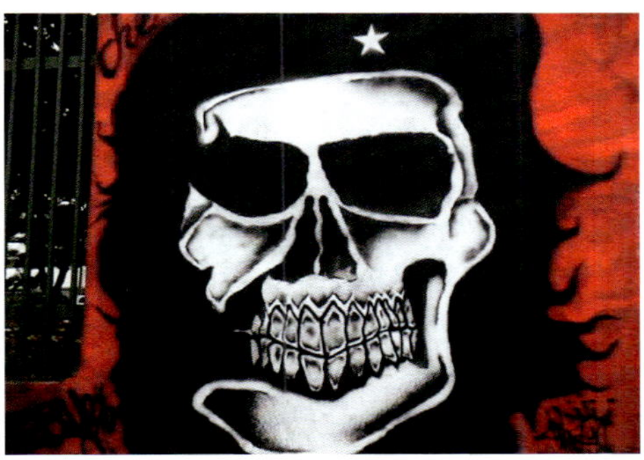

Carlos Motta, *Ideological Graffiti* (from *The Good Life*), 2005–2011, Ché Guevara mural, Managua, Nicaragua, 2007, digital C-Print, ca. 28 × 35 cm

MTL

Nitasha Dhillon (*1985, Rangareddy, India) is an artist based in New York and New Delhi. She has an honors BA in mathematics from St. Stephen's College, University of Delhi, and attended the School of the International Center of Photography (2009–2010) and the Whitney Independent Study Program (2011–2012), both in New York. Dhillon is a founder and editor of *Tidal. Occupy Theory, Occupy Strategy* (tidalmag.org), a strategic movement platform that weaves together the voices of on-the-ground organizers with those of long-standing theorists to explore the possibilities created by the rupture of the Occupy movement and its aftermath. Dhillon is also a cofounder of MTL with Amin Husain, a collective that combines research, aesthetics, and organizing activism in its practice.

Amin Husain (*1975) is a Palestinian-American lawyer, artist, and activist. He has a BA in philosophy and political science, a JD from Indiana University Law School, Bloomington, Indiana, and an LLM in law from Columbia University in New York. He practiced at a law firm for five years before leaving law for art, studying at the School of the International Center of Photography (2009–2010) and at the Whitney Independent Study Program (2011–2012). Amin Husain is a founder and editor of *Tidal. Occupy Theory, Occupy Strategy*, a printed magazine and an online and in-person conversation that facilitates movement-generated theory, strategy, and action (tidalmag.org). He is also a part-time lecturer at The New School in New York where he teaches a graduate course entitled "Race, Class, and Ethnicity in Media," and he is cofounder of MTL.

Yates McKee is an art critic and organizer. His work has appeared in venues which include *October*, *Grey Room*, *The Nation*, and *Waging Nonviolence*. He is coeditor of the book *Sensible Politics. The Visual Cultures of Nongovernmental Activism* (2012), as well as the magazine *Tidal. Occupy Theory, Occupy Strategy* (tidalmag.org). McKee is a member of the MTL collective.

Nitasha Dhillon, Amin Husain, and Yates McKee

#OCCUPYWALLST: A Possible Story

إنها لثورة حتى النصر

> "And this is the domain of the strange, the marvelous, and the fantastic, a domain scorned by people of certain inclinations. Here is the freed image, dazzling and beautiful, with a beauty that could not be more unexpected and overwhelming. Here are the poet, the painter, and the artist, presiding over the metamorphoses and the inversions of the world under the sign of hallucinations and madness."
>
> Suzanne Césaire, *Tropiques*, 1941

Strike ~~Art~~

Art as we know it is corrupt, exhausted, and weak. We see works of postmodern masters sold to bankers for millions of dollars as signs of cultural capital and objects of financial investment. We see shimmering edifices of cultural wealth erected on the backs of hyper-exploited labor – the pyramids and coliseums of the twenty-first century. We see museums, galleries, and public art projects serving as the avant-garde of racialized gentrification and displacement. We see ruthless competition between indebted cultural workers in pursuit of the hollow dream of appearing in *Artforum*. We see so-called "social practice," the well-funded bureaucratization of alienated people's desire for community. And we see theoretically savvy "discursive platforms" that speak of radical democracy, militant ecology, and even communization, while recoiling at the prospect of deploying their considerable resources, skills, and potentials for the purposes of building a movement. This is no longer acceptable

When we speak of art after Occupy, we put art under erasure. We strike art to liberate art from itself. Not to end art, but to unleash its powers of direct action and radical imagination. Art does not dissolve into so-called real life. It revitalizes real life by making it *surreal*. Our surreal spirit is less that of André Breton's European vanguardism than Suzanne Césaire's freedom dream, informed as it is by the ongoing histories of slavery, imperialism, and debt. Art defamiliarizes life, asking us: *How do we live?* Art challenges us to respond to this question with direct action for which we ourselves are responsible rather than any preexisting institution. We strike art as training in the practice of freedom.

When we strike art, imagine a refugee camp collaged into the symbolic heart of finance capital. Imagine a self-organized commons installed at ground zero of empire. Imagine an empty minimalist plaza flooded with bodies and voices and cameras, blasting a collective cry to the world: *We are sorry it took so long, we are awake now!* Imagine a general strike in New York City. And imagine a never-ending process of experimentation, learning and undoing, resisting and building in the unexplored terrain of an historic rupture.

Before Beginning

MTL is in the West Bank. We are visiting friends and family, and retracing memories of the first Palestinian uprising. We are traveling, listening, recording, and translating. Land, life, liberation are on our minds. Then Mohamed Bouazizi ends his life through self-immolation. Tunisia breaks.

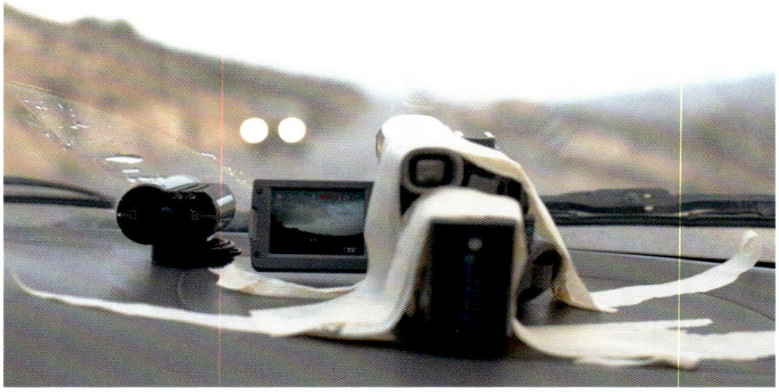

Somewhere in occupied Palestine, documenting the roads and geographies leading to conversation, 2010

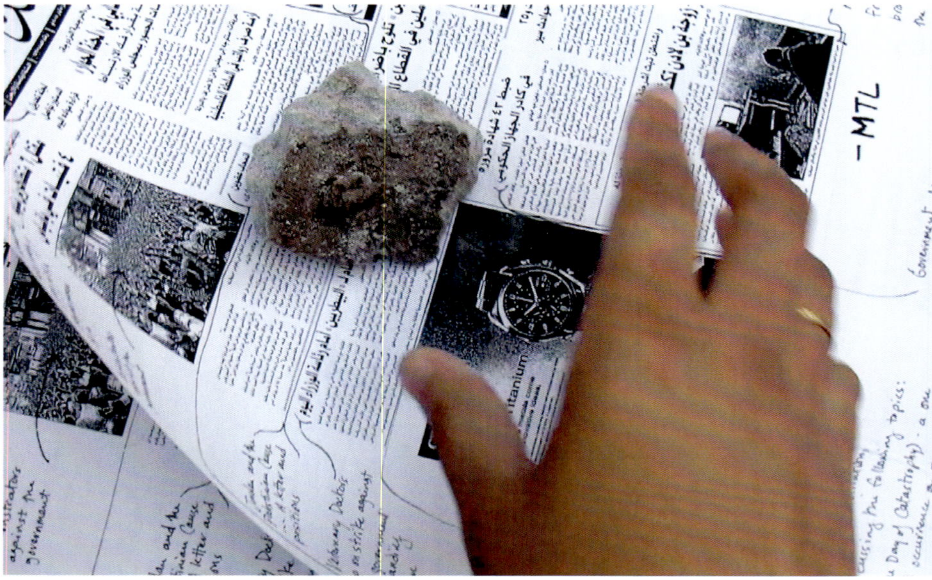

MTL, *Newspaper Action*, translating headlines of front pages of Arabic language newspapers with a wide circulation in occupied Palestine and other Arabic-speaking countries during the Arab Spring and distributing in and around New York, 2011

We return to New York. The city looks and feels different. Things are buzzing; we are watching closely. Soon Egypt breaks. We see revolutionary people power from below. But it doesn't seem to apply to the United States, even though we know it is all connected in an expanded field of empire. We say to ourselves, "That is a revolution against decades of brutal military dictatorship backed by the USA; those are not the same conditions faced by those living in the heart of the empire itself." But then Greece breaks: here is a nominal democracy and yet people are rising up, taking to the streets and holding the squares. Then Spain. A Western nation with an advanced economy in the midst of elections. With the crisis people are compelled to occupy, throwing into question the legitimacy of the entire political process: *Basta ya! No nos representan*.

We start to feel something is possible in the United States. The Wisconsin capitol building is occupied, and the occupiers invoke Egypt; labor and community groups set up the Bloombergville camp in New York to protest urban austerity, making reference to the

Spanish *indignados*. Cracks are forming. The power of the powerless is beginning to show itself.

The Artist as Organizer

We are meeting regularly. In light of the global economic disaster, we know we have the chance to push things further in the United States. The crisis has produced an opportunity. We are privileged to be in New York. We carry our cameras and our notebooks to document things, but we end up participating. The art we had imagined making for so long is starting to happen in real life. We do not have time to agonize about representation. We are making images, writing texts, having conversations, and developing relationships out of necessity and urgency. Aesthetics, research, organizing; it is all coming together in the creation of a new public space in the heart of the empire. It embodies imagination with implications on the ground. #occupywallst.

At this time, occupy is a verb rather than a noun. People meet every Sunday at 5 p.m. for hours to plan for the occupation on September 17, 2011. First at the Wall Street Bull sculpture a few blocks from the New York Stock Exchange on August 2. Then at the Irish Potato Famine Memorial in the Financial District on August 9. Then at the same time every week at Tompkins Square Park in the East Village. A horizontal process is used in meetings. Facilitation allows for the maximum number of diverse voices to be heard. No one can speak on behalf of others. Organizations cannot participate as such, only as people speaking on behalf of themselves. The slogan "We are the 99 Percent" is proposed to invite others to join. Everyone is interested in creating space, not deciding an agenda or specifying demands. Folks are in minimal but fundamental agreement on the need to reorganize social, political, and economic life in a manner that is just and equitable.

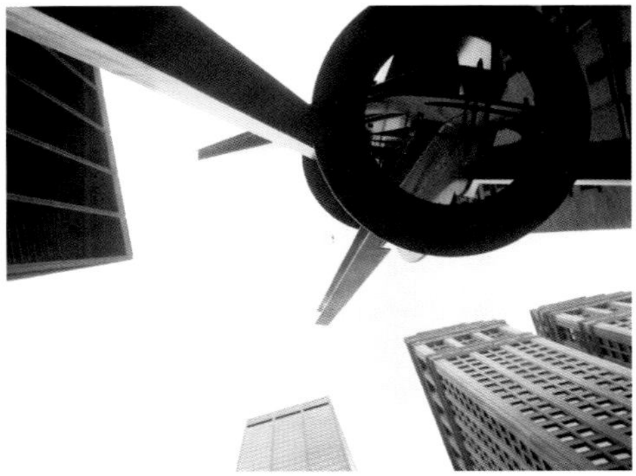

Zuccotti Park, New York City, during the occupation of Wall Street, 2011

Liberating Spaces, Cracking Capitalism

We occupy on September 17. A tweet goes out to gather at One Chase Manhattan Plaza in front of the Jean Dubuffet sculpture. It's a few blocks from the New York Stock Exchange. We find the plaza barricaded, so we go to plan B: Zuccotti Park is wide open.

Our backs are on pizza boxes. Our bodies warm the concrete. You look up, the buildings cease to dominate the horizon as figures against a ground; instead, they frame a threshold of freedom opening onto the sky. Mark di Suvero's "weird red thing" watches over us. We dumpster-dive. *If we have food, people will stay*. The kitchen is born. When the police prohibit amplification devices, we institute the People's Mic: we repeat what people say so others can hear, and in the process we internalize each other's words. General assemblies are held daily. Rather than issue demands, we articulate principles of solidarity. We begin the process of mapping capitalism with our bodies. We take direct action to communicate injustice. The park is now everyone's open wound. We realize how much needs to be undone. We address racism, colonialism, patriarchy, and other forms of oppression head-on. At the epicenter of financial terrorism, we establish a community of care and healing – a people's refuge in the belly of the beast.

We are sparking imagination. Occupations are spreading. Momentum is building. But they evict us from Zuccotti Park. Attempts to occupy Duarte Square at Sixth Avenue and Canal Street do not succeed. We are arrested and brutalized by the NYPD. A police state fears everything that does not follow its script. Our greatest threat is that we speak openly about inequality while establishing a self-organized community, a community grounded in the commons.

May Day Comes and Goes

Winter is hard. The camps are gone. Police repression has taken a toll. We realize we have to work differently to create conversations and actions in the absence of the park. We organize towards a future date and choose May Day – a day of global labor solidarity that has been suppressed in the United States. We come together: labor and student organizers, folks from Occupy Wall Street, undocumented workers' centers, inspired academics, and insurrectionist friends. We have weekly planning meetings. We debate what constitutes a general strike. Who can make the call? Who can participate? What does strike mean for precarious, undocumented, or nonunionized workers? What are the consequences of a call to strike that goes unheeded?

Finally, people agree on the following language:

OCCUPY WALL STREET
STANDS IN SOLIDARITY
WITH THE CALLS FOR
A DAY WITHOUT THE 99%,
A GENERAL STRIKE
AND MORE!! ON MAY DAY,
WHEREVER YOU ARE,
WE ARE CALLING FOR:
NO WORK, NO SCHOOL,
NO HOUSEWORK,
NO SHOPPING, NO BANKING.
TAKE THE STREETS!!!!!

After months of planning and preparation that yield thousands in the streets, a movement is not yet born. We realize unionized workers cannot break from the chains of their bosses and their leadership. So much has changed. Wages are stagnant, unions are busted, municipal austerity has set in; the exploitation of the worker increasingly overlaps with the experience of being in debt. We are all forced into servitude to Wall Street as we try to make ends meet. We articulate the indebted as a political subject.

Debt Is a Time Machine

We focus on debt and touch a nerve. The new American dream is to get out of debt. Education debt, medical debt, credit card debt, mortgage debt, payday loans. We meet people where they are at, where global finance touches our lives in the most immediate ways. We gather and tell stories. The feeling of strength in weakness. The power of refusal – *can't pay, won't pay*. The smell of the bills going up in smoke as we testify together. The images become actions and back again. We perform our shared reality to break the silence, the shame, the isolation, and build community. We imagine debt as more than a set of "issues." We imagine debt as a placeholder for a dehumanizing system in its totality; debt as an amplifier of other oppressions; debt as a racist war machine; debt as a distillation of non-freedom. We imagine other debts and other bonds: to friends, family, community, rather than to the banks. Debts owed from immemorial histories of slavery and colonization. Debts that are both immeasurable and singular, debts that mark each of our lives and relations in different ways.

...and Other Racist Bullshit

The identity of the debtor gains traction, but primarily among middle-class white people. We know that debt impacts poor communities of color the hardest,

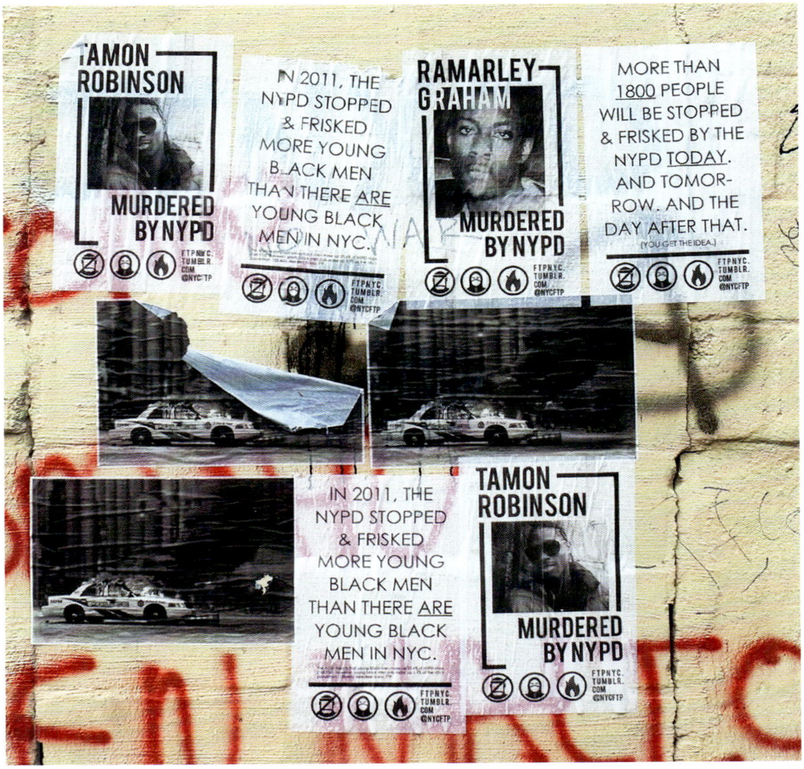

A wall in Bushwick, Brooklyn, New York City, 2012

from subprime mortgages to payday loans to urban austerity. Debt intersects with racialized state violence on an everyday basis. All roads lead to Wall Street, but they pass through the precinct, the prison, and the morgue. As we reimagine resistance to capitalism at an urban level, we think of those killed by the NYPD, private security forces, and racist vigilantes around the country:

AMADOU DIALLO
MANUEL DIAZ
SHANTEL DAVIS
RAMARLEY GRAHAM
SEAN BELL
TRAYVON MARTIN
OSCAR GRANT
KIMANI GRAY

…and so it goes.

Climate Strike

Climate strikes back against Wall Street, and we all get flooded. The banks are under water. The ocean in the streets, block by block. The boardwalk is in ruins. We convert churches into hubs for mutual aid. In the void left by the state, we must make a calculation. Lives are lives. There is no hesitation. We step in, we take the risk. It is a crisis and an opportunity. We are reminded that our struggle against the concentration of wealth and power in the hands of a few is also a struggle for life – and that an obsession with growth and firing up a sputtering economy misses the larger ecological questions confronting the planet at large.

We offset the negligence of the city and the agencies just so everything won't fall further apart. A gray area between emergency relief and political resistance. *Can we pivot in that space?* Can we align our responsibility to act with what we are working toward? How do we link climate to debt, to work, to sustainable living?

We go to Detroit with these questions.

It Does Not Resemble a City

Detroit is a mythic wasteland of romantic ruins and vacant space. This post-industrial picturesque effaces those living and struggling in what used to be the city. Capital and the state have withdrawn from massive swathes of territory. Every square inch is a Wall Street crime scene. In both its devastation and possibility, Detroit is an outpost from our collective future.

Long-term struggles on the ground throw everything into a new light: our own cities, our own work, our own lives. Racial, economic, and environmental justice understood in a global context of empire, neoliberalism, and climate disaster. People thinking of revolutionary time in decades and centuries, rather than in days and months. Non-monetary economies; community-based agriculture; work beyond jobs; education beyond school; culture beyond art; life beyond capitalism. In Detroit, we hear over and over: how do we live?

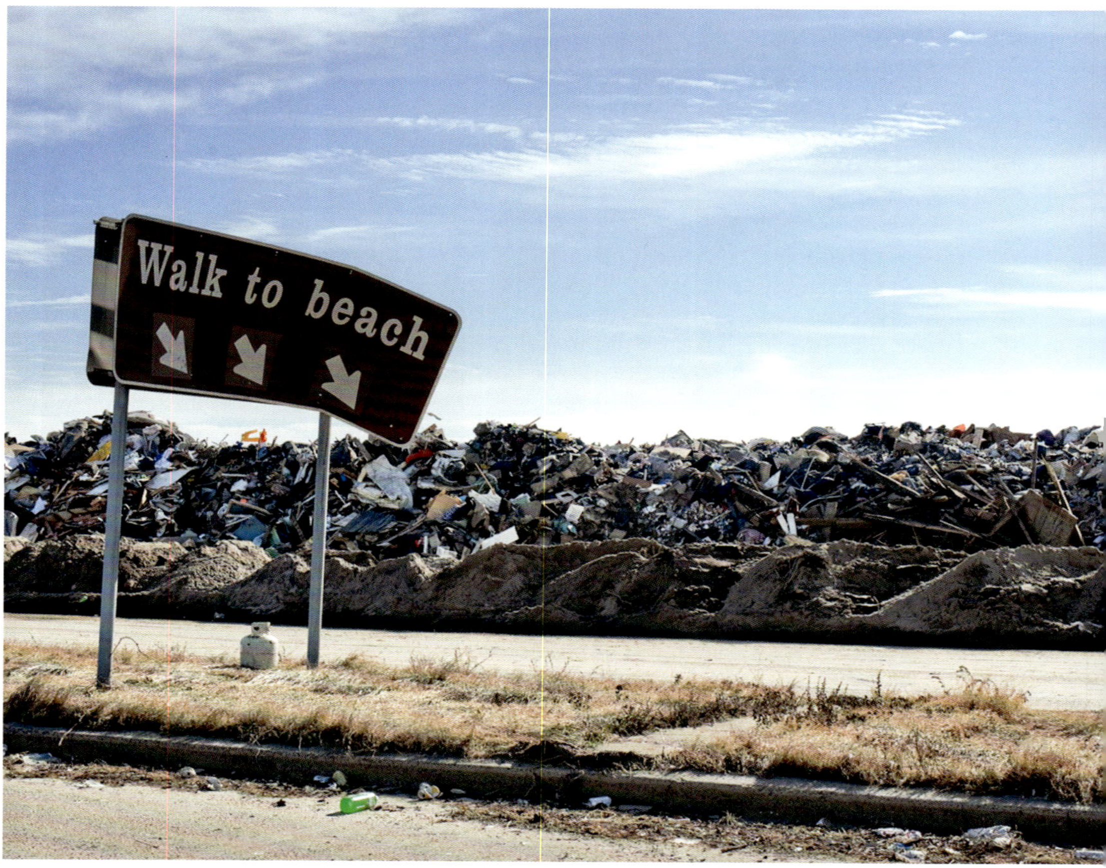

Somewhere in Far Rockaway, Queens, New York City, after Hurricane Sandy had struck, 2012

Beautiful Disruptions

MTL is called to participate in an ongoing solidarity initiative with South Asian migrant workers in Abu Dhabi placed into debt servitude as they pursue the so-called "Gulf dream." Yearly, thousands of workers arrive to Saadiyat "Happiness" Island to build a complex of luxury cultural amenities for the global 1% who will take up residence there: New York University, Guggenheim, the Louvre. The collusion of art and capitalist injustice is exemplified here, but it also offers an opportunity to escalate and amplify through direct action.

We begin by mapping the transnational chain of debt involved in Saadiyat Island. The migrant worker, the student, and the artist are all part of this chain, woven together through student loans, precarity, indebted labor in the art world, and the debt incurred by the migrant workers as "recruitment fees" to travel to Abu Dhabi. *What does solidarity of the indebted look like across national borders and lines of class privilege?*

Developing the analysis and organizing a principled boycott of Guggenheim Abu Dhabi by artists are crucial steps. But they remain on low boil for months while the institution drags its feet and offers empty promises of reform. We assemble a crew of old and new friends to form the Global Ultra Luxury Faction (G.U.L.F.), and within weeks unleash an unrelenting sequence of actions at the iconic flagship of the Guggenheim itself.

Beautiful disruptions cause collective gasps. The museum is unprepared, taken off guard. Banners are dropped in the photogenic rotunda to chant:

"WHO IS BUILDING THE GUGGENHEIM ABU DHABI?"

"1% GLOBAL MUSEUM"

is projected onto the facade of the iconic edifice in the stealth of night. A fake website at globalguggenheim.org representing the Guggenheim as an ethical and sustainable museum is circulated to the press. We return to the museum to make it rain thousands of fake dollar bills from atop of the Guggenheim's spiral. A Futurism exhibition at the museum is supplemented by plastering the pristine walls with modular machine-age icons displaying kinetic slogans directed at the trustees:

G.U.L.F. JUSTICE NOW!
INTO THE FUTURE
WITH DIGNITY!
NO JUSTICE, NO ART!

Our actions string together over time a sense of how capitalism is located in concrete institutions, using a specific place as a physical platform, aesthetic theater, and media force multiplier. The boundaries between art, media, and organizing are dissolving once again. We are applying the lessons of Occupy, while adapting them to a specific struggle.

Everything Is Common

Acts of protest leverage the visibility of an art institution, but we know that no matter how big our protests get they will remain ephemeral. To both sustain resistance and move into the construction of alternatives – at home and in a global frame – we must build bases for community, mutual support, and education at the level of the city in which we ourselves struggle to live. We return to the challenges of Zuccotti Park and the lessons of Sandy and Detroit – block by block, brick by brick.

We need space and find it immediately on offer from our friends in the radical faith community. Faith spaces are numerous throughout the city, and largely underutilized. They have a ready-made physical infrastructure and local community roots. We begin cultivating a network of spaces for building communities of resistance and experimenting with noncapitalist economic systems capable of reproducing themselves.

We declare Jubilee House! In numerous faith traditions around the world, Jubilee names the cancellation of debts, the redistribution of land, and the liberation of slaves. One version of the story emphasizes the generosity of the rulers from on high. But another celebrates the power of the enslaved, the exploited, the indebted, and the evicted to declare their own jubilee, one that calls for the sharing of all things in common. Looking to militant struggles from the origins of capitalism itself, our motto is: *Omnia sunt communia! Everything is common!*

Jubilee House is always and forever being built, like a multidimensional dwelling with twists, turns, and secret tunnels all over the globe – a new chapter in the story of the "mole" of communism celebrated by Karl Marx. Imagine Jubilee Houses opening halls of fellowship in an episcopal church in Brooklyn, a mosque in Bay Ridge, a burned-out shopping mall in Buffalo, a shuttered school in Detroit, a community center in Cleveland. This would be the work not only for our activists, organizers, and clergy, but for our poets, musicians, and workers. Over time the lines continue to blur.

Jubilee House makes use of what we learn from our ancestors and traditions. It thrives on knowledges and spirits of the past to build structures that have the flexibility and capacity to endure. Jubilee House is a choice in the land of no-choice. Art will play a critical role in unlocking this potential.

Do you remember when they said it was the end of history?

Do you remember when we couldn't imagine?

Do you remember when a borderless world wasn't possible?

Do you remember when the crack opened beneath our feet?

The liberated territories are coming…

حتى النصر
حتى النصر

This is a living document which first appeared in the exhibition *Arbeidstiden* [The Worktime], Henie Onstad Kunstsenter, Oslo, Norway, 2013.

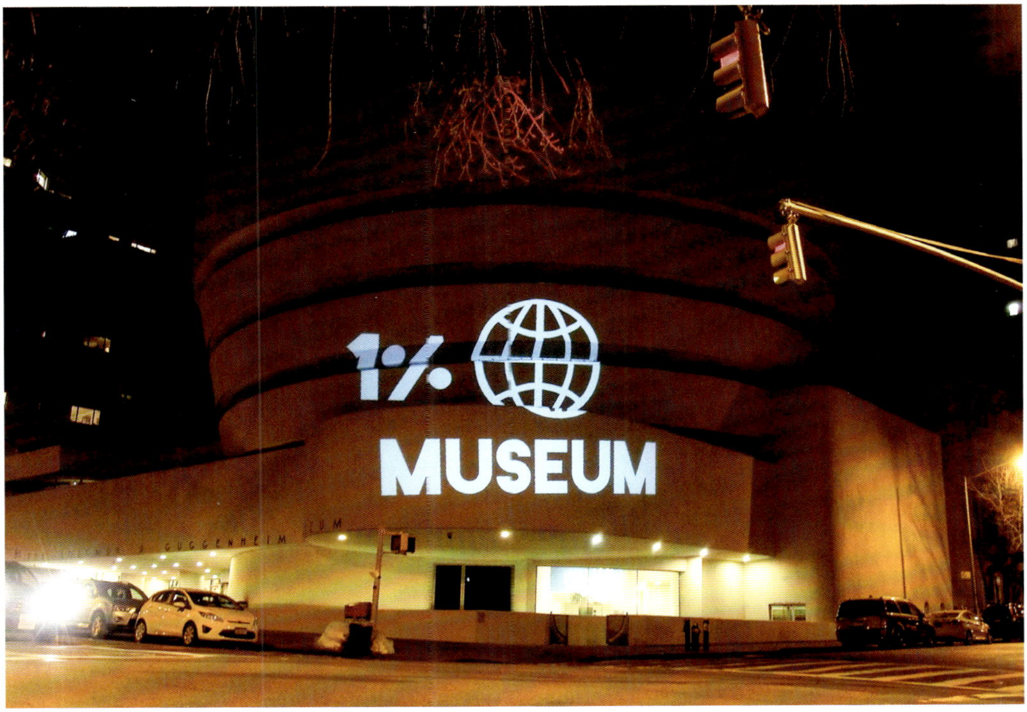

G.U.L.F., *Illumination Action* targeting the facade of the Guggenheim Museum in New York City, March 24, 2014

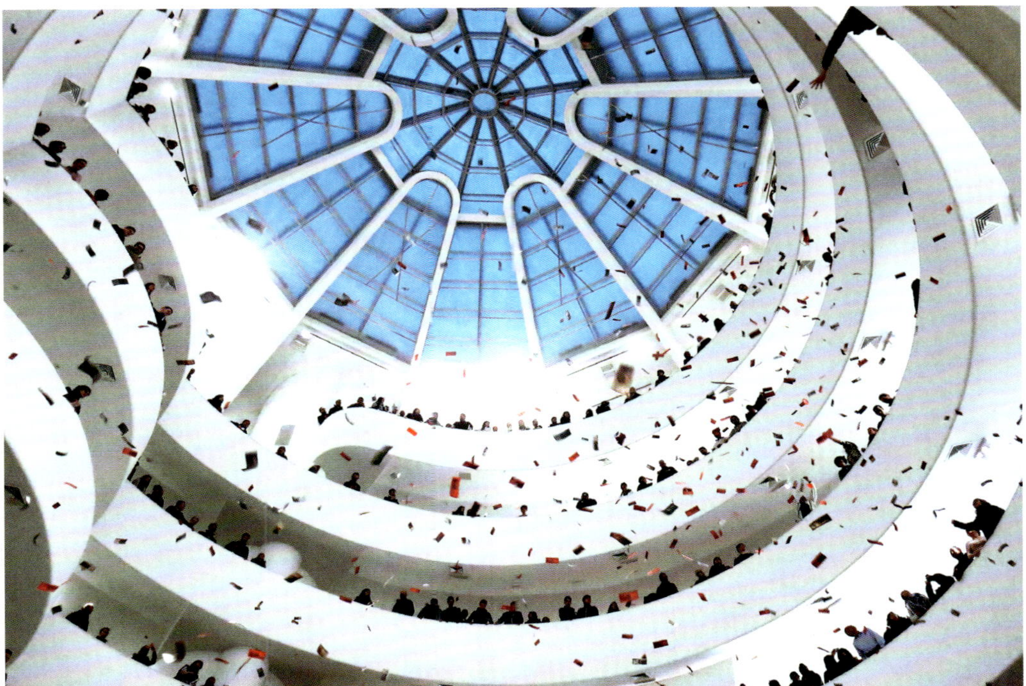

G.U.L.F., *Fake Dollar Bills Action* inside the Guggenheim Museum in New York City, March 29, 2014

NEOZOON

NEOZOON is a collective of female artists based in Paris and Berlin that has become known for its artistic interventions in urban space to explore the relationship between humans and animals, dead or alive.

For their series *Nos espaces cuisine* (2011), NEOZOON modified advertising posters to draw attention to the ambivalence of how we deal with domesticated animals. By relocating the act of slaughter to posters and thus to the public realm, the artists force the public to remember the act of killing, which is often forgotten when consuming meat. NEOZOON draws on the aesthetics of mainstream advertising campaigns and subverts their logic by integrating disturbing elements in their artworks.

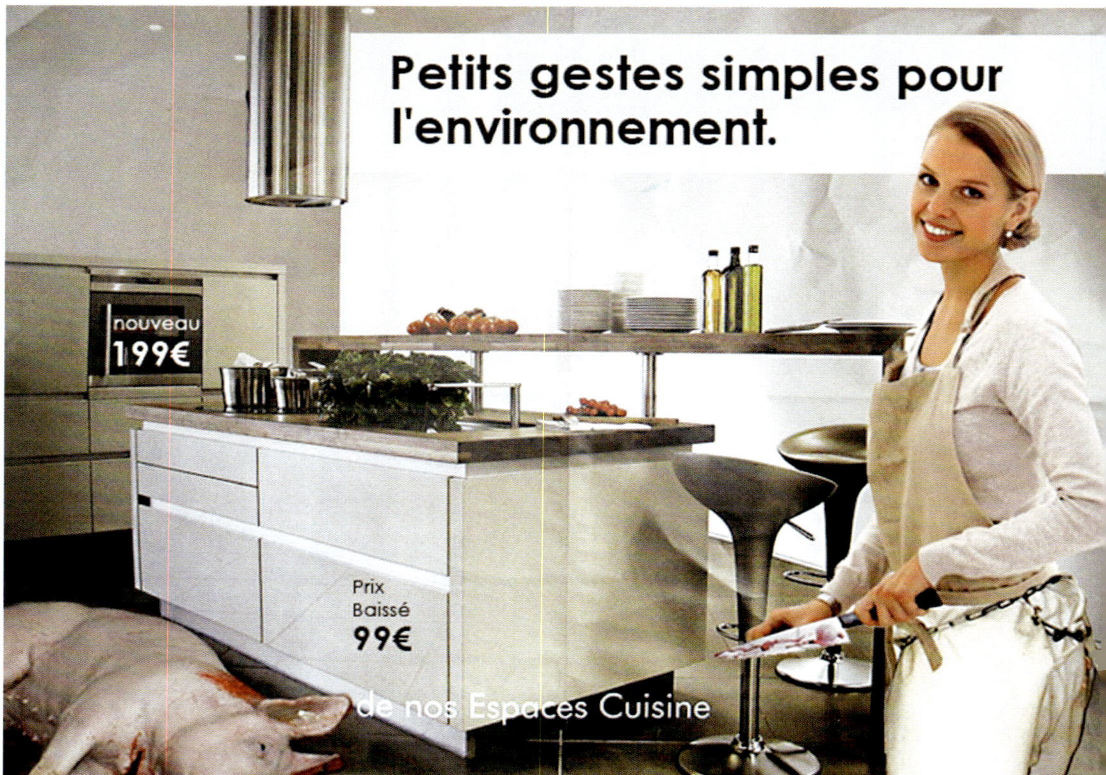

NEOZOON, *L'espace cuisine II*, from the series *Nos espaces cuisine*, 2011, poster, Fototex, 2 × 3 m

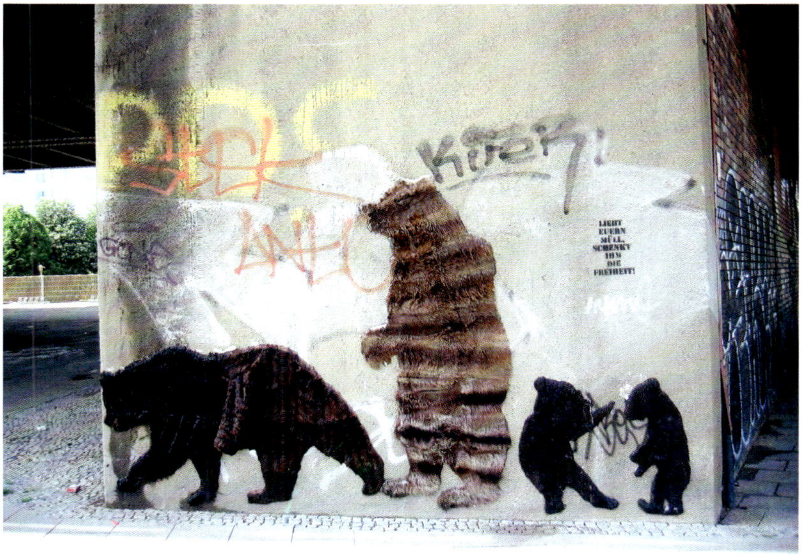

NEOZOON, *Berlin Bears*, 2009, installation, fur coat recycling, bears in the streets of Berlin

In another series of works, NEOZOON stages a protest against the use of animal furs in fashion: fur coats are transformed into street art graffiti by juxtaposing fur cutouts and different urban landscapes. These new creatures, made of dead animals but seemingly alive, populate urban space and create startling effects, especially when they seem to interact with passersby. In a way, they have been given back and now haunt the space from whence they were forced out by humans and human civilization. For their work *Bah Bah Black Sheep* (2010), NEOZOON created a site-specific installation of one hundred lamb silhouettes made from fur coats, attached to the walls of a former slaughterhouse in Dresden. At certain intervals, a children's choir could be heard singing the nursery rhyme "Baa Baa Black Sheep." In a further variant of their concept, NEOZOON developed three-dimensional installations made of fur objects which were, for example, displayed on trees. They have also produced several video works. In their fur collages and installation works the principle of recycling is quite apparent, and it is also used in their YouTube collages.

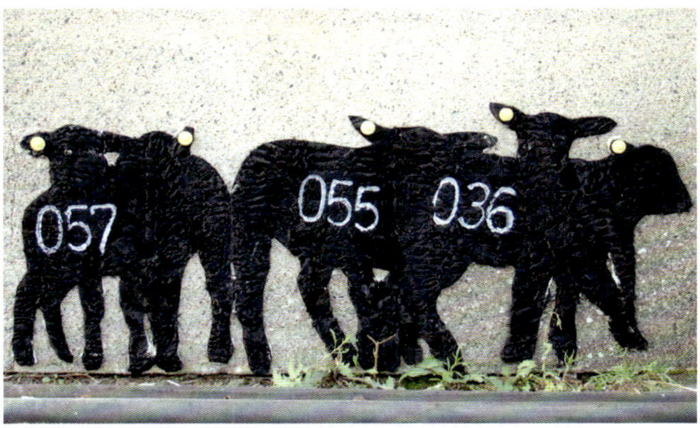

NEOZOON, *Bah Bah Black Sheep*, 2010, installation, fur coat recycling, 100 lamb silhouettes made from old fur coats along the outer wall of the former slaughterhouse in Dresden, Germany

Christof Nüssli *1986 and Christoph Oeschger *1984

Christof Nüssli is cofounder of the Swiss graphic design studio typo-salon, and, together with media artist Christoph Oeschger, cofounder of cpress publishers. Both Nüssli and Oeschger have been engaged in political art projects.

In the comprehensive artist book dedicated to Miklós Klaus Rózsa, born in 1956 in Hungary, Christof Nüssli and Christoph Oeschger not only portray a period in the life and career of a leftist photographer who worked both for traditional and leftist media, but also significant events in Swiss cultural history: the leftist movements of the 1970s and 1980s that made Zurich tremble.

Rózsa grew up in Zurich; he soon joint the leftist movement, became a political activist (protesting against the Vietnam War, for instance) and worked as a photographer and journalist: for Rózsa, taking photos was a political activity. He documented demonstrations, clashes between masked protesters and the police, brutal incidents, the 1980 youth uprising, and police actions, including operations with tear gas, rubber bullets, and water cannon – he soon became a target of the police himself, he was interrogated, arrested, and attacked. A (hi)story of observation and counterobservation began. It was only in 1989 that it became known that, from 1971 to 1989, the Swiss state security service had established and built up an immense archive of documents and images, targeting individuals and organizations. While all file cards and dossiers (approximately 800,000) can be consulted upon request since 1989, the image archive is still not accessible. Rózsa's political activities, his work as a journalist, and the details and banalities of his private life were painstakingly documented: the archive contains more than 3,200 records on Rózsa, from typewritten reports on political activities, images, and press clippings to transcripts of bugged phone calls. Formal in tone, the reports still reveal personal judgment, and are at times even involuntarily humorous.

The publication *Miklós Klaus Rózsa* (2014) documents two counter-movements chronologically, which is also reflected in the design of the book. Numerous police files, records, and dossiers, which characterize Rózsa as a dangerous individual who transgresses Swiss laws, are contrasted with Rózsa's photos of police operations, capturing the dynamics, spirit, and brutality of the events. The book offers a rich and rigorous visual narrative about observation and surveillance, and about the interpretability of images and documents: Both layers of the narrative tell a different story and form a subjective collage. There is conflict and interference, and there are blanks: for instance, numerous names and passages of documents were blacked out by the state security. Miklós Klaus Rózsa is witness, documentarist, and key protagonist of politically agitated times and places in Swiss history.

Via the Swiss crowdfunding platform wemakeit.com, it is possible to make a financial contribution to covering the production costs of the book.

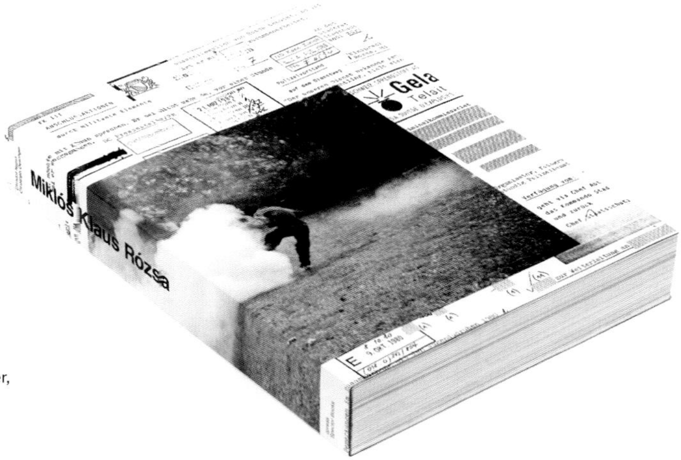

Christof Nüssli and Christoph Oeschger, *Miklós Klaus Rózsa*, 2014, artist book, 624 pages, 450 b/w images, cpress, Zurich, Spector Books, Leipzig

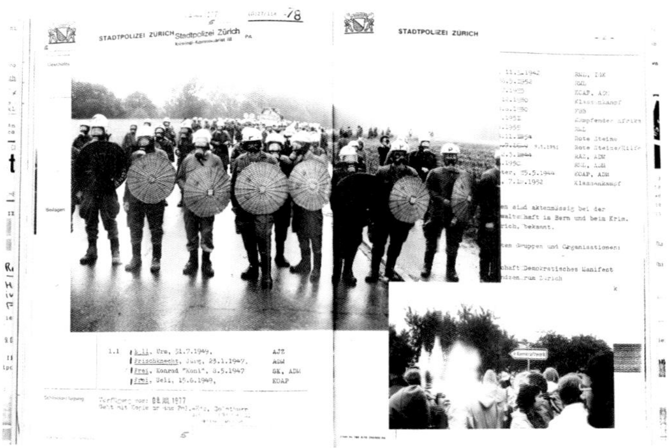

Pages from *Miklós Klaus Rózsa*, 2014; Swiss antinuclear protesters are confronted by a large contingent of police in riot gear.

Pages from *Miklós Klaus Rózsa*, 2014; The violent clashes between police and citizens in front of Zurich's opera house in the summer of 1980 marked the start of Zurich's youth movement; policemen running away from stones being thrown at them.

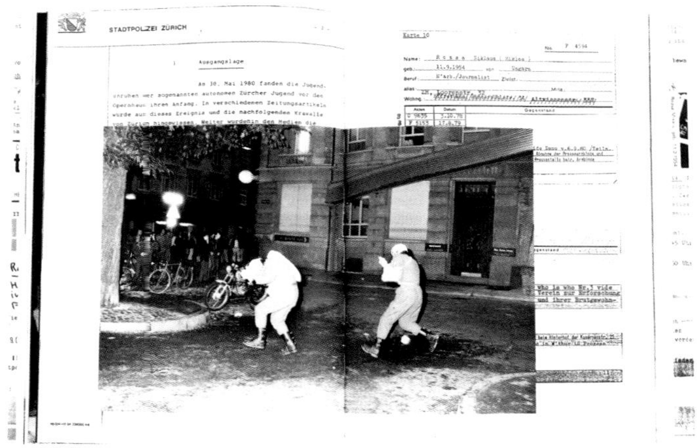

Jean-Gabriel Périot *1974

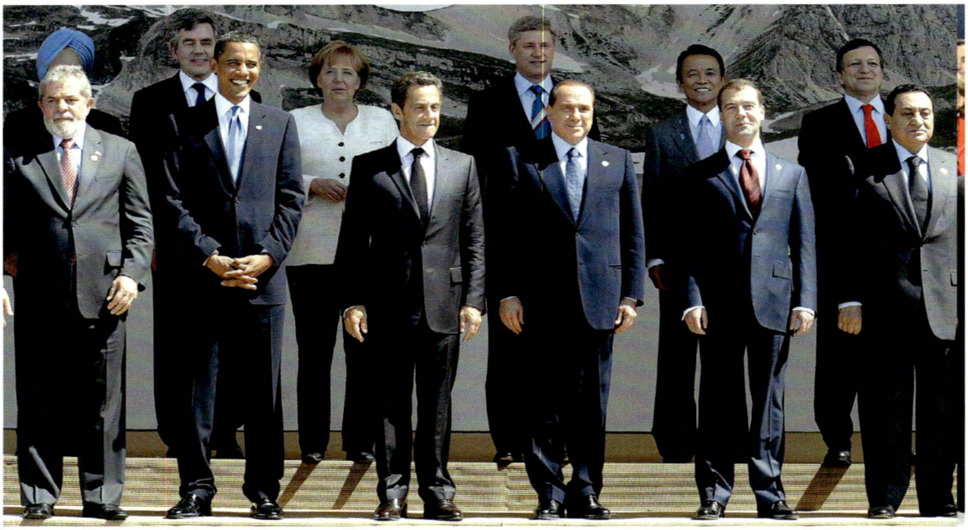

Jean-Gabriel Périot, *The Barbarians*, 2010, video, color, stereo, 5:00 min, video still

Jean-Gabriel Périot is an artist and filmmaker with a special focus on the innovative and precise editing of archival material. He uses films and photos, recordings from television, drawings, animation and graphic elements, websites, songs, and audio recordings to create his dense political narratives that often capture moments of crisis and engage with violence and human rights. In an approximation of and search for reality, he juxtaposes, manipulates, edits, implements, and stages his raw material and found footage.

In his video work *The Barbarians* (2010), Périot shows an abundance of posed group photos of political events, such as heads of state attending the G8 Summit, alternated by photos of military and police groups, sports teams, and family pictures. Progressively, in Périot's whiplash montage, the order is dissolved by meshing and juxtaposing images and scenes, and new scenes and orders appear. Faces of activists are highlighted not even for a second, their faces often covered, and images of agitation and protest are shown, leading up to scenes of violence. Périot places special emphasis on the sound design and often cuts his work to the tempo of a piece of music. In *The Barbarians*, as the rhythm of the score and the montage slows down, the scenes become more and more dramatic: street fights, destroyed areas, burning objects and people. By the end, everything is in flames. The narrative unfolds without a commentary and relies solely on the composition of images and sounds.

The Barbarians ends with an insert, a statement by French philosopher Alain Brossat from his book *La résistance infinie* (2006): "If politics were to come back, it could only be from its savage and disreputable fringe. Then, a muffled rumor shall arise whence that roar is heard: 'We are scum! We are barbarian!'"

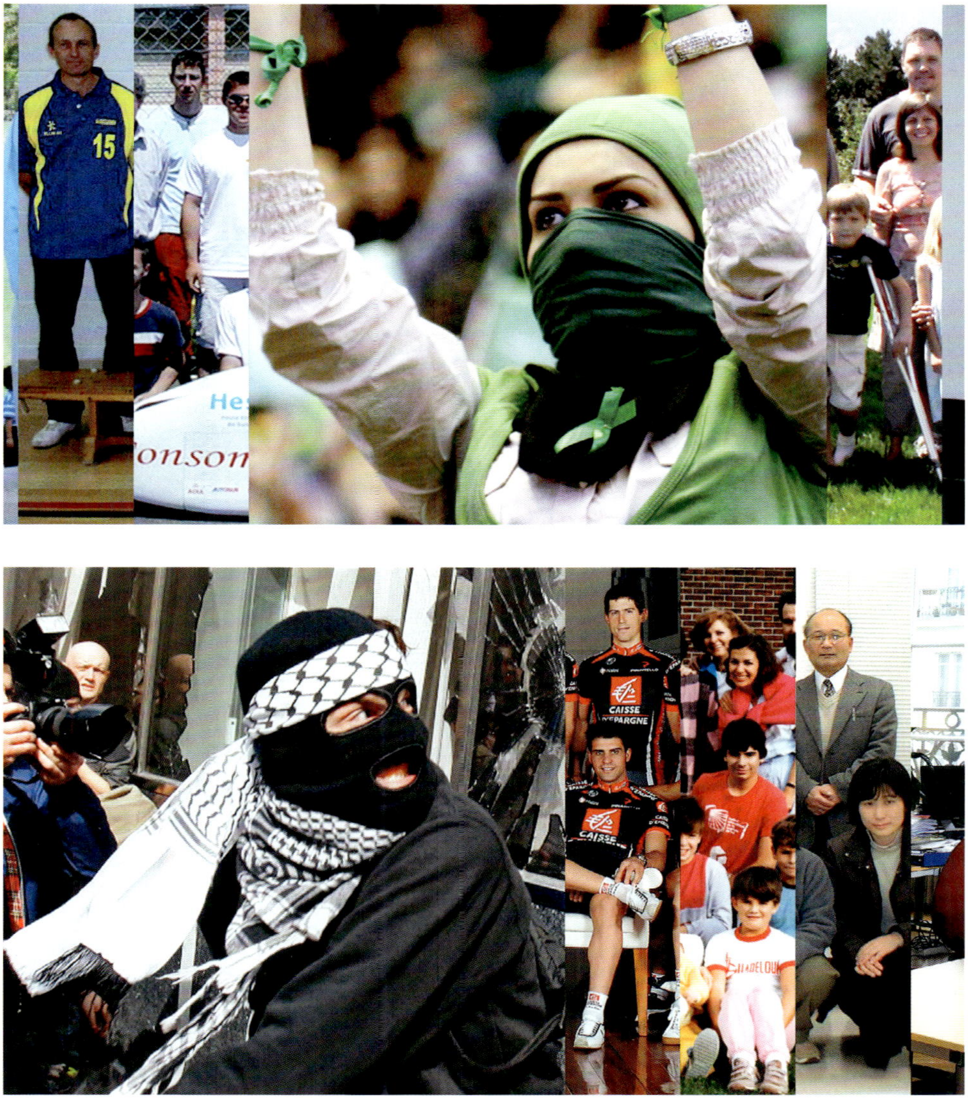

Jean-Gabriel Périot, *The Barbarians*, 2010, video, color, stereo, 5:00 min, video stills

Founded in 1983
UK

http://platformlondon.org

Platform

The nonprofit organization Platform, which comprises multiple strands of activity, namely, the arts, activism, education, and research, was founded in London in 1983. Platform organizes exhibitions, events, publications, and seminars, which focus especially on the social, economic, and ecopolitical effects of the global oil industry. Platform operates through collective decision-making and has implemented a social justice waging system that foresees the same core salary for all members and takes into account factors such as the number of dependents and inherited wealth. It comprises activists, artists, and researchers who collaborate on long-term projects and have been engaged in artistic, activist, and political movements.

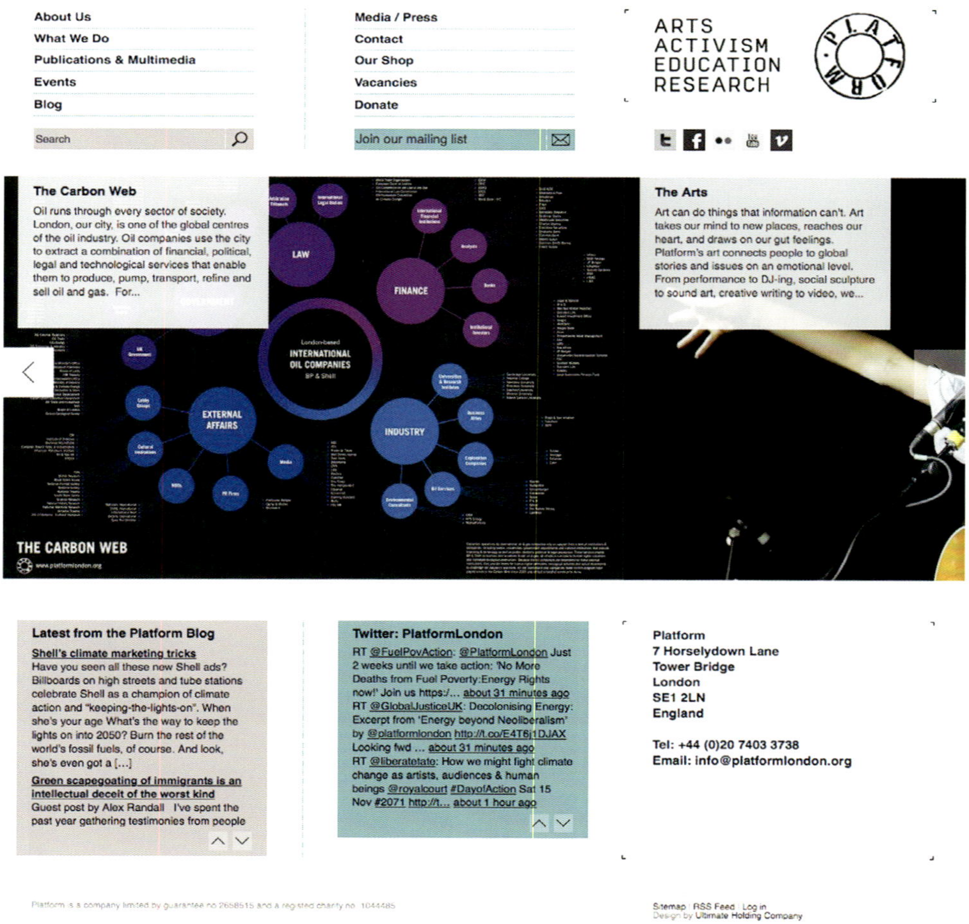

Platform, screenshot from the website, 11/14/2014

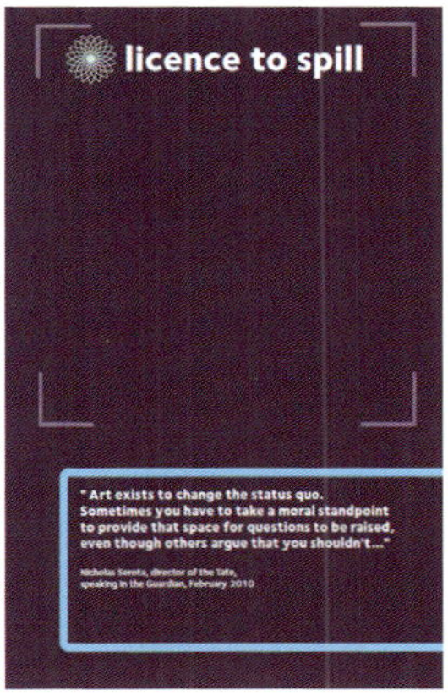

Platform, *Licence to Spill*, 2010, cover of the brochure

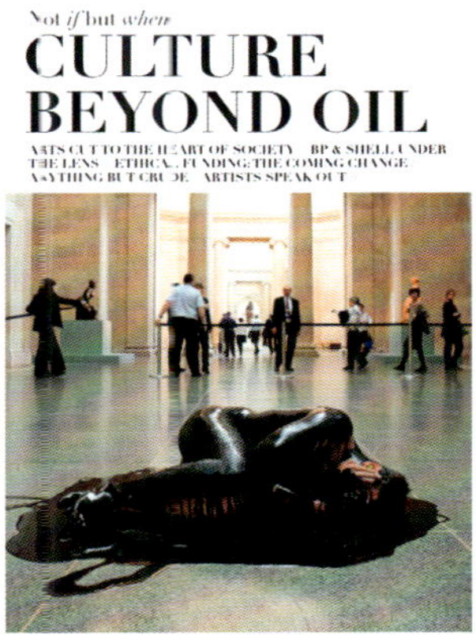

Platform, *Not If but When. Culture Beyond Oil*, 2011, cover of the publication

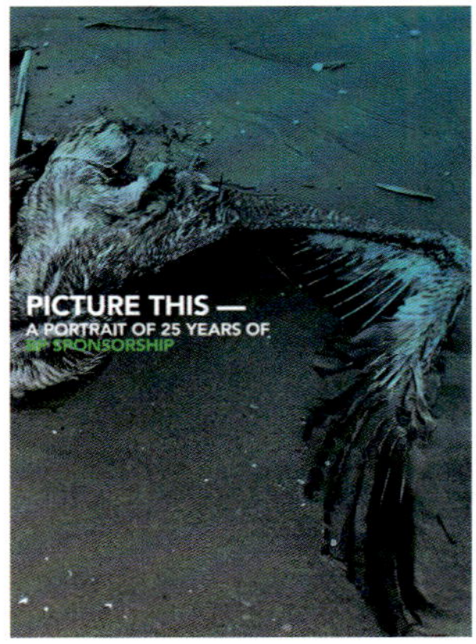

Platform, *Picture This – A Portrait of 25 Years of BP Sponsorship*, 2014, cover of the report

Platform seeks to “combine the transformatory power of art with the tangible goals of campaigning, the rigor of in-depth research with the vision to promote futures beyond oil.”

Early on, Platform was engaged in street theater and chose an agitprop approach. In the 1980s, Platform supported striking hospital cleaners and their trade union as well as antinuclear protests, and campaigned against cuts in the higher education system. In the late 1980s, environmental issues became a new focus, and Platform established a dialog and exchange with representatives of the German Green activists and direct democracy movements. In the 1990s, Platform carried out the *Still Waters* project, which proposed the activation of London’s buried rivers to generate hydropower. When environmental and human rights activist Ken Saro-Wiwa, together with eight collaborators, was executed by the Nigerian government because of his activist engagement against the destruction of the homeland of the Ogoni people in the Niger Delta by powerful global oil companies, Platform set new priorities: since then, Platform assesses the impact of the operations of oil companies such as BP and Shell on the environment and human rights.

In their long-term project *The Carbon Web*, Platform has been mapping and analyzing the global network of relationships between oil and gas companies, regulators, banks, governmental and cultural institutions, with London being one of the key global centers of the oil industry. Based on this work, carried out for more than a decade, numerous campaigns have been launched, tackling, for instance, the financing of fossil fuel projects by banks and BP’s sponsorship of Tate. In the latter case, Platform sought to find out more about the relationship between Tate and BP that spans more than two decades; BP is Tate’s longest-standing sponsor, with a former BP chief executive serving as chairman of the Tate’s Board of Trustees. In 2010, Platform launched the project *Licence to Spill* and, together with the activist group Art Not Oil, supported several events and a publication of the Liberate Tate collective, dealing with oil sponsorship of the arts. In times of economic crisis, when cultural institutions undergo severe public funding cuts, sponsorship becomes increasingly important; in terms of social responsibility, it can be a delicate issue.

Pussy Riot

Pussy Riot is a Russian feminist punk rock band and activist collective, with variable membership of up to fifteen women, which is critical of the government and the church and the ties between them. Pussy Riot was formed by the members of a short-lived group called Pisya Riot, and two Pussy Riot members, Nadezhda (Nadya) Tolokonnikova and Yekaterina (Kat) Samutsevich, were originally part of the art collective Voina. Voina split up in two eponymous groups in 2009, which resulted in bitter conflicts between the Saint Petersburg group and the Moscow faction, the latter represented by Tolokonnikova and Samutsevich before they joined Pussy Riot.

Pussy Riot became known through their provocative performances and artistic interventions in public spaces that captivated an international audience: they performed in the streets, on Red Square, and they gate-crashed a fashion show. Due to numerous arrests at their illegal performances, for their videos Pussy Riot often recorded songs in advance and filmed on makeshift sets, later combining this material with the footage from the actual performance. Pussy Riot's performances reflect their political views: anti-Putin, feminist, environmentalist, anticapitalist, and advocating the rights of the LGBT community. Their hallmarks are gaudy dresses and colorful woolen balaclavas. Pussy Riot members name punk bands and the Riot Grrrl movement of the 1990s as significant influences. In Russia, Pussy Riot emerged with and inspired a new generation of Russian activist artist groups.

Release the Cobblestones was Pussy Riot's first public performance, which took place on scaffolding in a subway station in Moscow in November 2011, where they tore apart feather pillows and encouraged Russians to protest the upcoming parliamentary elections. The video of the performance garnered strong media interest. In December 2011, Pussy Riot performed an illegal show on top of a detention center where political prisoners were being held because of their participation in a protest against the elections. The band hung up a banner and sang their song *Death to Prison, Freedom to Protests*, which the detainees were able to watch. A YouTube video of the show reached more than 60,000 viewers.

After the punk prayer "Mother of God, Chase Putin Away!" performed by five members of Pussy Riot in the Cathedral of Christ the Savior (a highly symbolic building, destroyed in the 1930s during the rule of Joseph Stalin) in Moscow near the Kremlin in February 2012, in which they also commented on the close ties of the Russian Orthodox Church to President Vladimir Putin, three Pussy Rioters were arrested: Maria (Masha) Alyokhina, Nadezhda Tolokonnikova, and Yekaterina Samutsevich. They pleaded not guilty, claiming that their performance was a political, not an antireligious statement. While the sentence against Samutsevich was suspended, her fellow protesters were convicted to two years in penal colonies for hooliganism motivated by religious hatred. Their imprisonment caused reactions from U.S. and European foreign ministries, calling the conviction disproportionate, and was on the news for several months. People from all over the world declared their solidarity with the activists in public demonstrations. While the overall public opinion in Russia has been rather critical towards

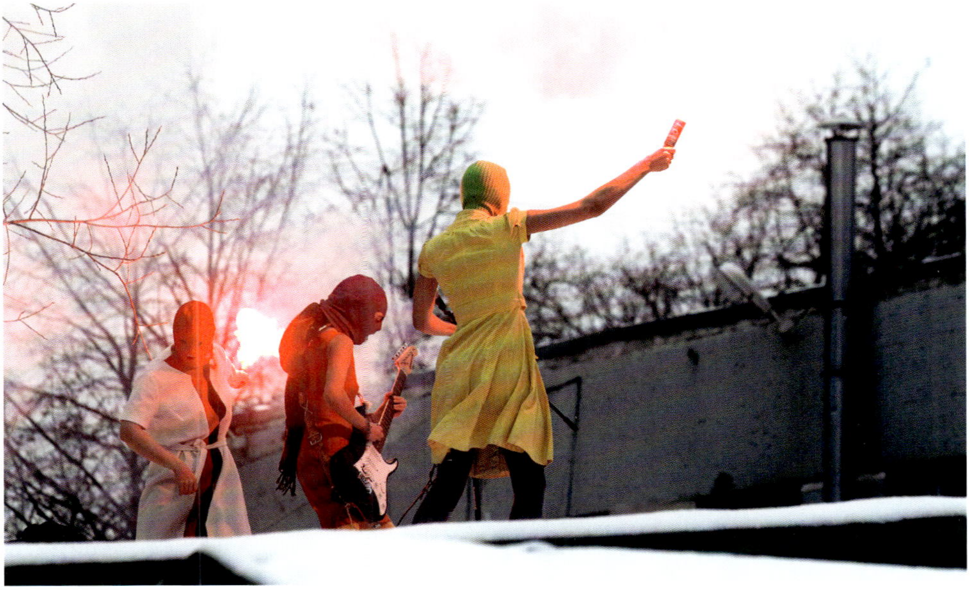

Pussy Riot, *Death to Prison, Freedom to Protests*, December 2011, performance on the rooftop of a detention center in Moscow

Pussy Riot and Russians seem to remain distinctly uncomfortable with the feminist activists, including liberal opposition leaders, Pussy Riot has become the "flagship group" of Russian art activism: They became pop stars with mass appeal especially in Western countries, and many prominent politicians, artists, and human rights organizations expressed their support and concern. In August 2012, near the end of the court case, Pussy Riot released *Putin Lights Up the Fires*, which was about the arrests and trial. Alyokhina and Tolokonnikova were released because of a presidential amnesty in December 2013, but have remained under the close surveillance of the state security services. They filed suit at the European Court of Human Rights against their arrest and detention.

In February 2014 an anonymous statement on behalf of several Pussy Riot members was published, announcing that Alyokhina and Tolokonnikova were not members of the group anymore. Yet both of them attempted to perform as Pussy Riot alongside the Winter Olympics in Sotchi where they were attacked with pepper spray and whips by Cossack security staff when singing their song *Putin Will Teach You to Love the Motherland*. To date, this was their last performance; as Tolokonnikova stated in an interview with the *Guardian*, currently, in view of the Ukraine crisis, ironic performance does not seem to be an appropriate means of protest. Tolokonnikova and Alyokhina set up the prison reform project Zona Prava [Justice Zone] and launched the independent news agency website MediaZona, and in September 2014 Tolokonnikova's correspondence with philosopher Slavoj Žižek during her imprisonment was published.

From October to December 2014, the Garage Museum of Contemporary Art in Moscow presented the exhibition *Russian Performance: A Cartography of Its History* that contextualized contemporary activist artist groups in the long lineage and history of Russian performance art, from the Futurists to Pussy Riot.

R.E.P.

R.E.P. stands for "Revolutionary Experimental Space" and is a Ukrainian collective of six young artists, founded in 2004. Since 2006 its members are Ksenia Gnylitska, Nikita Kadan, Zhanna Kadyrova, Lesia Khomenko, Volodymyr Kuznetsov, and Lada Nakonechna. Besides their independent and collective artistic projects, R.E.P. members work as curators, especially featuring artists who are engaged in sociopolitical activism. Members of R.E.P. are also co-founders or members of the Ukrainian curatorial and activist group Hudrada [Creative Committee] and the Art Workers' Self-Defense Initiative ICTM.

When the R.E.P. group was founded, all of its members had already developed their own artistic style, and they have continued in the same vein ever since. However, in all these years the artists have also engaged in collective art practices, thus maintaining their small art community. The political events of the Orange Revolution were a key element in establishing the group. The first collective actions of the R.E.P. took place in the crowd of protesters in Kiev's Maidan Square: it was the collective action of broad masses of society struggling for a common political cause that brought these Ukrainian artists to work together. Another reason for maintaining the group, which is still a factor today, is the weak infrastructure of the Kiev art scene. Lacking an extensive institutional network to support experimental art, artists form associations that substitute for nonexistent institutions. This development is typical not only of the Kiev art community, but for the entire post-Soviet territories, and many other peripheral countries as well. In keeping with the wide and diverse social background of the R.E.P. group, the artists have decided not only to "practice collectivity, but also thematize it." Since 2007 they have been involving other groups in joint projects, presenting various forms of collaboration in one space together.

We Will R.E.P. You (2005) is a documentation of an early action of the R.E.P. group in public space, as a part of their "Intervention" series. Filmed with a shaky hand camera, it shows R.E.P. members during the celebrations to mark the anniversary of the October Revolution on Maidan Square, staging a demonstration and presenting themselves as political activists, alongside communist and nationalist demonstrators. The artists wear absurd black-and-white costumes and make random pronouncements that refer to art ("Does anybody love Andy Warhol like I do?"), which leads to moments of irritation amongst passers-by and other demonstrators and creates peculiar interactions. When right-wing demonstrators from the Ukrainian National Assembly and Ukrainian National Self-Defense party, including an Orthodox priest, enter the scene and R.E.P. try to join the Communist march, the atmosphere becomes tense, and conflicts between "real" and "fake" demonstrators arise.

In a similar performance in 2006, during the election campaigns for the parliamentary elections, the group performed another action in public space in Kiev: *R.E.P. Party*. The group put up its own information stand, and dressed in odd costumes, reminiscent of painters' clothing and radiation protection suits, they presented themselves as a political party. By proclaiming an absurd election program, R.E.P. mocked the superficiality of political slogans and campaigns.

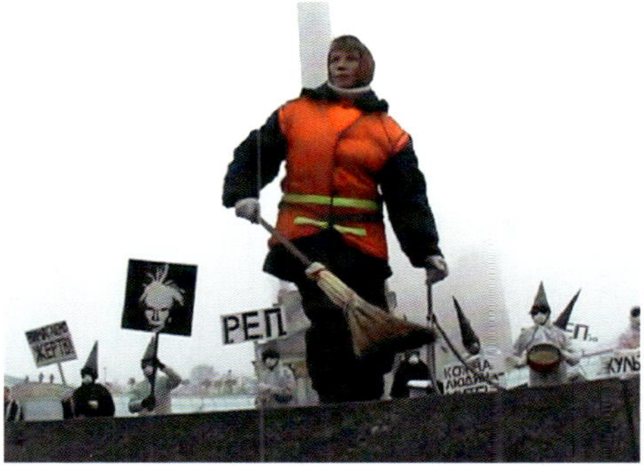

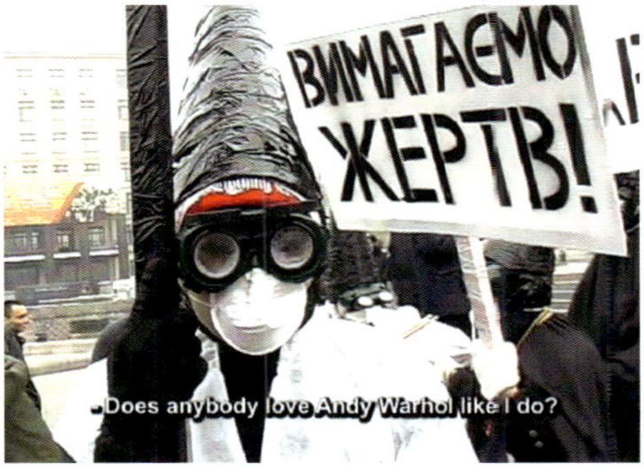

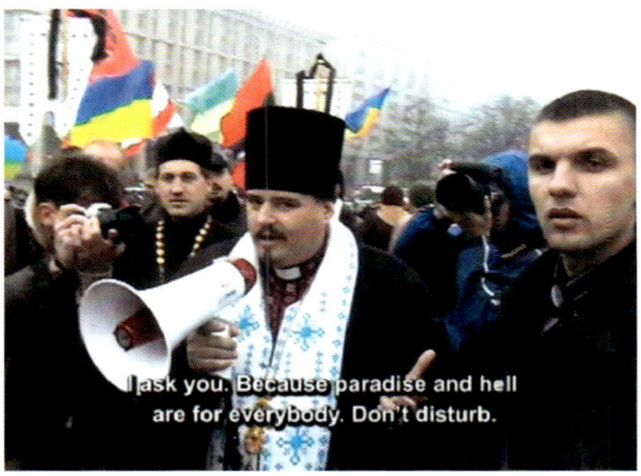

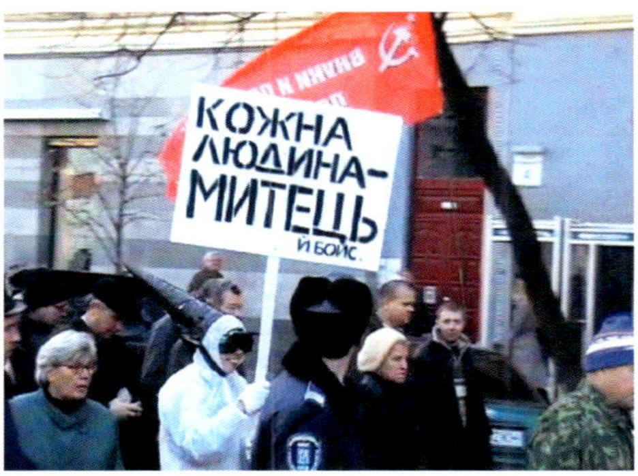

R.E.P., *We Will R.E.P. You*, 2005,
video, color, sound, 10:59 min, video stills

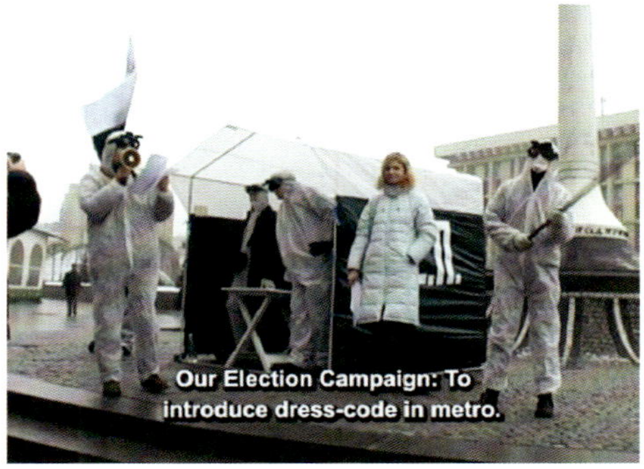

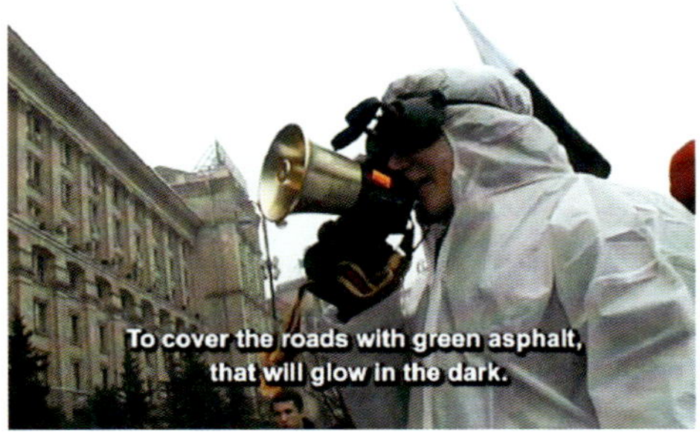

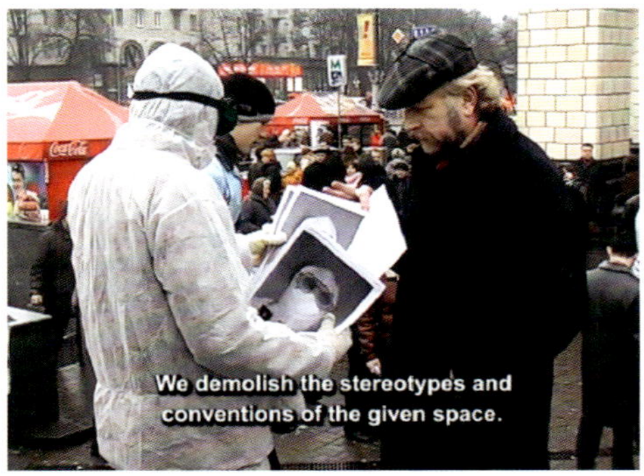

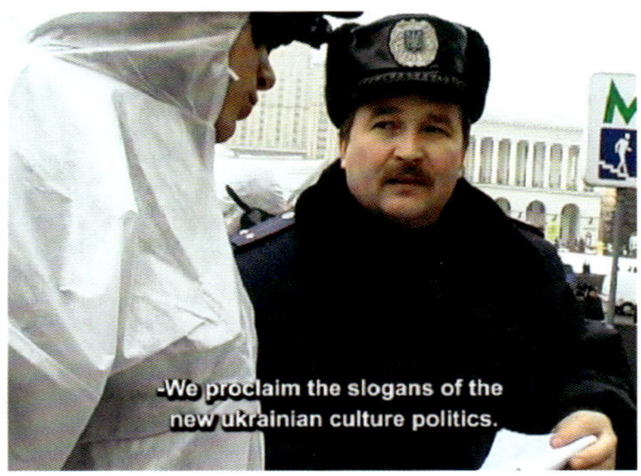

R.E.P., *R.E.P. Party*, 2006,
video, color, sound, 3:42 min, video stills

Itamar Rose *1979 and Yossi Atia *1979

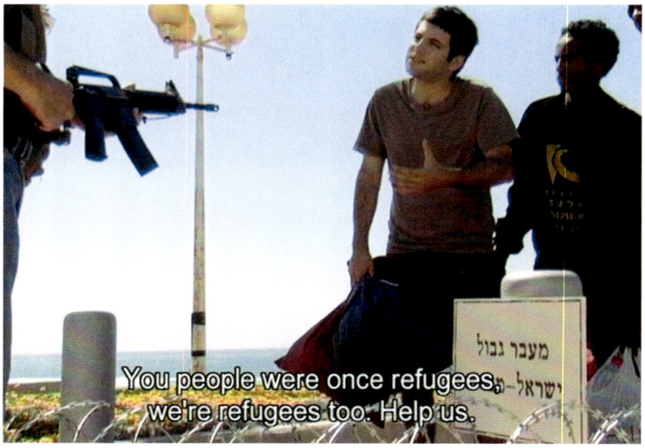

Itamar Rose and Yossi Atia, *Darfur*, 2008, video, color, sound, 4:01 min, video still

The two Israeli video artists and filmmakers Itamar Rose and Yossi Atia started their artistic collaboration in 2005, when they created four satirical films about the Israeli disengagement from the Gaza Strip. Since then, they have made numerous short films together. Combining documentary and strategies of reenactment, Rose and Atia take a satirical approach to charged sociopolitical themes such as racism and immigration, militarization and war. They are fond of engaging with and breaking taboos. Their staged role plays are disturbing, yet not without humor: Rose and Atia aim at making people laugh in order to make them think and create a shift of perspective. Itamar Rose also produces solo works, such as *Israeli Kids in the Army Museum* (2012), a video about the impact of militarization and military education on children that was shot in Israel, but could take place in any country or region at war.

Itamar Rose and Yossi Atia's video work *Darfur* (2008) is a documentary compilation of an artistic intervention in Bat Yam in which they animated passersby in a public space to participate in a theater action and play border guards who turn away refugees from Darfur. The two artists asked passersby about their opinion towards the admission of Sudanese immigrants by the Israeli government. In several cases the answer was, "Put them right back there." When asked to participate in a "little game," "ordinary citizens" volunteered to become actors in an absurd scenario, carefully designed to reveal prejudice, indifference, and aggression in their actions and improvised sets of arguments. Equipped with uniforms and arms, they were supposed to guard the Israeli–Egyptian border, marked on the street by razor wire. An elderly lady, with a sunhat, a striped pink sweater, and a machine gun, asked:

"Who is responsible for what I do?"
"You are."
"Shoot them only in the head?"
"You don't have to kill."
"Can I?"

When a group of actors, including Rose and Atia, playing the Sudanese immigrants, entered the scene, they were stopped and interrogated by the "guards," and when they crossed the symbolic line, a simulated shooting and a disturbing play of law and order began. While one man refused them access ("I have a heart, but these are my orders"), another man agreed to let them in ("Because we are Jews") – and welcomed them with a kiss on the cheek. They walked away, to the tune of *Our Vast Country*.

The subject tackled by Rose and Atia has not lost its relevance: the Israeli government under Benjamin Netanyahu launched a series of strict and controversial immigration policies that also reflect public sentiment, turning increasingly against immigrants from Sudan and Eritrea, with numerous public protests and attacks against them. The government erected a high-tech fence alongside the Egyptian border where most immigrants enter, carried out repatriations via third-party states and arrests, and passed a new amendment to the "Prevention of Infiltration Law" in December 2013 – despite Israel being a signatory party to the UN Refugee Convention – which authorizes the imprisonment of asylum seekers for one year without trial, followed by indefinite detention in "open prison" facilities. The new laws sparked mass acts of civil disobedience and hunger strikes among asylum seekers, and UN Refugee Convention warned that Israel could be breaking international law.

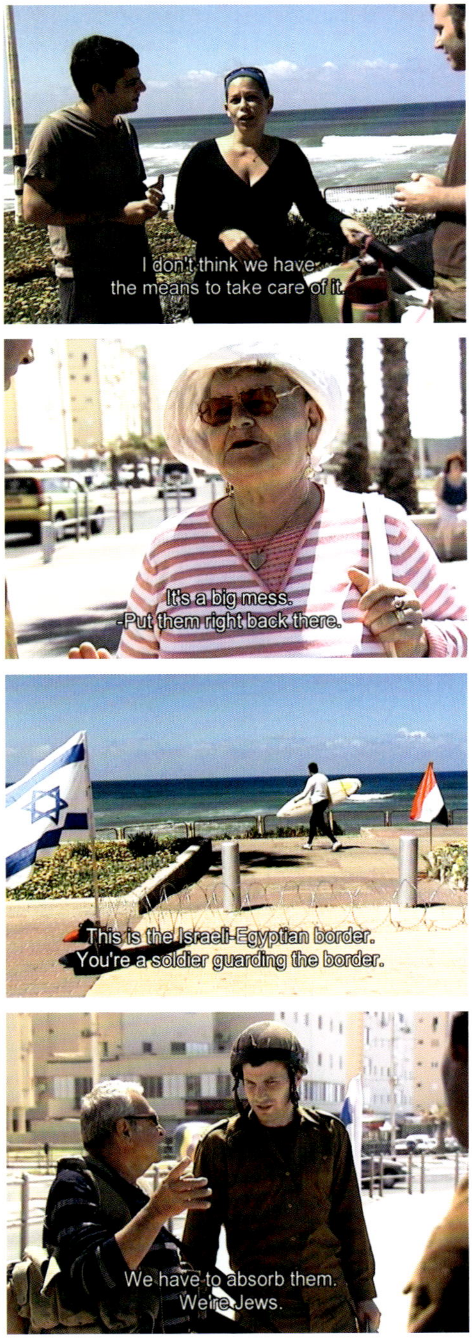

Itamar Rose and Yossi Atia, *Darfur*, 2008, video, color, sound, 4:01 min, video stills

Bahia Shehab *1977

Bahia Shehab is a Lebanese art historian, designer, and artist based in Cairo whose work centers on the history of Arabic script, communication, and design. She is associate professor at The American University in Cairo, executive director of the graphic design agency MI7-Cairo, and currently working on a PhD thesis on Fatimid Kufic inscriptions on portable items in the Mediterranean basin and beyond. In 2011 she published a comprehensive book on the history, significance, and development of *lam-alif*, the Arabic script for "no," and the rich visual cultural heritage of the Arab world, *A Thousand Times NO. The Visual History of Lam-Alif.* During the Egyptian revolution in 2011, she started a street art campaign to raise awareness of political, social, and economic injustices and received international acclaim. Mostly during the night, Shehab sprayed her messages as signs of protest of an Arab citizen, a woman, an artist:

"No to dictatorship,"
"No to violence,"
"No to military rule," and
"No to the stripping of people"

– the latter, together with a tag of a blue bra, alludes to the shameful public beating and stripping of a young veiled woman by the Egyptian military, the images of which became iconic as symbols for violence against women during the Egyptian uprising.

In her series *The Story of a Wall in Cairo* (2011–2013), Bahia Shehab captured the tags and works of several street artists in Cairo. Their work has become part of the city, its culture, and spirit; in her projection series, Shehab records and documents these ephemeral works that tell different stories about Cairo, the revolution, and beyond.

Bahia Shehab wrote about her series in November 2013:

"On the walls of Cairo we constantly hold ongoing conversations with each other and with the people on the street. Even when our work is erased, it is a form of conversation; you say something and another person says: 'I don't want to hear it.' Like many of the street artists in Cairo, I chose to tell stories on the city's walls. We try to document Egypt's ongoing struggle for justice and freedom. Most of the time different factions erase our work, but that does not stop us from going down to the streets over and over again. I chose to share the story of one wall in Cairo and the stories and work of the various artists who have contributed to the wall and whose works no longer exist. Every wall we spray becomes a conversation – an open invitation for people to comment on or just look at and contemplate or ignore completely. Each and every thing we paint becomes an idea that has a life of its own, where passersby have the right to add, take away, or eventually eliminate altogether. On the streets our work is alive; people pass by it every day on their way to work, or when they go to buy groceries. By posting our work online we give it a new form of life and a new meaning. We share our messages not just with the inhabitants of Cairo or the inhabitants of Egypt, but send our messages to the whole world. We keep telling the story of the revolution on the streets in the hope that we can change our future and the future of an entire nation. The fact that the work gets covered over is insignificant; keeping the conversation going is what is important."

Bahia Shehab, *The Story of a Wall in Cairo*, 2011–2013, photos for the projection of a PowerPoint slideshow

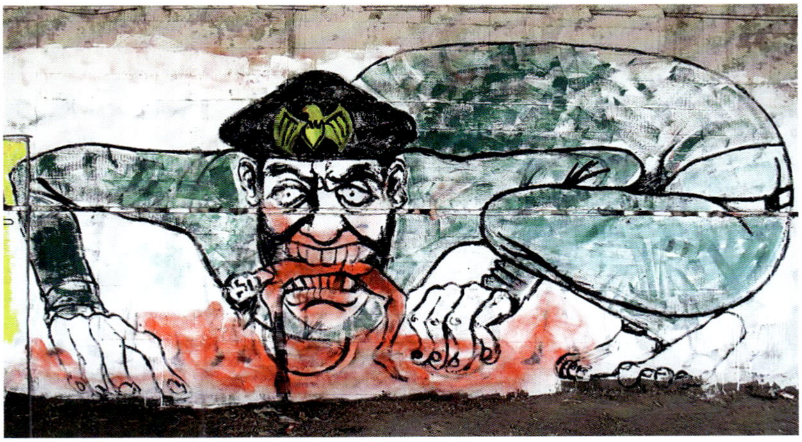

Mohamed Khalid, *Tantawi Maiden-Eating Monster* (closeup), January 2012

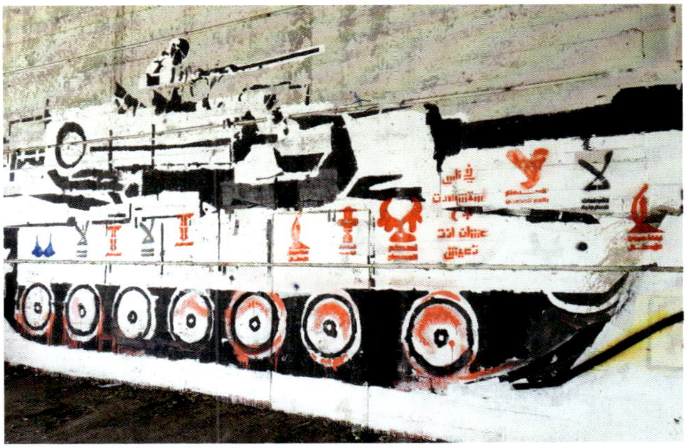

Bahia Shehab, *A Thousand Times No* (closeup), March 2012

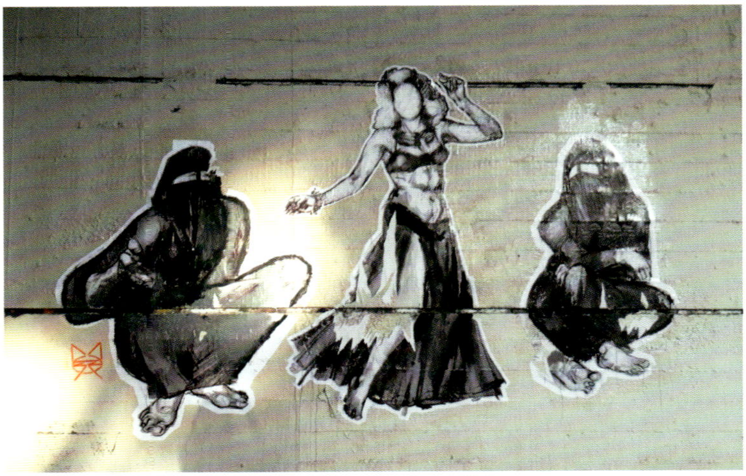

Anonymous, *Damaged Belly Dancer*, June 2013

Founded in 2005
Ukraine

www.soskagroup.com

SOSka group

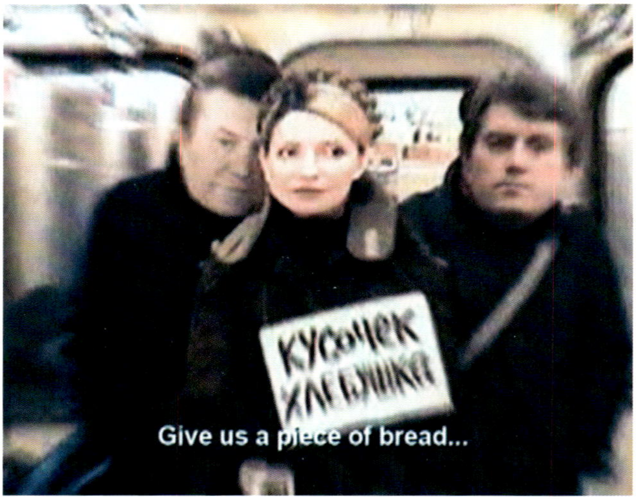

SOSka group, *They Trapped on Streets*, 2006, video, color, sound, 1:28 min, video still

SOSka group is part of a post-Soviet wave of socially engaged artists and was founded in October 2005 by Ukrainian artists Mykola Ridnyi (*1985), Serhiy Popov (*1978), and Ganna Kriventsova (*1985) in Kharkiv – the city that still cherishes the memory of the bygone days when it was the capital of the Ukrainian Soviet Socialist Republic, and takes special pride in its artistic traditions which reach back to the cultural avant-garde and political utopian period of the 1920s. Currently, SOSka group's members include Mykola Ridnyi and Serhiy Popov. Social and political issues and inequalities are the main themes of SOSka group's projects that are often situated between art and activism.
At the center of SOSka group's work is the notion that the processes and problems of the contemporary art system are strongly connected to the social environment and the political context. SOSka group explores problems of the binary nature of neoliberalism, taking the example of relations between society and art: poverty of the people and commercialization of art objects; street protests and the attractiveness of contemporary art exhibitions.

SOSka group creates performances, does research, participates in exhibitions, and is engaged in curatorial activities and activist practices that focus on self-organization and community building, as alternatives to the principles and models deriving from the current neoliberal system. From 2005 to 2012, SOSka group ran the SOSka gallery-lab, an art space and independent cultural platform based on do-it-yourself principles to foster and develop the local contemporary art scene in Kharkiv, where the group curated exhibitions and hosted a regular events program. SOSka group curated the exhibition *The New History* (2009) at the Kharkiv Art Museum, an intervention of contemporary art in a traditional museum that caused a veritable scandal: because of the controversial nature of several exhibits, the museum director closed the show and destroyed an artwork by David Ter-Oganyan. From 2011 to 2013

SOSka group co-organized the Days of Apartment Exhibitions, a festival of self-organized exhibitions in Kharkiv.

In their early video work *They Trapped on Streets* (2006), documenting a series of actions in public places on the eve of the Ukraine parliamentary elections in Kiev and Kharkiv in 2006, SOSka group played homeless people and wore masks with the faces of major Ukrainian politicians: the president, the prime minister, and the opposition leader. The process of asking passersby for money can be seen as both a direct metaphor for the electoral spectacle of winning votes by means of the glut of political campaigning in the media, and as a subversive action that not only deconstructs the image of powerful political leaders, but also addresses the problem of homelessness and poverty, as well as the divide between the electoral masses and political leaders.

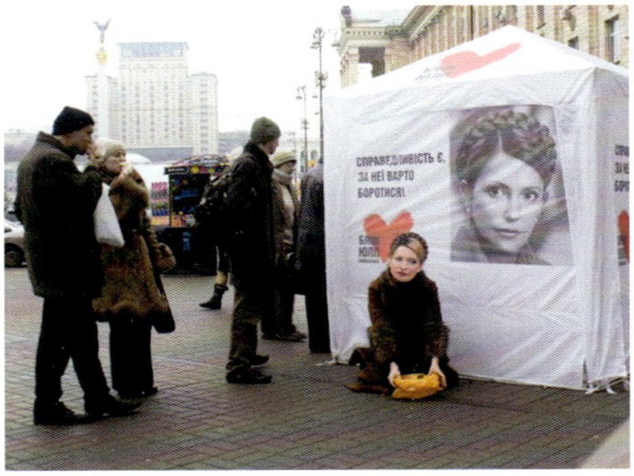

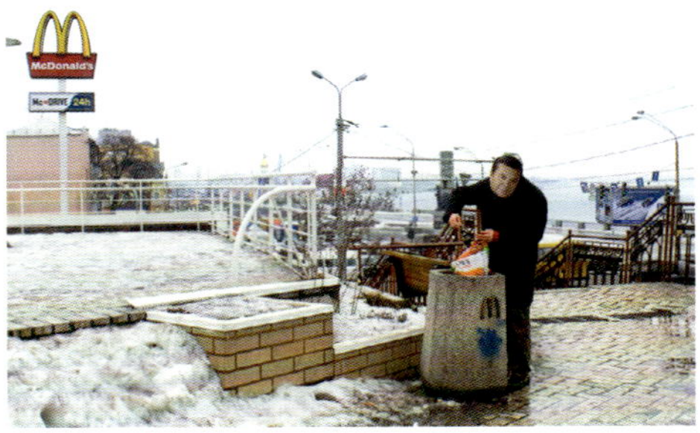

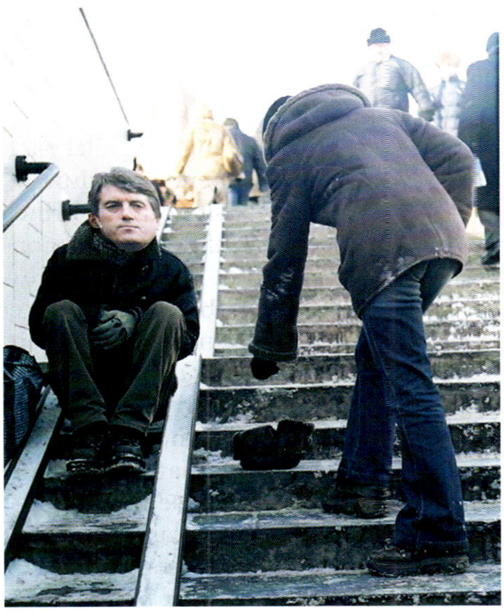

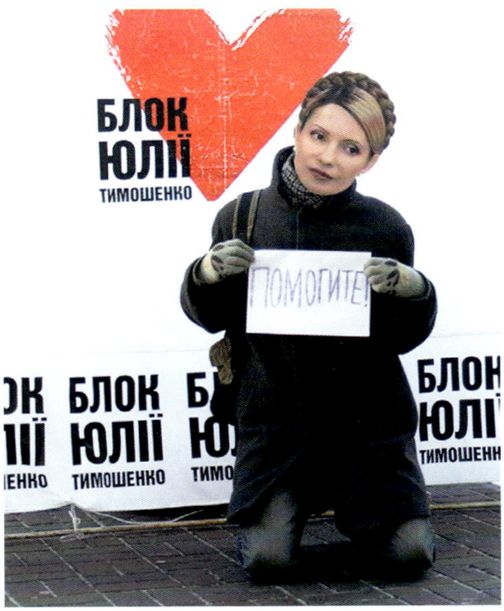

SOSka group, *They Trapped on Streets*, 2006, video, color, sound, 1:28 min, video stills

Joulia Strauss *1974 with Moritz Mattern *1981

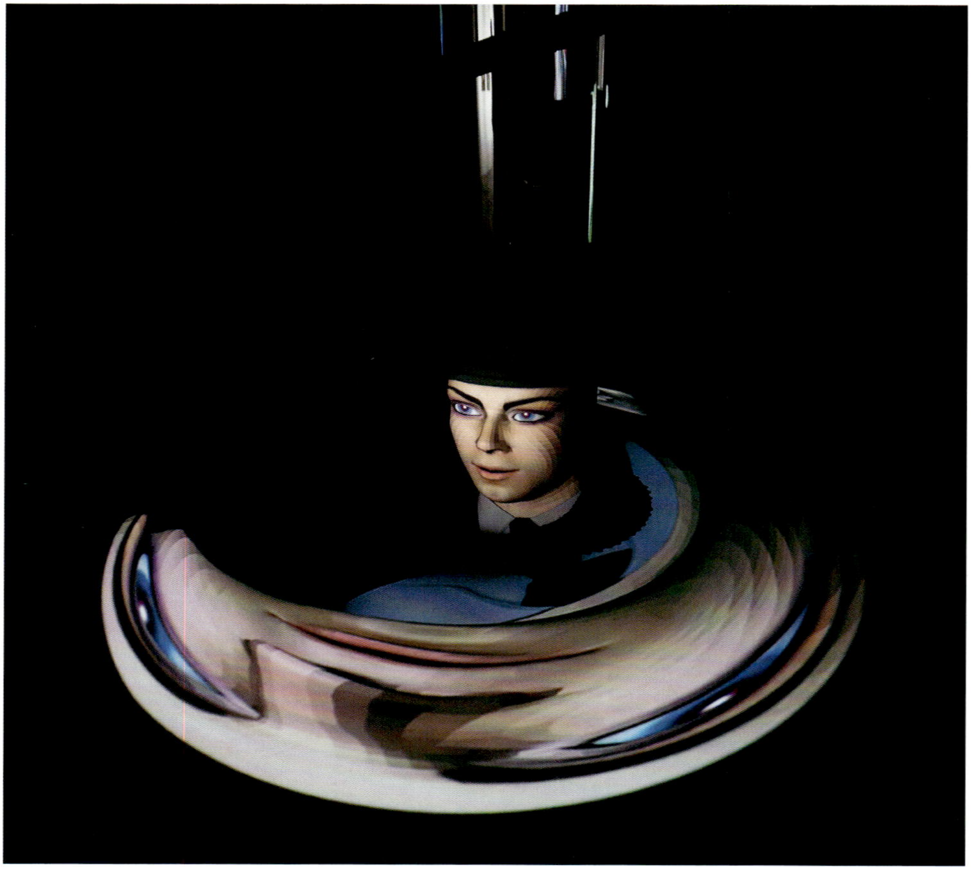

Joulia Strauss with Moritz Mattern, *Anamorphous Monument to Chelsea Manning*, 2010/2013, installation, mixed media, installation view, ZKM | Karlsruhe, 2014

Joulia Strauss is a Berlin-based artist and activist who is originally from the Mari El Republic in the Volga Federal District of the Russian Federation, a minority community of approximately 700,000 people with a rich tradition in performing arts. Strauss studied at the New Academy of Fine Arts in Saint Petersburg (as the only woman in an exclusively male environment) where she was classically trained as a sculptor. She contributed significantly to the Russian Neoacademist art movement in the 1990s, before relocating to study at the Berlin University of the Arts. From 2000 to 2005 she was involved in the artist-run platform art_science which fosters interdisciplinary artistic research projects and exchanges between scientists and artists. In her works she creates "sculptural systems" that embody archaic knowledge structures, which she develops with digital simulation technologies. Together with music scientist and media philosopher Martin Carlé, Strauss worked on a project called *Cat-Notation*, dedicated to the reconstruction of excavated fragments of Ancient Greek music notations and their translation into 3-D animal sculptures which embody mathematical operations. For a video for the reconstruction and performance of the *First Delphic Hymn to Apollon* from ca 138 B.C.E., Strauss collaborated with 3-D artist Moritz Mattern, who is an expert in the modeling of 3-D interiors for real-time analysis.

The mixed-media installation *Anamorphous Monument to Chelsea Manning* (2010/2013) was created when whistle-blower Chelsea (then Bradley) Manning – who leaked classified documents to the disclosure portal WikiLeaks in 2010, was arrested in the same year, and convicted of violations of the U.S. Espionage Act and other offenses in 2013 – was portrayed as traitor in the U.S. media. The 3-D video sculpture dedicated to Manning was produced for the 2011 Moscow Biennale and sought to create a counterportrait to the biased, distorted media representations. Its sound track, a quote by Manning, explains Manning's motivation and puts it in a new perspective; in the background, a reconstruction of the musical fragment of *Orestes* by Euripides, played by Strauss, can be heard. The 3-D sculpture has female features and also simulates the process and progress of Manning's gender transformation.

Manning had already started to give her gender identity a digital presence on social media before the WikiLeaks scandal broke. After Manning was sentenced to 35 years of confinement, she published a press release: "As I transition into this next phase of my life, I want everyone to know the real me. I am Chelsea Manning. I am a female." Manning wants to undergo hormone therapy, a treatment commonly available for civilians diagnosed with gender identity disorders but not for U.S. military prisoners. Although Manning's name was officially and legally changed to Chelsea Elizabeth Manning in 2014, and Bradley Manning ceased to exist, the army does not acknowledge transgender individuals who are ineligible to serve. For the military, only Bradley Manning exists.

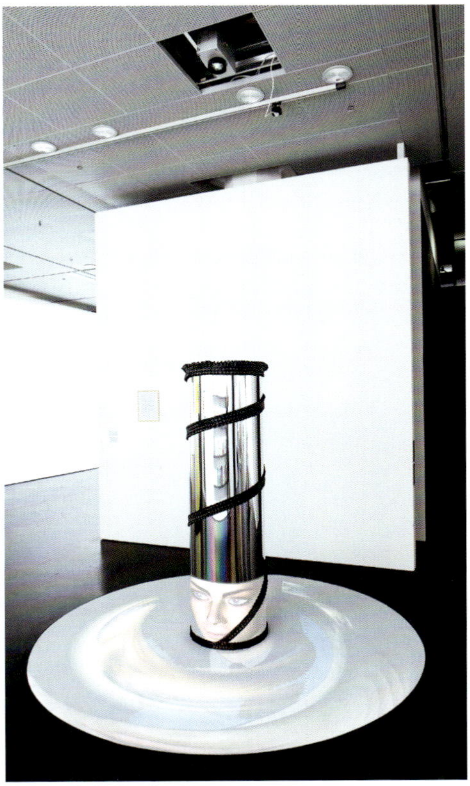

Joulia Strauss with Moritz Mattern, *Anamorphous Monument to Chelsea Manning*, 2010/2013, installation, mixed media

Jackie Sumell *1973

Jackie Sumell is a New Orleans-based artist and activist who engages with America's history of institutionalized racism and its culture of torture in her artistic interventions, workshops, and lectures. Her work focuses on the practice of long-term solitary confinement and fosters dialog around the overuse of this practice and the cruel, unusual, and inhumane punishment in American prisons. Sumell became known through her decade-long collaboration with U.S. human rights activist and long-term prisoner Herman Wallace (1941–2013); her work received widespread critical acclaim, and she was awarded the 2013 Soros Justice Fellowship of the Open Society Foundations.

Herman Wallace was a U.S. human rights activist and member of the Black Panther movement; for a conviction based on questionable evidence he spent over 41 years in solitary confinement in Louisiana State Penitentiary – the longest period of solitary confinement in the history of the U.S. penal system. In 2001, the year her project began, Sumell worked as an environmental organizer in San Francisco; when she met a member of the inmate crew known as "Angola 3," fighting for prisoners' rights, she initiated a correspondence with Angola 3 member Herman Wallace that would last for more than a decade. For an architecture assignment at Stanford University, she explored the following question: "What kind of house does a man who has lived in a six-foot-by-nine-foot box for over thirty years dream of?" Wallace, confined to a tiny cell and isolated for 23 hours a day, started to imagine a house, his house: He began with ideas and details such as a garden with flowers and a swimming pool. Over the years, Wallace and Sumell created drawings, plans, and designs for a complete house (including a hot tub of exactly the size of his cell). Wallace said, "[This project] helps me to maintain what little sanity I have left, to maintain my humanity and dignity."

Sumell drew blueprints, built models, and produced 3-D renderings. For her installation, she also created a model of Herman Wallace's cell so that visitors could experience physical confinement. She initiated an awareness campaign and fundraising activities to actually build Herman Wallace's house.

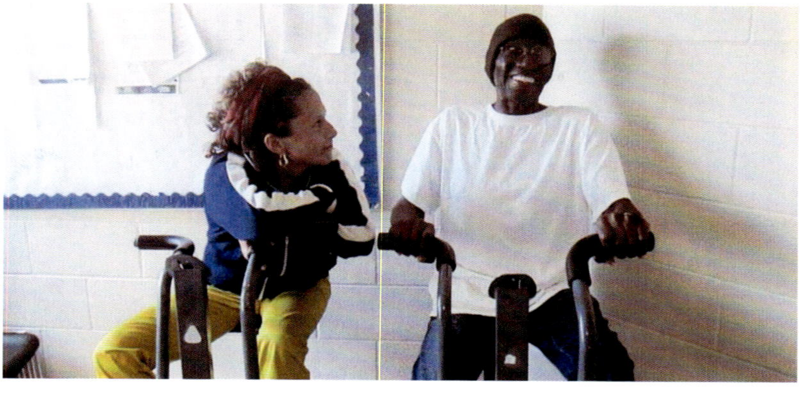

Jackie Sumell and Herman Wallace, Elayn Hunt Prison, Louisiana, August 2013

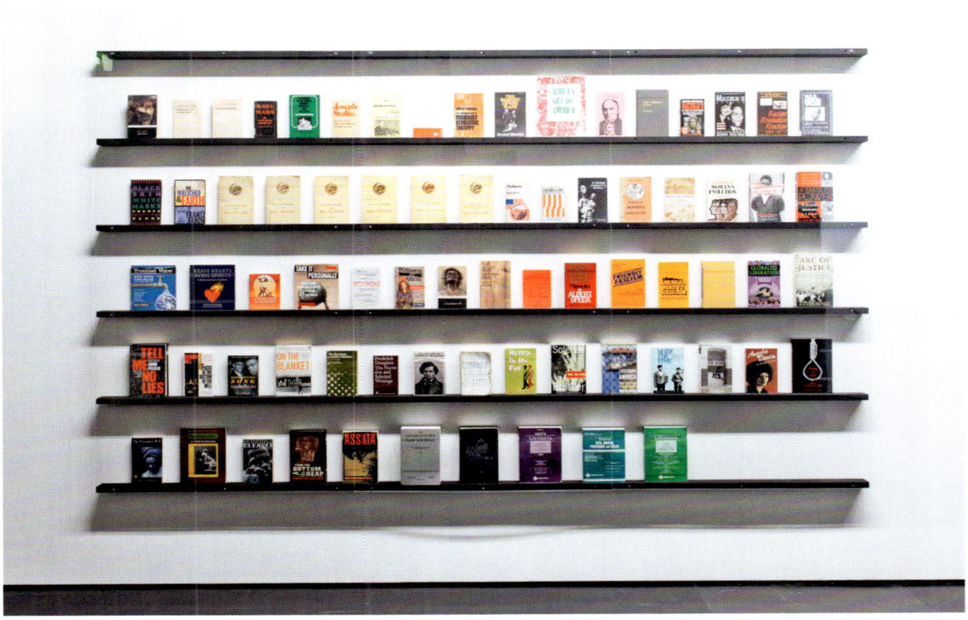

Jackie Sumell, *The House That Herman Built: Herman's Library*, 2010, installation, mixed media, installation view, ZKM | Karlsruhe, 2014

In October 2013, Wallace's conviction was overturned, and he was released from prison. He died only a few days later. After his death, Sumell has continued to pursue her plans to build the house: to honor Wallace and to create a symbol of resistance and the power of imagination. Herman's House should become a community center in New Orleans.

Sumell's correspondence and collaboration with Herman Wallace was documented in a book, published in 2006, and in numerous exhibitions; it is also the subject of Angad Singh Bhalla's debut feature documentary *Herman's House* (2013). An interactive documentary in the form of a Web-based platform, *Inside Herman's House*, is in production. Herman's House was first exhibited at Akademie Schloss Solitude in Stuttgart, Germany, in 2006, and in 2010, the library of the planned house *(The House That Herman Built: Herman's Library)* was installed there.

Jackie Sumell

The Best Activism Is Always Equal Parts Love and Equal Parts Anger

In capitalist societies, particularly in the West, historical social patterning, consumer pressure, and hierarchical power structures reduce the wonderful complexities of personal experience to a system of relative binaries. This simplification provides the theoretical foundations and social mechanisms for systems of mass incarceration, wrongful conviction, oversentencing, and abuses of power such as solitary confinement. The decade-long collaborative work of political prisoner and Black Panther Herman Wallace and Jackie Sumell has become an entry point for critical analysis – exposing preconceived notions of justice and punishment as binaries (guilty/innocent, good/bad, right/wrong).

At present, more than 80,000 people are held in isolation in U.S. jails, prisons, and detention centers. Solitary confinement places prisoners in single cell isolation for a minimum of twenty-three hours a day, seven days a week. The context of this struggle is informed by the reality that the United States is the greatest incarcerator in the world, maintaining 5 percent of the world's population and 25 percent of its prison population. 97 percent of those who are incarcerated will be released back into our communities.

The U.S. Correctional System is a mechanism of the empire that returns prisoners to society more damaged than when they entered, and thus perpetuates a profit-based system of incarceration that is relegated by patriarchal power structure and a fetishized culture of punishment. We must examine the entire culture of punishment in order to contextualize the significance of solitary confinement within a prison, and the prison as solitary confinement to society.

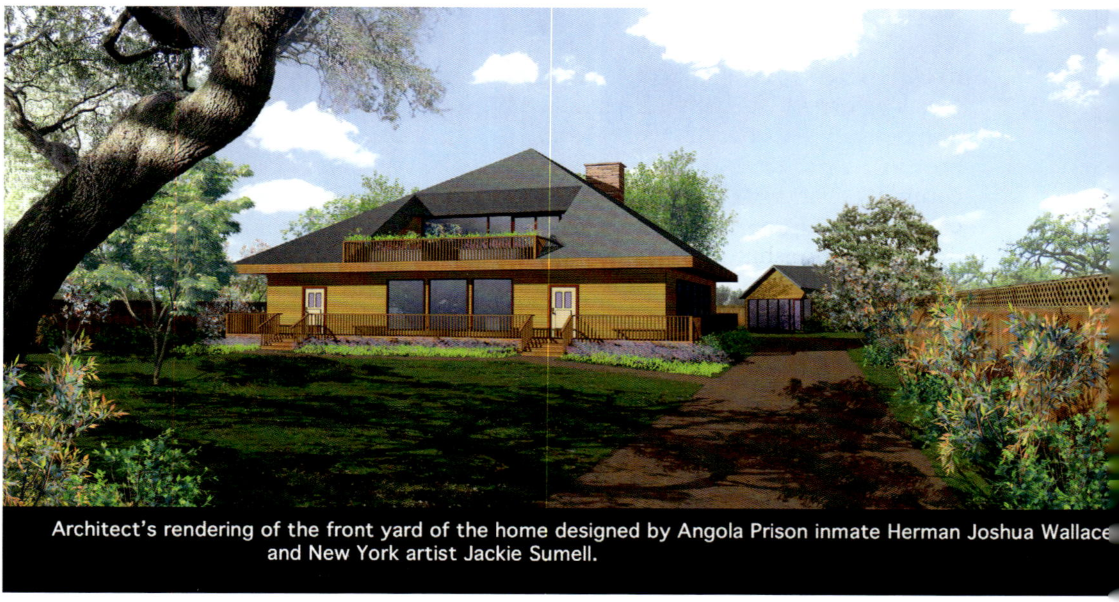

Architect's rendering of the front yard of the home designed by Angola Prison inmate Herman Joshua Wallace and New York artist Jackie Sumell.

CAD still of Herman's House, 2007

The work we do (as artists, activists, parents, teachers, attorneys, bankers, ice cream makers, human doings, or human beings) should interrupt the status quo's binary system and repair the collective imagination. All too often the space of wonder and invention is consumed by a flavor of ego or confusion – thus rendering society so creatively impotent that it defaults to patterns of exclusion and capital hierarchy. Those that have access are responsible to further the momentum of compassion and social justice. We have a responsibility to expose the multiple dimensions of inequality by putting forth creative-visible-powerful arguments surrounding decarceration and prison abolition. We need to steward meaningful relationships that cultivate the compassion, education, and debate needed to transform public perceptions of (invisible) prisoners into (visible) persons. As human doings (formerly known as activists), it is important not to let our disciplines become our identity and ultimately discipline our activity. By dissolving the prescribed binary structure of personal identity, we radicalize an understanding of the prison industrial complex, climate of punishment, and can transform these practices into a deeper relationship to universal compassion, reform, and rehabilitation.

The heart of our work will engage a provocative debate that questions the landscape of prisons, punishment, and the climate of torture such that it challenges preconceived notions of justice as a system of binaries. To do so, this conversation must confront linear readings of history by making visible a shared blueprint of racialized inequality. Today our prisons, jails, and detention centers house more than twice as many people suffering from mental illness than all the psychiatric hospitals in the United States combined. From the creative positioning of compassion, we must implicitly question why the only solution for social problems such as mental illness, addiction, illiteracy, and poverty has become the prison industrial complex.

Herman Wallace wrongfully spent almost 42 years in solitary confinement before being released in October 2013 – he died less than four days later. Herman's story is at the center of *The House That Herman Built*. The process of this project manifested a complex, thirteen-year friendship between Herman Wallace and Jackie Sumell, ultimately exposing the inside of the prison industrial complex. This led to a revealing critique of mass incarceration as well as introductions to many people who have survived the impossible burden of wrongful conviction, solitary confinement, and cruel and unusual punishment. This project has become a contemporary Trojan horse, making visible the active and inactive (through complacency) participation of viewers into these systems worldwide. Herman's House has thus infiltrated the museum industrial complex with an illuminating view of the prison industrial complex. Now that these similarities in power structure have been established, we must ask ourselves why we allow them to continue.

All Power to the People

VII

OK, as you see I tried to put the cell together to give you some idea of how we live in CCR- The front is actually a cage as you see it. The window in my cell is actually that large allowing me to open & close the 2 ~~bott~~ bottom windows. There is the table, bed, locker box, sink & toilet. Oops! I fucked up again! I forgot to add the Tray hatch. I put a patch on it! :3 There are cells ajoining, I just did one. You see one you see all.

Don't worry about the P.C. being denied we can over come that.

One More Thing about Rig/ Albert Visiting. When you guys come you all with be able to swap while you are. with me, he will be with Albert and Vice Versa so don't

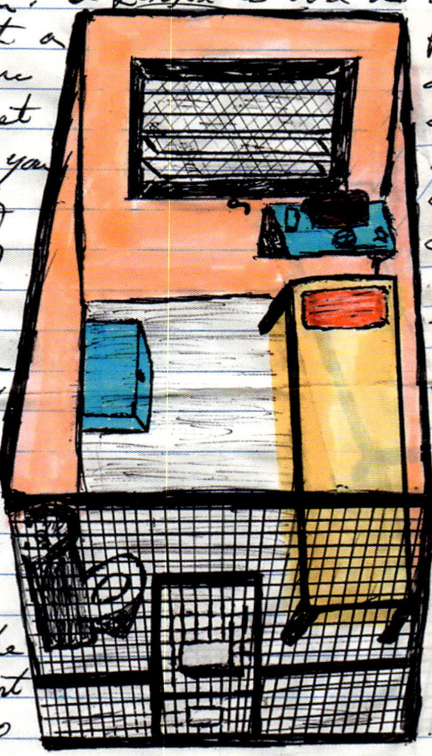

Letter from Herman Wallace to Jackie Sumell, 2003

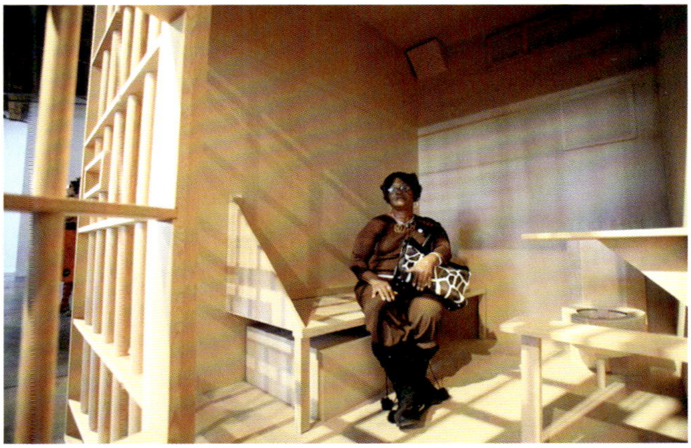

Herman Wallace's sister Vicky sits in Jackie Sumell's installation, a reconstruction of his cell, at the Prospect1 Biennial, New Orleans, 2010

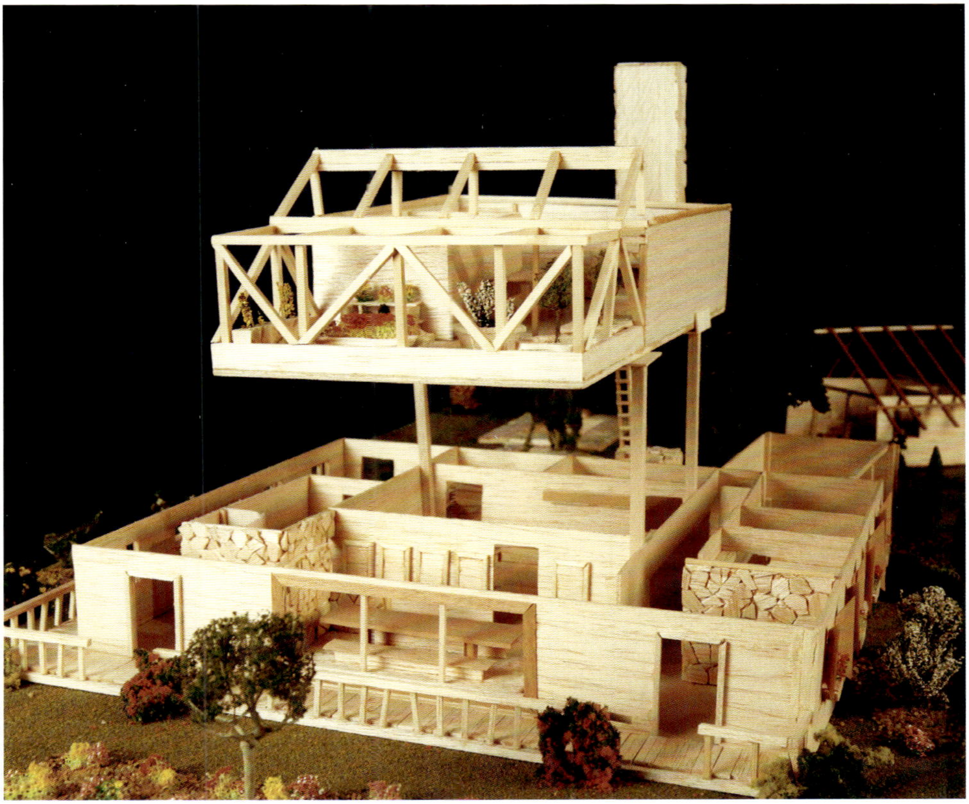

Wooden model of Herman's House, 2007

Founded in 2011
Italy

www.teatrovalleoccupato.it

Teatro Valle Occupato

Teatro Valle is the oldest operating theater in Rome. It was closed in 2011 due to budget cuts in government-run arts and culture programs, but a few months later, it was occupied by a group of art activists with professional backgrounds in theater and cinema and since then has been turned into a center for producing and presenting new culture. Ever since, the activists have put on their own theater program and performances, and travel as a group to international activist events such as Blockupy Frankfurt in Germany. They define occupation as a collective political practice, a gesture of reappropriation which institutes an open space, a project to share with companies, artists, and operators from Italy and Europe in order to activate a different way of making politics without delegation and to practice a different way of working, creating, and producing. Their main aim is to connect activists, institutions, artists, and persons who organize resistance and self-governance everywhere; persons who do not conform but create different modalities of production, persons who fight for the common good.

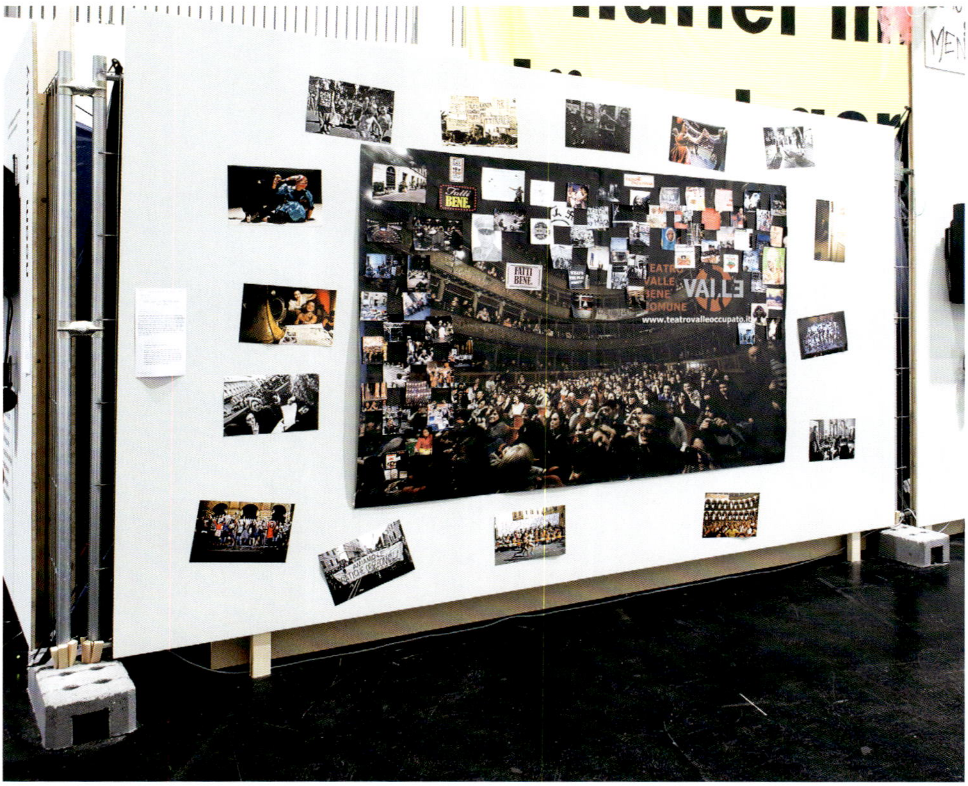

Teatro Valle Occupato, *Dal 14 giugno 2011 per sempre*, 2011–2013, installation, mixed media, installation view, ZKM | Karlsruhe, 2014

Ugo Mattei

The Valle Theater Commons Foundation: How to Deploy the Law in Current and Future Struggles

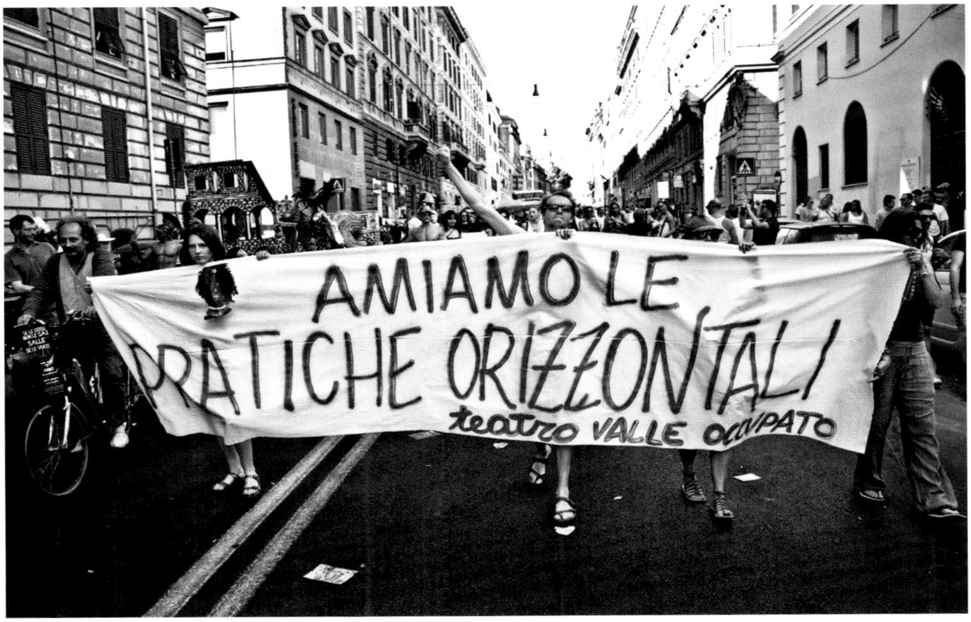

Teatro Valle Occupato, photo from the mixed-media installation *Dal 14 giugno 2011 per sempre*, 2011–2013

Introduction

I have often written that the commons are not specific kinds of goods (*Sachen*), inanimate objects of the outside world. Any positivistic attitude that separates the world of the subject from that of the object, that of *being* from that of the *should be*, is ill-suited to understand their nature.[1] Every common inextricably links a collective subjectivity (made up of needs, sounds, scents, and desires) with its vital space, often but not necessarily a sharable physical object. Thus, it is best to understand the commoning as a quality relationship comparable to that linking every living organism to its ecosystem.

The commons emerge from a constituent collective struggle for their recognition and defense.[2] A collective of individuals is the interpreter of commoning practices whose aim is to universalize access and save the recognized commons from the clutches of the state and private ownership. These two dominant capitalist institutions, since the dawn of modernity, have crushed the existence and unfolding of commoning, transforming a qualitative relationship into extractive capitalist accumulation. Once saved (through struggle) from its sad destiny of being exploited and destroyed, every common must, from a social and institutional point of view, be interpreted in a way coherent with its nature.

No challenge today is more fascinating and complex for the jurist than

1 See: Ugo Mattei, *Beni Comuni. Un Manifesto*, Laterza, Rome, Bari, 2011.

2 See: Antonio Negri and Michael Hardt, *Commonwealth*, Belknap Press of Harvard University Press, Cambridge (MA), 2009.

providing a legal structure coherent with the need to manage the different commons in a generative rather than extractive fashion.[3] Such a legal structure, far from being universalistic, must necessarily be contextual, because only contexts (places of conflicts and relationships) provide a soul to that great abstraction that otherwise is the law.[4] From these contexts of commoning stems a new *constituent legality*, one that challenges the mechanistic and formalistic reductionism of the formal legal system. This does not mean that this "new legality of the commons," grounded in a profound feeling of collective justice, emancipation, and intergenerational obligation, cannot find, in the traditional jurist's toolbox, legal forms capable of representing and legitimizing it within the established legal order. When this is the case, a commoning experience can thus realize its own transformative potential with the weapons of law and not only with its political force.

The Valle Theater, occupied in Rome from June 14, 2011 to August 11, 2014, is a case study of extraordinary value. That commoning experience, initiated by a conscious break of the legal order, is to the best of my knowledge the first struggle for the commons that has produced a legal form from the bottom up. This collective production of legal subjectivity, the Fondazione Teatro Valle Bene Comune [The Valle Theater Commons Foundation], has produced the most formidable weapon, which the occupants have been able to deploy to transform the occupation into an entirely new process of constructing a public–commons partnership, the outcome of which will be seen in the coming months.[5]

In what way can we consider the Valle Theater, the oldest and most prestigious of Rome, a common? What have been and will be the implications of its being a common for the legal forms of its management? In what measure has the Valle Theater Commons Foundation forged a "constituent legality" and is not just an ordinary act of private autonomy, as such recognized by Italian private law as by any other legal system? What is the juridical itinerary that the commoners should undertake now, after having negotiated to avoid police-managed eviction after more than three years of uninterrupted, public, and widely tolerated occupation? What are the rights and duties of the institution that has "risen" from the three-years-long struggle to avoid privatization of this magnificent theater located in the very heart of Rome?

Any unbiased observer must recognize that the commoning struggle carried on within the premises of the Valle Theater, running it successfully as an internationally recognized experience,[6] has been an extraordinary constituent laboratory of a new legality, as much an alternative to the established logic of (private) profit as that of (public) power. For the jurist, the Valle Theater as a common is especially meaningful for it is the originating venue of a great constituent design, destined to produce evident intergenerational consequences, that goes well beyond the contingent motivation of securing for Italy an avant-garde center dedicated to drama and music. The recognition and construction of culture as a common, a legacy of the past that we must project into the future, is at stake here. It is the protection and guarantee of culture as a common by

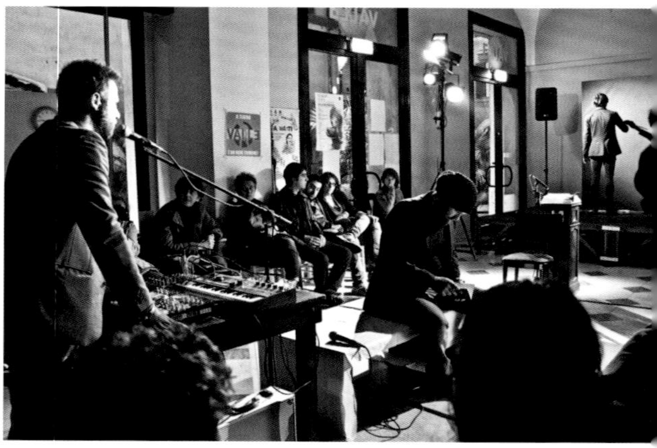

Teatro Valle Occupato, photo from the mixed-media installation *Dal 14 giugno 2011 per sempre*, 2011–2013

means of an institutional system that is effectively insulated from the whim of the political majority in power and/or from the arrogance and might of private capital, which today throughout Europe controls a progressively starved public sector.

This importance of the Valle for the jurist is twofold. In the first place there is, possibly for the first time in the history of radical political movements, a genuine constituent effort to use and modify the law in carrying on a political struggle. The occupiers did not fear the law exclusively as a foe, but also pursued its transformation as a political experience and as an ally in the long-term struggle. It became clear, soon after the occupation, that this was the only strategy to make the results possibly achieved permanent. Given the location and the historical importance of the theater, any other strategy not supported by a claim of legitimacy in the law would have brought about certain eviction with no standing to negotiate the future. Secondly, by originating the "constituent for the commons" discussed in chapter I of this book,[7] the Valle Theater Commons Foundation has proved capable of gathering nationwide attention on the use of law in constituent political struggles that will be extremely useful in the months to come.

1. Some Background

The occupation started on June 14, 2011, the day after the national referendum on water as a common's historic victory. The occupation interrupted a complex ongoing procedure of transferring responsibility for the Valle Theater, technically an historical immovable in the domain of the state (Article 822 of the Italian Civil Code), from the Ministry of Cultural Heritage and Activities to the municipality of Rome. The central government and the municipality completed the procedure, spelled out in a convention on June 15, 2011. The aim of this transfer, frustrated by the occupation, was to gain flexibility in order to auction off the management of the theater to private actors or perhaps even to put this public property up for sale. The aim of the first occupiers, a few dozen actors and activists who initially planned a symbolic and short-term occupation, was to oppose rumors of privatization and at the same time to draw public attention to the precarious conditions of the workers in the entertainment business, reduced to a new form of intellectual proletariat. The occupiers believed that there is a duty for current political institutions to sustain the culture of the performing arts, so that future generations can also maintain our collective identity just as we are able to do now thanks to the efforts of our ancestors. This long-term perspective gives content to the idea that *culture is a common*, a head-on critique of the logic of "here and now" that has taken control of the dominant narrative of neoliberalism.

This "good civic action" of the theater's occupants, like that of numerous other citizens risking the consequences of breaking the law to protect the commons, shows the new awareness already reached in Italy when the water referendum took place. A sort of hegemony of the commons discourse, discussed in chapter I, legitimizes this sort of radical critique in the public perception.

3 For the opposition of generative and extracting property, see: Marjorie Kelly, *Owning Our Future. The Emerging Ownership Revolution. Journeys to a Generative Economy*, Berrett-Koehler, San Francisco (CA), 2012.

4 See: Laura Nader, *The Life of the Law. Anthropological Projects*, University of California Press, Berkeley (CA), 2002.

5 See: David Bollier, "The Teatro Valle Occupation Ends – and a New Theater Commons Begins," August 11, 2014, available online at: http://bollier.org/blog/teatro-valle-occupation-ends-and-new-theater-commons-begins, accessed 09/10/2014.

6 In 2014, the Valle received the prestigious Princess Margriet Award from the European Cultural Foundation. See: www.culturalfoundation.eu/pma-2014, accessed 09/10/2014. During the occupation four other prizes were awarded.

7 For further information on the Italian political background, see the author's essay "Institutionalizing the Commons: An Italian Primer," this volume, pp. 85–99.

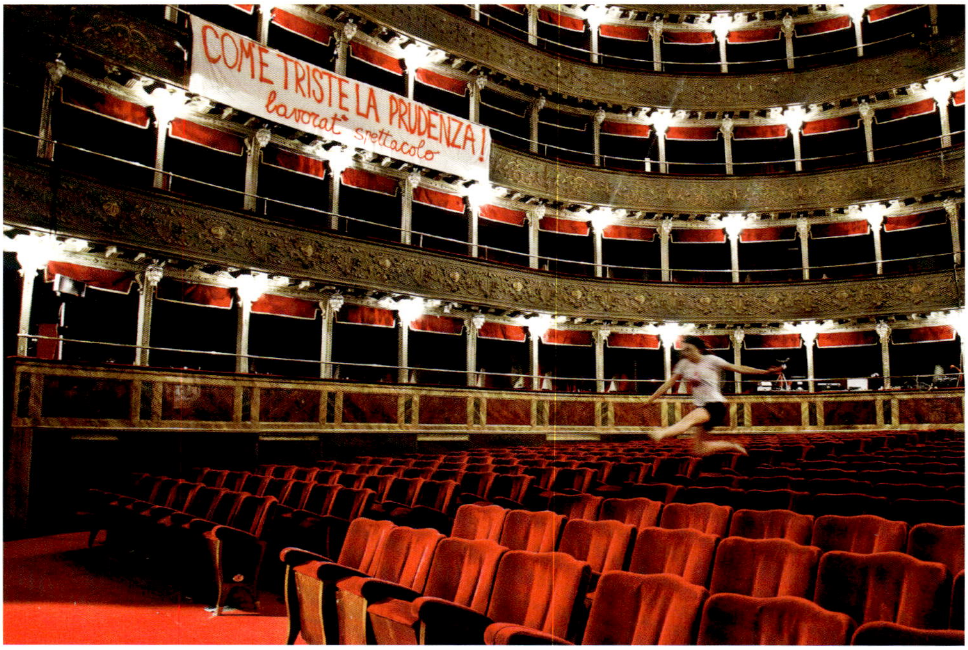

Teatro Valle Occupato, photo from the mixed-media installation *Dal 14 giugno 2011 per sempre*, 2011–2013

This new hegemony took on a new shape at the Valle occupation as a mixture of politics, drama, and law. It may even be capable of redeeming the international image of Italian culture, devastated by the particularly shameful way in which the *bel paese* [Beautiful Country] has interpreted the "end of history" over the last quarter of a century.[8] The occupied Valle Theater's contribution to this recovery of Italy's international image culminated in March 2014, with the aforementioned award of the prize from the European Cultural Foundation, an event that was extremely embarrassing for Italian diplomacy.

In Italy, the contribution of the Valle's resilience has been invaluable, especially due to the "contagion" capable of generating a network of occupied cultural spaces (Rome, Venice, Milan, Naples, Catania, Palermo, Messina, Pisa, and Turin, just to mention the best-known) claiming culture as a common against its complete commodification, which has long been part of bipartisan policy. The Valle managed to become the hub of a rich experimentation on democratic management of cultural spaces. This experience has certainly benefitted from a relative calm with regard to the police brutality used against other struggles for the commons (for example, No TAV in the Susa Valley[9]). At the Valle there has been enough time to develop crucial alliances and to show in practice, by opening the theater to the public, that an alternative and better management was possible.

The circumstances of this struggle have been rather lucky. The Valle is Rome's oldest theater, located in the city center behind the Senate. Right from day one, the occupation has involved important personalities from both the cultural and the art world, and has been the beneficiary of widespread media coverage, though often distorted. The occupation began immediately after the success of the referendum for "water as a common" on June 13, 2011, a rather unique moment in recent Italian history. Furthermore, the occupants of the Valle immediately demonstrated an incredible talent in interpreting the theater as an "open common," offering to citizens, in consideration of a voluntary offer, a program of the highest quality and a venue that is always open for political and cultural debate. Moreover (particularly important), compared to the above-mentioned initiative in the Susa Valley where a public project of tens of billions is involved (with all the pork thus generated), the stakes at the Valle Theater were relatively low, so politicians were less motivated to use police force to defeat opposition. A military-style attack on the Valle Theater would not have yielded much political (or economic) return for anybody, which explains the long inactivity of the Roman authorities and their current willingness to negotiate with the Valle Theater Commons Foundation about the future of the venue. Finally, a change in the political color of the Rome administration, with a center-left mayor taking over the administration from a postfascist, has removed many of the political impediments for negotiations that finally started in July 2014. In fact, the occupants were not willing to talk to postfascists, nor were the latter willing to talk to rebellious occupiers.

2. The Valle Theater Commons Foundation

Paradoxically, given the highly complex and unstable political context of former Italian Prime Minister Silvio Berlusconi's final years in office, conditions of relative stability have facilitated the work at the Valle. The political conditions allowed the occupation enough time to "upgrade" its legal status. It was thus possible for the occupiers to move all the way from the openly illegal and de facto status of possessors in bad faith of a public property to the Valle Theater Commons Foundation, an entity claiming that the occupation was justified within a different kind of legality. This foundation, established with a public notarial act executed in Rome in September 2013, has formally linked to the occupation some 5,000 citizens, who together have collected more than 150,000 euros in cash and a similar amount in donated artworks.

The prefect eventually refused government recognition of the foundation for lack of sufficient means to reach its purpose in the absence of a legal title to the theater. However, as we shall see in more detail, the nonrecognized foundation is certainly a legal reality in Italian law governed by the Civil Code provisions devoted to "nonrecognized associations" as, for example, all political parties and trade unions are. Thus the creation of the Valle Theater Commons Foundation, a participatory process involving large numbers of people and many quite distinguished jurists for more than a year, has provided the occupants with a formidable legal and political tool. Not only is it the foundation that negotiates on behalf of the former occupants now that the occupation has ended, but it became clear that the occupiers, shortly before just de facto possessors of the theater, have been and still are trustees of the commons in the interests of the population at large, of culture, and of future generations. Clearly, the political price of evicting a foundation made of thousands of citizen trustees of the commons and of the public interest was just too high to pay.

While the foundation still lacks "juridical personality" (that is, the perfect patrimonial autonomy with full separation of the social patrimony from that of those people who act on behalf of the said foundation), over 5,000 founding members make it an important "juridical reality," despite lacking the prefect's stamp of approval.

8 Francis Fukuyama's book *The End of History and the Last Man* (1992) had a major impact on the convergence of the political discourse both of the center right and of the center left toward neoliberalism. While the years of Silvio Berlusconi made this option more clear, the center left and technical governments of Carlo Azeglio Ciampi, Giuliano Amato, Romano Prodi, Mario Monti, Enrico Letta, and Matteo Renzi carried on substantially nondistinguishable economic and social policies.

9 See: "No TAV," this volume, pp. 170–171.

Tens of open assemblies and the development of an innovative open access Internet platform have crafted the bylaws of the foundation in an impressive bottom-up effort. The bylaws eventually agreed upon and notarized are rich in important and significant institutional innovations.

The discussion about the law and its role in the occupation commenced within two weeks of the occupation.[10] It soon produced the first legal instrument (in August 2011): the Committee for the Valle as a Common was entered into by a handful of occupants and registered in Turin. The main task of the committee was to attract new members (in the end more than 5,000) and to generate sufficient capital to transform itself into a foundation, which eventually happened in September 2013.

In the civil law tradition, committees and foundations are typical and very traditional legal forms stemming from the so-called principle of "private autonomy" of the individuals. Thus, at the very beginning of the discussion it seemed rather paradoxical to deploy such a typical instrument of private law to fight against the privatization of a public property. Indeed quite a few of the detractors of the Valle experience pointed out the paradox of an act of occupation, which is a private acquisition of possession, claiming to be protection of the public. However, such criticism only shows the lack in traditional legal taxonomy of the notion of the "commons," which is neither public nor private in the usual legal meaning. A legal institution of the commons can only result from a transformation, either from the public or from the private. The context of each struggle determines the legal path, necessarily counterhegemonic, that one has to follow. The occupation thus used a typical act of private autonomy recognized by the law in a counterhegemonic way to produce a collective legal subjectivity reflecting the spirit of the occupation. Abandoning the spirit of the self, the individual subjectivity that since modernity has become the fundamental building block of private law, the commons foundation provides a legal form for the spirit of "us" stemming from the occupation. Sharing, collectivism, solidarity, pluralism, and ecology, dimensions of a collective subjectivity

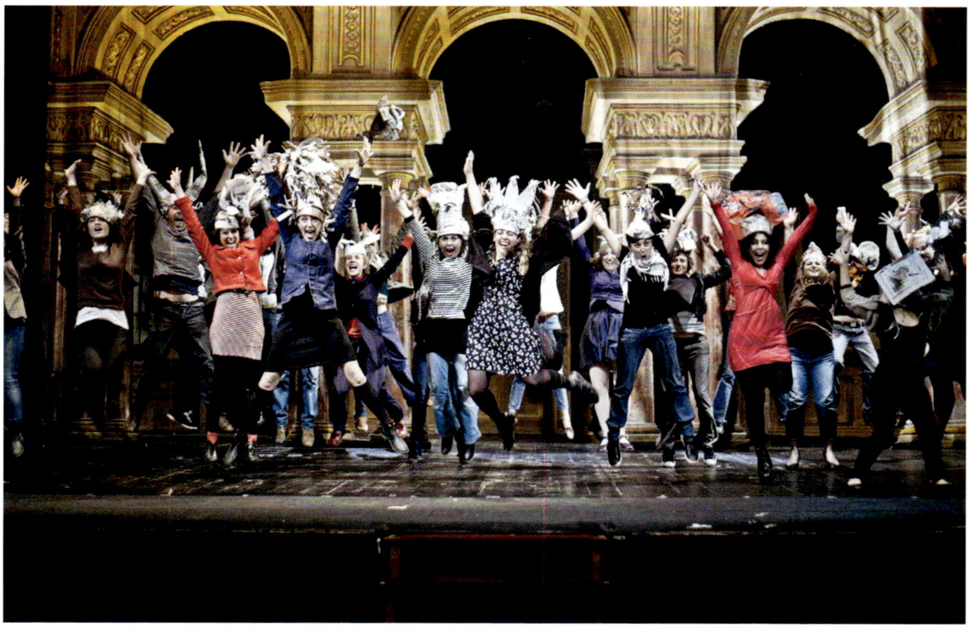

Teatro Valle Occupato, photo from the mixed-media installation *Dal 14 giugno 2011 per sempre*, 2011–2013

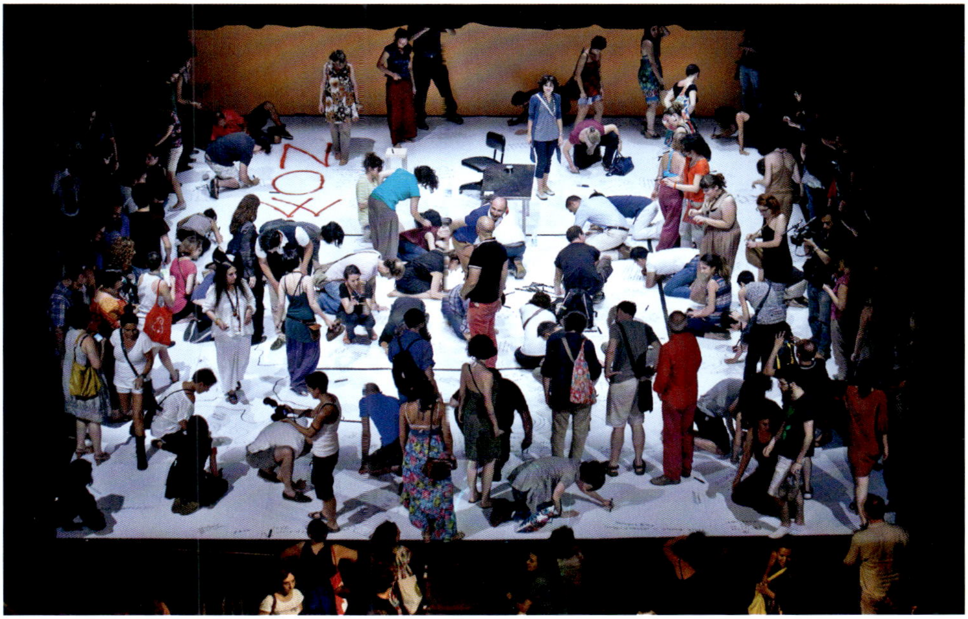

Teatro Valle Occupato, photo from the mixed-media installation *Dal 14 giugno 2011 per sempre*, 2011–2013

always careful not to clip the wings of free spirits, were thus enshrined in the bylaws of the Valle Theater Commons Foundation.

This spirit of "us," produced by the collective experience of breaking a legal order made illegitimate by neoliberal unconstitutional policy oblivious of the obligations of the public sphere toward the people, can generate a commons institution. Commoning develops into a physical place, shielded from the market logic, transformed into the ecological community of reference in the interest of the fundamental constitutional rights of the people and of future generations. The Valle Theater Commons Foundation generates and transforms into law such an ecological community, providing a legal tool coherent with the definition of the Rodotà Commission and of the Supreme Court of Cassation.[11] So conceived the foundation is neither private nor public but is indeed a common.[12]

The foundation is thus a new form of legal participatory governance of the commons. By constructing a legitimate form of governance over a usurped title, the occupants have been mocking the formalistic distinction between title and management, which in neoliberal times is based so much on the massive de facto privatizations of the public sector – again a use of irony in the law as form of counter-hegemony. The experience provided by the referendum against the privatization of water and public services inspired this strategy. In that campaign the government, defeated along with its neoliberal allies, had claimed that water and public services would anyway keep a public title, and that its aim was only to privatize the management. Similarly, at the Valle we were saying that irrespective of the title on the theater, the management should be an experience of commoning.

The bylaws contain effective guarantees that a spirit of openness, transparency, and supportive political-cultural coresponsibility will forever inspire the management of Valle Theater. The collective legal structure realized

10 The discussion can be seen online at: www.youtube.com/watch?v=732TP9wTtXQ, accessed 09/10/2014.

11 For further information, see the author's essay "Institutionalizing the Commons: An Italian Primer," this volume, pp. 85–99.

12 See: Supreme Court of Cassation S.U. 14-2-2011 no. 3665.

appears capable of intimately connecting the Valle Theater as a cultural property in the public domain to a "workers' or users' association" that, according to Article 43 of the Italian Constitution, can be called upon to manage issues of "general interest." The community of the Valle has thus found a neglected article of the Constitution to claim a legal base for its struggle. Commoning, we claim, is a subjective right of a constitutional nature removed from the variable contingencies of representative politics. It entitles communities to claim in the preeminent general interest a long-term fair and transparent public financing.

3. Three Legal Phases

From the legal point of view, the struggle for the recognition of the Valle Theater as a common has just concluded the first two phases and has now entered the third decisive one. The first phase was *occupation*, which occurred without violence of any type, through which a "workers' or users' association" (Article 43 of the Constitution) from the entertainment business took *possession* of the Valle Theater during the extremely dangerous "transition" from the Ministry of Cultural Heritage and Activities to the municipality of Rome. This transition between public entities was a consequence of the abolition (by Law 78, 31-05-2010) of the Ente Teatrale Italiano (ETI), the Italian Theatrical Corporation, the public entity controlled by the ministry, which since its inception was responsible for coordinating the management of Italian publicly owned theaters by Law 365, 19-03-1942. The reader will recall that the "shift of responsibility" from the central government to the municipality under austerity pressure exponentially increases the risks of privatization. In the absence of a satisfactory legal framework governing public property (whose discipline, drawn up by the Rodotà Commission, was never discussed in the Senate), there was a concrete risk that any private businessman could propose a *business plan* at odds with the nature of an old-established theater. The municipalities, strapped for cash in times of austerity, often surrender to such ideas as happened at the Teatro Smeraldo in Milan, which was transformed into an eatery by the tycoon Oscar Farinetti of Eataly.[13] The occupation (and the media attention it generated) protected the Valle from the risk of succumbing to such a Disneyland concept of culture.

The first beneficiaries of this act of revolt are "future generations," who have the right to live in a world in which historical memory is not obliterated by a consumer subculture, even one accompanied by a brushstroke of green. The occupation of the Valle Theater impeded such a transformation and has been successful, after three years, to maintain it in a genuinely public sphere. The theater will keep providing the fundamental right to culture, a moral asset that may avoid everyone being transformed into a brutish customer.[14]

The second relevant juridical phase was the constitution, on August 2, 2011, of the "Open social committee to promote the Valle Theater as a common," registered on October 6 of the same year. This legal form, whose first objective was the institution of the "Valle Theater Commons Foundation for Contemporary and Italian Drama," became the subject capable of producing over the following two years the political and economic conditions to give life to the foundation. The committee eventually established the foundation with a public act executed in Rome by the prominent notary Professor Gennaro Mariconda on September 16, 2013.

The process was therefore gradual, with progressive consolidation of the juridical effects, by means of a strategy of inclusion and access, whose challenge was to combine the artistic praxis with the juridical-political one to

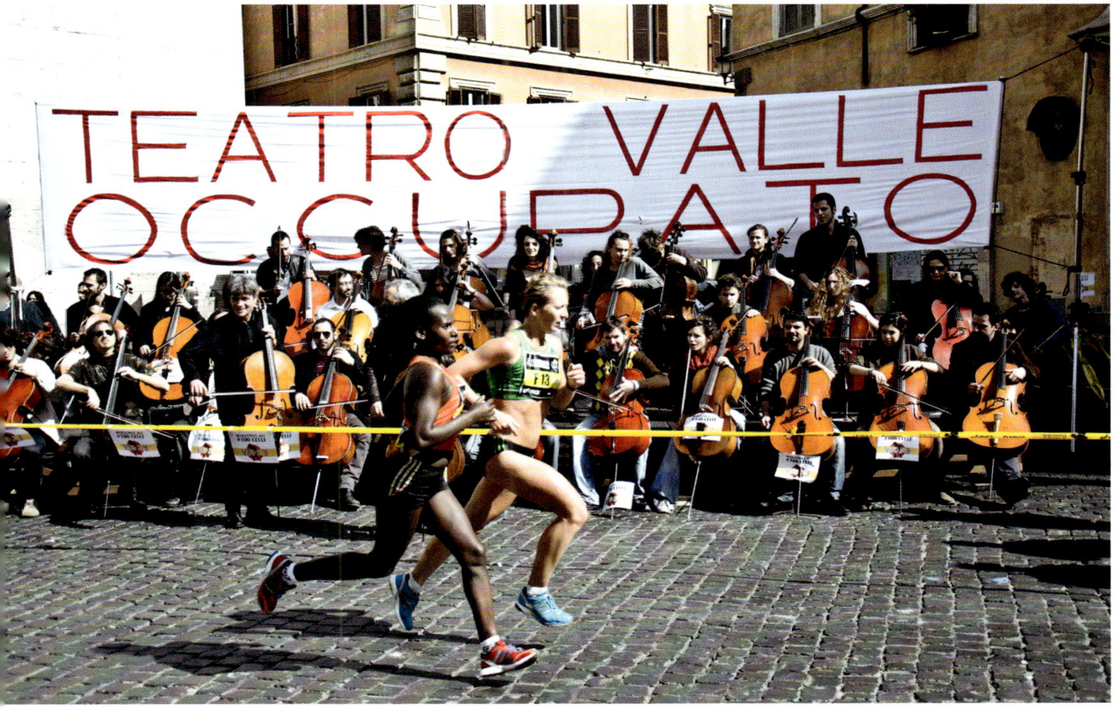

Teatro Valle Occupato, photo from the mixed-media installation *Dal 14 giugno 2011 per sempre*, 2011–2013

produce a model of direct action and active citizenry. It is worth noting that this very process of creating a collective subjectivity in the making already gives rise to a more beautiful world that is capable of denouncing the sadness and unsustainability of our materialistic "reality." We are not talking about a mere aesthetic experience. The Valle Theater bylaws immediately exhibit politically demanding passages. Especially Article 3 points to methodology for struggle based upon: "Organization of the conflict strategy dedicated to the genuine fulfillment of the foundation by means of every legal and political means, radically nonviolent unless called upon to legitimately defend itself, including the occupation of new spaces recognized as public properties by the city of Rome and elsewhere."

Other indications of great interest regarding the militant refusal to separate art, politics, and law (such a separation is a strategy created by the mechanistic thinking of modernity) are found in Article 4 of the foundation's bylaws. For example: "Promotion, in legal and political form, of all the connections with other struggles about the commons, necessary for the full recognition of culture as a common, of the full juridical and political subjectivity of part-time workers, and of the full appreciation of culture as a common." And again, point (d): "The active and artistic practice of repudiating war and any form of dominion, exploitation and oppression, including precarious work in form." Moreover: "the struggle by means of every artistic, political and legal means, including the promotion of abrogative referendums according to Art. 75 of the Constitution, for the reconversion of every resource dedicated to practices described in clause (d) in favor of culture and of the common."

13 See: www.lifegate.it/persone/news/inaugurato-eataly-allex-teatro-smeraldo-milano, accessed 09/10/2014.

14 See: Saki Bailey, Gilda Farrell, and Ugo Mattei, *Protecting Future Generations through Commons*, Trends in Social Cohesion, vol. 26, Council of Europe Publishing, Strasbourg, 2014.

The bylaws of the foundation are formulated in fully awareness that it is a clearly antagonistic model with respect to the current hegemonic conceptions. For this reason they propose the "promotion of solidarity and cooperation aimed at offering a virtuous example of commons governance of the Teatro Valle, in order to promote it at the international level as an example of Italian talent in the dramatic arts as well as to promote creative practices of commoning culture."

Beyond the language, which transmits deep civic values pursued with the necessary irony and levity (the members are defined after the Paris Commune as *communards*, hoping that things work out better this time…), there are numerous elements of great legal interest in the bylaws. In the first place, the awareness of the *constituent* value of this experience.

The bylaws attempt a *genuine implementation* of the principles present in the Italian Constitution that too often have remained at the level of good intentions (Articles 1, 2, 3, 4, 9, 18, 21, 33, 34, 36, 43, 46 are expressly mentioned). The bylaws self-confidently aim at being a contribution to the production of "fundamental and constituent principles of ecological justice and international and intergenerational solidarity."

The bylaws do not limit themselves to the formal discipline of just the foundation. They also seek to establish bases for a *first legal discipline of culture as a common*. From this ambition stems the intimate link between the juridical dimension of *having* and that of *being*, which is clearly and succinctly expressed in the two most significant patrimonial sources of income. "The Foundation's patrimony is constituted *by the full utilities produced by the Valle Theater as a common, and by the cognitive patrimony and the work of all the communards* capable of having recognized and restored life to the Valle Theater during its occupation and of having planned and put into operation the political and cultural objectives of the present bylaws."

The foundation institutes the principle of *radical substantial equality* as a political and legal precondition to the expression of commoning as a qualitative relationship. In the determination of the quota of participation the principle is: "from each one according to their possibilities," while at the same time "all the participants have the same duties and rights to a vote in the assembly regardless of the quota paid."

The bylaws also recognize their own nature of a "living" DNA of the foundation that is capable of adapting to the contexts of its operation. Accordingly, the bylaws are articulated in three separate parts, different at the semantic level, but united in their long-term function. The communards continuously monitor the *preamble*, the *text*, and the *political code* for their coherence with the real practices carried out at the theater and in their capacity to keep the commoning alive in its genuine long-term political meaning. These flexible features, which required some precise and skillful wording in the making of the foundation's legal architecture, should avoid the hypocritical phenomenon of the non-applied law. Thus, the bylaws institutionalize forms that are able "to guarantee *the living nature* of the foundation" and its "capacity to guarantee that the objectives of the governing community of the Valle Theater are coherent with the nature of the commons."

Moreover, it is *the duty of the communards*, whose relationship with the place is physical and not only abstract, to participate in the deliberative process of the assembly, whose decisions are consensually made with no majority vote, regardless of the number of those present. Although anyone can become a communard just by participating in a number of consecutive assemblies, communards can lose this status due to nonfulfillment of social obligations.

Of vital importance is the way in which the bylaws structure the commoning practice in order to defeat *the dynamics of concentrated power.*

The election of the executive organ must be coherent with two principles: that of "*people's broadest participation* and of workers' self-government." Accordingly, the executive organ is stable as a collective organ, but mutable in its physical membership by means of a complex system of taking turns in office.

Finally, the bylaws pursue full political integration between the managerial function and the artistic component. The executive body launches a variety of "calls for proposals," which become the tools of mediation between the communards' collective body and the needs of free artistic creativity for those artists who are in charge of running a specific program.

A noteworthy aspect of the bylaws is also the presence of a board of guardians, made of three individuals selected from high-profile artists or academics who have been recognized as being close to the values of the commons movement, which serves as an ultimate consulting and dispute resolution body, and as a guardian of the purpose of the foundation.

Moreover, the foundation goes beyond a vision of the Valle as a mere theater. A very important aspect of its success, recognized also in the current phase of negotiation on the future of the place, has been the development of a highly advanced educational mission at many levels for people interested in the world of acting and drama as well as being a center for dramatic productions. The premiere of a major play by the well-known dramatist and communard Fausto Paravidino will take place in Brussels in October 2015.

4. The Commons Foundation Model and the Break with the Legal Logic of the Status Quo

As mentioned above, the Valle Theater Commons Foundation passed the control of legality, which in Italian law belongs to the notary, but did not obtain the final recognition (act of registration) by the government.

Prefect Giuseppe Pecoraro, in a letter addressed to the president of the Valle Theater Commons Foundation (thus giving a first implicit recognition of the occupation) on January 28, 2014, refused the registration because of the lack of a valid title by the foundation over the theater itself. According to the prefect, in the absence of such a title the resources collected by the committee that gave life to the foundation (valued at roughly 250,000 euros) would not be sufficient to fulfill the social aim of valorizing the theater in the interest of future generations.

Of course, the Italian media did their best to persuade public opinion that the prefectorial refusal meant the "death" of the Valle Theater Commons Foundation experience.[15] Notwithstanding, the reality is far more nuanced and complex as it was made clear at an important seminar held at the Valle Theater on March 14, 2014. Among the participants were the notary Professor Gennaro Mariconda, whose act had certified the legal validity of the foundation, as well as other well-known civil law scholars, including Stefano Rodotà and Pietro Rescigno, perhaps the most prestigious emeritus professor of civil law in Italy.

There is no doubt that the notarial deed was perfectly legal. The issue is with the legal effect of the prefectorial refusal – not on the existence of the legal entity as such, but on its "legal personality." In fact, the notarial deed, although followed by the prefect's refusal of its registration, nevertheless constitutes a notable step forward with respect to the previous hypothesis of *unrecognized foundations*. In the past Italian legal scholars have discussed the issue for the hypothesis in which, following the private agreement on the bylaws, the notarial deed does not happen

15 See, for example: "Valle occupato, la grande bruttezza del premio europeo all'illegalità" [The Occupied Valle and the Sheer Ugliness of the Euro Award to Illegality], in: *Il Messaggero*, 03/15/2014, pp. 1 and 13.

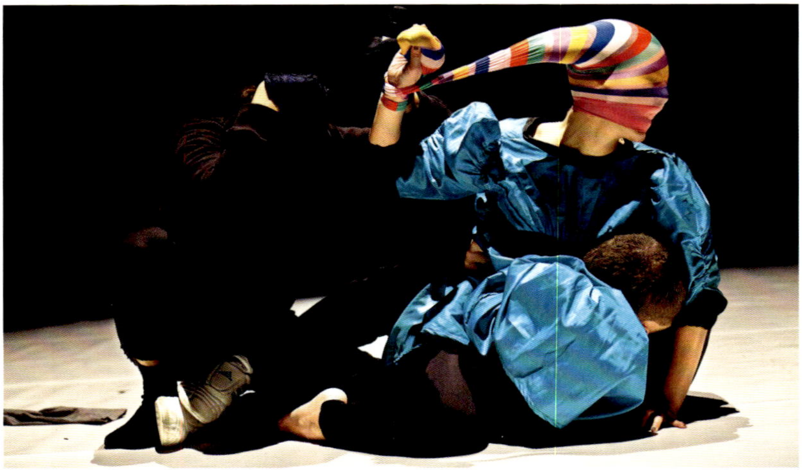

Teatro Valle Occupato, photo from the mixed-media installation *Dal 14 giugno 2011 per sempre*, 2011–2013

(no matter for what reason). Italian legal writings and case law has followed since the 1970s the opinion of the illustrious late scholar Francesco Galgano, who acknowledged the existence of the *unrecognized foundation* in the case of a lacking public notarial act.[16] Galgano suggested that the Civil Code rules on committees and associations (Articles 36–42 of the Civil Code) which, according to the Civil Code, do not require recognition apply to the *unrecognized foundation*. Thus, the *unrecognized foundation* is a kind of nonrecognized association, perfectly valid among its members, but lacking the so-called legal personality (or limited responsibility); that is, the separation of the entity's patrimony from that of its members acting on its behalf. The reader must keep in mind that in our system the political parties, which dominate the political and constitutional life of the country, are indeed "unrecognized associations." The Valle Theater Commons Foundation, thus, is as much a valid legal entity as the Italian Democratic Party, which highlights the deceit and ignorance of those journalists who wrote about the defeat and demise of the Valle Theater Commons Foundation experience.

At the conclusion of the seminar on the legal status of the unrecognized Valle Theater Commons Foundation the participants circulated the following text:

"An in-depth seminar of legal scholarship was held on March 14, 2014, at Rome's Valle Theater to study and discuss:

1. The constitutive act of the Valle Theater Commons Foundation of September 16, 2013.
2. The letter from Prefect Pecoraro to the president of the foundation of January 2014.
3. The convention between the Ministry of Cultural Heritage and Activities and the municipality of Rome of June 15, 2011.

From analysis of the legal documents, despite differences of doctrinal opinion regarding theoretical admissibility and the practical effects of the *unrecognized foundation*, the participating jurists were in agreement on the following points:

(a) Prefect Pecoraro's letter does not declare the nullity of the constitutive public act drafted by the notary Professor Mariconda, but limits itself to denying the transcription of the same due to the foundation's lack of title on the theater, which appears as its legal seat on the bylaws.

(b) The current theater's qualified possession cannot be presumed *contra ius*, being held neither in a violent nor in a clandestine way since the moment immediately after its acquisition on June 14, 2011. There are, to the contrary, elements that might point to tolerance in the absence of any formal act by the owner to stop the occupation.

(c) The current formal ownership of the property appears in doubt because the convention between the municipality of Rome and the Ministry of Cultural Heritage and Activities appears to have expired and not been honored. In the absence of its renewal, the Valle Theater is part of the state's domain under the responsibility of the ministry and not of the municipality.

(d) The bylaws, whatever is the legal nature and the value towards third parties of the Valle Theater Commons Foundation, are not legally inexistent. To the contrary, from the civil law point of view they are an interesting and advanced experiment in collective private autonomy capable of giving juridical form to the sharing of an asset that has remained open to the public for nearly three years.

(e) It is both possible and beneficial to reach a consensual agreement relative to the title allowing its correction in order to recognize the foundation. Such agreement could take on the innovative form of a public–common partnership that the foundation and the municipality of Rome could suggest to the ministry. This "management pact" to run the Valle according to democratic and participatory values shall be a concrete application of the constitutional principle of subsidiarity.

(f) Nonetheless, a unilateral formal transformation of the foundation's bylaws in order to reach legal personality appears possible in a legal way.[17] The foundations organ's can unanimously deliberate and make into the public knowledge by reasonable advertising a transformation of the *unrecognized foundation* into a *charitable trust* governed by the law of a common law jurisdiction. Such transformation, to be studied in its details, would make it possible to reach *limited responsibility* and thus would be a functional substitute to the prefectorial recognition. The Hague Convention on the Law Applicable to Trusts and on Their Recognition, of which Italy is a signatory, allows this possibility. This strategy, if followed, allows perfect patrimonial autonomy of the *unrecognized foundation* transformed into a trust, even if the current title to the theater is not upgraded in agreement with the ministry.

In the light of the above principles, the jurists recommend the immediate setting up of a round table attended by the Valle Theater Commons Foundation and the public authority holding title to the theater in order to study a definitive juridical solution for the running of the Valle Theater in line with its continuous and protracted recognition as a common.

Rome, March 15, 2014"

16 See: Francesco Galgano, *Delle persone giuridiche. Disposizioni generali, delle associazioni e delle fondazioni* [On Legal Persons. General Provisions, Associations, and Foundations], Commentario del Codice Civile, Antonio Scialoja and Giuseppe Branca (eds.), vols. 11–35, Zanichelli, Bologna, Foro italiano, Rome, 1969, p. 149.

17 At the Roman seminar, I personally suggested the formal steps that could be carried out, in a context of counterhegemonic use of transnational legality, to obtain juridical personality while removing the Valle Theater from the bureaucratic control of the police-minded Italian prefecture. It requires quite simply a public (notarial) act, a so-called "heterogeneous" transformation of the Valle Theater Commons Foundation to have it become a *trust* (in the interest of future generations), governed by an appropriate legal system of a common law jurisdiction. It is a legal scheme not different from the one pursued to transform the Naples water company from a stock corporation into a common (see also the author's essay "Institutionalizing the Commons: An Italian Primer," this volume, pp. 85–99).

In the months following the seminar, in which it was agreed that the foundation would be available for negotiations thus overturning the previous position of no discussions with the postfascist mayor, complex, reluctant, preliminary negotiations began with the authorities of the municipality of Rome. In a first move, the Assessor to Culture appointed five facilitators to talk with all the stakeholders and come up with a proposal to solve the standoff. Unfortunately, after only one meeting, because of the unfathomable alchemy of Italian politics, the assessor, in spite of belonging to the Democratic Party, resigned (or was fired) at the end of May following the victory of the same Democratic Party at the European elections. For over a month, Rome had to live with the embarrassment of being without someone responsible for cultural policy!

The most interesting factor that emerged from these first timid and abortive attempts to discuss the future of the occupied Valle Theater with the political institutions having legal ownership of it is the radical disagreement on how to assign public cultural areas. The authorities, embedded in a neoliberal competitive mindset, were sticking to the idea of an auction, a sort of public contest in which different candidates compete, one against the other, for management of the theater. In this *competitive* logic, the Valle Theater Commons Foundation could be one of the *competitors* on equal standing with any other private association or corporation, with a total de facto erasure of the occupation experience. Of course, the very opposite, inclusive, and *noncompetitive* logic permeates a *commons* institution like the one that the occupation has created by notarizing the Valle Theater Commons Foundation. As part of a process of political struggle in the making, for three years a commons institution has been the legal framework through which anyone wanting to take charge and manage the Valle Theater could do so. It was sufficient for anybody to attend on a regular basis the assembly of communards that met every Monday at the Valle's premises. Beginning with this very concrete commoning practice, any citizen who so wishes, without the bureaucracy of a public contest, may give her contribution, according to her own possibilities and talents, to the management of this magnificent theater, symbol of civility. Thus, on the occupants' side, there was no availability to participate in a contest, a symbol of neoliberal vision and at odds with the institution-building process carried out there.

The negotiations stalled until late June 2014. The facilitators had prepared a lengthy document on the Valle that was never made public by the municipality, but arrived in the public domain via a scoop by the national newspaper *Il Fatto Quotidiano*.[18] At the same time, in a couple of declarations to the public media, Ignazio Marino, the mayor of Rome, used fierce language and threatened the use of public force to vacate the place.[19] The most likely explanation of this sudden change of attitude by an otherwise reasonable politician, a well-known doctor and former democratic senator sometimes teaching in the United States, was pressure from Matteo Renzi and the Rome Democratic Party's establishment. Renzi himself had delivered an attack on the Valle Theater Commons Foundation right after his seizure of power in February 2014, later confirmed by a landslide electoral success in the European elections of May. At the end of June the political climate around the Valle, a living defiance of the new law-and-order platform of the government, was very hot,[20] and international solidarity reached its peak.[21]

As jurists of the "constituent for the commons"[22] we offered our help in the resumption of negotiations.[23] After a couple of meetings with high officials in the Marino administration, and the appointment in the first days of July 2014 of a new Assessor to

Culture whose first important public task was the solution of the Valle "political problem," an agreement was reached to open direct negotiations between the Valle Theater Commons Foundation and the Teatro di Roma. The municipality pledged to withdraw the plan to auction off the theater and accepted to assign it to the Teatro di Roma, the public entity controlled by the municipality that runs the most important theaters in the Italian capital. This was a first important result for the occupation, which has effectively defeated privatization. Moreover, Marino Sinibaldi, president of the Teatro di Roma and director of the more progressive third channel of Italian public radio (Rai Radio 3), an intellectual respected by many of the communards, became the chief negotiator for the municipality. In quite a dramatic month of negotiations, with the Valle communards, foundation members, and ordinary citizens in permanent assembly at the theater, the release of the Valle for the purpose of remodeling, refurbishing, and upgrading of the infrastructure was agreed upon and became effective on August 11, 2014.[24] The political agreement reached was to work out a public–common partnership in the running of an experimental participatory theater, open for long hours and capable of maintaining the spirit and the international profile created by its commoning in more than three years of occupation.

While the table for the discussion of the terms of the partnership, as recommended by the jurists right after the seminar of March 15, was officially opened on September 2, 2014, it is too early to say how far the experimentation will be able to go and how long the process will take.[25] In this process of negotiation the Valle Theater Commons Foundation needs the attention and the solidarity of the international commons movement.

This paper deploys a personal narrative on events that I have shared with many comrades and friends. The communards of the Valle became to me a collective entity that I have most enjoyed and that I wish all to thank. Among those who became more close to me in the three years of the occupation, who may or may not agree with my political conclusions, but with whom I have most discussed the technical and political issues of the Valle Theater Commons Foundation, I need to mention: Ilenia Caleo, Benedetta Cappon, Alessandra Quarta, Fulvio Molena, Guido De Togni, Andrea Gropplero, Chiara Giorgi, Giuliana Aliberti, Simona Panzino, and Daniela Festa. Special thanks to Freddy Paul Grunert, who initiated the occasion for writing this paper by inviting a large Valle crowd to ZKM | Karlsruhe, and also for physically taking me there in spite of my overdose of traveling. Translated from the Italian by Robert Booth.

18 See: www.ilfattoquotidiano.it/2014/07/09/questo-il-futuro-del-teatro-valle-ma-marino-nasconde-il-dossier/1054486/, accessed 09/10/2014.

19 See: http://m.lastampa.it/2014/07/05/italia/cronache/roma-scontro-a-sinistra-sul-teatro-valle-marino-peggio-di-alemanno-IBynb2XMMbEJJgOcd1Z9dC/pagina.html, accessed 09/10/2014.

20 The media declarations released on the Valle Theater by Prime Minister Matteo Renzi are available online at: www.ilmessaggero.it/ROMA/CRONACA/renzi_teatro_wvalle_occupato/notizie/526269.shtml, http://roma.repubblica.it/cronaca/2014/02/18/news/renzi_il_valle_non_un_esempio_ma_lui_ama_la_cultura_disneyland-78888060/, accessed 09/10/2014.

21 See: David Bollier, "Save the Teatro Valle Commons in Rome," July 8, 2014, available online at: http://bollier.org/blog/save-teatro-valle-commons-rome, accessed 09/10/2014.

22 See the author's essay "Institutionalizing the Commons: An Italian Primer," this volume, pp. 85–99.

23 I personally offered the help of the constituent jurists to Ignazio Marino, an old political acquaintance of mine, with a text message on July 3, 2014.

24 See: Bollier, August 11, 2014.

25 The latest news on the process of refurbishing released by the press on September 16, 2014 are not encouraging. See: www.iltempo.it/cultura-spettacoli/2014/09/16/teatro-valle-senza-pace-ora-c-e-il-giallo-dei-lavori-1.1309115, accessed 09/16/2014.

Patricia K. Triki *1964 and Christine Bruckbauer *1969

Patricia K. Triki was born in Paris and works as a photographer and artist in Tunis. Together with Malek Sebaï and Sondos Belhassen, she created several choreographic installations and performances. Her performance *Prison des délits de cœur* about a phenomenon and symbol of Tunisian patriarchy, *Dar Joued*, educational, prison-like institutions, where disobedient women are confined, was presented at the Centre national de la danse in Pantin, France, in 2011. Triki joined the protests in Tunisia and participated in the founding of an association of Tunisian visual artists (UAPT). Christine Bruckbauer is an Austrian art historian, art critic, and curator based in Tunis, with a special focus on contemporary art from South Asia and North Africa. She lectures at the University of Mantouba in Tunis.

Triki and Bruckbauer collaborated on the exhibition *Rosige Zukunft. Aktuelle Kunst aus Tunesien* [Rosy Future. Contemporary Art from Tunisia], which was presented in Berlin and Stuttgart in 2012 and 2013. The artworks exhibited demonstrate how Tunisian artists deal with the social and political changes since Tunisian president Ben Ali, who governed the country autocratically until January 2011 and is widely considered a dictator, was forced to resign following massive popular protests. Tunisia's rather modest contemporary art scene flourished after the so-called "Jasmine Revolution" and achieved a new visibility, also internationally, and many artists left the closed realm of private galleries and chose public space or the Internet to show their works. Their artworks often deal with conflicts that could not be addressed due to censorship or self-censorship, with hope, and (disappointed) expectations.

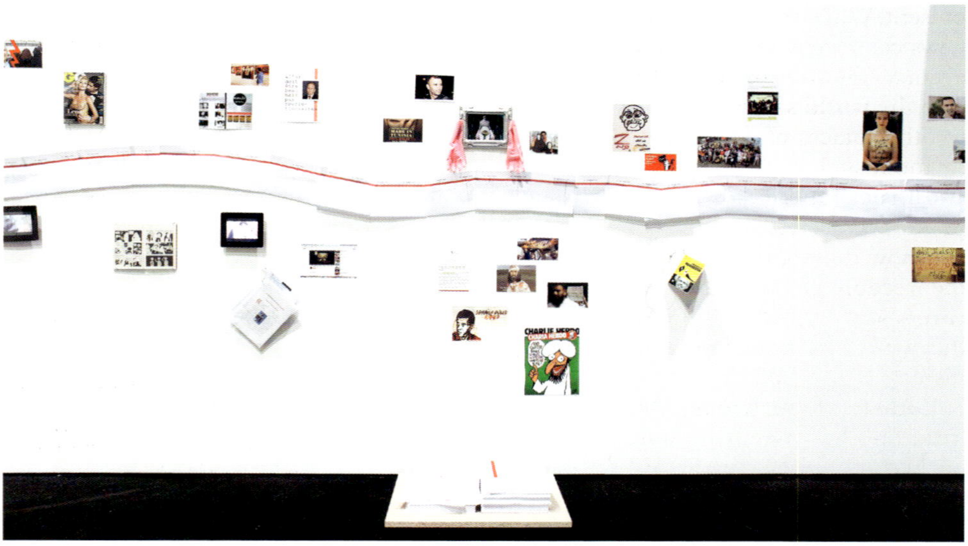

Patricia K. Triki and Christine Bruckbauer, *Chronology*, 2011–2013, installation, mixed media, installation view, ZKM | Karlsruhe, 2014

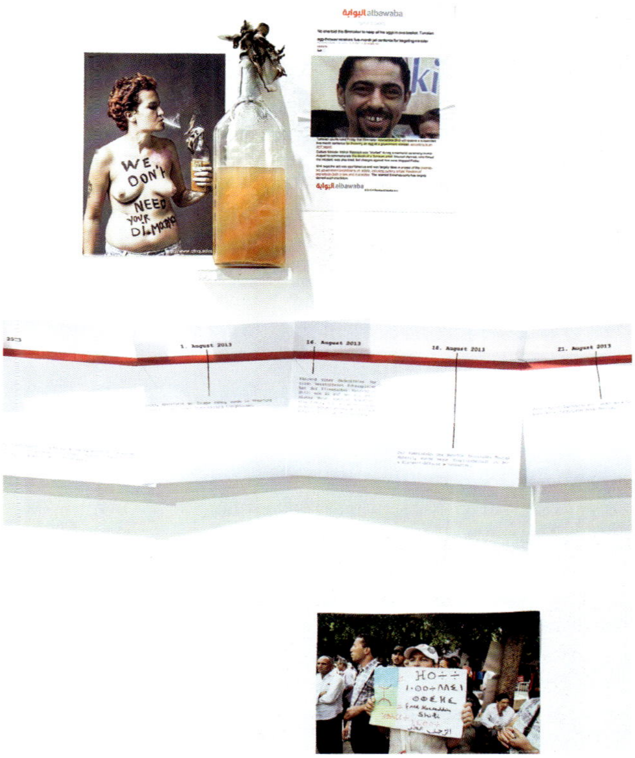

Patricia K. Triki and
Christine Bruckbauer,
Chronology, 2011–2013,
installation, mixed media,
installation view,
ZKM | Karlsruhe, 2014

Triki and Bruckbauer's collaborative work *Chronology* (2011–2013) is a time line that documents and shows events from the Tunisian revolution to the present. While the focus of international news coverage was on macropolitical events, and after the end of Ben Ali's rule the world's eyes turned away to other places of political and civil turmoil, such as Egypt and Syria, Triki and Bruckbauer focus on the micropolitics of postrevolutionary Tunisia and how the political changes affected the freedom of expression. With their chronology, which starts in March 2011, they tell a heterogeneous and personal history of the violations of artistic, cultural, and creative freedom in Tunisia. They highlight conservative backlashes under the Islamist-led government that hinders the work of artists and cultural activists and curbs their freedom of expression both with laws and in practice: Clashes between students and Salafists occurred, critical university staff were fired, and artists and activists faced attacks, legal investigations, and arrests because of supposedly blasphemous artworks. In 2012, participants of the Printemps des Arts show were attacked and received death threats from radical Islamists, backed in their actions by the government. These incidents, outlined in writing on a timeline, are illustrated with artistic and cultural artifacts or documents: images, videos, cartoons, postcards, printed quotes, screenshots, and objects. The information about the release of the arrested Tunisian Femen member Amina Tyler (Sbouï) is accompanied by the reconstruction of a Molotov cocktail and an image that became iconic: Tyler, posing with a cigarette that she lights with a Molotov cocktail, with the writing on her bare torso: "We don't need your democracy."

Voina

Voina is an activist collective, which opposes the authoritarian Russian state with provocative actions, and has had a strong influence on a new generation of Russian activist and performance artists. Whereas in the first phase of their work they focused on political performances and art pranks, over time their actions became more radical, eventually escalating to confrontations and vandalism, which caused major controversies. Voina consider themselves as an anarchist militant underground gang; they reject the use of money and chose a do-it-yourself scavenging ethic, including squatting and shoplifting. Contrary to other activist groups, they do not hide their identities. As their activities have spawned many legends and myths, Voina's statements are not devoid of ambiguity (for instance, they distance themselves from the institutionalized art world but participate in art events), and the group has become the object of projections and assumptions, which makes it difficult to pin down Voina's artistic and activist approach. Their activities are documented on the website en.free-voina.org, maintained by the collective and/or its supporters.

In 2005 Oleg Vorotnikov (called Vor, "thief"), a philosophy graduate from Moscow State University, and his wife Natalia Sokol (called Kozol, "goat"), later joined by members of the art group Bombily, formed a collective called Sokoleg, a predecessor of Voina. In 2007, Voina ("war") was founded by Vorotnikov and Sokol. As Voina consider each and every participant in their actions as a group member, to date they have approximately two hundred members. In 2009, Nadezhda Tolokonnikova and her husband Peter Verzilov, both members from the early years, were expelled, or split, from the group (the accounts vary); while Vorotnikov and other members continued their public actions in Saint Petersburg, Tolokonnikova, who later became famous as a member of Pussy Riot, and Verzilov staged performance art actions in Moscow, with both factions operating under the name Voina. Later, at the time when Pussy Riot caught the international media's attention, a controversy arose over which faction should take credit for which actions.

Mordovian Hour is an early action, staged on May Day in 2007, a celebration of the International Workers' Day, in which the activists threw living cats over the counters of a McDonald's restaurant in Moscow. In 2008, on the day before the election of Russian President Dmitry Medvedev, Voina achieved notoriety with their action *Fuck for the Heir Puppy Bear!* in which several couples held a public orgy at the Timiryazev State Museum of Biology. In the same year, in an action called *Storm of White House*, Voina gained access to a hotel across from the government building of the Russian Federation and projected a skull and crossbones onto the facade of the Russian White House. In 2009 Voina performed a punk concert in a courtroom, disrupting a federal court hearing: a formula later also used by Pussy Riot.

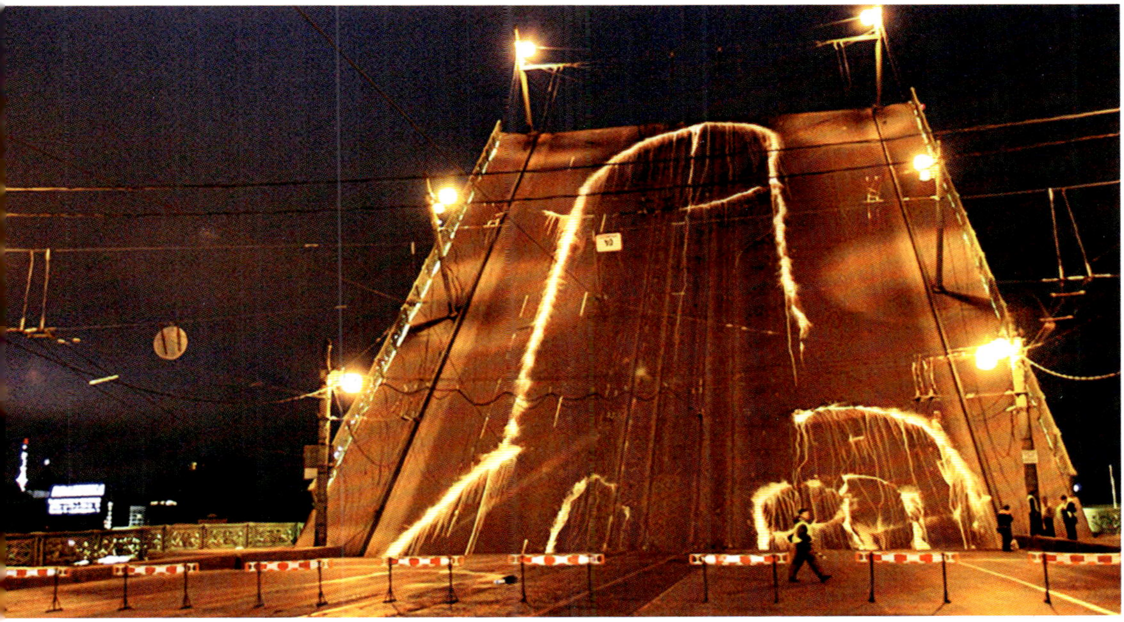

Voina, *Dick Captured by the FSB*, 2010, action in Saint Petersburg, photo

In one of their most monumental actions, *Dick Captured by the FSB* from 2010, Voina painted a 65-meter-high and 27-meter-wide phallus on the Liteyny Bridge in Saint Petersburg, opposite the headquarters of the KGB's successor, the Federal Security Service. Voina had studied traffic patterns, as they only had thirty seconds to complete the painting. For this action, Voina was awarded the Innovation Prize for contemporary visual art by the Russian Ministry of Culture. Voina did not attend the ceremony, claiming that their work does not need formal approval, and the prize money was given to Agora, an NGO defending prisoners' rights.

To date, more than twenty criminal investigations have been launched against Voina members. When Peter Vorotnikov and core member Leonid Nikolayev were arrested in 2011 on charges of hooliganism, British graffiti artist Banksy donated £80,000 from a print sale to Voina; Vorotnikov and Nikolayev were released on bail. In 2011, Vorotnikov and Sokol were declared wanted fugitives, and an international arrest warrant was issued against Vorotnikov. In response to this, "Voina Wanted" banners were displayed on museum facades and in public places also internationally, as an artistic intervention by Voina supporters and activists. In December 2011, Voina set a police van used to transport prisoners on fire.

In 2012, the artist Artur Żmijewski, who curated the 7th Berlin Biennale, invited Voina to be cocurators of the event. In late 2012/early 2013, Vorotnikov, Sokol, and their two small children – whom they consider as the youngest Voina members – fled to Italy from Russia. Since then Voina participates in public actions and events only infrequently.

Alexander Volodarsky *1987

Alexander Volodarsky is a Ukrainian artist-activist who studied computer science in Germany and became known as a blogger under the pseudonym Shiitman on the platform Livejournal. In 2010 he was arrested after a performance with a female activist in front of the Ukrainian parliament Verkhovna Rada, in which he imitated the act of sexual intercourse to protest against censorship by Ukraine's National Expert Commission for Protecting Public Morality. This commission leads investigations into all activities by media and legal subjects who create products with sexual, erotic, or violent content, and has targeted, for instance, films with Sacha Baron Cohen and artworks by Damien Hirst.

Volodarsky was held in pretrial detention for one and a half months. In 2011 he was sentenced under § 296 (2) of the Ukrainian criminal code for hooliganism to one year of prison in a "secure treatment center." Violators of § 296 can be sentenced to up to five years of imprisonment.

During his incarceration he produced handwritten texts which were smuggled out and posted on a blog called "Anarchy and Other Shit." On the more comprehensive website free.shiitman.net, news on the trial, press coverage, and information about solidarity campaigns and how to help can be accessed. The publication of Volodarsky's texts on a blog also affected Volodarsky's life in prison.

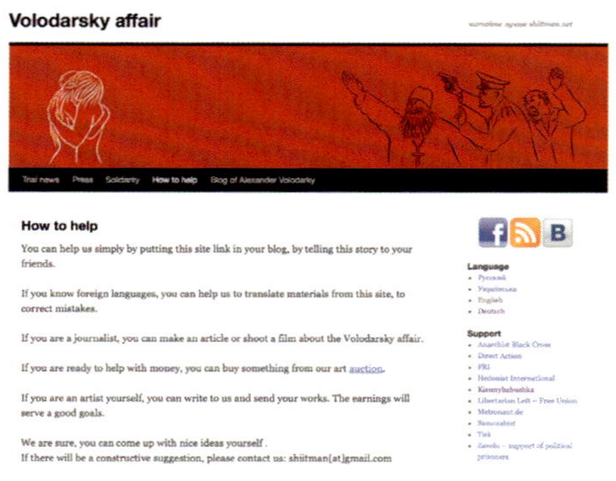

Screenshot from the website on the Alexander Volodarsky affair free.shiitman.net, 11/18/2014

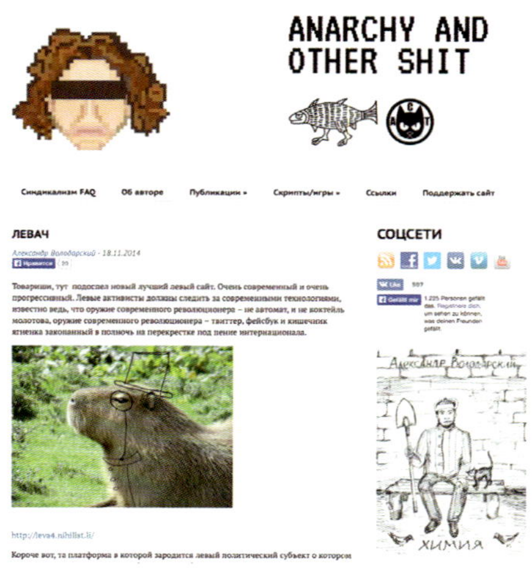

Alexander Volodarsky, screenshot from his personal blog shiitman.net, 11/18/2014

Here is an extract from Volodarsky's prison notes (part of the mixed-media installation *Prison Notes* from 2007):

Prison Rules

6:00 a.m. – Wake-up time

6:45 a.m. – Breakfast. Tea and porridge, sometimes broth.

7:00 a.m. – Roll call. The prisoners are sorted according to departments, and they are counted. After the roll call, all working prisoners go to their workplaces (some to the factory in the grounds, others are accompanied to their workplaces in the city). Most prisoners do not have a job and go to their rooms to continue to sleep.

11:45 a.m. – Supper. Colorless soup that can be spiced up with some dried pepper, as a second course: porridge with a hint of meat, a big piece of bread, and watery, sweet tea.

12:00 noon – Roll call. We are counted again and split up again; some to work, some to their rooms to watch TV, or some other simple pleasure/pastime.

5:00 p.m. – Roll call. We are very carefully counted; the names are called out.

5:15 p.m. (or right after the roll call) – Dinner. Tea and porridge. One time we had fried caplin (an arctic fish that is common in Eastern Europe) on bread, and everyone was waiting for it like a feast day treat. There wasn't any fish for several months, and our diet only became more varied thanks to the interest of a commission from the departments. After dinner, the workers return from the factory.

8:00 p.m. – Last roll call. By then everyone has to be back, including those who work outside of the detention center.

10:00 p.m. – Curfew. The guards walk through the rooms, turn off the lights, and count the prisoners.

3:00 a.m. – Control. At night the cops come into the rooms quietly and count the prisoners once again; they try not to wake anyone, since the daily routine stipulates "uninterrupted sleep."

At 6:00 a.m. Everything starts again. Fridays and Saturdays the curfew is 11:00 p.m., and the wake-up call is postponed to 7:00 a.m. This is how people are allowed to get a taste of holiday.

February 5, 2011

Aalam Wassef *1970

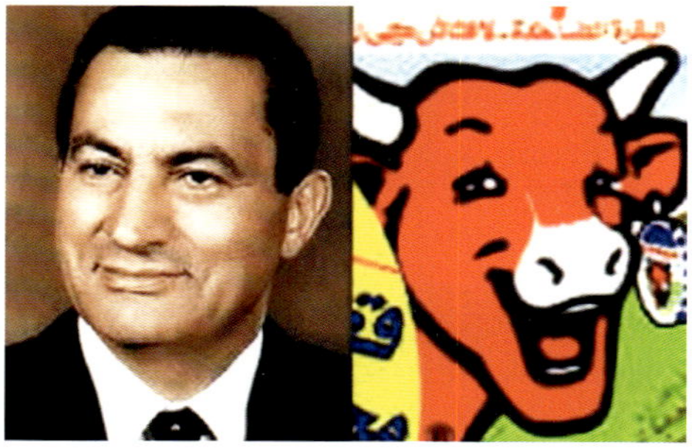

Aalam Wassef, *Egyptian Postcard #1*, 2006, video, color, sound, 0:35 min, video still

Aalam Wassef was born in Cairo, Egypt, and lived in France for over twenty years where he studied fine arts and new technologies. He advised publishers and public institutions about their strategies for digital cross-platform dissemination, distribution, and publishing and is founder of the platform PeerEvaluation.org. In 2007, Wassef returned to Cairo and focused on his artistic work, which has two strands: As an artist and activist, he works under several pseudonyms, as well as under his real name. In 2008, Wassef opened the 000-001 project space in Cairo and developed site-specific installations and art projects in the ancient Sayyeda Zeinab neighborhood. Wassef is also part of the Mosireen video activist collective.

From 2006 to 2011, Wassef adopted several identities, such as Mohamed Michael, the impossible combination of a Muslim and a Christian name, and, most notably, Ahmad Sherif. Choosing pseudonyms and the alleged anonymity of the Internet allowed him to pursue his work that was critical of President Hosni Mubarak. Under the Egyptian emergency laws, critical artists faced the possibility of being arrested, imprisoned, and tortured. Wassef's blog ahmadsherif.wordpress.com about the political and cultural situation in Egypt assembled political commentaries, images, flyers, and artworks and became widely known amongst supporters of the Egyptian revolution. Via his blog and YouTube, Wassef also published his own video works, combining documentary material, texts, and songs, such as *Actor of the Year* (2007) about a torture case ("President Mubarak, The world is watching you") and *Dictatorships for Dummies* (2008) ("I avoid free press – lies, lies lies; I do not travel – it corrupts me"). His aim was to raise awareness of the hypocrisy, the injustices, and human rights violations of the Mubarak regime and the constraints placed on the artistic and political freedom of expression: by gathering

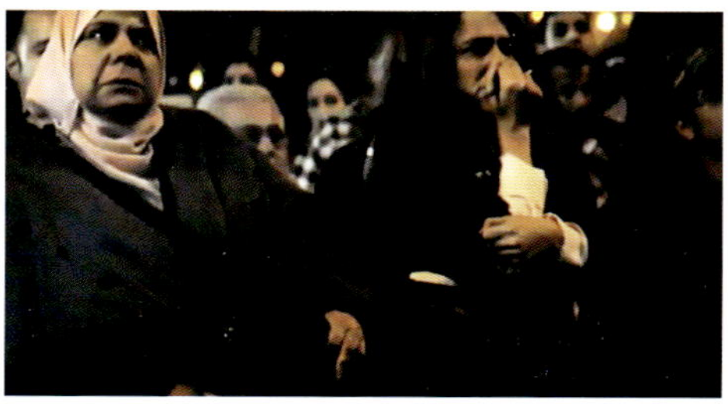

Aalam Wassef, *Watch Being Killed*, 2012, video, color, sound, 1:52 min, video still

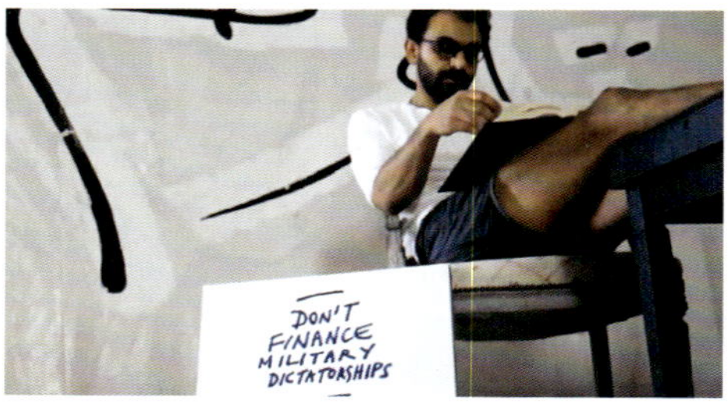

Aalam Wassef, *Speaking of Which*, 2013, video, color, sound, 1:31 min, video still

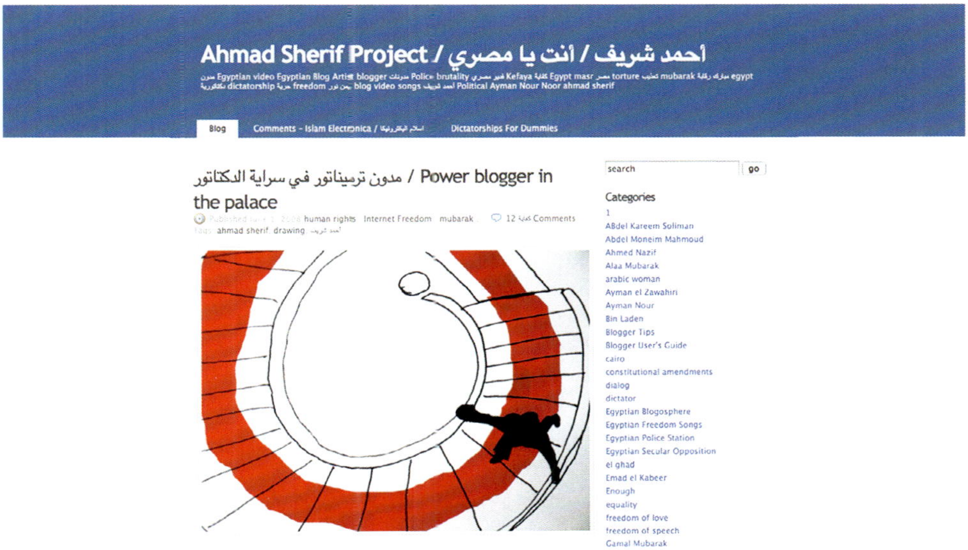

Aalam Wassef, screenshot of the blog he ran under the pseudonym Ahmad Sherif, http://ahmadsherif.wordpress.com

information, evidence, and proof from "the inside" by a collective of Egyptian bloggers, Wassef sought to foster a revolutionary culture and a language of dissent, and to encourage people to fight for democracy. Humor and references to popular culture were employed as a dissemination strategy to extend the outreach. When a torture video was published on ahmadsherif.wordpress.com, it was also covered widely in the news and was supporting material to a court case. For Wassef, "democracy is not something you get, it is something you aim at," and with his campaigns he sought to contribute to this process.

Wassef used subversive and viral strategies to create a counterpublic: In 2007, he began to purchase Google ads, and every time a search for "Mubarak," "Nile cruise," or "Egypt" was performed, ads with critical messages or mocking President Hosni Mubarak appeared. Wassef's campaign worked well for several months. His activities as an Internet activist reached a massive audience – but they also attracted the attention of Egypt's State Security Investigations Service who, for instance, started to bid against him for Google ads. In 2011, after the fall of President Mubarak, Wassef decided to reveal his identity and to continue to launch activist and art projects under his real name. In 2011 and 2012, Wassef blogged for the French newspaper *Libération* (crisdegypte.blogs.liberation.fr). For a documentation of his work as Ahmad Sherif, Aalam Wassef received an honorary mention in the Hybrid Art category at the Austrian media arts festival Ars Electronica in 2008.

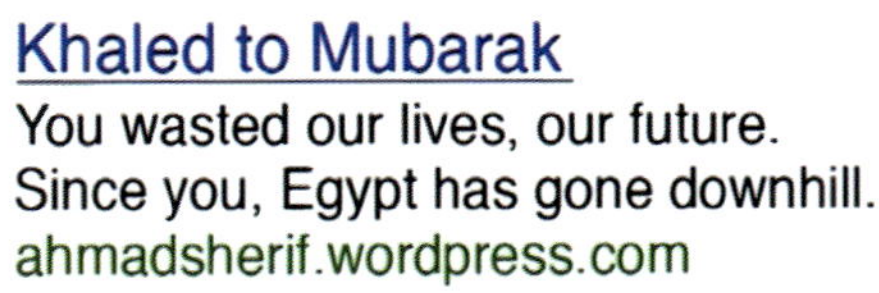

Aalam Wassef, *Mr Mubarak, You've Got Mail*, 2007, collaborative online happening, Google ad

Peter Weibel *1944

Since the early 1960s, media artist Peter Weibel has concentrated on establishing a concept of recognizing the political as the decisive field of action, thus developing an own sense of political performance, and thereby especially focusing on the audience. As a result, he conquered not only the exhibition space, but also addressed the audience in the public space – on the streets, at the university, in front of the TV screen.

As part of a group exhibition on students' day in 1968 Weibel staged the text action *Das Recht mit Füßen treten* [Trampling on the Law] to criticize and demonstrate the conditions prevailing in Austria after 1945, a post-fascist continuum. The entire floor of a room in the exhibition was inscribed with the word "Recht" [law] and the visitors only realized when they moved into the room what the title of the action meant: trampling on the law.

As a member of the Sozialistischer Österreichischer Studentenbund [Austrian Socialist Students' Association] Weibel co-organized *Kunst und Revolution* [Art and Revolution], an event which took place on June 7, 1968, in Lecture Hall 1 at Vienna University and in the course of which Weibel held his *Brandrede* [inflammatory speech], an attack on the then Austrian government, especially on Treasury Secretary Stephan Koren. Because of these and similar actions Weibel was repeatedly the target of police repression and in the end he fled to Sweden for a time.

Back in Vienna, he continued his actions in public places, for example, with his series *Anschläge* [attacks] (1970/1971). In *Polizei lügt* [Police lies] Weibel held up a slip of paper inscribed with the word "lügt" [lies] while standing under a sign with the word "Polizei" [Police] over the entrance of a Vienna police station (see this volume, page 243).

During the decades that followed his work has remained political; in recent years he has engaged with and commented repeatedly on themes such as surveillance, censorship, and whistle-blowing.

Thanks to the commitment of incredibly courageous and dedicated individuals, such as Bradley Manning and Edward Snowden, light has been thrown on the dark side of state-run data storage. Manning and Snowden defended democracy and civil rights against the encroachments of a security junta, which grasps policy in an ever tighter grip. This is the only explanation why Manning and Snowden, who have done nothing more than fulfill their civic duty, are imprisoned or forced to flee. The free world thanks Manning and Snowden for this enlightenment. If people like Snowden had not commented on military actions erupting into the privacy of citizens, the politicians responsible, like Obama, would have maintained their silence about this. NSA's PRISM program, the secret computer system Tempora used by the British Government Communications Headquarters, and other programs to control global data traffic: they all point to the distrust of the state towards its citizens. So, why should the citizens trust their states? In the name of informational self-determination (in German law the right to informational self-determination is the right of individuals to determine in principle the disclosure and use of his/her personal data) we call for a 20th fundamental right in the German Basic Law: The state should not spy on its citizens – freedom for the infosphere!

Bradley Manning / Invitation

Betreff: Bradley Manning / Invitation
Von: Peter Weibel <weibel@zkm.de>
Datum: 10.01.12 16:40
An: info@armycourtmartialdefense.com
Blindkopie (BCC): Joulia Strauss <jouliastrauss@gmx.de>

Dear Mr. David E. Coombs, Esq.,

I am Chairman and CEO of ZKM (Centre for Arts and Media Karlsruhe / Germany), which is one of the most renowned institutions for new media internationally.

I am contacting you concerning Bradley Manning. In my opinion Mr. Manning is a hero of the Information Age. In the tradition of enlightenment he distributed information to the public to protect human rights. He evidently understands that the internet, following the free press, is one of the best instruments to proclaim democracy. His example demonstrates that in the 21st century we are experiencing a shift from visual media to social media, in which the media are becoming the platform of individual agency as social engagement.

Therefore I would very much like to invite Bradley Manning to become a Fellow at my institution for a period of two years to share his competence and knowledge with us and to develop new projects.
Mr. Manning's Fellowship would entail a stipend and full access to our remarkable facilities. He would be at liberty to join our scientists and technology specialists in all areas of IT, proposing his own projects and/or participating in ongoing ones. Along with my colleagues, I would be honoured if Mr. Manning would accept my invitation to work at ZKM.

I am also pleased to inform you that as a curator of the Moscow Biennial 4, I had invited Berlin-based artist Joulia Strauss to participate with her media monument for Bradley Manning in this exhibition. Her media sculpture with Bradley Manning’s voice and face was a big success. I selected this project as a Western counterpart to the position of Ai Weiwei, whose video work "Beijing" was also shown at the Biennial.

I wish you and Bradley Manning the very best for 2012 and look forward to your answer.

Yours sincerely,

Peter Weibel

--
Prof. Dr. h.c. Peter Weibel
Vorstand / Chairman and CEO

1 von 2 10.01.12 16:41

On January 10, 2012, Weibel sent a letter of invitation to the whistle-blower Chelsea Manning (then: Bradley Manning), who is serving a 35-year jail sentence because of passing classified documents, including video recordings of the shooting of Iraqi civilians and internal diplomatic cables from U.S. embassies, to the whistle-blower website WikiLeaks in 2010. Weibel invited Manning to become a fellow at ZKM | Karlsruhe and share his competence and knowledge and develop new projects.

Facing page: Statement from Peter Weibel on the cases of Edward Snowden and Bradley Manning, released on the ZKM blog in 2014, translated from the German

Founded in 2002
Spain

http://yomango.net

Yomango

On July 5, 2002, a strange new brand began cropping up in the streets of Barcelona, Spain. On that day, at the height of the sales season, more than fifty people rushed through the center of Barcelona to the Bershka clothing store to put on the very first Yomango fashion show, documented in the video *YOMANGO: Official Presentation of the Brandname*. The show lived up to its "magical" billing: a simple object was turned into a symbol of another way of living. To be more precise, a ten-euro dress was spirited from the store, later to show up as a work of art at one of the most important art museums in the city. All the activities of Yomango were open, public, and publicized.

The name "Yomango" and the lifestyle it celebrates refers to *mangar*, a Spanish slang term meaning "to shoplift," particularly from multinational corporations. The concept of ethical shoplifting has suddenly acquired public visibility. The Yomango brand is itself a reappropriation, or *détournement*, of the widely popular brand Mango. By adding a pronominal prefix (*yo* means "I" in Spanish) to the clothing company's name, the modified brand takes on a different meaning entirely: "I swipe." On beautifultrouble.org, the website of an international network of artist-activist trainers, Leónidas Martín Saura explains: "Yomango disrupts the primary goal of the original brand, turning it into a new direct-action practice based on the widespread habit of shoplifting. At first glance, this may seem like simply surrender to the greedy logic of capitalism, but nothing could be further from the truth. As Yomango states on its website, its only interest in commodities is 'to make something new happen in their midst, to push them to the point of turning them into something else, something that has nothing to do with producing a way of life that is dedicated to consumption, but rather moves toward inventing new possible ways of living.' Through its actions and its philosophy, but also through its style and design, Yomango turns the impulse to shoplift into a movement, a method, an art form." (Leónidas Martín Saura, "Case Study: Yomango," available online at: http://beautifultrouble.org/case/yomango/, accessed 03/12/2015)

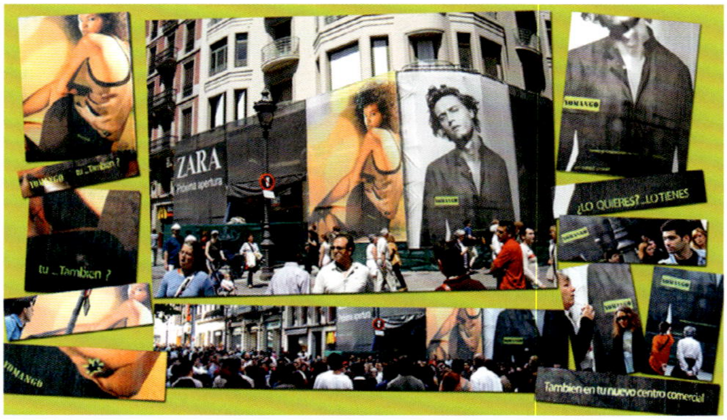

Yomango, poster, 2002

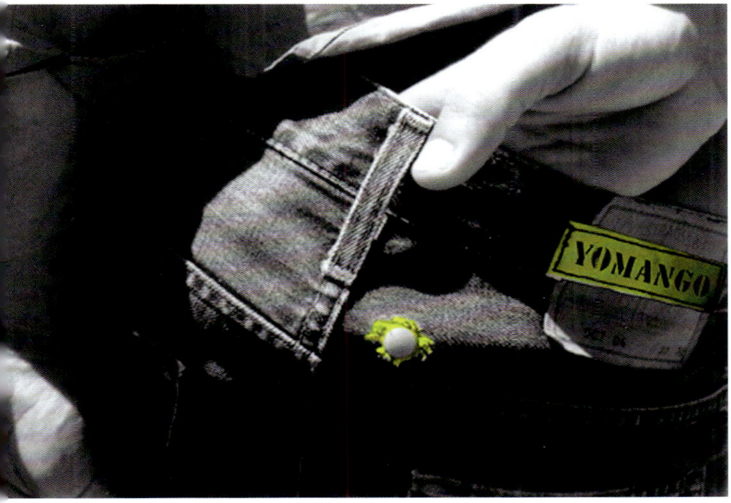

Yomango, poster, 2002

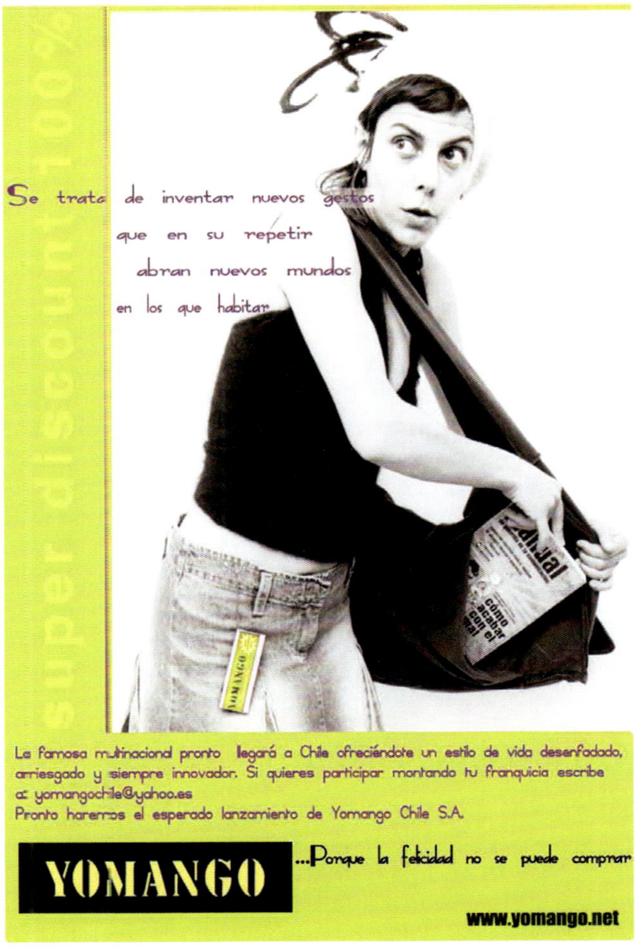

Yomango, poster, 2002

Authors' Biographies

Can Altay (*1975) is an artist and assistant professor in the Faculty of Architecture at Istanbul Bilgi University. He studies and investigates the functions, meaning, organization, and reconfiguration of public space. His "settings" facilitate critical reflection on urban phenomena and artistic activity. His work traverses sculpture, photography, and installation, and is staged and manifested in the spaces, exhibitions, and publications he produces. His public projects include: *Inner Space Station* (New York, 2013) *Distributed* (London, 2012), *The Church Street Partners' Gazette* (The Showroom, London, 2010), and *PARK: bir ihtimal* (Istanbul, 2010). Altay is the editor of *Ahali: An Anthology for Setting a Setting*, 2013 published by Bedford Press, London.

http://can-altay.com

Sruti Bala (*1973) is assistant professor at the Department of Theatre Studies, University of Amsterdam. Her research interests are in the fields of participatory art, theater and conflict, feminist theory, and pedagogy. Together with Veronika Zangl, she coordinates a research project on humorous approaches to art and activism in conflict at the Amsterdam School for Cultural Analysis (ASCA). Following her doctoral study on *The Performativity of Nonviolent Protest in South Asia (1918–1948)* (2009), her essays have appeared in the journals *Theatre Research International*, *Research in Drama Education*, *Peace & Change*, and the *Dutch Yearbook for Women's History*, as well as in anthologies in German and English. In 2014–2015 she is research fellow at the Free University of Berlin's International Research Centre Interweaving Performance Cultures.

Tatiana Bazzichelli (*1974) is a curator and researcher. She is director of the Disruption Network Lab, an experimental curatorial project on art, hacktivism, and disruption. She was program curator at the transmediale festival in Berlin from 2011 to 2014, initiating the yearround reSource transmedial culture berlin project. She was postdoctoral researcher in the Centre for Digital Cultures at the Leuphana University of Lüneburg, Germany (2012–2014). In 2011, she received her PhD in information and media studies from the Faculty of Arts of Aarhus University in Denmark. In 2009 she was a visiting scholar at the Human-Sciences and Technologies Advanced Research Institute (H-STAR) of Stanford University in California. She is author of the books *Networked Disruption* (DARC Press, Aarhus University, 2013) and *Networking* (Costa & Nolan, 2006 / DARC Press, Aarhus University, 2008). Her last book, coedited with Geoff Cox, is *Disrupting Business* (Autonomedia, 2013). Active in the Italian hacker community since the 1990s, her networking project AHA: Activism–Hacking–Artivism won the honorary mention for digital communities at Ars Electronica in 2007. She was born in Rome and since 2003 she lives in Berlin.

www.disruptionlab.org
http://networkingart.eu
http://disruptiv.biz

Youness Belghazi is a filmmaker and human rights activist from Salé, Morocco, who graduated with a degree in sound production. He is one of the founders of the February 20 Movement and codirector and coproducer of several short films and documentaries, which deal particularly with the right to freedom of expression, including the experimental documentary *L'Mask* (2012) and Nadir Bouhmouch's film *My Makhzen & Me* (2012), in which he also participated. Belghazi is a cofounder of Guerrilla Cinema, a group of resistance fighters, who seek to encourage the Moroccan people to question the ruling system. In Morocco it is prohibited to film without a license from the authorities. To independent film crews who want to pursue their passion, this permission is not granted and they are therefore forced to film illegally. If they are caught by the police, their equipment may be confiscated. The short documentary *Basta – The Film That Had Never Been Done* (2012), for example, was also shot illegally; it documents censorship and propaganda in Morocco and how challenging it is to shoot independent films. With his experiences, impressions, and reports of his own political commitment, Belghazi aims to offer an international audience a better understanding of the transformations taking place in Morocco.

Robin Celikates is associate professor of political and social philosophy at the University of Amsterdam, where he is also the vice director of the Amsterdam School for Cultural Analysis (ASCA) and a member of the Amsterdam Centre for Globalisation Studies (ACGS). He is the author of *Kritik als soziale Praxis* (Campus, 2009) and the coauthor of *Politische Philosophie* (Reclam, 2013) as well as coeditor of the journals *Krisis* and *Polar*.

Hadeer Elmahdawy is an Egyptian journalist and researcher, who took part in many events and some campaigns of the Egyptian revolution. She graduated from the Political Sciences Department of the Faculty of Economics and Political Science at Cairo University in 2006. She began working as a journalist in the same year, covering issues of health care, corruption, poverty, and political, social, and cultural aspects of Egyptian society She also worked for almost two years as a research assistant in various Egyptian research centers, and for almost three years in Egyptian independent theater. She now works as a freelance journalist for the Lebanese newspaper *As-Safir*, and the German magazine and website *Correspondents*. She is currently writing her master's thesis on political culture and protests at the European Mediterranean Studies Program of Cairo University.

Korhan Gümüş (*1954) is an architect and urban planner. He was director of urban and architectural projects for the Istanbul 2010 European Capital of Culture Agency. As a cofounder of the Taksim Platform, he supports the democratic right of citizens to have a say in the design of the Taksim Square, and was one of the initiators of the protests in Gezi Park at the end of May 2013.

Dietrich Heissenbüttel (*1956) studied literature (Italian, English, French, and Francophone literature) and history of art. His PhD thesis was on medieval frescoes in southern Italy. Since 1996 he has been making radio programs on jazz and improvised music for FRS, an independent radio station in Stuttgart, Germany. He also works for various daily newspapers and specialist journals (including *springerin – Hefte für Gegenwartskunst*, *Neue Zeitschrift für Musik*, *KONTEXT Wochenzeitung*). His main subjects are globalization, contemporary art, new music, architecture, and transport policy. Heissenbüttel was the recipient of scholarships at the Bibliotheca Hertziana in Rome and the Akademie Schloss Solitude in Stuttgart. From 2005 to 2006 he moderated an intercultural composers' workshop, "Global Interplay," at the ISCM festival World New Music Days. He has taught at the University of Stuttgart's History of Art Institute since 2008.
In 2010 he was cocurator of the exhibition, *Friedensschauplätze / Theater of Peace* for the Neue Gesellschaft für bildende Kunst (nGbK) in Berlin. Dietrich Heissenbüttel has written numerous articles on the subject of art and conflict

for various publications. He is also active in the campaigns to preserve the University of Stuttgart's History of Art Institute and Stuttgart's main railway station.
www.artwritings.de

Bruno Latour (*1947) is professor at Sciences Po Paris and director of the TARDE program (Theory of Actor-network and Research in Digital Environments). From 1982 to 2006 he was professor at the Centre de Sociologie de l'Innovation (CSI) at the École nationale supérieure des mines in Paris and, for various periods, visiting professor at University of California, San Diego (UCSD), at the London School of Economics and Political Science (LSE), and in the Department of the History of Science at Harvard University. In addition to work in philosophy, history, sociology, and anthropology of science, he has collaborated on many studies in science policy and research management. He has published various books and articles, including: *Laboratory Life. The Construction of Scientific Facts* (Princeton University Press, 1986); *Science in Action* (1987); *The Pasteurization of France* (1988); *Pandora's Hope. Essays in the Reality of Science Studies* (1999); *We Have Never Been Modern* (1993; all with Harvard University Press); *Reassembling the Social. An Introduction to Actor-Network-Theory* (Oxford University Press, 2005); *On the Modern Cult of the Factish Gods* (Duke University Press, 2010). Together with Peter Weibel he curated the major exhibitions *Iconoclash. Beyond the Image Wars in Science, Religion and Art* (2002) and *Making Things Public. The Atmospheres of Democracy* (2005) at ZKM | Center for Art and Media Karlsruhe, both accompanied by comprehensive publications with The MIT Press. In 2013 he received the Holberg Prize.
www.bruno-latour.fr

Sarah Lewison (*1960) is an artist, writer, and activist whose work centers on political ecology, intersubjectivity, and critical pedagogies. Her installation, performance, and media projects address relationships between human and nonhuman entities through play, dialog, and images. She has presented work and lectured in the USA and internationally; currently often in collaboration with Compass collective. Her essays appeared in: Pat Harrigan and Noah Wardrip-Fruin (eds.), *Third Person. Authoring and Exploring Vast Narratives* (The MIT Press, 2009); Alexis Bhagat and Lize Mogel (eds.), *An Atlas of Radical Cartography*, Journal of Aesthetics & Protest (2007); Nicole Antebi, Colin Dickey, and Robby Herbst (eds.), *Failure! Experiments in Aesthetic and Social Practices*, Journal of Aesthetics & Protest (2008); *Tema* (Denmark); *Journal of Northeast Issues* (Germany); *AREA* (Chicago); *Journal of Aesthetics & Protest* (Los Angeles). She is an associate professor in the College of Mass Communication and Media Arts at Southern Illinois University, has also taught at University of Chicago, University of California at Davis, and San Francisco State University.
www.carbonfarm.us

Sarah Maske is an art historian, economist, and curator based in Karlsruhe. In 2013, she completed her MA at the Johannes Gutenberg University in Mainz with a thesis on Wolf Vostell's television works. She currently works as a curatorial and research trainee at the ZKM | Museum of Contemporary Art in Karlsruhe, where she was project manager of the *global aCtIVISm* exhibition. She has contributed to various exhibitions including *Das Theater ist auf der Straße. Die Happenings von Wolf Vostell* at the Museum Morsbroich in Leverkusen in 2010, and *Fluxus at 50* at the Museum Wiesbaden in 2012. Her main research interests are art in public space, as well as performative and intermedia art and video art.

Ugo Mattei (*1961) attended the Law School of the University of Turin (JD, 1983), University of California Berkeley School of Law (LLM, Fulbright Fellow, 1989), the London School of

Economics, and the Faculté internationale de droit comparé, Strasbourg. He has been a visiting scholar at Yale Law School and the University of Cambridge, and a visiting professor in Oslo, Berkeley, Montpellier, and Macau. In 1997 he accepted a professorship at the University of Turin, Faculty of Law. As a lawyer and an activist, Mattei recently masterminded the Italian campaign against the privatization of water, which was successfully completed in June 2011 with a national referendum in which over 27 million Italians voted to endorse his scheme to recognize water as a common good. His highly interdisciplinary work has been published widely in many languages. *Beni comuni. Un manifesto,* which has been published in Italian in 2011 (Laterza) and in Spanish in 2013 (Editorial Trotta S.A.), provides a theoretical basis for the current wave of resistance against neoliberalism in Italy, and has reached its eighth edition in just six months. Mattei's most recent books are *Contro riforme* (Einaudi, 2013) and *"Senza proprietà non c'è libertà" Falso!* (Laterza, 2014).

Graham Meikle is professor of social media at the University of Westminster, London. His most recent book is *Media Convergence. Networked Digital Media in Everyday Life*, coauthored with Sherman Young (Palgrave Macmillan, 2011). His next book, *Social Media. Creativity, Sharing, Visibility* will be published by Routledge in 2015.

André Mesquita focuses his research on the relationship between art, politics, and activism. He holds a PhD in social history from the Faculty of Philosophy, Languages and Literature, and Human Sciences at the University of São Paulo, Brazil, and is the author of *Insurgências Poéticas: Arte Ativista e Ação Coletiva* (Annablume/FAPESP, 2011). Mesquita is a member of Red Conceptualismos del Sur, was one of the curators of the exhibition *Losing the Human Form. A Seismic Image of the 1980s in Latin America* (Museo Reina Sofía, Madrid, 2012), and cocurated the exhibition *Politicization of Friendship* (Museum of Contemporary Art Metelkova, Ljubljana, 2014).

Marcus Michaelsen (*1974) is a researcher specializing in digital media, democratization, and Iranian politics. He obtained his PhD in media and communication studies from the University of Erfurt, Germany, with a dissertation on the role of the Internet in Iran's political transformation (published in German: *Wir sind die Medien. Internet und politischer Wandel in Iran*, transcript, 2013). He is also the editor of a collection of articles by Iranian journalists on the 2009 election protests and their subsequent repression (*Election Fallout. Iran's Exiled Journalists on their Struggles for Democratic Change*, Schiler, 2011). From 2004 to 2006, Marcus Michaelsen lived in Tehran as a research fellow at the Institut Français de Recherche en Iran (IFRI).

Walter D. Mignolo (*1941) is William H. Wannamaker Distinguished Professor of Literature and Roman Studies and director of the Center for Global Studies and the Humanities at Duke University (Durham, New York) and holds an associated research position at the Andina Simón Bolívar University in Quito, Ecuador. He has been working for the past 25 years on the formation and transformation of the modern/colonial world system and on the idea of Western civilization. Among his major works are: *The Darker Side of The Renaissance. Literacy, Territoriality, and Colonization* (University of Michigan Press, 1995); *Local Histories / Global Designs. Coloniality, Subaltern Knowledge, and Border Thinking* (Princeton University Press, 2000); *The Idea of Latin America* (Blackwell, 2005); *The Darker Side of Western Modernity. Global Futures, Decolonial Options* (Duke University Press, 2011); *Learning to Unlearn. Decolonial Reflections from Eurasia and the Americas* (with Madina Tlostanova, Ohio State University Press, 2012). Mignolo has co-organized with Rolando Vázquez summer schools on

"Coloniality and Decoloniality" at the Roosevelt Academy of the University of Utrecht in Middelburg, Netherlands. He has coedited numerous books and edited a wide range of journals. He is a member of many international advisory boards, including the advisory board of the Hong Kong Advanced Institute for Cross-Disciplinary Studies, where he was a visiting fellow from January to June of 2012. He will be at the Centre for Indian Studies in Africa (CISA) at the University of the Witwatersrand, Johannesburg (ZA), at the invitation of the Wits Distinguished Scholars.

http://waltermignolo.com

Antonio Negri (*1933) studied philosophy at the University of Padova, Italy, at the École normale supérieure in Paris, and at the Istituto di Studi Storici Benedetto Croce in Naples, Italy. He became professor of state doctrine at the University of Padova. In 1969, in the aftermath of the workers' and student protests, in which he took an active part, he founded the political organization Potere Operaio [Workers' Power] together with Oreste Scalzone and Franco Piperno. From that moment he became one of the main points of reference within the Workers' Autonomy movement. In 1979, he was arrested in relation to the "April 7 trial," along with numerous other members of the extraparliamentary and academic Left, and charged with being the leader of a terrorist organization – a charge that was promptly dropped. In 1983, after four and a half years in prison awaiting trial, he was elected to the Italian parliament as a deputy with the Radical Party. Released thanks to parliamentary immunity, he escaped to Paris. In France, where he lived for the next fourteen years, he returned to teaching at the university level, at University of Paris 8 and the Collège international de philosophie. During his exile in France, Negri met up again with old intellectual friends (Louis Althusser, Félix Guattari, Gilles Deleuze, Michel Foucault), and started new friendships, in particular with a group of academics from the Paris 8, with whom he created a new magazine, *Futur antérieur* (1990–1997). During the 1990s, his original thirty-year prison sentence was reduced to eighteen. In July 1997, he returned to Italy to raise the political question of amnesty for political crimes committed during the "Years of Lead." He additionally served six years in prison. Negri now lives in Venice and Paris, and teaches at various foreign universities, particularly in Europe and Latin America.

Dimitris Papadopoulos is a reader in sociology and organization and director of the PhD program in the School of Management, University of Leicester, UK. His work in cultural studies of science and technology, politics and social theory, labor and transnational migration has been published in various journals and in several monographs, including *Escape Routes. Control and Subversion in the 21st Century* (Pluto Press, 2008), *Analysing Everyday Experience. Social Research and Political Change* (Palgrave Macmillian, 2006), and *Lev Vygotsky: Work and Reception* (Lehmanns 2010). He is currently completing *Crafting Politics. Technoscience, Organization and Material Culture* (Duke University Press, forthcoming), a study of alternative interventions in technoscientific culture.

Rita Raley is a researcher and lecturer at the University of California, Santa Barbara. She is the author of *Tactical Media* (University of Minnesota Press, 2009), coeditor of the *Electronic Literature Collection*, volume 2 (2011), and has more recently published articles on interventionist media arts practices, dataveillance, digital poetics, and global English. She has had fellowship appointments at the National Humanities Center, the University of California, Los Angeles (as part of a Mellon-funded project on the digital humanities), the University of Bergen (Fulbright), and the Dutch Foundation for Literature in Amsterdam. She has taught at the Rice University (Houston), the University of

Minnesota (Minneapolis), and the New York University, and she currently coedits the "Critical Media Aesthetics" book series for Bloomsbury and the "Electronic Mediations" book series for the University of Minnesota Press.
http://raley.english.ucsb.edu

Martha Rosler (*1943) is an artist whose work often focuses on the public sphere and landscapes of everyday life, especially as they affect women. Rosler has produced works for many years on war and the national security climate, connecting everyday experiences at home with the conduct of war abroad. She also writes about art and culture. Her most recent book is *Culture Class*, published by e-flux and Sternberg Press in 2013 from which the essay in this volume is drawn. Rosler has had numerous solo exhibitions at museums and galleries all over the world. In November 2012 she presented her performance and installation *Meta-Monumental Garage Sale* at the Museum of Modern Art, New York, and in 2014 her exhibition and project *Guide for the Perplexed: How to Succeed in the New Poland* was held at the Center for Contemporary Art in Warsaw.

Peter Sloterdijk (*1947) studied philosophy, German studies, and history in Munich and Hamburg from 1968 to 1974. In 1975, he received his PhD from Hamburg University with a dissertation on the philosophy and history of modern autobiographic literature. Since 1980, Sloterdijk has published countless essays on questions concerning time diagnostics, culture and religion, philosophy, art theory, and psychology. From 1989 to 2008 he was director of the Institute for Cultural Philosophy at the Academy of Fine Arts Vienna. In 1992, he became professor of philosophy and media theory at the Karlsruhe University of Arts and Design. One year later, he won the Ernst Robert Curtius Prize for essay writing. In the following years he received many prizes and honors including the Friedrich Märker Prize for essay writing (2000), the Christian Kellerer Prize for the future of philosophical thought (2001), the Sigmund Freud Prize for Scientific Prose (2005), the Commandeur de l'Ordre des Arts et des Lettres of the French Republic (2006), the International Mendelssohn Prize (2008), the BDA Architectural Critic Award (2009), as well as the Ludwig Börne Prize (2013). Since 2001, Sloterdijk is rector of the Karlsruhe University of Arts and Design. From 2002 to 2012, he cohosted the cultural talk show *Das Philosophische Quartett* on German public TV broadcaster ZDF together with Rüdiger Safranski. In 2012, he cofounded the Prix Mychkine. Sloterdijk was a guest lecturer at Bard College, New York, at the Collège international de philosophie, Paris, at the ETH, Zurich, and at the University of Strasbourg (Emmanuel Levinas Chair).
www.petersloterdijk.net

Karl-Peter Sommermann (*1956) is professor of public law, political theory, and comparative law. He studied law and history at the universities of Bonn, Germany, and Geneva, Switzerland, and administrative sciences at the German University of Administrative Sciences Speyer. This was followed by one year of research in Madrid at the Complutense University and at the Centre of Political and Constitutional Studies. In 1984, Sommermann received his Doctor of Law from the University of Bonn, and two years later he completed the Second State Examination in Law. He next became a lecturer at the Institute for Public International Law of the University of Bonn, and from 1989 to 1998 he was Secretary General of the Research Institute for Public Administration in Speyer. In 1996, he received the *venia legendi* from the Humboldt University of Berlin in public law, public constitutional history. Since 1998, he is a full professor of public law, political theory, and comparative law at the German University of Administrative Sciences Speyer. Additionally, he is visiting professor at the University of Paris 1 (Panthéon-Sorbonne), at the Sciences Po,

Paris, at the Andean University Simón Bolívar (La Paz / Sucre), and at the Fluminense Federal University (Rio de Janeiro). He is a former director of the Research Institute of Public Administration and rector of the German University of Administrative Sciences Speyer, and president of the Scientific Council of the Advisory Board of the Federal Academy of Public Administration.

Guido Strack studied law and political science in Trier, Germany. At first he worked as a lawyer for the Federal Ministry for Economic Affairs in Bonn. From 1995 to 2005 he was an officer in the European Commission in Luxemburg. There, he became a whistle-blower and informed the European Anti-Fraud Office (OLAF) about irregularities in his department. This resulted in a years-long court battle with the European Commission, which is documented on http://whistleblower-net.de.strack. After quitting active service, Guido Strack enrolled in postgraduate studies at the University of Cologne where he earned an MA in economic law, and completed a training course at the Friedensbildungswerk Cologne (state-approved adult education institute founded by members of the peace movement) to become a mediator. As chairperson of Whistleblower-Netzwerk e.V. (a registered association), Strack campaigns for effective protection of whistle-blowers, and as an expert has participated in hearings on the subject of whistle-blowing at the European Parliament, the Council of Europe, the German Bundestag, and the Landtag of North Rhine–Westphalia.

Joulia Strauss (*1974) is a Berlin artist and activist who unites art, science, technology, and politics, as well as different movements. Her most recent publication, *Modulating Politics* (Spree Athen, 2011), develops archaic structures of knowledge into a sculptural system as a political model that is opposed to the United States of Europe. Together with Daniel Mützel she coedits the Berlin issue of the activist magazine *Krytyka Polityczna*. Strauss studied at the New Academy of Fine Arts, Saint Petersburg and at the Berlin University of the Arts, class of Professor Georg Baselitz, where she received the Special Award of the president. She creates political monuments, such as the *Anamorphous Monument to Bradley Manning* (2010/2013). Her solo exhibitions include *Modulating Politics* (Kunsthalle Palazzo, Liestal, Switzerland, 2011), *Welcome to the Mediterranean Basin* (Beton7 Gallery, Athens, 2010), *Cat-Notation* (COMA, Berlin, 2008), *Medienspiritismus. Videokabinet* (Guelman Gallery, Moscow, 2003), and *Virtual Kingdom of Beauty* (Pergamonmuseum, Berlin, 2000). Her works have been shown in group exhibitions at the Martin-Gropius-Bau, Berlin, Hudson Valley Center for Contemporary Art, Peekskill, New York, Tirana Biennale, Oostende Museum of Modern Art, Stedelijk Museum, Amsterdam, 2nd Athens Biennale, Fourth Moscow Biennial, Tate Modern, London, ZKM | Center for Art and Media Karlsruhe, Perm Museum for Modern Art, Russia, and Museum Tinguely, Basel.

Zixue Tai is currently an associate professor in the School of Journalism and Telecommunications at the University of Kentucky, Lexington. His primary area of research pertains to the various aspects of the sociopolitical ramifications of Internet-based new media in China. He is the author of *The Internet in China. Cyberspace and Civil Society* (Routledge, 2006/2012), a pioneer scholarly work examining the social impact of the Internet in China. He has also published extensively in premier journal outlets in the fields of communication, new media, and journalism studies. Additionally, he has contributed numerous chapters to edited volumes focusing on the interplay of new media and Chinese society. He is currently completing two book-length projects, one focusing on online video games in China and the other concerning social media use and impact in China.

Vassilis Tsianos, PhD, is a lecturer in theoretical sociology and migration studies at the University of Hamburg He was previously a senior researcher at the Mig@Net research program and research fellow with the project Transit Migration (Goethe University, Frankfurt am Main, Germany) investigating the border regimes and structures of labor in southeast Europe. He has published numerous books, including, most recently, the coauthored monograph *Escape Routes. Control and Subversion in the 21st Century* (Pluto Press, 2008), and was coeditor of *Empire und die biopolitische Wende* (Campus, 2007) and *Turbulente Ränder. Neue Persektiven auf Migration an den Grenzen Europas* (transcript, 2007). His publications on mobility studies, critical urbanism, and antiracist movements have appeared in *Citizenship Studies, European Journal of Social Theory, Peripherie, darkmatter, Multitudes, Boundary 2, Sozialsysteme, 1999. Zeitschrift für Sozialgeschichte des 20. und 21. Jahrhunderts,* and *Texte zur Kunst,* amongst other journals.

Margarita Tsomou is a Greek writer, researcher, and artist based in Berlin. She publishes the pop feminist magazine *Missy Magazine* and holds a scholarship at the artistic research program Assemblies and Participation: Urban Publics and Performance (initiated by Hafen-City University, Kampnagel Theater, Fundus Theater) in Hamburg, where she is also working on her PhD on the Greek *indignados* movement of 2011, which focuses on issues of the "representation of the many." Her most recent academic publication dealt with solidarity networks in the Greek crisis as practices of exodus, and appeared in *WestEnd. Neue Zeitschrift für Sozialforschung* of the Frankfurt Institute for Social Research.

Tatiana Volkova has held curatorial positions at the Tsaritsyno Museum, State Tretyakov Gallery, Reflex Gallery, the Garage Center for Contemporary Culture, and the ZHIR project, Moscow. Since 2009 she has specialized in the research and development of Russian activist art. Tatiana curated a series of exhibitions of young Russian activist artists at the ZHIR project, Moscow (Winzavod Centre for Contemporary Art, 2009–2010) as well as the *Silence=Death* exhibition (Artplay Centre, Moscow, 2012). Since 2011 Tatiana has been an initiator and one of the moderators of the MediaImpact Festival of Activist Art that has been held in Moscow and other Russian cities, such as Novosibirsk, Murmansk, Nizhny Novgorod, and Saint Petersburg. She has written for exhibition catalogs, books, and the Web and given a course of lectures on Russian activist art.

Dan S. Wang (*1968) is a writer, organizer, blogger, and print media artist living in Madison, Wisconsin, USA. Wang's texts have been published internationally in journals, exhibition catalogs, and book collections. His art projects circulate constantly in functional activist settings and through artist-run networks. Along with seven others he cofounded Mess Hall, the renowned experimental cultural space in Chicago that operated from 2003 to 2013, and he regularly works with the art and research groups Compass and Red76. For the year 2013 Dan was named a Fellow in Arts and Culture Leadership at the Rockwood Leadership Institute of Oakland, California.

Peter Weibel (*1944) studied literature, medicine, logic, philosophy, and film in Paris and Vienna. He became a central figure in European media art on account of his various activities as artist, media theorist, curator, and as a nomad between art and science. Since 1984, he has been a professor at the University of Applied Arts Vienna. From 1984 to 1989, he was head of the digital arts laboratory at the Media Department of New York University in Buffalo, and in 1989 he founded the Institute of New Media at the Städelschule in

Frankfurt am Main, Germany, which he directed until 1995. Between 1986 and 1995, he was in charge of the Ars Electronica in Linz as artistic director, and from 1993 to 1999 he commissioned the Austrian pavilions at the Venice Biennale. He was artistic director of the Seville Biennial (Biacs3), in 2008 and of the Fourth Moscow Biennale of Contemporary Art in 2011. From 1993 to 2011 he was chief curator of the Neue Galerie Graz, and since 1999, Peter Weibel is Chairman and CEO of the ZKM | Center for Art and Media Karlsruhe. He was granted honorary doctorates by the University of Art and Design Helsinki in 2007 and by the University of Pécs, Hungary, in 2013. In 2008, he was awarded with the French distinction Officier dans l'Ordre des Arts et des Lettres. The following year he was appointed a full member of the Bavarian Academy of Fine Arts Munich, and he was awarded the Europäischer Kultur-Projektpreis of the European Foundation for Culture. In 2010, he was decorated with the Austrian Cross of Honour for Science and Art, First Class. In 2014, he received the Oskar Kokoschka Prize. From 2015 onwards, he is curator of the lichtsicht 5 – Projection Biennale in Bad Rothenfelde.

Veronika Zangl (*1962) is assistant professor at the Department of Theatre Studies, University of Amsterdam. Her research interests encompass theater, poetics, and memory studies, specifically Holocaust studies. Together with Sruti Bala she coordinates a research project on humorous approaches to art and activism in conflict at the Amsterdam School of Cultural Analysis (ASCA). She has taught literature, theater, and cultural studies at the Universitiy of Vienna and the New Design University in St. Pölten, Austria, and is a member of the COST European research network on memory studies. Her publications include *Poetik nach dem Holocaust. Erinnerungen – Tatsachen – Geschichten* (Fink, 2009), and *Körperkonstruktionen und Geschlechtermetaphern: Zum Zusammenhang vom Rhetorik und Embodiment*, coauthored with Marlen Bidwell-Steiner (StudienVerlag, 2009).

Ahmad Zatari is an independent journalist and writer living in Amman, Jordan. He has published two books and the third is on its way. He has worked as a cultural correspondent for the Lebanese newspaper *Al-Akhbar* and also as program coordinator for Freemuse foundation in the Middle East and North Africa to support freedom of expression in music. These experiences provided the foundation to set up and edit www.ma3azef.com, a website specializing in in-depth research articles and studies on music with the focus on the Arab world. Since its establishment in late 2012, Ma3azef.com has gained a great number of followers.

Bo Zheng grew up in Beijing. He has been making and writing about socially engaged art since 2003. He has worked with a wide range of communities, including the Queer Cultural Center in Beijing and Filipino domestic helpers in Hong Kong. His most recent project, *Plants Living in Shanghai*, combines a physical site with an open online course to explore historical, political, and cultural connections between plants and the city. His essays on Chinese socially engaged art have been published in journals and books. He teaches at the School of Creative Media, City University of Hong Kong, and is affiliated with the China Academy of Art in Hangzhou. He received his PhD in visual and cultural studies from the University of Rochester.

M. Ragıp Zık (*1981) holds a master's degree in cultural studies from Istanbul Bilgi University. He currently works at Columbia Global Centers in Turkey and occasionally serves at the Council of Europe as a trainer and expert. In the past, he worked for various civil society organizations in Turkey, Italy, and Greece. Zik is involved with a number of grassroots initiatives and takes part in international collaborations.

He is interested in minorities, linguistics, political art, historical dialog, and youth work.

Slavoj Žižek (*1949) received his Doctor of Arts in psychoanalysis from the University of Paris 8 in 1985 and was awarded a Doctor Causa Honoris from the National University of Cordoba, Argentina, in 2005. He was visiting professor at numerous universities: at the Department of Psychoanalysis, University of Paris 8 (1982–1983 and 1985–1986); at Columbia University, New York (1995); at Princeton University, New Jersey (1996); at the New School for Social Research, New York (1997); at the University of Michigan, Ann Arbor (1998); at Georgetown University, Washington DC (1999); and at the Film Department of New York University (2002). From 2005 onwards he was codirector of the Institute for the Humanities, Birkbeck College, University of London. Žižek is the founder and president of the Society for Theoretical Psychoanalysis, Ljubljana, and editor of the book series "Short Circuits" (The MIT Press), "Wo es war" (Verso), and "[sic]" (Duke University Press). His major works are: *The Sublime Object of Ideology* (Verso, 1989), *Tarrying with the Negative. Kant, Hegel, and the Critique of Ideology* (Duke University Press, 1993), *The Plague of Fantasies* (Verso, 1997), *The Ticklish Subject. The Absent Centre of Political Ontology* (Verso, 1999), *The Fragile Absolute – or, why is the christian legacy worth fighting for?* (Verso, 2000), *The Puppet and the Dwarf. The Perverse Core of Christianity* (The MIT Press, 2003), *The Parallax View* (The MIT Press, 2006), *Less Than Nothing. Hegel and the Shadow of Dialectical Materialism* (Verso, 2012).

global aCtIVISm

The Symposium

On the occasion of the exhibition *global aCtIVISm*, a research symposium and an activist summit with almost fifty participants from all over the world took place at ZKM | Karlsruhe from January 24–26, 2014. Here researchers, artists, and activists discussed how the forms and sociopolitical significance of civic engagement have evolved in the twenty-first century influenced by contemporary fine arts and communication media tools.

Concept: Peter Weibel
Organization Activist Summit: Joulia Strauss, Daniel Mützel, and Noah Fischer

Friday, January 24

Welcome, Peter Weibel (Karlsruhe)

Opening Speech, Ugo Mattei (Turin)
Commons and Cultural Political Agenda for Europe

Panel I: Activism and the Citizen

Robin Celikates (Amsterdam, Berlin)
Civil Disobedience as a Practice of Contestation

Bo Zheng (Hong Kong)
Nearby Facts to Trouble the Emperor

Olaf Bertram-Nothnagel (New York)
Word on the Street: Aspiring to Democracy in NYC

Jackie Sumell (New Orleans)
I Wish the Indians Won

Panel II: How to Do Activism

Rita Raley (Santa Barbara)
Care of the Community

Howard Barrell (Cardiff)
Nonviolent Force, Political Space, and the Uses of the Arts and Media

Youness Belghazi (Rabat)
Cracks in the Wall of the Palace: A Moroccan Spring

Bani Brusadin (Barcelona)
The Political Potential of Fiction: Experiments in Communication Guerrilla at The Influencers

Arman and Arash T. Riahi (Vienna)
Everyday Rebellion – The Art of Change

Saturday, January 25

Panel III: Tactical, Social, and Global Media

Zixue Tai (Lexington)
Finger Power and Smart Mob Politics: Social Activism and Grassroots Collaboration in China

Thameur Mekki (Tunis)
Social Media and Music as a Tool for Social and Political Mobilization

Martina Steis (Berlin)
Partisan 2.0 – On the Battlefield of Information, Propaganda, and Manipulation

Birgitta Jónsdóttir (Reykjavík)
Democracy Upgrade: 21st Century Lawmaking

Panel IV: Art and Activism

Olivier Krischer (Sydney)
Lateral Thinking: The Networked Ecology of Creative Activism in East Asia

Sruti Bala (Amsterdam) and Veronika Zangl (Vienna, Amsterdam)
Humor, Art, and Activism in the Global Moment

Sotirios Bahtsetzis (Athens, Berlin)
Image Wars: For a Novel Distribution of Semiopower

Tatiana Volkova (Moscow)
The Art Experience of Recent Protest Movements in Russia

M. Ragıp Zık (Istanbul)
Intervention through Art in New Social Movements

Jonas Staal (Rotterdam)
Art and the Democratic Experiment

Filmscreening *ART WAR* and Artist Talk with Marco Wilms, Ammar Abo Bakr, and Ganzeer

Sunday, January 26
Activist Summit

Introduction

Noah Fischer (New York), Daniel Mützel (Berlin), Joulia Strauss (Berlin)

Imani Jaqueline Brown (New Orleans), Antonio Calleja López (Madrid), Hadeer Elmahdawy (Cairo), Noah Fischer (New York), MTL (Nitasha Dhillon and Amin Husain, New York)

Daniel Mützel (Berlin), Napuli Paul Langa (Berlin), Lucas Oliveira (São Paulo), Joulia Strauss (Berlin), Alexander Volodarsky (Kiev, Erlangen), Artur Żmijewski (Warsaw)

Index

!Mediengruppe Bitnik
19, 242–245
#occupygezi
20, 438, 602
#StopWatchingUs
19, 246, 247
0.
20, 438
15M
85, 90, 152, 153, 231, 354, 360, 362, 543
3Nós3
497, 500, 501

A

A buon diritto
606
A Revolução Não Será Televisionada
501
Abbasgholizadeh, Mahboubeh
389
Abd El-Fattah, Alaa
545
Abo Bakr, Ammar
21, 544–551, 705
Abu-Kwaik, Tarek
532, 533, 534
ACT UP (AIDS Coalition to Unleash Power)
156, 157
Actipedia
20, 439
Adam al-Dhaib, Amna
159
Adams, Jason
485
Adams, Gavin
509
Adbusters
19, 132, 133, 284, 305
Adler, Laure
154
Adorno, Theodor W.
285
U.S. Civil Rights Movement
66, 313, 314, 540
Agha-Soltan, Neda
393
Agora
685
Aguerreberry, Rodolfo
504
Ahmadinejad, Mahmoud
276, 386, 388, 389, 391, 393
Ai, Weiwei
325, 326
Ai, Xiaoming
325
Akash, G.M.B.
21, 552, 553
Al Ghomous, Fatima
159
Al Naem, Kassar
158
Al Rousan, Yazan
532
Al-Assad, Bashar
240, 622, 623
Al-Ghazālī, Abū Hāmid
217, 218
Al Qasimi, Sheikha Hoor
220, 221
Al-Sisi, Abdel Fatah
546
Aladağ, Nevin
213, 222
Alawneh, Ahed
533
Albayrak, Mehmet Barış
210
Ali, Ben
462, 465, 682, 683
Ali, Muhsana
604
Aliberti, Giuliana
681
Almeida, Guilherme de
502
Altay, Can
19, 201–206, 694
Althusser, Louis
698
Alyokhina, Maria (Masha)
285, 648, 649
Alÿs, Francis
215, 223, 495
Amin, Ash
296
Amnesty International
19, 24, 58, 134, 135, 176
Andrade, Oswald de
452
Andrade Prado, Márcia Regina de
506
Andre, Carl
478
Angola 3
660
Anker, Steve
223
Anonymous
19, 20, 61, 136, 296, 313, 439, 457, 458, 655
Anonymous News Germany
20, 439
Antebi, Nicole
696
Anti-Apartheid Movement
479
Apostol, Corina L.
554
Appelbaum, Jacob
458, 459
April 6 Youth Movement
274
Aranda, Julieta
294
Arendt, Hannah
69, 100
Aristotle
35, 36, 37, 45
Art Not Oil
647
Art Workers‘ Self-Defense Initiative (ICTM)
650
ArtLeaks
21, 554, 555
Arts & Labor
299
Asendorf, Kim
602
Ashraf, Irfan
194
Assange, Julian
233, 234, 238, 240, 242, 245, 321, 323, 445
Atia, Yossi
21, 652, 653
Atoum, Zainab
159
Attac (Association for the Taxation of Financial Transactions and Aid to Citizens)
19, 137
Austin, John Langshaw
25, 35, 54
AvANa
456
Azazi, Ziya
540
Azzariti, Gaetano
88

B

Baan, Iwan
559
Bagad Penhars
540
Bailey, Stephanie
216
Baker, Dean
300
Bakhtin, Mikhail
449, 451, 452, 541
Bakri, Tarek
475
Bala, Sruti
21, 449–454, 694, 702, 705
Ball, Katherine
299
Balluch, Martin
20, 440
Banksy
685
Barbie Liberation Organization
284
Barmak, Siddiq
366
Baron Cohen, Sacha
686
Baroni, Vittore
460
Baselitz, Georg
700
Bashiriyeh, Hossein
392
Basurama
294
Baudelaire, Charles
451
BAVO
296
Bazzichelli, Tatiana
21, 57, 455–461, 694
Beallor, Angela
412, 413
Beck, Glenn
410
Begalskaya, Victoria
528
Begg, Zanny
20, 332, 333, 353, 510

Beieler, John
20, 334, 335
Belghazi, Youness
20, 271–278, 694, 695, 704
Belhassen, Sondos
682
Ben Ali, Zine el Abidine
462, 465, 682, 683
Benhnin, Abbas
215
Benjamin, Walter
509, 532
Bennett, W. Lance
398
Berardi, Franco
289, 296
Berlusconi, Silvio
85, 91, 92, 96, 671
Berman, Harold J.
43
Berners-Lee, Tim
374, 377, 378
Bertram-Nothnagel, Olaf
19, 138, 139, 704
Beuys, Joseph
57, 471, 472, 482
Bhalla, Angad Singh
661
Bichlbaum, Andy
190, 191, 624
Bicicletada
506
Bidin, Alexander
518
Biemann, Ursula
480, 481
BijaRi
501, 508
Birger, Irina
162
Bishop, Claire
54, 290, 294, 295, 297
Black, Rich
310
Black Mask
28
Black Panther movement
660
Blackberry
615
Blair, Tony
594
Blasquez, Jimena
215
Blissett, Luther
457
Blume, Félix
215
Bocara, Ivan
215
Boggs, James
485
Boggs, Grace Lee
485
Bois, Yve-Alain
597
Bombily
21, 519, 521, 529, 556, 557, 684
Bonadies, Ángela
21, 558–563
Bonanno, Mike
190, 191, 624
Booth, Robert
85–99, 667–681
Bosse, Abraham
44
Bouazizi, Mohamed
67, 631
Bouhmouch, Nadir
19, 140, 141, 695
Bourriaud, Nicolas
213, 22[illegible]
Bovay, Alvan E.
41
Boycott, Divestment, and Sanctions
140
Bozkurt, Osman
21, 464, 564, 565
Bradshaw, John
39
Brâncuși, Constantin
52
Brand, Dollar
479
Brandenburger, Elfe
366
Brecht, George
54
Brener, Alexander
516, 522
Bréton, André
631
Brillembourg, Alfredo
559
Brillembourg, David
558, 560
Bromberg, Ava
509, 510
Brossat, Alain
644
Brown, Bill
258, 259
Brown, Earle
53
Bruckbauer, Christine
21, 682, 683
Burns, David
291, 292, 293
Bush, George W.
143, 190, 235, 236, 478, 506, 571, 615
Bush, George H. W.
76
Buzzini Carvalho, Marilda
497

C

C.O.B.A.I.A.
501
Cabrujas, José Ignacio
563
Cacophony Society
457
Cage, John
53, 54
Caldana, Beatriz
497
Caldeira, Teresa
493, 494
Caldera, Rafael
560
Caleo, Ilenia
681
Callot, Jacques
476
Campact
20, 336, 337
Campbell, Thomas
514–530
Cancellieri, Annamaria
93
Canépa, Alfonso
450, 451
Canetti, Elias
44
CANVAS (Center for Applied Nonviolent Action and Strategies)
20, 338, 339
Cappon, Benedetta
681
Cardano, Gerolamo
49
Cárdenas, Micha
410, 411
Carey, James W.
373
Carlé, Martin
658
Carrière, Jean-Claude
154
Carroll, Amy Sara
410
Carter, Michael
258, 259
Carvalho, Flávio de
496, 497, 500
Casafranca, Augusto
450
Castelli, Leo
478
Castells, Manuel
374, 375, 378
Catadores de Histórias
508
Çatı Dance Group
586
Celikates, Robin
19, 65–72, 695, 704
Cengiz, Emrah
70
Center
523
Center for Artistic Activism
439
Centro de Livre Expressão
497
Certeau, Michel de
501, 563
Césaire, Suzanne
631
Chernyshevsky, Nikolay
568
Chim↑Pom
21, 566, 567
Chirac, Jacques
104
Chizhenkov, Vlad
523
Chomsky, Noam
19, 34, 61, 142, 143, 474
Christensen, Ralf
20, 340, 341
Christo
500
Chto Delat?
21, 554, 568, 569
Chubarov, Igor
526
Chunosov, Dmitry
526
Cia. Cachorra
508
Cirio, Paolo
19, 248–251
Clandestine Insurgent Rebel Clown Army
342
Clark, Lygia
497
Clinton, Bill
76, 380
Clinton, Hillary
430

Cohn-Bendit, Daniel
154
Colectivo Acciones de Arte
505
Colectivo Etcétera
21, 570, 571
Cólera
493
Coletivo Dragão da Gravura
508
Collective Thinking Work Group
354
Comando de Caça aos Comunistas
500
Compass
696, 701
Contrafilé
501, 502, 503, 510
Copyleft Movement
252
Correa, Ana
450
Coulthard, Glen
484, 489, 490
Cox, Geoff
456, 459, 694
Craighead, Alison
19, 260, 261, 262, 263
Creative Commons
19, 152, 252, 414, 419, 555
Critical Art Ensemble
295, 509
Cruz, Khavn De La
224
Custance, Isaac
161, 511–514
CyberGuerilla
266

D

D'Alembert
234
Dahl, Robert A.
29
Damascus Bureau, The
19, 197
Darsi, Hassan
19, 144, 145
Davies, Martyn
216
Davis, Shantel
635
De Togni, Guido
681
Debord, Guy
519
Debray, Régis
19, 148, 154
Delacroix, Eugène
535, 536
Deleuze, Gilles
698
Delfinov, Alexander
527
Dellaloğlu, Besim
543
Deller, Jeremy
591
Demand Progress
419
Demirbakan, Emre
540
Democritus
36
Demorand, Nicolas
154
Derrida, Jacques
106
Descartes, René
49
Devaux, Julien
215
Dewey, John
47, 48
Dhillon, Nitasha
21, 630, 631–639, 705
Diallo, Amadou
635
Diani, Mario
536
Diaz, Manuel
635
Dickey, Colin
696
Dieter, Michael
297
Digital Activism Research Project
443
Diogenes Laertius
36
Diretas Já
496
Djinović, Slobodan
338, 339
Doctors Without Borders
58, 588
Dollé, Jean-Paul
154
Dominguez, Ricardo
410
Domke, Johanna
20, 408, 409
Dorchester Projects
294
Dorokhov, Georgy
523
Douglas, Brian
590
Downey, Anthony
224
Draghi, Mario
91
Dreier, Ralf
125
Dubuffet, Jean
633
Duchamp, Marcel
52, 53, 587, 595

E

Echakhch, Latifa
216, 223
Eisenhower, Dwight D.
56
El Far3i
531, 532, 533
El Morabba3
534
El-Baradei, Mohamed
430
Elahi, Hasan
452, 453, 454
Electronic Disturbance Theater
20, 410, 411
Elefante
508
Elkoussy, Hala
220, 223
Ellick, Adam B.
194
Ellie
566, 567
Elmahdawy, Hadeer
20, 271–278, 695, 705
Enmedio
21, 572, 573
Enwezor, Okwui
213, 214, 479
Erdoğan, Recep Tayyip
201, 202, 204, 207, 208, 209, 426, 430, 539, 542, 584
Ertan, Ekmel
427
Esfandiari, Golnaz
429, 430
Espaço Coringa
508
Esqueleto Coletivo
508
Essam, Ramy
21, 574, 575
Euripides
659
Experiência Imersiva Ambiental
508

F

Facebook
20, 70, 140, 230, 248, 273, 283, 313, 363, 373, 375, 376, 377, 382, 383, 384, 391, 394, 395, 430, 436, 440, 469, 540, 543, 555, 584, 623, 626
Fach, Ole
602
Fadlabi, Mohamed Ali
215, 223
Faerman, Marcos
497
Fahlström, Öyvind
494, 510
Fairey, Shepard
313
Falkovsky, Ilya
518, 526, 527
Fallen Fruit
291–294, 296
Fanon, Frantz
490
Farinetti, Oscar
674
Fashutdinova, Tatyana
527
Fawkes, Guy
136, 313
February 20 Movement
140, 271, 275, 694
Felsenstein, Lee
458
Femen
285–289, 361, 527, 528, 683, 728, 729
Ferramenta
497
Ferrara, Gianni
88
Festa, Daniela
681
Figueiredo, João
500
Filali, Amina
140
Filippenko, Pavel
523
Finkelstein, Marina
279
Fischer, Noah
21, 512, 513, 576, 577, 704, 705

Floating Lab Collective
21, 578–581
Flores, Julio
504
Florida, Richard
306, 308, 309, 311–314
Forja
497
Foucault, Michel
49, 51, 107, 205, 433, 519, 698
França, Rafael
500
Francis, Nick
176
Frank, Andre Gunder
219
Franklin, Benjamin
41
Free Speech Movement
302
Freedom of the Press Foundation
20, 441
Freij, Muath
19, 146, 147
Freire, Cristina
499, 506
Freitas, Frederico
498
Fremeaux, Isabelle
20, 342, 343
Frente 3 de Fevereiro
501, 506, 508
Freyer, Conny
264, 265
Fuad, Arnold
168, 169

G

Gaines, Jeremy
23–27, 29–61, 111–118, 119–128, 279–288, 315–324, 463–482, 592–597
Galgano, Francesco
678, 679
Gandhi, Mahatma
65, 66, 124
Ganzeer
21, 544–551, 705
García Bernal, Gael
176, 177
Garrett, R. Kelly
398
Gaskarov, Alexei
525
Gates, Theaster
294
Gautel, Jakob
21, 582, 583
Geisel, Ernesto
496
Gell, Alfred
60
Genç Müminler
209
George, Susan
301
Ghazi, Fereshteh
392
Gilbert, Cass
311
Giorgi, Chiara
681
Girifna
278
Glaeser, Edward
309
Global Ultra Luxury Faction (G.U.L.F.)
637, 639
Gnil, Ira
527
Gnylitska, Ksenia
650
Goffman, Erving
537
Goldman, Emma
536
Goldman, Sacha
19, 148, 149, 154, 155
Gómez de la Serna, Ramón
451
Gottsberger, Rudolf
353, 355
Gould, Corrina
492
Goya, Francisco
476
Graeber, David
61, 305, 495, 507
Graham, Ramarley
635
Gramma
615
Gramsci, Antonio
385, 395
Granato, Ivald
496
Grant, Oscar
635
Gray, Kimani
635
Gray-Garcia, Lisa
353
Green Movement / Green Revolution
276, 386, 387, 390–393, 395, 429, 430, 463, 469
Greenpeace
19, 24, 58, 126, 127, 150, 151
Grohe, David
353
Gronas, Mikhail
521
Gropplero, Andrea
681
Group Center
28
Grueso, Stéphane M.
19, 152, 153
Grunert, Freddy Paul
27, 99, 681
Grupo de Arte Callejero
501
Grupo de Arte Experimental Cucaño
498
Grupo Rex
496
Guerrilla Cinema
140, 695
Gümüş, Korhan
19, 207–210, 695
Gündüz, Erdem
21, 464, 538, 584–589, 734
Güngör, Doğukan
538

H

Haacke, Hans
478
Habermas, Jürgen
30, 65, 385
Hacker, Jacob Stewart
32
Hadzi, Adnan
242
Hall, Ed
21, 590, 591
Hamidreza & Haleh
437
Hannibal
615
Hanson, Duane
478
Hardt, Michael
38, 61, 69, 93, 332, 667
Harrigan, Pat
696
Harrison, Sarah
445
Hartley, John
375, 376
Härtling, Peter
467, 468
Hartmann, Idis
21, 27, 592–597
Harvey, David
510
Hasegawa, Yuko
211, 214–217, 219, 220, 222
Hauriou, Maurice
119
Haw, Brian
21, 592–597
Hayashi, Yasutaka
566
Hayes, Sharon
20, 412, 413
Hebdige, Dick
302, 303
Hedonist International
19, 253
Hegel, Georg Wilhelm Friedrich
48, 50, 51, 490
Heinisch, Brigitte
320, 323
Heissenbüttel, Dietrich
21, 27, 462–482, 718
Herbst, Robby
696
Herman, Edward S.
34, 142, 474
Herold, Hannes
324, 719
Hesse, Eva
477
Hessel, Stéphane
19, 59, 154, 155
Heym, Georg
476
Hill, Julia "Butterfly"
19, 254, 255
Hiller, Kurt
476, 477, 482
Hirschhorn, Thomas
593
Hirst, Damien
686
Hobbes, Thomas
39, 44, 45, 58, 121
Hoddis, Jakob von
476
Hoffmann, Niklas
21, 598, 599
Höge, Helmut
514
Hollande, François
154
Hollar, Wenceslaus
44
Hsing, You-tien
397, 399

Hu, Huishan
325
Hubbard, Jim
19, 156, 157
Hudinilson, Jr.
500
Hudrada
650
Hulot, Nicolas
154
Human Rights Watch
19, 158, 159
Husain, Amin
21, 630, 631–639, 705
Hyde, Lewis
293

I

I.H.N.A.B.T.B.
523
Icy & Sot
365
Idle, Nadia
61, 423
Inaoka, Motomu
566
Independent Media Center
20, 441
Indignados
24, 33, 85, 102, 109, 302, 360, 361, 362, 462, 483, 542, 633, 701
Integração Sem Posse
508
International Encyclopedia of Revolution and Protest
20, 442
Invisible Children
379, 380
Iorsh, Alexey
21, 600, 601
Iranian Riots
20, 442

J

Jaafar, Ali
224
Jeanne-Claude
500
Jefferson, Thomas
40, 41
Johns, Jasper
478
Johnson, Simon H.
300
Jordan, John
20, 342, 343, 482
Joyce, Mary
443
Jud, Mathias
20, 426–435
Judd, Donald
477
JUST DO IT.
21, 602, 603
Justseeds Artists' Cooperative
299

K

Kachko, Alexandra
527
Kadan, Nikita
650
Kadi, Yassin Abdullah
126
Kadyrova, Zhanna
650
Kalı, Utku
240
Kambouri, Nelli
226
kanalB
20, 414, 415
Kandinsky, Wassily
51
Kane Sy (Kan-Si), Amadou
21, 604, 605
Kant, Immanuel
48, 237, 238, 473, 475, 703
Kaprow, Allan
54
Karaïndros, Jason
21, 582, 583
Karasek, Horst
468
Karasic, Carmin
410
Karroubi, Mehdi
386, 391
Kavecsprojects
624
Kefaya
274
Kein Mensch ist illegal
19, 160, 161
Kelly, Marjorie
90, 98, 669
Kentridge, William
479
Kerr, Clark
302, 309, 314
Kexel, Guillermo
504
Khaled, Said
547
Khalid, Mohamed
655
Khamenei, Ali
386
Khasawnih, Diala
534
Khatami, Mohammad
387, 390
Khomeini, Ayatollah
387
Khomenko, Lesia
650
Khotta Ba
531, 533
Kilpper, Thomas
21, 606–609
King, Jr., Martin Luther
65, 68, 124
Kiselev, Alexei
526
Kiseleva, Maria
610, 611
Kiss my Ba
21, 517, 610, 611
Kittler, Friedrich A.
49
Kläger, Florian
173
Klee, Paul
473
Klein, Naomi
342
Klein, Yves
53
Kleiner, Dmytri
459
Klock, John
486
Kluitenberg, Eric
519
Klumpner, Hubert
559
Kolbowski, Silvia
290
Kolektif Istanbul
540
kom.post
624
König, Thomas
537
Kony, Joseph
379, 380, 382
Kooning, Elaine de
477
Kosolapov, Alexander
470
Kotányi, Attila
493
Kouri, Maro
228
Kreativer Straßenprotest
20, 368
Kriventsova, Ganna
656
Krugman, Paul Robin
32, 237, 300, 301
Krylov, Matvei
525
Kuball, Mischa
21, 612, 613
Kučan, Milan
154, 155
Kuiper, Jan Jaap
19, 162, 163
Kulik, Oleg
516
Kunanbaev, Abay
523
Kurmaz, Sasha
20, 344, 345, 522
Kuznetsov, Volodymyr
650

L

La r.O.n.c.e.
342
Lacan, Jacques
235
LaMarca, Christopher
21, 614, 615, 725
Laouli, Mohammed
21, 616, 617
Lasn, Kalle
132
Latour, Bruno
19, 38, 73–84, 596, 597, 696
Lauterbach, Lynn
19, 136, 164, 165
Lazzarato, Maurizio
296
Le Pen, Jean-Marie
104
Lee, Ching Kwan
397, 399
Lee, Wesley Duke
496
Leirner, Nelson
496
Lenin
312, 477, 522, 523, 611
Leser, Julia
20, 346, 347

Let's Do It! World
19, 166, 167
Letta, Enrico
92, 671
Leverdier, Roger
110, 154, 719
Lévi-Strauss, Claude
499
Levine, Jack
477
Levitt, Theodore
299, 303, 304, 308
Lewison, Sarah
21, 483–492, 696
Liberate Tate
647
Lichen
615
Lichtenstein, Roy
477
Ligresti, Salvatore
93
Lincoln, Abraham
41, 512
Lippard, Lucy
478
Lippmann, Walter
46, 47, 48, 75
Liu, Hung
490, 491, 492
Liu, Jiakun
325
Locke, John
39, 121
Lomasko, Viktoria
21, 523, 525, 527, 618, 619
Los Angeles Urban Rangers
294, 296
Loskutov, Artem
517, 525, 610, 611
Lovink, Geert
297
Lowry, Glenn D.
612
Lucarelli, Alberto
88, 94, 95, 96, 99
Lucena, Cibele
502
LulzSec
313
Luntz, Frank
75, 78
Luo, Xiaoming
330, 403
Luther, Martin
65, 68, 124, 143, 457

M

McGregor, Chris
479
Machiavelli, Niccolò di Bernardo dei
107
Magistris, Luigi de
95, 96
Mahbubani, Kishore
211, 212
maiz
452, 453
Makeba, Miriam
479
Makhacheva, Taus
217, 223
Makhmalbaf, Mohsen
366
Malevich, Kazimir
51, 344
Man Ray
52
Mandela, Nelson
66
Mandindi, Billy
479
Manga Rosa
497
Manning, Chelsea (formerly Bradley)
233, 235, 236, 238, 239, 240, 319, 321, 323, 445, 512, 514, 658, 659, 690, 691
Mao, Zedong
326, 397, 399, 485
Mappus, Stefan
465, 466
Maraka, Aziz
532
Marcuse, Herbert
67
Marea Alta
452
Mariconda, Gennaro
674, 677, 678
Marighella, Carlos
496, 497
Marino, Ignazio
680, 681
Marjanović, Mirko
338
Marshall, Thomas Humphrey
30, 31, 34, 374, 375
Martello, Davide
540
Martens, Renzo
21, 620, 621
Martin, Trayvon
635
Martín Saura, Leónidas
692
Marx, Karl
50, 107, 234, 237, 298, 312, 473, 484, 638
Masasit Mati
21, 622, 623
Masekela, Hugh
479
Masha, Umnaya
527
Mashakel
574
Maske, Sarah
20, 27, 279–288, 589, 696
Mastella, Clemente
87
Mathieu, Georges
53
Mattei, Ugo
19, 21, 27, 85–99, 667–681, 696, 697, 704
Mattern, Moritz
21, 514, 658, 659
Matuck, Carlos
496
Mavromatti, Oleg
516
Maximova, Elena
527
McGuirk, Justin
204, 559
McKee, Yates
21, 630, 631–639
McNeill, David
353
MediaImpact
21, 526, 529, 530, 600, 610, 624, 625, 701
Medvedev, Dmitry
684
Medvedev, Kirill
517
Meetup
20, 284, 443
Mehrmand, Elle
410
Meidner, Ludwig
476
Meikle, Graham
20, 373–383, 697
Meining, Rebecca
21, 598, 599
Meirelles, Márcia
497
Melucci, Alberto
282, 295
Mendieta, Eduardo
212
Merkel, Angela
32
Mernissi, Fatima
218
Mesquita, André
21, 493–510, 697
Meta-Activism
20, 443
Metahaven
202, 438
Michaelsen, Marcus
20, 384–395, 697
Mignolo, Walter D.
19, 211–224, 697, 698
Mikaela
19, 256, 257, 287, 527
Mill, John Stuart
39
Miller, Toby
373, 375
Millî Görüş
207, 208, 209
Milner, Jean-Claude
235, 236
Milošević, Slobodan
338
MindBomb
21, 626, 627
Mir-Hosseini, Ziba
391
Mizuno, Toshinori
566
Modi, Mehelli
224
Mogel, Lize
352, 353, 696
Mohsen, Bassem
546
Mokhnatkin, Sergei
525
Molena, Fulvio
681
Montaigne, Michel de
49
Montesquieu
30
Monti, Mario
91, 96, 671
Moosa, Ebrahim
217
MootiroMaps
20, 416, 417
Morais, Frederico
496, 497
Morgan, Edmund S.
42
Morin, Edgar
154
Morozov, Evgeny
429, 430

Morris, Robert
478
Morsi, Mohamed
168, 272, 726
Moscow Feminist Group
527, 618
Mothers of the Plaza de Mayo
504
Motherwell, Robert
477
Motta, Carlos
21, 628, 629
Moussa, Amr
545
Movimento Passe Livre
503, 504, 505
Movimento Sem-Teto do Centro
507, 508
Mubarak, Hosni
4, 168, 272, 273, 274, 395, 420, 421, 422, 423, 462, 465, 545, 574, 688, 689
Mukařovský, Jan
481
Müller, Gin
452
Museum of the Revolution
19, 168, 169
Mustafin, Denis
523
Mützel, Daniel
271–278, 700, 704, 705

N

Nafeer
278
Nakonechna, Lada
650
Napolitano, Giorgio
91, 92
Narcophobia
524, 525, 527
Negri, Antonio
19, 38, 61, 69, 93, 100–110, 332, 667, 698
NEOZOON
21, 640, 641
Nerval, Gérard de
451
Neto, Alcino Leite
224
Nicklaus, Jack
487
Nikolaev, Anton
521, 525, 556, 618
Nikolayev, Leonid
685
Nivarra, Luca
88
No TAV
19, 90, 170, 171, 670, 671
Noel, Sebastien
264
Noisebridge
457, 459
Nova Pasta
508
Nunns, Alex
61, 423
Nüssli, Christof
21, 642, 643

O

Obama, Barack
143, 194, 235, 236, 313, 690
Occupy Abay
523, 524
Occupy Auckland
311
Occupy Frankfurt
301
Occupy Gezi
71
Occupy Oakland
309, 310, 492
Occupy Toronto
310
Occupy Wall Street
24, 33, 65, 68, 69, 90, 131, 132, 142, 148, 154, 232, 261, 266, 289, 293, 294, 298, 299, 302, 305, 307, 312, 314, 353, 354, 361, 363, 364, 378, 433, 462, 464, 465, 483, 485, 492, 512, 542, 576, 630, 631, 634, 637, 724
Oeschger, Christoph
21, 642, 643
Office for Anti-propaganda
463, 464
Oiticica, Hélio
497
Okada, Masataka
566
Okamoto, Taro
566
Olavarría, Juan José
21, 558–563
Omara, Marouan
20, 408, 409
Ono, Yoko
52, 54
Open access movement
419
Oppenheim, Meret
52
Orbán, Viktor
237
organ of critical arts
624
Orr, Jackie
225
Ortega, Julio
450, 451
Ortega, Rafael
215
Orwell, George
237, 258
Osborne, George
424
Osipova, Taisiya
525
Osmolovsky, Anatoly
516, 517, 522
Ostolski, Adam
352
Otero, Alejandro
558
Otpor!
338

P

Paik, Nam June
53
Paine, Thomas
40
Panagos, Nikos
353
Pandit, Vikram
299
Panofsky, Erwin
473
Panzino, Simona
681
Papadopoulos, Dimitris
19, 225–232, 698
Papandreou, Georgios
226, 227
Paravidino, Fausto
677
Parb, Thomas
355
Partizaning
20, 348, 349, 518, 522
Pavlensky, Petr
523
Pearson, Paul
32
Pecoraro, Giuseppe
677, 678
Peet, Roger
299
Peil, Chelsea
299
Pereira de Mello, Roberto
497
Périot, Jean-Gabriel
21, 644, 645
Perjovschi, Dan
468
Pershina, Natalya
527
Petty, Maximilian
39
Pfemfert, Franz
476, 477
PG
517, 518
Pisapia, Giuliano
93
Piketty, Thomas
32
Pinkney, Edward
488
Piperno, Franco
698
Pisya Riot
648
Pivetta da Mota, Caroline
495
Pizarro, Francisco
450
Platform
21, 646, 647
Plato
35, 36
Plungian, Nadia
527
Poe, Edgar Allan
451
Politics Outdoors
20, 368
Politkovskaya, Anna
517
Polsky, Anton
522
Popov, Serhiy
656
Popović, Srdja
338, 363
Popper, Karl
35
Prodi, Romano
87, 671
Professional Union of Street Art
556

Project Row Houses
294
Pussy Riot
17, 21, 240, 284, 285, 287, 288, 462, 517, 519, 520, 521, 523, 528, 600, 611, 618, 648, 649, 684, 730
Putin, Vladimir
17, 78, 285, 519, 520, 521, 528, 556, 648, 649, 730

Q

Quarta, Alessandra
88, 681
Quéau, Philippe
56
Quilombo dos Palmares
508

R

R.E.P.
21, 650, 651
Raabe, Paul
476, 477
rabble
19, 174, 175
Ragnole, Luiz Sergio
497
Raley, Rita
20, 289–297, 698, 699, 704
Ramiro, Mario
497, 500, 501
Ramos, Plínio
508
Rawls, John
33, 65, 124, 125
Reagan, Ronald
76, 298
Rebelodrom
452, 453
Reclaim the Streets
342
Red Brigade
282
Red76
701
Reed, T. V.
540
Refugee Strike Berlin
518
Rehm, Jean-Pierre
224
Reinhardt, Ad
477
Renzi, Matteo
92, 671, 680, 681
Repina, Anna
527
Rescigno, Pietro
677
Resist
19, 176, 177
Ressler, Oliver
20, 352–359
Rettet die KMB
612, 613
Reviglio, Edoardo
87
Rey, Begoña
215
Rheingold, Howard
400
Riahi, Arman T.
20, 360–365, 704, 719
Riahi, Arash T.
20, 360–365, 704, 719
Rice, Condoleezza
190
Richter, Gerhard
612
Ridnyi, Mykola
19, 178, 179, 656
Riot Grrrl
648
ROBIN WOOD
19, 180, 181
Rocard, Michel
154
Rodchenko, Alexander
52
Rodotà, Stefano
87, 88, 92, 93, 677
Romano Svato
452
Rommel, Peter
173
Romney, Mitt
378
Roosevelt, Franklin D.
300
Rose, Itamar
21, 652, 653
Rosenquist, James
477
Rosler, Martha
20, 298–314, 507, 509, 699
Rossihin, Alexander
556
Roubini, Nouriel
298, 299, 300
Rouissi, Faten
19, 182, 183
Rousseau, Jean-Jacques
39, 47, 48, 49, 121, 126
Rózsa, Miklós Klaus
642, 643
Rúa, Fernando de la
227
Rubalcava, Roberto
215
Rubiner, Ludwig
476
Rucki, Eva
264
Russian Feminist Initiative
256
Ryser, Daniel
242

S

Safranski, Rüdiger
699
Saharkhiz, Mehdi
393
Said, Edward
474
Said, Khaled
430, 547
Saint Phalle, Niki de
54
Samodurov, Yuri
524, 525
Sampsa
551
Samutsevich, Yekaterina (Kat)
648
Sandel, Michael J.
33
Sanguinovo group
497
Sant'Ana, Flavio
506
Sarkisyan, Oxana
519, 528
Sarkozy, Nicholas
604
Saro-Wiwa, Ken
647
Sartre, Jean-Paul
69, 77
Sassen, Saskia
25, 58, 205, 288
Satyarthi, Kailash
194
Scalzone, Oreste
698
Schäfer, Sandra
20, 366, 367
Scheeren, Ole
221
Schlingensief, Christoph
593
Schmalz, Bill
132
Schmitt, Carl
81
Schröder, Gerhard
32
Schulman, Sarah
156, 157
Schumpeter, Joseph A.
30
Scotti, Luigi
87
Searle, John
77
Sebaï, Malek
682
Seidel, Clarissa
20, 346, 347
Sen, Amartya
31, 33, 119
Servin, Jacques
190, 191, 624
Shakespeare, William
112
Sharp, Gene
279, 281, 282, 284, 287, 338, 380
Shawky, Wael
218, 223
Shehab, Bahia
21, 654, 655
Shihadeh, Firas
532
Shirky, Clay
407
Sholette, Gregory
294, 506, 509
Sieyès, Emmanuel Joseph
122
Silver, Marc
176, 177
Simon, Taryn
20, 418, 419
Sinibaldi, Marino
681
Situationist International
519
Sloterdijk, Peter
19, 24, 25, 111–118, 154, 155, 596, 597, 699
Smetanina, Yana
527
Smirnov, Alexei
525
Smith, Adam
31, 121
Smith, Mike
594
Smith, Rogers M.
374

Smith, Neil
484
Smoljo, Domagoj
242
Snow, David A.
537
Snowden, Edward
56, 233, 236, 238, 239, 240, 241, 246, 321, 323, 377, 433, 690, 691
Société Réaliste
554
Sokol, Natalia
684, 685
Sokoleg
684
Sokolova, Katja
19, 162, 163
Solitary Watch
20, 444
Solopov, Maxim
525
Sommermann, Karl-Peter
19, 119–128, 699
Sony, Warrick
479
SOSka group
21, 178, 656, 657
Souza Melo, Marli de
497
Spengler, Oswald
113
Sperling, Lisa
173
Spinoza, Baruch
38, 107, 110
Squibb, Stephen
314
Staal, Jonas
438, 705
Stalbaum, Brett
410
Stalin, Joseph
469, 648
Stam, Robert
541
Stein, Lorenz von
535
Stella, Frank
478
Stiglitz, Joseph E.
32, 300
Stockhausen, Karlheinz
479, 521
Stop the Traffik
19, 184, 185
Strack, Guido
20, 315–324, 700
Strano Network
456
Strauss, Joulia
21, 27, 275, 278, 511–514, 517, 624, 658, 659, 700, 704, 705, 718
Stuttgart 21
19, 116, 170, 172, 173, 433, 735
Sumell, Jackie
21, 660–665, 704
Surveillance Camera Players
19, 258, 259
Sushenkova, Tanya
19, 186, 187, 518
Suvero, Mark di
477, 478, 633
Svensson, Jörgen
293
Swartz, Aaron
20, 418, 419
Swinton, Tilda
224
Szpiro, George G.
33

T

Tai, Zixue
20, 396–407, 700, 704
Take the Square
20, 369
Taller de Investigaciones Teatrales
498
Tang, Weijie
330
Tao, Yuanming
492
Tavakoli, Ahmad
388
Tavakoli, Majid
390, 436
Teatro Valle Occupato
21, 27, 90, 93, 94, 95, 666–681
Telekommunisten
457, 459, 461
Telestreet movement
456
Ter-Oganyan, Avdei
516
Ter-Oganyan, David
656
Terre des Hommes
19, 188, 189
Terreform ONE
296
Thatcher, Margaret
32, 86, 233, 298, 299, 590
The Church of the SubGenius
457
The Laboratory of Insurrectionary Imagination (Labofii)
342, 482
The Yes Men
19, 190, 191, 624
Thomson, Jon
19, 260, 261
Thoreau, Henry David
65, 124
Thrift, Nigel
296
Tinguely, Jean
54
Tlostanova, Madina
529, 697
Tolokonnikova, Nadezhda (Nadya)
17, 285, 648, 649, 684
Tönnies, Ferdinand
46
Topbaş, Kadir
208
Torabyeh
531, 532, 533
Tozzi, Claudio
496
Trakl, Georg
451
Tranca Rua
508
Transparency International
19, 24, 192, 193
Traoré, Aminata
604
traschq
452
Trichet, Jean-Claude
91
Triki, Patricia K.
21, 682, 683
Tripper, Jay
310
Troika
19, 264, 265
Tsianos, Vassilis
19, 225–232, 701
Tsomou, Margarita
19, 225–232, 701
TupiNãoDá
496
Turner, Fred
456, 458, 459
Tweets from Tahrir
20, 61, 420–423
Twitter
20, 70, 140, 202, 204, 230, 273, 313, 326, 362, 363, 364, 373, 384, 392, 393, 420, 426, 427, 429, 430, 432, 433, 438, 444, 467, 469, 539, 543, 584, 588, 623
Tyler (Sbouï), Amina
683

U

UK Uncut
20, 424, 425
Up Against the Wall Motherfucker
28
Ushiro, Ryuta
566

V

Vallauri, Alex
496
Vamos, Igor
190
Vaneigem, Raoul
493, 541
Vázquez, Rolando
221, 697
Vendola, Nichi
96
Venizelos, Evangelos
226, 227
Verzilov, Peter
684
Viajou Sem Passaporte
497, 498
Vidokle, Anton
294
Viegener, Matias
291, 292, 293
Voina
21, 517, 520, 521, 556, 600, 648, 684, 685
Volans, Kevin
479
Volgina, Sasha
163
Volkova, Tatiana
21, 27, 515–530, 624, 701, 705
Volodarsky, Alexander
21, 686, 687, 705
Vorotnikov, Oleg
684, 685
Vostell, Wolf
53, 54, 696

W

Wachter, Christoph
20, 426–435
Wacquant, Loïc
61, 488
Wade, Abdoulaye
462

Wallace, Herman
660–665
Wallace, Victory
665
Wallinger, Mark
21, 592–597
Walther, Franz Erhard
52
Wang, Dan S.
21, 483–492, 701
Wang Jiahao
330
WANGO (World Association of Non-governmental Organizations)
19, 196
Waorani
614
Wardrip-Fruin, Noah
696
Warhol, Andy
586, 650
Warren, Mark E.
31, 397, 407
Washko, Angela
284
Wassef, Aalam
21, 688, 689
We are all Majid
20, 390, 436, 437
We are the 99 Percent
19, 267, 313, 379, 633
Weber, Max
41
Weerasethakul, Apichatpong
221, 223, 224
Weibel, Peter
19, 21, 23–27, 29–61, 242, 243, 511, 512, 518, 519, 592–597, 624, 690, 691, 696, 701, 702, 704
Weiss, Peter
476
Weisskopf, Carmen
242
Wesselman, Tom
477
Westerwelle, Guido
111
Whistleblower-Netzwerk e.V.
315, 324, 700
Wiener, Oswald
451
Wiener Gruppe
451, 452, 454
WikiLeaks
20, 234, 235, 237, 240, 242, 323, 324, 438, 445, 659, 691
Williamson, Sue
479
Wolf, Florian
275
Women2Drive
283
Wray, Stefan
410
Wu, Xian
402
Wu, Ping
400, 401
Wu, Wenguang
326, 327, 328

X

Xi, Chen
397, 399
Xu, Zhiyong
325

Y

Yang, Dacai
404, 405
Yang, Wu
400, 401, 404, 405
Yeltsin, Boris
522
Yerofeyev, Andrei
520, 524, 525
Yes Lab
190, 439
Yezzi
19, 197
Yomango
21, 692, 693
Young, Austin
291, 293
Young, Sherman
697
Young, La Monte
53
Yousafzai, Malala
19, 194, 195
YouTube
20, 140, 204, 250, 325, 379, 384, 394, 426, 427, 428, 436, 445, 469, 480, 519, 532, 574, 588, 623, 648, 688
Yusuf, Ahmed Ali
126
Yuyachkani
450, 451, 454

Z

Zaidler, Waldemar
496
Zaitseva, Anna
521, 522
Zalev, Susanne
284
Zamyatin, Yevgeny
470
Zangl, Veronika
21, 449–454, 694, 702, 705
Zapata, Miguel Rubio
450
Zapatistas
274, 410
Zaslavskaya, Polina
528
Zatari, Ahmad
21, 531–534, 702
Zheng, Bo
20, 325–331, 702, 704
Zhou, Shuguang (“Zola”)
401
Žižek, Slavoj
19, 129, 130, 131, 233–241, 521, 649, 703
Zık, M. Ragıp
21, 535–543, 702, 705
Żmijewski, Artur
685, 705
Zola, Émile
476
Zou, Xueping
327, 328
Zukin, Sharon
313, 314
Zumbi dos Palmares
508
Аркадий Коц [Arkady Kots]
517, 523
Верхотура и друзья [Verkhotura and Friends]
527
Ганди [Gandhi]
522
Жена [Wife]
527
Рисуем суд [Drawing the Court]
525
СВОИ 2000 [SVOI 2000]
517
Серое Фиолетовое [Gray Violet]
528
Феминистская кухня. Профоюз сексуальных работников [Feminist Kitchen: A Trade Union of Sex Workers]
528
ЭТИ [E.T.I. – Expropriation of the Territory of Art]
515, 516

Photocredit

Icons of Revolution
2–3 © Jeff Widener / Associated Press 4–5 © REUTERS / Yannis Behrakis 6–7 © AP Photo / Mahesh Kumar A. 8–9 © REUTERS / Osman Orsal 10–11 © Fred Dufour / AFP / Getty Images 12–13 © REUTERS / Yannis Behrakis 14 © Mark Ralston / AFP / Getty Images 15 © EPA / Sergei Chirikov 28 © Larry Fink 45 Public domain

Chapter I
64 CC BY 3.0 Stefano Bolognini 66 (top) http://occupygezipics.tumblr.com 66 (bottom) © REUTERS / Marko Djurica 67 © REUTERS / Murad Sezer 69 © Gürsel Göncü, © Metis Yayınları 70 © REUTERS / Murad Sezer 71 © Emrah Cengiz 101 © ZKM | Karlsruhe 120 © ZKM | Karlsruhe, photo: ONUK 131 © 2014, Impose Magazine 132–133 © Adbusters Magazine 134, 135 © Amnesty International, campaign: walker advertising agency, Zurich, www.walker.ag 136 © Lynn Lauterbach 137 © Kai Horstmann / www.attac.de 139 © Liz Starin 141 © Nadir Bouhmouch 2012 142, 143 © ZKM | Karlsruhe, photo: Felix Grünschloss 144 © Archives Hermitage park / La Source du Lion 2010 145 (top) Photo: La Source du Lion 145 (bottom) Courtesy the artist 146, 147 © Muath Freij 149 © Sacha Goldmann 150 © Bert Bostelmann / Greenpeace 151 © ZKM | Karlsruhe, photo: Tobias Wootton 152, 153 © 2013 Some Rights Reserved. Creative Commons License Attribution – ShareAlike 3.0 ES 154, 155 © 2012 ZKM | Karlsruhe and Sacha Goldman 156, 157 © ACT UP Oral History Project / Jim Hubbard 158, 159 © 2012 Samer Muscati / Human Rights Watch 160 © Fabrizio Casaburi, 2006 162, 163 © ThankEve Productions 164, 165 © Lynn Lauterbach 167 © Let's Do It! World 168, 169 © Arnold Fuad 171 © Pro Natura Piemonte 172 © Haus der Geschichte Baden-Württemberg, photo © ZKM | Karlsruhe, photo: Tobias Wootton 173 © 2011 Home Run Pictures / Rommel Film 174, 175 © rabble 176, 177 © Marc Silver 179 Courtesy the artist 180, 181 © ROBIN WOOD-Magazin 182, 183 Courtesy the artist 184, 185 © STOP THE TRAFFIK / www.stopthetraffik.org, Duval Guillaume Modem 186, 187 © Tanya Sushenkova 188 © Theo Dom 189 (top) © B. Rasing / terre des hommes 189 (bottom) © C. Kovermann / terre des hommes 190 © Common Decency, LLC / Article Z / Arte France 2009 191 © The Yes Men 192, 193 © 2014 Transparency International. All rights reserved. 195 © Claude Truong-Ngoc / Wikimedia Commons CC BY-SA 3.0

Chapter II
200 CC BY-SA 3.0 Mstyslav Chernov 203, 204, 205 Photo: Can Altay, Istanbul, 2013 209 Photo: Bertil Videt / Wikimedia Commons 212, 215, 218, 220 © Photo: Haupt & Binder, Universes in Universe 213 Courtesy the artist 216 © Photo: Haupt & Binder, Universes in Universe, courtesy the artist and Kamel Mennour, Paris, image courtesy Sharjah Art Foundation 217 courtesy of the artist and Laura Bulian Gallery, image courtesy Sharjah Art Foundation 221 Photo © Sharjah Art Foundation 234 © WILL OLIVER / AFP / Getty Images 235 © Mark Wilson / Getty Images 240 www.youtube.com/user/TheWikiLeaksChannel 243 (top), 243 (bottom), 244 (top right and bottom), 245 (bottom) Courtesy !Mediengruppe Bitnik 243 (middle) Photo © Archiv Peter Weibel 244 (top left) Courtesy Maxime Dufour 245 (top) Courtesy Helmhaus, Zurich 246 © #StopWatchingUs 247 © ZKM | Karlsruhe, photo: Tobias Wootton 249, 250–251 (bottom) © Paolo Cirio 250 (top) © Paolo Cirio, photo © ZKM | Karlsruhe, photo: Tobias Wootton 253 © Hedonist International 254, 255 © Thomas DeSoto 256, 257 © Mikaela, photo © ZKM | Karlsruhe, photo: Tobias Wootton 258 © Surveillance Camera Players 260 © Thomson & Craighead 261–263 © Thomson & Craighead, photo © ZKM | Karlsruhe, photo: Tobias Wootton 264, 265 © Troika

Chapter III
270 CC BY 2.0 Jonathan Rashad 275 © Joulia Strauss and Florian Wolf 282 © Red Brigade 283 youtu.be/nHsuzhd-1Fc 284 © Adbusters, courtesy Igor Vamos 285 © Pussy Riot, photo: Denis Bochkarev 286 © Arman and Arash T. Riahi 287 © Mikaela 291, 293 © Fallen Fruit 299 (top left) © Martha Rosler 299 (top right) CC BY-SA 2.0 Michael Fleshman 299 (bottom) © Chelsea Peil, Roger Peet, Katherine Ball 300 (top) © REUTERS / Juan Medina 300 (bottom) © Jacopo Quaranta 301 (top) © Maxi Failla / AFP / Getty Images 301 (bottom) © Bernd Kammerer 302 © Alfredo de la Rosa, 2011 303 (top) Bureau of Labor Statistics, Real Hourly Compensation, Business Sector, Series ID number: PRS84006153; Bureau of Labor Statistics, Output Per Hour, Business Sector, Series ID number: PRS84006093; online source: www.dollarsandsense.org 303 (bottom) Facundo Alvaredo, Anthony B. Atkinson, Thomas Piketty, and Emmanuel Saez, The World Top Incomes Database, http://topincomes.parisschoolofeconomics.eu, Paris School of Economics 304 CC BY 2.0 Nathan Jongewaar 305 Shared by Mark Hughes via Twitter, October 31, 2011, #occupy #infographic #ows #OLSX #OccupyLondon 307 (top) www.occupyboston.org 307 (bottom) CC BY-SA 2.0 Michael Fleshman 309 http://pix.toile-libre.org/upload/original/1308899279.jpg 310 (left) © Rich Black 310 (right) © Jay Tripper 311 CC BY-NC-ND 2.0 Jen Corbet 312 CC BY 2.0 David Shankbone 317 © ZKM | Karlsruhe, photo: ONUK 317 © Whistleblower Netzwerk e.V., www.whistleblower-net.de 326, 327 © The Folk Memory Project 328, 330 Creative Commons, photo: Bo Zheng 329 Creative Commons, photo: Bo Zheng and Jinghua Zhang 332, 333 Courtesy the artist 334, 335 © John Beieler 336, 337 © Campact 339 © Canvas 340, 341 © Ralf Christensen 343 © The Laboratory of Insurrectionary Imagination, courtesy the artists 344, 345 Courtesy the artist 346, 347 © Julia Leser and Clarissa Seidel 348–351 © Partizaning 352, 353 Courtesy the artist, ZKM_Collection 354, 355 Courtesy the artist 356, 357 Courtesy the artist, ZKM_Collection, photo © ZKM | Karlsruhe, photo: Tobias Wootton 358, 359 Courtesy the artist, photo © ZKM | Karlsruhe, photo: Tobias Wootton 360–365 © Arash and Arman T. Riahi

Chapter IV
372 CC BY-SA 3.0 Essam Sharaf 379 (top) www.occupywallst.org 379 (bottom) www.occupytogether.org 380 http://invisiblechildren.com/kony-2012 381 www.bitcoinfoundation.org 382 www.joindiaspora.com 386 © sabzphoto / Flickr 390 youtu.be/3QIVwHsrsvg#t=67 392 © Mark Ralston / AFP / Getty Images 393 © Pietro Masturzo / OnOff Picture 400 Photo © Derek R. Kolb 402 © Sophie Chen 403 © REUTERS/Stringer 405 Photo © Weibo 408, 409 © Johanna Domke, Marouan Omara 410, 411 (bottom) Courtesy Electronic Disturbance Theater 411 (top) Photo © ZKM | Karlsruhe, photo: Tobias Wootton 412, 413 Courtesy the artist and Tanya Leighton, Berlin; and Louis Cisneroz; Imani Henry; Sam Tylicki; Beth Vild; Provin Collection, Bancroft Library (Banc MSS 2011/128); University of Washington Library, Special Collections; Labadie Collection, University of Michigan; UCLA Charles E. Young Research Library Department of Special Collections, Los Angeles Times Photographic Archive, Copyright the Regents of the University of California, UCLA Library; Tamiment Archives, NYU; Hoover Institution Library and Archives, Stanford University; May 4 Collection, Kent State University Libraries Special Collections and Archives; The National Archive of Lesbian, Gay, Bisexual, & Transgender History; The Lesbian, Gay, Bisexual & Transgender Community Center, NYC; Lesbian Herstory Archives; Downtown Collection, Fales Library, NYU; Minnesota Historical Society; Smith College Archives and Sofia Smith Archive, photo © ZKM | Karlsruhe, photo: Tobias Wootton 414, 415 © kanalB 416, 417 © MootiroMaps 418, 419 www.imageatlas.org 425 © UK Uncut

427, 428, 432, 435 © Christoph Wachter & Mathias Jud 431 © Christoph Wachter & Mathias Jud, photo © ZKM | Karlsruhe, photo: Tobias Wootton 437 youtu.be/3QIVwHsrsvg#t=67

Chapter V

448 © Gerard Waillson Or 450 Photo: Elsa Estremaydoro 453 Photo © Rebelodrom/maiz 454 Photo © Hasan Elahi 458 © Tatiana Bazzichelli 459 Logo: Jonas Frankki 460 Photo: Juan Quinones 463 © Office for Anti-propaganda 465, 466 Photo: Dietrich Heissenbüttel 468 © Dan Perjovschi 470 Courtesy Galerie Volker Diehl, Berlin 472 Photo © ZKM | Karlsruhe, photo: Barbara von Woellwarth 475 © Tarek Bakri 478 Charles Brittin Archive, The Getty Research Institute, Los Angeles, (2005.M.11). Photo: Charles Brittin. © J. Paul Getty Trust 480, 481 © Ursula Biemann 486 Photo: Dan S. Wang 487 © Library of Congress 490, 491 Courtesy Alexander Ochs Galleries Berlin | Beijing, Trillium Graphics, and the artist 498 Courtesy Frederico Freitas 498 Photo: Daigo Oliva, courtesy Daigo Oliva 501, 503 Courtesy Contrafilé 504 Photo: Caiuá Franco, courtesy Caiuá Franco 505 Courtesy André Mesquita 513 © Noah Fischer, photo © ZKM | Karlsruhe, photo: Tobias Wootton 514 © Joulia Strauss, photo © ZKM | Karlsruhe, photo: Tobias Wootton 516 © Archive of the Garage Centre for Contemporary Culture, Moscow 521 © Pussy Riot 523 © Viktoria Lomasko 524 Photo: Mikhail Tikhonov 526 Photo: Yuri Timofeyev 530 Photo: Tanya Sushenkova 532–534 Photo: Ali Saadi 538 (top) http://thecalifornial.com/post/84825917256 538 (bottom) © REUTERS / Marko Djurica 539 http://twicsy.com/i/nhCFMd 540 © Emre Demirbakan 546 Photo: Mehri Khalil 547 (top) Photo: Beshoy Fayez 547 (bottom) Photo: Abdelrhman Zin Eldin 548 Photo: Ammar Abo Bakr 550 Photo: Mostafa Hussein 551 © Ganzeer 552, 553 Photo © G.M.B. Akash 554, 555 © ArtLeaks 557 © Bombily 558–563 © Ángela Bonadies & Juan José Olavarría 564 © Osman Bozkurt, photo © ZKM | Karlsruhe, photos: Tobias Wootton 565 © Osman Bozkurt 567 © Chim↑Pom, Courtesy MUJIN-TO Production, Tokyo 569 © Van Abbemuseum / SMART Project Space / Chto Delat? (video realized by: Tsaplya [Olga Egorova], Dmitry Vilensky, Gluklya (Natalia Pershina) and Nina Gasteva; directed by: Tsaplya [Olga Egorova]; A Van Abbemuseum Production / A SMART Project Space Production; supported by: Van Abbemuseum, SMART Circle Trust, SKOR | Foundation for Art and Public Domain) 570, 571 © Colectivo Etcétera 573 © Enmedio 574, 575 (top) Photo © Mark LeVine, courtesy Freemuse, photo: Mark LeVine 575 © Ramy Essam 576 © Noah Fischer, photo © ZKM | Karlsruhe, photo: Tobias Wootton 577 © Noah Fischer 578, 580 © Floating Lab Collective 579 © Floating Lab Collective, photo: Sue Wrbican 581 © Floating Lab Collective, photo: Sue Wrbican 582, 583 © Jakob Gautel and Jason Karaïndros / ADAGP, courtesy the artists; with the support of the municipality of Nisyros and the participation of the mayor, M. Nikos Karakonstaninos. Heartful thanks to Thymios and Maria Assimakopoulou, Giorgos Kantilis, Virginia Mastrogiannaki, and to all the people who helped us 585 © REUTERS / Marko Djuric 587, 588 Photo © ZKM | Karlsruhe, photo: Tobias Wootton 590, 591 © Ed Hall, courtesy British Council Collection, photo © ZKM | Karlsruhe, photo: Tobias Wootton 592 CC BY 2.0 Laura Hadden 593 CC BY-SA 2.0 Salim Fadhley 594 (top left) CC BY-ND 2.0 Phil 594 (top right) Photo © Danielle Carrick 594 (bottom), 595, 596, 597 Courtesy the artist, Hauser and Wirth, London, and carlier | gebauer, Berlin, photo © ZKM | Karlsruhe, photos: Tobias Wootton 598 © Niklas Hoffmann and Rebecca Meining, photo © ZKM | Karlsruhe, photo: Tobias Wootton 599 (top, middle left) © Niklas Hoffmann and Rebecca Meining, photo © Rebecca Meining 599 (middle right, bottom) © Niklas Hoffmann and Rebecca Meining 600, 601 © Alexey Iorsh 603 © JUST DO IT. 604 © Kan-si, photo © ZKM | Karlsruhe, photos: Tobias Wootton 605 © Kan-si 606 © Thomas Kilpper, courtesy Galerie Nagel Draxler, Berlin/Köln, and private collection, Berlin, photo © ZKM | Karlsruhe, photos: Tobias Wootton 607–609 © Thomas Kilpper, courtesy Galerie Nagel Draxler, Berlin/Köln 610, 611 © Kiss my Ba, photo: Evgeny Ivanov 614, 615 Photo © Christopher LaMarca / Redux / laif 616 © Mohammed Laouli, photo © iRRi ART, photo: Fayssal Ajouz Sanhaji 617 © Mohammed Laouli 618, 619 © Viktoria Lomasko 620, 621 © Renzo Martens, courtesy Galerie Fons Welters and Wilkinson Gallery 622, 623 Courtesy Masasit Mati 624 Photo © MediaImpact International Festival of Activist Art, photo: Tatyana Sushenkova 625 © Media Impact International Festival of Activist Art, cover illustrations: Alexandra Galkina, Garadja, and Tiurya, 2011 626, 627 CC BY-NC-ND MindBomb 628, 629 Courtesy the artist, Galeria Filomena Soares, Lisbon, and Fundación Rosón Arte Contemporaneo, Pontevedra, Spain 632–636 Courtesy MTL 639 Courtesy G.U.L.F. 640, 641 © NEOZOON 643 © Christof Nüssli and Christoph Oeschger, photo © Christoph Oeschger 644, 645 © Jean-Gabriel Périot, Sacrebleu Productions 646, 647 © Platform – www.platformlondon.org 649 © Pussy Riot 651 © R.E.P. 652, 653 © Itamar Rose and Yossi Atia 655 Photo © Bahia Shehab 656, 657 © SOSka group, courtesy the artists 658 © Joulia Strauss, courtesy the artist 659 © Joulia Strauss, photo © ZKM | Karlsruhe, photo: Tobias Wootton 660 Photo © jackie sumell 661 © jackie sumell, photo © ZKM | Karlsruhe, photo: Tobias Wootton 662 Photo © Dan Hatch, courtesy jackie sumell 664 photo © jackie sumell 665 (top) photo © jackie sumell, photo: Nicolas Krebill 665 (bottom) Photo: Mizue Aizeki, courtesy jackie sumell 666 Photo © ZKM | Karlsruhe, photo: Tobias Wootton 667, 668, 672, 673 Photo © Teatro Valle Occupato, photo: Tiziana Tomasulo 670, 675, 678 Photo © Teatro Valle Occupato, photo: Valeria Tomasulo 682, 683 © Patricia K. Triki and Christine Bruckbauer, photo © ZKM | Karlsruhe, photo: Tobias Wootton 685 © Voina 686 © Alexander Volodarsky 688, 689 © Aalam Wassef, courtesy Galerie Conradi, Hamburg 691 Photo © ZKM | Karlsruhe, photo: Tobias Wootton 692, 693 © Yomango

Icons of Revolution

720–721 © REUTERS / Juan Medina 722–723 © REUTERS / Ivan Alvarado 724 © AP Photo / Stephanie Keith 725 © Christopher LaMarca / Redux / laif 726–727 © AP Photo / Khalil Hamra 728–729 © 20 MINUTES / SIPA / 1209181752 730–731 © Pussy Riot 732–733 © REUTERS/ Stringer 734 © EPA / Marijan Murat 735 © REUTERS / Marko Djurica

VG Bild-Kunst, Bonn 2015 for:

472 Joseph Beuys 582, 583 Jakob Gautel 606–609 Thomas Kilpper 470 Alexander Kosolapov 612, 613 Mischa Kuball, Düsseldorf 640, 641 NEOZOON 644, 645 Jean-Gabriel Périot 367 Sandra Schäfer

global activism

The Exhibition

December 14, 2013–March 30, 2014

Curator:
Peter Weibel
Curatorial Staff:
Andreas Beitin, Andrea Buddensieg, Elisabeth Klotz, Joulia Strauss, Tatiana Volkova, Philipp Ziegler
Project Management Exhibition:
Sarah Maske
Project Assistance:
Sabiha Keyif, Linnea Semmerling with assistance of Annika Etter, Elisa Kaiser
Editor Blog:
Dietrich Heissenbüttel
Project Management Symposia:
Linnea Semmerling, Idis Hartmann
Editorial Staff:
Martina Hofmann, Caroline Jansky, Jens Lutz
Website Programming:
Axel Heide
Website Main Editing:
Heike Borowski
Graphic Design:
Jan Kiesswetter, Niko Singer
Design Social Media Space:
Gloria Hasnay, Moritz Nebenführ, Maxim Weirich
Modular Connecting Tool:
Marlene Oeken
Registrar:
Marianne Meister, Nina Fernandez
Museum and Exhibition Technical Services:
Stefan Wessels
Technical Management:
Anne Däuper, Henrike Mall
Technical Staff:
Volker Becker, Claudius Böhm, Mirco Fraß, Rainer Gabler, Gregor Gaissmaier, Ronny Haas, Dirk Heesakker, Christof Hierholzer, Werner Hutzenlaub, Gisbert Laaber, Marco Preitschopf
External Companies:
Concern Art, DNH-Artsupport GBR, Essential Art Solutions
Conservation:
Nahid Matin Pour, Verena Bolz, Wibke Ottweiler, Morgane Stricot
Public Relations:
Dominika Szope, Constanze Heidt, Verena Noack, Julia Wicky, Siemke Hanßen
Museum Communication:
Janine Burger, Banu Beyer, Justin Humm, Eva Lusch, Marianne Spencer, Stephanie Syring
Event Technology and Event Management:
Hartmut Bruckner, Viola Gaiser, Hans Gass, Monika Weimer, Wolfgang Knapp, Manuel Weber
Library:
Petra Zimmermann, Christiane Minter, Stephanie Mayer
Media Library:
Andreas Brehmer, Claudia Gehrig, Hartmut Jörg
IT Support:
Elena Lorenz, Joachim Schütze, Volker Sommerfeld

In cooperation with
Goethe-Institut Egypt
Goethe-Institut Tunisia

GOETHE INSTITUT
Sprache. Kultur. Deutschland.

Supported by
the Federal Foreign Office
German-Egyptian/-Tunisian
Transformation Partnership

Federal Foreign Office

The Book

Editor:
Peter Weibel
Editorial Staff:
Jens Lutz, Martina Hofmann (editors), Katharina Holas, Caroline Jansky (assistant editors), with Eva-Maria Höllerer
Copyediting:
Martina Hofmann, Katharina Holas, Jens Lutz, Gloria Custance
Translations:
Robert Booth, Thomas Campbell, Cinescript Berlin, Isaac Custance, Dijital Tercüme, Jeremy Gaines, Roger Leverdier
Work Descriptions / Artist Pages:
Martina Hofmann, Katharina Holas, and the artists
Transcription:
Hannes Herold
Design:
Jan Kiesswetter, Niko Singer
Lithography:
COMYK Roland Merz, Karlsruhe
Printed and bound:
e&b engelhardt und bauer – a company of Kraft Druck GmbH, Ettlingen (Germany)
Paper:
GardaMatt Art: 135 g/m², 400 g/m²
This book was set in:
Neutral Std, Plantin MT
Thanks to:
Banu Beyer, Andrea Buddensieg, Anett Holzheid, Idis Hartmann, Sabiha Keyif, Adela Kim, Sarah Maske, Arman and Arash T. Riahi, Linnea Semmerling, Joulia Strauss

ZKM | Karlsruhe
Chairman an CEO:
Peter Weibel
General Manager:
Christiane Riedel
Head of Administration:
Boris Kirchner

Printed and bound in Germany

ISBN 978-0-262-52689-0

Library of Congress Control Number 2015943521

zkm karlsruhe

Founders
Baden-Württemberg
MINISTERIUM FÜR WISSENSCHAFT, FORSCHUNG UND KUNST
Karlsruhe

Partner
EnBW

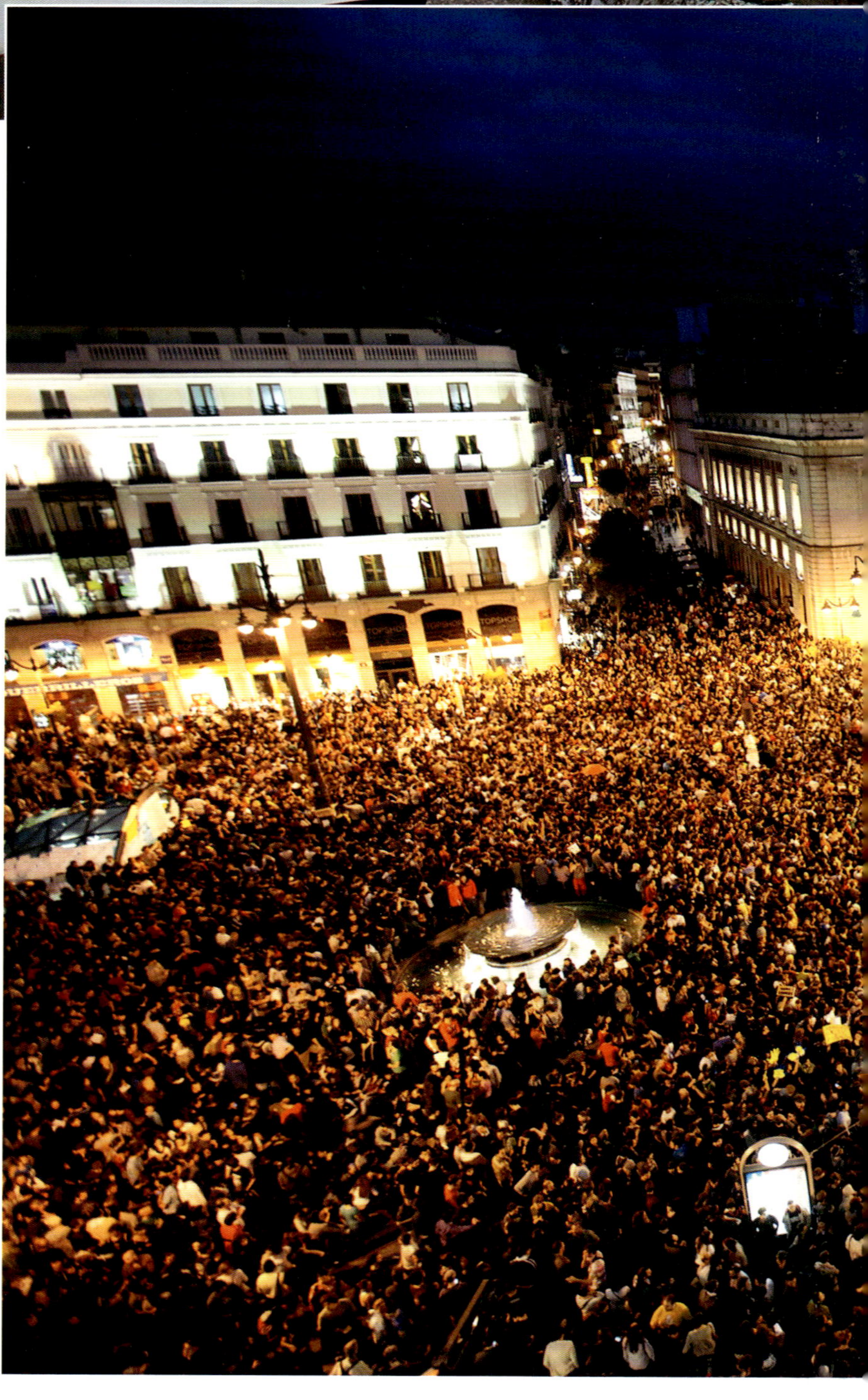

Spain

Demonstrators gather and shout slogans in Madrid's famous landmark Puerta del Sol against politicians', bankers', and authorities' handling of the economic crisis on May 18, 2011. The demonstrations began on May 15, 2011, when thousands of people gathered in several cities in Spain to demand what they called "real democracy," and protesters vowed to occupy central squares in several Spanish cities until the local elections on May 22.

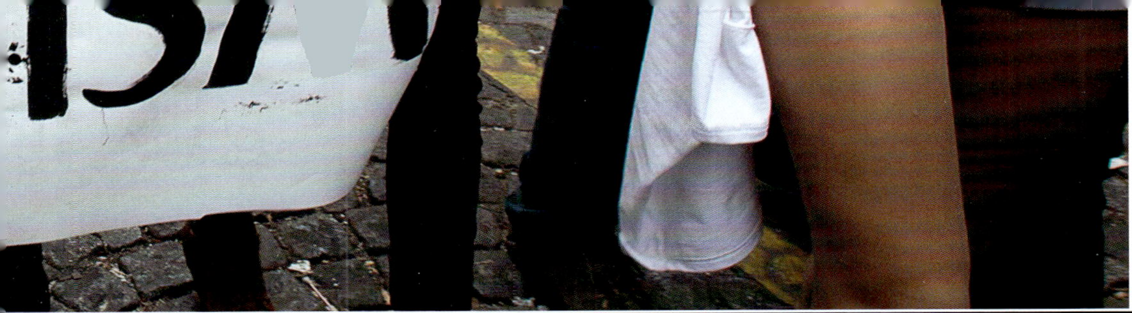

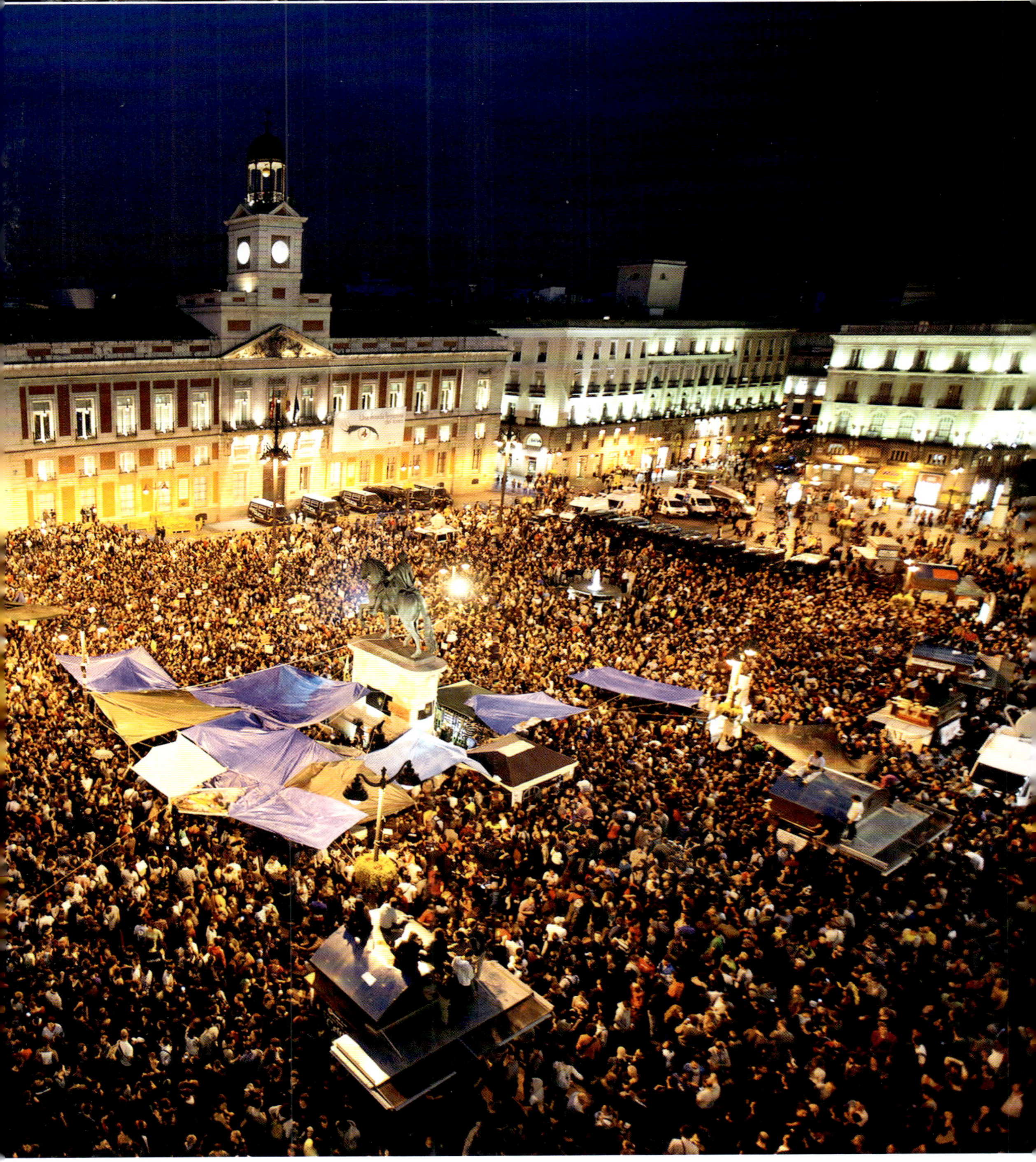

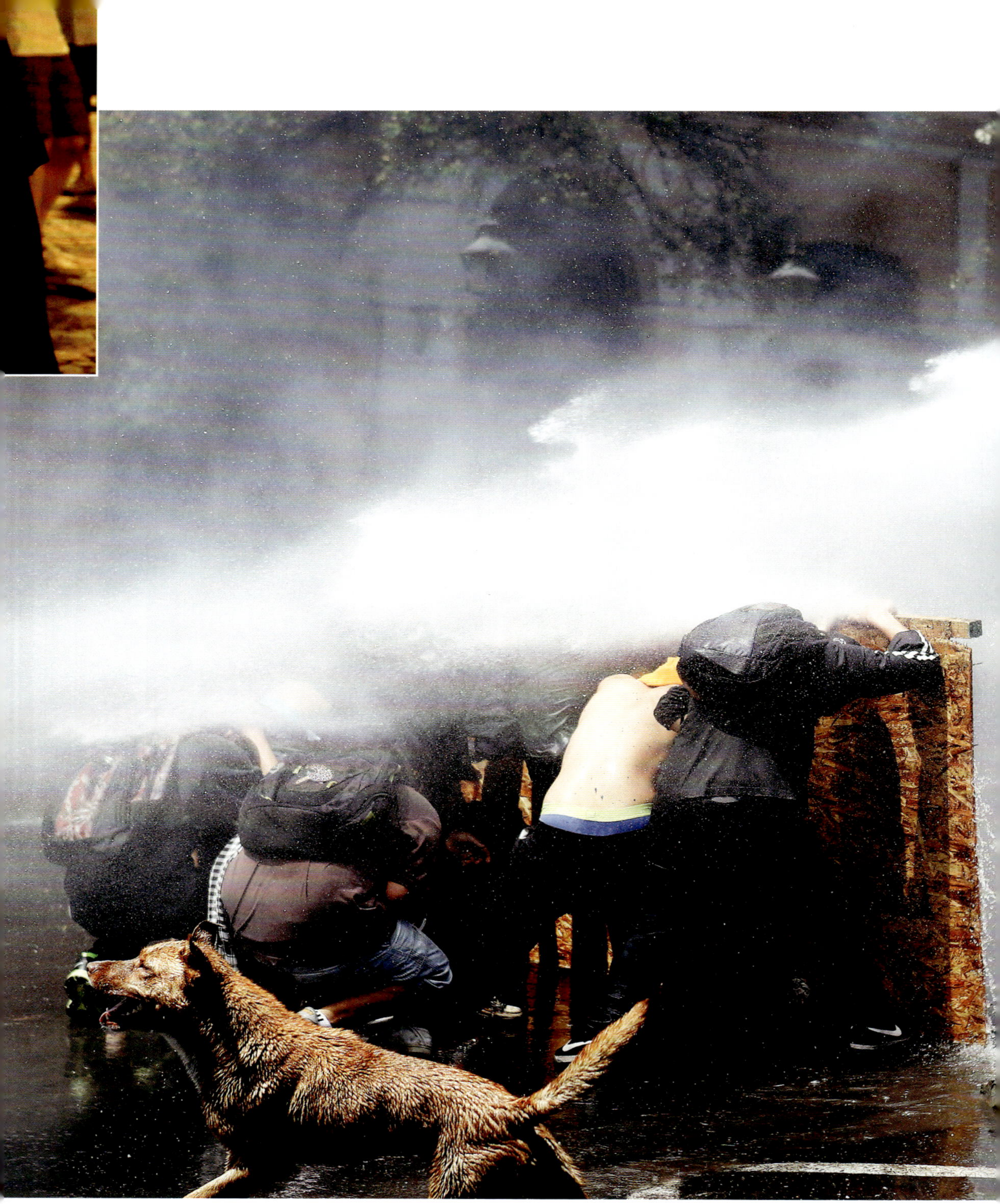

Chile

Student protesters take cover from a jet of water from a riot police vehicle during a demonstration against the government to demand changes in the public state education system in Santiago de Chile on October 17, 2013. Chilean students protested against what they say is profiteering by the state education system.

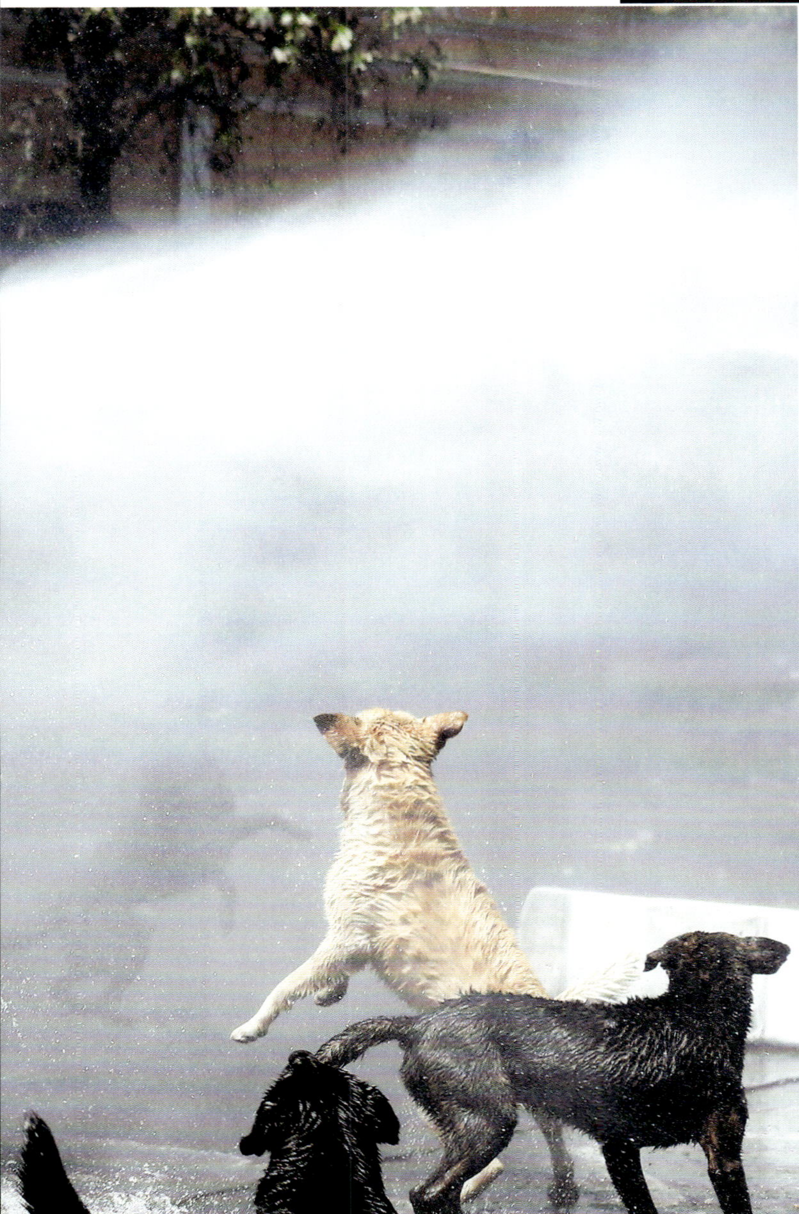

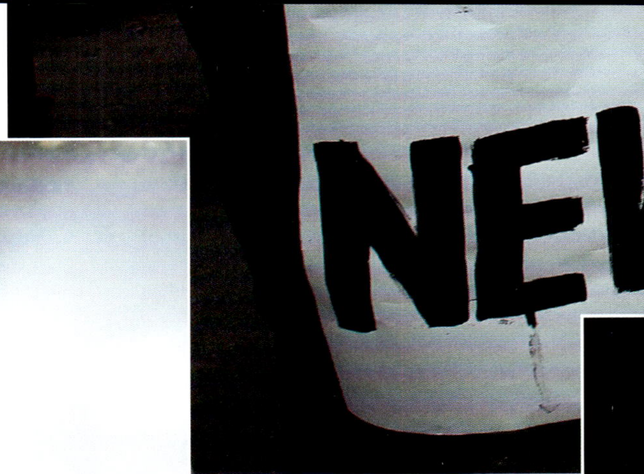
NE

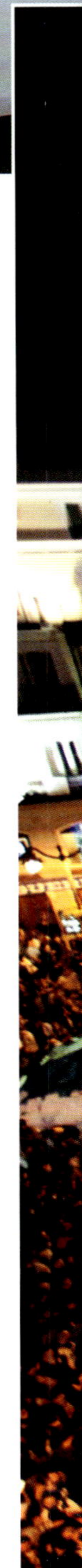

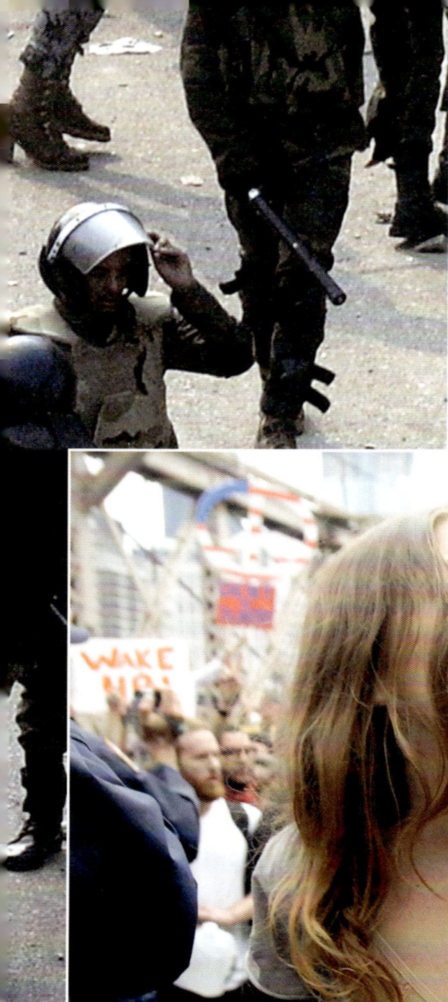

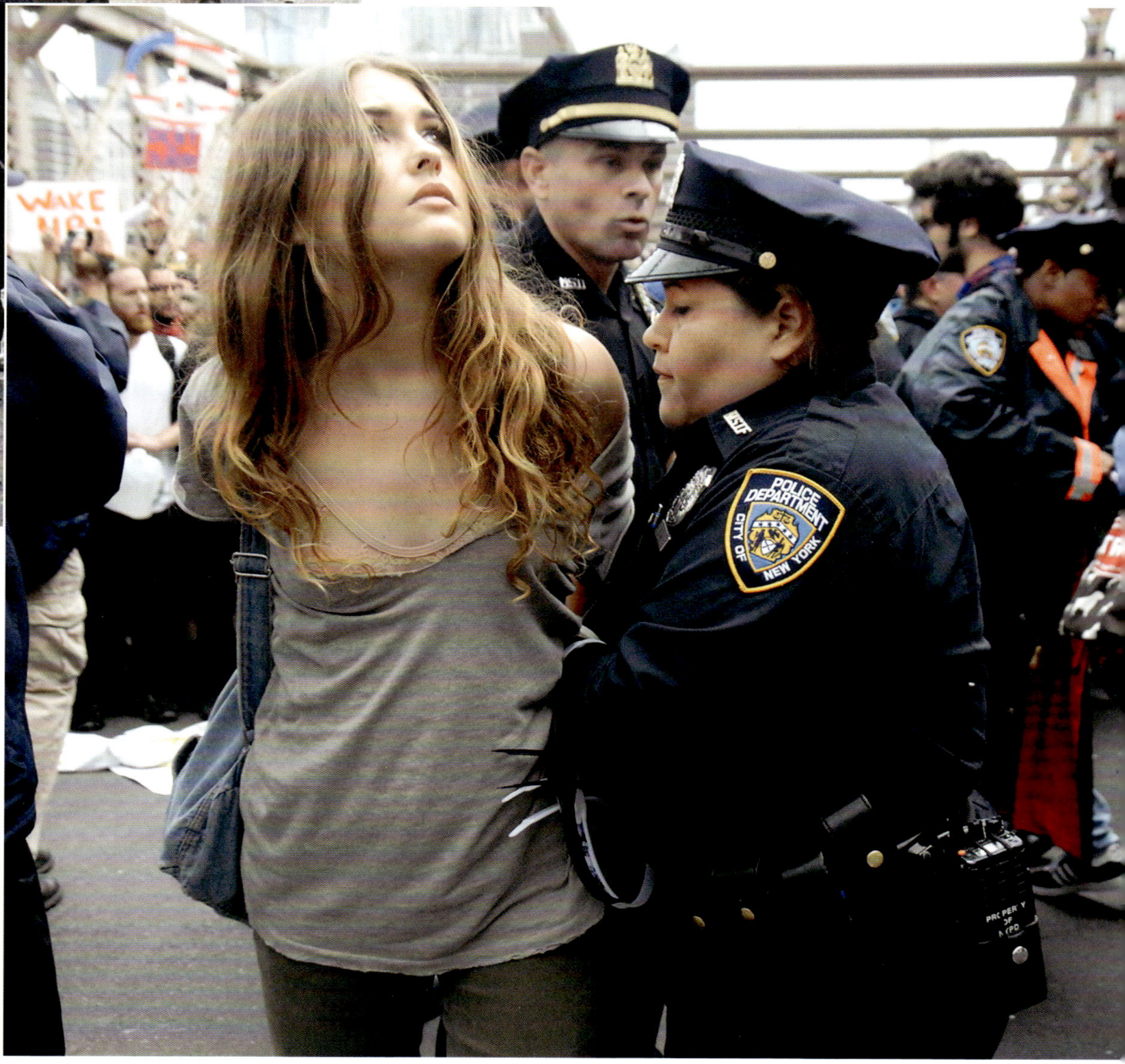

USA

Police arrest a protester on New York's Brooklyn Bridge during a march by Occupy Wall Street on October 1, 2011. Protesters speaking out against corporate greed and other grievances attempted to walk over the bridge from Manhattan, resulting in the arrest of more than 700 during a tense confrontation with police. The majority of those arrested were given citations for disorderly conduct and were released.

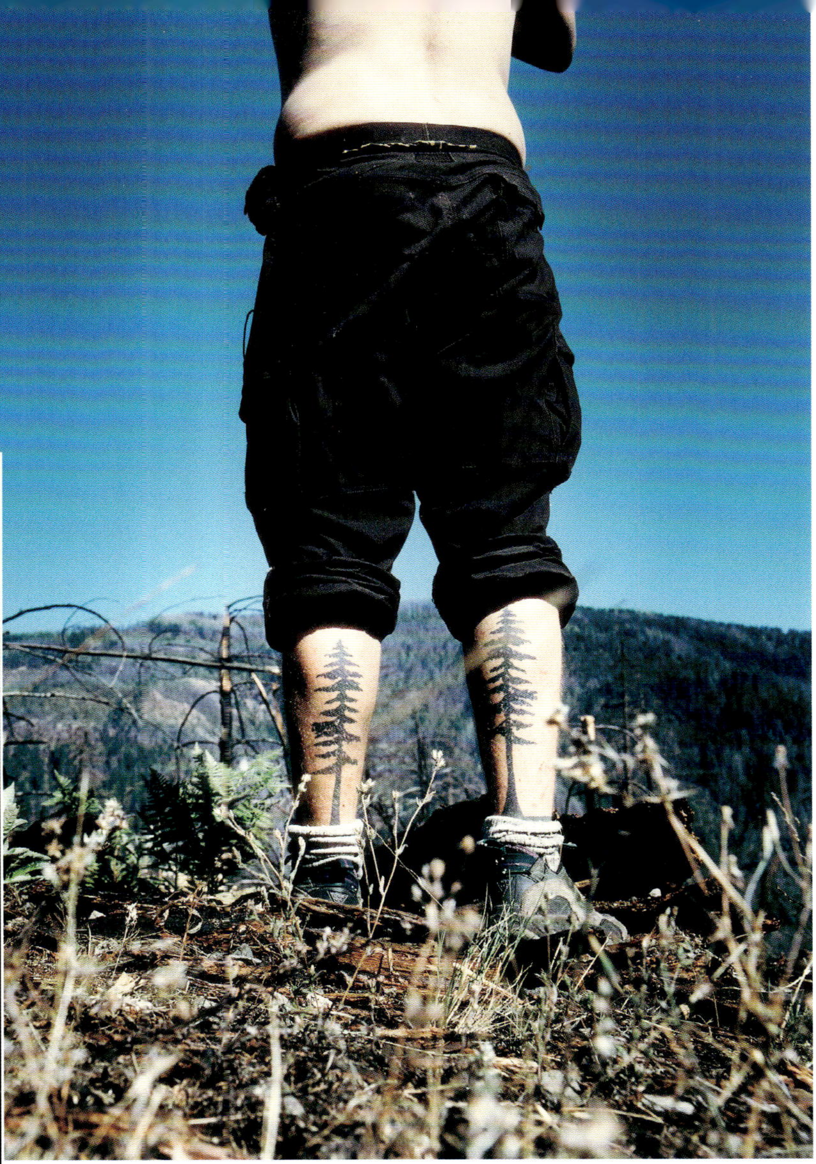

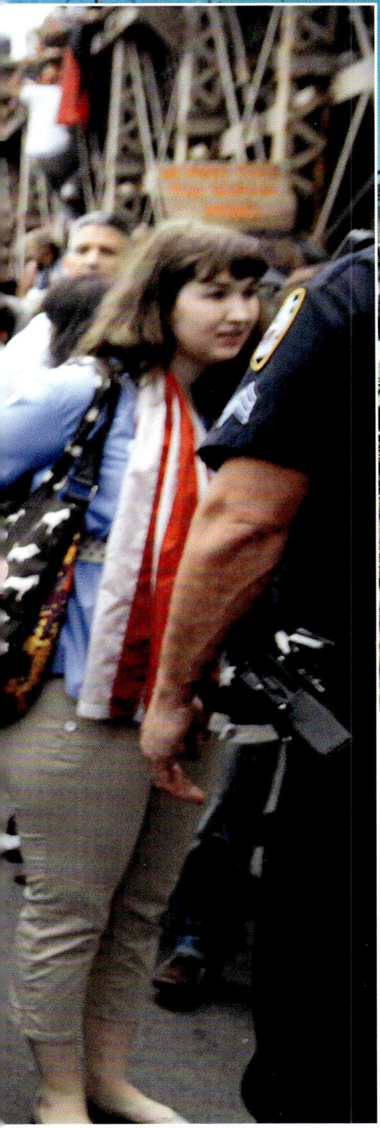

USA

Forest defender and activist Gedden looks over the Biscuit Fire Timber Sale in Oregon, captured by photographer Christopher LaMarca. Gedden patrols the surrounding timber sales looking for Forest Service activity.

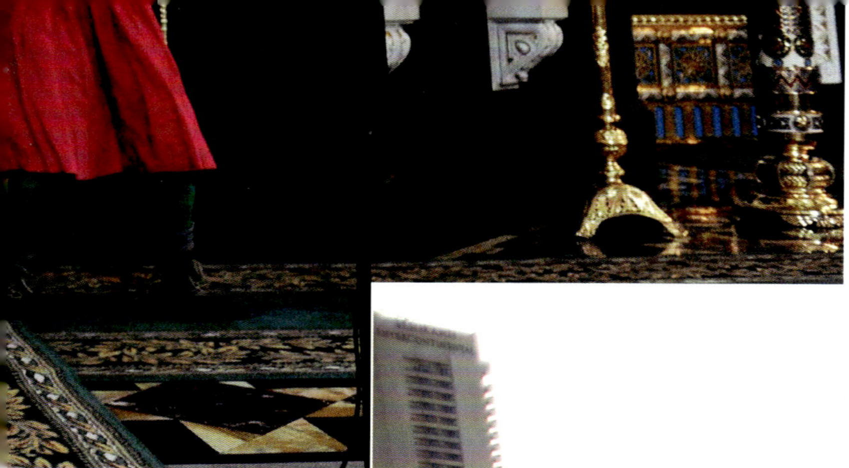

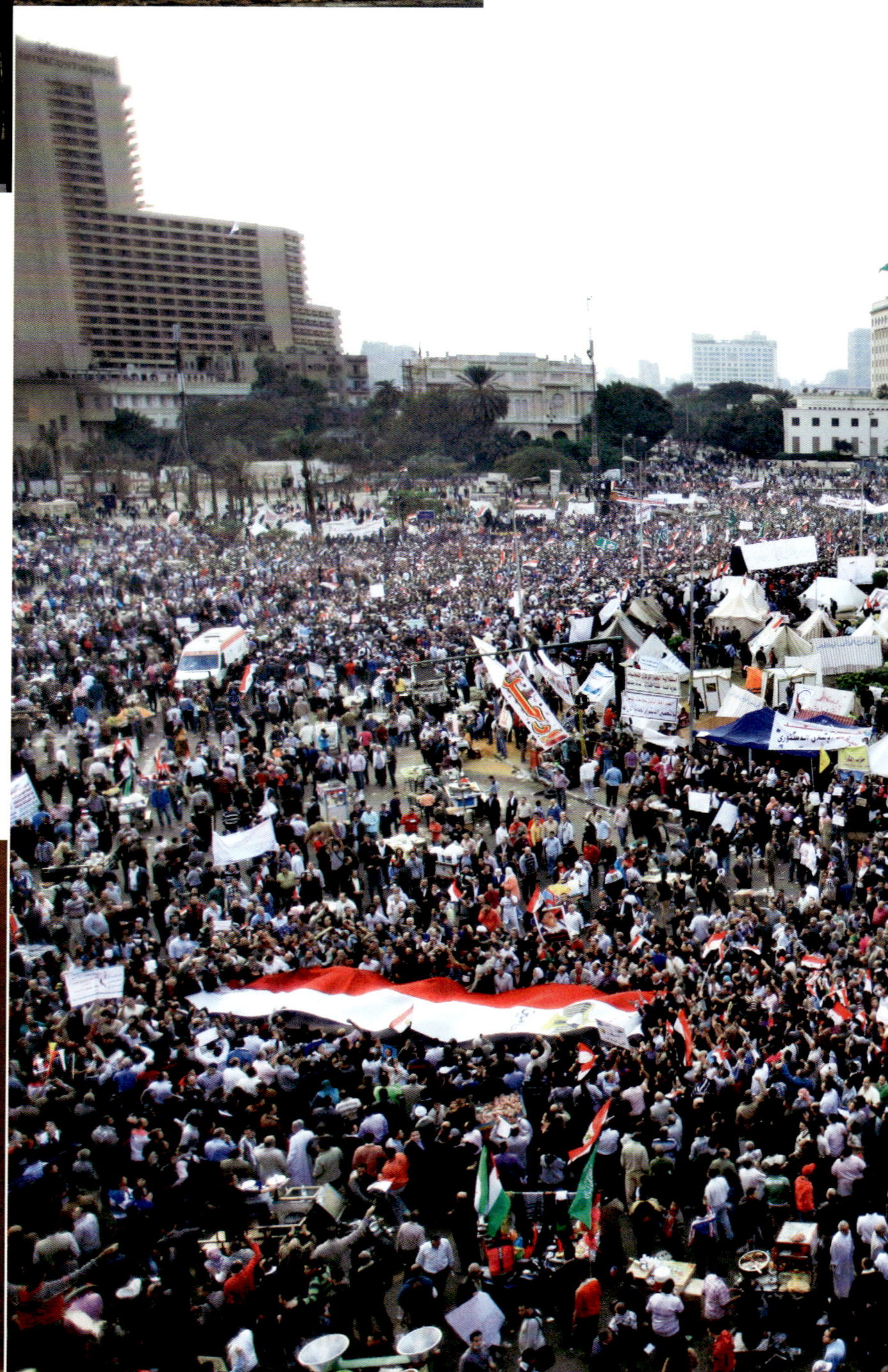

Egypt

Egyptian protesters attend an opposition rally in Tahrir Square in Cairo, on November 27, 2012. Thousands flocked to Cairo's central Tahrir Square for the protest against Egypt's then president Mohamed Morsi in a significant test of whether the opposition could rally the street behind it in a confrontation aimed at forcing Morsi to rescind decrees that granted him near-absolute powers.

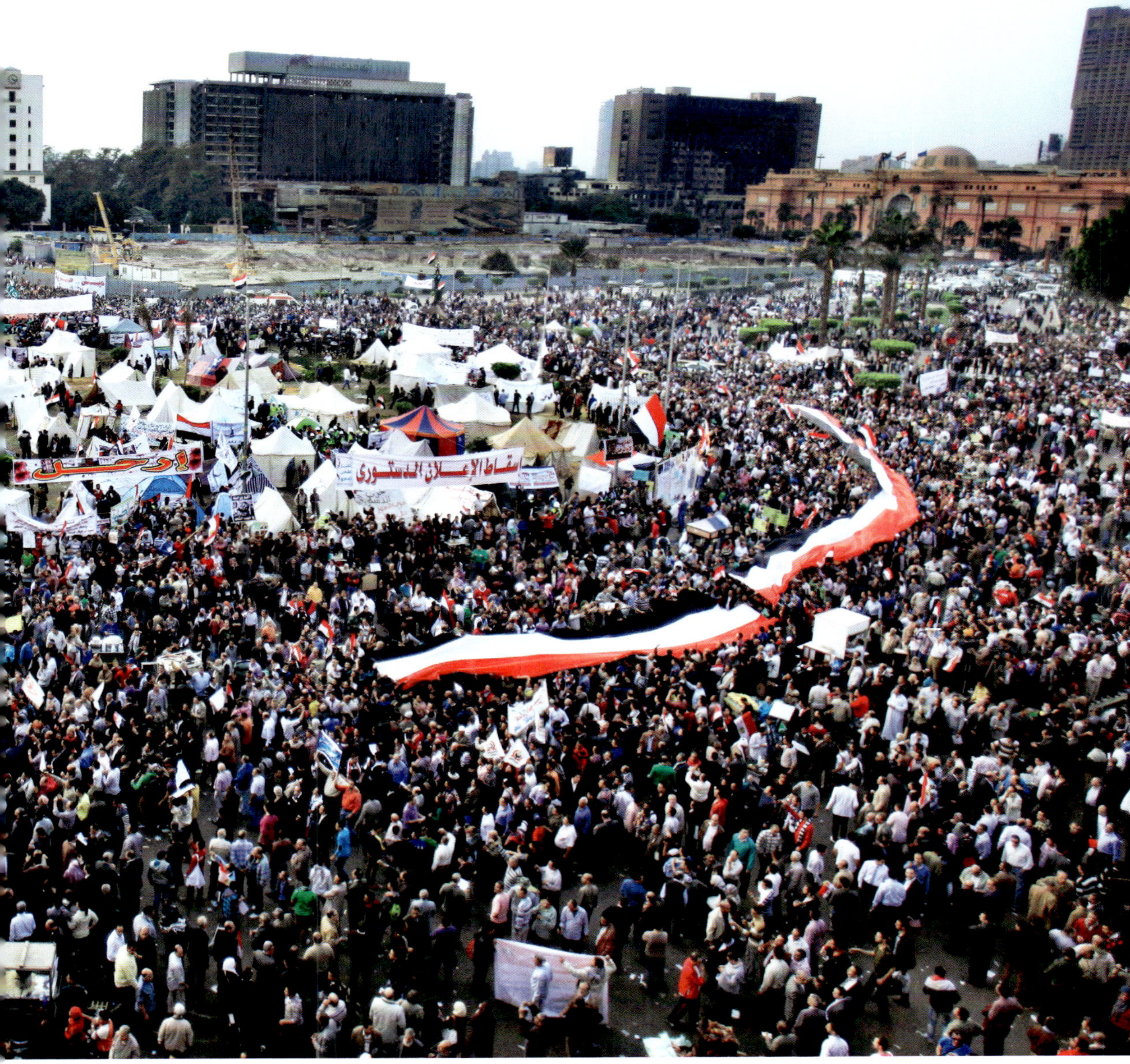
ارحل
اسقاط الإعلان الدستوري

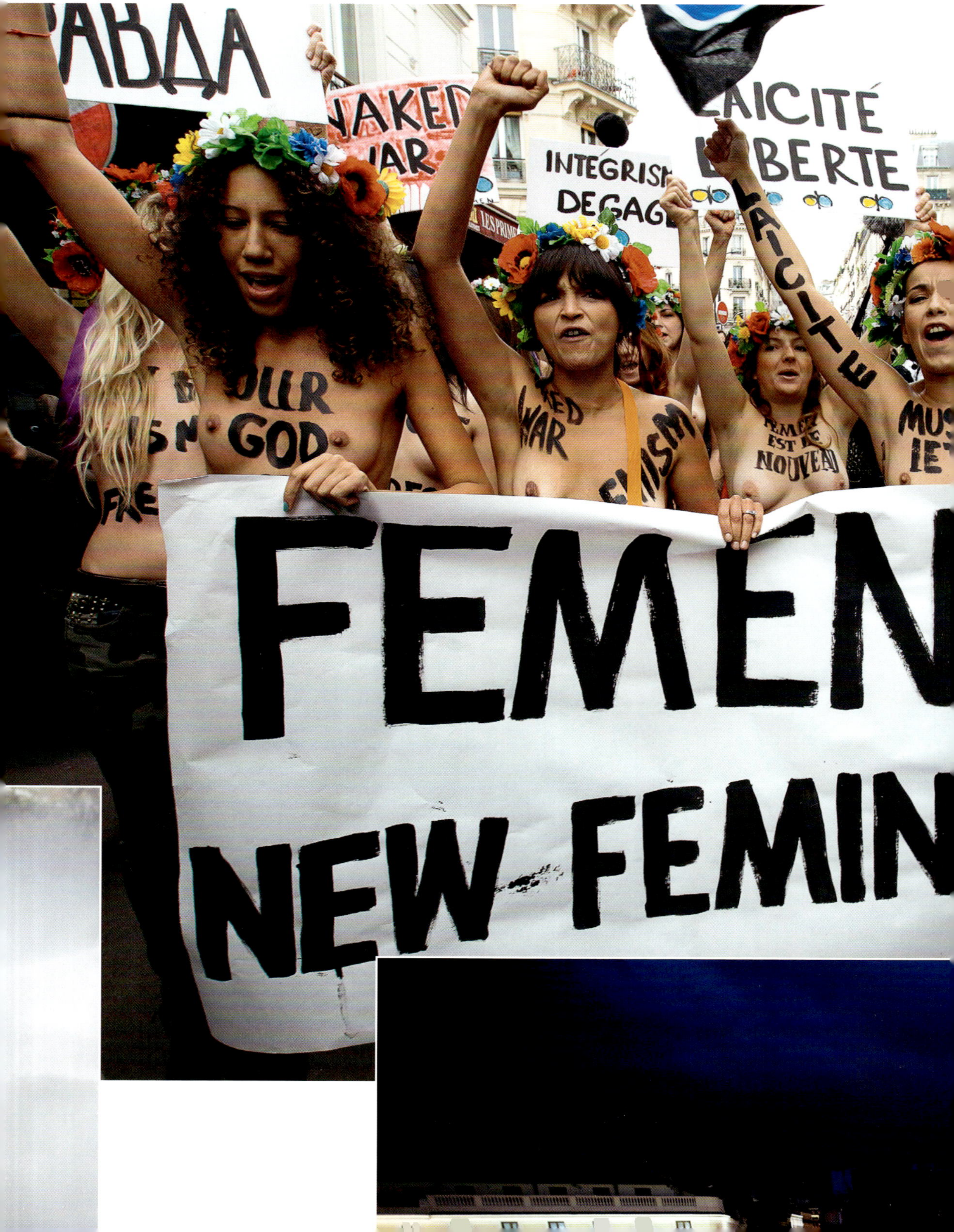

РАВДА
NAKED
WAR
INTEGRISM
DEGAGE
AICITÉ
BERTE
LAICITE
GOD
FEMEN EST LE NOUVEAU
FEMEN
NEW FEMIN

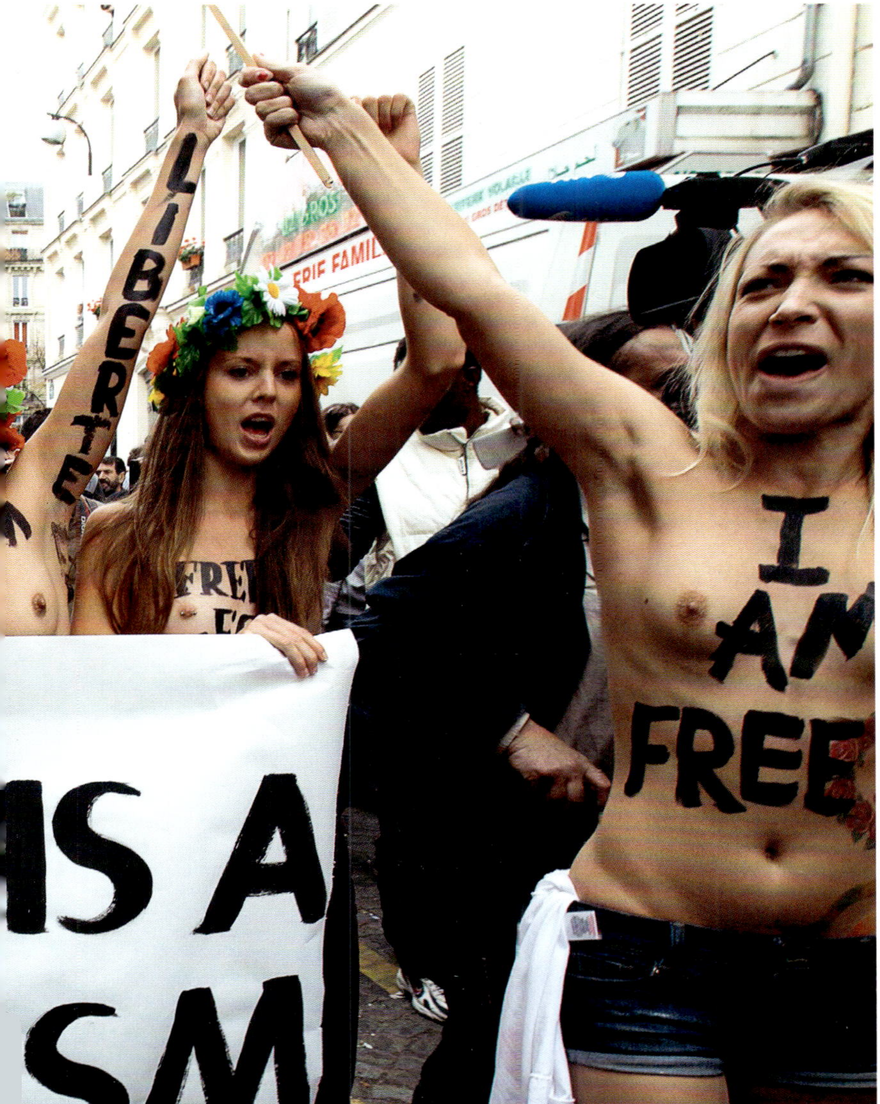

Global

Members from the Ukrainian women's rights group Femen, with messages written on their chests, including "Muslims let's get naked," take part topless in a demonstration near their "training camp" at the Lavoir Moderne Parisien (LMP) in Paris on September 18, 2012. Femen members moved to France to "recruit soldiers" in their fight against the discrimination of women.

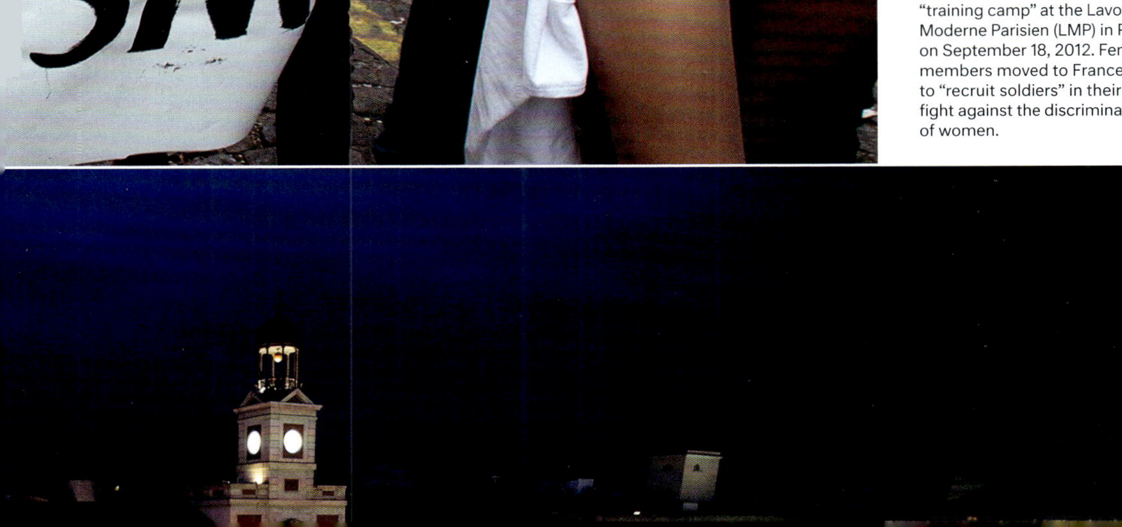

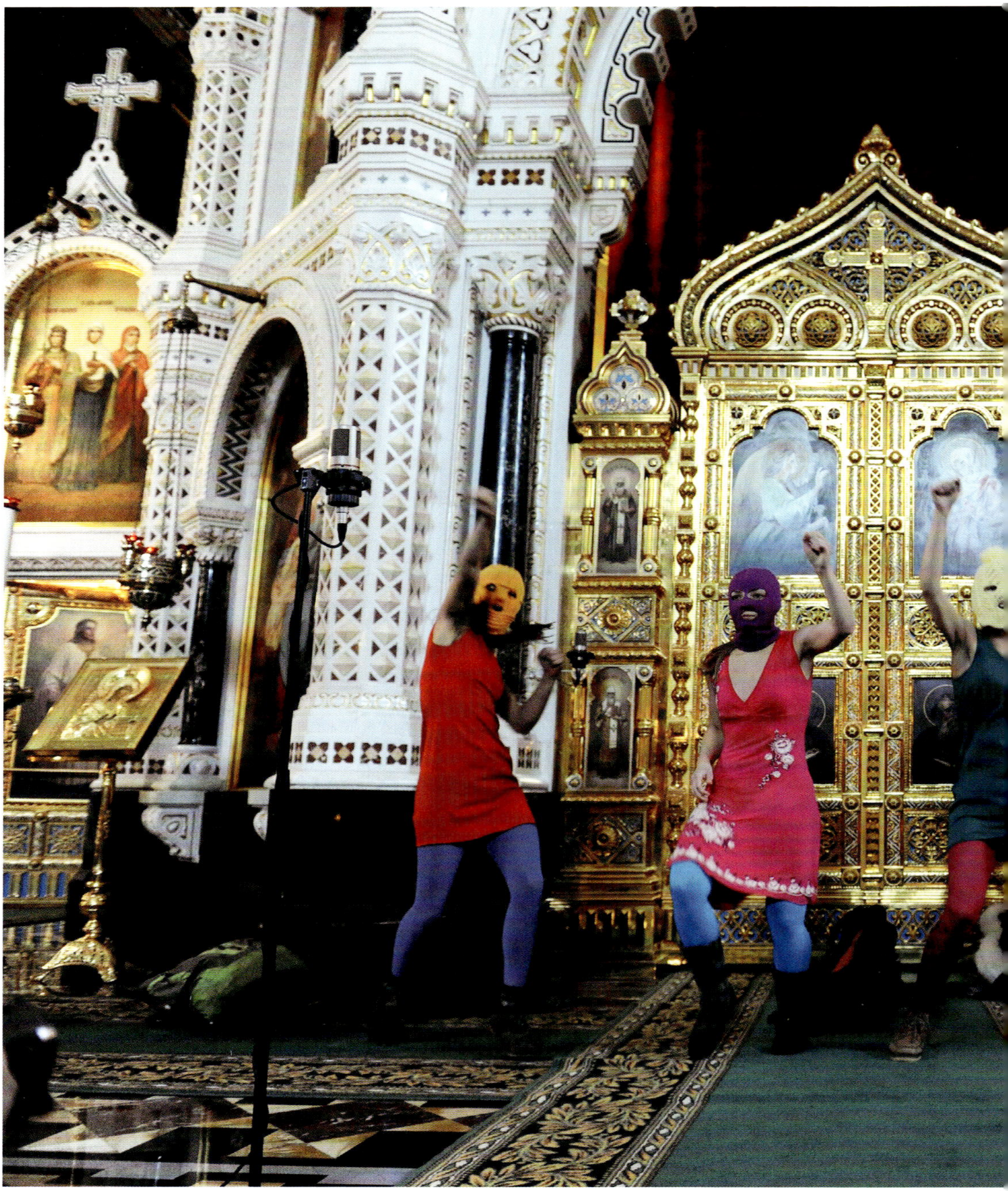

Russia

On February 21, 2012 the Russian feminist punk band Pussy Riot performed the "punk prayer" Богородица, Путина прогони! [Mother of God, Chase Putin Away!] at the Cathedral of Christ the Savior in Moscow. Three members of the group were arrested for public hooliganism. After their imprisonment people from all over the world declared their solidarity with the activists.

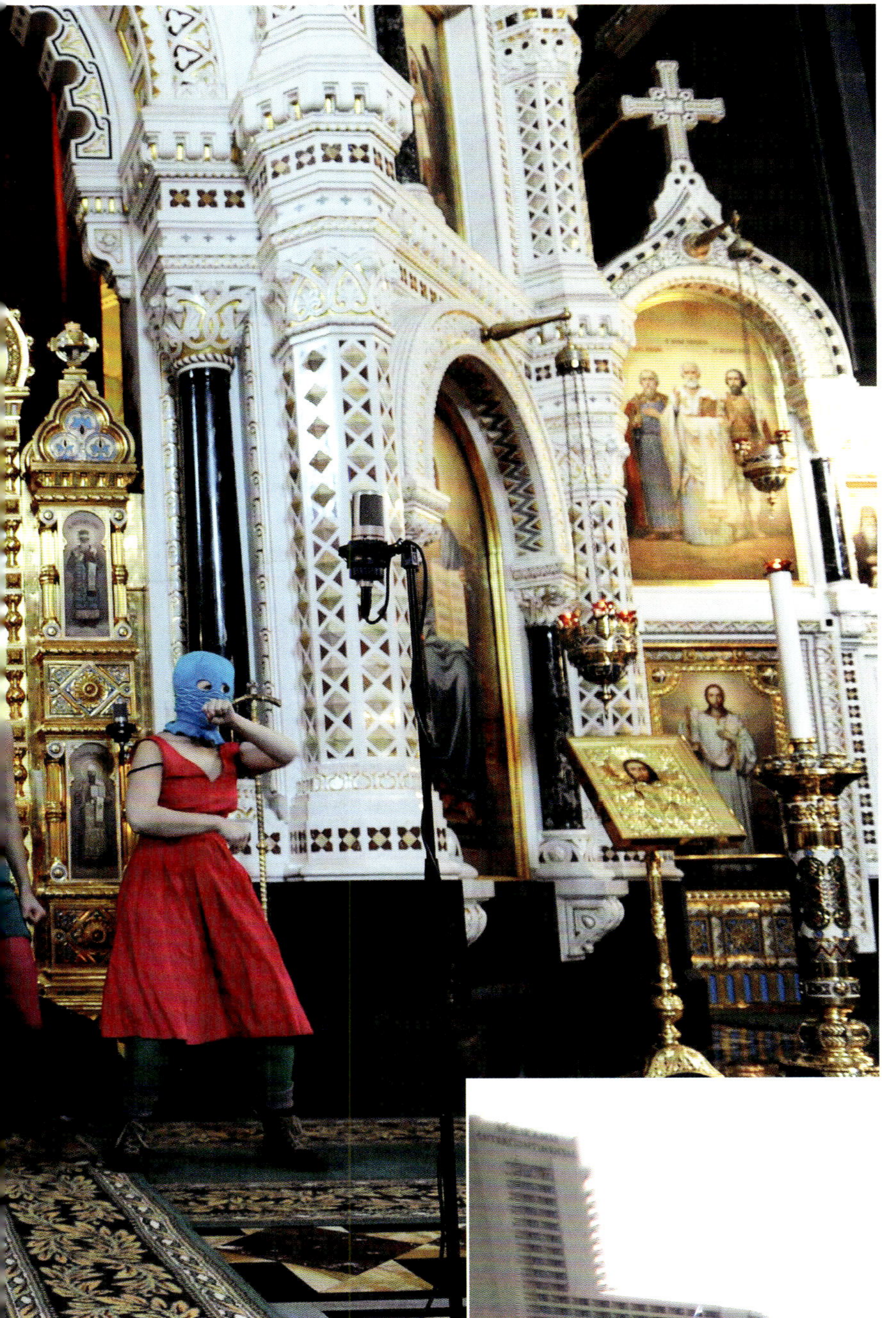

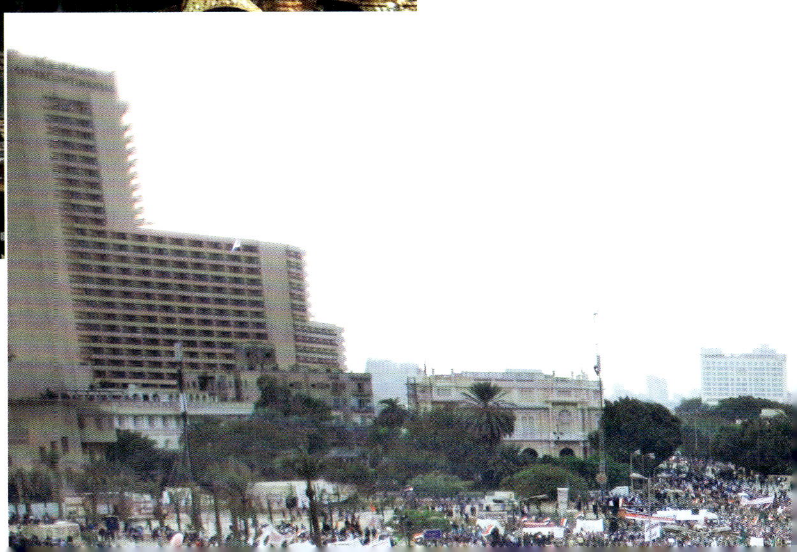

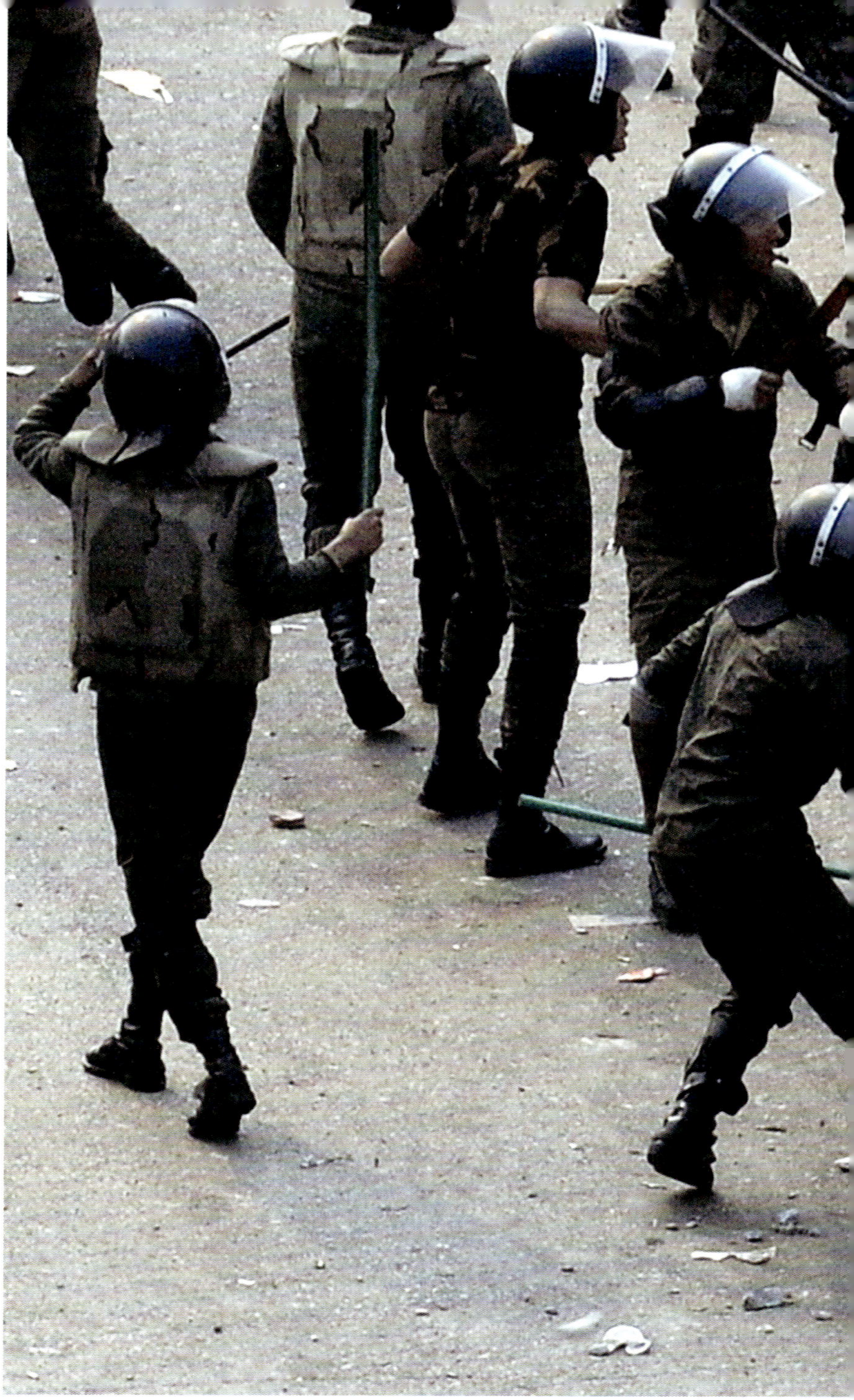

Egypt

Egyptian army soldiers pull off a female protester's abaya, drag her down a street just off Tahrir Square in Cairo, and arrest her on December 17, 2011. Soldiers beat demonstrators with batons in Tahrir Square in a second day of clashes in December 2011 that killed nine people and wounded more than 300, marring the first free election most Egyptians can remember. The "girl in the blue bra" became a symbol of the struggle for equality and freedom.

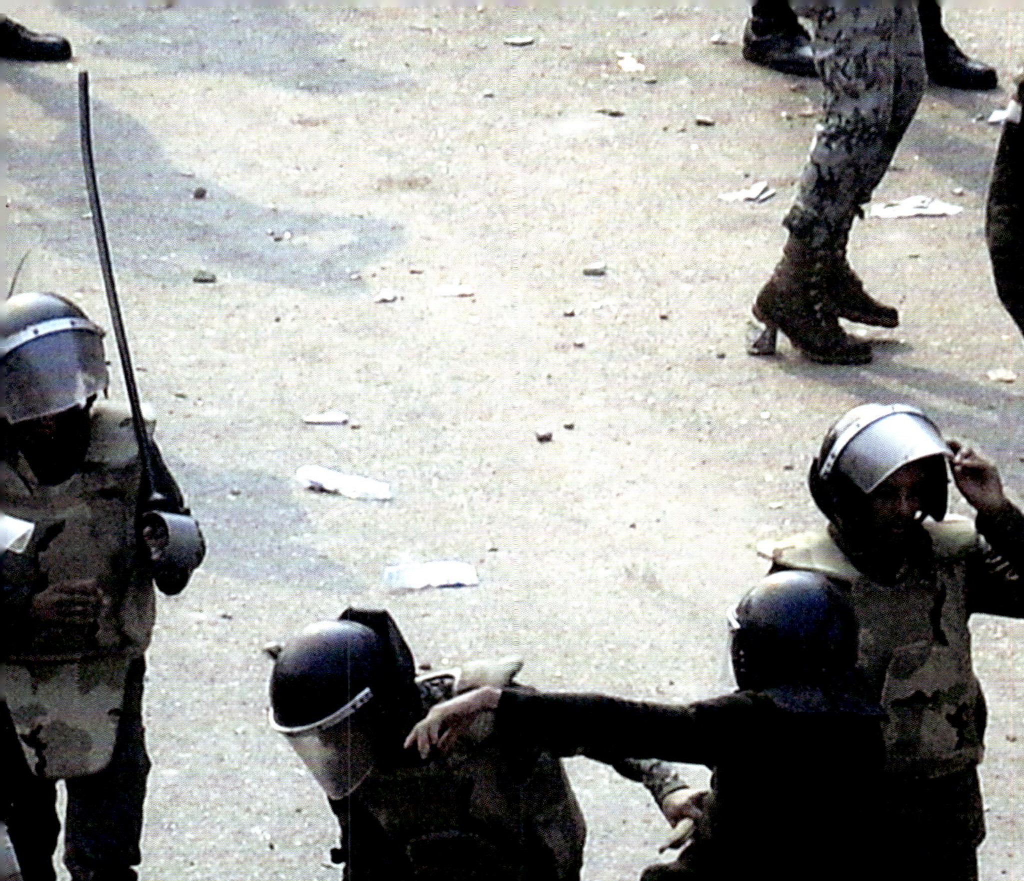

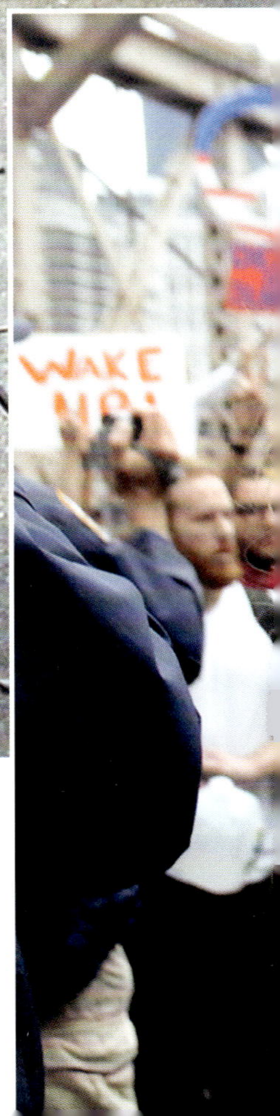
WAKE

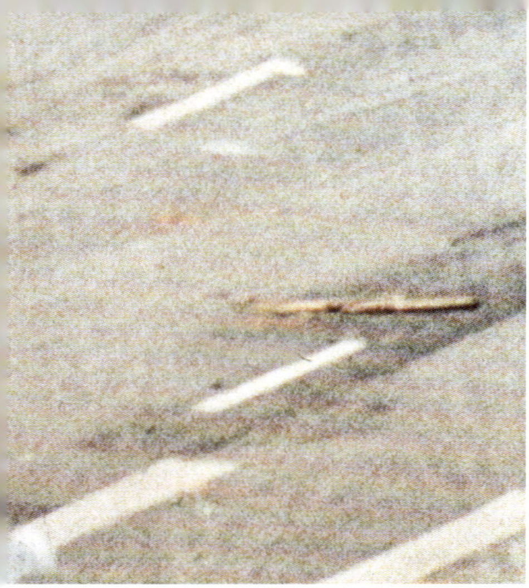

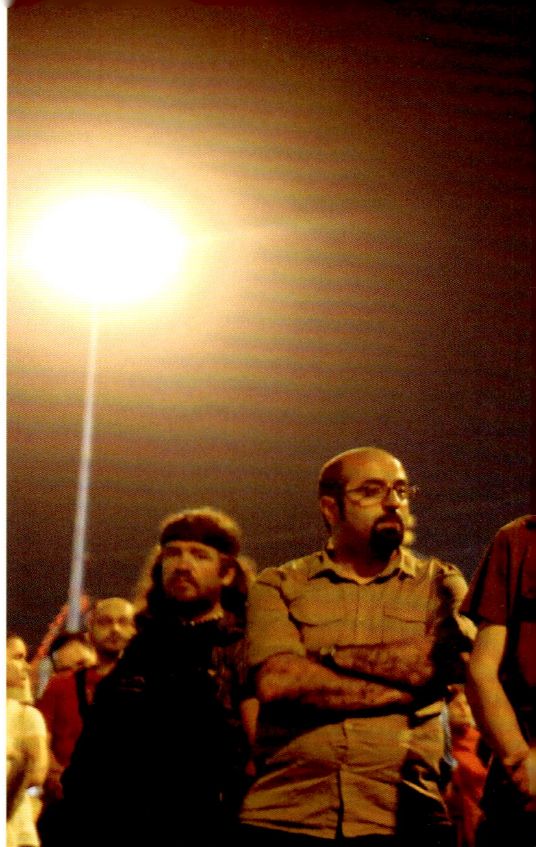

Turkey

Erdem Gündüz, along with other people, stands in a silent protest at Taksim Square in Istanbul on June 17, 2013. Gündüz staged an eight-hour silent vigil on Istanbul's Taksim Square, scene of violent clashes between police and antigovernment protesters since May 2013, inspiring hundreds of others to follow his lead.

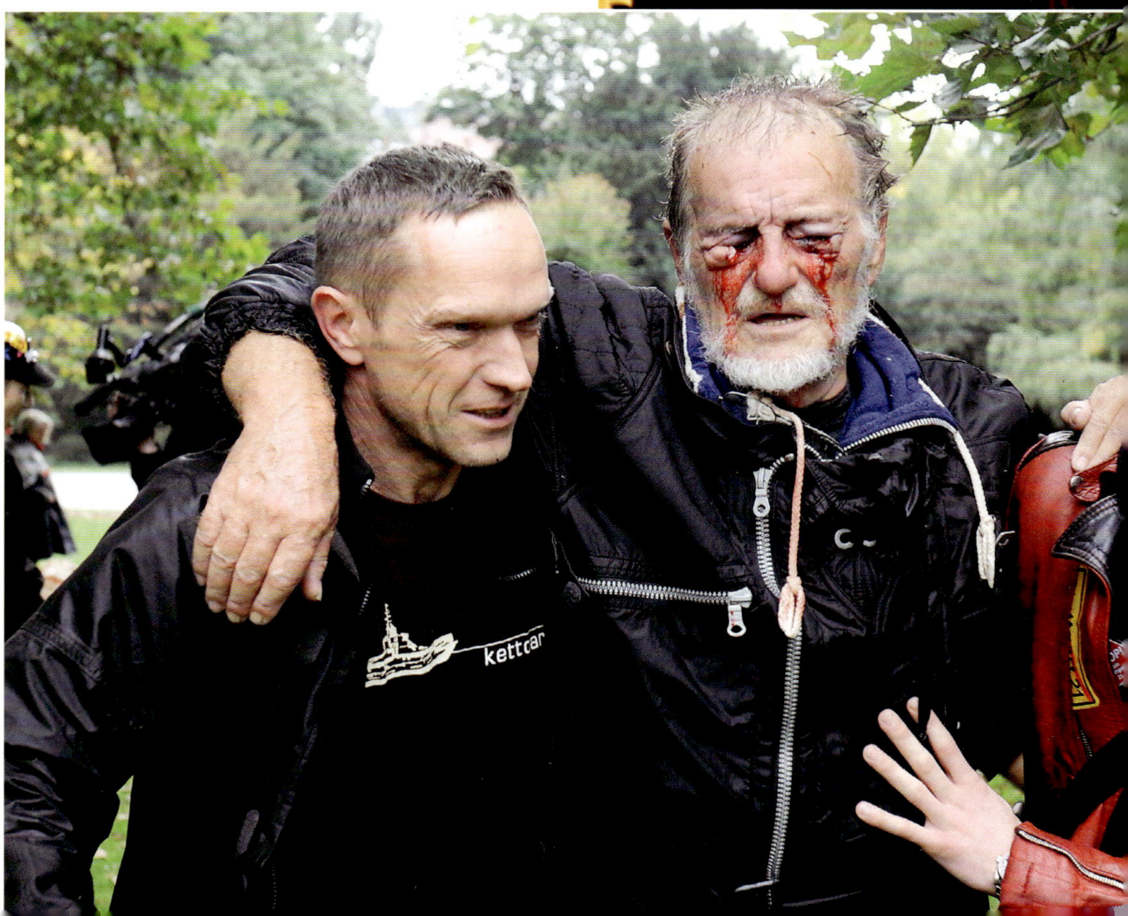

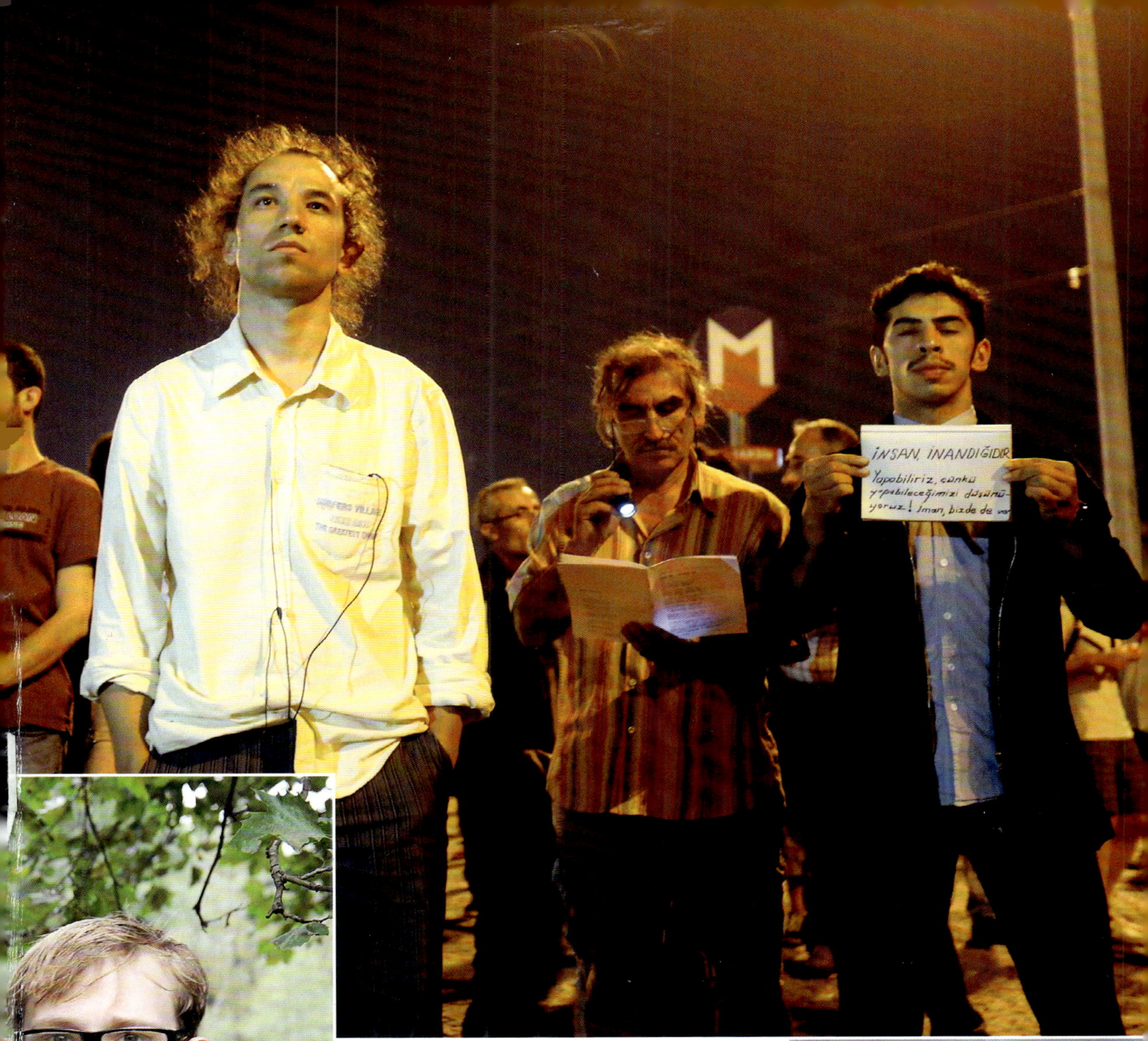

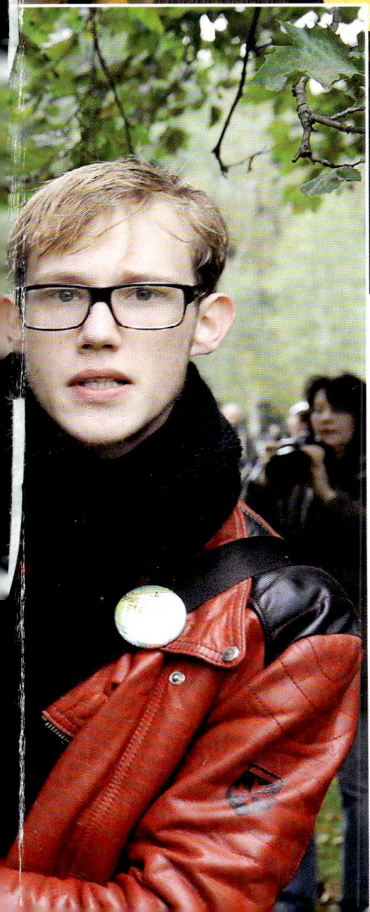

Germany

Dietrich Wagner is helped by protesters during a protest against heavily disputed railway station project Stuttgart 21 in Stuttgart, Germany, on September 30, 2010. Media reports stated in October 2010 that Dietrich Wagner will stay blind in one eye according to a speaker of the Katharinen Hospital and the German Press Agency dpa.

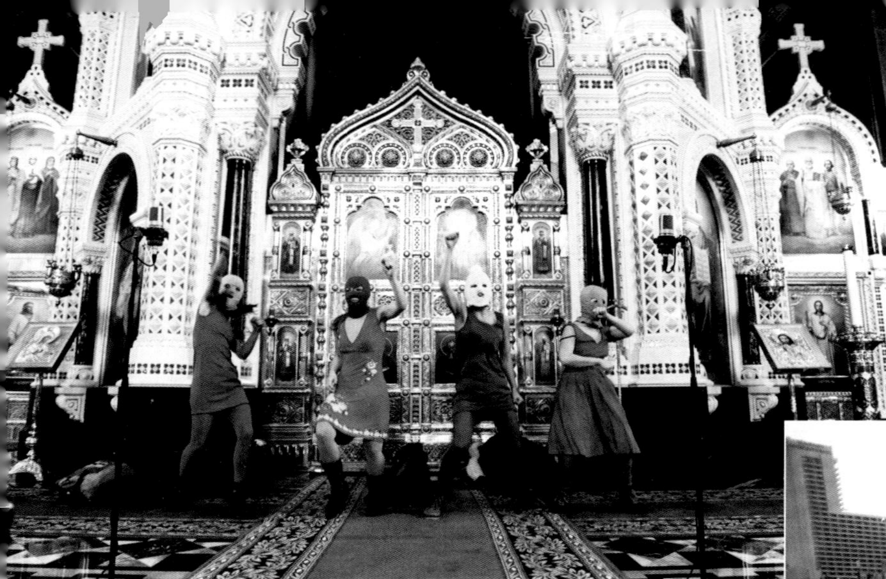

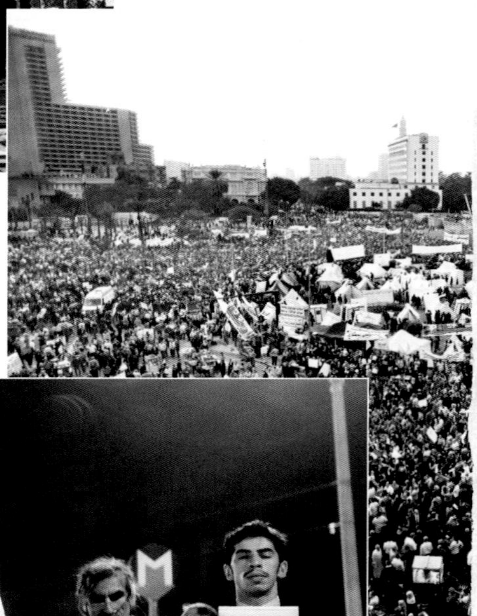

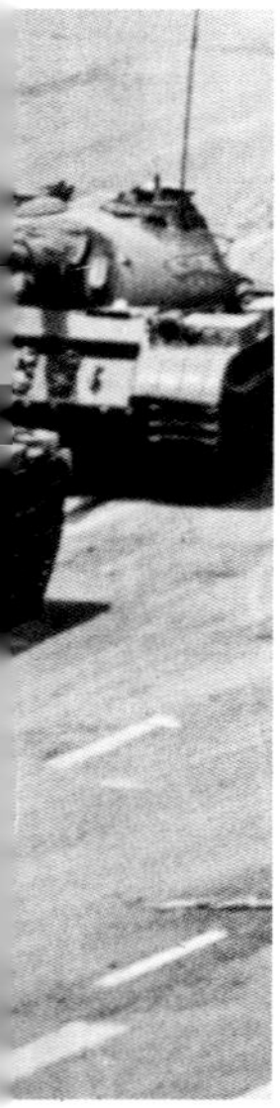

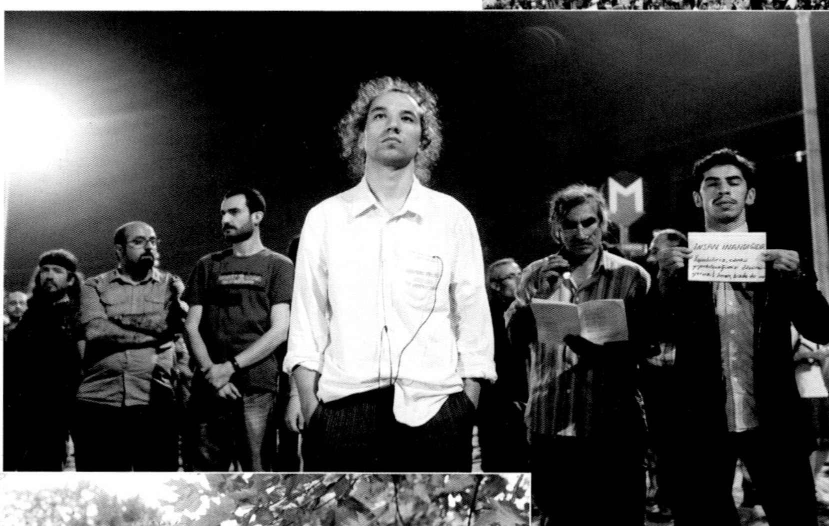

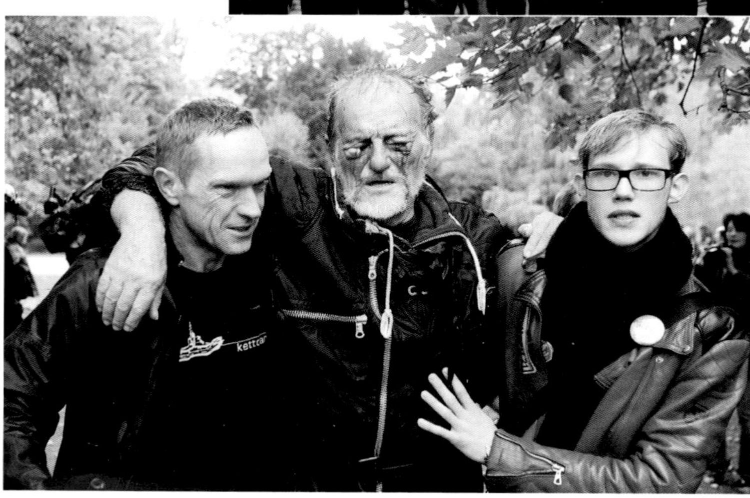